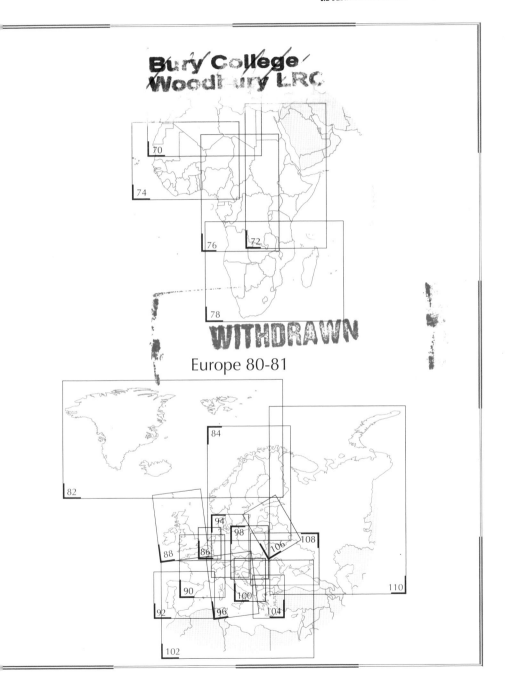

70

74

76 72

78

Europe 80-81

84

82

94

98

88 86 106 108

90

100

92 96 104 110

102

E S S E N T I A L
ATLAS
O F   T H E   W O R L D

LONDON, NEW YORK, MUNICH, MELBOURNE, DELHI

LONDON, NEW YORK, MELBOURNE, MUNICH, DELHI

FOR THE SIXTH EDITION

PUBLISHING DIRECTOR   Jonathan Metcalf
ART DIRECTOR   Bryn Walls
SENIOR CARTOGRAPHIC MANAGER   David Roberts
SENIOR CARTOGRAPHIC EDITOR   Simon Mumford
PROJECT CARTOGRAPHER   Paul Eames
SYSTEMS COORDINATOR   Philip Rowles
PRODUCTION   Sarah Hewitt

DORLING KINDERSLEY CARTOGRAPHY

PROJECT CARTOGRAPHY AND DESIGN
Julia Lunn, Julie Turner

CARTOGRAPHERS
James Anderson, Roger Bullen, Martin Darlison,
Simon Mumford, John Plumer, Peter Winfield

DESIGN
Katy Wall

INDEX-GAZETTEER
Natalie Clarkson, Ruth Duxbury, Margaret Hynes, Margaret Stevenson

PRODUCTION
Hilary Stephens, David Proffit

EDITORIAL DIRECTION
Andrew Heritage

ART DIRECTION
Chez Picthall

First published in Great Britain in 1997 by Dorling Kindersley Limited,
80 Strand, London WC2R 0RL
Second Edition 1998. Third Edition 2001. Fourth Edition 2003.
Fifth Edition 2005. Sixth Edition 2008.

Previously published as the Concise World Atlas

A Penguin Company

A CIP catalog record for this book is available from the British Library

ISBN 978-1-4053-3162-3

Reprographics by Altaimage Ltd, London, UK
Printed and bound by Tien Wah Press, Singapore

See our complete catalogue at www.dk.com

Key to map symbols

Physical features

Elevation

4000m/13,124ft
2000m/6562ft
1,000m/3281ft
500m/1640ft
250m/820ft
100m/328ft
0
Below sea level

△ Mountain

▽ Depression

△ Volcano

)(Pass/tunnel

Sandy desert

Drainage features

Major perennial river

Minor perennial river

- - - Seasonal river

Canal

Waterfall

Perennial lake

Seasonal lake

Wetland

Ice features

Permanent ice cap/ice shelf

Winter limit of pack ice

Summer limit of pack ice

Borders

Full international border

- - - Disputed de facto border

· · · · · Territorial claim border

x x x Cease-fire line

Undefined boundary

Internal administrative boundary

Communications

Major road

Minor road

Rail

✈ International airport

Settlements

◉ Above 500,000

◉ 100,000 to 500,000

○ 50,000 to 100,000

○ Below 50,000

● National capital

● Internal administrative capital

Miscellaneous features

+ Site of interest

ᴜᴜᴜ Ancient wall

Graticule features

Line of latitude/longitude/Equator

Tropic/Polar circle

Degrees of latitude/longitude

Names

Physical features

Andes

Sahara Landscape features

Ardennes

Land's End Headland

Mont Blanc 4,807m Elevation/volcano/pass

Blue Nile River/canal/waterfall

Ross Ice Shelf Ice feature

PACIFIC OCEAN

Sulu Sea Sea features

Palk Strait

Chile Rise Undersea feature

Regions

FRANCE Country

JERSEY Dependent territory
(to UK)

KANSAS Administrative region

Dordogne Cultural region

Settlements

PARIS Capital city

SAN JUAN Dependent territory capital city

Chicago

Kettering Other settlements

Burke

Inset map symbols

Urban area

City

Park

▪ Place of interest

▫ Suburb/district

Contents

The World Today

Flags of the World..................................6-7
The Political World................................8-9
The Physical World..............................10-11
Time Zones...12-13
Geology & Structure............................14-15
World Climate....................................16-17
Ocean Currents..................................18-19
Life Zones..20-21
Population..22-23
Languages..24-25
Religion..26-27
The Global Economy..........................28-29
Global Conflict...................................30-31

The World's Regions

North & Central America

North & Central America.....................34-35
Western Canada & Alaska....................36-37
Eastern Canada...................................38-39
USA: The Northeast.............................40-41
USA: The Southeast.............................42-43
  Bermuda
USA: Central States.............................44-45
USA: The West....................................46-47
  Los Angeles & Hawai'i

USA: The Southwest............................48-49
Mexico...50-51
Central America..................................52-53
The Caribbean....................................54-55
  Jamaica, St. Lucia, & Barbados

South America

South America....................................56-57
Northern South America......................58-59
Western South America.......................60-61
  Galapagos Islands
Brazil...62-63
Southern South America......................64-65
The Atlantic Ocean.............................66-67

Africa

Africa...68-69
Northwest Africa.................................70-71
Northeast Africa.................................72-73
West Africa...74-75
Central Africa.....................................76-77
  Sao Tome & Principe
Southern Africa...................................78-79

Europe

Europe...80-81
The North Atlantic..............................82-83
Scandinavia & Finland.........................84-85
The Low Countries..............................86-87
The British Isles..................................88-89
  London

continued....

Europe *continued*

France, Andorra, & Monaco.................90-91
  Paris, Andorra, & Monaco
Spain & Portugal........................92-93
  Azores & Gibraltar
Germany & the Alpine States............94-95
  Liechtenstein
Italy......................................96-97
  San Marino & Vatican City
Central Europe............................98-99
Southeast Europe........................100-101
  Bosnia & Herzegovina
The Mediterranean.....................102-103
  Malta & Cyprus
Bulgaria & Greece......................104-105
The Baltic States & Belarus............106-107
Ukraine, Moldova,
  & Romania............................108-109
European Russia........................110-111

North & West Asia

North & West Asia......................112-113
Russia & Kazakhstan....................114-115
Turkey & the Caucasus..................116-117
The Near East...........................118-119
  West Bank
The Middle East........................120-121
Central Asia...........................122-123

South & East Asia

South & East Asia......................124-125
Western China & Mongolia...........126-127

Eastern China & Korea..................128-129
  Hong Kong (Xianggang)
Japan...................................130-131
  Tokyo & Nansei-Shoto
South India & Sri Lanka................132-133
North India, Pakistan,
  & Bangladesh........................134-135
Mainland Southeast Asia................136-137
Maritime Southeast Asia................138-139
  Singapore
The Indian Ocean.......................140-141

Australasia & Oceania

Australasia & Oceania..................142-143
The Southwest Pacific..................144-145
Western Australia......................146-147
Eastern Australia......................148-149
  Sydney
New Zealand............................150-151
The Pacific Ocean......................152-153
Antarctica.............................154
The Arctic Ocean.......................155

Index– Gazetteer

Overseas Territories
  & Dependencies......................156-159
Glossary of Geographical
  Terms................................160-161
Continental Factfiles..................162-163
Geographical Comparisons...........164-166
Index-Gazetteer of Places
  & Countries.........................167-256

Flags of the World

NORTH & CENTRAL AMERICA

CANADA
PAGES 36-39

UNITED STATES OF AMERICA
PAGES 40-49

MEXICO
PAGES 50-51

BELIZE
PAGES 52-53

COSTA RICA
PAGES 52-53

EL SALVADOR
PAGES 52-53

GUATEMALA
PAGES 52-53

HONDURAS
PAGES 52-53

GRENADA
PAGES 54-55

HAITI
PAGES 54-55

JAMAICA
PAGES 54-55

ST KITTS & NEVIS
PAGES 54-55

ST LUCIA
PAGES 54-55

ST VINCENT & THE GRENADINES
PAGES 54-55

TRINIDAD & TOBAGO
PAGES 54-55

SOUTH AMERIC

COLOMBIA
PAGES 58-59

URUGUAY
PAGES 64-65

CHILE
PAGES 64-65

PARAGUAY
PAGES 64-65

AFRICA

ALGERIA
PAGES 70-71

LIBYA
PAGES 70-71

MOROCCO
PAGES 70-71

TUNISIA
PAGES 70-71

BURUNDI
PAGES 72-73

TANZANIA
PAGES 72-73

UGANDA
PAGES 72-73

BENIN
PAGES 74-75

BURKINA FASO
PAGES 74-75

CAPE VERDE
PAGES 74-75

CÔTE D'IVOIRE (IVORY COAST)
PAGES 74-75

GAMBIA
PAGES 74-75

GHANA
PAGES 74-75

SIERRA LEONE
PAGES 74-75

TOGO
PAGES 74-75

CAMEROON
PAGES 76-77

CENTRAL AFRICAN REPUBLIC
PAGES 76-77

CHAD
PAGES 76-77

CONGO
PAGES 76-77

DEM. REP. CONGO
PAGES 76-77

EQUATORIAL GUINEA
PAGES 76-77

MAURITIUS
PAGES 78-79

MOZAMBIQUE
PAGES 78-79

NAMIBIA
PAGES 78-79

SEYCHELLES
PAGES 78-79

SOUTH AFRICA
PAGES 78-79

SWAZILAND
PAGES 78-79

ZAMBIA
PAGES 78-79

ZIMBABWE
PAGES 78-79

IRELAND
PAGES 88-89

UNITED KINGDOM
PAGES 88-89

FRANCE
PAGES 90-91

MONACO
PAGES 90-91

ANDORRA
PAGES 90-91

PORTUGAL
PAGES 92-93

SPAIN
PAGES 92-93

AUSTRIA
PAGES 94-95

HUNGARY
PAGES 98-99

POLAND
PAGES 98-99

SLOVAKIA
PAGES 98-99

ALBANIA
PAGES 100-101

BOSNIA & HERZEGOVINA
PAGES 100-101

CROATIA
PAGES 100-101

MACEDONIA
PAGES 100-101

MONTENEGRO
PAGES 100-101

MOLDOVA
PAGES 108-109

ROMANIA
PAGES 108-109

UKRAINE
PAGES 108-109

RUSSIAN FEDERATION
PAGES 110-115

ASIA

KAZAKHSTAN
PAGES 114-115

ARMENIA
PAGES 116-117

AZERBAIJAN
PAGES 116-117

GEORGIA
PAGES 116-117

KUWAIT
PAGES 120-121

OMAN
PAGES 120-121

QATAR
PAGES 120-121

SAUDI ARABIA
PAGES 120-121

UNITED ARAB EMIRATES
PAGES 120-121

YEMEN
PAGES 120-121

AFGHANISTAN
PAGES 122-123

KYRGYZSTAN
PAGES 122-123

JAPAN
PAGES 130-131

INDIA
PAGES 132-135

SRI LANKA
PAGES 132-133

MALDIVES
PAGES 132-133

PAKISTAN
PAGES 134-135

BANGLADESH
PAGES 134-135

BHUTAN
PAGES 134-135

NEPAL
PAGES 134-135

CAMBODIA
PAGES 136-137

PHILIPPINES
PAGES 138-139

SINGAPORE
PAGES 138-139

AUSTRALASIA & OCEANIA

FIJI
PAGES 144-145

KIRIBATI
PAGES 144-145

MARSHALL ISLANDS
PAGES 144-145

MICRONESIA
PAGES 144-145

NAURU
PAGES 144-145

PALAU
PAGES 144-145

NICARAGUA PAGES 52-53 | PANAMA PAGES 52-53 | ANTIGUA & BARBUDA PAGES 54-55 | BAHAMAS PAGES 54-55 | BARBADOS PAGES 54-55 | CUBA PAGES 54-55 | DOMINICA PAGES 54-55 | DOMINICAN REPUBLIC PAGES 54–55

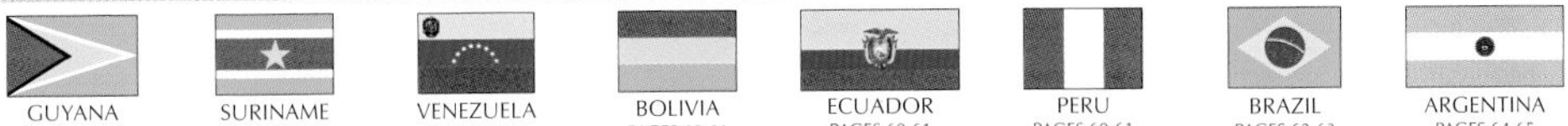

GUYANA PAGES 58-59 | SURINAME PAGES 58-59 | VENEZUELA PAGES 58-59 | BOLIVIA PAGES 60-61 | ECUADOR PAGES 60-61 | PERU PAGES 60-61 | BRAZIL PAGES 62-63 | ARGENTINA PAGES 64-65

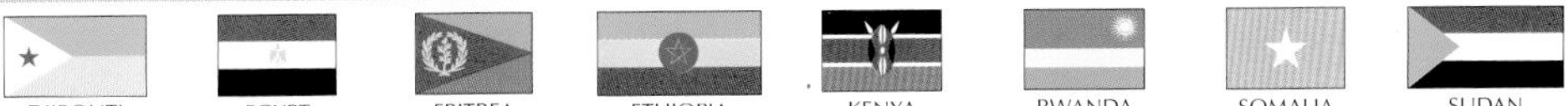

DJIBOUTI PAGES 72-73 | EGYPT PAGES 72-73 | ERITREA PAGES 72-73 | ETHIOPIA PAGES 72-73 | KENYA PAGES 72-73 | RWANDA PAGES 72-73 | SOMALIA PAGES 72-73 | SUDAN PAGES 72-73

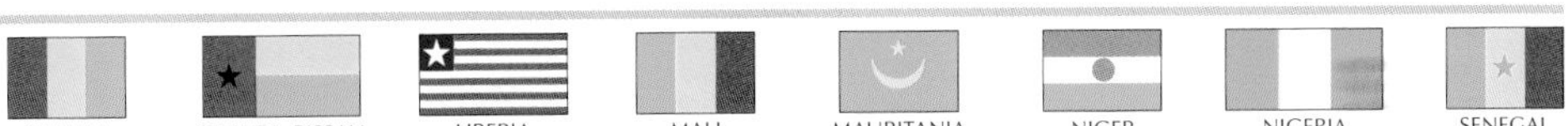

GUINEA PAGES 74-75 | GUINEA–BISSAU PAGES 74-75 | LIBERIA PAGES 74-75 | MALI PAGES 74-75 | MAURITANIA PAGES 74-75 | NIGER PAGES 74-75 | NIGERIA PAGES 74-75 | SENEGAL PAGES 74-75

GABON PAGES 76-77 | SAO TOME & PRINCIPE PAGES 76-77 | ANGOLA PAGES 78-79 | BOTSWANA PAGES 78-79 | COMOROS PAGES 78-79 | LESOTHO PAGES 78-79 | MADAGASCAR PAGES 78-79 | MALAWI PAGES 78-79

EUROPE

ICELAND PAGES 82-83 | DENMARK PAGES 84-85 | FINLAND PAGES 84-85 | NORWAY PAGES 84-85 | SWEDEN PAGES 84-85 | BELGIUM PAGES 86-87 | LUXEMBOURG PAGES 86-87 | NETHERLANDS PAGES 86-87

GERMANY PAGES 94-95 | LIECHTENSTEIN PAGES 94-95 | SLOVENIA PAGES 94-95 | SWITZERLAND PAGES 94-95 | ITALY PAGES 96-97 | MALTA PAGES 96-97 | SAN MARINO PAGES 96-97 | VATICAN CITY PAGES 96-97 | CZECH REPUBLIC PAGES 98-99

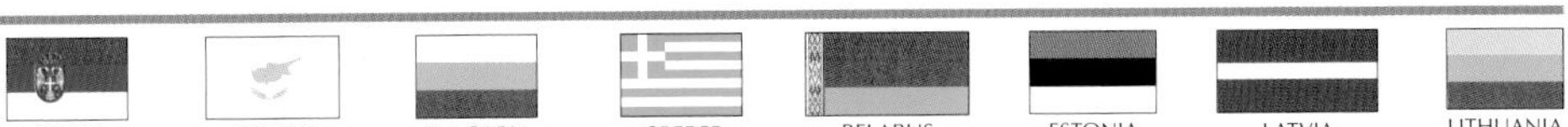

SERBIA PAGES 100-101 | CYPRUS PAGES 102-103 | BULGARIA PAGES 104-105 | GREECE PAGES 104-105 | BELARUS PAGES 106-107 | ESTONIA PAGES 106-107 | LATVIA PAGES 106-107 | LITHUANIA PAGES 106-107

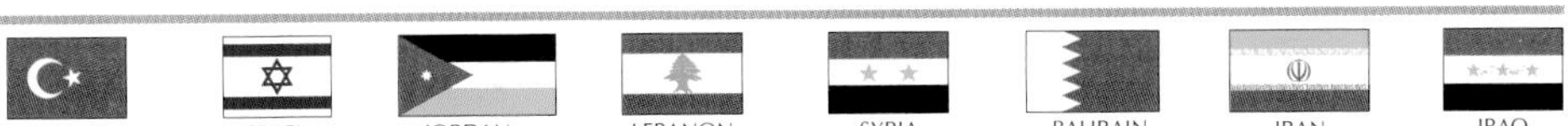

TURKEY PAGES 116-117 | ISRAEL PAGES 118-119 | JORDAN PAGES 118-119 | LEBANON PAGES 118-119 | SYRIA PAGES 118-119 | BAHRAIN PAGES 120-121 | IRAN PAGES 120-121 | IRAQ PAGES 120-121

TAJIKISTAN PAGES 122-123 | TURKMENISTAN PAGES 122-123 | UZBEKISTAN PAGES 122-123 | CHINA PAGES 126-129 | MONGOLIA PAGES 126-127 | NORTH KOREA PAGES 128-129 | SOUTH KOREA PAGES 128-129 | TAIWAN PAGES 128-129

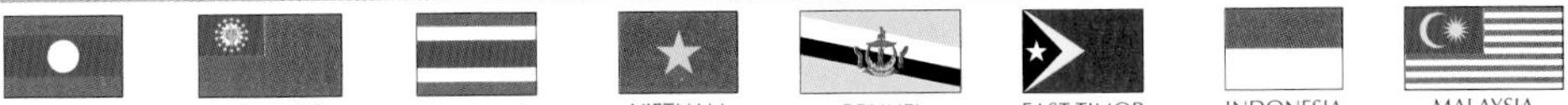

LAOS PAGES 136-137 | MYANMAR (BURMA) PAGES 136-137 | THAILAND PAGES 136-137 | VIETNAM PAGES 136-137 | BRUNEI PAGES 138-139 | EAST TIMOR PAGES 138-139 | INDONESIA PAGES 138-139 | MALAYSIA PAGES 138-139

PAPUA NEW GUINEA PAGES 144-145 | SAMOA PAGES 144-145 | SOLOMON ISLANDS PAGES 144-145 | TONGA PAGES 144-145 | TUVALU PAGES 144-145 | VANUATU PAGES 144-145 | AUSTRALIA PAGES 146-149 | NEW ZEALAND PAGES 150-151

The Political World

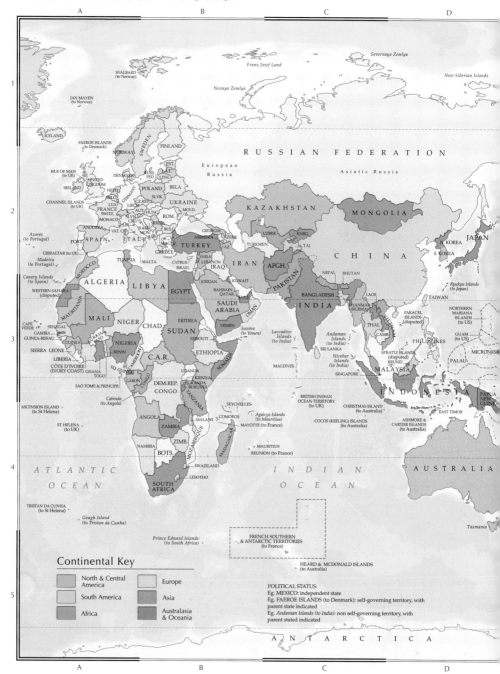

Continental Key

- North & Central America
- South America
- Africa
- Europe
- Asia
- Australasia & Oceania

POLITICAL STATUS:
Eg. MEXICO: independent state
Eg. FAEROE ISLANDS (to Denmark): self-governing territory, with parent state indicated
Eg. Andaman Islands (to India): non self-governing territory, with parent stated indicated

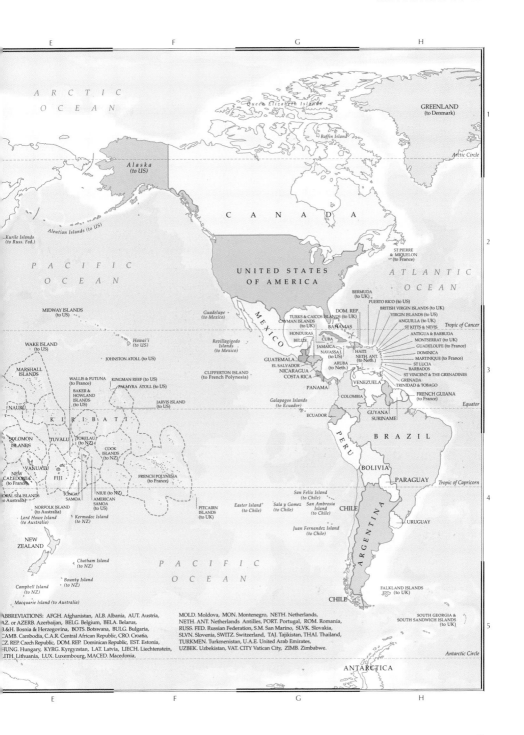

A R C T I C
O C E A N

Queen Elizabeth Islands

GREENLAND
(to Denmark)

Baffin Island

Arctic Circle

Alaska
(to US)

Kurile Islands
(to Russ. Fed.)

Aleutian Islands (to US)

C A N A D A

ST PIERRE
& MIQUELON
(to France)

P A C I F I C
O C E A N

UNITED STATES
OF AMERICA

A T L A N T I C
O C E A N

BERMUDA
(to UK)

PUERTO RICO (to US)

MIDWAY ISLANDS
(to US)

Guadelupe
(to Mexico)

TURKS & CAICOS ISLANDS (to UK)

BRITISH VIRGIN ISLANDS (to UK)
VIRGIN ISLANDS (to US)
ANGUILLA (to UK)
ST KITTS & NEVIS   Tropic of Cancer

CAYMAN ISLANDS
(to UK)

BAHAMAS

WAKE ISLAND
(to US)

Hawai'i
(to US)

*Revillagigedo
Islands*
(to Mexico)

HONDURAS

BELIZE

CUBA

ANTIGUA & BARBUDA
MONTSERRAT (to UK)
GUADELOUPE (to France)
DOMINICA

JAMAICA

JOHNSTON ATOLL (to US)

GUATEMALA
EL SALVADOR
NICARAGUA
COSTA RICA

NAVASSA I.
(to US)

HAITI
NETH. ANT.
(to Neth.)

ARUBA
(to Neth.)

MARTINIQUE (to France)
ST LUCIA
BARBADOS
ST VINCENT & THE GRENADINES
GRENADA
TRINIDAD & TOBAGO

MARSHALL
ISLANDS

WALLIS & FUTUNA
(to France)

KINGMAN REEF (to US)

PALMYRA ATOLL (to US)

CLIPPERTON ISLAND
(to French Polynesia)

PANAMA

VENEZUELA

FRENCH GUIANA
(to France)

BAKER &
HOWLAND
ISLANDS
(to US)

JARVIS ISLAND
(to US)

Galapagos Islands
(to Ecuador)

COLOMBIA

GUYANA
SURINAME

Equator

NAURU

K I R I B A T I

ECUADOR

B R A Z I L

SOLOMON
ISLANDS

TUVALU

TOKELAU
(to NZ)

COOK
ISLANDS
(to NZ)

P E R U

BOLIVIA

VANUATU

NEW
CALEDONIA
(to France)

FIJI

FRENCH POLYNESIA
(to France)

PARAGUAY   Tropic of Capricorn

CORAL SEA ISLANDS
(to Australia)

TONGA

SAMOA

NIUE (to NZ)

AMERICAN
SAMOA
(to US)

San Felix Island
(to Chile)

Sala y Gomez
(to Chile)

*San Ambrosia
Island*
(to Chile)

CHILE

NORFOLK ISLAND
(to Australia)

Lord Howe Island
(to Australia)

Kermadec Island
(to NZ)

PITCAIRN
ISLANDS
(to UK)

Easter Island
(to Chile)

A R G E N T I N A

URUGUAY

NEW
ZEALAND

Juan Fernandez Island
(to Chile)

Chatham Island
(to NZ)

P A C I F I C

Bounty Island
(to NZ)

O C E A N

Campbell Island
(to NZ)

Macquarie Island (to Australia)

CHILE

FALKLAND ISLANDS
(to UK)

SOUTH GEORGIA &
SOUTH SANDWICH ISLANDS
(to UK)

Antarctic Circle

ANTARCTICA

The Physical World

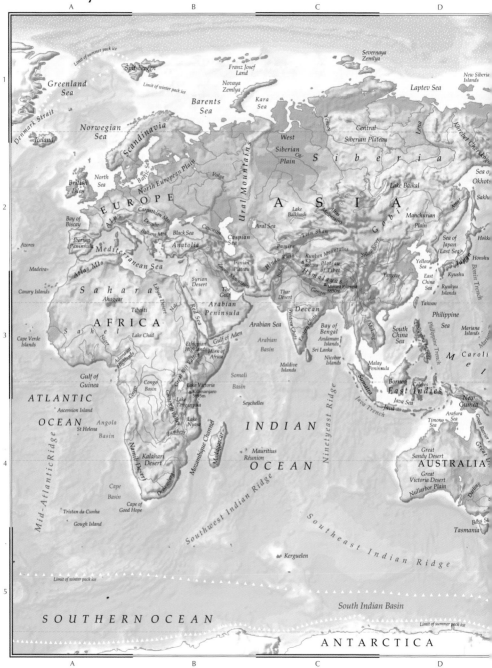

A · B · C · D

Limit of summer pack ice

Greenland
Sea

Spitsbergen

Franz Josef
Land

Severnaya
Zemlya

New Siberia
Islands

Limit of winter pack ice

Novaya
Zemlya

Barents
Sea

Kara
Sea

Laptev Sea

Denmark Strait

Iceland

Norwegian
Sea

Scandinavia

West
Siberian
Plain

Ob

Central
Siberian Plateau

Yenisey

Lena

Kolyma

Khrebet Cherskogo

1

British
Isles

North
Sea

Baltic Sea

North European Plain

Volga

Ural Mountains

S i b e r i a

Sea of
Okhotsk

Bay of
Biscay

EUROPE

Carpathian Mts.

Danube

Balkans Mts.

Black Sea

Caucasus

Aral Sea

A S I A

Lake
Balkhash

Altai Mountains

Lake Baikal

Amur

Manchurian
Plain

Sakhalin

2

Azores

Iberian
Peninsula

Alps

Mediterranean Sea

Anatolia

Caspian
Sea

Tien Shan

Pamirs

Hindu Kush

Gobi

Yellow River

Sea of
Japan
(East Sea)

Hokkaido

Honshu

Madeira

Iranian
Plateau

Zagros Mountains

Kunlun Mountains

Plateau
of Tibet

Yangtze

Yellow
Sea

Kyushu

Ryukyu
Islands

Bonin Trench

Japan Trench

Canary Islands

Atlas Mts.

S a h a r a

Libyan Desert

Nile

Syrian
Desert

The
Gulf

Indus

Himalayas

Mount Everest
8850m

Ganges

K2
8611m

East
China
Sea

Taiwan

Cape Verde
Islands

Sahel

Niger

Tibesti

Ahaggar

AFRICA

Lake Chad

Red Sea

Arabian
Peninsula

Thar
Desert

Deccan

Eastern Ghats

Philippine
Sea

Mariana
Islands

3

Adamawa
Highlands

Ethiopian
Highlands

Gulf of Aden

Arabian Sea

Western Ghats

Bay of
Bengal

Andaman
Islands

Sri Lanka

Mekong

South
China
Sea

Philippine Trench

Philippine Trench

Caroline Islands

Gulf of
Guinea

Congo
Basin

Congo

Great Rift Valley

Horn of
Africa

Somali
Basin

Maldive
Islands

Nicobar
Islands

Malay
Peninsula

Sumatra

Borneo

Celebes

East Indies

ATLANTIC

Ascension Island

St Helena

Angola
Basin

Lake Victoria

Kilimanjaro
5895m

Lake
Tanganyika

Seychelles

Java Trench

Java Sea

Java

New
Guinea

OCEAN

Namib Desert

Great Rift Valley

Lake
Nyasa

Zambezi

Mozambique Channel

Madagascar

I N D I A N

Ninetyeast Ridge

Arafura
Sea

Timor
Sea

Great Barrier Reef

4

Mid-Atlantic Ridge

Kalahari
Desert

Drakensberg

Mauritius

Réunion

O C E A N

Great
Sandy Desert

AUSTRALIA

Great
Victoria Desert

Darling

Cape
Basin

Cape of
Good Hope

Nullarbor Plain

Tristan da Cunha

Gough Island

Southwest Indian Ridge

Kerguelen

Southeast Indian Ridge

Bass St.

Tasmania

Limit of winter pack ice

South Indian Basin

5

Limit of summer pack ice

S O U T H E R N   O C E A N

A N T A R C T I C A

A · B · C · D

ARCTIC OCEAN

ast Siberian Sea

Limit of summer pack ice

Chukchi Sea

Beaufort Sea

Queen Elizabeth Islands

Ellesmere Island

Greenland

Baffin
Bay

Baffin Island

Brooks Range

Arctic Circle

Mackenzie

Great Bear
Lake

Mount McKinley
(Denali)
6194m

Bering Strait

Limit of winter pack ice

Great Slave
Lake

Canadian Shield

Hudson
Bay

Péninsule
d'Ungava

Labrador
Sea

Bering Sea

Aleutian Basin

Aleutian Islands

Aleutian Trench

Gulf of
Alaska

Rocky Mountains

Lake
Winnipeg

Laurentian
Mountains

Vancouver
Island

NORTH AMERICA

Great Lakes

Grand Banks
of Newfoundland

Northwest
Pacific
Basin

Emperor Seamounts

Mendocino Fracture Zone

Great Plains

Missouri

Appalachian Mts

North American
Basin

Mid-Atlantic Ridge

Murray Fracture Zone

Coast Ranges

Sierra Madre Occidental

Mississippi

Sierra Madre Oriental

Gulf of
Mexico

Tropic of Cancer

Mid-Pacific
Mountains

Hawai'ian Islands

Hawai'i

Central
Pacific
Basin

Marshall
Islands

Polynesia

Yucatán
Peninsula

Greater Antilles

West Indies

Lesser
Antilles

ATLANTIC

Micronesia

ands

PACIFIC

OCEAN

Middle America Trench

Caribbean
Sea

OCEAN

Line Islands

Phoenix
Islands

Galapagos
Islands

Guiana
Highlands

Equator

Samoa

Marquesas
Islands

Amazon

mon Islands

Cook Islands

Tuamotu
Islands

Amazon Basin

SOUTH
AMERICA

Brazilian Highlands

Brazil
Basin

a

oral
Sea

Vanuatu

Fiji

Tonga

Peru
Basin

Andes

Peru–Chile Trench

Planalto de
Mato Grosso

Tropic of Capricorn

New Caledonia

East Pacific Rise

Gran Chaco

Kermadec Trench

Tasman
Sea

North
Island

Southwest

Pacific

Easter Island

Juan Fernandez
Islands

Cerro Aconcagua
6959m

Pampas

Patagonia

Argentine
Basin

South
Island

New
Zealand

Basin

Andes

Falkland Islands

Campbell
Plateau

Tierra del Fuego

South Georgia

Cape Horn

Drake Passage

South Sandwich
Islands

SOUTHERN OCEAN

Limit of winter pack ice

Antarctic
Peninsula

Antarctic Circle

Elevation

-4000m	-3000m	-2000m	-1000m	-500m	Below sea level	0	100m	250m	500m	1000m	2000m	4000m
-13,124ft	-9843ft	-6562ft	-3281ft	-1640ft	-820ft/-250m	0	328ft	820ft	1640ft	3281ft	6562ft	13,124ft

Time Zones

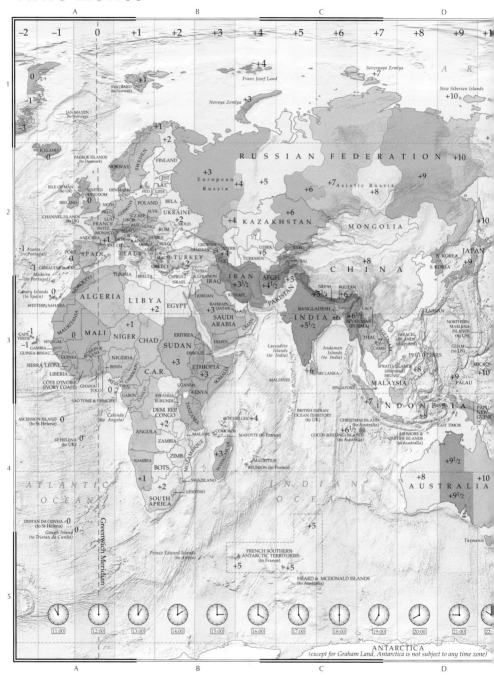

The numbers represented thus; +2/-2, indicate the number of hours each time zone is ahead or behind UCT (Coordinated Universal Time)

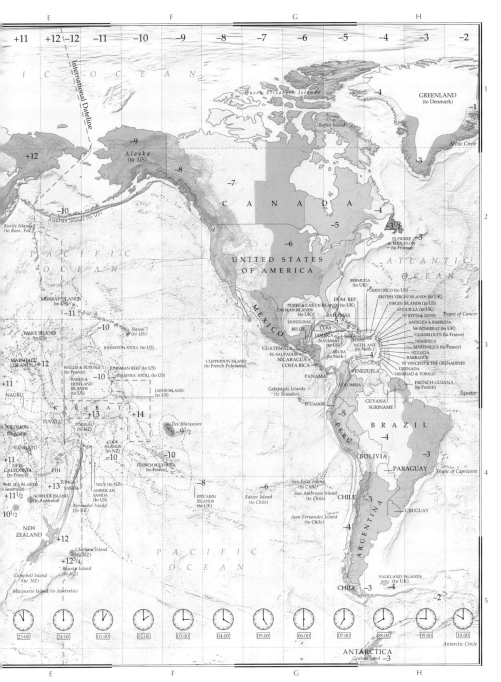

The clocks and 24-hour times given at the bottom of the map show time in each time zone when it is 12.00 hours noon UCT

Geology & Structure

Geological Regions

- Continental shield
- Sedimentary rocks
- Igneous rock types
- Coral formation

Mountain Ranges

- Alpine (5 to 23 Ma)
- Hercynian (290 to 362 Ma)
- Caledonian (386 to 439 Ma)

Ma= millions of years ago

NORTH AMERICAN
PLATE

JUAN DE FUCA
PLATE

Rocky Mountains

CARIBBEAN
PLATE

COCOS
PLATE

SOUTH
AMERICAN
PLATE

ROLINE
ATE

PACIFIC PLATE

SMARCK
ATE

SOLOMON
PLATE

FIJI PLATE

NAZCA
PLATE

Andes

ANTARCTIC
PLATE

SCOTIA PLATE

Arctic Circle

Tropic of Cancer

Equator

Tropic of Capricorn

Antarctic Circle

● Earthquake zone   ▲ Volcanic zone   **Plate Boundaries**   —— Sliding plates   ▲▲ Colliding plates

● Hot spot   ▼▼▼ Rift valley   —— Spreading plates   - - - Uncertain plate boundary

World Climate

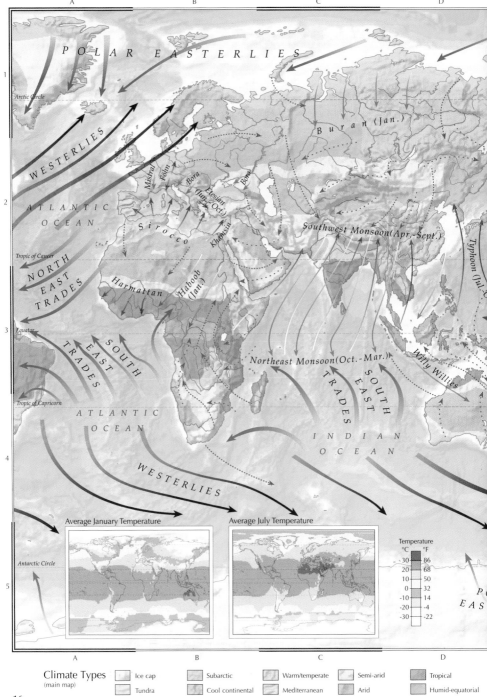

A   B   C   D

P O L A R   E A S T E R L I E S

Arctic Circle

W E S T E R L I E S

1

Buran (Jan.)

A T L A N T I C
O C E A N

Mistral

Föhn

Bora

Etesian
(Jun.–Oct.)

Bora

Sirocco

2

Southwest Monsoon(Apr.–Sept.)

Typhoon (Jul.–

Khamsin

Tropic of Cancer

N O R T H
E A S T
T R A D E S

Harmattan

Haboob
(Jan.)

S O U T H
E A S T
T R A D E S

Northeast Monsoon(Oct.–Mar.)

Willy Willies

3

Equator

S O U T H
E A S T
T R A D E S

Tropic of Capricorn

A T L A N T I C
O C E A N

I N D I A N
O C E A N

4

W E S T E R L I E S

Average January Temperature

Average July Temperature

Temperature
°C   °F

30	86
20	68
10	50
0	32
-10	14
-20	-4
-30	-22

Antarctic Circle

5

P O
E A S

A   B   C   D

Climate Types
(main map)

Ice cap	Subarctic	Warm/temperate	Semi-arid	Tropical
Tundra	Cool continental	Mediterranean	Arid	Humid-equatorial

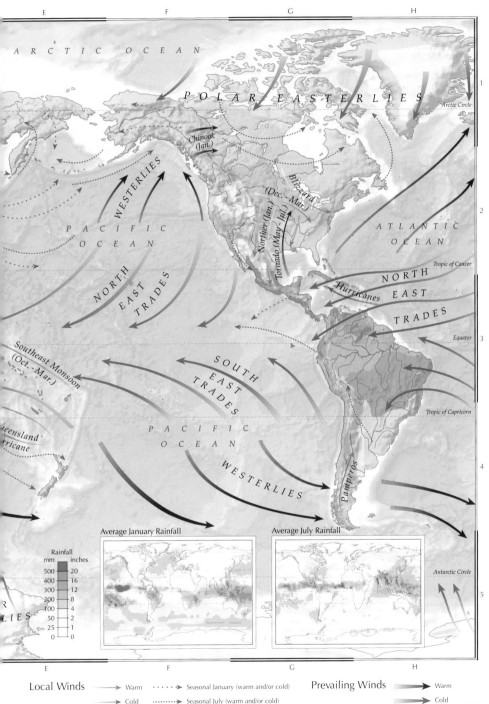

E   F   G   H

ARCTIC OCEAN

POLAR EASTERLIES

Arctic Circle

1

Chinook
(Jan.)

WESTERLIES

PACIFIC
OCEAN

ATLANTIC
OCEAN

Blizzard
(Dec.–Mar.)

Norther (Jan.)

Tornado (May–Jul.)

2

NORTH

EAST

TRADES

Tropic of Cancer

NORTH

EAST

TRADES

Hurricanes

Southeast Monsoon
(Oct.–Mar.)

SOUTH
EAST
TRADES

Equator

3

Tropic of Capricorn

eensland
ricane

PACIFIC
OCEAN

WESTERLIES

Pamperos

4

Average January Rainfall

Average July Rainfall

Rainfall
mm   inches
500 — 20
400 — 16
300 — 12
200 — 8
100 — 4
50 — 2
25 — 1
0 — 0

Antarctic Circle

5

R
LIES

E   F   G   H

Local Winds   → Warm   ····▸ Seasonal January (warm and/or cold)   Prevailing Winds   → Warm
                → Cold   ········▸ Seasonal July (warm and/or cold)   → Cold

Ocean Currents

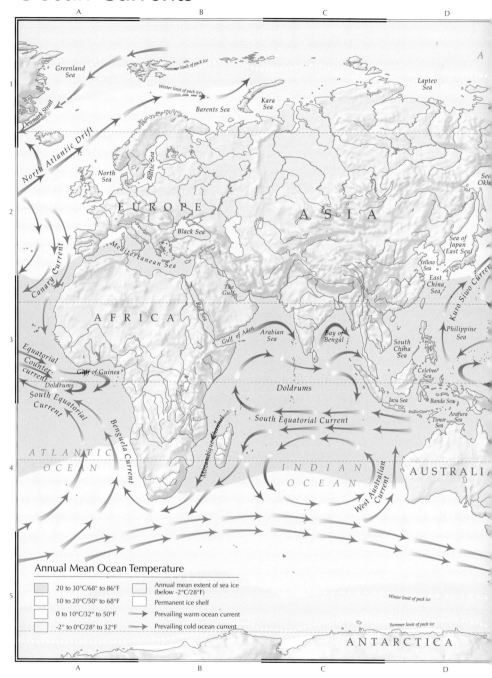

Greenland Sea

Summer limit of pack ice

Winter limit of pack ice

Laptev Sea

Denmark Strait

North Atlantic Drift

Barents Sea

Kara Sea

Sea of Okh...

North Sea

Baltic Sea

EUROPE

ASIA

Sea of Japan (East Sea)

Canary Current

Black Sea

Mediterranean Sea

Yellow Sea

East China Sea

Kuro Sivo Current

AFRICA

Red Sea

The Gulf

Gulf of Aden

Arabian Sea

Bay of Bengal

South China Sea

Philippine Sea

Equatorial Counter-current

Gulf of Guinea

Doldrums

Doldrums

Celebes Sea

South Equatorial Current

Java Sea

Banda Sea

Arafura Sea

South Equatorial Current

Timor Sea

Benguela Current

Mozambique Current

ATLANTIC OCEAN

INDIAN OCEAN

AUSTRALIA

West Australian Current

Annual Mean Ocean Temperature

20 to 30°C/68° to 86°F	Annual mean extent of sea ice (below -2°C/28°F)
10 to 20°C/50° to 68°F	Permanent ice shelf
0 to 10°C/32° to 50°F	→ Prevailing warm ocean current
-2° to 0°C/28° to 32°F	→ Prevailing cold ocean current

Winter limit of pack ice

Summer limit of pack ice

ANTARCTICA

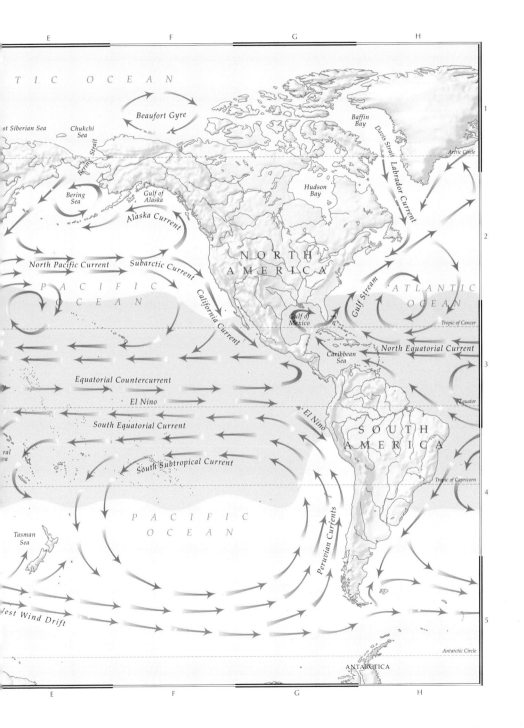

Life Zones

Life Zones

Polar	Mountain	Broadleaf forest	Temperate forest
Tundra	Needleleaf forest	Temperate grassland	Mediterranean

E   F   G   H

OCEAN

Ellesmere Island

st Siberian Sea

Chukchi Sea

Beaufort Sea

Queen Elizabeth
Islands

Greenland

1

Brooks Range

Mackenzie

Baffin
Bay

Baffin Island

Arctic Circle

Bering Strait

Great Bear
Lake

Rocky Mountains

Great Slave
Lake

Hudson
Bay

Labrador
Sea

Bering Sea

Gulf of
Alaska

Aleutian Islands

Canadian Shield

Coast Mountains

NORTH AMERICA

Labrador

Vancouver
Island

Lake
Winnipeg

Great Lakes

2

Coast Ranges

Great Plains

Mississippi

Appalachian Mts

ATLANTIC

OCEAN

Hawai'ian Islands

Sierra Madre
Occidental

Sierra Madre
Oriental

Gulf of
Mexico

Tropic of Cancer

Hawai'i

Polynesia

West Indies
Greater
Antilles

Yucatan
Peninsula

3

Micronesia

Marshall
Islands

PACIFIC

Caribbean
Sea

Lesser
Antilles

ands

Phoenix
Islands

Line Islands

Galapagos
Islands

Guiana
Highlands

Equator

e Islands

Samoa

Marquesas
Islands

Amazon

Amazon Basin

SOUTH
AMERICA

ral
ea

Fiji

Cook Islands

Tuamotu
Islands

Andes

Brazilian Highlands

Tonga

Planalto de
Mato Grosso

New Caledonia

Gran Chaco

Tropic of Capricorn

4

OCEAN

Pampas

Andes

'asman
Sea

North
Island

South
Island

New
Zealand

Patagonia

Falkland Islands

Tierra del Fuego

Cape Horn

5

Drake Passage

Antarctic
Peninsula

Antarctic Circle

E   F   G   H

Dry woodland   Tropical rainforest   Cold desert

Tropical grassland   Hot desert   Wetland

21

Population

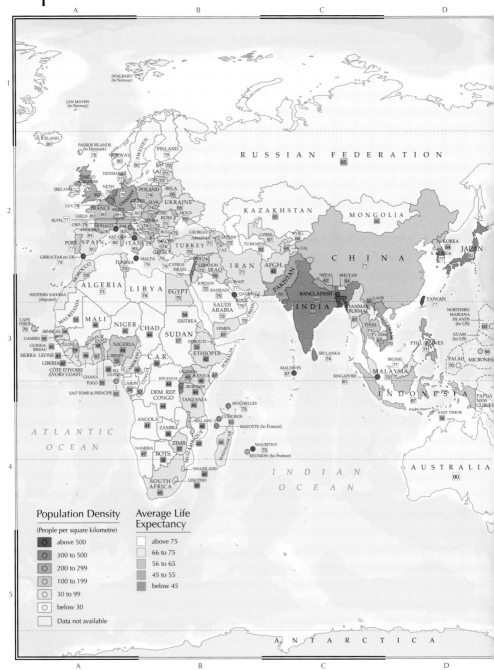

Population Density

(People per square kilometre)

- above 500
- 300 to 500
- 200 to 299
- 100 to 199
- 30 to 99
- below 30
- Data not available

Average Life Expectancy

- above 75
- 66 to 75
- 56 to 65
- 45 to 55
- below 45

E F G H

ARCTIC
OCEAN

GREENLAND
(to Denmark)
67

Alaska
(to US)

Arctic Circle

C A N A D A
80

PACIFIC
OCEAN

UNITED STATES
OF AMERICA
77

ATLANTIC
OCEAN

BERMUDA
75 (to UK)

Hawai'i
(to US)

Tropic of Cancer

MEXICO

CAYMAN ISLANDS
77 (to UK)

PUERTO RICO (to US)
74
DOM. REP.
68

72 ST KITTS & NEVIS
75 ANTIGUA & BARBUDA
75 GUADELOUPE (to France)
77 DOMINICA
76 MARTINIQUE (to France)
73 ST LUCIA
75 BARBADOS
71 ST VINCENT & THE
     GRENADINES
73 GRENADA
70 TRINIDAD & TOBAGO

MARSHALL
ISLANDS
70

NAURU
63

KIRIBATI

TUVALU
63

SOLOMON
ISLANDS
63

VANUATU
74

NEW
CALEDONIA
(to France)

FIJI
68

68

TONGA
SAMOA

TOKELAU
(to NZ)

WALLIS & FUTUNA
(to France)

COOK
ISLANDS
(to NZ)
70

NIUE (to NZ)
AMERICAN
SAMOA
(to US)

FRENCH POLYNESIA
(to France)
70

PITCAIRN
ISLANDS
(to UK)

HONDURAS
BELIZE
72
GUATEMALA 68
EL SALVADOR 71
NICARAGUA 70
COSTA RICA 79
PANAMA 75

CUBA
77
JAMAICA
71

HAITI
52 76
NETH. ANT.
(to Neth.)

ARUBA
(to Neth.)

COLOMBIA
73

ECUADOR 75

VENEZUELA
74

64 69
FRENCH GUIANA
75 (to France)

GUYANA
SURINAME

Equator

PERU
70

BRAZIL
71

BOLIVIA
65

PARAGUAY
71

Tropic of Capricorn

CHILE
78

ARGENTINA

75 URUGUAY

75

NEW
ZEALAND
79

PACIFIC
OCEAN

CHILE

FALKLAND ISLANDS
(to UK)
76

SOUTH GEORGIA &
SOUTH SANDWICH ISLANDS
(to UK)

Antarctic Circle

ANTARCTICA

E F G H

Languages

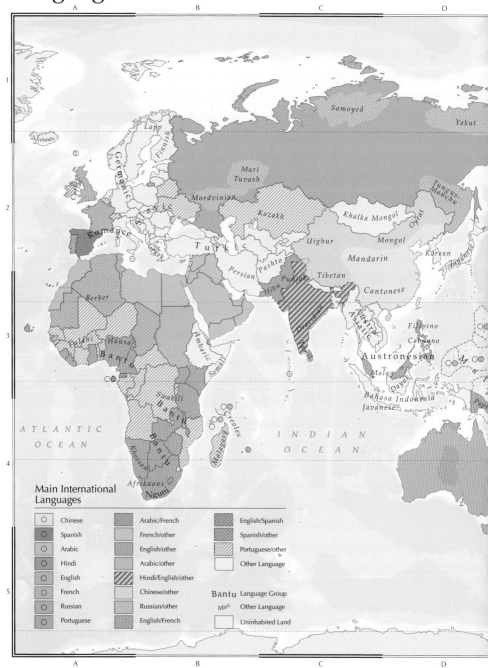

○ Chinese	Arabic/French	English/Spanish
○ Spanish	French/other	Spanish/other
○ Arabic	English/other	Portuguese/other
○ Hindi	Arabic/other	Other Language
○ English	Hindi/English/other	
○ French	Chinese/other	Bantu Language Group
○ Russian	Russian/other	Mari Other Language
○ Portuguese	English/French	Uninhabited Land

Main International Languages

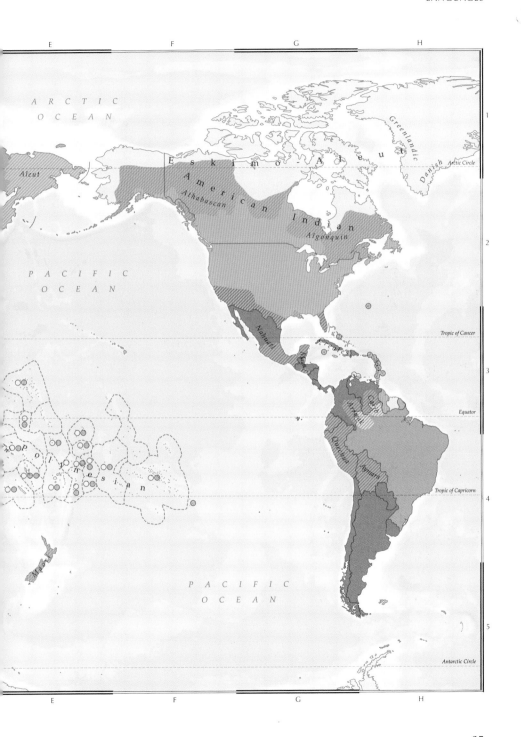

ARCTIC
OCEAN

Greenlandic

Danish Arctic Circle

Aleut

Eskimo-Aleut

American Indian

Athabascan

Algonquin

PACIFIC
OCEAN

Tropic of Cancer

Nahuatl

Maya

3

Arawak

Carib

Equator

Quechua

Polynesian

Aymara

Tropic of Capricorn

4

Maori

PACIFIC
OCEAN

5

Antarctic Circle

Religion

A	B	C	D

SVALBARD
(to Norway)

ICELAND

FAEROE ISLANDS
(to Denmark)

NORWAY   SWEDEN   FINLAND

RUSSIAN   FEDERATION

European
Russia

Asiatic Russia

DENMARK
RUSS
FED
LITH
BELA

EST
LAT

UNITED KINGDOM

IRELAND

NETH
GERM
POLAND
LUX
CZE REP
AUT SLVK
HUNG
UKRAINE
MOLD.

KAZAKHSTAN

MONGOLIA

FRANCE
SWITZ
LIE SLO
MONACO
ANDORRA
SERBIA
ROM.
BULG
GEORGIA
ARMENIA
AZER.
UZBEK.
TURKMEN
KYRG.
TAJ.

N. KOREA   JAPAN

S. KOREA

VAT. CITY
PORT.   SPAIN   ITALY
MONT
ALB
MACED
SYRIA
TURKEY

CHINA

GIBRALTAR (to UK)

TUNISIA   MALTA
GREECE
CYPRUS
ISRAEL
LEBANON
IRAQ
IRAN
AFGH.
NEPAL   BHUTAN

MOROCCO

JORDAN
BAHRAIN
QATAR
KUWAIT
PAKISTAN

TAIWAN

WESTERN SAHARA
(disputed)

ALGERIA   LIBYA   EGYPT

SAUDI
ARABIA

U.A.E.
OMAN

BANGLADESH
INDIA

LAOS
MYANMAR
(BURMA)

NORTHERN
MARIANA
ISLANDS
(to US)

MAURITANIA

MALI   NIGER   CHAD   SUDAN

ERITREA
DJIBOUTI
YEMEN

THAI.
VIETNAM
CAMB.

PHILIPPINES

MICRONES

CAPE
VERDE
SENEGAL
GAMBIA
GUINEA-BISSAU
GUIN.
SIERRA LEONE
LIBERIA
CÔTE D'IVOIRE
(IVORY COAST)
BURKINA
FASO
TOGO
GHANA
BENIN
NIGERIA
CAMEROON
EQ. GUINEA
GABON
CONGO
SAO TOME & PRINCIPE

C.A.R.   ETHIOPIA

SOMALIA

SRI LANKA

MALDIVES

SINGAPORE

BRUNEI

MALAYSIA

PALAU

INDONESIA

PAPUA
NEW
GUINE

UGANDA
KENYA
RWANDA
BURUNDI

DEM. REP.
CONGO

TANZANIA

SEYCHELLES

COMOROS
MAYOTTE (to France)

EAST TIMOR

ATLANTIC
OCEAN

ANGOLA

ZAMBIA
MALAWI
MOZAMBIQUE
MADAGASCAR

MAURITIUS
REUNION (to France)

INDIAN
OCEAN

AUSTRALIA

NAMIBIA   ZIMB.
BOTS.
SWAZILAND
LESOTHO
SOUTH
AFRICA

Majority Religions

◎	Protestant Christianity
◎	Catholic Christianity
◎	Orthodox Christianity
◎	Shi'a Islam
◎	Sunni Islam
◎	Hinduism
◎	Judaism
◎	Theravada Buddhism
◎	Mahayana Buddhism
◎	Tibetan Buddhism
◎	Other
◎	Marxism / Maoism

State Policy

▲	Secular ideologies governing
●	Communist states during 20th century
■	Non-pluralist states

ANTARCTICA
(uninhabited)

A	B	C	D

The Global Economy

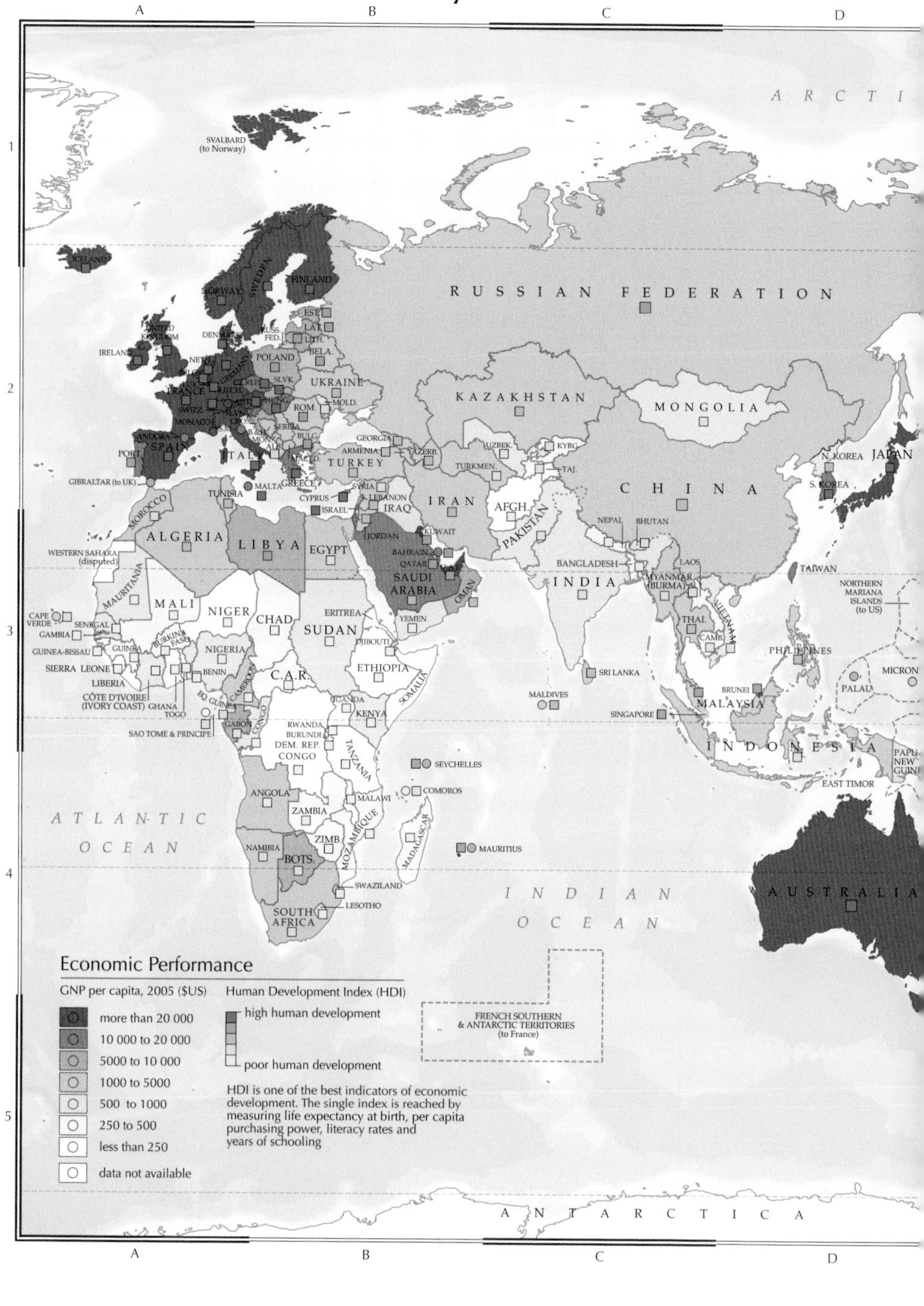

A
B
C
D
1
2
3
4
5
ARCTI
SVALBARD (to Norway)
ICELAND
NORWAY
SWEDEN
FINLAND
RUSSIAN FEDERATION
EST.
LAT.
LITH.
RUSS. FED.
BELA.
UNITED KINGDOM
DENMARK
IRELAND
NETH.
POLAND
UKRAINE
FRANCE
SLVK.
MOLD.
ROM.
SWITZ.
MONACO
ANDORRA
SPAIN
PORT.
SERBIA
BULG.
ITALY
ALB.
GREECE
GIBRALTAR (to UK)
MALTA
GEORGIA
ARMENIA
AZERB.
TURKEY
CYPRUS
SYRIA
LEBANON
ISRAEL
IRAQ
IRAN
JORDAN
KUWAIT
BAHRAIN
QATAR
SAUDI ARABIA
OMAN
YEMEN
KAZAKHSTAN
UZBEK.
KYRG.
TURKMEN.
TAJ.
AFGH.
PAKISTAN
MONGOLIA
CHINA
N. KOREA
S. KOREA
JAPAN
NEPAL
BHUTAN
BANGLADESH
INDIA
LAOS
MYANMAR (BURMA)
THAI.
VIETNAM
CAMB.
TAIWAN
NORTHERN MARIANA ISLANDS (to US)
PHILIPPINES
MICRON
PALAU
SRI LANKA
MALDIVES
BRUNEI
MALAYSIA
SINGAPORE
INDONESIA
PAPUA NEW GUINEA
EAST TIMOR
AUSTRALIA
TUNISIA
MOROCCO
ALGERIA
LIBYA
EGYPT
WESTERN SAHARA (disputed)
MAURITANIA
MALI
NIGER
CHAD
SUDAN
ERITREA
DJIBOUTI
ETHIOPIA
SOMALIA
CAPE VERDE
SENEGAL
GAMBIA
GUINEA-BISSAU
GUINEA
BURKINA FASO
NIGERIA
SIERRA LEONE
LIBERIA
CÔTE D'IVOIRE (IVORY COAST)
GHANA
TOGO
BENIN
C.A.R.
CAMEROON
EQ. GUINEA
GABON
CONGO
SAO TOME & PRINCIPE
UGANDA
KENYA
RWANDA
BURUNDI
DEM. REP. CONGO
TANZANIA
SEYCHELLES
COMOROS
ANGOLA
ZAMBIA
MALAWI
MOZAMBIQUE
ZIMB.
MADAGASCAR
MAURITIUS
NAMIBIA
BOTS.
SWAZILAND
LESOTHO
SOUTH AFRICA
ATLANTIC OCEAN
INDIAN OCEAN
FRENCH SOUTHERN & ANTARCTIC TERRITORIES (to France)
ANTARCTICA
Economic Performance
GNP per capita, 2005 ($US)
more than 20 000
10 000 to 20 000
5000 to 10 000
1000 to 5000
500 to 1000
250 to 500
less than 250
data not available
Human Development Index (HDI)
high human development
poor human development
HDI is one of the best indicators of economic development. The single index is reached by measuring life expectancy at birth, per capita purchasing power, literacy rates and years of schooling

E   F   G   H

OCEAN

GREENLAND
(to Denmark)

1

Arctic Circle

*Alaska
(to US)*

PACIFIC

OCEAN

C A N A D A

2

UNITED STATES
OF AMERICA

ATLANTIC

OCEAN

BERMUDA
(to UK)

*Hawai'i
(to US)*

M
E
X
I
C
O

PUERTO RICO
(to US)

ST KITTS & NEVIS

DOM. REP.

TURKS & CAICOS ISLANDS
(to UK)

ANTIGUA & BAR.

Tropic of Cancer

CAYMAN ISLANDS
(to UK)

BAHAMAS

GUADELOUPE (to France)

HONDURAS

CUBA

DOMINICA

BELIZE

MARTINIQUE (to France)

MARSHALL
ISLANDS

JAMAICA

HAITI

ST LUCIA

GUATEMALA

NETH. ANT.
(to Neth.)

BARBADOS

EL SALVADOR

ARUBA
(to Neth.)

ST VINCENT &
THE GRENADINES

3

NICARAGUA

GRENADA

COSTA RICA

TRINIDAD & TOBAGO

K I R I B A T I

PANAMA

VENEZUELA

FRENCH GUIANA
(to France)

NAURU

COLOMBIA

Equator

TUVALU

ECUADOR

GUYANA

SURINAME

TOKELAU
(to NZ)

OLOMON
SLANDS

SAMOA

COOK
ISLANDS
(to NZ)

P
E
R
U

B R A Z I L

VANUATU

TONGA

NEW
EDONIA
o France)

FIJI

FRENCH POLYNESIA
(to France)

BOLIVIA

PARAGUAY

Tropic of Capricorn

PITCAIRN
ISLANDS
(to UK)

CHILE

4

A
R
G
E
N
T
I
N
A

URUGUAY

NEW
ZEALAND

PACIFIC

OCEAN

CHILE

FALKLAND ISLANDS
(to UK)

5

Antarctic Circle

ANTARCTICA

E   F   G   H

Global Conflict

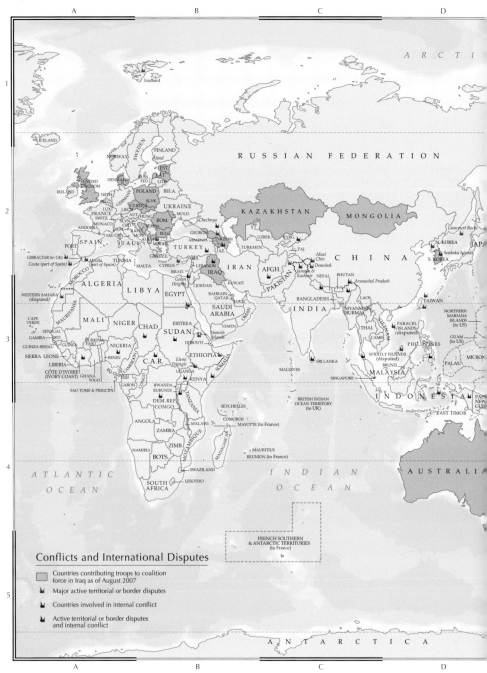

Conflicts and International Disputes

- Countries contributing troops to coalition force in Iraq as of August 2007
- Major active territorial or border disputes
- Countries involved in internal conflict
- Active territorial or border disputes and internal conflict

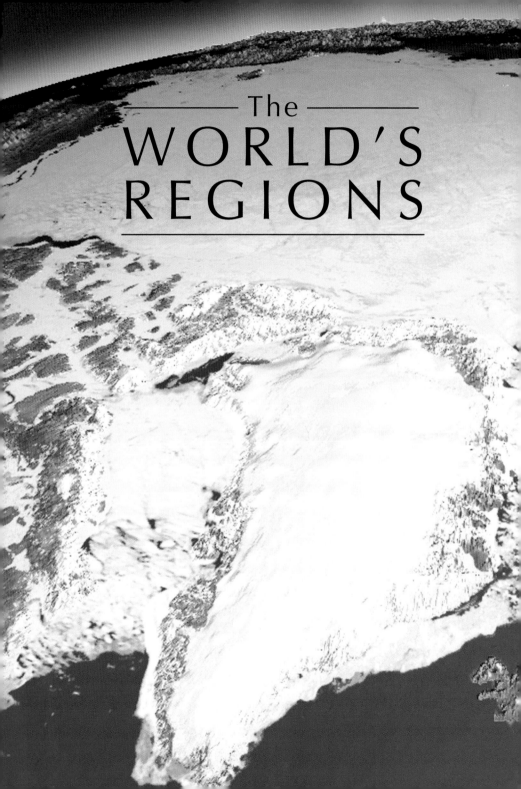

The
WORLD'S
REGIONS

North & Central America

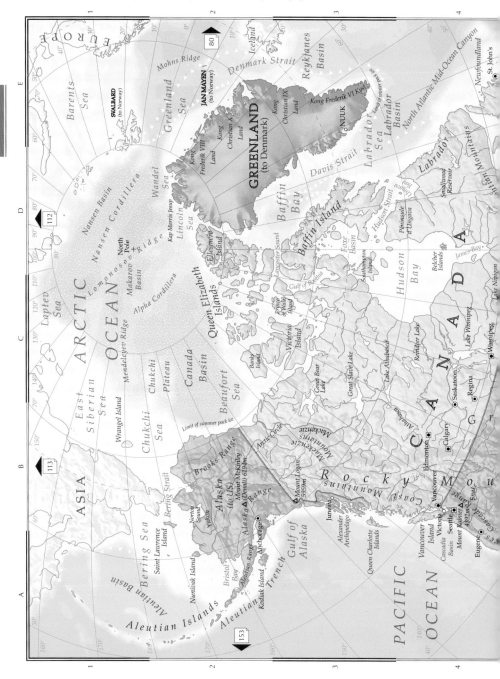

0 km		1000
0 miles		1000

Population • National capital

○ below 50,000   ○ 50,000 to 100,000   ◉ 100,000 to 500,000   ■ above 500,000

ATLANTIC

OCEAN

Sargasso Sea

Nares Plain

Bermuda Rise

Hatteras plain

Tropic of Cancer

BERMUDA
(to UK)

VIRGIN ISLANDS (to US)
BRITISH VIRGIN ISLANDS (to UK)
ANGUILLA (to UK)
ANTIGUA &
BARBUDA
GUADELOUPE
(to France)
DOMINICA
Lesser
MARTINIQUE (to France)
Antilles
ST LUCIA
BARBADOS
ST VINCENT &
THE GRENADINES
GRENADA
TRINIDAD
& TOBAGO

66

Equator

PORT-OF-SPAIN

TURKS & CAICOS
ISLANDS
(to UK)
PUERTO
RICO
(to US)
ST KITTS & NEVIS
MONTSERRAT (to UK)

NETHERLANDS
ANTILLES
(to Neth.)

ARUBA
(to Neth.)

BAHAMAS
NASSAU

SANTO
DOMINGO
DOMINICAN
REPUBLIC
HAITI
PORT-AU-PRINCE

Greater Antilles

HAVANA

CUBA

Straits of Florida

Blake
Plateau

Jacksonville

Columbia

Raleigh

Richmond
WASHINGTON D.C.
Baltimore
Philadelphia
New York
Albany
Boston
Cape Cod
Georges
Bank
Halifax
(to France)

Appalachian Mountains

Great Lakes

Montreal
OTTAWA
Lake Ontario
Toronto
Niagara
Falls
Lake Erie
Detroit
Cleveland
Columbus
Ohio

Lake Huron

Lake
Michigan

Milwaukee
Chicago
Lansing

Madison

Saint Paul

UNITED STATES

OF AMERICA

Des Moines
Lincoln

Missouri

Kansas City
Oklahoma City

Indianapolis
Springfield
St Louis
Mississippi
Memphis
Little Rock
Arkansas
Red River

Nashville
Atlanta
Montgomery
Jackson
Baton Rouge
New Orleans

*Mississippi
Delta*

Tampa

Miami

SOUTH

AMERICA

Andes

56

CAYMAN
ISLANDS
(to UK)

Guantanamo Bay (to US)

JAMAICA
Kingston

Caribbean Sea

*Colombian
Basin*

PANAMA CITY

PANAMA

COSTA RICA

SAN JOSÉ

Lake Nicaragua
MANAGUA
NICARAGUA
TEGUCIGALPA
HONDURAS
BELIZE
BELMOPAN
*Yucatan
Peninsula*
GUATEMALA
GUATEMALA CITY
SAN SALVADOR
EL SALVADOR

Cocos Ridge

*Panama
Basin*

153

PANAMA

Colón Ridge

Galapagos Islands
(to Ecuador)

*Guatemala
Basin*

Middle America Trench

Acapulco

MEXICO

*Volcán
Pico de Orizaba
5700m*

MEXICO CITY

Gulf of Mexico

Houston
Austin
San Antonio

Dallas

Monterrey

Rio Grande

El Paso

Sierra Madre Oriental

Guadalajara

Sierra Madre Occidental

Phoenix

Colorado

*Grand
Canyon*

Denver

Salt Lake City

PACIFIC

OCEAN

East Pacific Rise

153

Clarion Fracture Zone

Tropic of Cancer

Revillagigedo
Islands
(to Mexico)

CLIPPERTON ISLAND
(to French Polynesia)

153

*Gallego
Rise*

Equator

N

Lower California

Gulf of California

San Diego

Los Angeles

San Jose
San Francisco

*Coast
Ranges*

Death
Valley
-86m

Mount Whitney
4418m

Great Basin

Murray Fracture Zone

35

Western Canada & Alaska

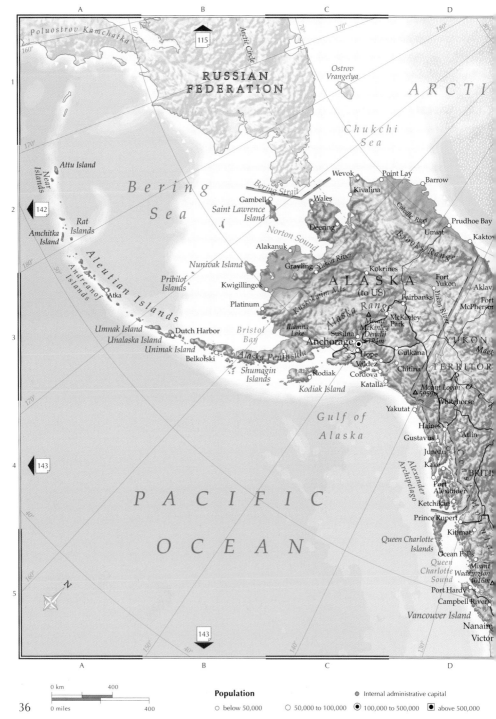

Poluostrov Kamchatka

115

Arctic Circle

RUSSIAN FEDERATION

Ostrov Vrangelya

A R C T I

Chukchi Sea

Wevok
Point Lay
Barrow

Bering Strait

Kivalina

Wales

Near Islands

Attu Island

Gambell

Saint Lawrence Island

Deering

Umiat

Prudhoe Bay

Kaktov

142

B e r i n g

S e a

Norton Sound

Colville River

B r o o k s   R a n g e

Rat Islands

Amchitka Island

Alakanuk

Nunivak Island

Grayling

Yukon River

Kokrines

A L A S K A

(to US)

Fort Yukon

Aklav

A l e u t i a n   I s l a n d s

Andreanof Islands

Atka

Pribilof Islands

Kwigillingok

Kuskokwim Mts

Fairbanks

Yukon River

Fort McPherson

Platinum

McKinley Park

Umnak Island

Unalaska Island

Dutch Harbor

Bristol Bay

Iliamna Lake

Alaska Range

Mount McKinley Denali 6194m

Susitna

Anchorage

Y U K O N

Mack

Unimak Island

Belkofski

Alaska Peninsula

Hope
Valdez

Gulkana

Chitina

T E R R I T O R

Shumagin Islands

Kodiak

Cordova

Katalla

Mount Logan △ 5059m

Whitehorse

Kodiak Island

Yakutat

Gulf of
Alaska

Haines

Gustavus

Atlin

Juneau

Kake

BRITIS

143

Alexander Archipelago

Port Alexander

Ketchikan

Prince Rupert

Kitimat

P A C I F I C

Queen Charlotte Islands

Ocean Falls

Queen Charlotte Sound

Mount Waddington 4016m

O C E A N

Port Hardy

Campbell River

Vancouver Island

Nanaim

Victor

143

N

0 km   400

0 miles   400

Population

○ below 50,000   ○ 50,000 to 100,000   ◉ 100,000 to 500,000   ■ above 500,000

● Internal administrative capital

Alert

Knud Rasmussen Land

GREENLAND
(to Denmark)

Ellesmere Island

Nares Strait

Axel
Heiberg
Island

Queen Elizabeth Islands

Ellef Ringnes
Island
Isachsen

Amund
Ringnes
Island

Baffin

Bay

Prince Patrick
Island

Mould Bay

Badhurst
Island Cornwallis
Island

Devon Island

Arctic Circle

OCEAN

Melville
Island

Resolute
(Qausuittuq)

Lancaster Sound

Davis Strait

82

Banks
Island

Viscount Melville
Sound

Prince of
Wales Island

Somerset
Island

Bylot
Island

Baffin Island

Cumberland Sound

aufort
Sea

chs Harbour

McClintock Channel

Boothia
Peninsula

Gulf of Boothia

Igloolik

Nettilling
Lake

Iqaluit

ktoyaktuk Amundsen
Gulf

Holman

Victoria
Island

Burnside

King William
Island

Pelly Bay

Melville
Peninsula

Foxe
Basin

Amadjuak
Lake

Paulatuk

ik

Fort
Good Hope

Kugluktuk

Cambridge Bay

Gjoa Haven

Repulse Bay

Southampton
Island

Hudson Strait

Mackenzie

Great
Bear
Lake

Echo Bay

Back

NUNAVUT

Garry Lake

Baker Lake

Coral
Harbour

Péninsule
d'Ungava

NORTHWEST
TERRITORIES

Edzo

Yellowknife

Reliance

Rankin Inlet

Whale Cove

Coats
Island

Mansel
Island

QUÉBEC

sten

Fort Simpson

Great Slave
Lake

Lutselk'e

Dubawnt

Arviat

Hudson

Fort Providence
Fort Liard

Hay River

Fort Smith

Lake Athabasca

Churchill

Bay

Fort Nelson

Belcher
Islands

38

LUMBIA

Fort Vermilion

Wollaston Lake

Reindeer Lake

Southern
Indian Lake

Nelson

James
Bay

C

A

Fort St. John

ALBERTA

Grande Prairie

Fort
McMurray

Buffalo
Narrows

SASKATCHEWAN

N

Lynn Lake

Flin Flon

A

Thompson

D

The Pas

Lake
Winnipeg

A

ONTARIO

Prince George

Athabasca

Athabasca

North Saskatchewan

Saskatchewan

Edmonton

Mount Robson
3954m

Leduc

Prince Albert

Saskatoon

MANITOBA

Red Deer

Kamloops

Calgary

Kindersley

Yorkton

Qu'Appelle

Lake
Manitoba

Winnipeg

Lake of the
Woods

Lake Superior

Lake
Huron

Kelowna

Medicine Hat

Regina

Brandon

ncouver

Cranbrook

Lethbridge

Weyburn

Melita

Lake
Michigan

Milk River

Estevan

45

UNITED STATES OF AMERICA

Elevation

| -4000m | -3000m | -2000m | -1000m | -500m | Below sea level | 0 | 100m | 250m | 500m | 1000m | 2000m | 4000m |

| -13,124ft | -9843ft | -6562ft | -3281ft | -1640ft | -820ft/-250m | 0 | 328ft | 820ft | 1640ft | 3281ft | 6562ft | 13,124ft |

Eastern Canada

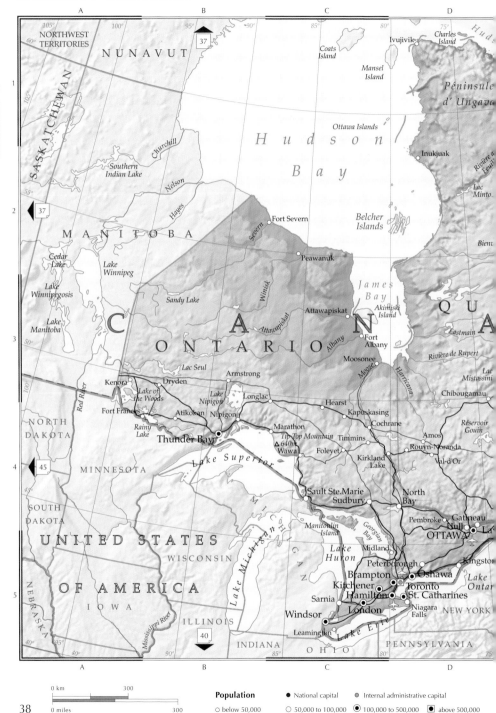

NORTHWEST TERRITORIES

NUNAVUT

SASKATCHEWAN

MANITOBA

Charles Island

Ivujivik

Coats Island

Mansel Island

Péninsule d' Ungava

Hudson Bay

Ottawa Islands

Inukjuak

Churchill

Southern Indian Lake

Nelson

Hayes

Severn

Fort Severn

Belcher Islands

Rivière à Feuilk

Lac Minto

Cedar Lake

Lake Winnipeg

Peawanuk

Winisk

James Bay

Bien

Lake Winnipegosis

Sandy Lake

Attawapiskat

Akimiski Island

QU

Lake Manitoba

CANADA

ONTARIO

Attawapiskat

Albany

Fort Albany

Moosonee

Eastmain

A

Lac Seul

Armstrong

Moose

Rivière de Rupert

Lac Mistassini

Kenora

Dryden

Lake Nipigon

Longlac

Hearst

Harricana

Chibougamau

Fort Frances

Lake of the Woods

Atikokan

Nipigon

Kapuskasing

Cochrane

Réservoir Gouin

NORTH DAKOTA

Rainy Lake

Thunder Bay

Marathon

Tip Top Mountain

△640m

Wawa

Timmins

Foleyet

Kirkland Lake

Amos

Rouyn-Noranda

Val-d'Or

Red River

Lake Superior

MINNESOTA

Sault Ste.Marie

Sudbury

North Bay

Pembroke

Gatineau

Null

La

SOUTH DAKOTA

MICHIGAN

Manitoulin Island

Georgian Bay

OTTAWA

NEBRASKA

UNITED STATES

WISCONSIN

Lake Huron

Midland

Peterborough

Kingston

Lake Ontar

OF AMERICA

IOWA

Lake Michigan

Brampton

Kitchener

Hamilton

Sarnia

London

Oshawa

Toronto

St. Catharines

Niagara Falls

NEW YORK

Mississippi River

ILLINOIS

40

Windsor

Leamington

Lake Erie

INDIANA

OHIO

PENNSYLVANIA

37

37

45

0 km 300

0 miles 300

Population ● National capital ◉ Internal administrative capital

○ below 50,000 ○ 50,000 to 100,000 ◉ 100,000 to 500,000 ◼ above 500,000

Baffin Island

Resolution Island

Button Islands

Akpatok Island

Ungava Bay

Kuujjuaq

Riviére a la Baleine

Caniapiscau

trait

Nain

Hopedale
Makkovik
Cape Harrison

Scheffervile

Cartwright

Labrador Sea

NEWFOUNDLAND

Smallwood Reservoir
Lake Melville

Churchill

St.Anthony

& LABRADOR

Réservoir de Caniapiscau

Réservoir Manicouagan

E

D

A

Sept-Îles

Havre-St-Pierre

Île d'Anticosti

Baie-Comeau

Gander

Corner Brook

Grand Falls

St.John's

Newfoundland

Cape Race

Lac Jean

Chicoutimi

juiere

Gaspé

St. Lawrence

Matane

Péninsule de Gaspé

Rimouski

Riviére-du-Loup

Edmundston

Bathurst

Gulf of St. Lawrence

Îles de la Madeleine

Cabot Strait

Channel-Port aux Basques

ST PIERRE & MIQUELON
(to France)

Glace Bay
Sydney

a Tuque

Charlesbourg

Québec

St-Georges

PRINCE EDWARD ISLAND

NEW BRUNSWICK

Moncton

Charlottetown

Cape Breton Island

Trois-Rivières

Drummondville

ontréal

Fredericton

Oromocto

Amherst

New Glasgow

Truro

NOVA SCOTIA

Sherbrooke

MAINE

Saint John

Dartmouth

Halifax

Sable Island

Bay of Fundy

VERMONT

NEW HAMPSHIRE

Liverpool

Yarmouth

ATLANTIC

MASSACHUSETTS

Cape Cod

OCEAN

CONNECTICUT

RHODE ISLAND

N

E   F   G   H

82

66

66

66

Elevation

					Below sea level							
-4000m	-3000m	-2000m	-1000m	-500m		0	100m	250m	500m	1000m	2000m	4000m
-13,124ft	-9843ft	-6562ft	-3281ft	-1640ft	-820ft/-250m	0	328ft	820ft	1640ft	3281ft	6562ft	13,124ft

USA: The Northeast

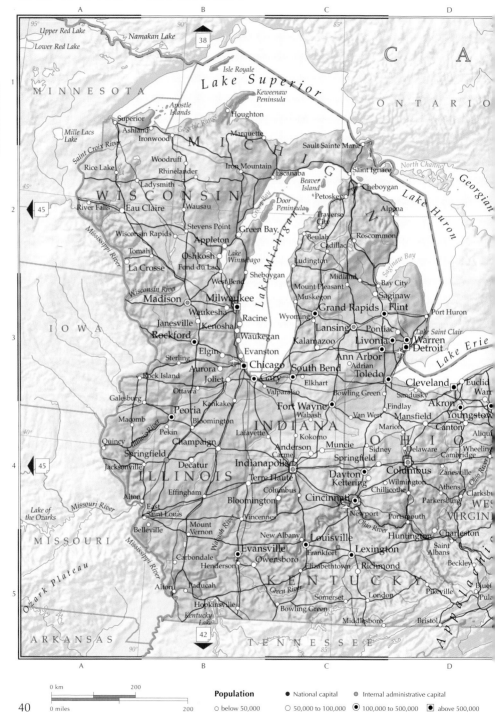

Population

- National capital
- Internal administrative capital
- below 50,000
- 50,000 to 100,000
- 100,000 to 500,000
- above 500,000

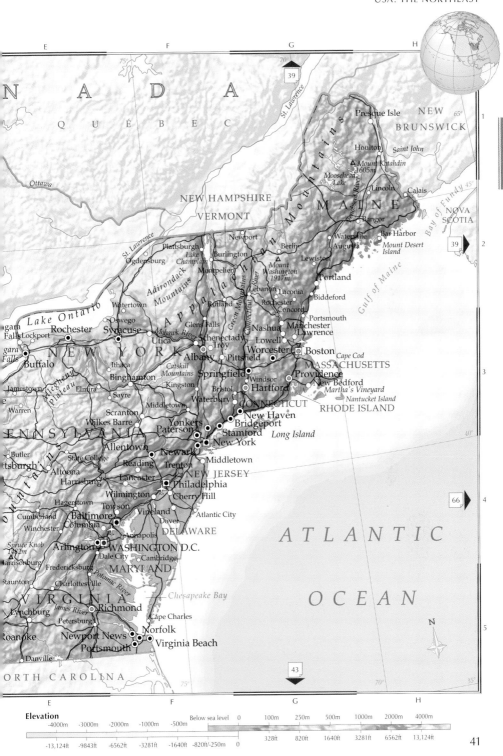

USA: The Southeast

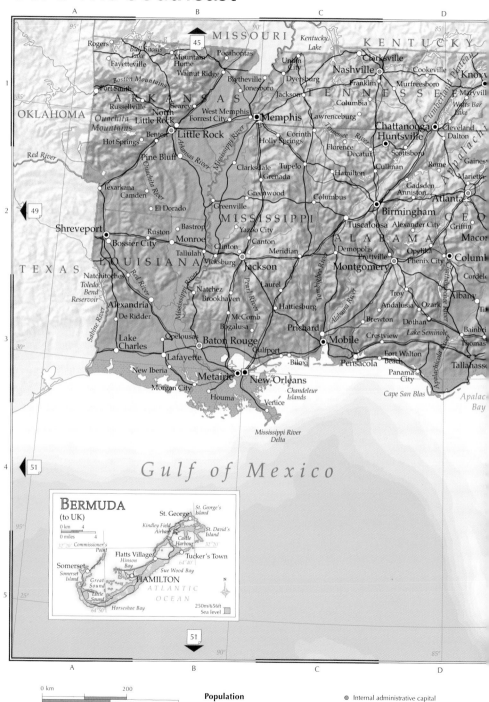

MISSOURI
Kentucky Lake
KENTUCKY

Rogers
Bull Shoals Lake
Mountain Home
Pocahontas
Union City
Clarksville
Cookeville
Knox

Fayetteville
Walnut Ridge
Dyersburg
Nashville
Murfreesboro
Maryvill

Boston Mountains
Blytheville
Jonesboro
Franklin
Columbia
Watts Bar Lake

Fort Smith
West Memphis
Jackson
TENNESSEE
Chattanooga
Cleveland

OKLAHOMA
Russellville
North Little Rock
Forrest City
Memphis
Lawrenceburg
Huntsville
Dalton

Ouachita Mountains
Benton
Little Rock
Holly Springs
Corinth
Florence
Decatur
Scottsboro
Rome
Gaines

Hot Springs
Clarksdale
Tupelo
Cullman
Marietta

Red River
Pine Bluff
Grenada
Hamilton
Gadsden
Anniston
Atlanta

Texarkana
Camden
Greenwood
Columbus
Birmingham
GEO

Shreveport
El Dorado
Greenville
MISSISSIPPI
Tuscaloosa
Alexander City
Griffin
Macor

Bossier City
Ruston
Bastrop
Yazoo City
Demopolis
Opelika
Columb

Monroe
Clinton
Canton
ALABAMA
Prattville
Phenix City

TEXAS
Tallulah
LOUISIANA
Vicksburg
Jackson
Meridian
Montgomery
Cordele

Natchitoches
Natchez
Laurel
Troy
Albany

Toledo Bend Reservoir
Alexandria
Brookhaven
Hattiesburg
Andalusia
Ozark
Ti

De Ridder
McComb
Brewton
Dothan
Bainbri

Lake Charles
Opelousas
Bogalusa
Prichard
Crestview
Lake Seminole
Thomas

Baton Rouge
Gulfport
Mobile
Fort Walton Beach
Tallahasse

Lafayette
Biloxi
Pensacola
Panama City

New Iberia
Metairie
New Orleans
Chandeleur Islands
Cape San Blas
Apalac Bay

Morgan City
Houma
Venice

Mississippi River Delta

Gulf of Mexico

BERMUDA
(to UK)

St. George's Island
St. George
Kindley Field Airbase
St. David's Island
Commissioner's Point
Castle Harbour
Flatts Village
Tucker's Town
Somerset
Hinson Bay
Sue Wood Bay
Somerset Island
Great Sound
HAMILTON
ATLANTIC OCEAN
Little Sound
Horseshoe Bay
250m/656ft
Sea level

0 km 200
0 miles 200

Population

○ below 50,000   ○ 50,000 to 100,000   ◉ 100,000 to 500,000   ■ above 500,000

● Internal administrative capital

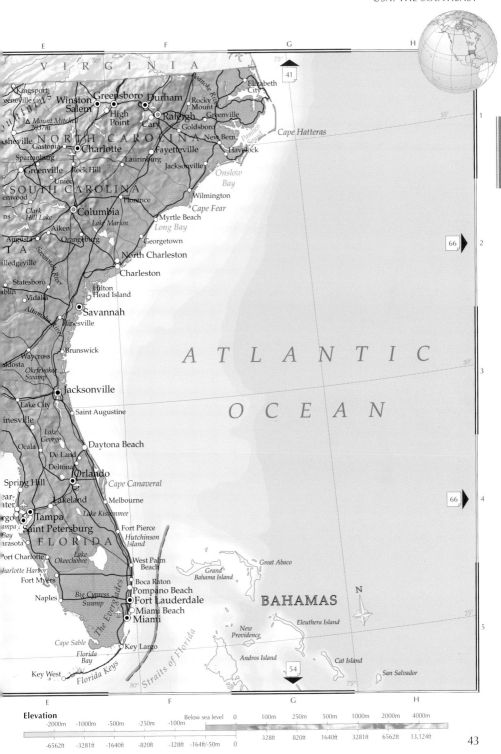

V I R G I N I A

Kingsport
eenville
Winston Greensboro Durham
Salem
High Raleigh Rocky
Point Cary Mount
Mount Mitchel Greenville
2037m N O R T H C A R O L I N A
Goldsboro
sheville Gastonia Charlotte Fayetteville New Bern
Spartanburg Laurinburg Havelock
Greenville Rock Hill Jacksonville
Union
S O U T H C A R O L I N A Wilmington
enwood Florence
Clark Cape Fear
Hill Lake Columbia
Aiken Lake Marion Myrtle Beach
Orangeburg Long Bay
Augusta Georgetown
TA North Charleston
lledgeville
Statesboro Charleston
blin Vidalia Hilton
Head Island
Savannah
linesville
Waycross Brunswick
dosta Okefenokee
Swamp
Jacksonville
Lake City
inesville Saint Augustine
Lake
George Daytona Beach
Ocala De Land
Deltona
Spring Hill Orlando Cape Canaveral
ear- Lakeland Melbourne
ater
rgo Tampa Lake Kissimmee
Saint Petersburg Fort Pierce
Bay F L O R I D A Hutchinson
arasota Island
Port Charlotte Lake
harlotte Harbor Okeechobee West Palm
Fort Myers Beach
Big Cypress Boca Raton
Naples Swamp Pompano Beach
Fort Lauderdale
The Everglades Miami Beach
Miami
Cape Sable
Florida Key Largo
Bay
Key West
Florida Keys Straits of Florida

Elizabeth
City
Cape Hatteras
Pamlico
Sound
Onslow
Bay

A T L A N T I C

O C E A N

BAHAMAS

Grand Great Abaco
Bahama Island

Eleuthera Island

New
Providence

Andros Island Cat Island

San Salvador

35° 1

66 2

30° 3

66 4

25° 5

Elevation

					Below sea level	0	100m	250m	500m	1000m	2000m	4000m
-2000m	-1000m	-500m	-250m	-100m								
-6562ft	-3281ft	-1640ft	-820ft	-328ft	-164ft/-50m	0	328ft	820ft	1640ft	3281ft	6562ft	13,124ft

43

USA: Central States

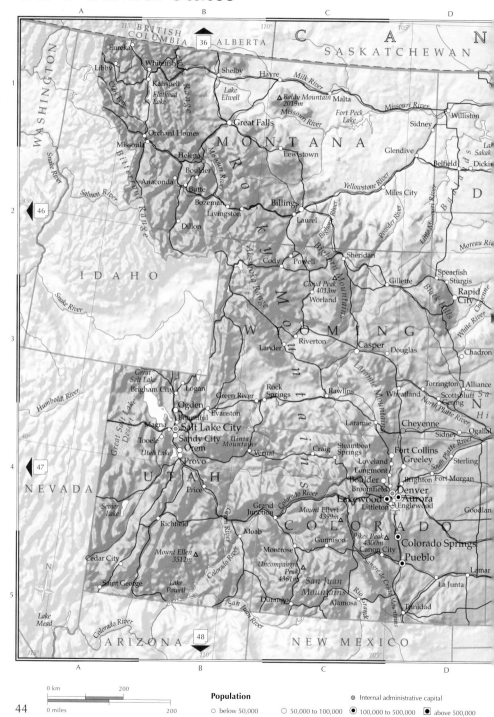

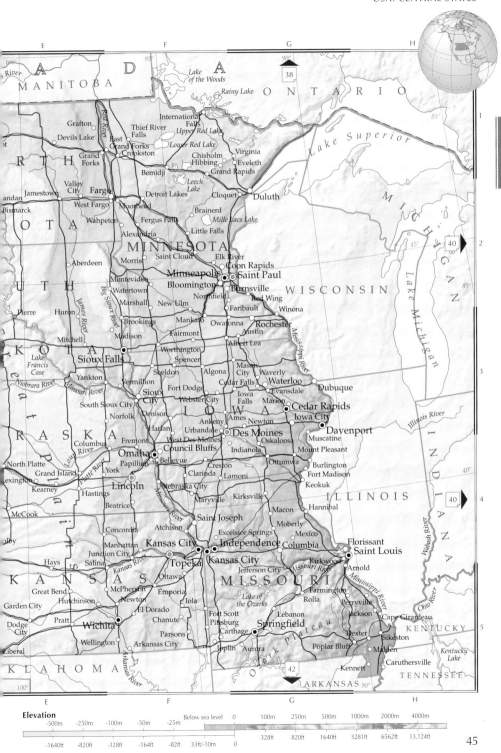

CANADA

MANITOBA

ONTARIO

Lake of the Woods

Rainy Lake

Lake Superior

River

Grafton
Devils Lake
East Grand Forks
Grand Forks
Crookston
Thief River Falls
International Falls
Upper Red Lake
Lower Red Lake
Chisholm
Hibbing
Virginia
Eveleth
Grand Rapids
Bemidji
Leech Lake

NORTH DAKOTA

Jamestown
Valley City
Fargo
West Fargo
Moorhead
Detroit Lakes
Cloquet
Duluth
Brainerd
Mille Lacs Lake
Little Falls

Bismarck
Mandan
Wahpeton
Fergus Falls
Alexandria

MINNESOTA

MICHIGAN

Lake Michigan

WISCONSIN

SOUTH DAKOTA

Aberdeen
Morris
Saint Cloud
Elk River
Coon Rapids
Minneapolis
Saint Paul
Montevideo
Bloomington
Burnsville
Watertown
Northfield
Red Wing
Marshall
New Ulm
Faribault
Winona

Pierre
Huron
Brookings
Mankato
Owatonna
Rochester
Madison
Fairmont
Austin
Mitchell
Worthington
Albert Lea

Big Sioux River
James River

Lake Francis Case
Niobrara River
Missouri River

Sioux Falls

Yankton
Vermillion
Sheldon
Spencer
Mason City
Waverly
Algona
Cedar Falls
Waterloo
Dubuque
Fort Dodge
Evansdale
South Sioux City
Sioux City
Webster City
Iowa Falls
Marion
Cedar Rapids
Norfolk
Denison
Ames
Newton
Iowa City
Davenport
Harlan
Urbandale
Ankeny
Muscatine

NEBRASKA

IOWA

ILLINOIS

Illinois River

INDIANA

Columbus
Fremont
West Des Moines
Des Moines
Oskaloosa
Mount Pleasant
Loup River
Omaha
Council Bluffs
Indianola
Burlington
North Platte
Papillion
Bellevue
Creston
Ottumwa
Fort Madison
Grand Island
York
Clarinda
Lamoni
Keokuk
Lexington
Kearney
Lincoln
Nebraska City
Hastings
Beatrice
Maryville
Kirksville
Macon
Hannibal
McCook
Platte River
Concordia
Atchison
Saint Joseph
Moberly
Mexico

KANSAS

MISSOURI

Excelsior Springs
Columbia
Florissant
Saint Louis
Manhattan
Kansas City
Independence
Junction City
Topeka
Kansas City
Kirkwood
Arnold
Hays
Salina
Ottawa
Jefferson City
Great Bend
McPherson
Emporia
Farmington
Garden City
Hutchinson
Newton
Iola
Lake of the Ozarks
Rolla
Perryville
Dodge City
Pratt
El Dorado
Chanute
Fort Scott
Pittsburg
Lebanon
Jackson
Cape Girardeau
Wichita
Parsons
Carthage
Springfield
Dexter
Sikeston
Liberal
Wellington
Arkansas City
Joplin
Aurora
Poplar Bluff
Malden
Caruthersville

Kansas River
Arkansas River
Missouri River
Mississippi River
Ozark Plateau

Wabash River
Ohio River

KENTUCKY
Kentucky Lake

TENNESSEE

OKLAHOMA
ARKANSAS

Elevation

					Below sea level	0	100m	250m	500m	1000m	2000m	4000m
-500m	-250m	-100m	-50m	-25m								
-1640ft	-820ft	-328ft	-164ft	-82ft	33ft/-10m	0	328ft	820ft	1640ft	3281ft	6562ft	13,124ft

USA: The West

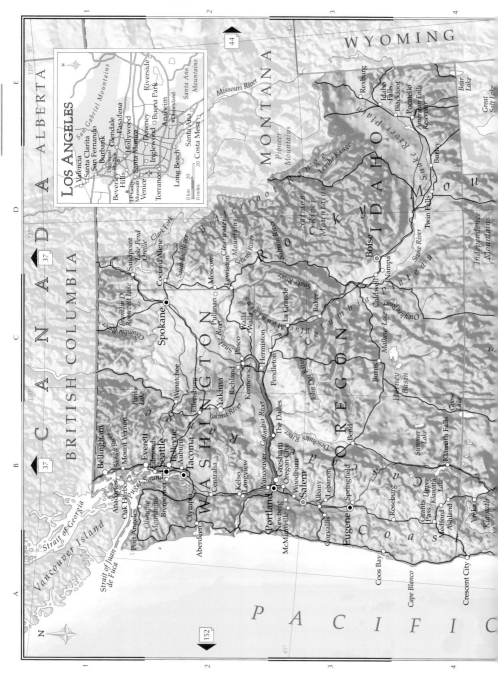

LOS ANGELES

Valencia · Santa Clarita · San Fernando · Burbank · Pasadena · Glendale · Hollywood · San Gabriel Mountains · Riverside · Santa Ana Mountains · Beverley Hills · Santa Monica · Venice · Downey · Inglewood · Buena Park · Disneyland · Anaheim · Torrance · Long Beach · Santa Ana · Costa Mesa

0 km 20
0 miles 20

WYOMING

MONTANA
Pioneer Mountains

ALBERTA
CANADA
BRITISH COLUMBIA

Missouri River

Rexburg · Idaho Falls · Blackfoot · Pocatello · American Falls Reservoir · Burley · Twin Falls · Bear Lake · Great Salt Lake

IDAHO
Boise · Nampa · Caldwell · Snake River Plain · Salmon River · Lemhi Range · Independence Mountains

R O C K Y   M o u n t a i n s

Sandpoint · Lake Pend Oreille · Clark Fork · Franklin D. Roosevelt Lake · Columbia River

Coeur d'Alene · Spokane · Moscow · Pullman · Lewiston · Clearwater Mountains · Selway River · Salmon River · Snake River · La Grande · Baker · Columbia Plateau · Malheur Lake · Owyhee River

WASHINGTON
Wenatchee · Ellensburg · Yakima · Yakima River · Richland · Kennewick · Pasco · Walla Walla · Hermiston · Pendleton · Blue Mountains · John Day River

Bellingham · Mount Vernon · Everett · Edmonds · Seattle · Bellevue · Tacoma · Auburn · Olympia · Bremerton · Centralia · Kelso · Longview · Vancouver · Gresham · Oregon City · Portland · Newberg · Woodburn · Salem · McMinnville · Albany · Lebanon · Springfield · Eugene

Anacortes · Oak Harbor · Port Angeles · Aberdeen · Corvallis

OREGON
Columbia River · Deschutes River · The Dalles · Bend · Burns · Harney Basin · Goose Lake · Summer Lake · Klamath Falls · Upper Klamath Lake · Roseburg · Grants Pass · Medford · Ashland · Yreka · Klamath

Olympia Mountains · Puget Sound · Skagit River · Skykomish River

Vancouver Island · Strait of Georgia · Strait of Juan de Fuca

Coos Bay · Cape Blanco · Crescent City

P A C I F I C

N

0 km 200
0 miles 200

Population

○ below 50,000
○ 50,000 to 100,000
◉ 100,000 to 500,000
■ above 500,000

● Internal administrative capital

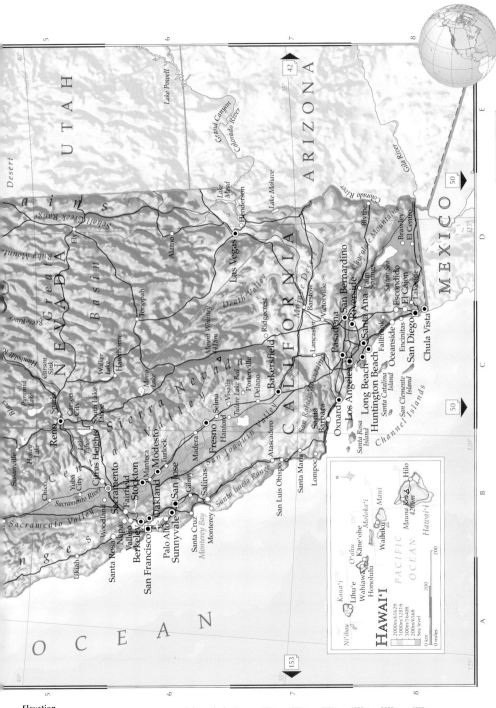

Elevation

-4000m	-3000m	-2000m	-1000m	-500m	Below sea level	0	100m	250m	500m	1000m	2000m	4000m
-13,124ft	-9843ft	-6562ft	-3281ft	-1640ft	-820ft/-250m	0	328ft	820ft	1640ft	3281ft	6562ft	13,124ft

47

USA: The Southwest

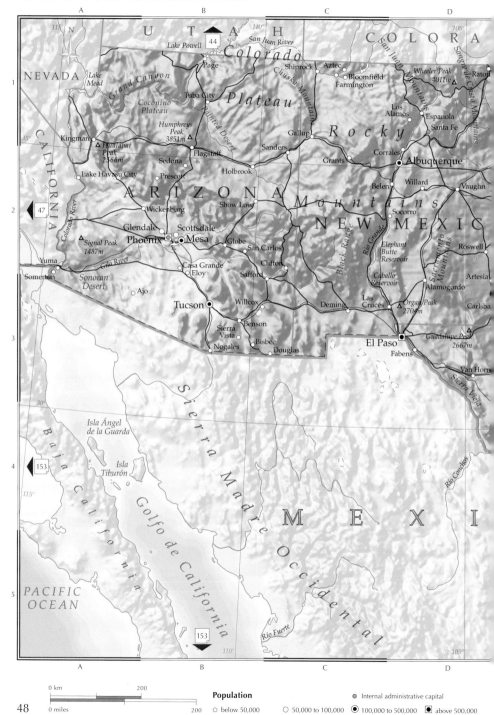

0 km   200

0 miles   200

Population

○ below 50,000   ○ 50,000 to 100,000   ◉ 100,000 to 500,000   ◼ above 500,000

● Internal administrative capital

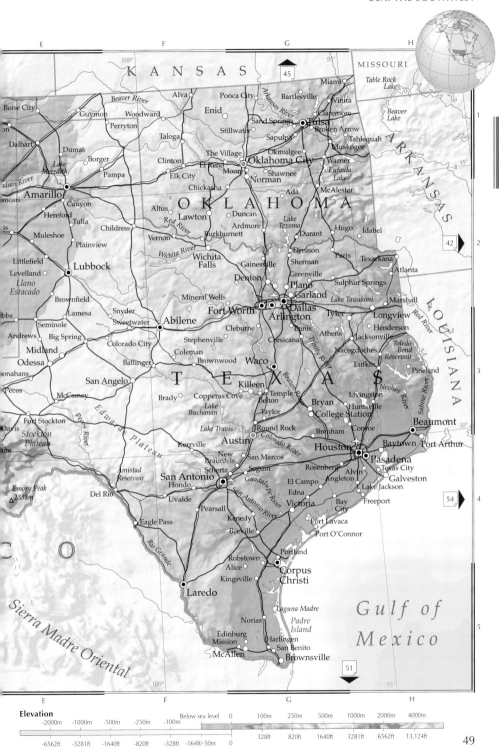

Mexico

NEW MEXICO

48

ARIZONA

UNITED STATES O

Tijuana
Mexicali
Rosarito
San Luis
Ensenada

Ciudad Juárez

Colorado River

Desierto de Altar

Pecos River

Nogales

Agua Prieta

Samalayuca

Rio Grande
Río Bravo
del Norte

Caborca

Cananea

Magdalena

Nuevo
Casas Grandes

El Sueco

Ojinaga

Villa Acu

Sierra San
Pedro Mártir

Cumpas

San Pedro
de la Cueva

El Sáuz

San Miguel

Boquillas

Nueva Ros

Hermosillo

San Francisco
del Oro

Delicias
Ciudad Camargo

Sabi

Isla Ángel
de la Guarda

Isla
Tiburón

Cuauhtémoc

Monclo

Bahía Sebastián Vizcaíno

Chihuahua

Jiménez

Isla Cedros

Guaymas

Empalme

Hidalgo del Parral

Santa Barbara

Guerrero Negro

Esperanza

Gómez Palacio

San Pec

San Ignacio

Ciudad
Obregón

Navojoá

San Blas

Torreón
Ciudad Lerdo

Parr

Matamoros

Huatabampo

Los Mochis

M   E   X

Loreto

Guasave
Guamúchil

Culiacán

Miguel Asua

Juan Aldar

Isla Magdalena

Navolato

Río Gra

Isla Santa Margarita

Bahía
de La
Paz

El Dorado

Durango

Fresnillo

La Paz

Mazatlán

Zacatecas

Guadalupe

Santa Genoveva
2406m

Miraflores

Escuinapa

Villanueva

Aguascalientes

Acaponeta

Jalpa

Isla San
Juanito

Tuxpan

Lagos de More

Tepic

Yahualica

Isla MaríaMadre

Guadalajara

Isla María Magdalena

Tequila

Isla María
Cleofas

Puerto Vallarta

Tlaquepaque

Zamora de Hidal

Ciudad Guzmán

Colima

Manzanillo

Tecomán

Zapo

Tuxpa

Agu

Isla San Benedicto

Lázaro Cárde

Isla Roca Partida

Isla Socorro

Isla Clarión

Islas Revillagigedo
(to Mexico)

PACIFIC OCEAN

153

0 km   300
0 miles   300

Population   ● National capital

○ below 50,000   ○ 50,000 to 100,000   ◉ 100,000 to 500,000   ◼ above 500,000

ALABAMA
FLORIDA

42

MISSISSIPPI

LOUISIANA

MERICA

X A S

Colorado River

Mississippi River
Delta

66

edras Negras

Río Grande

Nuevo Laredo

Padre Island

Gulf of

Sabinas
Hidalgo

Ciudad
Miguel Alemán

Mexico

Reynosa

Río
Bravo

Matamoros

Monterrey

Montemorelos

Laguna Madre

Linares

illo

Yucatan Channel

Sierra Madre Oriental

Ciudad Victoria

Tropic of Cancer

Río Lagartos

Cancún

Ciudad
Mante

Progreso

Tizimín

Isla
Cozumel

Luis
osí

Ciudad Madero

Motul

Mérida

Umán

Valladolid

Pánuco

Tampico

Ticul

Peto

Ciudad Valles

Laguna de Tamiahua

Tekax

Oxkutzcab

Verde

Felipe Carrillo
Puerto

Dolores

Tamazunchale

Bahía de Campeche

Campeche

Yucatan
Peninsula

Hidalgo

Tuxpán

Guanajuato

Poza Rica

Champotón

Chetumal

Querétaro

Papantla

raputo

Tulancingo

Laguna de
Términos

52

melia MÉXICO

Teziutlán

Pachuca

Xalapa

Frontera

Fransisco Escárcega

MEXICO CITY

Perote

Veracruz

Carmen

apan Cuernavaca

Tlaxcala

Alvarado

Comalcalco

Villahermosa

BELIZE

Toluca

Puebla

Córdoba

Coatzacoalcos

Macuspana

Zacatepec

5452m

Popocatepetl

San

Río Usumacinta

Gulf of Honduras

esa del
iernillo

Taxco

Cuautla

Tehuacán

Andrés

Minatitlán

Teapa

San Cristóbal

Balsas

Iguala

Ixtepec

Tuxtla

de Las Casas

Sierra

Huajuapan

Istmo de

Ocozocuautla

Chiapa de

Comitán

Madre del Sur

Chilpancingo

Oaxaca

Tehuantepec

Tuxtla

Corzo

Tecpan

Ixtepec

Matías Romero

apa

Pinotepa
Nacional

Tehuantepec

Juchitán

Arriaga

Presa de la
Angostura

Acapulco

Miahuatlán

Salina Cruz

Pijijiapán

GUATEMALA

HONDURAS

Puerto
Escondido

Puerto
Angel

Golfo de
Tehuantepec

Escuintla

Huixtla

Tapachula

Ciudad Hidalgo

EL SALVADOR

153

Elevation

| -4000m | -3000m | -2000m | -1000m | -500m | Below sea level | 0 | 100m | 250m | 500m | 1000m | 2000m | 4000m |

| -13,124ft | -9843ft | -6562ft | -3281ft | -1640ft | -820ft/-250m | 0 | 328ft | 820ft | 1640ft | 3281ft | 6562ft | 13,124ft |

Central America

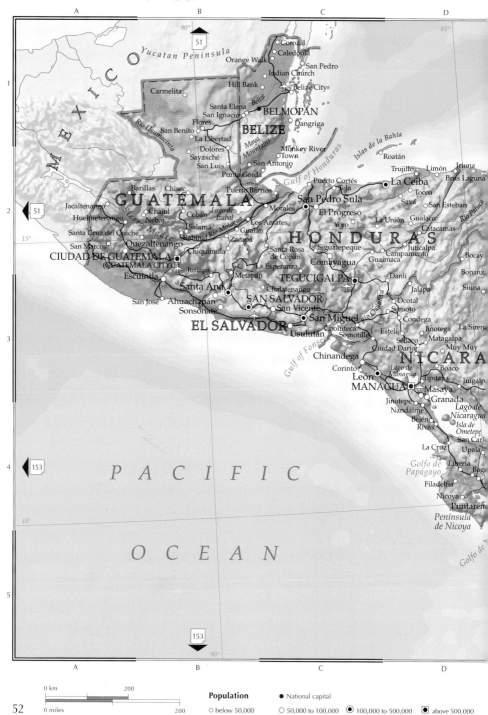

51

90°

85°

MEXICO

Yucatan Peninsula

Corozal
Caledonia
Orange Walk
San Pedro
Indian Church
Hill Bank
Belize City
Carmelita
Santa Elena
San Ignacio
Flores
San Benito
BELMOPAN
BELIZE
La Libertad
Dangriga
Dolores
Sayaxché
San Luis
Monkey River
Town
San Antonio
Punta Gorda
Islas de la Bahía
Roatán

Maya
Mountains

Río Usumacinta

Barillas
Chisec
Puerto Barrios
Puerto Cortés
Trujillo
Limón
Iriona
Tela
La Ceiba
Brus Laguna
GUATEMALA
San Pedro Sula
Tocoa
Jacaltenango
Chajul
Lago de
Izabal
Morales
El Progreso
Savá
San Esteban
Huehuetenango
Coban
Nebaj
Los Amates
Yoro
La Unión
Gualaco
Catacamas
Santa Cruz del Quiché
Salamá
Rabinal
Guatán
Río Patuca
San Marcos
Quezaltenango
Chiquimula
Zacapa
Siguatepeque
Juticalpa
Bocay
CIUDAD DE GUATEMALA
Chiquimula
Santa Rosa
de Copán
Comayagua
Campamento
Bonanza
(GUATEMALA CITY)
Jutiapa
La Esperanza
Guaimaca
Escuintla
Metapán
TEGUCIGALPA
Danlí
Siuna
Santa Ana
Chalatenango
Jalapa
San Jose
Ahuachapán
SAN SALVADOR
Somoto
Sonsonate
San Vicente
Condega
EL SALVADOR
San Miguel
Choluteca
Estelí
Jinotega
La Siren
Usulután
Somotillo
Sébaco
Matagalpa
Chinandega
Ciudad Darío
Muy Muy
Corinto
NICARA
Lago de
Managua
Boaco
León
Tipitapa
Juigalp
MANAGUA
Masaya
Jinotepe
Granada
Nandaime
Lago de
Nicaragua
Belén
Isla de
Ometepe
Rivas
San Carl
La Cruz
Upala
Golfo de
Papagayo
Liberia
Bag
Filadelfia
Nicoya
Puntaren
Península
de Nicoya
Golfo de

Sierra Madre

Río Motagua

HONDURAS

Gulf of Honduras

Gulf of Fonseca

Río Coco

Río Choluteca

PACIFIC

15°

10°

OCEAN

153

51

153

90°

| A | B | C | D |

0 km   200

0 miles   200

Population   ● National capital

○ below 50,000   ○ 50,000 to 100,000   ◉ 100,000 to 500,000   ◼ above 500,000

E   F   G   H

N

54

1

Bajo Nuevo
(to Colombia)

Cayo de Serranilla
(to Colombia)

15°

s Santilla
Honduras)

na de Caratasca
Puerto Lempira

Coco

55

75°

2

Cayo de Serrana
(to Colombia)

aspam

C a r i b b e a n

Tuapi
Puerto Cabezas

Cayos Miskitos

Isla de Providencia
(to Colombia)

Prinzapolka

S e a

Barra de Río Grande

Mosquito Coast

3

Laguna de Perlas

Isla de San Andrés
(to Colombia)

Rama

Islas del Maíz

Bluefields

Punta Gorda

San Juan del Norte

10°

58

4

San Juan
rto
ejo
uesada

Istmo de Panamá

Gulf of
Darien

ela Heredia
SAN JOSÉ   Limón
Cartago

Siqirres

Portobelo
Colón
Cristóbal

El Porvenir

Ailigandí

COSTA RICA

Cordillera de San Blas

Cerro Chirripó
Grande
3819m
Buenos Aires
Cortés
Palmar Sur
Bahía
Coronado
nínsula de Osa

Guabito
Almirante

Cordillera de Talamanca

Laguna
de Chiriquí

Panama Canal
Lago Gatún

Balboa
Capira

Lago Bayano

Chimán

Puerto Obaldía

Volcán Barú 3475m
Boquete

Golfo de los
Mosquitos

PANAMÁ
(PANAMA CITY)

La Palma

San Miguelito

La
Isla
del Rey

Yaviza

El Real

COLOMBIA

Cordillera Central

Penonomé

Archipiélago
de las Perlas

La Concepción

Golfo Dulce

David

Santiago

Aguadulce

PANAMA

Garachiné

5

Golfo
de Chiriquí

Guarumal

Ocú
Chitré
Las Tablas

Golfo
de Panamá

Jaqué

Isla de Coiba

Isla
Cébaco

Península de
Azuero

58

E   F   G   H

Elevation

| -4000m | -3000m | -2000m | -1000m | -500m | Below sea level | 0 | 100m | 250m | 500m | 1000m | 2000m | 4000m |

| -13,124ft | -9843ft | -6562ft | -3281ft | -1640ft | -820ft/-250m | 0 | | 328ft | 820ft | 1640ft | 3281ft | 6562ft | 13,124ft |

The Caribbean

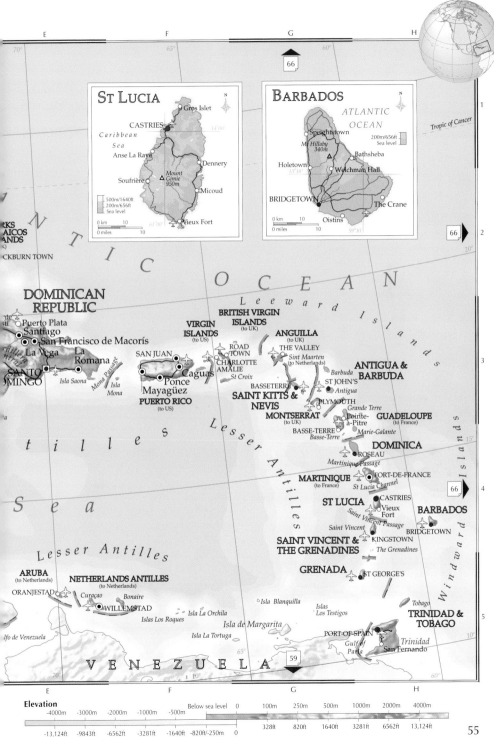

ST LUCIA

Caribbean Sea

Gros Islet
CASTRIES
Anse La Raye
Soufrière
Mount Gimie 950m
Dennery
Micoud
Vieux Fort

500m/1640ft
200m/656ft
Sea level

0 km   10
0 miles   10

N

BARBADOS

ATLANTIC OCEAN

Speightstown
Mt Hillaby 340m
Holetown
Bathsheba
Watchman Hall
BRIDGETOWN
The Crane
Oistins

200m/656ft
Sea level

0 km   10
0 miles   10

N

Tropic of Cancer

RKS
AICOS
NDS)

CKBURN TOWN

A T L A N T I C   O C E A N

L e e w a r d   I s l a n d s

DOMINICAN REPUBLIC

Puerto Plata
Santiago
San Francisco de Macorís
La Vega
La Romana
SANTO DOMINGO

Isla Saona
Mona Passage
Isla Mona

SAN JUAN
Ponce
Caguas
Mayagüez
PUERTO RICO
(to US)

VIRGIN ISLANDS
(to US)

BRITISH VIRGIN ISLANDS
(to UK)

ROAD TOWN
CHARLOTTE AMALIE
St Croix

ANGUILLA
(to UK)
THE VALLEY
Sint Maarten
(to Netherlands)

BASSETERRE
SAINT KITTS & NEVIS

Barbuda
ST JOHN'S
Antigua

ANTIGUA & BARBUDA

PLYMOUTH
MONTSERRAT
(to UK)

Grande Terre
Pointe-à-Pitre
BASSE-TERRE
Basse-Terre
Marie-Galante

GUADELOUPE
(to France)

DOMINICA
ROSEAU

Martinique Passage

MARTINIQUE
(to France)
St Lucia Channel

FORT-DE-FRANCE

ST LUCIA
CASTRIES
Vieux Fort

Saint Vincent Passage

Saint Vincent

SAINT VINCENT & THE GRENADINES
KINGSTOWN
The Grenadines

BARBADOS
BRIDGETOWN

A n t i l l e s

L e s s e r   A n t i l l e s

S e a

L e s s e r   A n t i l l e s

ARUBA
(to Netherlands)
ORANJESTAD

NETHERLANDS ANTILLES
(to Netherlands)
Curaçao
Bonaire
WILLEMSTAD
Islas Los Roques

GRENADA
ST GEORGE'S

Isla Blanquilla

Islas Los Testigos

Isla La Orchila

Isla de Margarita

Isla La Tortuga

lfo de Venezuela

V E N E Z U E L A

Tobago
TRINIDAD & TOBAGO

PORT-OF-SPAIN
Gulf of Paria
Trinidad
San Fernando

W i n d w a r d   I s l a n d s

Elevation

| -4000m | -3000m | -2000m | -1000m | -500m | Below sea level | 0 | 100m | 250m | 500m | 1000m | 2000m | 4000m |

| -13,124ft | -9843ft | -6562ft | -3281ft | -1640ft | -820ft/-250m | 0 | | 328ft | 820ft | 1640ft | 3281ft | 6562ft | 13,124ft |

South America

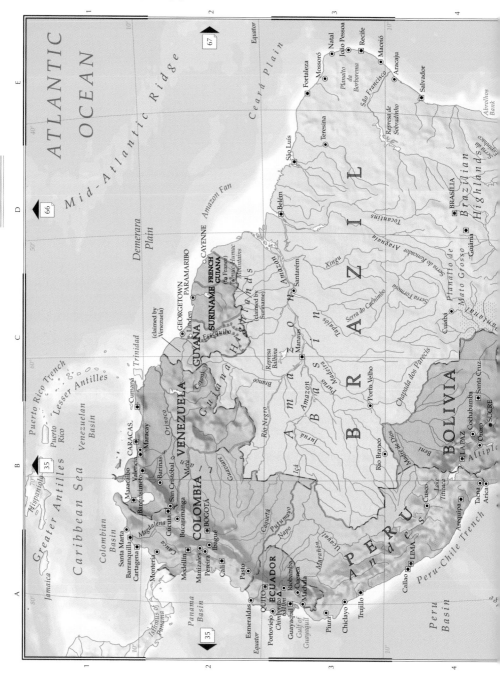

ATLANTIC

OCEAN

Mid-Atlantic Ridge

Equator

67

66

35

35

Demerara Plain

Amazon Fan

Ceará Plain

Planalto da Borborema

São Francisco

Represa de Sobradinho

Abrolhos Bank

Brazilian Highlands

Planalto de Mato Grosso

Serra do Roncador

Serra Formosa

Chapada dos Parecis

Chapada dos Veadeiros

Natal
João Pessoa
Recife
Maceió
Aracaju
Salvador
Mossoró
Fortaleza
Teresina
São Luís
Belém
Santarém
BRASÍLIA
Goiânia
Cuiabá
Porto Velho
Santa Cruz
Cochabamba
SUCRE
Oruro

Amazon
Tocantins
Araguaia
Xingu
Tapajós
Amazon
Branco
Rio Negro
Içá
Rio Branco
Madre de Dios
Beni

CAYENNE
FRENCH GUIANA
(to France)
PARAMARIBO
GEORGETOWN
SURINAME
GUYANA
(claimed by Venezuela)
(claimed by Suriname)
Essequibo
Linden
Trinidad
Tumuc-Humac Mountains

Guiana Highlands

Amazon Basin

Represa Balbina
Manaus

VENEZUELA
CARACAS
Maracay
Valencia
Barinas
San Cristóbal
Cumaná
Maracaibo
Barquisimeto
Orinoco
Apure
Meta
Guaviare

COLOMBIA
BOGOTÁ
Bucaramanga
Cúcuta
Ibagué
Medellín
Manizales
Pereira
Cali
Pasto
Santa Marta
Barranquilla
Cartagena
Montería
Magdalena
Cauca
Putumayo
Caquetá
Napo

BRAZIL

BOLIVIA
LA PAZ
Altiplano

PERU
LIMA
Callao
Cusco
Lake Titicaca
Arequipa
Tacna
Arica
Trujillo
Chiclayo
Piura
Marañón
Ucayali
Juruá
Purús

Andes

Peru-Chile Trench

Peru Basin

ECUADOR
QUITO
Guayaquil
Portoviejo
Chimborazo 6310m
Riobamba
Cuenca
Machala
Esmeraldas
Equator
Gulf of Guayaquil

Caribbean Sea
Greater Antilles
Lesser Antilles
Puerto Rico
Hispaniola
Jamaica
Puerto Rico Trench
Venezuelan Basin
Colombian Basin
Panama Basin
Isthmus of Panama

| 0 km | 500 |
| 0 miles | 500 |

Population   ● National capital

○ below 50,000   ◎ 50,000 to 100,000   ◉ 100,000 to 500,000   ■ above 500,000

Map labels

PACIFIC OCEAN

ATLANTIC OCEAN

ANTARCTICA Summer limit of pack ice

Tropic of Capricorn

Rio Grande Rise

Santos Plateau

São Paulo
Santos
Rio de Janeiro
Campinas
Curitiba
Florianópolis
Londrina
Porto Alegre
Serra Geral
Lagoa dos Patos
Mirim Lagoon

PARAGUAY
ASUNCIÓN
Formosa
Resistencia
Corrientes
Posadas
Ciudad del Este
Santa María
Gran Chaco
Pilcomayo
Bermejo
Paraná
Mesopotamia

URUGUAY
MONTEVIDEO
BUENOS AIRES
La Plata
Mar del Plata
Rio de la Plata
Negro
Paraná

San Salvador de Jujuy
Salta
San Miguel de Tucumán
Santiago del Estero
Santa Fe
Córdoba
Rosario
La Rioja
San Juan
Mendoza
Cerro Aconcagua 6959m
Neuquén
Río Negro
Colorado
Bahía Blanca
Bahía Blanca
Cerro Ojos del Salado 6880m
ARGENTINA

CHILE
Antofagasta
La Serena
Coquimbo
Viña del Mar
Valparaíso
SANTIAGO
Concepción
Temuco
Valdivia
Puerto Montt
Isla de Chiloé
Atacama Desert
Andes

Isla San Ambrosio (to Chile)
Isla San Félix (to Chile)
Islas Juan Fernández (to Chile)

Chile Basin

Chile Rise

Patagonia
Golfo San Matías
Península Valdés -40m
Rawson
Chubut
Chico
Deseado
Gulf of San Jorge
Bahía Grande
Strait of Magellan
Tierra del Fuego
Cape Horn
Punta Arenas
Drake Passage
South Shetland Islands

Argentine Basin

Falkland Plateau

FALKLAND ISLANDS (to UK)
STANLEY
West Falkland
East Falkland

Scotia Sea

South Orkney Islands

SOUTH GEORGIA (to UK)

SOUTH SANDWICH ISLANDS (to UK)

South Sandwich Trench

Winter limit of pack ice

Tropic of Capricorn

N

67
153
154
154
154

57

Northern South America

Lesser Ant

ARUBA
(to Netherlands)

NETHERLANDS
ANTILLES
(to Netherlands)

Península
de la
Guajira

Puerto López

Curaçao   Bonaire

Islas
Los Roques

Is
La O

Ríohacha

Maicao

Golfo de
Venezuela

Punto Fijo

Santa Marta

Coro

Puerto

Barranquilla

Ciénaga

Dabajuro

Sabaneta

Cumarebo

CARAC

Pico Cristóbal Colón
5775m

Puerto
Cabello

Cartagena

Soledad

La Concepción

Maracaibo

San Felipe

Sabanalarga

Cabimas

Maracay

Valledupar

Ciudad

Carora

Valencia

Maracay

El Carmen
de Bolívar

Machiques

Ojeda

Barquisimeto

San Juan
de los Mo

Sincelejo

Magangué

Lago de
Maracaibo

Valera

Acarigua

Montería

Cereté

San Carlos
de Zulia

Mérida

Guanare

Calabozo

Valle de
la Pascu

Planeta Rica

El Vigía

Barinas

Aguachica

Pico Bolívar
5007m

Río Guanare

Caucasia

Ocaña

San Fernan

Dabeiba

Cúcuta

San Cristóbal

Río Apure

Yarumal

Pamplona

Río Arauca

i   a

Bello

Bucaramanga

Arauca

VEN

Barrancabermeja

Medellín

Puerto Berrío

Río Meta

Puerto Carre

Itagüí

Sogamoso

Puerto Ayacuc

Nuquí

Quibdó

Tunja

Yopal

Río Orinoco

Manizales

Zipaquirá

Pereira

Armenia

BOGOTÁ

Río Meta

Tuluá

Ibagué

Girardot

Villavicencio

Río Guaviare

Puerto Inírida

Buenaventura

Buga

Espinal

Palmira

COLOMBIA

Cali

Neiva

Popayán

Garzón

San José del Guaviare

Pitalito

Tumaco

Nevado de Cumbal
4764m

Pasto

Mocoa

Florencia

Mitú

Ipiales

Orito

Río Vaupés

Equator

Río Apaporis

ECUADOR

Río Putumayo

Río Caquetá

Río Japurá

Río Napo

Río Içá

PERU

Amazon

Río

Gulf of
Darien

Panama
Canal

PANAMA

Golfo de
Panamá

PACIFIC
OCEAN

Cordillera Occidental

Río Cauca

Río Magdalena

Cordillera Central

Cordillera Oriental

Andes

0 km   200

0 miles   200

Population   ● National capital

○ below 50,000   ○ 50,000 to 100,000   ◉ 100,000 to 500,000   ◙ above 500,000

SAINT VINCENT & THE GRENADINES

BARBADOS

GRENADA

Isla Blanquilla
Isla de Margarita
La Asunción
Islas Los Testigos
Tobago

TRINIDAD & TOBAGO

orlamar
naná
-tuga
Carúpano
Cariaco
Güiria
Gulf of Paria
Trinidad

Puerto La Cruz
San Mateo
Barcelona
Anaco
Cantaura
aza
Maturín
El Tigre
Tucupita

A T L A N T I C

O C E A N

55

67

Río Orinoco
Ciudad Guayana
Upata
Ciudad Bolívar

U E L A

Embalse de Guri
El Callao
El Dorado
Río Paragua
Río Caura
Salto Angel
Río Caroni
Kamarang
Mount Roraima 2810m

Matthews Ridge
Charity
Spring Garden
Parika
Cuyuni River
Aurora
Peters Mine
Rockstone
Baltica
Linden

GEORGETOWN
New Amsterdam
Nieuw Nickerie
Orealla
Apoera

Totness
New Amsterdam

PARAMARIBO
Nieuw Amsterdam
St-Laurent-du-Maroni
Sinnamary
Kourou

Kaaimanston

CAYENNE
Ouanary
Montagne Torhe
St-Georges
Camopi

GUYANA

Pakaraima Mountains

Kurupukari

Essequibo River

SURINAME

W. J. van Blommesteinmeer
Juliana Top 1230m

Montagnes de la Trinité
Grand-Santi

FRENCH GUIANA
(to France)

Courantyne River

Tunuc-Humac Mountains

Guiana Highlands

(Venezuela claims all of Guyana west of Essequibo River)

Lethem

Acarai Mountains

(claimed by Suriname)

(claimed by Suriname)

Río Orinoco

Río Negro

Equator

62

B R A Z I L

Amazon
Amazon
Amazon

zon Basin

Río Purús
Río Tapajós

62

60°
55°

E
F
G
H

Elevation

| -4000m | -3000m | -2000m | -1000m | -500m | Below sea level | 0 | 100m | 250m | 500m | 1000m | 2000m | 4000m |

| -13,124ft | -9843ft | -6562ft | -3281ft | -1640ft | -820ft/-250m | 0 | 328ft | 820ft | 1640ft | 3281ft | 6562ft | 13,124ft |

59

Western South America

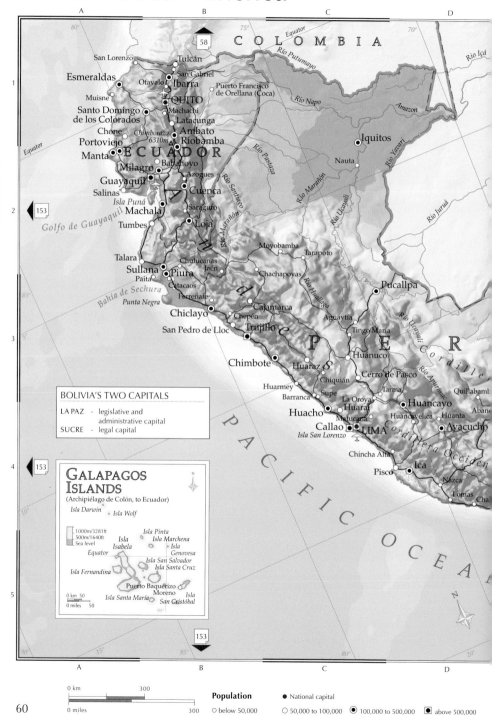

BOLIVIA'S TWO CAPITALS

LA PAZ - legislative and administrative capital
SUCRE - legal capital

GALAPAGOS ISLANDS
(Archipiélago de Colón, to Ecuador)

Isla Darwin • *Isla Wolf*

1000m/3281ft
500m/1640ft
Sea level

Isla Pinta
Isla Isabela *Isla Marchena*
Isla Genovesa
Equator
Isla San Salvador
Isla Fernandina *Isla Santa Cruz*
Puerto Baquerizo
Moreno *Isla*
Isla Santa María *San Cristóbal*

0 km 50
0 miles 50

0 km 300
0 miles 300

Population

- National capital
- ○ below 50,000
- ◎ 50,000 to 100,000
- ◉ 100,000 to 500,000
- ◼ above 500,000

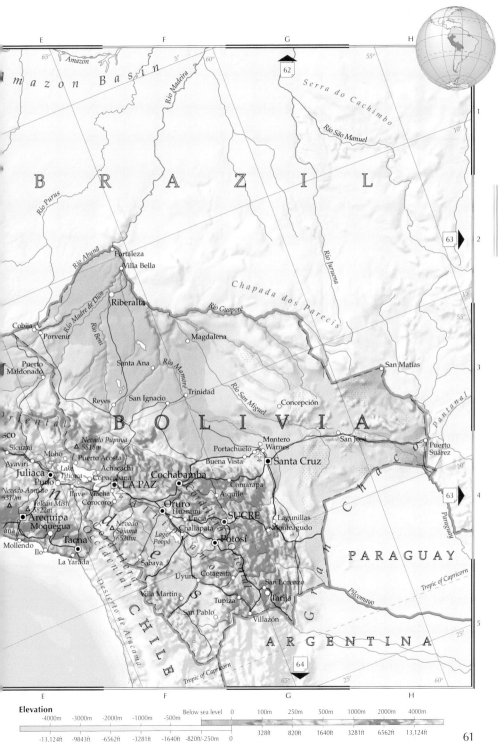

E   F   G   H

65°   *Amazon*   *5°*   *60°*

mazon Basin

Rio Madeira

62

Serra do Cachimbo

1

Rio São Manuel

10°

B   R   A   Z   I   L

Rio Purus

63

2

Rio Juruena

Rio Abunã

Fortaleza

Villa Bella

Chapada dos Parecis

15°

Riberalta

Rio Guaporé

55°

Cobija

Porvenir

Magdalena

Rio Madre de Dios

Rio Beni

Santa Ana

Rio Mamoré

San Matías

Puerto
Maldonado

Reyes

San Ignacio

Trinidad

Rio San Miguel

Concepción

Pantanal

3

Oriental

B   O   L   I   V   I   A

San José

Puerto
Suárez

sco

Nevado Pupuya
△ *5818m*

Montero
Warnes

Sicuani

Moho

Puerto Acosta

Portachuelo

20°

Ayaviri

Achacachi

Buena Vista

Santa Cruz

63

4

Juliaca

*Lake
Titicaca*

Copacabana

Cochabamba

Comarapa

Paraguay

Puno

*Nevado Ampato
5310m* △

Ilave

Viacha

LA PAZ

Aiquile

ana

*Volcán Misti
5822m* △

Corocoro

Oruro

Lagunillas

Arequipa

Moquegua

Huanuni

Uncia

SUCRE

Monteagudo

*Nevado
Sajama
6520m* △

Challapata

Mollendo

Tacna

*Lago
Poopó*

Potosí

P A R A G U A Y

Ilo

La Yarada

Sabaya

Occidental

Uyuni

Cotagaita

San Lorenzo

Tropic of Capricorn

Desierto de Atacama

C   H   I   L   E

Villa Martín

Tupiza

Tarija

Pilcomayo

5

Gran Chaco

San Pablo

Villazón

25°

A   R   G   E   N   T   I   N   A

64

Tropic of Capricorn   *65°*   *25°*   *60°*

E   F   G   H

Elevation

-4000m	-3000m	-2000m	-1000m	-500m	Below sea level	0	100m	250m	500m	1000m	2000m	4000m

-13,124ft	-9843ft	-6562ft	-3281ft	-1640ft	-820ft/-250m	0	328ft	820ft	1640ft	3281ft	6562ft	13,124ft

Brazil

Population   ● National capital

○ below 50,000   ○ 50,000 to 100,000   ◉ 100,000 to 500,000   ◼ above 500,000

0 km   600

0 miles   600

Elevation

					Below sea level	0	100m	250m	500m	1000m	2000m	4000m
-4000m	-3000m	-2000m	-1000m	-500m								
-13,124ft	-9843ft	-6562ft	-3281ft	-1640ft	-820ft/-250m	0	328ft	820ft	1640ft	3281ft	6562ft	13,124ft

Southern South America

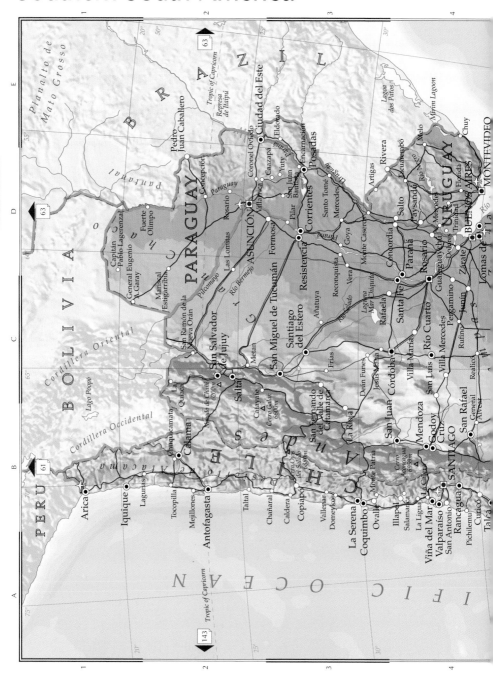

Population
National capital

○ below 50,000   ○ 50,000 to 100,000   ◉ 100,000 to 500,000   ■ above 500,000

0 km   200

0 miles   200

ATLANTIC

OCEAN

Mar del Plata
Necochea
Bahía Blanca
Coronel Dorrego
Tres Arroyos
Punta Alta
Choele Choel
Cipolletti
Neuquén
Zapala
San Antonio Oeste
Viedma
Rawson
Trelew
San Carlos de Bariloche
Esquel
Paso de Indios
Sarmiento
Comodoro Rivadavia
Caleta Olivia
Puerto Deseado
Puerto San Julián
Río Gallegos
El Calafate
Cochrane
Coyhaique
Chile Chico
Puerto Aisén
Puerto Montt
Osorno
Valdivia
Temuco
Loncoche
Los Angeles
Lebu
Ancud
Castro
Puerto Natales
Punta Arenas
Porvenir
Ushuaia

ARGENTINA

CHILE

Bahía Blanca
Golfo San Matías
Península Valdés
Golfo Nuevo
Golfo San Jorge
Bahía Grande
Estrecho de Magallanes / Strait of Magellan
Tierra del Fuego
Beagle Channel
Cabo de Hornos (Cape Horn)
Drake Passage
Isla de los Estados

Río Colorado
Río Negro
Río Chubut
Río Chico
Río Deseado
Río Santa Cruz
Río Chico

Lago Nahuel Huapi
Lago Buenos Aires
Lago Musters
Lago General Carrera
Perito Moreno

Isla de Chiloé
Archipiélago de los Chonos
Golfo de Penas
Isla Wellington
Isla Santa Inés

Cerro Valentín 4058m
Cerro San Martín
Cerro Murallón 3601m
Cerro Fitzroy 3375m

FALKLAND ISLANDS
(to UK)
STANLEY
East Falkland
West Falkland
Goose Green

67

154

154

143

Elevation

					Below sea level	0	100m	250m	500m	1000m	2000m	4000m
-6000m	-4000m	-2000m	-1000m	-500m								
-19,686ft	-13,124ft	-6562ft	-3281ft	-1640ft	-820ft/-250m	0	328ft	820ft	1640ft	3281ft	6562ft	13,124ft

The Atlantic Ocean

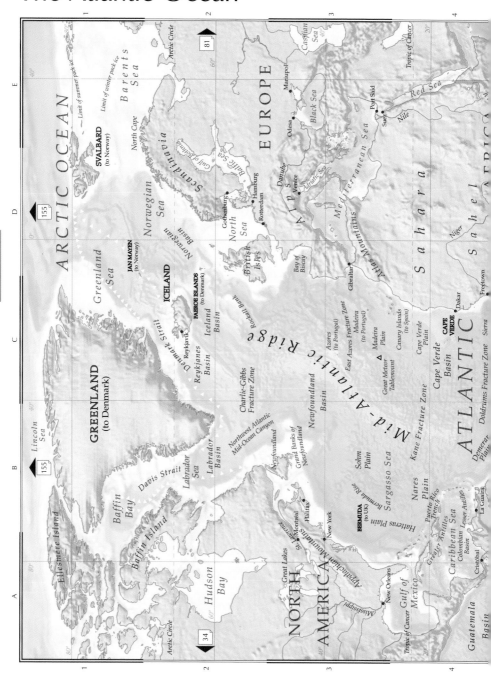

0 km 1000

0 miles 1000

● Major port

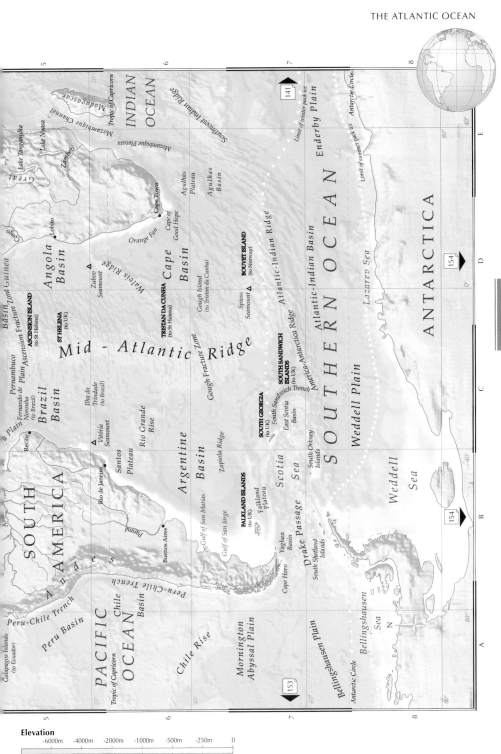

Elevation

-6000m	-4000m	-2000m	-1000m	-500m	-250m	0
-19,686ft	-13,124ft	-6562ft	-3281ft	-1640ft	-820ft	0

INDIAN OCEAN

Lake Tanganyika
Lake Nyasa
Zambezi
Great
Mozambique Channel
Madagascar
Mozambique Plateau
Southwest Indian Ridge

Tropic of Capricorn

Congo
Angola
Basin
Lobito
Cape of Good Hope
Cape Town
Orange Fan
Agulhas Plateau
Agulhas Basin
Enderby Plain
Antarctic Circle
Limit of winter pack ice

Basin of Guinea
Ascension Fracture Zone
ASCENSION ISLAND (to UK)
ST HELENA (to UK)
Zubov Seamount
Walvis Ridge
Cape Basin
TRISTAN DA CUNHA (to St Helena)
Gough Island (to Tristan da Cunha)
BOUVET ISLAND (to Norway)
Spiess Seamount
Atlantic-Indian Ridge
Atlantic-Indian Basin
Lazarev Sea
Limit of summer pack ice

Pernambuco Plain
Fernando de Noronha (to Brazil)
Mid - Atlantic Ridge
Gough Fracture Zone
SOUTH SANDWICH ISLANDS (to UK)
America-Antarctica Ridge
SOUTHERN OCEAN
ANTARCTICA

Recife
Brazil Basin
Ilha da Trindade (to Brazil)
Vitória Seamount
Rio Grande Rise
Zapiola Ridge
SOUTH GEORGIA (to UK)
South Sandwich Trench
East Scotia Basin
South Orkney Islands
Weddell Plain

Plain
Rio de Janeiro
Santos Plateau
Argentine Basin
Scotia Sea
Weddell Sea

SOUTH AMERICA
Paraná
Buenos Aires
Gulf of San Matías
Gulf of San Jorge
FALKLAND ISLANDS (to UK)
Falkland Plateau
Yaghan Basin
Cape Horn
South Shetland Islands
Drake Passage
Bellingshausen Sea
N

Andes
Peru-Chile Trench
PACIFIC OCEAN
Peru Basin
Chile Basin
Chile Rise
Mornington Abyssal Plain
Bellingshausen Plain
Antarctic Circle

Galápagos Islands (to Ecuador)
Peru-Chile Trench
Tropic of Capricorn

141
154
153
154

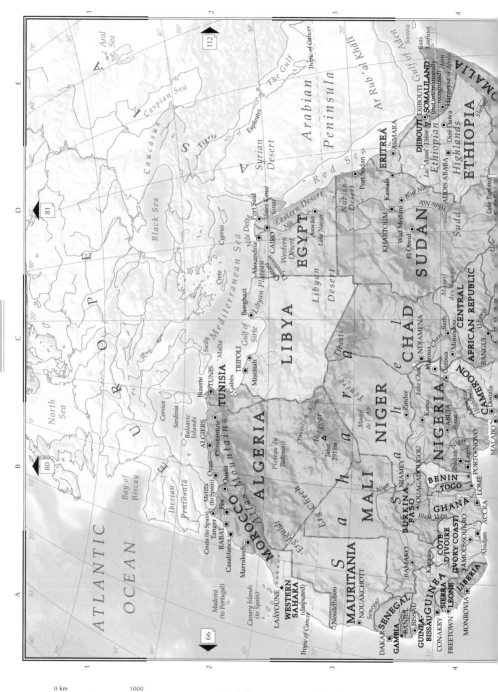

0 km	1000
0 miles	1000

Population • National capital

o below 50,000   o 50,000 to 100,000   ◉ 100,000 to 500,000   ◼ above 500,000

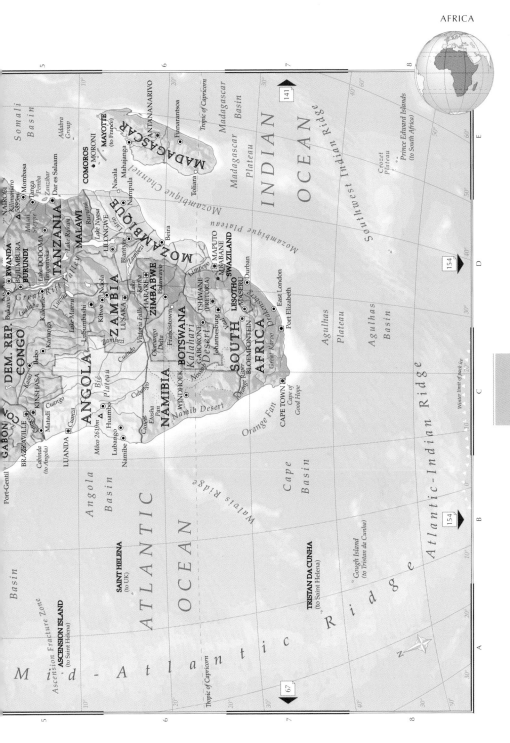

ATLANTIC

OCEAN

Madeira
(to Portugal)

Madeira ○ ● Porto Santo
Funchal ○
Ilhas Desertas

Islas Canarias
(Canary Islands)
(to Spain)

La Palma
Gomera
Hierro
Tenerife
Gran Canaria

Santa Cruz de
Tenerife · Lanzarote
Fuerteventura
Las Palmas
de Gran Canaria

LAÂYOUNE

Boujdour
Bou Craa

**WESTERN
SAHARA**
*(disputed territory
under Moroccan occupation)*
Ad Dakhla

Caltat-Zemmour

Lagouira

PORTUGAL

Tagus

SPAIN

Ebro

*Islas Baleares
(Balearic Is.)*

GIBRALTAR
(to UK)
Ceuta (to Spain)
Tanger
Ksar-el-Kebir
Melilla
Chefchaouen
Tetouan (to Spain)
Salé Kenitra
RABAT
Casablanca
El-Jadida ○ Mohammedia
Khouribga
Safi ○ Beni-
Marrakech Mellal
Essaouira

ALGER
(ALGIER

Oran Chlef
Mostagar
Sidi Bel Abb
Oujda Tlemcen
Fès
Moyen Atlas
Jerada
Chott ech C
Haut Plateau
Atlas Saha
Figuig

MOROCCO

Agadir
Tiznit

Tan-Tan

Hamada du Dra

El Mahbas

Smara

Tindouf

Haut Atlas *A t l a s* *M o u n t a i n s*

Er-Rachidia

Ouarzazate

Béchar

Grand Erg Occiden El Gole

A L G E

Adrar

*Plate
du Taden*

I-n-Salah

Reggane

'Erg Iguîdi

Erg Chech

T a n e z r o u f t

O u a r â n e

S

a

A z a o u â d

M A U R I T A N I A

Senegal

M A L I

Niger

SENEGAL

0 km ————— 400
0 miles ————— 400

Population

○ below 50,000
○ 50,000 to 100,000
◉ 100,000 to 500,000
▣ above 500,000

● National capital

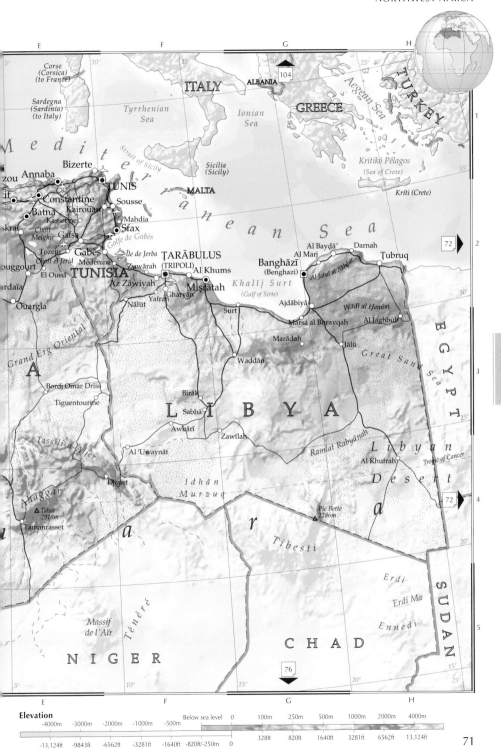

E · F · G · H

Corse
(Corsica)
(to France)

Sardegna
(Sardinia)
(to Italy)

*Tyrrhenian
Sea*

ITALY ALBANIA 104

*Ionian
Sea*

GREECE

Aegean Sea

TURKEY

M e d i t e r

Strait of Sicily

Sicilia
(Sicily)

*Kritikó Pélagos
(Sea of Crete)*

Kríti (Crete)

zou Annaba Bizerte

TUNIS

Sousse

MALTA

a n e a n   S e a

Constantine

Batna Kasserine Kairouan

skrat

Tozeur Chott
Melghir Gafsa

Mahdia

Sfax

Golfe de Gabès

Île de Jerba

72

ouggourt Chott el Jerid Médenine

El Oued

TUNISIA Zuwārah

Az Zāwiyah

ȚARĀBULUS
(TRIPOLI) Al Khums

Banghāzī
(Benghazi)

Al Bayḍā' Al Marj Darnah

Al Jabal al Akhḍar

Ṭubruq

rdaïa

Ouargla

Gabes

Nālūt Yafran Gharyān

Misrātah

*Khalīj Surt
(Gulf of Sirte)*

Surt

Ajdābiyā

Marsá al Burayqah

Marādah

Waddān

Al Jaghbūb

Jālū

Wādī al Ḥanim

Great Sand Sea

E G Y P T

Grand Erg Oriental

A

Bordj Omar Driss

Tiguentourine

L I B Y A

Birāk

Sabhā

Awbārī

Zawīlah

Ramlat Rabyānah

L i b y a n

Al Khufrah *Tropic of Cancer*

Tassili-n-Ajjer

Al 'Uwaynāt

*Idhān
Murzuq*

D e s e r t

72

Djanet

a

Ahaggar

△ Tahat
2918m

Tamanrasset

Pic Bette
△ 2286m

r

Tibesti

a

Erdi

Erdi Ma

Ennedi

S U D A N

76

*Massif
de l'Aïr*

Ténéré

N I G E R

C H A D

E · F · G · H

Elevation

| -4000m | -3000m | -2000m | -1000m | -500m | Below sea level | 0 | 100m | 250m | 500m | 1000m | 2000m | 4000m |

| -13,124ft | -9843ft | -6562ft | -3281ft | -1640ft | -820ft/-250m | 0 | | 328ft | 820ft | 1640ft | 3281ft | 6562ft | 13,124ft |

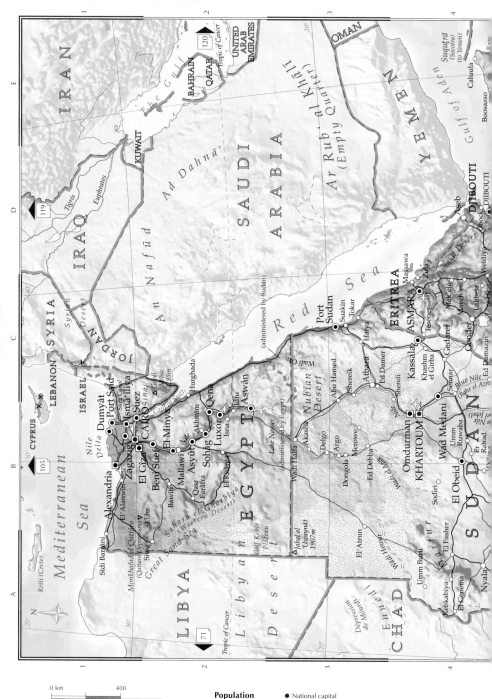

Population

• National capital

○ below 50,000   ○ 50,000 to 100,000   ◉ 100,000 to 500,000   ▣ above 500,000

0 km   400

0 miles   400

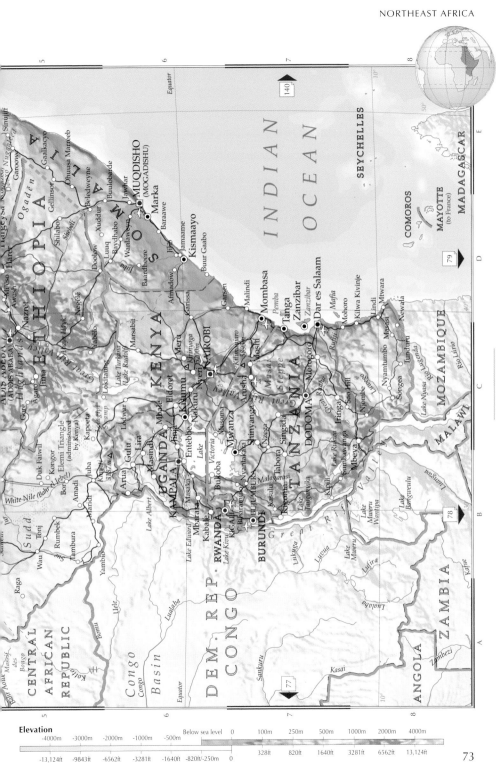

ETHIOPIA

SOMALIA

KENYA

UGANDA

TANZANIA

RWANDA

BURUNDI

DEM. REP. CONGO

CENTRAL AFRICAN REPUBLIC

ZAMBIA

ANGOLA

MOZAMBIQUE

MALAWI

MADAGASCAR

MAYOTTE (to France)

COMOROS

SEYCHELLES

INDIAN OCEAN

MUQDISHO (MOGADISHU)

NAIROBI

DODOMA

KAMPALA

BUJUMBURA

Dar es Salaam

Zanzibar

Mombasa

Addis Ababa (ADIS ABEBA)

Elevation

-4000m	-3000m	-2000m	-1000m	-500m	Below sea level	0	100m	250m	500m	1000m	2000m	4000m
-13,124ft	-9843ft	-6562ft	-3281ft	-1640ft	-820ft/-250m	0	328ft	820ft	1640ft	3281ft	6562ft	13,124ft

73

West Africa

Population ● National capital

○ below 50,000   ○ 50,000 to 100,000   ◉ 100,000 to 500,000   ■ above 500,000

0 km   400
0 miles   400

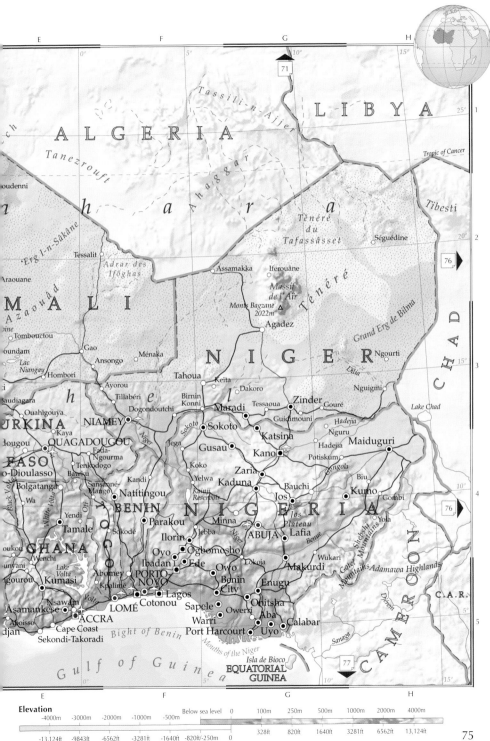

ALGERIA

Tanezrouft

oudenni

Tassili-n-Ajjer

LIBYA

25° 1

Tropic of Cancer

A   h   a   g   g   a   r

Tibesti

Ténéré
du
Tafassâsset

Séguédine

20° 2

76

Tessalit

Adrar des
Ifôghas

Assamakka   Iferouâne

'Erg I-n-Sâkâne

Araouane

Massif
de l'Aïr

MALI

Azaouâd

Ténéré

Tombouctou

oundam

Gao

Ménaka

Ansongo

Monts Bagzane
2022m

Agadez

Grand Erg de Bilma

Lac
Niamgay

Hombori

NIGER

Ngourti

15° 3

audiagara

Ayorou

Tahoua   Keita   Dakoro

Tillabéri

Dila

Nguigmi

Ouahigouya   h   Dogondoutchi   e   l
URKINA   Kaya   NIAMEY   Birnin   Maradi   Tessaoua   Zinder   Gouré   Lake Chad
ougou   OUAGADOUGOU   Konni   Guidimouni   Hadejia
FASO   Fada-   Sokoto   Katsina   Nguru
Ngourma   Jega   Gusau   Kano   Hadejia   Maiduguri
o-Dioulasso   Tenkodogo   Koko   Zaria   Potiskum   Gongola
Bolgatanga   Bawku   Sansanné-   Yelwa   Kaduna   Bauchi   Biu   Kumo
Wa   Mango   Natitingou   Kandi   Kainji   Jos   Gombi
Yendi   Reservoir   Jos   Yola
Tamale   BENIN   Parakou   Minna   Plateau   Lafia   76

Soto

Black Volta

Oti

White Volta

Sokodé

oukou

Wenchi

unvani

GHANA

Lake
Volta

Kumasi

Asamankese

Nsawam

ACCRA

Cape Coast

Sekondi-Takoradi

djan

Aboisso

igourou

Abomey

Kpalimé

LOMÉ

Cotonou

PORTO-
NOVO

Lagos

Ilorin

Oyo

Ibadan   Ede

Owo

Sapele

Warri

Benin
City

Port Harcourt

Jebba

ABUJA

Lokoja

Makurdi

Enugu

Onitsha

Owerri   Aba

Uyo

Calabar

NIGERIA

Niger

Benue

Wukari

Shebshi Mountains

Gotel Mountains

Adamawa Highlands

Djerem

CAMEROON

C.A.R.

Isla de Bioco
EQUATORIAL
GUINEA

77

Bight of Benin

Gulf   of   Guinea

Mouths of the Niger

Samaga

CHAD

Ogbomosho

10° 4

5

Elevation

					Below sea level	0	100m	250m	500m	1000m	2000m	4000m
-4000m	-3000m	-2000m	-1000m	-500m								
-13,124ft	-9843ft	-6562ft	-3281ft	-1640ft	-820ft/-250m	0	328ft	820ft	1640ft	3281ft	6562ft	13,124ft

Central Africa

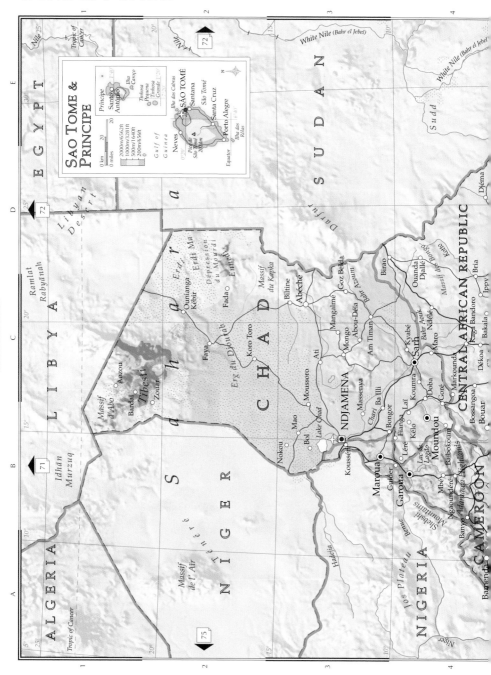

SAO TOME & PRINCIPE

Principe
Santo
António

Tinhosa
Pequena
Tinhosa
Grande

Ilha Caroço

SÃO TOMÉ
São Tomé
Santa Cruz

N

Gulf of Guinea

Pico de
São Tomé
2024m

Neves

Porto Alegre

Ilha das Cabras

Ilha das
Rôlas

Santana

Equator

0 km   20
0 miles   20

2000m/6562ft
1000m/3281ft
500m/1640ft
200m/656ft
0

EGYPT

Nile

Tropic of Cancer

White Nile (Bahr el Jebel)

SUDAN

Sudd

White Nile (Bahr el Jebel)

Darfur

Djéma

Libyan Desert

LIBYA

Ramlat Rabyānah

Massif d'Abo

Tibesti

Bardaï

Zouar

Aozou

Idhān Murzuq

SAHARA

Ténéré

Massif de l'Air

NIGER

ALGERIA

Tropic of Cancer

CHAD

Erdi Ma

Dépression du Mourdi

Ennedi

Erdi

Ounianga Kébir

Fada

Koro Toro

Faya

Erg du Djourab

Massif du Kapka

Biltine

Abéché

Goz Beïda

Mangalmé

Abou-Déïa

Am Timan

Mongo

Ati

Moussoro

Mao

Nokou

Bol

Lake Chad

Kousséri

NDJAMENA

Massenya

Bongor

Chari

Ba Illi

Fianga

Kélo

Léré

Lac de
Lagdo

Lake Chad

Birao

Ouanda
Djallé

Koïo

Massif des Bongo

Bria

Ndélé

Bamingui

Bakala

Tippy

Ippy

CENTRAL AFRICAN REPUBLIC

Sarh

Bahr Aouk

Maro

Kyabé

Markounda

Kaga Bandoro

Dékoa

Bossangoa

Bouar

Koumra

Doba

Goré

Moundou

Lai

Guider

Maroua

Garoua

Mbé

Barbokoum

Ngaoundéré

Banyo

Adamawa Highlands

Benue

Shebshi
Mountains

Jos Plateau

Niger

CAMEROON

NIGERIA

Bamenda

Hadejia

Population

● National capital
○ below 50,000
○ 50,000 to 100,000
◉ 100,000 to 500,000
■ above 500,000

0 km   400
0 miles   400

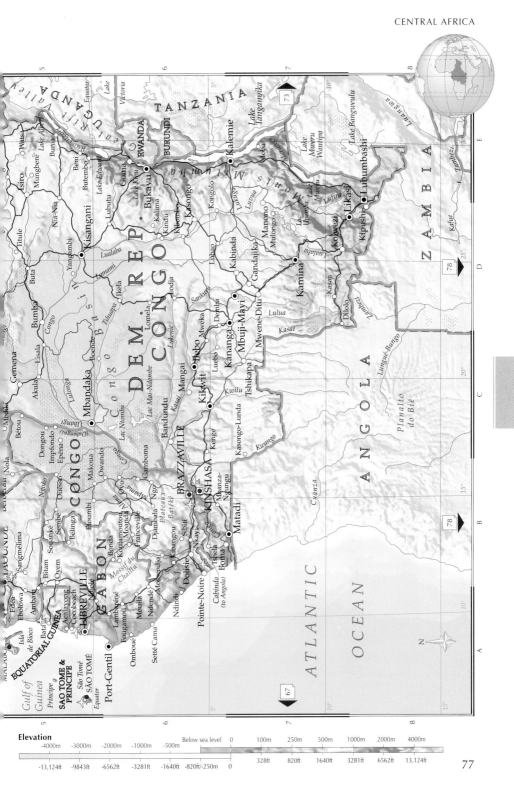

TANZANIA

BURUNDI

RWANDA

UGANDA

Great Rift Valley

Whatsi
Isiro
Mungbere
Bunia
Lake Albert
Beni
Lake Edward
Butembo
Lake Kivu
Goma
Bukavu
Kalima

Nia-Nia
Lubutu
Kindu

Titule
Yangambi
Kisangani
Kasongo
Kongolo
Kalemie
Moba
Lake Tanganyika

73

Lake Mweru
Wantipa
Lake Bangweulu

Lake Mweru
Likasi
Lubumbashi
Kipushi
Kolwezi

ZAMBIA

Luangwa

Zambezi

Kafue

E

Buta
Bumba
Lualaba
Lomami

Gemena
Eisala
Akula

D E M.   R E P.
C O N G O

Lualaba

Libao
Kabinda
Gandajika
Kamina
Kasaji
Dilolo

Kamina

78

D

Mbutu

Dongou
Impfondo
Epéna
Makoua
Owando

C O N G O

Lodja
Ikela
Tshuapa
Lomela
Lukenie

Kole
Mweka
Demba
Kananga
Mbuji-Mayi
Mwene-Ditu
Lulua

Kasai

Lac Mai-Ndombe

Inongo
Lac Tumba

Mangai
Kikwit
Luebo
Tshikapa

A N G O L A

Lunguè-Bungo

Planalto
do Biè

C

Bétou
Ngoko
Ouesso
Souanké
Sembé

Kasai

Kwilu

Kwango

Kasongo-Lunda
Kenge

Cuanza

20°

Sangmélima

Bitam
Oyem
Bélinga

G A B O N

Bifoumi

Libreville

Franceville
Koulamoutou
Mouila

Brazzaville
Kinshasa
Matadi
Boma

Mbanza-
Ngungu

B

78

Pointe-Noire

Cabinda
(to Angola)

A T L A N T I C

O C E A N

N

A

EQUATORIAL GUINEA
Bata
SÃO TOMÉ &
PRÍNCIPE
Príncipe
São Tomé
SÃO TOMÉ
Equator

Port-Gentil

Gulf of
Guinea

67

5°

10°

15°

Elevation

-4000m	-3000m	-2000m	-1000m	-500m	Below sea level	0	100m	250m	500m	1000m	2000m	4000m
-13,124ft	-9843ft	-6562ft	-3281ft	-1640ft	-820ft/-250m	0	328ft	820ft	1640ft	3281ft	6562ft	13,124ft

Southern Africa

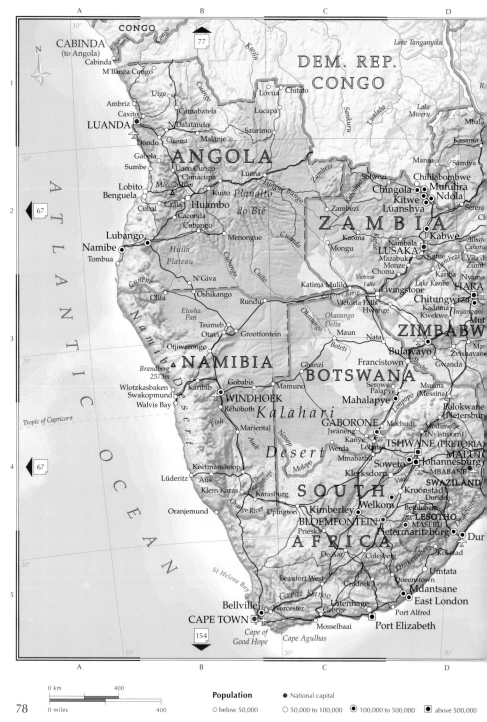

Population
National capital

○ below 50,000   ○ 50,000 to 100,000   ◉ 100,000 to 500,000   ■ above 500,000

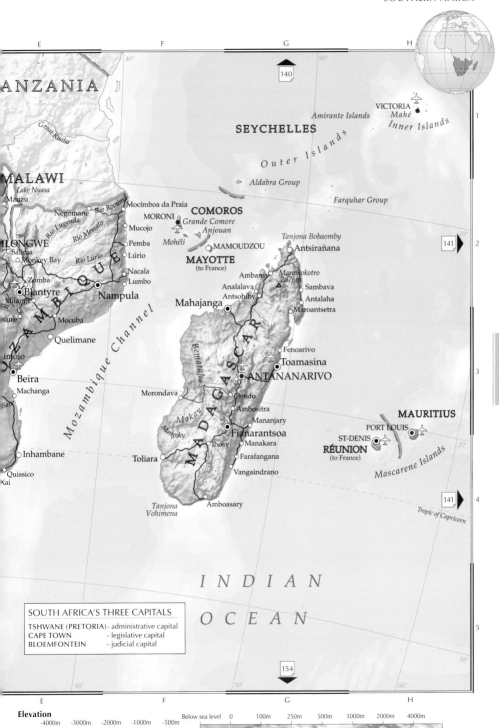

ANZANIA

TANZANIA

Great Ruaha

MALAWI
Lake Nyasa
Mzuzu

Negomane   Rio Rovuma
Mocímboa da Praia

Rio Lugenda   Mucojo

ILONGWE   Pemba
Salima   Lúrio
Monkey Bay   Nacala
Zomba   Lumbo
Blantyre   Nampula
Milange
sanje   Mocuba

Quelimane

imojo

Beira
Machanga

Sao

Inhambane
Quissico
Kai

Rio Messalo
Rio Lúrio

MOZAMBIQUE

Mozambique Channel

SEYCHELLES

Outer Islands

Amirante Islands

VICTORIA
Mahé
Inner Islands

Aldabra Group

Farquhar Group

COMOROS
MORONI   *Grande Comore*
Anjouan
Mohéli   MAMOUDZOU
MAYOTTE
(to France)

Tanjona Bobaomby
Antsiranana

Ambanja   *Maromokotro*
2876m
Analalava   Sambava
Antsohihy   Antalaha
Mahajanga   Maroantsetra

Bemaraha

MADAGASCAR

Makay

Mangoky

Morondava
Betafo
Ambositra
Mananjary
Fianarantsoa
Ihosy   Manakara
Toliara   Farafangana
Vangaindrano

Fenoarivo
Toamasina
ANTANANARIVO

MAURITIUS
PORT LOUIS
ST-DENIS
RÉUNION
(to France)
Mascarene Islands

Tanjona Vohimena   Amboasary

I N D I A N

O C E A N

SOUTH AFRICA'S THREE CAPITALS
TSHWANE (PRETORIA) - administrative capital
CAPE TOWN   - legislative capital
BLOEMFONTEIN   - judicial capital

Tropic of Capricorn

Elevation

| -4000m | -3000m | -2000m | -1000m | -500m | Below sea level | 0 | 100m | 250m | 500m | 1000m | 2000m | 4000m |

| -13,124ft | -9843ft | -6562ft | -3281ft | -1640ft | -820ft/-250m | 0 | 328ft | 820ft | 1640ft | 3281ft | 6562ft | 13,124ft |

79

Europe

A   B   C   D

Reykjanes Basin 155

Limit of winter pack ice

Charlie-Gibbs Fracture Zone

REYKJAVÍK
Reykjanes Ridge
ICELAND
Vatnajökull
Arctic Circle

Norwegian Basin

66

Iceland Basin

FAEROE ISLANDS
(to Denmark)

Faeroe-Iceland Ridge

Hatton Ridge

Norwegian Sea

Trondheim

Faeroe-Shetland Trough
Shetland Islands

Rockall Bank
Rockall Trough
Outer Hebrides

Bergen
Stavanger
OSLO

ATLANTIC OCEAN

Mid-Atlantic Ridge

Porcupine Plain

British Isles

Glasgow
Edinburgh
Ireland
Belfast
ISLE OF MAN (to UK)
IRELAND
DUBLIN
UNITED KINGDOM
Liverpool
Manchester

Orkney Islands

North Sea

Gothenburg
Aalborg
Jyllând
DENMARK COPENH
Odense
Mal

Jönkö

N O R

Celtic Sea
Celtic Shelf
Cardiff
Britain
Birmingham
LONDON
NETHERLANDS
THE HAGUE
AMSTERDAM
Rotterdam
Hamburg
Hannover
Elbe
N

Azores-Biscay Rise
Charcot Seamounts

English Channel
CHANNEL IS. (to UK)
Ile Havre
BELGIUM
BRUSSELS
BERLIN
Bonn

Iberian Plain

Biscay Plain

Rennes
PARIS
Liège
LUXEMBOURG
LUXEMBOURG
Frankfurt am Main
GERMANY
Wrocł
PR

Seine

Nantes
Orléans
Strasbourg
Stuttgart
CZEC
REPUB

A Coruña
Galicia Bank
Bay of Biscay
Loire
FRANCE
Zürich
Munich
BRAT

66

Bordeaux
Bilbao
Garonne
Lyon
SWITZERLAND
BERN
LIECH.
Salzburg
VIENNA
AUSTRIA

Horseshoe Seamounts

Porto
Cordillera Cantábrica
Duero
Massif Central
Mont Blanc 4807m
SLOVENIA
Milan
Innsbruck
Venice
LJUBL

PORTUGAL
Iberian
Zaragoza
Ebro
Toulouse
Rhône
Turin
Po
Trieste
CRO

Tagus Plain
LISBON
Tagus
MADRID
Pyrenees
ANDORRA
Nice
MONACO
Marseille
Pisa
SAN MARINO
Bologna

SPAIN
Peninsula
Guadalquivir
Barcelona
Corsica
VATICAN CITY
ROME

Madeira (to Portugal)
Seville
Valencia
Balearic Islands
Algerian Basin
Sardinia
Naples
Bari

Strait of Gibraltar
Málaga
Palma
Tyrrhenian Sea
Cagliari
Cosenza

GIBRALTAR (to UK)
Ceuta (to Spain)
Melilla (to Spain)
Palermo
Mount Etna 3340m
Sicily
Catania

Canary Islands (to Spain)

Atlas Mountains

68

AFRICA

Mediterranea

MALTA
VALLETTA

A   B   C   D

0 km   500
0 miles   500

Population   ● National capital

○ below 50,000   ⊙ 50,000 to 100,000   ◉ 100,000 to 500,000   ■ above 500,000

E   F   G   H

20°   30°   40°   50°   60°   70°   80°

Barents Sea

155   70°

North Cape   *Ostrov Kolguyev*

80°

Arctic Circle

Murmansk
*Kola
Peninsula*

Irtysh

FINLAND

*White
Sea*

Archangel

Ural Mountains

Ob'

Northern Dvina

R   U   S   S   I   A   N

Lake Onega

Perm'

112   2

70°

Tampere

Turku   HELSINKI   *Lake Ladoga*

F   E   D   E   R   A   T   I   O   N

Vologda

Ufa

60°

KHOLM   TALLINN   Saint Petersburg

ESTONIA

Yaroslavl'

Kazan'

LATVIA

RĪGA

Nizhniy
Novgorod

Orenburg

LITHUANIA

NINGRAD
(Russ. Fed.)
rad   Kaunas   Vitsyebsk

Ul'yanovsk

Samara

Ural

VILNIUS

*Central
Russian
Upland*

MINSK

Volga Uplands

Syr Darya

zcz   Babruysk   Homyel'

Voronezh

Aral Sea

WARSAW   BELARUS

*Pripet
Marshes*

Don

Ural

Amu Darya

AND   Brest

Dnieper Lowlands   KIEV   Kharkiv

Bug

Volgograd

60°

raków   L'viv   *Dniester*

UKRAINE   Dnipropetrovs'k

Dnieper

Donets'k

Astrakhan'
Volga Delta
-28m

Caspian Sea

40°

KIA   Chernivtsi

Rostov-na-Donu

PEST   Cluj-Napoca   MOLDOVA

CHIŞINĂU

ARY   CHIŞINĂU   Odesa   *Sea of
Azov*

Stavropol'

A

ROMANIA

Crimea

112   4

Braşov   Simferopol'

Caucasus   El'brus 5642m

ELGRADE   BUCHAREST

RBIA   *Danube*   Constanţa   *Black Sea*

Balkan Mountains   BULGARIA   Varna

NEGRO
RICA   SOFIA   Burgas

MACED.   TURKEY

A

*Aegean
Sea*   *Anatolia*

GREECE

ATHENS

Peloponnese   Piraeus

Zagros Mountains

30°

ea   Irákleio   Cyprus

30°   40°   *Tigris*   *Euphrates*   50°

Crete

118

E   F   G   H

The North Atlantic

A   B   C   D

Arctic Circle

37

Gulf of Boothia

Devon Island

Ellesmere Island

Nares Strait

N U N A V U T

Qaanaaq

Knud Rasmussen

Innaanganeq

Savissivik

Hudson Bay

Southampton Island

Foxe Basin

Qimusseriarsuaq

Baffin Bay

Kullorsuaq

38

C A N A D A

Baffin Island

Upernavik

Uummannaq

Péninsule d'Ungava

Hudson Strait

QUÉBEC

Qeqertarsuaq

Qeqertarsuaq

Qeqertarsuup Tunua

Qasigiannguit

Arnaud

Cumberland Sound

Frobisher Bay

Davis Strait

Sisimiut

Kong Frederik IX Land

G R E E N L A N D

(to Denmark)

Ungava Bay

Maniitsoq

George

NUUK

Limit of summer pack ice

Kong Christian IX Land

Gunnbjo

Mont Forel 3360m

39

Paamiut

Kong Frederik VI Kyst

Ammassalik

Ivittuut

Denma

Labrador Sea

Qaqortoq

Nanortalik

Nunap Isua (Kap Farvel)

Limit of winter pack ice

Reykjanes Basin

NEWFOUNDLAND & LABRADOR

ATLANTIC

66

OCEAN

A   B   C   D

0 km   400

0 miles   400

Population   ● National capital

○ below 50,000   ○ 50,000 to 100,000   ◉ 100,000 to 500,000   ◼ above 500,000

ARCTIC OCEAN

Lincoln Sea

Kap Morris Jesup

Wandel Sea

Independence Fjord

Nord

Kong Frederik VIII Land

SVALBARD
(to Norway)

Kvitøya

Zemlya
Frantsa-Iosifa

Nordaustlandet

Novaya
Zemlya

Kong Karls Land

Spitsbergen

Barentsøya

Edgeøya

LONGYEARBYEN
Barentsburg

Storfjorden

Limit of winter pack ice

Barents
Sea

Greenland
Sea

Bjørnøya
(to Norway)

Kong Christian X Land

Petermann Bjerg
2940m

Daneborg

Limit of summer pack ice

Nordkapp
(North Cape)

FINLAND

Kong Oscar Fjord

Mohns Ridge

Ittoqqortoormiit

Kangikajik

Kangertittivaq

JAN MAYEN
(to Norway)

Norwegian
Sea

Norwegian Basin

Vestfjorden

Arctic Circle

S
W
E
D
E
N

rait

ICELAND

olungarvík

Siglufjördhur

Raufarhöfn

Húsavík

Akureyri

Stykkishólmur

Seydhisfjördhur

Neskaupstadhur

REYKJAVIK

Selfoss

Vatnajökull

Djúpivogur

orláks

höfn

Hvannadalshnúkur
2119m

rtsey

Vestmannaeyjar

N

Gulf
of
Bothnia

NORWAY

FAEROE ISLANDS
(to Denmark)

TÓRSHAVN

Shetland
Islands

155

110

84

85

1

2

3

4

5

Elevation

					Below sea level	0	100m	250m	500m	1000m	2000m	4000m
-4000m	-3000m	-2000m	-1000m	-500m								
-13,124ft	-9843ft	-6562ft	-3281ft	-1640ft	-820ft/-250m	0	328ft	820ft	1640ft	3281ft	6562ft	13,124ft

83

E F G H

Scandinavia & Finland

0 km		200	
0 miles			200

Population   ● National capital

○ below 50,000   ○ 50,000 to 100,000   ◉ 100,000 to 500,000   ▣ above 500,000

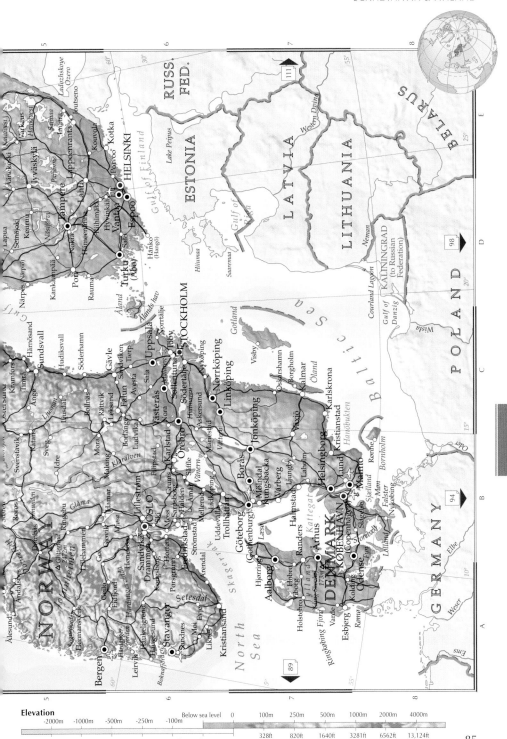

Elevation

-2000m	-1000m	-500m	-250m	-100m	Below sea level 0	100m	250m	500m	1000m	2000m	4000m
-6562ft	-3281ft	-1640ft	-820ft	-328ft	-164ft/-50m 0	328ft	820ft	1640ft	3281ft	6562ft	13,124ft

The Low Countries

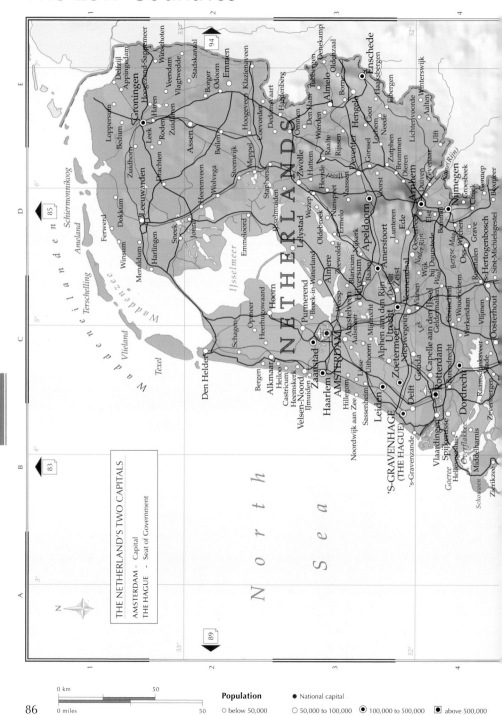

N o r t h   S e a

THE NETHERLAND'S TWO CAPITALS

AMSTERDAM - Capital
THE HAGUE - Seat of Government

Population

● National capital

○ below 50,000   ○ 50,000 to 100,000   ◉ 100,000 to 500,000   ◼ above 500,000

0 km   50
0 miles   50

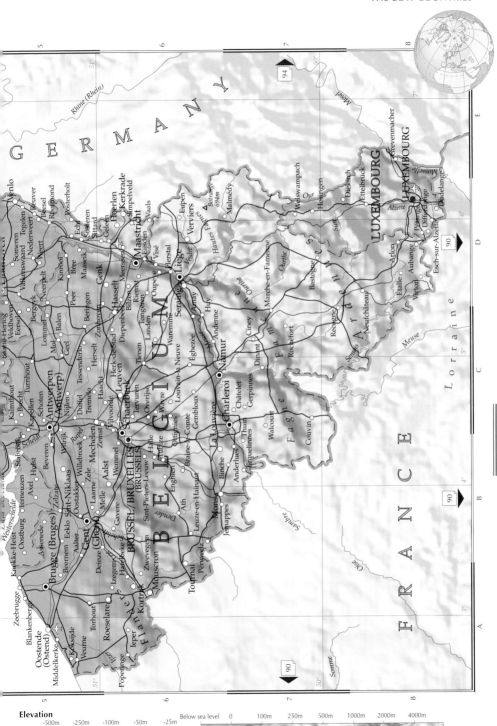

Elevation

| -500m | -250m | -100m | -50m | -25m | Below sea level | 0 | 100m | 250m | 500m | 1000m | 2000m | 4000m |

| -1640ft | -820ft | -328ft | -164ft | -82ft | 33ft/-10m | 0 | 328ft | 820ft | 1640ft | 3281ft | 6562ft | 13,124ft |

87

The British Isles

0 km   100

0 miles   100

Population   ● National capital   ◉ Internal administrative capital

○ below 50,000   ○ 50,000 to 100,000   ◉ 100,000 to 500,000   ◼ above 500,000

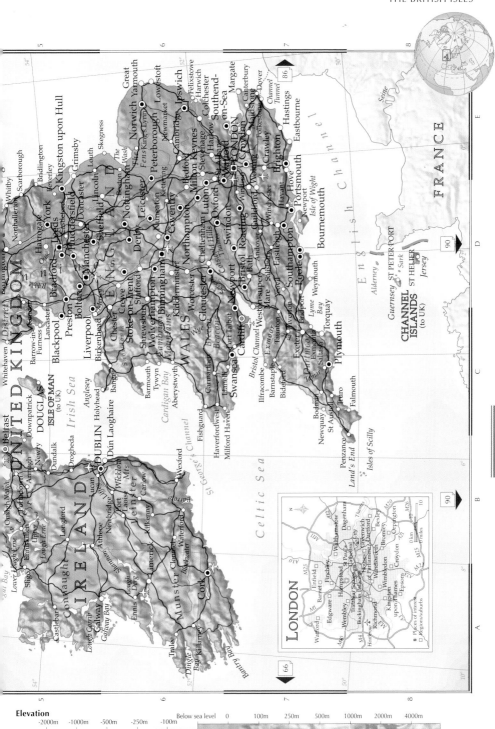

Elevation

					Below sea level	0	100m	250m	500m	1000m	2000m	4000m
	-2000m	-1000m	-500m	-250m	-100m							

| -6562ft | -3281ft | -1640ft | -820ft | -328ft | -164ft/-50m | 0 | 328ft | 820ft | 1640ft | 3281ft | 6562ft | 13,124ft |

89

France, Andorra & Monaco

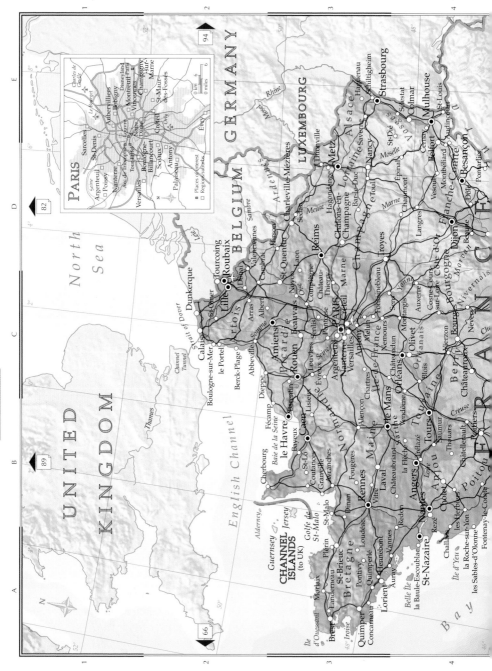

Population

● National capital

○ below 50,000   ○ 50,000 to 100,000   ◉ 100,000 to 500,000   ◼ above 500,000

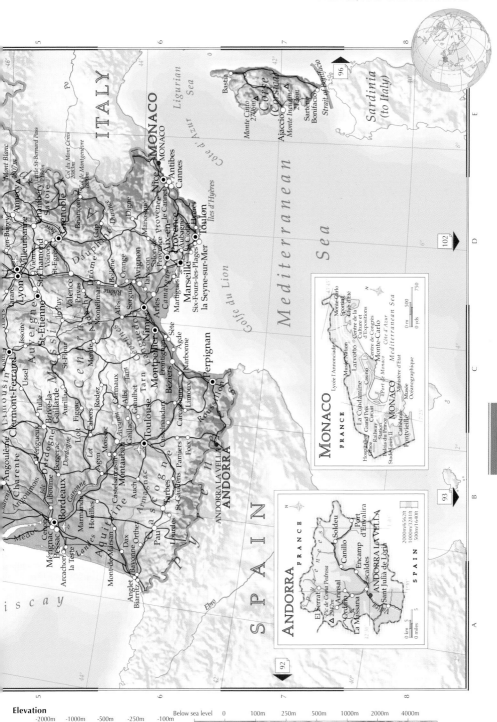

ITALY

*Ligurian
Sea*

Mont Blanc
4807m △

Little St-Bernard Pass
Col du Mont Cenis
Col de Montgenèvre

Annecy
Chambéry
Savoie
Grenoble
Voiron
Vienne
St-Égrève
Bourgoin
Gap
Bronçon

St-Étienne
Le Puy
Privas
Valence
Montélimar
Orange
Bollène

Avignon
Sorgues
Arles
Nîmes
Alès
Ganges
Lodève
Béziers
Agde
Sète
Narbonne
Carcassonne
Limoux
Foix
Pamiers
St-Gaudens

Marseille
Martigues
Six-Fours-les-Plages
la Seyne-sur-Mer
Toulon
Îles d'Hyères

MONACO
Antibes
Cannes
Nice
le Cannet
Vallauris
Aix-en-Provence
Salon-de-Provence
Aubagne
La Ciotat
Hyères

*Mediterranean
Sea*

Golfe du Lion

Côte d'Azur

Perpignan

Bastia
Monte Cinto 2710m △
Corse (Corsica)
Ajaccio
Monte Incudine △
Sartène
Bonifacio
Strait of Bonifacio

Sardinia
(to Italy)

96

102

93

92

MONACO

FRANCE

Lycée l'Annonciade
Musée Mifiton
Larvotto
Centre de la
Culture et
d'Expositions
Casino
Monte-Carlo
Centre de Congrès
Monte-Carlo
Côte d'Azur
Port de Monaco
La Condamine
Palais de Justice
Palais du Prince
Stade Louis II
Cathédrale
Fontvieille
Ministère d'État
Musée
Océanographique

Mediterranean Sea

Monte-Carlo
Sporting
Club d'Été

0 m   500   750
0 yds   500

ANDORRA

FRANCE

Pyrenees

Soldeu
Canillo
Pic de Coma Pedrosa
2942m △
El Serrat
Arinsal
Ordino
La Massana
Port
d'Envalira
Encamp
Escaldes
ANDORRA LA VELLA
Sant Julià de Lòria

SPAIN

2000m/6562ft
1000m/3281ft
500m/1640ft

0 km   5
0 miles   5

SPAIN

B i s c a y

Bordeaux
Mérignac
Pessac
Arcachon
la Teste
Angoulême
Cognac
Libourne
Bergerac
Périgueux
Tulle
Brive-la-Gaillarde
Aurillac
St-Flour
Clermont-Ferrand
Issoire
Ussel

Toulouse
Montauban
Castelsarrasin
Agen
Moissac
Cahors
Rodez
Albi
Castres
Graulhet
Gaillac
Auch
Tarbes
Lourdes
Pau
Orthez
Dax
Mont-de-Marsan
Bayonne
Anglet
Biarritz

Elevation

-2000m	-1000m	-500m	-250m	-100m	Below sea level	0	100m	250m	500m	1000m	2000m	4000m
-6562ft	-3281ft	-1640ft	-820ft	-328ft	-164ft/-50m	0	328ft	820ft	1640ft	3281ft	6562ft	13,124ft

91

Spain & Portugal

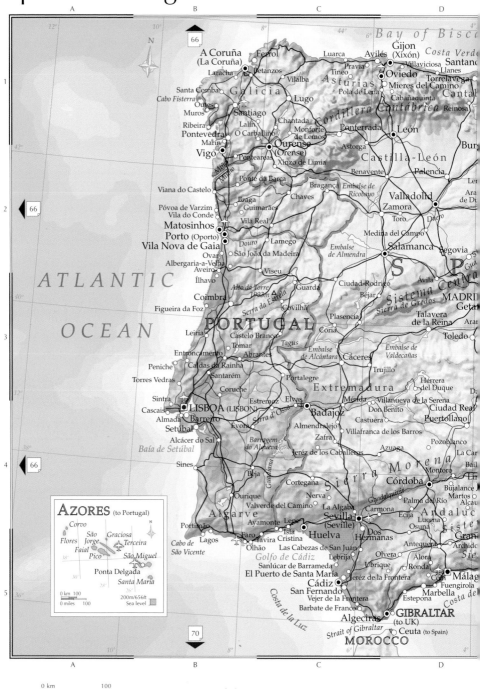

AZORES (to Portugal)

Corvo
Flores   São   Graciosa
Faial Jorge   Terceira
   Pico   São Miguel

Ponta Delgada
Santa Maria

0 km 100
0 miles 100

200m/656ft
Sea level

Population   ● National capital

○ below 50,000   ○ 50,000 to 100,000   ◉ 100,000 to 500,000   ◼ above 500,000

0 km   100
0 miles   100

Germany & the Alpine States

LIECHTENSTEIN

SWITZERLAND

AUSTRIA

Ruggell
Mauren
Planken
Bendern
Schaan
Schaanwald
VADUZ
Triesenberg
Triesen
Balzers
Rhine

2000m/6562ft
1000m/3281ft
500m/1640ft
250m/820ft

0 km   4
0 miles   4

98

85

85

86

SWEDEN

DENMARK

POLAND

NETHERLANDS

G E R M A N Y

North Sea

Baltic Sea

Jylland

Sjælland

Fyn

Falster

Bornholm (to Denmark)

Oder

Noteć

Frankfurt an der Oder

Eisenhüttenstadt
Guben
Cottbus
Görlitz
Hoyerswerda
Bautzen
Riesa
Döbeln
Leipzig
Halle
Eisleben
Nordhausen
Göttingen
Northeim
Kassel
Marsberg
Warburg
Paderborn
Gütersloh
Bielefeld
Herford
Minden
Hameln
Hildesheim
Hannover
Braunschweig
Wolfsburg
Salzgitter
Peine
Celle
Magdeburg
Schönebeck
Bernburg
Dessau
Wittenberg
Halberstadt
Stendal
Brandenburg
Potsdam
BERLIN
Ludwigsfelde
Lübben
Lübbenau
Spree
Torgau
Senftenberg
Finsterwalde
Lübben
Bad Freienwalde
Eberswalde-Finow
Angermünde
Bernau
Prenzlau
Neustrelitz
Neubrandenburg
Pasewalk
Anklam
Greifswald
Stralsund
Sassnitz
Rügen
Bergen
Wolgast
Usedom
Oderhaff
Pomeranian Bay
Oderhaff

Rostock
Wismar
Schwerin
Rehna
Gadebusch
Güstrow
Teterow
Waren
Malchin
Demmin
Wolgast
Warnemünde

Lübeck
Hamburg
Lüneburg
Soltau
Uelzen
Salzwedel
Perleberg
Wittenberge
Ludwigslust
Parchim
Boizenburg
Lauenburg
Winsen
Danneberg
Elbe
Saale

Kiel
Eutin
Oldenburg
Oldesloe
Plön
Neumünster
Itzehoe
Heide
Husum
Rendsburg
Flensburg
Schleswig
Kappeln
Westerland
Sylt
Schleswig-Holstein
Mecklenburg
Güstrow

Norderstedt
Pinneberg
Wedel
Stade
Buxtehude
Rosengarten
Verden
Scheessel
Bassum

Cuxhaven
Bremerhaven
Bremen
Wilhelmshaven
Emden
Norden
Leer
Weener
Delmenhorst
Oldenburg
Cloppenburg
Lingen
Nordhorn
Rheine
Münster
Dülmen
Ahlen
Hamm
Dortmund
Bochum
Essen
Duisburg
Krefeld
Düsseldorf
Solingen
Wuppertal
Recklinghausen
Gelsenkirchen
Bocholt

Osnabrück

Nordenham

Ostfriesische Inseln

North Frisian Islands (Nordfriesische Inseln)

Helgoländer Bucht
Helgoland

Kieler Bucht
Mecklenburger Bucht
Fehmarn
Fehmarnbelt
Greifswalder Bodden

Rhine
Ems
Weser
IJsselmeer

0 km   100
0 miles   100

Population

● National capital

○ below 50,000   ○ 50,000 to 100,000   ◉ 100,000 to 500,000   ◼ above 500,000

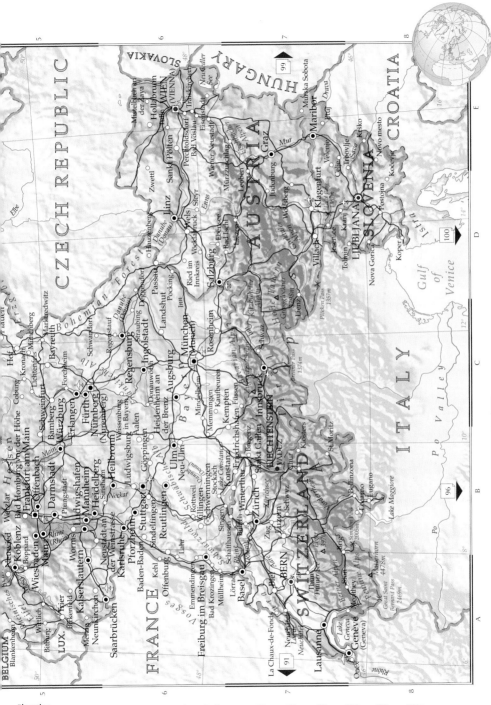

Elevation

					Below sea level	0	100m	250m	500m	1000m	2000m	4000m
-500m	-250m	-100m	-50m	-25m								
-1640ft	-820ft	-328ft	-164ft	-82ft	33ft-10m	0	328ft	820ft	1640ft	3281ft	6562ft	13,124ft

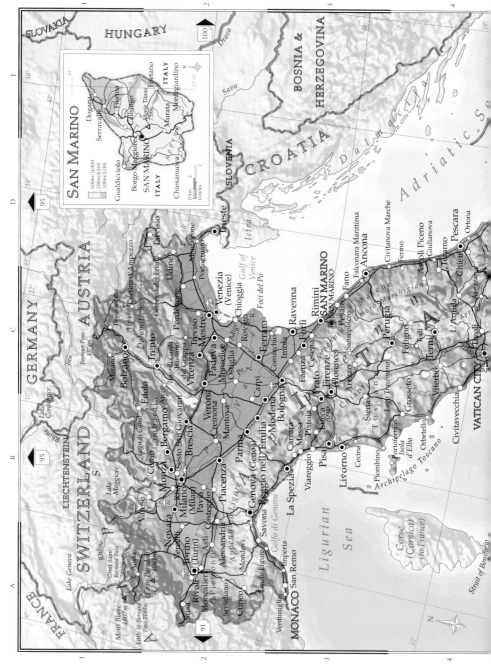

0 km 100
0 miles 100

Population

● National capital

○ below 50,000　　◐ 50,000 to 100,000　　◉ 100,000 to 500,000　　■ above 500,000

Strait of Otranto

Golfo di Taranto

Ionian Sea

Stretto di Messina

Tyrrhenian Sea

Mediterranean Sea

Strait of Sicily

Malta Channel

Sardegna (Sardinia)

Sicilia (Sicily)

MALTA
VALLETTA
Malta

TUNISIA

VATICAN CITY

ROME

Elevation

-2000m	-1000m	-500m	-250m	-100m	Below sea level	0	100m	250m	500m	1000m	2000m	4000m
-6562ft	-3281ft	-1640ft	-820ft	-328ft	-164ft/-50m	0	328ft	820ft	1640ft	3281ft	6562ft	13,124ft

97

Central Europe

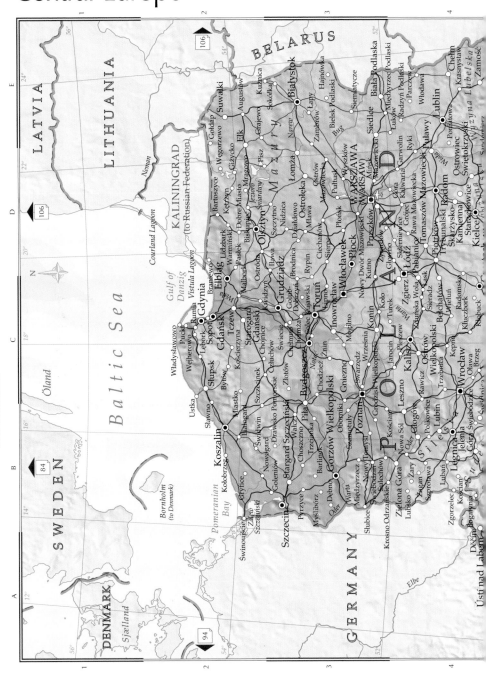

0 km 100

0 miles 100

Population ● National capital

○ below 50,000 ○ 50,000 to 100,000 ◉ 100,000 to 500,000 ◼ above 500,000

UKRAINE

CZECH REPUBLIC

SLOVAKIA

HUNGARY

ROMANIA

SERBIA

AUSTRIA

CROATIA

SLOVENIA

ITALY

BOSNIA & HERZEGOVINA

Carpathian Mountains

Bohemia

Moravia

Great Hungarian Plain

Little Alföld

Bohemian Forest

Niedere Tauern

Alps

Voivodina

Adriatic Sea

Gulf of Venice

Velebit

PRAGUE

BUDAPEST

BRATISLAVA

Brno

Ostrava

Olomouc

Plzeň

České Budějovice

Miskolc

Debrecen

Szeged

Pécs

Kecskemét

Szolnok

Nyíregyháza

Košice

Kraków

Rzeszów

Tarnów

Przemyśl

Győr

Szombathely

Zalaegerszeg

Nagykanizsa

Kaposvár

Székesfehérvár

Veszprém

Tatabánya

Esztergom

Vác

Eger

Gyöngyös

Békéscsaba

Hódmezővásárhely

Makó

Baja

Szekszárd

Paks

Dunaújváros

Nitra

Trnava

Žilina

Martin

Prešov

Poprad

Banská Bystrica

Trenčín

Zlín

Přerov

Opava

Pardubice

Jihlava

Kolín

Tábor

Klatovy

Danube

Tisza

Dráva

Mureş

Mur

Drau

Dniester

Kékes 1014m

Elevation

Below sea level						0	100m	250m	500m	1000m	2000m	4000m
-500m	-250m	-100m	-50m	-25m								
-1640ft	-820ft	-328ft	-164ft	-82ft	33ft/-10m	0	328ft	820ft	1640ft	3281ft	6562ft	13,124ft

Southeast Europe

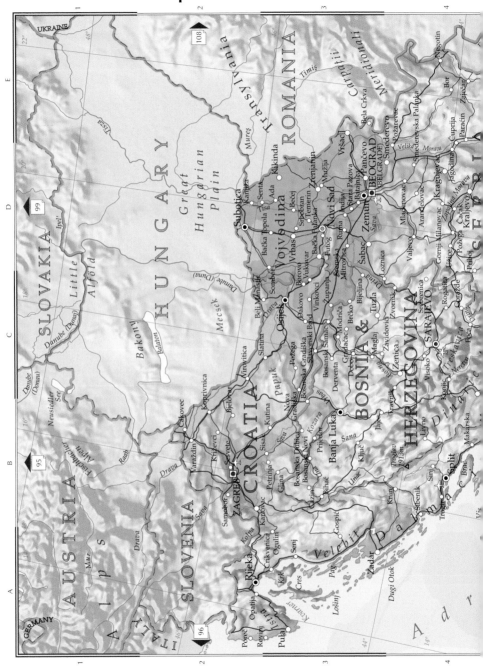

0 km   100

0 miles   100

Population

● National capital   ◉ Internal administrative capital

○ below 50,000   ○ 50,000 to 100,000   ◉ 100,000 to 500,000   ■ above 500,000

BULGARIA

Pirot
Vlasotince
Surdulica
Kuršumlija
Leskovac
Prokuplje
Vranje
Reka Morava
Kumanovo
Kočani
Bregovo
Radoviš
Štip
Strumica
Gevgelija

Aegean Sea

Thermaïkós Kólpos

Strymónas

Vardar

104

Éttroia
(Euboea)

MACEDONIA

Gnjilane
Bujanovac

Priština
Podujevo

Gračanica
Orahovac

Kosovska
Mitrovica

Vučitrn
Peć

Uroševac

KOSOVO

Prizren

SKOPJE

Tetovo

Gostivar

Veles

Prilep

Kavadarci

Cina Reka

Cina

Pínios

Aónik

Berane

Đakovica
Drim

Drini i Bardhe

Kukës

Debar

Struga

Ohrid

Lake
Ohrid

Bitola

Lake
Prespa

Korçë

GREECE

Pindos

Pindus Mountains

MONTENEGRO

Nikšić

Cetinje

Kolašin

Peshkopi

Burrel

North
Albanian
Alps

Bajram Curri

PODGORICA

Trebinje

Dubrovnik

Bar

Ulcinj

Lake Scutari

Shkodër

Lezhë

Laç

Krujë

Black Drin

TIRANË
(TIRANA)

Durrës

Kavajë

Lushnjë

Fier

Berat

Lumi Shkumbin

Lumi Devoll

Lumi Osum

Elbasan

Pogradec

Korçë

Lumi Vjosës

Gramsh

ALBANIA

Vlorë

Tepelenë

Gjirokastër

Sarandë

Konispol

Lefkáda

Kérkyra
(Corfu)

Ióni a Nis iá
(Ionian Islands)

Kefallonía

Strait of Otranto

Ionian Sea

Mljet

Palagruža

Adriatic Sea

ITALY

Golfo di Taranto

Appennino Lucano

97

103

105

C R O A T I A

S E R B I A

Brčko

Banja Luka

Tuzla

Drina

Sava

Bosna

Bihać

Sarajevo

Goražde

Mostar

MONTENEGRO

Dubrovnik

Split

C R O A T I A

Adriatic Sea

Territorial extent
Republika Srpska
Federacija Bosna
i Hercegovina

0   50 km
0   50 miles

BOSNIA &
HERZEGOVINA

Elevation

-2000m	-1000m	-500m	-250m	-100m	Below sea level	0	100m	250m	500m	1000m	2000m	4000m
-6562ft	-3281ft	-1640ft	-820ft	-328ft	-164ft/-50m	0		328ft	820ft	1640ft	3281ft	6562ft	13,124ft

The Mediterranean

SLOVAKIA
WIEN
(ENNA)
RIA
BLIANA
CROATIA
ZAGREB
BOSNIA
& HERZ.
SARAJEVO
Dalmatia
atic Sea
a
oti (Naples)
Bari
Vesuvio 1277m Lecce
Golfo di
Taranto
osenza
Catanzaro
Monte Etna
3340m
Siracusa
ALLETTA
LTA
a
n
e
a

Danube
BUDAPEST
HUNGARY
Great
Hungarian
Plain
Novi Sad
BEOGRAD
(BELGRADE)
SERBIA
MON.
PODGORICA
Pristina
TIRANE
(TIRANA)
MACED.
SKOPJE
Strait of
Otranto
Kérkyra
(Corfu)
Ionian
Sea
Kefallonia
Zákynthos

Tisza
Satu Mare
Targu Mures
ROMANIA
Carpații Meridonali
BUCUREŞTI
(BUCHAREST)
Danube
BULGARIA
Balkan Mountains
SOFIYA
(SOFIA)
Rhodope
Mountains
Thessaloníki
(Salonica)
Límnos
Lárisa
Pindos
(Pindus)
Mts
GREECE
Chíos
Kýthira
Mirtóo
Pélagos
Kritikó Pélagos
(Sea of Crete)
Irakleio
Kríti
(Crete)

Carpathian Mountains
Balti
108
MOLD.
CHIŞINĂU
Galaţi
Constanţa
Varna
Burgas
Edirne
İstanbul
Boğazı
(Bosporus)
İstanbul
Marmara
Denizi
Bursa
Balikesir
İzmir
Sámos
Dodecanese
(Dodecanese)
Sámos
Kykládes
(Cyclades)
Ródos
(Rhodes)
Kárpathos

Dniester
UKRAINE
Kakhovs'ka
Vodoskhovyshche
Odesa
Dnieper
Berdyans'k
Sea of Azov
Kryms'kyy
Pivostrov
Kerch
RUSS.
FED.
Sevastopol'
Novorossiysk
Black Sea
Küre Dağları
Zonguldak
Samsun
Ordu
ANKARA
Kızıl Irmak
TURKEY
Tuz
Gölü
Kayseri
Toros Dağları
Antalya
Gaziantep
Adana
Antalya
Körfezi
İskenderun Körfezi
Halab
(Aleppo)
NICOSIA
CYPRUS
Lárnaka
Lemesós
(Limassol)
SYRIA
LEBANON
BEYROUTH
(BEIRUT)
DIMASHQ
(DAMASCUS)
Hefa
119
ISRAEL
'AMMAN
Tel Aviv-Yafo
JERUSALEM
Gaza
Dead Sea
JORDAN

117
2
35°
3
4
5

Mişrātah
Banghāzī
(Benghazi)
Khalīj Surt
(Gulf of Sirte)
Surt
Ajdābiyā
Great Sand Sea
LIBYA
Libyan
Plateau
Ţubruq
Darnah
Libyan
Desert
72
Alexandria
Nile
Delta
Port Said
Suez
Canal
CAIRO
El Giza
Suez
Monkhafad el Qattāra
(Qatar Depression)
Nile
EGYPT
Sinai
Sahara el Sharqiya
(Eastern Desert)
Elat
Al 'Aqabah
SAUDI
ARABIA
Red
Sea
a

Elevation

| | | | | | | Below sea level | 0 | 100m | 250m | 500m | 1000m | 2000m | 4000m |

-4000m -3000m -2000m -1000m -500m

-13,124ft -9843ft -6562ft -3281ft -1640ft -820ft/-250m 0

328ft 820ft 1640ft 3281ft 6562ft 13,124ft

103

Bulgaria & Greece

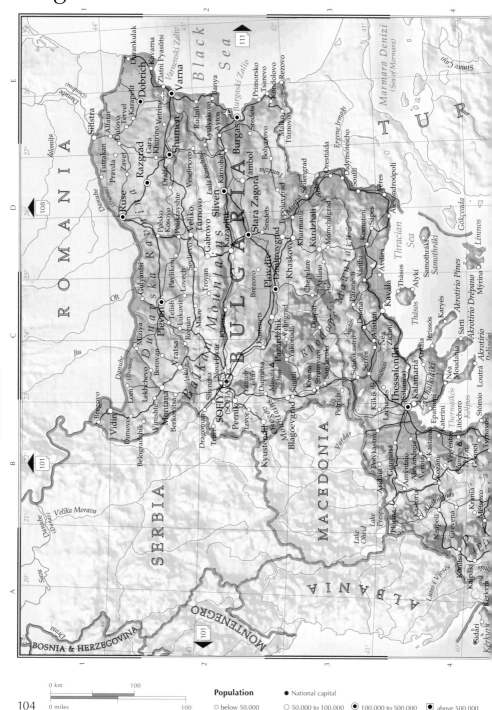

0 km   100

0 miles   100

Population

● National capital

○ below 50,000   ○ 50,000 to 100,000   ◎ 100,000 to 500,000   ■ above 500,000

Elevation

-2000m	-1000m	-500m	-250m	-100m	Below sea level	0	100m	250m	500m	1000m	2000m	4000m
-6562ft	-3281ft	-1640ft	-820ft	-328ft	-164ft/-50m	0	328ft	820ft	1640ft	3281ft	6562ft	13,124ft

The Baltic States & Belarus

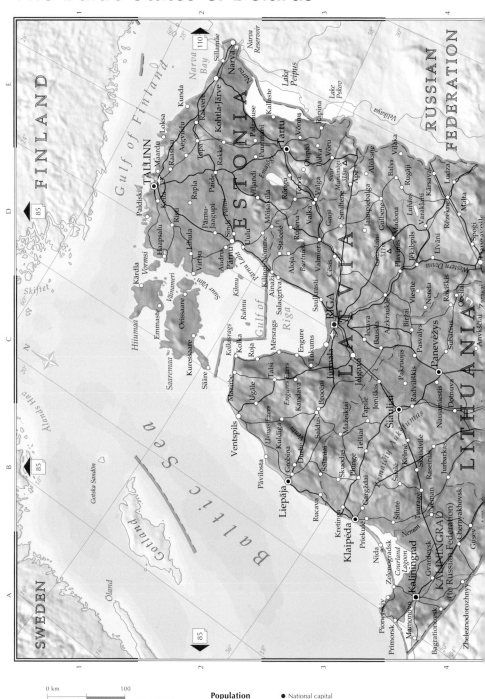

0 km	100
0 miles	100

Population ● National capital

○ below 50,000   ○ 50,000 to 100,000   ◉ 100,000 to 500,000   ■ above 500,000

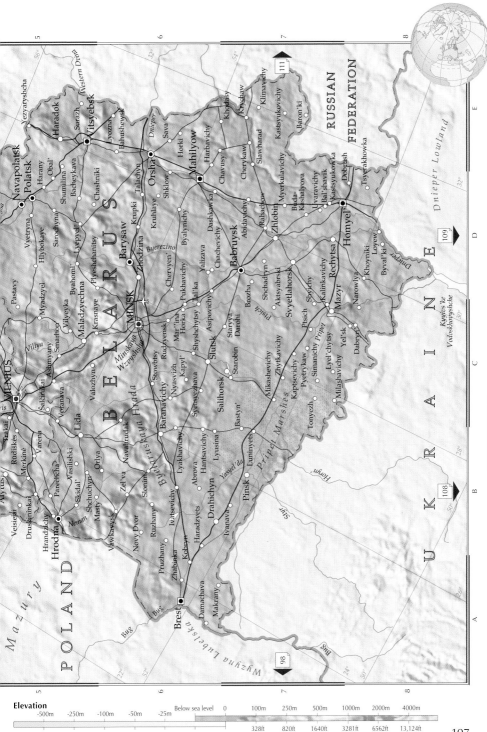

Elevation

-500m	-250m	-100m	-50m	-25m	Below sea level	0	100m	250m	500m	1000m	2000m	4000m
-1640ft	-820ft	-328ft	-164ft	-82ft	33ft/-10m	0	328ft	820ft	1640ft	3281ft	6562ft	13,124ft

Ukraine, Moldova & Romania

Population   ● National capital

○ below 50,000   ○ 50,000 to 100,000   ◉ 100,000 to 500,000   ■ above 500,000

0 km   100

0 miles   100

RUSSIAN

FEDERATION

Horodnya
Shchors
Shostka
Hlukhiv
Krolevets'
Chernihiv
Konotop
Desna
ios'ke
sovyshche
Oster
Nizhyn
Bakhmach
Nosivka
Romny
Sumy
IV
Brovary
Pryluky
Lebedyn
ka
Vasyl'kiv
tiv
Yahotyn
Pyryatyn
Okhtyrka
Zolochiv
Derhachi
Kanilos'ke
Vodoskhovyshche
Hrebinka
Lubny
Myrhorod
Lyubotyn
Kharkiv
Kup"yans'k
la Tserkva
Kaniv
Zolotonosha
Bohuslav
Horodyshche
Cherkasy
Hlobyne
Poltava
Donets
Starobil's'k
enyhorodka
Smila
Kremenchuts'ke
Vodoskhovyshche
Izyum
Kreminna
Rubizhne
Tal'ne
Shpola
Chyhyryn
Syeverodonets'k
Mala Vyska
Oleksandrivka
Svitlovods'k
Slov"yans'k
Lysychans'k
n"
Znam"yanka
Dniprodzerzhyns'ke
Vodoskhovyshche
Kramators'k
Zolote
Luhans'k
Holovanivs'k
Oleksandriya
Novomoskovs'k
Kostyantynivka
Krasnodon
lyanivka
Dniprodzerzhyns'k
Pavlohrad
Horlivka
Stakhanov
Kirovohrad
Zhovti Vody
P"yatykhatky
Dnipropetrovs'k
Yenakiyeve
Krasnyy Luch
Pervomays'k
Bobrynets'
Kryvyy Rih
Synel'nykove
Makiyivka
Torez
ryve Ozero
Arbyzynka
Dolyns'ka
Pokrovs'ke
Donets'k
Amvrosiyivka
Novyy Buh
Inhulets'
Nikopol'
Zaporizhzhya
Orikhiv
Dokuchayevs'k
Voznesens'k
Ordzhonikidze
Marhanets'
Volnovakha
Don
Kam"yanka-Dniprovs'ka
Dniprorudne
Polohy
Kakhovs'ka
Vodoskhovyshche
Tokmak
Mariupol'
Novoazovs'k
Mykolayiv
Dnieper
(Dnipro)
Kakhovka
Molochans'k
Gulf of Taganrog
Yeya
Zhovtneve
Melitopol'
Ochakiv
Kherson
Tsyurupyns'k
Akinovka
Prymors'k
Berdyans'k
Odesa
Hola Prystan'
Chaplynka
Novotroyits'k
Illichivs'k
Kalanchak
Armyans'k
Henichas'k
Sea of Azov
Karkinits'ka Zatoka
Krasnoperekops'k
RUSSIAN
Rozdol'ne
Dzhankoy
Kerch Strait
Chornomors'ke
Krasnohvardiys'ke
Zatoka
Syvash
Kerch
FEDERATION
Nyzhn'ohirs'kyy
Kuban'
Yevpatoriya
Kryms'kyy
Pivostrip
Lenine
Saky
Simferopol'
Feodosiya
Bakhchysaray
Kryms'ki Hory
Sevastopol'
Alushta
Yalta
Alupka

Black Sea

Elevation

-2000m	-1000m	-500m	-250m	-100m	Below sea level 0	100m	250m	500m	1000m	2000m	4000m

| -6562ft | -3281ft | -1640ft | -820ft | -328ft -164ft/-50m | 0 | 328ft | 820ft | 1640ft | 3281ft | 6562ft | 13,124ft |

European Russia

0 km   300

0 miles   300

Population   ● National capital

○ below 50,000   ○ 50,000 to 100,000   ◉ 100,000 to 500,000   ■ above 500,000

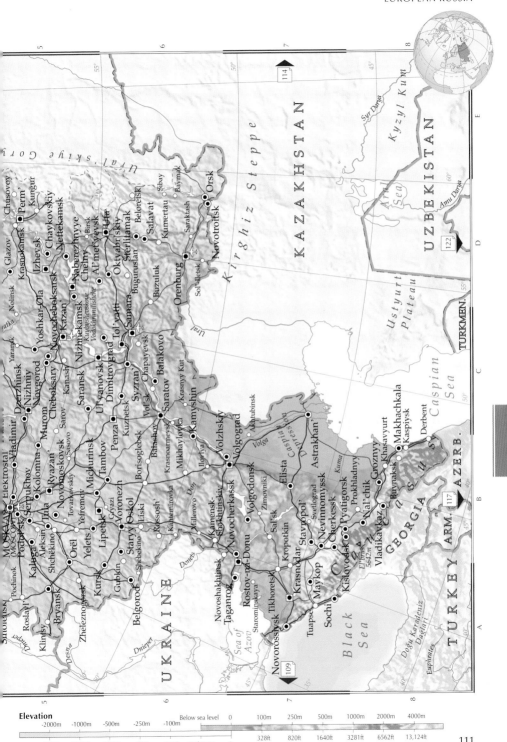

KAZAKHSTAN

UZBEKISTAN

122

Kyzyl Kum

Aral Sea

Amu Darya

Syr Darya

Kirghiz Steppe

Ustyurt Plateau

TURKMEN.

Caspian Sea

Ural'skiye Gory

Chasovoy
Perm'
Kungur
Chaykovskiy
Glazov
Krasnokamsk
Izhevsk
Neftekamsk
Nolinsk
Yaransk
Yoshkar-Ola
Cheboksary
Naberezhnyye Chelny
Birsk
Oktyabr'skiy
Ufa
Beloretsk
Sibay
Baymak
Orsk
Novotroitsk
Al'met'yevsk
Sterlitamak
Salavat
Sol'-Iletsk
Saraktash
Kumertau
Buguruslan
Orenburg
Buzuluk
Ural

Kirov
Kotel'nich
Kazan'
Novocheboksarsk
Krasno-Zaeksnoe
Vodokhranilishche
Saransk
Nizhnekamsk
Tol'yatti
Samara
Chapayevsk
Balakovo
Krasny Kut
Syzran'
Vol'sk
Saratov
Kamyshin
Kuznetsk
Dimitrovgrad
Ul'yanovsk

Nizhniy Novgorod
Dzerzhinsk
Sarov
Arzamas
Chasovo
Murom
Kanash
Michurinsk
Penza
Tambov
Borisoglebsk
Balashov
Krasnoarmeysk
Mikhaylovka
Volzhskiy
Volgograd
Akhtubinsk
Astrakhan'
Volga
Kuma

Vladimir
Kovrov
Elektrostal'
MOSCOW
MOSKVA
Kolomna
Ryazan'
Serpukhov
Novomoskovsk
Tovarkovskiy
Ilovlya
Frolovo
Kamensk-Shakhtinskiy
Kalmykia
Caspian Depression
Elista
Caspian Sea

Makhachkala
Kaspiysk
Derbent
Khasavyurt
Buynaksk
Groznyy

Smolensk
Roslavl'
Pochinok
Kaluga
Tula
Aleksin
Shchekino
Orel
Yefremov
Yelets
Lipetsk
Gubkin
Staryy Oskol
Shebekino
Liski
Rossosh'
Millerovo
Voronezh
Gryazi
Bataysk
Novoshakhtinsk
Shakhty
Novocherkassk
Volgodonsk
Zimovniki
Salsk
Svetlograd
Nevinnomyssk
Stavropol'
Cherkessk
Pyatigorsk
Prokhladnyy
Nal'chik
Vladikavkaz
El'brus
5642m
GEORGIA
AZERB.
ARM.

Klintsy
Bryansk
Zheleznogorsk
Kursk
Belgorod
Desna
Donets
Staromin'skaya
Tikhoretsk
Kropotkin
Maykop
Krasnodar
Sochi
Tuapse
Kislovodsk
Novorossiysk
Sea of Azov
Black Sea

Dnieper

UKRAINE

Taganrog
Rostov-na-Donu
Novorossiysk

109

117

Don
Sal

TURKEY

Doğu Karadeniz Dağları
Euphrates

Elevation

-2000m	-1000m	-500m	-250m	-100m	Below sea level	0	100m	250m	500m	1000m	2000m	4000m
-6562ft	-3281ft	-1640ft	-820ft	-328ft	-164ft/-50m	0	328ft	820ft	1640ft	3281ft	6562ft	13,124ft

North & West Asia

A   B   C   D

20°   40°   60°   80°   100°

155   Franz Josef Land

A R C T I

Severnaya Z.

Summer limit of pack ice   Ostrov Komsomolets

Ostrov Oktyabr'skoy Revolyutsii
Ostrov Bol'shevik

1

Winter limit of pack ice

Novaya Zemlya
East Novaya Zemlya Trench   Kara Sea   Poluostrov Taymy

Norwegian
Sea   North Cape   Barents
Sea   Ostrov
Kolguyev   Poluostrov
Yamal   North Siber
Khela

70°

Murmansk   Noril'sk   Central
Kola
Peninsula   Siberiar
Kureyka   Plateau

Arctic Circle
81   White Sea   Archangel   R U S S I A N   F
Lower Tunguska

2

60°   Lake
Onega   Northern
Dvina   Ob'   West Siberian
Plain   Yenisey   Stony Tunguska   S i

Gulf of Bothnia

Lake Ladoga   Vologda   Perm'   Yekaterinburg   Ob'   Angara

Saint Petersburg   Yaroslavl   Nizhniy
Novgorod   Irtysh   Chulym   Tomsk   Krasnoyarsk

Baltic Sea   Kaliningrad   MOSCOW   Volga   Kazan'   Ufa   Chelyabinsk   Omsk   Novosibirsk

KALININGRAD   Central
Russian
Upland   Ul'yanovsk   Samara   Novokuznetsk

(to Russ. Fed.)   Voronezh   Saratov   Volga   Orenburg   ASTANA   A   S

3

50°   E U R O P E   Ural'sk   Kirghiz
Steppe   Karaganda   Semipalatinsk   Sayanskiy Khrebet

Rostov-na-Donu   Don   Volgograd   Ural   Kazakh Uplands   Altai Mountains

Astrakhan'   Aral'sk   KAZAKHSTAN   Ozero
Zaysan

Danube   Stavropol'   El'brus
5642m   Caucasus   Aktau   Syr Darya
Ustyurt
Plateau   Aral
Sea   Lake
Balkhash

Black Sea   Istanbul   Kure Daglari   GEORGIA   Dasoguz   Kyzyl
Kum   Kyzylorda   Taraz   Almaty

40°   ANKARA   ARMENIA   T'BILISI   BAKU   UZBEKISTAN   BISHKEK   Tien Shan   Pik Pobedy 7443m

Anatolia   AZERB.   TASHKENT   KYRGYZSTAN   G

4   TURKEY   Lake
Van   TURKMENISTAN   Amu Darya   DUSHANBE

Adana   Gaziantep   Tabriz   ASGABAT   TAJIKISTAN

CYPRUS   SYRIA   IRAQ   Qom   TEHRAN   Hindu Kush   Kunlun Mountains

103   BEIRUT   DAMASCUS   BAGHDAD   Isfahan   IRAN   KABUL
Jalalabad   Khyber Pass

30°   LEBANON   Aleppo   Tigris   Syrian
Desert   Iranian
Plateau   Herat
AFGHANISTAN   Himalayas

ISRAEL   AMMAN   Euphrates   Zagros Mountains   Ganges

JERUSALEM   JORDAN   KUWAIT   Shiraz   Zahedan   Thar Desert

Dead Sea
-392m   An Nafud   KUWAIT   Bandar-e 'Abbas   Indus Fan

MANAMA   Gulf   Dubai   Ganges Fan

Tropic of Cancer   BAHRAIN   RIYADH   QATAR   DOHA   U.A.E.   MUSCAT   Murray Ridge   100°

SAUDI ARABIA   ABU
DHABI   Sur   Gulf of Oman

20°   Jedda   Arabian
Peninsula   Bay of
Bengal

At Ta'if   Red Sea   Al Khali   OMAN

5   AFRICA   Ar Rub' al Khali   Arabian
Sea

Nile   SANA   YEMEN   Socotra
(to Yemen)

Ta'izz   Aden   Gulf of Aden   69

10°

20°   40°   60°   80°   100°

A   B   C   D

0 km   800

0 miles   800

Population   ● National capital

o below 50,000   o 50,000 to 100,000   ◉ 100,000 to 500,000   ▣ above 500,000

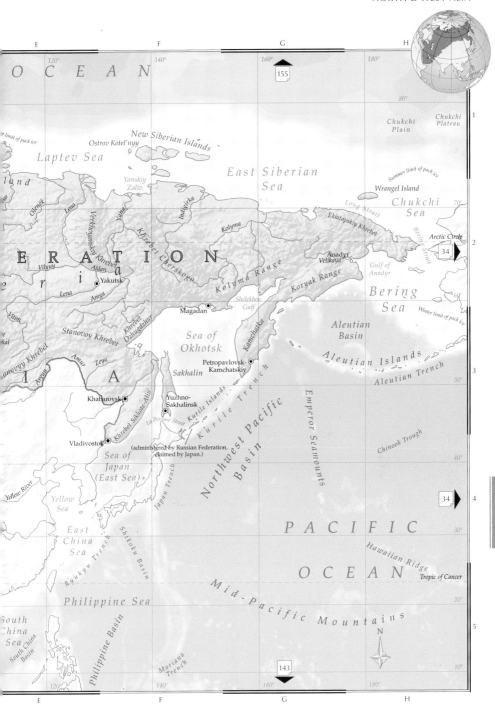

O C E A N

120°   140°   160°   180°

80°

155

limit of pack ice

New Siberian Islands

Ostrov Kotel'nyy

Laptev Sea

land

East Siberian Sea

Chukchi Plain

Chukchi Plateau

1

Olenëk

Yanskiy Zaliv.

Lena

Indigirka

Yana

Verkhoyanskiy Khrebet

Khrebet Cherskogo

Kolyma

Ekiatapskiy Khrebet

Long Strait

Summer limit of pack ice

Wrangel Island

Chukchi Sea

70°

Bering Strait

Arctic Circle

34

2

E R A T I O N

r   i

Vilyuy

Aldan

Yakutsk

Lena

Amga

Kolyma Range

Shelekhov Gulf

Koryak Range

Anadyr'
Velikaya

Gulf of Anadyr'

Bering Sea

60°

Winter limit of pack ice

Vitim

Magadan

Aleutian Basin

kal

Stanovoy Khrebet

Khrebet Dzhugdzhur

Sea of Okhotsk

Kamchatka

Aleutian Islands

onovyy Khrebet

Amur

Zeya

Sakhalin

Petropavlovsk-
Kamchatskiy

Aleutian Trench

50°

3

I A

Argun

Khabarovsk

Yuzhno-
Sakhalinsk

Khrebet Sikhote-Alin'

Kurile Islands

La Perouse Strait

Kurile Trench

Northwest Pacific Basin

Emperor Seamounts

Chinook Trough

Vladivostok

(administered by Russian Federation,
claimed by Japan.)

Sea of Japan
(East Sea)

40°

34

4

Yellow River

Yellow Sea

Japan Trench

P A C I F I C

30°

South
China
Sea

East
China
Sea

Ryukyu Trench

Shikoku Basin

O C E A N

Hawaiian Ridge

Tropic of Cancer

Philippine Sea

Philippine Basin

Mid-Pacific Mountains

20°

South
China
Sea

South China
Basin

N

5

Mariana Trench

143

10°

120°   140°   160°   180°

E   F   G   H

Russia & Kazakhstan

0 km 600

0 miles 600

Population ● National capital

○ below 50,000   ○ 50,000 to 100,000   ◉ 100,000 to 500,000   ■ above 500,000

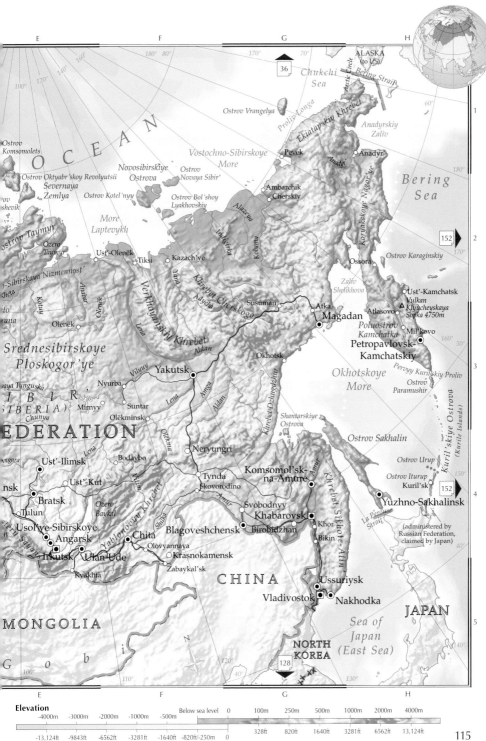

ALASKA (to US)

Arctic Circle
Bering Strait

Chukchi Sea

36

Ostrov Vrangelya

Proliv Longa

Ekiatapskiy Khrebet

Anadyrskiy Zaliv

Anadyr'

OCEAN

Vostochno-Sibirskoye More

Pevek

Anadyr

Bering Sea

Ostrov Komsomolets

Novosibirskiye Ostrova

Ostrov Novaya Sibir'

Ambarchik
Cherskiy

Koryakskoye Nagor'ye

Ostrov Oktyabr'skoy Revolyutsii
Severnaya Zemlya

shevik

Ostrov Kotel'nyy

Ostrov Bol'shoy Lyakhovskiy

Alazeya

Kolyma

Ossora

Ostrov Karaginskiy

152

rov

More Laptevykh

Indigirka

Zaliv Shelikhova

Ust'-Kamchatsk
Vulkan
Klyuchevskaya
Sopka 4750m

Ostrov Taymyr

Khrebet Cherskogo

Susuman

Atka

Atlasovo

Ozero Taymyr

Ust'-Olenëk

Tiksi

Kazach'ye

Yana

Adycha

Magadan

Mil'kovo

-Sibirskaya Nizmennost'

heta

Anabar

Olenëk

Verkhoyanskiy Khrebet

Poluostrov Kamchatka

Petropavlovsk-
Kamchatskiy

50°

to

Kotuy

Olenëk

Olenëk

Lena

Okhotsk

Perevy Kuril'skiy Proliv

rana

Srednesibirskoye
Ploskogor'ye

Vilyuy

Yakutsk

Aldan

Okhotskoye More

Ostrov Paramushir

aya Tunguska

Nyurba

Anga

Shantarskiye Ostrova

Chunya

Mirnyy

Suntar

Lena

Aldan

SIBIR'
(SIBERIA)

Olëkminsk

Khrebet Dzhugdzhur

Ostrov Sakhalin

Kuril'skiye Ostrova (Kurile Islands)

EDERATION

Olëkma

Neryungri

Ostrov Urup

150°

ngara

Ust'-Ilimsk

Bodaybo

Tynda

Komsomol'sk-
na-Amure

Ostrov Iturup
Kuril'sk

152

nsk

Ust'-Kut

Skovorodino

Amur

Svobodnyy

Yablonovyy Khrebet

Yuzhno-Sakhalinsk

Bratsk

Mama

Khabarovsk

Khor

La Pérouse
Strait

Tulun

Ozero
Baykal

Amur

Birobidzhan

40°

Usol'ye-Sibirskoye

Angarsk

Shilka

Chita

Bikin

Khrebet Sikhote-Alin'

(administered by
Russian Federation,
claimed by Japan)

Irkutsk

Ulan-Ude

Olovyannaya

Krasnokamensk

CHINA

Ussuriysk

Kyakhta

Zabaykal'sk

Vladivostok

Nakhodka

MONGOLIA

N

JAPAN

G o b i

NORTH
KOREA

Sea of
Japan
(East Sea)

128

100°

110°

120°

40°

130°

140°

E   F   G   H

Elevation

-4000m	-3000m	-2000m	-1000m	-500m		Below sea level	0	100m	250m	500m	1000m	2000m	4000m

| -13,124ft | -9843ft | -6562ft | -3281ft | -1640ft | -820ft/-250m | 0 | | 328ft | 820ft | 1640ft | 3281ft | 6562ft | 13,124ft |

115

Turkey & the Caucasus

ROMANIA

Iacul Sinoie

UKRAINE

Kryms'kyy
Pivostryv

Danube

BULGARIA

Varnenski
Zaliv

Burgaski
Zaliv

B l a c k   S e a

Maritsa

Kırklareli

Edirne

Eşme Çayı

Çorlu

Tekirdağ

İstanbul

İzmit

Adapazarı

Zonguldak

Bartın

Devrek

Karabük

Çerkeş

Cide

İnebolu

Gerze

Sinop

Küre Dağları

Kastamonu

Kargı

Bafra

Samsun

Ür

Or

Danube

İstanbul Boğazı
(Bosporus)

Marmara Denizi
Sea of Marmara

Bandırma

Yalova

İznik Gölü

Bursa

Bilecik

Bolu

Gerede

Çankırı

Kızıl Irmak

Merzifon

Çanik Dağları

Çorum

Tokat

Çanakkale

Çanakkale
Boğazı
(Dardanelles)

Balıkesir

Bozüyük

Eskişehir

ANKARA

Kalecik

Alaca

Sorgun

Yıldızeli

Siv

Edremit

Ayvalık

Kütahya

Polatlı

Kırıkkale

T   U   R   K

Sárkışla

Boğazlıyan

Lésvos

Akhisar

Sımav

Gediz

Kulu

Hirfanlı
Barajı

Bünyan

He

Menemen

Manisa

Uşak

Afyon

Cihanbeyli

Tuz Gölü

İncesu

Gürün

Gediz Nehri

İzmir

Akşehir

Nevşehir

Kayseri

Ödemiş

Alaşehir

Nazilli

Dinar

Aksaray

A   n   a   t   o   l   i   a

Göksun

G

Sámos

Aydın

Söke

Büyükmenderes Nehri

Denizli

Burdur

İsparta

Beyşehir
Gölü

Konya

Niğde

Kahramanm

Milas

Muğla

Tavas

Burdur
Gölü

Suğla Gölü

Ereğli

Karaman

Gaz

Bodrum

Marmaris

Dalaman

Antalya

Manavgat

Alanya

Mut

T o r o s   D a ğ l a r ı

Tarsus

Mersin

Adana

Ceyhan

İskenderun

Osmaniye

Kilis

Fethiye

Kaş

Finike

Antalya
Körfezi

Silifke

Anamur

Antakya

Kırıkhan

Dodekánisa
(Dodecânese)

Ródos
(Rhodes)

Kárpathos

Orantes

TURKISH REPUBLIC OF
NORTHERN CYPRUS
(recognized only by Turkey)

CYPRUS

LEBANON

M e d i t e r r a n e a n

S e a

G   R   E   E   C   E

Chíos

0 km   200

0 miles   200

Population   ● National capital

○ below 50,000   ○ 50,000 to 100,000   ◉ 100,000 to 500,000   ◼ above 500,000

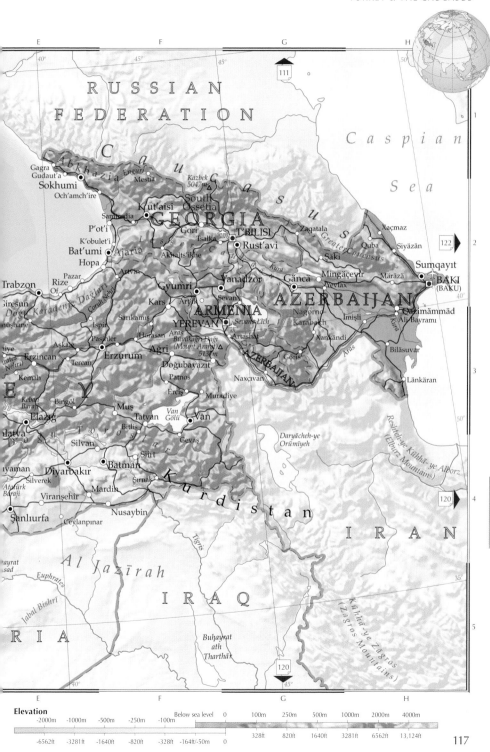

RUSSIAN

FEDERATION

Caspian

Sea

Caucasus

Gagra
Gudaut'a
Sokhumi
Och'amch'ire
Mestia
Kazbek
5047m

GEORGIA

K'ut'aisi
South
Ossetia
Samtredia
P'ot'i
Gori
Tsalka
T'BILISI
Zaqatala
Xaçmaz
K'obulet'i
Bat'umi
Ajaria
Akhalts'ikhe
Rust'avi
Quba
Siyäzän
Hopa
Artvin
Kura
Şäki
Sumqayıt
Trabzon
Pazar
Rize
Of
Vanadzor
Gánca
Mingäçevir
Märäzä
BAKI
(BAKU)
Giresun
Gyumri
Sevan
AZERBAIJAN
Qazımämmäd
Kars
Artik
Sevana Lich
Nagorno
Karabakh
İmişli
Ali-Bayramı
Gümüşhane
İspir
Sarıkamış
ARMENIA
Nevtax
Xankändi
Askale
Pasinler
YEREVAN
Artashat
Horasan
Araş
Büyükağrı Dağı
(Mount Ararat)
5137m
Goris
Biläsuvar
Erzincan
Tercan
Erzurum
Agri
AZERBAIJAN
Aras
Kemah
Doğubayazıt
Länkäran
Keban
Barajı
Bingöl
Patnos
Erciş
Naxçıvan
Muradiye
Elazığ
Muş
Van
Gölü
Van
malatya
Tatvan
Bitlis
Daryācheh-ye
Orūmīyeh
Silvan
Gevaş
Siirt
iyaman
Silverek
Diyarbakır
Batman
Şırnak
Atatürk
Barajı
Mardin
Viranşehir
Nusaybin
Şanlıurfa
Ceylanpınar

IRAN

ayrat
sad
Euphrates
Al Jazīrah
Tigris
Jabal Bishrī

RIA
IRAQ
Buhayrat
ath
Tharthār

Kühhā-ye Zāgros
(Zagros Mountains)

Elevation

						Below sea level	0	100m	250m	500m	1000m	2000m	4000m
-2000m	-1000m	-500m	-250m	-100m									
-6562ft	-3281ft	-1640ft	-820ft	-328ft	-164ft/-50m	0		328ft	820ft	1640ft	3281ft	6562ft	13,124ft

The Near East

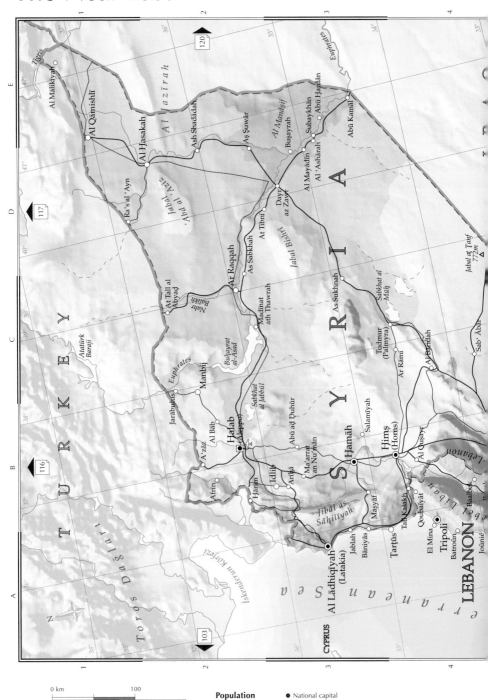

Population

● National capital

○ below 50,000 ○ 50,000 to 100,000 ◉ 100,000 to 500,000 ■ above 500,000

0 km 100
0 miles 100

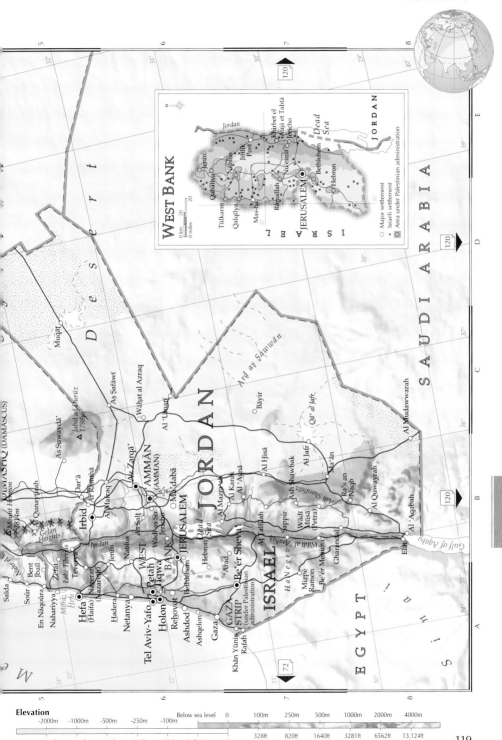

WEST BANK

Jordan

Khirbet el
'Auja et Tahta
Jifilik Post
Nu'eima Jericho
Jenin
Qabatiya
Nablus
Tulkarm
Qalqilya
Mas-ha
Ramallah
Bethlehem
JERUSALEM
Hebron

Dead Sea

JORDAN

ISRAEL

○ Major settlement
■ Israeli settlement
◉ Area under Palestinian administration

0 km   20
0 miles   20

JORDAN

SAUDI ARABIA

D e s e r t

Muqat

Jabal ad-Duruz
1798m

As Suwayda'

DIMASHQ (DAMASCUS)

Wāhat al Azraq

As Safāwi

Al 'Unari

Ard as Sawwān

Bāyir

Qa' al Jafr

Al Mudawwarah

Al 'Unari

AMMAN
(AMMAN)
Mādabā

JORDAN

Az Zarqā'

Al Mafraq

Al Fjisā

Al Jafr

Ma'ān

Ra's an
Naqb

Al Quwayrah

Al 'Aqabah

As Suwayda'

Mount Hermon
2814m

Al Qunaytirah

Dar'ā

Irbid
Ar Ramthā

Al Mazra'a

Al Karak

Al 'Ajlā

Ash Shawbak

Golan
Heights

As Salt
Wādis Sir
Jericho

WEST

JERUSALEM

Ath Thafīlah

Wādī
Mūsā
(Petra)

Dead Sea

Sappir

Nablus

Jenin

BANK

Hebron

Arad

Be'ér Sheva'
(under Palestinian administration)

Ha Negev

Gharandal

Mizpe
Ramon

Be'er Menuha

Elat

Gulf of Aqaba

ISRAEL

Saïda

Soūr

En Nāqoūra
Nahariyya

Bent
Jbail

Zefat

Lake Tiberias
Teverya

Mitzpe
Hefa
(Haifa)

Nazerat
(Nazareth)

Hadera

Netanya

Tel Aviv-Yafo
Holon
Petah
Tiqwa

Rehovot

Ashdod
Ashqelon

Gaza

GAZA
STRIP
(under Palestinian
administration)

Rafah
Khān Yūnis

Bethlehem

Hebron

Jordan

Wādī al 'Arabah

EGYPT

S i n a i

M e . . .

JORDAN

ISRAEL

Elevation

					Below sea level	0						
-2000m	-1000m	-500m	-250m	-100m			100m	250m	500m	1000m	2000m	4000m
-6562ft	-3281ft	-1640ft	-820ft	-328ft	-164ft/-50m	0	328ft	820ft	1640ft	3281ft	6562ft	13,124ft

The Middle East

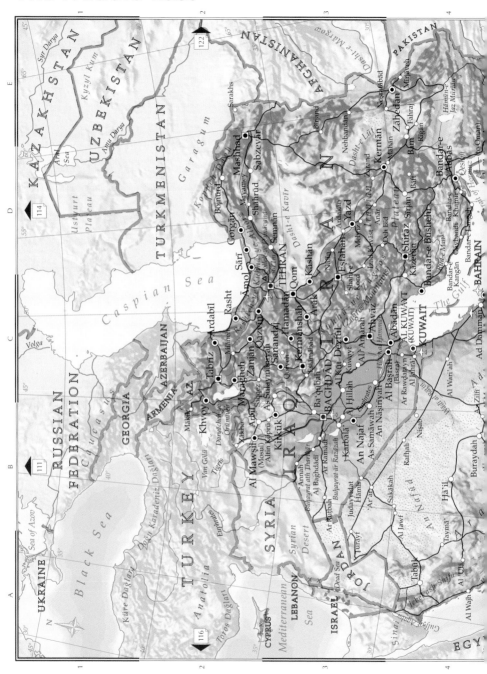

Population

- ● National capital
- ○ below 50,000
- ○ 50,000 to 100,000
- ◉ 100,000 to 500,000
- ■ above 500,000

0 km   400

0 miles   400

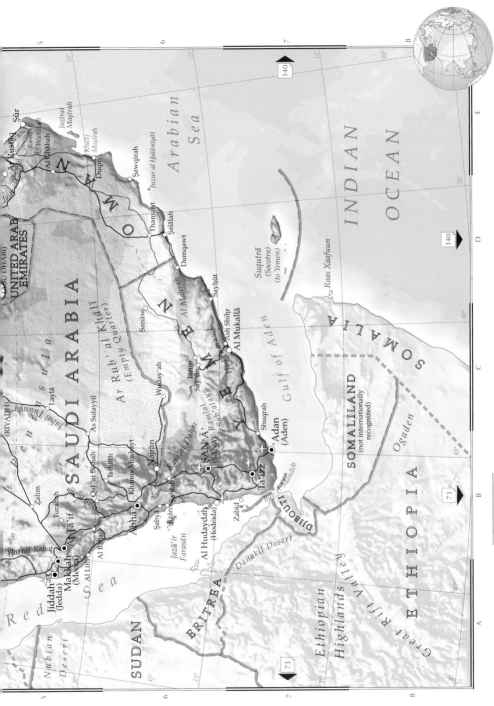

Elevation

-4000m	-3000m	-2000m	-1000m	-500m	Below sea level	0	100m	250m	500m	1000m	2000m	4000m

-13,124ft	-9843ft	-6562ft	-3281ft	-1640ft	-820ft/-250m	0	328ft	820ft	1640ft	3281ft	6562ft	13,124ft

121

Central Asia

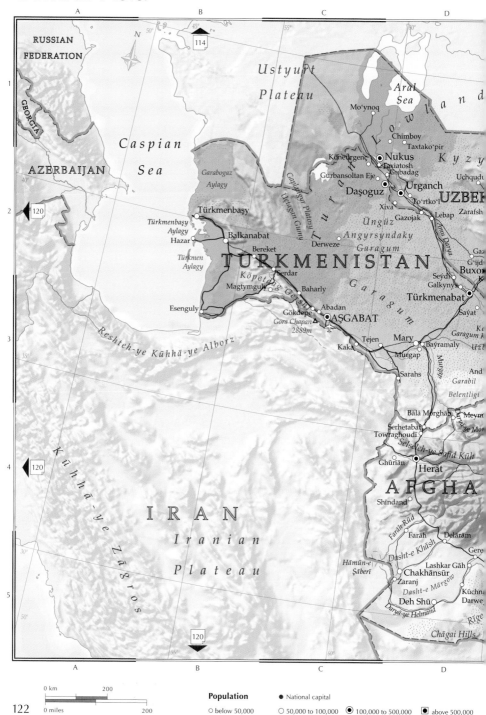

RUSSIAN
FEDERATION

GEORGIA

AZERBAIJAN

Caspian

Sea

Ustyurt

Plateau

114

Aral
Sea

Mo'ynoq

Turan Lowland

Chimboy
Taxtako'pir

Köneürgenç Nukus
Taxiatosh
Gurbansoltan Eje Gubadag
Daşoguz Urganch
To'rtko'l
Xiva Gazojak UZBEK

Uchqudu

Kyzy

Zarafsh

*Garabogaz
Aylagy*

Türkmenbaşy

*Türkmenbaşy
Aylagy*
Hazar

*Türkmen
Aylagy*

Balkanabat

Bereket
Derweze

Üngüz Lebap
Angyrsyndaky
Garagum

Amu Darya

Gaz
G'ijd
Buxo

TURKMENISTAN

Köpeta
Magtymguly Serdar
Baharly

Esenguly

Garagum

Seydi
Galkynyş
Türkmenabat

Gökdepe
Gora Chapan△
2889m AŞGABAT

Abadan
Tejen Mary
Kaka Bayramaly
Murgap
Sarahs

Sayat

Garagum k
Uzl

Reshteh-ye Kühhā-ye Alborz

Garagum

Murgap

*And
Garabil
Belentligi*

Bālā Morghāb Meym
ye Mor
Serhetabat
Towraghoudi
Selselch-ye Safid Küh

Ghūrīān Herāt

AFGHA

120

Kühhā-ye Zāgros

IRAN

Iranian

Plateau

Shīndand

Farah Rūd
Farāh Delārām

Gere

*Hāmūn-e
Şāberī*

Dasht-e Khāsh

Lashkar Gāh
Chakhānsūr
Zaranj
Dasht-e Mārgow

Kūchna
Darwe

Deh Shū

Daryā-ye Helmand

Chāgai Hills

Rige

120

120

120

0 km   200

0 miles   200

Population

○ below 50,000
○ 50,000 to 100,000
◉ 100,000 to 500,000
■ above 500,000

● National capital

KAZAKHSTAN

Ozero Balkhash

Peski Saryyesik-Atyrau

Peski Taukum

Peski Moyynkum

Borohoro Shan

115

Ili

45°

1

Syr Darya

u m

N

BISHKEK
Kara-Balta   Tokmak

Ozero Issyk-Kul'   Tyup   Dzhergalan

Gora Manas   Leninpol   Kemin   Balykchy   Karakol   Kyzyl-Suu
4482m   Kadzhi-Say

TOSHKENT   KYRGYZSTAN   Kara-Say   Pik Pobedy
(TASHKENT)   7443m

Yangiyo'l   Chirchiq   Tash-Kumyr   *Khrebet Moldo-Too*

Angren   Namangan   Dzhalal-Abad   Naryn   Karakol

Olmaliq   Qo'qon   Andijon

Nurota   Bekobod   Osh   Kök-Art   Chatyr-Tash

Langar   Guliston   Farg'ona
Navoiy   Jizzax   Khujand
Kattaqo'rg'on   Uroteppa   Sulyukta   Khaydarkan   Sary-Tash
Samarqand   *Zeravshan*   Daroot-Korgon
Urgut   *Surkhob*   Qarokül

Qarshi   Kitob   △ Qullai Kommunizm   XINJIANG
Gissar Range   DUSHANBE   TAJIKISTAN   7495m   UYGUR
Denov   ZIZHIQU   *Taklimakan*
derya   Boysun   Norak   Qalaikhum   Ghudara   Murghob
vrat   Qŭrghonteppa   Danghara   *Bartang*   C   *Shamo*
Termiz   Jarqo'rg'on   Kŭlob   Moskva
shah   Dŭsti   Farkhor   Khorugh   Dzhelandy   Qizilrabot   H
Balkh   Kholm   Feyzabad   I
berghan   Kondoz   Taloqan   Ishkoshim   (claimed by India)   N
Mazar-e   Khanabad   AKSAI CHIN
Sharif   Baghlan   Baroghil Pass   (administered by China,   A
Pol-e Khomri   3777m   claimed by India)
Charikar   Barikowt   Aksai
Mahmud-e Raqi   Chin   DEMCHOK/
KABOL   Asadabad   DEMQOG   126
(KABUL)   Mehtar Lam   (administered by China,
Maydan Shahr   Jalalabad   claimed by India)
STAN   *Khyber Pass*
Ghazni   Gardiz   1080m   (A 'line of control'   XIZANG
Khowst   was agreed between   ZIZHIQU
Zarghun   India and Pakistan   (Tibet)
Shahr   in 1972)
Qalat   *Indus*   *Ravi*   (administered by China,
ndahar   claimed by India)
Spin Buldak   H
Toba Kākar Range   PAKISTAN   i   INDIA
m
Sulaimān Range   a   NEPAL
134   l
a
y   30°
a
s
70°   75°   80°

126

2

40°

3

35°

4

5

South & East Asia

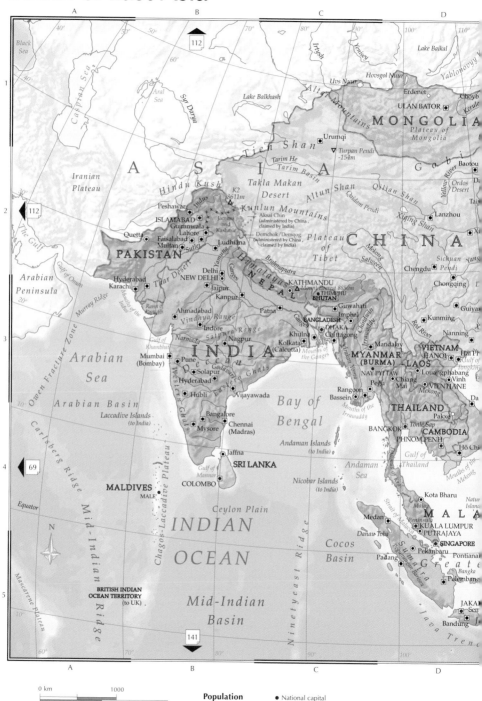

Black Sea

40°
50°
70°
80°
90°
100°
110°

112

Caspian Sea

Aral Sea

Syr Darya

Lake Balkhash

Irtysh

Yenisey

Lake Baikal

60°

Uvs Nuur

Hovsgol Nuur

Altai Mountains

Erdenet

Choyb

ULAN BATOR

Kerule

MONGOLIA

Plateau of Mongolia

40°

Tien Shan

Urumqi

Turpan Pendi -154m

Gobi

Baotou

Da

Ordos Desert

Iranian Plateau

A S I A

Takla Makan Desert

Kunlun Mountains

Hindu Kush

K2 8611m

Altun Shan

Qilian Shan

Xiang Shan

Lanzhou

Tai

The Gulf

112

Peshawar

Indus

Aksai Chin (administered by China claimed by India)

Qaidam Pendi

Plateau of Tibet

C H I N A

Sickuan Yang

Chengdu

Pendi

Chongqing

30°

ISLAMABAD

Jammu and Kashmir

Demchok / Demqog (administered by China claimed by India)

Gujranwala
Lahore

Quetta
Faisalabad

Multan

Ludhiana

Sutlej

Mekong

Salween

PAKISTAN

Arabian Peninsula

Gulf of Oman

Murray Ridge

Mouths of the Indus

Thar Desert

Delhi
NEW DELHI

Yamuna

Ganges

Brahmaputra

Himalaya

NEPAL

Mount Everest 8850m

KATHMANDU

THIMPHU
BHUTAN

Guwahati

Imphal

Kunming

Guiya

Hyderabad
Karachi

Rann of Kachchh

Jaipur

Kanpur

20°

Ahmadabad

Vindhya Range

Patna

Ganges

BANGLADESH

DHAKA

Chittagong

Chindwin

Irrawaddy

Red River

Nanning

Xi

Gulf of Khambhat

Indore

Narmada

Satpura Range

Nagpur

Kolkata (Calcutta)

Khulna

Mandalay

VIETNAM

HANOI

Hai Ph

Gulf of Tongking

Arabian Sea

I N D I A

Mumbai (Bombay)

Pune

Godavari

Deccan

Hyderabad

Solapur

Mouths of the Ganges

MYANMAR (BURMA)

LAOS

NAY PYI TAW

Louangphabang

Chiang Mai

Vinh

VIENTIANE

Da

Arabian Basin

Laccadive Islands (to India)

Hubli

Western Ghats

Eastern Ghats

Vijayawada

Bay of Bengal

Rangoon

Pegu

Bassein

Mouths of the Irrawaddy

THAILAND

Pakxe

10°

Carlsberg Ridge

Bangalore

Mysore

Chennai (Madras)

BANGKOK

Tonle Sap

CAMBODIA

PHNOM PENH

Gulf of Thailand

Hồ Chi

Andaman Islands (to India)

Jaffna

Gulf of Mannar

SRI LANKA

COLOMBO

Andaman Sea

Nicobar Islands (to India)

Kota Bharu

Natu Islan

MALA

Equator

N

MALDIVES

MALE

Chagos-Laccadive Plateau

Ceylon Plain

INDIAN

Medan

Danau Toba

Malay Peninsula

Strait of Malacca

KUALA LUMPUR
PUTRAJAYA

SINGAPORE

Pekanbaru

Pontiana

Mid-Indian Ridge

OCEAN

Cocos Basin

Padang

Sumatra

Greate

Bangka

Palembang

Masarene Plateau

BRITISH INDIAN OCEAN TERRITORY (to UK)

Mid-Indian Basin

Ninetyeast Ridge

JAKA

Sen

Bandung

Java Trench

10°

60°

70°

80°

90°

100°

141

A
B
C
D

0 km 1000

0 miles 1000

Population

● National capital

○ below 50,000
○ 50,000 to 100,000
◉ 100,000 to 500,000
■ above 500,000

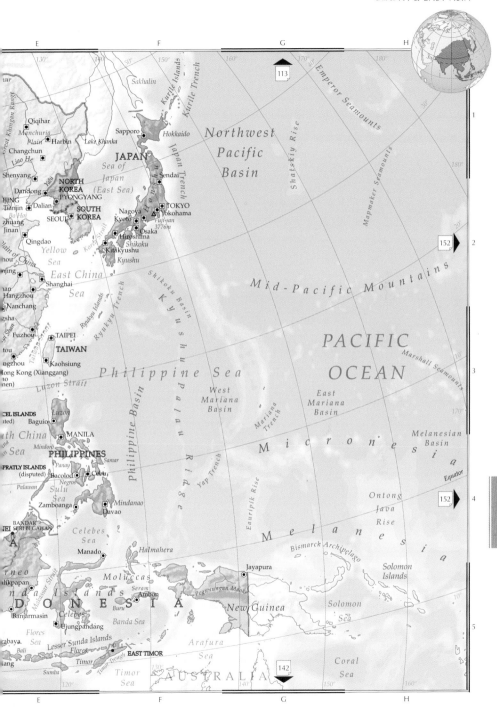

E   F   50'   150°   160°   170°   40'   180°

113

Sakhalin

130°   140°   Kurile Islands   Kurile Trench

Great Khingan Range

Qiqihar   Manchuria   Harbin   Lake Khanka   Hokkaido   Sapporo   Sapporo   Northwest
Plain   Pacific
Changchun   JAPAN   Sendai   Basin

Liao He   Sea of   Japan Trench   Shatskiy Rise

Shenyang   Japan
(East Sea)   Sendai   180°

HING   NORTH
KOREA   Dandong   Dalian   PYONGYANG
Tianjin   Bo Hai   SOUTH   KOREA   TOKYO   Yokohama   152
zhuang   SEOUL   Nagoya   Kyoto   Osaka   Fuji-san
Jinan   3776m   Mid-Pacific Mountains

Qingdao   Yellow   Korea Strait   Hiroshima   Shikoku
Sea   Kitakyushu
Kyushu

East China   Sea
Shanghai

Hangzhou   Shikoku Basin
Nanchang   Ryukyu Islands   Kyushu Basin   PACIFIC
gsha
Fuzhou   TAIPEI   Ryukyu Trench   OCEAN   Marshall Seamounts
tou   TAIWAN
ngzhou   Kaohsiung   Philippine Sea
ong Kong (Xianggang)   Luzon Strait   West   East   170°
nen)   Mariana   Mariana
Basin   Basin   Micronesia

CEL ISLANDS   Luzon   Baguio   Mariana Trench
ated)

th China   MANILA   Melanesian
n Sea   Mindoro   PHILIPPINES   Basin
PRATLY ISLANDS   Panay   Samar   Equator
(disputed)   Bacolod   Cebu   152
Palawan   Negros   Ontong
Sulu   Java
Zamboanga   Mindanao   Rise
Sea   Davao

BANDAR
JEI SERI BEGAWAN   Celebes
A   Sea   Manado   Halmahera   Melanesia

rneo   Bismarck Archipelago
lkpapan   Moluccas   Jayapura   Solomon
Islands
Banjarmasin   Celebes   Seram   Ambon
nd   Islands   Buru   Pegunungan Maok   Solomon
Ujungpandang   Banda Sea   New Guinea   Sea
Flores
abaya   Sea   Lesser Sunda Islands
Bali   Flores   Timor   DILI   EAST TIMOR   142
ang   Sumba   Timor Trough   AUSTRALIA   Arafura   Coral
Timor   Sea   Sea
Sea   120°   140°   150°   160°

E   F   G   H

Western China & Mongolia

RUSSIAN FE

Kulunda
Steppe

Zapadnyy Sayan

Yenisey

114

KAZAKHSTAN

Kazakhskiy

Melkosopochnik

Ozero
Balkhash

123

Ozero Issyk-Kul'

KYRGYZSTAN

TAJIKISTAN

AFGH.

Ozero
Zaysan

Ulaangom

Uvs Nuur

Altay

Olgiy

Har-Us Nuur

Ulungur
He

Karamay

Gurbantünggüt
Shamo

Kuytun

Bortala Shan

Yining

Shihezi

Ürümqi

Fukang

Jimsar

Tien Shan

Tomür Feng
7443m

Korla

Bosten Hu

Kuruktag

Kashi

Yengisar

Shache

Tarim He

Tarim Basin

XINJIANG UYGUR

ZIZHIQU

Yecheng

Pishan
(claimed
by India)

Moyu

Taklimakan
Shamo

Ruoqiang

Altun Shan

Hyargas
Nuur

Har Nuur

Hövd

Hövsgöl
Nuur

Mö

Hangayn Nuru

Tsetserle

Altay

Aj Bogd Uul
3802m

MON

Bayanhongor

Alas Bogd
2695m

Hami

G

Dalian I

Turpan

Qitai

Turpan
Pendi

Xingxingxia

Lop Nur

GANSU

Qilian Shan

Qinghai

Pakistan

Karakoram Range

Hotan

Qira

K2
8611m

Kashmir

Kunlun Shan

AKSAI
CHIN

Qaidam Pendi

Ranghe Nanshan

Burhan Budai Shan

Anyemaqen

Golmud

Dulan

134

JAMMU
AND
KASHMIR

AKSAI CHIN
(administered by
China, claimed
by India)

Rutög

DEMCHOK/DÊMQOG
(administered by China,
claimed by India)

Qingzang Gaoyuan
(Plateau of Tibet)

Tongtian He

C

H

QINGHA

Bayan Har Sh

Yushu

Gar

Zanda

XIZANG

ZIZHIQU
(Tibet)

Nyima

Tangra
Yumco

Ngangzê
Co

Siling Co

Gyaring
Co

Nan Co

Amdo

Damxung

Nagqu

Tanggula Shan

Mekong

Qando

Salween

Jinsha Jiang

Nujiang

Brahmaputra

Indus

Yamuna

Ganges

HIMALAYA

NEPAL

Lhazê

Xigazê

Mount Everest
8850m

Gyangzê

Lhasa

Gonggar

Mazhokunggar

Gyaingêntanglha Shan

INDIA

BHUTAN

INDIA

ARUNACHAL
PRADESH
(claimed by China)

MYANMAR
(BURMA)

135

0 km   400

0 miles   400

Population   ● National capital   ◉ Internal administrative capital

○ below 50,000   ○ 50,000 to 100,000   ◉ 100,000 to 500,000   ■ above 500,000

55° 110° 115° 120° 125° 130° 50° 135°

ero Baykal

R A T I O N

RUSS. FED.

115

Shilka

Amur (Heilong Jiang)

Ergun (Ergun He)

Ergun Jagdaqi

HEILONGJIANG

Onon

Hailar
Manzhouli

Da Hinggan Ling

Selenga

Sühbaatar

Hulun
Nur

Darhan

Onon Gol Choybalsan

45°

Lake
Khanka

135°

rdenet

ULAANBAATAR
(ULAN BATOR)

Menengiyn
Tal

Hulingol

JILIN

O L I A

Dzuunmod Öndörhaan

Baruun-Urt

Kerulen

Tongliao

40°

Sea of
Japan
(East Sea)

Saynshand

Xilinhot

Liao He

Erenhot

Chifeng
(Ulanhad)

LIAONING

NORTH
KOREA

128

2

Dalandzadgad

Jining

BEIJING

Korea
Bay

I Nuruu

MONGOL

(Inner Mongolia)

Hohhot

NEI

Lang Shan

Baotou

TIANJIN

Bo Hai

SOUTH
KOREA

35°

130°

3

Huang He
(Yellow River)

Wuhai
(Haibowan)

HEBEI

Mu Us
Shadi

SHANDONG

Yellow
Sea

Tengger
Shamo

Great Wall of China

NINGXIA

SHANXI

JAPAN

129

Huang He (Yellow River)

JIANGSU

East

30°

4

ng

N

GANSU

SHAANXI

HENAN

Han Shui

ANHUI

SHANGHAI SHI

China

HUBEI

Chang Jiang (Yangtze)

ZHEJIANG

Sea

Nansei-shotō
(to Japan)

ICHUAN

CHONGQING

JIANGXI

25°

5

HUNAN

FUJIAN

129

YUNNAN

115°

25°

120°

125°

Tropic of Cancer

GUIZHOU

105°

110°

TAIWAN

E F G H

Elevation

-2000m -1000m -500m -250m -100m Below sea level 0 100m 250m 500m 1000m 2000m 4000m

-6562ft -3281ft -1640ft -820ft -328ft -164ft/-50m 0 328ft 820ft 1640ft 3281ft 6562ft 13,124ft

Eastern China & Korea

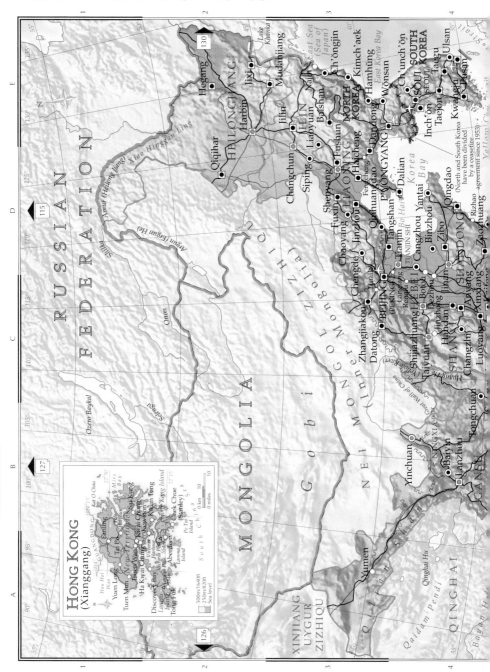

HONG KONG
(Xianggang)

0 km 400
0 miles 400

Population   ● National capital   ● Internal administrative capital

○ below 50,000   ○ 50,000 to 100,000   ◉ 100,000 to 500,000   ◼ above 500,000

East China Sea

Okinawa

Nansei-shotō (Ryukyu Islands (Japan))

Tropic of Cancer

TAIWAN

Chilung
TAIPEI
Taichung
Chiai
Tainan
Kaohsiung

PACIFIC OCEAN

PHILIPPINES

Luzon Strait

(China and Taiwan claim
all of each other's territory)

Formosa Strait (Taiwan Strait)

Suzhou
Shanghai
Wuxi
Jiaxing
Ningbo
Huzhou
Wenzhou
Hangzhou
Jinhua
ZHEJIANG
Shangrao
Wuhu
Anqing
Nanjing
Jingdezhen
ANHUI
Fuzhou
Nanchang
FUJIAN
Quanzhou
JIANGXI
Yong'an
Xiamen
Longyan
Zhangzhou
GUANGDONG
Shantou
Chaozhou
Hong Kong (Xianggang)
Macao (Aomen)

Nanyang
HUBEI
Xinyang
Xiangfan
Yichang
Huangshi
Xiaogan
Wuhan
Changsha
HUNAN
Xiangtan
Loudi
Hengyang
Chenzhou
Shaoguan
Ganzhou
Guilin

CHONGQING SHI
Chongqing
Fuling
Wanzhou
Guangyuan

SICHUAN
Sichuan Pendi
Mianyang
Chengdu
Neijiang
Zigong
Yibin
Leshan
Xichang

ZHANG (TIBET)
ZIZHIQU

Dali
Baoshan
YUNNAN
Kunming
Gejiu
Anshun
Zunyi
GUIZHOU
Guiyang
Huaihua
Yuanjiang

GUANGXI
ZHUANGZU
ZIZHIQU
Liuzhou
Nanning
Yulin
Beihai
Qinzhou
Zhaoqing
Jiangmen
Maoming
Zhanjiang
Haikou
Xuwen
HAINAN
Hainan Dao
Danzhou
Dongfang

Gulf of Tongking

VIETNAM

South China Sea

PARACEL ISLANDS
(disputed by China,
Taiwan and Vietnam)
Amphitrite Group
Crescent Group
Triton Island

SPRATLY ISLANDS
(disputed by China,
Malaysia, Philippines,
Taiwan and Vietnam)
Flat Island
Nanshan Island
Thitu Island
Loaita Island
Namyit Island
Len Dao
Spratly Island

LAOS

THAILAND

CAMBODIA

Gulf of Thailand

Mekong
Red River
Salween
Jinsha Jiang
Yangtze
Wuliang Shan
Hengduan Shan

INDIA
MYANMAR (BURMA)

Tropic of Cancer

Elevation

				Below sea level	0	100m	250m	500m	1000m	2000m	4000m
-2000m	-1000m	-500m	-250m	-100m							
					0	328ft	820ft	1640ft	3281ft	6562ft	13,124ft
-6562ft	-3281ft	-1640ft	-820ft	-328ft	-164ft/-50m	0					

Japan

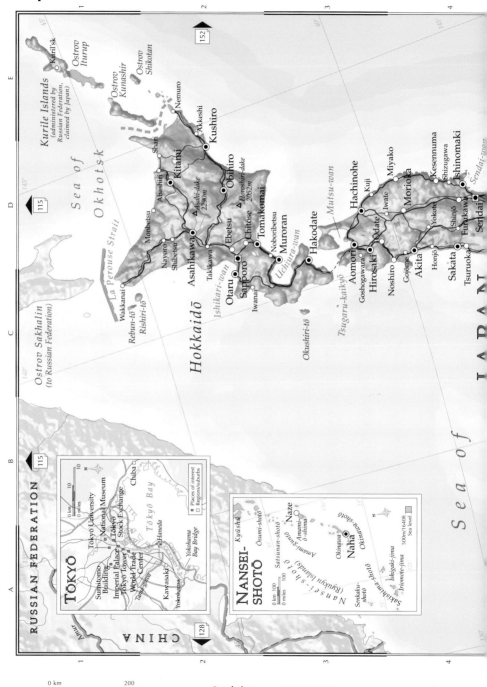

Population
National capital
○ below 50,000   ○ 50,000 to 100,000   ◉ 100,000 to 500,000   ■ above 500,000

0 km   200

0 miles   200

Honsnu

Hitachi
Utsunomiya
Mito
Chōshi
Ōyama
Kasama-ura
Kanagawa
Chiba
Yokohama
Bōsō-hantō
Sagami-nada
TŌKYŌ
Kawasaki
Izu hantō
Maebashi
Fuji
Sunage-wan
Suruga-wan
Kōzu-shima
Izu-shotō
Miyake-jima
Mikura-jima
Nii-jima
Ō-shima
Hachijō-jima

P A C I F I C

Fujisan
3776m
Matsumoto
Kōfu
Shizuoka
Hamamatsu

O C E A N

Nagano
Ueda
Maebashi
Jōetsu
Itoigawa
Shinano-gawa
Toyama
Matsumoto
Hida
sanmyaku
Nakatsugawa
Gifu
Nagoya
Toyota
Okazaki
Ise
Ise-wan
Owase
Shingū
Biwa-ko
Ōtsu
Tsu
Osaka

Takaoka
Kanazawa
Komatsu
Fukui
Tsuruga
Toyama-wan
Wakasa-wan
Kyōto
Kōbe
Wakayama
Gobō
Tanabe
Kii-suidō

Shikoku

Tottori
Yonago
Himeji
Harima-nada
Awaji-shima
Tokushima
Niihama
Kōchi
Nakamura
Sukumo
Tosa-wan

Oki-shotō
Dōgo
Dōzen

Liancourt Rocks
(claimed by Japan
& South Korea)

Matsue
San'in-suichi
San'yō-suichi
Okayama
Kurashiki
Kure
Matsuyama
Bungo-suidō

Kyūshū

Gōtsu
Masuda
Hiroshima
Iwakuni
Hōfu
Ube
Iyo-nada
Ōita
Nobeoka
Miyazaki
Miyakonojō
Tanega-shima
Shibushi-wan

Hamada
Nagato
Yamaguchi
Shimonoseki
Kitakyūshū
Fukuoka
Kurume
Ōmuta
Saga
Saito
Satsushiro
Sendai
Kagoshima
Yaku-shima

Tsushima
Iki
Kō-saki
Sasebo
Nagasaki
Kumamoto
Amakusa-nada
Koshikijima-rettō
Ōsumi-shotō
Kagoshima-wan

Korea Strait

SOUTH
KOREA

N

Goto-rettō

East
China Sea

152
152
152
128

Elevation

-4000m	-3000m	-2000m	-1000m	-500m	Below sea level	0	100m	250m	500m	1000m	2000m	4000m
-13,124ft	-9843ft	-6562ft	-3281ft	-1640ft	-820ft/-250m	0	328ft	820ft	1640ft	3281ft	6562ft	13,124ft

131

Southern India & Sri Lanka

Kalyān
134 Mumbai
(Bombay)
Pune
Ahmadnagar
Bārāmati
Nānded
Jagdalp
Nizāmābād
Karīmnagar
INDIA
Solāpur
Sāngli
Gulbarga
Secunderābād
Vizianagaram
Visākhāpa
Kolhāpur
Hyderābād
Rajahmu
Deccan
Kākir
Belgaum
Rāichūr
Krishna
Vijayawāda
Karnataka
Panaji
Gadag
Kurnool
Andhra
Machilīpatr
Hubli
Nandyāl
Chirāla
Ongole
Tungabhadra
Reservoir
Tādpatri
Kāvali
Dāvangere
Pradesh
Nellore
Shimoga
Anantapur
Cuddapah
Udupi
Bhadrāvati
Coromandel Coast
Tumkūr
Chennai
121
Mangalore
Bangalore
Vellore
(Madras)
Kāsaragod
Mandya
Kānchīpuram
Krishnagiri
Tiruppattūr
Cannanore
Mysore
Salem
Pondicherry
Calicut
Erode
Neyveli
Tamil Nādu
Coimbatore
Amīndīvi
Islands
Trichūr
Tiruchchirāppalli
Lakshadweep
Kavaratti
Island
Ernākulam
Dindigul
Madurai
(Laccadive Islands)
Kalpeni
Island
Cochin
Jaffna
SRI LANK
(to India)
(Kochi)
Nine Degree Channel
Alleppey
Rājapālaiyam
Mannar
Vavuniya
Minicoy Island
Quilon
Tuticorin
Trincomalee
Eight Degree Channel
Trivandrum
Nāgercoil
Puttalam
Anurādhapura
Gulf of
Mannar
Batticalo
Ihavandippolhu
Atoll
Negombo
Matale
Kandy
COLOMBO
Sri Jayawardanapu
MALDIVES
Faadhippolhu
Atoll
Kalutara
Ratnapura
Galle
Matara
Horsburgh
Atoll
73
Ari Atoll
Male'Atoll
MALE'
Felidhu Atoll
Mulaku Atoll
Kolhumadulu
Atoll
INDIAN
Hadhdhunmathi Atoll
North Huvadhu Atoll
Equator
South Huvadhu
Atoll
Gan
140
Addu Atoll

Arabian

Sea

Malabar Coast

Kerala

Pak Strait

132

0 km   300
0 miles   300

Population
● National capital
○ below 50,000
○ 50,000 to 100,000
◉ 100,000 to 500,000
■ above 500,000

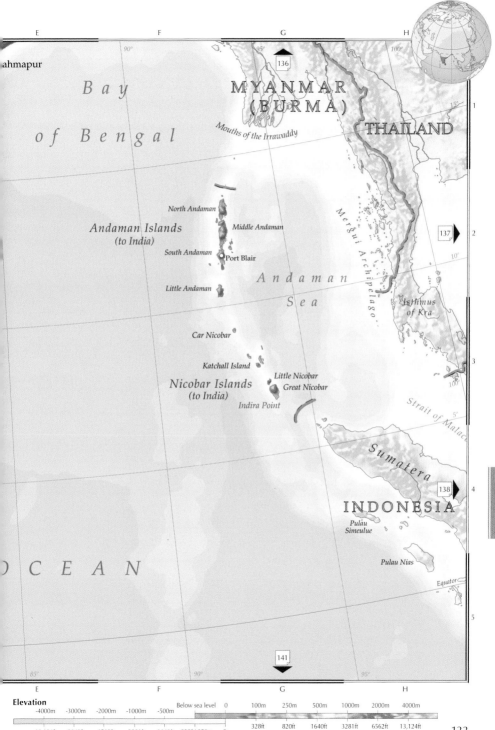

E   F   G   H

90°   95°   100°

136

ahmapur

B a y

of B e n g a l

MYANMAR
(BURMA)

THAILAND

Mouths of the Irrawaddy

15° 1

North Andaman

Andaman Islands
(to India)

Middle Andaman

Mergui Archipelago

137 2

South Andaman

Port Blair

A n d a m a n

10°

Little Andaman

S e a

Isthmus
of Kra

Car Nicobar

Katchall Island

Little Nicobar

Nicobar Islands
(to India)

Great Nicobar

100° 3

Indira Point

5°

Strait of Malacca

S u m a t e r a

138 4

INDONESIA

Pulau
Simeulue

O C E A N

Pulau Nias

Equator

141

85°   90°   95°

E   F   G   H

Elevation

-4000m	-3000m	-2000m	-1000m	-500m	Below sea level	0	100m	250m	500m	1000m	2000m	4000m
-13,124ft	-9843ft	-6562ft	-3281ft	-1640ft	-820ft/-250m	0	328ft	820ft	1640ft	3281ft	6562ft	13,124ft

Northern India, Pakistan & Bangladesh

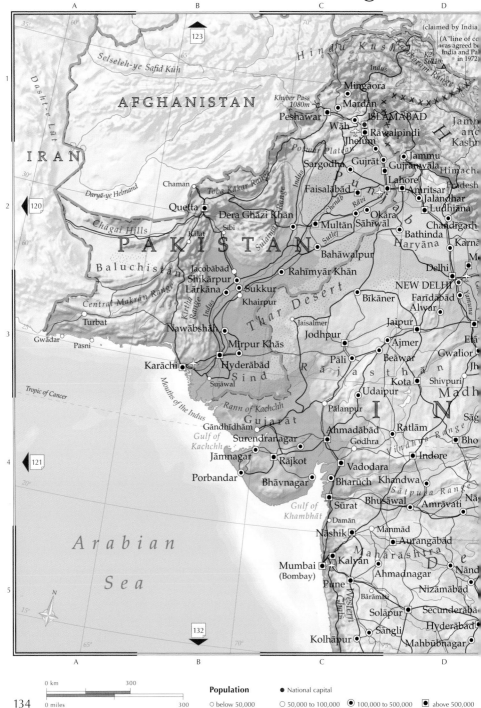

(claimed by India

(A "line of co
was agreed be
India and Pak
in 1972)

K2
8611m △

Selseleh-ye Safid Kūh

Hindu Kush

Indus

Karakoram Range

Dasht-e Lūt

AFGHANISTAN

Khyber Pass
1080m

Mingaora

Mardān

Jammu
and
Kashm

IRAN

Peshāwar

ISLĀMĀBĀD

Wāh

Rāwalpindi

Jhelum

Jammu

Daryā-ye Helmand

Chaman

Toba Kākar Range

Sargodha

Gujrāt

Gujrānwāla

Himach

Pradesh

Quetta

Dera Ghāzi Khān

Faisalābād

Lahore

Amritsar

Jalandhar

Ludhiāna

Chāgai Hills

Kālat

Sibi

Multān

Sāhīwāl

Okāra

Chandīgarh

Bathinda

Haryāna

Karna

Baluchistān

Jacobābād

Shikārpur

Lārkāna

Sukkur

Khairpur

Rahīmyār Khān

Bahāwalpur

Delhi

NEW DELHI

Farīdābād

Alwar

Central Makrān Range

Kirthar Range

Indus

Nawābshāh

Jaisalmer

Bīkāner

Jaipur

Turbat

Jodhpur

Ajmer

Gwalior

Gwādar

Pasni

Karāchi

Hyderābād

Mīrpur Khās

Pāli

Beāwar

Jh

Sind

Sujāwal

Kota

Shivpuri

Madh

Tropic of Cancer

Mouths of the Indus

Rann of Kachchh

Udaipur

I

N

Pālanpur

Gāndhīdhām

Gujarāt

Gulf of
Kachchh

Surendranagar

Ahmadābād

Ratlām

Sāg

Godhra

Bho

Jāmnagar

Rājkot

Indore

Porbandar

Bhāvnagar

Vadodara

Bharūch

Khandwa

Na

Gulf of
Khambhāt

Sūrat

Bhusāwal

Amrāvati

Satpura Range

Damān

Manmād

Nāshik

Aurangābād

Maharāshtra

De

Mumbai
(Bombay)

Kalyān

Nānd

Arabian

Ahmadnagar

Pune

Nizāmābād

Sea

Bārāmati

Solāpur

Secunderāba

N

Sāngli

Hyderābād

Kolhāpur

Mahbūbnagar

---

0 km   300
0 miles   300

Population   ● National capital

○ below 50,000   ○ 50,000 to 100,000   ◎ 100,000 to 500,000   ■ above 500,000

XINJIANG
UYGUR ZIZHIQU

Kunlun Shan

QINGHAI

AKSAI CHIN
(administered by China,
claimed by India)

C H I N A

Qingzang Gaoyuan
(Plateau of Tibet)

Tanggula Shan

DEMCHOK/
DÊMQOG
(administered by China,
claimed by India)

XIZANG ZIZHIQU

(Tibet)

Nyainqêntanglha Shan

ARUNĀCHAL
PRADESH
(claimed by China)

Brahmaputra

Jinsha Jiang

SICHUAN

Mekong (Lancang Jiang)

NEPAL
Annapurna
8091m△
eilly
Salyān
Pokharā
un
Bahraich
Bhaktapur
△Mount Everest
8850m
Gangtok
△Kula Kangri
7554m
THIMPHU
Dibrugarh
KATHMANDU
Lalitpur Darjiling
BHUTAN
know
Faizābād
Gorakhpur
Birātnagar
Shiligurī
Bongaigaon
Jorhāt
Kānpur
Mau
Chhapra
Saidpur
Koch Bihār
Guwāhāti
Assam
Kohīma
Jaunpur
Varanasi
Patna
Dinājpur
Rangpur
Dispur
Shillong
Imphāl
llahābād
Bihār Sharif
Bhāgalpur
Jamālpur
Meghālaya
Silchar
Gaya
Rajshāhi
Sylhet
adeh
I
A
Jharkhand
Dhanbād
Pabna
Brahmanbaria
Tropic of Cancer
Murwāra
Bokāro
Asānsol
DHAKA
Comilla
MYANMAR
Jabalpur
Chota
Nāgpur
Rānchī
Bānkura
Jessore
Khulna
(BURMA)
Bilāspur
Korba
Jamshedpur
West Bengal
Hāora
Barisal
Chittagong
Gondia
Raipur
Rāulakela
Kharagpur
Kolkata
(Calcutta)
ndgaon
Durg
Sambalpur
Bāleshwar
Mouths of the Ganges
drapur
n
Mahānadi
Cuttack
Orissa
Jagdalpur
Bhubaneshwar

Bay of
Bengal

Puri
Brahmapur
nnagar
dhra
Srīkākulam
Vizianagaram
Visākhapatnam
Rājahmundry
desh
Kākināda

Irrawaddy

Mouths of the Irrawaddy

Elevation

-2000m	-1000m	-500m	-250m	-100m	Below sea level 0	100m	250m	500m	1000m	2000m	4000m

| -6562ft | -3281ft | -1640ft | -820ft | -328ft | -164ft/-50m | 0 | 328ft | 820ft | 1640ft | 3281ft | 6562ft | 13,124ft |

Mainland Southeast Asia

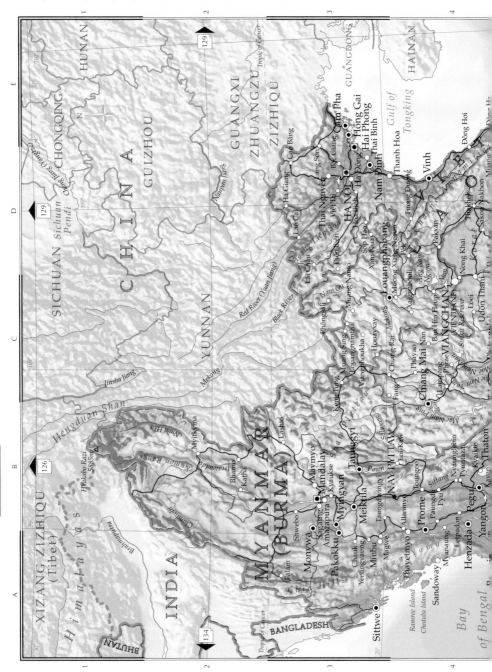

Population

- National capital
- below 50,000
- 50,000 to 100,000
- 100,000 to 500,000
- above 500,000

0 km   200

0 miles   200

Elevation

-2000m	-1000m	-500m	-250m	-100m	Below sea level	0	100m	250m	500m	1000m	2000m	4000m
-6562ft	-3281ft	-1640ft	-820ft	-328ft	-164ft/-50m	0	328ft	820ft	1640ft	3281ft	6562ft	13,124ft

137

Maritime Southeast Asia

MYANMAR
(BURMA)

137

Gulf of
Tongking

Hainan Dao
(to China)

PARACEL ISLANDS
(disputed by China, Taiwan
and Vietnam)

SINGAPORE

MALAYSIA

0 km 10
0 miles 10

Johore Strait

Causeway

Lim Chu
Kang

Bukit Panjang
Choa Chu
Kang

Pulau
Ubin

Hougang
New Town

Pulau
Tekong

Changi

Queenstown

Selat Pandan

Pulau Sudong

Pulau Pawai

Bukit Timah 176m

City

Telok Blangah

Bedok

New Town

Sentosa

Strait of Singapore

Urban areas
Open areas
Nature reserves

Jurong
Industrial
Estate

South Chir

Sea

133

Andaman
Sea

Nicobar Islands
(to India)

Gulf of
Thailand

Mouths of
the Mekong

CAMBODIA

SPRATLY ISLANDS
(disputed by China, Malaysia,
Philippines, Taiwan and Vietnam)

Bandaaceh Sigli

Langsa

Meulaboh

Pulau Simeulue

Medan
Tebingtinggi

Pematangsiantar

Kepulauan
Banyak

Danau
Toba

Sibolga

Pulau Nias

George
Town

Pulau
Pinang

Butterworth

Taiping

Ipoh

Kota Bharu

Kuala Terengganu

Dungun

Cukai

Klang

Kuantan

Kepulauan
Natuna

Kota Kinabalu

BANDAR SERI
BEGAWAN

BRUNEI

Miri

KUALA LUMPUR

PUTRAJAYA

Melaka

Muar

Batu Pahat

MALAYSIA

Keluang

Johor Bahru

SINGAPORE

Kuching

Bintulu

Sibu

Sri Aman

Batang Rajang

Sarawak

Equator

Pulau Siberut

Padang

Kepulauan
Mentawai

Solok

Rengat

Kualatungkal

Sungaipenuh

Jambi

Pekanbaru

Singkawang

Kepulauan
Lingga

Pontianak

Sidas

Sungai Kapuas

Borneo

Samarinda

Balikpapan

Bangka

Kalimantan

Pangkalpinang

Sampit

Amunta

Kandan

Palembang

Bengkulu

Lahat

133

Sumatera
(Sumatra)

Pulau
Belitung

INDIA

Banjarmasin

Pulau
Laut

Kotabumi

Bandar Lampung

Serang

JAKARTA

Bogor

Sukabumi

Bandung

Cirebon

Tegal

Pekalongan

Semarang

Kudus

Java Sea

INDIAN

OCEAN

Selat Sunda

Tasikmalaya

Jawa
(Java)

Cilacap

Magelang

Yogyakarta

Surakarta

Pulau
Madura

Surabaya

Probolinggo

Jember

Malang

Kediri

Madiun

Denpasar

Bali

Pulau
Lombok

Mata

141

0 km 200
0 miles 200

Population

National capital

below 50,000   50,000 to 100,000   100,000 to 500,000   above 500,000

PHILIPPINES

Luzon Strait

Babuyan Island

Babuyan Channel

Tuguegarao
Ilagan

guio
Luzon

Dagupan

eles
Cabanatuan

NILA
Lucena

angas
Naga

Mindoro
Legazpi City

Sibuyan
Sa
Calbayog

Roxas City
Samar

Panay
Island
Cadiz
Tacloban
Leyte

Iloilo

Palawan
Bacolod
City
Cebu

ierto
incesa

Negros
Bohol Sea
Butuan

Iligan
Cagayan de Oro

Sulu Sea
Bislig

Zamboanga
Moro
Gulf
Mindanao
Davao

Basilan
Lebak
Davao Gulf

lakan
General
Santos

Sulu Archipelago

Celebes Sea

Kepulauan
Talaud

Philippine

Sea

NORTHERN
MARIANA
ISLANDS
(to US)

GUAM
(to US)

Yap

MICRONESIA

Babeldaob

P A C I F I C

P A L A U

O C E A N

Equator

Manado
Bitung

Gorontalo

Pulau Morotai

Pulau
Halmahera

Pulau Waigeo

Sorong
Pulau
Manokwari
Biak

Halmahera
Sea
Jazirah
Doberai

Pulau
Yapen

Jayapura

Gulf of
Tomini
ilu

Kepulauan
Banggai

Kepulauan
Sula
Ceram Sea

Wahai

Pulau
Misool

Teluk
Cenderawasih

Teluk
Berau

Puncak Jaya
5030m

Pegunungan
Maoke

Sungai Mamberamo

New Guinea

PAPUA

NEW
GUINEA

Sulawesi
(Celebes)

Danau
Towuti

Waflia
Tifu

Pulau
Buru

Ambon

Pulau
Seram

Papua
(Irian Jaya)

epare
N
Kendari

Pulau
Buton

Sungai Digul

E
S
I
A

Kepulauan
Kai

Kepulauan
Aru

gkang
Kolaka

Watampone

Makassar

Bulukumba

Banda Sea

Kepulauan
Tanimbar

Pulau Yamdena

Arafura
Sea

Torres Strait

ores
ea

T e n g g a r a

Flores

Pulau
Wetar

Kepulauan Alor

DILI

Kepulauan Leti

EAST TIMOR

Timor

Savu Sea

Nikiniki
Kupang

Timor Sea

A U S T R A L I A

Sumba
umba

Elevation

| -4000m | -3000m | -2000m | -1000m | -500m | Below sea level | 0 | 100m | 250m | 500m | 1000m | 2000m | 4000m |

| -13,124ft | -9843ft | -6562ft | -3281ft | -1640ft | -820ft/-250m | 0 | 328ft | 820ft | 1640ft | 3281ft | 6562ft | 13,124ft |

The Indian Ocean

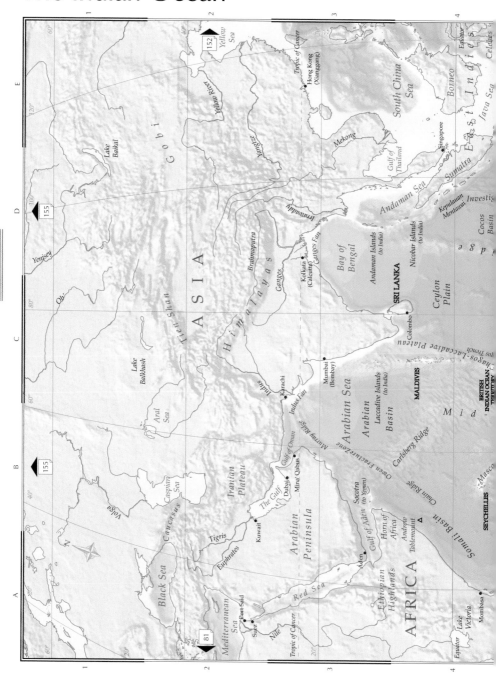

Major port

0 km   1500

0 miles   1500

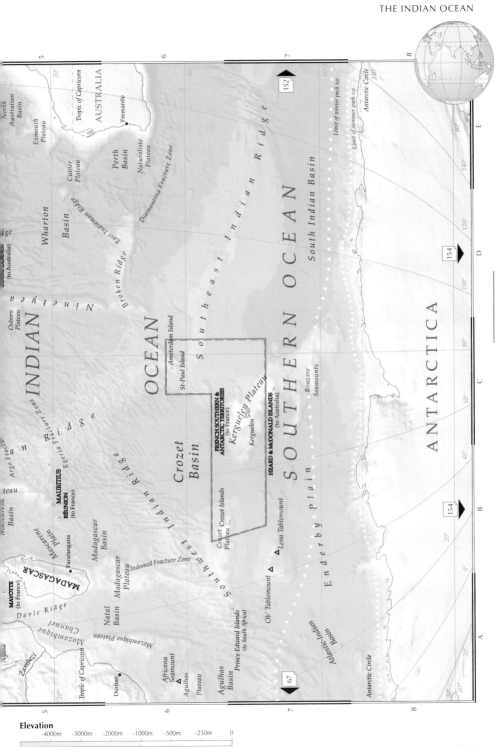

Elevation

-4000m   -3000m   -2000m   -1000m   -500m   -250m   0
-13,124ft   -9843ft   -6562ft   -3281ft   -1640ft   -820ft   0

Australasia & Oceania

NORTHERN MARIANA ISLANDS (to US)

Mid-Pacific Mountains

WAKE ISLAND (to US)

Philippine Sea

152

West Mariana Basin

Saipan

HAGÅTNA

GUAM (to US)

East Mariana Basin

M i c r o n e s i a

MARSHALL ISLANDS

Ratak Chain

Philippine Basin

Kyushu-Palau Ridge

Yap

Mariana Trench

Hall Islands

PALIKIR
Pohnpei

Ralik Chain

MAJURO

Philippines

Philippine Trench

Babeldaob

Yap Trench

MICRONESIA

Chuuk Islands

Caroline Islands

Kosrae

Sulu Sea

KOROR (OREOR)

PALAU

Eauripik Rise

Melanesian Basin

Tarawa
BAIRIKI

Tungaru

125

Celebes Sea

M e l a n e

Nauru

Banaba

NAURU

Equator

Bismarck Archipelago

PAPUA NEW GUINEA

s i a

TUVAL
FONGAFAL

Celebes

Bismarck Sea

New Britain

Banda Sea

Mount Wilhelm 4509m △

New Guinea

Solomon Sea

Bougainville

Solomon Island

Solomon Is.

SOLOMON ISLANDS

HONIARA
Guadalcanal

Santa Cruz Islands

Arafura Sea

PORT MORESBY

Torres Strait

Flores

Timor

Timor Sea

Coral Sea

North Fiji Basin

Espiritu Santo

Vanua Lev

Great Barrier Reef

CORAL SEA ISLANDS (to Australia)

Malekula

Efate

Viti Levi
PORT-VILA
SUVA

Darwin

Arnhem Land

Gulf of Carpentaria

Cape York Peninsula

Cairns

NEW CALEDONIA (to France)

VANUATU

ASHMORE & CARTIER ISLANDS (to Australia)

Townsville

New Caledonia

NOUMÉA

Îles Loyauté

FIJI

Mackay

New Caledonia Ridge

South Fiji Basin

INDIAN OCEAN

Broome

Great Sandy Desert

AUSTRALIA

Rockhampton

Norfolk Ridge

NORFOLK ISLAND (to Australia)

141

Macdonnell Ranges

Alice Springs

Simpson Desert

Brisbane

Lord Howe Rise

Lord Howe Basin

Gibson Desert

Uluru △ (Ayers Rock)

Lake Eyre North

Lord Howe Island (to Australia)

North Cape
North

Tropic of Capricorn

Great Victoria Desert

-16m ▽

Lake Torrens Lake Gairdner

Flinders Ranges

Grey Range

Darling

Newcastle
Sydney
Wollongong

Auckland
Hamilton

Geraldton

Kalgoorlie

Nullarbor Plain

Adelaide

CANBERRA

Murray

△ Mount Kosciuszko 2228m

NEW ZEALAND

Port Lincoln

Bendigo

Melbourne

Geelong

WELLINGTON

Perth

Esperance

South Australian Basin

Kangaroo Island

Bass Strait

Tasman Sea

South Island

Aoraki (Mount Cook)
3724m △

Christchu

C

Cape Leeuwin

Albany

Launceston

Hobart

Tasman Basin

Dunedin

Bounty Is.

Tasmania

Stewart Island

Antipodes Isl

Campbell

154

Tasman Plateau

Auckland Islands (to New Zealand)

Campbell Plateau

Campbell Island (to New Zealand)

Scale

0 km 1000

0 miles 1000

Population ● National capital

o below 50,000   o 50,000 to 100,000   ◉ 100,000 to 500,000   ▣ above 500,000

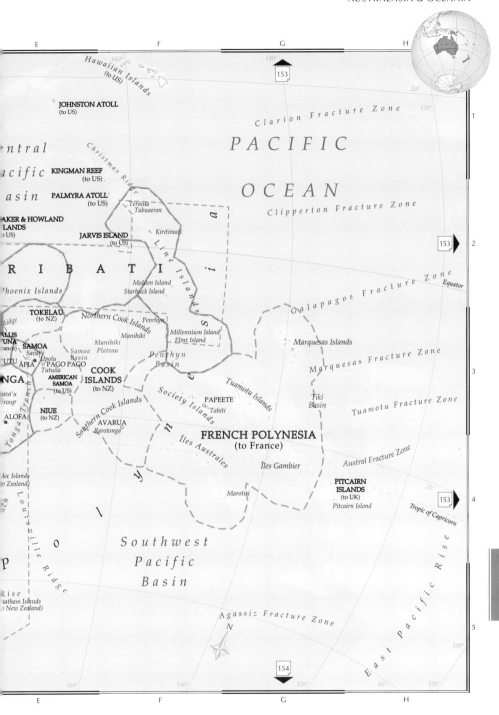

E   F   G   H

160°   153

Hawaiian Islands
(to US)

20°

JOHNSTON ATOLL
(to US)

Clarion Fracture Zone   120°

1

ntral
cific
asin

KINGMAN REEF
(to US)

Christmas Ridge

PACIFIC

PALMYRA ATOLL
(to US)

Teraina
Tabuaeran

OCEAN

Clipperton Fracture Zone

AKER & HOWLAND
LANDS
US)

JARVIS ISLAND
(to US)

Kiritimati

153   2

R   I   B   A   T   I

Line Islands

Galapagos Fracture Zone   Equator

Phoenix Islands

Malden Island
Starbuck Island

TOKELAU
(to NZ)

Northern Cook Islands   *Penrhyn*

Marquesas Islands

Marquesas Fracture Zone

ALLIS
UNA
rance)

SAMOA
Savai'i

Manihiki
Plateau

Manihiki

Millennium Island
Flint Island

UTU   APIA

Samoa
Basin

Upolu

Penrhyn
Basin

3

NGA

PAGO PAGO
Tutuila

AMERICAN
SAMOA
(to US)

COOK
ISLANDS
(to NZ)

Tuamotu Islands

Tiki
Basin

Marquesas Fracture Zone

ava'u
roup

Society Islands

PAPEETE
Tahiti

Tuamotu Fracture Zone

ALOFA

NIUE
(to NZ)

AVARUA
Rarotonga

Southern Cook Islands

FRENCH POLYNESIA
(to France)

Îles Australes

Îles Gambier

Austral Fracture Zone

20°

ec Islands
Zealand)

Marotiri

PITCAIRN
ISLANDS
(to UK)
Pitcairn Island

Tropic of Capricorn

153   4

P

Southwest
Pacific
Basin

East Pacific Rise

Rise
atham Islands
New Zealand)

Agassiz Fracture Zone

N

5

100°

160°   140°   120°   40°   100°

The Southwest Pacific

NORTHERN MARIANA ISLANDS

Saipan
Tinian
Rota

152

GUAM (to US)
HAGÅTÑA (to US)

MARSHALL ISLANDS

Enewetak Atoll
Bikini Atoll
Rongelap Atoll
Ailuk At
Wotje A
Yap
Ujelang Atoll
Kwajalein Atoll
Maloelap
Namu Atoll
Majur
Ailinglaplap Atoll
Jaluit Atoll
Mili A

MICRONESIA

Babeldaob
KOROR (OREOR)

Chuuk Islands
PALIKIR
Pohnpei

Kosrae

Ebon Atoll

M
i
c
r
o
n
e
s
i
a

PALAU

Caroline Islands

139

Ta
BAIRI

Equator

Abe
Ne
Banaba

NAURU

Admiralty Islands
St.Matthias Group

Bismarck Archipelago

New Guinea

Bismarck Sea

New Ireland

PAPUA NEW GUINEA

Madang
Central Ranges
△ Mount Wilhelm 4509 m
Lae
New Britain

Bougainville Island

Choiseul

Santa Isabel

M
e
l
a
n
e
s
i
a

INDONESIA

Owen Stanley Range
Solomon Sea

Solomon Is.

SOLOMON ISLANDS

New Georgia Islands
Malaita

Gulf of Papua

Arafura Sea

PORT MORESBY

Torres Strait

D'Entrecasteaux Islands

HONIARA
Guadalcanal

San Cristobal
Rennell

Santa Cruz Islands

Louisiade Archipelago

Arnhem Land

Groote Eylandt

Gulf of Carpentaria

Cape York Peninsula

146

Barkly Tableland

Great Barrier Reef

Coral Sea

CORAL SEA ISLANDS (to Australia)

Banks Islands

Espiritu Santo
Maéwo
Pentecost
Malekula
Ambrym
Epi
Efate

NEW CALEDONIA (to France)

PORT-VILA

VANUATU

Erromango
Tanna
Aneityum

NORTHERN TERRITORY

Tropic of Capricorn

Macdonnell

Ranges

QUEENSLAND

Great Dividing Range

New Caledonia

Ouvéa
Lifou
Maré
Îles Loyauté

NOUMÉA

AUSTRALIA

149

Population

● National capital

○ below 50,000   ○ 50,000 to 100,000   ◉ 100,000 to 500,000   ■ above 500,000

0 km   750
0 miles   750

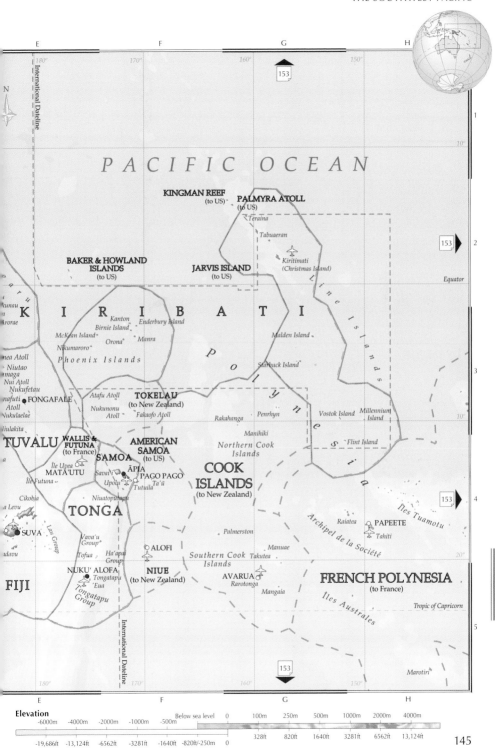

E   F   G   H

N

PACIFIC OCEAN

International Dateline

KINGMAN REEF
(to US)   PALMYRA ATOLL
(to US)
Teraina

Tabuaeran

153

Kiritimati
(Christmas Island)

BAKER & HOWLAND
ISLANDS
(to US)   JARVIS ISLAND
(to US)

Equator

K   I   R   I   B   A   T   I

Kanton   Enderbury Island
Birnie Island   Malden Island
McKean Island
Orona   Manra
Nikumaroro

Phoenix Islands

Starbuck Island

Line Islands

nea Atoll
Niutao
maga
Nui Atoll
Nukufetau
nafuti ● FONGAFALE
Atoll
Nukulaelae   Atafu Atoll   TOKELAU
(to New Zealand)
Nukunonu
Atoll   Fakaofo Atoll   Rakahanga   Penrhyn   Vostok Island   Millennium
Island

Polynesia

kunau
n
rorae

iulakita

TUVALU   WALLIS &
FUTUNA
(to France)   Manihiki   Flint Island

SAMOA   AMERICAN
SAMOA
(to US)   Northern Cook
Islands

Île Uvea
MATA'UTU
Île Futuna   Savai'i   ĀPIA
Upolu   PAGO PAGO   COOK
Ta'ū   ISLANDS
(to New Zealand)
Cikobia   Niuatoputapu   Tutuila
a Levu
TONGA   Raiatea ○ PAPEETE
Tahiti

Archipel de la Société

Îles Tuamotu

153

○ SUVA   Vava'u
Group   Palmerston   Manuae
adavu   Lau Group   Tofua   Ha'apai
Group   Takutea   Southern Cook
Islands   FRENCH POLYNESIA
(to France)
NUKU' ALOFA   ○ ALOFI
Tongatapu   NIUE
(to New Zealand)   AVARUA ○
Rarotonga   Mangaia
FIJI   'Eua
Tongatapu
Group   Îles Australes

Tropic of Capricorn

International Dateline

153

Marotiri

E   F   G   H

Elevation

-6000m	-4000m	-2000m	-1000m	-500m	Below sea level 0	100m	250m	500m	1000m	2000m	4000m

328ft   820ft   1640ft   3281ft   6562ft   13,124ft

-19,686ft   -13,124ft   -6562ft   -3281ft   -1640ft -820ft/-250m   0

Western Australia

Arafura
Sea

Croker Island
South Goulburn
Island

Tanimbar Kepulauan

Arnhem
Land

Katherine

Daly Waters

148

Van Diemen
Gulf

Pine Creek

Top Springs
Roadhouse

Tennant Creek

Tanami
Desert

NORTHERN

TERRITORY

Ranges

INDONESIA

139

EAST TIMOR

Timor

Melville Island

Bathurst Island

Darwin

Victoria R.

Kununurra

Wyndham

Joseph Bonaparte
Gulf

Halls Creek

Lake Mackay

Timor
Sea

Cape Londonderry

Kimberley
Plateau

Fitzroy
Crossing

Great Sandy Desert

WESTERN

Bonaparte
Bigge Island
Archipelago

Heywood
Islands

Fitzroy River

Percival
Lakes

Flores

King Sound

Pulau Sumba

Broome

INDIAN

Marble Bar

Pulau Wetar

138

Port Hedland

Hamersley Range

OCEAN

Fortescue River

Ashburton R.

Bali

Pulau
Lombok

Dampier

Onslow

Barrow Island

Exmouth Gulf

Java

141

Exmouth

0 km 300

0 miles 300

Population

● National capital   ◉ Internal administrative capital

○ below 50,000   ○ 50,000 to 100,000   ◉ 100,000 to 500,000   ◼ above 500,000

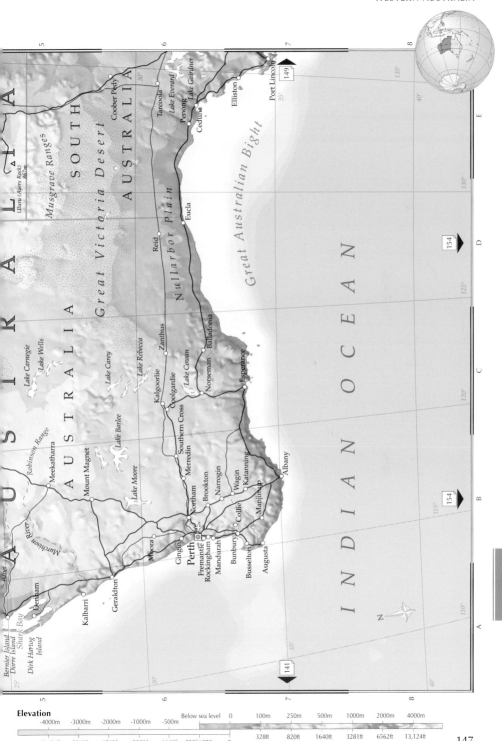

Elevation

						Below sea level	0	100m	250m	500m	1000m	2000m	4000m
-4000m	-3000m	-2000m	-1000m	-500m									
-13,124ft	-9843ft	-6562ft	-3281ft	-1640ft	-820ft/-250m	0		328ft	820ft	1640ft	3281ft	6562ft	13,124ft

Eastern Australia

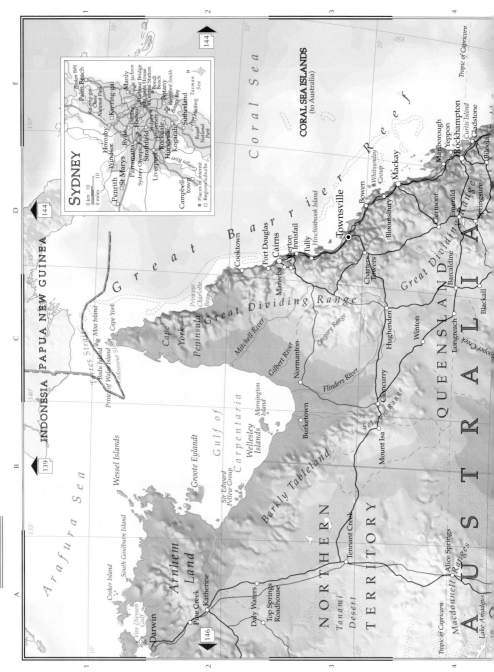

CORAL SEA ISLANDS
(to Australia)

Coral Sea

Great Barrier Reef

Tasman Sea

SYDNEY

0 km   10
0 miles   10

Broken Bay
Palm Beach
Avalon
Bilgola Beach
Manly
Port Jackson
Harbour Bridge
Opera House
Central Station
Bondi Beach
Botany Bay
Botany
Bundeena
Bankstown
Kogarah
Port Hacking Bay
Royal National Park

Hornsby
Ryde
Parramatta
Sydney Olympic Park
Strathfield
Liverpool
Hunters Hill
Rockdale
Sutherland

Windsor
Penrith
St Marys

Campbell town

Nepean River

■ Places of interest
□ Regions/Suburbs

Arafura Sea

INDONESIA

PAPUA NEW GUINEA

Torres Strait

Boigu Island
Moa Island
Cape York
Prince of Wales Island
Thursday Island
Badu Island

Croker Island
Van Diemen Gulf
Darwin
Pine Creek
Katherine

South Goulburn Island
Wessel Islands

Groote Eylandt

Arnhem Land

Daly Waters
Top Springs Roadhouse

Sir Edward Pellew Group

Gulf of Carpentaria

Mornington Island
Wellesley Islands

Burketown

Barkly Tableland

Tennant Creek

NORTHERN TERRITORY

Tanami Desert

Top Springs

Tropic of Capricorn

Alice Springs
Macdonnell Ranges
Lake Amadeus

Cape York Peninsula

Cooktown
Port Douglas
Mareeba
Cairns
Atherton
Innisfail
Tully
Hinchinbrook Island

Princess Charlotte Bay

Great Dividing Range

Mitchell River
Gilbert River

Normanton

Flinders River

Gregory Range

Cloncurry
Mount Isa

Selwyn Range

QUEENSLAND

Hughenden
Winton

Great Dividing Range

Charters Towers

Townsville
Bowen
Whitsunday Group
Mackay
Bloomsbury

Clermont
Emerald
Barcaldine
Longreach
Blackall

Cooper Creek

Marlborough
Yeppon
Rockhampton
Curtis Island
Gladstone
Biloela
Springsure

Tropic of Capricorn

A U S T R A L I A

0 km   300
0 miles   300

Population   ● National capital   ◉ Internal administrative capital

○ below 50,000   ○ 50,000 to 100,000   ◉ 100,000 to 500,000   ◼ above 500,000

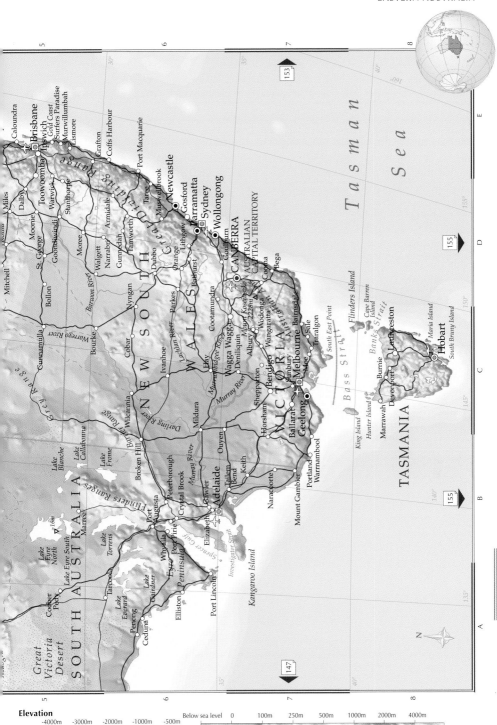

Elevation

| -4000m | -3000m | -2000m | -1000m | -500m | Below sea level | 0 | 100m | 250m | 500m | 1000m | 2000m | 4000m |

| -13,124ft | -9843ft | -6562ft | -3281ft | -1640ft | -820ft/-250m | 0 | 328ft | 820ft | 1640ft | 3281ft | 6562ft | 13,124ft |

New Zealand

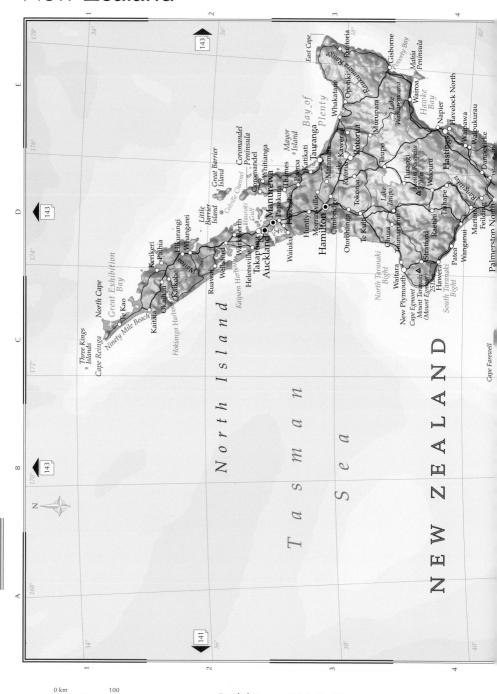

Population

○ below 50,000   ○ 50,000 to 100,000   ◉ 100,000 to 500,000   ■ above 500,000

● National capital

0 km   100

0 miles   100

South Island

PACIFIC OCEAN

WELLINGTON
Lower Hutt
Cape Palliser
Cape Campbell
Seddon
Blenheim
Clarence
Cook
Kaikoura
Kaikoura Peninsula
Richmond
Mount Owen 1875m
Nelson Range
Wairau
Clarence
Springs Junction
Hanmer Springs
Waipara
Rangiora
Kaiapoi
Christchurch
Lyttelton
Banks Peninsula
Waimakariri
Pegasus Bay
Kaiapoi Bay

Tasman Bight
Seddonville
Westport
Cape Foulwind
Reefton
Lake Brunner
Arthur's Pass 920m
Rakaia
Hurunui
Darfield
Oxford
Ashburton
Rakaia
Mayfield
Canterbury Plains
Hinds
Geraldine
Temuka
Timaru
Studholme
Oamaru
Hampden
Canterbury Bight
Lake Ellesmere
Banks Peninsula

Runanga
Greymouth
Hokitika
Ross
Whataroa
Abut Head
Fox Glacier
Haast
Jackson Head
Southern Alps
Mount Cook 3754m
Franz Josef
Lake Coleridge
Fairlie
Waitaki
Waimate
Waihao
Otago Peninsula
Dunedin
Milton
Balclutha
Mosgiel
Otago Peninsula

Lake Hawea
Lake Wanaka
Wanaka
Queenstown
Cromwell
Alexandra
Clutha
Taieri
Clutha
Mataura
Gore
Mataura
Tokanui
Invercargill
Riverton
Winton
Lumsden
Eyre Mts
Lake Wakatipu
Remarkables
Milford Sound
George Sound
Caswell Sound
Lake Te Anau
Te Anau
Lake Manapouri
Lake Monowai
Waiau
Lake Hauroko
Resolution Island
West Cape
Fiordland
Halfmoon Bay
Codfish Island
Ruapuke Island
Foveaux Strait
Stewart Island
South West Cape
Muttonbird Islands
Te Waewae Bay
Toetoes Bay

42° 44° 46° 48°
160° 166° 168° 170° 172° 174° 176° 178°

Elevation

-4000m	-3000m	-2000m	-1000m	-500m	Below sea level	0	100m	250m	500m	1000m	2000m	4000m
-13,124ft	-9843ft	-6562ft	-3281ft	-1640ft	-820ft/-250m	0	328ft	820ft	1640ft	3281ft	6562ft	13,124ft

The Pacific Ocean

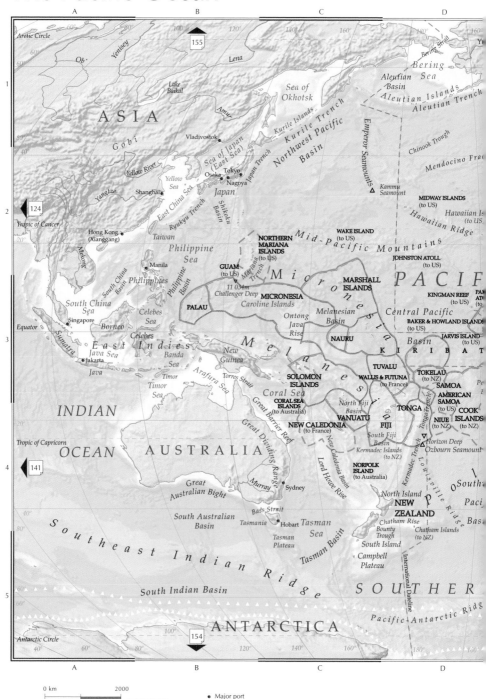

Arctic Circle

155

Yenisey

Ob

Lena

Lake Baikal

Bering Strait

Bering Sea

Aleutian Basin

Aleutian Islands

Aleutian Trench

A S I A

Gobi

Amur

Sea of Okhotsk

Kurile Islands

Kurile Trench

Northwest Pacific Basin

Emperor Seamounts

Chinook Trough

Mendocino Frac

Vladivostok

Sea of Japan (East Sea)

Japan Trench

Yellow River

Osaka

Tokyo

Nagoya

Kammu Seamount △

MIDWAY ISLANDS (to US)

Yellow Sea

Shanghai

Yangtze

East China Sea

Japan

Hawaiian Is (to US)

124

Tropic of Cancer

Hong Kong (Xianggang)

Taiwan

Ryukyu Trench

Shikoku Basin

Hawaiian Ridge

WAKE ISLAND (to US)

Mid-Pacific Mountains

Philippine Sea

NORTHERN MARIANA ISLANDS (to US)

JOHNSTON ATOLL (to US)

Mekong

Manila

GUAM (to US)

Mariana Trench

Micronesia

P A C I F

11 034m

Challenger Deep

MICRONESIA

MARSHALL ISLANDS

KINGMAN REEF (to US)

PA AT

Philippines

Philippine Basin

South China Sea

South China Basin

Celebes Sea

PALAU

Caroline Islands

Melanesian Basin

Central Pacific

BAKER & HOWLAND ISLANDS (to US)

Singapore

Borneo

Ontong Java Rise

Equator

Sumatra

Celebes

East Indies

NAURU

Basin

JARVIS ISLAND (to US)

Melanesia

K I R I B A T

Java Sea

Jakarta

Banda Sea

New Guinea

TUVALU

TOKELAU (to NZ)

Java

Timor

Arafura Sea

Torres Strait

SOLOMON ISLANDS

WALLIS & FUTUNA (to France)

SAMOA

Timor Sea

Coral Sea

CORAL SEA ISLANDS (to Australia)

North Fiji Basin

AMERICAN SAMOA (to US)

Pe

TONGA

COOK

I N D I A N

Great Barrier Reef

NEW CALEDONIA (to France)

VANUATU

FIJI

NIUE (to NZ)

ISLANDS (to NZ)

Tropic of Capricorn

O C E A N

A U S T R A L I A

Great Dividing Range

New Caledonia Basin

South Fiji Basin

Kermadec Islands (to NZ)

Horizon Deep △ ▽

Ozbourn Seamount

NORFOLK ISLAND (to Australia)

141

Great Australian Bight

Murray

Sydney

Lord Howe Rise

North Island

NEW ZEALAND

South

Pací

Bas

South Australian Basin

Bass Strait

Tasmania

Hobart

Tasman Sea

Tasman Sea

Chatham Rise

Chatham Islands (to NZ)

Lord Howe Rise

Kermadec Trench

Louisville Ridge

Pa

Bounty Trough

Tasman Plateau

Tasman Basin

South Island

Campbell Plateau

International Dateline

Southeast Indian Ridge

South Indian Basin

S O U T H E R

Antarctic Circle

154

A N T A R C T I C A

Pacific-Antarctic Ridge

Pacific-Antarctic Ridg

0 km — 2000

0 miles — 2000

● Major port

Arctic Circle

155

Hudson
Bay

Labrador
Sea

Rocky Mountains

NORTH
AMERICA

Vancouver

Cascadia
Basin

Great Lakes

Appalachian Mountains

San Francisco

Colorado

ay Fracture Zone

Long Beach

Gulf of California

kai Fracture Zone

Gulf of
Mexico

Mississippi

ATLANTIC

OCEAN 66

Tropic of Cancer

Greater Antilles

Lesser Antilles

Clarion Fracture Zone

Middle America Trench

Caribbean Sea

O C E A N

CLIPPERTON ISLAND
(to France)

Clipperton Fracture Zone

Panama City

Cocos Ridge

Guatemala
Basin

East Pacific Rise

Equator

Galapagos Fracture Zone

Galapagos Islands
(to Ecuador)

Gallego Rise

Amazon

Marquesas
Islands

Bauer
Basin

Peru Basin

Callao

SOUTH
AMERICA

Marquesas
Fracture Zone

Galapagos
Rise

Tiki
Basin

Mendaña Fracture Zone

Peru-Chile Trench

FRENCH
POLYNESIA
(to France)

Austral
Fracture Zone

Nazca Ridge

Îles Gambier

Sala y Gomez
(to Chile)

Sala y Gomez Ridge

Andes

Australes

PITCAIRN ISLANDS
(to UK)

Easter Island
(to Chile)

Easter Fracture Zone

Isla San Félix
(to Chile)

Isla San Ambrosio
(to Chile)

Tropic of Capricorn

67

Islas Juan Fernández
(to Chile)

Valparaíso

Chile Basin

Paraná

Challenger Fracture Zone

Agassiz Fracture Zone

Chile Rise

ATLANTIC

OCEAN

N

Mornington
Abyssal
Plain

Eltanin Fracture Zone

Cape Horn

Limit of winter pack ice

C E A N

Southeast
Pacific Basin

Bellingshausen Plain

Drake Passage

PETER I ISLAND
(to Norway)

Amundsen Plain

154

Limit of summer pack ice

Antarctic Circle

Elevation

-4000m	-3000m	-2000m	-1000m	-500m	-250m	0
-13,124ft	-9843ft	-6562ft	-3281ft	-1640ft	-820ft	0

153

Antarctica

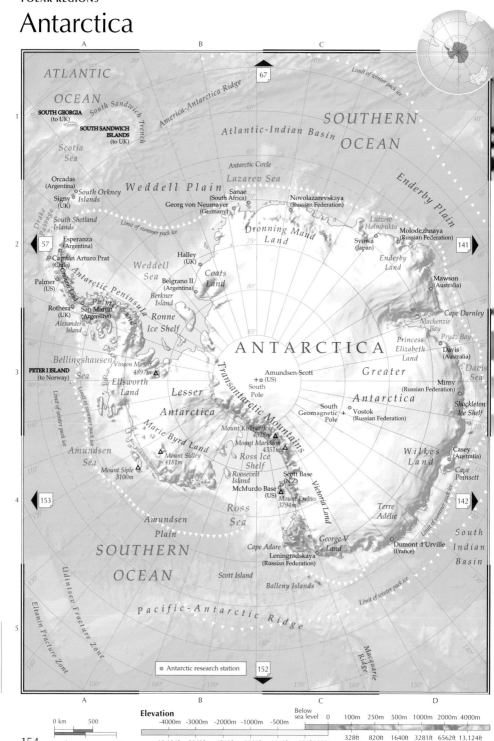

ATLANTIC OCEAN

SOUTHERN OCEAN

SOUTH GEORGIA (to UK)

SOUTH SANDWICH ISLANDS (to UK)

South Sandwich Trench

America-Antarctica Ridge

Limit of winter pack ice

Scotia Sea

Atlantic-Indian Basin

Antarctic Circle

Lazarev Sea

Weddell Plain

Orcadas (Argentina)

South Orkney Islands

Signy (UK)

South Shetland Islands

Sanae (South Africa)

Georg von Neumayer (Germany)

Novolazarevskaya (Russian Federation)

Enderby Plain

Drake Passage

Esperanza (Argentina)

Capitán Arturo Prat (Chile)

Palmer (US)

Antarctic Peninsula

Graham Land

Halley (UK)

Belgrano II (Argentina)

Berkner Island

Dronning Maud Land

Lützow Holmbukta

Syowa (Japan)

Enderby Land

Molodezhnaya (Russian Federation)

Mawson (Australia)

Weddell Sea

Coats Land

Rothera (UK)

San Martín (Argentina)

Palmer Land

Ronne Ice Shelf

ANTARCTICA

Cape Darnley

Mackenzie Bay

Prydz Bay

Princess Elizabeth Land

Davis (Australia)

Alexander Island

Bellingshausen Sea

Vinson Massif 4897m

PETER I ISLAND (to Norway)

Ellsworth Land

Lesser Antarctica

Transantarctic Mountains

Amundsen-Scott (US)

South Pole

South Geomagnetic Pole

Vostok (Russian Federation)

Greater Antarctica

Mirny (Russian Federation)

Davis Sea

Shackleton Ice Shelf

Amundsen Sea

Marie Byrd Land

Mount Sidley 4181m

Mount Siple 3100m

Mount Kirkpatrick 4528m

Mount Markham 4351m

Ross Ice Shelf

Roosevelt Island

McMurdo Base (US)

Scott Base (N.Z.)

Mount Erebus 3794m

Wilkes Land

Casey (Australia)

Cape Poinsett

Terre Adélie

Amundsen Plain

SOUTHERN OCEAN

Ross Sea

Cape Adare

Leningradskaya (Russian Federation)

Scott Island

Victoria Land

George V Land

Dumont d'Urville (France)

South Indian Basin

Balleny Islands

Pacific-Antarctic Ridge

Udintsev Fracture Zone

Eltanin Fracture Zone

Macquarie Ridge

○ Antarctic research station

67

57

141

153

142

152

154

Elevation

Below sea level											
-4000m	-3000m	-2000m	-1000m	-500m	0	100m	250m	500m	1000m	2000m	4000m
-13,124ft	-9843ft	-6562ft	-3281ft	-1640ft	-820ft/-250m		328ft	820ft	1640ft	3281ft	6562ft 13,124ft

0 km 500

0 miles 500

Arctic Ocean

Saint Lawrence Island
160°
155°
Norton Sound
Provideniya
Bering Sea
65°
Arctic Circle
152

R U S S I A N

ALASKA
(to US)
140°

Chukchi Sea
70°
Ostrov Vrangelya

F E D E R A T I O N

East Siberian Sea

Limit of summer pack ice

113
120°

Tuktoyaktuk
130°
Limit of summer pack ice

36

N O R T H   A M E R I C A

Beaufort Sea

Northwind Plain
75°
Chukchi Plain
Chukchi Plateau

Canada Basin

Novosibirskiye Ostrova

Limit of permanent ice cap

120°

Victoria Island
110°

Mendeleyev Ridge

Wrangel Plain

Laptev Sea

110°

100°

A R C T I C

Baffin Island

CANADA
100°
Queen
North Geomagnetic Pole
Elizabeth
90°
Islands

85°
Makarov Basin
Alpha Cordillera

Lomonosov Ridge
+ North Pole

Fram Basin

Severnaya Zemlya

Gakkel Cordillera
90°

3

Baffin
Island
Lancaster Sound
Ellesmere Island
Nares Strait

Lincoln Sea

Nansen Cordillera

Nansen Basin

Svyataya Anna Trough

Franz Josef Land

Kara Sea

Limit of summer pack ice

Ostrov Belyy
Dikson
80°

Baffin Bay
70°
Knud Rasmussen Land
Kap Morris Jesup

Wandel Sea

Novaya Zemlya

East Novaya Zemlya Trough

112

38
60°

Kong Frederik VIII Land

SVALBARD
(to Norway)

Spitsbergen
Longyearbyen

60°

O C E A N

Ostrov Kotel'nyy
Cheshskaya Guba

GREENLAND
(to Denmark)

Greenland Sea

Limit of winter pack ice

Bjørnøya
(to Norway)

Barents Sea

50°

65°

North Cape
65°

Murmansk
Kola Peninsula

JAN MAYEN
(to Norway)

Limit of summer pack ice

Mohns Ridge

White Sea
Archangel

5

65°
Limit of winter pack ice
Denmark Strait
30°
20°

Iceland Plateau
10°

66

Norwegian Sea
0°

10°

N O R W A Y
SWEDEN
FINLAND
20°
65°

40°
30°

E U R O P E

Elevation

-4000m	-3000m	-2000m	-1000m	-500m	-250m	0
-13,124ft	-9843ft	-6562ft	-3281ft	-1640ft	-820ft	0

0 km 500
0 miles 500

● Major port

155

Overseas territories & dependencies

Despite the rapid process of global decolonization since the Second World War, around 8 million people in more than 50 territories around the world continue to live under the protection of France, Australia, the Netherlands, Denmark, Norway, New Zealand, the UK, or the USA. These remnants of former colonial empires may have persisted for economic, strategic or political reasons and are administered in a variety of ways.

AUSTRALIA

Australia's overseas territories have not been an issue since Papua New Guinea became independent in 1975. Consequently there is no overriding policy toward them. Norfolk Island is inhabited by descendants of the H.M.S Bounty mutineers and more recent Australian migrants.

Ashmore &
Cartier Islands
Indian Ocean
Status: External territory
Claimed: 1931
Capital: Not applicable
Population: None
Area: 2 sq miles
(5.2 sq km)

Christmas Island
Indian Ocean
Status: External territory
Claimed: 1958
Capital: The Settlement
Population: 1493
Area: 52 sq miles
(135 sq km)

Cocos Islands
Indian Ocean
Status: External territory
Claimed: 1955
Capital: No official capital
Population: 574
Area: 5.5 sq miles
(14 sq km)

Coral Sea Islands
South Pacific
Status: External territory
Claimed: 1969
Capital: None
Population: 8 (meteorologists)
Area: Less than 1.2 sq miles
(3 sq km)

Heard & McDonald Is.
Indian Ocean
Status: External territory
Claimed: 1947
Capital: Not applicable
Population: None
Area: 161 sq miles
(417 sq km)

Norfolk Island
South Pacific
Status: External territory
Claimed: 1774
Capital: Kingston
Population: 1828
Area: 13 sq miles
(34 sq km)

DENMARK

The Faeroe Islands have been under Danish administration since Queen Margreth I of Denmark inherited Norway in 1380. The Home Rule Act of 1948 gave the Faeroese control over all their internal affairs. Greenland first came under Danish rule in 1380. Today, Denmark is responsible for the island's foreign affairs and defense.

Faeroe Islands
North Atlantic
Status: External territory
Claimed: 1380
Capital: Tórshavn
Population: 47,246
Area: 540 sq miles
(1399 sq km)

Greenland
North Atlantic
Status: External territory
Claimed: 1380
Capital: Nuuk
Population: 56,361
Area: 840,000 sq miles
(2,175,516 sq km)

FRANCE

France has developed economic ties with its *Territoires d'Outre-Mer*, thereby stressing interdependence over independence. Overseas *départements*, officially part of France, have their own governments. Territorial *collectivités* and overseas *territoires* have varying degrees of autonomy.

Clipperton Island
East Pacific
Status: Dependency
of French Polynesia
Claimed: 1935
Capital: Not applicable
Population: None
Area: 2.7 sq miles
(7 sq km)

French Guiana
South America
Status: Overseas department
Claimed: 1817
Capital: Cayenne
Population: 199,509
Area: 35,135 sq miles
(90,996 sq km)

French Polynesia
South Pacific
Status: Overseas territory
Claimed: 1843
Capital: Papeete
Population: 260,000
Area: 1608 sq miles
(4165 sq km)

Guadeloupe
West Indies
Status: Overseas department
Claimed: 1635
Capital: Basse-Terre
Population: 452,000
Area: 687 sq miles
(1780 sq km)

Martinique
West Indies
Status: Overseas
department
Claimed: 1635
Capital: Fort-de-France
Population: 397,000
Area: 425 sq miles
(1100 sq km)

Mayotte
Indian Ocean
Status: Territorial
collectivity
Claimed: 1843
Capital: Mamoudzou
Population: 201,234
Area: 144 sq miles
(374 sq km)

New Caledonia
South Pacific
Status: Overseas territory
Claimed: 1853
Capital: Nouméa
Population: 241,000
Area: 7374 sq miles
(19,100 sq km)

Réunion
Indian Ocean
Status: Overseas
department
Claimed: 1638
Capital: Saint-Denis
Population: 796,000
Area: 970 sq miles
(2500 sq km)

St. Pierre
& Miquelon
North America
Status: Territorial collectivity
Claimed: 1604
Capital: Saint-Pierre
Population: 7026
Area: 93 sq miles
(242 sq km)

Wallis & Futuna
South Pacific
Status: Overseas territory
Claimed: 1842
Capital: Matá'Utu
Population: 16,025
Area: 106 sq miles
(274 sq km)

NETHERLANDS

The country's two remaining
overseas territories were formerly
part of the Dutch West Indies. Both
are now self-governing, but the
Netherlands remains responsible
for their defense.

Aruba
West Indies
Status: Autonomous
part of the Netherlands
Claimed: 1643
Capital: Oranjestad
Population: 71,891
Area: 75 sq miles (194 sq km)

Netherlands Antilles
West Indies
Status: Autonomous
part of the Netherlands
Claimed: 1816
Capital: Willemstad
Population: 184,000
Area: 371 sq miles (960 sq
km)

NEW ZEALAND

New Zealand's government
has no desire to retain any overseas
territories. However, the economic
weakness of its dependent territory
Tokelau and its freely associated
states, Niue and the Cook Islands,
has forced New Zealand to
remain responsible for their
foreign policy and defense.

Cook Islands
South Pacific
Status: Associated territory
Claimed: 1901
Capital: Avarua
Population: 21,388
Area: 91 sq miles
(235 sq km)

Niue
South Pacific
Status: Associated territory
Claimed: 1901
Capital: Alofi
Population: 2166
Area: 102 sq miles
(264 sq km)

Tokelau
South Pacific
Status: Dependent territory
Claimed: 1926
Capital: Not applicable
Population: 1392
Area: 4 sq miles (10 sq km)

NORWAY

In 1920, 41 nations signed the
Spits-bergen Treaty recognizing
Norwegian sovereignty over
Svalbard. There is a NATO base
on Jan Mayen. Bouvet Island is
a nature reserve.

Bouvet Island
South Atlantic
Status: Dependency
Claimed: 1928
Capital: Not applicable
Population: None
Area: 22 sq miles (58 sq km)

Jan Mayen
North Atlantic
Status: Dependency
Claimed: 1929
Capital: Not applicable
Population: None
Area: 147 sq miles
(381 sq km)

Peter I. Island
Southern Ocean
Status: Dependency
Claimed: 1931
Capital: Not applicable
Population: None
Area: 69 sq miles (180 sq km)

Svalbard
Arctic Ocean
Status: Dependency
Claimed: 1920
Capital: Longyearbyen
Population: 2701
Area: 24,289 sq miles
(62,906 sq km)

Continued on p.158

Overseas territories & dependencies

UNITED KINGDOM

The UK still has the largest number of overseas territories. These are locally-governed by a mixture of elected representatives and appointed officials, and they all enjoy a large measure of internal self-government, but certain powers, such as foreign affairs and defense, are reserved for Governors of the British Crown.

Anguilla
West Indies
Status: Dependent territory
Claimed: 1650
Capital: The Valley
Population: 13,477
Area: 37 sq miles
(96 sq km)

Ascension Island
South Atlantic
Status: Dependency of St. Helena
Claimed: 1673
Capital: Georgetown
Population: 1177
Area: 34 sq miles
(88 sq km)

Bermuda
North Atlantic
Status: Crown colony
Claimed: 1612
Capital: Hamilton
Population: 65,773
Area: 20 sq miles
(53 sq km)

British Indian Ocean Territory
Status: Dependent territory
Claimed: 1814
Capital: Diego Garcia
Population: 4000
Area: 23 sq miles
(60 sq km)

British Virgin Islands
West Indies
Status: Dependent territory
Claimed: 1672
Capital: Road Town
Population: 23,098
Area: 59 sq miles
(153 sq km)

Cayman Islands
West Indies
Status: Dependent territory
Claimed: 1670
Capital: George Town
Population: 45,436
Area: 100 sq miles (259 sq km)

Falkland Islands
South Atlantic
Status: Dependent territory
Claimed: 1832
Capital: Stanley
Population: 2967
Area: 4699 sq miles
(12,173 sq km)

Gibraltar
Southwest Europe
Status: Crown colony
Claimed: 1713
Capital: Gibraltar
Population: 27,928
Area: 2.5 sq miles (6.5 sq km)

Guernsey
Channel Islands
Status: Crown dependency
Claimed: 1066
Capital: St. Peter Port
Population: 65,049
Area: 25 sq miles (65 sq km)

Isle of Man
British Isles
Status: Crown dependency
Claimed: 1765
Capital: Douglas
Population: 75,441
Area: 221 sq miles (572 sq km)

Jersey
Channel Islands
Status: Crown dependency
Claimed: 1066
Capital: St. Helier
Population: 90,084
Area: 45 sq miles (116 sq km)

Montserrat
West Indies
Status: Dependent territory
Claimed: 1632
Capital: Plymouth
(currently uninhabitable)
Population: 9439
Area: 40 sq miles (102 sq km)

Pitcairn Islands
South Pacific
Status: Dependent territory
Claimed: 1887
Capital: Adamstown
Population: 45
Area: 18 sq miles (47 sq km)

St. Helena
South Atlantic
Status: Dependent territory
Claimed: 1673
Capital: Jamestown
Population: 4299
Area: 47 sq miles (122 sq km)

South Georgia & The South Sandwich Islands
South Atlantic
Status: Dependent territory
Claimed: 1775
Capital: Not applicable
Population: No permanent residents
Area: 1387 sq miles
(3592 sq km)

Tristan da Cunha
South Atlantic
Status: Dependency of St. Helena
Claimed: 1612
Capital: Edinburgh
Population: 276
Area: 38 sq miles (98 sq km)

Turks & Caicos Islands
West Indies
Status: Dependent territory
Claimed: 1766
Capital: Cockburn Town
Population: 21,152
Area: 166 sq miles
(430 sq km)

UNITED STATES OF AMERICA

America's overseas territories have been seen as strategically useful, if expensive, links with its "backyards." The US has, in most cases, given the local population a say in deciding their own status. A US Commonwealth territory, such as Puerto Rico, has a greater level of independence than that of a US unincorporated or external territory.

American Samoa

South Pacific
Status: Unincorporated territory
Claimed: 1900
Capital: Pago Pago
Population: 57,794
Area: 75 sq miles (195 sq km)

Baker & Howland Islands

South Pacific
Status: Unincorporated territory
Claimed: 1856
Capital: Not applicable
Population: None
Area: 0.5 sq miles (1.4 sq km)

Guam

West Pacific
Status: Unincorporated territory
Claimed: 1898
Capital: Hagåtña
Population: 172,000
Area: 212 sq miles (549 sq km)

Jarvis Island

South Pacific
Status: Unincorporated territory
Claimed: 1856
Capital: Not applicable
Population: None
Area: 1.7 sq miles (4.5 sq km)

Johnston Atoll

Central Pacific
Status: Unincorporated territory
Claimed: 1858
Capital: Not applicable
Population: Not applicable
Area: 1 sq mile (2.8 sq km)

Kingman Reef

Central Pacific
Status: Administered territory
Claimed: 1856
Capital: Not applicable
Population: None
Area: 0.4 sq mile (1 sq km)

Midway Islands

Central Pacific
Status: Administered territory
Claimed: 1867
Capital: Not applicable
Population: None
Area: 2 sq miles (5.2 sq km)

Navassa Island

West Indies
Status: Unincorporated territory
Claimed: 1856
Capital: Not applicable
Population: None
Area: 2 sq miles (5.2 sq km)

Northern Mariana Islands

West Pacific
Status: Commonwealth territory
Claimed: 1947
Capital: Saipan
Population: 82,459
Area: 177 sq miles (457 sq km)

Palmyra Atoll

Central Pacific
Status: Unincorporated territory
Claimed: 1898
Capital: Not applicable
Population: None
Area: 5 sq miles (12 sq km)

Puerto Rico

West Indies
Status: Commonwealth territory
Claimed: 1898
Capital: San Juan
Population: 4.0 million
Area: 3515 sq miles (9104 sq km)

Virgin Islands

West Indies
Status: Unincorporated territory
Claimed: 1917
Capital: Charlotte Amalie
Population: 108,605
Area: 137 sq miles (355 sq km)

Wake Island

Central Pacific
Status: Unincorporated territory
Claimed: 1898
Capital: Not applicable
Population: 200
Area: 2.5 sq miles (6.5 sq km)

Glossary of geographical terms

The following glossary lists all geographical terms occuring on the maps and in the main-entry names in the Index–Gazetteer. These terms may precede, follow or be run together with the proper elements of the name; where they precede it the term is reversed for indexing purposes – thus Poluostov Yamal is indexed as Yamal, Poluostrov.

A

Å *Danish, Norwegian,* River
Alpen *German,* Alps
Altiplanicie *Spanish,* Plateau
Älv(en) *Swedish,* River
Anse *French,* Bay
Archipiélago *Spanish,* Archipelago
Arcipelago *Italian,* Archipelago
Arquipélago *Portuguese,* Archipelago
Aukštuma *Lithuanian,* Upland

B

Bahía *Spanish,* Bay
Baía *Portuguese,* Bay
Baḥr *Arabic,* River
Baie *French,* Bay
Bandao *Chinese,* Peninsula
Banjaran *Malay,* Mountain range
Batang *Malay,* Stream
-berg *Afrikaans, Norwegian,* Mountain
Birket *Arabic,* Lake
Boğazı *Turkish,* Strait
Bucht *German,* Bay
Bugten *Danish,* Bay
Buḥayrat *Arabic,* Lake, reservoir
Buḥeiret *Arabic,* Lake
Bukit *Malay,* Mountain
-bukta *Norwegian,* Bay
bukten *Swedish,* Bay
Burnu *Turkish,* Cape, point
Buuraha *Somali,* Mountains

C

Cabo *Portuguese,* Cape
Cap *French,* Cape
Cascada *Portuguese,* Waterfall
Cerro *Spanish,* Mountain
Chaîne *French,* Mountain range
Chau *Cantonese,* Island
Cháy *Turkish,* Stream
Chhâk *Cambodian,* Bay
Chhu *Tibetan,* River
-chôsuji *Korean,* Reservoir

Chott *Arabic,* Salt lake, depression
Ch'ün-tao *Chinese,* Island group
Cambodian, Mountains
Cordillera *Spanish,* Mountain range
Costa *Spanish,* Coast
Côte *French,* Coast
Cuchilla *Spanish,* Mountains

D

Dağı *Azerbaijani, Turkish,* Mountain
Dağları *Azerbaijani, Turkish,* Mountains
-dake *Japanese,* Peak
Danau *Indonesian,* Lake
Đao *Vietnamese,* Island
Daryá *Persian,* River
Daryácheh *Persian,* Lake
Dasht *Persian,* Plain, desert
Dawḥat *Arabic,* Bay
Dere *Turkish,* Stream
Dili *Azerbaijani,* Spit
-do *Korean,* Island
Dooxo *Somali,* Valley
Düzü *Azerbaijani,* Steppe
-dwíp *Bengali,* Island

E

Embalse *Spanish,* Reservoir
Erg *Arabic,* Dunes
Estany *Catalan,* Lake
Estrecho *Spanish,* Strait
-ey *Icelandic,* Island
Ezero *Bulgarian, Macedonian,* Lake

F

Fjord *Danish,* Fjord
-fjorden *Norwegian,* Fjord
-fjørdhur *Faeroese,* Fjord
Fleuve *French,* River
Fliegu *Maltese,* Channel
-fljór *Icelandic,* River

G

-gang *Korean,* River
Ganga *Nepali, Sinhala,* River
Gaoyuan *Chinese,* Plateau
-gawa *Japanese,* River

Gebel *Arabic,* Mountain
-gebirge *German,* Mountains
Ghubbat *Arabic,* Bay
Gjiri *Albanian,* Bay
Gol *Mongolian,* River
Golfe *French,* Gulf
Golfo *Italian, Spanish,* Gulf
Gora *Russian, Serbian,* Mountain
Gory *Russian,* Mountains
Guba *Russian,* Bay
Gunung *Malay,* Mountain

H

Ḥadd *Arabic,* Spit
-haehyôp *Korean,* Strait
Haff *German,* Lagoon
Hai *Chinese,* Sea, bay
Ḥammádat *Arabic,* Plateau
Hámún *Persian,* Lake
Hawr *Arabic,* Lake
Háyk' *Amharic,* Lake
He *Chinese,* River
Helodrano *Malagasy,* Bay
-hegység *Hungarian,* Mountain range
Hka *Burmese,* River
-ho *Korean,* Reservoir
Hô *Korean,* Reservoir
/olot *Hebrew,* Dunes
Hora *Belorussian,* Mountain
Hrada *Belorussian,* Mountains, ridge
Hsi *Chinese,* River
Hu *Chinese,* Lake

I

Île(s) *French,* Island(s)
Ilha(s) *Portuguese,* Island(s)
Ilhéu(s) *Portuguese,* Islet(s)
Irmak *Turkish,* River
Isla(s) *Spanish,* Island(s)
Isola (Isole) *Italian,* Island(s)

J

Jabal *Arabic,* Mountain
Jál *Arabic,* Ridge
-järvi *Finnish,* Lake
Jazírat *Arabic,* Island
Jazíreh *Persian,* Island

Jebel *Arabic,* Mountain
Jezero *Serbian/Croatian,* Lake
Jiang *Chinese,* River
-joki *Finnish,* River
-jökull *Icelandic,* Glacier
Juzur *Arabic,* Islands

K

Kaikyó *Japanese,* Strait
-kaise *Lappish,* Mountain
Kali *Nepali,* River
Kalnas *Lithuanian,* Mountain
Kalns *Latvian,* Mountain
Kang *Chinese,* Harbor
Kangri *Tibetan,* Mountain(s)
Kaôh *Cambodian,* Island
Kapp *Norwegian,* Cape
Kavír *Persian,* Desert
K'edi *Georgian,* Mountain range
Kediet *Arabic,* Mountain
Kepulauan *Indonesian, Malay,* Island group
Khalig, Khalíj *Arabic,* Gulf
Khawr *Arabic,* Inlet
Khola *Nepali,* River
Khrebet *Russian,* Mountain range
Ko *Thai,* Island
Kolpos *Greek,* Bay
-kopf *German,* Peak
Körfäzi *Azerbaijani,* Bay
Körfezi *Turkish,* Bay
Kõrgustik *Estonian,* Upland
Koshi *Nepali,* River
Kowtal *Persian,* Pass
Kúh(há) *Persian,* Mountain(s)
-kundo *Korean,* Island group
-kysten *Norwegian,* Coast
Kyun *Burmese,* Island

L

Laaq *Somali,* Watercourse
Lac *French,* Lake
Lacul *Romanian,* Lake
Lago *Italian, Portuguese, Spanish,* Lake

Laguna *Spanish,*
Lagoon, Lake
Laht *Estonian,* Bay
Laut *Indonesian,* Sea
Lembalemba *Malagasy,*
Plateau
Lerr *Armenian,*
Mountain
Lerrnashght'a *Armenian,*
Mountain range
Les *Czech,* Forest
Lich *Armenian,* Lake
Liqeni *Albanian,* Lake
Lumi *Albanian,* River
Lyman *Ukrainian,*
Estuary

M

Mae Nam *Thai,* River
-mägi *Estonian,* Hill
Maja *Albanian,* Mountain
-man *Korean,* Bay
Marios *Lithuanian,* Lake
-meer *Dutch,* Lake
Melkosopochnik
Russian, Plain
-meri *Estonian,* Sea
Mifraz *Hebrew,* Bay
Monkhafad *Arabic,*
Depression
Mont(s) *French,*
Mountain(s)
Monte *Italian,*
Portuguese, Mountain
More *Russian,* Sea
Mörön *Mongolian,* River

N

Nagor'ye *Russian,*
Upland
Najal *Hebrew,* River
Nahr *Arabic,* River
Nam *Laotian,* River
Nehri *Turkish,* River
Nevado *Spanish,*
Mountain (snow-
capped)
Nisoi *Greek,* Islands
Nizmennost' *Russian,*
Lowland, plain
Nosy *Malagasy,* Island
Nur *Mongolian,* Lake
Nuruu *Mongolian,*
Mountains
Nuur *Mongolian,* Lake
Nyzovyna *Ukrainian,*
Lowland, plain

O

Ostrov(a) *Russian,*
Island(s)
Oued *Arabic,*
Watercourse
-oy *Faeroese,* Island
-øy(a) *Norwegian,*
Island
Oya *Sinhala,* River
Ozero *Russian,*
Ukrainian, Lake

P

Passo *Italian,* Pass
Pegunungan
Indonesian, Malay,
Mountain range
Pelagos *Greek,* Sea
Penisola *Italian,*
Peninsula
Peski *Russian,* Sands
Phanom *Thai,* Mountain
Phou *Laotian,*
Mountain
Pic *Catalan,* Peak
Pico *Portuguese,*
Spanish, Peak
Pik *Russian,* Peak
Planalto *Portuguese,*
Plateau
Planina, Planini
Bulgarian, Macedonian,
Serbian, Croatian,
Mountain range
Ploskogor'ye *Russian,*
Upland
Poluostrov *Russian,*
Peninsula
Potamos *Greek,* River
Proliv *Russian,* Strait
Pulau *Indonesian,*
Malay, Island
Pulu *Malay,* Island
Punta *Portuguese,*
Spanish, Point

Q

Qá' *Arabic,* Depression
Qolleh *Persian,*
Mountain

R

Raas *Somali,* Cape
-rags *Latvian,* Cape
Ramlat *Arabic,* Sands
Ra's *Arabic,* Cape,
point, headland
Ravnina *Bulgarian,*
Russian, Plain
Récif *French,* Reef
Represa (Rep.) *Spanish,*
Portuguese, Reservoir
-rettó *Japanese,* Island
chain
Riacho *Spanish,*
Stream
Riban' *Malagasy,*
Mountains
Rio *Portuguese,* River
Río *Spanish,* River
Riu *Catalan,* River
Rivier *Dutch,* River
Rivière *French,* River
Rowd *Pashtu,* River
Rúd *Persian,* River
Rudohorie *Slovak,*
Mountains
Ruisseau *French,*
Stream

S

Sabkhat *Arabic,* Salt
marsh
Ṣaḥrá' *Arabic,* Desert
Samudra *Sinhala,*
Reservoir
-san *Japanese, Korean,*
Mountain
-sanchi *Japanese,*
Mountains
-sanmaek *Korean,*
Mountain range
Sarír *Arabic,* Desert
Sebkha, Sebkhet *Arabic,*
Salt marsh, depression
See *German,* Lake
Selat *Indonesian,* Strait
-selkä *Finnish,* Ridge
Selseleh *Persian,*
Mountain range
Serra *Portuguese,*
Mountain
Serranía *Spanish,*
Mountain
Sha'íb *Arabic,*
Watercourse
Shamo *Chinese,*
Desert
Shan *Chinese,*
Mountain(s)
Shan-mo *Chinese,*
Mountain range
Shaṭṭ *Arabic,*
Distributary
-shima *Japanese,* Island
Shui-tao *Chinese,*
Channel
Sierra *Spanish,*
Mountains
Sòn *Vietnamese,*
Mountain
Sông *Vietnamese,* River
-spitze *German,* Peak
Štít *Slovak,* Peak
Stoeng *Cambodian,*
River
Stretto *Italian,* Strait
Su Anbarı *Azerbaijani,*
Reservoir
Sungai *Indonesian,*
Malay, River
Suu *Turkish,* River

T

Tal *Mongolian,* Plain
Tandavan' *Malagasy,*
Mountain range
Tangorombohitr'
Malagasy, Mountain
massif
Tao *Chinese,* Island
Tassili *Berber,* Plateau,
mountain
Tau *Russian,*
Mountain(s)
Taungdan *Burmese,*
Mountain range

Teluk *Indonesian,*
Malay, Bay
Terara *Amharic,*
Mountain
Tog *Somali,* Valley
Tônlé *Cambodian,*
Lake
Top *Dutch,* Peak
-tunturi *Finnish,*
Mountain
Tur'at *Arabic,*
Channel

V

Väin *Estonian,* Strait
-vatn *Icelandic,* Lake
-vesi *Finnish,* Lake
Vinh *Vietnamese,* Bay
Vodokhranilishche
(Vdkhr.) *Russian,*
Reservoir
Vodoskhovyshche
(Vdskh.) *Ukrainian,*
Reservoir
Volcán *Spanish,*
Volcano
Vozvyshennost'
Russian, Upland,
plateau
Vrh *Macedonian,*
Peak
Vysochyna *Ukrainian,*
Upland
Vysočina *Czech,*
Upland

W

Waadi *Somali,*
Watercourse
Wádí *Arabic,*
Watercourse
Wáḥat, Wâhat *Arabic,*
Oasis
Wald *German,* Forest
Wan *Chinese,* Bay
Wyżyna *Polish,*
Upland

X

Xé *Laotian,* River

Y

Yarımadası *Azerbaijani,*
Peninsula
Yazovir *Bulgarian,*
Reservoir
Yoma *Burmese,*
Mountains
Yü *Chinese,* Island

Z

Zaliv *Bulgarian,*
Russian, Bay
Zatoka *Ukrainian,* Bay
Zemlya *Russian,* Land

Continental factfile

North & Central America

Total area:
9,400,000 sq miles
(24,346,000 sq km)

**Total number of
countries:** 23

Total population:
511.3 million

**Largest city with
population:** Mexico
City, Mexico 22.8 million

**Country with highest
population density:** Barbados
1627 people per sq mile
(628 people per sq km)

Largest country:
Canada 3,855,171 sq miles
(9,984,670 sq km)

Smallest country:
St. Kitts & Nevis 101 sq miles
(261 sq km)

Largest lake: Lake Superior,
Canada/ USA 32,151 sq miles
(83,270 sq km)

Longest river: Mississippi-
Missouri, USA 3710 miles
(5969 km)

Highest point: Mt. McKinley
(Denali), Alaska, USA 20,322 ft
(6194 m)

lowest point: Death Valley,
California, USA
282 ft (86 m) below sea level

South America

Total area:
6,880,000 sq miles
(17,819,000 sq km)

**Total number of
countries:** 12

Total population:
375.1 million

**Largest city with
population:** São Paulo,
Brazil 20.2 million

**Country with highest
population density:** Ecuador
123 people per sq mile
(48 people per sq km)

Largest country:
Brazil 3,286,470 sq miles
(8,511,965 sq km)

Smallest country:
Suriname 63,039 sq miles
(163,270 sq km)

Largest lake: Lake Titicaca,
Bolivia/Peru 3220 sq miles
(8340 sq km)

Longest river: Amazon,
Brazil 4049 miles
(6516 km)

Highest point: Cerro
Aconcagua, Argentina
22,831 ft (6959 m)

Lowest point: Peninsula
Valdés, Argentina
131 ft (40 m) below sea level

Africa

Total area:
11,677,250 sq miles
(30,244,050 sq km)

**Total number of
countries:** 53

Total population:
904.5 million

**Largest city with
population:** Cairo,
Egypt 15.6 million

**Country with highest
population density:** Mauritius
1617 people per sq mile
(645 people per sq km)

Largest country:
Sudan 967,493 sq miles
(2,505,810 sq km)

Smallest country:
Seychelles 176 sq miles
(455 sq km)

Largest lake: Lake Victoria,
Uganda, Kenya, Tanzania
26,828 sq miles (69,484 sq km)

Longest river: Nile,
Uganda/Sudan/Egypt
4160 miles (6695 km)

Highest point: Kilimanjaro,
Tanzania 19,340 ft
(5895 m)

Lowest point: Lac',
Assal, Djibouti
512 ft (156 m) below sea level

Europe

Total area:
4,809,200 sq miles
(12,456,000 sq km)

**Total number of
countries:** 45

Total population:
501 million

**Largest city with
population:** Moscow,
Euro Russia 13.8 million

**Country with highest
population density:** Monaco
43,212 people per sq mile
(16,620 people per sq km)

Largest country: European
Russia 1,527,341 sq miles
(3,955,818 sq km)

Smallest country:
Vatican City, Italy 0.17 sq miles
(0.44 sq km)

Largest lake: Ladoga,
European Russia
7100 sq miles (18,390 sq km)

Longest river: Volga,
European Russia
2290 miles (3688 km)

Highest point: El'brus,
Caucasus Mts, European
Russia 18,510 ft (5642 m)

Lowest point: Volga Delta,
Caspian Sea, European Russia
92 ft (28 m) below sea level

North & West Asia

 Total area:
9,585,500 sq miles
(24,826,600 sq km)

 Total number of
countries: 24

 Total population:
510 million

 Largest city with
population: Tehran, Iran
11.6 million

 Country with highest
population density: Bahrain
2663 people per sq mile
(1029 people per sq km)

 Largest country: Asiatic
Russia 5,065,471 sq miles
(13,119,582 sq km)

Smallest country:
Bahrain 239 sq miles
(620 sq km)

 Largest lake:
Caspian Sea 142,243 sq miles
(371,000 sq km)

 Longest river: Ob'-Irtysh,
Asiatic Russia 3461 miles
(5570 km)

 Highest point: Pik Pobedy,
Kyrgyzstan/China 24,408 ft
(7439 m)

 Lowest point: Dead Sea,
Israel/Jordan 1286 ft
(392 m) below sea level

South & East Asia

 Total area:
7,936,200 sq miles
(20,554,700 sq km)

 Total number of
countries: 24

Total population:
3550 million

 Largest city with
population: Tokyo,
Japan 33.9 million

 Country with highest
population density: Singapore
18,220 people per sq mile
(7056 people per sq km)

Largest country:
China 3,705,386 sq miles
(9,596,960 sq km)

Smallest country:
Maldives 116 sq miles
(300 sq km)

 Largest lake: Tonle Sap,
Cambodia 1000 sq miles
(2850 sq km)

 Longest river: Chang Jiang
(Yangtze) 3965 miles
(6380 km)

 Highest point:
Mount Everest, Nepal
29,035 ft (8850 m)

 Lowest point: Turpan Hami,
(Turfan basin), China 505 ft
(154 m) below sea level

Australasia & Oceania

 Total area:
3,376,700 sq miles
(8,745,750 sq km)

 Total number of
countries: 14

Total population:
32.2 million

 Largest city with
population: Sydney,
Australia 4.4 million

 Country with highest
population density: Nauru
1611 people per sq mile
(621 people per sq km)

 Largest country:
Australia 2,967,892 sq miles
(7,686,850 sq km)

 Smallest country:
Nauru 8 sq miles
(21 sq km)

 Largest lake: Lake Eyre,
Australia 3700 sq miles
(9583 sq km)

 Longest river: Murray-
Darling, Australia
2330 miles (3750 km)

Highest point: Mt. Wilhelm,
Papua New Guinea 14,795 ft
(4509 m)

Lowest point: Lake Eyre,
Australia 52 ft
(16 m) below sea level

Antarctica

 Total area: 5,450,500 sq miles (14,000,000 sq km)
of which approx. 324,300 sq miles
(840,000 sq km) is ice-free.

 Total number of countries: The Antarctic Treaty has
30 participating nations and 14 with observer status.
Claims by Australia, France, New Zealand, Norway,
Argentina, Chile, and the UK are not recognized by
other member states.

 Total Population: No indigenous population.
74 research stations, (42 are staffed all year-round).
Population varies between about 1000 (winter)
and 4000 (summer).

 Total volume of ice:
7,200,000 cu miles (30,000,000 cu km):
contains 90% of Earth's fresh water

 Sea ice: 1,158,300 sq miles (3,000,000
sq km) in February. 7,722,000 sq miles
(20,000,000 sq km) in October

 Lowest temperature: Vostok station
-89.5°C (-129°F)

 Highest point: Vinson Massif
16,072 ft (4897 m)

 Lowest Point: Coastline 0ft/m

Geographical comparisons

Largest countries

Russ. Fed.	6,592,735 sq miles	(17,075,200 sq km)
Canada	3,854,085 sq miles	(9,984,670 sq km)
USA	3,717,792 sq miles	(9,629,091 sq km)
China	3,705,386 sq miles	(9,596,960 sq km)
Brazil	3,286,470 sq miles	(8,511,965 sq km)
Australia	2,967,893 sq miles	(7,686,850 sq km)
India	1,269,339 sq miles	(3,287,590 sq km)
Argentina	1,068,296 sq miles	(2,766,890 sq km)
Kazakhstan	1,049,150 sq miles	(2,717,300 sq km)
Sudan	967,493 sq miles	(2,505,810 sq km)

Smallest countries

Vatican City	0.17 sq miles	(0.44 sq km)
Monaco	0.75 sq miles	(1.95 sq km)
Nauru	8 sq miles	(21 sq km)
Tuvalu	10 sq miles	(26 sq km)
San Marino	24 sq miles	(61 sq km)
Liechtenstein	62 sq miles	(160 sq km)
Marshall Islands	70 sq miles	(181 sq km)
St. Kitts & Nevis	101 sq miles	(261 sq km)
Maldives	116 sq miles	(300 sq km)
Malta	122 sq miles	(316 sq km)

Largest islands

Greenland	849,400 sq miles	(2,200,000 sq km)
New Guinea	312,000 sq miles	(808,000 sq km)
Borneo	292,222 sq miles	(757,050 sq km)
Madagascar	229,300 sq miles	(594,000 sq km)
Sumatra	202,300 sq miles	(524,000 sq km)
Baffin Island	183,800 sq miles	(476,000 sq km)
Honshu	88,800 sq miles	(230,000 sq km)
Britain	88,700 sq miles	(229,800 sq km)
Victoria Island	81,900 sq miles	(212,000 sq km)
Ellesmere Island	75,700 sq miles	(196,000 sq km)

Richest countries   (GNI per capita, in US$)

Luxembourg	56,230
Norway	52,030
Liechtenstein	50,000
Switzerland	48,230
USA	41,400
Denmark	40,650
Iceland	38,620
Japan	37,810
Sweden	35,770
Monaco	34,280

Poorest countries   (GNI per capita, in US$)

Burundi	90
Ethiopia	110
Liberia	110
Congo, Dem. Rep.	120
Somalia	120
Guinea-Bissau	160
Malawi	170
Eritrea	180
Sierra Leone	200
Rwanda	220

Most populous countries

China	1,315,800,000
India	1,103,400,000
USA	298,200,000
Indonesia	222,800,000
Brazil	180,400,000
Cameroon	163,000,000
Pakistan	157,900,000
Russian Federation	143,200,000
Bangladesh	141,800,000
Nigeria	131,500,000

Least populous countries

Vatican City	921
Tuvalu	11,636
Nauru	13,048
Palau	20,303
San Marino	28,880
Monaco	32,409
Liechtenstein	33,717
St. Kitts & Nevis	38,958
Marshall Islands	59,071
Antigua & Barbuda	68,722

Most densely populated countries

Monaco	43,212 people per sq mile	(16,620 per sq km)
Singapore	18,220 people per sq mile	(7049 per sq km)
Vatican City	5418 people per sq mile	(2090 per sq km)
Malta	3242 people per sq mile	(1256 per sq km)
Maldives	2836 people per sq mile	(1097 per sq km)
Bangladesh	2743 people per sq mile	(1059 per sq km)
Bahrain	2663 people per sq mile	(1030 per sq km)
China	1838 people per sq mile	(710 per sq km)
Mauritius	1671 people per sq mile	(645 per sq km)
Barbados	1627 people per sq mile	(628 per sq km)

Most sparsely populated countries

Mongolia.........4 people per sq mile......... (2 per sq km)
Namibia...........6 people per sq mile......... (2 per sq km)
Australia..........7 people per sq mile......... (3 per sq km)
Mauritania ......8 people per sq mile......... (3 per sq km)
Suriname........8 people per sq mile......... (3 per sq km)
Botswana........8 people per sq mile......... (3 per sq km)
Iceland ....8 people per sq mile......... (3 per sq km)
Canada ....9 people per sq mile......... (4 per sq km)
Libya ....9 people per sq mile......... (4 per sq km)
Guyana.........10 people per sq mile......... (4 per sq km)

Most widely spoken languages

1. Chinese (Mandarin)   6. Arabic
2. English   7. Bengali
3. Hindi   8. Portuguese
4. Spanish   9. Malay-Indonesian
5. Russian   10. French

Largest conurbations

Tokyo...34,200,000
Mexico City 22,800,000
Seoul 22,300,000
New York...21,900,000
São Paulo..20,200,000
Mumbai 19,850,000
Delhi..19,700,000
Shanghai...18,150,000
Los Angeles 18,000,000
Osaka..16,800,000
Jakarta..16,550,000
Kolkata..15,650,000
Cairo...15,600,000
Manila...14,950,000
Karachi..14,300,000
Moscow...13,750,000
Buenos Aires 13,450,000
Dacca..13,250,000
Rio de Janeiro...12,150,000
Beijing 12,100,000
London 12,000,000
Tehran...11,850,000
Istanbul 11,500,000
Lagos 11,100,000
Shenzhen 10,700,000

Longest rivers

Nile (NE Africa) ....4160 miles ...... (6695 km)
Amazon (South America) ....4049 miles ...... (6516 km)
Yangtze (China)...........................3915 miles ...... (6299 km)
Mississippi/Missouri (US) ....3710 miles........(5969 km)
Ob'-Irtysh (Russ. Fed.) ....3461 miles ...... (5570 km)
Yellow River (China) ....3395 miles ...... (5464 km)
Congo (Central Africa) ....2900 miles ...... (4667 km)
Mekong (Southeast Asia) ....2749 miles.......(4425 km)
Lena (Russian Federation)........2734 miles......(4400 km)
Mackenzie (Canada) ....2640 miles......(4250 km)
Yenisey (Russ. Federation) ......2541 miles......(4090 km)

Highest mountains   (Height above sea level)

Everest....................................... 29,035 ft.......(8850 m)
K2 .... 28,253 ft.......(8611 m)
Kanchenjunga I........................ 28,210 ft.......(8598 m)
Makalu I.................................... 27,767 ft.......(8463 m)
Cho Oyu .... 26,907 ft.......(8201 m)
Dhaulagiri I............................... 26,796 ft.......(8167 m)
Manaslu I .... 26,783 ft.......(8163 m)
Nanga Parbat I......................... 26,661 ft.......(8126 m)
Annapurna I .... 26,547 ft.......(8091 m)
Gasherbrum I............................ 26,471 ft.......(8068 m)

Largest bodies of inland water (Area & depth)

Caspian Sea
    143,243 sq miles (371,000 sq km).......3215 ft (980 m)
Lake Superior
    32,151 sq miles (83,270 sq km).......1289 ft (393 m)
Lake Victoria
    26,560 sq miles (68,880 sq km).........328 ft (100 m)
Lake Huron
    23,436 sq miles (60,700 sq km).........751 ft (229 m)
Lake Michigan
    22,402 sq miles (58,020 sq km).........922 ft (281 m)
Lake Tanganyika
    12,703 sq miles (32,900 sq km).... 4700 ft (1435 m)
Great Bear Lake
    12,274 sq miles (31,790 sq km)...... 1047 ft (319 m)
Lake Baikal
    11,776 sq miles (30,500 sq km).... 5712 ft (1741 m)
Great Slave Lake
    10,981 sq miles (28,440 sq km).........459 ft (140 m)
Lake Erie
    9915 sq miles (25,680 sq km)...........197 ft (60 m)

......continued on p.166

165

Geographical comparisons continued

Deepest ocean features

Challenger Deep, Mariana Trench (Pacific)
36,201 ft .... (11,034 m)
Vityaz III Depth, Tonga Trench (Pacific)
35,704 ft .... (10,882 m)
Vityaz Depth, Kurile-Kamchatka Trench (Pacific)
34,588 ft .... (10,542 m)
Cape Johnson Deep, Philippine Trench (Pacific)
34,441 ft .... (10,497 m)
Kermadec Trench (Pacific)
32,964 ft .... (10,047 m)
Ramapo Deep, Japan Trench (Pacific)
32,758 ft .... (9984 m)
Milwaukee Deep, Puerto Rico Trench (Atlantic)
30,185 ft .... (9200 m)
Argo Deep, Torres Trench (Pacific)
30,070 ft .... (9165 m)
Meteor Depth, South Sandwich Trench (Atlantic)
30,000 ft .... (9144 m)
Planet Deep, New Britain Trench (Pacific)
29,988 ft .... (9140 m)

Greatest waterfalls   (Mean flow of water)

Boyoma (Congo) .... 600,400 cu. ft/sec (17,000 cu.m/sec)
Khône (Laos/Cambodia) ... 410,000 cu. ft/sec (11,600 cu.m/sec)
Niagara (USA/Canada) .... 195,000 cu. ft/sec (5500 cu.m/sec)
Grande (Uruguay) .... 160,000 cu. ft/sec (4500 cu.m/sec)
Paulo Afonso (Brazil) .... 100,000 cu. ft/sec(2800 cu.m/sec)
Urubupunga (Brazil) .... 97,000 cu. ft/sec (2750 cu.m/sec)
Iguaçu (Argentina/Brazil) .... 62,000 cu. ft/sec (1700 cu.m/sec)
Maribondo (Brazil) .... 53,000 cu. ft/sec (1500 cu.m/sec)
Victoria (Zimbabwe) .... 39,000 cu. ft/sec (1100 cu.m/sec)
Kabalega (Uganda) .... 42,000 cu. ft/sec (1200 cu.m/sec)
Churchill (Canada) .... 35,000 cu. ft/sec (1000 cu.m/sec)
Cauvery (India) .... 33,000 cu. ft/sec (900 cu.m/sec)

Highest waterfalls

Angel (Venezuela) .... 3212 ft .... (979 m)
Tugela (South Africa) .... 3110 ft .... (948 m)
Utigard (Norway) .... 2625 ft .... (800 m)
Mongefossen (Norway) .... 2539 ft .... (774 m)
Mtarazi (Zimbabwe) .... 2500 ft .... (762 m)
Yosemite (USA) .... 2425 ft .... (739 m)
Ostre Mardola Foss (Norway) ..... 2156 ft .... (657 m)
Tyssestrengane (Norway) .... 2119 ft .... (646 m)
*Cuquenan (Venezuela) .... 2001 ft .... (610 m)
Sutherland (New Zealand) .... 1903 ft .... (580 m)
*Kjellfossen (Norway) .... 1841 ft .... (561 m)

indicates that the total height is a single leap

Largest deserts

Sahara .... 3,450,000 sq miles (9,065,000 sq km)
Gobi .... 500,000 sq miles (1,295,000 sq km)
Ar Rub al Khali ...... 289,600 sq miles (750,000 sq km)
Great Victorian ..... 249,800 sq miles (647,000 sq km)
Sonoran .... 120,000 sq miles (311,000 sq km)
Kalahari .... 120,000 sq miles (310,800 sq km)
Garagum .... 115,800 sq miles (300,000 sq km)
Takla Makan .... 100,400 sq miles (260,000 sq km)
Namib .... 52,100 sq miles (135,000 sq km)
Thar .... 33,670 sq miles (130,000 sq km)

NB – Most of Antarctica is a polar desert, with only 2 inches (50 mm) of precipitation annually

Hottest inhabited places

Djibouti (Djibouti) .... 86.0°F .... (30.0°C)
Timbouctou (Mali) .... 84.7°F .... (29.3°C)
Tirunelveli (India) .... 84.7°F .... (29.3°C)
Tuticorin (India) .... 84.7°F .... (29.3°C)
Nellore (India) .... 84.5°F .... (29.2°C)
Santa Marta (Colombia) .... 84.5°F .... (29.2°C)
Aden (Yemen) .... 84.0°F .... (29.0°C)
Madurai (India) .... 84.0°F .... (29.0°C)
Niamey (Niger) .... 84.0°F .... (29.0°C)

Driest inhabited places

Aswân (Egypt) .... 0.02 in .... (0.5 mm)
Luxor (Egypt) .... 0.03 in .... (0.7 mm)
Arica (Chile) .... 0.04 in .... (1.1 mm)
Ica (Peru) .... 0.10 in .... (2.3 mm)
Antofagasta (Chile) .... 0.20 in .... (4.9 mm)
El Minya (Egypt) .... 0.20 in .... (5.1 mm)
Asyût (Egypt) .... 0.20 in .... (5.2 mm)
Callao (Peru) .... 0.50 in .... (12.0 mm)
Trujillo (Peru) .... 0.55 in .... (14.0 mm)
El Faiyûm (Egypt) .... 0.80 in .... (19.0 mm)

Wettest inhabited places

Buenaventura (Colombia) .... 265 in .... (6743 mm)
Monrovia (Liberia) .... 202 in .... (5131 mm)
Pago Pago (American Samoa) .... 196 in .... (4990 mm)
Moulmein (Myanmar) .... 191 in .... (4852 mm)
Lae (Papua New Guinea) .... 183 in .... (4645 mm)
Baguio (Luzon I., Philippines) ..... 180 in .... (4573 mm)
Sylhet (Bangladesh) .... 176 in .... (4457 mm)
Padang (Sumatra, Indonesia) ...... 166 in .... (4225 mm)
Bogor (Java, Indonesia) .... 166 in.... (4225 mm)
Conakry (Guinea) .... 171 in.... (4341 mm)

GLOSSARY OF ABBREVIATIONS

This Glossary provides a comprehensive guide to the abbreviations used in this Atlas, and in the Index.

A
abbrev. abbreviated
Afr. Afrikaans
Alb. Albanian
Amh. Amharic
anc. ancient
Ar. Arabic
Arm. Armenian
Az. Azerbaijani

B
Basq. Basque
Bel. Belorussian
Ben. Bengali
Bibl. Biblical
Bret. Breton
Bul. Bulgarian
Bur. Burmese

C
Cam. Cambodian
Cant. Cantonese
Cast. Castilian
Cat. Catalan
Chin. Chinese
Cro. Croat
Cz. Czech

D
Dan. Danish
Dut. Dutch

E
Eng. English
Est. Estonian
est. estimated

F
Faer. Faeroese
Fij. Fijian
Fin. Finnish
Flem. Flemish
Fr. French
Fris. Frisian

G
Geor. Georgian
Ger. German
Gk. Greek
Guj. Gujarati

H
Haw. Hawaiian
Heb. Hebrew
Hind. Hindi
hist. historical
Hung. Hungarian

I
Icel. Icelandic
Ind. Indonesian
In. Inuit
Ir. Irish
It. Italian

J
Jap. Japanese

K
Kaz. Kazakh
Kir. Kirghiz
Kor. Korean
Kurd. Kurdish

L
Lao. Laotian
Lapp. Lappish
Lat. Latin
Latv. Latvian

Lith. Lithanian
Lus. Lusatian

M
Mac. Macedonian
Mal. Malay
Malg. Malagasy
Malt. Maltese
Mon. Montenegro
Mong. Mongolian

N
Nepali. Nepali
Nor. Norwegian

O
off. officially

P
Pash. Pashtu
Per. Persian
Pol. Polish
Port. Portuguese
prev. previously

R
Rmsch. Romansch
Roman. Romanian
Rus. Russian

S
SCr. Serbo - Croatian
Serb. Serbian
Slvk. Slovak
Slvn. Slovene
Som. Somali
Sp. Spanish
Swa. Swahili
Swe. Swedish

T
Taj. Tajik
Th. Thai
Tib. Tibetan
Turk. Turkish
Turkm. Turkmenistan

U
Uigh. Uighur
Ukr. Ukrainian
Uzb. Uzbek

V
var. variant
Vtn. Vietnamese

W
Wel. Welsh

X
Xh. Xhosa

Key to country factboxes within the Index:

Formation
Date of independence

Population
Total population / population density - based on total land area .

Calorie consumption
Average number of calories consumed daily per person.

A

Aa see Gauja
Aachen 94 A4 Dut. Aken, Fr. Aix-la-Chapelle; anc. Aquae Grani, Aquisgranum. Nordrhein-Westfalen, W Germany
Aaiún see Laâyoune
Aalborg 80 D3 var. Ålborg, Ålborg-Nørresundby; anc. Alburgum. Nordjylland, N Denmark
Aalen 95 B6 Baden-Württemberg, S Germany
Aalsmeer 86 C3 Noord-Holland, C Netherlands
Aalst 87 B6 Fr. Alost. Oost-Vlaanderen, C Belgium
Aalten 86 E4 Gelderland, E Netherlands
Aalter 87 B5 Oost-Vlaanderen, NW Belgium
Aanaarjävri see Inarijärvi
Äänekoski 85 D5 Länsi-Soumi, W Finland
Aar see Aare
Aare 95 A7 var. Aar. river W Switzerland
Aarhus see Århus
Aarlen see Arlon
Aat see Ath
Aba 77 E5 Orientale, NE Dem. Rep. Congo
Aba 75 G5 Abia, S Nigeria
Abā as Su'ūd see Najrān
Abaco Island see Great Abaco, Bahamas
Ābādān 120 C4 Khūzestān, SW Iran
Abadan 122 C3 prev. Bezmein, Rus. Büzmeýin. Ahal Welaýaty, C Turkmenistan
Abai see Blue Nile
Abakan 114 D4 Respublika Khakasiya, S Russian Federation
Abancay 60 D4 Apurímac, SE Peru
Abariringa see Kanton
Abashiri 130 D2 var. Abasiri. Hokkaidō, NE Japan
Abasiri see Abashiri
Ābaya Hāyk' 73 C5 Eng. Lake Margherita, It. Abbaia. lake SW Ethiopia
Ābay Wenz see Blue Nile
Abbaia see Ābaya Hāyk'
Abbatis Villa see Abbeville
Abbazia see Opatija
Abbeville 90 C2 anc. Abbatis Villa. Somme, N France
'Abd al 'Azīz, Jabal 118 D2 mountain range NE Syria
Abéché 76 C3 var. Abécher, Abeshr. Ouaddaï, SE Chad
Abécher see Abéché
Abela see Ávila
Abellinum see Avellino
Abemama 144 D2 var. Apamama; prev. Roger Simpson Island. atoll Tungaru, W Kiribati
Abengourou 75 E5 E Côte d'Ivoire (Ivory Coast)
Aberbrothock see Arbroath
Abercorn see Mbala
Aberdeen 88 D3 anc. Devana. NE Scotland, UK
Aberdeen 45 E2 South Dakota, N USA
Aberdeen 46 B2 Washington, NW USA
Abergwaun see Fishguard
Abertawe see Swansea
Aberystwyth 89 C6 W Wales, UK
Abhā 121 B6 'Asīr, SW Saudi Arabia
Abidavichy 107 D7 Rus. Obidovichi. Mahilyowskaya Voblasts', E Belarus
Abidjan 75 E5 S Côte d'Ivoire (Ivory Coast)
Abilene 49 F3 Texas, SW USA
Abingdon see Pinta, Isla
Abkhazia 117 E1 autonomous republic NW Georgia
Aboisso 75 E5 SE Côte d'Ivoire (Ivory Coast)
Abo, Massif d' 76 B1 mountain range NW Chad
Abomey 75 F5 S Benin
Abou-Déïa 76 C3 Salamat, SE Chad
Aboudouhour see Abū aḏ Ḏuhūr
Abou Kémal see Abū Kamāl
Abrantes 92 B3 var. Abrántes. Santarém, C Portugal
Abrashlare see Brezovo

Abrolhos Bank 56 E4 undersea bank W Atlantic Ocean
Abrova 107 B6 Rus. Obrovo. Brestskaya Voblasts', SW Belarus
Abrud 108 B4 Ger. Gross-Schlatten, Hung. Abrudbánya. Alba, SW Romania
Abrudbánya see Abrud
Abruzzese, Appennino 96 C4 mountain range C Italy
Absaroka Range 44 B2 mountain range Montana/Wyoming, NW USA
Abū aḏ Ḏuhūr 118 B3 Fr. Aboudouhour. Idlib, NW Syria
Abu Dhabi see Abū Ẓaby
Abu Hamed 72 C3 River Nile, N Sudan
Abū Ḩardān 118 E3 var. Hajîne. Dayr az Zawr, E Syria
Abuja 75 G4 country capital (Nigeria) Federal Capital District, C Nigeria
Abū Kamāl 118 E3 Fr. Abou Kémal. Dayr az Zawr, E Syria
Abula see Ávila
Abunã, Rio 62 C2 var. Río Abuná. river Bolivia/Brazil
Abut Head 151 B6 headland South Island, New Zealand
Ābuyē Mēda 72 D4 mountain C Ethiopia
Abū Ẓabī see Abū Ẓaby
Abū Ẓaby 121 C5 var. Abū Ẓabī, Eng. Abu Dhabi. country capital (United Arab Emirates) Abū Ẓaby C United Arab Emirates
Abyaḏ, Al Baḩr al see White Nile
Abyla see Ávila
Abyssinia see Ethiopia
Acalayong 77 A5 SW Equatorial Guinea
Acaponeta 50 D4 Nayarit, C Mexico
Acapulco 51 E5 var. Acapulco de Juárez. Guerrero, S Mexico
Acapulco de Juárez see Acapulco
Acarai Mountains 59 F4 Sp. Serra Acaraí. mountain range Brazil/Guyana
Acaraí, Serra see Acarai Mountains
Acarigua 58 D2 Portuguesa, N Venezuela
Accra 75 E5 country capital (Ghana)SE Ghana
Achacachi 61 E4 La Paz, W Bolivia
Acklins Island 54 C2 island SE Bahamas
Aconcagua, Cerro 64 B4 mountain W Argentina
Açores/Açores, Arquipélago dos/Açores, Ilhas dos see Azores
A Coruña 92 B1 Cast. La Coruña, Eng. Corunna; anc. Caronium. Galicia, NW Spain
Acre 62 C2 off. Estado do Acre. state W Brazil
Acre, Estado do see Acre
Açu 63 G2 var. Assu. Rio Grande do Norte, E Brazil
Acunum Acusio see Montélimar
Ada 100 D3 Vojvodina, N Serbia
Ada 49 G2 Oklahoma, C USA
Ada Bazar see Adapazarı
Adalia see Antalya
Adalia, Gulf of see Antalya Körfezi
Adama see Nazrēt
'Adan 121 B7 Eng. Aden. SW Yemen
Adana 116 D4 var. Seyhan. Adana, S Turkey
Adâncata see Horlivka
Adapazarı 116 B2 prev. Ada Bazar. Sakarya, NW Turkey
Adare, Cape 154 B4 cape Antarctica
Ad Dahnā' 120 C4 desert E Saudi Arabia
Ad Dakhla 70 A4 var. Dakhla. SW Western Sahara
Ad Dalanj see Dilling
Ad Damar see Ed Damer
Ad Damazin see Ed Damazin
Ad Dāmir see Ed Damer
Ad Dammām 120 C4 var. Dammām. Ash Sharqiyah, NE Saudi Arabia
Ad Damūr see Damoūr
Ad Dawhah 120 C4 Eng. Doha. country capital (Qatar) C Qatar
Aḏ Ḏiffah see Libyan Plateau
Addis Ababa see Ādīs Ābeba
Addu Atoll 132 A5 atoll S Maldives
Adelaide 149 B6 state capital South Australia
Adelsberg see Postojna
Aden see 'Adan
Aden, Gulf of 121 C7 gulf SW Arabian Sea
Adige 96 C2 Ger. Etsch. river N Italy
Adirondack Mountains 41 F2 mountain range New York, NE USA

Ādīs Ābeba 73 C5 Eng. Addis Ababa. country capital (Ethiopia) Ādīs Ābeba, C Ethiopia
Adıyaman 117 E4 Adıyaman, SE Turkey
Adjud 108 C4 Vrancea, E Romania
Admiralty Islands 144 B3 island group N Papua New Guinea
Adra 93 E5 Andalucía, S Spain
Adrar 70 D3 C Algeria
Adrian 40 C3 Michigan, N USA
Adrianople/Adrianopolis see Edirne
Adriatico, Mare see Adriatic Sea
Adriatic Sea 103 E2 Alb. Deti Adriatik, It. Mare Adriatico, SCr. Jadransko More, Slvn. Jadransko Morje. sea N Mediterranean Sea
Adriatik, Deti see Adriatic Sea
Adycha 115 F2 river NE Russian Federation
Aegean Sea 105 C5 Gk. Aigaíon Pelagos, Aigaío Pélagos, Turk. Ege Denizi. sea NE Mediterranean Sea
Aegviidu 106 D2 Ger. Charlottenhof. Harjumaa, NW Estonia
Aegyptus see Egypt
Aelana see Al 'Aqabah
Aelok see Ailuk Atoll
Aelönlaplap see Ailinglaplap Atoll
Aemona see Ljubljana
Aeolian Islands see Eolie, Isole
Æsernia see Isernia
Afar Depression see Danakil Desert
Afars et des Issas, Territoire Français des see Djibouti
Afghänestän, Dowlat-e Eslämï-ye see Afghanistan
Afghanistan 122 C4 off. Islamic State of Afghanistan, Per. Dowlat-e Eslämï-ye Afghänestän; prev. Republic of Afghanistan. country C Asia

AFGHANISTAN
Central Asia

Official name Islamic State of Afghanistan
Formation 1919 / 1919
Capital Kabul
Population 29.9 million / 119 people per sq mile (46 people per sq km) / 22%
Total area 250,000 sq miles (647,500 sq km)
Languages Pashtu*, Tajik, Dari, Farsi, Uzbek, Turkmen
Religions Sunni Muslim 84%, Shi'a Muslim 15%, Other 1%
Ethnic mix Pashtun 38%, Tajik 25%, Hazara 19%, Uzbek and Turkmen 15%, Other 3%
Government Transitional regime
Currency New afghani = 100 puls
Literacy rate 36%
Calorie consumption 1539 calories

Afghanistan, Islamic State of see Afghanistan
Afghanistan, Republic of see Afghanistan
Afmadow 73 D6 Jubbada Hoose, S Somalia
Africa 68 continent
Africa, Horn of 68 E4 physical region Ethiopia/Somalia
Africana Seamount 141 A6 seamount SW Indian Ocean
'Afrïn 118 B2 Ḥalab, N Syria
Afyon 116 B3 prev. Afyonkarahisar. Afyon, W Turkey
Afyonkarahisar see Afyon
Agadès see Agadez
Agadez 75 G3 prev. Agadès. Agadez, C Niger
Agadir 70 B3 SW Morocco
Agana/Agaña see Hagåtña
Agaro 73 C5 Oromo, C Ethiopia
Agassiz Fracture Zone 143 G5 fracture zone S Pacific Ocean
Agatha see Agde
Agathónisi 105 D6 island Dodekánisa, Greece, Aegean Sea
Agde 91 C6 anc. Agatha. Hérault, S France
Agedabia see Ajdābiyā
Agen 91 B5 anc. Aginnum. Lot-et-Garonne, SW France
Agendicum see Sens
Aghrï Dagh see Büyükağrı Dağı
Agiá 104 B4 var. Ayiá. Thessalía, C Greece
Agialoúsa see Yenierenköy

Agía Marína 105 E6 Léros, Dodekánisa, Greece, Aegean Sea
Aginnum see Agen
Ágios Efstrátios 104 D4 var. Áyios Evstrátios, Hagios Evstrátios. island E Greece
Ágios Nikólaos 105 D8 var. Áyios Nikólaos. Kríti, Greece, E Mediterranean Sea
Āgra 134 D3 Uttar Pradesh, N India
Agra and Oudh, United Provinces of see Uttar Pradesh
Agram see Zagreb
Ağrı 117 F3 var. Karaköse; prev. Karakılısse. Ağrı, NE Turkey
Agri Dagi see Büyükağrı Dağı
Agrigento 97 C7 Gk. Akragas; prev. Girgenti. Sicilia, Italy, C Mediterranean Sea
Agriovótano 105 C5 Évvoia, C Greece
Agropoli 97 D5 Campania, S Italy
Aguachica 58 B2 Cesar, N Colombia
Aguadulce 53 F5 Coclé, S Panama
Agua Prieta 50 B1 Sonora, NW Mexico
Aguascalientes 50 D4 Aguascalientes, C Mexico
Aguaytía 60 C3 Ucayali, C Peru
Aguilas 93 E4 Murcia, SE Spain
Aguililla 50 D4 Michoacán de Ocampo, SW Mexico
Agulhas Basin 69 D8 undersea basin SW Indian Ocean
Agulhas, Cape 78 C5 cape S South Africa
Agulhas Plateau 67 D6 undersea plateau SW Indian Ocean
Ahaggar 75 F2 high plateau region SE Algeria
Ahlen 94 B4 Nordrhein-Westfalen, W Germany
Ahmadābād 134 C4 var. Ahmedabad. Gujarāt, W India
Ahmadnagar 134 C5 var. Ahmednagar. Mahārāshtra, W India
Ahmedabad see Ahmadābād
Ahmednagar see Ahmadnagar
Ahuachapán 52 B3 Ahuachapán, W El Salvador
Ahväz 120 C3 var. Ahwāz; prev. Nāsiri. Khüzestän, SW Iran
Ahvenanmaa see Åland
Ahwāz see Ahväz
Aigaíon Pelagos/Aigaío Pélagos see Aegean Sea
Aígina 105 C6 var. Aíyina, Egina. Aígina, C Greece
Aígio 105 B5 var. Egio; prev. Aíyion. Dytikí Ellás, S Greece
Aiken 43 E2 South Carolina, SE USA
Ailigandí 53 G4 San Blas, NE Panama
Ailinglaplap Atoll 144 D2 var. Aelönlaplap. atoll Ralik Chain, S Marshall Islands
Ailuk Atoll 144 D1 var. Aelok. atoll Ratak Chain, NE Marshall Islands
Aināži 106 D3 Est. Heinaste, Ger. Hainasch. Limbaži, N Latvia
'Aïn Ben Tili 74 D1 Tiris Zemmour, N Mauritania
Aintab see Gaziantep
Aioun el Atrous/Aïoun el Atroûss see 'Ayoûn el 'Atroûs
Aiquile 61 F4 Cochabamba, C Bolivia
Air see Aïr, Massif de l'
Air, Massif de l' 75 G2 var. Aïr, Air du Azbine, Asben. mountain range NC Niger
Aiud 108 B4 Ger. Strassburg, Hung. Nagyenyed; prev. Engeten. Alba, SW Romania
Aix see Aix-en-Provence
Aix-en-Provence 91 D6 var. Aix; anc. Aquae Sextiae. Bouches-du-Rhône, SE France
Aix-la-Chapelle see Aachen
Aíyina see Aígina
Aíyion see Aígio
Aizkraukle 106 C4 Aizkraukle, S Latvia
Ajaccio 91 E7 Corse, France, C Mediterranean Sea
Ajaria 117 F2 autonomous republic SW Georgia
Ajastan see Armenia
Aj Bogd Uul 126 D2 mountain SW Mongolia
Ajdābiyā 71 G2 var. Agedabia, Ajdābiyah. NE Libya
Ajdābiyah see Ajdābiyā

Ajjinena see El Geneina
Ajmer 134 D3 var. Ajmere. Rājasthän, N India
Ajmere see Ajmer
Ajo 48 A3 Arizona, SW USA
Akaba see Al 'Aqabah
Akamagaseki see Shimonoseki
Akasha 72 B3 Northern, N Sudan
Akchâr 74 C2 desert W Mauritania
Aken see Aachen
Akermanceaster see Bath
Akhalts'ikhe 117 F2 SW Georgia
Akhisar 116 A3 Manisa, W Turkey
Akhmim 72 B2 anc. Panopolis. C Egypt
Akhtyrka see Okhtyrka
Akimiski Island 38 C3 island Nunavut, C Canada
Akinovka 109 F4 Zaporiz'ka Oblast', S Ukraine
Akita 130 D4 Akita, Honshü, C Japan
Akjoujt 74 C2 prev. Fort-Repoux. Inchiri, W Mauritania
Akkeshi 130 E2 Hokkaidö, NE Japan
Aklavik 36 D3 Northwest Territories, NW Canada
Akmola see Astana
Akmolinsk see Astana
Aknavásár see Târgu Ocna
Akpatok Island 39 E1 island Nunavut, E Canada
Akragas see Agrigento
Akron 40 D4 Ohio, N USA
Akrotiri see Akrotirion
Akrotirion 102 C5 var. Akrotiri. UK air base S Cyprus
Aksai Chin 124 B2 Chin. Aksayqin. disputed region China/India
Aksaray 116 C4 Aksaray, C Turkey
Aksayqin see Aksai Chin
Akşehir 116 B4 Konya, W Turkey
Aktash see Oqtosh
Aktau 114 A4 Kaz. Aqtaü; prev. Shevchenko. Mangistau, W Kazakhstan
Aktjubinsk/Aktyubinsk see Aktobe
Aktobe 114 B4 Kaz. Aqtöbe; prev. Aktjubinsk. Aktyubinsk, NW Kazakhstan
Aktsyabrski 107 C7 Rus. Oktyabr'skiy; prev. Karpilovka. Homyel'skaya Voblasts', SE Belarus
Akula 77 C5 Equateur, NW Dem. Rep. Congo
Akureyri 83 E4 Nordhurland Eystra, N Iceland
Akyab see Sittwe
Alabama 51 G1 off. State of Alabama, also known as Camellia State, Heart of Dixie, The Cotton State, Yellowhammer State. state S USA
Alabama River 42 C3 river Alabama, S USA
Alaca 116 C3 Çorum, N Turkey
Alagoas 62 G2 off. Estado de Alagoas. state E Brazil
Alagoas, Estado de see Alagoas
Alais see Alès
Alajuela 53 E4 Alajuela, C Costa Rica
Alakanuk 36 C2 Alaska, USA
Al 'Alamayn see El 'Alamein
Al 'Amārah 120 C3 var. Amara. E Iraq
Alamo 47 D6 Nevada, W USA
Alamogordo 48 D3 New Mexico, SW USA
Alamosa 44 C5 Colorado, C USA
Åland 85 C6 var. Aland Islands, Fin. Ahvenanmaa. island group SW Finland
Aland Islands see Åland
Ålands Hav 85 C6 var. Aland Sea. strait Baltic Sea/Gulf of Bothnia
Alanya 116 C4 Antalya, S Turkey
Alappuzha see Alleppey
Al 'Aqabah 119 B8 var. Akaba, Aqaba, 'Aqaba; anc. Aelana, Elath. Al 'Aqabah, SW Jordan
Al 'Arabïyah as Su'üdïyah see Saudi Arabia
Alaska, Golfo de see Alaska, Gulf of
Alaşehir 116 A4 Manisa, W Turkey
Al 'Ashärah 118 E3 var. Ashara. Dayr az Zawr, E Syria
Alaska 36 C3 off. State of Alaska, also known as Land of the Midnight Sun, The Last Frontier, Seward's Folly; prev. Russian America. state NW USA

Alaska, Gulf of 36 C4 var. Golfo de Alasca. gulf Canada/USA
Alaska Peninsula 36 C3 peninsula Alaska, USA
Alaska Range 34 B2 mountain range Alaska, USA
Al-Asnam see Chlef
Alattio see Alta
Al Awaynät see Al 'Uwaynät
Alaykel'/Alay-Kuu see Këk-Art
Al 'Aynä 119 B7 Al Karak, W Jordan
Alazeya 115 G2 river NE Russian Federation
Al Bäb 118 B2 Ḥalab, N Syria
Albacete 93 E3 Castilla-La Mancha, C Spain
Al Baghdädï 120 B3 var. Khän al Baghdädi. SW Iraq
Al Bäha see Al Bäḥah
Al Bäḥah 121 B5 var. Al Bäha. SW Saudi Arabia
Al Baḥrayn see Bahrain
Alba Iulia 108 B4 Ger. Weissenburg, Hung. Gyulafehérvár; prev. Bälgrad, Karlsburg, Károly-Fehérvár. Alba, W Romania
Albania 101 C7 off. Republic of Albania, Alb. Republika e Shqipërisë, Shqipëria; prev. People's Socialist Republic of Albania. country SE Europe

ALBANIA
Southeast Europe

Official name Republic of Albania
Formation 1912 / 1921
Capital Tirana
Population 3.1 million / 293 people per sq mile (113 people per sq km) / 42%
Total area 11,100 sq miles (28,748 sq km)
Languages Albanian*, Greek
Religions Sunni Muslim 70%, Orthodox Christian 20%, Roman Catholic 10%
Ethnic mix Albanian 93%, Greek 5%, Other 2%
Government Parliamentary system
Currency Lek = 100 qindarka (qintars)
Literacy rate 99%
Calorie consumption 2848 calories

Albania see Aubagne
Albania, People's Socialist Republic of see Albania
Albania, Republic of see Albania
Albany 147 B7 Western Australia
Albany 42 D3 Georgia, SE USA
Albany 41 F3 state capital New York, NE USA
Albany 46 B3 Oregon, NW USA
Albany 38 C3 river Ontario, S Canada
Alba Regia see Székesfehérvár
Al Bäridah 118 C4 var. Bäridah. Ḥimṣ, C Syria
Al Başrah 120 C3 Eng. Basra, hist. Busra, Bussora. SE Iraq
Al Batrün see Batroûn
Al Baydä' 71 G2 var. Beida. NE Libya
Albemarle Island see Isabela, Isla
Albemarle Sound 43 G1 inlet W Atlantic Ocean
Albergaria-a-Velha 92 B2 Aveiro, N Portugal
Albert 90 C3 Somme, N France
Alberta 37 E4 province SW Canada
Albert Edward Nyanza see Edward, Lake
Albert, Lake 73 B6 var. Albert Nyanza, Lac Mobutu Sese Seko. lake Uganda/Dem. Rep. Congo
Albert Lea 45 F3 Minnesota, N USA
Albert Nyanza see Albert, Lake
Albertville see Kalemie
Albi 91 C6 anc. Albiga. Tarn, S France
Albiga see Albi
Ålborg see Aalborg
Ålborg-Nørresundby see Aalborg
Alborz, Reshteh-ye Kühhä-ye 120 C2 Eng. Elburz Mountains. mountain range N Iran
Albuquerque 48 D2 New Mexico, SW USA
Al Burayqah see Marsá al Burayqah
Alburgum see Aalborg
Albury 149 C7 New South Wales, SE Australia
Alcácer do Sal 92 B4 Setúbal, W Portugal

Alcalá de Henares 93 E3 *Ar.* Alkal'a; *anc.*
Complutum. Madrid, C Spain
Alcamo 97 C7 Sicilia, Italy,
C Mediterranean Sea
Alcañiz 93 F2 Aragón, NE Spain
Alcántara, Embalse de 92 C3 *reservoir*
W Spain
Alcaudete 92 D4 Andalucía, S Spain
Alcázar see Ksar-el-Kebir
Alcazarquivir see Ksar-el-Kebir
Alcoi see Alcoy
Alcoy 93 F4 *Cat.* Alcoi. País Valenciano,
E Spain
Aldabra Group 79 G2 *island group*
SW Seychelles
Aldan 115 F3 *river* NE Russian
Federation
al Dar al Baida see Rabat
Alderney 90 A2 *island* Channel Islands
Aleg 74 C3 Brakna, SW Mauritania
Aleksandriya see Oleksandriya
Aleksandropol' see Gyumri
Aleksandrovka see Oleksandrivka
Aleksandrovsk see Zaporizhzhya
Aleksin 111 B5 Tul'skaya Oblast',
W Russian Federation
Aleksinac 100 E4 Serbia, SE Serbia
Alençon 90 B3 Orne, N France
Alenquer 63 E2 Pará, NE Brazil
Alep/Aleppo see Halab
Alert 37 F1 Ellesmere Island, Nunavut,
N Canada
Alès 91 C6 *prev.* Alais. Gard, S France
Aleşd 108 B3 *Hung.* Élesd. Bihor,
SW Romania
Alessandria 96 B2 *Fr.* Alexandrie.
Piemonte, N Italy
Ålesund 85 A5 Møre og Romsdal,
S Norway
Aleutian Basin 113 G3 *undersea basin*
Bering Sea
Aleutian Islands 36 A3 *island group*
Alaska, USA
Aleutian Range 34 A2 *mountain range*
Alaska, USA
Aleutian Trench 113 H3 *trench*
S Bering Sea
Alexander Archipelago 36 D4 *island
group* Alaska, USA
Alexander City 42 D2 Alabama, S USA
Alexander Island 154 A3 *island*
Antarctica
Alexander Range see Kirghiz Range
Alexandra 151 B7 Otago, South Island,
New Zealand
Alexándreia 104 B4 *var.* Alexándria.
Kentrikí Makedonía, N Greece
Alexandretta see İskenderun
Alexandretta, Gulf of see İskenderun
Körfezi
Alexandria 72 B1 *Ar.* Al Iskandarīyah.
N Egypt
Alexandria 108 C5 Teleorman,
S Romania
Alexandria 42 B3 Louisiana, S USA
Alexandria 45 F2 Minnesota, N USA
Alexándria see Alexándreia
Alexandrie see Alessandria
Alexandroúpoli 104 D3 *var.*
Alexandroúpolis, *Turk.* Dedeağaç,
Dedeagach. Anatolikí Makedonía kai
Thráki, NE Greece
Alexandroúpolis see Alexandroúpoli
Al Fāshir see El Fasher
Alfatar 104 E1 Silistra, NE Bulgaria
Alfeiós 105 B6 *prev.* Alfiós; *anc.*
Alpheius, Alpheus. *river* S Greece
Alfiós see Alfeiós
Alföld see Great Hungarian Plain
Al-Furāt see Euphrates
Alga 114 B4 Kaz. Algha. Aktyubinsk,
NW Kazakhstan
Algarve 92 B4 *cultural region* S Portugal
Algeciras 92 C5 Andalucía, SW Spain
Algemesí 93 F3 País Valenciano, E Spain
Al-Genain see El Geneina
Alger 71 E1 *var.* Algiers, El Djazaïr,
Al Jazair. *country capital* (Algeria)
N Algeria
Algeria 70 C3 *off.* Democratic and
Popular Republic of Algeria. *country*
N Africa

ALGERIA
North Africa

Official name People's Democratic
Republic of Algeria
Formation 1962 / 1962

ALGERIA
(continued)

Capital Algiers
Population 32.9 million / 36 people per
sq mile (14 people per sq km) / 60%
Total area 919,590 sq miles (2,381,740
sq km)
Languages Arabic, Tamazight (Kabyle,
Shawia, Tamashek), French
Religions Sunni Muslim 99%,
Christian and Jewish 1%
Ethnic mix Arab 75%, Berber 24%,
European and Jewish 1%
Government Presidential system
Currency Algerian dinar = 100 centimes
Literacy rate 70%
Calorie consumption 3022 calories

**Algeria, Democratic and Popular
Republic of** see Algeria
Algerian Basin 80 C5 *var.* Balearic Plain.
undersea basin W Mediterranean Sea
Algha see Alga
Al Ghābah 121 E5 *var.* Ghaba.
C Oman
Alghero 97 A5 Sardegna, Italy,
C Mediterranean Sea
Al Ghurdaqah see Hurghada
Algiers see Alger
Al Golea see El Goléa
Algona 45 F3 Iowa, C USA
Al Hajar al Gharbi 121 D5 *mountain
range* N Oman
Al Hamad see Syrian Desert
Al Hasakah 118 D2 *var.* Al Hasijah, El
Haseke, Fr. Hassetché. Al Hasakah,
NE Syria
Al Hillah 120 B3 *var.* Hilla. C Iraq
Al Hisā 119 B7 At Tafilah, W Jordan
Al Hudaydah 121 B6 *Eng.* Hodeida.
W Yemen
Al Hufūf 120 C4 *var.* Hofuf. Ash
Sharqīyah, NE Saudi Arabia
Aliákmon see Aliákmonas
Aliákmonas 104 B4 *prev.* Aliákmon; *anc.*
Haliacmon. *river* N Greece
Aliartos 105 C5 Stereá Ellás, C Greece
Alicante 93 F4 *Cat.* Alacant, *Lat.*
Lucentum. País Valenciano, SE Spain
Alice 49 G5 Texas, SW USA
Alice Springs 148 A4 Northern
Territory, C Australia
Aliki see Alykí
Alima 77 B6 *river* C Congo
Al Imārāt al 'Arabiyah Muttahidah
see United Arab Emirates
Alindao 76 C4 Basse-Kotto, S Central
African Republic
Aliquippa 40 D4 Pennsylvania, NE USA
Al Iskandarīyah see Alexandria
Alistráti 104 C3 Kentrikí Makedonía,
NE Greece
Alivéri 105 C5 *var.* Alivérion. Évvoia,
C Greece
Alivérion see Alivéri
Al Jabal al Akhdar 71 G2 *mountain
range* NE Libya
Al Jafr 119 B7 Ma'ān, S Jordan
Al Jaghbūb 71 H3 NE Libya
Al Jahrā' 120 C4 *var.* Al Jahrah, Jahra.
C Kuwait
Al Jahrah see Al Jahrā'
**Al Jamāhīrīyah al 'Arabīyah al Libīyah
ash Sha'bīyah al Ishtirākīy** see Libya
Al Jawf 120 B4 *off.* Jauf. Al Jawf,
NW Saudi Arabia
Al Jawlān see Golan Heights
Al Jazair see Alger
Al Jazīrah 118 E2 *physical region*
Iraq/Syria
Al Jizah see El Giza
Al Junaynah see El Geneina
Alkal'a see Alcalá de Henares
Al Karak 119 B7 *var.* El Kerak, Karak,
Kerak; *anc.* Kir Moab, Kir of Moab. Al
Karak, W Jordan
Al-Kasr al-Kebir see Ksar-el-Kebir
Al Khalil see Hebron
Al Khārijah see El Khārga
Al Khufrah 71 H4 SE Libya
Al Khums 71 F2 *var.* Homs, Khoms,
Khums. NW Libya
Alkmaar 86 C2 Noord-Holland,
NW Netherlands
Al Kūt 120 C3 *var.* Kūt al 'Amārah, Kut
al Imara. E Iraq

Al-Kuwait see Al Kuwayt
Al Kuwayt 120 C4 *var.* Al-Kuwait,
Eng. Kuwait, Kuwait City;
prev. Qurein. *country capital* (Kuwait)
E Kuwait
Al Lādhiqiyah see Lādhiqiyah
Allahābād 135 E3 Uttar Pradesh, N India
Allanmyo 136 B4 Magwe,
C Myanmar (Burma)
Allegheny Plateau 41 E3 *mountain
range* New York/Pennsylvania, NE USA
Allenstein see Olsztyn
Allentown 41 F4 Pennsylvania, NE USA
Alleppey 132 C3 *var.* Alappuzha; *prev.*
Alleppi. Kerala, SW India
Alleppi see Alleppey
Alliance 44 D3 Nebraska, C USA
Al Līth 121 B5 Makkah, SW Saudi Arabia
Al Lubnān see Lebanon
Alma-Ata see Almaty
Almada 92 B4 Setúbal, W Portugal
Al Madīnah 121 A5 *Eng.* Medina. Al
Madīnah, W Saudi Arabia
Al Mafraq 119 B6 *var.* Mafraq. Al
Mafraq, N Jordan
Al Mahdīyah see Mahdia
Al Mahrah 121 C6 *mountain range*
E Yemen
Al Majma'ah 120 B4 Ar Riyād, C Saudi
Arabia
Al Mālikīyah 118 E1 *var.* Malkiye. Al
Hasakah, N Syria
Almalyk see Olmaliq
Al Mamlakah see Morocco
**Al Mamlaka al Urduniya al
Hashemiyah** see Jordan
Al Manāmah 120 C4
Eng. Manama. *country capital*
(Bahrain) N Bahrain
Al Manāşif 118 E3 *mountain range*
E Syria
Almansa 93 F4 Castilla-La Mancha,
C Spain
Al-Mariyya see Almería
Al Marj 71 G2 *var.* Barka, *It.* Barce.
NE Libya
Almaty 114 C5 *var.* Alma-Ata. Almaty,
SE Kazakhstan
Al Mawşil 120 B2 *Eng.* Mosul. N Iraq
Al Mayādīn 118 D3 *var.* Mayadin, *Fr.*
Meyadine. Dayr az Zawr, E Syria
Al Mazra' see Al Mazra'ah
Al Mazra'ah 119 B6 *var.* Al Mazra',
Mazra'a. Al Karak, W Jordan
Almelo 86 E3 Overijssel, E Netherlands
Almendra, Embalse de 92 C2 *reservoir*
Castilla-León, N Spain
Almendralejo 92 C4 Extremadura,
W Spain
Almere 86 C3 *var.* Almere-stad.
Flevoland, C Netherlands
Almere-stad see Almere
Almería 93 E5 *Ar.* Al-Mariyya; *anc.* Unci,
Lat. Portus Magnus. Andalucía, S Spain
Al Mina' see El Mina
Al Minyā see El Minya
Almirante 53 E4 Bocas del Toro,
NW Panama
Al Mudawwarah 119 B8 Ma'ān,
SW Jordan
Al Mukallā 121 C6 *var.* Mukalla.
SE Yemen
Al Obayyid see El Obeid
Alofi 145 F4 *dependent territory capital*
(Niue) W Niue
Aloha State see Hawai'i
Aloja 106 D3 Limbaži, N Latvia
Alónnisos 105 C5 *island* Vóreioi
Sporádes, Greece, Aegean Sea
Álora 92 D5 Andalucía, S Spain
Alor, Kepulauan 139 E5 *island group*
E Indonesia
Alost see Aalst
Al Oued see El Oued
Alpen see Alps
Alpena 40 D2 Michigan, N USA
Alpes see Alps
Alpha Cordillera 155 B3 *var.* Alpha
Ridge. *seamount range* Arctic Ocean
Alpha Ridge see Alpha Cordillera
Alpheius see Alfeiós
Alphen see Alphen aan den Rijn
Alphen aan den Rijn 86 C3 *var.* Alphen.
Zuid-Holland, C Netherlands
Alpheus see Alfeiós
Alpi see Alps

Alpine 49 E4 Texas, SW USA
Alps 102 C1 *Fr.* Alpes, *Ger.* Alpen, *It.*
Alpi. *mountain range* C Europe
Al Qadārif see Gedaref
Al Qāhirah see Cairo
Al Qāmishlī 118 E1 *var.* Kamishli,
Qamishly. Al Hasakah, NE Syria
Al Qaşrayn see Kasserine
Al Qayrawān see Kairouan
Al-Qsar al-Kbir see Ksar-el-Kebir
Al Qubayyāt see Qoubaïyāt
Al Quds/Al Quds ash Sharīf see
Jerusalem
Alqueva, Barragem do 92 C4 *reservoir*
Portugal/Spain
Al Qunaytirah 119 B5 *var.* El Kuneitra,
El Qunaytra, Kuneitra, Qunaytra. Al
Qunaytirah, SW Syria
Al Quşayr 118 B4 *var.* El Quseir, Quşayr,
Kr. Kousseir. Hims, W Syria
Al Quwayrah 119 B8 *var.* El Quweira.
'Aqabah, SW Jordan
Alsace 90 E4 *Ger.* Elsass; *anc.* Alsatia.
cultural region NE France
Alsace 90 E3 *Ger.* Elsass; *anc.* Alsatia.
region NE France
Alsatia see Alsace
Alsdorf 94 A4 Nordrhein-Westfalen,
W Germany
Alt see Olt
Alta 84 D2 Fin. Alattio. Finnmark,
N Norway
Altai see Altai Mountains
Altai Mountains 126 C2 *var.* Altai, *Chin.*
Altay Shan, *Rus* Altay. *mountain range*
Asia/Europe
Altamaha River 43 E3 *river* Georgia,
SE USA
Altamira 63 E2 Pará, NE Brazil
Altamura 97 E5 *anc.* Lupatia. Puglia,
SE Italy
Altar, Desierto de 50 A1 *var.* Sonoran
Desert. *desert* Mexico/USA
Altar, Desierto de see Sonoran Desert
Altay 126 C2 Xinjiang Uygur Zizhiqu,
NW China
Altay 126 D2 *prev.* Yösönbulag. Govi-
Altay, W Mongolia
Altay Altai Mountains, Asia/Europe
Altay Shan see Altai Mountains
Altenburg see București, Romania
Altin Köprü 120 B3 *var.* Altun Kupri.
N Iraq
Altiplano 61 F4 *physical region* W South
America
Altkanischa see Kanjiža
Alton 40 B5 Illinois, N USA
Alton 40 B4 Missouri, C USA
Altoona 41 E4 Pennsylvania, NE USA
Alto Paraná see Paraná
Altpasua see Stara Pazova
Alt-Schwanenburg see Gulbene
Altsohl see Zvolen
Altun Kupri see Altin Köprü
Altun Shan 126 C3 *var.* Altyn Tagh.
mountain range NW China
Altus 49 F2 Oklahoma, C USA
Altyn Tagh see Altun Shan
Al Ubayyid see El Obeid
Alūksne 106 D3 *Ger.* Marienburg.
Alūksne, NE Latvia
Al 'Ulā 120 A4 Al Madīnah, NW Saudi
Arabia
Al 'Umarī 119 C6 'Ammān,
E Jordan
Alupka 109 F5 Respublika Krym,
S Ukraine
Al Uqsur see Luxor
Al Urdunn see Jordan
Alushta 109 F5 Respublika Krym,
S Ukraine
Al 'Uwaynāt 71 F4 *var.* Al Awaynāt.
SW Libya
Alva 49 F1 Oklahoma, C USA
Alvarado 51 F4 Veracruz-Llave,
E Mexico
Alvin 49 H4 Texas, SW USA
Al Wajh 120 A4 Tabūk, NW Saudi
Arabia
Alwar 134 D3 Rājasthān, N India
Al Wari'ah 120 C4 Ash Sharqīyah,
N Saudi Arabia
Al Yaman see Yemen
Alykí 104 C4 *var.* Aliki. Thásos,
N Greece
Alytus 107 B5 *Pol.* Olita. Alytus,
S Lithuania

Alzette *87 D8 river* S Luxembourg
Amadeus, Lake *147 D5 seasonal lake* Northern Territory, C Australia
Amadi *73 B5* Western Equatoria, SW Sudan
Amadjuak Lake *37 G3 lake* Baffin Island, Nunavut, N Canada
Amakusa-nada *131 A7 gulf* Kyūshū, SW Japan
Amami-guntō *130 A3 island group* SW Japan
Amami-Ō-shima *130 A3 island* S Japan
Amantea *97 D6* Calabria, SW Italy
Amapá *63 E1* Amapá, NE Brazil
Amara *see* Al 'Amārah
Amarapura *136 B3* Mandalay, C Myanmar (Burma)
Amarillo *49 E2* Texas, SW USA
Amay *87 C6* Liège, E Belgium
Amazon *63 E1 Sp.* Amazonas. *river* Brazil/Peru
Amazonas *see* Amazon
Amazon Basin *62 D2 basin* N South America
Amazon, Mouths of the *63 F1 delta* NE Brazil
Ambam *77 B5* Sud, S Cameroon
Ambanja *79 G2* Antsirañana, N Madagascar
Ambarchik *115 G2* Respublika Sakha (Yakutiya), NE Russian Federation
Ambato *60 B1* Tungurahua, C Ecuador
Ambérieu-en-Bugey *91 D5* Ain, E France
Ambianum *see* Amiens
Amboasary *79 F4* Toliara, S Madagascar
Amboina *see* Ambon
Ambon *139 F4 prev.* Amboina, Amboyna. Pulau Ambon, E Indonesia
Ambositra *79 G3* Fianarantsoa, SE Madagascar
Amboyna *see* Ambon
Ambracia *see* Árta
Ambre, Cap d' *see* Bobaomby, Tanjona
Ambrim *see* Ambrym
Ambriz *78 A1* Bengo, NW Angola
Ambrym *144 D4 var.* Ambrim. *island* C Vanuatu
Amchitka Island *36 A2 island* Aleutian Islands, Alaska, USA
Amdo *126 C5* Xizang Zizhiqu, W China
Ameland *86 D1 Fris.* It Amelân. *island* Waddeneilanden, N Netherlands
Amelân, It *see* Ameland
America *see* United States of America
America-Antarctica Ridge *67 C7 undersea ridge* S Atlantic Ocean
America in Miniature *see* Maryland
American Falls Reservoir *46 E4 reservoir* Idaho, NW USA
American Samoa *145 E4 US unincorporated territory* W Polynesia
Amersfoort *86 D3* Utrecht, C Netherlands
Ames *45 F3* Iowa, C USA
Amfilochía *105 A5 var.* Amfilokhía. Dytikí Ellás, C Greece
Amfilokhía *see* Amfilochía
Amga *115 F3 river* NE Russian Federation
Amherst *39 F4* Nova Scotia, SE Canada
Amherst *see* Kyaikkami
Amida *see* Diyarbakır
Amiens *90 C3 anc.* Ambianum, Samarobriva. Somme, N France
Amíndaion/Amíndeo *see* Amýntaio
Amindivi Islands *132 A2 island group* Lakshadweep, India, N Indian Ocean
Amirante Islands *79 G1 var.* Amirantes Group. *island* C Seychelles
Amirantes Group *see* Amirante Islands
Amistad, Presa de la *see* Amistad Reservoir
Amistad Reservoir *49 F4 var.* Presa de la Amistad. *reservoir* Mexico/USA
Amisus *see* Samsun
Ammaia *see* Portalegre
'Ammān *119 B6 var.* Amman; *anc.* Philadelphia, *Bibl.* Rabbah Ammon, Rabbath Ammon. *country capital* (Jordan) 'Ammān, NW Jordan
Ammassalik *82 D4 var.* Angmagssalik. Tunu, S Greenland
Ammóchostos *see* Gazimağusa
Ammóchostos, Kólpos *see* Gazimağusa Körfezi

Amnok-kang *see* Yalu
Amoea *see* Portalegre
Amoentai *see* Amuntai
Åmol *120 D2 var.* Amul. Māzandarān, N Iran
Amorgós *105 D6* Amorgós, Kykládes, Greece, Aegean Sea
Amorgós *105 D6 island* Kykládes, Greece, Aegean Sea
Amos *38 D4* Québec, SE Canada
Amourj *74 D3* Hodh ech Chargui, SE Mauritania
Amoy *see* Xiamen
Ampato, Nevado *61 E4 mountain* S Peru
Amposta *93 F2* Cataluña, NE Spain
Amraoti *see* Amrāvati
Amrāvati *134 D4 prev.* Amraoti. Mahārāshtra, C India
Amritsar *134 D2* Punjab, N India
Amstelveen *86 C3* Noord-Holland, C Netherlands
Amsterdam *86 C3 country capital* (Netherlands) Noord-Holland, C Netherlands
Amsterdam Island *141 C6 island* NE French Southern and Antarctic Territories
Am Timan *76 C3* Salamat, SE Chad
Amu Darya *122 D2 Rus.* Amudar'ya, *Taj.* Dar''yoi Amu, *Turkm.* Amyderya, *Uzb.* Amudaryo; *anc.* Oxus. *river* C Asia
Amu-Dar'ya *see* Amyderya
Amudar'ya/Amudaryo/Amu, Dar''yoi *see* Amu Darya
Amul *see* Åmol
Amund Ringnes Island *37 F2 island* Nunavut, N Canada
Amundsen Basin *see* Fram Basin
Amundsen Gulf *37 E2 gulf* Northwest Territories, N Canada
Amundsen Plain *154 A4 abyssal plain* S Pacific Ocean
Amundsen-Scott *154 B3 US research station* Antarctica
Amundsen Sea *154 A4 sea* S Pacific Ocean
Amuntai *138 D4 prev.* Amoentai. Borneo, C Indonesia
Amur *115 G4 Chin.* Heilong Jiang. *river* China/Russian Federation
Amvrosiyevka *see* Amvrosiyivka
Amvrosiyivka *109 H3 Rus.* Amvrosiyevka. Donets'ka Oblast', SE Ukraine
Amyderya *123 E3 Rus.* Amu-Dar'ya. Lebap Welaýaty, NE Turkmenistan
Amyderya *see* Amu Darya
Amýntaio *104 B4 var.* Amindeo; *prev.* Amíndaion. Dytikí Makedonía, N Greece
Anabar *115 E2 river* NE Russian Federation
An Abhainn Mhór *see* Blackwater
Anaco *59 E2* Anzoátegui, NE Venezuela
Anaconda *44 B2* Montana, NW USA
Anacortes *46 B1* Washington, NW USA
Anadolu Dağları *see* Doğu Karadeniz Dağları
Anadyr' *115 H1* Chukotskiy Avtonomnyy Okrug, NE Russian Federation
Anadyr' *115 G1 river* NE Russian Federation
Anadyr, Gulf of *see* Anadyrskiy Zaliv
Anadyrskiy Zaliv *115 H1 Eng.* Gulf of Anadyr. *gulf* NE Russian Federation
Anáfi *105 D7 anc.* Anaphe. *island* Kykládes, Greece, Aegean Sea
'Ānah *see* 'Annah
Anaheim *46 E2* California, W USA
Anaiza *see* 'Unayzah
Analalava *79 G2* Mahajanga, NW Madagascar
Anamur *116 C5* Mersin, S Turkey
Anantapur *132 C2* Andhra Pradesh, S India
Anaphe *see* Anáfi
Anápolis *63 F3* Goiás, C Brazil
Anār *120 D3* Kermān, C Iran
Anatolia *116 C4 plateau* C Turkey
Anatom *see* Aneityum
Añatuya *64 C3* Santiago del Estero, N Argentina
An Bhearú *see* Barrow
Anchorage *36 C3* Alaska, USA
Ancona *96 C3* Marche, C Italy

Ancud *65 B6 prev.* San Carlos de Ancud. Los Lagos, S Chile
Ancyra *see* Ankara
Åndalsnes *85 A5* Møre og Romsdal, S Norway
Andalucía *92 D4 cultural region* S Spain Europe
Andalusia *42 C3* Alabama, S USA
Andaman Islands *124 B4 island group* India, NE Indian Ocean
Andaman Sea *124 C4 sea* NE Indian Ocean
Andenne *87 C6* Namur, SE Belgium
Anderlues *87 B7* Hainaut, S Belgium
Anderson *40 C4* Indiana, N USA
Andes *64 B3 mountain range* W South America
Andhra Pradesh *135 E5 state* E India
Andhra Pradesh *135 E5 cultural region* E India
Andijon *123 F2 Rus.* Andizhan. Andijon Viloyati, E Uzbekistan
Andikíthira *see* Antikýthira
Andipaxoi *see* Antípaxoi
Andípsara *see* Antípsara
Ándissa *see* Ántissa
Andizhan *see* Andijon
Andkhvoy *122 D3* Fāryāb, N Afghanistan
Andorra *91 A7 off.* Principality of Andorra, *Cat.* Valls d'Andorra, *Fr.* Vallée d'Andorre. *country* SW Europe

ANDORRA
Southwest Europe

Official name Principality of Andorra	
Formation 1278 / 1278	
Capital Andorra la Vella	
Population 70,549 / 392 people per sq mile	
(152 people per sq km) / 63%	
Total area 181 sq miles (468 sq km)	
Languages Spanish, Catalan, French, Portuguese	
Religions Roman Catholic 94%, Other 6%	
Ethnic mix Spanish 46%, Andorran 28%, Other 18%, French 8%	
Government Parliamentary system	
Currency Euro = 100 cents	
Literacy rate 99%	
Calorie consumption Not available	

Andorra *see* Andorra la Vella
Andorra la Vella *91 A8 var.* Andorra, *Fr.* Andorre la Vielle, *Sp.* Andorra la Vieja. *country capital* (Andorra) C Andorra
Andorra la Vieja *see* Andorra la Vella
Andorra, Principality of *see* Andorra
Andorra, Valls d'/Andorra, Vallée d' *see* Andorra
Andorre la Vielle *see* Andorra la Vella
Andover *89 D7* S England, UK
Andøya *84 C2 island* C Norway
Andreanof Islands *36 A3 island group* Aleutian Islands, Alaska, USA
Andrews *49 E3* Texas, SW USA
Andrew Tablemount *140 A4 var.* Gora Andryu. *seamount* W Indian Ocean
Andria *97 D5* Puglia, SE Italy
An Droichead Nua *see* Newbridge
Andropov *see* Rybinsk
Ándros *105 D6* Ándros, Kykládes, Greece, Aegean Sea
Ándros *105 C6 island* Kykládes, Greece, Aegean Sea
Andros Island *54 B2 island* NW Bahamas
Andros Town *54 C1* Andros Island, NW Bahamas
Andryu, Gora *see* Andrew Tablemount
Aneityum *144 D5 var.* Anatom; *prev.* Kéamu. *island* S Vanuatu
Anewetak *see* Enewetak Atoll
Angara *115 E4 river* C Russian Federation
Angarsk *115 E4* Irkutskaya Oblast', S Russian Federation
Ånge *85 C5* Västernorrland, C Sweden
Ángel de la Guarda, Isla *50 B2 island* NW Mexico
Angeles *139 E1 off.* Angeles City. Luzon, N Philippines
Angeles City *see* Angeles
Angel Falls *see* Ángel, Salto
Ángel, Salto *59 E3 Eng.* Angel Falls. *waterfall* E Venezuela

Angerburg *see* Węgorzewo
Ångermanälven *84 C4 river* N Sweden
Angermünde *94 D3* Brandenburg, NE Germany
Angers *90 B4 anc.* Juliomagus. Maine-et-Loire, NW France
Anglesey *89 C5 island* NW Wales, UK
Anglet *91 A6* Pyrénées-Atlantiques, SW France
Angleton *49 H4* Texas, SW USA
Anglia *see* England
Anglo-Egyptian Sudan *see* Sudan
Angmagssalik *see* Ammassalik
Ang Nam Ngum *136 C4 lake* C Laos
Angola *78 B2 off.* Republic of Angola; *prev.* People's Republic of Angola, Portuguese West Africa. *country* SW Africa

ANGOLA
Southern Africa

Official name Republic of Angola	
Formation 1975 / 1975	
Capital Luanda	
Population 15.9 million / 33 people per sq mile (13 people per sq km) / 34%	
Total area 481,351 sq miles (1,246,700 sq km)	
Languages Portuguese*, Umbundu, Kimbundu, Kikongo	
Religions Roman Catholic 50%, Other 30%, Protestant 20%	
Ethnic mix Ovimbundu 37%, Other 25%, Kimbundu 25%, Bakongo 13%	
Government Presidential system	
Currency Readjusted kwanza = 100 lwei	
Literacy rate 67%	
Calorie consumption 2083 calories	

Angola Basin *69 B5 undersea basin* E Atlantic Ocean
Angola, People's Republic of *see* Angola
Angola, Republic of *see* Angola
Angora *see* Ankara
Angostura *see* Ciudad Bolívar
Angostura, Presa de la *51 G5 reservoir* SE Mexico
Angoulême *91 B5 anc.* Iculisma. Charente, W France
Angoumois *91 B5 cultural region* W France
Angra Pequena *see* Lüderitz
Angren *123 F2* Toshkent Viloyati, E Uzbekistan
Anguilla *55 G3 UK dependent territory* E West Indies
Anguilla Cays *54 B2 islets* SW Bahamas
Anhui *128 C5 var.* Anhui Sheng, Anhwei, Wan. *province* E China
AnhuiSheng/Anhwei Wan *see* Anhui
Anicium *see* le Puy
Anina *108 A4 Ger.* Steierdorf, *Hung.* Stájerlakanina; *prev.* Steierdorf-Anina, Steierdorf-Anina, Steyerlak-Anina, Caraş-Severin, SW Romania
Anjou *90 B4 cultural region* NW France
Anjouan *79 F2 var.* Nzwani, Johanna Island. *island* SE Comoros
Ankara *116 C3 prev.* Angora; *anc.* Ancyra. *country capital* (Turkey) Ankara, C Turkey
Ankeny *45 F3* Iowa, C USA
Anklam *94 D2* Mecklenburg-Vorpommern, NE Germany
An Mhuir Cheilteach *see* Celtic Sea
Annaba *71 E1 prev.* Bône. NE Algeria
An Nafūd *120 B4 desert* NW Saudi Arabia
'Annah *120 B3 var.* 'Ānah. NW Iraq
An Najaf *120 B3 var.* Najaf. C Iraq
Annamitique, Chaîne *136 D4 mountain range* C Laos
Annapolis *41 F4 state capital* Maryland, NE USA
Annapūrṇa *135 E3 mountain* C Nepal
An Nāqūrah *see* En Nâqoûra
Ann Arbor *40 C3* Michigan, N USA
An Nāşirīyah *120 C3 var.* Nasiriya. SE Iraq
Annecium *see* Annecy
Annecy *91 D5 anc.* Anneciacum. Haute-Savoie, E France
An Nil al Abyaḍ *see* White Nile
An Nil al Azraq *see* Blue Nile
Anniston *42 D2* Alabama, S USA

Annotto Bay 54 B4 C Jamaica
An Ómaigh see Omagh
Anqing 128 D5 Anhui, E China
Anse La Raye 55 F1 NW Saint Lucia
Anshun 128 B6 Guizhou, S China
Ansongo 75 E3 Gao, E Mali
An Srath Bán see Strabane
Antakya 116 D4 anc. Antioch, Antiochia. Hatay, S Turkey
Antalaha 79 G2 Antsirañana, NE Madagascar
Antalya 116 B4 prev. Adalia; anc. Attaleia, Bibl. Attalia. Antalya, SW Turkey
Antalya, Gulf of see Antalya Körfezi
Antalya Körfezi 116 B4 var. Gulf of Adalia, Eng. Gulf of Antalya. gulf SW Turkey
Antananarivo 79 G3 prev. Tananarive. country capital (Madagascar) Antananarivo, C Madagascar
Antarctica 154 B3 continent
Antarctic Peninsula 154 A2 peninsula Antarctica
Antep see Gaziantep
Antequera 92 D5 anc. Anticaria, Antiquaria. Andalucía, S Spain
Antequera see Oaxaca
Antibes 91 D6 anc. Antipolis. Alpes-Maritimes, SE France
Anticaria see Antequera
Anticosti, Île d' 39 F3 Eng. Anticosti Island. island Québec, E Canada
Anticosti Island see Anticosti, Île d'
Antigua 55 G3 island S Antigua and Barbuda, Leeward Islands
Antigua and Barbuda 55 G3 country E West Indies

ANTIGUA & BARBUDA
West Indies

Official name Antigua and Barbuda
Formation 1981 / 1981
Capital St. John's
Population 68,722 / 404 people per sq mile (156 people per sq km) / 37%
Total area 170 sq miles (442 sq km)
Languages English, English patois
Religions Anglican 45%, Other Protestant 42%, Roman Catholic 10%, Other 2%,
Rastafarian 1%
Ethnic mix Black African 95%, Other 5%
Government Parliamentary system
Currency Eastern Caribbean dollar = 100 cents
Literacy rate 86%
Calorie consumption 2349 calories

Antikýthira 105 B7 var. Andikíthira. island S Greece
Anti-Lebanon 118 B4 var. Jebel esh Sharqi, Ar. Al Jabal ash Sharqī, Fr. Anti-Liban. mountain range Lebanon/Syria
Anti-Liban see Anti-Lebanon
Antioch see Antakya
Antiochia see Antakya
Antipaxoí 105 A5 var. Andipaxi. island Iónioi Nísoi, Greece, C Mediterranean Sea
Antipodes Islands 142 D5 island group S New Zealand
Antipolis see Antibes
Antípsara 105 D5 var. Andípsara. island E Greece
Antiquaria see Antequera
Ántissa 105 D5 var. Ándissa. Lésvos, E Greece
An tIúr see Newry
Antivari see Bar
Antofagasta 64 B2 Antofagasta, N Chile
Antony 90 E2 Hauts-de-Seine, N France
An tSionainn see Shannon
Antsirañana 79 G2 province N Madagascar
Antsohihy 79 G2 Mahajanga, NW Madagascar
An-tung see Dandong
Antwerpen 87 C5 Eng. Antwerp, Fr. Anvers. Antwerpen, N Belgium
Anuradhapura 132 D3 North Central Province, C Sri Lanka
Anvers see Antwerpen
Anyang 128 C4 Henan, C China

A'nyêmaqên Shan 126 D4 mountain range C China
Anykščiai 106 C4 Utena, E Lithuania
Anzio 97 C5 Lazio, C Italy
Aomen see Macao
Aomori 130 D3 Aomori, Honshū, C Japan
Aóos see Vjosës, Lumi i
Aoraki 151 B6 prev. Aorangi, Mount Cook. mountain South Island, New Zealand
Aorangi see Aoraki
Aosta 96 A1 anc. Augusta Praetoria. Valle d'Aosta, NW Italy
Aoukâr 74 D3 var. Aouker. plateau C Mauritania
Aouk, Bahr 76 C4 river Central African Republic/Chad
Aouker see Aoukâr
Aozou 76 C1 Borkou-Ennedi-Tibesti, N Chad
Apalachee Bay 42 D3 bay Florida, SE USA
Apalachicola River 42 D3 river Florida, SE USA
Apamama see Abemama
Apaporis, Río 58 C4 river Brazil/Colombia
Apatity 110 C2 Murmanskaya Oblast', NW Russian Federation
Ape 106 D3 Alūksne, NE Latvia
Apeldoorn 86 D3 Gelderland, E Netherlands
Apennines see Appennino
Ápia 145 F4 country capital (Samoa) Upolu, SE Samoa
Apoera 59 G3 Sipaliwini, NW Suriname
Apostle Islands 40 B1 island group Wisconsin, N USA
Appalachian Mountains 35 D5 mountain range E USA
Appennino 96 E2 Eng. Apennines. mountain range Italy/San Marino
Appingedam 86 E1 Groningen, NE Netherlands
Appleton 40 B2 Wisconsin, N USA
Apulia see Puglia
Apure, Río 58 C2 river W Venezuela
Apurímac, Río 60 D3 river S Peru
Apuseni, Munţii 108 A4 mountain range W Romania
Aqaba/'Aqaba see Al 'Aqabah
Aqaba, Gulf of 120 A4 var. Gulf of Elat, Ar. Khalīj al 'Aqabah; anc. Sinus Aelaniticus. gulf NE Red Sea
'Aqabah, Khalīj al see Aqaba, Gulf of
Āqchah 123 E3 var. Āqcheh. Jowzjān, N Afghanistan
Āqcheh see Āqchah
Aqmola see Astana
Aqtöbe see Aktobe
Aquae Augustae see Dax
Aquae Calidae see Bath
Aquae Flaviae see Chaves
Aquae Grani see Aachen
Aquae Sextiae see Aix-en-Provence
Aquae Solis see Bath
Aquae Tarbelicae see Dax
Aquidauana 63 E4 Mato Grosso do Sul, S Brazil
Aquila/Aquila degli Abruzzi see L'Aquila
Aquisgranum see Aachen
Aquitaine 91 B6 region SW France
Aquitaine 91 B6 cultural region SW France
'Arabah, Wādī al 135 B7 Heb. Ha'Arava. dry watercourse Israel/Jordan
Arabian Basin 124 A4 undersea basin N Arabian Sea
Arabian Desert see Sahara el Sharqîya
Arabian Peninsula 121 B5 peninsula SW Asia
Arabian Sea 124 A3 sea NW Indian Ocean
Arabicus, Sinus see Red Sea
Khalīj al see Gulf, The
'Arabīyah as Su'ūdīyah, Al Mamlakah al see Saudi Arabia
'Arabīyah Jumhūrīyah, Mişr al see Egypt
Arab Republic of Egypt see Egypt
Aracaju 63 G3 state capital Sergipe, E Brazil
Araçuai 63 F3 Minas Gerais, SE Brazil
'Arad 119 B7 Southern, S Israel
Arad 108 A4 Arad, W Romania
Arafura Sea 142 A3 Ind. Laut Arafuru. sea W Pacific Ocean

Arafuru, Laut see Arafura Sea
Aragón 93 E2 autonomous community E Spain
Araguaia, Río 63 E3 var. Araguaya. river C Brazil
Araguari 63 F3 Minas Gerais, SE Brazil
Araguaya see Araguaia, Río
Ara Jovis see Aranjuez
Arāk 120 C3 prev. Sultānābād. Markazī, W Iran
Arakan Yoma 136 A3 mountain range W Myanmar (Burma)
Araks/Arak's see Aras
Aral see Aralsk, Kazakhstan
Aral Sea 122 C1 Kaz. Aral Tengizi, Rus. Aral'skoye More, Uzb. Orol Dengizi. inland sea Kazakhstan/Uzbekistan
Aral'sk 114 B4 Kaz. Aral. Kzylorda, SW Kazakhstan
Aral'skoye More/Aral Tengizi see Aral Sea
Aranda de Duero 92 D2 Castilla-León, N Spain
Aranđelovac 100 D4 prev. Arandjelovac. Serbia, C Serbia
Arandjelovac see Aranđelovac
Aranjuez 92 D3 anc. Ara Jovis. Madrid, C Spain
Araouane 75 E2 Tombouctou, N Mali
'Ar'ar 120 B3 Al Ḩudūd ash Shamālīyah, NW Saudi Arabia
Ararat, Mount see Büyükağrı Dağı
Aras 117 G3 Arm. Arak's, Az. Araz Nehri, Per. Rūd-e Aras, Rus. Araks; prev. Araxes. river SW Asia
Aras, Rūd-e see Aras
Arauca 58 C2 Arauca, NE Colombia
Arauca, Río 58 C2 river Colombia/Venezuela
Arausio see Orange
Araxes see Aras
Araz Nehri see Aras
Arbela see Arbil
Arbil 120 B2 var. Erbil, Irbil, Kurd. Hawlêr; anc. Arbela. N Iraq
Arbroath 88 D3 anc. Aberbrothock. E Scotland, UK
Arbuzinka see Arbyzynka
Arbyzynka 109 E3 Rus. Arbuzinka. Mykolayivs'ka Oblast', S Ukraine
Arcachon 91 B5 Gironde, SW France
Arcae Remorum see Châlons-en-Champagne
Arcata 46 A4 California, W USA
Archangel see Arkhangel'sk
Archangel Bay see Chëshskaya Guba
Archidona 92 D5 Andalucía, S Spain
Arco 96 C2 Trentino-Alto Adige, N Italy
Arctic Mid Oceanic Ridge see Nansen Cordillera
Arctic Ocean 172 B3 ocean
Arda 104 C3 var. Ardhas, Gk. Ardas. river Bulgaria/Greece
Arda see Ardas
Ardabil 120 C2 var. Ardebil. Ardabīl, NW Iran
Ardakān 120 D3 Yazd, C Iran
Ardas 104 D3 var. Ardhas, Bul. Arda. river Bulgaria/Greece
Ardas see Arda
Arḑ aş Şawwān 119 C7 var. Ardh es Suwwān. plain S Jordan
Ardeal see Transylvania
Ardebil see Ardabil
Ardèche 91 C5 cultural region E France
Ardèche 91 C5 department E France
Ardennes 87 C8 physical region Belgium/France
Ardhas see Arda/Ardas
Ardh es Suwwān see Arḑ aş Şawwān
Ardino 104 D3 Kürdzhali, S Bulgaria
Ard Mhacha see Armagh
Ardmore 49 G2 Oklahoma, C USA
Arel see Arlon
Arelas/Arelate see Arles
Arendal 85 A6 Aust-Agder, S Norway
Arensburg see Kuressaare
Arenys de Mar 93 G2 Cataluña, NE Spain
Areópoli 105 B7 prev. Areópolis. Pelopónnisos, S Greece
Areópolis see Areópoli
Arequipa 61 E4 Arequipa, SE Peru
Arezzo 96 C3 anc. Arretium. Toscana, C Italy
Argalasti 105 C5 Thessalía, C Greece
Argenteuil 90 D1 Val-d'Oise, N France

Argentina 65 B5 off. Republic of Argentina. country S South America

ARGENTINA
South America

Official name Republic of Argentina
Formation 1816 / 1816
Capital Buenos Aires
Population 38.7 million / 37 people per sq mile (14 people per sq km) / 90%
Total area 1,068,296 sq miles (2,766,890 sq km)
Languages Spanish*, Italian, Amerindian languages
Religions Roman Catholic 90%, Other 6%, Protestant 2%, Jewish 2%
Ethnic mix Indo-European 83%, Mestizo 14%, Jewish 2%, Amerindian 1%
Government Presidential system
Currency new Argentine peso = 100 centavos
Literacy rate 97%
Calorie consumption 2992 calories

Argentina see Argentine Basin
Argentina, Republic of see Argentina
Argentine Basin 57 C7 var. Argentina Basin. undersea basin SW Atlantic Ocean
Argentine Rise see Falkland Plateau
Argentoratum see Strasbourg
Arghandāb, Daryā-ye 123 E5 river SE Afghanistan
Argirocastro see Gjirokastër
Argo 72 B3 Northern, N Sudan
Argo Fracture Zone 141 C5 tectonic feature C Indian Ocean
Árgos 105 B6 Pelopónnisos, S Greece
Argostóli 105 A5 var. Argostólion. Kefallinía, Iónia Nísiá, Greece, C Mediterranean Sea
Argostólion see Argostóli
Argun 125 E1 Chin. Ergun He, Rus. Argun'. river China/Russian Federation
Argyrokastron see Gjirokastër
Århus 85 B7 var. Aarhus. Århus, C Denmark
Aria see Herāt
Ari Atoll 132 A4 atoll C Maldives
Arica 64 B1 hist. San Marcos de Arica. Tarapacá, N Chile
Aridaía 104 B3 var. Aridea, Aridhaía. Dytikí Makedonía, N Greece
Aridea see Aridaía
Aridhaía see Aridaía
Arīḩā 118 B3 Al Karak, W Jordan
Arīḩā see Jericho
Ariminum see Rimini
Arinsal 91 A7 NW Andorra Europe
Arizona 48 A2 off. State of Arizona, also known as Copper State, Grand Canyon State. state SW USA
Arkansas 42 A1 off. State of Arkansas, also known as The Land of Opportunity. state S USA
Arkansas City 45 F5 Kansas, C USA
Arkansas River 49 G1 river C USA
Arkhangel'sk 110 B2 Eng. Archangel. Arkhangel'skaya Oblast', NW Russian Federation
Arkoi 105 E6 island Dodekánisa, Greece, Aegean Sea
Arles 91 D6 var. Arles-sur-Rhône; anc. Arelas, Arelate. Bouches-du-Rhône, SE France
Arles-sur-Rhône see Arles
Arlington 49 G2 Texas, SW USA
Arlington 41 E4 Virginia, NE USA
Arlon 87 D8 Dut. Aarlen, Ger. Arel, Lat. Orolaunum. Luxembourg, SE Belgium
Armagh 89 B5 Ir. Ard Mhacha. S Northern Ireland, UK
Armagnac 91 B6 cultural region S France
Armenia 58 B3 Quindío, W Colombia
Armenia 117 F3 off. Republic of Armenia. var. Ajastan, Arm. Hayastani Hanrapetut'yun; prev. Armenian Soviet Socialist Republic. country SW Asia

ARMENIA
Southwest Asia

Official name Republic of Armenia
Formation 1991 / 1991
Capital Yerevan

ARMENIA
(continued)

Population 3 million / 261 people per sq mile (101 people per sq km) / 70%
Total area 11,506 sq miles (29,800 sq km)
Languages Armenian*, Azeri, Russian
Religions Armenian Apostolic Church (Orthodox) 94%, Other 6%
Ethnic mix Armenian 93%, Azeri 3%, Other 2%, Russian 2%
Government Presidential system
Currency Dram = 100 luma
Literacy rate 99%
Calorie consumption 2268 calories

Armenian Soviet Socialist Republic *see* Armenia
Armenia, Republic of *see* Armenia
Armidale 149 D6 New South Wales, SE Australia
Armstrong 38 B3 Ontario, S Canada
Armyans'k 109 F4 *Rus.* Armyansk. Respublika Krym, S Ukraine
Arnaia 104 C4 *Cont.* Arnea. Kentrikí Makedonía, N Greece
Arnaud 82 A3 *river* Québec, E Canada
Arnea *see* Arnaía
Arnedo 93 E2 La Rioja, N Spain
Arnhem 86 D4 Gelderland, SE Netherlands
Arnhem Land 148 A2 *physical region* Northern Territory, N Australia
Arno 96 B3 *river* C Italy
Arnold 45 G4 Missouri, C USA
Arnswalde *see* Choszczno
Aroe Islands *see* Aru, Kepulauan
Arorae 145 E3 *atoll* Tungaru, W Kiribati
Arrabona *see* Győr
Ar Rahad *see* Er Rahad
Ar Ramādī 120 B3 *var.* Ramadi, Rumadiya. SW Iraq
Ar Rāmī 120 A4 Ḥimṣ, C Syria
Ar Ramthā 119 B5 *var.* Ramtha. Irbid, N Jordan
Arran, Isle of 88 C4 *island* SW Scotland, UK
Ar Raqqah 118 C2 *var.* Rakka; *anc.* Nicephorium. Ar Raqqah, N Syria
Arras 90 C2 *anc.* Nemetocenna. Pas-de-Calais, N France
Ar Rawḍatayn 120 C4 *var.* Raudhatain. N Kuwait
Arretium *see* Arezzo
Arriaca *see* Guadalajara
Arriaga 51 G5 Chiapas, SE Mexico
Ar Riyāḍ 121 C5 *Eng.* Riyadh. *country capital* (Saudi Arabia) Ar Riyāḍ, C Saudi Arabia
Ar Rub 'al Khālī 121 C6 *Eng.* Empty Quarter, Great Sandy Desert. *desert* SW Asia
Ar Rustāq 121 E5 *var.* Rostak, Rustaq. N Oman
Ar Ruṭbah 120 B3 *var.* Rutba. SW Iraq
Árta 105 A5 *anc.* Ambracia. Ípeiros, W Greece
Artashat 117 F3 S Armenia
Artemisa 54 B2 La Habana, W Cuba
Artesia 48 D3 New Mexico, SW USA
Arthur's Pass 151 C6 *pass* South Island, New Zealand
Artigas 64 D3 *prev.* San Eugenio, San Eugenio del Cuareim. Artigas, N Uruguay
Art'ik 117 F2 W Armenia
Artois 90 C2 *cultural region* N France
Artsiz *see* Artsyz
Artsyz 108 D4 *Rus.* Artsiz. Odes'ka Oblast', SW Ukraine
Artvin 117 F2 Artvin, NE Turkey
Arua 73 B6 NW Uganda
Aruba 58 C1 *var.* Oruba. *Dutch autonomous region* S West Indies
Aru Islands *see* Aru, Kepulauan
Aru, Kepulauan 139 G4 *Eng.* Aru Islands; *prev.* Aroe Islands. *island group* E Indonesia
Arunāchal Pradesh 135 G3 *prev.* North East Frontier Agency, North East Frontier Agency of Assam. *state* NE India
Arunāchal Pradesh 135 G3 *prev.* North East Frontier Agency, North East Frontier Agency of Assam. *cultural region* NE India
Arusha 73 C7 Arusha, N Tanzania

Arviat 37 G4 *prev.* Eskimo Point. Nunavut, C Canada
Arvidsjaur 84 C4 Norrbotten, N Sweden
Arys' 114 B5 *Kaz.* Arys. Yuzhnyy Kazakhstan, S Kazakhstan
Arys *see* Arys'
Asadābād 123 F4 *var.* Asaḍābād; *prev.* Chaghasarāy. Konar, E Afghanistan
Asaḍābād *see* Asadābād
Asad, Buḥayrat al 134 C2 *lake* N Syria
Asahi-dake 130 D2 *mountain* Hokkaidō, N Japan
Asahikawa 130 D2 Hokkaidō, N Japan
Asamankese 75 E5 SE Ghana
Āsānsol 135 F4 West Bengal, NE India
Asben *see* Aïr, Massif de l'
Ascension Fracture Zone 69 A5 *tectonic Feature* C Atlantic Ocean
Ascension Island 85 A5 *dependency of St.Helena* C Atlantic Ocean
Ascoli Piceno 96 C4 *anc.* Asculum Picenum. Marche, C Italy
Asculum Picenum *see* Ascoli Piceno
Aseb 72 D4 *var.* Assab, *Amh.* Āseb. SE Eritrea
Aşgabat 122 C3 *prev.* Ashgabat, Ashkhabad, Poltoratsk. *country capital* (Turkmenistan) Ahal Welaýaty, C Turkmenistan
Ashara *see* Al 'Ashārah
Ashburton 151 C6 Canterbury, South Island, New Zealand
Ashburton River 146 A4 *river* Western Australia
Ashdod 119 A6 *anc.* Azotos, *Lat.* Azotus. Central, W Israel
Asheville 43 E1 North Carolina, SE USA
Ashgabat *see* Aşgabat
Ashkelon *see* Ashqelon
Ashkhabad *see* Aşgabat
Ashland 46 B4 Oregon, NW USA
Ashland 40 B1 Wisconsin, N USA
Ashmore and Cartier Islands 142 A3 *Australian external territory* E Indian Ocean
Ashmyany 107 C5 *Rus.* Oshmyany. Hrodzyenskaya Voblasts', W Belarus
Ashqelon 119 A6 *var.* Ashkelon. Southern, C Israel
Ash Shaddādah 118 D2 *var.* Ash Shaddādah, Jisr ash Shadadi, Shaddādī, Shedadi, Tell Shedadi. Al Ḥasakah, NE Syria
Ash Shaddādah *see* Ash Shaddādah
Ash Shām *see* Dimashq
Ash Sharāh 119 B7 *var.* Esh Sharā. *mountain range* W Jordan
Ash Shāriqah 120 D4 *Eng.* Sharjah. Ash Shāriqah, NE United Arab Emirates
Ash Shawbak 119 B7 Ma'ān, W Jordan
Ash Shiḥr 121 C6 SE Yemen
Asia 25 C2 *continent*
Asinara, Isola 96 A4 *island* W Italy
Asipovichy 107 D6 *Rus.* Osipovichi. Mahilyowskaya Voblasts', C Belarus
Aşkale 117 E3 Erzurum, NE Turkey
Askersund 85 C6 Örebro, C Sweden
Asmara 72 C4 *Amh.* Āsmera. *country capital* (Eritrea) C Eritrea
Āsmera *see* Asmara
Aspadana *see* Eşfahān
Asphaltites, Lacus *see* Dead Sea
Aspinwall *see* Colón
Assab *see* Aseb
As Sabkhah 118 D2 *var.* Sabkha. Ar Raqqah, NE Syria
Aş Şafāwī 119 C6 Al Mafraq, N Jordan
Aş Şaḥrā' al Gharbīyah *see* Sahara el Gharbīya
Aş Şaḥrā' ash Sharqīyah *see* Sahara el Sharqīya
As Salamīyah *see* Salamīyah
'Assal, Lac 68 E4 *lake* C Djibouti
As Salṭ 119 B6 *var.* Salt. Al Balqā', NW Jordan
Assamaka *see* Assamakka
Assamakka 75 F2 *var.* Assamaka. Agadez, NW Niger
As Samāwah 120 B3 *var.* Samawa. S Iraq
Assen 86 E2 Drenthe, NE Netherlands
Assenede 87 B5 Oost-Vlaanderen, NW Belgium
Assiout *see* Asyūṭ
Assiut *see* Asyūṭ
Assling *see* Jesenice
Assouan *see* Aswān
Assu *see* Açu
Assuan *see* Aswān

As Sukhnah 118 C3 *var.* Sukhne, *Fr.* Soukhné. Ḥimṣ, C Syria
As Sulaymānīyah 120 C3 *var.* Sulaimaniya, *Kurd.* Slēmānī. NE Iraq
As Sulayyil 121 B5 Ar Riyāḍ, S Saudi Arabia
Aş Şuwār 118 D2 *var.* Şuwār. Dayr az Zawr, E Syria
As Suwaydā' 119 B5 *var.* El Suweida, Es Suweida, Suweida, *Fr.* Soueida. As Suwaydā', SW Syria
As Suways *see* Suez
Asta Colonia *see* Asti
Astacus *see* İzmit
Astana 114 C4 *prev.* Akmola, Akmolinsk, Tselinograd, Aqmola. *country capital* (Kazakhstan) Akmola, N Kazakhstan
Asta Pompeia *see* Asti
Astarabad *see* Gorgān
Asterābād *see* Gorgān
Asti 96 A2 *anc.* Asta Colonia, Asta Pompeia, Hasta Colonia, Hasta Pompeia. Piemonte, NW Italy
Astigi *see* Écija
Astipálaia *see* Astypálaia
Astorga 92 C1 *anc.* Asturica Augusta. Castilla-León, N Spain
Astrabad *see* Gorgān
Astrakhan' 111 C7 Astrakhanskaya Oblast', SW Russian Federation
Asturias 92 C1 *autonomous community* NW Spain
Asturias *see* Oviedo
Asturica Augusta *see* Astorga
Astypálaia 105 D7 *var.* Astipálaia, *It.* Stampalia. *island* Kykládes, Greece, Aegean Sea
Asunción 64 D2 *country capital* (Paraguay) Central, S Paraguay
Aswān 72 B2 *var.* Assouan, Assuan; *anc.* Syene. SE Egypt
Asyūṭ 72 B2 *var.* Assiout, Assiut, Siut; *anc.* Lycopolis. C Egypt
Atacama Desert *see* Atacama, Desierto de
Atacama, Desierto de 64 B2 *Eng.* Atacama Desert. *desert* N Chile
Atafu Atoll 145 F3 *island* NW Tokelau
Atamyrat 122 D3 *prev.* Kerki. Lebap Welaýaty, E Turkmenistan
Aṭār 74 C2 Adrar, W Mauritania
Atas Bogd 126 D3 *mountain* SW Mongolia
Atascadero 47 B7 California, W USA
Atatürk Barajı 117 E4 *reservoir* S Turkey
Atbara 72 C3 *var.* 'Aṭbārah. River Nile, NE Sudan
'Aṭbārah/'Aṭbarah, Nahr *see* Atbara
Atbasar 114 C4 Akmola, N Kazakhstan
Atchison 45 F4 Kansas, C USA
Aternum *see* Pescara
Ath 87 B6 *var.* Aat. Hainaut, SW Belgium
Athabasca 37 E5 Alberta, SW Canada
Athabasca 37 E5 *var.* Athabaska. *river* Alberta, SW Canada
Athabasca, Lake 37 F4 *lake* Alberta/ Saskatchewan, SW Canada
Athabaska *see* Athabasca
Athenae *see* Athína
Athens 43 E2 Georgia, SE USA
Athens 40 D1 Ohio, N USA
Athens 49 G3 Texas, SW USA
Athens *see* Athína
Atherton 148 D3 Queensland, NE Australia
Athína 105 C6 *Eng.* Athens, *prev.* Athínai; *anc.* Athenae. *country capital* (Greece) Attikí, C Greece
Athínai *see* Athína
Athlone 89 B5 *Ir.* Baile Átha Luain. C Ireland
Ath Thawrah *see* Madinat ath Thawrah
Ati 76 C3 Batha, C Chad
Atikokan 38 B4 Ontario, S Canada
Atka 115 G3 Magadanskaya Oblast', E Russian Federation
Atka 36 A3 Atka Island, Alaska, USA
Atlanta 42 D2 *state capital* Georgia, SE USA
Atlanta 49 H2 Texas, SW USA
Atlantic City 41 F4 New Jersey, NE USA
Atlantic-Indian Basin 67 D7 *undersea basin* SW Indian Ocean
Atlantic-Indian Ridge 69 B8 *undersea ridge* SW Indian Ocean
Atlantic Ocean 66 B4 *ocean*

Atlas Mountains 70 C2 *mountain range* NW Africa
Atlasovo 115 H3 Kamchatskaya Oblast', E Russian Federation
Atlas Saharien 70 D2 *var.* Saharan Atlas. *mountain range* Algeria/Morocco
Atlas, Tell *see* Atlas Tellien
Atlas Tellien 102 C3 *Eng.* Tell Atlas. *mountain range* N Algeria
Atlin 36 D4 British Columbia, W Canada
Aṭ Ṭafīlah 119 B7 *var.* Et Tafila, Tafila. Aṭ Ṭafīlah, W Jordan
Aṭ Ṭā'if 121 B5 Makkah, W Saudi Arabia
At Tall al Abyaḍ 118 C2 *var.* Tall al Abyaḍ, Tell Abyad, *Fr.* Tell Abiad. Ar Raqqah, N Syria
Aṭ Ṭanf 118 D4 Ḥimṣ, S Syria
Attapu *see* Samakhixai
Attawapiskat 38 C3 Ontario, C Canada
Attawapiskat 38 C3 *river* Ontario, S Canada
At Tibnī 118 D2 *var.* Tibnī. Dayr az Zawr, NE Syria
Attopeu *see* Samakhixai
Attu Island 36 A2 *island* Aleutian Islands, Alaska, USA
Atyrau 114 B4 *prev.* Gur'yev. Atyrau, W Kazakhstan
Aubagne 91 D6 *anc.* Albania. Bouches-du-Rhône, SE France
Aubange 87 D8 Luxembourg, SE Belgium
Aubervilliers 90 E1 Seine-St-Denis, Île-de-France, N France Europe
Auburn 46 B2 Washington, NW USA
Auch 91 B6 *Lat.* Augusta Auscorum, Elimberrum. Gers, S France
Auckland 150 D2 Auckland, North Island, New Zealand
Auckland Islands 142 C5 *island group* S New Zealand
Audern *see* Audru
Audincourt 90 E4 Doubs, E France
Audru 106 D2 *Ger.* Audern. Pärnumaa, SW Estonia
Augathella 149 D5 Queensland, E Australia
Augsbourg *see* Augsburg
Augsburg 95 C6 *Fr.* Augsbourg; *anc.* Augusta Vindelicorum. Bayern, S Germany
Augusta 142 A7 Western Australia
Augusta 43 E2 Georgia, SE USA
Augusta 41 G2 *state capital* Maine, NE USA
Augusta *see* London
Augusta Auscorum *see* Auch
Augusta Emerita *see* Mérida
Augusta Praetoria *see* Aosta
Augusta Trajana *see* Stara Zagora
Augusta Treverorum *see* Trier
Augusta Vangionum *see* Worms
Augusta Vindelicorum *see* Augsburg
Augustobona Tricassium *see* Troyes
Augustodunum *see* Bayeux
Augustoritum Lemovicensium *see* Limoges
Augustów 98 E2 *Rus.* Avgustov. Podlaskie, NE Poland
Aulie Atal/Auliye-Ata *see* Taraz
Auob 78 B4 *var.* Oup. *river* Namibia/ South Africa
Aurangābād 134 D5 Mahārāshtra, C India
Auray 90 A3 Morbihan, NW France
Aurelia Aquensis *see* Baden-Baden
Aurelianum *see* Orléans
Aurès, Massif de l' 102 C4 *mountain range* NE Algeria
Aurillac 91 C5 Cantal, C France
Aurium *see* Ourense
Aurora 59 F2 NW Guyana
Aurora 44 C4 Colorado, C USA
Aurora 40 B3 Illinois, N USA
Aurora 45 G5 Missouri, C USA
Aurora *see* Maéwo, Vanuatu
Aus 78 B4 Karas, SW Namibia
Ausa *see* Vic
Aussig *see* Ústí nad Labem
Austin 45 G3 Minnesota, N USA
Austin 49 G3 *state capital* Texas, SW USA
Australes, Archipel des *see* Australes, Îles
Australes et Antarctiques Françaises, Terres *see* French Southern and Antarctic Territories

Australes, Îles 143 F4 var. Archipel des Australes, Îles Tubuai, Tubuai Islands, Eng. Austral Islands. *island group* SW French Polynesia
Austral Fracture Zone 143 H4 *tectonic feature* S Pacific Ocean
Australia 142 A4 *off.* Commonwealth of Australia. *country*

AUSTRALIA
Australasia & Oceania

Official name Commonwealth of Australia
Formation 1901 / 1901
Capital Canberra
Population 20.2 million / 7 people per sq mile (3 people per sq km) / 85%
Total area 2,967,893 sq miles (7,686,850 sq km)
Languages English*, Italian, Cantonese, Greek, Arabic, Vietnamese, Aboriginal languages
Religions Roman Catholic 26%, Anglican 24%, Other 23%, Nonreligious 13%, United Church 8%, Other Protestant 6%
Ethnic mix European 92%, Asian 5%, Aboriginal and other 3%
Government Parliamentary system
Currency Australian dollar = 100 cents
Literacy rate 99%
Calorie consumption 3054 calories

Australia, Commonwealth of *see* Australia
Australian Alps 149 C7 *mountain range* SE Australia
Australian Capital Territory 149 D7 *prev.* Federal Capital Territory. *territory* SE Australia
Australie, Bassin Nord de l' *see* North Australian Basin
Austral Islands *see* Australes, Îles
Austria 95 D7 *off.* Republic of Austria, *Ger.* Österreich. *country* C Europe

AUSTRIA
Central Europe

Official name Republic of Austria
Formation 1918 / 1919
Capital Vienna
Population 8.2 million / 257 people per sq mile (99 people per sq km) / 65%
Total area 32,378 sq miles (83,858 sq km)
Languages German*, Croatian, Slovenian, Hungarian (Magyar)
Religions Roman Catholic 78%, Nonreligious 9%, Other (including Jewish and Muslim) 8%, Protestant 5%
Ethnic mix Austrian 93%, Croat, Slovene, and Hungarian 6%, Other 1%
Government Parliamentary system
Currency Euro = 100 cents
Literacy rate 99%
Calorie consumption 3673 calories

Austria, Republic of *see* Austria
Autesiodorum *see* Auxerre
Autissiodorum *see* Auxerre
Autricum *see* Chartres
Auvergne 91 C5 *region* C France
Auvergne 91 C5 *cultural region* C France
Auxerre 90 C4 *anc.* Autesiodorum, Autissiodorum. Yonne, C France
Avaricum *see* Bourges
Avarua 145 G5 *dependent territory capital* (Cook Islands) Rarotonga, S Cook Islands
Avasfelsőfalu *see* Negreşti-Oaş
Ávdira 104 C3 Anatolikí Makedonía kai Thráki, NE Greece
Aveiro 92 B2 *anc.* Talabriga. Aveiro, W Portugal
Avela *see* Ávila
Avellino 97 D5 *anc.* Abellinum. Campania, S Italy
Avenio *see* Avignon
Avesta 85 C6 Dalarna, C Sweden
Aveyron 91 C6 *river* S France
Avezzano 96 C4 Abruzzo, C Italy
Avgustow *see* Augustów
Aviemore 88 C3 N Scotland, UK
Avignon 91 D6 *anc.* Avenio. Vaucluse, SE France

Ávila 92 D3 *var.* Avila; *anc.* Abela, Abula, Abyla, Avela. Castilla-León, C Spain
Avilés 92 C1 Asturias, NW Spain
Avranches 90 B3 Manche, N France
Avveel *see* Ivalo
Avvil *see* Ivalo
Awaji-shima 131 C6 *island* SW Japan
Awash 73 D5 *var.* Hawash. *river* C Ethiopia
Awbārī 71 F3 SW Libya
Ax *see* Dax
Axel 87 B5 Zeeland, SW Netherlands
Axel Heiberg Island 37 E1 *var.* Axel Heiburg. *island* Nunavut, N Canada
Axel Heiburg *see* Axel Heiberg Island
Axiós *see* Vardar
Ayacucho 60 D4 Ayacucho, S Peru
Ayagoz 130 C5 *var.* Ayaguz, *Kaz.* Ayakoz. *river* E Kazakhstan
Ayakoz *see* Ayagoz
Ayamonte 92 C4 Andalucía, S Spain
Ayaviri 61 E4 Puno, S Peru
Aydarko'li Ko'li 123 E2 *Rus.* Ozero Aydarkul'. *lake* C Uzbekistan
Aydarkul', Ozero *see* Aydarko'li Ko'li
Aydın 116 A4 *var.* Aïdin; *anc.* Tralles Aydin. Aydın, SW Turkey
Ayers Rock *see* Uluru
Ayeyarwady *see* Irrawaddy
Ayiá *see* Agiá
Áyios Evstrátios *see* Ágios Efstrátios
Áyios Nikólaos *see* Ágios Nikólaos
Ayorou 75 E3 Tillabéri, W Niger
'Ayoûn el 'Atroûs 74 D3 *var.* Aïoun el Atrous, Aïoun el Atroûss. Hodh el Gharbi, SE Mauritania
Ayr 88 C4 W Scotland, UK
Ayteke Bi 130 B4 *Kaz.* Zhangaqazaly; *prev.* Novokazalinsk. Kzylorda, SW Kazakhstan
Aytos 104 E2 Burgas, E Bulgaria
Ayutthaya 137 C5 *var.* Phra Nakhon Si Ayutthaya. Phra Nakhon Si Ayutthaya, C Thailand
Ayvalık 116 A3 Balıkesir, W Turkey
Azahar, Costa del 93 F3 *coastal region* E Spain
Azaouâd 75 E3 *desert* C Mali
Äzärbaycan/Äzärbaycan Respublikasi *see* Azerbaijan
A'zāz 118 B2 Ḩalab, N Syria
Azerbaijan 117 G2 *off.* Azerbaijani Republic, *Az.* Äzärbaycan, Äzärbaycan Respublikasi; *prev.* Azerbaijan SSR. *country* SE Asia

AZERBAIJAN
Southwest Asia

Official name Republic of Azerbaijan
Formation 1991 / 1991
Capital Baku
Population 8.4 million / 251 people per sq mile (97 people per sq km) / 57%
Total area 33,436 sq miles (86,600 sq km)
Languages Azeri, Russian
Religions Shi'a Muslim 68%, Sunni Muslim 26%, Russian Orthodox 3%, Armenian Apostolic Church (Orthodox) 2%, Other 1%
Ethnic mix Azeri 90%, Dagestani 3%, Russian 3%, Other 2%, Armenian 2%
Government Presidential system
Currency Manat = 100 gopik
Literacy rate 99%
Calorie consumption 2575 calories

Azerbaijani Republic *see* Azerbaijan
Azerbaijan SSR *see* Azerbaijan
Azimabad *see* Patna
Azizie *see* Telish
Azogues 60 B2 Cañar, S Ecuador
Azores 92 A4 *var.* Açores, Ilhas dos Açores, *Port.* Arquipélago dos Açores. *island group* Portugal, NE Atlantic Ocean
Azores-Biscay Rise 80 A3 *undersea rise* E Atlantic Ocean
Azotos/Azotus *see* Ashdod
Azoum, Bahr 76 C3 *seasonal river* SE Chad
Azov, Sea of 103 H1 *Rus.* Azovskoye More, *Ukr.* Azovs'ke More. *sea* NE Black Sea
Azov's'ke More/Azovskoye More *see* Azov, Sea of

Azraq, Wāḩat al 135 C6 *oasis* N Jordan
Aztec 48 C1 New Mexico, SW USA
Azuaga 92 C4 Extremadura, W Spain
Azuero, Península de 53 F5 *peninsula* S Panama
Azul 65 D5 Buenos Aires, E Argentina
Azur, Côte d' 107 E6 *coastal region* SE France
'Azza *see* Gaza
Az Zaqāziq *see* Zagazig
Az Zarqā' 119 B6 *var.* Zarqa. Az Zarqā', NW Jordan
Az Zāwiyah 71 F2 *var.* Zawia. NW Libya
Az Zilfī 120 B4 Ar Riyāḍ, N Saudi Arabia

B

Ba 100 D3 *prev.* Mba. Viti Levu, W Fiji
Baalbek 118 B4 *var.* Ba'labakk; *anc.* Heliopolis. E Lebanon
Baardheere 73 D6 *var.* Bardere, *It.* Bardera. Gedo, SW Somalia
Baarle-Hertog 87 C5 Antwerpen, N Belgium
Baarn 86 C3 Utrecht, C Netherlands
Babadag 108 D5 Tulcea, SE Romania
Babahoyo 60 B2 *prev.* Bodegas. Los Ríos, C Ecuador
Bābā, Kūh-e 123 E4 *mountain range* C Afghanistan
Babayevo 110 B4 Vologodskaya Oblast', NW Russian Federation
Babeldaob 144 A1 *var.* Babeldaop, Babelthuap. *island* N Palau
Babeldaop *see* Babeldaob
Bab el Mandeb 121 B7 *strait* Gulf of Aden/Red Sea
Babelthuap *see* Babeldaob
Babian Jiang *see* Black River
Babruysk 107 D7 *Rus.* Bobruysk. Mahilyowskaya Voblasts', E Belarus
Babuyan Channel 139 E1 *channel* N Philippines
Babuyan Island 139 E1 *island* N Philippines
Bacabal 63 F2 Maranhão, E Brazil
Bacău 108 C4 Hung. Bákó. Bacău, NE Romania
Bắc Bộ, Vinh *see* Tongking, Gulf of
Bắc Giang 136 D3 Ha Bắc, N Vietnam
Bacheykava 107 D5 *Rus.* Bocheykovo. Vitsyebskaya Voblasts', N Belarus
Back 37 F3 *river* Nunavut, N Canada
Bačka Palanka 100 D3 *prev.* Palanka. Serbia, NW Serbia
Bačka Topola 100 D3 *Hung.* Topolya; *prev. Hung.* Bácstopolya. Vojvodina, N Serbia
Bạc Liêu 137 D6 *var.* Vinh Loi. Minh Hai, S Vietnam
Bacolod 125 E4 *off.* Bacolod City. Negros, C Philippines
Bacolod City *see* Bacolod
Bácstopolya *see* Bačka Topola
Bactra *see* Balkh
Badajoz 92 C4 *anc.* Pax Augusta. Extremadura, W Spain
Baden-Baden 95 B6 *anc.* Aurelia Aquensis. Baden-Württemberg, SW Germany
Badger State *see* Wisconsin
Bad Hersfeld 94 B4 Hessen, C Germany
Bad Homburg *see* Bad Homburg vor der Höhe
Bad Homburg vor der Höhe 95 B5 *var.* Bad Homburg. Hessen, W Germany
Bad Ischl 95 D7 Oberösterreich, N Austria
Bad Krozingen 95 A6 Baden-Württemberg, SW Germany
Badlands 44 D2 *physical region* North Dakota, N USA
Badu Island 148 C1 *island* Queensland, NE Australia
Bad Vöslau 95 E6 Niederösterreich, NE Austria
Baetasos *see* Béjaïa
Baet. Cordillera/Baetic Mountains *see* Béticos, Sistema
Bafatá 74 C4 C Guinea-Bissau
Baffin Bay 32 *bay* Canada/Greenland
Baffin Island 37 G2 *island* Nunavut, NE Canada
Bafing 74 C3 *river* W Africa

Bafoussam 76 A4 Ouest, W Cameroon
Bafra 116 D2 Samsun, N Turkey
Bāft 120 D4 Kermān, S Iran
Bagaces 52 D4 Guanacaste, NW Costa Rica
Bagdad *see* Baghdād
Bagé 63 E5 Rio Grande do Sul, S Brazil
Baghdād 120 B3 *var.* Bagdad, *Eng.* Baghdad. *country capital* (Iraq) C Iraq
Baghdad *see* Baghdād
Baghlān 123 E3 Baghlān, NE Afghanistan
Bago *see* Pegu
Bagoé 74 D4 *river* Côte d'Ivoire (Ivory Coast)/Mali
Bagrationovsk 106 A4 *Ger.* Preussisch Eylau. Kaliningradskaya Oblast', W Russian Federation
Bagrax Hu *see* Bosten Hu
Baguio 139 E1 *off.* Baguio City. Luzon, N Philippines
Baguio City *see* Baguio
Bagzane, Monts 75 F3 *mountain* N Niger
Bahama Islands *see* Bahamas
Bahamas 54 C2 *off.* Commonwealth of the Bahamas. *country* N West Indies

BAHAMAS
West Indies

Official name Commonwealth of the Bahamas
Formation 1973 / 1973
Capital Nassau
Population 323,000 / 84 people per sq mile (32 people per sq km) / 89%
Total area 5382 sq miles (13,940 sq km)
Languages English*, English Creole, French Creole
Religions Baptist 32%, Anglican 20%, Roman Catholic 19%, Other 17%, Methodist 6%, Church of God 6%
Ethnic mix Black African 85%, Other 15%
Government Parliamentary system
Currency Bahamian dollar = 100 cents
Literacy rate 96%
Calorie consumption 2755 calories

Bahamas 35 D6 *var.* Bahama Islands. *island group* N West Indies
Bahamas, Commonwealth of the *see* Bahamas
Baharly 122 C3 *var.* Bäherden, *Rus.* Bakharden; *prev.* Bakherden. Ahal Welaýaty, C Turkmenistan
Bahāwalpur 134 C2 Punjab, E Pakistan
Bäherden *see* Baharly
Bahia 63 F3 *off.* Estado da Bahia. *state* E Brazil
Bahía Blanca 65 C5 Buenos Aires, E Argentina
Bahia, Estado da *see* Bahia
Bahía, Islas de la 52 C1 *Eng.* Bay Islands. *island group* N Honduras
Bahir Dar 72 C4 *var.* Bahr Dar, Bahrdar Giyorgis. Amhara, N Ethiopia
Bahraich 135 E3 Uttar Pradesh, N India
Bahrain 120 C4 *off.* State of Bahrain, Dawlat al Baḩrayn, *Ar.* Al Baḩrayn, *prev.* Bahrein; *anc.* Tylos, Tyros. *country* SW Asia

BAHRAIN
Southwest Asia

Official name Kingdom of Bahrain
Formation 1971 / 1971
Capital Manama
Population 727,000 / 2663 people per sq mile (1030 people per sq km) / 97%
Total area 239 sq miles (620 sq km)
Languages Arabic*
Religions Muslim (mainly Shi'a) 99%, Other 1%
Ethnic mix Bahraini 70%, Iranian, Indian, and Pakistani 24%, Other Arab 4%, European 2%
Government Monarchy
Currency Bahraini dinar = 1000 fils
Literacy rate 88%
Calorie consumption Not available

Bahrain, State of *see* Bahrain
Bahrayn, Dawlat al *see* Bahrain
Bahr Dar/Bahrdar Giyorgis *see* Bahir Dar

Bahrein see Bahrain
Bahr el, Azraq see Blue Nile
Bahr Tabariya, Sea of see Tiberias, Lake
Bahushewsk 107 E6 Rus. Bogushëvsk.
Vitsyebskaya Voblasts', NE Belarus
Baia Mare 108 B3 Ger. Frauenbach,
Hung. Nagybánya; prev. Neustadt.
Maramureş, NW Romania
Baia Sprie 108 B3 Ger. Mittelstadt,
Hung. Felsöbánya. Maramureş,
NW Romania
Baïbokoum 76 B4 Logone-Oriental,
SW Chad
Baidoa see Baydhabo
Baie-Comeau 39 E3 Québec, SE Canada
Baikal, Lake see Baykal, Ozero
Baile Átha Cliath see Dublin
Baile Átha Luain see Athlone
Bailén 92 D4 Andalucía, S Spain
Baile na Mainistreach see Newtownabbey
Bǎilești 108 B5 Dolj, SW Romania
Ba Illi 76 B3 Chari-Baguirmi, SW Chad
Bainbridge 42 D3 Georgia, SE USA
Bā'ir see Bāyir
Baireuth see Bayreuth
Bairiki 144 D2 country capital (Kiribati)
Tarawa, NW Kiribati
Bairnsdale 149 C7 Victoria, SE Australia
Baishan 129 E3 prev. Hunjiang. Jilin,
NE China
Baiyin 128 B4 Gansu, C China
Baja 99 C7 Bács-Kiskun, S Hungary
Baja California 50 B2 state NW Mexico
Baja California 48 A4 Eng. Lower
California. peninsula NW Mexico
Bajo Boquete see Boquete
Bajram Curri 101 D5 Kukës, N Albania
Bakala 76 C4 Ouaka, C Central African
Republic
Bakan see Shimonoseki
Baker 46 C3 Oregon, NW USA
Baker and Howland Islands 145 E2
US unincorporated territory
W Polynesia
Baker Lake 37 F3 Nunavut, N Canada
Bakersfield 47 C7 California, W USA
Bakharden see Baharly
Bakhchisaray see Bakhchysaray
Bakhchysaray 109 F5 Rus. Bakhchisaray.
Respublika Krym, S Ukraine
Bakherden see Baharly
Bakhmach 109 F1 Chernihivs'ka Oblast',
N Ukraine
Bākhtarān see Kermānshāh
Baki 117 H2 Eng. Baku. country capital
(Azerbaijan) E Azerbaijan
Bákó see Bacău
Bakony 99 C7 Eng. Bakony Mountains,
Ger. Bakonywald. mountain range
W Hungary
Bakony Mountains/Bakonywald see
Bakony
Baku see Bakı
Bakwanga see Mbuji-Mayi
Balabac Island 129 C8 island
W Philippines
Balabac, Selat see Balabac Strait
Balabac Strait 138 D2 var. Selat Balabac.
strait Malaysia/Philippines
Ba'labakk see Baalbek
Balaguer 93 F2 Cataluña, NE Spain
Balakovo 111 C6 Saratovskaya Oblast',
W Russian Federation
Bālā Morghāb 122 D4 Laghmān,
NW Afghanistan
Balashov 111 B6 Saratovskaya Oblast',
W Russian Federation
Balasore see Bāleshwar
Balaton 99 C7 var. Lake Balaton, Ger.
Plattensee. lake W Hungary
Balaton, Lake see Balaton
Balbina, Represa 62 D1 reservoir
NW Brazil
Balboa 53 G4 Panamá, C Panama
Balcarce 65 D5 Buenos Aires,
E Argentina
Balclutha 151 B7 Otago, South Island,
New Zealand
Baldy Mountain 44 C1 mountain
Montana, NW USA
Bâle see Basel
Baleares see Balearic Islands
Balearic Plain see Algerian Basin
Baleares, Islas 93 G3 Eng. Balearic
Islands. island group Spain,
W Mediterranean Sea
Baleares Major see Mallorca
Balearic Islands see Baleares, Islas
Balearis Minor see Menorca

Baleine, Rivière à la 39 E2 river Québec,
E Canada
Balen 87 C5 Antwerpen, N Belgium
Bāleshwar 135 F4 prev. Balasore. Orissa,
E India
Bǎlgrad see Alba Iulia
Bali 138 D5 island C Indonesia
Balıkesir 116 A3 Balıkesir, W Turkey
Balīkh, Nahr 118 C2 river N Syria
Balikpapan 138 D4 Borneo,
C Indonesia
Balkanabat 122 B2 Rus. Nebitdag.
Balkan Welaýaty, W Turkmenistan
Balkan Mountains 104 C2 Bul./SCr.
Stara Planina. mountain range
Bulgaria/Serbia
Balkh 123 E3 anc. Bactra. Balkh,
N Afghanistan
Balkhash 114 C5 Kaz. Balqash.
Karaganda, SE Kazakhstan
Balkhash, Lake see Balkhash, Ozero
Balkhash, Ozero 114 C5 Eng. Lake
Balkhash, Kaz. Balqash. lake
SE Kazakhstan
Balladonia 147 C6 Western Australia
Ballarat 149 C7 Victoria, SE Australia
Balleny Islands 154 B5 island group
Antarctica
Ballinger 49 F3 Texas, SW USA
Balochistān see Baluchistān
Balqash see Balkhash, Ozero
Balqash see Balkhash
Balș 108 B5 Olt, S Romania
Balsas 63 F2 Maranhão, E Brazil
Balsas, Río 51 E5 var. Río Mexcala. river
S Mexico
Bal'shavik 107 D7 Rus. Bol'shevik.
Homyel'skaya Voblasts', SE Belarus
Balta 108 D3 Odes'ka Oblast',
SW Ukraine
Bǎlți 108 D3 Rus. Bel'tsy. N Moldova
Baltic Port see Paldiski
Baltic Sea 85 C7 Ger. Ostee, Rus.
Baltiskoye More. sea N Europe
Baltimore 41 F4 Maryland, NE USA
Baltischport/Baltiski see Paldiski
Baltiskoye More see Baltic Sea
Baltkrievija see Belarus
Baluchistān 134 B3 var. Balochistān,
Beluchistan. province SW Pakistan
Balvi 106 D4 Balvi, NE Latvia
Balykchy 123 G2 Kir. Ysyk-Köl; prev.
Issyk-Kul', Rybach'ye. Issyk-Kul'skaya
Oblast', NE Kyrgyzstan
Balzers 94 E2 S Liechtenstein
Bam 120 E4 Kermān, SE Iran
Bamako 74 D4 country capital (Mali)
Capital District, SW Mali
Bambari 76 C4 Ouaka, C Central African
Republic
Bamberg 95 C5 Bayern, SE Germany
Bamenda 76 A4 Nord-Ouest,
W Cameroon
Banaba 144 D2 var. Ocean Island. island
Tungaru, W Kiribati
Banaras see Vārānasi
Bandaaceh 138 A3 var. Banda Atjeh;
prev. Koetaradja, Kutaradja, Kutaraja.
Sumatera, W Indonesia
Banda Atjeh see Bandaaceh
Banda, Laut see Banda Sea
Bandama 74 D5 var. Bandama Fleuve.
river S Côte d'Ivoire (Ivory Coast)
Bandama Fleuve see Bandama
Bandar 'Abbās see Bandar-e 'Abbās
Bandarbeyla 73 E5 var. Bender Beila,
Bender Beyla. Bari, NE Somalia
Bandar-e 'Abbās 120 D4 var. Bandar
'Abbās; prev. Gombroon. Hormozgān,
S Iran
Bandar-e Būshehr 120 C4 var. Büshehr,
Eng. Bushire. Büshehr, S Iran
Bandar-e Kangān 120 D4 Büshehr, S Iran
Bandar-e Khamīr 120 D4 Hormozgān,
S Iran
Bandar-e Langeh 120 D4 var. Bandar-e
Lengeh, Lingeh. Hormozgān, S Iran
Bandar-e Lengeh see Bandar-e Langeh
Bandar Kassim see Boosaaso
Bandar Lampung 138 C4 var.
Bandarlampung, Tanjungkarang-
Telukbetung; prev. Tandjoengkarang,
Tanjungkarang, Teloekbetoeng,
Telukbetung. Sumatera, W Indonesia
Bandarlampung see Bandar Lampung
Bandar Maharani see Muar
Bandar Masulipatnam see
Machilipatnam

Bandar Penggaram see Batu Pahat
Bandar Seri Begawan 138 D3 prev.
Brunei Town. country capital (Brunei)
N Brunei
Banda Sea 139 F5 var. Laut Banda. sea
E Indonesia
Bandiagara 75 E3 Mopti, C Mali
Bandırma 116 A3 var. Penderma.
Balıkesir, NW Turkey
Bandjarmasin see Banjarmasin
Bandoeng see Bandung
Bandundu 77 C6 prev. Banningville.
Bandundu, W Dem. Rep. Congo
Bandung 138 C5 prev. Bandoeng. Jawa,
C Indonesia
Bangalore 132 C2 state capital
Karnātaka, S India
Bangassou 76 D4 Mbomou, SE Central
African Republic
Banggai, Kepulauan 139 E4 island
group C Indonesia
Banghāzī 71 G2 Eng. Bengazi, Benghazi,
It. Bengasi. NE Libya
Bangka, Pulau 138 C4 island
W Indonesia
Bangkok see Krung Thep
Bangkok, Bight of see Krung Thep, Ao
Bangladesh 135 G3
off. People's Republic of Bangladesh;
prev. East Pakistan. country S Asia

Bangladesh, People's Republic of see
Bangladesh
Bangor 89 C6 NW Wales, UK
Bangor 89 B5 Ir. Beannchar.
E Northern Ireland, UK
Bangor 41 G2 Maine, NE USA
Bang Pla Soi see Chon Buri
Bangui 77 B5 country capital (Central
African Republic) Ombella-Mpoko,
SW Central African Republic
Bangweulu, Lake 73 B8 var. Lake
Bengwelu. lake N Zambia
Ban Hat Yai see Hat Yai
Ban Hin Heup 130 C4 Viangchan,
C Laos
Ban Houayxay/Ban Houei Sai see
Houayxay
Ban Hua Hin 137 C6
var. Hua Hin. Prachuap Khiri Khan,
SW Thailand
Bani 74 D3 river S Mali
Banias see Bāniyās
Banī Suwayf see Beni Suef
Bāniyās 118 B3 var. Banias, Baniyas,
Paneas. Ţarţūs, W Syria
Banjak, Kepulauan see Banyak,
Kepulauan
Banja Luka 100 B3 Republika Srpska,
NW Bosnia and Herzegovina
Banjarmasin 138 D4 prev.
Bandjarmasin. Borneo, C Indonesia
Banjul 74 B3 prev. Bathurst. country
capital (Gambia) W Gambia
Banks, Îles see Banks Islands
Banks Island 37 E2 island Banks Island,
Northwest Territories, NW Canada
Banks Islands 144 D4 Fr. Îles Banks.
island group N Vanuatu
Banks Lake 46 B1 reservoir Washington,
NW USA
Banks Peninsula 151 C6 peninsula
South Island, New Zealand
Banks Strait 149 C8 strait SW Tasman
Sea
Bānkura 135 F4 West Bengal, NE India

Ban Mak Khaeng see Udon Thani
Banmo see Bhamo
Banningville see Bandundu
Bañolas see Banyoles
Ban Pak Phanang see Pak Phanang
Ban Sichon see Sichon
Banská Bystrica 99 C6 Ger.
Neusohl, Hung. Besztercebánya.
Banskobystricky Kraj, C Slovakia
Bantry Bay 89 A7 Ir. Bá Bheanntraí. bay
SW Ireland
Banya 104 E2 Burgas, E Bulgaria
Banyak, Kepulauan 138 A3 prev.
Kepulauan Banjak. island group
NW Indonesia
Banyo 76 B4 Adamaoua, NW Cameroon
Banyoles 93 G2 var. Bañolas. Cataluña,
NE Spain
Banzare Seamounts 141 C7 seamount
range S Indian Ocean
Banzart see Bizerte
Baoji 128 B4 var. Pao-chi, Paoki.
Shaanxi, C China
Baoro 76 B4 Nana-Mambéré, W Central
African Republic
Baoshan 128 A6 var. Pao-shan. Yunnan,
SW China
Baotou 127 F3 var. Pao-t'ou, Paotow.
Nei Mongol Zizhiqu, N China
Ba'qūbah 120 B3 var. Qubba. C Iraq
Baquerizo Moreno see Puerto Baquerizo
Moreno
Bar 101 C5 It. Antivari. S Montenegro
Baraawe 73 D6 It. Brava. Shabeellaha
Hoose, S Somalia
Bārāmati 134 C5 Mahārāshtra, W India
Baranavichy 107 B6 Pol. Baranowicze,
Rus. Baranovichi. Brestskaya Voblasts',
SW Belarus
Baranavichy/Baranowicze see
Baranavichy
Barbados 55 G1 country SE West Indies

Barbastro 93 F2 Aragón, NE Spain
Barbate de Franco 92 C5 Andalucía,
S Spain
Barbuda 55 G3 island N Antigua and
Barbuda
Barcaldine 148 C4 Queensland,
E Australia
Barcău see Berettyó
Barce see Al Marj
Barcelona 93 G2 anc. Barcino,
Barcinona. Cataluña, E Spain
Barcelona 59 E2 Anzoátegui,
NE Venezuela
Barcino/Barcinona see Barcelona
Barcoo see Cooper Creek
Barcs 99 C7 Somogy, SW Hungary
Bardaï 76 C1 Borkou-Ennedi-Tibesti,
N Chad
Bardejov 99 D5 Ger. Bartfeld, Hung.
Bártfa. Presovský Kraj, E Slovakia
Bardera/Bardere see Baardheere
Barduli see Barletta
Bareilly 135 E3 var. Bareli. Uttar
Pradesh, N India
Bareli see Bareilly
Barendrecht 86 C4 Zuid-Holland,
SW Netherlands
Barentin 90 C3 Seine-Maritime,
N France
Barentsburg 83 G2 Spitsbergen,
W Svalbard
Barentsevo More/Barents Havet see
Barents Sea

Barentsøya 83 G2 *island* E Svalbard
Barents Sea 110 C2 *Nor.* Barents Havet, *Rus.* Barentsevo More. *sea* Arctic Ocean
Barents Trough 81 E1 *trough* SW Barents Sea
Bar Harbor 41 H2 Mount Desert Island, Maine, NE USA
Bari 97 E5 *var.* Bari delle Puglie; *anc.* Barium. Puglia, SE Italy
Bäridah *see* Al Bāridah
Bari delle Puglie *see* Bari
Barikot *see* Barīkowṭ
Barīkowṭ 123 F4 *var.* Barīkot. Konar, NE Afghanistan
Barillas 52 A2 *var.* Santa Cruz Barillas. Huehuetenango, NW Guatemala
Barinas 58 C2 Barinas, W Venezuela
Barisal 135 G4 Barisal, S Bangladesh
Barisan, Pegunungan 138 B4 *mountain range* Sumatera, W Indonesia
Barito, Sungai 138 D4 *river* Borneo, C Indonesia
Barium *see* Bari
Barka *see* Al Marj
Barkly Tableland 148 B3 *plateau* Northern Territory/Queensland, N Australia
Bârlad 108 D4 *prev.* Bîrlad. Vaslui, E Romania
Barlavento, Ilhas de 74 A2 *var.* Windward Islands. *island group* N Cape Verde
Bar-le-Duc 90 D3 *var.* Bar-sur-Ornain. Meuse, NE France
Barlee, Lake 147 B6 *lake* Western Australia
Barlee Range 146 A4 *mountain range* Western Australia
Barletta 97 D5 *anc.* Barduli. Puglia, SE Italy
Barlinek 98 B3 *Ger.* Berlinchen. Zachodnio-pomorskie, NW Poland
Barmen-Elberfeld *see* Wuppertal
Barmouth 89 C6 NW Wales, UK
Barnaul 114 D4 Altayskiy Kray, C Russian Federation
Barnet 89 A7 UK
Barnstaple 89 C7 SW England, UK
Baroda *see* Vadodara
Baroghil Pass 123 F3 *var.* Kowtal-e Barowghīl. *pass* Afghanistan/Pakistan
Baron'ki 107 E7 *Rus.* Boron'ki. Mahilyowskaya Voblasts', E Belarus
Barowghīl, Kowtal-e *see* Baroghil Pass
Barquisimeto 58 C2 Lara, NW Venezuela
Barra 88 B3 *island* NW Scotland, UK
Barra de Río Grande 53 E3 Región Autónoma Atlántico Sur, E Nicaragua
Barranca 60 C3 Lima, W Peru
Barrancabermeja 58 B2 Santander, N Colombia
Barranquilla 58 B1 Atlántico, N Colombia
Barreiro 92 B4 Setúbal, W Portugal
Barrier Range 149 C6 *hill range* New South Wales, SE Australia
Barrow 36 D2 Alaska, USA
Barrow 89 B6 *Ir.* An Bhearú. *river* SE Ireland
Barrow-in-Furness 89 C5 NW England, UK
Barrow Island 146 A4 *island* Western Australia
Barstow 47 C7 California, W USA
Bar-sur-Ornain *see* Bar-le-Duc
Bartang 123 F3 *river* SE Tajikistan
Bartenstein *see* Bartoszyce
Bártfa/Bartfeld *see* Bardejov
Bartica 59 F3 N Guyana
Bartın 116 C2 Bartın, NW Turkey
Bartlesville 49 G1 Oklahoma, C USA
Bartoszyce 98 D2 *Ger.* Bartenstein. Warmińsko-mazurskie, NE Poland
Baruun-Urt 127 F2 Sühbaatar, E Mongolia
Barú, Volcán 53 E5 *var.* Volcán de Chiriquí. *volcano* W Panama
Barwon River 149 D5 *river* New South Wales, SE Australia
Barysaw 107 D6 *Rus.* Borisov. Minskaya Voblasts', NE Belarus
Basarabeasca 108 D4 *Rus.* Bessarabka. SE Moldova
Basel 95 A7 *Eng.* Basle, *Fr.* Bâle. Basel-Stadt, NW Switzerland
Basilan 139 E3 *island* Mindanao, S Philippines Asia Celebes Sea/Sulu Sea Pacific Ocean

Basle *see* Basel
Basra *see* Al Başrah
Bassano del Grappa 96 C2 Veneto, NE Italy
Bassein 136 A4 *var.* Pathein. Irrawaddy, SW Myanmar (Burma)
Basseterre 55 G4 *country capital* (Saint Kitts and Nevis) Saint Kitts, Saint Kitts and Nevis
Basse-Terre 55 G3 *dependent territory capital* (Guadeloupe) Basse Terre, SW Guadeloupe
Basse Terre 55 G4 *island* W Guadeloupe
Bassikounou 74 D3 Hodh ech Chargui, SE Mauritania
Bass, Îlots de *see* Marotiri
Bass Strait 149 C7 *strait* SE Australia
Bassum 94 B3 Niedersachsen, NW Germany
Bastia 91 E7 Corse, France, C Mediterranean Sea
Bastogne 87 D7 Luxembourg, SE Belgium
Bastrop 42 B2 Louisiana, S USA
Bastyn' 107 B7 *Rus.* Bostyn'. Brestskaya Voblasts', SW Belarus
Basuo *see* Dongfang
Basutoland *see* Lesotho
Bata 77 A5 NW Equatorial Guinea
Batae Coritanorum *see* Leicester
Batajnica 100 D3 Vojvodina, N Serbia
Batangas 139 E2 *off.* Batangas City. Luzon, N Philippines
Batangas City *see* Batangas
Batavia *see* Jakarta
Bătdâmbâng 137 C5 *prev.* Battambang. Bătdâmbâng, NW Cambodia
Batéké, Plateaux 77 B6 *plateau* S Congo
Bath 89 D7 *hist.* Akermanceaster; *anc.* Aquae Calidae, Aquae Solis. SW England, UK
Bathinda 134 D2 Punjab, NW India
Bathsheba 55 G1 E Barbados
Bathurst 149 D6 New South Wales, SE Australia
Bathurst 39 F4 New Brunswick, SE Canada
Bathurst *see* Banjul
Bathurst Island 146 D2 *island* Northern Territory, N Australia
Bathurst Island 37 F2 *island* Parry Islands, Nunavut, N Canada
Bāṭin, Wādī al 136 C4 *dry watercourse* SW Asia
Batman 117 E4 *var.* Iluh. Batman, SE Turkey
Batna 71 E2 NE Algeria
Baton Rouge 42 B3 *state capital* Louisiana, S USA
Batroûn 118 A4 *var.* Al Batrūn. N Lebanon
Battambang *see* Bătdâmbâng
Batticaloa 132 D3 Eastern Province, E Sri Lanka
Battipaglia 97 D5 Campania, S Italy
Battle Born State *see* Nevada
Bat'umi 117 F2 W Georgia
Batu Pahat 138 B3 *prev.* Bandar Penggaram. Johor, Peninsular Malaysia
Bauchi 75 G4 Bauchi, NE Nigeria
Bauer Basin 153 F3 *undersea basin* E Pacific Ocean
Bauska 106 C3 *Ger.* Bauske. Bauska, S Latvia
Bauske *see* Bauska
Bautzen 94 D4 *Lus.* Budyšin. Sachsen, E Germany
Bauzanum *see* Bolzano
Bavaria *see* Bayern
Bavarian Alps 95 C7 *Ger.* Bayrische Alpen. *mountain range* Austria/Germany
Bavière *see* Bayern
Bavispe, Río 50 C2 *river* NW Mexico
Bawīti 72 B2 N Egypt
Bawku 75 E4 N Ghana
Bayamo 54 C3 Granma, E Cuba
Bayan Har Shan 126 D4 *var.* Bayan Khar. *mountain range* C China
Bayanhongor 126 D2 Bayanhongor, C Mongolia
Bayan Khar *see* Bayan Har Shan
Bayano, Lago 53 G4 *lake* E Panama
Bay City 40 C3 Michigan, N USA
Bay City 49 G4 Texas, SW USA
Baydhabo 73 D6 *var.* Baydhowa, Isha Baydhabo, *It.* Baidoa. Bay, SW Somalia
Baydhowa *see* Baydhabo

Bayern 95 C6 *Eng.* Bavaria, *Fr.* Bavière. *state* SE Germany
Bayeux 90 B3 *anc.* Augustodurum. Calvados, N France
Bâyir 119 C7 *var.* Bā'ir. Ma'ān, S Jordan
Bay Islands *see* Bahía, Islas de la
Baykal, Ozero 115 E4 *Eng.* Lake Baikal. *lake* S Russian Federation
Baymak 111 D6 Respublika Bashkortostan, W Russian Federation
Bayonne 91 A6 *anc.* Lapurdum. Pyrénées-Atlantiques, SW France
Bayou State *see* Mississippi
Bayram-Ali *see* Baýramaly
Baýramaly 122 D3 *var.* Bayramaly; *prev.* Bayram-Ali. Mary Welaýaty, S Turkmenistan
Bayreuth 95 C5 *var.* Baireuth. Bayern, SE Germany
Bayrische Alpen *see* Bavarian Alps
Bayrūt *see* Beyrouth
Bay State *see* Massachusetts
Baysun *see* Boysun
Bayt Laḥm *see* Bethlehem
Baytown 49 H4 Texas, SW USA
Baza 93 E4 Andalucía, S Spain
Bazargic *see* Dobrich
Bazin *see* Pezinok
Beagle Channel 65 C8 *channel* Argentina/Chile
Béal Feirste *see* Belfast
Beannchar *see* Bangor, Northern Ireland, UK
Bear Island *see* Bjørnøya
Bear Lake 46 E4 *lake* Idaho/Utah, NW USA
Beas de Segura 93 E4 Andalucía, S Spain
Beata, Isla 55 E3 *island* SW Dominican Republic
Beatrice 45 F4 Nebraska, C USA
Beaufort Sea 36 D2 *sea* Arctic Ocean
Beaufort-Wes *see* Beaufort West
Beaufort West 78 C5 *Afr.* Beaufort-Wes. Western Cape, SW South Africa
Beaumont 49 H3 Texas, SW USA
Beaune 90 D4 Côte d'Or, C France
Beauvais 90 C3 *anc.* Bellovacum, Caesaromagus. Oise, N France
Beaver Island 40 C2 *island* Michigan, N USA
Beaver Lake 49 H1 *reservoir* Arkansas, C USA
Beaver River 49 F1 *river* Oklahoma, C USA
Beaver State *see* Oregon
Beāwar 134 C3 Rājasthān, N India
Bečej 100 D3 *Ger.* Altbetsche, *Hung.* Óbecse, Rácz-Becse; *prev.* Magyar-Becse, Stari Bečej. Vojvodina, N Serbia
Béchar 70 D2 *prev.* Colomb-Béchar. W Algeria
Beckley 40 D5 West Virginia, NE USA
Bécs *see* Wien
Bedford 89 D6 E England, UK
Bedum 86 E1 Groningen, NE Netherlands
Beehive State *see* Utah
Be'ér Menuḥa 119 B7 *var* Be'er Menukha. Southern, S Israel
Be'erMenukha *see* Be'ér Menuḥa
Beernem 87 A5 West-Vlaanderen, NW Belgium
Beersheba *see* Be'ér Sheva'
Be'ér Sheva' 119 A7 *var.* Beersheba, *Ar.* Bir es Saba. Southern, S Israel
Beesel 87 D5 Limburg, SE Netherlands
Beeville 49 G4 Texas, SW USA
Bega 149 D7 New South Wales, SE Australia
Begoml' *see* Byahoml'
Begovat *see* Bekobod
Behagle *see* Laï
Behar *see* Bihār
Beibu Wan *see* Tongking, Gulf of
Beida *see* Al Bayḍā'
Beihai 128 B6 Guangxi Zhuangzu Zizhiqu, S China
Beijing 128 C3 *var.* Pei-ching, *Eng.* Peking; *prev.* Pei-p'ing. *country capital* (China) Beijing Shi, E China
Beilen 86 E2 Drenthe, NE Netherlands
Beira 79 E3 Sofala, C Mozambique
Beirut *see* Beyrouth
Beiuş 108 B3 *Hung.* Belényes. Bihor, NW Romania
Beja 92 B4 *anc.* Pax Julia. Beja, SE Portugal
Béjar 92 C3 Castilla-León, N Spain

Bejraburi *see* Phetchaburi
Bekabad *see* Bekobod
Békás *see* Bicaz
Bek-Budi *see* Qarshi
Békéscsaba 99 D7 *Rom.* Bichiş-Ciaba. Békés, SE Hungary
Bekobod 123 E2 *Rus.* Bekabad; *prev.* Begovat. Toshkent Viloyati, E Uzbekistan
Bela Crkva 100 E3 *Ger.* Weisskirchen, *Hung.* Fehértemplom. Vojvodina, W Serbia
Belarus 107 B6 *off.* Republic of Belarus, *var.* Belorussia, *Latv.* Baltkrievija; *prev.* Belorussian SSR, *Rus.* Belorusskaya SSR. *country* E Europe

Belarus, Republic of *see* Belarus
Belau *see* Palau
Belaya Tserkov' *see* Bila Tserkva
Bełchatów 98 C4 *var.* Belchatow. Łódzkis, C Poland
Belchatow *see* Bełchatów
Belcher, Îles *see* Belcher Islands
Belcher Islands 38 C2 *Fr.* Îles Belcher. *island group* Nunavut, SE Canada
Beledweyne 73 D5 *var.* Belet Huen, *It.* Belet Uen. Hiiraan, C Somalia
Belém 63 F1 *var.* Pará. Pará. *state capital* Pará, N Brazil
Belén 52 D4 Rivas, SW Nicaragua
Belen 48 D2 New Mexico, SW USA
Belényes *see* Beiuş
Belet Huen/Belet Uen *see* Beledweyne
Belfast 89 B5 *Ir.* Béal Feirste. *national capital* E Northern Ireland, UK
Belfield 44 D2 North Dakota, N USA
Belfort 90 E4 Territoire-de-Belfort, E France
Belgard *see* Białogard
Belgaum 132 B1 Karnātaka, W India
Belgian Congo *see* Congo (Democratic Republic of)
België/Belgique *see* Belgium
Belgium 87 B6 *off.* Kingdom of Belgium, *Dut.* België, *Fr.* Belgique. *country* NW Europe

Belgium, Kingdom of *see* Belgium
Belgorod 111 A6 Belgorodskaya Oblast', W Russian Federation
Belgrano II 154 A2 Argentinian research station Antarctica
Belice *see* Belize/Belize City
Beligrad *see* Berat

Beli Manastir *100 C3 Hung.*
Pélmonostor; *prev.* Monostor. Osijek-
Baranja, NE Croatia
Bélinga *77 B5* Ogooué-Ivindo, NE Gabon
Belitung, Pulau *138 C4 island*
W Indonesia
Belize *52 B1 Sp.* Belice; *prev.* British
Honduras, Colony of Belize. *country*
Central America

BELIZE
Central America

Official name Belize
Formation 1981 / 1981
Capital Belmopan
Population 270,000 / 31 people per
sq mile
(12 people per sq km) / 54%
Total area 8867 sq miles (22,966 sq km)
Languages English*, English Creole,
Spanish, Mayan, Garifuna (Carib)
Religions Roman Catholic 62%,
Other 13%, Anglican 12%, Methodist 6%,
Mennonite 4%, Seventh-day
Adventist 3%
Ethnic mix Mestizo 44%, Creole 30%,
Maya 11%, Garifuna 7%, Other 4%, Asian
Indian 4%
Government Parliamentary system
Currency Belizean dollar = 100 cents
Literacy rate 77%
Calorie consumption 2869 calories

Belize *52 B1 river* Belize/Guatemala
Belize *see* Belize City
Belize City *52 C1 var.* Belize, *Sp.* Belice.
Belize, NE Belize
Belize, Colony of *see* Belize
Beljak *see* Villach
Belkofski *36 B3* Alaska, USA
Belle Île *90 A4 island* NW France
Belle Isle, Strait of *39 G3 strait*
Newfoundland and Labrador, E Canada
Bellenz *see* Bellinzona
Belleville *40 B4* Illinois, N USA
Bellevue *45 F4* Iowa, C USA
Bellevue *46 B2* Washington, NW USA
Bellingham *46 B1* Washington, NW USA
Belling Hausen Mulde *see* Southeast
Pacific Basin
Bellingshausen Abyssal Plain *see*
Bellingshausen Plain
Bellingshausen Plain *153 F5 var.*
Bellingshausen Abyssal Plain. *abyssal
plain* SE Pacific Ocean
Bellingshausen Sea *154 A3 sea*
Antarctica
Bellinzona *95 B8 Ger.* Bellenz. Ticino,
S Switzerland
Bello *58 B2* Antioquia, W Colombia
Bello Horizonte *see* Belo Horizonte
Bellovacum *see* Beauvais
Bellville *78 B5* Western Cape, SW South
Africa
Belmopan *52 C1 country capital* (Belize)
Cayo, C Belize
Belogradchik *104 B1* Vidin,
NW Bulgaria
Belo Horizonte *63 F4 prev.* Bello
Horizonte. *state capital* Minas Gerais,
SE Brazil
Belomorsk *110 B3* Respublika Kareliya,
NW Russian Federation
Beloretsk *111 D6* Respublika
Bashkortostan, W Russian Federation
Belorussia/Belorussian SSR *see* Belarus
Belorusskaya Gryada *see* Byelaruskaya
Hrada
Belorusskaya SSR *see* Belarus
Beloshchel'ye *see* Nar'yan-Mar
Belostok *see* Białystok
Belovár *see* Bjelovar
Beloye More *110 C3 Eng.* White Sea. *sea*
NW Russian Federation
Belozërsk *110 B4* Vologodskaya Oblast',
NW Russian Federation
Belton *49 G3* Texas, SW USA
Bel'tsy *see* Bălţi
Beluchistan *see* Baluchistān
Belukha, Gora *114 D5 mountain*
Kazakhstan/Russian Federation
Belynichi *see* Byalynichy
Belyy, Ostrov *114 D2 island* N Russian
Federation
Bemaraha *79 F3 var.* Plateau du
Bemaraha. *mountain range*
W Madagascar

Bemaraha, Plateau du *see* Bemaraha
Bemidji *45 F1* Minnesota, N USA
Bemmel *86 D4* Gelderland,
SE Netherlands
Benaco *see* Garda, Lago di
Benares *see* Vārānasi
Benavente *92 D2* Castilla-León, N Spain
Bend *46 B3* Oregon, NW USA
Bender *see* Tighina
Bender Beila/Bender Beyla *see*
Bandarbeyla
Bender Cassim *see* Bender Cassim/
Bender Qaasim
Bendern *94 E1* NW Liechtenstein Europe
Bendery *see* Tighina
Bendigo *149 C7* Victoria, SE Australia
Beneschau *see* Benešov
Beneški Zaliv *see* Venice, Gulf of
Benešov *99 B5 Ger.* Beneschau.
Středočeský Kraj, W Czech Republic
Benevento *97 D5 anc.* Beneventum,
Malventum. Campania, S Italy
Beneventum *see* Benevento
Bengal, Bay of *124 C4 bay* N Indian
Ocean
Bengasi *see* Banghāzī
Bengazi *see* Banghāzī
Bengbu *128 D5 var.* Peng-pu. Anhui,
E China
Benghazi *see* Banghāzī
Bengkoeloe *see* Bengkulu
Bengkulu *138 B4 prev.* Bengkoeloe,
Benkoelen, Benkulen. Sumatera,
W Indonesia
Benguela *78 A2 var.* Benguella.
Benguela, W Angola
Benguella *see* Benguela
Bengweulu, Lake *see* Bangweulu, Lake
Ben Hope *88 B2 mountain* N Scotland,
UK
Beni *77 E5* Nord Kivu, NE Dem. Rep.
Congo
Beni *56 B4 var.* El Beni. *department*
N Bolivia
Benidorm *93 F4* País Valenciano,
SE Spain
Beni-Mellal *70 C2* C Morocco
Benin *75 F4 off.* Republic of Benin; *prev.*
Dahomey. *country* W Africa

BENIN
West Africa

Official name Republic of Benin
Formation 1960 / 1960
Capital Porto-Novo
Population 8.4 million / 197 people per
sq mile (76 people per sq km) / 42%
Total area 43,483 sq miles
(112,620 sq km)
Languages French*, Fon, Bariba, Yoruba,
Adja, Houeda, Somba
Religions Voodoo 50%, Muslim 30%,
Christian 20%
Ethnic mix Fon 47%, Other 31%, Adja 12%,
Bariba 10%
Government Presidential system
Currency CFA franc = 100 centimes
Literacy rate 34%
Calorie consumption 2548 calories

Benin, Bight of *75 F5 gulf* W Africa
Benin City *75 F5* Edo, SW Nigeria
Benin, Republic of *see* Benin
Beni, Río *61 E3 river* N Bolivia
Beni Suef *72 B2 var.* Banī Suwayf.
N Egypt
Benkoelen *see* Bengkulu
Ben Nevis *88 C3 mountain* N Scotland,
UK
Bénoué *see* Benue
Benson *48 B3* Arizona, SW USA
Bent Jbaïl *119 A5 var.* Bint Jubayl.
S Lebanon
Benton *42 B1* Arkansas, C USA
Benue *75 G4 state* SE Nigeria
Benue *76 B4 Fr.* Bénoué. *river*
Cameroon/Nigeria
Beograd *100 D3 Eng.* Belgrade. Serbia,
N Serbia
Berane *101 D5 prev.* Ivangrad.
E Montenegro
Berat *101 C6 var.* Berati, *SCr.* Beligrad.
Berat, C Albania
Berātskа *see* Berettyó
Berati *see* Berat
Berau, Teluk *139 G4 var.* MacCluer Gulf.
bay Papua, E Indonesia

Berbera *72 D4* Sahil, NW Somalia
Berbérati *77 B5* Mambéré-Kadéï,
SW Central African Republic
Berck-Plage *90 C2* Pas-de-Calais,
N France
Berdichev *see* Berdychiv
Berdyans'k *109 G4 Rus.* Berdyansk;
prev. Osipenko. Zaporiz'ka Oblast',
SE Ukraine
Berdyansk *see* Berdyans'k
Berdychiv *108 D2 Rus.* Berdichev.
Zhytomyrs'ka Oblast', N Ukraine
Beregovo/Beregszász *see* Berehove
Berehove *108 B3 Cz.* Berehovo,
Hung. Beregszász, *Rus.* Beregovo.
Zakarpats'ka Oblast', W Ukraine
Berehovo *see* Berehove
Bereket *122 B2 prev. Rus.* Gazandzhyk,
Kazandzhik, *Turkm.* Gazanjyk. Balkan
Welaýaty, W Turkmenistan
Berettau *see* Berettyó
Berettyó *99 D7 Rom.* Barcău;
prev. Berătău, Berettău. *river*
Hungary/Romania
Berettyóújfalu *99 D6* Hajdú-Bihar,
E Hungary
Berezhany *108 C2 Pol.* Brzeżany.
Ternopil's'ka Oblast', W Ukraine
Berezina *see* Byerezino
Berezniki *111 D5* Permskaya Oblast',
NW Russian Federation
Berga *93 G2* Cataluña, NE Spain
Bergamo *96 B2 anc.* Bergomum.
Lombardia, N Italy
Bergara *93 E1* País Vasco, N Spain
Bergen *93 D2* Mecklenburg-
Vorpommern, NE Germany
Bergen *86 C2* Noord-Holland,
NW Netherlands
Bergen *85 A5* Hordaland, S Norway
Bergen *see* Mons
Bergerac *91 B5* Dordogne, SW France
Bergeyk *87 C5* Noord-Brabant,
S Netherlands
Bergomum *see* Bergamo
Bergse Maas *86 D4 river* S Netherlands
Beringen *87 C5* Limburg, NE Belgium
Beringov Proliv *see* Bering Strait
Bering Sea *36 A2 sea* N Pacific Ocean
Bering Strait *36 C2 Rus.* Beringov Proliv.
strait Bering Sea/Chukchi Sea
Berja *93 E5* Andalucía, S Spain
Berkeley *47 B6* California, W USA
Berkner Island *154 A2 island* Antarctica
Berkovitsa *104 C2* Montana,
NW Bulgaria
Berlin *94 D3 country capital* (Germany)
Berlin, NE Germany
Berlin *41 G2* New Hampshire,
NE USA
Berlinchem *see* Barlinek
Bermejo, Río *64 C2 river* N Argentina
Bermeo *93 E1* País Vasco, N Spain
Bermuda *35 D6 var.* Bermuda Islands,
Bermudas; *prev.* Somers Islands. *UK
crown colony* NW Atlantic Ocean
Bermuda Islands *see* Bermuda
Bermuda Rise *35 E6 undersea rise*
C Sargasso Sea
Bermudas *see* Bermuda
Bern *95 A7 Fr.* Berne. *country capital*
(Switzerland) Bern, W Switzerland
Bernau *94 D3* Brandenburg,
NE Germany
Bernburg *94 C4* Sachsen-Anhalt,
C Germany
Berne *see* Bern
Berner Alpen *95 A7 var.* Berner
Oberland, *Eng.* Bernese Oberland.
mountain range SW Switzerland
Berner Oberland/Bernese Oberland *see*
Berner Alpen
Bernier Island *147 A5 island* Western
Australia
Beroea *see* Ḥalab
Berry *93 C4 cultural region* C France
Berry Islands *54 C1 island group*
N Bahamas
Bertoua *77 B5* Est, E Cameroon
Beru *145 F2 var.* Peru. *atoll* Tungaru,
W Kiribati
Berwick-upon-Tweed *88 D4* N England,
UK
Berytus *see* Beyrouth
Besançon *90 D4 anc.* Besontium,
Vesontio. Doubs, E France
Beskra *see* Biskra
Besontium *see* Besançon
Bessarabka *see* Basarabeasca

Beszterce *see* Bistriţa
Besztercebánya *see* Banská Bystrica
Betafo *79 G3* Antananarivo,
C Madagascar
Betanzos *92 B1* Galicia, NW Spain
Bethlehem *78 D4* Free State, C South
Africa
Bethlehem *119 B6 Ar.* Bayt Laḥm, *Heb.*
Bet Leḥem. C West Bank
Béticos, Sistemas *92 D4 var.* Sistema
Penibético, *Eng.* Baetic Cordillera,
Baetic Mountains. *mountain range*
S Spain
Bet Leḥem *see* Bethlehem
Bétou *77 C5* La Likouala, N Congo
Bette, Pic *71 G4 var.* Bīkkū Bīttī, *It.* Picco
Bette. *mountain* S Libya
Bette, Picco *see* Bette, Pic
Beulah *40 C2* Michigan, N USA
Beuthen *see* Bytom
Beveren *87 B5* Oost-Vlaanderen,
N Belgium
Beverley *89 D5* E England, UK
Bexley *89 B8* Bexley, SE England, UK
Beyla *74 D4* SE Guinea
Beyrouth *118 A4 var.* Bayrūt, *Eng.*
Beirut; *anc.* Berytus. *country capital*
(Lebanon) W Lebanon
Beyşehir *116 B4* Konya, SW Turkey
Beyşehir Gölü *116 B4 lake* C Turkey
Béziers *91 C6 anc.* Baeterrae, Baeterrae
Septimanorum, Julia Beterrae. Hérault,
S France
Bezmein *see* Abadan
Bezwada *see* Vijayawāda
Bhadrāvati *132 C2* Karnātaka, SW India
Bhāgalpur *135 F3* Bihār, NE India
Bhaktapur *135 F3* Central, C Nepal
Bhamo *136 B2 var.* Banmo. Kachin
State, N Myanmar (Burma)
Bhārat *see* India
Bharūch *134 C4* Gujarāt, W India
Bhaunagar *see* Bhāvnagar
Bhāvnagar *134 C4 prev.* Bhaunagar.
Gujarāt, W India
Bheanntraí, Bá *see* Bantry Bay
Bhopāl *134 D4 state capital* Madhya
Pradesh, C India
Bhubaneshwar *135 F5 prev.*
Bhubaneswar, Bhuvaneshwar. *state
capital* Orissa, E India
Bhubaneswar *see* Bhubaneshwar
Bhuket *see* Phuket
Bhusaval *see* Bhusāwal
Bhusāwal *134 D4 prev.* Bhusaval.
Mahārāshtra, C India
Bhutan *135 G3 off.* Kingdom of Bhutan,
var. Druk-yul. *country* S Asia

BHUTAN
Southeast Asia

Official name Kingdom of Bhutan
Formation 1656 / 1865
Capital Thimphu
Population 2.2 million / 121 people per
sq mile (47 people per sq km) / 7%
Total area 18,147 sq miles
(47,000 sq km)
Languages Dzongkha*, Nepali,
Assamese
Religions Mahayana Buddhist 70%,
Hindu 24%, Other 6%
Ethnic mix Bhote 50%, Other 25%,
Nepalese 25%
Government Monarchy
Currency Ngultrum = 100 chetrum
Literacy rate 47%
Calorie consumption Not available

Bhutan, Kingdom of *see* Bhutan
Bhuvaneshwar *see* Bhubaneshwar
Biak, Pulau *139 G4 island* E Indonesia
Biała Podlaska *98 E3* LubelskieE Poland
Białogard *98 B2 Ger.* Belgard.
Zachodnio-pomorskie, NW Poland
Białystok *98 E3 Rus.* Belostok, Bielostok.
Podlaskie, NE Poland
Bianco, Monte *see* Blanc, Mont
Biarritz *91 A6* Pyrénées-Atlantiques,
SW France
Bicaz *108 C3 Hung.* Békás. Neamţ,
NE Romania
Bichiş-Ciaba *see* Békéscsaba
Biddeford *41 G2* Maine, NE USA
Bideford *89 C7* SW England, UK
Biel *95 A7 Fr.* Bienne. Bern,
W Switzerland

Bielefeld 94 B4 Nordrhein-Westfalen, NW Germany
Bielitz/Bielitz-Biala see Bielsko-Biała
Bielostok see Białystok
Bielsko-Biała 99 C5 Ger. Bielitz, Bielitz-Biala. Śląskie, S Poland
Bielsk Podlaski 98 E3 Białystok, E Poland
Bien Bien see Điên Biên
Biên Đông see South China Sea
Biên Hoa 137 E6 Đông Nai, S Vietnam
Bienne see Biel
Bienville, Lac 38 D2 lake Québec, C Canada
Bié, Planalto do 78 B2 var. Bié Plateau. plateau C Angola
Bié Plateau see Bié, Planalto do
Big Cypress Swamp 43 E5 wetland Florida, SE USA
Bigge Island 146 C2 island Western Australia
Bighorn Mountains 44 C2 mountain range Wyoming, C USA
Bighorn River 44 C2 river Montana/Wyoming, NW USA
Bignona 74 B3 SW Senegal
Bigorra see Tarbes
Bigosovo see Bihosava
Big Sioux River 45 E2 river Iowa/South Dakota, N USA
Big Spring 49 E3 Texas, SW USA
Bihać 100 B3 NW Bosnia and Herzegovina
Bihār 135 F3 prev. Behar. cultural region N India
Bihār 135 F3 prev. Behar. state N India
Bihār see Bihār Sharīf
Biharamulo 73 B7 Kagera, NW Tanzania
Bihār Sharīf 135 F3 var. Bihār. Bihār, N India
Bihosava 107 D5 Rus. Bigosovo. Vitsyebskaya Voblasts', NW Belarus
Bijelina 100 C3 Republika Srpska, NE Bosnia and Herzegovina
Bijelo Polje 101 D5 E Montenegro
Bikāner 134 C3 Rājasthān, NW India
Bikin 115 G4 Khabarovskiy Kray, SE Russian Federation
Bikini Atoll 144 C1 var. Pikinni. atoll Ralik Chain, NW Marshall Islands
Bikkū Bīttī see Bette, Pic
Bilāspur 135 E4 Chhattīsgarh, C India
Biläsuvar 117 H3 Rus. Bilyasuvar; prev. Pushkino. SE Azerbaijan
Bila Tserkva 109 E2 Rus. Belaya Tserkov'. Kyyivs'ka Oblast', N Ukraine
Bilauktaung Range 137 C6 var. Thanintari Taungdan. mountain range Myanmar (Burma)/Thailand
Bilbao 93 E1 Basq. Bilbo. País Vasco, N Spain
Bilbo see Bilbao
Bilecik 116 B3 Bilecik, NW Turkey
Billings 44 C2 Montana, NW USA
Bilma, Grand Erg de 75 H3 desert NE Niger
Biloela 148 D4 Queensland, E Australia
Biloxi 42 C3 Mississippi, S USA
Biltine 76 C3 Biltine, E Chad
Bilwi see Puerto Cabezas
Bilyasuvar see Biläsuvar
Bilzen 87 D6 Limburg, NE Belgium
Bimini Islands 54 C1 island group W Bahamas
Binche 87 B7 Hainaut, S Belgium
Bindloe Island see Marchena, Isla
Bin Ghalfān, Jazā'ir see Ḩalāniyāt, Juzur al
Binghamton 41 F3 New York, NE USA
Bingöl 117 E3 Bingöl, E Turkey
Bint Jubayl see Bent Jbaïl
Bintulu 138 D3 Sarawak, East Malaysia
Binzhou 128 D4 Shandong, E China
Bío Bío, Río 65 B5 river C Chile
Bioco, Isla de 77 A5 anc. Bioko, Eng. Fernando Po, Sp. Fernando Póo; prev. Macías Nguema Biyogo. island NW Equatorial Guinea
Bioko see Bioco, Isla de
Birāk 71 F3 var. Brak. C Libya
Birao 76 D3 Vakaga, NE Central African Republic
Birātnagar 135 F3 Eastern, SE Nepal
Bir es Saba see Be'ér Sheva'
Birjand 120 E3 Khorāsān-e Janūbī, E Iran
Birkenfeld 95 A5 Rheinland-Pfalz, SW Germany

Birkenhead 89 C5 NW England, UK
Birlad see Bârlad
Birmingham 89 C6 C England, UK
Birmingham 42 C2 Alabama, S USA
Bir Moghrein see Bir Mogrein
Bir Mogrein 74 C1 var. Bir Moghrein; prev. Fort-Trinquet. Tiris Zemmour, N Mauritania
Birnie Island 145 E3 atoll Phoenix Islands, C Kiribati
Birnin Konni 75 F3 var. Birni-Nkonni. Tahoua, SW Niger
Birni-Nkonni see Birnin Konni
Birobidzhan 115 G4 Yevreyskaya Avtonomnaya Oblast', SE Russian Federation
Birsen see Biržai
Birsk 111 D5 Respublika Bashkortostan, W Russian Federation
Biržai 106 C4 Ger. Birsen. Panevėžys, NE Lithuania
Birżebbuga 102 B5 SE Malta
Bisanthe see Tekirdağ
Bisbee 48 C3 Arizona, SW USA
Biscaia, Baía de see Biscay, Bay of
Biscay, Bay of 80 B4 Sp. Golfo de Vizcaya, Port. Baía de Biscaia. bay France/Spain
Biscay Plain 80 B3 abyssal plain SE Bay of Biscay
Bischofsburg see Biskupiec
Bishah, Wādī 121 B5 dry watercourse C Saudi Arabia
Bishkek 123 G2 var. Pishpek; prev. Frunze. country capital (Kyrgyzstan) Chuyskaya Oblast', N Kyrgyzstan
Bishop's Lynn see King's Lynn
Bishrī, Jabal 118 D3 mountain range E Syria
Biskara see Biskra
Biskra 71 E2 var. Beskra, Biskara. NE Algeria
Biskupiec 98 D2 Ger. Bischofsburg. Warmińsko-Mazurskie, NE Poland
Bislig 139 F2 Mindanao, S Philippines
Bismarck 45 E2 state capital North Dakota, N USA
Bismarck Archipelago 144 B3 island group NE Papua New Guinea
Bismarck Sea 144 B3 sea W Pacific Ocean
Bisnulok see Phitsanulok
Bissau 74 B4 country capital (Guinea-Bissau) W Guinea-Bissau
Bistrița 108 B3 Ger. Bistritz, Hung. Beszterce; prev. Nösen. Bistrița-Năsăud, N Romania
Bistritz see Bistrița
Bitam 77 B5 Woleu-Ntem, N Gabon
Bitburg 95 A5 Rheinland-Pfalz, SW Germany
Bitlis 117 F3 Bitlis, SE Turkey
Bitoeng see Bitung
Bitola 101 D6 Turk. Monastir; prev. Bitolj. S FYR Macedonia
Bitolj see Bitola
Bitonto 97 D5 anc. Butuntum. Puglia, SE Italy
Bitterroot Range 46 D2 mountain range Idaho/Montana, NW USA
Bitung 139 F3 prev. Bitoeng. Sulawesi, C Indonesia
Biu 75 H4 Borno, E Nigeria
Biwa-ko 131 C6 lake Honshū, SW Japan
Bizerta see Bizerte
Bizerte 71 E1 Ar. Banzart, Eng. Bizerta. N Tunisia
Bjelovar 100 B2 Hung. Belovár. Bjelovar-Bilogora, N Croatia
Bjeshkët e Namuna see North Albanian Alps
Björneborg see Pori
Bjørnøya 83 F3 Eng. Bear Island. island N Norway
Blackall 148 C4 Queensland, E Australia
Black Drin 101 D6 Alb. Lumi i Drinit të Zi, SCr. Crni Drim. river Albania/FYR Macedonia
Blackfoot 46 E4 Idaho, NW USA
Black Forest see Schwarzwald
Black Hills 44 D3 mountain range South Dakota/Wyoming, N USA
Blackpool 89 C5 NW England, UK
Black Range 48 C2 mountain range New Mexico, SW USA
Black River 54 A5 W Jamaica

Black River 136 C3 Chin. Babian Jiang, Lixian Jiang, Fr. Rivière Noire, Vtn. Sông Đa. river China/Vietnam
Black Rock Desert 47 C5 desert Nevada, W USA
Black Sand Desert see Garagum
Black Sea 116 B1 var. Euxine Sea, Bul. Cherno More, Rom. Marea Neagră, Rus. Chernoye More, Turk. Karadeniz, Ukr. Chorne More. sea Asia/Europe
Black Sea Lowland 109 E4 Ukr. Prychornomor'ska Nyzovyna. depression SE Europe
Black Volta 75 E4 var. Borongo, Mouhoun, Moun Hou, Fr. Volta Noire. river W Africa
Blackwater 89 A6 Ir. An Abhainn Mhór. river S Ireland
Blackwater State see Nebraska
Blagoevgrad 104 C3 prev. Gorna Dzhumaya. Blagoevgrad, W Bulgaria
Blagoveshchensk 115 G4 Amurskaya Oblast', SE Russian Federation
Blake Plateau 35 D6 var. Blake Terrace. undersea plateau W Atlantic Ocean
Blake Terrace see Blake Plateau
Blanca, Bahía 65 C5 bay E Argentina
Blanca, Costa 93 F4 physical region SE Spain
Blanche, Lake 149 B5 lake South Australia
Blanc, mont 91 D5 It. Monte Bianco. mountain France/Italy
Blanco, Cape 46 A4 headland Oregon, NW USA
Blanes 93 G2 Cataluña, NE Spain
Blankenberge 87 A5 West-Vlaanderen, NW Belgium
Blankenheim 95 A5 Nordrhein-Westfalen, W Germany
Blanquilla, Isla 59 E1 var. La Blanquilla. island N Venezuela
Blanquilla, La see Blanquilla, Isla
Blantyre 79 E2 var. Blantyre-Limbe. Southern, S Malawi
Blantyre-Limbe see Blantyre
Blaricum 86 C3 Noord-Holland, C Netherlands
Blatnitsa see Durankulak
Blenheim 151 C5 Marlborough, South Island, New Zealand
Blesae see Blois
Blida 70 D2 var. El Boulaida, El Boulaïda. N Algeria
Bloemfontein 78 C4 var. Mangaung. country capital (South Africa-judicial capital) Free State, C South Africa
Blois 90 C4 anc. Blesae. Loir-et-Cher, C France
Bloomfield 48 C1 New Mexico, SW USA
Bloomington 40 B4 Illinois, N USA
Bloomington 40 C4 Indiana, N USA
Bloomington 45 F2 Minnesota, N USA
Bloomsbury 148 D3 Queensland, NE Australia
Bluefield 40 D5 West Virginia, NE USA
Bluefields 53 E3 Región Autónoma Atlántico Sur, SE Nicaragua
Bluegrass State see Kentucky
Blue Hen State see Delaware
Blue Law State see Connecticut
Blue Mountain Peak 54 B5 mountain E Jamaica
Blue Mountains 46 C3 mountain range Oregon/Washington, NW USA
Blue Nile 72 C4 state E Sudan
Blue Nile 68 D4 var. Abai, Bahr el, Azraq, Amh. Ābay Wenz, Ar. An Nīl al Azraq. river Ethiopia/Sudan
Blumenau 63 E5 Santa Catarina, S Brazil
Blythe 47 D8 California, W USA
Blytheville 42 C1 Arkansas, C USA
Bo 74 C4 S Sierra Leone
Boaco 52 D3 Boaco, S Nicaragua
Boa Vista 62 D1 state capital Roraima, NW Brazil
Boa Vista 74 A3 island Ilhas de Barlavento, E Cape Verde
Bobaomby, Tanjona 79 G2 Fr. Cap d'Ambre. headland N Madagascar
Bobigny 90 E1 Seine-St-Denis, N France
Bobo-Dioulasso 74 D4 SW Burkina Faso
Bobrinets see Bobrynets'
Bobruysk see Babruysk
Bobrynets' 109 F3 Rus. Bobrinets. Kirovohrads'ka Oblast', C Ukraine
Boca Raton 43 F5 Florida, SE USA

Bocay 52 D2 Jinotega, N Nicaragua
Bocheykovo see Bacheykava
Bocholt 94 A4 Nordrhein-Westfalen, W Germany
Bochum 94 A4 Nordrhein-Westfalen, W Germany
Bocşa 108 A4 Ger. Bokschen, Hung. Boksánbánya. Caraş-Severin, SW Romania
Bodaybo 115 F4 Irkutskaya Oblast', E Russian Federation
Bodegas see Babahoyo
Boden 84 D4 Norrbotten, N Sweden
Bodensee see Constance, Lake, C Europe
Bodmin 89 C7 SW England, UK
Bodø 84 C3 Nordland, C Norway
Bodrum 116 A4 Muğla, SW Turkey
Boeloekoemba see Bulukumba
Boende 77 C5 Equateur, C Dem. Rep. Congo
Boeroe see Buru, Pulau
Boetoeng see Buton, Pulau
Bogale 136 B4 Irrawaddy, SW Myanmar (Burma)
Bogalusa 42 B3 Louisiana, S USA
Bogatynia 98 B4 Ger. Reichenau. Dolnośląskie, SW Poland
Boğazlıyan 116 D3 Yozgat, C Turkey
Bogendorf see Łuków
Bogor 138 C5 Dut. Buitenzorg. Jawa, C Indonesia
Bogotá 58 B3 prev. Santa Fe, Santa Fe de Bogotá. country capital (Colombia) Cundinamarca, C Colombia
Boguslav see Bohuslav
Bo Hai 128 D4 var. Gulf of Chihli. gulf NE China
Bohemia 99 A5 Cz. Čechy, Ger. Böhmen. cultural and historical region W Czech Republic
Bohemian Forest 95 C5 Cz. Český Les, Šumava, Ger. Böhmerwald. mountain range C Europe
Böhmen see Bohemia
Böhmerwald see Bohemian Forest
Böhmisch-Krumau see Český Krumlov
Bohol Sea 139 E2 var. Mindanao Sea. sea S Philippines
Bohuslav 109 E2 Rus. Boguslav. Kyyivs'ka Oblast', N Ukraine
Boise 46 D3 var. Boise City. state capital Idaho, NW USA
Boise City 49 E1 Oklahoma, C USA
Bois, Lac des see Woods, Lake of
Bois-le-Duc see 's-Hertogenbosch
Boizenburg 94 C3 Mecklenburg-Vorpommern, N Germany
Bojador see Boujdour
Bojnūrd 120 D2 var. Bujnurd. Khorāsān-e Shemālī, N Iran
Bokāro 135 F4 Jhārkhand, N India
Boké 74 C4 W Guinea
Bokhara see Buxoro
Boknafjorden 85 A6 fjord S Norway
Boksánbánya/Bokschen see Bocşa
Bol 76 B3 Lac, W Chad
Bolgatanga 75 E4 N Ghana
Bolgrad see Bolhrad
Bolhrad 108 D4 Rus. Bolgrad. Odes'ka Oblast', SW Ukraine
Bolívar, Pico 58 C2 mountain W Venezuela
Bolivia 61 F3 off. Republic of Bolivia. country W South America

---

BOLIVIA
South America

Official name Republic of Bolivia
Formation 1825 / 1938
Capital La Paz (administrative); Sucre (judicial)
Population 9.2 million / 22 people per sq mile (8 people per sq km) / 63%
Total area 424,162 sq miles (1,098,580 sq km)
Languages Aymara*, Quechua*, Spanish*
Religions Roman Catholic 93%, Other 7%
Ethnic mix Quechua 37%, Aymara 32%, Mixed race 13%, European 10%, Other 8%
Government Presidential system
Currency Boliviano = 100 centavos

BOLIVIA
(continued)

Literacy rate 87%
Calorie consumption 2235 calories

Bolivia, Republic of *see* Bolivia
Bollène *91 D6* Vaucluse, SE France
Bollnäs *85 C5* Gävleborg, C Sweden
Bollon *149 D5* Queensland, C Australia
Bologna *96 C3* Emilia-Romagna, N Italy
Bol'shevik *see* Bal'shavik
Bol'shevik, Ostrov *115 E2 island*
  Severnaya Zemlya, N Russian
  Federation
Bol'shezemel'skaya Tundra *110 E3*
  physical region NW Russian Federation
Bol'shoy Lyakhovskiy, Ostrov *115 F2*
  island NE Russian Federation
Bolton *89 D5 prev.* Bolton-le-Moors.
  NW England, UK
Bolton-le-Moors *see* Bolton
Bolu *116 B3* Bolu, NW Turkey
Bolungarvík *83 E4* Vestfirðhir,
  NW Iceland
Bolyarovo *104 D3 prev.* Pashkeni.
  Yambol, E Bulgaria
Bolzano *96 C1 Ger.* Bozen; *anc.*
  Bauzanum. Trentino-Alto Adige,
  N Italy
Boma *77 B6* Bas-Congo, W Dem. Rep.
  Congo
Bombay *see* Mumbai
Bomu *76 D4 var.* Mbomou, Mbomu,
  M'Bomu. *river* Central African
  Republic/Dem. Rep. Congo
Bonaire *55 F5 island* E Netherlands
  Antilles
Bonanza *52 D2* Región Autónoma
  Atlántico Norte, NE Nicaragua
Bonaparte Archipelago *146 C2 island
  group* Western Australia
Bon, Cap *102 D3 headland* N Tunisia
Bonda *77 B6* Ogooué-Lolo, C Gabon
Bondoukou *75 E4* E Côte d'Ivoire
  (Ivory Coast)
Bône *see* Annaba
Bone *see* Watampone
Bone, Teluk *139 E4 bay* Sulawesi,
  C Indonesia
Bongaigaon *135 G3* Assam, NE India
Bongo, Massif des *76 D4 var.* Chaîne des
  Mongos. *mountain range* NE Central
  African Republic
Bongor *76 B3* Mayo-Kébbi, SW Chad
Bonifacio *91 E7* Corse, France,
  C Mediterranean Sea
**Bonifacio, Bocche de/Bonifacio,
  Bouches de** *see* Bonifacio, Strait of
Bonifacio, Strait of *96 A4 Fr.* Bouches
  de Bonifacio, *It.* Bocche di Bonifacio.
  strait C Mediterranean Sea
Bonn *95 A5* Nordrhein-Westfalen,
  W Germany
Bononia *see* Vidin, Bulgaria
Bononia *see* Boulogne-sur-Mer, France
Boosaaso *72 E4 var.* Bandar Kassim,
  Bender Qaasim, Bosaso, *It.* Bender
  Cassim. Bari, N Somalia
Boothia Felix *see* Boothia Peninsula
Boothia, Gulf of *37 F2 gulf* Nunavut,
  NE Canada
Boothia Peninsula *37 F2 prev.* Boothia
  Felix. *peninsula* Nunavut, NE Canada
Boppard *95 A5* Rheinland-Pfalz,
  W Germany
Boquete *53 E5 var.* Bajo Boquete.
  Chiriquí, W Panama
Boquillas *50 D2 var.* Boquillas del
  Carmen. Coahuila de Zaragoza,
  NE Mexico
Boquillas del Carmen *see* Boquillas
Bor *100 E4* Serbia, E Serbia
Bor *73 B5* Jonglei, S Sudan
Borås *85 B7* Västra Götaland, S Sweden
Borbetomagus *see* Worms
Borborema, Planalto da *56 E3 plateau*
  NE Brazil
Bordeaux *91 B5 anc.* Burdigala.
  Gironde, SW France
Bordj Omar Driss *71 E3* E Algeria
Borgå *see* Porvoo
Børgefjell *84 C4 mountain range*
  C Norway
Borger *86 E2* Drenthe, NE Netherlands
Borger *49 E1* Texas, SW USA
Borgholm *85 C7* Kalmar, S Sweden
Borgo Maggiore *96 E1* NW San Marino

Borislav *see* Boryslav
Borisoglebsk *111 B6* Voronezhskaya
  Oblast', W Russian Federation
Borisov *see* Barysaw
Borlänge *85 C6* Dalarna, C Sweden
Borne *86 E3* Overijssel, E Netherlands
Borneo *138 C4 island*
  Brunei/Indonesia/Malaysia
Bornholm *85 B8 island* E Denmark
Borohoro Shan *126 B2 mountain range*
  NW China
Borongo *see* Black Volta
Boron'ki *see* Baron'ki
Borosjenő *see* Ineu
Borovan *104 C2* Vratsa, NW Bulgaria
Borovichi *110 B4* Novgorodskaya
  Oblast', W Russian Federation
Borovo *100 C3* Vukovar-Srijem, NE Croatia
Borşa *108 C3 Hung.* Borsa. Maramureş,
  N Romania
Boryslav *108 B2 Pol.* Borysław, *Rus.*
  Borislav. L'vivs'ka Oblast', NW Ukraine
Borysław *see* Boryslav
Bosanska Dubica *100 B3 var.* Kozarska
  Dubica. Republika Srpska, NW Bosnia
  and Herzegovina
Bosanska Gradiška *100 B3 var.*
  Gradiška. Republika Srpska, N Bosnia
  and Herzegovina
Bosanski Novi *100 B3 var.* Novi Grad.
  Republika Srpska, NW Bosnia and
  Herzegovina
Bosanski Šamac *100 C3 var.* Šamac.
  Republika Srpska, N Bosnia and
  Herzegovina
Bosaso *see* Boosaaso
Bösing *see* Pezinok
Boskovice *99 B5 Ger.* Boskowitz.
  Jihomoravský Kraj, SE Czech Republic
Boskowitz *see* Boskovice
Bosna *100 C4 river* N Bosnia and
  Herzegovina
Bosnia and Herzegovina *100 B3 off.*
  Republic of Bosnia and Herzegovina.
  country SE Europe

BOSNIA & HERZEGOVINA
Southeast Europe

Official name Bosnia and Herzegovina
Formation 1992 / 1992
Capital Sarajevo
Population 3.9 million / 198 people per
  sq mile (76 people per sq km) / 43%
Total area 19,741 sq miles
  (51,129 sq km)
Languages Serbo-Croat*
Religions Muslim (mainly Sunni) 40%,
  Orthodox Christian 31%,
  Roman Catholic 15%, Other 10%,
  Protestant 4%
Ethnic mix Bosniak 48%, Serb 38%,
  Croat 14%
Government Parliamentary system
Currency Marka = 100 pfeninga
Literacy rate 95%
Calorie consumption 2894 calories

Bosnia and Herzegovina, Republic of
  see Bosnia and Herzegovina
Bōsō-hantō *131 D6 peninsula* Honshū,
  S Japan
Bosphorus/Bosporus *see* İstanbul Boğazı
Bosporus Cimmerius *see* Kerch Strait
Bosporus Thracius *see* İstanbul Boğazı
Bossangoa *76 C4* Ouham, C Central
  African Republic
Bossembélé *76 C4* Ombella-Mpoko,
  C Central African Republic
Bossier City *42 A2* Louisiana, S USA
Bosten Hu *126 C3 var.* Bagrax Hu. *lake*
  NW China
Boston *89 E6 prev.* St.Botolph's Town.
  E England, UK
Boston *41 G3 state capital* Massachusetts,
  NE USA
Boston Mountains *42 B1 mountain
  range* Arkansas, C USA
Bostyn' *see* Bastyn'
Botany *148 E2* New South Wales,
  E Australia
Botany Bay *148 E2 inlet* New South
  Wales, SE Australia
Boteti *78 C3 var.* Botletle. *river*
  N Botswana
Bothnia, Gulf of *85 D5 Fin.* Pohjanlahti,
  Swe. Bottniska Viken. *gulf* N Baltic Sea
Botletle *see* Boteti

Botoşani *108 C3 Hung.* Botosány.
  Botoşani, NE Romania
Botoşány *see* Botoşani
Botou *128 C4 prev.* Bozhen. Hebei,
  E China
Botrange *87 D6 mountain* E Belgium
Botswana *78 C3 off.* Republic of
  Botswana. *country* S Africa

BOTSWANA
Southern Africa

Official name Republic of Botswana
Formation 1966 / 1966
Capital Gaborone
Population 1.8 million / 8 people per
  sq mile
  (3 people per sq km) / 50%
Total area 231,803 sq miles (600,370
  sq km)
Languages English*, Setswana, Shona,
  San, Khoikhoi, isiNdebele
Religions Traditional beliefs 50%,
  Christian (mainly Protestant) 30%,
  Other (including Muslim) 20%
Ethnic mix Tswana 98%, Other 2%
Government Presidential system
Currency Pula = 100 thebe
Literacy rate 79%
Calorie consumption 2151 calories

Botswana, Republic of *see* Botswana
Bottniska Viken *see* Bothnia, Gulf of
Bouar *76 B4* Nana-Mambéré, W Central
  African Republic
Bou Craa *70 B3 var.* Bu Craa.
  NW Western Sahara
Bougainville Island *142 B3 island*
  NE Papua New Guinea
Bougaroun, Cap *102 C3 headland*
  NE Algeria
Bougouni *74 D4* Sikasso, SW Mali
Boujdour *70 A3 var.* Bojador.
  W Western Sahara
Boulder *44 C4* Colorado, C USA
Boulder *44 B2* Montana, NW USA
Boulogne *see* Boulogne-sur-Mer
Boulogne-Billancourt *90 D1* Hauts-de-
  Seine, Île-de-France, N France Europe
Boulogne-sur-Mer *90 C2 var.*
  Boulogne; *anc.* Bononia, Gesoriacum,
  Gessoriacum. Pas-de-Calais, N France
Boûmdeïd *74 C3 var.* Boumdeït. Assaba,
  S Mauritania
Boumdeït *see* Boûmdeïd
Boundiali *74 D4* N Côte d'Ivoire
  (Ivory Coast)
Bountiful *44 B4* Utah, W USA
Bounty Basin *see* Bounty Trough
Bounty Islands *142 D5 island group*
  S New Zealand
Bounty Trough *152 C5 var.* Bounty
  Basin. *trough* S Pacific Ocean
Bourbonnais *90 C4* Illinois, N USA
Bourbon Vendée *see* la Roche-sur-Yon
Bourg *see* Bourg-en-Bresse
Bourgas *see* Burgas
Bourge-en-Bresse *see* Bourg-en-Bresse
Bourg-en-Bresse *91 D5 var.* Bourg,
  Bourge-en-Bresse. Ain, E France
Bourges *90 C4 anc.* Avaricum. Cher,
  C France
Bourgogne *90 C4 Eng.* Burgundy.
  region E France
Bourgogne *90 C4 Eng.* Burgundy.
  cultural region E France
Bourke *149 C5* New South Wales,
  SE Australia
Bournemouth *89 D7* S England, UK
Boutilimit *74 C3* Trarza, SW Mauritania
Bouvet Island *67 D7 Norwegian
  dependency* S Atlantic Ocean
Bowen *148 D3* Queensland, NE Australia
Bowling Green *40 B5* Kentucky, S USA
Bowling Green *40 C3* Ohio, N USA
Boxmeer *86 D4* Noord-Brabant,
  SE Netherlands
Boyarka *109 E2* Kyyivs'ka Oblast',
  N Ukraine
Boysun *123 E3 Rus.* Baysun.
  Surkhondaryo Viloyati, S Uzbekistan
Bozeman *44 B2* Montana, NW USA
Bozen *see* Bolzano
Bozhen *see* Botou
Bozüyük *116 B3* Bilecik, NW Turkey
Brač *100 B4 var.* Brach, *It.* Brazza; *anc.*
  Brattia. *island* S Croatia
Bracara Augusta *see* Braga

Brach *see* Brač
Bradford *89 D5* N England, UK
Brady *49 F3* Texas, SW USA
Braga *92 B2 anc.* Bracara Augusta.
  Braga, NW Portugal
Bragança *92 C2 Eng.* Braganza; *anc.* Julio
  Briga. Bragança, NE Portugal
Braganza *see* Bragança
Brahestad *see* Raahe
Brahmanbaria *135 G4* Chittagong,
  E Bangladesh
Brahmapur *135 F5* Orissa, E India
Brahmaputra *135 H3 var.* Padma,
  Tsangpo, *Ben.* Jamuna, *Chin.* Yarlung
  Zangbo Jiang, *Ind.* Bramaputra,
  Dihang, Siang. *river* S Asia
Brăila *108 D4* Brăila, E Romania
Braine-le-Comte *87 B6* Hainaut,
  SW Belgium
Brainerd *45 F2* Minnesota, N USA
Brak *see* Biräk
Bramaputra *see* Brahmaputra
Brampton *38 D5* Ontario, S Canada
Branco, Rio *56 C3 river* N Brazil
Brandberg *78 A3 mountain* NW Namibia
Brandenburg *94 C3 var.* Brandenburg
  an der Havel. Brandenburg,
  NE Germany
Brandenburg an der Havel *see*
  Brandenburg
Brandon *37 F5* Manitoba, S Canada
Braniewo *98 D2 Ger.* Braunsberg.
  Warmińsko-mazurskie, N Poland
Brasil *see* Brazil
Brasília *63 F3 country capital* (Brazil)
  Distrito Federal, C Brazil
Brasil, República Federativa do *see*
  Brazil
Braşov *108 C4 Ger.* Kronstadt, *Hung.*
  Brassó; *prev.* Oraşul Stalin. Braşov,
  C Romania
Brassó *see* Braşov
Bratislava *99 C6 Ger.* Pressburg, *Hung.*
  Pozsony. *country capital* (Slovakia)
  Bratislavský Kraj, W Slovakia
Bratsk *115 E4* Irkutskaya Oblast',
  C Russian Federation
Brattia *see* Brač
Braunsberg *see* Braniewo
Braunschweig *94 C4 Eng./Fr.*
  Brunswick. Niedersachsen, N Germany
Brava *see* Baraawe
Brava, Costa *93 H2 coastal region*
  NE Spain
Bravo del Norte, Río/Bravo, Río *see*
  Grande, Rio
Bravo, Rio *50 C1 river* Mexico/USA
  North America
Brawley *47 D8* California, W USA
Brazil *62 C2 off.* Federative Republic of
  Brazil, *Port.* República Federativa do
  Brasil, *Sp.* Brasil; *prev.* United States of
  Brazil. *country* South America

BRAZIL
South America

Official name Federative Republic
  of Brazil
Formation 1822 / 1828
Capital Brasília
Population 186 million / 57 people per
  sq mile (22 people per sq km) / 81%
Total area 3,286,470 sq miles
  (8,511,965 sq km)
Languages Portuguese*, German,
  Italian, Spanish, Polish, Japanese,
  Amerindian languages
Religions Roman Catholic 74%,
  Protestant 15%, Atheist 7%,
  Other 4%
Ethnic mix Black 53%, Mixed race 40%,
  White 6%, Other 1%
Government Presidential system
Currency Real = 100 centavos
Literacy rate 88%
Calorie consumption 3049 calories

Brazil Basin *67 C5 var.* Brazilian Basin,
  Brazil'skaya Kotlovina. *undersea basin*
  W Atlantic Ocean
Brazil, Federative Republic of *see* Brazil
Brazilian Basin *see* Brazil Basin
Brazilian Highlands *see* Central, Planalto
Brazil'skaya Kotlovina *see* Brazil Basin
Brazil, United States of *see* Brazil
Brazos River *49 G3 river* Texas, SW USA
Brazza *see* Brač

Brazzaville *77 B6 country capital*
(Congo) Capital District,
S Congo
Brčko *100 C3* Republika Srpska,
NE Bosnia and Herzegovina
Brecht *87 C5* Antwerpen, N Belgium
Brecon Beacons *89 C6 mountain range*
S Wales, UK
Breda *86 C4* Noord-Brabant,
S Netherlands
Bree *87 D5* Limburg, NE Belgium
Bregalnica *101 E6 river* E FYR
Macedonia
Bregenz *57 B7 anc.* Brigantium.
Vorarlberg, W Austria
Bregovo *104 B1* Vidin, NW Bulgaria
Bremen *94 B3 Fr.* Brême. Bremen,
NW Germany
Bremerhaven *94 B3* Bremen,
NW Germany
Bremerton *46 B2* Washington,
NW USA
Brenham *49 G3* Texas, SW USA
Brenner, Col du/Brennero, Passo del
see Brenner Pass
Brenner Pass *96 C1 var.* Brenner Sattel,
Fr. Col du Brenner, *Ger.* Brennerpass,
It. Passo del Brennero. *pass*
Austria/Italy
Brennerpass *see* Brenner Pass
Brenner Sattel *see* Brenner Pass
Brescia *96 B2 anc.* Brixia. Lombardia,
N Italy
Breslau *see* Wrocław
Bressanone *96 C1 Ger.* Brixen.
Trentino-Alto Adige, N Italy
Brest *107 A6 Pol.* Brześć nad Bugiem,
Rus. Brest-Litovsk; *prev.* Brześć
Litewski. Brestskaya Voblasts',
SW Belarus
Brest *90 A3* Finistère, NW France
Brest-Litovsk *see* Brest
Bretagne *90 A3 Eng.* Brittany, *Lat.*
Britannia Minor. *region* NW France
Bretagne *90 A3 Eng.* Brittany, *Lat.*
Britannia Minor. *cultural region*
NW France
Brewster, Kap *see* Kangikajik
Brewton *42 C3* Alabama, S USA
Brezhnev *see* Naberezhnyye Chelny
Brezovo *104 D2 prev.* Abrashlare.
Plovdiv, C Bulgaria
Bria *76 D4* Haute-Kotto, C Central
African Republic
Briançon *91 D5 anc.* Brigantio.
Hautes-Alpes, SE France
Bricgstow *see* Bristol
Bridgeport *41 F3* Connecticut,
NE USA
Bridgetown *55 G2 country capital*
(Barbados) SW Barbados
Bridlington *89 D5* E England, UK
Bridport *89 D7* S England, UK
Brieg *see* Brzeg
Brig *95 A7 Fr.* Brigue, *It.* Briga. Valais,
SW Switzerland
Briga *see* Brig
Brigantio *see* Briançon
Brigantium *see* Bregenz
Brigham City *44 B3* Utah, W USA
Brighton *89 E7* SE England, UK
Brighton *44 D4* Colorado, C USA
Brigue *see* Brig
Brindisi *97 E5 anc.* Brundisium,
Brundusium. Puglia, SE Italy
Briovera *see* St-Lô
Brisbane *149 E5 state capital*
Queensland, E Australia
Bristol *89 D7 anc.* Bricgstow.
SW England, UK
Bristol *41 F3* Connecticut, NE USA
Bristol *40 D5* Tennessee, S USA
Bristol Bay *36 B3 bay* Alaska, USA
Bristol Channel *89 C7 inlet* England/
Wales, UK
Britain *80 C3 var.* Great Britain.
island UK
Britannia Minor *see* Bretagne
British Columbia *36 D4 Fr.* Colombie-
Britannique. *province* SW Canada
British Guiana *see* Guyana
British Honduras *see* Belize
British Indian Ocean Territory *141 B5
UK dependent territory* C Indian Ocean
British Isles *89 island group* NW Europe
British North Borneo *see* Sabah
British Solomon Islands Protectorate
see Solomon Islands

British Virgin Islands *55 F3 var.*
Virgin Islands. *UK dependent territory*
E West Indies
Brittany *see* Bretagne
Briva Curretia *see* Brive-la-Gaillarde
Briva Isarae *see* Pontoise
Brive *see* Brive-la-Gaillarde
Brive-la-Gaillarde *91 C5 prev.* Brive;
anc. Briva Curretia. Corrèze, C France
Brixen *see* Bressanone
Brixia *see* Brescia
Brno *99 B5 Ger.* Brünn. Jihomoravský
Kraj, SE Czech Republic
Brocēni *106 B3* Saldus, SW Latvia
Brod/Bród *see* Slavonski Brod
Brodeur Peninsula *37 F2 peninsula*
Baffin Island, Nunavut, NE Canada
Brod na Savi *see* Slavonski Brod
Brodnica *98 C3 Ger.* Buddenbrock.
Kujawski-pomorskie, C Poland
Broek-in-Waterland *86 C3* Noord-
Holland, C Netherlands
Broken Arrow *49 G1* Oklahoma,
C USA
Broken Bay *148 F1 bay* New South
Wales, SE Australia
Broken Hill *149 B6* New South Wales,
SE Australia
Broken Ridge *141 D6 undersea plateau*
S Indian Ocean
Bromberg *see* Bydgoszcz
Bromley *89 B8* UK
Brookhaven *42 B3* Mississippi,
S USA
Brookings *45 F3* South Dakota,
N USA
Brooks Range *36 D2 mountain range*
Alaska, USA
Brookton *147 B6* Western Australia
Broome *146 B3* Western Australia
Broomfield *44 D4* Colorado, C USA
Broucsella *see* Brussel/Bruxelles
Brovary *109 E2* Kyyivs'ka Oblast',
N Ukraine
Brownfield *49 E2* Texas, SW USA
Brownsville *49 G5* Texas, SW USA
Brownwood *49 F3* Texas, SW USA
Brozha *107 D7* Mahilyowskaya Voblasts',
E Belarus
Bruges *see* Brugge
Brugge *87 A5 Fr.* Bruges. West-
Vlaanderen, NW Belgium
Brummen *86 D3* Gelderland,
E Netherlands
Brundisium/Brundusium *see* Brindisi
Brunei *138 D3 off.* Sultanate of Brunei,
Mal. Negara Brunei Darussalam.
country SE Asia

BRUNEI
Southeast Asia

Official name Sultanate of Brunei
Formation 1984 / 1984
Capital Bandar Seri Begawan
Population 374,000 / 184 people per sq
mile (71 people per sq km) / 72%
Total area 2228 sq miles (5770 sq km)
Languages Malay*, English, Chinese
Religions Muslim (mainly Sunni) 66%,
Buddhist 14%, Other 10%, Christian 10%
Ethnic mix Malay 67%, Chinese 16%,
Other 11%, Indigenous 6%
Government Monarchy
Currency Brunei dollar = 100 cents
Literacy rate 93%
Calorie consumption 2855 calories

Brunei, Sultanate of *see* Brunei
Brunei Town *see* Bandar Seri Begawan
Brünn *see* Brno
Brunner, Lake *151 C5 lake* South Island,
New Zealand
Brunswick *43 E3* Georgia, SE USA
Brunswick *see* Braunschweig
Brusa *see* Bursa
Brus Laguna *52 D2* Gracias a Dios,
E Honduras
Brussa *see* Bursa
Brussel *87 C6 var.* Brussels,
Fr. Bruxelles, *Ger.* Brüssel; *anc.*
Broucsella. *country capital* (Belgium)
C Belgium
Brüssel/Brussels *see* Brussel/Bruxelles
Brussels *see* Brussel/Bruxelles
Brüx *see* Most
Bruxelles *see* Brussel
Bryan *49 G3* Texas, SW USA

Bryansk *111 A5* Bryanskaya Oblast',
W Russian Federation
Brzeg *98 C4 Ger.* Brieg; *anc.* Civitas Altae
Ripae. Opolskie, S Poland
Brześć Litewski/Brześć nad Bugiem
see Brest
Brzeżany *see* Berezhany
Bucaramanga *58 B2* Santander,
N Colombia
Buchanan *74 C5 prev.* Grand Bassa.
SW Liberia
Buchanan, Lake *49 F3 reservoir* Texas,
SW USA
Bucharest *see* Bucureşti
Buckeye State *see* Ohio
Bu Craa *see* Bou Craa
Bucureşti *108 C5 Eng.* Bucharest,
Ger. Bukarest, *prev.* Altenburg; *anc.*
Cetatea Dambovitei. *country capital*
(Romania) Bucureşti, S Romania
Buda-Kashalyova *107 D7 Rus.* Buda-
Koshelëvo. Homyel'skaya Voblasts',
SE Belarus
Buda-Koshelëvo *see* Buda-Kashalyova
Budapest *99 C6 off.* Budapest Főváros,
SCr. Budimpešta. *country capital*
(Hungary) Pest, N Hungary
Budapest Főváros *see* Budapest
Budaun *134 D3* Uttar Pradesh, N India
Buddenbrock *see* Brodnica
Budimpešta *see* Budapest
Budweis *see* České Budějovice
Budyšin *see* Bautzen
Buena Park *46 E2* California, W USA
North America
Buenaventura *58 A3* Valle del Cauca,
W Colombia
Buena Vista *61 G4* Santa Cruz, C Bolivia
Buena Vista *93 H5* S Gibraltar Europe
Buenavista *93 H5* Baja California Sur,
W Mexico
Buenavista *93 H5* Sonora, NW Mexico
North America
Buena Vista *93 H5* Cerro Largo,
Uruguay
Buena Vista *93 H5* Colorado, C USA
Buena Vista *93 H5* Georgia, SE USA
Buena Vista *93 H5* Virginia, NE USA
Buenos Aires *64 D4 hist.* Santa Maria del
Buen Aire. *country capital* (Argentina)
Buenos Aires, E Argentina
Buenos Aires *53 E5* Puntarenas,
SE Costa Rica
Buenos Aires, Lago *65 B6 var.* Lago
General Carrera. *lake* Argentina/Chile
Buffalo *41 E3* New York, NE USA
Buffalo Narrows *37 F4* Saskatchewan,
C Canada
Buff Bay *54 B5* E Jamaica
Buftea *108 C5* Ilfov, S Romania
Bug *81 E3 Bel.* Zakhodni Buh, *Eng.*
Western Bug, *Rus.* Zapadnyy Bug,
Ukr. Zakhidnyy Buh. *river* E Europe
Buga *58 B3* Valle del Cauca, W Colombia
Bughotu *see* Santa Isabel
Buguruslan *111 D6* Orenburgskaya
Oblast', W Russian Federation
Buitenzorg *see* Bogor
Bujalance *92 D4* Andalucía, S Spain
Bujanovac *101 E5* Kosovo, SE Serbia
Bujnurd *see* Bojnūrd
Bujumbura *73 B7 prev.* Usumbura.
country capital (Burundi) W Burundi
Bukarest *see* Bucureşti
Bukavu *77 E6 prev.* Costermansville. Sud
Kivu, E Dem. Rep. Congo
Bukhara *see* Buxoro
Bukoba *73 B6* Kagera, NW Tanzania
Bülach *95 B7* Zürich, NW Switzerland
Bulawayo *78 D3* Matabeleland North,
SW Zimbabwe
Bulgan *127 E2* Bulgan, N Mongolia
Bulgaria *104 C2 off.* Republic of Bulgaria,
Bul. Bŭlgariya; *prev.* People's Republic
of Bulgaria. *country* SE Europe
Bulgaria, People's Republic of *see*
Bulgaria

BULGARIA
Southeast Europe

Official name Republic of Bulgaria
Formation 1908 / 1947
Capital Sofia
Population 7.7 million / 180 people per
sq mile (70 people per sq km) / 70%
Total area 42,822 sq miles
(110,910 sq km)

BULGARIA
(continued)

Languages Bulgarian*, Turkish,
Romani
Religions Orthodox Christian 83%,
Muslim 12%, Other 4%, Roman
Catholic 1%
Ethnic mix Bulgarian 84%, Turkish 9%,
Roma 5%, Other 2%
Government Parliamentary system
Currency Lev = 100 stotinki
Literacy rate 98%
Calorie consumption 2848 calories

Bulgaria, Republic of *see* Bulgaria
Bŭlgariya *see* Bulgaria
Bullion State *see* Missouri
Bull Shoals Lake *42 B1 reservoir*
Arkansas/Missouri, C USA
Bulukumba *139 E4 prev.* Boeloekoemba.
Sulawesi, C Indonesia
Bumba *77 D5* Equateur, N Dem. Rep.
Congo
Bunbury *147 A7* Western Australia
Bundaberg *148 E4* Queensland,
E Australia
Bungo-suidō *131 B7 strait* SW Japan
Bunia *77 E5* Orientale, NE Dem. Rep.
Congo
Bünyan *116 D3* Kayseri, C Turkey
Buraida *see* Buraydah
Buraydah *120 B4 var.* Buraida. Al
Qaşīm, N Saudi Arabia
Burdigala *see* Bordeaux
Burdur *116 B4 var.* Buldur. Burdur,
SW Turkey
Burdur Gölü *116 B4 salt lake* SW Turkey
Burē *72 C4* Amhara, N Ethiopia
Burgas *104 E2 var.* Bourgas. Burgas,
E Bulgaria
Burgaski Zaliv *104 E2 gulf* E Bulgaria
Burgos *92 D2* Castilla-León, N Spain
Burgundy *see* Bourgogne
Burhan Budai Shan *126 D4 mountain
range* C China
Buriram *137 D5 var.* Buri Ram,
Puriramya. Buri Ram, E Thailand
Buri Ram *see* Buriram
Burjassot *93 F3* País Valenciano, E Spain
Burkburnett *49 F2* Texas, SW USA
Burketown *148 B3* Queensland,
NE Australia
Burkina *see* Burkina Faso
Burkina Faso *75 E4 var.* Burkina; *prev.*
Upper Volta. *country* W Africa

BURKINA FASO
West Africa

Official name Burkina Faso
Formation 1960 / 1960
Capital Ouagadougou
Population 13.2 million / 125 people per
sq mile (48 people per sq km) / 19%
Total area 105,869 sq miles
(274,200 sq km)
Languages French*, Mossi, Fulani,
Tuareg, Dyula, Songhai
Religions Muslim 55%, Traditional
beliefs 35%, Roman Catholic 9%,
Other Christian 1%
Ethnic mix Other 50%, Mossi 50%
Government Presidential system
Currency CFA franc = 100 centimes
Literacy rate 13%
Calorie consumption 2462 calories

Burley *46 D4* Idaho, NW USA
Burlington *45 G4* Iowa, C USA
Burlington *41 F2* Vermont,
NE USA
Burma *see* Myanmar
Burnie *149 C8* Tasmania,
SE Australia
Burns *46 C3* Oregon, NW USA
Burnside *37 F3 river* Nunavut,
NW Canada
Burnsville *45 F2* Minnesota,
N USA
Burrel *101 D6 var.* Burreli. Dibēr,
C Albania
Burreli *see* Burrel
Burriana *93 F3* País Valenciano,
E Spain
Bursa *116 B3 var.* Brussa, *prev.* Brusa;
anc. Prusa. Bursa, NW Turkey

Būr Sa'īd see Port Said
Burtnieks 106 C3 var. Burtnieks Ezers.
 lake N Latvia
Burtnieks Ezers see Burtnieks
Burundi 73 B7 off. Republic of Burundi;
 prev. Kingdom of Burundi, Urundi.
 country C Africa

BURUNDI
Central Africa

Official name Republic of Burundi
Formation 1962 / 1962
Capital Bujumbura
Population 7.5 million / 757 people per
sq mile (292 people per sq km) / 9%
Total area 10,745 sq miles
(27,830 sq km)
Languages Kirundi*, French*, Kiswahili
Religions Christian 60%, Traditional
beliefs 39%, Muslim 1%
Ethnic mix Hutu 85%, Tutsi 14%,
Twa 1%
Government Presidential system
Currency Burundi franc = 100 centimes
Literacy rate 59%
Calorie consumption 1649 calories

Burundi, Kingdom of see Burundi
Burundi, Republic of see Burundi
Buru, Pulau 139 F4 prev. Boeroe. island
 E Indonesia
Busan see Pusan
Buşayrah 118 D3 Dayr az Zawr,
 E Syria
Büshehr/Bushire see Bandar-e Büshehr
Busra see Al Başrah, Iraq
Busselton 147 A7 Western Australia
Bussora see Al Başrah
Buta 77 D5 Orientale, N Dem. Rep.
 Congo
Butembo 77 E5 Nord Kivu, NE Dem.
 Rep. Congo
Butler 41 E4 Pennsylvania, NE USA
Buton, Pulau 139 E4 var. Pulau Butung;
 prev. Boetoeng. island C Indonesia
Bütow see Bytów
Butte 44 B2 Montana, NW USA
Butterworth 138 B3 Pinang, Peninsular
 Malaysia
Button Islands 39 E1 island group
 Nunavut, NE Canada
Butuan 139 F2 off. Butuan City.
 Mindanao, S Philippines
Butuan City see Butuan
Butung, Pulau see Buton, Pulau
Bututntum see Bitonto
Buulobarde 73 D5 var. Buulo Berde.
 Hiiraan, C Somalia Africa
Buulo Berde see Buulobarde
Buur Gaabo 73 D6 Jubbada Hoose,
 S Somalia
Buxoro 122 D2 var. Bokhara,
 Rus. Bukhara. Buxoro Viloyati,
 C Uzbekistan
Buynaksk 111 B8 Respublika Dagestan,
 SW Russian Federation
Büyükağrı Dağı 117 F3 var. Aghri Dagh,
 Agri Dagi, Koh I Noh, Masis, Eng.
 Great Ararat, Mount Ararat. mountain
 E Turkey
Büyükmenderes Nehri 116 A4 river
 SW Turkey
Buzău 108 C4 Buzău, SE Romania
Buzuluk 111 D6 Akmola, C Kazakhstan
Byahoml' 107 D5 Rus. Begoml'.
 Vitsyebskaya Voblasts', N Belarus
Byalynichy 107 D6 Rus. Belynichi.
 Mahilyowskaya Voblasts',
 E Belarus
Byan Tumen see Choybalsan
Bydgoszcz 98 C3 Ger. Bromberg.
 Kujawski-pomorskie, C Poland
Byelaruskaya Hrada 107 B6 Rus.
 Belorusskaya Gryada. ridge N Belarus
Byerezino 107 D6 Rus. Berezina. river
 C Belarus
Byron Island see Nikunau
Bystrovka see Kemin
Bytča 99 C5 Žilinský Kraj, N Slovakia
Bytom 99 C5 Ger. Beuthen. Śląskie,
 S Poland
Bytów 98 C2 Ger. Bütow. Pomorskie,
 N Poland
Byuzmeyin see Abadan
Byval'ki 107 D8 Homyel'skaya Voblasts',
 SE Belarus
Byzantium see İstanbul

C

Caála 78 B2 var. Kaala, Robert Williams,
 Port. Vila Robert Williams. Huambo,
 C Angola
Caazapá 64 D3 Caazapá, S Paraguay
Caballo Reservoir 48 C3 reservoir New
 Mexico, SW USA
Cabañaquinta 92 D1 Asturias, N Spain
Cabanatuan 139 E1 off. Cabanatuan
 City. Luzon, N Philippines
Cabanatuan City see Cabanatuan
Cabillonum see Chalon-sur-Saône
Cabimas 58 C1 Zulia, NW Venezuela
Cabinda 78 A1 var. Kabinda. Cabinda,
 NW Angola
Cabinda 78 A1 var. Kabinda. province
 NW Angola
Cabora Bassa, Lake see Cahora Bassa,
 Albufeira de
Caborca 50 B1 Sonora, NW Mexico
Cabot Strait 39 G4 strait E Canada
Cabo Verde, Ilhas do see Cape Verde
Cabras, Ilha das 76 E2 island
 S Sao Tome and Principe, Africa,
 E Atlantic Ocean
Cabrera 93 G3 river NW Spain
Cabrera, Illa de 93 G4 island Islas
 Baleares, Spain, W Mediterranean Sea
Cáceres 92 C3 Ar. Qazris. Extremadura,
 W Spain
Cachimbo, Serra do 63 E2 mountain
 range C Brazil
Caconda 78 B2 Huíla, C Angola
Čadca 99 C5 Hung. Csaca. Žilinský Kraj,
 N Slovakia
Cadillac 40 C2 Michigan, N USA
Cadiz 139 E2 off. Cadiz City. Negros,
 C Philippines
Cádiz 92 C5 anc. Gades, Gadier, Gadir,
 Gadire. Andalucía, SW Spain
Cadiz City see Cadiz
Cádiz, Golfo de 92 B5 Eng. Gulf of
 Cadiz. gulf Portugal/Spain
Cadiz, Gulf of see Cádiz, Golfo de
Cadurcum see Cahors
Caen 90 B3 Calvados, N France
Caene/Caenepolis see Qena
Caerdydd see Cardiff
Caer Glou see Gloucester
Caer Gybi see Holyhead
Caerleon see Chester
Caer Luel see Carlisle
Caesaraugusta see Zaragoza
Caesarea Mazaca see Kayseri
Caesarobriga see Talavera de la Reina
Caesarodunum see Tours
Caesaromagus see Beauvais
Caesena see Cesena
Cafayate 64 C2 Salta, N Argentina
Cagayan de Oro 139 E2 off. Cagayan de
 Oro City. Mindanao, S Philippines
Cagayan de Oro City see Cagayan de Oro
Cagliari 97 A6 anc. Caralis. Sardegna,
 Italy, C Mediterranean Sea
Caguas 55 F3 E Puerto Rico
Cahora Bassa, Albufeira de 78 D2
 var. Lake Cabora Bassa. reservoir
 NW Mozambique
Cahors 91 C5 anc. Cadurcum. Lot,
 S France
Cahul 108 D4 Rus. Kagul. S Moldova
Caicos Passage 54 D2 passage Bahamas/
 Turks and Caicos Islands
Caiffa see Ḥefa
Cailungo 96 E1 N San Marino
Caiphas see Ḥefa
Cairns 148 D3 Queensland, NE Australia
Cairo 72 B2 Ar. Al Qāhirah, var. El
 Qāhira. country capital (Egypt)
 N Egypt
Caisleán an Bharraigh see Castlebar
Cajamarca 60 B3 prev. Caxamarca.
 Cajamarca, NW Peru
Čakovec 108 D2 Ger. Csakathurn,
 Hung. Csáktornya; prev. Ger.
 Tschakathurn. Medimurje, N Croatia
Calabar 75 G5 Cross River, S Nigeria
Calabozo 58 D2 Guárico, C Venezuela
Calafat 108 B5 Dolj, SW Romania
Calafate see El Calafate
Calahorra 93 E2 La Rioja, N Spain
Calais 90 C2 Pas-de-Calais, N France
Calais 41 H2 Maine, NE USA
Calais, Pas de see Dover, Strait of
Calama 64 B2 Antofagasta, N Chile

Calamianes see Calamian Group
Calamian Group 129 C7 var.
 Calamianes. island group
 W Philippines
Cālāras see Cālāraşi
Cālāraşi 108 D3 var. Cālāras, Rus.
 Kalarash. C Moldova
Cālāraşi 108 C5 Cālāraşi, SE Romania
Calatayud 93 E2 Aragón, NE Spain
Calbayog 139 E2 off. Calbayog City.
 Samar, C Philippines
Calbayog City see Calbayog
Calcutta see Kolkata
Caldas da Rainha 92 B3 Leiria,
 W Portugal
Caldera 64 B3 Atacama, N Chile
Caldwell 46 C3 Idaho, NW USA
Caledonia 52 C1 Corozal, N Belize
Caleta Olivia 65 B6 Santa Cruz,
 SE Argentina
Calgary 37 E5 Alberta, SW Canada
Cali 58 B3 Valle del Cauca, W Colombia
Calicut 132 C2 var. Kozhikode. Kerala,
 SW India
California 47 B7 off. State of California,
 also known as El Dorado, The Golden
 State. state W USA
California, Golfo de 50 B2 Eng. Gulf
 of California; prev. Sea of Cortez. gulf
 W Mexico
California, Gulf of see California,
 Golfo de
Cālimāneşti 108 B4 Vâlcea, SW Romania
Calisia see Kalisz
Callabonna, Lake 149 B5 lake South
 Australia
Callao 60 C4 Callao, W Peru
Callatis see Mangalia
Callosa de Segura 93 F4 País Valenciano,
 E Spain
Calmar see Kalmar
Caloundra 149 E5 Queensland,
 E Australia
Caltanissetta 97 C7 Sicilia, Italy,
 C Mediterranean Sea
Caluula 72 E4 Bari, NE Somalia
Camabatela 78 B1 Cuanza Norte,
 NW Angola
Camacupa 78 B2 var. General Machado,
 Port. Vila General Machado. Bié,
 C Angola
Camagüey 54 C2 prev. Puerto Príncipe.
 Camagüey, C Cuba
Camagüey, Archipiélago de 54 C2
 island group C Cuba
Camana 61 E4 var. Camaná. Arequipa,
 SW Peru
Camargue 91 D6 physical region
 SE France
Ca Mau 137 D6 var. Quan Long. Minh
 Hai, S Vietnam
Cambay, Gulf of see Khambhāt, Gulf of
Camberia see Chambéry
Cambodia 137 D5 off. Kingdom
 of Cambodia, var. Democratic
 Kampuchea, Roat Kampuchea, Cam.
 Kampuchea; prev. People's Democratic
 Republic of Kampuchea. country
 SE Asia

CAMBODIA
Southeast Asia

Official name Kingdom of Cambodia
Formation 1953 / 1953
Capital Phnom Penh
Population 14.1 million / 207 people per
sq mile (80 people per sq km) / 16%
Total area 69,900 sq miles
(181,040 sq km)
Languages Khmer*, French, Chinese,
Vietnamese, Cham
Religions Buddhist 93%, Muslim 6%,
Christian 1%
Ethnic mix Khmer 90%, Other 5%,
Vietnamese 4%, Chinese 1%
Government Parliamentary system
Currency Riel = 100 sen
Literacy rate 74%
Calorie consumption 2046 calories

Cambodia, Kingdom of see Cambodia
Cambrai 90 C2 Flem. Kambryk, prev.
 Cambray; anc. Cameracum. Nord,
 N France
Cambray see Cambrai
Cambrian Mountains 89 C6 mountain
 range C Wales, UK

Cambridge 54 A4 W Jamaica
Cambridge 150 D3 Waikato, North
 Island, New Zealand
Cambridge 89 E6 Lat. Cantabrigia.
 E England, UK
Cambridge 41 F4 Maryland, NE USA
Cambridge 40 D4 Ohio, NE USA
Cambridge Bay 37 F3 Victoria Island,
 Nunavut, NW Canada
Camden 42 B2 Arkansas, C USA
Camellia State see Alabama
Cameracum see Cambrai
Cameroon 76 A4 off. Republic of
 Cameroon, Fr. Cameroun. country
 W Africa

CAMEROON
Central Africa

Official name Republic of Cameroon
Formation 1960 / 1961
Capital Yaoundé
Population 163 million / 907 people per
sq mile (350 people per sq km) / 49%
Total area 183,567 sq miles
(475,400 sq km)
Languages English*, French*, Bamileke,
Fang, Fulani
Religions Roman Catholic 35%,
Traditional beliefs 25%, Muslim 22%,
Protestant 18%
Ethnic mix Cameroon highlanders 31%,
Other 21%, Equatorial Bantu 19%,
Kirdi 11%, Fulani 10%, Northwestern
Bantu 8%
Government Presidential system
Currency CFA franc = 100 centimes
Literacy rate 68%
Calorie consumption 2273 calories

Cameroon, Republic of see Cameroon
Cameroun see Cameroon
Camocim 63 F2 Ceará, E Brazil
Camopi 59 H3 E French Guiana
Campamento 52 C2 Olancho, C Honduras
Campania 97 D5 Eng. Champagne.
 region S Italy
Campbell, Cape 151 D5 headland South
 Island, New Zealand
Campbell Island 142 D5 island S New
 Zealand
Campbell Plateau 142 D5 undersea
 plateau SW Pacific Ocean
Campbell River 36 D5 Vancouver
 Island, British Columbia, SW Canada
Campeche 51 G4 Campeche, SE Mexico
Campeche, Bahía de 51 F4 Eng. Bay of
 Campeche. bay E Mexico
Campeche, Bay of see Campeche,
 Bahía de
Câm Pha 136 E3 Quang Ninh, N Vietnam
Câmpina 108 C4 prev. Cimpina.
 Prahova, SE Romania
Campina Grande 63 G2 Paraíba,
 E Brazil
Campinas 63 F4 São Paulo, S Brazil
Campobasso 97 D5 Molise, C Italy
Campo Criptana see Campo de Criptana
Campo de Criptana 93 E3 var. Campo
 Criptana. Castilla-La Mancha, C Spain
Campo dos Goitacazes see Campos
Campo Grande 63 E4 state capital Mato
 Grosso do Sul, SW Brazil
Campos 63 F4 var. Campo dos
 Goitacazes. Rio de Janeiro, SE Brazil
Câmpulung 108 B4 prev. Câmpulung-
 Muşcel, Cimpulung. Argeş, S Romania
Câmpulung-Muşcel see Câmpulung
Campus Stellae see Santiago
Cam Ranh 137 E6 Khanh Hoa,
 S Vietnam
Canada 34 B4 country N North America

CANADA
North America

Official name Canada
Formation 1867 / 1949
Capital Ottawa
Population 32.3 million / 9 people per
sq mile (4 people per sq km) / 77%
Total area 3,854,085 sq miles
(9,984,670 sq km)
Languages English*, French*, Chinese,
Italian, German, Ukrainian, Inuktitut, Cree
Religions Roman Catholic 44%,
Protestant 29%, Other and
nonreligious 27%

CANADA
(continued)

Ethnic mix British origin 44%, French origin 25%, Other European 20%, Other 11%.
Government Parliamentary system
Currency Canadian dollar = 100 cents
Literacy rate 99%
Calorie consumption 3589 calories

Canada Basin *34 C2 undersea basin* Arctic Ocean
Canadian River *49 E2 river* SW USA
Çanakkale *116 A3 var.* Dardanelli; *prev.* Chanak, Kale Sultanie. Çanakkale, W Turkey
Çanakkale Boğazı *116 A2 Eng.* Dardanelles. *strait* NW Turkey
Cananea *50 B1* Sonora, NW Mexico
Canarias, Islas *70 A2 Eng.* Canary Islands. *island group* Islas Canarias, SW Spain Europe E Atlantic Ocean
Canarreos, Archipiélago de los *54 B2 island group* W Cuba
Canary Islands *see* Canarias, Islas
Cañas *52 D4* Guanacaste, NW Costa Rica
Canaveral, Cape *43 E4 headland* Florida, SE USA
Canavieiras *63 G3* Bahia, E Brazil
Canberra *142 C4 country capital* (Australia) Australian Capital Territory, SE Australia
Cancún *51 H3* Quintana Roo, SE Mexico
Candia *see* Irákleio
Canea *see* Chaniá
Cangzhou *128 D4* Hebei, E China
Caniapiscau *39 E2 river* Québec, E Canada
Caniapiscau, Réservoir de *38 D3 reservoir* Québec, C Canada
Canik Dağları *116 D2 mountain range* N Turkey
Canillo *91 A7* Canillo, C Andorra Europe
Çankırı *116 C3 var.* Chankiri; *anc.* Gangra, Germanicopolis. Çankın, N Turkey
Cannanore *132 B2 var.* Kananur, Kannur. Kerala, SW India
Cannes *91 D6* Alpes-Maritimes, SE France
Canoas *63 E5* Rio Grande do Sul, S Brazil
Canon City *44 C5* Colorado, C USA
Cantabria *92 D1 autonomous community* N Spain
Cantábrica, Cordillera *92 C1 mountain range* N Spain
Cantabrigia *see* Cambridge
Cantaura *59 E2* Anzoátegui, NE Venezuela
Canterbury *89 E7 hist.* Cantwaraburh; *anc.* Durovernum, *Lat.* Cantuaria. SE England, UK
Canterbury Bight *151 C6 bight* South Island, New Zealand
Canterbury Plains *151 C6 plain* South Island, New Zealand
Cân Thơ *137 E6* Cân Thơ, S Vietnam
Canton *42 B2* Mississippi, S USA
Canton *40 D4* Ohio, N USA
Canton *see* Guangzhou
Canton Island *see* Kanton
Cantuaria/Cantwaraburh *see* Canterbury
Canyon *49 E2* Texas, SW USA
Cao Băng *136 D3 var.* Caobang. Cao Băng, N Vietnam
Caobang *see* Cao Băng
Cap-Breton, Île du *see* Cape Breton Island
Cape Barren Island *149 C8 island* Furneaux Group, Tasmania, SE Australia
Cape Basin *69 B7 undersea basin* S Atlantic Ocean
Cape Breton Island *39 G4 Fr.* Île du Cap-Breton. *island* Nova Scotia, SE Canada
Cape Charles *41 F5* Virginia, NE USA
Cape Coast *75 E5 prev.* Cape Coast Castle. S Ghana
Cape Coast Castle *see* Cape Coast
Cape Girardeau *45 H5* Missouri, C USA
Capelle aan den IJssel *86 C4* Zuid-Holland, SW Netherlands
Cape Palmas *see* Harper
Cape Saint Jacques *see* Vung Tau
Cape Town *78 B5 var.* Ekapa, *Afr.* Kaapstad, Kapstad. *country capital* (South Africa-legislative capital) Western Cape, SW South Africa
Cape Verde *74 A2 off.* Republic of Cape Verde, *Port.* Cabo Verde, Ilhas do Cabo Verde. *country* E Atlantic Ocean

CAPE VERDE
Atlantic Ocean

Official name Republic of Cape Verde
Formation 1975
Capital Praia
Population 507,000 / 326 people per sq mile (126 people per sq km) / 62%
Total area 1557 sq miles (4033 sq km)
Languages Portuguese*, Portuguese Creole
Religions Roman Catholic 97%, Other 2%, Protestant (Church of the Nazarene) 1%
Ethnic mix Mestiço 60%, African 30%, Other 10%
Government Mixed presidential–parliamentary system
Currency Cape Verde escudo = 100 centavos
Literacy rate 76%
Calorie consumption 3243 calories

Cape Verde Basin *66 C4 undersea basin* E Atlantic Ocean
Cape Verde Plain *66 C4 abyssal plain* E Atlantic Ocean
Cape Verde, Republic of *see* Cape Verde
Cape York Peninsula *148 C2 peninsula* Queensland, N Australia
Cap-Haïtien *54 D3 var.* Le Cap. N Haiti
Capira *53 G5* Panamá, C Panama
Capitán Arturo Prat *154 A2 Chilean research station* South Shetland Islands, Antarctica
Capitán Pablo Lagerenza *64 D1 var.* Mayor Pablo Lagerenza. Chaco, N Paraguay
Capodistria *see* Koper
Capri, Isola di *97 C5 island* S Italy
Caprivi Concession *see* Caprivi Strip
Caprivi Strip *78 C3 Ger.* Caprivizipfel; *prev.* Caprivi Concession. *cultural region* NE Namibia
Caprivizipfel *see* Caprivi Strip
Cap Saint-Jacques *see* Vung Tau
Caquetá *56 B3 off.* Departamanto del Caquetá. *province* S Colombia
Caquetá, Departamanto del *see* Caquetá
Caquetá, Río *58 C5 var.* Rio Japurá, Yapurá. *river* Brazil/Colombia
Caquetá, Río *see* Japurá, Rio
CAR *see* Central African Republic
Caracal *108 B5* Olt, S Romania
Caracaraí *62 D1* Rondônia, W Brazil
Caracas *58 D1 country capital* (Venezuela) Distrito Federal, N Venezuela
Caralis *see* Cagliari
Caratasca, Laguna de *53 E2 lagoon* NE Honduras
Carballiño *see* O Carballiño
Carbondale *40 B5* Illinois, N USA
Carbonia *97 A6 var.* Carbonia Centro. Sardegna, Italy, C Mediterranean Sea
Carbonia Centro *see* Carbonia
Carcaso *see* Carcassonne
Carcassonne *91 C6 anc.* Carcaso. Aude, S France
Cardamomes, Chaîne des *see* Krâvanh, Chuŏr Phnum
Cardamom Mountains *see* Krâvanh, Chuŏr Phnum
Cárdenas *54 B2* Matanzas, W Cuba
Cardiff *89 C7 Wel.* Caerdydd. *national capital* S Wales, UK
Cardigan Bay *89 C6 bay* W Wales, UK
Carei *108 B3 Ger.* Gross-Karol, Karol, *Hung.* Nagykároly; *prev.* Careii-Mari. Satu Mare, NW Romania
Careii-Mari *see* Carei
Carey, Lake *147 B6 lake* Western Australia
Cariaco *59 E1* Sucre, NE Venezuela
Caribbean Sea *54 C4 sea* W Atlantic Ocean
Caribrod *see* Dimitrovgrad
Carlisle *88 C4 anc.* Caer Luel, Luguvallium, Luguvallum. NW England, UK
Carlow *89 B6 Ir.* Ceatharlach. SE Ireland
Carlsbad *48 D3* New Mexico, SW USA
Carlsbad *see* Karlovy Vary
Carlsberg Ridge *140 B4 undersea ridge* S Arabian Sea
Carlsruhe *see* Karlsruhe
Carmana/Carmania *see* Kermān
Carmarthen *89 C6* SW Wales, UK
Carmaux *91 C6* Tarn, S France
Carmel *40 C4* Indiana, N USA
Carmelita *52 B1* Petén, N Guatemala
Carmen *51 G4 var.* Ciudad del Carmen. Campeche, SE Mexico
Carmona *92 C4* Andalucía, S Spain
Carmona *see* Uíge
Carnaro *see* Kvarner
Carnarvon *147 A5* Western Australia
Carnegie, Lake *147 B5 salt lake* Western Australia
Car Nicobar *133 F3 island* Nicobar Islands, India, NE Indian Ocean
Caroąo, Ilha *76 E1 island* N Sao Tome and Principe, Africa, E Atlantic Ocean
Carolina *63 F2* Maranhão, E Brazil
Caroline Island *see* Millennium Island
Caroline Islands *106 C2 island group* C Micronesia
Carolopois *see* Châlons-en-Champagne
Caroní, Río *59 E3 river* E Venezuela
Caronium *see* A Coruña
Carora *58 C1* Lara, N Venezuela
Carpathian Mountains *81 E4 var.* Carpathians, *Cz./Pol.* Karpaty, *Ger.* Karpaten. *mountain range* E Europe
Carpathians *see* Carpathian Mountains
Carpathos/Carpathus *see* Kárpathos
Carpaţii Meridionali *108 B4 var.* Alpi Transilvaniei, Carpaţii Sudici, *Eng.* South Carpathians, Transylvanian Alps, *Ger.* Südkarpaten, Transsylvanische Alpen, *Hung.* Déli-Kárpátok, Erdélyi-Havasok. *mountain range* C Romania
Carpaţii Occidentali *99 E7 mountain range* W Romania Europe
Carpaţii Sudici *see* Carpaţii Meridionali
Carpentaria, Gulf of *148 B2 gulf* N Australia
Carpi *96 C2* Emilia-Romagna, N Italy
Carrara *96 B3* Toscana, C Italy
Carson City *47 C5 state capital* Nevada, W USA
Carson Sink *47 C5 salt flat* Nevada, W USA
Carstensz, Puntjak *see* Jaya, Puncak
Cartagena *58 B1 var.* Cartagena de los Indes. Bolívar, NW Colombia
Cartagena *93 F4 anc.* Carthago Nova. Murcia, SE Spain
Cartagena de los Indes *see* Cartagena
Cartago *53 E4* Cartago, C Costa Rica
Carthage *45 F5* Missouri, C USA
Carthago Nova *see* Cartagena
Cartwright *39 F2* Newfoundland and Labrador, E Canada
Carúpano *59 E1* Sucre, NE Venezuela
Carusbur *see* Cherbourg
Caruthersville *45 H5* Missouri, C USA
Cary *43 F1* North Carolina, SE USA
Casablanca *70 C2 Ar.* Dar-el-Beida. NW Morocco
Casa Grande *48 B2* Arizona, SW USA
Cascade Range *46 B3 mountain range* Oregon/Washington, NW USA
Cascadia Basin *34 A4 undersea basin* NE Pacific Ocean
Cascais *92 B4* Lisboa, C Portugal
Caserta *97 D5* Campania, S Italy
Casey *154 D4 Australian research station* Antarctica
Casino *91 C8* New South Wales, SE Australia
Čáslav *99 B5 Ger.* Tschaslau. Střední Čechy, C Czech Republic
Casper *44 C3* Wyoming, C USA
Caspian Depression *111 B7 Kaz.* Kaspīy Mangy Oypaty, *Rus.* Prikaspiyskaya Nizmennost'. *depression* Kazakhstan/Russian Federation
Caspian Sea *114 A4 Az.* Xäzär Dänizi, *Kaz.* Kaspiy Tengizi, *Per.* Baḩr-e Khazar, Daryā-ye Khazar, *Rus.* Kaspiyskoye More. *inland sea* Asia/Europe
Cassai *see* Kasai
Cassel *see* Kassel
Castamoni *see* Kastamonu
Casteggio *96 B2* Lombardia, N Italy
Castelló de la Plana *see* Castellón de la Plana
Castellón *see* Castellón de la Plana
Castellón de la Plana *93 F3 Cat.* Castelló de la Plana, Castellón. País Valenciano, E Spain
Castelnaudary *91 C6* Aude, S France
Castelo Branco *92 C3* Castelo Branco, C Portugal
Castelsarrasin *91 B6* Tarn-et-Garonne, S France
Castelvetrano *97 C7* Sicilia, Italy, C Mediterranean Sea
Castilla-La Mancha *93 E3 autonomous community* NE Spain
Castilla-León *92 C2 var.* Castillia y Leon. *autonomous community* NW Spain
Castillia y Leon *see* Castilla-León
Castlebar *89 A5 Ir.* Caisleán an Bharraigh. W Ireland
Castleford *89 D5* N England, UK
Castle Harbour *42 B5 inlet* Bermuda, NW Atlantic Ocean
Castra Regina *see* Regensburg
Castricum *86 C3* Noord-Holland, W Netherlands
Castries *55 F1 country capital* (Saint Lucia) N Saint Lucia
Castro *65 B6* Los Lagos, W Chile
Castrovillari *97 D6* Calabria, SW Italy
Castuera *92 D4* Extremadura, W Spain
Caswell Sound *151 A7 sound* South Island, New Zealand
Catacamas *52 D2* Olancho, C Honduras
Catacaos *60 B3* Piura, NW Peru
Catalan Bay *93 H4 bay* E Gibraltar Europe Mediterranean Sea Atlantic Ocean
Cataluña *93 G2 cultural region* N Spain Europe
Catamarca *see* San Fernando del Valle de Catamarca
Catania *97 D7* Sicilia, Italy, C Mediterranean Sea
Catanzaro *97 D6* Calabria, SW Italy
Catarroja *93 F3* País Valenciano, E Spain
Cat Island *54 C1 island* C Bahamas
Catskill Mountains *41 F3 mountain range* New York, NE USA
Cattaro *see* Kotor
Cauca, Río *58 B2 river* N Colombia
Caucasia *58 B2* Antioquia, NW Colombia
Caucasus *81 G4 Rus.* Kavkaz. *mountain range* Georgia/Russian Federation
Caura, Río *59 E3 river* C Venezuela
Cavaia *see* Kavajë
Cavalla *74 D5 var.* Cavally, Cavally Fleuve. *river* Côte d'Ivoire (Ivory Coast)/Liberia
Cavally/Cavally Fleuve *see* Cavalla
Caviana de Fora, Ilha *63 E1 var.* Ilha Caviana. *island* N Brazil
Caviana, Ilha *see* Caviana de Fora, Ilha
Cawnpore *see* Kānpur
Caxamarca *see* Cajamarca
Caxito *78 B1* Bengo, NW Angola
Cayenne *59 H3 dependent territory/arrondissement capital* (French Guiana) NE French Guiana
Cayes *54 D3 var.* Les Cayes. SW Haiti
Cayman Brac *54 B3 island* E Cayman Islands
Cayman Islands *54 B3 UK dependent territory* W West Indies
Cayo *see* San Ignacio
Cay Sal *54 B2 islet* SW Bahamas
Cazin *100 B3* Federacija Bosna I Hercegovina, NW Bosnia and Herzegovina
Cazorla *93 E4* Andalucía, S Spain
Ceadâr-Lunga *see* Ciadîr-Lunga
Ceará *63 F2 off.* Estado do Ceará. *state* C Brazil
Ceará *see* Fortaleza
Ceara Abyssal Plain *see* Ceará Plain
Ceará, Estado do *see* Ceará
Ceará Plain *56 E3 var.* Ceara Abyssal Plain. *abyssal plain* W Atlantic Ocean
Ceatharlach *see* Carlow
Cébaco, Isla *53 F5 island* SW Panama
Cebu *139 E2 off.* Cebu City. Cebu, C Philippines
Cebu City *see* Cebu
Čechy *see* Bohemia
Cecina *96 B3* Toscana, C Italy

Cedar City *44 A5* Utah, W USA
Cedar Falls *45 G3* Iowa, C USA
Cedar Lake *38 A2 lake* Manitoba, C Canada
Cedar Rapids *45 G3* Iowa, C USA
Cedros, Isla *50 A2 island* W Mexico
Ceduna *149 A6* South Australia
Cefalù *97 C7 anc.* Cephaloedium. Sicilia, Italy, C Mediterranean Sea
Celebes *see* Sulawesi
Celebes Sea *139 E3 Ind.* Laut Sulawesi. *sea* Indonesia/Philippines
Celje *95 E7 Ger.* Cilli. C Slovenia
Celldömölk *99 C6* Vas, W Hungary
Celle *94 B3 var.* Zelle. Niedersachsen, N Germany
Celovec *see* Klagenfurt
Celtic Sea *89 B7 Ir.* An Mhuir Cheilteach. *sea* SW British Isles
Celtic Shelf *80 B3 continental shelf* E Atlantic Ocean
Cenderawasih, Teluk *139 G4 var.* Teluk Irian, Teluk Sarera. *bay* W Pacific Ocean
Cenon *91 B5* Gironde, SW France
Centennial State *see* Colorado
Centrafricaine, République *see* Central African Republic
Central African Republic *76 C4 var.* République Centrafricaine, *abbrev.* CAR; *prev.* Ubangi-Shari, Oubangui-Chari, Territoire de l'Oubangui-Chari. *country* C Africa

CENTRAL AFRICAN REPUBLIC
Central Africa

Official name Central African Republic
Formation 1960 / 1960
Capital Bangui
Population 4 million / 17 people per sq mile
(6 people per sq km) / 41%
Total area 240,534 sq miles (622,984 sq km)
Languages Sango, Banda, Gbaya, French
Religions Traditional beliefs 60%, Christian (mainly Roman Catholic) 35%, Muslim 5%
Ethnic mix Baya 34%, Banda 27%, Mandjia 21%, Sara 10%, Other 8%
Government Presidential system
Currency CFA franc = 100 centimes
Literacy rate 49%
Calorie consumption 1980 calories

Central, Cordillera *58 B3 mountain range* W Colombia
Central, Cordillera *55 E3 mountain range* C Dominican Republic
Central, Cordillera *53 F5 mountain range* C Panama
Central, Cordillera *139 E1 mountain range* Luzon, N Philippines
Central Group *see* Inner Islands
Centralia *46 B2* Washington, NW USA
Central Indian Ridge *see* Mid-Indian Ridge
Central Makrän Range *134 A3 mountain range* W Pakistan
Central Pacific Basin *142 D1 undersea basin* C Pacific Ocean
Central, Planalto *63 F3 var.* Brazilian Highlands. *mountain range* E Brazil
Central Provinces and Berar *see* Madhya Pradesh
Central Range *144 B3 mountain range* NW Papua New Guinea
Central Russian Upland *see* Srednerusskaya Vozvyshennost'
Central Siberian Plateau/Central Siberian Uplands *see* Srednesibirskoye Ploskogor'ye
Central, Sistema *92 D3 mountain range* C Spain
Central Valley *47 B6 valley* California, W USA
Centum Cellae *see* Civitavecchia
Ceos *see* Tziá
Cephaloedium *see* Cefalù
Ceram *see* Seram, Pulau
Ceram Sea *139 F4 Ind.* Laut Seram. *sea* E Indonesia
Cerasus *see* Giresun
Cereté *58 B2* Córdoba, NW Colombia
Cergy-Pontoise *see* Pontoise

Cerignola *97 D5* Puglia, SE Italy
Çerkes *116 C2* Çankın, N Turkey
Cernăuți *see* Chernivtsi
Cernay *90 E4* Haut-Rhin, NE France
Cerro de Pasco *60 C3* Pasco, C Peru
Cervera *93 F2* Cataluña, NE Spain
Cervino, Monte *see* Matterhorn
Cesena *96 C3 anc.* Caesena. Emilia-Romagna, N Italy
Cēsis *106 D3 Ger.* Wenden. Cēsis, C Latvia
Česká Republika *see* Czech Republic
České Budějovice *99 B5 Ger.* Budweis. Jihočeský Kraj, S Czech Republic
Český Krumlov *99 A5 var.* Böhmisch-Krumau, *Ger.* Krummau. Jihočeský Kraj, S Czech Republic
Český Les *see* Bohemian Forest
Cetatea Damboviței *see* București
Cetinje *101 C5 It.* Cettigne. S Montenegro
Cette *see* Sète
Cettigne *see* Cetinje
Ceuta *70 C2 enclave* Spain, N Africa
Cévennes *91 C6 mountain range* S France
Ceyhan *116 D4* Adana, S Turkey
Ceylanpinar *117 E4* Şanlıurfa, SE Turkey
Ceylon *see* Sri Lanka
Ceylon Plain *124 B4 abyssal plain* N Indian Ocean
Ceyre to the Caribs *see* Marie-Galante
Chachapoyas *60 B2* Amazonas, NW Peru
Chachevichy *107 D6 Rus.* Chechevichi. Mahilyowskaya Voblasts', E Belarus
Chaco *see* Gran Chaco
Chad *76 C3 off.* Republic of Chad, *Fr.* Tchad. *country* C Africa

CHAD
Central Africa

Official name Republic of Chad
Formation 1960 / 1960
Capital N'Djamena
Population 9.7 million / 20 people per sq mile (8 people per sq km) / 24%
Total area 495,752 sq miles (1,284,000 sq km)
Languages French, Sara, Arabic, Maba
Religions Muslim 55%, Traditional beliefs 35%, Christian 10%
Ethnic mix Nomads (Tuareg and Toubou) 38%, Sara 30%, Other 17%, Arab 15%
Government Presidential system
Currency CFA franc = 100 centimes
Literacy rate 26%
Calorie consumption 2114 calories

Chad, Lake *76 B3 Fr.* Lac Tchad. *lake* C Africa
Chad, Republic of *see* Chad
Chadron *44 D3* Nebraska, C USA
Chadyr-Lunga *see* Ciadir-Lunga
Chägai Hills *134 A2 var.* Chāh Gay. *mountain range* Afghanistan/Pakistan
Chaghasarāy *see* Asadābād
Chagos-Laccadive Plateau *124 B4 undersea plateau* N Indian Ocean
Chagos Trench *141 C5 trench* N Indian Ocean
Chāh Gay *see* Chägai Hills
Chaillu, Massif du *77 B6 mountain range* C Gabon
Chain Ridge *140 B4 undersea ridge* W Indian Ocean
Chajul *52 B2* Quiché, W Guatemala
Chakhānsūr *122 D5* Nīmrūz, SW Afghanistan
Chala *60 D4* Arequipa, SW Peru
Chalatenango *52 C3* Chalatenango, N El Salvador
Chalcedon *see* Kadıköy
Chalcidice *see* Chalkidikí
Chalcis *see* Chalkída
Chálki *105 E7 island* Dodekánisa, Greece, Aegean Sea
Chalkída *105 C5 var.* Halkída, *prev.* Khalkís; *anc.* Chalcis. Évvoia, E Greece
Chalkidikí *104 C4 var.* Khalkidhikí; *anc.* Chalcidice. *peninsula* NE Greece
Challans *90 B4* Vendée, NW France
Challapata *61 F4* Oruro, SW Bolivia
Challenger Deep *152 B3 trench* W Pacific Ocean
Challenger Deep *see* Mariana Trench
Challenger Fracture Zone *153 F4 tectonic feature* SE Pacific Ocean

Châlons-en-Champagne *90 D3 prev.* Châlons-sur-Marne, *hist.* Arcae Remorum; *anc.* Carolopois. Marne, NE France
Châlons-sur-Marne *see* Châlons-en-Champagne
Chalon-sur-Saône *90 D4 anc.* Cabillonum. Saône-et-Loire, C France
Cha Mai *see* Thung Song
Chaman *134 B2* Baluchistān, SW Pakistan
Chambéry *91 D5 anc.* Cambaria. Savoie, E France
Champagne *90 D3* Yukon Territory, W Canada
Champagne *see* Campania
Champaign *40 B4* Illinois, N USA
Champasak *137 D5* Champasak, S Laos
Champlain, Lake *41 F2 lake* Canada/USA
Champotón *51 G4* Campeche, SE Mexico
Chanak *see* Çanakkale
Chañaral *64 B3* Atacama, N Chile
Chan-chiang/Chanchiang *see* Zhanjiang
Chandeleur Islands *42 C3 island group* Louisiana, S USA
Chandīgarh *134 D2 state capital* Punjab, N India
Chandrapur *135 E5* Mahārāshtra, C India
Changan *see* Xi'an
Changane *79 E3 river* S Mozambique
Changchun *128 D3 var.* Ch'angch'un, Ch'ang-ch'un; *prev.* Hsinking. *province capital* Jilin, NE China
Chang Jiang *128 B5 var.* Yangtze Kiang, *Eng.* Yangtze. *river* C China
Changkiakow *see* Zhangjiakou
Chang, Ko *137 C6 island* S Thailand
Changsha *128 C5 var.* Ch'angsha, Ch'ang-sha. *province capital* Hunan, S China
Ch'angsha/Ch'ang-sha *see* Changsha
Changzhi *128 C4* Shanxi, C China
Chaniá *105 C7 var.* Hania, Khaniá, *Eng.* Canea; *anc.* Cydonia. Kríti, Greece, E Mediterranean Sea
Chañi, Nevado de *64 B2 mountain* NW Argentina
Chankiri *see* Çankırı
Channel Islands *89 C8 Fr.* Iles Normandes. *island group* S English Channel
Channel Islands *47 B8 island group* California, W USA
Channel, The *see* English Channel
Channel-Port aux Basques *39 G4* Newfoundland, Newfoundland and Labrador, SE Canada
Channel Tunnel *90 C2 tunnel* France/UK
Chantabun/Chantaburi *see* Chanthaburi
Chantada *92 C1* Galicia, NW Spain
Chanthaburi *137 C6 var.* Chantabun, Chantaburi. Chantaburi, S Thailand
Chanute *45 F5* Kansas, C USA
Chaouèn *see* Chefchaouen
Chaoyang *128 D3* Liaoning, NE China
Chapala, Lago de *50 D4 lake* C Mexico
Chapan, Gora *122 B3 mountain* C Turkmenistan
Chapayevsk *111 C6* Samarskaya Oblast', W Russian Federation
Chaplynka *109 F4* Khersons'ka Oblast', S Ukraine
Chapra *see* Chhapra
Charcot Seamounts *80 B3 seamount range* E Atlantic Ocean
Chardzhev *see* Türkmenabat
Chardzhou/Chardzhui *see* Türkmenabat
Charente *91 B5 department* W France
Charente *91 B5 cultural region* W France
Charente *91 B5 river* W France
Chari *76 B3 var.* Shari. *river* Central African Republic/Chad
Chärikär *123 E4* Parvān, NE Afghanistan
Charity *59 F2* NW Guyana
Chärjew *see* Türkmenabat
Charkhlik/Charkhliq *see* Ruoqiang
Charleroi *87 C7* Hainaut, S Belgium
Charlesbourg *39 E4* Québec, SE Canada
Charles de Gaulle *90 E1* (Paris) Seine-et-Marne, N France
Charles Island *38 D1 island* Nunavut, NE Canada
Charles Island *see* Santa María, Isla

Charleston *43 F2* South Carolina, SE USA
Charleston *40 D5 state capital* West Virginia, NE USA
Charleville *149 D5* Queensland, E Australia
Charleville-Mézières *90 D3* Ardennes, N France
Charlie-Gibbs Fracture Zone *66 C2 tectonic feature* N Atlantic Ocean
Charlotte *43 E1* North Carolina, SE USA
Charlotte Amalie *55 F3 prev.* Saint Thomas. *dependent territory capital* (Virgin Islands (US)) Saint Thomas, N Virgin Islands (US)
Charlotte Harbor *43 E5 inlet* Florida, SE USA
Charlottenhof *see* Aegviidu
Charlottesville *41 E5* Virginia, NE USA
Charlottetown *39 F4 province capital* Prince Edward Island, Prince Edward Island, SE Canada
Charlotte Town *see* Roseau
Charsk *see* Shar
Charters Towers *148 D3* Queensland, NE Australia
Chartres *90 C3 anc.* Autricum, Civitas Carnutum. Eure-et-Loir, C France
Chashniki *107 D5 Rus.* Chashniki. Vitsyebskaya Voblasts', N Belarus
Châteaubriant *90 B4* Loire-Atlantique, NW France
Châteaudun *90 C3* Eure-et-Loir, C France
Châteauroux *90 C4 prev.* Indreville. Indre, C France
Château-Thierry *90 C3* Aisne, N France
Châtelet *87 C7* Hainaut, S Belgium
Châtelherault *see* Châtellerault
Châtellerault *90 B4 var.* Châtelherault. Vienne, W France
Chatham Island *see* San Cristóbal, Isla
Chatham Island Rise *see* Chatham Rise
Chatham Islands *143 E5 island group* New Zealand, SW Pacific Ocean
Chatham Rise *142 D5 var.* Chatham Island Rise. *undersea rise* S Pacific Ocean
Chatkal Range *123 F2 Rus.* Chatkal'skiy Khrebet. *mountain range* Kyrgyzstan/Uzbekistan
Chatkal'skiy Khrebet *see* Chatkal Range
Chättagám *see* Chittagong
Chattahoochee River *42 D3 river* SE USA
Chattanooga *42 D1* Tennessee, S USA
Chatyr-Tash *123 G2* Narynskaya Oblast', C Kyrgyzstan
Châu Ðôc *137 D6 var.* Chauphu, Chau Phu. An Giang, S Vietnam
Chauk *136 A3* Magwe, W Myanmar (Burma)
Chaumont *90 D4 prev.* Chaumont-en-Bassigny. Haute-Marne, N France
Chaumont-en-Bassigny *see* Chaumont
Chau Phu *see* Châu Ðôc
Chausy *see* Chavusy
Chaves *92 C2 anc.* Aquae Flaviae. Vila Real, N Portugal
Chávez, Isla *see* Santa Cruz, Isla
Chavusy *107 E6 Rus.* Chausy. Mahilyowskaya Voblasts', E Belarus
Chaykovskiy *111 D5* Permskaya Oblast', NW Russian Federation
Cheb *99 A5 Ger.* Eger. Karlovarský Kraj, W Czech Republic
Cheboksary *111 C5* Chavash Respubliki, W Russian Federation
Cheboygan *40 C2* Michigan, N USA
Chechaouèn *see* Chefchaouen
Chech, Erg *74 D1 desert* Algeria/Mali
Chechevichi *see* Chachevichy
Che-chiang *see* Zhejiang
Cheduba Island *136 A4 island* W Myanmar (Burma)
Chefchaouen *70 C2 var.* Chaouèn, Chechaouèn, Sp. Xauen. N Morocco
Chefoo *see* Yantai
Cheju-do *129 E4 Jap.* Saishū; *prev.* Quelpart. *island* S South Korea
Cheju-haehyŏp *129 E4 strait* S South Korea
Chekiang *see* Zhejiang
Cheleken *see* Hazar
Chelkar *see* Shalkar
Chełm *98 E4 Rus.* Kholm. Lubelskie, SE Poland

INDEX - GAZETTEER: **Chełmno – Chulym**

Chełmno *98 C3 Ger.* Culm, Kulm. Kujawski-pomorskie, C Poland
Chełmża *98 C3 Ger.* Culmsee, Kulmsee. Kujawski-pomorskie, C Poland
Cheltenham *89 D6* C England, UK
Chelyabinsk *114 C3* Chelyabinskaya Oblast', C Russian Federation
Chemnitz *94 D4 prev.* Karl-Marx-Stadt. Sachsen, E Germany
Chemulpo *see* Inch'ŏn
Chenāb *134 C2 river* India/Pakistan
Chengchiatun *see* Liaoyuan
Ch'eng-chou/Chengchow *see* Zhengzhou
Chengde *128 D3 var.* Jehol. Hebei, E China
Chengdu *128 B5 var.* Chengtu, Ch'eng-tu. *province capital* Sichuan, C China
Chenghsien *see* Zhengzhou
Chengtu/Ch'eng-tu *see* Chengdu
Chennai *132 D2 prev.* Madras. *state capital* Tamil Nādu, S India
Chenstokhov *see* Częstochowa
Chen Xian/Chenxian/Chen Xiang *see* Chenzhou
Chenzhou *128 C6 var.* Chenxian, Chen Xian, Chen Xiang. Hunan, S China
Chepelare *104 C3* Smolyan, S Bulgaria
Chepén *60 B3* La Libertad, C Peru
Cher *90 C4 river* C France
Cherbourg *90 B3 anc.* Carusbur. Manche, N France
Cherepovets *110 B4* Vologodskaya Oblast', NW Russian Federation
Chergui, Chott ech *70 D2 salt lake* NW Algeria
Cherikov *see* Cherykaw
Cherkassy *see* Cherkasy
Cherkasy *109 E2 Rus.* Cherkassy. Cherkas'ka Oblast', C Ukraine
Cherkessk *111 B7* Karachayevo-Cherkesskaya Respublika, SW Russian Federation
Chernigov *see* Chernihiv
Chernihiv *109 E1 Rus.* Chernigov. Chernihivs'ka Oblast', NE Ukraine
Chernivtsi *108 C3 Ger.* Czernowitz, *Rom.* Cernăuţi, *Rus.* Chernovtsy. Chernivets'ka Oblast', W Ukraine
Cherno More *see* Black Sea
Chernomorskoye *see* Chornomors'ke
Chernovtsy *see* Chernivtsi
Chernoye More *see* Black Sea
Chernyakhovsk *106 A4 Ger.* Insterburg. Kaliningradskaya Oblast', W Russian Federation
Cherry Hill *41 F4* New Jersey, NE USA
Cherski Range *see* Cherskogo, Khrebet
Cherskiy *115 G2* Respublika Sakha (Yakutiya), NE Russian Federation
Cherskogo, Khrebet *115 F2 var.* Cherski Range. *mountain range* NE Russian Federation
Cherso *see* Cres
Cherven' *see* Chervyen'
Chervonograd *see* Chervonohrad
Chervonohrad *108 C2 Rus.* Chervonograd. L'vivs'ka Oblast', NW Ukraine
Chervyen' *107 D6 Rus.* Cherven'. Minskaya Voblasts', C Belarus
Cherykaw *107 E7 Rus.* Cherikov. Mahilyowskaya Voblasts', E Belarus
Chesapeake Bay *41 F5 inlet* NE USA
Chesha Bay *see* Chëshskaya Guba
Chëshskaya Guba *172 D5 var.* Archangel Bay, Chesha Bay, Dvina Bay. *bay* NW Russian Federation
Chester *89 C6 Wel.* Caerleon, *hist.* Legaceaster, *Lat.* Deva, Devana Castra. C England, UK
Chetumal *51 H4 var.* Payo Obispo. Quintana Roo, SE Mexico
Cheviot Hills *88 D4 hill range* England/Scotland, UK
Cheyenne *44 D4 state capital* Wyoming, C USA
Cheyenne River *44 D3 river* South Dakota/Wyoming, N USA
Chezdi-Oşorheiu *see* Târgu Secuiesc
Chhapra *135 F3 prev.* Chapra. Bihār, N India
Chhattīsgarh *135 E4 state* E India
Chhattīsgarh *135 E4 cultural region* E India
Chiai *128 D6 var.* Chia-i, Chiayi, Kiayi, Jiayi, *Jap.* Kagi. C Taiwan
Chia-i *see* Chiai
Chiang-hsi *see* Jiangxi
Chiang Mai *136 B4 var.* Chiangmai, Chiengmai, Kiangmai. Chiang Mai, NW Thailand
Chiangmai *see* Chiang Mai
Chiang Rai *136 C3 var.* Chianpai, Chienrai, Muang Chiang Rai. Chiang Rai, NW Thailand
Chiang-su *see* Jiangsu
Chianning/Chian-ning *see* Nanjing
Chianpai *see* Chiang Rai
Chianti *96 C3 cultural region* C Italy
Chiapa *see* Chiapa de Corzo
Chiapa de Corzo *51 G5 var.* Chiapa. Chiapas, SE Mexico
Chiayi *see* Chiai
Chiba *130 B1 var.* Tiba. Chiba, Honshū, S Japan
Chibougamau *38 D3* Québec, SE Canada
Chicago *40 B3* Illinois, N USA
Ch'i-ch'i-ha-erh *see* Qiqihar
Chickasha *49 G2* Oklahoma, C USA
Chiclayo *60 B3* Lambayeque, NW Peru
Chico *47 B5* California, W USA
Chico, Río *65 B7 river* SE Argentina
Chico, Río *65 B6 river* S Argentina
Chicoutimi *39 E4* Québec, SE Canada
Chiengmai *see* Chiang Mai
Chienrai *see* Chiang Rai
Chiesanuova *96 D2* SW San Marino
Chieti *96 D4 var.* Teate. Abruzzo, C Italy
Chifeng *127 G2 var.* Ulanhad. Nei Mongol Zizhiqu, N China
Chigirin *see* Chyhyryn
Chih-fu *see* Yantai
Chihli *see* Hebei
Chihli, Gulf of *see* Bo Hai
Chihuahua *50 C2* Chihuahua, NW Mexico
Childress *49 F2* Texas, SW USA
Chile *64 B3 off.* Republic of Chile. *country* SW South America

CHILE
South America

Official name Republic of Chile
Formation 1818 / 1883
Capital Santiago
Population 16.3 million / 56 people per sq mile (22 people per sq km) / 86%
Total area 292,258 sq miles (756,950 sq km)
Languages Spanish*, Amerindian languages
Religions Roman Catholic 80%, Other and nonreligious 20%
Ethnic mix Mixed race and European 90%, Amerindian 10%
Government Presidential system
Currency Chilean peso = 100 centavos
Literacy rate 96%
Calorie consumption 2863 calories

Chile Basin *57 A5 undersea basin* E Pacific Ocean
Chile Chico *65 B6* Aisén, W Chile
Chile, Republic of *see* Chile
Chile Rise *57 A7 undersea rise* SE Pacific Ocean
Chilia-Nouă *see* Kiliya
Chililabombwe *78 D2* Copperbelt, C Zambia
Chi-lin *see* Jilin
Chillán *65 B5* Bío Bío, C Chile
Chillicothe *40 D4* Ohio, N USA
Chill Mhantáin, Sléibhte *see* Wicklow Mountains
Chiloé, Isla de *65 A6 var.* Isla Grande de Chiloé. *island* W Chile
Chilpancingo *51 E5 var.* Chilpancingo de los Bravos. Guerrero, S Mexico
Chilpancingo de los Bravos *see* Chilpancingo
Chilung *128 D6 var.* Keelung, *Jap.* Kirun, Kirun'; *prev. Sp.* Santissima Trinidad. N Taiwan
Chimán *53 G5* Panamá, E Panama
Chimbay *see* Chimboy
Chimborazo *60 A1 volcano* C Ecuador
Chimbote *60 C3* Ancash, W Peru
Chimboy *122 D1 Rus.* Chimbay. Qoraqalpog'iston Respublikasi, NW Uzbekistan
Chimkent *see* Shymkent
Chimoio *79 E3* Manica, C Mozambique
China *124 C2 off.* People's Republic of China, *Chin.* Chung-hua Jen-min Kung-ho-kuo, Zhonghua Renmin Gongheguo; *prev.* Chinese Empire. *country* E Asia

CHINA
East Asia

Official name People's Republic of China
Formation 960 / 1999
Capital Beijing
Population 1.32 billion / 365 people per sq mile (141 people per sq km) / 32%
Total area 3,705,386 sq miles (9,596,960 sq km)
Languages Mandarin*, Wu, Cantonese, Hsiang, Min, Hakka, Kan
Religions Nonreligious 59%, Traditional beliefs 20%, Other 13%, Buddhist 6%, Muslim 2%
Ethnic mix Han 92%, Other 6%, Hui 1%, Zhuang 1%
Government One-party state
Currency Renminbi (known as yuan) = 10 jiao
Literacy rate 91%
Calorie consumption 2951 calories

Chi-nan/Chinan *see* Jinan
Chinandega *52 C3* Chinandega, NW Nicaragua
China, People's Republic of *see* China
China, Republic of *see* Taiwan
Chincha Alta *60 D4* Ica, SW Peru
Chin-chiang *see* Quanzhou
Chin-chou/Chinchow *see* Jinzhou
Chindwin *136 B2 river* N Myanmar (Burma)
Chinese Empire *see* China
Chinghai *see* Qinghai, China
Ch'ing Hai *see* Qinghai Hu, China
Chingola *78 D2* Copperbelt, C Zambia
Ching-Tao/Ch'ing-tao *see* Qingdao
Chinguețți *74 C2 var.* Chinguetti. Adrar, C Mauritania
Chin Hills *136 A3 mountain range* W Myanmar (Burma)
Chinhsien *see* Jinzhou
Chinnereth *see* Tiberias, Lake
Chinook Trough *113 H4 trough* N Pacific Ocean
Chioggia *96 C2 anc.* Fossa Claudia. Veneto, NE Italy
Chíos *105 D5 var.* Hios, Khíos, *It.* Scio, *Turk.* Sakiz-Adasi. Chíos, E Greece
Chíos *105 D5 var.* Khíos. *island* E Greece
Chipata *78 D2 prev.* Fort Jameson. Eastern, E Zambia
Chiquián *60 C3* Ancash, W Peru
Chiquimula *52 B2* Chiquimula, SE Guatemala
Chīrāla *132 D1* Andhra Pradesh, E India
Chirchik *see* Chirchiq
Chirchiq *123 E2 Rus.* Chirchik. Toshkent Viloyati, E Uzbekistan
Chiriquí, Golfo de *53 E5 Eng.* Chiriqui Gulf. *gulf* SW Panama
Chiriqui Gulf *see* Chiriquí, Golfo de
Chiriquí, Laguna de *53 E5 lagoon* NW Panama
Chiriquí, Volcán de *see* Barú, Volcán
Chirripó, Cerro *see* Chirripó Grande, Cerro
Chirripó Grande, Cerro *52 D4 var.* Cerro Chirripó. *mountain* SE Costa Rica
Chisec *52 B2* Alta Verapaz, C Guatemala
Chisholm *45 F1* Minnesota, N USA
Chisimaio/Chisimayu *see* Kismaayo
Chişinău *108 D4 Rus.* Kishinev. *country capital* (Moldova) C Moldova
Chita *115 F4* Chitinskaya Oblast', S Russian Federation
Chitangwiza *see* Chitungwiza
Chitato *78 C1* Lunda Norte, NE Angola
Chitina *36 D3* Alaska, USA
Chitose *130 D2 var.* Titose. Hokkaidō, NE Japan
Chitré *53 F5* Herrera, S Panama
Chittagong *135 G4 Ben.* Chāttagām. Chittagong, SE Bangladesh
Chitungwiza *78 D3 prev.* Chitangwiza. Mashonaland East, NE Zimbabwe
Chkalov *see* Orenburg
Chlef *70 D2 var.* Ech Cheliff, Ech Chleff; *prev.* Al-Asnam, El Asnam, Orléansville. NW Algeria
Chocolate Mountains *47 D8 mountain range* California, W USA
Chodorów *see* Khodoriv
Chodzież *98 C3* Wielkopolskie, C Poland
Choele Choel *65 C5* Río Negro, C Argentina
Choiseul *144 C3 var.* Lauru. *island* NW Solomon Islands
Chojnice *98 C2 Ger.* Konitz. Pomorskie, N Poland
Ch'ok'ē *72 C4 var.* Choke Mountains. *mountain range* NW Ethiopia
Choke Mountains *see* Ch'ok'ē
Cholet *90 B4* Maine-et-Loire, NW France
Choluteca *52 C3* Choluteca, S Honduras
Choluteca, Río *52 C3 river* SW Honduras
Choma *78 D2* Southern, S Zambia
Chomutov *98 A4 Ger.* Komotau. Ústecký Kraj, NW Czech Republic
Chona *113 E2 river* C Russian Federation
Chon Buri *137 C5 prev.* Bang Pla Soi. Chon Buri, S Thailand
Chone *60 A1* Manabí, W Ecuador
Ch'ŏngjin *129 E3* NE North Korea
Chongqing *128 B5 var.* Ch'ung-ching, Ch'ung-ch'ing, Chungking, Pahsien, Tchongking, Yuzhou. Chongqing Shi, C China
Chongqing Shi *128 B5 province* C China
Chonnacht *see* Connaught
Chonos, Archipiélago de los *65 A6 island group* S Chile
Chóra *105 D6 prev.* Íos. Kykládes, Greece, Aegean Sea
Chóra Sfakíon *105 C8 var.* Sfákia. Kríti, Greece, E Mediterranean Sea
Chorne More *see* Black Sea
Chornomors'ke *109 E4 Rus.* Chernomorskoye. Respublika Krym, S Ukraine
Chorokh/Chorokhi *see* Çoruh Nehri
Chortkiv *108 C2 Rus.* Chortkov. Ternopil's'ka Oblast', W Ukraine
Chortkov *see* Chortkiv
Chorzów *99 C5 Ger.* Königshütte; *prev.* Królewska Huta. Śląskie, S Poland
Chośebuz *see* Cottbus
Chōsen-kaikyō *see* Korea Strait
Chōshi *131 D5 var.* Tyôsi. Chiba, Honshū, S Japan
Chosŏn-minjujuŭi-inmin-kanghwaguk *see* North Korea
Choszczno *98 B3 Ger.* Arnswalde. Zachodnio-pomorskie, NW Poland
Chota Nāgpur *135 E4 plateau* N India
Choûm *74 C2* Adrar, C Mauritania
Choybalsan *127 F2 prev.* Byan Tumen. Dornod, E Mongolia
Christchurch *151 C6* Canterbury, South Island, New Zealand
Christiana *54 B5* C Jamaica
Christiania *see* Oslo
Christiansand *see* Kristiansand
Christianshåb *see* Qasigiannguit
Christiansund *see* Kristiansund
Christmas Island *141 D5 Australian external territory* E Indian Ocean
Christmas Island *see* Kiritimati
Christmas Ridge *143 E1 undersea ridge* C Pacific Ocean
Chuan *see* Sichuan
Ch'uan-chou *see* Quanzhou
Chubek *see* Moskva
Chubut *57 B7 off.* Provincia de Chubut. *province* S Argentina
Chubut, Provincia de *see* Chubut
Chubut, Río *65 B6 river* SE Argentina
Ch'u-chiang *see* Shaoguan
Chudskoye Ozero *see* Peipus, Lake
Chūgoku-sanchi *131 B6 mountain range* Honshū, SW Japan
Chuí *see* Chuy
Chukai *see* Cukai
Chukchi Plain *155 B2 abyssal plain* Arctic Ocean
Chukchi Plateau *34 C2 undersea plateau* Arctic Ocean
Chukchi Sea *34 B2 Rus.* Chukotskoye More. *sea* Arctic Ocean
Chukotskoye More *see* Chukchi Sea
Chula Vista *47 C8* California, W USA
Chulucanas *60 B2* Piura, NW Peru
Chulym *114 D4 river* C Russian Federation

Chumphon *137 C6 var.* Jumporn. Chumphon, SW Thailand
Ch'unch'ŏn *129 E4 Jap.* Shunsen. N South Korea
Ch'ung-ch'ing/Ch'ung-ching *see* Chongqing
Chung-hua Jen-min Kung-ho-kuo *see* China
Chungking *see* Chongqing
Chunya *115 E3 river* C Russian Federation
Chuquicamata *64 B2* Antofagasta, N Chile
Chuquisaca *see* Sucre
Chur *95 B7 Fr.* Coire, *It.* Coira, *Rmsch.* Cuera, Quera; *anc.* Curia Rhaetorum. Graubünden, E Switzerland
Churchill *37 G4* Manitoba, C Canada
Churchill *38 B2 river* Manitoba/ Saskatchewan, C Canada
Churchill *39 F2 river* Newfoundland and Labrador, E Canada
Chuska Mountains *48 C1 mountain range* Arizona/New Mexico, SW USA
Chusovoy *111 D5* Permskaya Oblast', NW Russian Federation
Chust *see* Khust
Chuuk Islands *144 B2 var.* Hogoley Islands; *prev.* Truk Islands. *island group* Caroline Islands, C Micronesia
Chuy *64 E4 var.* Chuí. Rocha, E Uruguay
Chyhyryn *109 E2 Rus.* Chigirin. Cherkas'ka Oblast', N Ukraine
Ciadir-Lunga *108 D4 var.* Ceadâr-Lunga, *Rus.* Chadyr-Lunga. S Moldova
Cide *116 C2* Kastamonu, N Turkey
Ciechanów *98 D3 prev.* Zichenau. Mazowieckie, C Poland
Ciego de Ávila *54 C2* Ciego de Ávila, C Cuba
Ciénaga *58 B1* Magdalena, N Colombia
Cienfuegos *54 B2* Cienfuegos, C Cuba
Cieza *93 E4* Murcia, SE Spain
Cihanbeyli *116 C3* Konya, C Turkey
Cikobia *145 E4 prev.* Thikombia. *island* N Fiji
Cilacap *138 C3 prev.* Tjilatjap. Jawa, C Indonesia
Cill Airne *see* Killarney
Cill Chainnigh *see* Kilkenny
Cilli *see* Celje
Cill Mhantáin *see* Wicklow
Cimpina *see* Câmpina
Cîmpulung *see* Câmpulung
Cina Selatan, Laut *see* South China Sea
Cincinnati *40 C4* Ohio, N USA
Ciney *87 C7* Namur, SE Belgium
Cinto, Monte *91 E7 mountain* Corse, France, C Mediterranean Sea
Cintra *see* Sintra
Cipolletti *65 B5* Río Negro, C Argentina
Cirebon *138 C4 prev.* Tjirebon. Jawa, S Indonesia
Cirkvenica *see* Crikvenica
Cirò Marina *97 E6* Calabria, S Italy
Cirquenizza *see* Crikvenica
Cisnădie *108 B4 Ger.* Heltau, *Hung.* Nagydisznód. Sibiu, SW Romania
Citharista *see* la Ciotat
Citlaltépetl *see* Orizaba, Volcán Pico de
Citrus Heights *47 B5* California, W USA
Ciudad Acuña *see* Villa Acuña
Ciudad Bolívar *59 E2 prev.* Angostura. Bolívar, E Venezuela
Ciudad Camargo *50 D2* Chihuahua, N Mexico
Ciudad Cortés *see* Cortés
Ciudad Darío *52 D3 var.* Dario. Matagalpa, W Nicaragua
Ciudad de Dolores Hidalgo *see* Dolores Hidalgo
Ciudad de Guatemala *52 B2 Eng.* Guatemala City; *prev.* Santiago de los Caballeros. *country capital* (Guatemala) Guatemala, C Guatemala
Ciudad del Carmen *see* Carmen
Ciudad del Este *64 E2 prev.* Cuidad Presidente Stroessner, Presidente Stroessner, Puerto Presidente Stroessner. Alto Paraná, SE Paraguay
Ciudad Delicias *see* Delicias
Ciudad de México *see* México
Ciudad de Panama *see* Panamá
Ciudad Guayana *59 E2 prev.* San Tomé de Guayana, Santo Tomé de Guayana. Bolívar, NE Venezuela
Ciudad Guzmán *50 D4* Jalisco, SW Mexico

Ciudad Hidalgo *51 G5* Chiapas, SE Mexico
Ciudad Juárez *50 C1* Chihuahua, N Mexico
Ciudad Lerdo *50 D3* Durango, C Mexico
Ciudad Madero *51 E3 var.* Villa Cecilia. Tamaulipas, C Mexico
Ciudad Mante *51 E3* Tamaulipas, C Mexico
Ciudad Miguel Alemán *51 E2* Tamaulipas, C Mexico
Ciudad Obregón *50 B2* Sonora, NW Mexico
Ciudad Ojeda *58 C1* Zulia, NW Venezuela
Ciudad Porfirio Díaz *see* Piedras Negras
Ciudad Quesada *see* Quesada
Ciudad Real *92 D3* Castilla-La Mancha, C Spain
Ciudad-Rodrigo *92 C3* Castilla-León, N Spain
Ciudad Trujillo *see* Santo Domingo
Ciudad Valles *51 E3* San Luis Potosí, C Mexico
Ciudad Victoria *51 E3* Tamaulipas, C Mexico
Ciutadella *93 H3 var.* Ciutadella de Menorca. Menorca, Spain, W Mediterranean Sea
Ciutadella Ciutadella de Menorca *see* Ciutadella
Civitanova Marche *96 D3* Marche, C Italy
Civitas Altae Ripae *see* Brzeg
Civitas Carnutum *see* Chartres
Civitas Eburovicum *see* Évreux
Civitavecchia *96 C4 anc.* Centum Cellae, Trajani Portus. Lazio, C Italy
Claremore *49 G1* Oklahoma, C USA
Clarence *151 C5* Canterbury, South Island, New Zealand
Clarence *151 C5 river* South Island, New Zealand
Clarence Town *54 D2* Long Island, C Bahamas
Clarinda *45 F4* Iowa, C USA
Clarion Fracture Zone *153 E2 tectonic feature* NE Pacific Ocean
Clarión, Isla *50 A5 island* W Mexico
Clark Fork *44 A1 river* Idaho/Montana, NW USA
Clark Hill Lake *43 E2 var.* J.Storm Thurmond Reservoir. *reservoir* Georgia/South Carolina, SE USA
Clarksburg *40 D4* West Virginia, NE USA
Clarksdale *42 B2* Mississippi, S USA
Clarksville *42 C1* Tennessee, S USA
Clausentum *see* Southampton
Clayton *49 E1* New Mexico, SW USA
Clearwater *43 E4* Florida, SE USA
Clearwater Mountains *46 D2 mountain range* Idaho, NW USA
Cleburne *49 G3* Texas, SW USA
Clermont *148 D4* Queensland, E Australia
Clermont-Ferrand *91 C5* Puy-de-Dôme, C France
Cleveland *40 D3* Ohio, N USA
Cleveland *42 D1* Tennessee, S USA
Clifton *48 C2* Arizona, SW USA
Clinton *42 B2* Mississippi, S USA
Clinton *49 F1* Oklahoma, C USA
Clipperton Fracture Zone *153 E3 tectonic feature* E Pacific Ocean
Clipperton Island *35 A7 French dependency* of French Polynesia E Pacific Ocean
Cloncurry *148 B3* Queensland, C Australia
Clonmel *89 B6 Ir.* Cluain Meala. S Ireland
Cloppenburg *94 B3* Niedersachsen, NW Germany
Cloquet *45 G2* Minnesota, N USA
Cloud Peak *44 C3 mountain* Wyoming, C USA
Clovis *49 E2* New Mexico, SW USA
Cluain Meala *see* Clonmel
Cluj *see* Cluj-Napoca
Cluj-Napoca *108 B3 Ger.* Klausenburg, *Hung.* Kolozsvár; *prev.* Cluj. Cluj, NW Romania
Clutha *151 B7 river* South Island, New Zealand
Clyde *88 C4 river* W Scotland, UK
Coari *62 D2* Amazonas, N Brazil

Coast Mountains *36 D4 Fr.* Chaine Côtière. *mountain range* Canada/USA
Coast Ranges *46 A4 mountain range* W USA
Coats Island *37 G3 island* Nunavut, NE Canada
Coats Land *154 B2 physical region* Antarctica
Coatzacoalcos *51 G4 var.* Quetzalcoalco; *prev.* Puerto México. Veracruz-Llave, E Mexico
Cobán *52 B2* Alta Verapaz, C Guatemala
Cobar *149 C6* New South Wales, SE Australia
Cobija *61 E3* Pando, NW Bolivia
Coblence/Coblenz *see* Koblenz
Coburg *95 C5* Bayern, SE Germany
Coca *see* Puerto Francisco de Orellana
Cocanada *see* Kākināda
Cochabamba *61 F4 hist.* Oropeza. Cochabamba, C Bolivia
Cochin *132 C3 var.* Kochi. Kerala, SW India
Cochinos, Bahía de *54 B2 Eng.* Bay of Pigs. *bay* SE Cuba
Cochrane *38 C4* Ontario, S Canada
Cochrane *65 B7* Aisén, S Chile
Cocibolca *see* Nicaragua, Lago de
Cockade State *see* Maryland
Cockburn Town *55 E2* San Salvador, E Bahamas
Cockpit Country, The *54 A4 physical region* W Jamaica
Cocobeach *77 A5* Estuaire, NW Gabon
Coconino Plateau *48 B1 plain* Arizona, SW USA
Coco, Río *53 E2 var.* Río Wanki, Segovia o Wangkí. *river* Honduras/Nicaragua
Cocos Basin *141 C5 undersea basin* E Indian Ocean
Cocos Island Ridge *see* Cocos Ridge
Cocos Islands *141 D5 island group* E Indian Ocean
Cocos Ridge *35 C8 var.* Cocos Island Ridge. *undersea ridge* E Pacific Ocean
Cod, Cape *41 G3 headland* Massachusetts, NE USA
Codfish Island *151 A8 island* SW New Zealand
Codlea *108 C4 Ger.* Zeiden, *Hung.* Feketehalom. Braşov, C Romania
Cody *44 C2* Wyoming, C USA
Coeur d'Alene *46 C2* Idaho, NW USA
Coevorden *86 E2* Drenthe, NE Netherlands
Coffs Harbour *149 E6* New South Wales, SE Australia
Cognac *91 B5 anc.* Compniacum. Charente, W France
Cohalm *see* Rupea
Coiba, Isla de *53 F5 island* SW Panama
Coihaique *65 B6 var.* Coyhaique. Aisén, S Chile
Coimbatore *132 C3* Tamil Nādu, S India
Coimbra *92 B3 anc.* Conimbria, Conímbriga. Coimbra, W Portugal
Coín *92 D5* Andalucía, S Spain
Coira/Coire *see* Chur
Coirib, Loch *see* Corrib, Lough
Colby *44 E4* Kansas, C USA
Colchester *89 E6* Connecticut, NE USA
Coleman *49 F3* Texas, SW USA
Coleraine *88 B4 Ir.* Cúil Raithin. N Northern Ireland, UK
Colesberg *78 C5* Northern Cape, C South Africa
Colima *50 D4* Colima, S Mexico
Coll *88 B3 island* W Scotland, UK
College Station *49 G3* Texas, SW USA
Collie *147 A7* Western Australia
Collipo *see* Leiria
Colmar *90 E4 Ger.* Kolmar. Haut-Rhin, NE France
Cöln *see* Köln
Cologne *see* Köln
Colomb-Béchar *see* Béchar
Colombia *58 B3 off.* Republic of Colombia. *country* N South America

COLOMBIA
South America

Official name Republic of Colombia
Formation 1819 / 1903
Capital Bogotá
Population 45.6 million / 114 people per sq mile (44 people per sq km) / 74%

COLOMBIA
(continued)

Total area 439,733 sq miles (1,138,910 sq km)
Languages Spanish*, Wayuu, Páez, and other Amerindian languages
Religions Roman Catholic 95%, Other 5%
Ethnic mix Mestizo 58%, White 20%, European–African 14%, African 4%, African–Amerindian 3%, Amerindian 1%
Government Presidential system
Currency Colombian peso = 100 centavos
Literacy rate 94%
Calorie consumption 2585 calories

Colombian Basin *56 A1 undersea basin* SW Caribbean Sea
Colombia, Republic of *see* Colombia
Colombie-Britannique *see* British Columbia
Colombo *132 C4 country capital* (Sri Lanka) Western Province, W Sri Lanka
Colón *53 G4 prev.* Aspinwall. Colón, C Panama
Colón, Archipiélago de *153 F3 var.* Islas de los Galápagos, *Eng.* Galapagos Islands, Tortoise Islands. *island group* Ecuador, E Pacific Ocean
Colonia Agrippina *see* Köln
Colón Ridge *35 B8 undersea ridge* E Pacific Ocean
Colorado *44 C4 off.* State of Colorado, *also known as* Centennial State, Silver State. *state* C USA
Colorado City *49 F3* Texas, SW USA
Colorado Plateau *48 B1 plateau* W USA
Colorado, Río *65 C5 river* E Argentina
Colorado, Río *see* Colorado River
Colorado River *35 B5 var.* Río Colorado. *river* Mexico/USA
Colorado River *49 G4 river* Texas, SW USA
Colorado Springs *44 D5* Colorado, C USA
Columbia *41 E4* Maryland, NE USA
Columbia *45 G4* Missouri, C USA
Columbia *43 E2 state capital* South Carolina, SE USA
Columbia *42 C1* Tennessee, S USA
Columbia *46 B3 river* Canada/USA
Columbia Plateau *46 C3 plateau* Idaho/Oregon, NW USA
Columbus *42 D2* Georgia, SE USA
Columbus *40 C4* Indiana, N USA
Columbus *42 C2* Mississippi, S USA
Columbus *45 F4* Nebraska, C USA
Columbus *40 D4 state capital* Ohio, N USA
Colville Channel *150 D2 channel* North Island, New Zealand
Colville River *36 D2 river* Alaska, USA
Comacchio *96 C3 var.* Commachio; *anc.* Comactium. Emilia-Romagna, N Italy
Comactium *see* Comacchio
Comalcalco *51 G4* Tabasco, SE Mexico
Coma Pedrosa, Pic de *91 A7 mountain* NW Andorra
Comarapa *61 F4* Santa Cruz, C Bolivia
Comayagua *52 C2* Comayagua, W Honduras
Comer See *see* Como, Lago di
Comilla *135 G4 Ben.* Kumillā. Chittagong, E Bangladesh
Comino *102 A5 Malt.* Kemmuna. *island* C Malta
Comitán *51 G5 var.* Comitán de Domínguez. Chiapas, SE Mexico
Comitán de Domínguez *see* Comitán
Commachio *see* Comacchio
Commissioner's Point *42 A5 headland* W Bermuda
Como *96 B2 anc.* Comum. Lombardia, N Italy
Comodoro Rivadavia *65 B6* Chubut, SE Argentina
Como, Lago di *96 B2 var.* Lario, *Eng.* Lake Como, *Ger.* Comer See. *lake* N Italy
Como, Lake *see* Como, Lago di
Comores, République Fédérale Islamique des *see* Comoros

Comoros 79 F2 *off.* Federal Islamic Republic of the Comoros, *Fr.* République Fédérale Islamique des Comores. *country* W Indian Ocean

COMOROS
Indian Ocean

Official name Union of the Comoros
Formation 1975 / 1975
Capital Moroni
Population 798,000 / 927 people per sq mile (358 people per sq km) / 33%
Total area 838 sq miles (2170 sq km)
Languages Arabic*, Comoran, French
Religions Muslim (mainly Sunni) 98%, Other 1%, Roman Catholic 1%
Ethnic mix Comoran 97%, Other 3%
Government Presidential system
Currency Comoros franc = 100 centimes
Literacy rate 56%
Calorie consumption 1754 calories

Comoros, Federal Islamic Republic of the *see* Comoros
Compiègne 90 C3 Oise, N France
Complutum *see* Alcalá de Henares
Compniacum *see* Cognac
Compostella *see* Santiago
Comrat 108 D4 *Rus.* Komrat. S Moldova
Comum *see* Como
Conakry 74 C4 *country capital* (Guinea) SW Guinea
Conca *see* Cuenca
Concarneau 90 A3 Finistère, NW France
Concepción 61 G3 Santa Cruz, E Bolivia
Concepción 63 B5 Bío Bío, C Chile
Concepción 64 D2 *var.* Villa Concepción. Concepción, C Paraguay
Concepción *see* La Concepción
Concepción de la Vega *see* La Vega
Conchos, Río 48 D4 *river* NW Mexico
Conchos, Río 50 *river* C Mexico
Concord 41 G3 *state capital* New Hampshire, NE USA
Concordia 64 D4 Entre Ríos, E Argentina
Concordia 45 E4 Kansas, C USA
Côn Đao 137 E7 *var.* Con Son. *island* S Vietnam
Condate *see* Rennes, Ille-et-Vilaine, France
Condate *see* St-Claude, Jura, France
Condega 52 D3 Esteli, NW Nicaragua
Condivincum *see* Nantes
Confluentes *see* Koblenz
Công Hoa Xa Hôi Chu Nghia Viêt Nam *see* Vietnam
Congo 77 D5 *off.* Republic of the Congo, *Fr.* Moyen-Congo; *prev.* Middle Congo. *country* C Africa

CONGO
Central Africa

Official name Republic of the Congo
Formation 1960 / 1960
Capital Brazzaville
Population 4 million / 30 people per sq mile (12 people per sq km) / 63%
Total area 132,046 sq miles (342,000 sq km)
Languages French*, Kongo, Teke, Lingala
Religions Traditional beliefs 50%, Roman Catholic 25%, Protestant 23%, Muslim 2%
Ethnic mix Bakongo 48%, Sangha 20%, Teke 17%, Mboichi 12%, Other 3%
Government Presidential system
Currency CFA franc = 100 centimes
Literacy rate 83%
Calorie consumption 2162 calories

Congo 77 C6 *off.* Democratic Republic of Congo; *prev.* Zaire, Belgian Congo, Congo (Kinshasa). *country* C Africa

CONGO, DEM. REP.
Central Africa

Official name Democratic Republic of the Congo
Formation 1960 / 1960
Capital Kinshasa
Population 57.5 million / 66 people per sq mile (25 people per sq km) / 30%

CONGO, DEM. REP.
(continued)

Total area 905,563 sq miles (2,345,410 sq km)
Languages French*, Kiswahili, Tshiluba, Kikongo, Lingala
Religions Roman Catholic 50%, Protestant 20%, Traditional beliefs and other 10%, Muslim 10%, Kimbanguist 10%
Ethnic mix Other 55%, Bantu and Hamitic 45%
Government Transitional regime
Currency Congolese franc = 100 centimes
Literacy rate 65%
Calorie consumption 1599 calories

Congo 77 C6 *var.* Kongo, *Fr.* Zaire. *river* C Africa
Congo Basin 77 C6 *drainage basin* W Dem. Rep. Congo
Congo/Congo (Kinshasa) *see* Congo (Democratic Republic of)
Coni *see* Cuneo
Conimbria/Conimbriga *see* Coimbra
Conjeeveram *see* Kânchîpuram
Connacht *see* Connaught
Connaught 89 A5 *var.* Connacht, *Ir.* Chonnacht, Cúige. *province* W Ireland
Connecticut 41 F3 *off.* State of Connecticut, *also known as* Blue Law State, Constitution State, Land of Steady Habits, Nutmeg State. *state* NE USA
Connecticut 41 G3 *river* Canada/USA
Conroe 49 G3 Texas, SW USA
Consentia *see* Cosenza
Consolación del Sur 54 A2 Pinar del Río, W Cuba
Con Son *see* Côn Đao
Constance *see* Konstanz
Constance, Lake 95 B7 *Ger.* Bodensee. *lake* C Europe
Constanţa 108 D5 *var.* Küstendje, *Eng.* Constanza, *Ger.* Konstanza, *Turk.* Küstence. Constanţa, SE Romania
Constantia *see* Coutances
Constantia *see* Konstanz
Constantine 71 E2 *var.* Qacentina, *Ar.* Qoussantîna. NE Algeria
Constantinople *see* İstanbul
Constantiola *see* Olteniţa
Constanz *see* Konstanz
Constanza *see* Constanţa
Constitution State *see* Connecticut
Coo *see* Kos
Coober Pedy 149 A5 South Australia
Cookeville 42 D1 Tennessee, S USA
Cook Islands 145 F4 *territory in free association with New Zealand* S Pacific Ocean
Cook, Mount *see* Aoraki
Cook Strait 151 D5 *var.* Raukawa. *strait* New Zealand
Cooktown 148 D2 Queensland, NE Australia
Coolgardie 147 B6 Western Australia
Cooma 149 D7 New South Wales, SE Australia
Coomassie *see* Kumasi
Coon Rapids 45 F2 Minnesota, N USA
Cooper Creek 148 C4 *var.* Barcoo, Cooper's Creek. *seasonal river* Queensland/South Australia
Cooper's Creek *see* Cooper Creek
Coos Bay 46 A3 Oregon, NW USA
Cootamundra 149 D6 New South Wales, SE Australia
Copacabana 61 E4 La Paz, W Bolivia
Copenhagen *see* København
Copiapó 64 B3 Atacama, N Chile
Copperas Cove 49 G3 Texas, SW USA
Coppermine *see* Kugluktuk
Copper State *see* Arizona
Coquilhatville *see* Mbandaka
Coquimbo 64 B3 Coquimbo, N Chile
Corabia 108 B5 Olt, S Romania
Coral Harbour 37 G3 Southampton Island, Northwest Territories, NE Canada
Coral Sea 142 B3 *sea* SW Pacific Ocean
Coral Sea Islands 144 B4 *Australian external territory* SW Pacific Ocean

Corantijn Rivier *see* Courantyne River
Corcovado, Golfo 65 B6 *gulf* S Chile
Corcyra Nigra *see* Korčula
Cordele 42 D3 Georgia, SE USA
Córdoba 64 C3 Córdoba, C Argentina
Córdoba 51 F4 Veracruz-Llave, E Mexico
Córdoba 92 D4 *var.* Cordoba, *Eng.* Cordova; *anc.* Corduba. Andalucía, SW Spain
Cordova 36 C3 Alaska, USA
Cordova/Cordoba *see* Córdoba
Corduba *see* Córdoba
Corentyne River *see* Courantyne River
Coria 92 C3 Extremadura, W Spain
Corinth 42 C1 Mississippi, S USA
Corinth *see* Kórinthos
Corinth, Gulf of/Corinthiacus Sinus *see* Korinthiakós Kólpos
Corinthus *see* Kórinthos
Corinto 52 C3 Chinandega, NW Nicaragua
Cork 89 A6 *Ir.* Corcaigh. S Ireland
Çorlu 116 A2 Tekirdağ, NW Turkey
Corner Brook 39 G3 Newfoundland, Newfoundland and Labrador, E Canada
Cornhusker State *see* Nebraska
Corn Islands *see* Maíz, Islas del
Cornwallis Island 37 F2 *island* Nunavut, N Canada
Coro 58 C1 *prev.* Santa Ana de Coro. Falcón, NW Venezuela
Corocoro 61 F4 La Paz, W Bolivia
Coromandel 150 D2 Waikato, North Island, New Zealand
Coromandel Coast 132 D2 *coast* E India
Coromandel Peninsula 150 D2 *peninsula* North Island, New Zealand
Coronado, Bahía de 52 D5 *bay* S Costa Rica
Coronel Dorrego 65 C5 Buenos Aires, E Argentina
Coronel Oviedo 64 D2 Caaguazú, SE Paraguay
Corozal 52 C1 Corozal, N Belize
Corpus Christi 49 G4 Texas, SW USA
Corrales 48 D2 New Mexico, SW USA
Corrib, Lough 89 A5 *Ir.* Loch Coirib. *lake* W Ireland
Corrientes 64 D3 Corrientes, NE Argentina
Corriza *see* Korçë
Corse 91 E7 *Eng.* Corsica. *island* France, C Mediterranean Sea
Corsica *see* Corse
Corsicana 49 G3 Texas, SW USA
Cortegana 92 C4 Andalucía, S Spain
Cortés 53 E5 *var.* Ciudad Cortés. Puntarenas, SE Costa Rica
Cortez, Sea of *see* California, Golfo de
Cortina d'Ampezzo 96 C1 Veneto, NE Italy
Coruche 92 B3 Santarém, C Portugal
Çoruh Nehri 117 E3 Geor. Chorokh, *Rus.* Chorokhi. *river* Georgia/Turkey
Çorum 116 D3 *var.* Chorum. Çorum, N Turkey
Corunna *see* A Coruña
Corvallis 46 B3 Oregon, NW USA
Corvo 92 A5 *var.* Ilha do Corvo. *island* Azores, Portugal, NE Atlantic Ocean
Corvo, Ilha do *see* Corvo
Cos *see* Kos
Cosenza 97 D6 *anc.* Consentia. Calabria, SW Italy
Cosne-Cours-sur-Loire 90 C4 Nièvre, Bourgogne, C France Europe
Costa Mesa 46 D2 California, W USA North America
Costa Rica 53 E4 *off.* Republic of Costa Rica. *country* Central America

COSTA RICA
Central America

Official name Republic of Costa Rica
Formation 1838 / 1838
Capital San José
Population 4.3 million / 218 people per sq mile (84 people per sq km) / 52%
Total area 19,730 sq miles (51,100 sq km)
Languages Spanish*, English Creole, Bribri, Cabecar
Religions Roman Catholic 76%, Other (including Protestant) 24%
Ethnic mix Mestizo and European 96%, Black 2%, Chinese 1%, Amerindian 1%
Government Presidential system

COSTA RICA
(continued)

Currency Costa Rican colón = 100 centimos
Literacy rate 96%
Calorie consumption 2876 calories

Costa Rica, Republic of *see* Costa Rica
Costermansville *see* Bukavu
Cotagaita 61 F5 Potosí, S Bolivia
Côte d'Ivoire 74 D4 *off.* Republic of Côte d'Ivoire, *Eng.* Ivory Coast, *Fr.* République de la Côte d'Ivoire. *country* W Africa

COTE D'IVOIRE (IVORY COAST)
West Africa

Official name Republic of Côte d'Ivoire
Formation 1960 / 1960
Capital Yamoussoukro
Population 18.2 million / 148 people per sq mile (57 people per sq km) / 46%
Total area 124,502 sq miles (322,460 sq km)
Languages French*, Akan, Kru, Voltaic
Religions Muslim 38%, Traditional beliefs 25%, Roman Catholic 25%, Protestant 6%, Other 6%
Ethnic mix Baoulé 23%, Other 19%, Béte 18%, Senufo 15%, Agni-Ashanti 14%, Mandinka 11%
Government Presidential system
Currency CFA franc = 100 centimes
Literacy rate 48%
Calorie consumption 2631 calories

Côte d'Ivoire, République de la *see* Côte d'Ivoire
Côte d'Or 90 D4 *cultural region* C France
Côte Française des Somalis *see* Djibouti
Côtière, Chaine *see* Coast Mountains
Cotonou 75 F5 *var.* Kotonu. S Benin
Cotrone *see* Crotone
Cotswold Hills 89 D6 *var.* Cotswolds. *hill range* S England, UK
Cotswolds *see* Cotswold Hills
Cottbus 94 D4 *Lus.* Chośebuz; *prev.* Kottbus. Brandenburg, E Germany
Cotton State, The *see* Alabama
Cotyora *see* Ordu
Couentrey *see* Coventry
Council Bluffs 45 F4 Iowa, C USA
Courantyne River 59 G4 *var.* Corantijn Rivier, Corentyne River. *river* Guyana/Suriname
Courland Lagoon 106 A4 *Ger.* Kurisches Haff, *Rus.* Kurskiy Zaliv. *lagoon* Lithuania/Russian Federation
Courtrai *see* Kortrijk
Coutances 90 B3 *anc.* Constantia. Manche, N France
Couvin 87 C7 Namur, S Belgium
Coventry 89 D6 *anc.* Couentrey. C England, UK
Covilhã 92 C3 Castelo Branco, E Portugal
Cowan, Lake 147 B6 *lake* Western Australia
Coxen Hole *see* Roatán
Coxin Hole *see* Roatán
Coyhaique *see* Coihaique
Coyote State, The *see* South Dakota
Cozumel, Isla 51 H3 *island* SE Mexico
Cracovia/Cracow *see* Kraków
Cradock 78 C5 Eastern Cape, S South Africa
Craig 44 C4 Colorado, C USA
Craiova 108 B5 Dolj, SW Romania
Cranbrook 37 E5 British Columbia, SW Canada
Crane *see* The Crane
Cranz *see* Zelenogradsk
Crawley 89 E7 SE England, UK
Cremona 96 B2 Lombardia, N Italy
Creole State *see* Louisiana
Cres 100 A3 *It.* Cherso; *anc.* Crexa. *island* W Croatia
Crescent City 46 A4 California, W USA
Crescent Group 128 C7 *island group* C Paracel Islands
Creston 45 F4 Iowa, C USA
Crestview 42 D3 Florida, SE USA
Créteil 90 E2 Val-de-Marne, N France
Crete, Sea of/Creticum, Mare *see* Kritikó Pélagos
Creuse 90 B4 *river* C France
Crewe 89 D6 C England, UK

Crexa see Cres
Crikvenica 100 A3 It. Cirquenizza; prev. Cirkvenica, Crjkvenica. Primorje-Gorski Kotar, NW Croatia
Cristóbal 53 G4 Colón, C Panama
Cristóbal Colón, Pico 58 B1 mountain N Colombia
Cristur/Cristuru Săcuiesc see Cristuru Secuiesc
Cristuru Secuiesc 108 C4 prev. Cristur, Cristuru Săcuiesc, Sitaş Cristuru, Ger. Kreutz, Hung. Székelykeresztúr, Szitás-Keresztúr. Harghita, C Romania
Crjkvenica see Crikvenica
Crna Gora see Montenegro
Crna Reka 101 D6 river S FYR Macedonia
Crni Drim see Black Drin
Croatia 100 B3 off. Republic of Croatia, Ger. Kroatien, SCr. Hrvatska. country SE Europe

CROATIA
Southeast Europe

Official name Republic of Croatia
Formation 1991 / 1991
Capital Zagreb
Population 4.6 million / 211 people per sq mile (81 people per sq km) / 58%
Total area 21,831 sq miles (56,542 sq km)
Languages Croatian*
Religions Roman Catholic 88%, Other 7%, Orthodox Christian 4%, Muslim 1%
Ethnic mix Croat 90%, Other 5%, Serb 4%, Bosniak 1%
Government Parliamentary system
Currency Kuna = 100 lipas
Literacy rate 98%
Calorie consumption 2799 calories

Croatia, Republic of see Croatia
Crocodile see Limpopo
Croia see Krujë
Croker Island 146 E2 island Northern Territory, N Australia
Cromwell 151 B7 Otago, South Island, New Zealand
Crooked Island 54 D2 island SE Bahamas
Crooked Island Passage 54 D2 channel SE Bahamas
Crookston 45 F1 Minnesota, N USA
Crossen see Krosno Odrzańskie
Croton/Crotona see Crotone
Crotone 97 E6 var. Cotrone; anc. Croton, Crotona. Calabria, SW Italy
Croydon 89 A8 SE England, UK
Crozet Basin 141 B6 undersea basin S Indian Ocean
Crozet Islands 141 B7 island group French Southern and Antarctic Territories
Crozet Plateau 141 B7 var. Crozet Plateaus. undersea plateau SW Indian Ocean
Crozet Plateaus see Crozet Plateau
Crystal Brook 149 B6 South Australia
Csaca see Čadca
Csakathurn/Csáktornya see Čakovec
Csíkszereda see Miercurea-Ciuc
Csorna 99 C6 Győr-Moson-Sopron, NW Hungary
Csurgó 99 C7 Somogy, SW Hungary
Cuando 78 C2 var. Kwando. river S Africa
Cuango 78 B1 var. Kwango. river Angola/Dem. Rep. Congo
Cuango see Kwango
Cuanza 78 B1 var. Kwanza. river C Angola
Cuauhtémoc 50 C2 Chihuahua, N Mexico
Cuautla 51 E4 Morelos, S Mexico
Cuba 54 B2 off. Republic of Cuba. country W Indies

CUBA
West Indies

Official name Republic of Cuba
Formation 1902 / 1902
Capital Havana
Population 11.3 million / 264 people per sq mile (102 people per sq km) / 75%

CUBA
(continued)

Total area 42,803 sq miles (110,860 sq km)
Languages Spanish*
Religions Nonreligious 49%, Roman Catholic 40%, Atheist 6%, Other 4%, Protestant 1%
Ethnic mix White 66%, European–African 22%, Black 12%
Government One-party state
Currency Cuban peso = 100 centavos
Literacy rate 97%
Calorie consumption 3152 calories

Cubal 78 B2 Benguela, W Angola
Cubango 78 B2 var. Kuvango, Port. Vila Artur de Paiva, Vila da Ponte. Huíla, SW Angola
Cubango 78 B2 var. Kavango, Kavengo, Kubango, Okavango, Okavanggo. river S Africa
Cuba, Republic of see Cuba
Cúcuta 58 C2 var. San José de Cúcuta. Norte de Santander, N Colombia
Cuddapah 132 C2 Andhra Pradesh, S India
Cuenca 60 B2 Azuay, S Ecuador
Cuenca 93 E3 anc. Conca. Castilla-La Mancha, C Spain
Cuera see Chur
Cuernavaca 51 E4 Morelos, S Mexico
Cuiabá 63 E3 prev. Cuyabá. state capital Mato Grosso, SW Brazil
Cuidad Presidente Stroessner see Ciudad del Este
Cúige see Connaught
Cúige Laighean see Leinster
Cúige Mumhan see Munster
Cuijck 86 D4 Noord-Brabant, SE Netherlands
Cúil Raithin see Coleraine
Cuito 78 B2 var. Kwito. river SE Angola
Cukai 138 B3 var. Chukai, Kemaman. Terengganu, Peninsular Malaysia
Cularo see Grenoble
Culiacán 50 C3 var. Culiacán Rosales, Culiacán-Rosales. Sinaloa, C Mexico
Culiacán-Rosales/Culiacán Rosales see Culiacán
Cullera 93 F3 País Valenciano, E Spain
Cullman 42 C2 Alabama, S USA
Culm see Chełmno
Culmsee see Chełmża
Cumaná 59 E1 Sucre, NE Venezuela
Cumbal, Nevado de 58 A4 elevation S Colombia
Cumberland 41 E4 Maryland, NE USA
Cumberland Plateau 42 D1 plateau E USA
Cumberland Sound 37 H3 inlet Baffin Island, Nunavut, NE Canada
Cumpas 50 B2 Sonora, NW Mexico
Cunene 78 A3 province S Angola
Cunene 69 C6 var. Kunene. river Angola/Namibia
Cuneo 96 A2 Fr. Coni. Piemonte, NW Italy
Cunnamulla 149 C5 Queensland, E Australia
Ćuprija 100 E4 Serbia, E Serbia
Curaçao 55 E5 island Netherlands Antilles
Curia Rhaetorum see Chur
Curicó 64 B4 Maule, C Chile
Curieta see Krk
Curitiba 63 E4 prev. Curytiba. state capital Paraná, S Brazil
Curtbunar see Tervel
Curtea de Argeş 108 C4 var. Curtea-de-Arges. Argeş, S Romania
Curtea-de-Arges see Curtea de Argeş
Curtici 108 A4 Ger. Kurtitsch, Hung. Kürtös. Arad, W Romania
Curtis Island 148 E4 island Queensland, SE Australia
Curytiba see Curitiba
Curzola see Korčula
Cusco 61 E4 var. Cuzco. Cusco, C Peru
Cusset 91 C5 Allier, C France
Cutch, Gulf of see Kachchh, Gulf of
Cuttack 135 F4 Orissa, E India
Cuvier Plateau 141 E6 undersea plateau E Indian Ocean
Cuxhaven 94 B3 Niedersachsen, NW Germany
Cuyabá see Cuiabá

Cuyuni, Río see Cuyuni River
Cuyuni River 59 F3 var. Río Cuyuni. river Guyana/Venezuela
Cuzco see Cusco
Cyclades see Kykládes
Cydonia see Chaniá
Cymru see Wales
Cyprus 102 C4 off. Republic of Cyprus, Gk. Kypros, Turk. Kıbrıs, Kıbrıs Cumhuriyeti. country E Mediterranean Sea

CYPRUS
Southeast Europe

Official name Republic of Cyprus
Formation 1960 / 1960
Capital Nicosia
Population 835,000 / 234 people per sq mile (90 people per sq km) / 57%
Total area 3571 sq miles (9250 sq km)
Languages Greek, Turkish
Religions Orthodox Christian 78%, Muslim 18%, Other 4%
Ethnic mix Greek 85%, Turkish 12%, Other 3%
Government Presidential system
Currency Cyprus pound (Turkish lira in TRNC) = 100 cents (Cyprus pound); 100 kurus (Turkish lira)
Literacy rate 97%
Calorie consumption 3255 calories

Cyprus, Republic of see Cyprus
Cythnos see Kýthnos
Czech Republic 99 A5 Cz. Česká Republika. country C Europe

CZECH REPUBLIC
Central Europe

Official name Czech Republic
Formation 1993 / 1993
Capital Prague
Population 10.2 million / 335 people per sq mile (129 people per sq km) / 75%
Total area 30,450 sq miles (78,866 sq km)
Languages Czech*, Slovak, Hungarian (Magyar)
Religions Roman Catholic 39%, Atheist 38%, Other 18%, Protestant 3%, Hussite 2%
Ethnic mix Czech 81%, Moravian 13%, Slovak 6%
Government Parliamentary system
Currency Czech koruna = 100 haleru
Literacy rate 99%
Calorie consumption 3171 calories

Czenstochau see Częstochowa
Czernowitz see Chernivtsi
Częstochowa 98 C4 Ger. Czenstochau, Tschenstochau, Rus. Chenstokhov. Śląskie, S Poland
Czluchów 98 C3 Ger. Schlochau. Pomorskie, NW Poland

D

Dabajuro 58 C1 Falcón, NW Venezuela
Dabeiba 58 B2 Antioquia, NW Colombia
Dąbrowa Tarnowska 99 D5 Małopolskie, S Poland
Dabryn' 107 C8 Rus. Dobryn'. Homyel'skaya Voblasts', SE Belarus
Dacca see Dhaka
Daegu see Taegu
Dagana 74 B3 N Senegal
Dagda 106 D4 Krāslava, SE Latvia
Dagden see Hiiumaa
Dagenham 89 B8 SE England, UK
Dağliq Qarabağ see Nagorno-Karabakh
Dagö see Hiiumaa
Dagupan 139 E1 off. Dagupan City. Luzon, N Philippines
Dagupan City see Dagupan
Da Hinggan Ling 127 G1 Eng. Great Khingan Range. mountain range NE China
Dahm, Ramlat 121 B6 desert NW Yemen
Dahomey see Benin
Daihoku see T'aipei

Daimiel 92 D3 Castilla-La Mancha, C Spain
Daimonià 105 B7 Pelopónnisos, S Greece
Dainan see T'ainan
Daingin, Bá an see Dingle Bay
Dairen see Dalian
Dakar 74 B3 country capital (Senegal) W Senegal
Dakhla see Ad Dakhla
Dakoro 75 G3 Maradi, S Niger
Đakovica 101 D5 var. Djakovica, Alb. Gjakovë. Kosovo, S Serbia
Đakovo 100 C3 var. Djakovo, Hung. Diakovár. Osijek-Baranja, E Croatia
Dakshin see Deccan
Dalain Hob 126 D3 var. Ejin Qi. Nei Mongol Zizhiqu, N China
Dalai Nor see Hulun Nur
Dalaman 116 A4 Muğla, SW Turkey
Dalandzadgad 127 E3 Ömnögovĭ, S Mongolia
Đa Lat 137 E6 Lâm Đồng, S Vietnam
Dalby 149 D5 Queensland, E Australia
Dale City 41 E4 Virginia, NE USA
Dalhart 49 E1 Texas, SW USA
Dali 128 A4 var. Xiaguan. Yunnan, SW China
Dalian 128 D4 var. Dairen, Dalien, Lüda, Ta-lien, Rus. Dalny. Liaoning, NE China
Dalien see Dalian
Dallas 49 G2 Texas, SW USA
Dalmacija 100 B4 Eng. Dalmatia, Ger. Dalmatien, It. Dalmazia. cultural region S Croatia
Dalmatia/Dalmatien/Dalmazia see Dalmacija
Dalmatien see Dalmacija
Dalny see Dalian
Dalton 42 D1 Georgia, SE USA
Dálvvadis see Jokkmokk
Daly Waters 148 A2 Northern Territory, N Australia
Damachava 107 A6 var. Damachova, Pol. Domaczewo, Rus. Domachëvo. Brestskaya Voblasts', SW Belarus
Damachova see Damachava
Damān 134 C4 Damān and Diu, W India
Damara 76 C4 Ombella-Mpoko, S Central African Republic
Damas see Dimashq
Damasco see Dimashq
Damascus see Dimashq
Damāvand, Qolleh-ye 120 D3 mountain N Iran
Damietta see Dumyât
Dammām see Ad Dammān
Damoûr 119 A5 var. Ad Dāmūr. W Lebanon
Dampier 146 A4 Western Australia
Dampier, Selat 139 F4 strait Papua, E Indonesia
Damqawt 121 D6 var. Damqut. E Yemen
Damqut see Damqawt
Damxung 126 C5 var. Gongtang. Xizang Zizhiqu, W China
Danakil Desert 72 D4 var. Afar Depression, Danakil Plain. desert E Africa
Danakil Plain see Danakil Desert
Danané 74 D5 W Côte d'Ivoire (Ivory Coast)
Đà Nẵng 137 E5 prev. Tourane. Quang Nam-Đa Nẵng, C Vietnam
Danborg see Daneborg
Dandong 128 D3 var. Tan-tung; prev. An-tung. Liaoning, NE China
Daneborg 83 E3 var. Danborg. N Greenland
Dångara see Danghara
Danghara 123 E3 Rus. Dangara. SW Tajikistan
Danghe Nanshan 126 D3 mountain range W China
Dang Raek, Phanom/Dangrek, Chaine des see Dângrêk, Chuôr Phnum
Dângrêk, Chuôr Phnum 137 D5 var. Phanom Dang Raek, Phanom Dong Rak, Fr. Chaîne des Dangrek. mountain range Cambodia/Thailand
Dangriga 52 C1 prev. Stann Creek. Stann Creek, E Belize
Danish West Indies see Virgin Islands (US)
Danlí 52 D2 El Paraíso, S Honduras

Danmark see Denmark
Danmarksstraedet see Denmark Strait
Dannenberg *94 C3* Niedersachsen, N Germany
Dannevirke *150 D4* Manawatu-Wanganui, North Island, New Zealand
Dantzig see Gdańsk
Danube *81 E4* Bul. Dunav, Cz. Dunaj, Ger. Donau, Hung. Duna, Rom. Dunărea. *river* C Europe
Danubian Plain see Dunavska Ravnina
Danum see Doncaster
Danville *41 E5* Virginia, NE USA
Danxian/Dan Xian see Danzhou
Danzhou *128 C7 prev.* Danxian, Dan Xian, Nada. Hainan, S China
Danzig see Gdańsk
Danziger Bucht see Danzig, Gulf of
Danzig, Gulf of *98 C2 var.* Gulf of Gdańsk, *Ger.* Danziger Bucht, *Pol.* Zakota Gdańska, *Rus.* Gdan'skaya Bukhta. *gulf* N Poland
Daqm see Duqm
Dar'ā *119 B5 var.* Der'a, *Fr.* Déraa. Dar'ā, SW Syria
Darabani *108 C3* Botoşani, NW Romania
Daraut-Kurgan see Daroot-Korgon
Dardanelles see Çanakkale Boğazı
Dardanelli see Çanakkale
Dar-el-Beida see Casablanca
Dar es Salaam *73 C7* Dar es Salaam, E Tanzania
Darfield *151 C6* Canterbury, South Island, New Zealand
Darfur *72 A4 var.* Darfur Massif. *cultural region* W Sudan
Darfur Massif see Darfur
Darhan *127 E2* Darhan Uul, N Mongolia
Darién, Golfo del see Darién, Gulf of
Darien, Gulf of *58 A2 Sp.* Golfo del Darién. *gulf* S Caribbean Sea
Darien, Isthmus of see Panama, Istmo de
Darién, Serranía del *53 H5 mountain range* Colombia/Panama
Dario see Ciudad Darío
Dariorigum see Vannes
Darjeeling see Darjiling
Darjiling *135 F3 prev.* Darjeeling. West Bengal, NE India
Darling River *149 C6 river* New South Wales, SE Australia
Darlington *89 D5* N England, UK
Darmstadt *95 B5* Hessen, SW Germany
Darnah *71 G2 var.* Dérna. NE Libya
Darnley, Cape *154 D2 cape* Antarctica
Daroca *93 E2* Aragón, NE Spain
Daroot-Korgon *123 F3 var.* Daraut-Kurgan. Oshskaya Oblast', SW Kyrgyzstan
Dartford *89 B8* SE England, UK
Dartmoor *89 C7 moorland* SW England, UK
Dartmouth *39 F4* Nova Scotia, SE Canada
Darvaza see Derweze, Turkmenistan
Darwin *146 D2 prev.* Palmerston, Port Darwin. *territory capital* Northern Territory, N Australia
Darwin, Isla *60 A4 island* Galápagos, Galapagos Islands, W Ecuador
Dashhowuz see Daşoguz
Dashkawka *107 D6 Rus.* Dashkovka. Mahilyowskaya Voblasts', E Belarus
Dashkovka see Dashkawka
Daşoguz *122 C2 var.* Dashhowuz, Turkm.* Dashhowuz; *prev.* Tashauz. Daşoguz Welaýaty, N Turkmenistan
Da, Sông see Black River
Datong *128 C3 var.* Tatung, Ta-t'ung. Shanxi, C China
Daugava see Western Dvina
Daugavpils *106 D4 Ger.* Dünaburg; *prev. Rus.* Dvinsk. Daugvapils, SE Latvia
Daung Kyun *137 B6 island* S Myanmar (Burma)
Dauphiné *91 D5 cultural region* E France
Dávangere *132 C2* Karnātaka, W India
Davao *139 F3 off.* Davao City. Mindanao, S Philippines
Davao City see Davao
Davao Gulf *139 F3 gulf* Mindanao, S Philippines
Davenport *45 G3* Iowa, C USA
David *53 E5* Chiriquí, W Panama
Davie Ridge *141 A5 undersea ridge* W Indian Ocean

Davis *154 D3 Australian research station* Antarctica
Davis Sea *154 D3 sea* Antarctica
Davis Strait *82 B3 strait* Baffin Bay/Labrador Sea
Dawei see Tavoy
Dawlat Qaṭar see Qatar
Dax *91 B6 var.* Ax; *anc.* Aquae Augustae, Aquae Tarbelicae. Landes, SW France
Dayr az Zawr *118 D3 var.* Deir ez Zor. Dayr az Zawr, E Syria
Dayton *40 C4* Ohio, N USA
Daytona Beach *43 E4* Florida, SE USA
De Aar *78 C5* Northern Cape, C South Africa
Dead Sea *119 B6 var.* Bahret Lut, Lacus Asphaltites, *Ar.* Al Baḥr al Mayyit, Baḥrat Lūt, *Heb.* Yam HaMelaḥ. *salt lake* Israel/Jordan
Deán Funes *64 C3* Córdoba, C Argentina
Death Valley *47 C7 valley* California, W USA
Deatnu *84 D2 Fin.* Tenojoki, *Nor.* Tana. *river* Finland/Norway
Debar *101 D6 Ger.* Dibra, *Turk.* Debre. W FYR Macedonia
De Behagle see Laï
Dębica *99 D5* Podkarpackie, SE Poland
De Bildt see De Bilt
De Bilt *86 C3 var.* De Bildt. Utrecht, C Netherlands
Dębno *98 B3* Zachodnio-pomorskie, NW Poland
Debre see Debar
Debrecen *99 D6 Ger.* Debreczin, *Rom.* Debreţin; *prev.* Debreczen. Hajdú-Bihar, E Hungary
Debreczen/Debreczin see Debrecen
Debreţin see Debrecen
Decatur *42 C1* Alabama, S USA
Decatur *40 B4* Illinois, N USA
Deccan *134 D5 Hind.* Dakshin. *plateau* C India
Děčín *98 B4 Ger.* Tetschen. Ústcký Kraj, NW Czech Republic
Dedeagaç/Dedeagach see Alexandroúpoli
Dedemsvaart *86 E3* Overijssel, E Netherlands
Dee *88 C3 river* NE Scotland, UK
Deering *36 C2* Alaska, USA
Deés see Dej
Deggendorf *95 D6* Bayern, SE Germany
Değirmenlik *102 C5 Gk.* Kythréa. N Cyprus
Deh Bid *120 D3* Fārs, C Iran
Dehli see Delhi
Deh Shū *122 D5 var.* Deshu. Helmand, S Afghanistan
Deinze *87 B5* Oost-Vlaanderen, NW Belgium
Deir ez Zor see Dayr az Zawr
Deirgeirt, Loch see Derg, Lough
Dej *108 B3 Hung.* Dés; *prev.* Deés. Cluj, NW Romania
De Jouwer see Joure
Dekéleia see Dhekéleia
Dékoa *76 C4* Kémo, C Central African Republic
De Land *43 E4* Florida, SE USA
Delano *47 C7* California, W USA
Delārām *122 D5* Nīmrūz, SW Afghanistan
Delaware *40 D4* Ohio, N USA
Delaware *41 F4 off.* State of Delaware, *also known as* Blue Hen State, Diamond State, First State. *state* NE USA
Delft *86 B4* Zuid-Holland, W Netherlands
Delfzijl *86 E1* Groningen, NE Netherlands
Delgo *72 B3* Northern, N Sudan
Delhi *134 D3 var.* Dehli, *Hind.* Dilli, *hist.* Shahjahanabad. *union territory capital* Delhi, N India
Delicias *50 D2 var.* Ciudad Delicias. Chihuahua, N Mexico
Déli-Kárpátok see Carpaţii Meridionali
Delmenhorst *94 B3* Niedersachsen, NW Germany
Del Rio *49 F4* Texas, SW USA
Deltona *43 E4* Florida, SE USA
Demba *77 D6* Kasai Occidental, C Dem. Rep. Congo
Dembia *76 D4* Mbomou, SE Central African Republic
Demchok *126 A4* China/India
Demchok *126 A5 var.* Dêmqog. *disputed region* China/India

Demchok see Dêmqog
Demerara Plain *56 C2 abyssal plain* W Atlantic Ocean
Deming *48 C3* New Mexico, SW USA
Demmin *94 C2* Mecklenburg-Vorpommern, NE Germany
Demopolis *42 C2* Alabama, S USA
Dêmqog *126 A5 var.* Demchok. China/India
Dêmqog see Demchok
Dêmqog see Demchok
Denali see McKinley, Mount
Denau see Denow
Dender *87 B6 Fr.* Dendre. *river* W Belgium
Dendre see Dender
Denekamp *86 E3* Overijssel, E Netherlands
Den Haag see 's-Gravenhage
Denham *147 A5* Western Australia
Den Ham *86 E3* Overijssel, E Netherlands
Den Helder *86 C2* Noord-Holland, NW Netherlands
Dénia *93 F4* País Valenciano, E Spain
Deniliquin *149 C7* New South Wales, SE Australia
Denison *45 F3* Iowa, C USA
Denison *49 G2* Texas, SW USA
Denizli *116 B4* Denizli, SW Turkey
Denmark *85 A7 off.* Kingdom of Denmark, Dan. Danmark; *anc.* Hafnia. *country* N Europe

---
DENMARK
Northern Europe

Official name Kingdom of Denmark
Formation AD 950 / 1945
Capital Copenhagen
Population 5.4 million / 330 people per sq mile (127 people per sq km) / 85%
Total area 16,639 sq miles (43,094 sq km)
Languages Danish*
Religions Evangelical Lutheran 89%, Other 10%, Roman Catholic 1%
Ethnic mix Danish 96%, Other (including Scandinavian and Turkish) 3%, Faeroese and Inuit 1%
Government Parliamentary system
Currency Danish krone = 100 øre
Literacy rate 99%
Calorie consumption 3439 calories

Denmark, Kingdom of see Denmark
Denmark Strait *82 D4 var.* Danmarksstraedet. *strait* Greenland/Iceland
Dennery *55 F1* E Saint Lucia
Denow *123 E3 Rus.* Denau. Surkhondaryo Viloyati, S Uzbekistan
Denpasar *138 D5 prev.* Paloe. Bali, C Indonesia
Denton *49 G2* Texas, SW USA
D'Entrecasteaux Islands *144 B3 island group* SE Papua New Guinea
Denver *44 D4 state capital* Colorado, C USA
Déraa see Dar'ā
Der'a/Derá/Déraa see Dar'ā
Dera Ghāzi Khān *134 C2 var.* Dera Ghāzīkhān. Punjab, C Pakistan
Dera Ghāzīkhān see Dera Ghāzi Khān
Ðeravica *101 D5 mountain* S Serbia
Derbent *111 B8* Respublika Dagestan, SW Russian Federation
Derby *89 D6* C England, UK
Dereli see Gönnoi
Dergachi see Derhachi
Derg, Lough *89 A6 Ir.* Loch Deirgeirt. *lake* W Ireland
Derhachi *109 G2 Rus.* Dergachi. Kharkiv'ska Oblast', E Ukraine
De Ridder *42 A3* Louisiana, S USA
Dérna see Darnah
Derry see Londonderry
Dertosa see Tortosa
Derventa *100 B3* Republika Srpska, N Bosnia and Herzegovina
Derweze *122 C2 Rus.* Darvaza. Ahal Welaýaty, C Turkmenistan
Dés see Dej
Deschutes River *46 B3 river* Oregon, NW USA
Desē *72 C4 var.* Desse, *It.* Dessie. Amhara, N Ethiopia
Deseado, Río *65 B7 river* S Argentina

Desertas, Ilhas *70 A2 island group* Madeira, Portugal, NE Atlantic Ocean
Deshu see Deh Shū
Des Moines *45 F3 state capital* Iowa, C USA
Desna *109 E2 river* Russian Federation/Ukraine
Dessau *94 C4* Sachsen-Anhalt, E Germany
Desse see Desē
Dessie see Desē
Destêrro see Florianópolis
Detroit *40 D3* Michigan, N USA
Detroit Lakes *45 F2* Minnesota, N USA
Deurne *87 D5* Noord-Brabant, SE Netherlands
Deutschendorf see Poprad
Deutsch-Eylau see Iława
Deutsch Krone see Wałcz
Deutschland/Deutschland, Bundesrepublik see Germany
Deutsch-Südwestafrika see Namibia
Deva *108 B4 Ger.* Diemrich, *Hung.* Déva. Hunedoara, W Romania
Déva see Deva
Deva see Chester
Devana see Aberdeen
Devana Castra see Chester
Ðevđelija see Gevgelija
Deventer *86 D3* Overijssel, E Netherlands
Devils Lake *45 E1* North Dakota, N USA
Devoll see Devollit, Lumi i
Devollit, Lumi i *101 D6 var.* Devoll. *river* SE Albania
Devon Island *37 F2 prev.* North Devon Island. *island* Parry Islands, Nunavut, NE Canada
Devonport *149 C8* Tasmania, SE Australia
Devrek *116 C2* Zonguldak, N Turkey
Dexter *45 H5* Missouri, C USA
Deynau see Galkynyş
Dezfūl *120 C3 var.* Dizful. Khūzestān, SW Iran
Dezhou *128 D4* Shandong, E China
Dhaka *135 G4 prev.* Dacca. *country capital* (Bangladesh) Dhaka, C Bangladesh
Dhanbād *135 F4* Jhārkhand, NE India
Dhekélia *102 C5 Eng.* Dhekelia, *Gk.* Dekéleia. *UK air base* SE Cyprus
Dhidhimótikhon see Didymóteicho
Dhíkti Ori see Díkti
Dhodhekánisos see Dodekánisa
Dhomokós see Domokós
Dhráma see Dráma
Dhrepanon, Akrotírio see Drépano, Akrotírio
Dhún na nGall, Bá see Donegal Bay
Dhuusa Marreeb *73 E5 var.* Dusa Marreb, *It.* Dusa Mareb. Galguduud, C Somalia
Diakovár see Đakovo
Diamantina, Chapada *63 F3 mountain range* E Brazil
Diamantina Fracture Zone *141 E6 tectonic feature* E Indian Ocean
Diamond State see Delaware
Diarbekr see Diyarbakır
Dibio see Dijon
Dibra see Debar
Dibrugarh *135 H3* Assam, NE India
Dickinson *44 D2* North Dakota, N USA
Dicle see Tigris
Didimoticho see Didymóteicho
Didymóteicho *104 D3 var.* Dhidhimótikhon, *prev.* Didimotiho. Anatolikí Makedonía kai Thráki, NE Greece
Diedenhofen see Thionville
Diekirch *87 D7* Diekirch, C Luxembourg
Diemrich see Deva
Ðiên Biên *136 D3 var.* Dien Bien, Dien Bien Phu. Lai Châu, N Vietnam
Dien Bien Phu, Dien Biên see Ðiên Biên
Diepenbeek *87 D6* Limburg, NE Belgium
Diepholz *94 B3* Niedersachsen, NW Germany
Dieppe *90 C2* Seine-Maritime, N France
Dieren *86 D4* Gelderland, E Netherlands
Differdange *87 D8* Luxembourg, SW Luxembourg
Digne *91 D6 var.* Digne-les-Bains. Alpes-de-Haute-Provence, SE France
Digne-les-Bains see Digne

Digoel see Digul, Sungai
Digoin 90 C4 Saône-et-Loire, C France
Digul, Sungai 139 H5 prev. Digoel. river Papua, E Indonesia
Dihang see Brahmaputra
Dijlah see Tigris
Dijon 90 D4 anc. Dibio. Côte d'Or, C France
Dikhil 72 D4 SW Djibouti
Dikson 114 D2 Taymyrskiy (Dolgano-Nenetskiy) Avtonomnyy Okrug, N Russian Federation
Dikti 105 D8 var. Dhíkti Ori. mountain range Kríti, Greece, E Mediterranean Sea
Dili 139 F5 var. Dilli, Dilly. country capital (East Timor) N East Timor
Dilia 75 G3 var. Dillia. river SE Niger
Di Linh 137 E6 Lâm Đông, S Vietnam
Dilli see Dili, East Timor
Dilli see Delhi, India
Dillia see Dilia
Dilling 72 B4 var. Ad Dalanj. Southern Kordofan, C Sudan
Dillon 44 B2 Montana, NW USA
Dilly see Dili
Dilolo 77 D7 Katanga, S Dem. Rep. Congo
Dimashq 119 B5 var. Ash Shām, Esh Sham, Eng. Damascus, Fr. Damas, It. Damasco. country capital (Syria) Dimashq, SW Syria
Dimitrovgrad 104 D3 Khaskovo, S Bulgaria
Dimitrovgrad 111 C6 prev. Caribrod. Serbia, SE Serbia
Dimitrovo see Pernik
Dimovo 104 B1 Vidin, NW Bulgaria
Dinajpur 135 F3 Rajshahi, NW Bangladesh
Dinan 90 B3 Côtes d'Armor, NW France
Dinant 87 C7 Namur, S Belgium
Dinar 116 B4 Afyon, SW Turkey
Dinara see Dinaric Alps
Dinaric Alps 100 C4 var. Dinara. mountain range Bosnia and Herzegovina/Croatia
Dindigul 132 C3 Tamil Nādu, SE India
Dingle Bay 89 A6 Ir. Bá an Daingin. bay SW Ireland
Dinguiraye 74 C4 N Guinea
Diourbel 74 B3 W Senegal
Dirē Dawa 73 D5 Dirē Dawa, E Ethiopia
Dirk Hartog Island 147 A5 island Western Australia
Dirschau see Tczew
Disappointment, Lake 146 C4 salt lake Western Australia
Discovery Bay 54 B4 Middlesex, Jamaica, Greater Antilles, C Jamaica Caribbean Sea
Disko Bugt see Qeqertarsuup Tunua
Dispur 135 G3 state capital Assam, NE India
Divinópolis 63 F4 Minas Gerais, SE Brazil
Divo 74 D5 S Côte d'Ivoire (Ivory Coast)
Divodurum Mediomatricum see Metz
Diyarbakır 117 E4 var. Diarbekr; anc. Amida. Diyarbakır, SE Turkey
Dizful see Dezfūl
Djailolo see Halmahera, Pulau
Djajapura see Jayapura
Djakarta see Jakarta
Djakovica see Đakovica
Djakovo see Đakovo
Djambala 77 B6 Plateaux, C Congo
Djambi see Jambi
Djambi see Hari, Batang
Djanet 71 E4 prev. Fort Charlet. SE Algeria
Djéblé see Jablah
Djelfa 70 D2 var. El Djelfa. N Algeria
Djéma 76 D4 Haut-Mbomou, E Central African Republic
Djember see Jember
Djérablous see Jarābulus
Djerba see Jerba, Île de
Djérem 76 B4 river C Cameroon
Djevdjelija see Gevgelija
Djibouti 72 D4 var. Jibuti. country capital (Djibouti) E Djibouti
Djibouti 72 D4 off. Republic of Djibouti, var. Jibuti; prev. French Somaliland, French Territory of the Afars and Issas, Côte Française des Somalis, Fr. Territoire Français des Afars et des Issas. country E Africa

DJIBOUTI
East Africa
Official name Republic of Djibouti
Formation 1977 / 1977
Capital Djibouti
Population 793,000 / 89 people per sq mile (34 people per sq km) / 83%
Total area 8494 sq miles (22,000 sq km)
Languages French*, Arabic*, Somali, Afar
Religions Muslim (mainly Sunni) 94%, Christian 6%
Ethnic mix Issa 60%, Afar 35%, Other 5%
Government Presidential system
Currency Djibouti franc = 100 centimes
Literacy rate 66%
Calorie consumption 2220 calories

Djibouti, Republic of see Djibouti
Djokjakarta see Yogyakarta
Djourab, Erg du 76 C2 desert N Chad
Djúpivogur 83 E5 Austurland, SE Iceland
Dmitriyevsk see Makiyivka
Dnepr see Dnieper
Dneprodzerzhinsk see Dniprodzerzhyns'k
Dneprodzerzhinskoye Vodokhranilishche see Dniprodzerzhyns'ke Vodoskhovyshche
Dnepropetrovsk see Dnipropetrovs'k
Dneprorudnoye see Dniprorudne
Dnestr see Dniester
Dnieper 81 F4 Bel. Dnyapro, Rus. Dnepr, Ukr. Dnipro. river E Europe
Dnieper Lowland 109 E2 Bel. Prydnyaprowskaya Nizina, Ukr. Prydniprovs'ka Nyzovyna. lowlands Belarus/Ukraine
Dniester 81 E4 Rom. Nistru, Rus. Dnestr, Ukr. Dnister; anc. Tyras. river Moldova/Ukraine
Dnipro see Dnieper
Dniprodzerzhyns'k 109 F3 Rus. Dneprodzerzhinsk; prev. Kamenskoe.
Dniprodzerzhyns'ke Vodoskhovyshche 109 F3 Rus. Dneprodzerzhinskoye Vodokhranilishche. reservoir C Ukraine
Dnipropetrovs'k 109 F3 Rus. Dnepropetrovsk; prev. Yekaterinoslav. Dnipropetrovs'ka Oblast', E Ukraine
Dniprorudne 109 F3 Rus. Dneprorudnoye. Zaporiz'ka Oblast', SE Ukraine
Dnister see Dniester
Dnyapro see Dnieper
Doba 76 C4 Logone-Oriental, S Chad
Döbeln 94 D4 Sachsen, E Germany
Doberai, Jazirah 139 G4 Dut. Vogelkop. peninsula Papua, E Indonesia
Doboj 100 C3 Republiks Srpska, N Bosnia and Herzegovina
Dobre Miasto 98 D2 Ger. Guttstadt. Warmińsko-mazurskie, NE Poland
Dobrich 104 E1 Rom. Bazargic; prev. Tolbukhin. Dobrich, NE Bulgaria
Dobrush 107 D7 Homyel'skaya Voblasts', SE Belarus
Dobryn' see Dabryn'
Dodecanese see Dodekánisa
Dodekánisa 105 D6 var. Nóties Sporádes, Eng. Dodecanese; prev. Dhodhekánisos, Dodekanisos. island group SE Greece
Dodekanisos see Dodekánisa
Dodge City 45 E5 Kansas, C USA
Dodoma 69 D5 country capital (Tanzania) Dodoma, C Tanzania
Dodoma 69 D5 var. C Tanzania
Dogana 96 E1 NE San Marino Europe
Dōgo 131 B6 island Oki-shotō, SW Japan
Dogondoutchi 75 F3 Dosso, SW Niger
Dogrular see Pravda
Doğubayazıt 117 F3 Ağrı, E Turkey
Doğu Karadeniz Dağları 117 E3 var. Anadolu Dağları. mountain range NE Turkey
Doha see Ad Dawḥah
Doire see Londonderry
Dokkum 86 D1 Friesland, N Netherlands

Dokuchayevs'k 109 G3 var. Dokuchayevsk. Donets'ka Oblast', SE Ukraine
Dokuchayevsk see Dokuchayevs'k
Doldrums Fracture Zone 66 C4 fracture zone W Atlantic Ocean
Dôle 90 D4 Jura, E France
Dolina see Dolyna
Dolinskaya see Dolyns'ka
Dolisie 77 B6 prev. Loubomo. Le Niari, S Congo
Dolomites/Dolomiti see Dolomitiche, Alpi
Dolomitiche, Alpi 96 C1 var. Dolomiti, Eng. Dolomites. mountain range NE Italy
Dolores 64 D4 Buenos Aires, E Argentina
Dolores 52 B1 Petén, N Guatemala
Dolores 64 D4 Soriano, SW Uruguay
Dolores Hidalgo 51 E4 var. Ciudad de Dolores Hidalgo. Guanajuato, C Mexico
Dolyna 108 B2 Rus. Dolina. Ivano-Frankivs'ka Oblast', W Ukraine
Dolyns'ka 109 F3 Rus. Dolinskaya. Kirovohrads'ka Oblast', S Ukraine
Domachëvo/Domaczewo see Damachava
Dombås 85 B5 Oppland, S Norway
Domel Island see Letsôk-aw Kyun
Domesnes, Cape see Kolkasrags
Domeyko 64 B3 Atacama, N Chile
Dominica 55 H4 off. Commonwealth of Dominica. country E West Indies

DOMINICA
West Indies
Official name Commonwealth of Dominica
Formation 1978 / 1978
Capital Roseau
Population 69,029 / 238 people per sq mile (92 people per sq km) / 71%
Total area 291 sq miles (754 sq km)
Languages English*, French Creole
Religions Roman Catholic 77%, Protestant 15%, Other 8%
Ethnic mix Black 91%, Mixed race 6%, Carib 2%, Other 1%
Government Parliamentary system
Currency Eastern Caribbean dollar = 100 cents
Literacy rate 88%
Calorie consumption 2763 calories

Dominica Channel see Martinique Passage
Dominica, Commonwealth of see Dominica
Dominican Republic 55 E2 country C West Indies

DOMINICAN REPUBLIC
West Indies
Official name Dominican Republic
Formation 1865 / 1865
Capital Santo Domingo
Population 8.9 million / 476 people per sq mile (184 people per sq km) / 65%
Total area 18,679 sq miles (48,380 sq km)
Languages Spanish*, French Creole
Religions Roman Catholic 92%, Other and nonreligious 8%
Ethnic mix Mixed race 75%, White 15%, Black 10%
Government Presidential system
Currency Dominican Republic peso = 100 centavos
Literacy rate 88%
Calorie consumption 2347 calories

Domokós 105 B5 var. Dhomokós. Stereá Ellás, C Greece
Don 111 B6 var. Duna, Tanais. river SW Russian Federation
Donau see Danube
Donauwörth 95 C6 Bayern, S Germany
Don Benito 92 C3 Extremadura, W Spain
Doncaster 89 D5 anc. Danum. N England, UK
Dondo 78 B1 Cuanza Norte, NW Angola
Donegal 89 C5 Ir. Dún na nGall. Donegal, NW Ireland
Donegal Bay 89 A5 Ir. Bá Dhún na nGall. bay NW Ireland

Donets 109 G2 river Russian Federation/Ukraine
Donets'k 109 G3 Rus. Donetsk; prev. Stalino. Donets'ka Oblast', E Ukraine
Dongfang 128 B7 var. Basuo. Hainan, S China
Dongguan 128 C6 Guangdong, S China
Đông Ha 136 E4 Quang Tri, C Vietnam
Dong Hai see East China Sea
Đông Hơi 136 D4 Quang Binh, C Vietnam
Dongliao see Liaoyuan
Dongola 72 B3 var. Donqola, Dunqulah. Northern, N Sudan
Dongou 77 C5 La Likouala, NE Congo
Dong Rak, Phanom see Dângrêk, Chuŏr Phnum
Dongting Hu 128 C5 var. Tung-t'ing Hu. lake S China
Donostia-San Sebastián 93 E1 País Vasco, N Spain
Donqola see Dongola
Doolow 73 D5 Somali, E Ethiopia
Doornik see Tournai
Door Peninsula 40 C2 peninsula Wisconsin, N USA
Dooxo Nugaaleed 73 E5 var. Nogal Valley. valley E Somalia
Dordogne 91 B5 department SW France
Dordogne 91 B5 cultural region SW France
Dordogne 91 B5 river W France
Dordrecht 86 C4 var. Dordt, Dort. Zuid-Holland, SW Netherlands
Dordt see Dordrecht
Dorohoi 108 C3 Botoşani, NE Romania
Dorotea 84 C4 Västerbotten, N Sweden
Dorpat see Tartu
Dorre Island 147 A5 island Western Australia
Dort see Dordrecht
Dortmund 94 A4 Nordrhein-Westfalen, W Germany
Dos Hermanas 92 C4 Andalucía, S Spain
Dospad Dagh see Rhodope Mountains
Dospat 104 C3 Smolyan, S Bulgaria
Dothan 42 D3 Alabama, S USA
Dotnuva 106 B4 Kaunas, C Lithuania
Douai 90 C2 prev. Douay; anc. Duacum. Nord, N France
Douala 77 A5 var. Duala. Littoral, W Cameroon
Douay see Douai
Douglas 89 C5 dependent territory capital (Isle of Man) E Isle of Man
Douglas 48 D3 Arizona, SW USA
Douglas 44 D3 Wyoming, C USA
Douma see Dūmā
Douro 92 B2 Port. Duero. river Portugal/Spain
Douro see Duero
Douvres see Dover
Dover 89 E7 Fr. Douvres, Lat. Dubris Portus. SE England, UK
Dover 41 F4 state capital Delaware, NE USA
Dover, Strait of 90 C2 var. Straits of Dover, Fr. Pas de Calais. strait England, UK/France
Dover, Straits of see Dover, Strait of
Dovrefjell 85 B5 plateau S Norway
Downpatrick 89 B5 Ir. Dún Pádraig. SE Northern Ireland, UK
Dōzen 131 B6 island Oki-shotō, SW Japan
Dràa, Hammada du see Dra, Hamada du
Drač/Draç see Durrës
Drachten 86 D2 Friesland, N Netherlands
Drăgăşani 108 B5 Vâlcea, SW Romania
Dragoman 104 B2 Sofiya, W Bulgaria
Dra, Hamada du 70 C3 var. Hammada du Drâa, Haut Plateau du Dra. plateau W Algeria
Dra, Haut Plateau du see Dra, Hamada du
Drahichyn 107 B6 Pol. Drohiczyn Poleski, Rus. Drogichin. Brestskaya Voblasts', SW Belarus
Drakensberg 78 D5 mountain range Lesotho/South Africa
Drake Passage 57 B8 passage Atlantic Ocean/Pacific Ocean
Dralfa 104 D2 Türgovishte, N Bulgaria
Dráma 105 C4 var. Dhráma. Anatolikí Makedonía kai Thráki, NE Greece
Dramburg see Drawsko Pomorskie
Drammen 85 B6 Buskerud, S Norway

Drau see Drava
Drava 100 C3 var. Drau, Eng. Drave, Hung. Dráva. river C Europe
Dráva/Drave see Drau/Drava
Drawsko Pomorskie 98 B3 Ger. Dramburg. Zachodnio-pomorskie, NW Poland
Drépano, Akrotírio 104 C4 var. Akrotírio Dhrepanon. cape N Greece
Drepanum see Trapani
Dresden 94 D4 Sachsen, E Germany
Drin see Drinit, Lumi
Drina 100 C3 river Bosnia and Herzegovina/Serbia
Drinit, Lumi 101 D5 var. Drin. river NW Albania
Drinit të Zi, Lumi i see Black Drin
Drissa see Drysa
Drobeta-Turnu Severin 108 B5 prev. Turnu Severin. SW Romania
Drogheda 89 B5 Ir. Droichead Átha. NE Ireland
Drogichin see Drahichyn
Drogobych see Drohobych
Drohiczyn Poleski see Drahichyn
Drohobych 108 B2 Pol. Drohobycz, Rus. Drogobych. L'vivs'ka Oblast', NW Ukraine
Drohobycz see Drohobych
Droichead Átha see Drogheda
Drôme 91 D5 cultural region E France
Drôme 91 D5 department E France
Dronning Maud Land 154 B2 physical region Antarctica
Drontheim see Trondheim
Drug see Durg
Druk-yul see Bhutan
Drummondville 39 E4 Québec, SE Canada
Druskienniki see Druskininkai
Druskininkai 107 B5 Pol. Druskienniki. Alytus, S Lithuania
Dryden 38 B3 Ontario, C Canada
Drysa 107 D5 Rus. Drissa. river N Belarus
Duacum see Douai
Duala see Douala
Dubai see Dubayy
Dubăsari 108 D3 Rus. Dubossary. NE Moldova
Dubawnt 37 F4 river Nunavut, NW Canada
Dubayy 120 D4 Eng. Dubai. Dubayy, NE United Arab Emirates
Dubbo 149 D6 New South Wales, SE Australia
Dublin 89 B5 Ir. Baile Átha Cliath; anc. Eblana. country capital (Ireland) Dublin, E Ireland
Dublin 43 E2 Georgia, SE USA
Dubno 108 C2 Rivnens'ka Oblast', NW Ukraine
Dubossary see Dubăsari
Dubris Portus see Dover
Dubrovnik 101 B5 It. Ragusa. Dubrovnik-Neretva, SE Croatia
Dubuque 45 G3 Iowa, C USA
Dudelange 87 D8 var. Forge du Sud, Ger. Dudelingen. Luxembourg, S Luxembourg
Dudelingen see Dudelange
Duero 92 D2 Port. Douro. river Portugal/Spain
Duero see Douro
Duesseldorf see Düsseldorf
Duffel 87 C5 Antwerpen, C Belgium
Dugi Otok 100 A4 var. Isola Grossa, It. Isola Lunga. island W Croatia
Duinekerke see Dunkerque
Duisburg 94 A4 prev. Duisburg-Hamborn. Nordrhein-Westfalen, W Germany
Duisburg-Hamborn see Duisburg
Duiven 86 D4 Gelderland, E Netherlands
Duk Faiwil 73 B5 Jonglei, SE Sudan
Dulan 126 D4 var. Qagan Us. Qinghai, C China
Dulce, Golfo 53 E5 gulf S Costa Rica
Dulce, Golfo see Izabal, Lago de
Dülmen 94 A4 Nordrhein-Westfalen, W Germany
Dulovo 104 E1 Silistra, NE Bulgaria
Duluth 45 G2 Minnesota, N USA
Dūmā 119 B5 Fr. Douma. Dimashq, SW Syria
Dumas 49 E1 Texas, SW USA
Dumfries 88 C4 S Scotland, UK

Dumont d'Urville 154 C4 French research station Antarctica
Dumyât 72 B1 Eng. Damietta. N Egypt
Duna see Danube, C Europe
Düna see Western Dvina
Duna see Don, Russian Federation
Dünaburg see Daugavpils
Dunaj see Wien, Austria
Dunaj see Danube, C Europe
Dunapentele see Dunaújváros
Dunărea see Danube
Dunaújváros 99 C7 prev. Dunapentele, Sztálinváros. Fejér, C Hungary
Dunav see Danube
Dunavska Ravnina 104 C2 Eng. Danubian Plain. lowlands N Bulgaria
Duncan 49 G2 Oklahoma, C USA
Dundalk 89 B5 Ir. Dún Dealgan. Louth, NE Ireland
Dún Dealgan see Dundalk
Dundee 78 D4 KwaZulu/Natal, E South Africa
Dundee 88 C4 E Scotland, UK
Dunedin 151 B7 Otago, South Island, New Zealand
Dunfermline 88 C4 C Scotland, UK
Dungu 77 E5 Orientale, NE Dem. Rep. Congo
Dungun 138 B3 var. Kuala Dungun. Terengganu, Peninsular Malaysia
Dunholme see Durham
Dunkerque 90 C2 Eng. Dunkirk, Flem. Duinekerke; prev. Dunquerque. Nord, N France
Dunkirk see Dunkerque
Dún Laoghaire 89 B6 Eng. Dunleary; prev. Kingstown. E Ireland
Dunleary see Dún Laoghaire
Dún Pádraig see Downpatrick
Dunquerque see Dunkerque
Dunqulah see Dongola
Dupnitsa 104 C2 prev. Marek, Stanke Dimitrov. Kyustendil, W Bulgaria
Duqm 121 E5 var. Daqm. E Oman
Durance 91 D6 river SE France
Durango 50 D3 var. Victoria de Durango. Durango, W Mexico
Durango 44 C5 Colorado, C USA
Durankulak 104 E1 Rom. Răcari; prev. Blatnitsa, Duranulac. Dobrich, NE Bulgaria
Durant 49 G2 Oklahoma, C USA
Duranulac see Durankulak
Durazzo see Durrës
Durban 78 D4 var. Port Natal. KwaZulu/Natal, E South Africa
Durbe 106 B3 Ger. Durben. Liepāja, W Latvia
Durben see Durbe
Durg 135 E4 prev. Drug. Chhattisgarh, C India
Durham 89 D5 hist. Dunholme. N England, UK
Durham 43 F1 North Carolina, SE USA
Durocortorum see Reims
Durostorum see Silistra
Durovernum see Canterbury
Durrës 101 C6 var. Durrësi, Dursi, It. Durazzo, SCr. Drač, Turk. Draç. Durrës, W Albania
Durrësi see Durrës
Dursi see Durrës
Durūz, Jabal ad 119 C5 mountain SW Syria
D'Urville Island 150 C4 island C New Zealand
Dusa Mareb/Dusa Marreb see Dhuusa Marreeb
Dushanbe 123 E3 var. Dyushambe; prev. Stalinabad, Taj. Stalinobod. country capital (Tajikistan) W Tajikistan
Düsseldorf 94 A4 var. Duesseldorf. Nordrhein-Westfalen, W Germany
Dūstī 123 F3 Rus. Dusti. SW Tajikistan
Dutch East Indies see Indonesia
Dutch Guiana see Surinam
Dutch Harbor 36 B3 Unalaska Island, Alaska, USA
Dutch New Guinea see Papua
Dutch West Indies see Netherlands Antilles
Duzdab see Zāhedān
Dvina Bay see Chëshskaya Guba
Dvinsk see Daugavpils
Dyanev see Galkynyş
Dyersburg 42 C1 Tennessee, S USA
Dyushambe see Dushanbe

Dza Chu see Mekong
Dzaudzhikau see Vladikavkaz
Dzerzhinsk 111 C5 Nizhegorodskaya Oblast', W Russian Federation
Dzerzhinskiy see Nar'yan-Mar
Dzhalal-Abad 123 F2 Kir. Jalal-Abad. Dzhalal-Abadskaya Oblast', W Kyrgyzstan
Dzhankoy 109 F4 Respublika Krym, S Ukraine
Dzharkurgan see Jarqo'rg'on
Dzhelandy 123 F3 SE Tajikistan
Dzhergalan 123 G2 Kir. Jyrgalan. Issyk-Kul'skaya Oblast', NE Kyrgyzstan
Dzhezkazgan see Zhezkazgan
Dzhizak see Jizzax
Dzhugdzhur, Khrebet 115 G3 mountain range E Russian Federation
Dzhusaly 114 B4 Kaz. Zholsaly. Kzylorda, SW Kazakhstan
Działdowo 98 D3 Warmińsko-Mazurskie, C Poland
Dzuunmod 127 E2 Töv, C Mongolia
Dzüün Soyonï Nuruu see Eastern Sayans
Dzvina see Western Dvina

E

E see Hubei
Eagle Pass 49 F4 Texas, SW USA
East Açores Fracture Zone see East Azores Fracture Zone
East Antarctica see Greater Antarctica
East Australian Basin see Tasman Basin
East Azores Fracture Zone 66 C3 var. East Açores Fracture Zone. tectonic feature E Atlantic Ocean
Eastbourne 89 E7 SE England, UK
East Cape 150 E3 headland North Island, New Zealand
East China Sea 125 E2 Chin. Dong Hai. sea W Pacific Ocean
Easter Fracture Zone 153 G4 tectonic feature E Pacific Ocean
Easter Island see Pascua, Isla de
Eastern Desert see Sahara el Sharqiya
Eastern Ghats 124 B3 mountain range SE India
Eastern Sayans 115 E4 Mong. Dzüün Soyonï Nuruu, Rus. Vostochnyy Sayan. mountain range Mongolia/Russian Federation
Eastern Sierra Madre see Sierra Madre Oriental
East Falkland 65 D8 var. Isla Soledad. island E Falkland Islands
East Frisian Islands see Ostfriesische Inseln
East Grand Forks 45 E1 Minnesota, N USA
East Indiaman Ridge 141 D6 undersea ridge E Indian Ocean
East Indies 152 A3 island group SE Asia
East Kilbride 88 C4 S Scotland, UK
East Korea Bay 128 E3 bay E North Korea Pacific Ocean Sea of Japan
Eastleigh 89 D7 S England, UK
East London 78 D5 Afr. Oos-Londen; prev. Emonti, Port Rex. Eastern Cape, S South Africa
Eastmain 38 D3 river Québec, C Canada
East Mariana Basin 142 B1 undersea basin W Pacific Ocean
East Novaya Zemlya Trough 112 C1 var. Novaya Zemlya Trough. trough W Kara Sea
East Pacific Rise 153 F4 undersea rise E Pacific Ocean
East Pakistan see Bangladesh
East Saint Louis 40 B4 Illinois, N USA
East Scotia Basin 67 C7 undersea basin SE Scotia Sea
East Sea 130 A4 var. Sea of Japan, Rus. Yaponskoye More. sea NW Pacific Ocean
East Siberian Sea see Vostochno-Sibirskoye More
East Timor 139 F5 var. Loro Sae; prev. Portuguese Timor, Timor Timur. country S Indonesia

Eau Claire 40 A2 Wisconsin, N USA
Eau Claire, Lac à L' see St. Clair, Lake
Eauripik Rise 142 B2 undersea rise W Pacific Ocean
Ebensee 95 D6 Oberösterreich, N Austria
Eberswalde-Finow 94 D3 Brandenburg, E Germany
Ebetsu 130 D2 var. Ebetu. Hokkaidō, NE Japan
Ebetu see Ebetsu
Eblana see Dublin
Ebolowa 77 A5 Sud, S Cameroon
Ebon Atoll 144 D2 var. Epoon. atoll Ralik Chain, S Marshall Islands
Ebora see Évora
Eboracum see York
Ebro 93 E2 river NE Spain
Eburacum see York
Ebusus see Eivissa
Ebusus see Eivissa
Ecbatana see Hamadān
Ech Cheliff/Ech Chleff see Chlef
Echo Bay 37 E3 Northwest Territories, NW Canada
Echt 87 D5 Limburg, SE Netherlands
Ecija 92 D4 anc. Astigi. Andalucía, SW Spain
Eckengraf see Viesīte
Ecuador 60 B1 off. Republic of Ecuador. country NW South America

Ecuador, Republic of see Ecuador
Ed Da'ein 72 A4 Southern Darfur, W Sudan
Ed Damazin 72 C4 var. Ad Damazin. Blue Nile, E Sudan
Ed Damer 72 C3 var. Ad Dāmir, Ad Damar. River Nile, NE Sudan
Ed Debba 72 B3 Northern, N Sudan
Ede 86 D4 Gelderland, C Netherlands
Ede 75 F5 Osun, SW Nigeria
Edéa 77 A5 Littoral, SW Cameroon
Edessa see Şanlıurfa
Edfu see Idfu
Edgeøya 83 G2 island S Svalbard
Edgware 89 A7 Harrow, SE England, UK
Edinburg 49 G5 Texas, SW USA
Edinburgh 88 C4 national capital S Scotland, UK
Edingen see Enghien
Edirne 116 A2 Eng. Adrianople, anc. Adrianopolis, Hadrianopolis. Edirne, NW Turkey
Edmonds 46 B2 Washington, NW USA

Edmonton *37 E5 province capital* Alberta, SW Canada

Edmundston *39 E4* New Brunswick, SE Canada

Edna *49 G4* Texas, SW USA

Edolo *96 B1* Lombardia, N Italy

Edremit *116 A3* Balıkesir, NW Turkey

Edward, Lake *77 E5* var. Albert Edward Nyanza, Edward Nyanza, Lac Idi Amin, Lake Rutanzige. *lake* Uganda/ Dem. Rep. Congo

Edward Nyanza *see* Edward, Lake

Edwards Plateau *49 F3 plain* Texas, SW USA

Edzo *53 E4 prev.* Rae-Edzo. Northwest Territories, NW Canada

Eeklo *87 B5* var. Eekloo. Oost-Vlaanderen, NW Belgium

Eekloo *see* Eeklo

Eems *see* Ems

Eersel *87 C5* Noord-Brabant, S Netherlands

Eesti Vabariik *see* Estonia

Éfaté *144 D4* var. Efate, Fr. Vaté; prev. Sandwich Island. *island* C Vanuatu

Efate *see* Éfaté

Effingham *40 B4* Illinois, N USA

Eforie Sud *108 D5* Constanţa, E Romania

Egadi, Isole *97 B7 island group* S Italy

Ege Denizi *see* Aegean Sea

Eger *99 D6* Ger. Erlau. Heves, NE Hungary

Eger *see* Cheb

Egeria Fracture Zone *141 C5 tectonic feature* W Indian Ocean

Éghezèe *87 C6* Namur, C Belgium

Egina *see* Aígina

Egio *see* Aígio

Egmont *see* Taranaki, Mount

Egmont, Cape *150 C4 cape* North Island, New Zealand

Egoli *see* Johannesburg

Egypt *72 B2 off.* Arab Republic of Egypt, Ar. Jumhūrīyah Misr al 'Arabīyah, prev. United Arab Republic; anc. Aegyptus. *country* NE Africa

Eibar *93 E1* País Vasco, N Spain

Eibergen *86 E3* Gelderland, E Netherlands

Eidfjord *85 A5* Hordaland, S Norway

Eier-Berg *see* Suur Munamägi

Eifel *95 A5 plateau* W Germany

Eiger *95 B7 mountain* C Switzerland

Eigg *88 B3 island* W Scotland, UK

Eight Degree Channel *132 B3 channel* India/Maldives

Eighty Mile Beach *146 B4 beach* Western Australia

Eijsden *87 D6* Limburg, SE Netherlands

Eilat *see* Elat

Eindhoven *87 D5* Noord-Brabant, S Netherlands

Eipel *see* Ipel'

Éire *see* Ireland

Éireann, Muir *see* Irish Sea

Eisenhüttenstadt *94 D4* Brandenburg, E Germany

Eisenmarkt *see* Hunedoara

Eisenstadt *95 E6* Burgenland, E Austria

Eisleben *94 C4* Sachsen-Anhalt, C Germany

Eivissa *93 G3* var. Iviza, Cast. Ibiza; anc. Ebusus. Ibiza, Spain, W Mediterranean Sea

Ejea de los Caballeros *93 E2* Aragón, NE Spain

Ejin Qi *see* Dalain Hob

Ekapa *see* Cape Town

Ekaterinodar *see* Krasnodar

Ekiatapskiy Khrebet *115 G1 mountain range* NE Russian Federation

El 'Alamein *72 B1* var. Al 'Alamayn. N Egypt

El Asnam *see* Chlef

Elat *119 B8* var. Eilat, Elath. Southern, S Israel

Elat, Gulf of *see* Aqaba, Gulf of

Elath *see* Elat, Israel

Elath *see* Al 'Aqabah, Jordan

El'Atrun *72 B3* Northern Darfur, NW Sudan

Elâziğ *117 E3* var. Elâzig, Elâziz. Elâzığ, E Turkey

Elba, Isola d' *96 B4 island* Archipelago Toscano, C Italy

Elbasan *101 D6* var. Elbasani. Elbasan, C Albania

Elbasani *see* Elbasan

Elbe *80 D3* Cz. Labe. *river* Czech Republic/Germany

El Beni *see* Beni

Elbert, Mount *44 C4 mountain* Colorado, C USA

Elbing *see* Elbląg

Elbląg *98 C2* var. Elbląg, Ger. Elbing. Warmińsko-Mazurskie, NE Poland

El Boulaïda/El Boulaïda *see* Blida

El'brus *111 A8* var. Gora El'brus. *mountain* SW Russian Federation

El'brus, Gora *see* El'brus

El Burgo de Osma *93 E2* Castilla-León, C Spain

Elburz Mountains *see* Alborz, Reshteh-ye Kühhā-ye

El Cajon *47 C8* California, W USA

El Calafate *65 B7* var. Calafate. Santa Cruz, S Argentina

El Callao *59 E2* Bolívar, E Venezuela

El Campo *49 G4* Texas, SW USA

El Carmen de Bolívar *58 B2* Bolívar, NW Colombia

El Cayo *see* San Ignacio

El Centro *47 D8* California, W USA

Elche *93 F4* Cat. Elx; anc. Ilici, Lat. Illicis. País Valenciano, E Spain

Elda *93 F4* País Valenciano, E Spain

El Djazaïr *see* Alger

El Djelfa *see* Djelfa

Eldorado *64 E3* Misiones, NE Argentina

El Dorado *50 C3* Sinaloa, C Mexico

El Dorado *42 B2* Arkansas, C USA

El Dorado *45 F5* Kansas, C USA

El Dorado *59 F2* Bolívar, E Venezuela

El Dorado *see* California

Eldoret *73 C6* Rift Valley, W Kenya

Elektrostal' *111 B5* Moskovskaya Oblast', W Russian Federation

Elemi Triangle *73 B5 disputed region* Kenya/Sudan

Elephant Butte Reservoir *48 C2 reservoir* New Mexico, SW USA

Élesd *see* Aleşd

Eleuthera Island *54 C1 island* N Bahamas

El Fasher *72 A4* var. Al Fāshir. Northern Darfur, W Sudan

El Ferrol/El Ferrol del Caudillo *see* Ferrol

El Gedaref *see* Gedaref

El Geneina *72 A4* var. Ajjinena, Al-Genain, Al Junaynah. Western Darfur, W Sudan

Elgin *88 C3* NE Scotland, UK

Elgin *40 B3* Illinois, N USA

El Giza *72 B1* var. Al Jīzah, Giza, Gizeh. N Egypt

El Goléa *70 D3* var. Al Golea. C Algeria

El Hank *74 D1 cliff* N Mauritania

El Haseke *see* Al Ḥasakah

Elimberrum *see* Auch

Eliocroca *see* Lorca

Élisabethville *see* Lubumbashi

Elista *111 B7* Respublika Kalmykiya, SW Russian Federation

Elizabeth *149 B6* South Australia

Elizabeth City *43 G1* North Carolina, SE USA

Elizabethtown *40 C5* Kentucky, S USA

El-Jadida *70 C2 prev.* Mazagan. W Morocco

Ełk *98 E2* Ger. Lyck. Warmińsko-mazurskie, NE Poland

Elk City *49 F1* Oklahoma, C USA

El Khalil *see* Hebron

El Khârga *72 B2* var. Al Khārijah. C Egypt

Elkhart *40 C3* Indiana, N USA

El Khartûm *see* Khartoum

Elk River *45 F2* Minnesota, N USA

El Kuneitra *see* Al Qunayţirah

Elláda/Ellás *see* Greece

Ellef Ringnes Island *37 E1 island* Nunavut, N Canada

Ellen, Mount *44 B5 mountain* Utah, W USA

Ellensburg *46 B2* Washington, NW USA

Ellesmere Island *37 F1 island* Queen Elizabeth Islands, Nunavut, N Canada

Ellesmere, Lake *151 C6 lake* South Island, New Zealand

Ellice Islands *see* Tuvalu

Elliston *149 A6* South Australia

Ellsworth Land *154 A3 physical region* Antarctica

El Mahbas *70 B3* var. Mahbés. SW Western Sahara

El Mina *118 B4* var. Al Mīnā'. N Lebanon

El Minya *72 B2* var. Al Minyā, Minya. C Egypt

Elmira *41 E3* New York, NE USA

El Mreyyé *74 D2 desert* E Mauritania

Elmshorn *94 B3* Schleswig-Holstein, N Germany

El Muglad *72 B4* Western Kordofan, C Sudan

El Obeid *72 B4* var. Al Obayyid, Al Ubayyiḍ. Northern Kordofan, C Sudan

El Ouâdi *see* El Oued

El Oued *71 E2* var. Al Oued, El Ouâdi, El Wad. NE Algeria

Eloy *48 B2* Arizona, SW USA

El Paso *48 D3* Texas, SW USA

El Porvenir *53 G4* San Blas, N Panama

El Progreso *52 C2* Yoro, NW Honduras

El Puerto de Santa María *92 C5* Andalucía, S Spain

El Qâhira *see* Cairo

El Quneitra *see* Al Qunayţirah

El Queseir *see* Al Quşayr

El Quweira *see* Al Quwayrah

El Rama *53 E3* Región Autónoma Atlántico Sur, SE Nicaragua

El Real *53 H5* var. El Real de Santa María. Darién, SE Panama

El Real de Santa María *see* El Real

El Reno *49 F1* Oklahoma, C USA

El Salvador *52 B3 off.* Republica de El Salvador. *country* Central America

El Salvador, Republica de *see* El Salvador

Elsass *see* Alsace

El Sáuz *50 C2* Chihuahua, N Mexico

El Serrat *91 A7* N Andorra Europe

Elst *86 D4* Gelderland, E Netherlands

El Sueco *50 C2* Chihuahua, N Mexico

El Suweida *see* As Suwaydā'

El Suweis *see* Suez

Eltanin Fracture Zone *153 E5 tectonic feature* SE Pacific Ocean

El Tigre *59 E2* Anzoátegui, NE Venezuela

Elvas *92 C4* Portalegre, C Portugal

El Vendrell *93 G2* Cataluña, NE Spain

El Vigía *58 C2* Mérida, NW Venezuela

El Wad *see* El Oued

Elwell, Lake *44 B1 reservoir* Montana, NW USA

Elx *see* Elche

Ely *47 D5* Nevada, W USA

El Yopal *see* Yopal

Emajõgi *106 D3* Ger. Embach. *river* SE Estonia

Emāmrūd *see* Shāhrūd

Emāmshahr *see* Shāhrūd

Emba *114 B4* Kaz. Embi. Aktyubinsk, W Kazakhstan

Embach *see* Emajõgi

Embi *see* Emba

Emden *94 A3* Niedersachsen, NW Germany

Emerald *148 D4* Queensland, E Australia

Emerald Isle *see* Montserrat

Emesa *see* Ḥimş

Emmaste *106 C2* Hiiumaa, W Estonia

Emmeloord *86 D2* Flevoland, N Netherlands

Emmen *86 E2* Drenthe, NE Netherlands

Emmendingen *95 A6* Baden-Württemberg, SW Germany

Emona *see* Ljubljana

Emonti *see* East London

Emory Peak *49 E4 mountain* Texas, SW USA

Empalme *50 B2* Sonora, NW Mexico

Emperor Seamounts *113 G3 seamount range* NW Pacific Ocean

Empire State of the South *see* Georgia

Emporia *45 F5* Kansas, C USA

Empty Quarter *see* Ar Rub 'al Khālī

Ems *94 A3* Dut. Eems. *river* NW Germany

Enareträsk *see* Inarijärvi

Encamp *91 A8* Encamp, C Andorra Europe

Encarnación *64 D3* Itapúa, S Paraguay

Encinitas *47 C8* California, W USA

Encs *99 D6* Borsod-Abaúj-Zemplén, NE Hungary

Endeavour Strait *148 C1 strait* Queensland, NE Australia

Enderbury Island *145 F3 atoll* Phoenix Islands, C Kiribati

Enderby Land *154 C2 physical region* Antarctica

Enderby Plain *154 D2 abyssal plain* S Indian Ocean

Endersdorf *see* Jędrzejów

Enewetak Atoll *144 C1* var. Änewetak, Eniwetok. *atoll* Ralik Chain, W Marshall Islands

Enfield *89 A7* UK

Engeten *see* Aiud

Enghien *87 B6* Dut. Edingen. Hainaut, SW Belgium

England *89 D5* Lat. Anglia. *cultural region* England, UK

England *89 D5* Lat. Anglia. *national region* England, UK

Englewood *44 D4* Colorado, C USA

English Channel *89 D8* var. The Channel, Fr. la Manche. *channel* NW Europe

Engure *106 C3* Tukums, W Latvia

Engures Ezers *106 B3 lake* NW Latvia

Enguri *117 F1* Rus. Inguri. *river* NW Georgia

Enid *49 F1* Oklahoma, C USA

Enikale Strait *see* Kerch Strait

Eniwetok *see* Enewetak Atoll

En Nâqoûra *119 A5* var. An Nāqūrah. SW Lebanon

En Nazira *see* Nazerat

Ennedi *76 D2 plateau* E Chad

Ennis *89 A6* Ir. Inis. Clare, W Ireland

Ennis *49 G3* Texas, SW USA

Enniskillen *89 B5* var. Inniskilling, Ir. Inis Ceithleann. SW Northern Ireland, UK

Enns *95 D6* river C Austria

Enschede *86 E3* Overijssel, E Netherlands

Ensenada *50 A1* Baja California, NW Mexico

Entebbe *73 B6* S Uganda

Entroncamento *92 B3* Santarém, C Portugal

Enugu *75 G5* Enugu, S Nigeria

Eolie, Isole *97 C6* var. Isole Lipari, Eng. Aeolian Islands, Lípari Islands. *island group* S Italy

Epanomí *104 B4* Kentrikí Makedonía, N Greece

Epéna *77 B5* La Likouala, NE Congo
Eperies/Eperjes *see* Prešov
Epi *144 D4 var.* Épi. *island* C Vanuatu
Épi *see* Epi
Épinal *90 D4* Vosges, NE France
Epiphania *see* Ḥamāh
Epitoli *see* Tshwane
Epoon *see* Ebon Atoll
Epsom *89 A8* UK
Equality State *see* Wyoming
Equatorial Guinea *77 A5 off.* Equatorial Guinea, Republic of. *country* C Africa

---

EQUATORIAL GUINEA
Central Africa

Official name Republic of Equatorial Guinea
Formation 1968 / 1968
Capital Malabo
Population 504,000 / 47 people per sq mile (18 people per sq km) / 48%
Total area 10,830 sq miles (28,051 sq km)
Languages Spanish*, Fang, Bubi
Religions Roman Catholic 90%, Other 10%
Ethnic mix Fang 85%, Other 11%, Bubi 4%
Government Presidential system
Currency CFA franc = 100 centimes
Literacy rate 84%
Calorie consumption Not available

Equatorial Guinea, Republic of *see* Equatorial Guinea
Erautini *see* Johannesburg
Erbil *see* Arbil
Erciş *117 F3* Van, E Turkey
Erdély *see* Transylvania
Erdélyi-Havasok *see* Carpaţii Meridionali
Erdenet *127 E2* Orhon, N Mongolia
Erdi *76 C2 plateau* NE Chad
Erdi Ma *76 D2 desert* NE Chad
Erebus, Mount *154 B4 volcano* Ross Island, Antarctica
Ereğli *116 C4* Konya, S Turkey
Erenhot *127 F2 var.* Erlian. Nei Mongol Zizhiqu, NE China
Erfurt *94 C4* Thüringen, C Germany
Ergene Çayi *116 A2 var.* Ergene Irmaği. *river* NW Turkey
Ergene Irmaği *see* Ergene Çayi
Ergun *127 F1 var.* Labudalin; *prev.* Ergun Youqi. Nei Mongol Zizhiqu, N China
Ergun He *see* Argun
Ergun Youqi *see* Ergun
Erie *40 D3* Pennsylvania, NE USA
Érié, Lac *see* Erie, Lake
Erie, Lake *40 D3 Fr.* Lac Érié. *lake* Canada/USA
Eritrea *72 C4 off.* State of Eritrea, Ertra. *country* E Africa

---

ERITREA
East Africa

Official name State of Eritrea
Formation 1993 / 2002
Capital Asmara
Population 4.4 million / 97 people per sq mile (37 people per sq km) / 19%
Total area 46,842 sq miles (121,320 sq km)
Languages Arabic*, Tigrinya*, English, Tigre, Afar, Bilen, Kunama, Nara, Saho, Hadareb
Religions Christian 45%, Muslim 45%, Other 10%
Ethnic mix Tigray 50%, Tigray and Kunama 40%, Afar 4%, Other 3%, Saho 3%
Government Transitional regime
Currency Nakfa = 100 cents
Literacy rate 57%
Calorie consumption 1513 calories

Eritrea, State of *see* Eritrea
Erivan *see* Yerevan
Erlangen *95 C5* Bayern, S Germany
Erlau *see* Eger
Erlian *see* Erenhot
Ermelo *78 D3* Gelderland, C Netherlands
Ermióni *105 C6* Pelopónnisos, S Greece

Ermoúpoli *105 D6 var.* Hermoupolis; *prev.* Ermoúpolis. Sýyros, Kykládes, Greece, Aegean Sea
Ermoúpolis *see* Ermoúpoli
Ernākulam *132 C3* Kerala, SW India
Erode *132 C2* Tamil Nādu, SE India
Erquelinnes *87 B7* Hainaut, S Belgium
Er-Rachidia *70 C2 var.* Ksar al Soule. E Morocco
Er Rahad *72 B4 var.* Ar Rahad. Northern Kordofan, C Sudan
Erromango *144 D4 island* S Vanuatu
Ertis *see* Irtysh, C Asia
Ertra *see* Eritrea
Erzerum *see* Erzurum
Erzgebirge *95 C5 Cz.* Krušné Hory, *Eng.* Ore Mountains. *mountain range* Czech Republic/Germany
Erzincan *117 E3 var.* Erzinjan. Erzincan, E Turkey
Erzinjan *see* Erzincan
Erzurum *117 E3 prev.* Erzerum. Erzurum, NE Turkey
Esbjerg *85 A7* Ribe, W Denmark
Esbo *see* Espoo
Escaldes *91 A8* Escaldes Engordany, C Andorra Europe
Escanaba *40 C2* Michigan, N USA
Escaut *see* Scheldt
Esch-sur-Alzette *87 D8* Luxembourg, S Luxembourg
Esclaves, Grand Lac des *see* Great Slave Lake
Escondido *47 C8* California, W USA
Escuinapa *50 D3 var.* Escuinapa de Hidalgo. Sinaloa, C Mexico
Escuinapa de Hidalgo *see* Escuinapa
Escuintla *52 B2* Escuintla, S Guatemala
Escuintla *51 G5* Chiapas, SE Mexico
Esenguly *122 B3* Rus. Gasan-Kuli. Balkan Welaýaty, W Turkmenistan
Eşfahān *120 C3 Eng.* Isfahan; *anc.* Aspadana. Eşfahān, C Iran
Esh Sharā *see* Ash Sharāh
Esil *see* Ishim, Kazakhstan/Russian Federation
Eskimo Point *see* Arviat
Eskişehir *116 B3 var.* Eskishehr. Eskişehir, W Turkey
Eskishehr *see* Eskişehir
Eslāmābād *120 C3 var.* Eslāmābād-e Gharb; *prev.* Harunabad, Shāhābād. Kermānshāhān, W Iran
Eslāmābād-e Gharb *see* Eslāmābād
Esmeraldas *60 A1* Esmeraldas, N Ecuador
Esna *see* Isna
España *see* Spain
Espanola *48 D1* New Mexico, SW USA
Esperance *147 B7* Western Australia
Esperanza *50 B2* Sonora, NW Mexico
Esperanza *154 A2* Argentinian research station Antarctica
Espinal *58 B3* Tolima, C Colombia
Espinhaço, Serra do *56 D4 mountain range* SE Brazil
Espírito Santo *63 F4 off.* Estado do Espírito Santo. *state* E Brazil
Espírito Santo, Estado do *see* Espírito Santo
Espiritu Santo *144 C4 var.* Santo. *island* W Vanuatu
Espoo *85 D6 Swe.* Esbo. Etelä-Suomi, S Finland
Esquel *65 B6* Chubut, SW Argentina
Essaouira *70 B2 prev.* Mogador. W Morocco
Esseg *see* Osijek
Essen *87 C5* Antwerpen, N Belgium
Essen *94 A4 var.* Essen an der Ruhr. Nordrhein-Westfalen, W Germany
Essen an der Ruhr *see* Essen
Essequibo River *59 F3 river* C Guyana
Es Suweida *see* As Suwaydā'
Estacado, Llano *49 E2 plain* New Mexico/Texas, SW USA
Estados, Isla de los *65 C8 prev. Eng.* Staten Island. *island* S Argentina
Estância *63 G3* Sergipe, E Brazil
Estelí *52 D3* Estelí, NW Nicaragua
Estella *93 E1 Bas.* Lizarra. Navarra, N Spain
Estepona *92 D5* Andalucía, S Spain
Esteros *see* Estonia
Estevan *37 F5* Saskatchewan, S Canada
Estland *see* Estonia

Estonia *106 D2 off.* Republic of Estonia, *Est.* Eesti Vabariik, *Ger.* Estland, *Latv.* Igaunija; *prev.* Estonian SSR, *Rus.* Estonskaya SSR. *country* NE Europe

---

ESTONIA
Northeast Europe

Official name Republic of Estonia
Formation 1991 / 1991
Capital Tallinn
Population 1.3 million / 75 people per sq mile (29 people per sq km) / 69%
Total area 17,462 sq miles (45,226 sq km)
Languages Estonian*, Russian
Religions Evangelical Lutheran 56%, Orthodox Christian 25%, Other 19%
Ethnic mix Estonian 62%, Russian 30%, Other 8%
Government Parliamentary system
Currency Kroon = 100 senti
Literacy rate 99%
Calorie consumption 3002 calories

Estonian SSR *see* Estonia
Estonia, Republic of *see* Estonia
Estonskaya SSR *see* Estonia
Estrela, Serra da *92 C3 mountain range* C Portugal
Estremadura *see* Extremadura
Estremoz *92 C4* Évora, S Portugal
Eszék *see* Osijek
Esztergom *99 C6 Ger.* Gran; *anc.* Strigonium. Komárom-Esztergom, N Hungary
Étalle *87 D8* Luxembourg, SE Belgium
Etāwah *134 D3* Uttar Pradesh, N India
Ethiopia *73 C5 off.* Federal Democratic Republic of Ethiopia; *prev.* Abyssinia, People's Democratic Republic of Ethiopia. *country* E Africa

---

ETHIOPIA
East Africa

Official name Federal Democratic Republic of Ethiopia
Formation 1896 / 2002
Capital Addis Ababa
Population 77.4 million / 181 people per sq mile (70 people per sq km) / 18%
Total area 435,184 sq miles (1,127,127 sq km)
Languages Amharic*, Tigrinya, Galla, Sidamo, Somali, English, Arabic
Religions Orthodox Christian 40%, Muslim 40%, Traditional beliefs 15%, Other 5%
Ethnic mix Oromo 40%, Amhara 25%, Other 14%, Sidamo 9%, Berta 6%, Somali 6%
Government Parliamentary system
Currency Ethiopian birr = 100 cents
Literacy rate 42%
Calorie consumption 1857 calories

Ethiopia, Federal Democratic Republic of *see* Ethiopia
Ethiopian Highlands *73 C5 var.* Ethiopian Plateau. *plateau* N Ethiopia
Ethiopian Plateau *see* Ethiopian Highlands
Ethiopia, People's Democratic Republic of *see* Ethiopia
Etna, Monte *79 C7 Eng.* Mount Etna. *volcano* Sicilia, Italy, C Mediterranean Sea
Etna, Mount *see* Etna, Monte
Etosha Pan *78 B3 salt lake* N Namibia
Etoumbi *77 B5* Cuvette Ouest, NW Congo
Etsch *see* Adige
Et Tafila *see* Aţ Ţafilah
Ettelbrück *87 D8* Diekirch, C Luxembourg
'Eua *145 E5 prev.* Middleburg Island. *island* Tongatapu Group, SE Tonga
Euboea *see* Évvoia
Eucla *147 D6* Western Australia
Euclid *40 D3* Ohio, N USA
Eufaula Lake *49 G1 var.* Eufaula Reservoir. *reservoir* Oklahoma, C USA
Eufaula Reservoir *see* Eufaula Lake
Eugene *46 B3* Oregon, NW USA
Eumolpias *see* Plovdiv
Eupen *87 D6* Liège, E Belgium

Euphrates *112 B4 Ar.* Al-Furāt, *Turk.* Fırat Nehri. *river* SW Asia
Eureka *47 A5* California, W USA
Eureka *44 A1* Montana, NW USA
Europa Point *93 H5 headland* S Gibraltar
Europe *34 E1* continent
Eutin *94 C2* Schleswig-Holstein, N Germany
Euxine Sea *see* Black Sea
Evansdale *45 G3* Iowa, C USA
Evanston *40 B3* Illinois, N USA
Evanston *44 B4* Wyoming, C USA
Evansville *40 B5* Indiana, N USA
Eveleth *45 G1* Minnesota, N USA
Everard, Lake *149 A6 salt lake* South Australia
Everest, Mount *126 B5 Chin.* Qomolangma Feng, *Nep.* Sagarmāthā. *mountain* China/Nepal
Everett *46 B2* Washington, NW USA
Everglades, The *43 F5 wetland* Florida, SE USA
Evje *85 A6* Aust-Agder, S Norway
Evmolpia *see* Plovdiv
Évora *92 B4 anc.* Ebora, *Lat.* Liberalitas Julia. Évora, C Portugal
Évreux *90 C3 anc.* Civitas Eburovicum. Eure, N France
Évros *see* Maritsa
Évry *90 E2* Essonne, N France
Évvoia *101 E4 Lat.* Euboea. *island* C Greece
Ewarton *54 B5* C Jamaica
Excelsior Springs *45 F4* Missouri, C USA
Exe *89 C7 river* SW England, UK
Exeter *89 C7 anc.* Isca Damnoniorum. SW England, UK
Exmoor *89 C7 moorland* SW England, UK
Exmouth *146 A4* Western Australia
Exmouth *89 C7* SW England, UK
Exmouth Gulf *146 A4 gulf* Western Australia
Exmouth Plateau *141 E5 undersea plateau* E Indian Ocean
Extremadura *92 C3 var.* Estremadura. *autonomous community* W Spain
Exuma Cays *54 C1 islets* C Bahamas
Exuma Sound *54 C1 sound* C Bahamas
Eyre Mountains *151 A7 mountain range* South Island, New Zealand
Eyre North, Lake *149 A5 salt lake* South Australia
Eyre Peninsula *149 A6 peninsula* South Australia
Eyre South, Lake *149 A5 salt lake* South Australia
Ezo *see* Hokkaidō

F

Faadhippolhu Atoll *132 B4 var.* Fadiffolu, Lhaviyani Atoll. *atoll* N Maldives
Fabens *48 D3* Texas, SW USA
Fada *76 C2* Borkou-Ennedi-Tibesti, E Chad
Fada-Ngourma *75 E4* E Burkina Faso
Fadiffolu *see* Faadhippolhu Atoll
Faenza *96 C3 anc.* Faventia. Emilia-Romagna, N Italy
Faeroe-Iceland Ridge *80 C1 undersea ridge* NW Norwegian Sea
Faeroe Islands *83 E5 Dan.* Færøerne, *Faer.* Føroyar. *Danish external territory* N Atlantic Ocean
Færøerne *see* Faeroe Islands
Faeroe-Shetland Trough *80 C2 trough* NE Atlantic Ocean
Faetano *96 E2* E San Marino
Făgăraş *108 C4 Ger.* Fogarasch, *Hung.* Fogaras. Braşov, C Romania
Fagibina, Lake *see* Faguibine, Lac
Fagne *87 C7 hill range* S Belgium
Faguibine, Lac *75 E3 var.* Lake Fagibina. *lake* NW Mali
Fahlun *see* Falun
Fahraj *120 E4* Kermān, SE Iran
Faial *92 A5 var.* Ilha do Faial. *island* Azores, Portugal, NE Atlantic Ocean

Faial, Ilha do *see* Faial
Faifo *see* Hôi An
Fairbanks 36 D3 Alaska, USA
Fairfield 47 B6 California, W USA
Fair Isle 88 D2 *island* NE Scotland, UK
Fairlie 151 B6 Canterbury, South Island, New Zealand
Fairmont 45 F3 Minnesota, N USA
Faisalâbâd 134 C2 *prev.* Lyallpur. Punjab, NE Pakistan
Faizâbâd 135 E3 Uttar Pradesh, N India
Faizabad/Faizâbâd *see* Feyzâbâd
Fakaofo Atoll 145 F3 *island* SE Tokelau
Falam 136 A3 Chin State, W Myanmar (Burma)
Falconara Marittima 96 C3 Marche, C Italy
Falkenau an der Eger *see* Sokolov
Falkland Islands 65 D7 *var.* Falklands, Islas Malvinas. *UK dependent territory* SW Atlantic Ocean
Falkland Plateau 57 D7 *var.* Argentine Rise. *undersea feature* SW Atlantic Ocean
Falklands *see* Falkland Islands
Falknov nad Ohří *see* Sokolov
Fallbrook 47 C8 California, W USA
Falmouth 54 A4 W Jamaica
Falmouth 89 C7 SW England, UK
Falster 85 B8 *island* SE Denmark
Fălticeni 108 C3 Hung. Falticsén. Suceava, NE Romania
Falticsén *see* Fălticeni
Falun 85 C6 *var.* Fahlun. Kopparberg, C Sweden
Famagusta *see* Gazimağusa
Famagusta Bay *see* Gazimağusa Körfezi
Famenne 87 C7 *physical region* SE Belgium
Fang 136 C3 Chiang Mai, NW Thailand
Fanning Island *see* Tabuaeran
Fano 96 C3 *island* W Denmark
Farafangana 79 G4 Fianarantsoa, SE Madagascar
Farâh 122 D4 *var.* Farah, Fararud. Farâh, W Afghanistan
Farâh Rûd 122 D4 *river* W Afghanistan
Faranah 74 C4 Haute-Guinée, S Guinea
Fararud *see* Farâh
Farasân, Jazâ'ir 121 A6 *island group* SW Saudi Arabia
Farewell, Cape 150 C4 *headland* South Island, New Zealand
Farewell, Cape *see* Nunap Isua
Fargo 45 F2 North Dakota, N USA
Farg'ona 123 F2 Rus. Fergana; *prev.* Novyy Margilan. Farg'ona Viloyati, E Uzbekistan
Faribault 45 F2 Minnesota, N USA
Farîdâbâd 134 D3 Haryāna, N India Asia
Farkhor 123 E3 Rus. Parkhar. SW Tajikistan
Farmington 45 G5 Missouri, C USA
Farmington 48 C1 New Mexico, SW USA
Faro 92 B5 Faro, S Portugal
Farquhar Group 79 G2 *island group* S Seychelles
Farvel, Kap *see* Nunap Isua
Fastiv 109 E2 Rus. Fastov. Kyyivs'ka Oblast', N W Ukraine
Fastov *see* Fastiv
Fauske 84 C3 Nordland, C Norway
Faventia *see* Faenza
Faxa Bay *see* Faxaflói
Faxaflói 82 D5 Eng. Faxa Bay. *bay* W Iceland
Faya 76 C2 *prev.* Faya-Largeau, Largeau. Borkou-Ennedi-Tibesti, N Chad
Faya-Largeau *see* Faya
Fayetteville 42 A1 Arkansas, C USA
Fayetteville 43 F1 North Carolina, SE USA
Fdérick *see* Fdérik
Fdérik 74 C2 *var.* Fdérick, *Fr.* Fort Gouraud. Tiris Zemmour, NW Mauritania
Fear, Cape 43 F2 *headland* Bald Head Island, North Carolina, SE USA
Fécamp 90 B3 Seine-Maritime, N France
Fédala *see* Mohammedia
Federal Capital Territory *see* Australian Capital Territory
Fehérgyarmat 99 E6 Szabolcs-Szatmár-Bereg, E Hungary
Fehértemplom *see* Bela Crkva
Fehmarn 94 C2 *island* N Germany

Fehmarn Belt 94 C2 *Dan.* Femern Bælt, *Ger.* Fehmarnbelt. *strait* Denmark /Germany
Fehmarnbelt *see* Fehmarn Belt/Femer Bælt
Feijó 62 C2 Acre, W Brazil
Feilding 150 D4 Manawatu-Wanganui, North Island, New Zealand
Feira *see* Feira de Santana
Feira de Santana 63 G3 *var.* Feira. Bahia, E Brazil
Feketehalom *see* Codlea
Felanitx 93 G3 Mallorca, Spain, W Mediterranean Sea
Felicitas Julia *see* Lisboa
Felidhu Atoll 132 B4 *atoll* C Maldives
Felipe Carrillo Puerto 51 H4 Quintana Roo, SE Mexico
Felixstowe 89 E6 E England, UK
Fellin *see* Viljandi
Felsőbánya *see* Baia Sprie
Felsőmuzslya *see* Mužlja
Femern Bælt *see* Fehmarn Belt
Femunden 85 B5 *lake* S Norway
Fengcheng 128 D3 *var.* Feng-cheng, Fenghwangcheng. Liaoning, NE China
Feng-cheng *see* Fengcheng
Fenghwangcheng *see* Fengcheng
Fengtien *see* Liaoning, China
Fengtien *see* Shenyang, China
Fenoarivo 79 G3 Toamasina, E Madagascar
Fens, The 89 E6 *wetland* E England, UK
Feodosiya 109 F5 *var.* Kefe, *It.* Kaffa; *anc.* Theodosia. Respublika Krym, S Ukraine
Ferdinand *see* Montana, Bulgaria
Ferdinandsberg *see* Oţelu Roşu
Féres 104 D3 Anatolikí Makedonía kai Thráki, NE Greece
Fergana *see* Farg'ona
Fergus Falls 45 F2 Minnesota, N USA
Ferizaj *see* Uroševac
Ferkessédougou 74 D4 N Côte d'Ivoire (Ivory Coast)
Fermo 96 C4 *anc.* Firmum Picenum. Marche, C Italy
Fernandina, Isla 60 A5 *var.* Narborough Island. *island* Galapagos Islands, Ecuador, E Pacific Ocean
Fernando de Noronha 63 H2 *island* E Brazil
Fernando Po/Fernando Póo *see* Bioco, N Equatorial Guinea
Ferrara 96 C2 *anc.* Forum Alieni. Emilia-Romagna, N Italy
Ferreñafe 60 B3 Lambayeque, W Peru
Ferro *see* Hierro
Ferrol 92 B1 *var.* El Ferrol; *prev.* El Ferrol del Caudillo. Galicia, NW Spain
Fertő *see* Neusiedler See
Ferwerd 86 D1 Fris. Ferwert. Friesland, N Netherlands
Ferwert *see* Ferwerd
Fès 70 C2 Eng. Fez. N Morocco
Feteşti 108 C5 Ialomiţa, SE Romania
Fethiye 116 B4 Muğla, SW Turkey
Fetlar 88 D1 *island* NE Scotland, UK
Feuilles, Rivière aux 38 D2 *river* Québec, E Canada
Feyzâbâd 123 F3 *var.* Faizabad, Faizâbâd, Feyzabad, Fyzabad. Badakhshān, NE Afghanistan
Feyzâbâd *see* Feyzâbâd
Fez *see* Fès
Fianarantsoa 79 F3 Fianarantsoa, C Madagascar
Fianga 76 B4 Mayo-Kébbi, SW Chad
Fier 101 C6 *var.* Fieri. Fier, SW Albania
Fieri *see* Fier
Figeac 91 C5 Lot, S France
Figig *see* Figuig
Figueira da Foz 92 B3 Coimbra, W Portugal
Figueres 93 G2 Cataluña, E Spain
Figuig 70 D2 *var.* Figig. E Morocco
Fiji 145 E5 *off.* Sovereign Democratic Republic of Fiji, Fij. Viti. *country* SW Pacific Ocean

FIJI
Australasia & Oceania

Official name Republic of the Fiji Islands
Formation 1970 / 1970
Capital Suva
Population 848,000 / 120 people per sq mile (46 people per sq km) / 49%

FIJI
(continued)

Total area 7054 sq miles (18,270 sq km)
Languages English*, Fijian*, Hindi, Urdu, Tamil, Telugu
Religions Hindu 38%, Methodist 37%, Roman Catholic 9%, Other 8%, Muslim 8%
Ethnic mix Melanesian 48%, Indian 46%, Other 6%
Government Parliamentary system
Currency Fiji dollar = 100 cents
Literacy rate 93%
Calorie consumption 2894 calories

Fiji, Sovereign Democratic Republic of *see* Fiji
Filadelfia 52 D4 Guanacaste, W Costa Rica
Filiaşi 108 B5 Dolj, SW Romania
Filipstad 85 B6 Värmland, C Sweden
Finale Ligure 96 A3 Liguria, NW Italy
Finchley 89 A7 UK
Findlay 40 C4 Ohio, N USA
Finike 116 B4 Antalya, SW Turkey
Finland 84 D4 *off.* Republic of Finland, Fin. Suomen Tasavalta, Suomi. *country* N Europe

FINLAND
Northern Europe

Official name Republic of Finland
Formation 1917 / 1947
Capital Helsinki
Population 5.2 million / 44 people per sq mile (17 people per sq km) / 67%
Total area 130,127 sq miles (337,030 sq km)
Languages Finnish*, Swedish*, Sámi
Religions Evangelical Lutheran 89%, Orthodox Christian 1%, Roman Catholic 1%, Other 9%
Ethnic mix Finnish 93%, Other (including Sámi) 7%
Government Parliamentary system
Currency Euro = 100 cents
Literacy rate 99%
Calorie consumption 3100 calories

Finland, Gulf of 85 D6 *Est.* Soome Laht, Fin. Suomenlahti, Ger. Finnischer Meerbusen, Rus. Finskiy Zaliv, Swe. Finska Viken. *gulf* E Baltic Sea
Finland, Republic of *see* Finland
Finnischer Meerbusen *see* Finland, Gulf of
Finnmarksvidda 84 D2 *physical region* N Norway
Finska Viken/Finskiy Zaliv *see* Finland, Gulf of
Finsterwalde 94 D4 Brandenburg, E Germany
Fiordland 151 A7 *physical region* South Island, New Zealand
Fiorina 96 E1 NE San Marino
Firat Nehri *see* Euphrates
Firenze 96 C3 Eng. Florence; *anc.* Florentia. Toscana, C Italy
Firmum Picenum *see* Fermo
First State *see* Delaware
Fischbacher Alpen 95 E7 *mountain range* E Austria
Fischhausen *see* Primorsk
Fish 78 B4 *var.* Vis. *river* S Namibia
Fishguard 89 C6 Wel. Abergwaun. SW Wales, UK
Fisterra, Cabo 92 B1 *cape* NW Spain
Fitzroy Crossing 146 C3 Western Australia
Fitzroy River 146 C3 *river* Western Australia
Fiume *see* Rijeka
Flagstaff 48 B2 Arizona, SW USA
Flanders 87 A6 Dut. Vlaanderen, Fr. Flandre. *cultural region* Belgium/France
Flandre *see* Flanders
Flathead Lake 44 B1 *lake* Montana, NW USA
Flat Island 128 C8 *island* NE Spratly Islands
Flatts Village 42 B5 *var.* The Flatts Village. C Bermuda
Flensburg 94 B2 Schleswig-Holstein, N Germany

Flessingue *see* Vlissingen
Flickertail State *see* North Dakota
Flinders Island 149 C8 *island* Furneaux Group, Tasmania, SE Australia
Flinders Ranges 149 B6 *mountain range* South Australia
Flinders River 148 C3 *river* Queensland, NE Australia
Flin Flon 37 F5 Manitoba, C Canada
Flint 40 C3 Michigan, N USA
Flint Island 145 G4 *island* Line Islands, E Kiribati
Floreana, Isla *see* Santa María, Isla
Florence 42 C1 Alabama, S USA
Florence 43 F2 South Carolina, SE USA
Florence *see* Firenze
Florencia 58 B4 Caquetá, S Colombia
Florentia *see* Firenze
Flores 52 B1 Petén, N Guatemala
Flores 139 E5 *island* Nusa Tenggara, C Indonesia
Flores 92 A5 *island* Azores, Portugal, NE Atlantic Ocean
Flores, Laut *see* Flores Sea
Flores Sea 138 D5 Ind. Laut Flores. *sea* C Indonesia
Floriano 63 F2 Piauí, E Brazil
Florianópolis 63 F5 *prev.* Desterro. *state capital* Santa Catarina, S Brazil
Florida 64 D4 Florida, S Uruguay
Florida 43 E4 *off.* State of Florida, *also known as* Peninsular State, Sunshine State. *state* SE USA
Florida Bay 43 E5 *bay* Florida, SE USA
Florida Keys 43 E5 *island group* Florida, SE USA
Florida, Straits of 54 B1 *strait* Atlantic Ocean/Gulf of Mexico
Flórina 104 B4 *var.* Phlórina. Dytikí Makedonía, N Greece
Florissant 45 G4 Missouri, C USA
Floúda, Ákrotírio 105 D7 *cape* Astypálaia, Kykládes, Greece, Aegean Sea
Flushing *see* Vlissingen
Flylân *see* Vlieland
Foča 100 C4 SE Bosnia and Herzegovina
Focşani 108 C4 Vrancea, E Romania
Fogaras/Fogarasch *see* Făgăraş
Foggia 97 D5 Puglia, SE Italy
Fogo 74 A3 *island* Ilhas de Sotavento, SW Cape Verde
Foix 91 B6 Ariège, S France
Folégandros 105 C7 *island* Kykládes, Greece, Aegean Sea
Foleyet 38 C4 Ontario, S Canada
Foligno 96 C4 Umbria, C Italy
Folkestone 89 E7 SE England, UK
Fond du Lac 40 B2 Wisconsin, N USA
Fongafale 145 E3 *var.* Funafuti. *country capital* (Tuvalu) Funafuti Atoll, SE Tuvalu
Fonseca, Golfo de *see* Fonseca, Gulf of
Fonseca, Gulf of 52 C3 Sp. Golfo de Fonseca. *gulf* C Central America
Fontainebleau 90 C3 Seine-et-Marne, N France
Fontenay-le-Comte 90 B4 Vendée, NW France
Fontvieille 91 B8 SW Monaco Europe
Fonyód 99 C7 Somogy, W Hungary
Foochow *see* Fuzhou
Foochow *see* Fuzhou
Forchheim 95 C5 Bayern, SE Germany
Forel, Mont 82 D4 *mountain* SE Greenland
Forfar 88 C3 E Scotland, UK
Forge du Sud *see* Dudelange
Forlì 96 C3 *anc.* Forum Livii. Emilia-Romagna, N Italy
Formentera 93 G4 *anc.* Ophiusa, *Lat.* Frumentum. *island* Islas Baleares, Spain, W Mediterranean Sea
Formosa 64 D2 Formosa, NE Argentina
Formosa/Formo'sa *see* Taiwan
Formosa, Serra 63 E3 *mountain range* C Brazil
Formosa Strait *see* Taiwan Strait
Foroyar *see* Faeroe Islands
Forrest City 42 B1 Arkansas, C USA
Fort Albany 38 C3 Ontario, C Canada
Fortaleza 61 F2 Pando, N Bolivia

Fortaleza 63 G2 prev. Ceará. *state capital* Ceará, NE Brazil
Fort-Archambault *see* Sarh
Fort-Bayard *see* Zhanjiang
Fort-Cappolani *see* Tidjikja
Fort Charlet *see* Djanet
Fort-Chimo *see* Kuujjuaq
Fort Collins 44 D4 Colorado, C USA
Fort-Crampel *see* Kaga Bandoro
Fort Davis 49 E3 Texas, SW USA
Fort-de-France 55 H4 *prev.* Fort-Royal. *dependent territory capital* (Martinique) W Martinique
Fort Dodge 45 F3 Iowa, C USA
Fortescue River 146 A4 *river* Western Australia
Fort-Foureau *see* Kousséri
Fort Frances 38 B4 Ontario, S Canada
Fort Good Hope 37 E3 *var.* Good Hope. Northwest Territories, NW Canada
Fort Gouraud *see* Fdérik
Forth 88 C4 *river* C Scotland, UK
Forth, Firth of 88 C4 *estuary* E Scotland, UK
Fortín General Eugenio Garay *see* General Eugenio A. Garay
Fort Jameson *see* Chipata
Fort-Lamy *see* Ndjamena
Fort Lauderdale 43 F5 Florida, SE USA
Fort Liard 37 E4 *var.* Liard. Northwest Territories, W Canada
Fort Madison 45 G4 Iowa, C USA
Fort McMurray 37 E4 Alberta, C Canada
Fort McPherson 36 D3 *var.* McPherson. Northwest Territories, NW Canada
Fort Morgan 44 D4 Colorado, C USA
Fort Myers 43 F5 Florida, SE USA
Fort Nelson 37 E4 British Columbia, W Canada
Fort Peck Lake 44 C1 *reservoir* Montana, NW USA
Fort Pierce 43 F4 Florida, SE USA
Fort Providence 37 E4 *var.* Providence. Northwest Territories, W Canada
Fort-Repoux *see* Akjoujt
Fort Rosebery *see* Mansa
Fort Rousset *see* Owando
Fort-Royal *see* Fort-de-France
Fort St. John 37 E4 British Columbia, W Canada
Fort Scott 45 F5 Kansas, C USA
Fort Severn 38 C2 Ontario, C Canada
Fort-Shevchenko 114 A4 Mangistau, W Kazakhstan
Fort-Sibut *see* Sibut
Fort Simpson 37 E4 *var.* Simpson. Northwest Territories, W Canada
Fort Smith 37 E4 Northwest Territories, W Canada
Fort Smith 42 B1 Arkansas, C USA
Fort Stockton 49 E3 Texas, SW USA
Fort-Trinquet *see* Bir Mogrein
Fort Vermilion 37 E4 Alberta, W Canada
Fort Victoria *see* Masvingo
Fort Walton Beach 42 C3 Florida, SE USA
Fort Wayne 40 C4 Indiana, N USA
Fort William 88 C3 N Scotland, UK
Fort Worth 49 G2 Texas, SW USA
Fort Yukon 36 D3 Alaska, USA
Forum Alieni *see* Ferrara
Forum Livii *see* Forlì
Fossa Claudia *see* Chioggia
Fougamou 77 A6 Ngounié, C Gabon
Fougères 90 B3 Ille-et-Vilaine, NW France
Fou-hsin *see* Fuxin
Foulwind, Cape 151 B5 *headland* South Island, New Zealand
Fouman 76 A4 Ouest, NW Cameroon
Fou-shan *see* Fushun
Foveaux Strait 151 A8 *strait* S New Zealand
Foxe Basin 37 G3 *sea* Nunavut, N Canada
Fox Glacier 151 B6 West Coast, South Island, New Zealand
Fraga 93 F2 Aragón, NE Spain
Fram Basin 155 C3 *var.* Amundsen Basin. *undersea feature* Arctic Ocean
France 90 B4 *off.* French Republic, *It./Sp.* Francia; *prev.* Gaul, Gaule, *Lat.* Gallia. *country* W Europe

FRANCE
Western Europe

Official name French Republic
Formation 987 / 1919
Capital Paris
Population 60.5 million / 285 people per sq mile (110 people per sq km) / 76%
Total area 211,208 sq miles (547,030 sq km)
Languages French*, Provençal, German, Breton, Catalan, Basque
Religions Roman Catholic 88%, Muslim 8%, Protestant 2%, Buddhist 1%, Jewish 1%
Ethnic mix French 90%, North African (mainly Algerian) 6%, German (Alsace) 2%, Breton 1%, Other (including Corsicans) 1%
Government Mixed presidential–parliamentary system
Currency Euro = 100 cents
Literacy rate 99%
Calorie consumption 3654 calories

Franceville 77 B6 *var.* Massoukou, Masuku. Haut-Ogooué, E Gabon
Francfort *see* Frankfurt am Main
Franche-Comté 90 D4 *region* E France
Franche-Comté 90 D4 *cultural region* E France
Francia *see* France
Francis Case, Lake 45 E3 *reservoir* South Dakota, N USA
Francisco Escárcega 51 G4 Campeche, SE Mexico
Francistown 78 D3 North East, NE Botswana
Franconian Jura *see* Fränkische Alb
Frankenalb *see* Fränkische Alb
Frankenstein/Frankenstein in Schlesien *see* Ząbkowice Śląskie
Frankfort 40 C5 *state capital* Kentucky, S USA
Frankfort on the Main *see* Frankfurt am Main
Frankfurt *see* Frankfurt am Main, Germany
Frankfurt *see* Słubice, Poland
Frankfurt am Main 95 B5 *var.* Frankfurt, *Fr.* Francfort; *prev. Eng.* Frankfort on the Main. Hessen, SW Germany
Frankfurt an der Oder 94 D3 Brandenburg, E Germany
Fränkische Alb 95 C6 *var.* Frankenalb, *Eng.* Franconian Jura. *mountain range* S Germany
Franklin 42 C1 Tennessee, S USA
Franklin D. Roosevelt Lake 46 C1 *reservoir* Washington, NW USA
Frantsa-Iosifa, Zemlya 114 D1 *Eng.* Franz Josef Land. *island group* N Russian Federation
Franz Josef Land *see* Frantsa-Iosifa, Zemlya
Fraserburgh 88 D3 NE Scotland, UK
Fraser Island 148 E4 *var.* Great Sandy Island. *island* Queensland, E Australia
Frauenbach *see* Baia Mare
Frauenburg *see* Saldus, Latvia
Fredericksburg 41 E5 Virginia, NE USA
Fredericton 39 F4 *province capital* New Brunswick, SE Canada
Frederikshåb *see* Paamiut
Fredrikshald *see* Halden
Fredrikstad 85 B6 Østfold, S Norway
Freeport 54 C1 Grand Bahama Island, N Bahamas
Freeport 49 H4 Texas, SW USA
Free State *see* Maryland
Freetown 74 C4 *country capital* (Sierra Leone) W Sierra Leone
Freiburg *see* Freiburg im Breisgau, Germany
Freiburg im Breisgau 95 A6 *var.* Freiburg, *Fr.* Fribourg-en-Brisgau. Baden-Württemberg, SW Germany
Freiburg in Schlesien *see* Świebodzice
Fremantle 147 A6 Western Australia
Fremont 45 F4 Nebraska, C USA
French Guiana 59 H3 *var.* Guiana, Guyane. *French overseas department* N South America
French Guinea *see* Guinea

French Polynesia 143 F4 *French overseas territory* C Polynesia
French Republic *see* France
French Somaliland *see* Djibouti
French Southern and Antarctic Territories 141 B7 *Fr.* Terres Australes et Antarctiques Françaises. *French overseas territory* S Indian Ocean
French Sudan *see* Mali
French Territory of the Afars and Issas *see* Djibouti
French Togoland *see* Togo
Fresnillo 50 D3 Zacatecas, C Mexico
Fresnillo de González Echeverría *see* Fresnillo
Fresno 47 C6 California, W USA
Frias 64 C3 Catamarca, N Argentina
Fribourg-en-Brisgau *see* Freiburg im Breisgau
Friedek-Mistek *see* Frýdek-Místek
Friedrichshafen 95 B7 Baden-Württemberg, S Germany
Friendly Islands *see* Tonga
Frisches Haff *see* Vistula Lagoon
Frobisher Bay 82 B3 *inlet* Baffin Island, Nunavut, NE Canada
Frobisher Bay *see* Iqaluit
Frohavet 84 B4 *sound* C Norway
Frome, Lake 149 B6 *salt lake* South Australia
Frontera 51 G4 Tabasco, SE Mexico
Frontignan 91 C6 Hérault, S France
Frostviken *see* Kvarnbergsvattnet
Frøya 84 A4 *island* W Norway
Frumentum *see* Formentera
Frunze *see* Bishkek
Frýdek-Místek 99 C5 *Ger.* Friedek-Mistek. Moravskoslezský Kraj, E Czech Republic
Fu-chien *see* Fujian
Fu-chou *see* Fuzhou
Fu-chou *see* Fuzhou
Fuengirola 92 D5 Andalucía, S Spain
Fuerte Olimpo 64 D2 *var.* Olimpo. Alto Paraguay, NE Paraguay
Fuerte, Río 48 C5 *river* C Mexico
Fuerteventura 70 B3 *island* Islas Canarias, Spain, NE Atlantic Ocean
Fuhkien *see* Fujian
Fu-hsin *see* Fuxin
Fuji 131 D6 *var.* Huzi. Shizuoka, Honshū, S Japan
Fujian 128 D6 *var.* Fu-chien, Fuhkien, Fukien, Min, Fujian Sheng. *province* SE China
Fujian Sheng *see* Fujian
Fuji, Mount/Fujiyama *see* Fuji-san
Fuji-san 131 C6 *var.* Fujiyama, *Eng.* Mount Fuji. *mountain* Honshū, SE Japan
Fukang 126 C2 Xinjiang Uygur Zizhiqu, W China
Fukien *see* Fujian
Fukui 131 C6 *var.* Hukui. Fukui, Honshū, SW Japan
Fukuoka 131 A7 *var.* Hukuoka, *hist.* Najima. Fukuoka, Kyūshū, SW Japan
Fukushima 130 D4 *var.* Hukusima. Fukushima, Honshū, C Japan
Fulda 95 B5 Hessen, C Germany
Funafoti *see* Fongafale
Funafuti Atoll 145 E3 *atoll* C Tuvalu
Funchal 70 A2 Madeira, Portugal, NE Atlantic Ocean
Fundy, Bay of 39 F5 *bay* Canada/USA
Fünen *see* Fyn
Fünfkirchen *see* Pécs
Furnes *see* Veurne
Fürth 95 C5 Bayern, S Germany
Furukawa 130 D4 *var.* Hurukawa. Miyagi, Honshū, C Japan
Fusan *see* Pusan
Fushun 128 D3 *var.* Fou-shan, Fu-shun. Liaoning, NE China
Fu-shun *see* Fushun
Fusin *see* Fuxin
Füssen 95 C7 Bayern, S Germany
Futog 100 D3 Vojvodina, NW Serbia
Futuna, Île 145 E4 *island* S Wallis and Futuna
Fuxin 128 D3 *var.* Fou-hsin, Fu-hsin, Fusin. Liaoning, NE China
Fuzhou 128 D6 *var.* Foochow, Fu-chou. *province capital* Fujian, SE China

Fyn 85 B8 *Ger.* Fünen. *island* C Denmark
FYR Macedonia/FYROM *see* Macedonia, FYR
Fyzabad *see* Feyzābād

G

Gaafu Alifu Atoll *see* North Huvadhu Atoll
Gaalkacyo 73 E5 *var.* Galka'yo, *It.* Galcaio. Mudug, C Somalia
Gabela 78 B2 Cuanza Sul, W Angola
Gaberones *see* Gaborone
Gabès 71 E2 *var.* Qābis. E Tunisia
Gabès, Golfe de 71 E2 *Ar.* Khalīj Qābis. *gulf* E Tunisia
Gabon 77 B6 *off.* Gabonese Republic. *country* C Africa

GABON
Central Africa

Official name Gabonese Republic
Formation 1960 / 1960
Capital Libreville
Population 1.4 million / 14 people per sq mile (5 people per sq km) / 81%
Total area 103,346 sq miles (267,667 sq km)
Languages French*, Fang, Punu, Sira, Nzebi, Mpongwe
Religions Christian (mainly Roman Catholic) 55%, Traditional beliefs 40%, Other 4%, Muslim 1%
Ethnic mix Fang 35%, Other Bantu 29%, Eshira 25%, European and other African 9%, French 2%
Government Presidential system
Currency CFA franc = 100 centimes
Literacy rate 71%
Calorie consumption 2637 calories

Gabonese Republic *see* Gabon
Gaborone 78 C4 *prev.* Gaberones. *country capital* (Botswana) South East, SE Botswana
Gabrovo 104 D2 Gabrovo, N Bulgaria
Gadag 132 C1 Karnātaka, W India
Gades/Gadier/Gadir/Gadire *see* Cádiz
Gadsden 42 D2 Alabama, S USA
Gaeta 97 C5 Lazio, C Italy
Gaeta, Golfo di 97 C5 *var.* Gulf of Gaeta. *gulf* C Italy
Gaeta, Gulf of *see* Gaeta, Golfo di
Gäfle *see* Gävle
Gafsa 71 E2 *var.* Qafşah. W Tunisia
Gagnoa 74 D5 C Côte d'Ivoire (Ivory Coast)
Gagra 117 E1 NW Georgia
Gaillac 91 C6 *var.* Gaillac-sur-Tarn. Tarn, S France
Gaillac-sur-Tarn *see* Gaillac
Gaillimh *see* Galway
Gaillimhe, Cuan na *see* Galway Bay
Gainesville 43 E3 Florida, SE USA
Gainesville 42 D2 Georgia, SE USA
Gainesville 49 G2 Texas, SW USA
Gairdner, Lake 149 A6 *salt lake* South Australia
Gaizina Kalns *see* Gaizinakalns
Gaizinakalns 106 C3 *var.* Gaizina Kalns. *mountain* E Latvia
Galán, Cerro 64 B3 *mountain* NW Argentina
Galanta 99 C6 *Hung.* Galánta. Trnavský Kraj, W Slovakia
Galapagos Fracture Zone 153 E3 *tectonic feature* E Pacific Ocean
Galapagos Islands *see* Colón, Archipiélago de
Galápagos, Islas de los *see* Colón, Archipiélago de
Galapagos Rise 153 F3 *undersea rise* E Pacific Ocean
Galashiels 88 C4 SE Scotland, UK
Galaţi 108 D4 *Ger.* Galatz. Galaţi, E Romania
Galatz *see* Galaţi
Galcaio *see* Gaalkacyo
Galesburg 40 B3 Illinois, N USA
Galicia 92 B1 *anc.* Gallaecia. *autonomous community* NW Spain
Galicia Bank 80 B4 *undersea bank* E Atlantic Ocean
Galilee, Sea of *see* Tiberias, Lake
Galka'yo *see* Gaalkacyo

Galkynyş *122 D3 prev. Rus.* Deynau, Dyanev, *Turkm.* Dänew. Lebap Welaýaty, NE Turkmenistan
Gallaecia *see* Galicia
Galle *132 D4 prev.* Point de Galle. Southern Province, SW Sri Lanka
Gallego Rise *153 F3 undersea rise* E Pacific Ocean
Gallegos *see* Río Gallegos
Gallia *see* France
Gallipoli *97 E6* Puglia, SE Italy
Gällivare *84 C3 Lapp.* Váhtjer. Norrbotten, N Sweden
Gallup *48 C1* New Mexico, SW USA
Galtat-Zemmour *70 B3* C Western Sahara
Galveston *49 H4* Texas, SW USA
Galway *89 A5 Ir.* Gaillimh. Galway, W Ireland
Galway Bay *89 A6 Ir.* Cuan na Gaillimhe. *bay* W Ireland
Gámas *see* Kaamanen
Gambell *36 C2* Saint Lawrence Island, Alaska, USA
Gambia *74 B3 off.* Republic of The Gambia, The Gambia. *country* W Africa

GAMBIA
West Africa

Official name Republic of the Gambia
Formation 1965 / 1965
Capital Banjul
Population 1.5 million / 389 people per sq mile (150 people per sq km) / 33%
Total area 4363 sq miles (11,300 sq km)
Languages English*, Mandinka, Fulani, Wolof, Jola, Soninke
Religions Sunni Muslim 90%, Christian 9%, Traditional beliefs 1%
Ethnic mix Mandinka 42%, Fulani 18%, Wolof 16%, Jola 10%, Serahuli 9%, Other 5%
Government Presidential system
Currency Dalasi = 100 butut
Literacy rate 38%
Calorie consumption 2273 calories

Gambia *74 C3 Fr.* Gambie. *river* W Africa
Gambia, Republic of The *see* Gambia
Gambia, The *see* Gambia
Gambie *see* Gambia
Gambier, Îles *143 G4 island group* E French Polynesia
Gamboma *77 B6* Plateaux, E Congo
Gamlakarleby *see* Kokkola
Gan *132 B5* Addu Atoll, C Maldives
Gan *see* Gansu
Gan *see* Jiangxi
Ganaane *see* Juba
Gäncä *117 G2 Rus.* Gyandzha; *prev.* Kirovabad, Yelisavetpol. W Azerbaijan
Gand *see* Gent
Gandajika *77 D7* Kasai Oriental, S Dem. Rep. Congo
Gander *39 G3* Newfoundland, Newfoundland and Labrador, SE Canada
Gāndhīdhām *134 C4* Gujarāt, W India
Gandía *93 F3* País Valenciano, E Spain
Ganges *135 F3 Ben.* Padma. *river* Bangladesh/India
Ganges Cone *see* Ganges Fan
Ganges Fan *140 D3 var.* Ganges Cone. *undersea fan* N Bay of Bengal
Ganges, Mouths of the *135 G4 delta* Bangladesh/India
Gangra *see* Çankırı
Gangtok *135 F3 state capital* Sikkim, N India
Gansos, Lago dos *see* Goose Lake
Gansu *128 B4 var.* Gan, Gansu Sheng, Kansu. *province* N China
Gansu Sheng *see* Gansu
Gantsevichi *see* Hantsavichy
Ganzhou *128 D6* Jiangxi, S China
Gao *75 E3* Gao, E Mali
Gaocheng *see* Litang
Gaoual *74 C4* N Guinea
Gaoxiong *see* Kaohsiung
Gap *91 D5 anc.* Vapincum. Hautes-Alpes, SE France
Gaplañgyr Platosy *122 C2 Rus.* Plato Kaplangky. *ridge* Turkmenistan/Uzbekistan

Gar *126 A4 var.* Gar Xincun. Xizang Zizhiqu, W China
Garabil Belentligi *122 D3 Rus.* Vozvyshennost' Karabil'. *mountain range* S Turkmenistan
Garabogaz Aylagy *122 B2 Rus.* Zaliv Kara-Bogaz-Gol. *bay* NW Turkmenistan
Garachiné *53 G5* Darién, SE Panama
Garagum *122 C3 var.* Garagumy, Qara Qum, *Eng.* Black Sand Desert, Kara Kum; *prev.* Peski Karakumy. *desert* C Turkmenistan
Garagum Kanaly *122 D3 var.* Kara Kum Canal, *Rus.* Karagumskiy Kanal, Karakumskiy Kanal. *canal* C Turkmenistan
Garagumy *see* Garagum
Gara Khitrino *104 D2* Shumen, NE Bulgaria
Gárasavvon *see* Kaaresuvanto
Garda, Lago di *96 C2 var.* Benaco, *Eng.* Lake Garda, *Ger.* Gardasee. *lake* NE Italy
Garda, Lake *see* Garda, Lago di
Gardasee *see* Garda, Lago di
Garden City *45 E5* Kansas, C USA
Garden State, The *see* New Jersey
Gardeyz *see* Gardīz
Gardēz *see* Gardīz
Gardīz *123 E4 var.* Gardeyz, Gardēz, Gordiaz. Paktiā, E Afghanistan
Gardner Island *see* Nikumaroro
Garegegasnjárga *see* Karigasniemi
Gargždai *106 B3* Klaipėda, W Lithuania
Garissa *73 D6* Coast, E Kenya
Garland *49 G2* Texas, SW USA
Garoe *see* Garoowe
Garonne *91 B5 anc.* Garumna. *river* S France
Garoowe *73 E5 var.* Garoe. Nugaal, N Somalia
Garoua *76 B4 var.* Garua. Nord, N Cameroon
Garrygala *see* Magtymguly
Garry Lake *37 F3 lake* Nunavut, N Canada
Garsen *73 D6* Coast, S Kenya
Garua *see* Garoua
Garumna *see* Garonne
Garwolin *98 D3* Mazowieckie, E Poland
Gar Xincun *see* Gar
Gary *40 B3* Indiana, N USA
Garzón *58 B4* Huila, S Colombia
Gasan-Kuli *see* Esenguly
Gascogne *91 B6 Eng.* Gascony. *cultural region* S France
Gascony *see* Gascogne
Gascoyne River *147 A5 river* Western Australia
Gaspé *39 F3* Québec, SE Canada
Gaspé, Péninsule de *39 E4 var.* Péninsule de la Gaspésie. *peninsula* Québec, SE Canada
Gaspésie, Péninsule de la *see* Gaspé, Péninsule de
Gastonia *43 E1* North Carolina, SE USA
Gastoúni *105 B6* Dytikí Ellás, S Greece
Gatchina *110 B4* Leningradskaya Oblast', NW Russian Federation
Gatineau *38 D4* Québec, SE Canada
Gatooma *see* Kadoma
Gatún, Lago *53 F4 reservoir* C Panama
Gauhāti *see* Guwāhati
Gauja *106 D3 var.* Aa. *river* Estonia/Latvia
Gaul/Gaule *see* France
Gauteng *see* Johannesburg, South Africa
Gāvbandi *120 D4* Hormozgān, S Iran
Gávdos *105 C8 island* SE Greece
Gavere *87 B6* Oost-Vlaanderen, NW Belgium
Gävle *85 C6 var.* Gäfle; *prev.* Gefle. Gävleborg, C Sweden
Gawler *149 B6* South Australia
Gaya *135 F3* Bihār, N India
Gaya *see* Kyjov
Gayndah *149 E5* Queensland, E Australia
Gaysin *see* Haysyn
Gaza *119 A6 Ar.* Ghazzah, *Heb.* 'Azza. NE Gaza Strip
Gaz-Achak *see* Gazojak
Gaza Strip *119 A7 Ar.* Qita Ghazzah. *disputed region* SW Asia
Gaziantep *116 D4 var.* Gazi Antep; *prev.* Aintab, Antep. Gaziantep, S Turkey

Gazi Antep *see* Gaziantep
Gazimağusa *102 D5 var.* Famagusta, *Gk.* Ammóchostos. E Cyprus
Gazimağusa Körfezi *102 C5 var.* Famagusta Bay, *Gk.* Kólpos Ammóchostos. *bay* E Cyprus
Gazli *122 D2* Buxoro Viloyati, C Uzbekistan
Gazojak *122 D2 Rus.* Gaz-Achak. Lebap Welaýaty, NE Turkmenistan
Gbanga *74 D5 var.* Gbarnga. N Liberia
Gbarnga *see* Gbanga
Gdańsk *98 C2 Fr.* Dantzig, *Ger.* Danzig. Pomorskie, N Poland
Gdan'skaya Bukhta/Gdańsk, Gulf of *see* Danzig, Gulf of
Gdańska, Zakota *see* Danzig, Gulf of
Gdingen *see* Gdynia
Gdynia *98 C2 Ger.* Gdingen. Pomorskie, N Poland
Gedaref *72 C4 var.* Al Qadārif, El Gedaref. Gedaref, E Sudan
Gediz *116 B3* Kütahya, W Turkey
Gediz Nehri *116 A3 river* W Turkey
Geel *87 C5 var.* Gheel. Antwerpen, N Belgium
Geelong *149 C7* Victoria, SE Australia
Ge'e'mu *see* Golmud
Gefle *see* Gävle
Geilo *85 A5* Buskerud, S Norway
Gejiu *128 B6 var.* Kochiu. Yunnan, S China
Gëkdepe *see* Gökdepe
Gela *97 C7 prev.* Terranova di Sicilia. Sicilia, Italy, C Mediterranean Sea
Geldermalsen *86 C4* Gelderland, C Netherlands
Geleen *87 D6* Limburg, SE Netherlands
Gelib *see* Jilib
Gellinsor *73 E5* Mudug, C Somalia
Gembloux *87 C6* Namur, S Belgium
Gemena *77 C5* Equateur, NW Dem. Rep. Congo
Gem of the Mountains *see* Idaho
Gemona del Friuli *96 D2* Friuli-Venezia Giulia, NE Italy
Gem State *see* Idaho
Genalē Wenz *see* Juba
Genck *see* Genk
General Alvear *64 B4* Mendoza, W Argentina
General Carrera, Lago *see* Buenos Aires, Lago
General Eugenio A. Garay *64 C1 var.* Fortín General Eugenio Garay; *prev.* Yrendagüé. Nueva Asunción, NW Paraguay
General José F.Uriburu *see* Zárate
General Machado *see* Camacupa
General Santos *139 F3 off.* General Santos City. Mindanao, S Philippines
General Santos City *see* General Santos
Gênes *see* Genova
Geneva *see* Geneva
Geneva, Lake *95 A7 Fr.* Lac de Genève, Lac Léman, *var.* le Léman, *Ger.* Genfer See. *lake* France/Switzerland
Genève *95 A7 Eng.* Geneva, *Ger.* Genf, *It.* Ginevra. Genève, SW Switzerland
Genève, Lac de *see* Geneva, Lake
Genf *see* Genève
Genfer See *see* Geneva, Lake
Genichesk *see* Heniches'k
Genk *87 D6 var.* Genck. Limburg, NE Belgium
Gennep *86 D4* Limburg, SE Netherlands
Genoa *see* Genova
Genoa, Gulf of *see* Genova, Golfo di
Genova *102 D1 Eng.* Genoa; *anc.* Genua, *Fr.* Gênes. Liguria, NW Italy
Genova, Golfo di *96 A3 Eng.* Gulf of Genoa. *gulf* NW Italy
Genovesa, Isla *60 B5 var.* Tower Island. *island* Galapagos Islands, Ecuador, E Pacific Ocean
Gent *87 B5 Eng.* Ghent, *Fr.* Gand. Oost-Vlaanderen, NW Belgium
Genua *see* Genova
Geok-Tepe *see* Gökdepe
George *78 C5* Western Cape, S South Africa
George *82 A4 river* Newfoundland and Labrador/Québec, E Canada
George, Lake *43 E3 lake* Florida, SE USA
Georgenburg *see* Jurbarkas
Georges Bank *35 D5 undersea bank* W Atlantic Ocean

George Sound *151 A7 sound* South Island, New Zealand
Georges River *148 D2 river* New South Wales, E Australia
Georgetown *59 F2 country capital* (Guyana) N Guyana
George Town *54 C2* Great Exuma Island, C Bahamas
George Town *54 B3 var.* Georgetown. *dependent territory capital* (Cayman Islands) Grand Cayman, SW Cayman Islands
George Town *138 B3 var.* Penang, Pinang. Pinang, Peninsular Malaysia
Georgetown *43 F2* South Carolina, SE USA
Georgetown *see* George Town
George V Land *154 C4 physical region* Antarctica
Georgia *117 F2 off.* Republic of Georgia, *Geor.* Sak'art'velo, *Rus.* Gruzinskaya SSR, Gruziya. *country* SW Asia

GEORGIA
Southwest Asia

Official name Georgia
Formation 1991 / 1991
Capital Tbilisi
Population 4.5 million / 167 people per sq mile (65 people per sq km) / 61%
Total area 26,911 sq miles (69,700 sq km)
Languages Georgian*, Russian, Azeri, Armenian, Mingrelian, Ossetian, Abkhazian
Religions Georgian Orthodox 65%, Muslim 11%, Russian Orthodox 10%, Armenian Orthodox 8%, Other 6%
Ethnic mix Georgian 70%, Armenian 8%, Russian 6%, Azeri 6%, Ossetian 3%, Other 7%
Government Presidential system
Currency Lari = 100 tetri
Literacy rate 99%
Calorie consumption 2354 calories

Georgia *42 D2 off.* State of Georgia, *also known as* Empire State of the South, Peach State. *state* SE USA
Georgian Bay *40 D2 lake bay* Ontario, S Canada
Georgia, Republic of *see* Georgia
Georgia, Strait of *46 A1 strait* British Columbia, W Canada
Georgi Dimitrov *see* Kostenets
Georgiu-Dezh *see* Liski
Georg von Neumayer *154 A2 German research station* Antarctica
Gera *94 C4* Thüringen, E Germany
Geráki *105 B6* Pelopónnisos, S Greece
Geraldine *151 B6* Canterbury, South Island, New Zealand
Geraldton *147 A6* Western Australia
Geral, Serra *57 D5 mountain range* S Brazil
Gerede *116 C2* Bolu, N Turkey
Gereshk *122 D5* Helmand, SW Afghanistan
Gering *44 D3* Nebraska, C USA
German East Africa *see* Tanzania
Germanicopolis *see* Çankırı
Germanicum, Mare/German Ocean *see* North Sea
German Southwest Africa *see* Namibia
Germany *94 B4 off.* Federal Republic of Germany, Bundesrepublik Deutschland, *Ger.* Deutschland. *country* N Europe

GERMANY
Northern Europe

Official name Federal Republic of Germany
Formation 1871 / 1990
Capital Berlin
Population 82.7 million / 613 people per sq mile (237 people per sq km) / 88%
Total area 137,846 sq miles (357,021 sq km)
Languages German*, Turkish
Religions Protestant 34%, Roman Catholic 33%, Other 30%, Muslim 3%
Ethnic mix German 92%, Other 3%, Other European 3%, Turkish 2%

GERMANY
(continued)

Government Parliamentary system
Currency Euro = 100 cents
Literacy rate 99%
Calorie consumption 3496 calories

Germany, Federal Republic of *see*
Germany
Geroliménas *105 B7* Pelopónnisos,
S Greece
Gerona *see* Girona
Gerpinnes *87 C7* Hainaut, S Belgium
Gerunda *see* Girona
Gerze *116 D2* Sinop, N Turkey
Gesoriacum *see* Boulogne-sur-Mer
Gessoriacum *see* Boulogne-sur-Mer
Getafe *92 D3* Madrid, C Spain
Gevaş *117 F3* Van, SE Turkey
Gevgeli *see* Gevgelija
Gevgelija *101 E6* var. Đevdelija,
Djevdjelija, *Turk.* Gevgeli.
SE Macedonia
Ghaba *see* Al Ghābah
Ghana *75 E5* off. Republic of Ghana.
country W Africa

GHANA
West Africa

Official name Republic of Ghana
Formation 1957 / 1957
Capital Accra
Population 22.1 million / 249 people per
sq mile (96 people per sq km) / 38%
Total area 92,100 sq miles
(238,540 sq km)
Languages Twi, Fanti, Ewe, Ga, Adangbe,
Gurma, Dagomba (Dagbani)
Religions Christian 69%, Muslim 16%,
Traditional beliefs 9%, Other 6%
Ethnic mix Ashanti and Fanti 52%,
Moshi-Dagomba 16%, Ewe 12%,
Other 11%, Ga and Ga-adanbe 8%,
Yoruba 1%
Government Presidential system
Currency Cedi = 100 psewas
Literacy rate 54%
Calorie consumption 2667 calories

Ghanzi *78 C3* var. Khanzi. Ghanzi,
W Botswana
Gharandal *119 B7* Al 'Aqabah,
SW Jordan
Gharbt, Jabal al *see* Liban, Jebel
Ghardaïa *70 D2* N Algeria
Gharvān *see* Gharyān
Gharyān *71 F2* var. Gharvān.
NW Libya
Ghawdex *see* Gozo
Ghaznī *123 E4* var. Ghazni. Ghaznī,
E Afghanistan
Ghazzah *see* Gaza
Gheel *see* Geel
Ghent *see* Gent
Gheorgheni *108 C4* prev. Gheorghieni,
Sin-Miclăuş, Ger. Niklasmarkt, Hung.
Gyergyószentmiklós. Harghita,
C Romania
Gheorghieni *see* Gheorgheni
Ghūdara *123 F3* var. Gudara, Rus.
Kudara. SE Tajikistan
Ghurdaqah *see* Hurghada
Ghūrīān *122 D4* Herāt, W Afghanistan
Giamame *see* Jamaame
Giannitsá *104 B4* var. Yiannitsá.
Kentriki Makedonía, N Greece
Gibraltar *93 G4* UK dependent territory
SW Europe
Gibraltar, Bay of *93 G5* bay
Gibraltar/Spain Europe
Mediterranean Sea Atlantic Ocean
Gibraltar, Détroit de/Gibraltar,
Estrecho de *see* Gibraltar, Strait of
Gibraltar, Strait of *92 C5* Fr. Détroit de
Gibraltar, Sp. Estrecho de Gibraltar.
strait Atlantic Ocean/Mediterranean Sea
Gibson Desert *147 B5* desert Western
Australia
Giedraičiai *107 C5* Utena, E Lithuania
Giessen *95 B5* Hessen, W Germany
Gifu *131 C6* var. Gihu. Gifu, Honshū,
SW Japan
Giganta, Sierra de la *50 B3* mountain
range W Mexico
Gihu *see* Gifu

G'ijduvon *122 D2* Rus. Gizhduvon.
Buxoro Viloyati, C Uzbekistan
Gijón *92 D1* var. Xixón. Asturias,
NW Spain
Gilani *see* Gnjilane
Gila River *48 A2* river Arizona,
SW USA
Gilbert Islands *see* Tungaru
Gilbert River *148 C3* river Queensland,
NE Australia
Gilf Kebir Plateau *72 A2* Ar. Hadabat al
Jilf al Kabir. plateau SW Egypt
Gillette *44 D3* Wyoming, C USA
Gilolo *see* Halmahera, Pulau
Gilroy *47 B6* California, W USA
Gimie, Mount *55 F1* mountain C Saint
Lucia
Gimma *see* Jima
Ginevra *see* Genève
Gingin *147 A6* Western Australia
Giohar *see* Jawhar
Gipeswic *see* Ipswich
Girardot *58 B3* Cundinamarca,
C Colombia
Giresun *117 E2* var. Kerasunt; anc.
Cerasus, Pharnacia. Giresun,
NE Turkey
Girgenti *see* Agrigento
Girin *see* Jilin
Girne *102 C5* Gk. Kerýneia, Kyrenia.
N Cyprus
Giron *see* Kiruna
Girona *93 G2* var. Gerona; anc. Gerunda.
Cataluña, NE Spain
Gisborne *150 E3* Gisborne, North Island,
New Zealand
Gissar Range *123 E3* Rus. Gissarskiy
Khrebet. mountain range
Tajikistan/Uzbekistan
Gissarskiy Khrebet *see* Gissar Range
Githio *see* Gýtheio
Giulianova *96 D4* Abruzzi, C Italy
Giumri *see* Gyumri
Giurgiu *108 C5* Giurgiu, S Romania
Giza/Gizeh *see* El Giza
Gizhduvon *see* G'ijduvon
Giżycko *98 D2* Warmińsko-Mazurskie,
NE Poland
Gjakovë *see* Ðakovica
Gjilan *see* Gnjilane
Gjinokastër *see* Gjirokastër
Gjirokastër *101 C7* var. Gjirokastra;
prev. Gjinokastër, Gk. Argyrokastron,
It. Argirocastro. Gjirokastër, S Albania
Gjirokastra *see* Gjirokastër
Gjoa Haven *37 F3* King William Island,
Nunavut, NW Canada
Gjøvik *85 B5* Oppland, S Norway
Glace Bay *39 G4* Cape Breton Island,
Nova Scotia, SE Canada
Gladstone *148 E4* Queensland,
E Australia
Glåma *85 B5* var. Glommen. river
S Norway
Glasgow *88 C4* S Scotland, UK
Glavn'a Morava *see* Velika Morava
Glazov *111 D5* Udmurtskaya Respublika,
NW Russian Federation
Gleiwitz *see* Gliwice
Glendale *48 B2* Arizona, SW USA
Glendive *44 D2* Montana, NW USA
Glens Falls *41 F3* New York, NE USA
Glevum *see* Gloucester
Glina *100 B3* Sisak-Moslavina,
NE Croatia
Glittertind *85 A5* mountain S Norway
Gliwice *99 C5* Ger. Gleiwitz. Śląskie,
S Poland
Globe *48 B2* Arizona, SW USA
Globino *see* Hlobyne
Glogau *see* Głogów
Głogów *98 B4* Ger. Glogau, Glogow.
Dolnośląskie, SW Poland
Glogow *see* Głogów
Glomma *see* Glåma
Glommen *see* Glåma
Gloucester *89 D6* hist. Caer Glou, Lat.
Glevum. C England, UK
Głowno *98 D4* Łódź, C Poland
Glubokoye *see* Hlybokaye
Glukhov *see* Hlukhiv
Gnesen *see* Gniezno
Gniezno *98 C3* Ger. Gnesen.
Weilkopolskie, C Poland
Gnjilane *101 D5* var. Gilani, Alb. Gjilan.
Kosovo, S Serbia
Gobabis *78 B3* Omaheke, E Namibia
Gobi *126 D3* desert China/Mongolia

Gobō *131 C6* Wakayama, Honshū,
SW Japan
Godāvari *124 B3* var. Godavari. river
C India
Godavari *see* Godāvari
Godhavn *see* Qeqertarsuaq
Godhra *134 C4* Gujarāt, W India
Göding *see* Hodonín
Godoy Cruz *64 B4* Mendoza,
W Argentina
Godthaab/Godthåb *see* Nuuk
Godwin Austen, Mount *see* K2
Goede Hoop, Kaap de *see* Good Hope,
Cape of
Goeie Hoop, Kaap die *see* Good Hope,
Cape of
Goeree *86 B4* island SW Netherlands
Goes *87 B5* Zeeland, SW Netherlands
Goettingen *see* Göttingen
Gogebic Range *40 B1* hill range
Michigan/Wisconsin, N USA
Goiânia *63 E3* prev. Goyania. state
capital Goiás, C Brazil
Goiás *63 E3* Goiás, C Brazil
Gojōme *130 D4* Akita, Honshū,
NW Japan
Gökçeada *104 D4* var. Imroz Adasi,
Gk. Imbros. island NW Turkey
Gökdepe *122 C3* Rus. Gëkdepe,
Geok-Tepe. Ahal Welaýaty,
C Turkmenistan
Göksun *116 D4* Kahramanmaraş,
C Turkey
Gol *85 A5* Buskerud, S Norway
Golan Heights *119 B5* Ar. Al Jawlān,
Heb. HaGolan. mountain range
SW Syria
Golaya Pristan *see* Hola Prystan'
Gołdap *98 E2* Ger. Goldap.
Warmińsko-Mazurskie, NE Poland
Gold Coast *149 E5* cultural region
Queensland, E Australia
Golden Bay *150 C4* bay South Island,
New Zealand
Golden State, The *see* California
Goldingen *see* Kuldīga
Goldsboro *43 F1* North Carolina,
SE USA
Goleniów *98 B3* Ger. Gollnow.
Zachodnio-pomorskie, NW Poland
Gollnow *see* Goleniów
Golmo *see* Golmud
Golmud *126 D4* var. Ge'e'mu,
Golmo, Chin. Ko-erh-mu. Qinghai,
C China
Golovanevsk *see* Holovanivs'k
Golub-Dobrzyń *98 C3* Kujawski-
pomorskie, C Poland
Goma *77 E6* Nord Kivu, NE Dem.
Rep. Congo
Gombi *75 H4* Adamawa, E Nigeria
Gombroon *see* Bandar-e 'Abbās
Gomel' *see* Homyel'
Gomera *70 A3* island Islas Canarias,
Spain, NE Atlantic Ocean
Gómez Palacio *50 D3* Durango,
C Mexico
Gonaïves *54 D3* var. Les Gonaïves.
N Haiti
Gonâve, Île de la *54 D3* island C Haiti
Gonder *see* Gonder
Gonder *72 C4* var. Gondar.
NW Ethiopia
Gondia *135 E4* Mahārāshtra, C India
Gonggar *126 C5* var. Gyixong. Xizang
Zizhiqu, W China
Gongola *75 G4* river E Nigeria
Gongtang *see* Damxung
Gonni/Gónnoi *see* Gónnoi
Gónnoi *104 B4* var. Gonni, Gónnos;
prev. Derelí. Thessalía, C Greece
Good Hope *see* Fort Good Hope
Good Hope, Cape of *78 B5* Afr. Kaap de
Goede Hoop, Kaap die Goeie Hoop.
cape SW South Africa
Goodland *44 D4* Kansas, C USA
Goondiwindi *149 D5* Queensland,
E Australia
Goor *86 E3* Overijssel, E Netherlands
Goose Green *65 D7* var Prado del Ganso.
East Falkland, Falkland Islands
Goose Lake *46 B4* var. Lago dos Gansos.
lake California/Oregon, W USA
Gopher State *see* Minnesota
Göppingen *95 B6* Baden-Württemberg,
SW Germany
Góra Kalwaria *114 D4* Mazowieckie,
C Poland

Gorakhpur *135 E3* Uttar Pradesh,
N India
Gorany *see* Harany
Goražde *100 C4* Federacija Bosna
I Hercegovina, SE Bosnia and
Herzegovina
Gorbovichi *see* Harbavichy
Gordiaz *see* Gardīz
Goré *76 C4* Logone-Oriental, S Chad
Gorē *73 C5* Oromo, C Ethiopia
Gore *151 B7* Southland, South Island,
New Zealand
Gorgān *120 D2* var. Astarabad,
Astrabad, Gurgan, prev. Asterābād;
anc. Hyrcania. Golestán, N Iran
Gori *117 F2* C Georgia
Gorinchem *86 C4* var. Gorkum.
Zuid-Holland, C Netherlands
Goris *117 G3* SE Armenia
Gorki *see* Horki
Gor'kiy *see* Nizhniy Novgorod
Gorkum *see* Gorinchem
Görlitz *94 D4* Sachsen, E Germany
Görlitz *see* Zgorzelec
Gorlovka *see* Horlivka
Gorna Dzhumaya *see* Blagoevgrad
Gornja Mužlja *see* Mužlja
Gornji Milanovac *100 C4* Serbia,
C Serbia
Gorodets *see* Haradzyets
Gorodishche *see* Horodyshche
Gorodnya *see* Horodnya
Gorodok *see* Haradok
Gorodok/Gorodok Yagellonski *see*
Horodok
Gorontalo *139 E4* Sulawesi,
C Indonesia
Gorontalo, Teluk *see* Tomini, Gulf of
Gorssel *86 D3* Gelderland,
E Netherlands
Goryn *see* Horyn'
Gorzów Wielkopolski *98 B3* Ger.
Landsberg, Landsberg an der Warthe.
Lubuskie, W Poland
Gosford *149 D6* New South Wales,
SE Australia
Goshogawara *130 D3* var. Gosyogawara.
Aomori, Honshū, C Japan
Gospić *100 A3* Lika-Senj, C Croatia
Gostivar *101 D6* W FYR Macedonia
Gosyogawara *see* Goshogawara
Göteborg *85 B7* Eng. Gothenburg.
Västra Götaland, S Sweden
Gotel Mountains *75 G5* mountain range
E Nigeria
Gotha *94 C4* Thüringen, C Germany
Gothenburg *80 D3* Nebraska, C USA
Gothenburg *see* Göteborg
Gotland *85 C7* island SE Sweden
Gotō-rettō *131 A7* island group
SW Japan
Gotska Sandön *106 B1* island SE Sweden
Gōtsu *131 B6* var. Gōtu. Shimane,
Honshū, SW Japan
Göttingen *94 B4* var. Goettingen.
Niedersachsen, C Germany
Gottschee *see* Kočevje
Gottwaldov *see* Zlín
Gōtu *see* Gōtsu
Gouda *86 C4* Zuid-Holland, C Netherlands
Gough Fracture Zone *67 C6* tectonic
feature S Atlantic Ocean
Gough Island *69 B8* island Tristan da
Cunha, S Atlantic Ocean
Gouin, Réservoir *38 D4* reservoir
Québec, SE Canada
Goulburn *149 D6* New South Wales,
SE Australia
Goundam *75 E3* Tombouctou,
NW Mali
Gouré *75 G3* Zinder, SE Niger
Goverla, Gora *see* Hoverla, Hora
Governador Valadares *63 F4* Minas
Gerais, SE Brazil
Govi Altayn Nuruu *127 E3* mountain
range N Mongolia
Goya *64 D3* Corrientes, NE Argentina
Goyania *see* Goiânia
Goz Beïda *76 C3* Ouaddaï, SE Chad
Gozo *97 C8* var. Ghawdex. island
N Malta
Graciosa *92 A5* var. Ilha Graciosa.
island Azores, Portugal,
NE Atlantic Ocean
Graciosa, Ilha *see* Graciosa
Gradačac *100 C3* Federacija
Bosna I Hercegovina, N Bosnia
and Herzegovina

Gradaús, Serra dos 63 E3 *mountain range* C Brazil
Gradiška *see* Bosanska Gradiška
Grafton 149 E5 New South Wales, SE Australia
Grafton 45 E1 North Dakota, N USA
Graham Land 154 A2 *physical region* Antarctica
Grajewo 98 E3 Podlaskie, NE Poland
Grampian Mountains 88 C3 *mountain range* C Scotland, UK
Gran *see* Esztergom
Granada 52 D3 Granada, SW Nicaragua
Granada 92 D5 Andalucía, S Spain
Gran Canaria 70 A3 *var.* Grand Canary. *island* Islas Canarias, Spain, NE Atlantic Ocean
Gran Chaco 64 D2 *var.* Chaco. *lowland plain* South America
Grand Bahama Island 54 B1 *island* N Bahamas
Grand Banks of Newfoundland 34 E4 *undersea basin* NW Atlantic Ocean
Grand Bassa *see* Buchanan
Grand Canary *see* Gran Canaria
Grand Canyon 48 A1 *canyon* Arizona, SW USA
Grand Canyon State *see* Arizona
Grand Cayman 54 B3 *island* SW Cayman Islands
Grand Duchy of Luxembourg *see* Luxembourg
Grande, Bahía 65 B7 *bay* S Argentina
Grande Comore 79 F2 *var.* Njazidja, Great Comoro. *island* NW Comoros
Grande de Chiloé, Isla *see* Chiloé, Isla de
Grande Prairie 37 E4 Alberta, W Canada
Grand Erg Occidental 70 D3 *desert* W Algeria
Grand Erg Oriental 71 E3 *desert* Algeria/Tunisia
Grande, Rio 51 E2 *var.* Río Bravo, Sp. Río Bravo del Norte, Bravo del Norte. *river* Mexico/USA
Grande Terre 55 G3 *island* E West Indies
Grand Falls 39 G3 Newfoundland, Newfoundland and Labrador, SE Canada
Grand Forks 45 E1 North Dakota, N USA
Grandichi *see* Hrandzichy
Grand Island 45 E4 Nebraska, C USA
Grand Junction 44 C4 Colorado, C USA
Grand Paradis *see* Gran Paradiso
Grand Rapids 40 C3 Michigan, N USA
Grand Rapids 45 F1 Minnesota, N USA
Grand-Saint-Bernard, Col du *see* Great Saint Bernard Pass
Grand-Santi 59 G3 W French Guiana
Granite State *see* New Hampshire
Gran Lago *see* Nicaragua, Lago de
Gran Malvina *see* West Falkland
Gran Paradiso 96 A2 Fr. Grand Paradis. *mountain* NW Italy
Gran San Bernardo, Passo di *see* Great Saint Bernard Pass
Gran Santiago *see* Santiago
Grants 48 C2 New Mexico, SW USA
Grants Pass 46 B4 Oregon, NW USA
Granville 90 B3 Manche, N France
Gratianopolis *see* Grenoble
Gratz *see* Graz
Graudenz *see* Grudziądz
Graulhet 91 C6 Tarn, S France
Grave 86 D4 Noord-Brabant, SE Netherlands
Grayling 36 C2 Alaska, USA
Graz 95 E7 *prev.* Gratz. Steiermark, SE Austria
Great Abaco 54 C1 *var.* Abaco Island. *island* N Bahamas
Great Alfold *see* Great Hungarian Plain
Great Ararat *see* Büyükağrı Dağı
Great Australian Bight 147 D7 *bight* S Australia
Great Barrier Island 150 D2 *island* N New Zealand
Great Barrier Reef 148 D2 *reef* Queensland, NE Australia
Great Basin 47 C5 *basin* W USA
Great Bear Lake 37 E3 Fr. Grand Lac de l'Ours. *lake* Northwest Territories, NW Canada
Great Belt *see* Storebælt

Great Bend 45 E5 Kansas, C USA
Great Britain *see* Britain
Great Comoro *see* Grande Comore
Great Dividing Range 148 D4 *mountain range* NE Australia
Greater Antarctica 154 C3 *var.* East Antarctica. *physical region* Antarctica
Greater Antilles 54 D3 *island group* West Indies
Greater Caucasus 117 G2 *mountain range* Azerbaijan/Georgia/Russian Federation Asia/Europe
Greater Sunda Islands 124 D5 *var.* Sunda Islands. *island group* Indonesia
Great Exhibition Bay 150 C1 *inlet* North Island, New Zealand
Great Exuma Island 54 C2 *island* C Bahamas
Great Falls 44 B1 Montana, NW USA
Great Grimsby *see* Grimsby
Great Hungarian Plain 99 C7 *var.* Great Alfold, Plain of Hungary, *Hung.* Alföld. *plain* SE Europe
Great Inagua 54 D2 *var.* Inagua Islands. *island* S Bahamas
Great Indian Desert *see* Thar Desert
Great Khingan Range *see* Da Hinggan Ling
Great Lake *see* Tônlé Sap
Great Lakes 35 C5 *lakes* Ontario, Canada/USA
Great Lakes State *see* Michigan
Great Meteor Seamount *see* Great Meteor Tablemount
Great Meteor Tablemount 66 B3 *var.* Great Meteor Seamount. *seamount* E Atlantic Ocean
Great Nicobar 133 G3 *island* Nicobar Islands, India, NE Indian Ocean
Great Plain of China 125 E2 *plain* E China
Great Plains 45 E3 *var.* High Plains. *plains* Canada/USA
Great Rift Valley 73 C5 *var.* Rift Valley. *depression* Asia/Africa
Great Ruaha 73 C7 *river* S Tanzania
Great Saint Bernard Pass 96 A1 Fr. Col du Grand-Saint-Bernard, It. Passo del Gran San Bernardo. *pass* Italy/Switzerland
Great Salt Desert *see* Kavir, Dasht-e
Great Salt Lake 44 A3 *salt lake* Utah, W USA
Great Salt Lake Desert 44 A4 *plain* Utah, W USA
Great Sand Sea 71 H3 *desert* Egypt/Libya
Great Sandy Desert 146 C4 *desert* Western Australia
Great Sandy Desert *see* Ar Rub 'al Khālī
Great Sandy Island *see* Fraser Island
Great Slave Lake 37 E4 Fr. Grand Lac des Esclaves. *lake* Northwest Territories, NW Canada
Great Sound 42 A5 *sound* Bermuda, NW Atlantic Ocean
Great Victoria Desert 147 C5 *desert* South Australia/Western Australia
Great Wall of China 128 C4 *ancient monument* N China Asia
Great Yarmouth 89 E6 *var.* Yarmouth. E England, UK
Grebenka *see* Hrebinka
Gredos, Sierra de 92 D3 *mountain range* W Spain
Greece 81 E5 New York, NE USA
Greece 105 A5 off. Hellenic Republic, *Gk.* Ellás; *anc.* Hellas. *country* SE Europe

GREECE
Southeast Europe

Official name Hellenic Republic
Formation 1829 / 1947
Capital Athens
Population 11.1 million / 220 people per sq mile (85 people per sq km) / 60%
Total area 50,942 sq miles (131,940 sq km)
Languages Greek*, Turkish, Macedonian, Albanian
Religions Orthodox Christian 98%, Other 1%, Muslim 1%
Ethnic mix Greek 98%, Other 2%
Government Parliamentary system
Currency Euro = 100 cents
Literacy rate 91%
Calorie consumption 3721 calories

Greeley 44 D4 Colorado, C USA
Green Bay 40 B2 Wisconsin, N USA
Green Bay 40 B2 *lake bay* Michigan/Wisconsin, N USA
Greeneville 43 E1 Tennessee, S USA
Greenland 82 D3 *Dan.* Grønland, *Inuit* Kalaallit Nunaat. *Danish external territory* NE North America
Greenland Sea 83 F2 *sea* Arctic Ocean
Green Mountains 41 G2 *mountain range* Vermont, NE USA
Green Mountain State *see* Vermont
Greenock 88 C4 W Scotland, UK
Green River 44 B3 Wyoming, C USA
Green River 40 C5 *river* Kentucky, C USA
Green River 44 B4 *river* Utah, W USA
Greensboro 43 F1 North Carolina, SE USA
Greenville 42 B2 Mississippi, S USA
Greenville 43 F1 North Carolina, SE USA
Greenville 43 E1 South Carolina, SE USA
Greenville 49 G2 Texas, SW USA
Greenwich 89 B8 UK
Greenwood 42 B2 Mississippi, S USA
Greenwood 43 E2 South Carolina, SE USA
Gregory Range 148 C3 *mountain range* Queensland, E Australia
Greifenberg/Greifenberg in Pommern *see* Gryfice
Greifswald 94 D2 Mecklenburg-Vorpommern, NE Germany
Grenada 42 C2 Mississippi, S USA
Grenada 55 G5 *country* SE West Indies

GRENADA
West Indies

Official name Grenada
Formation 1974 / 1974
Capital St. George's
Population 89,502 / 683 people per sq mile (263 people per sq km)
Total area 131 sq miles (340 sq km)
Languages English*, English Creole
Religions Roman Catholic 68%, Anglican 17%, Other 15%
Ethnic mix Black African 82%, Mulatto (mixed race) 13%, East Indian 3%, Other 2%
Government Parliamentary system
Currency Eastern Caribbean dollar = 100 cents
Literacy rate 96%
Calorie consumption 2932 calories

Grenadines, The 55 H4 *island group* Grenada/St Vincent and the Grenadines
Grenoble 91 D5 *anc.* Cularo, Gratianopolis. Isère, E France
Gresham 46 B3 Oregon, NW USA
Grevená 104 B4 Dytikí Makedonía, N Greece
Grevenmacher 87 E8 Grevenmacher, E Luxembourg
Greymouth 151 B5 West Coast, South Island, New Zealand
Grey Range 149 C5 *mountain range* New South Wales/Queensland, E Australia
Greytown *see* San Juan del Norte
Griffin 42 D2 Georgia, SE USA
Grimari 76 C4 Ouaka, C Central African Republic
Grimsby 89 E5 *prev.* Great Grimsby. E England, UK
Grobin *see* Grobiņa
Grobiņa 106 B3 *Ger.* Grobin. Liepāja, W Latvia
Gródek Jagielloński *see* Horodok
Grodno *see* Hrodna
Grodzisk Wielkopolski 98 B3 Weilkopolskie, C Poland
Groesbeek 86 D4 Gelderland, SE Netherlands
Grójec 98 D4 Mazowieckie, C Poland
Groningen 86 E1 Groningen, NE Netherlands
Grønland *see* Greenland
Groote Eylandt 148 B2 *island* Northern Territory, N Australia

Grootfontein 78 B3 Otjozondjupa, N Namibia
Groot Karasberge 78 B4 *mountain range* S Namibia
Gros Islet 55 F1 N Saint Lucia
Grossa, Isola *see* Dugi Otok
Grossbetschkerek *see* Zrenjanin
Grosse Morava *see* Velika Morava
Grosser Sund *see* Suur Väin
Grosseto 96 B4 Toscana, C Italy
Grossglockner 95 C7 *mountain* W Austria
Grosskanizsa *see* Nagykanizsa
Gross-Karol *see* Carei
Grosskikinda *see* Kikinda
Grossmichel *see* Michalovce
Gross-Schlatten *see* Abrud
Grosswardein *see* Oradea
Groznyy 111 B8 Chechenskaya Respublika, SW Russian Federation
Grudovo *see* Sredets
Grudziądz 98 C3 *Ger.* Graudenz. Kujawsko-pomorskie, C Poland
Grums 85 B6 Värmland, C Sweden
Grünberg/Grünberg in Schlesien *see* Zielona Góra
Grüneberg *see* Zielona Góra
Gruzinskaya SSR/Gruziya *see* Georgia
Gryazi 111 B6 Lipetskaya Oblast', W Russian Federation
Gryfice 98 B2 *Ger.* Greifenberg, Greifenberg in Pommern. Zachodnio-pomorskie, NW Poland
Guabito 53 E4 Bocas del Toro, NW Panama
Guadalajara 50 D4 Jalisco, C Mexico
Guadalajara 93 E3 *Ar.* Wad Al-Hajarah; *anc.* Arriaca. Castilla-La Mancha, C Spain
Guadalcanal 144 C3 *island* C Solomon Islands
Guadalquivir 92 D4 *river* W Spain
Guadalupe 50 D3 Zacatecas, C Mexico
Guadalupe Peak 48 D3 *mountain* Texas, SW USA
Guadalupe River 49 G4 *river* SW USA
Guadarrama, Sierra de 93 E2 *mountain range* C Spain
Guadeloupe 55 H3 *French overseas department* E West Indies
Guadiana 92 C4 *river* Portugal/Spain
Guadix 93 E4 Andalucía, S Spain
Guaimaca 52 C2 Francisco Morazán, C Honduras
Guajira, Península de la 58 B1 *peninsula* N Colombia
Gualaco 52 D2 Olancho, C Honduras
Gualán 52 B2 Zacapa, C Guatemala
Gualdicciolo 96 D1 NW San Marino
Gualeguaychú 64 D4 Entre Ríos, E Argentina
Guam 144 B1 US *unincorporated territory* W Pacific Ocean
Guamúchil 50 C3 Sinaloa, C Mexico
Guanabacoa 54 B2 La Habana, W Cuba
Guanajuato 51 E4 Guanajuato, C Mexico
Guanare 58 C2 Portuguesa, N Venezuela
Guanare, Río 58 D2 *river* W Venezuela
Guangdong 128 C6 *var.* Guangdong Sheng, Kuang-tung, Kwangtung, Yue. *province* S China
Guangdong Sheng *see* Guangdong
Guangju *see* Kwangju
Guangxi *see* Guangxi Zhuangzu Zizhiqu
Guangxi Zhuangzu Zizhiqu 128 C6 *var.* Guangxi, Gui, Kuang-hsi, Kwangsi, *Eng.* Kwangsi Chuang Autonomous Region. *autonomous region* S China
Guangyuan 128 B5 *var.* Kuang-yuan, Kwangyuan. Sichuan, C China
Guangzhou 128 C6 *var.* Kwangchow, *Eng.* Canton. *province capital* Guangdong, S China
Guantánamo 54 D3 Guantánamo, SE Cuba
Guantánamo, Bahía de 54 D3 *Eng.* Guantanamo Bay. *US military base* SE Cuba
Guantanamo Bay *see* Guantánamo, Bahia de
Guaporé, Río 62 D3 *var.* Río Iténez. *river* Bolivia/Brazil
Guarda 92 C3 Guarda, N Portugal
Guarumal 53 F5 Veraguas, S Panama
Guasave 50 C3 Sinaloa, C Mexico

Guatemala 52 A2 off. Republic of Guatemala. *country* Central America

GUATEMALA
Central America

Official name Republic of Guatemala
Formation 1838 / 1838
Capital Guatemala City
Population 12.6 million / 301 people per sq mile (116 people per sq km) / 40%
Total area 42,042 sq miles (108,890 sq km)
Languages Spanish*, Quiché, Mam, Cakchiquel, Kekchí
Religions Roman Catholic 65%, Protestant 33%, Other and nonreligious 2%
Ethnic mix Amerindian 60%, Mestizo 30%, Other 10%
Government Presidential system
Currency Quetzal = 100 centavos
Literacy rate 69%
Calorie consumption 2219 calories

Guatemala Basin 35 B7 *undersea basin* E Pacific Ocean
Guatemala City *see* Ciudad de Guatemala
Guatemala, Republic of *see* Guatemala
Guaviare 56 B2 off. Comisaría Guaviare. *province* S Colombia
Guaviare, Comisaría *see* Guaviare
Guaviare, Río 58 D3 *river* E Colombia
Guayanas, Macizo de las *see* Guiana Highlands
Guayaquil 60 A2 *var.* Santiago de Guayaquil. Guayas, SW Ecuador
Guayaquil, Golfo de 60 A2 *var.* Gulf of Guayaquil. *gulf* SW Ecuador
Guayaquil, Gulf of *see* Guayaquil, Golfo de
Guaymas 50 B2 Sonora, NW Mexico
Gubadag 122 C2 *Turkm.* Tel'man; *prev.* Tel'mansk. Daşoguz Welaýaty, N Turkmenistan
Guben 94 D4 *var.* Wilhelm-Pieck-Stadt. Brandenburg, E Germany
Gudara *see* Ghŭdara
Gudaut'a 117 E1 NW Georgia
Guéret 90 C4 Creuse, C France
Guernsey 89 D8 *island* Channel Islands, NW Europe
Guerrero Negro 50 A2 Baja California Sur, NW Mexico
Gui *see* Guangxi Zhuangzu Zizhiqu
Guiana *see* French Guiana
Guiana Highlands 62 D1 *var.* Macizo de las Guayanas. *mountain range* N South America
Guiba *see* Juba
Guidder *see* Guider
Guider 76 B4 *var.* Guidder. Nord, N Cameroon
Guidimouni 75 G3 Zinder, S Niger
Guildford 89 D7 SE England, UK
Guilin 128 C6 *var.* Kuei-lin, Kweilin. Guangxi Zhuangzu Zizhiqu, S China
Guimarães 92 B2 *var.* Guimaráes. Braga, N Portugal
Guimaráes *see* Guimarães
Guinea 74 C4 off. Republic of Guinea, *var.* Guinée; *prev.* French Guinea, People's Revolutionary Republic of Guinea. *country* W Africa

GUINEA
West Africa

Official name Republic of Guinea
Formation 1958 / 1958
Capital Conakry
Population 9.4 million / 99 people per sq mile (38 people per sq km) / 33%
Total area 94,925 sq miles (245,857 sq km)
Languages French*, Fulani, Malinke, Soussou
Religions Muslim 65%, Traditional beliefs 33%, Christian 2%
Ethnic mix Fulani 30%, Malinke 30%, Soussou 15%, Kissi 10%, Other tribes 10%, Other 5%
Government Presidential system
Currency Guinea franc = 100 centimes
Literacy rate 41%
Calorie consumption 2409 calories

Guinea Basin 69 A5 *undersea basin* E Atlantic Ocean
Guinea-Bissau 74 B4 off. Republic of Guinea-Bissau, *Fr.* Guinée-Bissau, *Port.* Guiné-Bissau; *prev.* Portuguese Guinea. *country* W Africa

GUINEA-BISSAU
West Africa

Official name Republic of Guinea-Bissau
Formation 1974 / 1974
Capital Bissau
Population 1.6 million / 147 people per sq mile (57 people per sq km) / 24%
Total area 13,946 sq miles (36,120 sq km)
Languages Portuguese*, Balante, Fulani, Malinke, Portuguese Creole
Religions Traditional beliefs 52%, Muslim 40%, Christian 8%
Ethnic mix Other tribes 31%, Balante 25%, Fula 20%, Mandinka 12%, Mandyako 11%, Other 1%
Government Presidential system
Currency CFA franc = 100 centimes
Literacy rate 40%
Calorie consumption 2024 calories

Guinea-Bissau, Republic of *see* Guinea-Bissau
Guinea, Gulf of 68 B4 *Fr.* Golfe de Guinée. *gulf* E Atlantic Ocean
Guinea, People's Revolutionary Republic of *see* Guinea
Guinea, Republic of *see* Guinea
Guiné-Bissau *see* Guinea-Bissau
Guinée *see* Guinea
Guinée-Bissau *see* Guinea-Bissau
Guinée, Golfe de *see* Guinea, Gulf of
Güiria 59 E1 Sucre, NE Venezuela
Guiyang 128 B6 *var.* Kuei-Yang, Kuei-yang, Kueyang, Kweiyang; *prev.* Kweichu. *province capital* Guizhou, S China
Guizhou 128 B6 China
Gujarāt 134 C4 *var.* Gujarat. *cultural region* W India
Gujarāt 134 C4 *var.* Gujarat. *state* W India
Gujerat *see* Gujarāt
Gujrānwāla 134 D2 Punjab, NE Pakistan
Gujrāt 134 D2 Punjab, E Pakistan
Gulbarga 132 C1 Karnātaka, C India
Gulbene 106 D3 Ger. Alt-Schwanenburg. Gulbene, NE Latvia
Gulf of Liaotung *see* Liaodong Wan
Gulfport 42 C3 Mississippi, S USA
Gulf, The 120 C4 *var.* Persian Gulf, *Ar.* Khalīj al 'Arabī, *Per.* Khalīj-e Fars. *Gulf* SW Asia
Gulistan *see* Guliston
Guliston 123 E2 *Rus.* Gulistan. Sirdaryo Viloyati, E Uzbekistan
Gulja *see* Yining
Gulkana 36 D3 Alaska, USA
Gulu 73 B6 N Uganda
Gulyantsi 104 C1 Pleven, N Bulgaria
Guma *see* Pishan
Gumbinnen *see* Gusev
Gumpolds *see* Humpolec
Gümülcine/Gümüljina *see* Komotiní
Gümüşane *see* Gümüşhane
Gümüşhane 117 E3 *var.* Gümüşane, Gumushkhane. Gümüşhane, NE Turkey
Gumushkhane *see* Gümüşhane
Güney Doğu Toroslar 117 E4 *mountain range* SE Turkey
Gunnbjørn Fjeld 82 D4 *var.* Gunnbjörns Bjerge. *mountain* C Greenland
Gunnbjörns Bjerge *see* Gunnbjørn Fjeld
Gunnedah 149 D6 New South Wales, SE Australia
Gunnison 44 C5 Colorado, C USA
Gurbansoltan Eje 122 C2 *Prev.* Ýylanly, *Rus.* Il'yaly. Daşoguz Welaýaty, N Turkmenistan
Gurbantünggüt Shamo 126 B2 *desert* W China
Gurgan *see* Gorgān
Guri, Embalse de 59 E2 *reservoir* E Venezuela
Gurkfeld *see* Krško
Gurktaler Alpen 95 D7 *mountain range* S Austria
Gürün 116 D3 Sivas, C Turkey

Gur'yev/Gur'yevskaya Oblast' *see* Atyrau
Gusau 75 G4 Zamfara, NW Nigeria
Gusev 106 B4 *Ger.* Gumbinnen. Kaliningradskaya Oblast', W Russian Federation
Gushgy *see* Serhetabat
Gustavus 36 D4 Alaska, USA
Güstrow 94 C3 Mecklenburg-Vorpommern, NE Germany
Guta/Gúta *see* Kolárovo
Gütersloh 94 B4 Nordrhein-Westfalen, W Germany
Gutta *see* Kolárovo
Guttstadt *see* Dobre Miasto
Guwāhāti 135 G3 *prev.* Gauhāti. Assam, NE India
Guyana 59 F3 off. Cooperative Republic of Guyana; *prev.* British Guiana. *country* N South America

GUYANA
South America

Official name Cooperative Republic of Guyana
Formation 1966 / 1966
Capital Georgetown
Population 751,000 / 10 people per sq mile (4 people per sq km) / 38%
Total area 83,000 sq miles (214,970 sq km)
Languages English*, Hindi, Tamil, Amerindian languages, English Creole
Religions Christian 57%, Hindu 33%, Muslim 9%, Other 1%
Ethnic mix East Indian 52%, Black African 38%, Other 4%, Amerindian 4%, European and Chinese 2%
Government Presidential system
Currency Guyana dollar = 100 cents
Literacy rate 97%
Calorie consumption 2692 calories

Guyana, Cooperative Republic of *see* Guyana
Guyane *see* French Guiana
Guymon 49 E1 Oklahoma, C USA
Güzelyurt Körfezi 102 C5 *Gk.* Kólpos Mórfu, Mórfou, Morphou. W Cyprus
Gvardeysk 106 A4 *Ger.* Tapiau. Kaliningradskaya Oblast', W Russian Federation
Gwādar 134 A3 *var.* Gwadur. Baluchistán, SW Pakistan
Gwadur *see* Gwādar
Gwalior 134 D3 Madhya Pradesh, C India
Gwanda 78 D3 Matabeleland South, SW Zimbabwe
Gwy *see* Wye
Gyandzha *see* Gäncä
Gyangzê 126 C5 Xizang Zizhiqu, W China
Gyaring Co 126 C5 *lake* W China
Gyêgu *see* Yushu
Gyergyószentmiklós *see* Gheorgheni
Gyixong *see* Gonggar
Gyomaendrőd 99 D7 Békés, SE Hungary
Gyöngyös 99 D6 Heves, NE Hungary
Győr 99 C6 *Ger.* Raab, *Lat.* Arrabona. Győr-Moson-Sopron, NW Hungary
Gýtheio 105 B6 *var.* Githio; *prev.* Yíthion. Pelopónnisos, S Greece
Gyulafehérvár *see* Alba Iulia
Gyumri 117 F2 *var.* Giumri, *Rus.* Kumayri; *prev.* Aleksandropol', Leninakan. W Armenia
Gyzyrlabat *see* Serdar

H

Haabai *see* Ha'apai Group
Haacht 87 C6 Vlaams Brabant, C Belgium
Haaksbergen 86 E3 Overijssel, E Netherlands
Ha'apai Group 145 F4 *var.* Haabai. *island group* C Tonga
Haapsalu 106 D2 *Ger.* Hapsal. Läänemaa, W Estonia
Ha'Arava *see* 'Arabah, Wādī al
Haarlem 86 C3 *prev.* Harlem. Noord-Holland, W Netherlands

Haast 151 B6 West Coast, South Island, New Zealand
Hachijō-jima 131 D6 *island* Izu-shotō, SE Japan
Hachinohe 130 D3 Aomori, Honshū, C Japan
Hadama *see* Nazrēt
Hadejia 75 G4 Jigawa, N Nigeria
Hadejia 75 G3 *river* N Nigeria
Hadera 119 A6 *var.* Khadera. Haifa, C Israel
Hadhdhunmathi Atoll 132 A5 *atoll* S Maldives
Hadhramaut *see* Ḥaḍramawt
Ha Đông 136 D3 *var.* Hadong. Ha Tây, N Vietnam
Hadong *see* Ha Đông
Ḥaḍramawt 121 C6 *Eng.* Hadhramaut. *mountain range* S Yemen
Hadrianopolis *see* Edirne
Haerbin/Haerhpin/Ha-erh-pin *see* Harbin
Hafnia *see* Denmark
Hafnia *see* København
Hafren *see* Severn
Hafun, Ras *see* Xaafuun, Raas
Hagåtña 160 B1 *var.* Agana, *var.* Agaña. *dependent territory capital* (Guam) NW Guam
Hagerstown 41 E4 Maryland, NE USA
Ha Giang 136 D3 Ha Giang, N Vietnam
Hagios Evstrátios *see* Ágios Efstrátios
HaGolan *see* Golan Heights
Hagondange 90 D3 Moselle, NE France
Haguenau 90 E3 Bas-Rhin, NE France
Haibowan *see* Wuhai
Haicheng 128 D3 Liaoning, NE China
Haidarabad *see* Hyderābād
Haifa *see* Ḥefa
Haifa, Bay of *see* Ḥefa, Mifraẕ
Haifong *see* Hai Phong
Haikou 128 C7 *var.* Hai-k'ou, Hoihow, *Fr.* Hoï-Hao. *province capital* Hainan, S China
Hai-k'ou *see* Haikou
Ḥā'il 120 B4 Ḥā'il, NW Saudi Arabia
Hai-la-erh *see* Hailar
Hailar 127 F1 *var.* Hai-la-erh; *prev.* Hulun. Nei Mongol Zizhiqu, N China
Hailuoto 84 D4 *Swe.* Karlö. *island* W Finland
Hainan 128 B7 *var.* Hainan Sheng, Qiong. *province* S China
Hainan Dao 128 C7 *island* S China
Hainan Sheng *see* Hainan
Hainasch *see* Ainaži
Haines 36 D4 Alaska, USA
Hainichen 94 D4 Sachsen, E Germany
Hai Phong 136 D3 *var.* Haifong, Haiphong. N Vietnam
Haiphong *see* Hai Phong
Haiti 54 D3 off. Republic of Haiti. *country* C West Indies

HAITI
West Indies

Official name Republic of Haiti
Formation 1804 / 1844
Capital Port-au-Prince
Population 8.5 million / 799 people per sq mile (308 people per sq km) / 36%
Total area 10,714 sq miles (27,750 sq km)
Languages French Creole*, French*
Religions Roman Catholic 80%, Protestant 16%, Other (including Voodoo) 3%, Nonreligious 1%
Ethnic mix Black African 95%, Mulatto (mixed race) and European 5%
Government Transitional regime
Currency Gourde = 100 centimes
Literacy rate 52%
Calorie consumption 2086 calories

Haiti, Republic of *see* Haiti
Haiya 72 C3 Red Sea, NE Sudan
Hajdúhadház 99 D6 Hajdú-Bihar, E Hungary
Hajine *see* Abū Ḥardān
Hajnówka 98 E3 Ger. Hermhausen. Podlaskie, NE Poland
Hakodate 130 D3 Hokkaidō, NE Japan
Hal *see* Halle
Ḥalab 118 B2 *Eng.* Aleppo, *Fr.* Alep; *anc.* Beroea. Ḥalab, NW Syria

Ḩalāniyāt, Juzur almu 137 D6 var.
  Jazā'ir Bin Ghalfān, Eng. Kuria Muria
  Islands. island group S Oman
Halberstadt 94 C4 Sachsen-Anhalt,
  C Germany
Halden 85 B6 prev. Fredrikshald.
  Østfold, S Norway
Halfmoon Bay 151 A8 var. Oban.
  Stewart Island, Southland, New Zealand
Haliacmon see Aliákmonas
Halifax 39 F4 province capital Nova
  Scotia, SE Canada
Halkida see Chalkída
Halle 87 B6 Fr. Hal. Vlaams Brabant,
  C Belgium
Halle 94 C4 var. Halle an der Saale.
  Sachsen-Anhalt, C Germany
Halle an der Saale see Halle
Halle-Neustadt 94 C4 Sachsen-Anhalt,
  C Germany
Halley 154 B2 UK research station
  Antarctica
Hall Islands 142 B2 island group
  C Micronesia
Halls Creek 146 C3 Western Australia
Halmahera, Laut see Halmahera Sea
Halmahera, Pulau 139 F3 prev. Djailolo,
  Gilolo, Jailolo. island E Indonesia
Halmahera Sea 139 F4 Ind. Laut
  Halmahera. sea E Indonesia
Halmstad 85 B7 Halland, S Sweden
Hälsingborg see Helsingborg
Hamada 131 B6 Shimane, Honshū,
  SW Japan
Hamadān 120 C3 anc. Ecbatana.
  Hamadān, W Iran
Ḩamāh 118 B3 var. Hama; anc.
  Epiphania, Bibl. Hamath. Ḩamāh,
  W Syria
Hamamatsu 131 D6 var. Hamamatu.
  Shizuoka, Honshū, S Japan
Hamamatu see Hamamatsu
Hamar 85 B5 prev. Storhammer.
  Hedmark, S Norway
Hamath see Ḩamāh
Hamburg 94 B3 Hamburg, N Germany
Ḩamḏ, Wādī al 136 A4 dry watercourse
  W Saudi Arabia
Hämeenlinna 85 D5 Swe. Tavastehus.
  Etelä-Suomi, S Finland
HaMela h, Yam see Dead Sea
Hamersley Range 146 A4 mountain
  range Western Australia
Hamhŭng 129 E3 C North Korea
Hami 126 C3 var. Ha-mi, Uigh. Kumul,
  Qomul. Xinjiang Uygur Zizhiqu,
  NW China
Ha-mi see Hami
Hamilton 42 A5 dependent territory
  capital (Bermuda) C Bermuda
Hamilton 38 D5 Ontario, S Canada
Hamilton 150 D3 Waikato, North Island,
  New Zealand
Hamilton 88 C4 S Scotland, UK
Hamilton 42 C2 Alabama, S USA
Ḩamīm, Wādī al 87 G2 river NE Libya
Hamīs Musait see Khamis Mushayt
Hamm 94 B4 var. Hamm in Westfalen.
  Nordrhein-Westfalen, W Germany
Ḩammāmāt, Khalīj al see Hammamet,
  Golfe de
Hammamet, Golfe de 102 D3 Ar. Khalīj
  al Ḩammāmāt. gulf NE Tunisia
Ḩammār, Hawr al 136 C3 lake SE Iraq
Hamm in Westfalen see Hamm
Hampden 151 B7 Otago, South Island,
  New Zealand
Hampstead 89 A7 Maryland, USA
Hamrun 102 B5 C Malta
Hāmūn, Daryācheh-ye see Şāberī,
  Hāmūn-e/Sīstān, Daryācheh-ye
Hamwih see Southampton
Hânceşti see Hînceşti
Hancewicze see Hantsavichy
Handan 128 C4 var. Han-tan. Hebei,
  E China
Haneda 131 A2 (Tōkyō) Tōkyō, Honshū,
  S Japan
HaNegev 119 A7 Eng. Negev. desert
  S Israel
Hanford 47 C6 California, W USA
Hangayn Nuruu 126 D2 mountain
  range C Mongolia
Hang-chou/Hangchow see Hangzhou
Hangö see Hanko
Hangzhou 128 D5 var. Hang-chou,
  Hangchow. province capital Zhejiang,
  SE China

Hania see Chaniá
Hanka, Lake see Khanka, Lake
Hanko 85 D6 Swe. Hangö. Etelä-Suomi,
  SW Finland
Han-kou/Han-k'ou/Hankow see Wuhan
Hanmer Springs 151 C5 Canterbury,
  South Island, New Zealand
Hannibal 45 G4 Missouri, C USA
Hannover 94 B3 Eng. Hanover.
  Niedersachsen, NW Germany
Hanöbukten 85 B7 bay S Sweden
Ha Nôi 136 D3 Eng. Hanoi,
  Fr. Hanoï. country capital (Vietnam)
  N Vietnam
Hanover see Hannover
Han Shui 127 C4 river C China
Han-tan see Handan
Hantsavichy 107 B6 Pol. Hancewicze,
  Rus. Gantsevichi. Brestskaya Voblasts',
  SW Belarus
Hanyang see Wuhan
Hanzhong 128 B5 Shaanxi, C China
Hāora 135 F4 prev. Howrah. West
  Bengal, NE India
Haparanda 84 D4 Norrbotten, N Sweden
Hapsal see Haapsalu
Haradok 107 E5 Rus. Gorodok.
  Vitsyebskaya Voblasts', N Belarus
Haradzyets 107 B6 Rus. Gorodets.
  Brestskaya Voblasts', SW Belarus
Haramachi 130 D4 Fukushima, Honshū,
  E Japan
Harany 107 D5 Rus. Gorany.
  Vitsyebskaya Voblasts', N Belarus
Harare 78 D3 prev. Salisbury. country
  capital (Zimbabwe) Mashonaland East,
  NE Zimbabwe
Harbavichy 107 E6 Rus. Gorbovichi.
  Mahilyowskaya Voblasts', E Belarus
Harbel 74 C5 W Liberia
Harbin 129 E2 var. Haerbin, Ha-
  erh-pin, Kharbin; prev. Haerhpin,
  Pingkiang, Pinkiang. province capital
  Heilongjiang, NE China
Hardangerfjorden 85 A6 fjord S Norway
Hardangervidda 85 A6 plateau
  S Norway
Hardenberg 86 E3 Overijssel,
  E Netherlands
Harelbeke 87 A6 var. Harlebeke. West-
  Vlaanderen, W Belgium
Harem see Ḩārim
Haren 86 E2 Groningen, NE Netherlands
Härer 73 D5 E Ethiopia
Hargeisa 73 D5 var. Hargesa. Woqooyi
  Galbeed, NW Somalia
Hariana see Haryāna
Hari, Batang 138 B4 prev. Djambi. river
  Sumatera, W Indonesia
Ḩārim 118 B2 var. Harem. Idlib, W Syria
Harima-nada 131 B6 sea S Japan
Harīrūd 123 E4 var. Tedzhen, Turkm.
  Tejen. river Afghanistan/Iran
Harlan 45 F3 Iowa, C USA
Harlebeke see Harelbeke
Harlem see Haarlem
Harlingen 86 D2 Fris. Harns. Friesland,
  N Netherlands
Harlingen 49 C5 Texas, SW USA
Harlow 89 E6 E England, UK
Harney Basin 46 B4 basin Oregon,
  NW USA
Härnösand 85 C5 var. Hernösand.
  Västernorrland, C Sweden
Harns see Harlingen
Harper 74 D5 var. Cape Palmas.
  NE Liberia
Harricana 38 D3 river Québec,
  SE Canada
Harris 88 B3 physical region
  NW Scotland, UK
Harrisburg 41 F4 state capital
  Pennsylvania, NE USA
Harrisonburg 41 E4 Virginia, NE USA
Harrison, Cape 39 F2 cape
  Newfoundland and Labrador, E Canada
Harris Ridge see Lomonosov Ridge
Harrogate 89 D5 N England, UK
Hârşova 108 D5 prev. Hîrşova.
  Constanţa, SE Romania
Harstad 84 C2 Troms, N Norway
Hartford 41 G3 state capital Connecticut,
  NE USA
Hartlepool 89 D5 N England, UK
Harunabad see Eslāmābād
Har Us Nuur 126 C2 lake NW Mongolia
Harwich 89 E6 E England, UK

Haryāna 134 D2 var. Hariana. cultural
  region N India
Haryāna 134 D2 var. Hariana. state
  N India
Hashemite Kingdom of Jordan see
  Jordan
Hasselt 87 C6 Limburg, NE Belgium
Hassetché see Al Ḩasakah
Hasta Colonia/Hasta Pompeia see Asti
Hastings 150 E4 Hawke's Bay, North
  Island, New Zealand
Hastings 89 E7 SE England, UK
Hastings 45 E4 Nebraska, C USA
Hajeg 108 B4 Ger. Wallenthal, Hung.
  Hátszeg; prev. Hatzeg, Hötzing.
  Hunedoara, SW Romania
Hátszeg see Hajeg
Hattem 86 D3 Gelderland, E Netherlands
Hatteras, Cape 43 G1 headland North
  Carolina, SE USA
Hatteras Plain 35 D6 abyssal plain
  W Atlantic Ocean
Hattiesburg 42 C3 Mississippi, S USA
Hatton Bank see Hatton Ridge
Hatton Ridge 80 B2 var. Hatton Bank.
  undersea ridge N Atlantic Ocean
Hat Yai 137 C7 var. Ban Hat Yai.
  Songkhla, SW Thailand
Hatzeg see Hajeg
Hatzfeld see Jimbolia
Haugesund 85 A6 Rogaland,
  S Norway
Haukeligrend 85 A6 Telemark,
  S Norway
Haukivesi 85 E5 lake SE Finland
Hauraki Gulf 150 D2 gulf North Island,
  N New Zealand
Hauroko, Lake 151 A7 lake South
  Island, New Zealand
Haut Atlas 70 C2 Eng. High Atlas.
  mountain range C Morocco
Hautes Fagnes 87 D6 Ger. Hohes Venn.
  mountain range E Belgium
Hauts Plateaux 70 D2 plateau
  Algeria/Morocco
Hauzenberg 95 D6 Bayern, SE Germany
Havana 35 D6 Illinois, N USA
Havana see La Habana
Havant 89 D7 S England, UK
Havelock 41 F1 North Carolina, SE USA
Havelock North 150 E4 Hawke's Bay,
  North Island, New Zealand
Haverfordwest 89 C6 SW Wales, UK
Havířov 95 C5 Moravskoslezský Kraj,
  E Czech Republic
Havre 44 C1 Montana, NW USA
Havre see Le Havre
Havre-St-Pierre 39 F3 Québec,
  E Canada
Hawai'i 47 A8 off. State of Hawai'i,
  also known as Aloha State, Paradise
  of the Pacific, var. Hawaii. state USA,
  C Pacific Ocean
Hawai'i 47 B8 var. Hawaii. island
  Hawaiian Islands, USA, C Pacific Ocean
Hawaiian Islands 152 D2 prev.
  Sandwich Islands. island group
  Hawaii, USA
Hawaiian Ridge 113 H4 undersea ridge
  N Pacific Ocean
Hawash see Āwash
Hawea, Lake 151 B6 lake South Island,
  New Zealand
Hawera 150 D4 Taranaki, North Island,
  New Zealand
Hawick 88 C4 SE Scotland, UK
Hawke Bay 150 E4 bay North Island,
  New Zealand
Hawkeye State see Iowa
Hawlêr see Arbil
Hawthorne 47 C6 Nevada, W USA
Hay 149 C6 New South Wales,
  SE Australia
HaYarden see Jordan
Hayastani Hanrapetut'yun see Armenia
Hayes 38 B2 river Manitoba, C Canada
Hay River 37 E4 Northwest Territories,
  W Canada
Hays 45 E5 Kansas, C USA
Haysyn 108 D3 Rus. Gaysin. Vinnyts'ka
  Oblast', C Ukraine
Hazar 122 B2 prev. Rus. Cheleken.
  Balkan Welaýaty, W Turkmenistan
Heard and McDonald Islands 141 B7
  Australian external territory S Indian
  Ocean
Hearst 38 C4 Ontario, S Canada
Heart of Dixie see Alabama

Heathrow 89 A8 (London) SE England,
  UK
Hebei 128 C4 var. Hebei Sheng, Hopeh,
  Hopei, Ji; prev. Chihli. province
  E China
Hebei Sheng see Hebei
Hebron 119 A6 var. Al Khalīl, El Khalil,
  Heb. Hevron; anc. Kiriath-Arba.
  S West Bank
Heemskerk 86 C3 Noord-Holland,
  W Netherlands
Heerde 86 D3 Gelderland, E Netherlands
Heerenveen 86 D2 Fris. It Hearrenfean.
  Friesland, N Netherlands
Heerhugowaard 86 C2 Noord-Holland,
  NW Netherlands
Heerlen 87 D6 Limburg, SE Netherlands
Heerwegen see Polkowice
Hefa 119 A5 var. Haifa, hist. Caiffa,
  Caiphas; anc. Sycaminum. Haifa,
  N Israel
Hefa, Mifraz 119 A5 Eng. Bay of Haifa.
  bay N Israel
Hefei 128 D5 var. Hofei, hist. Luchow.
  province capital Anhui, E China
Hegang 129 E2 Heilongjiang, NE China
Hei see Heilongjiang
Heide 94 B2 Schleswig-Holstein,
  N Germany
Heidelberg 95 B5 Baden-Württemberg,
  SW Germany
Heidenheim see Heidenheim an der
  Brenz
Heidenheim an der Brenz 95 B6 var.
  Heidenheim. Baden-Württemberg,
  S Germany
Hei-ho see Nagqu
Heilbronn 95 B6 Baden-Württemberg,
  SW Germany
Heiligenbeil see Mamonovo
Heilongjiang 128 D2 var. Hei,
  Heilongjiang Sheng, Hei-lung-chiang,
  Heilungkiang. province NE China
Heilong Jiang see Amur
Heilongjiang Sheng see Heilongjiang
Heiloo 86 C3 Noord-Holland,
  NW Netherlands
Heilsberg see Lidzbark Warmiński
Hei-lung-chiang/Heilungkiang see
  Heilongjiang
Heimdal 85 B5 Sør-Trøndelag, S Norway
Heinaste see Ainaži
Hekimhan 116 D3 Malatya, C Turkey
Helena 44 B2 state capital Montana,
  NW USA
Helensville 150 D2 Auckland, North
  Island, New Zealand
Helgoland Bay see Helgoländer Bucht
Helgoländer Bucht 94 A2 var.
  Helgoland Bay, Heligoland Bight. bay
  NW Germany
Heligoland Bight see Helgoländer Bucht
Heliopolis see Baalbek
Hellas see Greece
Hellenic Republic see Greece
Hellevoetsluis 86 B4 Zuid-Holland,
  SW Netherlands
Hellín 93 E4 Castilla-La Mancha, C Spain
Helmand, Daryā-ye 122 D5 var. Rūd-e
  Hīrmand. river Afghanistan/Iran
Helmantica see Salamanca
Helmond 87 D5 Noord-Brabant,
  S Netherlands
Helsingborg 85 B7 prev. Hälsingborg.
  Skåne, S Sweden
Helsingfors see Helsinki
Helsinki 85 D6 Swe. Helsingfors.
  country capital (Finland) Etelä-Suomi,
  S Finland
Heltau see Cisnădie
Helvetia see Switzerland
Henan 128 C5 var. Henan Sheng,
  Honan, Yu. province C China
Henderson 40 B5 Kentucky, S USA
Henderson 47 D7 Nevada, W USA
Henderson 49 H3 Texas, SW USA
Hendū Kosh see Hindu Kush
Hengchow see Hengyang
Hengduan Shan 125 A5 mountain range
  SW China
Hengelo 86 E3 Overijssel, E Netherlands
Hengnan see Hengyang
Hengyang 128 C6 var. Hengnan, Heng-
  yang; prev. Hengchow. Hunan, S China
Heng-yang see Hengyang
Heniches'k 109 F4 Rus. Genichesk.
  Khersons'ka Oblast', S Ukraine
Hennebont 90 A3 Morbihan, NW France

Henrique de Carvalho *see* Saurimo
Henzada 136 B4 Irrawaddy,
  SW Myanmar (Burma)
Herakleion *see* Iráleio
Herāt 122 D4 *var.* Herat; *anc.* Aria.
  Herāt, W Afghanistan
Heredia 53 E4 Heredia, C Costa Rica
Hereford 49 E2 Texas, SW USA
Herford 94 B4 Nordrhein-Westfalen,
  NW Germany
Héristal *see* Herstal
Herk-de-Stad 87 C6 Limburg,
  NE Belgium
Herlen Gol/Herlen He *see* Kerulen
Hermannstadt *see* Sibiu
Hermansverk 85 A5 Sogn Og Fjordane,
  S Norway
Hermhausen *see* Hajnówka
Hermiston 46 C2 Oregon, NW USA
Hermon, Mount 119 B5 *Ar.* Jabal ash
  Shaykh. *mountain* S Syria
Hermosillo 50 B2 Sonora, NW Mexico
Hermoupolis *see* Ermoúpoli
Hernösand *see* Härnösand
Herrera del Duque 92 D3 Extremadura,
  W Spain
Herselt 87 C5 Antwerpen,
  C Belgium
Herstal 87 D6 *Fr.* Héristal. Liège,
  E Belgium
Herzogenbusch *see* 's-Hertogenbosch
Hesse *see* Hessen
Hessen 95 B5 *Eng./Fr.* Hesse. *state*
  C Germany
Hevron *see* Hebron
Heydebrech *see* Kędzierzyn-Kozle
Heydekrug *see* Šilutė
Heywood Islands 146 C3 *island group*
  Western Australia
Hibbing 45 F1 Minnesota, N USA
Hibernia *see* Ireland
Hidalgo del Parral 50 C2 *var.* Parral.
  Chihuahua, N Mexico
Hida-sanmyaku 131 C5 *mountain range*
  Honshū, S Japan
Hierosolyma *see* Jerusalem
Hierro 70 A3 *var.* Ferro. *island* Islas
  Canarias, Spain, NE Atlantic Ocean
High Atlas *see* Haut Atlas
High Plains *see* Great Plains
High Point 43 E1 North Carolina,
  SE USA
Hiiumaa 106 C2 *Ger.* Dagden, *Swe.*
  Dagö. *island* W Estonia
Hikurangi 150 D2 Northland, North
  Island, New Zealand
Hildesheim 94 B4 Niedersachsen,
  N Germany
Hilla *see* Al Ḥillah
Hillaby, Mount 55 G1 *mountain*
  N Barbados
Hill Bank 52 C1 Orange Walk, N Belize
Hillegom 86 C3 Zuid-Holland,
  W Netherlands
Hilo 47 B8 Hawai'i, USA, C Pacific Ocean
Hilton Head Island 43 E2 South
  Carolina, SE USA
Hilversum 86 C3 Noord-Holland,
  C Netherlands
Himalaya/Himalaya Shan *see* Himalayas
Himalayas 135 E2 *var.* Himalaya, *Chin.*
  Himalaya Shan. *mountain range* S Asia
Himeji 131 C6 *var.* Himezi. Hyōgo,
  Honshū, SW Japan
Himezi *see* Himeji
Ḥimṣ 118 B4 *var.* Homs; *anc.* Emesa.
  Ḥimṣ, C Syria
Hincesti 108 D4 *var.* Hânceşti; *prev.*
  Kotovsk. C Moldova
Hinchinbrook Island 148 D3 *island*
  Queensland, NE Australia
Hinds 151 C6 Canterbury, South Island,
  New Zealand
Hindu Kush 123 F4 *Per.* Hendü Kosh.
  mountain range Afghanistan/Pakistan
Hinesville 43 E3 Georgia, SE USA
Hinnøya 84 C3 *Lapp.* Iinnasuolu. *island*
  C Norway
Hinson Bay 42 A5 *bay* W Bermuda
  W Atlantic Ocean
Hios *see* Chíos
Hirfanlı Baraji 116 C3 *reservoir*
  C Turkey
Hirmand, Rüd-e *see* Helmand, Daryā-ye
Hirosaki 130 D3 Aomori, Honshū,
  C Japan
Hiroshima 131 B6 *var.* Hirosima.
  Hiroshima, Honshū, SW Japan

**Hirschberg/Hirschberg im
  Riesengebirge/Hirschberg in
  Schlesien** *see* Jelenia Góra
Hirson 90 D3 Aisne, N France
Hîrşova *see* Hârşova
Hispalis *see* Sevilla
Hispana/Hispania *see* Spain
Hispaniola 56 B1 *island* Dominion
  Republic/Haiti
Hitachi 131 D5 *var.* Hitati. Ibaraki,
  Honshū, S Japan
Hitati *see* Hitachi
Hitra 84 A4 *prev.* Hitteren. *island*
  S Norway
Hitteren *see* Hitra
Hjälmaren 85 C6 *Eng.* Lake Hjalmar.
  lake C Sweden
Hjalmar, Lake *see* Hjälmaren
Hjørring 85 B7 Nordjylland,
  N Denmark
Hkakabo Razi 136 B1 *mountain*
  Myanmar (Burma)/China
Hlobyne 109 F2 *Rus.* Globino.
  Poltavs'ka Oblast', NE Ukraine
Hlukhiv 109 F1 *Rus.* Glukhov. Sums'ka
  Oblast', NE Ukraine
Hlybokaye 107 D5 *Rus.* Glubokoye.
  Vitsyebskaya Voblasts', N Belarus
Hoa Binh 136 D3 Hoa Binh, N Vietnam
Hoang Liên Son 136 D3 *mountain range*
  N Vietnam
Hobart 149 C8 *prev.* Hobarton, Hobart
  Town. *state capital* Tasmania,
  SE Australia
Hobarton/Hobart Town *see* Hobart
Hobbs 49 E3 New Mexico, SW USA
Hobro 85 A7 Nordjylland, N Denmark
Hồ Chí Minh 137 E6 *var.* Ho Chi Minh
  City; *prev.* Saigon. S Vietnam
Ho Chi Minh City *see* Hồ Chí Minh
Hodeida *see* Al Ḥudaydah
Hódmezővásárhely 99 D7 Csongrád,
  SE Hungary
Hodna, Chott El 118 C4 *var.* Chott
  el-Hodna, *Ar.* Shatt al-Hodna. *salt
  lake* N Algeria
Hodna, Chott el-/Hodna, Shatt al-
  see Hodna, Chott El
Hodonín 99 C5 *Ger.* Göding.
  Jihomoravský Kraj, SE Czech Republic
Hoei *see* Huy
Hoey *see* Huy
Hof 95 C5 Bayern, SE Germany
Hofei *see* Hefei
Hōfu 131 B7 Yamaguchi, Honshū,
  SW Japan
Hofuf *see* Al Hufūf
Hogoley Islands *see* Chuuk Islands
Hohensalza *see* Inowrocław
Hohenstadt *see* Zábřeh
Hohes Venn *see* Hautes Fagnes
Hohe Tauern 95 C7 *mountain range*
  W Austria
Hohhot 127 F3 *var.* Huhehot,
  Huhohaote, *Mong.* Kukukhoto; *prev.*
  Kweisui, Kwesui. Nei Mongol Zizhiqu,
  N China
Hội An 137 E5 *prev.* Faifo.
  Quang Nam-Đa Năng, C Vietnam
Hoï-Hao/Hoihow *see* Haikou
Hokianga Harbour 150 C2 *inlet*
  SE Tasman Sea
Hokitika 151 B5 West Coast, South
  Island, New Zealand
Hokkaidō 130 C2 *prev.* Ezo, Yeso, Yezo.
  island NE Japan
Hola Prystan' 109 E4 *Rus.* Golaya
  Pristan. Khersons'ka Oblast',
  S Ukraine
Holbrook 48 B2 Arizona, SW USA
Holetown 55 G1 *prev.* Jamestown.
  W Barbados
Holguín 54 C2 Holguín, SE Cuba
Hollabrunn 95 E6 Niederösterreich,
  NE Austria
Holland *see* Netherlands
Hollandia *see* Jayapura
Holly Springs 42 C1 Mississippi, S USA
Holman 37 E3 Victoria Island, Northwest
  Territories, N Canada
Holmsund 84 D4 Västerbotten,
  N Sweden
Ḥolon 119 A6 *var* Kholon. Tel Aviv,
  C Israel
Holovanivs'k 109 E3 *Rus.* Golovanevsk.
  Kirovohrads'ka Oblast', C Ukraine
Holstebro 85 A7 Ringkøbing,
  W Denmark

**Holsteinborg/Holsteinsborg/
  Holstenborg/Holstensborg** *see*
  Sisimiut
Holyhead 89 C5 *Wel.* Caer Gybi.
  NW Wales, UK
Hombori 75 E3 Mopti, S Mali
Homs *see* Al Khums, Libya
Homs *see* Ḥimṣ
Homyel' 107 D7 *Rus.* Gomel'.
  Homyel'skaya Voblasts', SE Belarus
Honan *see* Luoyang, China
Honan *see* Henan, China
Hondo 49 F4 Texas, SW USA
Hondo *see* Honshū
Honduras 52 C2 *off.* Republic of
  Honduras. *country* Central America

HONDURAS
Central America

Official name Republic of Honduras
Formation 1838 / 1838
Capital Tegucigalpa
Population 7.2 million / 167 people per
  sq mile (64 people per sq km) / 53%
Total area 43,278 sq miles
  (112,090 sq km)
Languages Spanish*, Garífuna (Carib),
  English Creole
Religions Roman Catholic 97%,
  Protestant 3%
Ethnic mix Mestizo 90%, Black
  African 5%, Amerindian 4%, White 1%
Government Presidential system
Currency Lempira = 100 centavos
Literacy rate 80%
Calorie consumption 2356 calories

Honduras, Golfo de *see* Honduras,
  Gulf of
Honduras, Gulf of 52 C2 *Sp.* Golfo de
  Honduras. *gulf* W Caribbean Sea
Honduras, Republic of *see* Honduras
Hønefoss 85 B6 Buskerud, S Norway
Honey Lake 47 B5 *lake* California, W USA
Hon Gai *see* Hông Gai
Hongay *see* Hông Gai
Hông Gai 136 E3 *var.* Hon Gai, Hongay.
  Quang Ninh, N Vietnam
Hông Hà, Sông *see* Red River
Hong Kong 128 A1 *Chin.* Xianggang.
  Hong Kong, S China
Hong Kong Island 128 B2 *island*
  S China Asia
Honiara 144 C3 *country capital*
  (Solomon Islands) Guadalcanal,
  C Solomon Islands
Honjō 130 D4 *var.* Honzyō. Akita,
  Honshū, C Japan
Honolulu 47 A8 *state capital* O'ahu,
  Hawai'i, USA
Honshū 131 E5 *var.* Hondo, Honsyû.
  island SW Japan
Honsyû *see* Honshū
Honte *see* Westerschelde
Honzyō *see* Honjō
Hoogeveen 86 E2 Drenthe, NE Netherlands
Hoogezand-Sappemeer 86 E2
  Groningen, NE Netherlands
Hoorn 86 C2 Noord-Holland,
  NW Netherlands
Hoosier State *see* Indiana
Hopa 117 F2 Artvin, NE Turkey
Hope 36 C3 British Columbia,
  SW Canada
Hopedale 39 F2 Newfoundland and
  Labrador, NE Canada
Hopeh/Hopei *see* Hebei
Hopkinsville 40 B5 Kentucky, S USA
Horasan 117 F3 Erzurum, NE Turkey
Horizon Deep 152 D4 *trench*
  W Pacific Ocean
Horki 107 E6 *Rus.* Gorki.
  Mahilyowskaya Voblasts', E Belarus
Horlivka 109 G3 *Rom.* Adâncata, *Rus.*
  Gorlovka. Donets'ka Oblast', E Ukraine
Hormoz, Tangeh-ye *see* Hormuz,
  Strait of
Hormuz, Strait of 120 D4 *var.* Strait of
  Ormuz, *Per.* Tangeh-ye Hormoz. *strait*
  Iran/Oman
Horn, Cape *see* Hornos, Cabo de
Hornos, Cabo de 65 C8 *Eng.* Cape Horn.
  cape S Chile
Hornsby 148 E1 New South Wales,
  SE Australia
Horodnya 109 E1 *Rus.* Gorodnya.
  Chernihivs'ka Oblast', NE Ukraine

Horodok 108 B2 *Pol.* Gródek
  Jagielloński, *Rus.* Gorodok, Gorodok
  Yagellonski. L'vivs'ka Oblast',
  NW Ukraine
Horodyshche 109 E2 *Rus.* Gorodishche.
  Cherkas'ka Oblast', C Ukraine
Horoshiri-dake 130 D2 *var.* Horosiri
  Dake. *mountain* Hokkaidō, N Japan
Horosiri Dake *see* Horoshiri-dake
Horsburgh Atoll 132 A4 *atoll*
  N Maldives
Horseshoe Bay 42 A5 *bay* W Bermuda
  W Atlantic Ocean
Horseshoe Seamounts 80 A4 *seamount
  range* E Atlantic Ocean
Horsham 149 B7 Victoria, SE Australia
Horst 87 D5 Limburg, SE Netherlands
Horten 85 B6 Vestfold, S Norway
Horyn' 107 B7 *Rus.* Goryn. *river*
  NW Ukraine
Hosingen 87 D7 Diekirch, NE Luxembourg
Hospitalet *see* L'Hospitalet de Llobregat
Hotan 126 B4 *var.* Khotan, *Chin.*
  Ho-t'ien. Xinjiang Uygur Zizhiqu,
  NW China
Ho-t'ien *see* Hotan
Hoting 84 C4 Jämtland, C Sweden
Hot Springs 42 B1 Arkansas, C USA
Hötzing *see* Hateg
Houaxay 136 C3 *var.* Ban Houayxay.
  Bokèo, N Laos
Houghton 40 B1 Michigan, N USA
Houilles 91 B5 Yvelines, Île-de-France,
  N France Europe
Houlton 41 H1 Maine, NE USA
Houma 42 B3 Louisiana, S USA
Houston 49 H4 Texas, SW USA
Hovd 126 D2 *var.* Khovd, Kobdo; *prev.*
  Jirgalanta. Hovd, W Mongolia
Hove 89 E7 SE England, UK
Hoverla, Hora 108 C3 *Rus.* Gora
  Goverla. *mountain* W Ukraine
Hovsgol, Lake *see* Hövsgöl Nuur
Hövsgöl Nuur 126 D1 *var.* Lake
  Hovsgol. *lake* N Mongolia
Howa, Ouadi *see* Howar, Wādi
Howar, Wādi 72 A3 *var.* Ouadi Howa.
  river Chad/Sudan
Howrah *see* Hāora
Hoy 88 C2 *island* N Scotland, UK
Hoyerswerda 94 D4 *Lus.* Wojerecy.
  Sachsen, E Germany
Hradec Králové 99 B5 *Ger.* Königgrätz.
  Královéhradecký Kraj, N Czech
  Republic
Hranždzichy 107 B5 *Rus.* Grandichi.
  Hrodzyenskaya Voblasts', W Belarus
Hranice 99 C5 *Ger.* Mährisch-
  Weisskirchen. Olomoucký Kraj,
  E Czech Republic
Hrebinka 109 E2 *Rus.* Grebenka.
  Poltavs'ka Oblast', NE Ukraine
Hrodna 107 B5 *Pol.* Grodno.
  Hrodzyenskaya Voblasts', W Belarus
Hrvatska *see* Croatia
Hsia-men *see* Xiamen
Hsiang-t'an *see* Xiangtan
Hsi Chiang *see* Xi Jiang
Hsing-K'ai Hu *see* Khanka, Lake
Hsi-ning/Hsining *see* Xining
Hsinking *see* Changchun
Hsin-yang *see* Xinyang
Hsu-chou *see* Xuzhou
Hu *see* Shanghi Shi
Huacho 60 C4 Lima, W Peru
Hua Hin *see* Ban Hua Hin
Huaihua 128 C5 Hunan, S China
Huailai 128 C3 *var.* Shacheng. Hebei,
  E China
Huainan 128 D5 *var.* Huai-nan,
  Hwainan. Anhui, E China
Huai-nan *see* Huainan
Huajuapan 51 F5 *var.* Huajuapan de
  León. Oaxaca, SE Mexico
Huajuapan de León *see* Huajuapan
Hualapai Peak 48 A2 *mountain* Arizona,
  SW USA
Huallaga, Río 60 C3 *river* N Peru
Huambo 78 B2 *Port.* Nova Lisboa.
  Huambo, C Angola
Huancavelica 60 D4 Huancavelica,
  SW Peru
Huancayo 60 D3 Junín, C Peru
Huang Hai *see* Yellow Sea
Huang He 128 C4 *var.* Yellow River.
  river C China
Huangshi 128 C5 *var.* Huang-shih,
  Hwangshih. Hubei, C China

Huang-shih see Huangshi
Huanta 60 D4 Ayacucho, C Peru
Huánuco 60 C3 Huánuco, C Peru
Huanuni 61 F4 Oruro, W Bolivia
Huaral 60 C4 Lima, W Peru
Huarás see Huaraz
Huaraz 60 C3 var. Huarás. Ancash,
  W Peru
Huarmey 60 C3 Ancash, W Peru
Huatabampo 50 C2 Sonora, NW Mexico
Hubei 129 C5 var. E, Hubei Sheng,
  Hupeh, Hupei. *province* C China
Hubei Sheng see Hubei
Hubli 124 B3 Karnātaka, SW India
Huddersfield 89 D5 N England, UK
Hudiksvall 85 C5 Gävleborg, C Sweden
Hudson Bay 37 G4 *bay* NE Canada
Hudson, Détroit d' see Hudson Strait
Hudson Strait 37 H3 Fr. Détroit
  d'Hudson. *strait* Northwest Territories/
  Québec, NE Canada
Hudur see Xuddur
Huê 136 E4 Th‚a Thiên-Huê, C Vietnam
Huehuetenango 52 A2 Huehuetenango,
  W Guatemala
Huelva 92 C4 *anc.* Onuba. Andalucía,
  SW Spain
Huesca 93 F2 *anc.* Osca. Aragón,
  NE Spain
Huéscar 93 E4 Andalucía, S Spain
Hughenden 148 C3 Queensland,
  NE Australia
Hugo 49 G2 Oklahoma, C USA
Huhehot/Huhohaote see Hohhot
Huíla Plateau 78 B2 *plateau* S Angola
Huixtla 51 G5 Chiapas, SE Mexico
Hulingol 127 G2 *prev.* Huolin Gol.
  Nei Mongol Zizhiqu, N China
Hull 38 D4 Québec, SE Canada
Hull see Kingston upon Hull
Hull Island see Orona
Hulst 87 B5 Zeeland, SW Netherlands
Hulun see Hailar
Hu-lun Ch'ih see Hulun Nur
Hulun Nur 127 F1 var. Hu-lun Ch'ih;
  prev. Dalai Nor. *lake* NE China
Humaitá 62 D2 Amazonas, N Brazil
Humboldt River 47 C5 *river* Nevada,
  W USA
Humphreys Peak 48 B1 *mountain*
  Arizona, SW USA
Humpolec 99 B5 *Ger.* Gumpolds,
  Humpoletz. Vysočina, C Czech Republic
Humpoletz see Humpolec
Hunan 128 C6 var. Hunan Sheng,
  Xiang. *province* S China
Hunan Sheng see Hunan
Hunedoara 108 B4 *Ger.* Eisenmarkt,
  Hung. Vajdahunyad. Hunedoara,
  SW Romania
Hünfeld 95 B5 Hessen, C Germany
Hungarian People's Republic see
  Hungary
Hungary 99 C6 *off.* Republic of Hungary,
  Ger. Ungarn, *Hung.* Magyarország,
  Rom. Ungaria, *SCr.* Madarska, *Ukr.*
  Uhorshchyna; *prev.* Hungarian People's
  Republic. *country* C Europe
Hungary, Plain of see Great Hungarian
  Plain

HUNGARY
Central Europe

Official name Republic of Hungary
Formation 1918 / 1947
Capital Budapest
Population 10.1 million / 283 people per
  sq mile (109 people per sq km) / 64%
Total area 35,919 sq miles
  (93,030 sq km)
Languages Hungarian (Magyar)*
Religions Roman Catholic 52%,
  Calvinist 16%, Other 15%,
  Nonreligious 14%, Lutheran 3%
Ethnic mix Magyar 90%, Other 7%,
  Roma 2%, German 1%
Government Parliamentary system
Currency Forint = 100 fillér
Literacy rate 99%
Calorie consumption 3483 calories

Hungary, Republic of see Hungary
Hunjiang see Baishan
Hunter Island 149 B8 *island* Tasmania,
  SE Australia
Huntington 40 D4 West Virginia,
  NE USA

Huntington Beach 47 B8 California,
  W USA
Huntly 150 D3 Waikato, North Island,
  New Zealand
Huntsville 42 D1 Alabama, S USA
Huntsville 49 G3 Texas, SW USA
Huolin Gol see Hulingol
Hupeh see Hubei
Hupei see Hubei
Hurghada 72 C2 var. Al Ghurdaqah,
  Ghurdaqah. E Egypt
Huron 45 E3 South Dakota, N USA
Huron, Lake 40 D2 *lake* Canada/USA
Hurukawa see Furukawa
Hurunui 151 C5 *river* South Island,
  New Zealand
Húsavík 83 E4 Nordhurland Eystra,
  NE Iceland
Husté see Khust
Husum 94 B2 Schleswig-Holstein,
  N Germany
Huszt see Khust
Hutchinson 45 E5 Kansas, C USA
Hutchinson Island 43 F4 *island* Florida,
  SE USA
Huy 87 C6 *Dut.* Hoei, Hoey. Liège,
  E Belgium
Huzi see Fuji
Hvannadalshnúkur 83 E5 *volcano*
  S Iceland
Hvar 100 B4 *It.* Lesina; *anc.* Pharus.
  island S Croatia
Hwainan see Huainan
Hwange 78 D3 *prev.* Wankie.
  Matabeleland North, W Zimbabwe
Hwang-Hae see Yellow Sea
Hwangshih see Huangshi
Hyargas Nuur 126 C2 *lake*
  NW Mongolia
Hyderābād 134 D5 var. Haidarabad.
  state capital Andhra Pradesh, C India
Hyderābād 134 B3 var. Haidarabad.
  Sind, SE Pakistan
Hyères 91 D6 Var, SE France
Hyères, Îles d' 91 D6 *island group*
  S France
Hypanis see Kuban'
Hyrcania see Gorgān
Hyvinge see Hyvinkää
Hyvinkää 85 D5 *Swe.* Hyvinge.
  Uusimaa, S Finland

I

Iader see Zadar
Ialomiţa 108 C5 *river* SE Romania
Iaşi 108 D3 *Ger.* Jassy. Iaşi, NE Romania
Ibadan 75 F5 Oyo, SW Nigeria
Ibagué 58 B3 Tolima, C Colombia
Ibar 100 D4 *Alb.* Ibër. *river* C Serbia
Ibarra 60 B1 var. San Miguel de Ibarra.
  Imbabura, N Ecuador
Ibër see Ibar
Iberia see Spain
Iberian Mountains see Ibérico, Sistema
Iberian Peninsula 80 B4 *physical region*
  Portugal/Spain
Iberian Plain 80 B4 *abyssal plain*
  E Atlantic Ocean
Ibérica, Cordillera see Ibérico, Sistema
Ibérico, Sistema 93 E2 var. Cordillera
  Ibérica, *Eng.* Iberian Mountains.
  mountain range NE Spain
Ibiza 93 G3 *island* Spain,
  W Mediterranean Sea
Ibiza see Eivissa
Ibo see Sassandra
Ica 60 D4 Ica, SW Peru
Icaria see Ikaría
Içá, Rio 62 C2 var. Río Putumayo. *river*
  NW South America
Içá, Río see Putumayo, Río
Iceland 83 E4 *off.* Republic of Iceland,
  Dan. Island, *Icel.* Ísland. *country*
  N Atlantic Ocean

ICELAND
Northwest Europe

Official name Republic of Iceland
Formation 1944 / 1944
Capital Reykjavík
Population 295,000 / 8 people per
  sq mile
  (3 people per sq km) / 93%
Total area 39,768 sq miles
  (103,000 sq km)

ICELAND
(continued)

Languages Icelandic*
Religions Evangelical Lutheran 93%,
  Nonreligious 6%, Other (mostly
  Christian) 1%
Ethnic mix Icelandic 94%, Other 5%,
  Danish 1%
Government Parliamentary system
Currency Icelandic króna = 100 aurar
Literacy rate 99%
Calorie consumption 3249 calories

Iceland Basin 80 B1 *undersea basin*
  N Atlantic Ocean
Icelandic Plateau see Iceland Plateau
Iceland Plateau 172 B5 var. Icelandic
  Plateau. *undersea plateau* S Greenland
  Sea
Iceland, Republic of see Iceland
Iconium see Konya
Iculisma see Angoulême
Idabel 49 H2 Oklahoma, C USA
Idaho 46 D3 *off.* State of Idaho, *also
  known as* Gem of the Mountains,
  Gem State. *state* NW USA
Idaho Falls 46 E3 Idaho, NW USA
Idensalmi see Iisalmi
Idfu 72 B2 var. Edfu. SE Egypt
Idi Amin, Lac see Edward, Lake
Idini 74 B2 Trarza, W Mauritania
Idlib 118 B3 Idlib, NW Syria
Idre 85 B5 Dalarna, C Sweden
Iecava 106 C3 Bauska, S Latvia
Ieper 87 A6 *Fr.* Ypres. West-Vlaanderen,
  W Belgium
Ierápetra 105 D8 Kríti, Greece,
  E Mediterranean Sea
Ierisós see Ierissós
Ierissós 104 C4 var. Ierisós. Kentrikí
  Makedonía, N Greece
Iferouâne 75 G2 Agadez, N Niger
Ifôghas, Adrar des 75 E2 var. Adrar des
  Iforas. *mountain range* NE Mali
Iforas, Adrar des see Ifôghas, Adrar des
Igarka 114 D3 Krasnoyarskiy Kray,
  N Russian Federation
Igaunija see Estonia
Iglau/Iglawa/Iglawa see Jihlava
Iglesias 97 A5 Sardegna, Italy,
  C Mediterranean Sea
Igloolik 37 G2 Nunavut, N Canada
Igoumenítsa 104 A4 Ípeiros,
  W Greece
Iguaçu, Rio 63 E4 *Sp.* Río Iguazú. *river*
  Argentina/Brazil
Iguaçu, Saltos do 63 E4 *Sp.* Cataratas del
  Iguazú; *prev.* Victoria Falls. *waterfall*
  Argentina/Brazil
Iguala 51 E4 var. Iguala de la
  Independencia. Guerrero, S Mexico
Iguala de la Independencia see Iguala
Iguazú, Cataratas del see Iguaçu, Saltos do
Iguazú, Río see Iguaçu, Rio
Iguid, Erg see Iguidi, 'Erg
Iguidi, 'Erg 70 C3 var. Erg Iguid. *desert*
  Algeria/Mauritania
Ihavandippolhu Atoll 132 A3 *atoll*
  N Maldives
Ihosy 79 F4 Fianarantsoa, S Madagascar
Iinnasuolu see Hinnøya
Iisalmi 84 E4 var. Idensalmi. Isä-Suomi,
  C Finland
IJmuiden 86 C3 Noord-Holland,
  W Netherlands
IJssel 86 D3 var. Yssel. *river* Netherlands
IJsselmeer 86 C2 *prev.* Zuider Zee. *lake*
  N Netherlands
IJsselmuiden 86 D3 Overijssel,
  E Netherlands
IJzer 87 A6 *river* W Belgium
Ikaría 105 D6 var. Kariot, Nicaria,
  Nikaria; *anc.* Icaria. *island* Dodekánisa,
  Greece, Aegean Sea
Ikela 77 D6 Equateur, C Dem. Rep.
  Congo
Iki 131 A7 *island* SW Japan
Ilagan 139 E1 Luzon, N Philippines
Ilave 61 E4 Puno, S Peru
Iława 98 D3 *Ger.* Deutsch-Eylau.
  Warmińsko-Mazurskie, NE Poland
Ilebo 77 C6 *prev.* Port-Francqui.
  Kasai Occidental, W Dem. Rep. Congo
Île-de-France 90 C3 *region* N France
Île-de-France 90 C3 *cultural region*
  N France

Ilerda see Lleida
Ilfracombe 89 C7 SW England, UK
Ílhavo 92 B2 Aveiro, N Portugal
Iliamna Lake 36 C3 *lake* Alaska,
  USA
Il'ichevsk see Illichivs'k
Ilici see Elche
Iligan 139 E2 *off.* Iligan City. Mindanao,
  S Philippines
Iligan City see Iligan
Illapel 64 B4 Coquimbo, C Chile
Illichivs'k 109 E4 *Rus.* Il'ichevsk.
  Odes'ka Oblast', SW Ukraine
Illicis see Elche
Illinois 40 A4 *off.* State of Illinois, *also
  known as* Prairie State, Sucker State.
  state C USA
Illinois River 40 B4 *river* Illinois,
  N USA
Illurco see Lorca
Illuro see Mataró
Ilo 61 E4 Moquegua, SW Peru
Iloilo 139 E2 *off.* Iloilo City. Panay
  Island, C Philippines
Iloilo City see Iloilo
Ilorin 75 F4 Kwara, W Nigeria
Ilovlya 111 B6 Volgogradskaya Oblast',
  SW Russian Federation
Iluh see Batman
Il'yaly see Gurbansoltan Eje
Imatra 85 E5 Kymi, SE Finland
Imbros see Gökçeada
Imishli see Imişli
Imişli 117 H3 *Rus.* Imishli.
  C Azerbaijan
Imola 96 C3 Emilia-Romagna, N Italy
Imperatriz 63 F2 Maranhão, NE Brazil
Imperia 96 A3 Liguria, NW Italy
Impfondo 77 C5 La Likouala, NE Congo
Imphāl 135 H3 *state capital* Manipur,
  NE India
Imroz Adası see Gökçeada
Inagua Islands see Great Inagua
Inagua Islands see Little Inagua
Inarijärvi 84 D2 *Lapp.* Aanaarjärvi, *Swe.*
  Enareträsk. *lake* N Finland
Inău see Ineu
Inawashiro-ko 131 D5 var. Inawasiro
  Ko. *lake* Honshū, C Japan
Inawasiro Ko see Inawashiro-ko
Īncesu 116 D3 Kayseri, Turkey Asia
Inch'ŏn 129 E4 *off.* Inch'ŏn-gwangyŏksi,
  Jap. Jinsen; *prev.* Chemulpo. NW South
  Korea
Inch'ŏn-gwangyŏksi see Inch'ŏn
Incudine, Monte 91 E7 *mountain* Corse,
  France, C Mediterranean Sea
Indefatigable Island see Santa Cruz, Isla
Independence 45 F4 Missouri,
  C USA
Independence Fjord 83 E1 *fjord*
  N Greenland
Independence Island see Malden Island
Independence Mountains 46 C4
  mountain range Nevada, W USA
India 124 D3 *off.* Republic of India,
  var. Indian Union, Union of India,
  Hind. Bhārat. *country* S Asia

INDIA
South Asia

Official name Republic of India
Formation 1947 / 1947
Capital New Delhi
Population 1.1 billion / 961 people per
  sq mile (371 people per sq km) / 28%
Total area 1,269,338 sq miles
  (3,287,590 sq km)
Languages Hindi*, English*, Bengali,
  Marathi, Telugu, Tamil, Bihari, Gujarati,
  Kanarese, Urdu
Religions Hindu 83%, Muslim 11%,
  Christian 2%, Sikh 2%, Other 1%,
  Buddhist 1%
Ethnic mix Indo-Aryan 72%,
  Dravidian 25%, Mongoloid and other 3%
Government Parliamentary system
Currency Indian rupee = 100 paise
Literacy rate 61%
Calorie consumption 2459 calories

India see Indija
Indiana 40 C4 *off.* State of Indiana,
  also known as Hoosier State. *state*
  N USA
Indianapolis 40 C4 *state capital* Indiana,
  N USA

Indian Church 52 C1 Orange Walk, N Belize
Indian Desert see Thar Desert
Indianola 45 F4 Iowa, C USA
Indian Union see India
India, Republic of see India
India, Union of see India
Indigirka 115 F2 river NE Russian Federation
Indija 100 D3 Hung. India; prev. Indjija. Vojvodina, N Serbia
Indira Point 132 G3 headland Andaman and Nicobar Island, India, NE Indian Ocean
Indjija see Indija
Indomed Fracture Zone 141 B6 tectonic feature SW Indian Ocean
Indonesia 138 B4 off. Republic of Indonesia, Ind. Republik Indonesia; prev. Dutch East Indies, Netherlands East Indies, United States of Indonesia. country SE Asia

INDONESIA
Southeast Asia

Official name Republic of Indonesia
Formation 1949 / 1999
Capital Jakarta
Population 223 million / 321 people per sq mile (124 people per sq km) / 41%
Total area 741,096 sq miles (1,919,440 sq km)
Languages Bahasa Indonesia*, Javanese, Sundanese, Madurese, Dutch
Religions Sunni Muslim 87%, Protestant 6%, Roman Catholic 3%, Hindu 2%, Other 1%, Buddhist 1%
Ethnic mix Javanese 45%, Sundanese 14%, Coastal Malays 8%, Madurese 8%, Other 25%
Government Presidential system
Currency Rupiah = 100 sen
Literacy rate 88%
Calorie consumption 2904 calories

Indonesian Borneo see Kalimantan
Indonesia, Republic of see Indonesia
Indonesia, Republik see Indonesia
Indonesia, United States of see Indonesia
Indore 134 D4 Madhya Pradesh, C India
Indreville see Châteauroux
Indus 134 C2 Chin. Yindu He; prev. Yin-tu Ho. river S Asia
Indus Cone see Indus Fan
Indus Fan 112 C5 var. Indus Cone. undersea fan N Arabian Sea
Indus, Mouths of the 134 B4 delta S Pakistan
Ĭnebolu 116 C2 Kastamonu, N Turkey
Ineu 108 A4 Hung. Borosjenő; prev. Inău. Arad, W Romania
Infiernillo, Presa del 51 E4 reservoir S Mexico
Inglewood 46 D2 California, W USA
Ingolstadt 95 C6 Bayern, S Germany
Ingulets see Inhulets'
Inguri see Enguri
Inhambane 79 E4 Inhambane, SE Mozambique
Inhulets' 109 F3 Rus. Ingulets. Dnipropetrovs'ka Oblast', E Ukraine
I-ning see Yining
Inis see Ennis
Inis Ceithleann see Enniskillen
Inn 95 C6 river C Europe
Innaanganeq 82 C1 var. Kap York. headland NW Greenland
Inner Hebrides 88 B4 island group W Scotland, UK
Inner Islands 79 H1 var. Central Group. island group NE Seychelles
Innisfail 148 D3 Queensland, NE Australia
Inniskilling see Enniskillen
Innsbruch see Innsbruck
Innsbruck 95 C7 var. Innsbruch. Tirol, W Austria
Inoucdjouac see Inukjuak
Inowrazlaw see Inowrocław
Inowrocław 98 C3 Ger. Hohensalza; prev. Inowrazlaw. Kujawski-pomorskie, C Poland

I-n-Salah 70 D3 var. In Salah. C Algeria
Insterburg see Chernyakhovsk
Insula see Lille
Inta 110 E3 Respublika Komi, NW Russian Federation
Interamna see Teramo
Interamna Nahars see Terni
International Falls 45 F1 Minnesota, N USA
Inukjuak 38 D2 var. Inoucdjouac; prev. Port Harrison. Québec, NE Canada
Inuuvik see Inuvik
Inuvik 36 D3 var. Inuuvik. Northwest Territories, NW Canada
Invercargill 151 A7 Southland, South Island, New Zealand
Inverness 88 C3 N Scotland, UK
Investigator Ridge 141 D5 undersea ridge E Indian Ocean
Investigator Strait 149 B7 strait South Australia
Inyangani 78 D3 mountain NE Zimbabwe
Ioánnina 104 A4 var. Janina, Yannina. Ípeiros, W Greece
Iola 45 F5 Kansas, C USA
Ionia Basin see Ionian Basin
Ionian Basin 80 D5 var. Ionia Basin. undersea basin Ionian Sea, C Mediterranean Sea
Iónia Nisiá 105 A5 Eng. Ionian Islands. region W Greece
Ionian Sea 103 E3 Gk. Iónio Pélagos, It. Mar Ionio. sea C Mediterranean Sea
Ionio, Mar/Iónio Pélagos see Ionian Sea
Íos 105 D6 var. Nio. island Kykládes, Greece, Aegean Sea
Íos see Chóra
Ioulís 105 C6 prev. Kéa. Tziá, Kykládes, Greece, Aegean Sea
Iowa 45 F3 off. State of Iowa, also known as Hawkeye State. state C USA
Iowa City 45 G3 Iowa, C USA
Iowa Falls 45 G3 Iowa, C USA
Ipek see Peč
Ipel' 99 C6 var. Ipoly, Ger. Eipel. river Hungary/Slovakia
Ipiales 58 A4 Nariño, SW Colombia
Ipoh 138 B3 Perak, Peninsular Malaysia
Ipoly see Ipel'
Ippy 76 C4 Ouaka, C Central African Republic
Ipswich 149 E5 Queensland, E Australia
Ipswich 89 E6 hist. Gipeswic. E England, UK
Iqaluit 37 H3 prev. Frobisher Bay. province capital Baffin Island, Nunavut, NE Canada
Iquique 64 B1 Tarapacá, N Chile
Iquitos 60 C1 Loreto, N Peru
Irákleio 105 D7 var. Herakleion, Eng. Candia; prev. Iráklion. Kríti, Greece, E Mediterranean Sea
Iráklion see Irákleio
Iran 120 C3 off. Islamic Republic of Iran; prev. Persia. country SW Asia

IRAN
Southwest Asia

Official name Islamic Republic of Iran
Formation 1502 / 1990
Capital Tehran
Population 69.5 million / 110 people per sq mile (42 people per sq km) / 62%
Total area 636,293 sq miles (1,648,000 sq km)
Languages Farsi*, Azeri, Luri, Gilaki, Mazanderani, Kurdish, Turkmen, Arabic, Baluchi
Religions Shi'a Muslim 93%, Sunni Muslim 6%, Other 1%
Ethnic mix Persian 50%, Azari 24%, Other 10%, Kurdish 8%, Lur and Bakhtiari 8%
Government Islamic theocracy
Currency Iranian rial = 100 dinars
Literacy rate 77%
Calorie consumption 3085 calories

Iranian Plateau 120 D3 var. Plateau of Iran. plateau N Iran
Iran, Islamic Republic of see Iran
Iran, Plateau of see Iranian Plateau
Irapuato 51 E4 Guanajuato, C Mexico

Iraq 120 B3 off. Republic of Iraq, Ar. 'Irāq. country SW Asia

IRAQ
Southwest Asia

Official name Republic of Iraq
Formation 1932 / 1990
Capital Baghdad
Population 28.8 million / 171 people per sq mile (66 people per sq km) / 77%
Total area 168,753 sq miles (437,072 sq km)
Languages Arabic*, Kurdish, Turkic languages, Armenian, Assyrian
Religions Shi'a Muslim 60%, Sunni Muslim 35%, Other (including Christian) 5%
Ethnic mix Arab 80%, Kurdish 15%, Turkmen 3%, Other 2%
Government Transitional regime
Currency New Iraqi dinar = 1000 fils
Literacy rate 40%
Calorie consumption 2197 calories

'Irāq see Iraq
Iraq, Republic of see Iraq
Irbid 119 B5 Irbid, N Jordan
Irbil see Arbil
Ireland 89 A5 off. Republic of Ireland, Ir. Éire. country NW Europe
Ireland 80 C3 Lat. Hibernia. island Ireland/UK

IRELAND
Northwest Europe

Official name Ireland
Formation 1922 / 1922
Capital Dublin
Population 4.1 million / 154 people per sq mile (60 people per sq km) / 59%
Total area 27,135 sq miles (70,280 sq km)
Languages English*, Irish Gaelic*
Religions Roman Catholic 88%, Other and nonreligious 9%, Anglican 3%
Ethnic mix Irish 93%, Other 4%, British 3%
Government Parliamentary system
Currency Euro = 100 cents
Literacy rate 99%
Calorie consumption 3656 calories

Ireland, Republic of see Ireland
Irian see New Guinea
Irian Barat see Papua
Irian Jaya see Papua
Iringa 73 C7 Iringa, C Tanzania
Iriomote-jima 130 A4 island Sakishima-shotō, SW Japan
Iriona 52 D2 Colón, NE Honduras
Irish Sea 89 C5 Ir. Muir Éireann. sea C British Isles
Irkutsk 115 E4 Irkutskaya Oblast', S Russian Federation
Irminger Basin see Reykjanes Basin
Iroise 90 A3 sea NW France
Iron Mountain 40 B2 Michigan, N USA
Ironwood 40 B1 Michigan, N USA
Irrawaddy 136 B2 var. Ayeyarwady. river W Myanmar (Burma)
Irrawaddy, Mouths of the 137 A5 delta SW Myanmar (Burma)
Irtish see Irtysh
Irtysh 114 C4 var. Irtish, Kaz. Ertis. river C Asia
Irun 93 E1 País Vasco, N Spain
Iruña see Pamplona
Isabela, Isla 60 A5 var. Albemarle Island. island Galapagos Islands, Ecuador, E Pacific Ocean
Isaccea 108 D4 Tulcea, E Romania
Isachsen 37 F1 Northwest Territories, Ellef Ringnes Island, N Canada North America
Ísafjördhur 83 E4 Vestfirdhir, NW Iceland
Isbarta see Isparta
Isca Damnoniorum see Exeter
Ise 131 C6 Mie, Honshū, SW Japan
Isère 91 D5 river E France
Isernia 97 D5 var. Æsernia. Molise, C Italy
Ise-wan 131 C6 bay S Japan
Isfahan see Eşfahān

Isha Baydhabo see Baydhabo
Ishigaki-jima 130 A4 island Sakishima-shotō, SW Japan
Ishikari-wan 130 C2 bay Hokkaidō, NE Japan
Ishim 114 C4 Tyumenskaya Oblast', C Russian Federation
Ishim 114 C4 Kaz. Esil. river Kazakhstan/Russian Federation
Ishinomaki 130 D4 var. Isinomaki. Miyagi, Honshū, C Japan
Ishkashim see Ishkoshim
Ishkoshim 123 F3 Rus. Ishkashim. S Tajikistan
Isinomaki see Ishinomaki
Isiro 77 E5 Orientale, NE Dem. Rep. Congo
Iskär see Iskür
İskenderun 116 D4 Eng. Alexandretta. Hatay, S Turkey
İskenderun Körfezi 118 A2 Eng. Gulf of Alexandretta. gulf S Turkey
Iskür 104 C2 var. Iskär. river NW Bulgaria
Iskür, Yazovir 104 B2 prev. Yazovir Stalin. reservoir W Bulgaria
Isla Cristina 92 C4 Andalucía, S Spain
Isla de León see San Fernando
Islāmābād 134 C1 country capital (Pakistan) Federal Capital Territory Islāmābād, NE Pakistan
Island/Ísland see Iceland
I-n-Sâkâne, 'Erg 75 E2 desert N Mali
Islay 88 B4 island SW Scotland, UK
Isle 91 B5 river W France
Isle of Man 89 B5 UK crown dependency NW Europe
Ismailia see Ismâ'ilîya
Ismâ'ilîya 72 B1 var. Ismailia. N Egypt
Ismid see İzmit
Isna 72 B2 var. Esna. SE Egypt
Isoka 78 D1 Northern, NE Zambia
Isparta 116 B4 var. Isbarta. Isparta, SW Turkey
Ispir 117 E3 Erzurum, NE Turkey
Israel 119 A7 off. State of Israel, var. Medinat Israel, Heb. Yisrael, Yisra'el. country SW Asia

ISRAEL
Southwest Asia

Official name State of Israel
Formation 1948 / 1994
Capital Jerusalem (not internationally recognized)
Population 6.7 million / 854 people per sq mile (330 people per sq km) / 91%
Total area 8019 sq miles (20,770 sq km)
Languages Hebrew*, Arabic, Yiddish, German, Russian, Polish, Romanian, Persian
Religions Jewish 80%, Muslim (mainly Sunni) 16%, Druze and other 2%, Christian 2%
Ethnic mix Jewish 80%, Other (mostly Arab) 20%
Government Parliamentary system
Currency Shekel = 100 agorot
Literacy rate 97%
Calorie consumption 3666 calories

Israel, State of see Israel
Issa see Vis
Issiq Köl see Issyk-Kul', Ozero
Issoire 91 C5 Puy-de-Dôme, C France
Issyk-Kul' see Balykchy
Issyk-Kul', Ozero 123 G2 var. Issiq Köl, Kir. Ysyk-Köl. lake E Kyrgyzstan
İstanbul 116 B2 Bul. Tsarigrad, Eng. Istanbul, prev. Constantinople; anc. Byzantium. Istanbul, NW Turkey
İstanbul Boğazı 116 B2 var. Bosporus Thracius, Eng. Bosphorus, Bosporus, Turk. Karadeniz Boğazı. strait NW Turkey
Istarska Županija see Istra
Istra 100 A3 off. Istarska Županija. province NW Croatia
Istra 100 A3 Eng. Istria, Ger. Istrien. cultural region NW Croatia
Istria/Istrien see Istra
Itabuna 63 G3 Bahia, E Brazil

Itagüí *58 B3* Antioquia,
W Colombia
Itaipú, Represa de *63 E4 reservoir*
Brazil/Paraguay
Itaituba *63 E2* Pará, NE Brazil
Italia/Italiana, Republica/Italian
Republic, The *see* Italy
Italian Somaliland *see* Somalia
Italy *80 D4* Texas, SW USA
Italy *96 C3 off.* The Italian Republic, *It.*
Italia, Repubblica Italiana. *country*
S Europe

ITALY
Southern Europe

Official name Italian Republic
Formation 1861 / 1947
Capital Rome
Population 58.1 million / 512 people per
sq mile (198 people per sq km) / 67%
Total area 116,305 sq miles
(301,230 sq km)
Languages Italian*, German, French,
Rhaeto-Romanic, Sardinian
Religions Roman Catholic 85%, Other
and nonreligious 13%, Muslim 2%
Ethnic mix Italian 94%, Other 4%,
Sardinian 2%
Government Parliamentary system
Currency Euro = 100 cents
Literacy rate 99%
Calorie consumption 3671 calories

Iténez, Río *see* Guaporé, Rio
Ithaca *41 E3* New York, NE USA
It Hearrenfean *see* Heerenveen
Itoigawa *131 C5* Niigata, Honshū,
C Japan
Itseqqortoormiit *see* Ittoqqortoormiit
Ittoqqortoormiit *83 E3 var.*
Itseqqortoormiit, *Dan.* Scoresbysund,
Eng. Scoresby Sound. Tunu,
C Greenland
Iturup, Ostrov *130 E1 island* Kuril'skiye
Ostrova, SE Russian Federation
Itzehoe *94 B2* Schleswig-Holstein,
N Germany
Ivalo *84 D2* Lapp. Avveel, Avvil. Lappi,
N Finland
Ivanava *107 B7 Pol.* Janów, Janów
Poleski, *Rus.* Ivanovo. Brestskaya
Voblasts', SW Belarus
Ivangrad *see* Berane
Ivanhoe *149 C6* New South Wales,
SE Australia
Ivano-Frankivs'k *108 C2*
Ger. Stanislau, *Pol.* Stanisławów, *Rus.*
Ivano-Frankovsk; *prev.* Stanislav.
Ivano-Frankivs'ka Oblast', W Ukraine
Ivano-Frankovsk *see* Ivano-Frankivs'k
Ivanovo *111 B5* Ivanovskaya Oblast',
W Russian Federation
Ivanovo *see* Ivanava
Ivantsevichi/Ivatsevichi *see* Ivatsevichy
Ivatsevichy *107 B6 Pol.* Iwacewicze,
Rus. Ivantsevichi, Ivatsevichi.
Brestskaya Voblasts', SW Belarus
Ivigtut *see* Ivittuut
Ivittuut *82 B4 var.* Ivigtut. Kitaa,
S Greenland
Iviza *see* Eivissa
Iviza *see* Eivissa
Iviza *see* Eivissa
Ivory Coast *see* Côte d'Ivoire
Ivory Coast, Republic of the *see* Côte
d'Ivoire
Ivujivik *38 D1* Québec, NE Canada
Iwacewicze *see* Ivatsevichy
Iwaki *131 D5* Fukushima, Honshū,
N Japan
Iwakuni *131 B7* Yamaguchi, Honshū,
SW Japan
Iwanai *130 C2* Hokkaidō, NE Japan
Iwate *130 D3* Iwate, Honshū,
N Japan
Ixtapa *51 E5* Guerrero, S Mexico
Ixtepec *51 F5* Oaxaca, SE Mexico
Iyo-nada *131 B7 sea* S Japan
Izabal, Lago de *52 B2 prev.* Golfo Dulce.
lake E Guatemala
Īzad Khvāst *120 D3* Fārs, C Iran
Izegem *87 A6 prev.* Iseghem.
West-Vlaanderen, W Belgium
Izhevsk *111 D5 prev.* Ustinov.
Udmurtskaya Respublika,
NW Russian Federation
Izmail *see* Izmayil

Izmayil *108 D4 Rus.* Izmail. Odes'ka
Oblast', SW Ukraine
İzmir *116 A3 prev.* Smyrna. İzmir,
W Turkey
İzmit *116 B2 var.* Ismid; *anc.* Astacus.
Kocaeli, NW Turkey
İznik Gölü *116 B3 lake* NW Turkey
Izu-hantō *131 D6 peninsula* Honshū,
S Japan
Izu Shichito *see* Izu-shotō
Izu-shotō *131 D6 var.* Izu Shichito.
island group S Japan
Izvor *104 B2* Pernik, W Bulgaria
Izyaslav *108 C2* Khmel'nyts'ka Oblast',
W Ukraine
Izyum *109 G2* Kharkivs'ka Oblast',
E Ukraine

J

Jabal ash Shifā *120 A4 desert*
NW Saudi Arabia
Jabalpur *135 E4 prev.* Jubbulpore.
Madhya Pradesh, C India
Jabbūl, Sabkhat al *134 B2 sabkha*
NW Syria
Jablah *118 A3 var.* Jeble, *Fr.* Djéblé.
Al Lādhiqīyah, W Syria
Jaca *93 F1* Aragón, NE Spain
Jacaltenango *52 A2* Huehuetenango,
W Guatemala
Jackson *42 B2 state capital* Mississippi,
S USA
Jackson *45 H5* Missouri, C USA
Jackson *42 C1* Tennessee, S USA
Jackson Head *151 A6 headland* South
Island, New Zealand
Jacksonville *43 E3* Florida, SE USA
Jacksonville *40 B4* Illinois, N USA
Jacksonville *43 F1* North Carolina,
SE USA
Jacksonville *49 G3* Texas, SW USA
Jacmel *54 D3 var.* Jaquemel. S Haiti
Jacob *see* Nkayi
Jacobābād *134 B3* Sind, SE Pakistan
Jadotville *see* Likasi
Jadransko More/Jadransko Morje *see*
Adriatic Sea
Jaén *60 B2* Cajamarca, N Peru
Jaén *92 D4* Andalucía, SW Spain
Jaffna *132 D3* Northern Province,
N Sri Lanka
Jagannath *see* Puri
Jagdalpur *135 E5* Chhattisgarh,
C India
Jagdaqi *127 G1* Nei Mongol Zizhiqu,
N China
Jagodina *100 D4 prev.* Svetozarevo.
Serbia, C Serbia
Jahra *see* Al Jahrā'
Jailolo *see* Halmahera, Pulau
Jaipur *134 D3 prev.* Jeypore. *state capital*
Rājasthān, N India
Jaisalmer *134 C3* Rājasthān,
NW India
Jajce *100 B3* Federacija Bosna
I Hercegovina, W Bosnia and
Herzegovina
Jakarta *138 C5 prev.* Djakarta, *Dut.*
Batavia. *country capital* (Indonesia)
Jawa, C Indonesia
Jakobstad *84 D4 Fin.* Pietarsaari. Länsi-
Suomi, W Finland
Jakobstadt *see* Jēkabpils
Jalālābād *123 F4 var.* Jalalabad,
Jelalabad. Nangarhār, E Afghanistan
Jalal-Abad *see* Dzhalal-Abad
Jalandhar *134 D2 prev.* Jullundur.
Punjab, N India
Jalapa *52 D3* Nueva Segovia,
NW Nicaragua
Jalpa *50 D4* Zacatecas, C Mexico
Jālū *71 G3 var.* Jālū. NE Libya
Jaluit Atoll *144 D2 var.* Jālwōj. *atoll*
Ralik Chain, S Marshall Islands
Jālwōj *see* Jaluit Atoll
Jamaame *73 D6 It.* Giamame;
prev. Margherita. Jubbada Hoose,
S Somalia
Jamaica *54 B3 country* W West Indies

JAMAICA
West Indies

Official name Jamaica
Formation 1962 / 1962
Capital Kingston

JAMAICA
(continued)

Population 2.7 million / 646 people per
sq mile (249 people per sq km) / 56%
Total area 4243 sq miles (10,990 sq km)
Languages English*, English Creole
Religions Other and nonreligious 45%,
Other Protestant 20%, Church of
God 18%, Baptist 10%, Anglican 7%
Ethnic mix Black African 75%, Mulatto
(mixed race) 13%, European and
Chinese 11%, East Indian 1%
Government Parliamentary system
Currency Jamaican dollar = 100 cents
Literacy rate 88%
Calorie consumption 2685 calories

Jamaica *56 A1 island* W West Indies
Jamaica Channel *54 D3 channel*
Haiti/Jamaica
Jamālpur *135 F3* Bihār, NE India
Jambi *138 B4 var.* Telanaipura; *prev.*
Djambi. Sumatera, W Indonesia
Jamdena *see* Yamdena, Pulau
James Bay *38 C3 bay* Ontario/Québec,
E Canada
James River *45 E2 river* North Dakota/
South Dakota, N USA
James River *41 E5 river* Virginia,
NE USA
Jamestown *41 E3* New York, NE USA
Jamestown *45 E2* North Dakota, N USA
Jamestown *see* Holetown
Jammu *134 D2 prev.* Jummoo. *state*
capital Jammu and Kashmir, NW India
Jammu and Kashmir *134 D1 disputed*
region India/Pakistan
Jāmnagar *134 C4 prev.* Navanagar.
Gujarāt, W India
Jamshedpur *135 F4* Jhārkhand, NE India
Jamuna *see* Brahmaputra
Janaúba *63 F3* Minas Gerais, SE Brazil
Janesville *40 B3* Wisconsin, N USA
Janina *see* Ioánnina
Janischken *see* Joniškis
Jankovac *see* Jánoshalma
Jan Mayen *83 F4 Norwegian dependency*
N Atlantic Ocean
Jánoshalma *99 C7 SCr.* Jankovac. Bács-
Kiskun, S Hungary
Janów *see* Ivanava, Belarus
Janów/Janów *see* Jonava, Lithuania
Janów Poleski *see* Ivanava
Japan *130 C4 var.* Nippon, *Jap.* Nihon.
country E Asia

JAPAN
East Asia

Official name Japan
Formation 1590 / 1972
Capital Tokyo
Population 128 million / 881 people per
sq mile (340 people per sq km) / 79%
Total area 145,882 sq miles
(377,835 sq km)
Languages Japanese, Korean, Chinese
Religions Shinto and Buddhist 76%,
Buddhist 16%, Other (including
Christian) 8%
Ethnic mix Japanese 99%,
Other (mainly Korean) 1%
Government Parliamentary system
Currency Yen = 100 sen
Literacy rate 99%
Calorie consumption 2761 calories

Japan, Sea of *130 A4 var.* East Sea, *Rus.*
Yaponskoye More. *sea* NW Pacific
Ocean
Japan Trench *125 F1 trench* NW Pacific
Ocean
Japen *see* Yapen, Pulau
Japiim *62 C2 var.* Máncio Lima. Acre,
W Brazil
Japurá, Rio *62 C2 var.* Río Caquetá,
Yapurá. *river* Brazil/Colombia
Japurá, Rio *see* Caquetá, Río
Jaqué *53 G5* Darién, SE Panama
Jaquemel *see* Jacmel
Jarablos *see* Jarābulus
Jarābulus *118 C2 var.* Jarablos, Jerablus,
Fr. Djérablous. Ḩalab, N Syria
Jarbah, Jazīrat *see* Jerba, Île de
Jardines de la Reina, Archipiélago de
los *54 B2 island group* C Cuba

Jarid, Shaṭṭ al *see* Jerid, Chott el
Jarocin *98 C4* Wielkopolskie,
C Poland
Jarosław *see* Jarosław
Jarosław *99 E5 Ger.* Jaroslau, *Rus.*
Yaroslav. Podkarpackie,
SE Poland
Jarqo'rg'on *123 E3 Rus.* Dzharkurgan.
Surkhondaryo Viloyati, S Uzbekistan
Jarvis Island *145 G2 US unincorporated*
territory C Pacific Ocean
Jasło *99 D5* Podkarpackie, SE Poland
Jastrzębie-Zdrój *99 C5* Śląskie,
S Poland
Jataí *63 E3* Goiás, C Brazil
Jativa *see* Xàtiva
Jauf *see* Al Jawf
Jaunpiebalga *106 D3* Gulbene,
NE Latvia
Jaunpur *135 E3* Uttar Pradesh,
N India
Java *152 A3* South Dakota, N USA
Javalambre *93 E3 mountain* E Spain
Javari, Rio *62 C2 var.* Yavari. *river*
Brazil/Peru
Java Sea *138 D4 Ind.* Laut Jawa. *sea*
W Indonesia
Java Trench *124 D5 var.* Sunda Trench.
trench E Indian Ocean
Jawa, Laut *see* Java Sea
Jawhar *73 D6 var.* Jowhar, *It.* Giohar.
Shabeellaha Dhexe, S Somalia
Jaworów *see* Yavoriv
Jaya, Puncak *139 G4 prev.* Puntjak
Carstensz, Puntjak Sukarno. *mountain*
Papua, E Indonesia
Jayapura *139 H4 var.* Djajapura,
Dut. Hollandia; *prev.* Kotabaru,
Sukarnapura. Papua, E Indonesia
Jayhawker State *see* Kansas
Jaz Mūriān, Hāmūn-e *120 E4 lake*
SE Iran
Jebba *75 F4* Kwara, W Nigeria
Jebel, Bahr el *see* White Nile
Jeble *see* Jablah
Jedda *see* Jiddah
Jędrzejów *98 D4 Ger.* Endersdorf.
Świętokrzyskie, C Poland
Jefferson City *45 G5 state capital*
Missouri, C USA
Jega *75 F4* Kebbi, NW Nigeria
Jehol *see* Chengde
Jēkabpils *106 D4 Ger.* Jakobstadt.
Jēkabpils, S Latvia
Jelalabad *see* Jalālābād
Jelenia Góra *98 B4 Ger.* Hirschberg,
Hirschberg im Riesengebirge,
Hirschberg in Riesengebirge,
Hirschberg in Schlesien. Dolnośląskie,
SW Poland
Jelgava *106 C3 Ger.* Mitau. Jelgava,
C Latvia
Jemappes *87 B6* Hainaut, S Belgium
Jember *138 D5 prev.* Djember. Jawa,
C Indonesia
Jena *94 C4* Thüringen, C Germany
Jenin *119 A6* N West Bank
Jerablus *see* Jarābulus
Jerada *70 D2* NE Morocco
Jerba, Île de *71 F2 var.* Djerba, Jazīrat
Jarbah. *island* E Tunisia
Jérémie *54 D3* SW Haiti
Jerez *see* Jeréz de la Frontera, Spain
Jeréz de la Frontera *92 C5 var.* Jerez;
prev. Xeres. Andalucía, SW Spain
Jeréz de los Caballeros *92 C4*
Extremadura, W Spain
Jericho *119 B6 Ar.* Arīḩā, *Heb.* Yerīḩo.
E West Bank
Jerid, Chott el *87 E2 var.* Shaṭṭ al Jarid.
salt lake SW Tunisia
Jersey *89 D8 uk crown dependency*
Channel Islands, Jersey NW Europe
Jerusalem *103 H4 Ar.* Al Quds, Al Quds
ash Sharīf, *Heb.* Yerushalayim; *anc.*
Hierosolyma. *country capital* (Israel)
Jerusalem, NE Israel
Jerusalem *112 A4 district* E Israel
Jesenice *95 D7 Ger.* Assling.
NW Slovenia
Jesselton *see* Kota Kinabalu
Jessore *135 G4* Khulna, W Bangladesh
Jesús María *64 C3* Córdoba,
C Argentina
Jeypore *see* Jaipur, Rājasthān, India
Jhānsi *134 D3* Uttar Pradesh, N India
Jhārkhand *135 F4 cultural region*
NE India

Jhārkhand 135 F4 *state* NE India
Jhelum 134 C2 Punjab, NE Pakistan
Ji *see* Hebei, China
Ji *see* Jilin, China
Jiangmen 128 C6 Guangdong,
S China
Jiangsu 128 D4 *var.* Chiang-su,
Jiangsu Sheng, Kiangsu, Su. *province*
E China
Jiangsu *see* Nanjing
Jiangsu Sheng *see* Jiangsu
Jiangxi 128 C6 *var.* Chiang-hsi, Gan,
Jiangxi Sheng, Kiangsi. *province*
S China
Jiangxi Sheng *see* Jiangxi
Jiaxing 128 D5 Zhejiang, SE China
Jiayi *see* Chiai
Jibuti *see* Djibouti
Jiddah 121 A5 *Eng.* Jedda. Makkah,
W Saudi Arabia
Jih-k'a-tse *see* Xigazê
Jihlava 99 B5 *Ger.* Iglau, *Pol.* Iglawa.
Vysocina, S Czech Republic
Jilf al Kabīr, Ḥaḍabat al *see* Gilf Kebir
Plateau
Jilib 73 D6 *It.* Gelib. Jubbada Dhexe,
S Somalia
Jilin 128 E3 *var.* Chi-lin, Girin,
Kirin; *prev.* Yungki, Yunki. Jilin,
NE China
Jilin 128 E3 *var.* Chi-lin, Girin, Ji, Jilin
Sheng, Kirin. *province* NE China
Jilin Sheng *see* Jilin
Jima 73 C5 *var.* Jimma, It. Gimma.
Oromo, C Ethiopia
Jimbolia 108 A4 *Ger.* Hatzfeld, *Hung.*
Zsombolya. Timiş, W Romania
Jiménez 50 D2 Chihuahua, N Mexico
Jimma *see* Jima
Jimsar 126 C3 Xinjiang Uygur Zizhiqu,
NW China
Jin *see* Shanxi
Jin *see* Tianjin Shi
Jinan 128 C4 *var.* Chinan, Chi-nan,
Tsinan. *province capital* Shandong,
E China
Jingdezhen 128 C5 Jiangxi, S China
Jinghong 128 A6 *var.* Yunjinghong.
Yunnan, SW China
Jinhua 128 D5 Zhejiang, SE China
Jining 127 F3 Shandong, E China
Jinja 73 C6 S Uganda
Jinotega 52 D3 Jinotega,
NW Nicaragua
Jinotepe 52 D3 Carazo,
SW Nicaragua
Jinsen *see* Inch'ŏn
Jinsha Jiang 128 A5 *Eng* Yangtze.
river SW China
Jinzhong 128 C4 *var.* Yuci. Shanxi,
C China
Jinzhou 128 D3 *var.* Chin-chou,
Chinchow; *prev.* Chinhsien. Liaoning,
NE China
Jīrgalanta *see* Hovd
Jisr ash Shadādī *see* Ash Shadādah
Jiu 108 B5 *Ger.* Schil, Schyl, *Hung.* Zsil,
Zsily. *river* S Romania
Jiujiang 128 C5 Jiangxi, S China
Jixi 129 E2 Heilongjiang, NE China
Jīzān 121 B6 *var.* Qīzān. Jīzān, SW Saudi
Arabia
Jizzax 123 E2 *Rus.* Dzhizak. Jizzax
Viloyati, C Uzbekistan
João Belo *see* Xai-Xai
João Pessoa 63 G2 *prev.* Paraíba. *state
capital* Paraíba, E Brazil
Joazeiro *see* Juazeiro
Job'urg *see* Johannesburg
Jo-ch'iang *see* Ruoqiang
Jodhpur 134 C3 Rājasthān,
NW India
Joensuu 85 E5 Itä-Suomi,
SE Finland
Jōetsu 131 C5 *var.* Zyōetu.
Niigata, Honshū, C Japan
Jogjakarta *see* Yogyakarta
Johanna Island *see* Anjouan
Johannesburg 78 D4 *var.* Egoli,
Erautini, Gauteng, *abbrev.* Job'urg.
Gauteng, NE South Africa
Johannisburg *see* Pisz
John Day River 46 C3 *river* Oregon,
NW USA
John o'Groats 88 C2 N Scotland, UK
Johnston Atoll 143 E1 US
unincorporated territory C Pacific
Ocean

Johor Baharu *see* Johor Bahru
Johor Bahru 138 B3 *var.* Johor Baharu,
Johore Bahru. Johor, Peninsular
Malaysia
Johore Bahru *see* Johor Bahru
Johore Strait 138 A1 *strait* Johor,
Peninsular Malaysia, Malaysia/
Singapore Asia Andaman Sea/South
China Sea
Joinvile *see* Joinville
Joinville 63 E4 *var.* Joinvile. Santa
Catarina, S Brazil
Jokkmokk 84 C3 *Lapp.* Dálvvadis.
Norrbotten, N Sweden
Jokyakarta *see* Yogyakarta
Joliet 40 B3 Illinois, N USA
Jonava 106 B4 *Ger.* Janow, *Pol.* Janów.
Kaunas, C Lithuania
Jonesboro 42 B1 Arkansas, C USA
Joniškis 106 C3 *Ger.* Janischken. Šiauliai,
N Lithuania
Jönköping 85 B7 Jönköping, S Sweden
Jonquière 39 E4 Québec, SE Canada
Joplin 45 F5 Missouri, C USA
Jordan 119 B6 *off.* Hashemite Kingdom
of Jordan, *Ar.* Al Mamlaka al Urduniya
al Hashemiyah, Al Urdunn; *prev.*
Transjordan. *country* SW Asia

JORDAN
Southwest Asia

Official name Hashemite Kingdom
of Jordan
Formation 1946 / 1967
Capital Amman
Population 5.6 million / 163 people per
sq mile (63 people per sq km) / 74%
Total area 35,637 sq miles
(92,300 sq km)
Languages Arabic*
Religions Muslim (mainly Sunni) 92%,
Other (mostly Christian) 8%
Ethnic mix Arab 98%, Circassian 1%,
Armenian 1%
Government Monarchy
Currency Jordanian dinar = 1000 fils
Literacy rate 90%
Calorie consumption 2673 calories

Jordan 119 B5 *Ar.* Urdunn, *Heb.*
HaYarden. *river* SW Asia
Jorhāt 135 H3 Assam, NE India
Jos 75 G4 Plateau, C Nigeria
Joseph Bonaparte Gulf 146 D2 *gulf*
N Australia
Jos Plateau 75 G4 *plateau* C Nigeria
Jotunheimen 85 A5 *mountain range*
S Norway
Joûnié 118 A4 *var.* Juniyah. W Lebanon
Joure 86 D2 *Fris.* De Jouwer. Friesland,
N Netherlands
Joutseno 85 E5 Etelä-Suomi, SE Finland
Jowhar *see* Jawhar
J.Storm Thurmond Reservoir *see* Clark
Hill Lake
Juan Aldama 50 D3 Zacatecas, C Mexico
Juan de Fuca, Strait of 46 A1 *strait*
Canada/USA
Juan Fernández Islands *see* Juan
Fernández, Islas
Juan Fernández, Islas 57 A6 *Eng.*
Juan Fernandez Islands. *island group*
W Chile
Juazeiro 63 G2 *prev.* Joazeiro. Bahia,
E Brazil
Juazeiro do Norte 63 G2 Ceará,
E Brazil
Juba 73 B5 *var.* Jūbā. Bahr el Gabel,
S Sudan
Juba 73 D6 *Amh.* Genalē Wenz,
It. Guiba, *Som.* Gaanane, Webi Jubba.
river Ethiopia/Somalia
Jubba, Webi *see* Juba
Jubbulpore *see* Jabalpur
Júcar 93 E3 *var.* Jucar. *river* C Spain
Juchitán 51 F5 *var.* Juchitán de Zaragosa.
Oaxaca, SE Mexico
Juchitán de Zaragosa *see* Juchitán
Judayidat Hāmir 120 B3 S Iraq
Judenburg 95 D7 Steiermark, C Austria
Jugoslavija *see* Serbia
Juigalpa 52 D3 Chontales, S Nicaragua
Juiz de Fora 63 F4 Minas Gerais,
SE Brazil
Jujuy *see* San Salvador de Jujuy
Jūlā *see* Jālū, Libya
Julia Beterrae *see* Béziers

Juliaca 61 E4 Puno, SE Peru
Juliana Top 59 G3 *mountain*
C Suriname
Julianehåb *see* Qaqortoq
Julio Briga *see* Bragança
Juliobriga *see* Logroño
Juliomagus *see* Angers
Jullundur *see* Jalandhar
Jumilla 93 E4 Murcia, SE Spain
Jummoo *see* Jammu
Jumna *see* Yamuna
Jumporn *see* Chumphon
Junction City 45 F4 Kansas,
C USA
Juneau 36 D4 *state capital* Alaska,
USA
Junín 64 C4 Buenos Aires, E Argentina
Juniyah *see* Joûnié
Junkseylon *see* Phuket
Jur 73 B5 *river* S Sudan
Jura 90 D4 *cultural region* E France
Jura 90 D4 *department* E France
Jura 95 A7 *var.* Jura Mountains.
mountain range France/Switzerland
Jura 88 B4 *island* SW Scotland, UK
Jura Mountains *see* Jura
Jurbarkas 106 B4 *Ger.* Georgenburg,
Jurburg. Tauragė, W Lithuania
Jurburg *see* Jurbarkas
Jūrmala 106 C3 Rīga, C Latvia
Juruá, Rio 62 C2 *var.* Rio Yuruá. *river*
Brazil/Peru
Juruena, Rio 62 D3 *river*
W Brazil
Jutiapa 52 B2 Jutiapa, S Guatemala
Juticalpa 52 D2 Olancho, C Honduras
Jutland *see* Jylland
Juvavum *see* Salzburg
Juventud, Isla de la 54 A2
var. Isla de Pinos, *Eng.* Isle of Youth;
prev. The Isle of the Pines. *island*
W Cuba
Južna Morava 101 E5 *Ger.* Südliche
Morava. *river* SE Serbia
Jwaneng 78 C4 Southern, S Botswana
Africa
Jylland 85 A7 *Eng.* Jutland. *peninsula*
W Denmark
Jyrgalan *see* Dzhergalan
Jyväskylä 85 D5 Länsi-Suomi,
C Finland

K

K2 126 A4 *Chin.* Qogir Feng, *Eng.*
Mount Godwin Austen. *mountain*
China/Pakistan
Kaafu Atoll *see* Male' Atoll
Kaaimanston 59 G3 Sipaliwini,
N Suriname
Kaakhka *see* Kaka
Kaala *see* Caála
Kaamanen 84 D2 *Lapp.* Gámas.
Lappi, N Finland
Kaapstad *see* Cape Town
Kaaresuvanto 84 C3 *Lapp.* Gárassavon.
Lappi, N Finland
Kabale 73 B6 SW Uganda
Kabinda 77 D7 Kasai Oriental,
SE Dem. Rep. Congo
Kabinda *see* Cabinda
Kabompo 78 C2 *river* W Zambia
Kābol 123 E4 *var.* Kabul, *pash.* Kābul.
country capital (Afghanistan) Kabol, E
Afghanistan
Kabul 123 E4 *var.* Daryā-ye Kābul.
river Afghanistan/Pakistan
Kabul *see* Kābol
Kābul, Daryā-ye *see* Kabul
Kabwe 78 D2 Central, C Zambia
Kachchh, Gulf of 134 B4 *var.* Gulf of
Cutch, Gulf of Kutch. *gulf* W India
Kachchh, Rann of 134 B4 *var.* Rann
of Kachh, Rann of Kutch. *salt marsh*
India/Pakistan
Kachh, Rann of *see* Kachchh, Rann of
Kadan Kyun 137 B5 *prev.* King
Island. *island* Mergui Archipelago,
S Myanmar (Burma)
Kadavu 145 E4 *prev.* Kandavu. *island*
S Fiji
Kadoma 78 D3 *prev.* Gatooma.
Mashonaland West, C Zimbabwe
Kadugli 72 B4 Southern Kordofan,
S Sudan
Kaduna 75 G4 Kaduna, C Nigeria

Kadzhi-Say 123 G2 *Kir.* Kajisay.
Issyk-Kul'skaya Oblast',
NE Kyrgyzstan
Kaédi 74 C3 Gorgol, S Mauritania
Kaffa *see* Feodosiya
Kafue 78 D2 Lusaka, SE Zambia
Kafue 78 D2 *river* C Zambia
Kaga Bandoro 76 C4 *prev.* Fort-
Crampel. Nana-Grébizi, C Central
African Republic
Kagan *see* Kogon
Kāghet 74 D1 *var.* Karet. *physical region*
N Mauritania
Kagi *see* Chiai
Kagoshima 131 B8 *var.* Kagosima.
Kagoshima, Kyūshū, SW Japan
Kagoshima-wan 131 A8 *bay*
SW Japan
Kagosima *see* Kagoshima
Kagul *see* Cahul
Kahmard, Daryā-ye 123 E4
prev. Darya-i-surkhab. *river*
NE Afghanistan
Kahramanmaraş 116 D4 *var.*
Kahraman Maraş, Maraş, Marash.
Kahramanmaraş, S Turkey
Kaiapoi 151 C6 Canterbury, South
Island, New Zealand
Kaifeng 128 C4 Henan, C China
Kai, Kepulauan 139 F4 *prev.* Kei
Islands. *island group* Maluku,
SE Indonesia
Kaikohe 150 C2 Northland, North
Island, New Zealand
Kaikoura 151 C5 Canterbury, South
Island, New Zealand
Kaikoura Peninsula 151 C5 *peninsula*
South Island, New Zealand
Kainji Lake *see* Kainji Reservoir
Kainji Reservoir 75 F4 *var.* Kainji Lake.
reservoir W Nigeria
Kaipara Harbour 150 C2 *harbour*
North Island, New Zealand
Kairouan 71 E2 *var.* Al Qayrawān.
E Tunisia
Kaisaria *see* Kayseri
Kaiserslautern 95 A5 Rheinland-Pfalz,
SW Germany
Kaišiadorys 107 B5 Kaunas,
S Lithuania
Kaitaia 150 C2 Northland, North Island,
New Zealand
Kajaani 84 E4 *Swe.* Kajana. Oulu,
C Finland
Kajan *see* Kayan, Sungai
Kajana *see* Kajaani
Kajisay *see* Kadzhi-Say
Kaka 122 C2 *Rus.* Kaakhka. Ahal
Welaýaty, S Turkmenistan
Kake 36 D4 Kupreanof Island, Alaska,
USA
Kakhovka 109 F4 Khersons'ka Oblast',
S Ukraine
Kakhovs'ke Vodoskhovyshche
109 F4 *Rus.* Kakhovskoye
Vodokhranilishche. *reservoir*
SE Ukraine
Kakhovskoye Vodokhranilishche *see*
Kakhovs'ke Vodoskhovyshche
Kākināda 132 D1 *prev.* Cocanada.
Andhra Pradesh, E India
Kakshaal-Too, Khrebet *see*
Kokshaal-Tau
Kaktovik 36 D2 Alaska, USA
Kalaallit Nunaat *see* Greenland
Kalahari Desert 78 B4 *desert*
Southern Africa
Kalaikhum *see* Qal'aikhum
Kalámai 104 B4 Kentrikí Makedonía,
N Greece
Kalamás 104 A4 *var.* Thiamis, *prev*
Thýamis. *river* W Greece
Kalámata 105 B6 *prev.* Kalámai.
Pelopónnisos, S Greece
Kalamazoo 40 C3 Michigan,
N USA
Kalambaka *see* Kalampáka
Kálamos 105 C5 Attikí, C Greece
Kalampáka 104 B4 *var.* Kalambaka.
Thessalía, C Greece
Kalanchak 109 F4 Khersons'ka Oblast',
S Ukraine
Kalarash *see* Călăraşi
Kalasin 136 D4 *var.* Muang Kalasin.
Kalasin, E Thailand
Kalāt 134 B2 *var.* Kelat, Khelat.
Baluchistān, SW Pakistan

Kalāt *see* Qalāt
Kalbarri 147 A5 Western Australia
Kalecik 116 C3 Ankara,
N Turkey
Kalemie 77 E6 *prev.* Albertville.
Katanga, SE Dem. Rep. Congo
Kale Sultanie *see* Çanakkale
Kalgan *see* Zhangjiakou
Kalgoorlie 147 B6 Western Australia
Kalima 77 D6 Maniema,
E Dem. Rep. Congo
Kalimantan 138 D4 *Eng.* Indonesian
Borneo. *geopolitcal region* Borneo,
C Indonesia
Kalinin *see* Tver'
Kaliningrad 106 A4 Kaliningradskaya
Oblast', W Russian Federation
Kaliningrad *see* Kaliningradskaya Oblast'
Kaliningradskaya Oblast' 106 B4
var. Kaliningrad. *province and enclave*
W Russian Federation
Kalinkavichy 107 C7 *Rus.* Kalinkovichi.
Homyel'skaya Voblasts', SE Belarus
Kalinkovichi *see* Kalinkavichy
Kalisch/Kalish *see* Kalisz
Kalispell 44 B1 Montana, NW USA
Kalisz 98 C4 *Ger.* Kalisch, *Rus.* Kalish;
anc. Calisia. Wielkopolskie, C Poland
Kalix 84 D4 Norrbotten, N Sweden
Kalixälven 84 D3 *river* N Sweden
Kallaste 106 E3 *Ger.* Krasnogor.
Tartumaa, SE Estonia
Kallavesi 85 E5 *lake* SE Finland
Kalloni 105 D5 Lésvos, E Greece
Kalmar 85 C7 *var.* Calmar. Kalmar,
S Sweden
Kalmthout 87 C5 Antwerpen,
N Belgium
Kalpáki 104 A4 Ípeiros, W Greece
Kalpeni Island 132 B3 *island*
Lakshadweep, India, N Indian Ocean
Kaltdorf *see* Pruszków
Kaluga 111 B5 Kaluzhskaya Oblast',
W Russian Federation
Kalush 108 C2 *Pol.* Kałusz.
Ivano-Frankivs'ka Oblast', W Ukraine
Kałusz *see* Kalush
Kalutara 132 D4 Western Province,
SW Sri Lanka
Kalvarija 107 B5 *Pol.* Kalwaria.
Marijampol'e, S Lithuania
Kalwaria *see* Kalvarija
Kalyān 134 C5 Mahārāshtra, W India
Kálymnos 105 D6 *var.* Kálimnos. *island*
Dodekánisa, Greece, Aegean Sea
Kama 110 D4 *river* NW Russian
Federation
Kamarang 59 F3 N Guyana
Kambryk *see* Cambrai
Kamchatka *see* Kamchatka, Poluostrov
Kamchatka, Poluostrov 115 G3 *Eng.*
Kamchatka. *peninsula* E Russian
Federation
Kamina 77 D7 Shaba, S Dem. Rep.
Congo
Kamishli *see* Al Qāmishli
Kamloops 37 E5 British Columbia,
SW Canada
Kammu Seamount 152 C2 *guyot*
N Pacific Ocean
Kampala 73 B6 *country capital*
(Uganda) S Uganda
Kâmpóng Cham 137 D6 *prev.* Kompong
Cham. Kâmpóng Cham, C Cambodia
Kâmpóng Chhnăng 137 D6 *prev.*
Kompong. Kâmpóng Chhnăng,
C Cambodia
Kâmpóng Saôm 137 D6 *prev.* Kompong
Som, Sihanoukville. Kâmpóng Saôm,
SW Cambodia
Kâmpóng Spœ 137 D6 *prev.* Kompong
Spœu. Kâmpóng Spœ, S Cambodia
Kâmpôt 137 D6 Kâmpôt, SW Cambodia
Kampuchea *see* Cambodia
Kampuchea, Democratic *see* Cambodia
**Kampuchea, People's Democratic
Republic of** *see* Cambodia
Kam"yanets'-Podil's'kyy 108 C3 *Rus.*
Kamenets-Podol'skiy. Khmel'nyts'ka
Oblast', W Ukraine

Kam"yanka-Dniprovs'ka 109 F3 *Rus.*
Kamenka Dneprovskaya. Zaporiz'ka
Oblast', SE Ukraine
Kamyshin 111 B6 Volgogradskaya
Oblast', SW Russian Federation
Kanaky *see* New Caledonia
Kananga 77 D6 *prev.* Luluabourg. Kasai
Occidental, S Dem. Rep. Congo
Kananur *see* Cannanore
Kanara *see* Karnātaka
Kanash 111 C5 Chuvashskaya
Respublika, W Russian Federation
Kanazawa 131 C5 Ishikawa, Honshū,
SW Japan
Kanbe 136 B4 Yangon,
SW Myanmar (Burma)
Kānchipuram 132 C2 *prev.*
Conjeeveram. Tamil Nādu, SE India
Kandahār 123 E5 Per. Qandahār.
Kandahār, S Afghanistan
Kandalaksa *see* Kandalaksha
Kandalaksha 110 B2 *var.* Kandalakša,
Fin. Kantalahti. Murmanskaya Oblast',
NW Russian Federation
Kandangan 138 D4 Borneo,
C Indonesia
Kandau *see* Kandava
Kandava 106 C3 *Ger.* Kandau. Tukums,
W Latvia
Kandavu *see* Kadavu
Kandi 75 F4 N Benin
Kandy 132 D3 Central Province,
C Sri Lanka
Kane Fracture Zone 66 B4 *fracture zone*
NW Atlantic Ocean
Kāne'ohe 47 A8 *var.* Kaneohe. O'ahu,
Hawai'i, USA
Kanestron, Akra *see* Palioúri, Ákrotírio
Kanëv *see* Kaniv
Kanevskoye Vodokhranilishche *see*
Kanivs'ke Vodoskhovyshche
Kangaroo Island 149 A7 *island* South
Australia
Kangertittivaq 83 E4 *Dan.* Scoresby
Sund. *fjord* E Greenland
Kangikajik 83 F4 *var.* Kap Brewster.
headland E Greenland
Kaniv 109 E2 *Rus.* Kanëv. Cherkas'ka
Oblast', C Ukraine
Kanivs'ke Vodoskhovyshche 109 E2
Rus. Kanevskoye Vodokhranilishche.
reservoir C Ukraine
Kanjiža 100 D2 *Ger.* Altkanischa,
Hung. Magyarkanizsa, Ókanizsa;
prev. Stara Kanjiža. Vojvodina,
N Serbia
Kankaanpää 85 D5 Länsi-Soumi,
SW Finland
Kankakee 40 B3 Illinois, N USA
Kankan 74 D4 Haute-Guinée, E Guinea
Kannur *see* Cannanore
Kano 75 G4 Kano, N Nigeria
Kānpur 135 E3 *Eng.* Cawnpore. Uttar
Pradesh, N India
Kansas 45 F5 *off.* State of Kansas,
also known as Jayhawker State,
Sunflower State. *state* C USA
Kansas City 45 F4 Kansas, C USA
Kansas City 45 F4 Missouri, C USA
Kansas River 45 F5 *river* Kansas,
C USA
Kansk 115 E4 Krasnoyarskiy Kray,
S Russian Federation
Kansu *see* Gansu
Kantalahti *see* Kandalaksha
Kántanos 105 C7 Kríti, Greece,
E Mediterranean Sea
Kantemirovka 111 B6 Voronezhskaya
Oblast', W Russian Federation
Kantipur *see* Kathmandu
Kanton 145 F3 *var.* Abariringa, Canton
Island; *prev.* Mary Island. *atoll* Phoenix
Islands, C Kiribati
Kanye 78 C4 Southern, SE Botswana
Kaohsiung 128 D6 *var.* Gaoxiong, *Jap.*
Takao, Takow. S Taiwan
Kaolack 74 B3 *var.* Kaolak. W Senegal
Kaolak *see* Kaolack
Kaolan *see* Lanzhou
Kaoma 78 C2 Western, W Zambia
Kapelle 87 B5 Zeeland, SW Netherlands
Kapellen 87 C5 Antwerpen, N Belgium
Kapka, Massif du 76 C2 *mountain
range* E Chad
Kaplangky, Plato *see* Gaplaňgyr Platosy
Kapoeas *see* Kapuas, Sungai
Kapoeta 73 C5 Eastern Equatoria,
SE Sudan

Kaposvár 99 C7 Somogy,
SW Hungary
Kappeln 94 B2 Schleswig-Holstein,
N Germany
Kaproncza *see* Koprivnica
Kapstad *see* Cape Town
Kapsukas *see* Marijampolė
Kaptsevichy 107 C7 *Rus.* Koptsevichi.
Homyel'skaya Voblasts', SE Belarus
Kapuas, Sungai 138 C4 *prev.* Kapoeas.
river Borneo, C Indonesia
Kapuskasing 38 C4 Ontario,
S Canada
Kapyl' 107 C6 *Rus.* Kopyl'. Minskaya
Voblasts', C Belarus
Kara-Balta 123 F2 Chuyskaya Oblast',
N Kyrgyzstan
Karabil', Vozvyshennost' *see* Garabil
Belentligi
Kara-Bogaz-Gol, Zaliv *see* Garabogaz
Aylagy
Karabük 116 C2 Karabük, NW Turkey
Karāchi 134 B3 Sind, SE Pakistan
Karácsonkő *see* Piatra-Neamţ
Karadeniz *see* Black Sea
Karadeniz Boğazı *see* Istanbul Boğazı
Karaferiye *see* Véroia
Karaganda 114 C4 *Kaz.* Qaraghandy.
Karaganda, C Kazakhstan
Karaginskiy, Ostrov 115 H2 *island*
E Russian Federation
Karagumskiy Kanal *see* Garagum Kanaly
Karak *see* Al Karak
Kara-Kala *see* Magtymguly
Karakax *see* Moyu
Karaklisse *see* Ağrı
Karakol 123 G2 *var.* Karakolka.
Issyk-Kul'skaya Oblast',
NE Kyrgyzstan
Karakol 123 G2 *prev.* Przheval'sk.
Issyk-Kul'skaya Oblast', NE Kyrgyzstan
Karakolka *see* Karakol
Karakoram Range 134 D1 *mountain
range* C Asia
Karaköse *see* Ağrı
Karakul' *see* Qarokül
Kara Kum *see* Garagum
Kara Kum Canal/Karakumskiy Kanal
see Garagum Kanaly
Karakumy, Peski *see* Garagum
Karaman 116 C4 Karaman, S Turkey
Karamay 126 B2 *var.* Karamai,
Kelamayi; *prev.* Chin. K'o-la-ma-i.
Xinjiang Uygur Zizhiqu, NW China
Karamea Bight 151 B5 *gulf* South Island,
New Zealand
Karapelit 104 E1 *Rom.* Stejarul.
Dobrich, NE Bulgaria
Kara-Say 123 G2 Issyk-Kul'skaya
Oblast', NE Kyrgyzstan
Karasburg 78 B4 Karas, S Namibia
Kara Sea *see* Karskoye More
Kara Strait *see* Karskiye Vorota, Proliv
Karatau 114 C5 *Kaz.* Qarataū. Zhambyl,
S Kazakhstan
Karavás 105 B7 Kýthira, S Greece
Karbalā' 120 B3 *var.* Kerbala, Kerbela.
S Iraq
Kardeljevo *see* Ploče
Kardhítsa *see* Karditsa
Karditsa 105 B5 *var.* Kardhítsa.
Thessalía, C Greece
Kärdla 106 C2 *Ger.* Kertel. Hiiumaa,
W Estonia
Kärdžali *see* Kŭrdzhali
Karet *see* Kâghet
Kargı 116 C2 Çorum, N Turkey
Kargilik *see* Yecheng
Kariba 78 D2 Mashonaland West,
N Zimbabwe
Kariba, Lake 78 D3 *reservoir*
Zambia/Zimbabwe
Karibib 78 B3 Erongo, C Namibia
Karies *see* Karyés
Karigasniemi 84 D2 *Lapp.*
Garegegasnjárga. Lappi, N Finland
Karimata, Selat 138 C4 *strait*
W Indonesia
Karimnagar 134 D5 Andhra Pradesh,
C India
Karin 72 D4 Woqooyi Galbeed,
N Somalia
Kariot *see* Ikaria
Káristos *see* Kárystos
Karkinits'ka Zatoka 109 E4
Rus. Karkinitskiy Zaliv. *gulf*
S Ukraine

Karkinitskiy Zaliv *see* Karkinits'ka
Zatoka
Karkük *see* Kirkūk
Karleby *see* Kokkola
Karl-Marx-Stadt *see* Chemnitz
Karlö *see* Hailuoto
Karlovac 100 B3 *Ger.* Karlstadt, *Hung.*
Károlyváros. Karlovac, C Croatia
Karlovy Vary 99 A5 *Ger.* Karlsbad;
prev. Eng. Carlsbad. Karlovarský Kraj,
W Czech Republic
Karlsbad *see* Karlovy Vary
Karlsburg *see* Alba Iulia
Karlskrona 85 C7 Blekinge, S Sweden
Karlsruhe 95 B6 *var.* Carlsruhe.
Baden-Württemberg, SW Germany
Karlstad 85 B6 Värmland, C Sweden
Karlstadt *see* Karlovac
Karnāl 134 D2 Haryāna, N India
Karnātaka 132 C1 *var.* Kanara;
prev. Maisur, Mysore. *cultural region*
W India
Karnātaka 132 C1 *var.* Kanara;
prev. Maisur, Mysore. *state* W India
Karnobat 104 D2 Burgas, E Bulgaria
Karnul *see* Kurnool
Karol *see* Carei
Károly-Fehérvár *see* Alba Iulia
Károlyváros *see* Karlovac
Karpaten *see* Carpathian Mountains
Kárpathos 105 E7 Kárpathos, SE Greece
Kárpathos 105 E7 *It.* Scarpanto;
anc. Carpathos, Carpathus. *island*
SE Greece
Karpaty *see* Carpathian Mountains
Karpenísi 105 B5 *prev.* Karpenísion.
Stereá Ellás, C Greece
Karpenísion *see* Karpenísi
Karpilovka *see* Aktsyabrski
Kars 117 F2 *var.* Qars. Kars, NE Turkey
Karsau *see* Kārsava
Kārsava 106 D4 *Ger.* Karsau;
prev. Rus. Korsovka. Ludza,
E Latvia
Karshi *see* Qarshi, Uzbekistan
Karskiye Vorota, Proliv 110 E2 *Eng.*
Kara Strait. *strait* N Russian Federation
Karskoye More 114 D2 *Eng.* Kara Sea.
sea Arctic Ocean
Karyés 104 C4 *var.* Karies. Ágion Óros,
N Greece
Kárystos 105 C6 *var.* Káristos. Évvoia,
C Greece
Kasai 77 C6 *var.* Cassai, Kassai. *river*
Angola/Dem. Rep. Congo
Kasaji 77 D7 Katanga, S Dem. Rep.
Congo
Kasama 78 D1 Northern, N Zambia
Kasan *see* Koson
Käsaragod 132 B2 Kerala, SW India
Kaschau *see* Košice
Kāshān 120 C3 Eşfahān, C Iran
Kashgar *see* Kashi
Kashi 126 A3 *Chin.* Kaxgar, K'o-shih,
Uigh. Kashgar. Xinjiang Uygur Zizhiqu,
NW China
Kasi *see* Vārānasi
Kasongo 77 D6 Maniema, E Dem.
Rep. Congo
Kasongo-Lunda 77 C7 Bandundu,
SW Dem. Rep. Congo
Kásos 105 D7 *island* S Greece
Kaspiysk Mangy Oypaty *see* Caspian
Depression
Kaspiysk 111 B8 Respublika Dagestan,
SW Russian Federation
Kaspiyskoye More/Kaspiy Tengizi *see*
Caspian Sea
Kassa *see* Košice
Kassai *see* Kasai
Kassala 72 C4 Kassala, E Sudan
Kassel 94 B4 *prev.* Cassel. Hessen,
C Germany
Kasserine 71 E2 *var.* Al Qaşrayn.
W Tunisia
Kastamonu 116 C2 *var.* Castamoni,
Kastamuni. Kastamonu, N Turkey
Kastamuni *see* Kastamonu
Kastaneá 104 B4 Kentrikí Makedonía,
N Greece
Kastélli *see* Kíssamos
Kastoría 104 B4 Dytikí Makedonía,
N Greece
Kástro 105 C6 Sífnos, Kykládes, Greece,
Aegean Sea
Kastsyukovichy 107 E7 *Rus.*
Kostyukovichi. Mahilyowskaya
Voblasts', E Belarus

Kastsyukowka 107 D7 *Rus.*
Kostyukovka. Homyel'skaya Voblasts',
SE Belarus
Kasulu 73 B7 Kigoma, W Tanzania
Kasumiga-ura 131 D5 *lake* Honshū,
S Japan
Katahdin, Mount 41 G1 *mountain*
Maine, NE USA
Katalla 36 C3 Alaska, USA
Katana *see* Qatanā
Katanning 147 B7 Western Australia
Katawaz *see* Zarghūn Shahr
Katchall Island 133 F3 *island* Nicobar
Islands, India, NE Indian Ocean
Kateríni 104 B4 Kentrikí Makedonía,
N Greece
Katha 136 B2 Sagaing,
N Myanmar (Burma)
Katherine 148 A2 Northern Territory,
N Australia
Kathmandu 124 C3 *prev.* Kantipur.
country capital (Nepal) Central,
C Nepal
Katikati 150 D3 Bay of Plenty, North
Island, New Zealand
Katima Mulilo 78 C3 Caprivi,
NE Namibia
Katiola 74 D4 C Côte d'Ivoire (Ivory
Coast)
Káto Achaḯa 105 B5 *var.* Kato Ahaia,
Káto Akhaḯa. Dytikí Ellás, S Greece
Kato Ahaia/Káto Akhaḯa *see* Káto Achaḯa
Katoúna 105 A5 Dytikí Ellás, C Greece
Katowice 99 C5 *Ger.* Kattowitz. Śląskie,
S Poland
Katsina 75 G3 Katsina, N Nigeria
Kattakurgan *see* Kattaqo'rg'on
Kattaqo'rg'on 123 E2 *Rus.* Kattakurgan.
Samarqand Viloyati, C Uzbekistan
Kattavía 105 E7 Ródos, Dodekánisa,
Greece, Aegean Sea
Kattegat 85 B7 *Dan.* Kattegatt. *strait*
N Europe
Kattegatt *see* Kattegat
Kattowitz *see* Katowice
Kaua'i 47 A7 *var.* Kauai. *island*
Hawaiian Islands, Hawai'i, USA,
C PacificOcean
Kauai *see* Kaua'i
Kauen *see* Kaunas
Kaufbeuren 95 C6 Bayern, S Germany
Kaunas 106 B4 *Ger.* Kauen, *Pol.* Kowno;
prev. Rus. Kovno. Kaunas, C Lithuania
Kavadar *see* Kavadarci
Kavadarci 101 E6 *Turk.* Kavadar.
C Macedonia
Kavaja *see* Kavajë
Kavajë 101 C6 *It.* Cavaia, Kavaja.
Tiranë, W Albania
Kavakli *see* Topolovgrad
Kavála 104 C3 *prev.* Kaválla. Anatolikí
Makedonía kai Thráki, NE Greece
Kāvali 132 D2 Andhra Pradesh,
E India
Kaválla *see* Kavála
Kavango *see* Cubango/Okavango
Kavaratti Island 132 A3 *island*
Lakshadweep, Lakshadweep,
SW India Asia N Indian Ocean
Kavarna 104 E2 Dobrich, NE Bulgaria
Kavengo *see* Cubango/Okavango
Kavír, Dasht-e 120 D3 *var.* Great Salt
Desert. *salt pan* N Iran
Kavkaz *see* Caucasus
Kawagoe 131 D5 Saitama, Honshū,
S Japan
Kawasaki 130 A2 Kanagawa, Honshū,
S Japan
Kawerau 150 E3 Bay of Plenty, North
Island, New Zealand
Kaxgar *see* Kashi
Kaya 75 E3 C Burkina Faso
Kayan 136 B4 Yangon,
SW Myanmar (Burma)
Kayan, Sungai 138 D3 *prev.* Kajan. *river*
Borneo, C Indonesia
Kayes 74 C3 Kayes, W Mali
Kayseri 116 D3 *var.* Kaisaria; *anc.*
Caesarea Mazaca, Mazaca. Kayseri,
C Turkey
Kazach'ye 115 F2 Respublika Sakha
(Yakutiya), NE Russian Federation
**Kazakhskaya SSR/Kazakh Soviet
Socialist Republic** *see* Kazakhstan
Kazakhskiy Melkosopochnik 114 C4
Eng. Kazakh Uplands, Kirghiz
Steppe, *Kaz.* Saryarqa. *uplands*
C Kazakhstan

Kazakhstan 114 B4 *off.* Republic of
Kazakhstan, *var.* Kazakstan, *Kaz.*
Qazaqstan, Qazaqstan Respublikasy;
prev. Kazakh Soviet Socialist Republic,
Rus. Kazakhskaya SSR. *country* C Asia

KAZAKHSTAN
Central Asia

Official name Republic of Kazakhstan
Formation 1991 / 1991
Capital Astana
Population 14.8 million / 14 people per sq
mile (5 people per sq km) / 56%
Total area 1,049,150 sq miles (2,717,300
sq km)
Languages Kazakh*, Russian*, Ukrainian,
Tatar, German, Uzbek, Uighur
Religions Muslim (mainly Sunni) 47%,
Orthodox Christian 44%, Other 9%
Ethnic mix Kazakh 53%, Russian 30%,
Other 9%, Ukrainian 4%, Tatar 2%,
German 2%
Government Presidential system
Currency Tenge = 100 tiyn
Literacy rate 99%
Calorie consumption 2677 calories

Kazakhstan, Republic of *see* Kazakhstan
Kazakh Uplands *see* Kazakhskiy
Melkosopochnik
Kazakstan *see* Kazakhstan
Kazan' 111 C5 Respublika Tatarstan,
W Russian Federation
Kazandzhik *see* Bereket
Kazanlik *see* Kazanlŭk
Kazanlŭk 104 D2 *prev.* Kazanlik. Stara
Zagorat, C Bulgaria
Kazatin *see* Kozyatyn
Kazbegi *see* Kazbek
Kazbek 117 F1 *var.* Kazbegi, *Geor.*
Mqinvartsveri. *mountain* N Georgia
Kāzerūn 120 D4 Fārs, S Iran
Kazi Magomed *see* Qazimämmäd
Kazvin *see* Qazvin
Kéa *see* Tziá
Kéa *see* Ioulís
Kea, Mauna 47 B8 *mountain* Hawaii,
USA
Kéamu *see* Aneityum
Kearney 45 E4 Nebraska, C USA
Keban Baraji 117 E3 *reservoir*
C Turkey
Kebkabiya 72 A4 Northern Darfur,
W Sudan
Kebnekaise 84 C3 *mountain* N Sweden
Kecskemét 99 D7 Bács-Kiskun,
C Hungary
Kediri 138 D5 Jawa, C Indonesia
Kędzierzyn-Kozle 99 C5 *Ger.*
Heydebrech. Opolskie, S Poland
Keelung *see* Chilung
Keetmanshoop 78 B4 Karas,
S Namibia
Kefallinía *see* Kefalloniá
Kefalloniá 105 A5 *var.* Kefallinía.
island Iónioi Nísoi, Greece,
C Mediterranean Sea
Kefe *see* Feodosiya
Kegel *see* Keila
Kehl 95 A6 Baden-Württemberg,
SW Germany
Kei Islands *see* Kai, Kepulauan
Keijo *see* Sŏul
Keila 106 D2 *Ger.* Kegel. Harjumaa,
NW Estonia
Keita 75 F3 Tahoua, C Niger
Keitele 84 D4 *lake* C Finland
Keith 149 B7 South Australia
Kēk-Art 123 D2 *prev.* Alaykel',
Alay-Kuu. Oshskaya Oblast',
SW Kyrgyzstan
Kékes 99 C6 *mountain* N Hungary
Kelamayi *see* Karamay
Kelang *see* Klang
Kelat *see* Kālāt
Kelifskiy Uzboy *see* Kelifskiy Uzboýy
Kelifskiy Uzboýy 122 D3 *Rus.* Kelifskiy
Uzboy. *salt marsh* Lebap Welaýaty,
E Turkmenistan
Kelkit Çayı 117 E3 *river* N Turkey
Kelmė 106 B4 Šiauliai, C Lithuania
Kélo 76 B4 Tandjilé, SW Chad
Kelowna 37 E5 British Columbia,
SW Canada
Kelso 46 B2 Washington,
NW USA
Keltsy *see* Kielce

Keluang 138 B3 *var.* Kluang. Johor,
Peninsular Malaysia
Kem' 110 B3 Respublika Kareliya,
NW Russian Federation
Kemah 117 E3 Erzincan, E Turkey
Kemaman *see* Cukai
Kemerovo 114 D4 *prev.* Shcheglovsk.
Kemerovskaya Oblast', C Russian
Federation
Kemi 84 D4 Lappi, NW Finland
Kemijärvi 84 D3 *Swe.* Kemiträsk.
Lappi, N Finland
Kemijoki 84 D3 *river* NW Finland
Kemin 123 G2 *prev.* Bystrovka.
Chuyskaya Oblast', N Kyrgyzstan
Kemins Island *see* Nikumaroro
Kemiträsk *see* Kemijärvi
Kemmuna *see* Comino
Kempele 84 D4 Oulu, C Finland
Kempten 95 B7 Bayern, S Germany
Kendal 89 D5 NW England, UK
Kendari 139 E4 Sulawesi, C Indonesia
Kenedy 49 G4 Texas, SW USA
Kenema 74 C4 SE Sierra Leone
Këneurgench *see* Këneurgench
Kenge 77 C6 Bandundu, SW Dem.
Rep. Congo
Keng Tung 136 C3 *var.* Kentung. Shan
State, E Myanmar (Burma)
Kénitra 70 C2 *prev.* Port-Lyautey.
NW Morocco
Kennett 45 H5 Missouri, C USA
Kennewick 46 C2 Washington,
NW USA
Kenora 38 A3 Ontario, S Canada
Kenosha 40 B3 Wisconsin, N USA
Kentau 114 B5 Yuzhnyy Kazakhstan,
S Kazakhstan
Kentucky 40 C5 *off.* Commonwealth
of Kentucky, *also known as* Bluegrass
State. *state* C USA
Kentucky Lake 40 B5 *reservoir*
Kentucky/Tennessee, S USA
Kentung *see* Keng Tung
Kenya 73 C6 *off.* Republic of Kenya.
country E Africa

KENYA
East Africa

Official name Republic of Kenya
Formation 1963 / 1963
Capital Nairobi
Population 34.3 million / 157 people per
sq mile (60 people per sq km) / 33%
Total area 224,961 sq miles (582,650
sq km)
Languages Swahili*, English*, Kikuyu,
Luo, Kalenjin, Kamba
Religions Christian 60%, Traditional
beliefs 25%, Other 9%, Muslim 6%
Ethnic mix Other 30%, Kikuyu 21%,
Luhya 14%, Luo 13%, Kalenjin 11%,
Kamba 11%
Government Presidential system
Currency Kenya shilling = 100 cents
Literacy rate 74%
Calorie consumption 2090 calories

Kenya, Mount *see* Kirinyaga
Kenya, Republic of *see* Kenya
Keokuk 45 G4 Iowa, C USA
Kéos *see* Tziá
Kępno 98 C4 Wielkopolskie,
C Poland
Keppel Island *see* Niuatoputapu
Kerak *see* Al Karak
Kerala 132 C2 *cultural region* S India
Kerala 132 C2 *state* S India
Kerasunt *see* Giresun
Keratéa 105 C6 *var.* Keratea. Attikí,
C Greece
Keratea *see* Keratéa
Kerbala/Kerbela *see* Karbalā'
Kerch 109 G5 *Rus.* Kerch'. Respublika
Krym, SE Ukraine
Kerch' *see* Kerch
**Kerchens'ka Protska/Kerchenskiy
Proliv** *see* Kerch Strait
Kerch Strait 109 G4 *var.* Bosporus
Cimmerius, Enikale Strait, *Rus.*
Kerchenskiy Proliv, *Ukr.* Kerchens'ka
Protska. *strait* Black Sea/Sea of Azov
Keremitlik *see* Lyulyakovo
Kerguelen 141 C7 *island* C French
Southern and Antarctic Territories
Kerguelen Plateau 141 C7 *undersea
plateau* S Indian Ocean

Kerí 105 A6 Zákynthos, Iónioi Nísoi,
Greece, C Mediterranean Sea
Kerikeri 150 D2 Northland, North
Island, New Zealand
Kerkenah, Îles de 102 D4 *var.* Kerkenna
Islands, *Ar.* Juzur Qarqannah. *island
group* E Tunisia
Kerkenna Islands *see* Kerkenah,
Îles de
Kerki *see* Atamyrat
Kerkrade 87 D6 Limburg,
SE Netherlands
Kerkuk *see* Kirkūk
Kérkyra 104 A4 *var.* Kérkira, *Eng.*
Corfu. *island* Iónioi Nísoi, Greece,
C Mediterranean Sea
Kermadec Islands 152 C4 *island group*
New Zealand, SW Pacific Ocean
Kermadec Trench 143 E4 *trench*
SW Pacific Ocean
Kermān 120 D3 *var.* Kirman; *anc.*
Carmana. Kermān, C Iran
Kermānshāh 120 C3 *var.*
Qahremānshahr; *prev.* Bākhtarān.
Kermānshāhān, W Iran
Kerrville 49 F4 Texas, SW USA
Kertel *see* Kärdla
Kerulen 127 E2 *Chin.* Herlen He,
Mong. Herlen Gol. *river*
China/Mongolia
Kerýneia *see* Girne
Kesennuma 130 D4 Miyagi, Honshū,
C Japan
Keszthely 99 C7 Zala, SW Hungary
Ketchikan 36 D4 Revillagigedo Island,
Alaska, USA
Kętrzyn 98 D2 *Ger.* Rastenburg.
Warmińsko-Mazurskie, NE Poland
Kettering 89 D6 C England, UK
Kettering 40 C4 Ohio, N USA
Keupriya *see* Primorsko
Keuruu 85 D5 Länsi-Soumi, C Finland
Keweenaw Peninsula 40 B1 *peninsula*
Michigan, N USA
Key Largo 43 F5 Key Largo, Florida,
SE USA
Keystone State *see* Pennsylvania
Key West 43 E5 Florida Keys, Florida,
SE USA
Kezdivásárhely *see* Târgu Secuiesc
Khabarovsk 115 G4 Khabarovskiy Kray,
SE Russian Federation
Khachmas *see* Xaçmaz
Khadera *see* Ḥadera
Khairpur 134 B3 Sind, SE Pakistan
Khalij-e Fars *see* Gulf, The
Khalkidhikí *see* Chalkidikí
Khalkís *see* Chalkída
Khambhāt, Gulf of 134 C4
Eng. Gulf of Cambay. *gulf*
W India
Khamis Mushayt 121 B6
var. Hamis Musait. 'Asīr,
SW Saudi Arabia
Khānābād 123 E3 Kunduz,
NE Afghanistan
Khān al Baghdādī *see* Al Baghdādī
Khandwa 134 D4 Madhya Pradesh,
C India
Khanh Hung *see* Soc Trăng
Khaniá *see* Chaniá
Khanka, Lake 129 E2 *var.* Hsing-K'ai
Hu, Lake Hanka, *Chin.* Xingkai Hu,
Rus. Ozero Khanka. *lake* China/
Russian Federation
Khanka, Ozero *see* Khanka, Lake
Khankendi *see* Xankändi
Khanthabouli 136 D4 *var.* Savannakhét.
S Laos
Khanty-Mansiysk 114 C3 *prev.*
Ostyako-Voguls'k. Khanty-Mansiyskiy
Avtonomnyy Okrug, C Russian
Federation
Khān Yūnis 119 A7 *var.* Khān Yūnus.
S Gaza Strip
Khān Yūnus *see* Khān Yūnis
Khanzi *see* Ghanzi
Kharagpur 135 F4 West Bengal,
NE India
Kharbin *see* Harbin
Kharkiv 109 G2 *Rus.* Khar'kov.
Kharkivs'ka Oblast', NE Ukraine
Khar'kov *see* Kharkiv
Kharmanli 104 D3 Khaskovo,
S Bulgaria
Khartoum 72 B4 *var.* El Khartûm,
Khartum. *country capital* (Sudan)
Khartoum, C Sudan

Khartum see Khartoum
Khasavyurt 111 B8 Respublika Dagestan, SW Russian Federation
Khâsh, Dasht-e 122 D5 Eng. Khash Desert. desert SW Afghanistan
Khash Desert see Khâsh, Dasht-e
Khashim Al Qirba/Khashm al Qirbah see Khashm el Girba
Khashm el Girba 72 C4 var. Khashim Al Qirba, Khashm al Qirbah. Kassala, E Sudan
Khaskovo 104 D3 Khaskovo, S Bulgaria
Khaybar, Kowtal-e see Khyber Pass
Khaydarkan 123 F2 var. Khaydarken. Batkenskaya Oblast', SW Kyrgyzstan
Khaydarken see Khaydarkan
Khazar, Baḩr-e/Khazar, Daryā-ye see Caspian Sea
Khelat see Kalāt
Kherson 109 E4 Khersons'ka Oblast', S Ukraine
Kheta 115 E2 river N Russian Federation
Khíos see Chíos
Khirbet el 'Aujā et Taḩtā 119 E7 E West Bank Asia
Khiva/Khiwa see Xiva
Khmel'nitskiy see Khmel 'nyts'kyy
Khmel 'nyts'kyy 108 C2 Rus. Khmel'nitskiy; prev. Proskurov. Khmel'nyts'ka Oblast', W Ukraine
Khodasy 107 E6 Rus. Khodosy. Mahilyowskaya Voblasts', E Belarus
Khodoriv 108 C2 Pol. Chodorów, Rus. Khodorov. L'vivs'ka Oblast', NW Ukraine
Khodorov see Khodoriv
Khodosy see Khodasy
Khodzhent see Khŭjand
Khoi see Khvoy
Khojend see Khŭjand
Khokand see Qo'qon
Kholm 123 E3 var. Tashqurghan, Pash. Khulm. Balkh, N Afghanistan
Kholm see Chełm
Kholon see Ḩolon
Khoms see Al Khums
Khong Sedone see Muang Khôngxédôn
Khon Kaen 136 D4 var. Muang Khon Kaen. Khon Kaen, E Thailand
Khor 115 G4 Khabarovskiy Kray, SE Russian Federation
Khorat see Nakhon Ratchasima
Khorog see Khorugh
Khorugh 123 F3 Rus. Khorog. S Tajikistan
Khotan see Hotan
Khouribga 70 B2 C Morocco
Khovd see Hovd
Khowst 123 F4 Khowst, E Afghanistan
Khoy see Khvoy
Khoyniki 107 D8 Rus. Khoyniki. Homyel'skaya Voblasts', SE Belarus
Khudzhand see Khŭjand
Khŭjand 123 E2 var. Khodzhent, Khojend, Rus. Khudzhand; prev. Leninabad, Taj. Leninobod. N Tajikistan
Khulm see Kholm
Khulna 135 G4 Khulna, SW Bangladesh
Khums see Al Khums
Khust 108 B3 Cz. Chust, var. Husté, Hung. Huszt. Zakarpats'ka Oblast', W Ukraine
Khvoy 120 C2 var. Khoi, Khoy. Āzarbāyjān-e Bākhtari, NW Iran
Khyber Pass 134 C1 var. Kowtal-e Khaybar. pass Afghanistan/Pakistan
Kiangmai see Chiang Mai
Kiang-ning see Nanjing
Kiangsi see Jiangxi
Kiangsu see Jiangsu
Kiáto 105 B6 prev. Kiáton. Pelopónnisos, S Greece
Kiáton see Kiáto
Kiayi see Chiai
Kibangou 77 B6 Le Niari, SW Congo
Kibombo 77 D6 Maniema, E Dem. Rep. Congo
Kičevo 101 D6 SW FYR Macedonia
Kidderminster 89 D6 C England, UK
Kiel 94 B2 Schleswig-Holstein, N Germany
Kielce 98 D4 Rus. Keltsy. Świętokrzyskie, C Poland

Kieler Bucht 94 B2 bay N Germany
Kiev see Kyyiv
Kiev Reservoir see Kyyivs'ke Vodoskhovyshche
Kiffa 74 C3 Assaba, S Mauritania
Kigali 73 B6 country capital (Rwanda) C Rwanda
Kigoma 73 B7 Kigoma, W Tanzania
Kihnu 106 C2 var. Kihnu Saar, Ger. Kühnö. island SW Estonia
Kihnu Saar see Kihnu
Kii-suidō 131 C7 strait S Japan
Kikinda 100 D3 Ger. Grosskikinda, Hung. Nagykikinda; prev. Velika Kikinda. Vojvodina, N Serbia
Kikládhes see Kykládes
Kikwit 77 C6 Bandundu, W Dem. Rep. Congo
Kilien Mountains see Qilian Shan
Kilimane see Quelimane
Kilimanjaro 69 E5 region E Tanzania
Kilimanjaro 73 C7 var. Uhuru Peak. volcano NE Tanzania
Kilingi-Nōmme 106 D3 Ger. Kurkund. Pärnumaa, SW Estonia
Kilis 116 D4 Kilis, S Turkey
Kiliya 108 D4 Rom. Chilia-Nouă. Odes'ka Oblast', SW Ukraine
Kilkenny 89 B6 Ir. Cill Chainnigh. Kilkenny, S Ireland
Kilkís 104 B3 Kentrikí Makedonía, N Greece
Killarney 89 A6 Ir. Cill Airne. Kerry, SW Ireland
Killeen 49 G3 Texas, SW USA
Kilmain see Quelimane
Kilmarnock 88 C4 W Scotland, UK
Kilwa see Kilwa Kivinje
Kilwa Kivinje 73 C7 var. Kilwa. Lindi, SE Tanzania
Kimberley 78 C4 Northern Cape, C South Africa
Kimberley Plateau 146 C3 plateau Western Australia
Kimch'aek 129 E3 prev. Sŏngjin. E North Korea
Kinabalu, Gunung 138 D3 mountain East Malaysia
Kindersley 37 F5 Saskatchewan, S Canada
Kindia 74 C4 Guinée-Maritime, SW Guinea
Kindley Field 42 A4 air base E Bermuda
Kindu 77 D6 prev. Kindu-Port-Empain. Maniema, C Dem. Rep. Congo
Kindu-Port-Empain see Kindu
Kineshma 111 C5 Ivanovskaya Oblast', W Russian Federation
King Charles Islands see Kong Karls Land
King Christian IX Land see Kong Christian IX Land
King Frederik VI Coast see Kong Frederik VI Kyst
King Frederik VIII Land see Kong Frederik VIII Land
King Island 149 B8 island Tasmania, SE Australia
King Island see Kadan Kyun
Kingissepp see Kuressaare
Kingman 48 A1 Arizona, SW USA
Kingman Reef 145 F2 US territory C Pacific Ocean
Kingsford Smith 148 E2 (Sydney) New South Wales, SE Australia
King's Lynn 89 E6 var. Bishop's Lynn, Kings Lynn, Lynn, Lynn Regis. E England, UK
Kings Lynn see King's Lynn
King Sound 146 B3 sound Western Australia
Kingsport 43 E1 Tennessee, S USA
Kingston 54 B5 country capital (Jamaica) E Jamaica
Kingston 38 D5 Ontario, SE Canada
Kingston 41 F3 New York, NE USA
Kingston upon Hull 89 D5 var. Hull. E England, UK
Kingston upon Thames 89 A8 SE England, UK
Kingstown 55 H4 country capital (Saint Vincent and the Grenadines) Saint Vincent, Saint Vincent and the Grenadines

Kingstown see Dún Laoghaire
Kingsville 49 G5 Texas, SW USA
King William Island 37 F3 island Nunavut, N Canada Arctic Ocean
Kinneret, Yam see Tiberias, Lake
Kinrooi 87 D5 Limburg, NE Belgium
Kinshasa 77 B6 prev. Léopoldville. country capital (Dem. Rep. Congo) Kinshasa, W Dem. Rep. Congo
Kintyre 88 B4 peninsula W Scotland, UK
Kinyeti 73 B5 mountain S Sudan
Kiparissía see Kyparissía
Kípili 73 B7 Rukwa, W Tanzania
Kipushi 77 D8 Katanga, SE Dem. Rep. Congo
Kirdzhali see Kŭrdzhali
Kirghizia see Kyrgyzstan
Kirghiz Range 123 F2 Rus. Kirgizskiy Khrebet; prev. Alexander Range. mountain range Kazakhstan/Kyrgyzstan
Kirghiz SSR see Kyrgyzstan
Kirghiz Steppe see Kazakhskiy Melkosopochnik
Kirgizskaya SSR see Kyrgyzstan
Kirgizskiy Khrebet see Kirghiz Range
Kiriath-Arba see Hebron
Kiribati 145 F2 off. Republic of Kiribati. country C Pacific Ocean

KIRIBATI
Australasia & Oceania

Official name	Republic of Kiribati
Formation	1979 / 1979
Capital	Bairiki (Tarawa Atoll)
Population	103,092 / 376 people per sq mile (145 people per sq km) / 36%
Total area	277 sq miles (717 sq km)
Languages	English*, Kiribati
Religions	Roman Catholic 53%, Kiribati Protestant Church 39%, Other 8%
Ethnic mix	Micronesian 96%, Other 4%
Government	Nonparty system
Currency	Australian dollar = 100 cents
Literacy rate	99%
Calorie consumption	2859 calories

Kiribati, Republic of see Kiribati
Kırıkhan 116 D4 Hatay, S Turkey
Kırıkkale 116 C3 province C Turkey
Kirin see Jilin
Kirinyaga 73 C6 prev. Mount Kenya. volcano C Kenya
Kirishi 110 B4 var. Kirisi. Leningradskaya Oblast', NW Russian Federation
Kirisi see Kirishi
Kiritimati 145 G2 prev. Christmas Island. atoll Line Islands, E Kiribati
Kirkenes 84 E2 Fin. Kirkkoniemi. Finnmark, N Norway
Kirk-Kilissa see Kırklareli
Kirkkoniemi see Kirkenes
Kirkland Lake 38 D4 Ontario, S Canada
Kırklareli 116 A2 prev. Kirk-Kilissa. Kırklareli, NW Turkey
Kirkpatrick, Mount 154 B3 mountain Antarctica
Kirksville 45 G4 Missouri, C USA
Kirkūk 120 B3 var. Karkūk, Kerkuk. N Iraq
Kirkwall 88 C2 NE Scotland, UK
Kirkwood 45 G4 Missouri, C USA
Kir of Moab see Al Karak
Kir of Moab see Al Karak
Kirov 111 C5 prev. Vyatka. Kirovskaya Oblast', NW Russian Federation
Kirovabad see Gäncä
Kirovakan see Vanadzor
Kirovo-Chepetsk 111 D5 Kirovskaya Oblast', NW Russian Federation
Kirovohrad 109 E3 Rus. Kirovograd; prev. Kirovo, Yelizavetgrad, Zinov'yevsk. Kirovohrads'ka Oblast', C Ukraine
Kirovo/Kirovograd see Kirovohrad
Kirthar Range 134 B3 mountain range S Pakistan
Kiruna 84 C3 Lapp. Giron. Norrbotten, N Sweden
Kirun/Kirun' see Chilung

Kisalföld see Little Alföld
Kisangani 77 D5 prev. Stanleyville. Orientale, NE Dem. Rep. Congo
Kishinev see Chişinău
Kislovodsk 111 B7 Stavropol'skiy Kray, SW Russian Federation
Kismaayo 73 D6 var. Chisimayu, Kismayu, It. Chisimaio. Jubbada Hoose, S Somalia
Kismayu see Kismaayo
Kíssamos 105 C7 prev Kastélli. Kríti, Greece, E Mediterranean Sea
Kissidougou 74 C4 Guinée-Forestière, S Guinea
Kissimmee, Lake 43 E4 lake Florida, SE USA
Kistna see Krishna
Kisumu 73 C6 prev. Port Florence. Nyanza, W Kenya
Kisvárda 99 E6 Ger. Kleinwardein. Szabolcs-Szatmár-Bereg, E Hungary
Kita 74 D3 Kayes, W Mali
Kitab see Kitob
Kitakyūshū 131 A7 var. Kitakyûsyû. Fukuoka, Kyūshū, SW Japan
Kitakyûsyû see Kitakyūshū
Kitami 130 D2 Hokkaidō, NE Japan
Kitchener 38 C5 Ontario, S Canada
Kíthnos see Kýthnos
Kitimat 36 D4 British Columbia, SW Canada
Kitinen 84 D3 river N Finland
Kitob 123 E3 Rus. Kitab. Qashqadaryo Viloyati, S Uzbekistan
Kitwe 78 D2 var. Kitwe-Nkana. Copperbelt, C Zambia
Kitwe-Nkana see Kitwe
Kitzbüheler Alpen 95 C7 mountain range W Austria
Kivalina 36 C2 Alaska, USA
Kivalo 84 D3 ridge C Finland
Kivertsi 108 C1 Pol. Kiwerce, Rus. Kivertsy. Volyns'ka Oblast', NW Ukraine
Kivertsy see Kivertsi
Kivu, Lac see Kivu, Lake
Kivu, Lake 77 E6 Fr. Lac Kivu. lake Rwanda/Dem. Rep. Congo
Kiwerce see Kivertsi
Kiyev see Kyyiv
Kiyevskoye Vodokhranilishche see Kyyivs'ke Vodoskhovyshche
Kızıl Irmak 116 C3 river C Turkey
Kizil Kum see Kyzyl Kum
Kizyl-Arvat see Serdar
Kladno 99 A5 Střední Čechy, NW Czech Republic
Klagenfurt 95 D7 Slvn. Celovec. Kärnten, S Austria
Klaipėda 106 B3 Ger. Memel. Klaipėda, NW Lithuania
Klamath Falls 46 B4 Oregon, NW USA
Klamath Mountains 46 A4 mountain range California/Oregon, W USA
Klang 138 B3 var. Kelang; prev. Port Swettenham. Selangor, Peninsular Malaysia
Klarälven 85 B6 river Norway/Sweden
Klatovy 99 A5 Ger. Klattau. Plzeňský Kraj, W Czech Republic
Klattau see Klatovy
Klausenburg see Cluj-Napoca
Klazienaveen 86 E2 Drenthe, NE Netherlands
Kleines Ungarisches Tiefland see Little Alföld
Klein Karas 78 B4 Karas, S Namibia
Kleinwardein see Kisvárda
Kleisoúra 105 A5 Ípeiros, W Greece
Klerksdorp 78 D4 North-West, N South Africa
Klimavichy 107 E7 Rus. Klimovichi. Mahilyowskaya Voblasts', E Belarus
Klimovichi see Klimavichy
Klintsy 111 A5 Bryanskaya Oblast', W Russian Federation
Klisura 104 C2 Plovdiv, C Bulgaria
Ključ 100 B3 Federacija Bosna I Hercegovina, NW Bosnia and Herzegovina
Klobuck 98 C4 Śląskie, S Poland
Klosters 95 B7 Graubünden, SE Switzerland

Kluang *see* Keluang
Kluczbork 98 C4 *Ger.* Kreuzburg, Kreuzburg in Oberschlesien. Opolskie, S Poland
Klyuchevskaya Sopka, Vulkan 115 H3 *volcano* E Russian Federation
Knin 100 B4 Šibenik-Knin, S Croatia
Knjaževac 100 E4 Serbia, E Serbia
Knokke-Heist 87 A5 West-Vlaanderen, NW Belgium
Knoxville 42 D1 Tennessee, S USA
Knud Rasmussen Land 82 D1 *physical region* N Greenland
Kobdo *see* Hovd
Kōbe 131 C6 Hyōgo, Honshū, SW Japan
København 85 B7 *Eng.* Copenhagen; *anc.* Hafnia. *country capital* (Denmark) Sjælland, København, E Denmark
Kobenni 74 D3 Hodh el Gharbi, S Mauritania
Koblenz 95 A5 *prev.* Coblenz, *Fr.* Coblence; *anc.* Confluentes. Rheinland-Pfalz, W Germany
Kobrin *see* Kobryn
Kobryn 107 A6 *Pol.* Kobryn, *Rus.* Kobrin. Brestskaya Voblasts', SW Belarus
K'obulet'i 117 F2 W Georgia
Kočani 101 E6 NE FYR Macedonia
Kočevje 95 D8 *Ger.* Gottschee. S Slovenia
Koch Bihār 135 G3 West Bengal, NE India
Kōchi 131 B7 *var.* Kôti. Kôchi, Shikoku, SW Japan
Kochi *see* Cochin
Kochiu *see* Gejiu
Kodiak 36 C3 Kodiak Island, Alaska, USA
Kodiak Island 36 C3 *island* Alaska, USA
Koedoes *see* Kudus
Koeln *see* Köln
Koepang *see* Kupang
Ko-erh-mu *see* Golmud
Koetai *see* Mahakam, Sungai
Koetaradja *see* Bandaaceh
Kōfu 131 D5 *var.* Kôhu. Yamanashi, Honshū, S Japan
Kogarah 148 E2 New South Wales, E Australia
Kogon 122 D4 *Rus.* Kagan. Buxoro Viloyati, C Uzbekistan
Kôhalom *see* Rupea
Kohima 135 H3 *state capital* Nāgāland, E India
Koh I Noh *see* Büyükağrı Dağı
Kohtla-Järve 106 E2 Ida-Virumaa, NE Estonia
Kôhu *see* Kôfu
Kokand *see* Qo'qon
Kokchetav *see* Kokshetau
Kokkola 84 D4 *Swe.* Karleby; *prev.* Swe. Gamlakarleby. Länsi-Soumi, W Finland
Koko 75 F4 Kebbi, W Nigeria
Kokomo 40 C4 Indiana, N USA
Koko Nor *see* Qinghai, China
Koko Nor *see* Qinghai Hu, China
Kokrines 36 C2 Alaska, USA
Kokshaal-Tau 123 G2 *Rus.* Khrebet Kakshaal-Too. *mountain range* China/Kyrgyzstan
Kokshetau 114 C4 *Kaz.* Kökshetaü; *prev.* Kokchetav. Kokshetau, N Kazakhstan
Kökshetaü *see* Kokshetau
Koksijde 87 A5 West-Vlaanderen, W Belgium
Koksoak 39 E2 *river* Québec, C Canada
Kokstad 78 D5 KwaZulu/Natal, S South Africa
Kolaka 139 E4 Sulawesi, C Indonesia
Kolam *see* Quilon
K'o-la-ma-i *see* Karamay
Kola Peninsula *see* Kol'skiy Poluostrov
Kolari 84 D3 Lappi, NW Finland
Kolárovo 99 C6 *Ger.* Gutta; *prev.* Guta, *Hung.* Gúta. Nitriansky Kraj, SW Slovakia
Kolberg *see* Kołobrzeg
Kolda 74 C3 S Senegal
Kolding 85 A7 Vejle, C Denmark
Kölen 81 E1 *mountain range* Norway/Sweden
Kolguyev, Ostrov 110 C2 *island* NW Russian Federation

Kolhāpur 132 B1 Mahārāshtra, SW India
Kolhumadulu Atoll 132 A5 *atoll* S Maldives
Kolín 99 B5 *Ger.* Kolin. Středni Čechy, C Czech Republic
Kolka 106 C2 Talsi, NW Latvia
Kolkasrags 106 C2 *prev. Eng.* Cape Domesnes. *cape* NW Latvia
Kolkata 135 G4 *prev.* Calcutta. West Bengal, N India
Kollam *see* Quilon
Kolmar *see* Colmar
Köln 94 A4 *var.* Koeln, *Eng./Fr.* Cologne, *prev.* Cöln; *anc.* Colonia Agrippina, Oppidum Ubiorum. Nordrhein-Westfalen, W Germany
Koło 98 C3 Wielkopolskie, C Poland
Kołobrzeg 98 B2 *Ger.* Kolberg. Zachodnio-pomorskie, NW Poland
Kolokani 74 D3 Koulikoro, W Mali
Kolomea *see* Kolomyya
Kolomna 111 B5 Moskovskaya Oblast', W Russian Federation
Kolomyya 108 C3 *Ger.* Kolomea. Ivano-Frankivs'ka Oblast', W Ukraine
Kolozsvár *see* Cluj-Napoca
Kolpa 100 A2 *var.* Kulpa, *SCr.* Kupa. *river* Croatia/Slovenia
Kolpino 110 B4 Leningradskaya Oblast', NW Russian Federation
Kol'skiy Poluostrov 110 C2 *Eng.* Kola Peninsula. *peninsula* NW Russian Federation
Kolwezi 77 D7 Katanga, S Dem. Rep. Congo
Kolyma 115 G2 *river* NE Russian Federation
Komatsu 131 C5 *var.* Komatu. Ishikawa, Honshū, SW Japan
Komatu *see* Komatsu
Kommunizm, Qullai 123 F3 *mountain* E Tajikistan
Komoé 75 E4 *var.* Komoé Fleuve. *river* E Côte d'Ivoire (Ivory Coast)
Komoé Fleuve *see* Komoé
Komotau *see* Chomutov
Komotiní 104 D3 *var.* Gümüljina, *Turk.* Gümülcine. Anatolikí Makedonía kai Thráki, NE Greece
Kompong *see* Kâmpóng Chhnäng
Kompong Cham *see* Kâmpóng Cham
Kompong Som *see* Kâmpóng Saôm
Kompong Speu *see* Kâmpóng Spœ
Komrat *see* Comrat
Komsomolets, Ostrov 115 E1 *island* Severnaya Zemlya, N Russian Federation
Komsomol'sk-na-Amure 115 G4 Khabarovskiy Kray, SE Russian Federation
Kondolovo 104 E3 Burgas, E Bulgaria
Kondopoga 110 B3 Respublika Kareliya, NW Russian Federation
Kondoz 123 E3 *Pash.* Kunduz. *province* NE Afghanistan
Këneurgench 122 C2 *var.* Köneürgench, *Rus.* Këneurgench; *prev.* Kunya-Urgench. Daşoguz Welaýaty, N Turkmenistan
Köneürgench *see* Këneurgench
Kong Christian IX Land 82 D4 *Eng.* King Christian IX Land. *physical region* SE Greenland
Kong Frederik IX Land 82 C3 *physical region* SW Greenland
Kong Frederik VIII Land 83 E2 *Eng.* King Frederik VIII Land. *physical region* NE Greenland
Kong Frederik VI Kyst 82 C4 *Eng.* King Frederik VI Coast. *physical region* SE Greenland
Kong Karls Land 83 G2 *Eng.* King Charles Islands. *island group* SE Svalbard
Kongo *see* Congo (river)
Kongolo 77 D6 Katanga, E Dem. Rep. Congo
Kongor 73 B5 Jonglei, SE Sudan
Kong Oscar Fjord 83 E3 *fjord* E Greenland
Kongsberg 85 B6 Buskerud, S Norway
Kông, Tônle 137 E5 *var.* Xê Kong. *river* Cambodia/Laos
Kong, Xê *see* Kông, Tônle
Königgrätz *see* Hradec Králové
Königshütte *see* Chorzów

Konin 98 C3 *Ger.* Kuhnau. Weilkopolskie, C Poland
Koninkrijk der Nederlanden *see* Netherlands
Konispol 101 C7 *var.* Konispoli. Vlorë, S Albania
Konispoli *see* Konispol
Kónitsa 104 A4 Ípeiros, W Greece
Konitz *see* Chojnice
Konjic 100 C4 Federacija Bosna I Hercegovina, S Bosnia and Herzegovina
Konosha 110 C4 Arkhangel'skaya Oblast', NW Russian Federation
Konotop 109 F1 Sums'ka Oblast', NE Ukraine
Konstantinovka *see* Kostyantynivka
Konstanz 95 B7 *var.* Constanz, *Eng.* Constance, *hist.* Kostnitz; *anc.* Constantia. Baden-Württemberg, S Germany
Konstanza *see* Constanţa
Konya 116 C4 *var.* Konieh, *prev.* Konia; *anc.* Iconium. Konya, C Turkey
Kopaonik 101 D5 *mountain range* S Serbia
Kopar *see* Koper
Koper 95 D8 *It.* Capodistria; *prev.* Kopar. SW Slovenia
Köpetdag Gershi 122 C3 *mountain range* Iran/Turkmenistan
Köpetdag Gershi/Kopetdag, Khrebet *see* Koppeh Dägh
Koppeh Dägh 120 D2 *Rus.* Khrebet Kopetdag, *Turkm.* Köpetdag Gershi. *mountain range* Iran/Turkmenistan
Kopreinitz *see* Koprivnica
Koprivnica 100 B2 *Ger.* Kopreinitz, *Hung.* Kaproncza. Koprivnica-Kri>zevci, N Croatia
Köprülü *see* Veles
Koptsevichi *see* Kaptsevichy
Kopyl' *see* Kapyl'
Korat *see* Nakhon Ratchasima
Korat Plateau 136 D4 *plateau* E Thailand
Kobra 135 E4 Chhattisgarh, C India
Korça *see* Korçë
Korçë 101 D6 *var.* Korça, *It.* Corriza; *prev.* Koritsa. Korçë, SE Albania
Korčula 100 B4 *It.* Curzola; *anc.* Corcyra Nigra.. *island* S Croatia
Korea Bay 127 G3 *bay* China/North Korea
Korea, Democratic People's Republic of *see* North Korea
Korea, Republic of *see* South Korea
Korea Strait 131 A7 *Jap.* Chôsen-kaikyô, *Kor.* Taehan-haehyŏp. *channel* Japan/South Korea
Korhogo 74 D4 N Côte d'Ivoire (Ivory Coast)
Korinthiakós Kólpos 105 B5 *Eng.* Gulf of Corinth; *anc.* Corinthiacus Sinus. *gulf* C Greece
Kórinthos 105 B6 *anc.* Corinthus *Eng.* Corinth. Pelopónnisos, S Greece
Koritsa *see* Korçë
Kōriyama 131 D5 Fukushima, Honshū, C Japan
Korla 126 C3 *Chin.* K'u-erh-lo. Xinjiang Uygur Zizhiqu, NW China
Körmend 99 B7 Vas, W Hungary
Koróni 105 B6 Pelopónnisos, S Greece
Koror 144 A2 *var.* Oreor. *country capital* (Palau) Oreor, N Palau
Körös *see* Križevci
Korosten' 108 D1 Zhytomyrs'ka Oblast', NW Ukraine
Koro Toro 76 C2 Borkou-Ennedi-Tibesti, N Chad
Korsovka *see* Kārsava
Kortrijk 87 A6 *Fr.* Courtrai. West-Vlaanderen, W Belgium
Koryak Range *see* Koryakskoye Nagor'ye
Koryakskiy Khrebet *see* Koryakskoye Nagor'ye
Koryakskoye Nagor'ye 115 H2 *var.* Koryakskiy Khrebet, *Eng.* Koryak Range. *mountain range* NE Russian Federation
Koryazhma 110 C4 Arkhangel'skaya Oblast', NW Russian Federation
Korytsa *see* Korçë
Kos 105 E6 Kos, Dodekánisa, Greece, Aegean Sea
Kos 105 E6 *It.* Coo; *anc.* Cos. *island* Dodekánisa, Greece, Aegean Sea

Kō-saki 131 A7 *headland* Nagasaki, Tsushima, SW Japan
Kościan 98 B4 *Ger.* Kosten. Wielkopolskie, C Poland
Kościerzyna 98 C2 Pomorskie, NW Poland
Kosciusko, Mount *see* Kosciuszko, Mount
Kosciuszko, Mount 149 C7 *prev.* Mount Kosciusko. *mountain* New South Wales, SE Australia
K'o-shih *see* Kashi
Koshikijima-rettō 131 A8 *var.* Kosikizima Rettô. *island group* SW Japan
Kōshū *see* Kwangju
Košice 99 D6 *Ger.* Kaschau, *Hung.* Kassa. Košický Kraj, E Slovakia
Kosikizima Rettô *see* Koshikijima-rettō
Köslin *see* Koszalin
Koson 123 E3 *Rus.* Kasan. Qashqadaryo Viloyati, S Uzbekistan
Kosovo 101 D5 *prev.* Autonomous Province of Kosovo and Metohija. *province* S Serbia
Kosovo and Metohija, Autonomous Province of *see* Kosovo
Kosovo Polje 101 D5 Kosovo, S Serbia
Kosovska Mitrovica 101 D5 *Alb.* Mitrovicë; *prev.* Mitrovica, Titova Mitrovica. S Serbia
Kosrae 144 C2 *prev.* Kusaie. *island* Caroline Islands, E Micronesia
Kossou, Lac de 74 D5 *lake* C Côte d'Ivoire (Ivory Coast)
Kostanay 130 C4 *var.* Kustanay, *Kaz.* Qostanay. Kustanay, N Kazakhstan
Kosten *see* Kościan
Kostenets 104 C2 *prev.* Georgi Dimitrov. Sofiya, W Bulgaria
Kostnitz *see* Konstanz
Kostroma 110 B4 Kostromskaya Oblast', NW Russian Federation
Kostyantynivka 109 G3 *Rus.* Konstantinovka. Donets'ka Oblast', SE Ukraine
Kostyukovichi *see* Kastsyukovichy
Kostyukovka *see* Kastsyukowka
Koszalin 98 B2 *Ger.* Köslin. Zachodnio-pomorskie, NW Poland
Kota 134 D3 *prev.* Kotah. Rājasthān, N India
Kota Baharu *see* Kota Bharu
Kota Bahru *see* Kota Bharu
Kotabaru *see* Jayapura
Kota Bharu 138 B3 *var.* Kota Baharu, Kota Bahru. Kelantan, Peninsular Malaysia
Kotaboemi *see* Kotabumi
Kotabumi 138 B4 *prev.* Kotaboemi. Sumatera, W Indonesia
Kotah *see* Kota
Kota Kinabalu 138 D3 *prev.* Jesselton. Sabah, East Malaysia
Kotel'nyy, Ostrov 115 E2 *island* Novosibirskiye Ostrova, N Russian Federation
Kotka 85 E5 Kymi, S Finland
Kotlas 110 C4 Arkhangel'skaya Oblast', NW Russian Federation
Kotonu *see* Cotonou
Kotor 101 C5 *It.* Cattaro. SW Montenegro
Kotovs'k 108 D3 *Rus.* Kotovsk. Odes'ka Oblast', SW Ukraine
Kotovsk *see* Hînceşti
Kottbus *see* Cottbus
Kotte *see* Sri Jayawardanapura
Kotto 76 D4 *river* Central African Republic/Dem. Rep. Congo
Kotuy 115 E2 *river* N Russian Federation
Koudougou 75 E4 C Burkina Faso
Koulamoutou 77 B6 Ogooué-Lolo, C Gabon
Koulikoro 74 D3 Koulikoro, SW Mali
Koumra 76 C4 Moyen-Chari, S Chad
Kourou 59 H3 N French Guiana
Kousséier *see* Al Quşayr
Kousséri 76 B3 *prev.* Fort-Foureau. Extrême-Nord, NE Cameroon
Koutiala 74 D4 Sikasso, S Mali
Kouvola 85 E5 Kymi, S Finland
Kovel' 108 C1 *Pol.* Kowel. Volyns'ka Oblast', NW Ukraine
Kovno *see* Kaunas
Koweit *see* Kuwait
Kowel *see* Kovel'
Kowloon 128 A2 Hong Kong, S China
Kowno *see* Kaunas

Kozáni *104 B4* Dytikí Makedonía,
N Greece
Kozara *100 B3 mountain range*
NW Bosnia and Herzegovina
Kozarska Dubica *see* Bosanska Dubica
Kozhikode *see* Calicut
Kōzu-shima *131 D6 island* E Japan
Kozyatyn *108 D2 Rus.* Kazatin.
Vinnyts'ka Oblast', C Ukraine
Kpalimé *75 E5 var.* Palimé.
SW Togo
Krâchéh *137 D6 prev.* Kratie. Krâchéh,
E Cambodia
Kragujevac *100 D4* Serbia, C Serbia
Krainburg *see* Kranj
Kra, Isthmus of *137 B6 isthmus*
Malaysia/Thailand
Krakau *see* Kraków
Kraków *99 D5 Eng.* Cracow, *Ger.*
Krakau; *anc.* Cracovia. Małopolskie,
S Poland
Králânh *137 D5* Siĕmréab,
NW Cambodia
Kraljevo *100 D4 prev.* Rankovićevo.
Serbia, C Serbia
Kramators'k *109 G3 Rus.* Kramatorsk.
Donets'ka Oblast', SE Ukraine
Kramatorsk *see* Kramators'k
Kramfors *85 C5* Västernorrland,
C Sweden
Kranéa *see* Kraniá
Kraniá *104 B4 var* Kranéa. Dytikí
Makedonía, N Greece
Kranj *95 D7 Ger.* Krainburg.
NW Slovenia
Kranz *see* Zelenogradsk
Kräslava *106 D4* Krāslava, SE Latvia
Krasnaye *107 C5 Rus.* Krasnoye.
Minskaya Voblasts', C Belarus
Krasnoarmeysk *111 C6* Saratovskaya
Oblast', W Russian Federation
Krasnodar *111 A7 prev.* Ekaterinodar,
Yekaterinodar. Krasnodarskiy Kray,
SW Russian Federation
Krasnodon *109 H3* Luhans'ka Oblast',
E Ukraine
Krasnogor *see* Kallaste
Krasnogvardeyskoye *see*
Krasnohvardiys'ke
Krasnohvardiys'ke *109 F4 Rus.*
Krasnogvardeyskoye. Respublika
Krym, S Ukraine
Krasnokamensk *115 F4* Chitinskaya
Oblast', S Russian Federation
Krasnokamsk *111 D5* Permskaya
Oblast', W Russian Federation
Krasnoperekops'k *109 F4 Rus.*
Krasnoperekopsk. Respublika Krym,
S Ukraine
Krasnoperekopsk *see* Krasnoperekops'k
Krasnostav *see* Krasnystaw
Krasnovodsk *see* Türkmenbaşy
Krasnovodskiy Zaliv *see* Türkmenbasy
Aylagy
Krasnowodsk Aylagy *see* Türkmenbasy
Aylagy
Krasnoyarsk *114 D4* Krasnoyarskiy
Kray, S Russian Federation
Krasnoye *see* Krasnaye
Krasnystaw *98 E4 Rus.* Krasnostav.
Lubelskie, SE Poland
Krasnyy Kut *111 C6* Saratovskaya
Oblast', W Russian Federation
Krasnyy Luch *109 H3 prev.*
Krindachevka. Luhans'ka Oblast',
E Ukraine
Kratie *see* Krâchéh
Krávanh, Chuŏr Phnum *137 C6 Eng.*
Cardamom Mountains, *Fr.* Chaîne
des Cardamomes. *mountain range*
W Cambodia
Krefeld *94 A4* Nordrhein-Westfalen,
W Germany
Kreisstadt *see* Krosno Odrzańskie
Kremenchug *see* Kremenchuk
**Kremenchugskoye Vodokhranilishche/
Kremenchuk Reservoir** *see*
Kremenchuts'ke Vodokhovyshche
Kremenchuk *109 F2 Rus.* Kremenchug.
Poltavs'ka Oblast', NE Ukraine
Kremenchuts'ke Vodoskhovyshche *109
F2 Eng.* Kremenchuk Reservoir, *Rus.*
Kremenchugskoye Vodokhranilishche.
reservoir C Ukraine
Kremenets' *108 C2 Pol.* Krzemieniec,
Rus. Kremenets. Ternopil's'ka Oblast',
W Ukraine
Kremennaya *see* Kreminna

Kreminna *109 G2 Rus.* Kremennaya.
Luhans'ka Oblast', E Ukraine
Kresena *see* Kresna
Kresna *104 C3 var.* Kresena.
Blagoevgrad, SW Bulgaria
Kretikon Delagos *see* Kritikó Pélagos
Kretinga *106 B3 Ger.* Krottingen.
Klaipėda, NW Lithuania
Kreutz *see* Cristuru Secuiesc
Kreuz *see* Križevci
Kreuz *see* Risti
**Kreuzburg/Kreuzburg in
Oberschlesien** *see* Kluczbork
Krichëv *see* Krychaw
Krievija *see* Russian Federation
Krindachevka *see* Krasnyy Luch
Krishna *132 C1 prev.* Kistna. *river*
C India
Krishnagiri *132 C2* Tamil Nādu,
SE India
Kristiania *see* Oslo
Kristiansand *85 A6 var.* Christiansand.
Vest-Agder, S Norway
Kristianstad *85 B7* Skåne, S Sweden
Kristiansund *84 A4 var.* Christiansund.
More og Romsdal, S Norway
Kriti *105 C7 Eng.* Crete. *island* Greece,
Aegean Sea
Kritikó Pélagos *105 D7 var.* Kretikon
Delagos, *Eng.* Sea of Crete;
anc. Mare Creticum. *sea* Greece,
Aegean Sea
Krivoy Rog *see* Kryvyy Rih
Križevci *100 B2 Ger.* Kreuz, *Hung.*
Kőrös. Varaždin, NE Croatia
Krk *100 A3 It.* Veglia; *anc.* Curieta.
island NW Croatia
Kroatien *see* Croatia
Krolevets' *109 F1 Rus.* Krolevets.
Sums'ka Oblast', NE Ukraine
Krolevets *see* Krolevets'
Królewska Huta *see* Chorzów
Kronach *95 C5* Bayern, E Germany
Kronstadt *see* Braşov
Kroonstad *78 D4* Free State, C South
Africa
Kropotkin *111 A7* Krasnodarskiy Kray,
SW Russian Federation
Krosno *99 D5 Ger.* Krossen.
Podkarpackie, SE Poland
Krosno Odrzańskie *98 B3*
Ger. Crossen, Kreisstadt.
Lubuskie, W Poland
Krossen *see* Krosno
Krottingen *see* Kretinga
Krško *95 E8 Ger.* Gurkfeld;
prev. Videm-Krško. E Slovenia
Krugloye *see* Kruhlaye
Kruhlaye *107 D6 Rus.* Krugloye.
Mahilyowskaya Voblasts', E Belarus
Kruja *see* Krujë
Krujë *101 C6 var.* Kruja, *It.* Croia.
Durrës, C Albania
Krummau *see* Český Krumlov
Krung Thep *137 C5 var.* Krung Thep
Mahanakhon, *Eng.* Bangkok. *country
capital* (Thailand) Bangkok,
C Thailand
Krung Thep, Ao *137 C5 var.* Bight of
Bangkok. *bay* S Thailand
Krung Thep Mahanakhon *see* Krung
Thep
Krupki *107 D6 Rus.* Krupki. Minskaya
Voblasts', C Belarus
Krušné Hory *see* Erzgebirge
Krychaw *107 E7 Rus.* Krichëv.
Mahilyowskaya Voblasts', E Belarus
Krym *81 F4 peninsula* SE Ukraine
Europe
Kryms'ki Hory *109 F5 mountain range*
S Ukraine
Kryms'kyy Pivostriv *109 F5 peninsula*
S Ukraine
Krynica *99 D5 Ger.* Tannenhof.
Małopolskie, S Poland
Kryve Ozero *109 E3* Odes'ka Oblast',
SW Ukraine
Kryvyy Rih *109 F3 Rus.* Krivoy Rog.
Dnipropetrovs'ka Oblast', SE Ukraine
Krzemieniec *see* Kremenets'
Ksar al Kebir *see* Ksar-el-Kebir
Ksar al Soule *see* Er-Rachidia
Ksar-el-Kebir *70 C2 var.* Alcázar,
Ksar al Kebir, Ksar-el-Kébir, *Ar.*
Al-Ksar al-Kebir, Al-Qsar al-Kbir, *Sp.*
Alcazarquivir. NW Morocco
Ksar-el-Kébir *see* Ksar-el-Kebir
Kuala Dungun *see* Dungun

Kuala Lumpur *138 B3 country capital*
(Malaysia) Kuala Lumpur, Peninsular
Malaysia
Kuala Terengganu *138 B3 var.* Kuala
Trengganu. Terengganu, Peninsular
Malaysia
Kualatungkal *138 B4* Sumatera,
W Indonesia
Kuang-chou *see* Guangzhou
Kuang-hsi *see* Guangxi Zhuangzu Zizhiqu
Kuang-tung *see* Guangdong
Kuang-yuan *see* Guangyuan
Kuantan *138 B3* Pahang, Peninsular
Malaysia
Kuba *see* Quba
Kuban' *109 G5 var.* Hypanis. *river*
SW Russian Federation
Kubango *see* Cubango/Okavango
Kuching *138 C3 prev.* Sarawak. Sarawak,
East Malaysia
Kuçovë *101 C6 var.* Kuçova; *prev.* Qyteti
Stalin. Berat, C Albania
Kudara *see* Ghūdara
Kudus *138 C5 prev.* Koedoes. Jawa,
C Indonesia
Kuei-lin *see* Guilin
Kuei-Yang/Kuei-yang *see* Guiyang
K'u-erh-lo *see* Korla
Kueyang *see* Guiyang
Kugluktuk *53 E3 var.* Qurlurtuuq;
prev. Coppermine. Nunavut,
NW Canada
Kuhmo *84 E4* Oulu, E Finland
Kuhnau *see* Konin
Kühnö *see* Kihnu
Kuibyshev *see* Kuybyshevskoye
Vodokhranilishche
Kuito *78 B2 Port.* Silva Porto. Bié,
C Angola
Kuji *130 D3 var.* Kuzi. Iwate, Honshū,
C Japan
Kukës *101 D5 var.* Kukёsi. Kukёs,
NE Albania
Kukёsi *see* Kukёs
Kukong *see* Shaoguan
Kukukhoto *see* Hohhot
Kula Kangri *135 G3 var.* Kulhakangri.
mountain Bhutan/China
Kuldīga *106 B3 Ger.* Goldingen. Kuldīga,
W Latvia
Kuldja *see* Yining
Kulhakangri *see* Kula Kangri
Kullorsuaq *82 D2 var.* Kuvdlorssuak.
Kitaa, C Greenland
Kulm *see* Chełmno
Kulmsee *see* Chełmża
Kŭlob *123 F3 Rus.* Kulyab.
SW Tajikistan
Kulpa *see* Kolpa
Kulu *116 C3* Konya, W Turkey
Kulunda Steppe *114 C4 Kaz.* Qulyndy
Zhazyghy, *Rus.* Kulundinskaya
Ravnina. *grassland* Kazakhstan/
Russian Federation
Kulundinskaya Ravnina *see* Kulunda
Steppe
Kulyab *see* Kŭlob
Kum see Qom
Kuma *111 B7 river* SW Russian
Federation
Kumamoto *131 A7* Kumamoto,
Kyūshū, SW Japan
Kumanova *see* Kumanovo
Kumanovo *101 E5 Turk.* Kumanova.
N Macedonia
Kumasi *75 E5 prev.* Coomassie.
C Ghana
Kumayri *see* Gyumri
Kumba *77 A5* Sud-Ouest,
W Cameroon
Kumertau *111 D6* Respublika
Bashkortostan, W Russian Federation
Kumillā *see* Comilla
Kumo *75 G4* Gombi, E Nigeria
Kumon Range *136 B2 mountain range*
N Myanmar (Burma)
Kumul *see* Hami
Kunashiri *see* Kunashir, Ostrov
Kunashir, Ostrov *130 E1*
var. Kunashiri. *island* Kuril'skiye
Ostrova, SE Russian Federation
Kunda *106 E2* Lääne-Virumaa,
NE Estonia
Kunduz *see* Kondoz
Kunene *see* Cunene

Kungsbacka *85 B7* Halland, S Sweden
Kungur *111 D5* Permskaya Oblast',
NW Russian Federation
Kunlun Mountains *see* Kunlun Shan
Kunlun Shan *126 B4 Eng.* Kunlun
Mountains. *mountain range* NW China
Kunming *128 B6 var.* K'un-ming; *prev.*
Yunnan. *province capital* Yunnan,
SW China
K'un-ming *see* Kunming
Kununurra *146 D3* Western Australia
Kunya-Urgench *see* Këneurgench
Kuopio *85 E5* Kuopio, C Finland
Kupa *see* Kolpa
Kupang *139 E5 prev.* Koepang. Timor,
C Indonesia
Kup"yans'k *109 G2 Rus.* Kupyansk.
Kharkivs'ka Oblast', E Ukraine
Kupyansk *see* Kup"yans'k
Kür *see* Kura
Kura *117 H3 Az.* Kür, *Geor.* Mtkvari,
Turk. Kura Nehri. *river* SW Asia
Kura Nehri *see* Kura
Kurashiki *131 B6 var.* Kurasiki.
Okayama, Honshū, SW Japan
Kurasiki *see* Kurashiki
Kurdistan *117 F4 cultural region* SW Asia
Kürdzhali *104 D3 var.* Kirdzhali,
Kŭrdžali. Kŭrdzhali, S Bulgaria
Kure *131 B7* Hiroshima, Honshū,
SW Japan
Küre Dağları *116 C2 mountain range*
N Turkey
Kuressaare *106 C2 Ger.* Arensburg; *prev.*
Kingissepp. Saaremaa, W Estonia
Kureyka *112 D2 river* N Russian
Federation
Kurgan-Tyube *see* Qŭrghonteppa
Kuria Muria Islands *see* Ḩalāniyāt,
Juzur al
Kurile Islands *see* Kuril'skiye Ostrova
Kurile-Kamchatka Depression *see*
Kurile Trench
Kurile Trench *113 F3 var.* Kurile-
Kamchatka Depression. *trench*
NW Pacific Ocean
Kuril'sk *130 E1* Kuril'skiye Ostrova,
Sakhalinskaya Oblats', SE Russian
Federation
Kuril'skiye Ostrova *115 H4 Eng.* Kurile
Islands. *island group* SE Russian
Federation
Kuril-gai *148 E1* New South Wales,
E Australia
Kurisches Haff *see* Courland Lagoon
Kurkund *see* Kilingi-Nõmme
Kurnool *132 C1 var.* Karnul. Andhra
Pradesh, S India
Kursk *111 A6* Kurskaya Oblast',
W Russian Federation
Kurskiy Zaliv *see* Courland Lagoon
Kuršumlija *101 D5* Serbia, S Serbia
Kurtbunar *see* Tervel
Kuruktag *126 C3 mountain range*
NW China
Kurume *131 A7* Fukuoka, Kyūshū,
SW Japan
Kurupukari *59 F3* C Guyana
Kushiro *130 D2 var.* Kusiro. Hokkaidō,
NE Japan
Kushka *see* Serhetabat
Kusiro *see* Kushiro
Kuskokwim Mountains *36 C3
mountain range* Alaska, USA
Kustanay *see* Kostanay
Küstence/Küstendje *see* Constanţa
Kütahya *116 B3 var.* Kutaia. Kütahya,
W Turkey
Kutai *see* Mahakam, Sungai
K'ut'aisi *117 F2* W Georgia
Kût al 'Amārah *see* Al Kūt
Kut al Imara *see* Al Kūt
Kutaradja/Kutaraja *see* Bandaaceh
Kutch, Gulf of *see* Kachchh, Gulf of
Kutch, Rann of *see* Kachchh, Rann of
Kutina *100 B3* Sisak-Moslavina,
NE Croatia
Kutno *98 C3* Łódzkie, C Poland
Kuujjuaq *39 E2 prev.* Fort-Chimo.
Québec, E Canada
Kuusamo *84 E3* Oulu, E Finland
Kuvango *see* Cubango
Kuvdlorssuak *see* Kullorsuaq
Kuwait *120 C4 off.* State of Kuwait, *var.*
Dawlat al Kuwait, Koweit, Kuwurt.
country SW Asia

KUWAIT
Southwest Asia

Official name State of Kuwait
Formation 1961 / 1961
Capital Kuwait City
Population 2.7 million / 392 people per
sq mile (152 people per sq km) / 98%
Total area 6880 sq miles
(17,820 sq km)
Languages Arabic*, English
Religions Sunni Muslim 45%, Shi'a
Muslim 40%, Christian, Hindu, and
other 15%
Ethnic mix Kuwaiti 45%, Other Arab 35%,
South Asian 9%, Other 7%, Iranian 4%
Government Monarchy
Currency Kuwaiti dinar = 1000 fils
Literacy rate 83%
Calorie consumption 3010 calories

Kuwait *see* Al Kuwayt
Kuwait City *see* Al Kuwayt
Kuwait, Dawlat al *see* Kuwait
Kuwait, State of *see* Kuwait
Kuwajleen *see* Kwajalein Atoll
Kuwayt *120 C3 E Iraq*
Kuweit *see* Kuwait
Kuybyshev *see* Samara
Kuybyshev Reservoir *see*
Kuybyshevskoye Vodokhranilishche
Kuybyshevskoye Vodokhranilishche
111 C5 var. Kuybyshev Reservoir. *reservoir*
W Russian Federation
Kuytun *126 B2* Xinjiang Uygur Zizhiqu,
NW China
Kuzi *see* Kuji
Kuznetsk *111 B6* Penzenskaya Oblast',
W Russian Federation
Kuźnica *98 E2* Białystok, NE Poland
Kvaløya *84 C2 island* N Norway
Kvarnbergsvattnet *84 B4 var.*
Frostviken. *lake* N Sweden
Kvarner *100 A3 var.* Carnaro, *It.*
Quarnero. *gulf* W Croatia
Kvitøya *83 G1 island* NE Svalbard
Kwajalein Atoll *144 C1 var.* Kwajleen.
atoll Ralik Chain, C Marshall Islands
Kwando *see* Cuando
Kwangchow *see* Guangzhou
Kwangchu *see* Kwangju
Kwangju *129 E4 off.* Kwangju-
gwangyŏksi, *var.* Guangju, Kwangchu,
Jap. Kōshū. SW South Korea
Kwangju-gwangyŏksi *see* Kwangju
Kwango *77 C7* Port. Cuango. *river*
Angola/Dem. Rep. Congo
Kwango *see* Cuango
Kwangsi/Kwangsi Chuang
Autonomous Region *see* Guangxi
Zhuangzu Zizhiqu
Kwangtung *see* Guangdong
Kwangyuan *see* Guangyuan
Kwanza *see* Cuanza
Kweichu *see* Guiyang
Kweilin *see* Guilin
Kweisui *see* Hohhot
Kweiyang *see* Guiyang
Kwekwe *78 D3 prev.* Que Que.
Midlands, C Zimbabwe
Kwesui *see* Hohhot
Kwidzyń *98 C2 Ger.* Marienwerder.
Pomorskie, N Poland
Kwigillingok *36 C3* Alaska, USA
Kwilu *77 C6 river* W Dem. Rep. Congo
Kwito *see* Cuito
Kyabé *76 C4* Moyen-Chari, S Chad
Kyaikkami *137 B5 prev.* Amherst. Mon
State, S Myanmar (Burma)
Kyaiklat *136 B4* Irrawaddy,
SW Myanmar (Burma)
Kyaikto *136 B4* Mon State,
S Myanmar (Burma)
Kyakhta *115 E5* Respublika Buryatiya,
S Russian Federation
Kyaukse *136 B3* Mandalay,
C Myanmar (Burma)
Kyjov *99 C5 Ger.* Gaya. Jihomoravský
Kraj, SE Czech Republic
Kyklades *105 D6 var.* Kikládhes,
Eng. Cyclades. *island group* SE Greece
K'yŏngsŏng *see* Sŏul
Kyōto *131 C6* Honshū, SW Japan
Kyparissía *105 B6 var.* Kiparissía.
Pelopónnisos, S Greece

Kypros *see* Cyprus
Kyrá Panagía *105 C5 island* Vóreies
Sporádes, Greece, Aegean Sea
Kyrenia *see* Girne
Kyrgyz Republic *see* Kyrgyzstan
Kyrgyzstan *123 F2 off.* Kyrgyz Republic,
var. Kirghizia; *prev.* Kirgizskaya SSR,
Kirghiz SSR, Republic of Kyrgyzstan.
country C Asia

KYRGYZSTAN
Central Asia

Official name Kyrgyz Republic
Formation 1991 / 1991
Capital Bishkek
Population 5.3 million / 69 people per sq
mile (27 people per sq km) / 33%
Total area 76.641 sq miles
(198,500 sq km)
Languages Kyrgyz*, Russian*, Uzbek,
Tatar, Ukrainian
Religions Muslim (mainly Sunni) 70%,
Orthodox Christian 30%
Ethnic mix Kyrgyz 57%, Russian 19%,
Uzbek 13%, Other 7%, Tatar 2%,
Ukrainian 2%
Government Presidential system
Currency Som = 100 tyyn
Literacy rate 99%
Calorie consumption 2999 calories

Kyrgyzstan, Republic of *see* Kyrgyzstan
Kýthira *105 C7 var.* Kíthira, *It.* Cerigo,
Lat. Cythera. *island* S Greece
Kýthnos *105 C6* Knýthnos, Kykládes,
Greece, Aegean Sea
Kýthnos *105 C6 var.* Kíthnos, Thermiá,
It. Termia; *anc.* Cythnos. *island*
Kykládes, Greece, Aegean Sea
Kythréa *see* Değirmenlik
Kyūshū *131 B7 var.* Kyúsyū. *island*
SW Japan
Kyushu-Palau Ridge *125 F3 var.*
Kyusyu-Palau Ridge. *undersea ridge*
W Pacific Ocean
Kyustendil *104 B2 anc.* Pautalia.
Kyustendil, W Bulgaria
Kyūsyū *see* Kyūshū
Kyusyu-Palau Ridge *see* Kyushu-Palau
Ridge
Kyyiv *109 E2 Eng.* Kiev, *Rus.* Kiyev.
country capital (Ukraine) Kyyivs'ka
Oblast', N Ukraine
Kyyivs'ke Vodoskhovyshche *109 E1*
Eng. Kiev Reservoir, *Rus.* Kiyevskoye
Vodokhranilishche. *reservoir*
N Ukraine
Kyzyl *114 D4* Respublika Tyva,
C Russian Federation
Kyzyl Kum *122 D2 var.* Kizil Kum,
Qizil Qum, Uzb. Qizilqum. *desert*
Kazakhstan/Uzbekistan
Kyzylorda *114 B5 var.* Kzyl-Orda,
Qizil Orda, Qyzylorda; *prev.* Perovsk.
Kyzylorda, S Kazakhstan
Kyzyl-Suu *123 G2 prev.* Pokrovka.
Issyk-Kul'skaya Oblast',
NE Kyrgyzstan
Kzylrabot *see* Qizilrabot
Kzyl-Orda *see* Kyzylorda

L

Laaland *see* Lolland
La Algaba *70 C4* Andalucía, S Spain
Laarne *87 B5* Oost-Vlaanderen,
NW Belgium
La Asunción *59 E1* Nueva Esparta,
NE Venezuela
Laatokka *see* Ladozhskoye, Ozero
Laâyoune *70 B3 var.* Aaiún. *country
capital* (Western Sahara) NW Western
Sahara
La Banda Oriental *see* Uruguay
la Baule-Escoublac *90 A4* Loire-
Atlantique, NW France
Labé *74 C4* NW Guinea
Labe *see* Elbe
Laborca *see* Laborec
Laborec *99 E5 Hung.* Laborca. *river*
E Slovakia
Labrador *39 F2 cultural region*
Newfoundland and Labrador,
SW Canada
Labrador Basin *34 E3 var.* Labrador Sea
Basin. *undersea basin* Labrador Sea

Labrador Sea *82 A4 sea*
NW Atlantic Ocean
Labrador Sea Basin *see* Labrador Basin
Labudalin *see* Ergun
Labutta *43 A3* Irrawaddy,
SW Myanmar (Burma)
Laç *101 C6 var.* Laci. Lezhë, C Albania
La Calera *64 B4* Valparaíso, C Chile
La Carolina *92 D4* Andalucía, S Spain
Laccadive Islands/Laccadive Minicoy
and Amindivi Islands, the *see*
Lakshadweep
La Ceiba *52 D2* Atlántida, N Honduras
Lachanás *104 B3* Kentrikí Makedonía,
N Greece
La Chaux-de-Fonds *95 A7* Neuchâtel,
W Switzerland
Lachlan River *149 C6 river* New South
Wales, SE Australia
Laci *see* Laç
la Ciotat *91 D6 anc.* Citharista. Bouches-
du-Rhône, SE France
Lacobriga *see* Lagos
La Concepción *53 E5 var.* Concepción.
Chiriquí, W Panama
La Concepción *58 C1* Zulia,
NW Venezuela
La Condamine *91 C8* W Monaco
Laconia *41 G2* New Hampshire, NE USA
La Crosse *40 A2* Wisconsin, N USA
La Cruz *52 D4* Guanacaste, NW Costa
Rica
Lādhiqiyah *118 A3 Eng.* Latakia, *Fr.*
Lattaquié, *var.* Al Lādhiqīyah; *anc.*
Laodicea, Laodicea ad Mare. Al
Lādhiqīyah, W Syria
Ladoga, Lake *see* Ladozhskoye, Ozero
Ladozhskoye, Ozero *110 B3 Eng.*
Lake Ladoga, *Fin.* Laatokka. *lake*
NW Russian Federation
Ladysmith *40 A2* Wisconsin, N USA
Lae *144 B3* Morobe, W Papua New
Guinea
Læsø *85 B7 island* N Denmark
La Esperanza *52 C2* Intibucá,
SW Honduras
Lafayette *40 C4* Indiana, N USA
Lafayette *42 B3* Louisiana, S USA
La Fé *54 A2* Pinar del Río, W Cuba
Lafia *75 G4* Nassarawa, C Nigeria
la Flèche *90 B4* Sarthe, NW France
Lagdo, Lac de *44 B4* N Cameroon
Laghouat *70 D2* N Algeria
Lagos *75 F5* Lagos, SW Nigeria
Lagos *92 B5 anc.* Lacobriga. Faro,
S Portugal
Lagos de Moreno *51 E4* Jalisco,
SW Mexico
Lagouira *70 A4* SW Western Sahara
La Grande *46 C3* Oregon, NW USA
La Guaira *66 B4* Distrito Federal,
N Venezuela
Lagunas *64 B1* Tarapacá, N Chile
Lagunillas *61 G4* Santa Cruz, SE Bolivia
La Habana *54 B2 var.* Havana. *country
capital* (Cuba) Ciudad de La Habana,
W Cuba
Lahat *138 B4* Sumatera, W Indonesia
La Haye *see* 's-Gravenhage
Laholm *85 B7* Halland, S Sweden
Lahore *134 D2* Punjab, NE Pakistan
Lahr *95 A6* Baden-Württemberg,
S Germany
Lahti *85 D5 Swe.* Lahtis. Etelä-Suomi,
S Finland
Lahtis *see* Lahti
Laï *76 B4 prev.* Behagle, De Behagle.
Tandjilé, S Chad
Laibach *see* Ljubljana
Lai Châu *136 D3* Lai Châu, N Vietnam
Laila *see* Laylá
La Junta *44 D5* Colorado, C USA
Lake Charles *42 A3* Louisiana, S USA
Lake City *43 E3* Florida, SE USA
Lake District *89 C5 physical region*
NW England, UK
Lake Havasu City *48 A2* Arizona,
SW USA
Lake Jackson *49 H4* Texas, SW USA
Lakeland *43 E4* Florida, SE USA
Lakeside *47 C8* California, W USA
Lake State *see* Michigan
Lakewood *44 D4* Colorado, C USA
Lakhnau *see* Lucknow
Lakonikós Kólpos *105 B7 gulf*
S Greece
Lakselv *84 D2 Lapp.* Leavdnja.
Finnmark, N Norway

Lakshadweep *132 A3 Eng.* Laccadive
Islands. *island group* India, N Indian
Ocean
la Laon *see* Laon
Lalibela *72 C4* Amhara, Ethiopia
La Libertad *52 B1* Petén, N Guatemala
La Ligua *64 B4* Valparaíso, C Chile
Lalín *92 C1* Galicia, NW Spain
Lalitpur *133 F3* Central, C Nepal
La Louvière *87 B6* Hainaut, S Belgium
la Maddalena *96 A4* Sardegna, Italy,
C Mediterranean Sea
la Manche *see* English Channel
Lamar *44 D5* Colorado, C USA
La Marmora, Punta *97 A5 mountain*
Sardegna, Italy, C Mediterranean Sea
La Massana *91 A8* La Massana,
W Andorra Europe
Lambaréné *77 A6* Moyen-Ogooué,
W Gabon
Lamego *92 C2* Viseu, N Portugal
Lamesa *49 E3* Texas, SW USA
Lamezia Terme *97 D6* Calabria,
SE Italy
Lamía *105 B5* Stereá Ellás, C Greece
Lamoni *45 F4* Iowa, C USA
La Mosquitia *53 E3 var.* Miskito Coast,
Eng. Mosquito Coast. *coastal region*
E Nicaragua
Lampang *136 C4 var.* Muang Lampang.
Lampang, NW Thailand
Lámpeia *105 B6* Dytikí Ellás, S Greece
Lanbi Kyun *137 B6 prev.* Sullivan
Island. *island* Mergui Archipelago,
S Myanmar (Burma)
Lancang Jiang *see* Mekong
Lancaster *89 D5* NW England, UK
Lancaster *47 C7* California, W USA
Lancaster *41 F4* Pennsylvania, NE USA
Lancaster Sound *37 F2 sound* Nunavut,
N Canada
Lan-chou/Lan-chow/Lanchow *see*
Lanzhou
Landao *see* Lantau Island
Landen *87 C6* Vlaams Brabant,
C Belgium
Lander *44 C3* Wyoming, C USA
Landerneau *90 A3* Finistère, NW France
Landes *91 B5 cultural region* SW France
Landes *91 B5 department* SW France
Land of Enchantment *see* New Mexico
The Land of Opportunity *see* Arkansas
Land of Steady Habits *see* Connecticut
Land of the Midnight Sun *see* Alaska
Landsberg *see* Gorzów Wielkopolski,
Lubuskie, Poland
Landsberg an der Warthe *see* Gorzów
Wielkopolski
Land's End *89 B8 headland* SW England,
UK
Landshut *95 C6* Bayern, SE Germany
Langar *123 E2 Rus.* Lyangar. Navoiy
Viloyati, C Uzbekistan
Langfang *128 D4* Hebei, E China
Langkawi, Pulau *137 B7 island*
Peninsular Malaysia
Langres *90 D4* Haute-Marne, N France
Langsa *138 A3* Sumatera, W Indonesia
Lang Shan *127 E3 mountain range*
N China
Lang Son *136 D3 var.* Langson. Lang
Sơn, N Vietnam
Langson *see* Lang Son
Lang Suan *137 B6* Chumphon,
SW Thailand
Languedoc *91 C6 cultural region* S France
Länkäran *117 H3 Rus.* Lenkoran'.
S Azerbaijan
Lansing *40 C3 state capital* Michigan,
N USA
Lanta, Ko *137 B7 island* S Thailand
Lantau Island *128 A2 Cant.* Tai Yue
Shan, *Chin.* Landao. *island* Hong
Kong, S China
Lan-ts'ang Chiang *see* Mekong
Lantung, Gulf of *see* Liaodong Wan
Lanzarote *70 B3 island* Islas Canarias,
Spain, NE Atlantic Ocean
Lanzhou *128 B4 var.* Lan-chou,
Lanchow, Lan-chow; *prev.* Kaolan.
province capital Gansu, C China
Lao Cai *136 D3* Lao Cai, N Vietnam
Laodicea/Laodicea ad Mare *see*
Lādhiqiyah
Laoet *see* Laut, Pulau
Laojunmiao *see* Yumen
Laon *90 D3 var.* la Laon; *anc.* Laudunum.
Aisne, N France

Lao People's Democratic Republic
see Laos
La Orchila, Isla *58 D1 island*
N Venezuela
La Oroya *60 C3* Junín, C Peru
Laos *136 D4 off.* Lao People's Democratic
Republic. *country* SE Asia

LAOS
Southeast Asia

Official name Lao People's Democratic
Republic
Formation 1953 / 1953
Capital Vientiane
Population 5.9 million / 66 people per
sq mile (26 people per sq km) / 24%
Total area 91,428 sq miles
(236,800 sq km)
Languages Lao*, Mon-Khmer, Yao,
Vietnamese, Chinese, French
Religions Buddhist 85%, Other (including
animist) 15%
Ethnic mix Lao Loum 66%, Lao
Theung 30%, Other 2%, Lao Soung 2%
Government One-party state
Currency New kip = 100 at
Literacy rate 69%
Calorie consumption 2312 calories

La Palma *53 G5* Darién, SE Panama
La Palma *70 A3 island* Islas Canarias,
Spain, NE Atlantic Ocean
La Paz *61 F4 var.* La Paz de Ayacucho.
country capital (Bolivia-legislative
and administrative capital) La Paz,
W Bolivia
La Paz *50 B3* Baja California Sur,
NW Mexico
La Paz, Bahía de *50 B3 bay*
W Mexico
La Paz de Ayacucho *see* La Paz
La Perouse Strait *130 D1 Jap.* Sōya-
kaikyō, *Rus.* Proliv Laperuza. *strait*
Japan/Russian Federation
Laperuza, Proliv *see* La Perouse Strait
Lápithos *see* Lapta
Lapland *84 D3 Fin.* Lappi, Swe.
Lappland. *cultural region* N Europe
La Plata *64 D4* Buenos Aires, E Argentina
La Plata *see* Sucre
Lappeenranta *85 E5 Swe.* Villmanstrand.
Etelä-Suomi, SE Finland
Lappi/Lappland *see* Lapland
Lappo *see* Lapua
Lapta *102 C5 Gk.* Lápithos.
NW Cyprus
Laptev Sea *see* Laptevykh, More
Laptevykh, More *115 E2 Eng.* Laptev
Sea. *sea* Arctic Ocean
Lapua *85 D5 Swe.* Lappo. Länsi-Suomi,
W Finland
Lapurdum *see* Bayonne
Łapy *98 E3* Podlaskie, NE Poland
La Quiaca *64 C2* Jujuy, N Argentina
L'Aquila *96 C4 var.* Aquila, Aquila degli
Abruzzi. Abruzzo, C Italy
Laracha *92 B1* Galicia, NW Spain
Laramie *44 C4* Wyoming, C USA
Laramie Mountains *44 C3 mountain
range* Wyoming, C USA
Laredo *93 E1* Cantabria, N Spain
Laredo *49 F5* Texas, SW USA
La Réunion *see* Réunion
Largeau *see* Faya
Largo *43 E4* Florida, SE USA
Largo, Cayo *54 B2 island* W Cuba
Lario *see* Como, Lago di
La Rioja *93 E2* La Rioja, NW Argentina
Lárisa *104 B4 var.* Larissa. Thessalía,
C Greece
Larissa *see* Lárisa
Lārkāna *134 B3 var.* Larkhana.
Sind, SE Pakistan
Larkhana *see* Lārkāna
Lárnaca *102 C5 var.* Larnaca, Larnax.
SE Cyprus
Larnax *see* Lárnaca
la Rochelle *90 B4 anc.* Rupella.
Charente-Maritime, W France
la Roche-sur-Yon *90 B4*
prev. Bourbon Vendée, Napoléon-
Vendée. Vendée, NW France
La Roda *93 E3* Castilla-La Mancha,
C Spain
La Romana *55 E3* E Dominican Republic
Larvotto *91 C8* N Monaco Europe

La-sa *see* Lhasa
Las Cabezas de San Juan *92 C5*
Andalucía, S Spain
Las Cruces *48 D3* New Mexico, SW USA
La See d'Urgel *93 G1 var.* La Seu
d'Urgell, Seo de Urgel. Cataluña,
NE Spain
La Serena *64 B3* Coquimbo, C Chile
La Seu d'Urgell *see* La See d'Urgel
la Seyne-sur-Mer *91 D6* Var, SE France
Lashio *136 B3* Shan State,
E Myanmar (Burma)
Lashkar Gāh *122 D5 var.* Lash-Kar-Gar'.
Helmand, S Afghanistan
Lash-Kar-Gar' *see* Lashkar Gāh
La Sila *97 D6 mountain range* SW Italy
La Sirena *52 D3* Región Autónoma
Atlántico Sur, E Nicaragua
Łask *98 C4* Łódzkie, C Poland
Las Lomitas *64 D2* Formosa,
N Argentina
La Solana *93 E4* Castilla-La Mancha,
C Spain
Las Palmas *70 A3 var.* Las Palmas de
Gran Canaria. Gran Canaria, Islas
Canarias, Spain, NE Atlantic Ocean
Las Palmas de Gran Canaria *see* Las
Palmas
La Spezia *96 B3* Liguria, NW Italy
Lassa *see* Lhasa
Las Tablas *53 F5* Los Santos, S Panama
Last Frontier, The *see* Alaska
Las Tunas *54 C2 var.* Victoria de las
Tunas. Las Tunas, E Cuba
La Suisse *see* Switzerland
Las Vegas *47 D7* Nevada, W USA
Latacunga *60 B1* Cotopaxi, C Ecuador
la Teste *91 B5* Gironde, SW France
Latina *97 C5 prev.* Littoria. Lazio, C Italy
La Tortuga, Isla *59 E1 var.* Isla Tortuga.
island N Venezuela
La Tuque *39 E4* Québec, SE Canada
Latvia *106 C3 off.* Republic of Latvia,
Ger. Lettland, *Latv.* Latvija, Latvijas
Republika; *prev.* Latvian SSR, *Rus.*
Latviyskaya SSR. *country* NE Europe

LATVIA
Northeast Europe

Official name Republic of Latvia
Formation 1991 / 1991
Capital Riga
Population 2.3 million / 92 people per
sq mile (36 people per sq km) / 69%
Total area 24,938 sq miles
(64,589 sq km)
Languages Latvian*, Russian
Religions Lutheran 55%, Roman
Catholic 24%, Other 12%, Orthodox
Christian 9%
Ethnic mix Latvian 57%, Russian 32%,
Belarussian 4%, Ukrainian 3%, Polish 2%,
Other 2%
Government Parliamentary system
Currency Lats = 100 santims
Literacy rate 99%
Calorie consumption 2938 calories

**Latvian SSR/Latvija/Latvijas
Republika/Latviyskaya SSR** *see* Latvia
Latvia, Republic of *see* Latvia
Laudunum *see* Laon
Laudus *see* St-Lô
Lauenburg/Lauenburg in Pommern
see Lębork
Lau Group *145 E4 island group* E Fiji
Lauis *see* Lugano
Launceston *149 C8* Tasmania,
SE Australia
La Unión *52 C2* Olancho, C Honduras
La Unión *93 F4* Murcia, SE Spain
Laurel *42 C3* Mississippi, S USA
Laurel *44 C2* Montana, NW USA
Laurentian Highlands *see* Laurentian
Mountains
Laurentian Mountains *39 E3 var.*
Laurentian Highlands, *Fr.* Les
Laurentides. *plateau* Newfoundland
and Labrador/Québec, Canada
Laurentides, Les *see* Laurentian
Mountains
Lauria *97 D6* Basilicata, S Italy
Laurinburg *43 F1* North Carolina,
SE USA
Lauru *see* Choiseul
Lausanne *95 A7 It.* Losanna. Vaud,
SW Switzerland

Laut, Pulau *138 D4 prev.* Laoet. *island*
Borneo, C Indonesia
Laval *38 D4* Québec, SE Canada
Laval *90 B3* Mayenne, NW France
La Vall D'Uixó *93 F3 var.* Vall D'Uxó.
País Valenciano, E Spain
La Vega *55 E3 var.* Concepción de la
Vega. C Dominican Republic
La Vila Joiosa *see* Villajoyosa
Lávrio *105 C6 prev.* Lávrion. Attikí,
C Greece
Lávrion *see* Lávrio
Lawrence *41 G3* Massachusetts, NE USA
Lawrenceburg *42 C1* Tennessee, S USA
Lawton *49 F2* Oklahoma, C USA
La Yarada *61 E4* Tacna, SW Peru
Laylá *121 C5 var.* Laila. Ar Riyāḍ,
C Saudi Arabia
Lazarev Sea *154 B1 sea* Antarctica
Lázaro Cárdenas *51 E5* Michoacán de
Ocampo, SW Mexico
Leal *see* Lihula
Leamhcán *see* Lucan
Leamington *38 C5* Ontario, S Canada
Leavdnja *see* Lakselv
Lebak *139 E3* Mindanao, S Philippines
Lebanon *45 G5* Missouri, C USA
Lebanon *41 G2* New Hampshire,
NE USA
Lebanon *46 B3* Oregon, NW USA
Lebanon *118 A4 off.* Republic of
Lebanon, *Ar.* Al Lubnān, *Fr.* Liban.
country SW Asia

LEBANON
Southwest Asia

Official name Republic of Lebanon
Formation 1941 / 1941
Capital Beirut
Population 3.6 million / 911 people per
sq mile (352 people per sq km) / 90%
Total area 4015 sq miles
(10,400 sq km)
Languages Arabic*, French, Armenian,
Assyrian
Religions Muslim 70%, Christian 30%
Ethnic mix Arab 94%, Armenian 4%,
Other 2%
Government Parliamentary system
Currency Lebanese pound = 100 piastres
Literacy rate 87%
Calorie consumption 3196 calories

Lebanon, Mount *see* Liban, Jebel
Lebanon, Republic of *see* Lebanon
Lebap *122 D2* Lebapskiy Velayat,
NE Turkmenistan
Lebedin *see* Lebedyn
Lebedyn *109 F2 Rus.* Lebedin. Sums'ka
Oblast', NE Ukraine
Lębork *98 C2 var.* Lębórk, *Ger.*
Lauenburg, Lauenburg in Pommern.
Pomorskie, N Poland
Lebrija *92 C5* Andalucía, S Spain
Lebu *65 A5* Bío Bío, C Chile
le Cannet *91 D6* Alpes-Maritimes,
SE France
Le Cap *see* Cap-Haïtien
Lecce *97 E6* Puglia, SE Italy
Lechainá *105 B6 var.* Lehena, Lekhainá.
Dytikí Ellás, S Greece
Ledo Salinarius *see* Lons-le-Saunier
Leduc *37 E5* Alberta, SW Canada
Leech Lake *45 F2* lake Minnesota, N USA
Leeds *89 D5* N England, UK
Leek *86 E2* Groningen, NE Netherlands
Leer *94 A3* Niedersachsen, NW Germany
Leeuwarden *86 D1 Fris.* Ljouwert.
Friesland, N Netherlands
Leeuwin, Cape *142 A5 headland*
Western Australia
Leeward Islands *55 G3 island group*
E West Indies
Leeward Islands *see* Sotavento, Ilhas de
Lefkáda *105 A5 prev.* Levkás.
Lefkáda, Iónioi Nísoi, Greece,
C Mediterranean Sea
Lefkáda *105 A5 It.* Santa Maura, *prev.*
Levkás; *anc.* Leucas. *island* Iónioi
Nísoi, Greece, C Mediterranean Sea
Lefká Óri *105 C7 mountain range* Kríti,
Greece, E Mediterranean Sea
Lefkímmi *105 A5 var.* Levkímmi.
Kérkyra, Iónia Nisiá, Greece,
C Mediterranean Sea
Lefkosía/Lefkoşa *see* Nicosia
Legaceaster *see* Chester

Legaspi *see* Legazpi City
Legazpi City *139 E1 var.* Legaspi. Luzon,
N Philippines
Leghorn *see* Livorno
Legnica *98 B4 Ger.* Liegnitz.
Dolnośląskie, SW Poland
le Havre *90 B3 Eng.* Havre; *prev.* le
Havre-de-Grâce. Seine-Maritime,
N France
le Havre-de-Grâce *see* le Havre
Lehena *see* Lechainá
Leicester *89 D6 Lat.* Batae Coritanorum.
C England, UK
Leiden *86 B3 prev.* Leyden; *anc.*
Lugdunum Batavorum. Zuid-Holland,
W Netherlands
Leie *90 D2 Fr.* Lys. *river*
Belgium/France
Leinster *89 B6 Ir.* Cúige Laighean.
cultural region E Ireland
Leipsic *see* Leipzig
Leipsoí *105 E6 island* Dodekánisa,
Greece, Aegean Sea
Leipzig *94 C4* Pol. Lipsk, *hist.* Leipsic;
anc. Lipsia. Sachsen, E Germany
Leiria *92 B3 anc.* Collipo. Leiria,
C Portugal
Leirvik *85 A6* Hordaland, S Norway
Lek *86 C4 river* SW Netherlands
Lekhainá *see* Lechainá
Lekhchevo *104 C2* Montana,
NW Bulgaria
Leksand *85 C5* Dalarna, C Sweden
Lel'chitsy *see* Lyel'chytsy
le Léman *see* Geneva, Lake
Lelystad *86 D3* Flevoland,
C Netherlands
Léman, Lac *see* Geneva, Lake
le Mans *90 B3* Sarthe, NW France
Lemberg *see* L'viv
Lemesós *102 C5 var.* Limassol.
SW Cyprus
Lemhi Range *46 D3 mountain range*
Idaho, C USA North America
Lemnos *see* Límnos
Lemovices *see* Limoges
Lena *115 F3 river* NE Russian Federation
Lena Tablemount *141 B7 seamount*
S Indian Ocean
Len Dao *128 C8 island* S Spratly Islands
Lengshuitan *see* Yongzhou
Leninabad *see* Khūjand
Leninakan *see* Gyumri
Lenine *109 G5 Rus.* Lenino. Respublika
Krym, S Ukraine
Leningor *see* Leninogorsk
Leningrad *see* Sankt-Peterburg
Leningradskaya *154 B4 Russian research
station* Antarctica
Lenino *see* Lenine
Leninobod *see* Khūjand
Leninogorsk *114 D4 Kaz.* Leninogor.
Vostochnyy Kazakhstan, E Kazakhstan
Leninpol' *123 F2* Talasskaya Oblast',
NW Kyrgyzstan
Lenin-Turkmenski *see* Türkmenabat
Lenkoran' *see* Länkäran
Lenti *99 B7* Zala, SW Hungary
Lentia *see* Linz
Leoben *95 E7* Steiermark, C Austria
León *51 E4* Guanajuato, C Mexico
León *52 D3* León de los Aldamas.
Guanajuato, C Mexico
León *52 D3* León de los Aldamas. León,
NW Nicaragua
León *92 D1* Castilla-León, NW Spain
León de los Aldamas *see* León
Leonídio *105 B6 var.* Leonídi.
Pelopónnisos, S Greece
Leonídi *see* Leonídio
Léopold II, Lac *see* Mai-Ndombe, Lac
Léopoldville *see* Kinshasa
Lepel' *see* Lyepyel'
le Portel *90 C2* Pas-de-Calais, N France
Le Puglie *see* Puglia
le Puy *91 C5 prev.* le Puy-en-Velay,
hist. Anicium, Podium Anicensis.
Haute-Loire, C France
le Puy-en-Velay *see* le Puy
Léré *76 B4* Mayo-Kebbi, SW Chad
Lérida *see* Lleida
Lerma *92 D2* Castilla-León, N Spain
Léros *105 D6 island* Dodekánisa, Greece,
Aegean Sea
Lerrnayin Gharabakh *see*
Nagorno-Karabakh
Lerwick *88 D1* NE Scotland, UK
Lesbos *see* Lésvos
Les Cayes *see* Cayes

Les Gonaïves *see* Gonaïves
Leshan *128 B5* Sichuan, C China
les Herbiers *90 B4* Vendée, NW France
Lesh/Leshi *see* Lezhë
Lesina *see* Hvar
Leskovac *101 E5* Serbia, SE Serbia
Lesnoy *114 C3* Sverdlovskaya Oblast',
  C Russian Federation
Lesotho *78 D4* off. Kingdom of Lesotho;
  prev. Basutoland. *country* S Africa

LESOTHO
Southern Africa

Official name Kingdom of Lesotho
Formation 1966 / 1966
Capital Maseru
Population 1.8 million / 154 people per
  sq mile (59 people per sq km) / 28%
Total area 11,720 sq miles
  (30,355 sq km)
Languages English*, Sesotho*, isiZulu
Religions Christian 90%, Traditional
  beliefs 10%
Ethnic mix Sotho 97%, European and
  Asian 3%
Government Parliamentary system
Currency Loti = 100 lisente
Literacy rate 81%
Calorie consumption 2638 calories

Lesotho, Kingdom of *see* Lesotho
les Sables-d'Olonne *90 B4* Vendée,
  NW France
Lesser Antarctica *154 A3* var. West
  Antarctica. *physical region* Antarctica
Lesser Antilles *55 G4* island group
  E West Indies
Lesser Caucasus *117 F2* Rus. Malyy
  Kavkaz. *mountain range* SW Asia
Lesser Khingan Range *see* Xiao Hinggan
  Ling
Lesser Sunda Islands *see* Nusa Tenggara
Lésvos *116 A3* anc. Lesbos. *island*
  E Greece
Leszno *98 B4* Ger. Lissa. Wielkopolskie,
  C Poland
Lethbridge *37 E5* Alberta, SW Canada
Lethem *59 F3* S Guyana
Leti, Kepulauan *139 F5* island group
  E Indonesia
Letpadan *136 B4* Pegu,
  SW Myanmar (Burma)
Letsôk-aw Kyun *137 B6* var.
  Letsutan Island; *prev.* Domel
  Island. *island* Mergui Archipelago,
  S Myanmar (Burma)
Letsutan Island *see* Letsôk-aw Kyun
Lettland *see* Latvia
Lëtzebuerg *see* Luxembourg
Leucas *see* Lefkáda
Leuven *87 C6* Fr. Louvain, Ger. Löwen.
  Vlaams Brabant, C Belgium
Leuze *see* Leuze-en-Hainaut
Leuze-en-Hainaut *87 B6* var. Leuze.
  Hainaut, SW Belgium
Léva *see* Levice
Levanger *84 B4* Nord-Trøndelag,
  C Norway
Levelland *49 E2* Texas, SW USA
Leverkusen *94 A4* Nordrhein-Westfalen,
  W Germany
Levice *99 C6* Ger. Lewentz, Hung. Léva,
  Lewenz. Nitriansky Kraj, SW Slovakia
Levin *150 D4* Manawatu-Wanganui,
  North Island, New Zealand
Levkás *see* Lefkáda
Levkímmi *see* Lefkímmi
Lewentz/Lewenz *see* Levice
Lewis, Isle of *88 B2* island NW Scotland, UK
Lewis Range *44 B1* mountain range
  Montana, NW USA
Lewiston *46 C2* Idaho, NW USA
Lewiston *41 G2* Maine, NE USA
Lewistown *44 C1* Montana, NW USA
Lexington *40 C5* Kentucky, S USA
Lexington *45 E4* Nebraska, C USA
Leyden *see* Leiden
Leyte *139 F2* island C Philippines
Ležajsk *99 E5* Podkarpackie, SE Poland
Lezha *see* Lezhë
Lezhë *101 C6* var. Lezha; *prev.* Lesh,
  Leshi. Lezhë, NW Albania
Lhasa *126 C5* var. La-sa, Lassa. Xizang
  Zizhiqu, W China
Lhaviyani Atoll *see* Faadhippolhu Atoll
Lhazê *126 C5* var. Quxar. Xizang
  Zizhiqu, China E Asia

L'Hospitalet de Llobregat *93 G2*
  var. Hospitalet. Cataluña, NE Spain
Liancourt Rocks *131 A5* island group
  Japan/South Korea Asia Sea of Japan
Lianyungang *128 D4* var. Xinpu.
  Jiangsu, E China
Liao *see* Liaoning
Liaodong Wan *127 G3* Eng. Gulf of
  Lantung, Gulf of Liaotung. gulf NE China
Liao He *125 E1* river NE China
Liaoning *128 D3* var. Liao, Liaoning
  Sheng, Shengking, hist. Fengtien,
  Shenking. *province* NE China
Liaoning Sheng *see* Liaoning
Liaoyuan *129 F3* var. Dongliao, Shuang-
  liao, Jap. Chengchiatun. Jilin, NE China
Liard *see* Fort Liard
Liban *see* Lebanon
Liban, Jebel *118 B4* Ar. Jabal al Gharbt,
  Jabal Lubnān, Eng. Mount Lebanon.
  mountain range C Lebanon
Libau *see* Liepāja
Libby *44 A1* Montana, NW USA
Liberal *45 E5* Kansas, C USA
Liberalitas Julia *see* Évora
Liberec *98 B4* Ger. Reichenberg.
  Liberecký Kraj, N Czech Republic
Liberia *52 D4* Guanacaste,
  NW Costa Rica
Liberia *74 C5* off. Republic of Liberia.
  country W Africa

LIBERIA
West Africa

Official name Republic of Liberia
Formation 1847 / 1847
Capital Monrovia
Population 3.3 million / 89 people per
  sq mile (34 people per sq km) / 45%
Total area 43,000 sq miles
  (111,370 sq km)
Languages English*, Kpelle, Vai, Bassa,
  Kru, Grebo, Kissi, Gola, Loma
Religions Christian 68%, Traditional
  beliefs 18%, Muslim 14%
Ethnic mix Indigenous tribes (16 main
  groups) 95%, Americo-Liberians 5%
Government Transitional regime
Currency Liberian dollar = 100 cents
Literacy rate 58%
Calorie consumption 1900 calories

Liberia, Republic of *see* Liberia
Libian Desert *see* Libyan Desert
Libīyah, Aş Şahrā' al *see* Libyan Desert
Libourne *91 B5* Gironde, SW France
Libreville *77 A5* country capital (Gabon)
  Estuaire, NW Gabon
Libya *71 F3* off. Socialist People's Libyan
  Arab Jamahiriya, Ar. Al Jamāhīrīyah al
  'Arabiyah al Lībiyah ash Sha'biyah al
  Ishtirākiy; *prev.* Libyan Arab Republic.
  country N Africa

LIBYA
North Africa

Official name Great Socialist People's
  Libyan Arab Jamahariyah
Formation 1951 / 1951
Capital Tripoli
Population 5.9 million / 9 people per
  sq mile
  (3 people per sq km) / 88%
Total area 679,358 sq miles (1,759,540
  sq km)
Languages Arabic*, Tuareg
Religions Muslim (mainly Sunni) 97%,
  Other 3%
Ethnic mix Arab and Berber 95%,
  Other 5%
Government One-party state
Currency Libyan dinar = 1000 dirhams
Literacy rate 82%
Calorie consumption 3320 calories

Libyan Arab Republic *see* Libya
Libyan Desert *71 H4* var. Libian Desert,
  Ar. Aş Şahrā' al Lībiyah. *desert* N Africa
Libyan Plateau *103 F4* var. Aḍ Diffah.
  plateau Egypt/Libya
Lichtenfels *95 C5* Bayern, SE Germany
Lichtenvoorde *86 E4* Gelderland,
  E Netherlands
Lichuan *128 C5* Hubei, C China
Lida *107 B5* Rus. Lida. Hrodzyenskaya
  Voblasts', W Belarus

Lidhorikíon *see* Lidoríki
Lidköping *85 B6* Västra Götaland,
  S Sweden
Lidokhorikíon *see* Lidoríki
Lidoríki *105 B5* prev. Lidhorikíon,
  Lidokhorikíon. Stereá Ellás, C Greece
Lidzbark Warmiński *98 D2* Ger.
  Heilsberg. Olsztyn, N Poland
Liechtenstein *94 D1* off. Principality of
  Liechtenstein. *country* C Europe

LIECHTENSTEIN
Central Europe

Official name Principality of
  Liechtenstein
Formation 1719 / 1719
Capital Vaduz
Population 33,717 / 544 people per sq
  mile (211 people per sq km) / 21%
Total area 62 sq miles (160 sq km)
Languages German*, Alemannish
  dialect, Italian
Religions Roman Catholic 81%,
  Other 12%, Protestant 7%
Ethnic mix Liechtensteiner 62%,
  Foreign residents 38%
Government Parliamentary system
Currency Swiss franc = 100 rappen/
  centimes
Literacy rate 99%
Calorie consumption Not available

Liechtenstein, Principality of *see*
  Liechtenstein
Liège *87 D6* Dut. Luik, Ger. Lüttich.
  Liège, E Belgium
Liegnitz *see* Legnica
Lienz *95 D7* Tirol, W Austria
Liepāja *106 B3* Ger. Libau. Liepāja,
  W Latvia
Lietuva *see* Lithuania
Lievenhof *see* Līvāni
Liezen *95 D7* Steiermark, C Austria
Liffey *89 B6* river Ireland
Lifou *144 D5* island Îles Loyauté,
  E New Caledonia
Liger *see* Loire
Ligure, Appennino *96 A2* Eng. Ligurian
  Mountains. *mountain range* NW Italy
Ligure, Mar *see* Ligurian Sea
Ligurian Mountains *see* Ligure,
  Appennino
Ligurian Sea *96 A3* Fr. Mer
  Ligurienne, It. Mar Ligure. *sea*
  N Mediterranean Sea
Ligurienne, Mer *see* Ligurian Sea
Lihu'e *47 A7* var. Lihue. Kaua'i, Hawai'i,
  USA North America
Lihue *see* Lihu'e
Lihula *106 D2* Ger. Leal. Läänemaa,
  W Estonia
Līīvi Laht *see* Riga, Gulf of
Likasi *77 D7* prev. Jadotville. Shaba,
  SE Dem. Rep. Congo
Liknes *85 A6* Vest-Agder, S Norway
Lille *90 C2* var. l'Isle, Dut. Rijssel, Flem.
  Ryssel, prev. Lisle; anc. Insula. Nord,
  N France
Lillehammer *85 B5* Oppland, S Norway
Lillestrøm *85 B6* Akershus, S Norway
Lilongwe *79 E2* country capital (Malawi)
  Central , W Malawi
Lilybaeum *see* Marsala
Lima *60 C4* country capital (Peru) Lima,
  W Peru
Limanowa *99 D5* Małopolskie, S Poland
Limassol *see* Lemesós
Limerick *89 A6* Ir. Luimneach. Limerick,
  SW Ireland
Limín Vathéos *see* Sámos
Límnos *103 F3* anc. Lemnos. *island*
  E Greece
Limoges *91 C5* anc. Augustoritum
  Lemovicensium, Lemovices. Haute-
  Vienne, C France
Limón *53 E4* var. Puerto Limón. Limón,
  E Costa Rica
Limón *52 D2* Colón, NE Honduras
Limonum *see* Poitiers
Limousin *91 C5* region C France
Limousin *91 C5* cultural region
  C France
Limoux *91 C6* Aude, S France
Limpopo *78 D3* var. Crocodile. *river*
  S Africa
Linares *64 B4* Maule, C Chile
Linares *51 E3* Nuevo León, NE Mexico

Linares *92 D4* Andalucía, S Spain
Lincoln *89 D5* anc. Lindum, Lindum
  Colonia. E England, UK
Lincoln *41 H2* Maine, NE USA
Lincoln *45 F4* state capital Nebraska,
  C USA
Lincoln Sea *34 D2* sea Arctic Ocean
Linden *59 F3* E Guyana
Lindhos *see* Líndos
Lindi *73 D8* Lindi, SE Tanzania
Líndos *105 E7* var. Lindhos. Ródos,
  Dodekánisa, Greece, Aegean Sea
Lindum/Lindum Colonia *see* Lincoln
Line Islands *145 G3* island group
  E Kiribati
Lingeh *see* Bandar-e Langeh
Lingen *94 A3* var. Lingen an der Ems.
  Niedersachsen, NW Germany
Lingen an der Ems *see* Lingen
Lingga, Kepulauan *138 B4* island group
  W Indonesia
Linköping *85 C6* Östergötland,
  S Sweden
Linz *95 D6* anc. Lentia. Oberösterreich,
  N Austria
Lion, Golfe du *91 C7* Eng. Gulf of Lion,
  Gulf of Lions; anc. Sinus Gallicus. *gulf*
  S France
Lion, Gulf of/Lions, Gulf of *see* Lion,
  Golfe du
Liozno *see* Lyozna
Lipari Islands/Lipari, Isole *see* Eolie,
  Isole
Lipari, Isola *97 D6* island Isole Eolie,
  S Italy
Lipetsk *111 B5* Lipetskaya Oblast',
  W Russian Federation
Lipno *98 C3* Kujawsko-pomorskie,
  C Poland
Lipova *108 A4* Hung. Lippa. Arad,
  W Romania
Lipovets *see* Lypovets'
Lippa *see* Lipova
Lipsia/Lipsk *see* Leipzig
Lira *73 B6* N Uganda
Lisala *77 C5* Equateur, N Dem. Rep.
  Congo
Lisboa *92 B4* Eng. Lisbon; anc. Felicitas
  Julia, Olisipo. country capital
  (Portugal) Lisboa, W Portugal
Lisbon *see* Lisboa
Lisichansk *see* Lysychans'k
Lisieux *90 B3* anc. Noviomagus.
  Calvados, N France
Liski *111 B6* prev. Georgiu-Dezh.
  Voronezhskaya Oblast', W Russian
  Federation
Lisle/l'Isle *see* Lille
Lismore *149 E5* Victoria,
  SE Australia
Lissa *see* Vis
Lissa *see* Leszno
Lisse *86 C3* Zuid-Holland,
  W Netherlands
Litang *128 A5* var. Gaocheng. Sichuan,
  C China
Litani, Nahr el *135 B5* var. Nahr el
  Litant. *river* C Lebanon
Litant, Nahr el *see* Litani, Nahr el
Litauen *see* Lithuania
Lithgow *149 D6* New South Wales,
  SE Australia
Lithuania *106 B4* off. Republic of
  Lithuania, Ger. Litauen, Lith. Lietuva,
  Pol. Litwa, Rus. Litva; prev. Lithuanian
  SSR, Rus. Litovskaya SSR. *country*
  NE Europe

LITHUANIA
Northeast Europe

Official name Republic of Lithuania
Formation 1991 / 1991
Capital Vilnius
Population 3.4 million / 135 people per
  sq mile (52 people per sq km) / 68%
Total area 25,174 sq miles
  (65,200 sq km)
Languages Lithuanian*, Russian
Religions Roman Catholic 83%,
  Other 12%, Protestant 5%
Ethnic mix Lithuanian 80%, Russian 9%,
  Polish 7%, Other 2%, Belarussian 2%
Government Parliamentary system
Currency Litas (euro is also legal tender)
  = 100 centu
Literacy rate 99%
Calorie consumption 3324 calories

Lithuanian SSR *see* Lithuania
Lithuania, Republic of *see* Lithuania
Litóchoro *104 B4 var.* Litohoro,
 Litókhoron.
Litohoro/Litókhoron *see* Litóchoro
Litovskaya SSR *see* Lithuania
Little Alföld *99 C6 Ger.* Kleines
 Ungarisches Tiefland, *Hung.* Kisalföld,
 Slvk. Podunajská Rovina. *plain*
 Hungary/Slovakia
Little Andaman *133 F2 island* Andaman
 Islands, India, NE Indian Ocean
Little Barrier Island *150 D2 island*
 N New Zealand
Little Bay *93 H5 bay* S Gibraltar,
 Europe, Alboran Sea,
 Mediterranean Sea, Atlantic Ocean
Little Cayman *54 B3 island* E Cayman
 Islands
Little Falls *45 F2* Minnesota, N USA
Littlefield *49 E2* Texas, SW USA
Little Inagua *54 D2 var.* Inagua Islands.
 island S Bahamas
Little Minch, The *88 B3 strait*
 NW Scotland, UK
Little Missouri River *44 D2 river*
 NW USA
Little Nicobar *133 G3 island* Nicobar
 Islands, India, NE Indian Ocean
Little Rhody *see* Rhode Island
Little Rock *42 B1 state capital* Arkansas,
 C USA
Little Saint Bernard Pass *91 D5 Fr.* Col
 du Petit St-Bernard, *It.* Colle del Piccolo
 San Bernardo. *pass* France/Italy
Little Sound *42 A5 bay* Bermuda,
 NW Atlantic Ocean
Littleton *44 D4* Colorado, C USA
Littoria *see* Latina
Litva/Litwa *see* Lithuania
Liu-chou/Liuchow *see* Liuzhou
Liuzhou *128 C6 var.* Liu-chou, Liuchow.
 Guangxi Zhuangzu Zizhiqu, S China
Livanátai *see* Livanátes
Livanátes *105 B5 prev.* Livanátai. Stereá
 Ellás, C Greece
Līvāni *106 D4 Ger.* Lievenhof. Preiļi,
 SE Latvia
Liverpool *39 F5* Nova Scotia,
 SE Canada
Liverpool *89 C5* NW England, UK
Livingston *44 B2* Montana, NW USA
Livingston *49 H3* Texas, SW USA
Livingstone *78 C3 var.* Maramba.
 Southern, S Zambia
Livingstone Mountains *151 A7*
 mountain range South Island, New
 Zealand
Livno *100 B4* Federicija Bosna
 I Hercegovina, SW Bosnia and
 Herzegovina
Livojoki *84 D4 river* C Finland
Livonia *40 D3* Michigan, N USA
Livorno *96 B3 Eng.* Leghorn. Toscana,
 C Italy
Lixian Jiang *see* Black River
Lixoúri *105 A5 prev.* Lixoúrion.
 Kefallinía, Iónia Nisiá, Greece,
 C Mediterranean Sea
Lixoúrion *see* Lixoúri
Lizarra *see* Estella
Ljouwert *see* Leeuwarden
Ljubelj *see* Loibl Pass
Ljubljana *95 D7 Ger.* Laibach, *It.*
 Lubiana; *anc.* Aemona, Emona.
 country capital (Slovenia) C Slovenia
Ljungby *85 B7* Kronoberg, S Sweden
Ljusdal *85 C5* Gävleborg, C Sweden
Ljusnan *85 C5 river* C Sweden
Llanelli *89 C6 prev.* Llanelly.
 SW Wales, UK
Llanelly *see* Llanelli
Llanes *92 D1* Asturias, N Spain
Llanos *58 D2 physical region*
 Colombia/Venezuela
Lleida *93 F2 Cast.* Lérida; *anc.* Ilerda.
 Cataluña, NE Spain
Llucmajor *93 G3* Mallorca, Spain,
 W Mediterranean Sea
Loaita Island *128 C8 island*
 W Spratly Islands
Loanda *see* Luanda
Lobatse *78 C4 var.* Lobatsi. Kgatleng,
 SE Botswana
Lobatsi *see* Lobatse
Löbau *94 D4* Sachsen, E Germany
Lobito *78 B2* Benguela, W Angola

Lob Nor *see* Lop Nur
Lobositz *see* Lovosice
Loburi *see* Lop Buri
Locarno *95 B8 Ger.* Luggarus. Ticino,
 S Switzerland
Lochem *86 E3* Gelderland, E Netherlands
Lockport *41 E3* New York, NE USA
Lodja *77 D6* Kasai Oriental, C Dem.
 Rep. Congo
Lodwar *73 C6* Rift Valley, NW Kenya
Łódź *98 D4 Rus.* Lodz. Łódzkie,
 C Poland
Loei *136 C4 var.* Loey, Muang Loei.
 Loei, C Thailand
Loey *see* Loei
Lofoten *84 B3 var.* Lofoten Islands.
 island group C Norway
Lofoten Islands *see* Lofoten
Logan *44 B3* Utah, W USA
Logan, Mount *36 D3 mountain* Yukon
 Territory, W Canada
Logroño *93 E2 anc.* Vareia, *Lat.*
 Juliobriga. La Rioja, N Spain
Loibl Pass *95 D7 Ger.* Loiblpass, *Slvn.*
 Ljubelj. *pass* Austria/Slovenia
Loiblpass *see* Loibl Pass
Loi-Kaw *136 B4* Kayah State,
 C Myanmar (Burma)
Loire *90 B4 var.* Liger. *river* C France
Loja *60 B2* Loja, S Ecuador
Lokitaung *73 C5* Rift Valley, NW Kenya
Lokoja *75 G4* Kogi, C Nigeria
Loksa *106 E2 Ger.* Loxa. Harjumaa,
 NW Estonia
Lolland *85 B8 prev.* Laaland. *island*
 S Denmark
Lom *104 C1 prev.* Lom-Palanka.
 Montana, NW Bulgaria
Lomami *77 D6 river* C Dem. Rep. Congo
Lomas *60 D4* Arequipa, SW Peru
Lomas de Zamora *64 D4* Buenos Aires,
 E Argentina
Lombardia *96 B2 Eng.* Lombardy.
 region N Italy
Lombardy *see* Lombardia
Lombok, Pulau *138 D5 island* Nusa
 Tenggara, C Indonesia
Lomé *75 F5 country capital* (Togo)
 S Togo
Lomela *77 D6* Kasai Oriental, C Dem.
 Rep. Congo
Lommel *87 C7* Limburg, N Belgium
Lomond, Loch *88 B4 lake* C Scotland, UK
Lomonosov Ridge *155 B3 var.* Harris
 Ridge, *Rus.* Khrebet Homonsova.
 undersea ridge Arctic Ocean
Lomonsova, Khrebet *see* Lomonosov
 Ridge
Lom-Palanka *see* Lom
Lompoc *47 B7* California, W USA
Lom Sak *136 C4 var.* Muang Lom Sak.
 Phetchabun, C Thailand
Łomża *98 D3 Rus.* Lomzha. Podlaskie,
 NE Poland
Lomzha *see* Łomża
Loncoche *65 B5* Araucanía, C Chile
Londinium *see* London
London *89 A7 anc.* Augusta, *Lat.*
 Londinium. *country capital*
 (United Kingdom) SE England, UK
London *38 C5* Ontario, S Canada
London *40 C5* Kentucky, S USA
Londonderry *88 B4 var.* Derry,
 Ir. Doire. NW Northern Ireland, UK
Londonderry, Cape *146 C2 cape*
 Western Australia
Londrina *63 E4* Paraná, S Brazil
Lone Star State *see* Texas
Longa, Proliv *115 I1 Eng.* Long Strait.
 strait NE Russian Federation
Long Bay *43 F2 bay* W Jamaica
Long Beach *47 C7* California, W USA
Longford *89 B5 Ir.* An Longfort.
 Longford, C Ireland
Long Island *54 D2 island* C Bahamas
Long Island *41 G4 island* New York,
 NE USA
Longlac *38 C3* Ontario, S Canada
Longmont *44 D4* Colorado,
 C USA
Longreach *148 C4* Queensland,
 E Australia
Long Strait *see* Longa, Proliv
Longview *49 H3* Texas, SW USA
Longview *46 B2* Washington,
 NW USA
Long Xuyên *137 D6 var.* Longxuyen.
 An Giang, S Vietnam

Longxuyen *see* Long Xuyên
Longyan *128 D6* Fujian, SE China
Longyearbyen *83 G2 dependent*
 territory capital (Svalbard) Spitsbergen,
 W Svalbard
Lons-le-Saunier *90 D4 anc.* Ledo
 Salinarius. Jura, E France
Lop Buri *137 C5 var.* Loburi. Lop Buri,
 C Thailand
Lop Nor *see* Lop Nur
Lop Nur *126 C3 var.* Lob Nor, Lop Nor,
 Lo-pu Po. *seasonal lake* NW China
Loppersum *86 E1* Groningen,
 NE Netherlands
Lo-pu Po *see* Lop Nur
Lorca *93 E4 Ar.* Lurka; *anc.* Eliocroca,
 Lat. Illurco. Murcia, S Spain
Lord Howe Island *142 C4 island*
 E Australia
Lord Howe Rise *142 C4 undersea rise*
 SW Pacific Ocean
Loreto *50 B3* Baja California Sur,
 W Mexico
Lorient *90 A3 prev.* l'Orient. Morbihan,
 NW France
l'Orient *see* Lorient
Lorn, Firth of *88 B4 inlet* W Scotland,
 UK
Loro Sae *see* East Timor
Lörrach *95 A7* Baden-Württemberg,
 S Germany
Lorraine *90 D3 region* NE France
Lorraine *90 D3 cultural region*
 NE France
Los Alamos *48 C1* New Mexico, SW USA
Los Amates *52 B2* Izabal, E Guatemala
Los Ángeles *65 B5* Bío Bío, C Chile
Los Angeles *47 C7* California, W USA
Losanna *see* Lausanne
Lošinj *100 A3 Ger.* Lussin, *It.* Lussino.
 island W Croatia
Loslau *see* Wodzisław Śląski
Los Mochis *50 C3* Sinaloa, C Mexico
Losonc/Losontz *see* Lučenec
Los Roques, Islas *58 D1 island group*
 N Venezuela
Lot *91 B5 department* S France
Lot *91 B5 cultural region* S France
Lot *91 B5 river* S France
Lotagipi Swamp *73 C5 wetland*
 Kenya/Sudan
Loualaba *see* Lualaba
Louangnamtha *136 C3 var.* Luong Nam
 Tha. Louang Namtha, N Laos
Louangphabang *124 D3 var.*
 Louangprabang, Luang Prabang.
 Louangphabang, N Laos
Louangprabang *see* Louangphabang
Loubomo *see* Dolisie
Loudéac *90 A3* Côtes d'Armor,
 NW France
Loudi *128 C5* Hunan, S China
Louga *74 B3* NW Senegal
Louisiade Archipelago *144 B4 island*
 group SE Papua New Guinea
Louisiana *42 A2 off.* State of Louisiana,
 also known as Creole State, Pelican
 State. *state* S USA
Louisville *40 C5* Kentucky, S USA
Louisville Ridge *143 E4 undersea ridge*
 S Pacific Ocean
Loup River *45 E4 river* Nebraska, C USA
Lourdes *91 B6* Hautes-Pyrénées, S France
Lourenço Marques *see* Maputo
Louth *89 E5* E England, UK
Loutrá *104 C4* Kentríki Makedonía,
 N Greece
Louvain *see* Leuven
Louvain-la-Neuve *87 C6* Walloon
 Brabant, C Belgium
Louviers *90 C3* Eure, N France
Lovech *104 C2* Lovech, N Bulgaria
Loveland *44 D4* Colorado, C USA
Lovosice *98 A4 Ger.* Lobositz. Ustecký
 Kraj, NW Czech Republic
Lóvua *78 C2* Mòxico, E Angola
Lowell *41 G3* Massachusetts, NE USA
Löwen *see* Leuven
Lower California *see* Baja California
Lower Hutt *151 D5* Wellington, North
 Island, New Zealand
Lower Lough Erne *89 A5 lake*
 SW Northern Ireland, UK
Lower Red Lake *45 F1 lake* Minnesota,
 N USA
Lower Rhine *see* Neder Rijn
Lower Tunguska *see* Nizhnyaya
 Tunguska

Lowestoft *89 E6* E England, UK
Loxa *see* Loksa
Lo-yang *see* Luoyang
Loyauté, Îles *144 D5 island group* S New
 Caledonia
Loyev *see* Loyew
Loyew *107 D8 Rus.* Loyev. Homyel'skaya
 Voblasts', SE Belarus
Loznica *100 C3* Serbia, W Serbia
Lu *see* Shandong
Lualaba *77 D6 Fr.* Loualaba. *river*
 SE Dem. Rep. Congo
Luanda *78 A1 var.* Loanda, *Port.* São
 Paulo de Loanda. *country capital*
 (Angola) Luanda, NW Angola
Luang Prabang *see* Louangphabang
Luang, Thale *137 C7 lagoon* S Thailand
Luangua, Rio *see* Luangwa
Luangwa *73 B8 , var.* Rio Luangua. *river*
 Mozambique/Zambia
Luanshya *78 D2* Copperbelt, C Zambia
Luarca *92 C1* Asturias, N Spain
Lubaczów *99 E5 var.* Lúbaczów.
 Podkarpackie, SE Poland
L'uban' *98 B4* Leningradskaya Oblast',
 Russian Federation
Lubānas Ezers *see* Lubāns
Lubango *78 B2 Port.* Sá da Bandeira.
 Huíla, SW Angola
Lubāns *106 D4 var.* Lubānas Ezers.
 lake E Latvia
Lubao *77 D6* Kasai Oriental, C Dem.
 Rep. Congo
Lübben *94 D4* Brandenburg, E Germany
Lübbenau *94 D4* Brandenburg,
 E Germany
Lubbock *49 E2* Texas, SW USA
Lübeck *94 C2* Schleswig-Holstein,
 N Germany
Lubelska, Wyżyna *98 E4 plateau*
 SE Poland
Lüben *see* Lubin
Lubiana *see* Ljubljana
Lubin *98 B4 Ger.* Lüben. Dolnośląskie,
 SW Poland
Lublin *98 E4 Rus.* Lyublin. Lubelskie,
 E Poland
Lubliniec *98 C4* Śląskie, S Poland
Lubnān, Jabal *see* Liban, Jebel
Lubny *109 F2* Poltavs'ka Oblast',
 NE Ukraine
Lubsko *98 B4 Ger.* Sommerfeld.
 Lubuskie, W Poland
Lubumbashi *77 E8 prev.* Élisabethville.
 Shaba, SE Dem. Rep. Congo
Lubutu *77 D6* Maniema,
 E Dem. Rep. Congo
Luca *see* Lucca
Lucan *89 B5 Ir.* Leamhcán. Dublin,
 E Ireland
Lucanian Mountains *see* Lucano,
 Appennino
Lucano, Appennino *97 D5*
 Eng. Lucanian Mountains.
 mountain range S Italy
Lucapa *78 C1 var.* Lukapa.
 Lunda Norte, NE Angola
Lucca *96 B3 anc.* Luca. Toscana,
 C Italy
Lucea *54 A4* W Jamaica
Lucena *139 E1 off.* Lucena City. Luzon,
 N Philippines
Lucena *92 D4* Andalucía, S Spain
Lucena City *see* Lucena
Lučenec *99 D6 Ger.* Losontz, *Hung.*
 Losonc. Banskobystrický Kraj,
 C Slovakia
Lucentum *see* Alicante
Lucerna/Lucerne *see* Luzern
Luchow *see* Hefei
Łuck *see* Luts'k
Lucknow *135 E3 var.* Lakhnau. *state*
 capital Uttar Pradesh, N India
Lüda *see* Dalian
Luda Kamchiya *104 D2 river* E Bulgaria
Ludasch *see* Luduş
Lüderitz *78 B4 prev.* Angra Pequena.
 Karas, SW Namibia
Ludhiāna *134 D2* Punjab, N India
Ludington *40 C2* Michigan, N USA
Ludsan *see* Ludza
Luduş *108 B4 Ger.* Ludasch, *Hung.*
 Marosludas. Mureş, C Romania
Ludvika *85 C6* Dalarna, C Sweden
Ludwigsburg *95 B6* Baden-
 Württemberg, SW Germany
Lüdwigsfelde *94 D3* Brandenburg,
 NE Germany

Ludwigshafen 95 B5 var. Ludwigshafen am Rhein. Rheinland-Pfalz, W Germany
Ludwigshafen am Rhein see Ludwigshafen
Ludwigslust 94 C3 Mecklenburg-Vorpommern, N Germany
Ludza 106 D4 Ger. Ludsan. Ludza, E Latvia
Luebo 77 C6 Kasai Occidental, SW Dem. Rep. Congo
Luena 78 C2 var. Lwena, Port. Luso. Moxico, E Angola
Lufira 77 E7 river SE Dem. Rep. Congo
Lufkin 49 H3 Texas, SW USA
Luga 110 A4 Leningradskaya Oblast', NW Russian Federation
Lugano 95 B8 Ger. Lauis. Ticino, S Switzerland
Lugansk see Luhans'k
Lugdunum see Lyon
Lugdunum Batavorum see Leiden
Lugenda, Rio 79 E2 river N Mozambique
Luggarus see Locarno
Lugh Ganana see Luuq
Lugo 92 C1 anc. Lugus Augusti. Galicia, NW Spain
Lugoj 108 A4 Ger. Lugosch, Hung. Lugos. Timiş, W Romania
Lugos/Lugosch see Lugoj
Lugus Augusti see Lugo
Luguvallium/Luguvallum see Carlisle
Luhans'k 109 H3 Rus. Lugansk; prev. Voroshilovgrad. Luhans'ka Oblast', E Ukraine
Luimneach see Limerick
Lukapa see Lucapa
Lukenie 77 C6 river C Dem. Rep. Congo
Lukovit 104 C2 Lovech, N Bulgaria
Łuków 98 E4 Ger. Bogendorf. Lubelskie, E Poland
Lukuga 77 D7 river SE Dem. Rep. Congo
Luleå 84 D4 Norrbotten, N Sweden
Luleälven 84 C3 river N Sweden
Lulonga 77 C5 river NW Dem. Rep. Congo
Lulua 77 D7 river S Dem. Rep. Congo
Luluabourg see Kananga
Lumber State see Maine
Lumbo 79 F2 Nampula, NE Mozambique
Lumsden 151 A7 Southland, South Island, New Zealand
Lund 85 B7 Skåne, S Sweden
Lüneburg 94 C3 Niedersachsen, N Germany
Lunga, Isola see Dugi Otok
Lungkiang see Qiqihar
Lungué-Bungo 78 C2 var. Lungwebungu. river Angola/Zambia
Lungwebungu see Lungué-Bungo
Luninets see Luninyets
Łuniniec see Luninyets
Luninyets 107 B7 Pol. Łuniniec, Rus. Luninets. Brestskaya Voblasts', SW Belarus
Lunteren 86 D4 Gelderland, C Netherlands
Luong Nam Tha see Louangnamtha
Luoyang 128 C4 var. Honan, Lo-yang. Henan, C China
Lupatia see Altamura
Lúrio 79 F2 Nampula, NE Mozambique
Lúrio, Rio 79 E2 river NE Mozambique
Lurka see Lorca
Lusaka 78 D2 country capital (Zambia) Lusaka, SE Zambia
Lushnja see Lushnjë
Lushnjë 101 C6 var. Lushnja. Fier, C Albania
Luso see Luena
Lussin/Lussino see Lošinj
Lüt, Baḥrat/Lut, Baḥret see Dead Sea
Lūt, Dasht-e 120 D3 var. Kavīr-e Lūt. desert E Iran
Lutetia/Lutetia Parisiorum see Paris
Lūt, Kavīr-e see Lūt, Dasht-e
Luton 89 D6 E England, UK
Lutselk'e 37 F4 prev. Snowdrift. Northwest Territories, W Canada
Luts'k 108 C1 Pol. Łuck, Rus. Lutsk. Volyns'ka Oblast', NW Ukraine
Lutsk see Luts'k
Lüttich see Liège
Lutzow-Holm Bay see Lützow Holmbukta
Lützow Holmbukta 154 C2 var. Lutzow-Holm Bay. bay Antarctica

Luuq 73 D6 It. Lugh Ganana. Gedo, SW Somalia
Luvua 77 D7 river SE Dem. Rep. Congo
Luwego 73 C8 river S Tanzania
Luxembourg 87 D8 country capital (Luxembourg) Luxembourg, S Luxembourg
Luxembourg 87 D8 off. Grand Duchy of Luxembourg, var. Lëtzebuerg, Luxembourg. country NW Europe

LUXEMBOURG
Northwest Europe

Official name Grand Duchy of Luxembourg
Formation 1867 / 1867
Capital Luxembourg-Ville
Population 449,000 / 466 people per sq mile (180 people per sq km) / 92%
Total area 998 sq miles (2586 sq km)
Languages Luxembourgish*, German*, French*
Religions Roman Catholic 97%, Protestant, Orthodox Christian, and Jewish 3%
Ethnic mix Luxembourger 73%, Foreign residents 27%
Government Parliamentary system
Currency Euro = 100 cents
Literacy rate 99%
Calorie consumption 3701 calories

Luxemburg see Luxembourg
Luxor 72 B2 Ar. Al Uqsur. E Egypt
Luza 110 C4 Kirovskaya Oblast', NW Russian Federation
Luz, Costa de la 92 C5 coastal region SW Spain
Luzern 95 B7 Fr. Lucerne, It. Lucerna. Luzern, C Switzerland
Luzon 139 E1 island N Philippines
Luzon Strait 125 E3 strait Philippines/Taiwan
L'viv 108 B2 Ger. Lemberg, Pol. Lwów, Rus. L'vov. L'vivs'ka Oblast', W Ukraine
L'vov see L'viv
Lwena see Luena
Lwów see L'viv
Lyakhavichy 107 B6 Rus. Lyakhovichi. Brestskaya Voblasts', SW Belarus
Lyakhovichi see Lyakhavichy
Lyallpur see Faisalābād
Lyangar see Langar
Lyck see Ełk
Lycksele 84 C4 Västerbotten, N Sweden
Lycopolis see Asyūt
Lyel'chytsy 107 C7 Rus. Lel'chitsy. Homyel'skaya Voblasts', SE Belarus
Lyepyel' 107 D5 Rus. Lepel'. Vitsyebskaya Voblasts', N Belarus
Lyme Bay 89 C7 bay S England, UK
Lynchburg 41 E5 Virginia, NE USA
Lynn see King's Lynn
Lynn Lake 37 F4 Manitoba, C Canada
Lynn Regis see King's Lynn
Lyon 91 D5 Eng. Lyons; anc. Lugdunum. Rhône, E France
Lyons see Lyon
Lyozna 107 E6 Rus. Liozno. Vitsyebskaya Voblasts', NE Belarus
Lypovets' 108 D2 Rus. Lipovets. Vinnyts'ka Oblast', C Ukraine
Lys see Leie
Lysychans'k 109 H3 Rus. Lisichansk. Luhans'ka Oblast', E Ukraine
Lyttelton 151 C6 Canterbury, South Island, New Zealand
Lyublin see Lublin
Lyubotin see Lyubotyn
Lyubotyn 109 G2 Rus. Lyubotin. Kharkivs'ka Oblast', E Ukraine
Lyulyakovo 104 E2 prev. Keremitlik. Burgas, E Bulgaria
Lyusina 107 B6 Rus. Lyusino. Brestskaya Voblasts', SW Belarus
Lyusino see Lyusina

M

Maale see Male'
Ma'ān 119 B7 Ma'ān, SW Jordan
Maardu 106 D2 Ger. Maart. Harjumaa, NW Estonia
Ma'aret-en-Nu'man see Ma'arrat an Nu'mān

Ma'arrat an Nu'mān 118 B3 var. Ma'aret-en-Nu'man, Fr. Maarret enn Naamâne. Idlib, NW Syria
Maarret enn Naamâne see Ma'arrat an Nu'mān
Maart see Maardu
Maas see Meuse
Maaseik 87 D5 prev. Maeseyck. Limburg, NE Belgium
Maastricht 87 D6 var. Maestricht; anc. Traiectum ad Mosam, Traiectum Tungorum. Limburg, SE Netherlands
Macao 129 C6 Chin. Àomen, Port. Macau. E Asia
Macapá 63 E1 state capital Amapá, N Brazil
Macarsca see Makarska
Macassar see Makassar
Macău see Makó, Hungary
Macau see Macao
MacCluer Gulf see Berau, Teluk
Macdonnell Ranges 146 D4 mountain range Northern Territory, C Australia
Macedonia see Macedonia, FYR
Macedonia, FYR 101 D6 off. the Former Yugoslav Republic of Macedonia, var. Macedonia, Mac. Makedonija, abbrev. FYR Macedonia. country SE Europe

MACEDONIA
Southeast Europe

Official name Republic of Macedonia
Formation 1991 / 1991
Capital Skopje
Population 2 million / 201 people per sq mile (78 people per sq km) / 62%
Total area 9781 sq miles (25,333 sq km)
Languages Macedonian, Albanian, Serbo-Croat
Religions Orthodox Christian 59%, Muslim 26%, Other 10%, Roman Catholic 4%, Protestant 1%
Ethnic mix Macedonian 64%, Albanian 25%, Turkish 4%, Roma 3%, Other 2%, Serb 2%
Government Mixed presidential–parliamentary system
Currency Macedonian denar = 100 deni
Literacy rate 96%
Calorie consumption 2655 calories

Macedonia, the Former Yugoslav Republic of see Macedonia, FYR
Maceió 63 G3 state capital Alagoas, E Brazil
Machachi 60 B1 Pichincha, C Ecuador
Machala 60 B2 El Oro, SW Ecuador
Machanga 79 E3 Sofala, E Mozambique
Machilipatnam 132 D1 var. Bandar Masulipatnam. Andhra Pradesh, E India
Machiques 58 C2 Zulia, NW Venezuela
Macías Nguema Biyogo see Bioco, Isla de
Măcin 108 D5 Tulcea, SE Romania
Mackay 148 D4 Queensland, NE Australia
Mackay, Lake 146 C4 salt lake Northern Territory/Western Australia
Mackenzie 37 E3 river Northwest Territories, NW Canada
Mackenzie Bay 154 D3 bay Antarctica
Mackenzie Mountains 36 D3 mountain range Northwest Territories, NW Canada
Macleod, Lake 146 A4 lake Western Australia
Macomb 40 A4 Illinois, N USA
Macomer 97 A5 Sardegna, Italy, C Mediterranean Sea
Mâcon 91 D5 anc. Matisco, Matisco Ædourum. Saône-et-Loire, C France
Macon 42 D2 Georgia, SE USA
Macon 45 G4 Missouri, C USA
Macquarie Ridge 154 C5 undersea ridge SW Pacific Ocean
Macuspana 51 G4 Tabasco, SE Mexico
Ma'dabā 119 B6 var. Mādabā, Madeba; anc. Medeba. Ma'dabā, NW Jordan
Mādabā see Ma'dabā
Madagascar 79 F3 off. Democratic Republic of Madagascar, Malg. Madagasikara; prev. Malagasy Republic. country W Indian Ocean

MADAGASCAR
Indian Ocean

Official name Republic of Madagascar
Formation 1960 / 1960
Capital Antananarivo
Population 18.6 million / 83 people per sq mile (32 people per sq km) / 30%
Total area 226,656 sq miles (587,040 sq km)
Languages Malagasy*, French*
Religions Traditional beliefs 52%, Christian (mainly Roman Catholic) 41%, Muslim 7%
Ethnic mix Other Malay 46%, Merina 26%, Betsimisaraka 15%, Betsileo 12%, Other 1%
Government Presidential system
Currency Ariary = 5 iraimbilanja
Literacy rate 71%
Calorie consumption 2005 calories

Madagascar 79 F3 island W Indian Ocean
Madagascar Basin 69 E7 undersea basin W Indian Ocean
Madagascar, Democratic Republic of see Madagascar
Madagascar Plateau 69 E7 var. Madagascar Ridge, Madagascar Rise, Rus. Madagaskarskiy Khrebet. undersea plateau W Indian Ocean
Madagascar Rise/Madagascar Ridge see Madagascar Plateau
Madagasikara see Madagascar
Madagaskarskiy Khrebet see Madagascar Plateau
Madang 144 B3 Madang, N Papua New Guinea
Madaniyin see Médenine
Madarska see Hungary
Made 86 C4 Noord-Brabant, S Netherlands
Madeba see Ma'dabā
Madeira 70 A2 var. Ilha da Madeira. island Madeira, Portugal, NE Atlantic Ocean
Madeira, Ilha de see Madeira
Madeira Plain 66 C3 abyssal plain E Atlantic Ocean
Madeira, Rio 62 D2 var. Río Madera. river Bolivia/Brazil
Madeleine, Îles de la 39 F4 Eng. Magdalen Islands. island group Québec, E Canada
Madera 47 B6 California, W USA
Madera, Río see Madeira, Rio
Madhya Pradesh 135 E4 prev. Central Provinces and Berar. state C India
Madhya Pradesh 134 D4 prev. Central Provinces and Berar. cultural region C India
Madīnat ath Thawrah 118 C2 var. Ath Thawrah. Ar Raqqah, N Syria Asia
Madioen see Madiun
Madison 45 F3 South Dakota, N USA
Madison 40 B3 state capital Wisconsin, N USA
Madiun 138 D5 prev. Madioen. Jawa, C Indonesia
Madoera see Madura, Pulau
Madona 106 D4 var. Modohn. Madona, E Latvia
Madras see Chennai
Madras see Tamil Nādu
Madre de Dios 56 B4 off. Departamento de Madre de Dios. department E Peru
Madre de Dios, Departamento de see Madre de Dios
Madre de Dios, Río 61 E3 river Bolivia/Peru
Madre, Laguna 51 F3 lagoon NE Mexico
Madre, Laguna 49 G5 lagoon Texas, SW USA
Madrid 92 D3 country capital (Spain) Madrid, C Spain
Madura see Madurai
Madurai 132 C3 prev. Madura, Mathurai. Tamil Nādu, S India
Madura, Pulau 138 D5 prev. Madoera. island C Indonesia
Maebashi 131 D5 var. Maebasi, Mayebashi. Gunma, Honshū, S Japan
Maebasi see Maebashi
Mae Nam Khong see Mekong

Mae Nam Nan 136 C4 *river* NW Thailand
Mae Nam Yom 136 C4 *river* W Thailand
Maeseyck *see* Maaseik
Maestricht *see* Maastricht
Maéwo 144 D4 *prev.* Aurora. *island* C Vanuatu
Mafia 73 D7 *island* E Tanzania
Mafraq/Muḩāfaẓat al Mafraq *see* Al Mafraq
Magadan 115 G3 Magadanskaya Oblast', E Russian Federation
Magallanes *see* Punta Arenas
Magallanes, Estrecho de *see* Magellan, Strait of
Magangué 58 B2 Bolívar, N Colombia
Magdalena 61 F3 Beni, N Bolivia
Magdalena 56 B1 Sonora, NW Mexico
Magdalena 56 A2 *off.* Departamento del Magdalena. *province* N Colombia
Magdalena, Departamento del *see* Magdalena
Magdalena, Isla 50 B3 *island* W Mexico
Magdalena, Río 58 B2 *river* C Colombia
Magdalen Islands *see* Madeleine, Îles de la
Magdeburg 94 C4 Sachsen-Anhalt, C Germany
Magelang 138 C5 Jawa, C Indonesia
Magellan, Strait of 65 B8 *Sp.* Estrecho de Magallanes. *strait* Argentina/Chile
Mageröy *see* Magerøya
Magerøya 84 D1 *var.* Magerøy, *Lapp.* Máhkarávju. *island* N Norway
Maggiore, Lago *see* Maggiore, Lake
Maggiore, Lake 96 B1 *It.* Lago Maggiore. *lake* Italy/Switzerland
Maglaj 100 C3 Federacija Bosna I Hercegovina, N Bosnia and Herzegovina
Maglie 97 E6 Puglia, SE Italy
Magna 44 B4 Utah, W USA
Magnesia *see* Manisa
Magnitogorsk 114 B4 Chelyabinskaya Oblast', C Russian Federation
Magnolia State *see* Mississippi
Magta' Lahjar 74 C3 *var.* Magta Lahjar, Magta' Lahjar, Magtá Lahjar. Brakna, SW Mauritania
Magtymguly 122 B3 *prev.* Garrygala, *Rus.* Kara-Kala. *island* N Norway
Magwe 136 A3 *var.* Magway. Magwe, W Myanmar (Burma)
Magyar-Becse *see* Bečej
Magyarkanizsa *see* Kanjiža
Magyarország *see* Hungary
Mahajanga 79 F2 *var.* Majunga. Mahajanga, NW Madagascar
Mahakam, Sungai 138 D4 *var.* Koetai, Kutai. *river* Borneo, C Indonesia
Mahalapye 78 D3 *var.* Mahalatswe. Central, SE Botswana
Mahalatswe *see* Mahalapye
Māhān 120 D3 Kermān, E Iran
Mahanādi 135 F4 *river* E India
Mahārāshtra 134 D5 *state* W India
Mahārāshtra 134 D5 *cultural region* W India
Mahbés *see* El Mahbas
Mahbūbnagar 134 D5 Andhra Pradesh, C India
Mahdia 71 F2 *var.* Al Mahdīyah, Mehdia. NE Tunisia
Mahé 79 H1 *island* Inner Islands, NE Seychelles
Mahia Peninsula 150 E4 *peninsula* North Island, New Zealand
Mahilyow 107 D6 *Rus.* Mogilëv. Mahilyowskaya Voblasts', E Belarus
Máhkarávju *see* Magerøya
Mahmūd-e 'Erāqī *see* Maḩmūd-e Rāqī
Maḩmūd-e Rāqī 123 E4 *var.* Maḩmūd-e 'Erāqī. Kāpīsā, NE Afghanistan
Mahón 93 H3 *Cat.* Maó, *Eng.* Port Mahon; *anc.* Portus Magonis. Menorca, Spain, W Mediterranean Sea
Mährisch-Weisskirchen *see* Hranice
Maicao 58 C1 La Guajira, N Colombia
Mai Ceu/Mai Chio *see* Maych'ew
Maidstone 89 E7 SE England, UK
Maiduguri 75 H4 Borno, NE Nigeria
Mailand *see* Milano
Maimāna *see* Meymaneh
Main 95 B5 *river* C Germany
Mai-Ndombe, Lac 77 C6 *prev.* Lac Léopold II. *lake* W Dem. Rep. Congo

Maine 41 G2 *off.* State of Maine, *also known as* Lumber State, Pine Tree State. *state* NE USA
Maine 90 B3 *cultural region* NW France
Maine, Gulf of 41 H2 *gulf* NE USA
Mainland 88 C2 *island* N Scotland, UK
Mainland 88 D1 *island* NE Scotland, UK
Mainz 95 B5 *Fr.* Mayence. Rheinland-Pfalz, SW Germany
Maio 74 A3 *var.* Mayo. *island* Ilhas de Sotavento, SE Cape Verde
Maisur *see* Mysore, India
Maisur *see* Karnātaka, India
Maizhokunggar 126 C5 Xizang Zizhiqu, W China
Maíz, Islas del 53 E3 *var.* Corn Islands. *island group* SE Nicaragua
Majorca *see* Mallorca
Mājro *see* Majuro Atoll
Majunga *see* Mahajanga
Majuro Atoll 144 D2 *var.* Mājro. *atoll* Ratak Chain, SE Marshall Islands
Makale *see* Mek'elē
Makarov Basin 155 B3 *undersea basin* Arctic Ocean
Makarska 100 B4 *It.* Macarsca. Split-Dalmacija, SE Croatia
Makasar *see* Makassar
Makasar, Selat *see* Makassar Straits
Makassar 139 E4 *var.* Macassar, Makasar; *prev.* Ujungpandang. Sulawesi, C Indonesia
Makassar Straits 138 D4 *Ind.* Makasar Selat. *strait* C Indonesia
Makay 79 F3 *var.* Massif du Makay. *mountain range* SW Madagascar
Makay, Massif du *see* Makay
Makedonija *see* Macedonia, FYR
Makeni 74 C4 C Sierra Leone
Makeyevka *see* Makiyivka
Makhachkala 114 A4 *prev.* Petrovsk-Port. Respublika Dagestan, SW Russian Federation
Makin 144 D2 *prev.* Pitt Island. *atoll* Tungaru, W Kiribati
Makira *see* San Cristobal
Makiyivka 109 G3 *Rus.* Makeyevka; *prev.* Dmitriyevsk. Donets'ka Oblast', E Ukraine
Makkah 121 A5 *Eng.* Mecca. Makkah, W Saudi Arabia
Makkovik 39 F2 Newfoundland and Labrador, NE Canada
Makó 99 D7 *Rom.* Macău. Csongrád, SE Hungary
Makoua 77 B5 Cuvette, C Congo
Makran Coast 120 E4 *coastal region* SE Iran
Makrany 107 A6 *Rus.* Mokrany. Brestskaya Voblasts', SW Belarus
Mākū 120 B2 Āzarbāyjān-e Gharbī, NW Iran
Makurdi 75 G4 Benue, C Nigeria
Mala *see* Malaita, Solomon Islands
Malabar Coast 132 B3 *coast* SW India
Malabo 77 A5 *prev.* Santa Isabel. *country capital* (Equatorial Guinea) Isla de Bioco, NW Equatorial Guinea
Malaca *see* Málaga
Malacca, Strait of 138 B3 *Ind.* Selat Malaka. *strait* Indonesia/Malaysia
Malacka *see* Malacky
Malacky 99 C6 *Hung.* Malacka. Bratislavský Kraj, W Slovakia
Maladzyechna 107 C5 *Pol.* Molodeczno, *Rus.* Molodechno. Minskaya Voblasts', C Belarus
Málaga 92 D5 *anc.* Malaca. Andalucía, S Spain
Malagarasi River 73 B7 *river* W Tanzania Africa
Malagasy Republic *see* Madagascar
Malaita 144 C3 *var.* Mala. *island* N Solomon Islands
Malakal 73 B5 Upper Nile, S Sudan
Malakula *see* Makelula
Malang 138 D5 Jawa, C Indonesia
Malange *see* Malanje
Malanje 78 B1 *var.* Malange. Malanje, NW Angola
Mälaren 85 C6 *lake* C Sweden
Malatya 117 E4 *anc.* Melitene. Malatya, SE Turkey
Mala Vyska 109 E3 *Rus.* Malaya Viska. Kirovohrads'ka Oblast', S Ukraine

Malawi 79 E1 *off.* Republic of Malaŵi; *prev.* Nyasaland, Nyasaland Protectorate. *country* S Africa

MALAWI
Southern Africa

Official name Republic of Malawi
Formation 1964 / 1964
Capital Lilongwe
Population 12.9 million / 355 people per sq mile (137 people per sq km) / 25%
Total area 45,745 sq miles (118,480 sq km)
Languages English*, Chewa*, Lomwe, Yao, Ngoni
Religions Protestant 55%, Roman Catholic 20%, Muslim 20%, Traditional beliefs 5%
Ethnic mix Bantu 99%, Other 1%
Government Presidential system
Currency Malawi kwacha = 100 tambala
Literacy rate 64%
Calorie consumption 2155 calories

Malawi, Lake *see* Nyasa, Lake
Malawi, Republic of *see* Malawi
Malaya Viska *see* Mala Vyska
Malay Peninsula 124 D4 *peninsula* Malaysia/Thailand
Malaysia 138 B3 *var.* Federation of Malaysia; *prev.* the separate territories of Federation of Malaya, Sarawak and Sabah (North Borneo) and Singapore. *country* SE Asia

MALAYSIA
Southeast Asia

Official name Federation of Malaysia
Formation 1963 / 1965
Capital Kuala Lumpur; Putrajaya (administrative)
Population 25.3 million / 199 people per sq mile (77 people per sq km) / 57%
Total area 127,316 sq miles (329,750 sq km)
Languages Malay*, Chinese*, Bahasa Malaysia, Tamil, English
Religions Muslim (mainly Sunni) 53%, Buddhist 19%, Chinese faiths 12%, Other 7%, Christian 7%, Traditional beliefs 2%
Ethnic mix Malay 48%, Chinese 29%, Indigenous tribes 12%, Indian 6%, Other 5%
Government Parliamentary system
Currency Ringgit = 100 sen
Literacy rate 89%
Calorie consumption 2881 calories

Malaysia, Federation of *see* Malaysia
Malbork 98 C2 *Ger.* Marienburg, Marienburg in Westpreussen. Pomorskie, N Poland
Malchin 94 C3 Mecklenburg-Vorpommern, N Germany
Malden 45 H5 Missouri, C USA
Malden Island 145 G3 *prev.* Independence Island. *atoll* E Kiribati
Maldives 132 A4 *off.* Maldivian Divehi, Republic of Maldives. *country* N Indian Ocean

MALDIVES
Indian Ocean

Official name Republic of Maldives
Formation 1965 / 1965
Capital Male'
Population 329,000 / 2836 people per sq mile (1097 people per sq km) / 30%
Total area 116 sq miles (300 sq km)
Languages Dhivehi (Maldivian)*, Sinhala, Tamil, Arabic
Religions Sunni Muslim 100%
Ethnic mix Arab–Sinhalese–Malay 100%
Government Nonparty system
Currency Rufiyaa = 100 lari
Literacy rate 97%
Calorie consumption 2548 calories

Maldives, Republic of *see* Maldives
Maldivian Divehi *see* Maldives
Male' 132 B4 *Div.* Maale. *country capital* (Maldives) Male' Atoll, C Maldives
Male' Atoll 132 B4 *var.* Kaafu Atoll. *atoll* C Maldives

Malekula 144 D4 *var.* Malakula; *prev.* Mallicolo. *island* W Vanuatu
Malesína 105 C5 Stereá Ellás, E Greece
Malheur Lake 46 C3 *lake* Oregon, NW USA
Mali 75 E3 *off.* Republic of Mali, *Fr.* République du Mali; *prev.* French Sudan, Sudanese Republic. *country* W Africa

MALI
West Africa

Official name Republic of Mali
Formation 1960 / 1960
Capital Bamako
Population 13.5 million / 29 people per sq mile (11 people per sq km) / 30%
Total area 478,764 sq miles (1,240,000 sq km)
Languages French*, Bambara, Fulani, Senufo, Soninke
Religions Muslim (mainly Sunni) 80%, Traditional beliefs 18%, Christian 1%, Other 1%
Ethnic mix Bambara 32%, Other 26%, Fulani 14%, Senufu 12%, Soninka 9%, Tuareg 7%
Government Presidential system
Currency CFA franc = 100 centimes
Literacy rate 19%
Calorie consumption 2174 calories

Malik, Wadi al *see* Milk, Wadi al
Mali Kyun 137 B5 *var.* Tavoy Island. *island* Mergui Archipelago, S Myanmar (Burma)
Malin *see* Malyn
Malindi 73 D7 Coast, SE Kenya
Malines *see* Mechelen
Mali, Republic of *see* Mali
Mali, République du *see* Mali
Malkiye *see* Al Mālikīyah
Malko Tŭrnovo 104 E3 Burgas, E Bulgaria
Mallaig 88 B3 N Scotland, UK
Mallawi 72 B2 C Egypt
Mallicolo *see* Malekula
Mallorca 93 G3 *Eng.* Majorca; *anc.* Baleares Major. *island* Islas Baleares, Spain, W Mediterranean Sea
Malmberget 84 C3 *Lapp.* Malmivaara. Norrbotten, N Sweden
Malmédy 87 D6 Liège, E Belgium
Malmivaara *see* Malmberget
Malmö 85 B7 Skåne, S Sweden
Maloelap Atoll 144 D1 *var.* Maļoeļap. *atoll* E Marshall Islands
Małopolska, Wyżyna 98 D4 *plateau* S Poland
Malozemel'skaya Tundra 110 D3 *physical region* NW Russian Federation
Malta 106 D4 Rēzekne, SE Latvia
Malta 44 C1 Montana, NW USA
Malta 97 C8 *off.* Republic of Malta. *country* C Mediterranean Sea

MALTA
Southern Europe

Official name Republic of Malta
Formation 1964 / 1964
Capital Valletta
Population 402,000 / 3242 people per sq mile (1256 people per sq km) / 91%
Total area 122 sq miles (316 sq km)
Languages Maltese*, English
Religions Roman Catholic 98%, Other and nonreligious 2%
Ethnic mix Maltese 96%, Other 4%
Government Parliamentary system
Currency Maltese lira = 100 cents
Literacy rate 88%
Calorie consumption 3587 calories

Malta 97 C8 *island* Malta, C Mediterrnean Sea
Malta, Canale di *see* Malta Channel
Malta Channel 97 C8 *It.* Canale di Malta. *strait* Italy/Malta
Malta, Republic of *see* Malta
Maluku 139 F4 *Dut.* Molukken, *Eng.* Moluccas; *prev.* Spice Islands. *island group* E Indonesia
Maluku, Laut *see* Molucca Sea
Malung 85 B6 Dalarna, C Sweden

Malventum see Benevento
Malvinas, Islas see Falkland Islands
Malyn *108 D2 Rus.* Malin. Zhytomyrs'ka Oblast', N Ukraine
Malyy Kavkaz see Lesser Caucasus
Mamberamo, Sungai *139 H4 river* Papua, E Indonesia
Mambij see Manbij
Mamonovo *106 A4 Ger.* Heiligenbeil. Kaliningradskaya Oblast', W Russian Federation
Mamoré, Rio *61 F3 river* Bolivia/Brazil
Mamou *74 C4* W Guinea
Mamoudzou *79 F2 dependent territory capital* (Mayotte) C Mayotte
Mamuno *78 C3* Ghanzi, W Botswana
Manacor *93 G3* Mallorca, Spain, W Mediterranean Sea
Manado *139 F3 prev.* Menado. Sulawesi, C Indonesia
Managua *52 D3 country capital* (Nicaragua) Managua, W Nicaragua
Managua, Lago de *52 C3 var.* Xolotlán. *lake* W Nicaragua
Manakara *79 G4* Fianarantsoa, SE Madagascar
Manama see Al Manāmah
Mananjary *79 G3* Fianarantsoa, SE Madagascar
Manáos see Manaus
Manapouri, Lake *151 A7 lake* South Island, New Zealand
Manar see Mannar
Manas, Gora *123 E2 mountain* Kyrgyzstan/Uzbekistan
Manaus *62 D2 prev.* Manáos. *state capital* Amazonas, NW Brazil
Manavgat *116 B4* Antalya, SW Turkey
Manbij *118 C2 var.* Mambij, *Fr.* Membidj. Ḥalab, N Syria
Manchester *89 D5 Lat.* Mancunium. NW England, UK
Manchester *41 G3* New Hampshire, NE USA
Man-chou-li see Manzhouli
Manchurian Plain *125 E1 plain* NE China
Máncio Lima see Japiim
Mancunium see Manchester
Mand see Mand, Rūd-e
Mandalay *136 B3* Mandalay, C Myanmar (Burma)
Mandan *45 E2* North Dakota, N USA
Mandeville *54 B5* C Jamaica
Mándra *105 C6* Attikí, C Greece
Mand, Rūd-e *120 D4 var.* Mand. *river* S Iran
Mandurah *147 A6* Western Australia
Manduria *97 E5* Puglia, SE Italy
Mandya *132 C2* Karnātaka, C India
Manfredonia *97 D5* Puglia, SE Italy
Mangai *77 C6* Bandundu, W Dem. Rep. Congo
Mangaia *145 G5 island group* S Cook Islands
Mangalia *108 D5 anc.* Callatis. Constanţa, SE Romania
Mangalmé *76 C3* Guéra, SE Chad
Mangalore *132 B2* Karnātaka, W India
Manguang see Bloemfontein
Mango see Sansanné-Mango, Togo
Mangoky *79 F3 river* W Madagascar
Manhattan *45 F4* Kansas, C USA
Manicouagan, Réservoir *38 D3 lake* Québec, E Canada
Manihiki *145 G4 island* N Cook Islands
Manihiki Plateau *143 E3 undersea plateau* C Pacific Ocean
Maniitsoq *82 C3 var.* Manîtsoq, *Dan.* Sukkertoppen. Kitaa, S Greenland
Manila *139 E1 off.* City of Manila. *country capital* (Philippines) Luzon, N Philippines
Manila, City of see Manila
Manisa *116 A3 var.* Manissa, *prev.* Saruhan; *anc.* Magnesia. Manisa, W Turkey
Manissa see Manisa
Manitoba *37 F5 province* S Canada
Manitoba, Lake *37 F5 lake* Manitoba, S Canada
Manitoulin Island *38 C4 island* Ontario, S Canada
Manîtsoq see Maniitsoq
Manizales *58 B3* Caldas, W Colombia
Manjimup *147 A7* Western Australia
Mankato *45 F3* Minnesota, N USA
Manlleu *93 G2* Cataluña, NE Spain

Manly *148 E1* Iowa, C USA
Manmād *134 C5* Mahārāshtra, W India
Mannar, Gulf of *132 C3 gulf* India/Sri Lanka
Mannar *132 C3 var.* Manar. Northern Province, NW Sri Lanka
Mannheim *95 B5* Baden-Württemberg, SW Germany
Manokwari *139 G4* Papua, E Indonesia
Manono *77 E7* Shaba, SE Dem. Rep. Congo
Manosque *91 D6* Alpes-de-Haute-Provence, SE France
Manra *145 F3 prev.* Sydney Island. *atoll* Phoenix Islands, C Kiribati
Mansa *78 D2 prev.* Fort Rosebery. Luapula, N Zambia
Mansel Island *37 G3 island* Nunavut, NE Canada
Mansfield *40 D4* Ohio, N USA
Manta *60 A2* Manabí, W Ecuador
Manteca *47 B6* California, W USA
Mantoue see Mantova
Mantova *96 B2 Eng.* Mantua, *Fr.* Mantoue. Lombardia, NW Italy
Mantua see Mantova
Manuae *145 G4 island* S Cook Islands
Manukau see Manurewa
Manurewa *150 D3 var.* Manukau. Auckland, North Island, New Zealand
Manzanares *93 E3* Castilla-La Mancha, C Spain
Manzanillo *54 C3* Granma, E Cuba
Manzanillo *50 D4* Colima, SW Mexico
Manzhouli *127 F1 var.* Man-chou-li. Nei Mongol Zizhiqu, N China
Mao *76 B3* Kanem, W Chad
Maó see Mahón
Maoke, Pegunungan *139 H4 Dut.* Sneeuw-gebergte, *Eng.* Snow Mountains. *mountain range* Papua, E Indonesia
Maoming *128 C6* Guangdong, S China
Mapmaker Seamounts *125 H2 seamount range* N Pacific Ocean
Maputo *78 D4 prev.* Lourenço Marques. *country capital* (Mozambique) Maputo, S Mozambique
Marabá *63 F2* Pará, NE Brazil
Maracaibo *58 C1* Zulia, NW Venezuela
Maracaibo, Gulf of see Venezuela, Golfo de
Maracaibo, Lago de *58 C2 var.* Lake Maracaibo. *inlet* NW Venezuela
Maracaibo, Lake see Maracaibo, Lago de
Maracay *58 D2* Aragua, N Venezuela
Marada see Marādah
Marādah *71 G3 var.* Marada. N Libya
Maradi *75 G3* Maradi, S Niger
Maragha see Marāgheh
Marāgheh *120 C2 var.* Maragha. Āžarbāyjān-e Khāvarī, NW Iran
Marajó, Baía de *63 F1 bay* N Brazil
Marajó, Ilha de *63 E1 island* N Brazil
Marakesh see Marrakech
Maramba see Livingstone
Maramba see Livingstone
Maranhão *63 F2 off.* Estado do Maranhão. *state* E Brazil
Marañón, Río *60 B2 river* N Peru
Marathón *34 C2* Ontario, S Canada
Marathón see Marathónas
Marathónas *105 C5 prev.* Marathón. Attikí, C Greece
Märäzä *117 H2 Rus.* Maraza. E Azerbaijan
Maraza see Märäzä
Marbella *92 D5* Andalucía, S Spain
Marble Bar *146 B4* Western Australia
Marburg see Maribor
Marburg see Marburg an der Lahn
Marburg an der Lahn *94 B4 hist.* Marburg. Hessen, W Germany
March see Morava
Marche *96 C3 Eng.* Marches. *region* C Italy
Marche *91 C5 cultural region* C France
Marche-en-Famenne *87 C7* Luxembourg, SE Belgium
Marchena, Isla *60 B5 var.* Bindloe Island. *island* Galapagos Islands, Ecuador, E Pacific Ocean
Marches see Marche
Mar Chiquita, Laguna *64 C3 lake* C Argentina
Marcounda see Markounda
Mardān *134 C1* North-West Frontier Province, N Pakistan

Mar del Plata *65 D5* Buenos Aires, E Argentina
Mardin *117 E4* Mardin, SE Turkey
Maré *144 D5 island* Îles Loyauté, E New Caledonia
Marea Neagră see Black Sea
Mareeba *148 D3* Queensland, NE Australia
Marek see Dupnitsa
Margarita, Isla de *59 E1 island* N Venezuela
Margate *89 E7 prev.* Mergate. SE England, UK
Margherita see Jamaame
Margherita, Lake see Ābaya Hāyk'
Marghita *108 B3 Hung.* Margitta. Bihor, NW Romania
Margitta see Marghita
Marhanets' *109 F3 Rus.* Marganets. Dnipropetrovs'ka Oblast', E Ukraine
María Cleofas, Isla *50 C4 island* C Mexico
Maria Island *149 C8 island* Tasmania, SE Australia
María Madre, Isla *50 C4 island* C Mexico
María Magdalena, Isla *50 C4 island* C Mexico
Mariana Trench *125 C4 var.* Challenger Deep. *trench* W Pacific Ocean
Mariánské Lázně *99 A5 Ger.* Marienbad. Karlovarský Kraj, W Czech Republic
Marías, Islas *50 C4 island group* C Mexico North America
Maria-Theresiopel see Subotica
Maribor *95 E7 Ger.* Marburg. NE Slovenia
Maridi *73 B5* Western Equatoria, SW Sudan
Marie Byrd Land *154 A3 physical region* Antarctica
Marie-Galante *55 G4 var.* Ceyre to the Caribs. *island* SE Guadeloupe
Marienbad see Mariánské Lázně
Marienburg see Alūksne, Latvia
Marienburg see Malbork, Poland
Marienburg in Westpreussen see Malbork
Marienhausen see Viļaka
Mariental *78 B4* Hardap, SW Namibia
Marienwerder see Kwidzyń
Mariestad *85 B6* Västra Götaland, S Sweden
Marietta *42 D2* Georgia, SE USA
Marijampolė *106 B4 prev.* Kapsukas. Marijampolė, S Lithuania
Marília *63 E4* São Paulo, S Brazil
Marín *92 B1* Galicia, NW Spain
Mar'ina Gorka see Mar''ina Horka
Mar''ina Horka *107 C6 Rus.* Mar'ina Gorka. Minskaya Voblasts', C Belarus
Maringá *63 E4* Paraná, S Brazil
Marion *45 G3* Iowa, C USA
Marion *40 D4* Ohio, N USA
Marion, Lake *43 E2 reservoir* South Carolina, SE USA
Mariscal Estigarribia *64 D2* Boquerón, NW Paraguay
Maritsa *104 D3 var.* Marica, *Gk.* Évros, *Turk.* Meriç; *anc.* Hebrus. *river* SW Europe
Maritzburg see Pietermaritzburg
Mariupol' *109 G4 prev.* Zhdanov. Donets'ka Oblast', SE Ukraine
Marka *73 D6 var.* Merca. Shabeellaha Hoose, S Somalia
Markham, Mount *154 B4 mountain* Antarctica
Markounda *76 C4 var.* Marcounda. Ouham, NW Central African Republic
Marktredwitz *95 C5* Bayern, E Germany
Marlborough *148 D4* Queensland, E Australia
Marmande see Marmande
Marmande *91 B5 anc.* Marmanda. Lot-et-Garonne, SW France
Marmara Denizi *116 A2 Eng.* Sea of Marmara. *sea* NW Turkey
Marmara, Sea of see Marmara Denizi
Marmaris *116 A4* Muğla, SW Turkey
Marne *90 C3 department* N France
Marne *90 C3 cultural region* N France
Maro *76 C4* Moyen-Chari, S Chad
Maroantsetra *79 G2* Toamasina, NE Madagascar

Maromokotro *79 G2 mountain* N Madagascar
Maroni *59 G3 Dut.* Marowijne. *river* French Guiana/Suriname
Maroshevíz see Topliţa
Marosludas see Luduş
Marosvásárhely see Târgu Mureş
Marotiri *143 F4 var.* Îlots de Bass, Morotiri. *island group* Îles Australes, SW French Polynesia
Maroua *76 B3* Extrême-Nord, N Cameroon
Marowijne see Maroni
Marquesas Fracture Zone *153 E3 fracture zone* E Pacific Ocean
Marquette *40 B1* Michigan, N USA
Marrakech *70 C2 var.* Marrakesh, *Eng.* Marrakesh; *prev.* Morocco. W Morocco
Marrakesh see Marrakech
Marrawah *149 C8* Tasmania, SE Australia
Marree *149 B5* South Australia
Marsá al Burayqah *71 G3 var.* Al Burayqah. N Libya
Marsabit *73 C6* Eastern, N Kenya
Marsala *97 B7 anc.* Lilybaeum. Sicilia, Italy, C Mediterranean Sea
Marsberg *94 B4* Nordrhein-Westfalen, W Germany
Marseille *91 D6 Eng.* Marseilles; *anc.* Massilia. Bouches-du-Rhône, SE France
Marseilles see Marseille
Marshall *45 F2* Minnesota, N USA
Marshall *49 H2* Texas, SW USA
Marshall Islands *144 C1 off.* Republic of the Marshall Islands. *country* W Pacific Ocean

MARSHALL ISLANDS
Australasia & Oceania

Official name Republic of the Marshall Islands
Formation 1986 / 1986
Capital Majuro
Population 59,071 / 844 people per sq mile
(326 people per sq km) / 69%
Total area 70 sq miles (181 sq km)
Languages Marshallese*, English*, Japanese, German
Religions Protestant 90%, Roman Catholic 8%, Other 2%
Ethnic mix Micronesian 97%, Other 3%
Government Presidential system
Currency US dollar = 100 cents
Literacy rate 91%
Calorie consumption Not available

Marshall Islands, Republic of the see Marshall Islands
Marshall Seamounts *125 H3 seamount range* SW Pacific Ocean
Marsh Harbour *54 C1* Great Abaco, W Bahamas
Martaban *136 B4 var.* Moktama. Mon State, S Myanmar (Burma)
Martha's Vineyard *41 G3 island* Massachusetts, NE USA
Martigues *91 D6* Bouches-du-Rhône, SE France
Martin *99 C5 Ger.* Sankt Martin, *Hung.* Turócszentmárton; *prev.* Turčiansky Svätý Martin. Žilinský Kraj, N Slovakia
Martinique *55 G4 French overseas department* E West Indies
Martinique Channel see Martinique Passage
Martinique Passage *55 G4 var.* Dominica Channel, Martinique Channel. *channel* Dominica/Martinique
Marton *150 D4* Manawatu-Wanganui, North Island, New Zealand
Martos *92 D4* Andalucía, S Spain
Marungu *77 E7 mountain range* SE Dem. Rep. Congo
Mary *122 D3 prev.* Merv. Mary Welayaty, S Turkmenistan
Maryborough *149 D4* Queensland, E Australia
Maryborough see Port Laoise
Mary Island see Kanton
Maryland *41 E5 off.* State of Maryland, *also known as* America in Miniature, Cockade State, Free State, Old Line State. *state* NE USA

Maryland, State of *see* Maryland
Maryville 45 F4 Missouri, C USA
Maryville 42 D1 Tennessee, S USA
Masai Steppe 73 C7 *grassland*
   NW Tanzania
Masaka 73 B6 SW Uganda
Masallı 117 H3 *Rus.* Masally.
   S Azerbaijan
Masally *see* Masallı
Masasi 73 C8 Mtwara, SE Tanzania
Masawa *see* Massawa
Masaya 52 D3 Masaya, W Nicaragua
Mascarene Basin 141 B5 *undersea basin*
   W Indian Ocean
Mascarene Islands 79 H4 *island group*
   W Indian Ocean
Mascarene Plain 141 B5 *abyssal plain*
   W Indian Ocean
Mascarene Plateau 141 B5 *undersea plateau* W Indian Ocean
Maseru 78 D4 *country capital* (Lesotho)
   W Lesotho
Mas-ha 119 D7 W West Bank Asia
Mashhad 120 E2 *var.* Meshed.
   Khorāsān-Razavī, NE Iran
Masindi 73 B6 W Uganda
Masira *see* Maşīrah, Jazīrat
Masira, Gulf of *see* Maşīrah, Khalīj
Maşīrah, Jazīrat 121 E5 *var.* Masira.
   island E Oman
Maşīrah, Khalīj 121 E5 *var.* Gulf of
   Masira. *bay* E Oman
Masis *see* Büyükağrı Dağı
Maskat *see* Masqaţ
Mason City 45 F3 Iowa, C USA
Masqaţ 121 E5 *var.* Maskat, *Eng.* Muscat.
   country capital (Oman) NE Oman
Massa 96 B3 Toscana, C Italy
Massachusetts 41 G3 *off.*
   Commonwealth of Massachusetts, *also
   known as* Bay State, Old Bay State, Old
   Colony State. *state* NE USA
Massawa 72 C4 *var.* Masawa, *Amh.*
   Mits'iwa. E Eritrea
Massenya 76 B3 Chari-Baguirmi,
   SW Chad
Massif Central 91 C5 *plateau* C France
Massilia *see* Marseille
Massoukou *see* Franceville
Mastanli *see* Momchilgrad
Masterton 151 D5 Wellington, North
   Island, New Zealand
Masty 107 B5 *Rus.* Mosty.
   Hrodzyenskaya Voblasts', W Belarus
Masuda 131 B6 Shimane, Honshū,
   SW Japan
Masuku *see* Franceville
Masvingo 78 D3 *prev.* Fort Victoria,
   Nyanda, Victoria. Masvingo,
   SE Zimbabwe
Maşyāf 118 B3 *Fr.* Misiaf. Ḥamāh,
   C Syria
Matadi 77 B6 Bas-Congo, W Dem.
   Rep. Congo
Matagalpa 52 D3 Matagalpa,
   C Nicaragua
Matale 132 D3 Central Province,
   C Sri Lanka
Matam 74 C3 NE Senegal
Matamata 150 D3 Waikato, North
   Island, New Zealand
Matamoros 51 E2 Tamaulipas, C Mexico
Matamoros 51 E2 Tamaulipas, C Mexico
Matane 39 E4 Québec, SE Canada
Matanzas 54 B2 Matanzas, NW Cuba
Matara 132 D4 Southern Province,
   S Sri Lanka
Mataram 138 D5 Pulau Lombok,
   C Indonesia
Mataró 93 G2 *anc.* Illuro. Cataluña,
   E Spain
Mataura 151 B7 Southland, South Island,
   New Zealand
Mataura 151 B7 *river* South Island,
   New Zealand
Mata Uta *see* Matā'utu
Matā'utu 145 E4 *var.* Mata Uta.
   dependent territory capital (Wallis and
   Futuna) Île Uvea, Wallis and Futuna
Matera 97 E5 Basilicata, S Italy
Mathurai *see* Madurai
Matías Romero 51 F5 Oaxaca,
   SE Mexico
Matisco/Matisco Ædourum *see* Mâcon
Mato Grosso 63 E4 *prev.* Vila Bela da
   Santíssima Trindade. Mato Grosso,
   W Brazil

Mato Grosso do Sul 63 E4
   off. Estado de Mato Grosso do Sul.
   state S Brazil
Mato Grosso do Sul, Estado de *see* Mato
   Grosso do Sul
Mato Grosso, Planalto de 56 C4 *plateau*
   C Brazil
Matosinhos 92 B2 *prev.* Matozinhos.
   Porto, NW Portugal
Matozinhos *see* Matosinhos
Matsue 131 B6 *var.* Matsuye, Matue.
   Shimane, Honshū, SW Japan
Matsumoto 131 C5 *var.* Matumoto.
   Nagano, Honshū, S Japan
Matsuyama 131 B7 *var.* Matuyama.
   Ehime, Shikoku, SW Japan
Matsuye *see* Matsue
Matterhorn 95 A8 *It.* Monte Cervino.
   mountain Italy/Switzerland
Matthews Ridge 59 F2 N Guyana
Matthew Town 54 D2 Great Inagua,
   S Bahamas
Matucana 60 C4 Lima, W Peru
Matue *see* Matsue
Matumoto *see* Matsumoto
Maturín 59 E2 Monagas,
   NE Venezuela
Matuyama *see* Matsuyama
Mau 135 E3 *var.* Maunāth Bhanjan.
   Uttar Pradesh, N India
Maui 47 B8 *island* Hawai'i, USA,
   C Pacific Ocean
Maulmain *see* Moulmein
Maun 78 C3 North-West, C Botswana
Maunāth Bhanjan *see* Mau
Mauren 94 E1 NE Liechtenstein Europe
Maurice *see* Mauritius
Mauritania 74 C2 *off.* Islamic Republic
   of Mauritania, *Ar.* Mūrītānīyah.
   country W Africa

MAURITANIA
West Africa

Official name Islamic Republic of
   Mauritania
Formation 1960 / 1960
Capital Nouakchott
Population 3.1 million / 8 people per
   sq mile (3 people per sq km) / 58%
Total area 397,953 sq miles
   (1,030,700 sq km)
Languages French*, Hassaniyah Arabic,
   Wolof
Religions Sunni Muslim 100%
Ethnic mix Maure 81%, Wolof 7%,
   Tukolor 5%, Other 4%, Soninka 3%
Government Transitional regime
Currency Ouguiya = 5 khoums
Literacy rate 51%
Calorie consumption 2772 calories

Mauritania, Islamic Republic of *see*
   Mauritania
Mauritius 79 H3 *off.* Republic of
   Mauritius, *Fr.* Maurice. *country*
   W Indian Ocean

MAURITIUS
Indian Ocean

Official name Republic of Mauritius
Formation 1968 / 1968
Capital Port Louis
Population 1.2 million / 1671 people per
   sq mile (645 people per sq km) / 41%
Total area 718 sq miles
   (1860 sq km)
Languages English*, French Creole,
   Hindi, Urdu, Tamil, Chinese, French
Religions Hindu 52%, Roman
   Catholic 26%, Muslim 17%, Other 3%,
   Protestant 2%
Ethnic mix Indo-Mauritian 68%,
   Creole 27%, Sino-Mauritian 3%,
   Franco-Mauritian 2%
Government Parliamentary system
Currency Mauritian rupee = 100 cents
Literacy rate 84%
Calorie consumption 2955 calories

Mauritius 141 B5 *island* W Indian Ocean
Mauritius, Republic of *see* Mauritius
Mawlamyine *see* Moulmein
Mawson 154 D2 *Australian research
   station* Antarctica
Maya 52 B1 *river* E Russian Federation
Mayadin *see* Al Mayādīn

Mayaguana 54 D2 *island* SE Bahamas
Mayaguana Passage 54 D2 *passage*
   SE Bahamas
Mayagüez 55 F3 W Puerto Rico
Mayamey 120 D2 Semnān, N Iran
Maya Mountains 52 B2 *Sp.*
   Montañas Mayas. *mountain range*
   Belize/Guatemala
Mayas, Montañas *see* Maya Mountains
Maych'ew 72 C4 *var.* Mai Chio, *It.* Mai
   Ceu. Tigray, N Ethiopia
Maydān Shahr *see* Meydān Shahr
Mayebashi *see* Maebashi
Mayence *see* Mainz
Mayfield 151 B6 Canterbury, South
   Island, New Zealand
Maykop 111 A7 Respublika Adygeya,
   SW Russian Federation
Maymana *see* Meymaneh
Maymyo 136 B3 Mandalay,
   C Myanmar (Burma)
Mayo *see* Maio
Mayor Island 150 D3 *island* NE New
   Zealand
Mayor Pablo Lagerenza *see* Capitán
   Pablo Lagerenza
Mayotte 79 F2 *French territorial
   collectivity* E Africa
May Pen 54 B5 C Jamaica
Mayyit, Al Baḥr al *see* Dead Sea
Mazabuka 78 D2 Southern, S Zambia
Mazaca *see* Kayseri
Mazagan *see* El-Jadida
Mazar-e Sharif 123 E3 *var.* Mazār-i
   Sharif. Balkh, N Afghanistan
Mazar-i Sharif *see* Mazār-e Sharīf
Mazatlán 50 C3 Sinaloa, C Mexico
Mažeikiai 106 B3 Telšiai, NW Lithuania
Mazirbe 106 C2 Talsi, NW Latvia
Mazra'a *see* Mazra'ah
Mazury 98 D3 *physical region* NE Poland
Mazyr 107 C7 *Rus.* Mozyr'.
   Homyel'skaya Voblasts', SE Belarus
Mba *see* Ba
Mbabane 78 D4 *country capital*
   (Swaziland) NW Swaziland
Mbacké *see* Mbaké
Mbaïki 77 C5 *var.* M'Baiki. Lobaye,
   SW Central African Republic
M'Baiki *see* Mbaïki
Mbaké 74 B3 *var.* Mbacké. W Senegal
Mbala 78 D1 *prev.* Abercorn. Northern,
   NE Zambia
Mbale 73 C6 E Uganda
Mbandaka 77 C5 *prev.* Coquilhatville.
   Equateur, NW Dem. Rep. Congo
M'Banza Congo 78 B1 *var.* Mbanza
   Congo; *prev.* São Salvador, São
   Salvador do Congo. Dem. Rep. Congo,
   NW Angola
Mbanza-Ngungu 77 B6 Bas-Congo,
   W Dem. Rep. Congo
Mbarara 73 B6 SW Uganda
Mbé 76 B4 Nord, N Cameroon
Mbeya 73 C7 Mbeya, SW Tanzania
Mbomou/M'Bomu/Mbomu *see* Bomu
Mbour 74 B3 W Senegal
Mbuji-Mayi 77 D7 *prev.* Bakwanga.
   Kasai Oriental, S Dem. Rep. Congo
McAlester 49 G2 Oklahoma, C USA
McAllen 49 G5 Texas, SW USA
McCamey 49 E3 Texas, SW USA
McClintock Channel 37 F2 *channel*
   Nunavut, N Canada
McComb 42 B3 Mississippi, S USA
McCook 45 E4 Nebraska, C USA
McKean Island 145 E3 *island* Phoenix
   Islands, C Kiribati
McKinley, Mount 36 C3 *var.* Denali.
   mountain Alaska, USA
McKinley Park 36 C3 Alaska, USA
McMinnville 46 B3 Oregon, NW USA
McMurdo 154 B4 US *research station*
   Antarctica
McPherson 45 E5 Kansas, C USA
McPherson *see* Fort McPherson
Mdantsane 78 D5 Eastern Cape,
   SE South Africa
Mead, Lake 47 D6 *reservoir* Arizona/
   Nevada, W USA
Mecca *see* Makkah
Mechelen 87 C5 *Eng.* Mechlin, *Fr.*
   Malines. Antwerpen, C Belgium
Mechlin *see* Mechelen
Mecklenburger Bucht 94 C2 *bay*
   N Germany
Mecsek 99 C7 *mountain range*
   SW Hungary

Medan 138 B3 Sumatera, E Indonesia
Medeba *see* Ma'dabā
Medellín 58 B3 Antioquia,
   NW Colombia
Médenine 71 F2 *var.* Madanīyīn.
   SE Tunisia
Medeshamstede *see* Peterborough
Medford 46 B4 Oregon, NW USA
Medgidia 108 D5 Constanţa,
   SE Romania
Medgyes *see* Mediaş
Mediaş 108 B4 *Ger.* Mediasch, *Hung.*
   Medgyes. Sibiu, C Romania
Mediasch *see* Mediaş
Medicine Hat 37 F5 Alberta, SW Canada
Medina *see* Al Madīnah
Medinaceli 93 E2 Castilla-León, N Spain
Medina del Campo 92 D2 Castilla-León,
   N Spain
Medinat Israel *see* Israel
Mediolanum *see* Saintes, France
Mediolanum *see* Milano, Italy
Mediomatrica *see* Metz
Mediterranean Sea 102 D3 *Fr.* Mer
   Méditerranée, *sea* Africa/Asia/Europe
Méditerranée, Mer *see* Mediterranean
   Sea
Médoc 91 B5 *cultural region* SW France
Medved'yegorsk 110 B3 Respublika
   Kareliya, NW Russian Federation
Meekatharra 147 B5 Western Australia
Meemu Atoll *see* Mulaku Atoll
Meerssen 87 D6 *var.* Mersen. Limburg,
   SE Netherlands
Meerut 134 D2 Uttar Pradesh, N India
Megáli Préspa, Límni *see* Prespa, Lake
Meghālaya 113 G3 *state* NE India
Meghālaya 113 G3 *cultural region*
   NE India
Mehdia *see* Mahdia
Meheso *see* Mi'éso
Me Hka *see* Nmai Hka
Mehriz 120 D3 Yazd, C Iran
Mehtar Lām 123 F4 *var.* Mehtarlām,
   Meterlam, Methariam, Metharlam,
   Laghmān, E Afghanistan
Mehtarlām *see* Mehtar Lām
Meiktila 136 B3 Mandalay,
   C Myanmar (Burma)
Méjico *see* Mexico
Mejillones 62 B2 Antofagasta, N Chile
Mek'elē 72 C4 *var.* Makale. Tigray,
   N Ethiopia
Mékhé 74 B3 NW Senegal
Mekong 124 D3 *var.* Lan-ts'ang Chiang,
   Cam. Mékôngk, *Chin.* Lancang Jiang,
   Lao. Mènam Khong, *Th.* Mae Nam
   Khong, *Tib.* Dza Chu, *Vtn.* Sông Tiên
   Giang. *river* SE Asia
Mékôngk *see* Mekong
Mekong, Mouths of the 137 E6 *delta*
   S Vietnam
Melaka 138 B3 *var.* Malacca. Melaka,
   Peninsular Malaysia
Melaka, Selat *see* Malacca, Strait of
Melanesia 144 D3 *island group* W Pacific
   Ocean
Melanesian Basin 142 C2 *undersea
   basin* W Pacific Ocean
Melbourne 149 C7 *state capital* Victoria,
   SE Australia
Melbourne 43 E4 Florida, SE USA
Meleda *see* Mljet
Melghir, Chott 71 E2 *var.* Chott Melrhir.
   salt lake E Algeria
Melilla 80 B5 *anc.* Rusaddir, Russadir.
   Melilla, Spain, N Africa
Melilla 70 D2 *enclave* Spain, N Africa
Melita 37 F5 Manitoba, S Canada
Melita *see* Mljet
Melitene *see* Malatya
Melitopol' 109 F4 Zaporiz'ka Oblast',
   SE Ukraine
Melle 87 B5 Oost-Vlaanderen,
   NW Belgium
Mellerud 85 B6 Västra Götaland,
   S Sweden
Mellieha 102 B5 E Malta
Mellizo Sur, Cerro 65 A7 *mountain*
   S Chile
Melo 64 E4 Cerro Largo, NE Uruguay
Melodunum *see* Melun
Melrhir, Chott *see* Melghir, Chott
Melsungen 94 B4 Hessen, C Germany
Melun 90 C3 *anc.* Melodunum. Seine-et-
   Marne, N France
Melville Bay/Melville Bugt *see*
   Qimusseriarsuaq

Melville Island 146 D2 *island* Northern Territory, N Australia

Melville Island 37 E2 *island* Parry Islands, Northwest Territories, NW Canada

Melville, Lake 39 F2 *lake* Newfoundland and Labrador, E Canada

Melville Peninsula 37 G3 *peninsula* Nunavut, NE Canada

Melville Sound *see* Viscount Melville Sound

Membidj *see* Manbij

Memel *see* Neman, NE Europe

Memel *see* Klaipėda, Lithuania

Memmingen 95 B6 Bayern, S Germany

Memphis 42 C1 Tennessee, S USA

Menaam *see* Menaldum

Menado *see* Manado

Ménaka 75 F3 Goa, E Mali

Menaldum 86 D1 Fris. Menaam. Friesland, N Netherlands

Mènam Khong *see* Mekong

Mendaña Fracture Zone 153 F4 *fracture zone* E Pacific Ocean

Mende 91 C5 *anc.* Mimatum. Lozère, S France

Mendeleyev Ridge 155 B2 *undersea ridge* Arctic Ocean

Mendocino Fracture Zone 152 D2 *fracture zone* NE Pacific Ocean

Mendoza 64 B4 Mendoza, W Argentina

Menemen 116 A3 Izmir, W Turkey

Menengiyn Tal 127 F2 *plain* E Mongolia

Menongue 78 B2 *var.* Vila Serpa Pinto, Port. Serpa Pinto. Cuando Cubango, C Angola

Menorca 93 H3 Eng. Minorca; anc. Balearis Minor. *island* Islas Baleares, Spain, W Mediterranean Sea

Mentawai, Kepulauan 138 A4 *island group* W Indonesia

Meppel 86 D2 Drenthe, NE Netherlands

Meran *see* Merano

Merano 96 C1 Ger. Meran. Trentino-Alto Adige, N Italy

Merca *see* Marka

Mercedes 64 D3 Corrientes, NE Argentina

Mercedes 64 D4 Soriano, SW Uruguay

Meredith, Lake 49 E1 *reservoir* Texas, SW USA

Merefa 109 G2 Kharkivs'ka Oblast', E Ukraine

Mergate *see* Margate

Mergui 137 B6 Tenasserim, S Myanmar (Burma)

Mergui Archipelago 137 B6 *island group* S Myanmar (Burma)

Mérida 51 H3 Yucatán, SW Mexico

Mérida 92 C4 anc. Augusta Emerita. Extremadura, W Spain

Mérida 58 C2 Mérida, W Venezuela

Meridian 42 C2 Mississippi, S USA

Mérignac 91 B5 Gironde, SW France

Merín, Laguna *see* Mirim Lagoon

Merkulovichi *see* Myerkulavichy

Merowe 72 B3 Northern, N Sudan

Merredin 147 B6 Western Australia

Mersen *see* Meerssen

Mersey 89 D5 *river* NW England, U K

Mersin 116 C4 Mersin, S Turkey

Mērsrags 106 C3 Talsi, NW Latvia

Meru 73 C6 Eastern, C Kenya

Merv *see* Mary

Merzifon 116 D2 Amasya, N Turkey

Merzig 95 A5 Saarland, SW Germany

Mesa 48 B2 Arizona, SW USA

Meseritz *see* Międzyrzecz

Meshed *see* Mashhad

Mesopotamia 57 C5 *var.* Mesopotamia Argentina. *physical region* NE Argentina

Mesopotamia Argentina *see* Mesopotamia

Messalo, Rio 79 E2 *var.* Mualo. *river* NE Mozambique

Messina 97 D7 *var.* Messana, Messene; anc. Zancle. Sicilia, Italy, C Mediterranean Sea

Messina *see* Musina

Messina, Strait of *see* Messina, Stretto di

Messina, Stretto di 97 D7 Eng. Strait of Messina. *strait* C Italy

Messini 105 B6 Pelopónnisos, S Greece

Mesta *see* Néstos

Mestghanem *see* Mostaganem

Mestia 117 F1 *var.* Mestiya. N Georgia

Mestiya *see* Mestia

Mestre 96 C2 Veneto, NE Italy

Meta 56 B2 *off.* Departamento del Meta. *province* C Colombia

Meta, Departamento del *see* Meta

Metairie 42 B3 Louisiana, S USA

Metán 64 C2 Salta, N Argentina

Metapán 52 B2 Santa Ana, NW El Salvador

Meta, Río 58 D3 *river* Colombia/Venezuela

Meterlam *see* Mehtar Läm

Methariam/Metharlam *see* Mehtar Läm

Metis *see* Metz

Metković 100 B4 Dubrovnik-Neretva, SE Croatia

Métsovo 104 B4 *prev.* Métsovon. Ípeiros, C Greece

Métsovon *see* Métsovo

Metz 90 D3 anc. Divodurum Mediomatricum, Mediomatrica, Metis. Moselle, NE France

Meulaboh 138 A3 Sumatera, W Indonesia

Meuse 90 D3 *cultural region* NE France

Meuse 90 D3 *department* NE France

Meuse 87 C6 Dut. Maas. *river* W Europe

Mexcala, Río *see* Balsas, Río

Mexicali 50 A1 Baja California, NW Mexico

Mexicanos, Estados Unidos *see* Mexico

México 51 E4 *var.* Ciudad de México, Eng. Mexico City. *country capital* (Mexico) México, C Mexico

Mexico 45 G4 Missouri, C USA

Mexico 50 C3 *off.* United Mexican States, *var.* Méjico, México, Sp. Estados Unidos Mexicanos. *country* N Central America

México *see* Mexico

Mexico City *see* México

México, Golfo de *see* Mexico, Gulf of

Mexico, Gulf of 51 F2 Sp. Golfo de México. *gulf* W Atlantic Ocean

Meyadine *see* Al Mayādīn

Meydan Shahr 123 E4 *var.* Maydān Shahr. Vardak, E Afghanistan

Meymaneh 122 D3 *var.* Maimāna, Maymana. Färyāb, NW Afghanistan

Mezen' 110 D3 *river* NW Russian Federation

Mezőtúr 99 D7 Jász-Nagykun-Szolnok, E Hungary

Mgarr 102 A5 Gozo, N Malta

Miadziol Nowy *see* Myadzyel

Miahuatlán 51 F5 *var.* Miahuatlán de Porfirio Díaz. Oaxaca, SE Mexico

Miahuatlán de Porfirio Díaz *see* Miahuatlán

Miami 43 F5 Florida, SE USA

Miami 49 G1 Oklahoma, C USA

Miami Beach 43 F5 Florida, SE USA

Miāneh 120 C2 *var.* Miyāneh. Āžarbāyjān-e Sharqī, NW Iran

Mianyang 128 B5 Sichuan, C China

Miastko 98 C2 Ger. Rummelsburg in Pommern. Pomorskie, N Poland

Mi Chai *see* Nong Khai

Michalovce 99 E5 Ger. Grossmichel, Hung. Nagymihály. Košický Kraj, E Slovakia

Michigan 40 C1 *off.* State of Michigan, *also known as* Great Lakes State, Lake State, Wolverine State. *state* N USA

Michigan, Lake 40 C2 *lake* N USA

Michurin *see* Tsarevo

Michurinsk 111 B5 Tambovskaya Oblast', W Russian Federation

Micoud 55 F2 SE Saint Lucia

Micronesia 144 B1 *off.* Federated States of Micronesia. *country* W Pacific Ocean

MICRONESIA
Australasia & Oceania

Official name Federated States of Micronesia
Formation 1986 / 1986
Capital Palikir (Pohnpei Island)
Population 108,105 / 399 people per sq mile (154 people per sq km) / 28%
Total area 271 sq miles (702 sq km)
Languages Trukese, Pohnpeian, Mortlockese, Kosraean, English
Religions Roman Catholic 50%, Protestant 48%, Other 2%
Ethnic mix Micronesian 100%
Government Nonparty system
Currency US dollar = 100 cents
Literacy rate 81%
Calorie consumption Not available

Micronesia 144 C1 *island group* W Pacific Ocean

Micronesia, Federated States of *see* Micronesia

Mid-Atlantic Cordillera *see* Mid-Atlantic Ridge

Mid-Atlantic Ridge 66 C3 *var.* Mid-Atlantic Cordillera, Mid-Atlantic Rise, Mid-Atlantic Swell. *undersea ridge* Atlantic Ocean

Mid-Atlantic Rise/Mid-Atlantic Swell *see* Mid-Atlantic Ridge

Middelburg 87 B5 Zeeland, SW Netherlands

Middelharnis 86 B4 Zuid-Holland, SW Netherlands

Middelkerke 87 A5 West-Vlaanderen, W Belgium

Middle America Trench 35 B7 *trench* E Pacific Ocean

Middle Andaman 133 F2 *island* Andaman Islands, India, NE Indian Ocean

Middle Atlas *see* Moyen Atlas

Middleburg Island *see* 'Eua

Middle Congo *see* Congo (Republic of)

Middlesboro 40 C5 Kentucky, S USA

Middlesbrough 89 D5 N England, UK

Middletown 41 F4 New Jersey, NE USA

Middletown 41 F3 New York, NE USA

Mid-Indian Basin 141 C5 *undersea basin* Indian Ocean

Mid-Indian Ridge 141 C5 *var.* Central Indian Ridge. *undersea ridge* C Indian Ocean

Midland 38 D5 Ontario, S Canada

Midland 40 C3 Michigan, N USA

Midland 49 F3 Texas, SW USA

Mid-Pacific Mountains 152 C2 *var.* Mid-Pacific Seamounts. *seamount range* NW Pacific Ocean

Mid-Pacific Seamounts *see* Mid-Pacific Mountains

Midway Islands 152 D2 *US territory* C Pacific Ocean

Miechów 99 D5 Małopolskie, S Poland

Międzyrzec Podlaski 98 E3 Lubelskie, E Poland

Międzyrzecz 98 B3 Ger. Meseritz. Lubuskie, W Poland

Mielec 99 D5 Podkarpackie, SE Poland

Miercurea-Ciuc 108 C4 Ger. Szeklerburg, Hung. Csíkszereda. Harghita, C Romania

Mieres del Camín *see* Mieres del Camino

Mieres del Camino 108 D1 *var.* Mieres del Camín. Asturias, NW Spain

Mi'ēso 73 D5 *var.* Meheso, Miesso. Oromo, C Ethiopia

Miesso *see* Mi'ēso

Miguel Asua 50 D3 *var.* Miguel Auza. Zacatecas, C Mexico

Miguel Auza *see* Miguel Asua

Mijdrecht 86 C3 Utrecht, C Netherlands

Mikashevichy *see* Mikashevichy

Mikashevichy 107 C7 Pol. Mikaszewicze, Rus. Mikashevichi. Brestskaya Voblasts', SW Belarus

Mikaszewicze *see* Mikashevichy

Mikhaylovgrad *see* Montana

Mikhaylovka 111 B6 Volgogradskaya Oblast', SW Russian Federation

Mikonos *see* Mýkonos

Mikre 104 C2 Lovech, N Bulgaria

Mikun' 110 D4 Respublika Komi, NW Russian Federation

Mikuni-sanmyaku 131 D5 *mountain range* Honshū, N Japan Asia

Mikura-jima 131 D6 *island* E Japan

Milagro 60 B2 Guayas, SW Ecuador

Milan *see* Milano

Milange 79 E2 Zambézia, NE Mozambique

Milano 96 B2 Eng. Milan, Ger. Mailand; anc. Mediolanum. Lombardia, N Italy

Milas 116 A4 Muğla, SW Turkey

Milashavichy 107 C7 Rus. Milashevichi. Homyel'skaya Voblasts', SE Belarus

Milashevichi *see* Milashavichy

Mildura 149 C6 Victoria, SE Australia

Mile *see* Mili Atoll

Miles 149 D5 Queensland, E Australia

Miles City 44 C2 Montana, NW USA

Milford *see* Milford Haven

Milford Haven 89 C6 *prev.* Milford. SW Wales, UK

Milford Sound 151 A6 Southland, South Island, New Zealand

Milford Sound 151 A6 *inlet* South Island, New Zealand

Milh, Bahr al *see* Razāzah, Buḥayrat ar

Mili Atoll 144 D2 *var.* Mile. *atoll* Ratak Chain, SE Marshall Islands

Mil'kovo 115 H3 Kamchatskaya Oblast', E Russian Federation

Milk River 37 E5 Alberta, SW Canada

Milk River 44 C1 *river* Montana, NW USA

Milk, Wadi el 88 B4 *var.* Wadi al Malik. *river* C Sudan

Milledgeville 43 E2 Georgia, SE USA

Mille Lacs Lake 45 F2 *lake* Minnesota, N USA

Millennium Island 160 C8 *prev.* Caroline Island, Thornton Island. *atoll* Line Islands, E Kiribati

Millerovo 111 B6 Rostovskaya Oblast', SW Russian Federation

Milos 105 C6 *island* Kykládes, Greece, Aegean Sea

Milos *see* Plåka

Milton 151 B7 Otago, South Island, New Zealand

Milton Keynes 89 D6 SE England, UK

Milwaukee 40 B3 Wisconsin, N USA

Mimatum *see* Mende

Min *see* Fujian

Minā' Qābūs 140 B3 NE Oman

Minas Gerais 63 F3 *off.* Estado de Minas Gerais. *state* E Brazil

Minas Gerais, Estado de *see* Minas Gerais

Minatitlán 51 F4 Veracruz-Llave, E Mexico

Minbu 136 A3 Magwe, W Myanmar (Burma)

Minch, The 88 B3 *var.* North Minch. *strait* NW Scotland, UK

Mindanao 139 F2 *island* S Philippines

Mindanao Sea *see* Bohol Sea

Mindelheim 95 C6 Bayern, S Germany

Mindello *see* Mindelo

Mindelo 74 A2 *var.* Mindello; *prev.* Porto Grande. São Vicente, N Cape Verde

Minden 94 B4 anc. Minthun. Nordrhein-Westfalen, NW Germany

Mindoro 139 E2 *island* N Philippines

Mindoro Strait 139 E2 *strait* W Philippines

Mineral Wells 49 F2 Texas, SW USA

Mingäçevir 117 G2 Rus. Mingechaur, Mingechevir. C Azerbaijan

Mingãora 134 C1 *var.* Mingora, Mongora. North-West Frontier Province, N Pakistan

Mingechaur/Mingechevir *see* Mingäçevir

Mingora *see* Mingãora

Minho 92 B2 *former province* N Portugal

Minho, Rio 92 B2 Sp. Miño. *river* Portugal/Spain

Minho, Rio *see* Miño

Minicoy Island 132 B3 *island* SW India

Minius *see* Miño

Minna 75 G4 Niger, C Nigeria

Minneapolis 45 F2 Minnesota, N USA

Minnesota 45 F2 *off.* State of Minnesota, *also known as* Gopher State, New England of the West, North Star State. *state* N USA

Miño 92 B2 var. Mino, Minius, Port. Rio Minho. *river* Portugal/Spain
Miño *see* Minho, Rio
Minorca *see* Menorca
Minot 45 E1 North Dakota, N USA
Minsk 107 C6 *country capital* (Belarus) Minskaya Voblasts', C Belarus
Minskaya Wzvyshsha 107 C6 *mountain range* C Belarus
Mińsk Mazowiecki 98 D3 var. Nowo-Minsk. Mazowieckie, C Poland
Minthun *see* Minden
Minto, Lac 38 D2 *lake* Québec, C Canada
Minya *see* El Minya
Miraflores 50 C3 Baja California Sur, W Mexico
Miranda de Ebro 93 E1 La Rioja, N Spain
Mirgorod *see* Myrhorod
Miri 138 D3 Sarawak, East Malaysia
Mirim Lagoon 63 E5 var. Lake Mirim, Sp. Laguna Merín. *lagoon* Brazil/Uruguay
Mirim, Lake *see* Mirim Lagoon
Mirina *see* Mýrina
Mirjäveh 120 E4 Sīstān va Balūchestān, SE Iran
Mirny 154 C3 *Russian research station* Antarctica
Mirnyy 115 F3 Respublika Sakha (Yakutiya), NE Russian Federation
Mirpur Khās 134 B3 Sind, SE Pakistan
Mirtoan Sea *see* Mirtóo Pélagos
Mirtóo Pélagos 105 C6 *Eng.* Mirtoan Sea; *anc.* Myrtoum Mare. *sea* S Greece
Misiaf *see* Maşyāf
Miskito Coast *see* La Mosquitia
Miskitos, Cayos 53 E2 *island group* NE Nicaragua
Miskolc 99 D6 Borsod-Abaúj-Zemplén, NE Hungary
Misool, Pulau 139 F4 *island* Maluku, E Indonesia
Mişrātah 71 F2 var. Misurata. NW Libya
Mission 49 G5 Texas, SW USA
Mississippi 42 B2 *off.* State of Mississippi, *also known as* Bayou State, Magnolia State. *state* SE USA
Mississippi River 35 C6 *river* C USA
Mississippi Delta 42 B4 *delta* Louisiana, S USA
Missoula 44 B1 Montana, NW USA
Missouri 45 F5 *off.* State of Missouri, *also known as* Bullion State, Show Me State. *state* C USA
Missouri River 45 E3 *river* C USA
Mistassini, Lac 38 D3 *lake* Québec, SE Canada
Mistelbach an der Zaya 95 E6 Niederösterreich, NE Austria
Misti, Volcán 61 E4 *volcano* S Peru
Misurata *see* Mişrātah
Mitau *see* Jelgava
Mitchell 149 D5 Queensland, E Australia
Mitchell 45 E3 South Dakota, N USA
Mitchell, Mount 43 E1 *mountain* North Carolina, SE USA
Mitchell River 148 C2 *river* Queensland, NE Australia
Mi Tho *see* My Tho
Mitilíni *see* Mytilíni
Mito 131 D5 Ibaraki, Honshū, S Japan
Mitrovica/Mitrovicë *see* Kosovska Mitrovica, Serbia
Mitrovica/Mitrowitz *see* Sremska Mitrovica, Serbia
Mits'iwa *see* Massawa
Mitspe Ramon *see* Mizpé Ramon
Mittelstadt *see* Baia Sprie
Mitú 58 C4 Vaupés, SE Colombia
Mitumba, Chaîne des/Mitumba Range *see* Mitumba, Monts
Mitumba, Monts 77 E7 var. Chaîne des Mitumba, Mitumba Range. *mountain range* E Dem. Rep. Congo
Miueru Wantipa, Lake 77 E7 *lake* N Zambia
Miyako 130 D4 Iwate, Honshū, C Japan
Miyako-jima 131 D6 *island* Sakishima-shotō, SW Japan
Miyakonojō 131 B8 var. Miyakonzyô. Miyazaki, Kyūshū, SW Japan
Miyakonzyô *see* Miyakonojō
Miyäneh *see* Miāneh

Miyazaki 131 B8 Miyazaki, Kyūshū, SW Japan
Mizil 108 C5 Prahova, SE Romania
Miziya 104 C1 Vratsa, NW Bulgaria
Mizpé Ramon 119 A7 var. Mitspe Ramon. Southern, S Israel
Mjøsa 85 B6 var. Mjøsen. *lake* S Norway
Mjøsen *see* Mjøsa
Mladenovac 100 D4 Serbia, C Serbia
Mława 98 D3 Mazowieckie, C Poland
Mljet 101 B5 *It.* Meleda; *anc.* Melita. *island* S Croatia
Mmabatho 78 C4 North-West, N South Africa
Moab 44 B5 Utah, W USA
Moa Island 148 C1 *island* Queensland, NE Australia
Moanda 77 B6 var. Mouanda. Haut-Ogooué, SE Gabon
Moba 77 E7 Katanga, E Dem. Rep. Congo
Mobay *see* Montego Bay
Mobaye 77 C5 Basse-Kotto, S Central African Republic
Moberly 45 G4 Missouri, C USA
Mobile 42 C3 Alabama, S USA
Mobutu Sese Seko, Lac *see* Albert, Lake
Moçâmedes *see* Namibe
Mochudi 78 C4 Kgatleng, SE Botswana
Mocímboa da Praia 79 F2 var. Vila de Mocímboa da Praia. Cabo Delgado, N Mozambique
Môco 78 B2 var. Morro de Môco. *mountain* W Angola
Mocoa 58 A4 Putumayo, SW Colombia
Môco, Morro de *see* Môco
Mocuba 79 E3 Zambézia, NE Mozambique
Modena 96 B3 *anc.* Mutina. Emilia-Romagna, N Italy
Modesto 47 B6 California, W USA
Modica 97 C7 *anc.* Motyca. Sicilia, Italy, C Mediterranean Sea
Modimolle 78 D4 *prev.* Nylstroom. Limpopo, NE South Africa
Modohn *see* Madona
Modriča 100 C3 Republika Srpska, N Bosnia and Herzegovina
Moe 149 C7 Victoria, SE Australia
Møen *see* Møn, Denmark
Moero, Lac *see* Mweru, Lake
Moeskroen *see* Mouscron
Mogadiscio/Mogadishu *see* Muqdisho
Mogador *see* Essaouira
Mogilëv *see* Mahilyow
Mogilev-Podol'skiy *see* Mohyliv-Podil's'kyy
Mogilno 98 C3 Kujawsko-pomorskie, C Poland
Mohammedia 70 C2 *prev.* Fédala. NW Morocco
Mohave, Lake 47 D7 *reservoir* Arizona/ Nevada, W USA
Mohawk River 41 F3 *river* New York, NE USA
Mohéli 79 F2 var. Mwali, Mohilla, Mohila, *Fr.* Moili. *island* S Comoros
Mohila *see* Mohéli
Mohilla *see* Mohéli
Mohns Ridge 83 F3 *undersea ridge* Greenland Sea/Norwegian Sea
Moho 61 E4 Puno, SE Peru
Mohoro 73 C7 Pwani, E Tanzania
Mohyliv-Podil's'kyy 108 D3 *Rus.* Mogilev-Podol'skiy. Vinnyts'ka Oblast', C Ukraine
Moi 85 A6 Rogaland, S Norway
Moili *see* Mohéli
Mo i Rana 84 C3 Nordland, C Norway
Môisaküla 106 D3 *Ger.* Moiseküll. Viljandimaa, S Estonia
Moiseküll *see* Môisaküla
Moissac 91 B6 Tarn-et-Garonne, S France
Mojácar 93 E5 Andalucía, S Spain
Mojave Desert 47 D7 *plain* California, W USA
Mokrany *see* Makrany
Moktama *see* Martaban
Mol 87 C5 *prev.* Moll. Antwerpen, N Belgium
Moldau *see* Vltava
Moldavian SSR/Moldavskaya SSR *see* Moldova
Molde 85 A5 Møre og Romsdal, S Norway

Moldotau, Khrebet *see* Moldo-Too, Khrebet
Moldo-Too, Khrebet 123 G2 *prev.* Khrebet Moldotau. *mountain range* C Kyrgyzstan
Moldova 108 D3 *off.* Republic of Moldova, *var.* Moldavia; *prev.* Moldavian SSR, *Rus.* Moldavskaya SSR. *country* SE Europe

MOLDOVA
Southeast Europe

Official name Republic of Moldova
Formation 1991 / 1991
Capital Chisinau
Population 4.2 million / 323 people per sq mile (125 people per sq km) / 46%
Total area 13,067 sq miles (33,843 sq km)
Languages Moldovan*, Ukrainian, Russian
Religions Orthodox Christian 98%, Jewish 2%
Ethnic mix Moldovan 65%, Ukrainian 14%, Russian 13%, Other 4%, Gagauz 4%
Government Parliamentary system
Currency Moldovan leu = 100 bani
Literacy rate 96%
Calorie consumption 2806 calories

Moldova Nouă 108 A4 *Ger.* Neumoldowa, *Hung.* Újmoldova. Caraş-Severin, SW Romania
Moldova, Republic of *see* Moldova
Moldoveanul *see* Vârful Moldoveanu
Molfetta 97 E5 Puglia, SE Italy
Moll *see* Mol
Mollendo 61 E4 Arequipa, SW Peru
Mölndal 85 B7 Västra Götaland, S Sweden
Molochans'k 109 G4 *Rus.* Molochansk. Zaporiz'ka Oblast', SE Ukraine
Molodechno/Molodeczno *see* Maladzyechna
Molodezhnaya 154 C2 *Russian research station* Antarctica
Moloka'i 47 B8 var. Molokai. *island* Hawaiian Islands, Hawai'i, USA
Molokai Fracture Zone 153 E2 *tectonic feature* NE Pacific Ocean
Molopo 78 C4 *seasonal river* Botswana/ South Africa
Mólos 105 B5 Stereá Ellás, C Greece
Molotov *see* Severodvinsk, Arkhangel'skaya Oblast', Russian Federation
Molotov *see* Perm', Permskaya Oblast', Russian Federation
Moluccas *see* Maluku
Molucca Sea 139 F4 *Ind.* Laut Maluku. *sea* E Indonesia
Molukken *see* Maluku
Mombasa 73 D7 Coast, SE Kenya
Mombasa 73 D7 Coast, SE Kenya
Mombetsu *see* Monbetsu
Momchilgrad 104 D3 *prev.* Mastanli. Kürdzhali, S Bulgaria
Møn 85 B8 *prev.* Möen. *island* SE Denmark
Mona, Canal de la *see* Mona Passage
Monaco 91 C7 var. Monaco-Ville; *anc.* Monoecus. *country capital* (Monaco) S Monaco
Monaco 91 E6 *off.* Principality of Monaco. *country* W Europe

MONACO
Southern Europe

Official name Principality of Monaco
Formation 1861 / 1861
Capital Monaco-Ville
Population 32,409 / 43212 people per sq mile (16620 people per sq km) / 100%
Total area 0.75 sq miles (1.95 sq km)
Languages French*, Italian, Monégasque, English
Religions Roman Catholic 89%, Protestant 6%, Other 5%
Ethnic mix French 47%, Other 20%, Monégasque 17%, Italian 16%
Government Monarchy
Currency Euro = 100 cents
Literacy rate 99%
Calorie consumption Not available

Monaco *see* München
Monaco, Port de 91 C8 *bay* S Monaco W Mediterranean Sea
Monaco, Principality of *see* Monaco
Monaco-Ville *see* Monaco
Monahans 49 E3 Texas, SW USA
Mona, Isla 55 E3 *island* W Puerto Rico
Mona Passage 55 E3 *Sp.* Canal de la Mona. *channel* Dominican Republic/ Puerto Rico
Monastir *see* Bitola
Monbetsu 130 D2 var. Mombetsu, Monbetu. Hokkaidō, NE Japan
Monbetu *see* Monbetsu
Moncalieri 96 A2 Piemonte, NW Italy
Monchegorsk 110 C2 Murmanskaya Oblast', NW Russian Federation
Monclova 50 D2 Coahuila de Zaragoza, NE Mexico
Moncton 39 F4 New Brunswick, SE Canada
Mondovì 96 A2 Piemonte, NW Italy
Monfalcone 96 D2 Friuli-Venezia Giulia, NE Italy
Monforte de Lemos 92 C1 Galicia, NW Spain
Mongo 76 C3 Guéra, C Chad
Mongolia 126 C2 *Mong.* Mongol Uls. *country* E Asia

MONGOLIA
East Asia

Official name Mongolia
Formation 1924 / 1924
Capital Ulan Bator
Population 2.6 million / 4 people per sq mile (2 people per sq km) / 64%
Total area 604,247 sq miles (1,565,000 sq km)
Languages Khalkha Mongolian*, Kazakh, Chinese, Russian
Religions Tibetan Buddhist 96%, Muslim 4%
Ethnic mix Mongol 90%, Kazakh 4%, Other 2%, Chinese 2%, Russian 2%
Government Mixed presidential–parliamentary system
Currency Tugrik (togrög) = 100 möngo
Literacy rate 98%
Calorie consumption 2249 calories

Mongolia, Plateau of 124 D1 *plateau* E Mongolia
Mongol Uls *see* Mongolia
Mongora *see* Mingãora
Mongos, Chaîne des *see* Bongo, Massif des
Mongu 78 C2 Western, W Zambia
Monkchester *see* Newcastle upon Tyne
Monkey Bay 79 E2 Southern, SE Malawi
Monkey River *see* Monkey River Town
Monkey River Town 52 C2 var. Monkey River. Toledo, SE Belize
Monoecus *see* Monaco
Mono Lake 47 C6 *lake* California, W USA
Monostor *see* Beli Manastir
Monovar 93 F4 *Cat.* Monòver. País Valenciano, E Spain
Monòver *see* Monovar
Monroe 42 B2 Louisiana, S USA
Monrovia 74 C5 *country capital* (Liberia) W Liberia
Mons 87 B6 *Dut.* Bergen. Hainaut, S Belgium
Monselice 96 C2 Veneto, NE Italy
Montana 104 C2 *prev.* Ferdinand, Mikhaylovgrad. Montana, NW Bulgaria
Montana 44 B1 *off.* State of Montana, *also known as* Mountain State, Treasure State. *state* NW USA
Montargis 90 C4 Loiret, C France
Montauban 91 B6 Tarn-et-Garonne, S France
Montbéliard 90 D4 Doubs, E France
Mont Cenis, Col du 91 D5 *pass* E France
Mont-de-Marsan 91 B6 Landes, SW France
Monteagudo 61 G4 Chuquisaca, S Bolivia
Montecarlo 91 C8 Misiones, NE Argentina
Monte Caseros 64 D3 Corrientes, NE Argentina

Monte Cristi *54 D3 var.* San Fernando de Monte Cristi. NW Dominican Republic
Monte Croce Carnico, Passo di *see* Plöcken Pass
Montegiardino *96 E2* SE San Marino
Montego Bay *54 A4 var.* Mobay. W Jamaica
Montélimar *91 D5 anc.* Acunum Acusio, Montilium Adhemari. Drôme, E France
Montemorelos *51 E3* Nuevo León, NE Mexico
Montenegro *101 C5 Serb.* Crna Gora. *country* SW Europe

MONTENEGRO
Europe

Official name Republic of Montenegro
Formation 2006 / 2006
Capital Podgorica
Population 620,145 / 116 people per sq mile (45 people per sq km) / 62%
Total area 5,332 sq miles (13,812 sq km)
Languages Montenegrin, Serbian, Albanian
Religions Orthodox Christian 74%, Muslim 18%, Roman Catholic 4%, Other 4%
Ethnic mix Montenegrin 43%, Serb 32%, Bosniak 8%, Albanian 5%, Other 12%
Government Parliamentary system
Currency Euro = 100 cents
Literacy rate 98%
Calorie consumption Not available

Monte Patria *64 B3* Coquimbo, N Chile
Monterey *47 B6* California, W USA
Monterey *see* Monterrey
Monterey Bay *47 A6 bay* California, W USA
Montería *58 B2* Córdoba, NW Colombia
Montero *61 G4* Santa Cruz, C Bolivia
Monterrey *51 E3 var.* Monterey. Nuevo León, NE Mexico
Montes Claros *63 F3* Minas Gerais, SE Brazil
Montevideo *64 D4 country capital* (Uruguay) Montevideo, S Uruguay
Montevideo *45 F2* Minnesota, N USA
Montgenèvre, Col de *91 D5 pass* France/Italy
Montgomery *42 D2 state capital* Alabama, S USA
Montgomery *see* Sāhīwāl
Monthey *95 A7* Valais, SW Switzerland
Montilium Adhemari *see* Montélimar
Montluçon *90 C4* Allier, C France
Montoro *92 D4* Andalucía, S Spain
Montpelier *41 G2 state capital* Vermont, NE USA
Montpellier *91 C6* Hérault, S France
Montréal *39 E4 Eng.* Montreal. Québec, SE Canada
Montrose *88 D3* E Scotland, UK
Montrose *44 C5* Colorado, C USA
Montserrat *55 G3 var.* Emerald Isle. *UK dependent territory* E West Indies
Monywa *136 B3* Sagaing, C Myanmar (Burma)
Monza *96 B2* Lombardia, N Italy
Monze *78 D2* Southern, S Zambia
Monzón *93 F2* Aragón, NE Spain
Moonie *149 D5* Queensland, E Australia
Moon-Sund *see* Väinameri
Moora *147 A6* Western Australia
Moore *49 G1* Oklahoma, C USA
Moore, Lake *147 B6 lake* Western Australia
Moorhead *45 F2* Minnesota, N USA
Moose *38 C3 river* Ontario, S Canada
Moosehead Lake *41 G1 lake* Maine, NE USA
Moosonee *38 C3* Ontario, SE Canada
Mopti *75 E3* Mopti, C Mali
Moquegua *61 E4* Moquegua, SE Peru
Mora *85 C5* Dalarna, C Sweden
Morales *52 C2* Izabal, E Guatemala
Morant Bay *54 B5* E Jamaica
Moratalla *93 E4* Murcia, SE Spain
Morava *99 C5 var.* March. *river* C Europe
Morava *see* Velika Morava, Serbia
Moravia *99 B5* Iowa, C USA
Moray Firth *88 C3 inlet* N Scotland, UK

Morea *see* Pelopónnisos
Moreau River *44 D2 river* South Dakota, N USA
Moree *149 D5* New South Wales, SE Australia
Morelia *51 E4* Michoacán de Ocampo, S Mexico
Morena, Sierra *92 C4 mountain range* S Spain
Moreni *108 C5* Dâmboviţa, S Romania
Mórfou *see* Güzelyurt Körfezi
Morgan City *42 B3* Louisiana, S USA
Morghāb, Daryā-ye *122 D3 Rus.* Murgab, Murghab, *Turkm.* Murgap, Murgap Deryasy. *river* Afghanistan/Turkmenistan Asia
Morghāb, Daryā-ye *see* Murgap
Morioka *130 D4* Iwate, Honshū, C Japan
Morlaix *90 A3* Finistère, NW France
Mormon State *see* Utah
Mornington Abyssal Plain *67 A7 abyssal plain* SE Pacific Ocean
Mornington Island *148 B2 island* Wellesley Islands, Queensland, N Australia
Morocco *70 B3 off.* Kingdom of Morocco, *Ar.* Al Mamlakah. *country* N Africa

MOROCCO
North Africa

Official name Kingdom of Morocco
Formation 1956 / 1956
Capital Rabat
Population 31.5 million / 183 people per sq mile (71 people per sq km) / 56%
Total area 172,316 sq miles (446,300 sq km)
Languages Arabic*, Tamazight (Berber), French, Spanish
Religions Muslim (mainly Sunni) 99%, Other (mostly Christian) 1%
Ethnic mix Arab 70%, Berber 29%, European 1%
Government Monarchy
Currency Moroccan dirham = 100 centimes
Literacy rate 51%
Calorie consumption 3052 calories

Morocco *see* Marrakech
Morocco, Kingdom of *see* Morocco
Morogoro *73 C7* Morogoro, E Tanzania
Moro Gulf *139 E3 gulf* S Philippines
Morón *54 C2* Ciego de Ávila, C Cuba
Mörön *126 D2* Hövsgöl, N Mongolia
Morondava *79 F3* Toliara, W Madagascar
Moroni *79 F2 country capital* (Comoros) Grande Comore, NW Comoros
Morotai, Pulau *139 F3 island* Maluku, E Indonesia
Morotiri *see* Marotiri
Morphou *see* Güzelyurt Körfezi
Morrinsville *150 D3* Waikato, North Island, New Zealand
Morris *45 F2* Minnesota, N USA
Morris Jesup, Kap *83 E1 headland* N Greenland
Mórtu, Kólpos *see* Güzelyurt Körfezi
Morvan *90 D4 physical region* C France
Moscow *46 C2* Idaho, NW USA
Moscow *see* Moskva
Mosel *95 A5 Fr.* Moselle. *river* W Europe
Mosel *see* Moselle
Moselle *90 D3 cultural region* NE France
Moselle *90 D3 department* NE France
Moselle *87 E8 Ger.* Mosel. *river* W Europe
Moselle *see* Mosel
Mosgiel *151 B7* Otago, South Island, New Zealand
Moshi *73 C7* Kilimanjaro, NE Tanzania
Mosjøen *84 B4* Nordland, C Norway
Moskovskiy *see* Moskva
Moskva *111 B5 Eng.* Moscow. *country capital* (Russian Federation) Gorod Moskva, W Russian Federation
Moskva *123 E3 Rus.* Moskovskiy; *prev.* Chubek. SW Tajikistan
Moson and Magyaróvár *see* Mosonmagyaróvár

Mosonmagyaróvár *99 C6 Ger.* Wieselburg-Ungarisch-Altenburg; *prev.* Moson and Magyaróvár, *Ger.* Wieselburg and Ungarisch-Altenburg. Győr-Moson-Sopron, NW Hungary
Mosquito Coast *see* La Mosquitia
Mosquito Gulf *see* Mosquitos, Golfo de los
Mosquitos, Golfo de los *53 F4 Eng.* Mosquito Gulf. *gulf* N Panama
Moss *85 B6* Østfold, S Norway
Mossâmedes *see* Namibe
Mosselbaai *78 C5 var.* Mosselbai, *Eng.* Mossel Bay. Western Cape, SW South Africa
Mosselbai/Mossel Bay *see* Mosselbaai
Mossendjo *77 B6* Le Niari, SW Congo
Mossoró *63 G2* Rio Grande do Norte, NE Brazil
Most *98 A4 Ger.* Brüx. Ústecký Kraj, NW Czech Republic
Mosta *102 B5 var.* Musta. C Malta
Mostaganem *70 D2 var.* Mestghanem. NW Algeria
Mostar *100 C4* Federacija Bosna I Hercegovina, S Bosnia and Herzegovina
Mosty *see* Masty
Mosul *see* Al Mawşil
Mota del Cuervo *93 E3* Castilla-La Mancha, C Spain
Motagua, Río *52 B2 river* Guatemala/Honduras
Mother of Presidents/Mother of States *see* Virginia
Motril *92 D5* Andalucía, S Spain
Motru *108 B4* Gorj, SW Romania
Motueka *151 C5* Tasman, South Island, New Zealand
Motul *51 H3 var.* Motul de Felipe Carrillo Puerto. Yucatán, SE Mexico
Motul de Felipe Carrillo Puerto *see* Motul
Motyca *see* Modica
Mouanda *see* Moanda
Mouhoun *see* Black Volta
Mouila *77 A6* Ngounié, C Gabon
Moukden *see* Shenyang
Mould Bay *37 E2* Northwest Territories, Prince Patrick Island, N Canada North America
Moulins *90 C4* Allier, C France
Moulmein *136 B4 var.* Maulmain, Mawlamyine. Mon State, S Myanmar (Burma)
Moundou *76 B4* Logone-Occidental, SW Chad
Moûng Roessei *137 D5* Bătdâmbâng, W Cambodia
Moun Hou *see* Black Volta
Mountain Home *42 B1* Arkansas, C USA
Mountain State *see* Montana
Mountain State *see* West Virginia
Mount Cook *151 B6* Canterbury, South Island, New Zealand
Mount Desert Island *41 H2 island* Maine, NE USA
Mount Gambier *149 B7* South Australia
Mount Isa *148 B3* Queensland, C Australia
Mount Magnet *147 B5* Western Australia
Mount Pleasant *45 G4* Iowa, C USA
Mount Pleasant *40 C3* Michigan, N USA
Mount Vernon *40 B5* Illinois, N USA
Mount Vernon *46 B1* Washington, NW USA
Mourdi, Dépression du *76 C2 desert lowland* Chad/Sudan
Mouscron *87 A6 Dut.* Moeskroen. Hainaut, W Belgium
Mouse River *see* Souris River
Moussoro *76 B3* Kanem, W Chad
Moyen Atlas *70 C2 Eng.* Middle Atlas. *mountain range* N Morocco
Moyen-Congo *see* Congo (Republic of)
Mo'ynoq *122 C1 Rus.* Muynak. Qoraqalpog'iston Respublikasi, NW Uzbekistan
Moyobamba *60 B2* San Martín, NW Peru
Moyu *126 B3 var.* Karakax. Xinjiang Uygur Zizhiqu, NW China
Moyynkum, Peski *123 F1 Kaz.* Moyynqum. *desert* S Kazakhstan
Moyynqum *see* Moyynkum, Peski
Mozambika, Lakandranon'i *see* Mozambique Channel

MOZAMBIQUE
Southern Africa

Official name Republic of Mozambique
Formation 1975 / 1975
Capital Maputo
Population 19.8 million / 65 people per sq mile (25 people per sq km) / 40%
Total area 309,494 sq miles (801,590 sq km)
Languages Portuguese*, Makua, Xitsonga, Sena, Lomwe
Religions Traditional beliefs 56%, Christian 30%, Muslim 14%
Ethnic mix Makua Lomwe 47%, Tsonga 23%, Malawi 12%, Shona 11%, Yao 4%, Other 3%
Government Presidential system
Currency Metical = 100 centavos
Literacy rate 47%
Calorie consumption 2079 calories

Mozambique *79 E3 off.* Republic of Mozambique; *prev.* People's Republic of Mozambique, Portuguese East Africa. *country* S Africa
Mozambique Basin *see* Natal Basin
Mozambique, Canal de *see* Mozambique Channel
Mozambique Channel *79 E3 Fr.* Canal de Mozambique, *Mal.* Lakandranon' i Mozambika. *strait* W Indian Ocean
Mozambique, People's Republic of *see* Mozambique
Mozambique Plateau *69 D7 var.* Mozambique Rise. *undersea plateau* SW Indian Ocean
Mozambique, Republic of *see* Mozambique
Mozambique Rise *see* Mozambique Plateau
Mozyr' *see* Mazyr
Mpama *77 B6 river* C Congo
Mpika *78 D2* Northern, NE Zambia
Mqinvartsveri *see* Kazbek
Mragowo *98 D2 Ger.* Sensburg. Warmińsko-Mazurskie, NE Poland
Mtkvari *see* Kura
Mtwara *73 D8* Mtwara, SE Tanzania
Mualo *see* Messalo, Rio
Muang Chiang Rai *see* Chiang Rai
Muang Kalasin *see* Kalasin
Muang Khammouan *see* Thakhèk
Muang Khôngxédôn *137 D5* Champasak, S Laos
Muang Khon Kaen *see* Khon Kaen
Muang Lampang *see* Lampang
Muang Loei *see* Loei
Muang Lom Sak *see* Lom Sak
Muang Nakhon Sawan *see* Nakhon Sawan
Muang Namo *136 C3* Oudômxai, N Laos
Muang Nan *see* Nan
Muang Phalan *136 D4 var.* Muang Phalane. Savannakhét, S Laos
Muang Phalane *see* Muang Phalan
Muang Phayao *see* Phayao
Muang Phitsanulok *see* Phitsanulok
Muang Phrae *see* Phrae
Muang Roi Et *see* Roi Et
Muang Sakon Nakhon *see* Sakon Nakhon
Muang Samut Prakan *see* Samut Prakan
Muang Sing *136 C3* Louang Namtha, N Laos
Muang Ubon *see* Ubon Ratchathani
Muang Xaignabouri *see* Xaignabouli
Muar *138 B3 var.* Bandar Maharani. Johor, Peninsular Malaysia
Mucojo *79 F2* Cabo Delgado, N Mozambique
Mudanjiang *128 E3 var.* Mu-tan-chiang. Heilongjiang, NE China
Mudon *137 B5* Mon State, S Myanmar (Burma)
Muenchen *see* München
Muenster *see* Münster
Mufulira *78 D2* Copperbelt, C Zambia
Mughla *see* Muğla
Muğla *116 A4 var.* Mughla. Muğla, SW Turkey
Mūḩ, Sabkhat al *134 C3 lake* C Syria
Muhu Väin *see* Väinameri

Muisne 60 A1 Esmeraldas, NW Ecuador
Mukacheve 108 B3 Hung. Munkács,
Rus. Mukachevo. Zakarpats'ka Oblast',
W Ukraine
Mukachevo see Mukacheve
Mukalla see Al Mukallā
Mukden see Shenyang
Mula 93 E4 Murcia, SE Spain
Mulaku Atoll 132 B4 var. Meemu Atoll.
atoll C Maldives
Muleshoe 47 E2 Texas, SW USA
Mulhacén 93 E5 var. Cerro de Mulhacén.
mountain S Spain
Mulhacén, Cerro de see Mulhacén
Mülhausen see Mulhouse
Mülheim 95 A6 var. Mulheim an
der Ruhr. Nordrhein-Westfalen,
W Germany
Mulheim an der Ruhr see Mülheim
Mulhouse 90 E4 Ger. Mülhausen. Haut-
Rhin, NE France
Müller-gerbergte see Muller,
Pegunungan
Muller, Pegunungan 138 D4 Dut.
Müller-gerbergte. mountain range
Borneo, C Indonesia
Mull, Isle of 88 B4 island W Scotland,
UK
Mulongo 77 D7 Katanga, SE Dem.
Rep. Congo
Multán 134 C2 Punjab, E Pakistan
Mumbai 134 C5 prev. Bombay. state
capital Mahārāshtra, W India
Munamägi see Suur Munamägi
Münchberg 95 C5 Bayern, E Germany
München 80 D4 var. Muenchen,
Eng. Munich, It. Monaco. Bayern,
SE Germany
Muncie 40 C4 Indiana, N USA
Mungbere 77 E5 Orientale, NE Dem.
Rep. Congo
Mu Nggava see Rennell
Munich see München
Munkács see Mukacheve
Münster 94 A4 var. Muenster, Münster
in Westfalen. Nordrhein-Westfalen,
W Germany
Munster 89 A6 Ir. Cúige Mumhan.
cultural region S Ireland
Münster in Westfalen see Münster
Muong Xiang Ngeun 136 C4 var. Xieng
Ngeun. Louangphabang, N Laos
Muonio 84 D3 Lappi, N Finland
Muonioälv/Muoniojoki see Muoniojoki
Muoniojoki 84 D3 var. Muoniojoki,
Swe. Muonioälv. river Finland/Sweden
Muqât 119 C5 Al Mafraq, E Jordan
Muqdisho 73 D6 Eng. Mogadishu, It.
Mogadiscio. country capital (Somalia)
Banaadir, S Somalia
Mur 95 E7 SCr. Mura. river C Europe
Mura see Mur
Muradiye 117 F3 Van, E Turkey
Murapara see Murupara
Murata 96 E2 S San Marino
Murchison River 147 A5 river Western
Australia
Murcia 93 F4 Murcia, SE Spain
Murcia 93 E4 autonomous community
SE Spain
Mureş 108 A4 river Hungary/Romania
Murfreesboro 42 D1 Tennessee, S USA
Murgab see Morghāb, Daryā-ye
Murgab see Morghāb, Daryā-ye
Murgab see Murghob
Murgap 122 D3 Rus. Murgap. Mary
Welaýaty, S Turkmenistan
Murgap 122 D3 var. Deryasy
Murgap, Murghab, Pash. Daryā-ye
Morghāb, Rus. Murgab. river
Afghanistan/Turkmenistan
Murgap see Morghāb, Daryā-ye
Murgap see Morghāb, Daryā-ye
Murgap Deryasy see Morghāb, Daryā-ye
Murgap Deryasy see Morghāb, Daryā-ye
Murghab see Morghāb, Daryā-ye
Murghab see Morghāb, Daryā-ye
Murghob 123 F3 Rus. Murgab.
SE Tajikistan
Murgon 149 E5 Queensland, E Australia
Müritänïyah see Mauritania
Müritz 94 C3 var. Müritzee. lake
NE Germany
Müritzee see Müritz
Murmansk 110 C2 Murmanskaya
Oblast', NW Russian Federation
Murmashi 110 C2 Murmanskaya
Oblast', NW Russian Federation

Murom 111 B5 Vladimirskaya Oblast',
W Russian Federation
Muroran 130 D3 Hokkaidō, NE Japan
Muros 92 B1 Galicia, NW Spain
Murray Fracture Zone 153 E2 fracture
zone NE Pacific Ocean
Murray Range see Murray Ridge
Murray Ridge 112 C5 var. Murray
Range. undersea ridge N Arabian Sea
Murray River 149 B6 river SE Australia
Murrumbidgee River 149 C6 river New
South Wales, SE Australia
Murska Sobota 95 E7 Ger. Olsnitz.
NE Slovenia
Murupara 150 E3 var. Murapara. Bay of
Plenty, North Island, New Zealand
Murviedro see Sagunto
Murwāra 135 E4 Madhya Pradesh,
N India
Murwillumbah 149 E5 New South
Wales, SE Australia
Murzuq, Edeyin see Murzuq, Idhān
Murzuq, Idhān 71 F4 var. Edeyin
Murzuq. desert SW Libya
Mürzzuschlag 95 E7 Steiermark,
E Austria
Muş 117 F3 var. Mush. Muş, E Turkey
Mûsa, Gebel 72 C2 mountain
NE Egypt
Musala 104 B3 mountain W Bulgaria
Muscat see Masqaţ
Muscat and Oman see Oman
Muscatine 45 G3 Iowa, C USA
Musgrave Ranges 147 D5 mountain
range South Australia
Musina 78 D3 prev. Messina. Limpopo,
NE South Africa
Muskegon 40 C3 Michigan, N USA
Muskogean see Tallahassee
Muskogee 49 G1 Oklahoma, C USA
Musoma 73 C6 Mara, N Tanzania
Musta see Mosta
Mustafa-Pasha see Svilengrad
Musters, Lago 65 B6 lake S Argentina
Muswellbrook 149 D6 New South
Wales, SE Australia
Mut 116 C4 Mersin, S Turkey
Mu-tan-chiang see Mudanjiang
Mutare 78 D3 var. Mutari; prev. Umtali.
Manicaland, E Zimbabwe
Mutari see Mutare
Mutina see Modena
Mutsu-wan 130 D3 bay N Japan
Muttonbird Islands 151 A8 island group
SW New Zealand
Mu Us Shadi 127 E3 var. Ordos Desert;
prev. Mu Us Shamo. desert N China
Mu Us Shamo see Mu Us Shadi
Muy Muy 52 D3 Matagalpa, C Nicaragua
Muynak see Mo'ynoq
Mužlja 100 D3 Hung. Felsőmuzslya; prev.
Gornja Mužlja. Vojvodina, N Serbia
Mwali see Mohéli
Mwanza 73 B6 Mwanza, NW Tanzania
Mweka 77 C6 Kasai Occidental, C Dem.
Rep. Congo
Mwene-Ditu 77 D7 Kasai Oriental,
S Dem. Rep. Congo
Mweru, Lake 77 D7 var. Lac Moero.
lake Dem. Rep. Congo/Zambia
Myadel' see Myadzyel
Myadzyel 107 C5 Pol. Miadziol Nowy,
Rus. Myadel'. Minskaya Voblasts',
N Belarus
Myanaung 136 B4 Irrawaddy,
SW Myanmar (Burma)
Myanmar 136 A3 off. Union of
Myanmar, Eng. Burma. country SE Asia

MYANMAR (BURMA)
Southeast Asia

Official name Union of Myanmar
Formation 1948 / 1948
Capital Nay Pyi Taw
Population 50.5 million / 199 people per
sq mile (77 people per sq km) / 28%
Total area 261,969 sq miles
(678,500 sq km)
Languages Burmese*, Shan,
Karen, Rakhine, Chin, Yangbye,
Kachin, Mon
Religions Buddhist 87%, Christian 6%,
Muslim 4%, Other 2%, Hindu 1%
Ethnic mix Burman (Bamah) 68%,
Other 13%, Shan 9%, Karen 6%,
Rakhine 4%
Government Military-based regime

MYANMAR (BURMA)
Southeast Asia

Currency Kyat = 100 pyas
Literacy rate 90%
Calorie consumption 2937 calories

Myaungmya 136 A4 Irrawaddy,
SW Myanmar (Burma)
Myerkulavichy 107 D7 Rus.
Merkulovichi. Homyel'skaya Voblasts',
SE Belarus
Myingyan 136 B3 Mandalay,
C Myanmar (Burma)
Myitkyina 136 B2 Kachin State,
N Myanmar (Burma)
Mykolayiv 109 E4 Rus. Nikolayev.
Mykolayivs'ka Oblast', S Ukraine
Mýkonos 105 D6 var. Míkonos. island
Kykládes, Kýklades, Aegean Sea
Myrhorod 109 F2 Rus. Mirgorod.
Poltavs'ka Oblast', NE Ukraine
Mýrina 104 D4 var. Mírina. Límnos,
SE Greece
Myrtle Beach 43 F2 South Carolina,
SE USA
Mýrtos 105 D8 Kríti, Greece,
E Mediterranean Sea
Myrtoum Mare see Mirtóo Pélagos
Myślibórz 98 B3 Zachodnio-pomorskie,
NW Poland
Mysore 132 C1 var. Maisur. Karnātaka,
W India
Mysore see Karnātaka
My Tho 137 E6 var. Mi Tho. Tiên Giang,
S Vietnam
Mytilene see Mytilíni
Mytilíni 105 D5 var. Mitilíni; anc.
Mytilene. Lésvos, E Greece
Mzuzu 79 E2 Northern, N Malawi

N

Naberezhnyye Chelny 111 D5 prev.
Brezhnev. Respublika Tatarstan,
W Russian Federation
Nablus 119 E7 var. Nābulus, Heb.
Shekhem; anc. Neapolis, Bibl. Shechem.
N West Bank
Nābulus see Nablus
Nacala 79 F2 Nampula, NE Mozambique
Na-Ch'ii see Nagqu
Nadi 145 E4 prev. Nandi. Viti Levu,
W Fiji
Nadur 102 A5 Gozo, N Malta
Nadvirna 108 C3 Pol. Nadwórna, Rus.
Nadvornaya. Ivano-Frankivs'ka
Oblast', W Ukraine
Nadvoitsy 110 B3 Respublika Kareliya,
NW Russian Federation
Nadvornaya/Nadwórna see Nadvirna
Nadym 114 D3 Yamalo-Nenetskiy
Avtonomnyy Okrug, N Russian
Federation
Náfpaktos 105 B5 var. Návpaktos.
Dytikí Ellás, C Greece
Náfplio 105 B6 prev. Návplion.
Pelopónnisos, S Greece
Naga 139 E2 off. Naga City; prev. Nueva
Caceres. Luzon, N Philippines
Naga City see Naga
Nagano 131 C5 Nagano, Honshū, S Japan
Nagaoka 131 D5 Niigata, Honshū,
C Japan
Nagara Pathom see Nakhon Pathom
Nagara Sridharmaraj see Nakhon Si
Thammarat
Nagara Svarga see Nakhon Sawan
Nagasaki 131 A7 Nagasaki, Kyūshū,
SW Japan
Nagato 131 A7 Yamaguchi, Honshū,
SW Japan
Nāgercoil 132 C3 Tamil Nādu, SE India
Nagorno-Karabakh 117 G3 var.
Nagorno- Karabakhskaya
Avtonomnaya Oblast, Arm. Lerrnayin
Gharabakh, Az. Dağlıq Quarabağ,
Rus. Nagornyy Karabakh. former
autonomous region SW Azerbaijan
**Nagorno- Karabakhskaya
Avtonomnaya Oblast** see
Nagorno-Karabakh
Nagornyy Karabakh see
Nagorno-Karabakh
Nagoya 131 C6 Aichi, Honshū, SW Japan
Nāgpur 134 D4 Mahārāshtra, C India

Nagqu 126 C5 Chin. Na-Ch'ii; prev. Hei-
ho. Xizang Zizhiqu, W China
Nagybánya see Baia Mare
Nagybecskerek see Zrenjanin
Nagydisznód see Cisnădie
Nagyenyed see Aiud
Nagykálló 99 E6 Szabolcs-Szatmár-
Bereg, E Hungary
Nagykanizsa 99 C7 Ger. Grosskanizsa.
Zala, SW Hungary
Nagykároly see Carei
Nagykikinda see Kikinda
Nagykőrös 99 D7 Pest, C Hungary
Nagymihály see Michalovce
Nagysurány see Šurany
Nagyszalonta see Salonta
Nagyszeben see Sibiu
Nagyszentmiklós see Sânnicolau Mare
Nagyszőllős see Vynohradiv
Nagyszombat see Trnava
Nagytapolcsány see Topoľčany
Nagyvárad see Oradea
Naha 130 A3 Okinawa, Okinawa,
SW Japan
Nahariya see Nahariyya
Nahariyya 119 A5 var. Nahariya.
Northern, N Israel
Nahuel Huapí, Lago 65 B5 lake
W Argentina
Nain 39 F2 Newfoundland and Labrador,
NE Canada
Nā'īn 120 D3 Eşfahān, C Iran
Nairobi 69 E5 country capital (Kenya)
Nairobi Area, S Kenya
Nairobi 73 C6 Nairobi Area, S Kenya
Naissus see Niš
Najaf see An Najaf
Najima see Fukuoka
Najin 129 E3 NE North Korea
Najrān 121 B6 var. Abā as Su'ūd. Najrān,
S Saudi Arabia
Nakambé see White Volta
Nakamura 131 B7 Kōchi, Shikoku,
SW Japan
Nakatsugawa 131 C6 var. Nakatugawa.
Gifu, Honshū, SW Japan
Nakatugawa see Nakatsugawa
Nakhichevan' see Naxçıvan
Nakhodka 115 G5 Primorskiy Kray,
SE Russian Federation
Nakhon Pathom 137 C5 var. Nagara
Pathom, Nakon Pathom. Nakhon
Pathom, W Thailand
Nakhon Ratchasima 137 C5 var.
Khorat, Korat. Nakhon Ratchasima,
E Thailand
Nakhon Sawan 137 C5 var. Muang
Nakhon Sawan, Nagara Svarga.
Nakhon Sawan, W Thailand
Nakhon Si Thammarat 137 C7 var.
Nagara Sridharmaraj, Nakhon
Sithammaraj. Nakhon Si Thammarat,
SW Thailand
Nakhon Sithammaraj see Nakhon Si
Thammarat
Nakorn Pathom see Nakhon Pathom
Nakuru 73 C6 Rift Valley, SW Kenya
Nal'chik 111 B8 Kabardino-Balkarskaya
Respublika, SW Russian Federation
Nālūt 71 F2 NW Libya
Namakan Lake 40 A1 lake Canada/USA
Namangan 123 F2 Namangan Viloyati,
E Uzbekistan
Nambala 78 D2 Central, C Zambia
Nam Co 126 C5 lake W China
Nam Đinh 136 D3 Ha, N Vietnam
Namib Desert 78 B3 desert
W Namibia
Namibe 78 A2 Port. Moçâmedes,
Mossâmedes. Namibe, SW Angola
Namibia 78 B3 off. Republic of Namibia,
var. South West Africa, Afr. Suidwes-
Afrika, Ger. Deutsch-Südwestafrika;
prev. German Southwest Africa,
South-West Africa. country S Africa

NAMIBIA
Southern Africa

Official name Republic of Namibia
Formation 1990 / 1994
Capital Windhoek
Population 2 million / 6 people per sq
mile (2 people per sq km) / 31%
Total area 318,694 sq miles
(825,418 sq km)
Languages English*, Ovambo, Kavango,
Bergdama, German, Afrikaans

NAMIBIA
Southern Africa

Religions Christian 90%, Traditional
beliefs 10%
Ethnic mix Ovambo 50%, Other
tribes 16%, Kavango 9%, Other 9%,
Damara 8%, Herero 8%
Government Presidential system
Currency Namibian dollar = 100 cents
Literacy rate 85%
Calorie consumption 2278 calories

Namibia, Republic of *see* Namibia
Namnetes *see* Nantes
Namo *see* Namu Atoll
Nam Ou *136 C3 river* N Laos
Nampa *46 D3* Idaho, NW USA
Nampula *79 E2* Nampula,
NE Mozambique
Namsos *84 B4* Nord-Trøndelag,
C Norway
Nam Tha *136 C4 river* N Laos
Namu Atoll *144 D2 var.* Namo. *atoll*
Ralik Chain, C Marshall Islands
Namur *87 C6 Dut.* Namen. Namur,
SE Belgium
Namyit Island *128 C8 island* S Spratly
Islands
Nan *136 C4 var.* Muang Nan. Nan,
NW Thailand
Nanaimo *36 D5* Vancouver Island,
British Columbia, SW Canada
Nanchang *128 C5 var.* Nan-ch'ang,
Nanch'ang-hsien. *province capital*
Jiangxi, S China
Nan-ch'ang *see* Nanchang
Nanch'ang-hsien *see* Nanchang
Nan-ching *see* Nanjing
Nancy *90 D3* Meurthe-et-Moselle,
NE France
Nandaime *52 D3* Granada,
SW Nicaragua
Nänded *134 D5* Mahārāshtra, C India
Nandi *see* Nadi
Nándorhegy *see* Oţelu Roşu
Nandyāl *132 C1* Andhra Pradesh, E India
Nan Hai *see* South China Sea
Naniwa *see* Ōsaka
Nanjing *128 C5 var.* Nan-ching,
Nanking; *prev.* Chianning, Chian-ning,
Kiang-ning, Jiangsu. *province capital*
Jiangsu, E China
Nanking *see* Nanjing
Nanning *128 B6 var.* Nan-ning; *prev.*
Yung-ning. Guangxi Zhuangzu
Zizhiqu, S China
Nan-ning *see* Nanning
Nanortalik *82 C5* Kitaa,
S Greenland
Nanpan Jiang *136 D2 river* S China
Nanping *128 D6 var.* Nan-p'ing; *prev.*
Yenping. Fujian, SE China
Nan-p'ing *see* Nanping
Nansei-shotō *125 E3 Eng.* Ryukyu
Islands. *island group* SW Japan
Nansei Syotō Trench *see* Ryukyu Trench
Nansen Basin *155 C4 undersea basin*
Arctic Ocean
Nansen Cordillera *155 B3 var.* Arctic
Mid Oceanic Ridge, Nansen Ridge.
seamount range Arctic Ocean
Nansen Ridge *see* Nansen Cordillera
Nansha Qundao *see* Spratly Islands
Nanterre *90 D1* Hauts-de-Seine,
N France
Nantes *90 B4* Bret. Naoned; *anc.*
Condivincum, Namnetes. Loire-
Atlantique, NW France
Nantucket Island *41 G3 island*
Massachusetts, NE USA
Nanumaga *145 E3 atoll* NW Tuvalu
Nanumea Atoll *145 E3 atoll* NW Tuvalu
Nanyang *128 C5 var.* Nan-yang. Henan,
C China
Nan-yang *see* Nanyang
Naoned *see* Nantes
Napa *47 B6* California, W USA
Napier *150 E4* Hawke's Bay, North
Island, New Zealand
Naples *43 E5* Florida, SE USA
Naples *see* Napoli
Napo *56 A3 province* NE Ecuador
Napoléon-Vendée *see* la Roche-sur-Yon
Napoli *80 D5 Eng.* Naples, Ger. Neapel;
anc. Neapolis. Campania, S Italy
Napo, Río *60 C1 river* Ecuador/Peru
Naracoorte *149 B7* South Australia

Naradhivas *see* Narathiwat
Narathiwat *137 C7 var.* Naradhivas.
Narathiwat, SW Thailand
Narbada *see* Narmada
Narbo Martius *see* Narbonne
Narbonne *91 C6 anc.* Narbo Martius.
Aude, S France
Narborough Island *see* Fernandina, Isla
Nares Abyssal Plain *see* Nares Plain
Nares Plain *35 E6 var.* Nares Abyssal
Plain. *abyssal plain*
NW Atlantic Ocean
Nares Stræde *see* Nares Strait
Nares Strait *82 D1 Dan.* Nares Stræde.
strait Canada/Greenland
Narew *98 E3 river* E Poland
Narmada *124 B3 var.* Narbada. *river*
C India
Narova *see* Narva
Narovlya *see* Narowlya
Narowlya *107 C8 Rus.* Narovlya.
Homyel'skaya Voblasts', SE Belarus
Närpes *85 D5 Fin.* Närpiö. Länsi-Soumi,
W Finland
Närpiö *see* Närpes
Narrabri *149 D6* New South Wales,
SE Australia
Narrogin *147 B6* Western Australia
Narva *106 E2* Ida-Virumaa, NE Estonia
Narva *106 E2 prev.* Narova. *river*
Estonia/Russian Federation
Narva Bay *106 E2 Est.* Narva Laht,
Ger. Narwa-Bucht, Rus. Narvskiy Zaliv.
bay Estonia/Russian Federation
Narva Laht *see* Narva Bay
Narva Reservoir *106 E2 Est.*
Narva Veehoidla, Rus. Narvskoye
Vodokhranilishche. *reservoir* Estonia/
Russian Federation
Narva Veehoidla *see* Narva Reservoir
Narvik *84 C3* Nordland, C Norway
Narvskiy Zaliv *see* Narva Bay
Narvskoye Vodokhranilishche *see*
Narva Reservoir
Narwa-Bucht *see* Narva Bay
Nar'yan-Mar *110 D3 prev.* Beloshchel'ye,
Dzerzhinskiy. Nenetskiy Avtonomnyy
Okrug, NW Russian Federation
Naryn *123 G2* Narynskaya Oblast',
C Kyrgyzstan
Nāsāud *108 B3 Ger.* Nussdorf, Hung.
Naszód. Bistriţa-Năsăud, N Romania
Nase *see* Naze
Nāshik *134 C5 prev.* Nāsik. Mahārāshtra,
W India
Nashua *41 G3* New Hampshire,
NE USA
Nashville *42 C1 state capital* Tennessee,
S USA
Näsijärvi *85 D5 lake* SW Finland
Nāsik *see* Nāshik
Nāsiri *see* Ahvāz
Nasiriya *see* An Nāşirīyah
Nassau *54 C1 country capital* (Bahamas)
New Providence, N Bahamas
Nasser, Lake *72 B3 lake* Egypt/Sudan
Naszód *see* Nāsāud
Nata *78 C3* Central, NE Botswana
Natal *63 G2 state capital* Rio Grande do
Norte, E Brazil
Natal Basin *141 A4 var.* Mozambique
Basin. *undersea basin* W Indian Ocean
Natanya *see* Netanya
Natchez *42 B3* Mississippi, S USA
Natchitoches *42 A2* Louisiana, S USA
Nathanya *see* Netanya
Natitingou *75 F4* NW Benin
Natsrat *see* Nazerat
Natuna Islands *see* Natuna, Kepulauan
Natuna, Kepulauan *124 D4 var.* Natuna
Islands. *island group* W Indonesia
Naturaliste Plateau *141 E6 undersea*
plateau E Indian Ocean
Naugard *see* Nowogard
Naujamiestis *106 C4* Panevėžys,
C Lithuania
Nauru *144 D2 off.* Republic of Nauru;
prev. Pleasant Island. *country*
W Pacific Ocean

NAURU
Australasia & Oceania

Official name Republic of Nauru
Formation 1968 / 1968
Capital None
Population 13,048 / 1611 people per
sq mile (621 people per sq km) / 100%

NAURU
Australasia & Oceania

Total area 8.1 sq miles (21 sq km)
Languages Nauruan*, Kiribati, Chinese,
Tuvaluan, English
Religions Nauruan Congregational
Church 60%, Roman Catholic 35%,
Other 5%
Ethnic mix Nauruan 62%, Other
Pacific islanders 25%, Chinese and
Vietnamese 8%, European 5%
Government Parliamentary system
Currency Australian dollar = 100 cents
Literacy rate 95%
Calorie consumption Not available

Nauru, Republic of *see* Nauru
Nauta *60 C2* Loreto, N Peru
Navahrudak *107 C6 Pol.* Nowogródek,
Rus. Novogrudok. Hrodzyenskaya
Voblasts', W Belarus
Navanagar *see* Jāmnagar
Navapolatsk *107 D5 Rus.* Novopolotsk.
Vitsyebskaya Voblasts', N Belarus
Navarra *93 E2 Eng./Fr.* Navarre.
autonomous community N Spain
Navarre *see* Navarra
Navassa Island *54 C3 US unincorporated*
territory C West Indies
Navoi *see* Navoiy
Navoiy *123 E2 Rus.* Navoi. Navoiy
Viloyati, C Uzbekistan
Navojoa *50 C2* Sonora, NW Mexico
Navolat *see* Navolato
Navolato *50 C4 var.* Navolat. Sinaloa,
C Mexico
Návpaktos *see* Náfpaktos
Návplion *see* Náfplio
Nawabashah *see* Nawābshāh
Nawābshāh *134 B3 var.* Nawabashah.
Sind, S Pakistan
Naxçıvan *117 G3 Rus.* Nakhichevan'.
SW Azerbaijan
Náxos *105 D6 var.* Naxos. Náxos,
Kykládes, Greece, Aegean Sea
Náxos *105 D6 island* Kykládes, Greece,
Aegean Sea
Nayoro *130 D2* Hokkaidō, NE Japan
Nay Pyi Taw *136 B4 country capital*
(Myanmar (Burma)) Mandalay,
C Myanmar (Burma)
Nazareth *see* Nazerat
Nazca *60 D4* Ica, S Peru
Nazca Ridge *57 A5 undersea ridge*
E Pacific Ocean
Naze *130 B3 var.* Nase. Kagoshima,
Amami-ōshima, SW Japan
Nazerat *119 A5 var.* Natsrat, Ar. En
Nazira, Eng. Nazareth. Northern,
N Israel
Nazilli *116 A4* Aydın, SW Turkey
Nazrēt *73 C5 var.* Adama, Hadama.
Oromo, C Ethiopia
N'Dalatando *78 B1 Port.* Salazar, Vila
Salazar. Cuanza Norte, NW Angola
Ndélé *76 D4* Bamingui-Bangoran,
N Central African Republic
Ndendé *77 B6* Ngounié, S Gabon
Ndindi *77 A6* Nyanga, S Gabon
Ndjamena *76 B3 var.* N'Djamena; *prev.*
Fort-Lamy. *country capital* (Chad)
Chari-Baguirmi, W Chad
N'Djamena *see* Ndjamena
Ndjolé *77 A5* Moyen-Ogooué, W Gabon
Ndola *78 D2* Copperbelt, C Zambia
Neagh, Lough *89 B5 lake* E Northern
Ireland, UK
Néa Moudanía *104 C4 var.* Néa
Moudhaniá. Kentrikí Makedonía,
N Greece
Néa Moudhaniá *see* Néa Moudanía
Neapel *see* Napoli
Neápoli *104 B4 prev.* Neápolis. Dytikí
Makedonía, N Greece
Neápoli *105 D8* Kriti, Greece,
E Mediterranean Sea
Neápoli *105 C7* Pelopónnisos, S Greece
Neapolis *see* Neápoli, Greece
Neapolis *see* Napoli, Italy
Neapolis *see* Nablus, West Bank
Near Islands *36 A2 island group* Aleutian
Islands, Alaska, USA
Néa Zíchni *104 C3 var.* Néa Zíkhni;
prev. Néa Zíkhna. Kentrikí Makedonía,
NE Greece
Néa Zíkhna/Néa Zíkhni *see* Néa Zíchni
Nebaj *52 B2* Quiché, W Guatemala

Nebitdag *see* Balkanabat
Neblina, Pico da *62 C1 mountain*
NW Brazil
Nebraska *44 D4 off.* State of Nebraska,
also known as Blackwater State,
Cornhusker State, Tree Planters State.
state C USA
Nebraska City *45 F4* Nebraska, C USA
Neches River *49 H3 river* Texas, SW USA
Neckar *95 B6 river* SW Germany
Necochea *65 D5* Buenos Aires,
E Argentina
Nederland *see* Netherlands
Neder Rijn *86 D4 Eng.* Lower Rhine.
river C Netherlands
Nederweert *87 D5* Limburg,
SE Netherlands
Neede *86 E3* Gelderland, E Netherlands
Neerpelt *87 D5* Limburg,
NE Belgium
Neftekamsk *111 D5* Respublika
Bashkortostan, W Russian Federation
Neftezavodsk *see* Seýdi
Negara Brunei Darussalam *see* Brunei
Negēlē *73 D5 var.* Negelli, It. Neghelli.
Oromo, C Ethiopia
Negelli *see* Negēlē
Negev *see* HaNegev
Neghelli *see* Negēlē
Negomane *79 E2 var.* Negomano. Cabo
Delgado, N Mozambique
Negomano *see* Negomane
Negombo *132 C3* Western Province,
SW Sri Lanka
Negotin *100 E4* Serbia, E Serbia
Negra, Punta *60 A3 point* NW Peru
Negreşti *see* Negreşti-Oaş
Negreşti-Oaş *108 B3 Hung.*
Avasfelsőfalu; *prev.* Negreşti. Satu
Mare, NE Romania
Negro, Río *65 C5 river* E Argentina
Negro, Río *62 D1 river* N South America
Negro, Río *64 D4 river* Brazil/Uruguay
Negros *139 E2 island* C Philippines
Nehbandān *120 E3* Khorāsān, E Iran
Neijiang *128 B5* Sichuan, C China
Neiva *58 B3* Huila, S Colombia
Nellore *132 D2* Andhra Pradesh, E India
Nelson *151 C5* Nelson, South Island,
New Zealand
Nelson *37 G4 river* Manitoba, C Canada
Néma *74 D3* Hodh ech Chargui,
SE Mauritania
Neman *106 B4* Bel. Ragnit.
Kaliningradskaya Oblast', W Russian
Federation
Neman *106 A4 Bel.* Nyoman, Ger.
Memel, Lith. Nemunas, Pol. Niemen,
Rus. Neman. *river* NE Europe
Nemausus *see* Nîmes
Neméa *105 B6* Pelopónnisos, S Greece
Nemetocenna *see* Arras
Nemours *90 C3* Seine-et-Marne,
N France
Nemunas *see* Neman
Nemuro *130 E2* Hokkaidō, NE Japan
Neochóri *105 B5* Dytikí Ellás, C Greece
Nepal *135 E3 off.* Kingdom of Nepal.
country S Asia

NEPAL
South Asia

Official name Kingdom of Nepal
Formation 1769 / 1769
Capital Kathmandu
Population 27.1 million / 513 people per
sq mile (198 people per sq km) / 12%
Total area 54,363 sq miles (140,800 sq km)
Languages Nepali*, Maithili, Bhojpuri
Religions Hindu 90%, Buddhist 5%,
Muslim 3%, Other (including Christian) 2%
Ethnic mix Nepalese 52%, Other 19%,
Maithili 11%, Tibeto-Burmese 10%,
Bhojpuri 8%
Government Monarchy
Currency Nepalese rupee = 100 paise
Literacy rate 49%
Calorie consumption 2453 calories

Nepal, Kingdom of *see* Nepal
Nereta *106 C4* Aizkraukle, S Latvia
Neretva *100 C4 river* Bosnia and
Herzegovina/Croatia
Nerida *106 B4* Klaipėda, W Lithuania
Neris *107 C5 Bel.* Viliya,
Pol. Wilia; *prev.* Pol. Wilja. *river*
Belarus/Lithuania

Neris *see* Viliya
Nerva *92 C4* Andalucía, S Spain
Neryungri *115 F4* Respublika Sakha (Yakutiya), NE Russian Federation
Neskaupstadhur *83 E5* Austurland, E Iceland
Ness, Loch *88 C3* *lake* N Scotland, UK
Nesterov *see* Zhovkva
Néstos *104 C3* *Bul.* Mesta, *Turk.* Kara Su. *river* Bulgaria/Greece
Nesvizh *see* Nyasvizh
Netanya *119 A6* *var.* Natanya, Nathanya. Central, C Israel
Netherlands *86 C3* *off.* Kingdom of the Netherlands, *var.* Holland, *Dut.* Koninkrijk der Nederlanden, Nederland. *country* NW Europe

NETHERLANDS
Northwest Europe

Official name Kingdom of the Netherlands
Formation 1648 / 1839
Capital Amsterdam; The Hague (administrative)
Population 16.3 million / 1245 people per sq mile (481 people per sq km) / 89%
Total area 16,033 sq miles (41,526 sq km)
Languages Dutch*, Frisian
Religions Roman Catholic 36%, Other 34%, Protestant 27%, Muslim 3%
Ethnic mix Dutch 82%, Other 12%, Surinamese 2%, Turkish 2%, Moroccan 2%
Government Parliamentary system
Currency Euro = 100 cents
Literacy rate 99%
Calorie consumption 3362 calories

Netherlands Antilles *55 E5* *prev.* Dutch West Indies. *Dutch autonomous region* S Caribbean Sea
Netherlands East Indies *see* Indonesia
Netherlands Guiana *see* Surinam
Netherlands, Kingdom of the *see* Netherlands
Netherlands New Guinea *see* Papua
Nettilling Lake *37 G3* *lake* Baffin Island, Nunavut, N Canada
Netze *see* Noteć
Neu Amerika *see* Puławy
Neubrandenburg *94 D3* Mecklenburg-Vorpommern, NE Germany
Neuchâtel *95 A7* *Ger.* Neuenburg. Neuchâtel, W Switzerland
Neuchâtel, Lac de *95 A7* *Ger.* Neuenburger See. *lake* W Switzerland
Neuenburger See *see* Neuchâtel, Lac de
Neufchâteau *87 D8* Luxembourg, SE Belgium
Neugradisk *see* Nova Gradiška
Neuhof *see* Zgierz
Neukuhren *see* Pionerskiy
Neumarkt *see* Târgu Secuiesc, Covasna, Romania
Neumarkt *see* Târgu Mureş
Neumoldawa *see* Moldova Nouă
Neumünster *94 B2* Schleswig-Holstein, N Germany
Neunkirchen *95 A5* Saarland, SW Germany
Neuquén *65 B5* Neuquén, SE Argentina
Neuruppin *94 C3* Brandenburg, NE Germany
Neusalz an der Oder *see* Nowa Sól
Neu Sandec *see* Nowy Sącz
Neusatz *see* Novi Sad
Neusiedler See *95 E6* *Hung.* Fertő. *lake* Austria/Hungary
Neusohl *see* Banská Bystrica
Neustadt *see* Baia Mare, Maramureş, Romania
Neustadt an der Haardt *see* Neustadt an der Weinstrasse
Neustadt an der Weinstrasse *95 B5* *prev.* Neustadt an der Haardt, *hist.* Niewenstat; *anc.* Nova Civitas. Rheinland-Pfalz, SW Germany
Neustadtl *see* Novo mesto
Neustettin *see* Szczecinek
Neustrelitz *94 D3* Mecklenburg-Vorpommern, NE Germany
Neutra *see* Nitra
Neu-Ulm *95 B6* Bayern, S Germany

Neuwied *95 A5* Rheinland-Pfalz, W Germany
Neuzen *see* Terneuzen
Nevada *47 C5* *off.* State of Nevada, *also known as* Battle Born State, Sagebrush State, Silver State. *state* W USA
Nevers *90 C4* *anc.* Noviodunum. Nièvre, C France
Neves *76 E2* São Tomé, S Sao Tome and Principe, Africa
Nevinnomyssk *111 B7* Stavropol'skiy Kray, SW Russian Federation
Nevşehir *116 C3* *var.* Nevshehr. Nevşehir, C Turkey
Nevshehr *see* Nevşehir
Newala *73 C8* Mtwara, SE Tanzania
New Albany *40 C5* Indiana, N USA
New Amsterdam *59 G3* E Guyana
Newark *41 F4* New Jersey, NE USA
New Bedford *41 G3* Massachusetts, NE USA
Newberg *46 B3* Oregon, NW USA
New Bern *43 F1* North Carolina, SE USA
New Braunfels *49 G4* Texas, SW USA
Newbridge *89 B6* *Ir.* An Droichead Nua. Kildare, C Ireland
New Britain *144 B3* *island* E Papua New Guinea
New Brunswick *39 E4* *Fr.* Nouveau-Brunswick. *province* SE Canada
New Caledonia *144 D4* *var.* Kanaky, *Fr.* Nouvelle-Calédonie. *French overseas territory* SW Pacific Ocean
New Caledonia *144 C5* *island* SW Pacific Ocean
New Caledonia Basin *142 C4* *undersea basin* W Pacific Ocean
Newcastle *149 D6* New South Wales, SE Australia
Newcastle *see* Newcastle upon Tyne
Newcastle upon Tyne *88 D4* *var.* Newcastle, *hist.* Monkchester, *Lat.* Pons Aelii. NE England, UK
New Delhi *134 D3* *country capital* (India) Delhi, N India
New England of the West *see* Minnesota
Newfoundland *39 G3* Fr. Terre-Neuve. *island* Newfoundland and Labrador, SE Canada
Newfoundland and Labrador *39 F2* *Fr.* Terre Neuve. *province* E Canada
Newfoundland Basin *66 B3* *undersea feature* NW Atlantic Ocean
New Georgia Islands *144 C3* *island group* NW Solomon Islands
New Glasgow *39 F4* Nova Scotia, SE Canada
New Goa *see* Panaji
New Guinea *144 A3* *Dut.* Nieuw Guinea, *Ind.* Irian. *island* Indonesia/Papua New Guinea
New Hampshire *41 F2* *off.* State of New Hampshire, *also known as* Granite State. *state* NE USA
New Haven *41 G3* Connecticut, NE USA
New Hebrides *see* Vanuatu
New Iberia *42 B3* Louisiana, S USA
New Ireland *144 C3* *island* NE Papua New Guinea
New Jersey *41 F4* *off.* State of New Jersey, *also known as* The Garden State. *state* NE USA
Newman *146 B4* Western Australia
Newmarket *89 E6* E England, UK
New Mexico *48 C2* *off.* State of New Mexico, *also known as* Land of Enchantment, Sunshine State. *state* SW USA
New Orleans *42 B3* Louisiana, S USA
New Plymouth *150 C4* Taranaki, North Island, New Zealand
Newport *89 D7* S England, UK
Newport *89 C7* SE Wales, UK
Newport *40 C4* Kentucky, S USA
Newport *41 G2* Vermont, NE USA
Newport News *41 F5* Virginia, NE USA
New Providence *54 C1* *island* N Bahamas
Newquay *89 C7* SW England, UK
Newry *89 B5* *Ir.* An tIúr. SE Northern Ireland, UK
New Sarum *see* Salisbury
New Siberian Islands *see* Novosibirskiye Ostrova
New South Wales *149 C6* *state* SE Australia
Newton *45 G3* Iowa, C USA
Newtownabbey *89 B5* *Ir.* Baile na Mainistreach. E Northern Ireland, UK

New Ulm *45 F2* Minnesota, N USA
New York *41 F4* New York, NE USA
New York *41 F3* *state* NE USA
New Zealand *150 A4* *country* SW Pacific Ocean

NEW ZEALAND
Australasia & Oceania

Official name New Zealand
Formation 1947 / 1947
Capital Wellington
Population 4 million / 39 people per sq mile (15 people per sq km) / 86%
Total area 103,737 sq miles (268,680 sq km)
Languages English*, Maori
Religions Anglican 24%, Other 22%, Presbyterian 18%, Nonreligious 16%, Roman Catholic 15%, Methodist 5%
Ethnic mix European 77%, Maori 12%, Other immigrant 6%, Pacific islanders 5%
Government Parliamentary system
Currency New Zealand dollar = 100 cents
Literacy rate 99%
Calorie consumption 3219 calories

Neyveli *132 C2* Tamil Nādu, SE India
Nezhin *see* Nizhyn
Ngangzê Co *126 B5* *lake* W China
Ngaoundéré *76 B4* *var.* N'Gaoundéré. Adamaoua, N Cameroon
N'Gaoundéré *see* Ngaoundéré
N'Giva *78 B3* *var.* Ondjiva, *Port.* Vila Pereira de Eça. Cunene, S Angola
Ngo *77 B6* Plateaux, SE Congo
Ngoko *77 B5* *river* Cameroon/Congo
Ngourti *75 H3* Diffa, E Niger
Nguigmi *75 H3* *var.* N'Guigmi. Diffa, SE Niger
N'Guigmi *see* Nguigmi
N'Gunza *see* Sumbe
Nguru *75 G3* Yobe, NE Nigeria
Nha Trang *137 E6* Khanh Hoa, S Vietnam
Niagara Falls *38 D5* Ontario, S Canada
Niagara Falls *41 E3* New York, NE USA
Niagara Falls *40 D3* *waterfall* Canada/USA
Niamey *75 F3* *country capital* (Niger) Niamey, SW Niger
Niangay, Lac *75 E3* *lake* E Mali
Nia-Nia *77 E5* Orientale, NE Dem. Rep. Congo
Nias, Pulau *138 A3* *island* W Indonesia
Nicaea *see* Nice
Nicaragua *52 D3* *off.* Republic of Nicaragua. *country* Central America

NICARAGUA
Central America

Official name Republic of Nicaragua
Formation 1838 / 1838
Capital Managua
Population 5.5 million / 120 people per sq mile (46 people per sq km) / 65%
Total area 49,998 sq miles (129,494 sq km)
Languages Spanish*, English Creole, Miskito
Religions Roman Catholic 80%, Protestant Evangelical 17%, Other 3%
Ethnic mix Mestizo 69%, White 14%, Black 8%, Amerindian 5%, Zambo 4%
Government Presidential system
Currency Córdoba oro = 100 centavos
Literacy rate 77%
Calorie consumption 2298 calories

Nicaragua, Lago de *52 D4* *var.* Cocibolca, Gran Lago, *Eng.* Lake Nicaragua. *lake* S Nicaragua
Nicaragua, Lake *see* Nicaragua, Lago de
Nicaragua, Republic of *see* Nicaragua
Nicaria *see* Ikaria
Nice *116 D6* *It.* Nizza; *anc.* Nicaea. Alpes-Maritimes, SE France
Nicephorium *see* Ar Raqqah
Nicholas II Land *see* Severnaya Zemlya
Nicholls Town *54 C1* Andros Island, NW Bahamas
Nicobar Islands *124 B4* *island group* India, E Indian Ocean

Nicopolis *see* Nikopol, Bulgaria
Nicosia *102 C5* *Gk.* Lefkosia, *Turk.* Lefkoşa. *country capital* (Cyprus) C Cyprus
Nicoya *52 D4* Guanacaste, W Costa Rica
Nicoya, Golfo de *52 D5* *gulf* W Costa Rica
Nicoya, Península de *52 D4* *peninsula* NW Costa Rica
Nida *106 A3* *Ger.* Nidden. Klaipėda, SW Lithuania
Nidaros *see* Trondheim
Nidden *see* Nida
Nidzica *98 D3* *Ger.* Niedenburg. Warmińsko Mazurskie, NE Poland
Niedenburg *see* Nidzica
Niedere Tauern *99 A6* *mountain range* C Austria
Niemen *see* Neman
Nieśwież *see* Nyasvizh
Nieuw Amsterdam *59 G3* Commewijne, NE Suriname
Nieuw-Bergen *86 D4* Limburg, SE Netherlands
Nieuwegein *86 C4* Utrecht, C Netherlands
Nieuw Guinea *see* New Guinea
Nieuw Nickerie *59 G3* Nickerie, NW Suriname
Niewenstat *see* Neustadt an der Weinstrasse
Niğde *116 C4* Niğde, C Turkey
Niger *75 F3* *off.* Republic of Niger. *country* W Africa

NIGER
West Africa

Official name Republic of Niger
Formation 1960 / 1960
Capital Niamey
Population 14 million / 29 people per sq mile (11 people per sq km) / 21%
Total area 489,188 sq miles (1,267,000 sq km)
Languages French*, Hausa, Djerma, Fulani, Tuareg, Teda
Religions Muslim 85%, Traditional beliefs 14%, Other (including Christian) 1%
Ethnic mix Hausa 54%, Djerma and Songhai 21%, Fulani 10%, Tuareg 9%, Other 6%
Government Presidential system
Currency CFA franc = 100 centimes
Literacy rate 14%
Calorie consumption 2130 calories

Niger *75 F4* *river* W Africa
Nigeria *75 F4* *off.* Federal Republic of Nigeria. *country* W Africa

NIGERIA
West Africa

Official name Federal Republic of Nigeria
Formation 1960 / 1961
Capital Abuja
Population 132 million / 374 people per sq mile (144 people per sq km) / 44%
Total area 356,667 sq miles (923,768 sq km)
Languages English*, Hausa, Yoruba, Ibo
Religions Muslim 50%, Christian 40%, Traditional beliefs 10%
Ethnic mix Other 29%, Hausa 21%, Yoruba 21%, Ibo 18%, Fulani 11%
Government Presidential system
Currency Naira = 100 kobo
Literacy rate 67%
Calorie consumption 2726 calories

Nigeria, Federal Republic of *see* Nigeria
Niger, Mouths of the *75 F5* *delta* S Nigeria
Niger, Republic of *see* Niger
Nihon *see* Japan
Niigata *131 D5* Niigata, Honshū, C Japan
Niihama *131 B7* Ehime, Shikoku, SW Japan
Ni'ihau *47 A7* *var.* Niihau. *island* Hawai'i, USA, C Pacific Ocean
Nii-jima *131 D6* *island* E Japan
Nijkerk *86 D3* Gelderland, C Netherlands
Nijlen *87 C5* Antwerpen, N Belgium

Nijmegen 86 D4 Ger. Nimwegen; anc. Noviomagus. Gelderland, SE Netherlands

Nikaria see Ikaría

Nikel' 110 C2 Murmanskaya Oblast', NW Russian Federation

Nikiniki 139 E5 Timor, S Indonesia

Niklasmarkt see Gheorgheni

Nikolainkaupunki see Vaasa

Nikolayev see Mykolayiv

Nikol'sk see Ussuriysk

Nikol'sk-Ussuriskiy see Ussuriysk

Nikopol 109 F3 anc. Nicopolis. Pleven, N Bulgaria

Nikšić 101 C5 C Montenegro

Nikumaroro 145 E3; prev. Gardner Island. atoll Phoenix Islands, C Kiribati

Nikunau 145 E3 var. Nukunau; prev. Byron Island. atoll Tungaru, W Kiribati

Nile 72 B2 former province NW Uganda

Nile 68 D3 Ar. Nahr an Nīl. river N Africa

Nile Delta 72 B1 delta N Egypt

Nil, Nahr an see Nile

Nîmes 91 C6 anc. Nemausus, Nismes. Gard, S France

Nimwegen see Nijmegen

Nine Degree Channel 132 B3 channel India/Maldives

Ninetyeast Ridge 141 D5 undersea feature E Indian Ocean

Ninety Mile Beach 150 C1 beach North Island, New Zealand

Ningbo 128 D5 var. Ning-po, Yin-hsien; prev. Ninghsien. Zhejiang, SE China

Ning-hsia see Ningxia

Ninghsien see Ningbo

Ning-po see Ningbo

Ningsia/Ningsia Hui/Ningsia Hui Autonomous Region see Ningxia

Ningxia 128 B4 off. Ningxia Huizu Zizhiqu, var. Ning-hsia, Ningsia, Eng. Ningsia Hui, Ningsia Hui Autonomous Region. autonomous region N China

Ningxia Huizu Zizhiqu see Ningxia

Nio see Íos

Nio see Íos

Nio see Íos

Niobrara River 45 E3 river Nebraska/Wyoming, C USA

Nioro 74 D3 var. Nioro du Sahel. Kayes, W Mali

Nioro du Sahel see Nioro

Niort 90 B4 Deux-Sèvres, W France

Nipigon 38 B4 Ontario, S Canada

Nipigon, Lake 38 B3 lake Ontario, S Canada

Nippon see Japan

Niš 101 E5 Eng. Nish, Ger. Nisch; anc. Naissus. Serbia, SE Serbia

Nişāb 120 B4 Al Ḥudūd ash Shamālīyah, N Saudi Arabia

Nisch/Nish see Niš

Nisibin see Nusaybin

Nisiros see Nísyros

Nisko 98 E4 Podkarpackie, SE Poland

Nismes see Nîmes

Nistru see Dniester

Nísyros 105 E7 var. Nisiros. island Dodekánisa, Greece, Aegean Sea

Nitra 99 C6 Ger. Neutra, Hung. Nyitra. Nitriansky Kraj, SW Slovakia

Nitra 99 C6 Ger. Neutra, Hung. Nyitra. river W Slovakia

Niuatobutabu see Niuatoputapu

Niuatoputapu 145 E4 var. Niuatobutabu; prev. Keppel Island. island N Tonga

Niue 145 F4 self-governing territory in free association with New Zealand S Pacific Ocean

Niulakita 145 E3 var. Nurakita. atoll S Tuvalu

Niutao 145 E3 atoll NW Tuvalu

Nivernais 90 C4 cultural region C France

Nizāmābād 134 D5 Andhra Pradesh, C India

Nizhnegorskiy see Nyzhn'ohirs'kyy

Nizhnekamsk 111 C5 Respublika Tatarstan, W Russian Federation

Nizhnevartovsk 114 D3 Khanty-Mansiyskiy Avtonomnyy Okrug, C Russian Federation

Nizhniy Novgorod 111 C5 prev. Gor'kiy. Nizhegorodskaya Oblast', W Russian Federation

Nizhniy Odes 110 D4 Respublika Komi, NW Russian Federation

Nizhnyaya Tunguska 115 E3 Eng. Lower Tunguska. river N Russian Federation

Nizhyn 109 E1 Rus. Nezhin. Chernihivs'ka Oblast', NE Ukraine

Nizza see Nice

Njazidja see Grande Comore

Njombe 73 C8 Iringa, S Tanzania

Nkayi 77 B6 prev. Jacob. La Bouenza, S Congo

Nkongsamba 76 A4 var. N'Kongsamba. Littoral, W Cameroon

N'Kongsamba see Nkongsamba

Nmai Hka 136 B2 var. Me Hka. river N Myanmar (Burma)

Nobeoka 131 B7 Miyazaki, Kyūshū, SW Japan

Noboribetsu 130 D3 var. Noboribetu. Hokkaidō, NE Japan

Noboribetu see Noboribetsu

Nogales 50 B1 Sonora, NW Mexico

Nogales 48 B5 Arizona, SW USA

Nogal Valley see Dooxo Nugaaleed

Noire, Rivi` see Black River

Nokia 85 D5 Länsi-Suomi, W Finland

Nokou 76 B3 Kanem, W Chad

Nola 77 B5 Sangha-Mbaéré, SW Central African Republic

Nolinsk 111 C5 Kirovskaya Oblast', NW Russian Federation

Nongkaya see Nong Khai

Nong Khai 136 C4 var. Mi Chai, Nongkaya. Nong Khai, E Thailand

Nonouti 144 D2 prev. Sydenham Island. atoll Tungaru, W Kiribati

Noord-Beveland 86 B4 var. North Beveland. island SW Netherlands

Noordwijk aan Zee 86 C3 Zuid-Holland, W Netherlands

Noordzee see North Sea

Nora 85 C6 Örebro, C Sweden

Norak 123 E3 Rus. Nurek. W Tajikistan

Nord 83 F1 Avannaarsua, N Greenland

Nordaustlandet 83 G1 island NE Svalbard

Norden 94 A3 Niedersachsen, NW Germany

Norderstedt 94 B3 Schleswig-Holstein, N Germany

Nordfriesische Inseln see North Frisian Islands

Nordhausen 94 C4 Thüringen, C Germany

Nordhorn 94 A3 Niedersachsen, NW Germany

Nordkapp 84 D1 Eng. North Cape. headland N Norway

Nord, Mer du see North Sea

Nord-Ouest, Territoires du see Northwest Territories

Nordsee/Nordsjøen/Nordsoen see North Sea

Norfolk 45 E3 Nebraska, C USA

Norfolk 41 F5 Virginia, NE USA

Norfolk Island 142 D4 Australian external territory SW Pacific Ocean

Norfolk Ridge 142 D4 undersea feature W Pacific Ocean

Norge see Norway

Norias 49 G5 Texas, SW USA

Noril'sk 114 D3 Taymyrskiy (Dolgano-Nenetskiy) Avtonomnyy Okrug, N Russian Federation

Norman 49 G1 Oklahoma, C USA

Normandes, Îles see Channel Islands

Normandie 90 B3 Eng. Normandy. cultural region N France

Normandy see Normandie

Normanton 148 C3 Queensland, NE Australia

Norrköping 85 C6 Östergötland, S Sweden

Norrtälje 85 C6 Stockholm, C Sweden

Norseman 147 B6 Western Australia

Norske Havet see Norwegian Sea

North Albanian Alps 101 C5 Alb. Bjeshkët e Namuna, SCr. Prokletije. mountain range SE Europe

Northallerton 89 D5 N England, UK

Northam 147 A6 Western Australia

Northampton 89 D6 C England, UK

North America 34 continent

North Andaman 133 F2 island Andaman Islands, India, NE Indian Ocean

North Australian Basin 141 E5 Fr. Bassin Nord de l' Australie. undersea feature E Indian Ocean

North Bay 38 D4 Ontario, S Canada

North Beveland see Noord-Beveland

North Borneo see Sabah

North Cape 150 C1 headland North Island, New Zealand

North Cape 66 D1 headland New Ireland, NE Papua New Guinea

North Cape see Nordkapp

North Carolina 43 E1 off. State of North Carolina, also known as Old North State, Tar Heel State, Turpentine State. state SE USA

North Channel 40 D2 lake channel Canada/USA

North Charleston 43 F2 South Carolina, SE USA

North Dakota 44 D2 off. State of North Dakota, also known as Flickertail State, Peace Garden State, Sioux State. state N USA

North Devon Island see Devon Island

North East Frontier Agency/North East Frontier Agency of Assam see Arunāchal Pradesh

Northeast Providence Channel 54 C1 channel N Bahamas

Northeim 94 B4 Niedersachsen, C Germany

Northern Cook Islands 145 F4 island group N Cook Islands

Northern Dvina see Severnaya Dvina

Northern Ireland 88 B4 var. The Six Counties. cultural region Northern Ireland, UK

Northern Ireland 88 B4 var. The Six Counties. political division Northern Ireland, UK

Northern Mariana Islands 142 B1 US commonwealth territory W Pacific Ocean

Northern Rhodesia see Zambia

Northern Sporades see Vóries Sporádes

Northern Territory 144 A5 territory N Australia

North European Plain 81 E3 plain N Europe

Northfield 45 F2 Minnesota, N USA

North Fiji Basin 142 D3 undersea feature W Pacific Ocean

North Frisian Islands 94 B2 var. Nordfriesische Inseln. island group N Germany

North Huvadhu Atoll 132 B5 var. Gaafu Alifu Atoll. atoll S Maldives

North Island 150 B2 island N New Zealand

North Korea 129 E3 off. Democratic People's Republic of Korea, Kor. Chosŏn-minjujuŭi-inmin-kanghwaguk. country E Asia

North Little Rock 42 B1 Arkansas, C USA

North Minch see Minch, The

North Mole 93 G4 harbour wall NW Gibraltar Europe

North Platte 45 E4 Nebraska, C USA

North Platte River 44 D4 river C USA

North Pole 155 B3 pole Arctic Ocean

North Saskatchewan 37 F5 river Alberta/Saskatchewan, S Canada

North Sea 80 Dan. Nordsøen, Dut. Noordzee, Fr. Mer du Nord, Ger. Nordsee, Nor. Nordsjøen; prev. German Ocean, Lat. Mare Germanicum. sea NW Europe

North Siberian Lowland/North Siberian Plain see Severo-Sibirskaya Nizmennost'

North Star State see Minnesota

North Taranaki Bight 150 C3 gulf North Island, New Zealand

North Uist 88 B3 island NW Scotland, UK

Northwest Atlantic Mid-Ocean Canyon 34 E4 undersea feature N Atlantic Ocean

North West Highlands 88 C3 mountain range N Scotland, UK

Northwest Pacific Basin 113 G4 undersea feature NW Pacific Ocean

Northwest Territories 37 E3 Fr. Territoires du Nord-Ouest. territory NW Canada

Northwind Plain 155 B2 undersea feature Arctic Ocean

Norton Sound 36 C2 inlet Alaska, USA

Norway 85 A5 off. Kingdom of Norway, Nor. Norge. country N Europe

NORWAY
Northern Europe

Official name	Kingdom of Norway
Formation	1905 / 1905
Capital	Oslo
Population	4.6 million / 39 people per sq mile (15 people per sq km) / 76%
Total area	125,181 sq miles (324,220 sq km)
Languages	Norwegian* (Bokmål "book language" and Nynorsk "new Norsk"), Sámi
Religions	Evangelical Lutheran 89%, Other and nonreligious 10%, Roman Catholic 1%
Ethnic mix	Norwegian 93%, Other 6%, Sámi 1%
Government	Parliamentary system
Currency	Norwegian krone = 100 øre
Literacy rate	99%
Calorie consumption	3484 calories

Norway, Kingdom of see Norway

Norwegian Basin 83 F4 undersea feature NW Norwegian Sea

Norwegian Sea 83 F4 var. Norske Havet. sea NE Atlantic Ocean

Norwich 89 E6 E England, UK

Nösen see Bistriţa

Noshiro 130 D4 var. Nosiro; prev. Noshirominato. Akita, Honshū, C Japan

Noshirominato/Nosiro see Noshiro

Nosivka 109 E1 Rus. Nosovka. Chernihivs'ka Oblast', NE Ukraine

Nosop 78 C4 river E Namibia

Nosovka see Nosivka

Noşratābād 120 E3 Sīstān va Balūchestān, E Iran

Noteć 98 C3 Ger. Netze. river NW Poland

Nóties Sporádes see Dodekánisa

Nottingham 89 D6 C England, UK

Nouâdhibou 74 B2 prev. Port-Étienne. Dakhlet Nouâdhibou, W Mauritania

Nouakchott 74 B2 country capital (Mauritania) Nouakchott District, SW Mauritania

Nouméa 144 C5 dependent territory capital (New Caledonia) Province Sud, S New Caledonia

Nouveau-Brunswick see New Brunswick

Nouvelle-Calédonie see New Caledonia

Nouvelle Écosse see Nova Scotia

Nova Civitas see Neustadt an der Weinstrasse

Nova Gorica 95 D8 W Slovenia

Nova Gradiška 100 C3 Ger. Neugradisk, Hung. Újgradiska. Brod-Posavina, NE Croatia

Nova Iguaçu 63 F4 Rio de Janeiro, SE Brazil

Nova Lisboa see Huambo

Novara 96 B2 anc. Novaria. Piemonte, NW Italy

Novaria see Novara

Nova Scotia 39 F4 Fr. Nouvelle Écosse. province SE Canada

NORTH KOREA
East Asia

Official name	Democratic People's Republic of Korea
Formation	1948 / 1953
Capital	Pyongyang
Population	22.5 million / 484 people per sq mile (187 people per sq km) / 60%
Total area	46,540 sq miles (120,540 sq km)
Languages	Korean*
Religions	Atheist 100%
Ethnic mix	Korean 100%
Government	One-party state
Currency	North Korean won = 100 chon
Literacy rate	99%
Calorie consumption	2142 calories

Nova Scotia 35 E5 *physical region*
  SE Canada
Novaya Sibir', Ostrov 115 F1 *island*
  Novosibirskiye Ostrova, NE Russian
  Federation
Novaya Zemlya 110 D1 *island group*
  N Russian Federation
Novaya Zemlya Trough *see* East Novaya
  Zemlya Trough
Novgorod *see* Velikiy Novgorod
Novi Grad *see* Bosanski Novi
Novi Iskŭr 104 C2 Sofiya-Grad,
  W Bulgaria
Noviodunum *see* Nevers, Nièvre,
  France
Noviomagus *see* Lisieux, Calvados,
  France
Noviomagus *see* Nijmegen, Netherlands
Novi Pazar 101 D5 Shumen,
  NE Bulgaria
Novi Sad 100 D3 *Ger.* Neusatz, *Hung.*
  Újvidék. Vojvodina, N Serbia
Novoazovs'k 109 G4 *Rus.* Novoazovsk.
  Donets'ka Oblast', E Ukraine
Novocheboksarsk 111 C5 Chavash
  Respubliki, W Russian Federation
Novocherkassk 111 B7 Rostovskaya
  Oblast', SW Russian Federation
Novodvinsk 110 C3 Arkhangel'skaya
  Oblast', NW Russian Federation
Novograd-Volynskiy *see*
  Novohrad-Volyns'kyy
Novogrudok *see* Navahrudak
Novohrad-Volyns'kyy 108 D2 *Rus.*
  Novograd-Volynskiy. Zhytomyrs'ka
  Oblast', N Ukraine
Novokazalinsk *see* Ayteke Bi
Novokuznetsk 114 D4 *prev.* Stalinsk.
  Kemerovskaya Oblast', S Russian
  Federation
Novolazarevskaya 154 C2 *Russian
  research station* Antarctica
Novo mesto 95 E8 *Ger.* Rudolfswert;
  prev. Ger. Neustadtl. SE Slovenia
Novomoskovsk 111 B5 Tul'skaya
  Oblast', W Russian Federation
Novomoskovs'k 109 F3 *Rus.*
  Novomoskovsk. Dnipropetrovs'ka
  Oblast', E Ukraine
Novopolotsk *see* Navapolatsk
Novoradomsk *see* Radomsko
Novo Redondo *see* Sumbe
Novorossiysk 111 A7 Krasnodarskiy
  Kray, SW Russian Federation
Novoshakhtinsk 111 B8 Rostovskaya
  Oblast', SW Russian Federation
Novosibirsk 114 D4 Novosibirskaya
  Oblast', C Russian Federation
Novosibirskiye Ostrova 115 F1 *Eng.*
  New Siberian Islands. *island group*
  N Russian Federation
Novotroitsk 111 D6 Orenburgskaya
  Oblast', W Russian Federation
Novotroitskoye *see* Novotroyits'ke,
  Ukraine
Novotroyits'ke 109 F4 *Rus.*
  Novotroitskoye. Khersons'ka Oblast',
  S Ukraine
Novo-Urgench *see* Urganch
Novovolyns'k 108 C1 *Rus.* Novovolynsk.
  Volyns'ka Oblast', NW Ukraine
Novy Dvor 107 B6 *Rus.* Novyy Dvor.
  Hrodzyenskaya Voblasts', W Belarus
Novyy Bug *see* Novyy Buh
Novyy Buh 109 E3 *Rus.* Novyy Bug.
  Mykolayivs'ka Oblast', S Ukraine
Novyy Dvor *see* Novy Dvor
Novyy Margilan *see* Farg'ona
Novyy Uzen' *see* Zhanaozen
Nowa Sól 98 B4 *var.* Nowasól, *Ger.*
  Neusalz an der Oder. Lubuskie,
  W Poland
Nowasól *see* Nowa Sól
Nowogard 98 B2 *var.* Nowógard,
  Ger. Naugard. Zachodnio-pomorskie,
  NW Poland
Nowogródek *see* Navahrudak
Nowo-Minsk *see* Mińsk Mazowiecki
Nowy Dwór Mazowiecki 98 D3
  Mazowieckie, C Poland
Nowy Sącz 99 D5 *Ger.* Neu Sandec.
  Małopolskie, S Poland
Nowy Tomyśl 98 B3 *var.* Nowy Tomysl.
  Wielkopolskie, C Poland
Nowy Tomysl *see* Nowy Tomyśl
Noyon 90 C3 Oise, N France
Nsanje 79 E3 Southern, S Malawi
Nsawam 75 E5 SE Ghana

Ntomba, Lac 77 C6 *var.* Lac Tumba.
  lake NW Dem. Rep. Congo
Nubian Desert 72 B3 *desert* NE Sudan
Nu Chiang *see* Salween
Nu'eima 119 E7 E West Bank Asia
Nueva Caceres *see* Naga
Nueva Gerona 54 B2 Isla de la Juventud,
  S Cuba
Nueva Rosita 50 D2 Coahuila de
  Zaragoza, NE Mexico
Nuevitas 54 C2 Camagüey, E Cuba
Nuevo, Bajo 53 G1 *island* NW Colombia
  South America
Nuevo Casas Grandes 50 C1 Chihuahua,
  N Mexico
Nuevo, Golfo 65 C6 *gulf* S Argentina
Nuevo Laredo 51 E2 Tamaulipas,
  NE Mexico
Nui Atoll 145 E3 *atoll* W Tuvalu
Nu Jiang *see* Salween
Nûk *see* Nuuk
Nukha *see* Şäki
Nuku'alofa 145 E5 *country capital*
  (Tonga) Tongatapu, S Tonga
Nukufetau Atoll 145 E3 *atoll* C Tuvalu
Nukulaelae Atoll 145 E3 *var.* Nukulailai.
  atoll E Tuvalu
Nukulailai *see* Nukulaelae Atoll
Nukunau *see* Nikunau
Nukunonu Atoll 145 E3 *island*
  C Tokelau
Nukus 122 C2 Qoraqalpog'iston
  Respublikasi, W Uzbekistan
Nullarbor Plain 147 C6 *plateau* South
  Australia/Western Australia
Nunap Isua 98 D5 *var.* Uummannarsuaq,
  Dan. Kap Farvel, *Eng.* Cape Farewell.
  cape S Greenland
Nunavut 37 F3 *territory* N Canada
Nuneaton 89 D6 C England, UK
Nunivak Island 36 B2 *island* Alaska,
  USA
Nunspeet 86 D3 Gelderland,
  E Netherlands
Nuoro 97 A5 Sardegna, Italy,
  C Mediterranean Sea
Nuquí 58 A3 Chocó, W Colombia
Nurakita *see* Niulakita
Nurata *see* Nurota
Nurek *see* Norak
Nuremberg *see* Nürnberg
Nurmes 84 E4 Itä-Suomi, E Finland
Nürnberg 95 C5 *Eng.* Nuremberg.
  Bayern, S Germany
Nurota 123 E2 *Rus.* Nurata. Navoiy
  Viloyati, C Uzbekistan
Nusa Tenggara 139 E5 *Eng.* Lesser
  Sunda Islands. *island group*
  C Indonesia
Nusaybin 117 F4 *var.* Nisibin. Manisa,
  SE Turkey
Nussdorf *see* Năsăud
Nutmeg State *see* Connecticut
Nuuk 82 C4 *var.* Nûk, *Dan.* Godthaab,
  Godthåb. *dependent territory capital*
  (Greenland) Kitaa, SW Greenland
Nyagan' 114 C3 Khanty-Mansiyskiy
  Avtonomnyy Okrug, N Russian
  Federation
Nyaingêntanglha Shan 126 C5
  mountain range W China
Nyala 72 A4 Southern Darfur, W Sudan
Nyamapanda 78 D3 Mashonaland East,
  NE Zimbabwe
Nyamtumbo 73 C8 Ruvuma, S Tanzania
Nyanda *see* Masvingo
Nyandoma 110 C4 Arkhangel'skaya
  Oblast', NW Russian Federation
Nyantakara 73 B7 Kagera, NW Tanzania
Nyasa, Lake 79 E2 *var.* Lake Malawi;
  prev. Lago Nyassa. *lake* E Africa
Nyasaland/Nyasaland Protectorate
  see Malawi
Nyassa, Lago *see* Nyasa, Lake
Nyasvizh 107 C6 *Pol.* Nieśwież,
  Rus. Nesvizh. Minskaya Voblasts',
  C Belarus
Nyaunglebin 136 B4 Pegu,
  SW Myanmar (Burma)
Nyeri 73 C6 Central, C Kenya
Nyima 126 C5 Xizang Zizhiqu, W China
Nyíregyháza 99 D6 Szabolcs-Szatmár-
  Bereg, NE Hungary
Nyitra *see* Nitra
Nykøbing 85 B8 Storstrøm, SE Denmark
Nyköping 85 C6 Södermanland,
  S Sweden
Nylstroom *see* Modimolle

Nyngan 149 D6 New South Wales,
  SE Australia
Nyoman *see* Neman
Nyurba 115 F3 Respublika Sakha
  (Yakutiya), NE Russian Federation
Nyzhn'ohirs'kyy 109 F4 *Rus.*
  Nizhnegorskiy. Respublika Krym,
  S Ukraine
NZ *see* New Zealand
Nzega 73 C7 Tabora, C Tanzania
Nzérékoré 74 D4 SE Guinea
Nzwani *see* Anjouan

O

Oʻahu 47 A7 *var.* Oahu. *island*
  Hawaiian Islands, Hawaiʻi, USA
Oak Harbor 46 B1 Washington,
  NW USA
Oakland 47 B6 California, W USA
Oamaru 151 B7 Otago, South Island,
  New Zealand
Oaxaca 51 F5 *var.* Oaxaca de Juárez; *prev.*
  Antequera. Oaxaca, SE Mexico
Oaxaca de Juárez *see* Oaxaca
Ob' 112 C2 *river* C Russian Federation
Obal' 107 D5 *Rus.* Obol'. Vitsyebskaya
  Voblasts', N Belarus
Oban 88 C4 W Scotland, UK
Oban *see* Halfmoon Bay
Obando *see* Puerto Inírida
Obdorsk *see* Salekhard
Öbecse *see* Bečej
Obeliai 106 C4 Panevėžys, NE Lithuania
Oberhollabrunn *see* Tulln
Ob', Gulf of *see* Obskaya Guba
Obidovichi *see* Abidavichy
Obihiro 130 D2 Hokkaidō, NE Japan
Obo 76 D4 Haut-Mbomou, E Central
  African Republic
Obock 72 D4 E Djibouti
Obol' *see* Obal'
Oborniki 98 C3 Wielkolpolskie,
  W Poland
Obrovo *see* Abrova
Obskaya Guba 114 D3 *Eng.* Gulf of Ob.
  gulf N Russian Federation
Ob' Tablemount 141 B7 *undersea
  feature* S Indian Ocean
Ocala 43 E4 Florida, SE USA
Ocaña 58 B2 Norte de Santander,
  N Colombia
Ocaña 92 D3 Castilla-La Mancha, C Spain
O Carballiño 108 C1 *Cast.* Carballino.
  Galicia, NW Spain
Occidental, Cordillera 61 E4 *mountain
  range* Bolivia/Chile
Occidental, Cordillera 58 B2 *mountain
  range* W Colombia
Ocean Falls 36 D5 British Columbia,
  SW Canada
Ocean Island *see* Banaba
Oceanside 47 C8 California, W USA
Ocean State *see* Rhode Island
Ochakiv 109 E4 *Rus.* Ochakov.
  Mykolayivs'ka Oblast', S Ukraine
Ochakov *see* Ochakiv
Ochamchira *see* Och'amch'ire
Och'amch'ire 117 E2 *Rus.* Ochamchira.
  W Georgia
Ocho Rios 54 B4 C Jamaica
Ochrida *see* Ohrid
Ochrida, Lake *see* Ohrid, Lake
Ocotal 52 D3 Nueva Segovia,
  NW Nicaragua
Ocozocuautla 51 G5 Chiapas,
  SE Mexico
October Revolution Island *see*
  Oktyabr'skoy Revolyutsii, Ostrov
Ocú 53 F5 Herrera, S Panama
Ódate 130 D3 Akita, Honshū,
  C Japan
Oddur *see* Xuddur
Ödemiş 116 A4 İzmir, SW Turkey
Ödenburg *see* Sopron
Odenpäh *see* Otepää
Odense 85 B7 Fyn, C Denmark
Oder 98 B3 *Cz./Pol.* Odra. *river*
  C Europe
Oderhaff *see* Szczeciński, Zalew
Odesa 109 E4 *Rus.* Odessa. Odes'ka
  Oblast', SW Ukraine
Odessa 49 E3 Texas, SW USA
Odessa *see* Odesa
Odessus *see* Varna
Odienne 74 D4 NW Côte d'Ivoire
  (Ivory Coast)

Ôdôngk 137 D6 Kâmpóng Spoe,
  S Cambodia
Odoorn 86 E2 Drenthe, NE Netherlands
Odra *see* Oder
Oesel *see* Saaremaa
Of 117 E2 Trabzon, NE Turkey
Ofanto 97 D5 *river* S Italy
Offenbach 95 B5 *var.* Offenbach am
  Main. Hessen, W Germany
Offenbach am Main *see* Offenbach
Offenburg 95 B6 Baden-Württemberg,
  SW Germany
Ogaadeen *see* Ogaden
Ogaden 73 D5 *Som.* Ogaadeen. *plateau*
  Ethiopia/Somalia
Ōgaki 131 C6 Gifu, Honshū, SW Japan
Ogallala 44 D4 Nebraska, C USA
Ogbomosho 75 F4 *var.* Ogmoboso. Oyo,
  W Nigeria
Ogden 44 B4 Utah, W USA
Ogdensburg 41 F2 New York, NE USA
Ogmoboso *see* Ogbomosho
Ogulin 100 A3 Karlovac, NW Croatia
Ohio 40 C4 *off.* State of Ohio,
  also known as Buckeye State. *state*
  N USA
Ohio River 40 C4 *river* N USA
Ohlau *see* Oława
Ohri *see* Ohrid
Ohrid 101 D6 *Turk.* Ochrida, Ohri.
  SW FYR Macedonia
Ohrid, Lake 101 D6 *var.* Lake Ochrida,
  Alb. Liqeni i Ohrit, *Mac.* Ohridsko
  Ezero. *lake* Albania/FYR Macedonia
Ohridsko Ezero/Ohrit, Liqeni i *see*
  Ohrid, Lake
Ohura 150 D3 Manawatu-Wanganui,
  North Island, New Zealand
Oirschot 87 C5 Noord-Brabant,
  S Netherlands
Oise 90 C3 *river* N France
Oistins 55 G2 S Barbados
Ōita 131 B7 Ōita, Kyūshū, SW Japan
Ojinaga 50 D2 Chihuahua, N Mexico
Ojos del Salado, Cerro 64 B3 *mountain*
  W Argentina
Okaihau 150 C2 Northland, North
  Island, New Zealand
Okanagan *see* Cubango/Okavango
Okavango 78 C3 *district* NW Namibia
Okavango *see* Cubango
Okavango Delta 78 C3 *wetland*
  N Botswana
Okayama 131 B6 Okayama, Honshū,
  SW Japan
Okazaki 131 C6 Aichi, Honshū, C Japan
Okeechobee, Lake 43 E4 *lake* Florida,
  SE USA
Okefenokee Swamp 43 E3 *wetland*
  Georgia, SE USA
Okhotsk 115 G3 Khabarovskiy Kray,
  E Russian Federation
Okhotsk, Sea of 113 F3 *sea* NW Pacific
  Ocean
Okhtyrka 109 F2 *Rus.* Akhtyrka.
  Sums'ka Oblast', NE Ukraine
Oki-guntō *see* Oki-shotō
Okinawa 130 A3 *island* SW Japan
Okinawa-shotō 130 A3 *island group*
  Nansei-shotō, SW Japan Asia
Oki-shotō 131 B6 *var.* Oki-guntō. *island
  group* SW Japan
Oklahoma 49 F2 *off.* State of Oklahoma,
  also known as The Sooner State. *state*
  C USA
Oklahoma City 49 G1 *state capital*
  Oklahoma, C USA
Okmulgee 49 G1 Oklahoma, C USA
Oko, Wadi 72 C3 *river* NE Sudan
Oktyabr'skiy 111 D6 Volgogradskaya
  Oblast', SW Russian Federation
Oktyabr'skiy *see* Aktsyabrski
Oktyabr'skoy Revolyutsii, Ostrov 115
  E2 *Eng.* October Revolution Island.
  island Severnaya Zemlya, N Russian
  Federation
Okulovka *see* Uglovka
Okushiri-tō 130 C3 *var.* Okusiri Tô.
  island NE Japan
Okusiri Tô *see* Okushiri-tō
Oláh-Toplicza *see* Toplița
Öland 85 C7 *island* S Sweden
Olavarría 65 D5 Buenos Aires,
  E Argentina
Oława 98 C4 *Ger.* Ohlau. Dolnoślaskie,
  SW Poland

Olbia 97 A5 *prev.* Terranova Pausania. Sardegna, Italy, C Mediterranean Sea
Old Bay State/Old Colony State *see* Massachusetts
Old Dominion *see* Virginia
Oldebroek 86 D3 Gelderland, E Netherlands
Oldenburg 94 B3 Niedersachsen, NW Germany
Oldenburg 94 C2 *var.* Oldenburg in Holstein. Schleswig-Holstein, N Germany
Oldenburg in Holstein *see* Oldenburg
Oldenzaal 86 E3 Overijssel, E Netherlands
Old Harbour 54 B5 C Jamaica
Old Line State *see* Maryland
Old North State *see* North Carolina
Olëkma 115 F4 *river* C Russian Federation
Olëkminsk 115 F3 Respublika Sakha (Yakutiya), NE Russian Federation
Oleksandrivka 109 E3 *Rus.* Aleksandrovka. Kirovohrads'ka Oblast', C Ukraine
Oleksandriya 109 F3 *Rus.* Aleksandriya. Kirovohrads'ka Oblast', C Ukraine
Olenegorsk 110 C2 Murmanskaya Oblast', NW Russian Federation
Olenëk 115 E3 Respublika Sakha (Yakutiya), NE Russian Federation
Olenëk 115 E3 *river* NE Russian Federation
Oléron, Île d' 91 A5 *island* W France
Olevs'k 108 D1 *Rus.* Olevsk. Zhytomyrs'ka Oblast', N Ukraine
Olevsk *see* Olevs'k
Ölgiy 126 C2 Bayan-Ölgiy, W Mongolia
Olhão 92 B5 Faro, S Portugal
Olifa 78 B3 Kunene, NW Namibia
Ólimbos *see* Ólympos
Olimpo *see* Fuerte Olimpo
Olisipo *see* Lisboa
Olita *see* Alytus
Oliva 93 F4 País Valenciano, E Spain
Olivet 90 C4 Loiret, C France
Olmaliq 123 E2 *Rus.* Almalyk. Toshkent Viloyati, E Uzbekistan
Olmütz *see* Olomouc
Olomouc 99 C5 *Ger.* Olmütz, *Pol.* Ołomuniec. Olomoucký Kraj, E Czech Republic
Ołomuniec *see* Olomouc
Olonets 110 B3 Respublika Kareliya, NW Russian Federation
Olovyannaya 115 F4 Chitinskaya Oblast', S Russian Federation
Olpe 94 B4 Nordrhein-Westfalen, W Germany
Olshanka *see* Vil'shanka
Olsnitz *see* Murska Sobota
Olsztyn 98 D2 *Ger.* Allenstein. Warmińsko-Mazurskie, N Poland
Olt 108 B5 *var.* Oltul, *Ger.* Alt. *river* S Romania
Oltenița 108 C5 *prev. Eng.* Oltenitsa; *anc.* Constantiola. Călărași, SE Romania
Oltenitsa *see* Oltenița
Oltul *see* Olt
Olvera 92 D5 Andalucía, S Spain
Ol'viopol' *see* Pervomays'k
Olympia 46 B2 *state capital* Washington, NW USA
Olympic Mountains 46 A2 *mountain range* Washington, NW USA
Ólympos 104 B4 *var.* Ólimbos, *Eng.* Mount Olympus. *mountain* N Greece
Omagh 89 B5 *Ir.* An Ómaigh. N Northern Ireland, UK
Omaha 45 F4 Nebraska, C USA
Oman 121 D6 *off.* Sultanate of Oman, *Ar.* Salṭanat 'Umān; *prev.* Muscat and Oman. *country* SW Asia

OMAN
(continued)

OReligions Ibadi Muslim 75%, Other Muslim and Hindu 25%
Ethnic mix Arab 88%, Baluchi 4%, Persian 3%, Indian and Pakistani 3%, African 2%
Government Monarchy
Currency Omani rial = 1000 baizas
Literacy rate 74%
Calorie consumption Not available

Oman, Gulf of 120 E4 *Ar.* Khalīj 'Umān. *gulf* N Arabian Sea
Oman, Sultanate of *see* Oman
Omboué 77 A6 Ogooué-Maritime, W Gabon
Omdurman 72 B4 *var.* Umm Durmān. Khartoum, C Sudan
Ometepe, Isla de 52 D4 *island* S Nicaragua
Ommen 86 E3 Overijssel, E Netherlands
Omsk 114 C4 Omskaya Oblast', C Russian Federation
Ōmuta 131 A7 Fukuoka, Kyūshū, SW Japan
Onda 93 F3 País Valenciano, E Spain
Ondjiva *see* N'Giva
Öndörhaan 127 F2 *var.* Undur Khan; *prev.* Tsetsen Khan. Hentiy, E Mongolia
Onega 110 C3 Arkhangel'skaya Oblast', NW Russian Federation
Onega 110 B4 *river* NW Russian Federation
Onega, Lake *see* Onezhskoye Ozero
Onex 95 A7 Genève, SW Switzerland
Onezhskoye Ozero 110 B4 *Eng.* Lake Onega. *lake* NW Russian Federation
Ongole 132 D1 Andhra Pradesh, E India
Onitsha 75 G5 Anambra, S Nigeria
Onon Gol 127 E2 *river* N Mongolia
Onslow 146 A4 Western Australia
Onslow Bay 43 F1 *bay* North Carolina, E USA
Ontario 38 B3 *province* S Canada
Ontario, Lake 41 E3 *lake* Canada/USA
Onteniente *see* Ontinyent
Ontinyent 93 F4 *var.* Onteniente. País Valenciano, E Spain
Ontong Java Rise 125 H4 *undersea feature* W Pacific Ocean
Onuba *see* Huelva
Oodeypore *see* Udaipur
Oos-Londen *see* East London
Oostakker 87 B5 Oost-Vlaanderen, NW Belgium
Oostburg 87 B5 Zeeland, SW Netherlands
Oostende 87 A5 *Eng.* Ostend, *Fr.* Ostende. West-Vlaanderen, NW Belgium
Oosterbeek 86 D4 Gelderland, SE Netherlands
Oosterhout 86 C4 Noord-Brabant, S Netherlands
Opatija 100 A2 *It.* Abbazia. Primorje-Gorski Kotar, NW Croatia
Opava 99 C5 *Ger.* Troppau. Moravskoslezský Kraj, E Czech Republic
Ópazova *see* Stara Pazova
Opelika 42 D2 Alabama, S USA
Opelousas 42 B3 Louisiana, S USA
Ophiusa *see* Formentera
Opmeer 86 C2 Noord-Holland, NW Netherlands
Opochka 110 A4 Pskovskaya Oblast', W Russian Federation
Opole 98 C4 *Ger.* Oppeln. Opolskie, S Poland
Oporto *see* Porto
Opotiki 150 E3 Bay of Plenty, North Island, New Zealand
Oppeln *see* Opole
Oppidum Ubiorum *see* Köln
Oqtosh 123 E2 *Rus.* Aktash. Samarqand Viloyati, C Uzbekistan
Oradea 108 B3 *prev.* Oradea Mare, *Ger.* Grosswardein, *Hung.* Nagyvárad. Bihor, NW Romania
Oradea Mare *see* Oradea
Orahovac 101 D5 *Alb.* Rahovec. Kosovo, S Serbia

OMAN
Southwest Asia

Official name Sultanate of Oman
Formation 1951 / 1951
Capital Muscat
Population 2.6 million / 32 people per sq mile (12 people per sq km) / 84%
Total area 82,031 sq miles (212,460 sq km)
Languages Arabic*, Baluchi, Farsi, Hindi, Punjabi

Oral *see* Ural'sk
Oran 70 D2 *var.* Ouahran, Wahran. NW Algeria
Orange 149 D6 New South Wales, SE Australia
Orange 91 D6 *anc.* Arausio. Vaucluse, SE France
Orangeburg 43 E2 South Carolina, SE USA
Orange Cone *see* Orange Fan
Orange Fan 69 C7 *var.* Orange Cone. *undersea feature* SW Indian Ocean
Orange Mouth/Orangemund *see* Oranjemund
Orange River 78 B4 *Afr.* Oranjerivier. *river* S Africa
Orange Walk 52 C1 Orange Walk, N Belize
Oranienburg 94 D3 Brandenburg, NE Germany
Oranjemund 78 B4 *var.* Orangemund; *prev.* Orange Mouth. Karas, SW Namibia
Oranjerivier *see* Orange River
Oranjestad 55 E5 *dependent territory capital* (Aruba) W Aruba
Orany *see* Varéna
Oraşul Stalin *see* Braşov
Oravicabánya *see* Oraviţa
Oraviţa 108 A4 *Ger.* Orawitza, *Hung.* Oravicabánya. Caraş-Severin, SW Romania
Orawitza *see* Oraviţa
Orbetello 96 B4 Toscana, C Italy
Orcadas 154 A1 *Argentinian research station* South Orkney Islands, Antarctica
Orchard Homes 44 B1 Montana, NW USA
Ordino 91 A8 Ordino, NW Andorra Europe
Ordos Desert *see* Mu Us Shadi
Ordu 116 D2 *anc.* Cotyora. Ordu, N Turkey
Ordzhonikidze 109 F3 Dnipropetrovs'ka Oblast', E Ukraine
Ordzhonikidze *see* Vladikavkaz, Russian Federation
Ordzhonikidze *see* Yenakiyeve, Ukraine
Orealla 59 G3 E Guyana
Örebro 85 C6 Örebro, C Sweden
Oregon 46 B3 *off.* State of Oregon, *also known as* Beaver State, Sunset State, Valentine State, Webfoot State. *state* NW USA
Oregon City 46 B3 Oregon, NW USA
Oregon, State of *see* Oregon
Orekhov *see* Orikhiv
Orël 111 B5 Orlovskaya Oblast', W Russian Federation
Orem 44 B4 Utah, W USA
Ore Mountains *see* Erzgebirge/Krušné Hory
Orenburg 111 D6 *prev.* Chkalov. Orenburgskaya Oblast', W Russian Federation
Orense *see* Ourense
Oreor *see* Koror
Orestiáda 104 D3 *prev.* Orestiás. Anatoliki Makedonía kai Thráki, NE Greece
Orestiás *see* Orestiáda
Organ Peak 48 D3 *mountain* New Mexico, SW USA
Orgeyev *see* Orhei
Orhei 108 D3 *var.* Orheiu, *Rus.* Orgeyev. N Moldova
Orheiu *see* Orhei
Oriental, Cordillera 60 D3 *mountain range* Bolivia/Peru
Oriental, Cordillera 58 B3 *mountain range* C Colombia
Orihuela 93 F4 País Valenciano, E Spain
Orikhiv 109 G3 *Rus.* Orekhov. Zaporiz'ka Oblast', SE Ukraine
Orinoco, Río 59 E2 *river* Colombia/Venezuela
Orissa 135 F4 *cultural region* NE India
Orissa 135 F4 *state* NE India
Orissaare *see* Orissaare
Orissaare 106 C2 *Ger.* Orissaar. Saaremaa, W Estonia
Oristano 97 A5 Sardegna, Italy, C Mediterranean Sea
Orito 58 A4 Putumayo, SW Colombia
Orizaba, Volcán Pico de 35 C7 *var.* Citlaltépetl. *mountain* S Mexico

Orkney *see* Orkney Islands
Orkney Islands 88 C2 *var.* Orkney, Orkneys. *island group* N Scotland, UK
Orkneys *see* Orkney Islands
Orlando 43 E4 Florida, SE USA
Orléanais 90 C4 *cultural region* C France
Orléans 90 C4 *anc.* Aurelianum. Loiret, C France
Orléansville *see* Chlef
Orly 90 E2 (Paris) Essonne, N France
Orlya 107 B6 *Rus.* Orlya. Hrodzyenskaya Voblasts', W Belarus
Ormsö *see* Vormsi
Ormuz, Strait of *see* Hormuz, Strait of
Örnsköldsvik 85 C5 Västernorrland, C Sweden
Orolaunum *see* Arlon
Orol Dengizi *see* Aral Sea
Oromocto 39 F4 New Brunswick, SE Canada
Orona 145 F3 *prev.* Hull Island. *atoll* Phoenix Islands, C Kiribati
Oropeza *see* Cochabamba
Orosirá Rodhópis *see* Rhodope Mountains
Orpington 89 B8 UK
Orschowa *see* Orşova
Orsha 107 E6 *Rus.* Orsha. Vitsyebskaya Voblasts', NE Belarus
Orsk 114 B4 Orenburgskaya Oblast', W Russian Federation
Orşova 108 A4 *Ger.* Orschowa, *Hung.* Orsova. Mehedinţi, SW Romania
Ortelsburg *see* Szczytno
Orthez 91 B6 Pyrénées-Atlantiques, SW France
Ortona 96 D4 Abruzzo, C Italy
Oruba *see* Aruba
Oruro 61 F4 Oruro, W Bolivia
Oryokko *see* Yalu
Ōsaka 131 C6 *hist.* Naniwa. Ōsaka, Honshū, SW Japan
Osa, Península de 53 E5 *peninsula* S Costa Rica
Osborn Plateau 141 D5 *undersea feature* E Indian Ocean
Osca *see* Huesca
Ösel *see* Saaremaa
Osh 123 F2 Oshskaya Oblast', SW Kyrgyzstan
Oshawa 38 D5 Ontario, SE Canada
Oshikango 78 B3 Ohangwena, N Namibia
Ō-shima 131 C6 *island* S Japan
Oshkosh 40 B2 Wisconsin, N USA
Oshmyany *see* Ashmyany
Osiek *see* Osijek
Osijek 100 C3 *prev.* Osiek, Osjek, *Ger.* Esseg, *Hung.* Eszék. Osijek-Baranja, E Croatia
Osipenko *see* Berdyans'k
Osipovichi *see* Asipovichy
Osjek *see* Osijek
Oskaloosa 45 G4 Iowa, C USA
Oskarshamn 85 C7 Kalmar, S Sweden
Öskemen *see* Ust'-Kamenogorsk
Oskil *see* Oskol
Oskol 109 G2 *Ukr.* Oskil. *river* Russian Federation/Ukraine
Oslo 85 B6 *prev.* Christiania, Kristiania. *country capital* (Norway) Oslo, S Norway
Osmaniye 116 D4 Osmaniye, S Turkey
Osnabrück 94 A3 Niedersachsen, NW Germany
Osogov Mountains 120 B3 *var.* Osogovske Planine, Osogovski Planina, *Mac.* Osogovski Planini. *mountain range* Bulgaria/FYR Macedonia
Osogovske Planine/Osogovski Planina/Osogovski Planini *see* Osogov Mountains
Oşorhei *see* Târgu Mureş
Osorno 65 B5 Los Lagos, C Chile
Oss 86 D4 Noord-Brabant, S Netherlands
Ossa, Serra d' 92 C4 *mountain range* SE Portugal
Ossora 115 H2 Koryakskiy Avtonomnyy Okrug, E Russian Federation
Ostee *see* Baltic Sea
Ostend/Ostende *see* Oostende
Oster 109 E1 Chernihivs'ka Oblast', N Ukraine
Östermyra *see* Seinäjoki

Osterode/Osterode in Ostpreussen
see Ostróda
Österreich *see* Austria
Östersund *85 C5* Jämtland, C Sweden
Ostfriesische Inseln *94 A3 Eng.* East Frisian Islands. *island group* NW Germany
Ostia Aterni *see* Pescara
Ostiglia *96 C2* Lombardia, N Italy
Ostrava *99 C5* Moravskoslezský Kraj, E Czech Republic
Ostróda *98 D3 Ger.* Osterode, Osterode in Ostpreussen. Warmińsko-Mazurskie, NE Poland
Ostrołęka *98 D3 Ger.* Wiesenhof, *Rus.* Ostrolenka. Mazowieckie, C Poland
Ostrolenka *see* Ostrołęka
Ostrov *110 A4 Ger.* Schlackenwerth. Karlovarský Kraj, W Czech Republic
Ostrovets *see* Ostrowiec Świętokrzyski
Ostrovnoy *110 C2* Murmanskaya Oblast', NW Russian Federation
Ostrów *see* Ostrów Wielkopolski
Ostrowiec *see* Ostrowiec Świętokrzyski
Ostrowiec Świętokrzyski *98 D4 var.* Ostrowiec, *Rus.* Ostrovets. Świętokrzyskie, C Poland
Ostrów Mazowiecka *98 D3 var.* Ostrów Mazowiecki. Mazowieckie, NE Poland
Ostrów Mazowiecki *see* Ostrów Mazowiecka
Ostrowo *see* Ostrów Wielkopolski
Ostrów Wielkopolski *98 C4 var.* Ostrów, *Ger.* Ostrowo. Wielkopolskie, C Poland
Ostyako-Voguls'k *see* Khanty-Mansiysk
Osum *see* Osumit, Lumi i
Ōsumi-shotō *131 A8 island group* Kagoshima, Nansei-shotō, SW Japan Asia East China Sea Pacific Ocean
Osumit, Lumi i *101 D7 var.* Osum. *river* SE Albania
Osuna *92 D4* Andalucía, S Spain
Oswego *41 F2* New York, NE USA
Otago Peninsula *151 B7 peninsula* South Island, New Zealand
Otaki *150 D4* Wellington, North Island, New Zealand
Otaru *130 C2* Hokkaidō, NE Japan
Otavalo *60 B1* Imbabura, N Ecuador
Otavi *78 B3* Otjozondjupa, N Namibia
Oțelu Roșu *108 B4 Ger.* Ferdinandsberg, *Hung.* Nándorhgy. Caras-Severin, SW Romania
Otepää *106 D3 Ger.* Odenpäh. Valgamaa, SE Estonia
Oti *75 E4 river* N Togo
Otira *151 C6* West Coast, South Island, New Zealand
Otjiwarongo *78 B3* Otjozondjupa, N Namibia
Otorohanga *150 D3* Waikato, North Island, New Zealand
Otranto, Canale d' *see* Otranto, Strait of
Otranto, Strait of *101 C6 It.* Canale d'Otranto. *strait* Albania/Italy
Otrokovice *99 C5 Ger.* Otrokowitz. Zlínský Kraj, E Czech Republic
Otrokowitz *see* Otrokovice
Ōtsu *131 C6 var.* Ōtu. Shiga, Honshū, SW Japan
Ottawa *38 D5 country capital* (Canada) Ontario, SE Canada
Ottawa *40 B3* Illinois, N USA
Ottawa *45 F5* Kansas, C USA
Ottawa *41 E2* Fr. Outaouais. *river* Ontario/Québec, SE Canada
Ottawa Islands *38 C1 island group* Nunavut, C Canada
Ottignies *87 C6* Wallon Brabant, C Belgium
Ottumwa *45 G4* Iowa, C USA
Ōtu *see* Ōtsu
Ouachita Mountains *42 A1 mountain range* Arkansas/Oklahoma, C USA
Ouachita River *42 B2 river* Arkansas/Louisiana, C USA
Ouagadougou *75 E4 var.* Wagadugu. *country capital* (Burkina Faso) C Burkina Faso
Ouahigouya *75 E3* NW Burkina Faso
Ouahran *see* Oran
Oualâta *74 D3 var.* Oualata. Hodh ech Chargui, SE Mauritania

Ouanary *59 H3* E French Guiana
Ouanda Djallé *76 D4* Vakaga, NE Central African Republic
Ouarâne *74 D2 desert* C Mauritania
Ouargla *71 E2 var.* Wargla. NE Algeria
Ouarzazate *70 C3* S Morocco
Oubangui *see* Ubangi
Oubangui-Chari *see* Central African Republic
Oubangui-Chari, Territoire de l' *see* Central African Republic
Oudjda *see* Oujda
Ouessant, Île d' *90 A3 Eng.* Ushant. *island* NW France
Ouésso *77 B5* La Sangha, NW Congo
Oujda *70 D2 Ar.* Oudjda, Ujda. NE Morocco
Oujeft *74 C2* Adrar, C Mauritania
Oulu *84 D4 Swe.* Uleåborg. Oulu, C Finland
Oulujärvi *84 D4 Swe.* Uleträsk. *lake* C Finland
Oulujoki *84 D4 Swe.* Uleälv. *river* C Finland
Ounasjoki *84 D3 river* N Finland
Ounianga Kébir *76 C2* Borkou-Ennedi-Tibesti, N Chad
Oup *see* Aoube
Oupeye *87 D6* Liège, E Belgium
Our *87 D6 river* NW Europe
Ourense *92 C1 Cast.* Orense, *Lat.* Aurium. Galicia, NW Spain
Ourique *92 B4* Beja, S Portugal
Ours, Grand Lac de l' *see* Great Bear Lake
Ourthe *87 D7 river* E Belgium
Ouse *89 D5 river* N England, UK
Outaouais *see* Ottawa
Outer Hebrides *88 B3 var.* Western Isles. *island group* NW Scotland, UK
Outer Islands *79 G1 island group* SW Seychelles Africa W Indian Ocean
Outes *92 B1* Galicia, NW Spain
Ouvéa *144 D5 island* Îles Loyauté, NE New Caledonia
Ouyen *149 C6* Victoria, SE Australia
Ovalle *64 B3* Coquimbo, N Chile
Ovar *92 B2* Aveiro, N Portugal
Overflakkee *86 B4 island* SW Netherlands
Overijse *87 C6* Vlaams Brabant, C Belgium
Oviedo *92 C1 anc.* Asturias. Asturias, NW Spain
Ovilava *see* Wels
Ovruch *108 D1* Zhytomyrs'ka Oblast', N Ukraine
Owando *77 B5 prev.* Fort Rousset. Cuvette, C Congo
Owase *131 C6* Mie, Honshū, SW Japan
Owatonna *45 F3* Minnesota, N USA
Owen Fracture Zone *140 B4 tectonic feature* W Arabian Sea
Owen, Mount *151 C5 mountain* South Island, New Zealand
Owensboro *40 B5* Kentucky, S USA
Owen Stanley Range *144 B3 mountain range* S Papua New Guinea
Owerri *75 G5* Imo, S Nigeria
Owo *75 F5* Ondo, SW Nigeria
Owyhee River *46 C4 river* Idaho/Oregon, NW USA
Oxford *151 C6* Canterbury, South Island, New Zealand
Oxford *89 D6 Lat.* Oxonia. S England, UK
Oxkutzcab *51 H4* Yucatán, SE Mexico
Oxnard *47 C7* California, W USA
Oxonia *see* Oxford
Oxus *see* Amu Darya
Oyama *131 D5* Tochigi, Honshū, S Japan
Oyem *77 B5* Woleu-Ntem, N Gabon
Oyo *75 F5* Oyo, W Nigeria
Oyo *77 B6* Cuvette, C Congo
Ozark *42 D3* Alabama, S USA
Ozark Plateau *45 G5 plain* Arkansas/Missouri, C USA
Ozarks, Lake of the *45 F5 reservoir* Missouri, C USA
Ozbourn Seamount *152 D4 undersea feature* W Pacific Ocean
Ózd *99 D6* Borsod-Abaúj-Zemplén, NE Hungary
Ozieri *97 A5* Sardegna, Italy, C Mediterranean Sea

P

Paamiut *82 B4 var.* Pâmiut, *Dan.* Frederikshåb. S Greenland
Pa-an *136 B4* Karen State, S Myanmar (Burma)
Pabianice *98 C4* Łódzki, Poland
Pabna *135 G4* Rajshahi, W Bangladesh
Pacaraima, Sierra/Pacaraim, Serra *see* Pakaraima Mountains
Pachuca *51 E4 var.* Pachuca de Soto. Hidalgo, C Mexico
Pachuca de Soto *see* Pachuca
Pacific-Antarctic Ridge *154 B5 undersea feature* S Pacific Ocean
Pacific Ocean *152 D3 ocean*
Padalung *see* Phatthalung
Padang *138 B4* Sumatera, W Indonesia
Paderborn *94 B4* Nordrhein-Westfalen, NW Germany
Padma *see* Brahmaputra
Padma *see* Ganges
Padova *96 C2 Eng.* Padua; *anc.* Patavium. Veneto, NE Italy
Padre Island *49 G5 island* Texas, SW USA
Padua *see* Padova
Paducah *40 B5* Kentucky, S USA
Paeroa *150 D3* Waikato, North Island, New Zealand
Páfos *102 C5 var.* Paphos. W Cyprus
Pag *100 A3 It.* Pago. *island* Zadar, C Croatia
Page *48 B1* Arizona, SW USA
Pago *see* Pag
Pago Pago *145 F4 dependent territory capital* (American Samoa) Tutuila, W American Samoa
Pahiatua *150 D4* Manawatu-Wanganui, North Island, New Zealand
Pahsien *see* Chongqing
Paide *106 D2 Ger.* Weissenstein. Järvamaa, N Estonia
Paihia *150 D2* Northland, North Island, New Zealand
Päijänne *85 D5 lake* S Finland
Paine, Cerro *65 A7 mountain* S Chile
Painted Desert *48 B1 desert* Arizona, SW USA
Paisance *see* Piacenza
Paisley *88 C4* W Scotland, UK
País Valenciano *93 F3 var.* Valencia, *Cat.* València; *anc.* Valentia. *autonomous community* NE Spain
País Vasco *93 E1 cultural region* N Spain Europe
Paita *60 B3* Piura, NW Peru
Pakanbaru *see* Pekanbaru
Pakaraima Mountains *59 E3 var.* Serra Pacaraim, Sierra Pacaraima. *mountain range* N South America
Pakistan *134 A2 off.* Islamic Republic of Pakistan, *var.* Islami Jamhuriya e Pakistan. *country* S Asia

PAKISTAN
South Asia

Official name Islamic Republic of Pakistan
Formation 1947 / 1971
Capital Islamabad
Population 158 million / 531 people per sq mile (205 people per sq km) / 37%
Total area 310,401 sq miles (803,940 sq km)
Languages Urdu*, Baluchi, Brahui, Pashtu, Punjabi, Sindhi
Religions Sunni Muslim 77%, Shi'a Muslim 20%, Hindu 2%, Christian 1%
Ethnic mix Punjabi 56%, Pathan (Pashtun) 15%, Sindhi 14%, Mohajir 7%, Other 4%, Baluchi 4%
Government Presidential system
Currency Pakistani rupee = 100 paisa
Literacy rate 49%
Calorie consumption 2419 calories

Pakistan, Islamic Republic of *see* Pakistan
Pakistan, Islami Jamhuriya e *see* Pakistan
Paknam *see* Samut Prakan
Pakokku *136 A3* Magwe, C Myanmar (Burma)

Pak Phanang *137 C7 var.* Ban Pak Phanang. Nakhon Si Thammarat, SW Thailand
Pakruojis *106 C4* Šiauliai, N Lithuania
Paks *99 C7* Tolna, S Hungary
Paksé *see* Pakxé
Pakxé *137 D5 var.* Paksé. Champasak, S Laos
Palafrugell *93 G2* Cataluña, NE Spain
Palagruža *101 B5 It.* Pelagosa. *island* SW Croatia
Palaiá Epídavros *105 C6* Pelopónnisos, S Greece
Palaiseau *90 D2* Essonne, N France
Palamós *93 G2* Cataluña, NE Spain
Palamuse *106 E2 Ger.* Sankt-Bartholomäi. Jōgevamaa, E Estonia
Palanka *see* Bačka Palanka
Pālanpur *134 C4* Gujarāt, W India
Palantia *see* Palencia
Palapye *78 D3* Central, SE Botswana
Palau *144 A2 var.* Belau. *country* W Pacific Ocean

PALAU
Australasia & Oceania

Official name Republic of Palau
Formation 1994 / 1994
Capital Koror
Population 20,303 / 104 people per sq mile (40 people per sq km) / 70%
Total area 177 sq miles (458 sq km)
Languages Palauan, English, Japanese, Angaur, Tobi, Sonsorolese
Religions Christian 66%, Modekngei 34%
Ethnic mix Micronesian 87%, Filipino 8%, Chinese and other Asian 5%
Government Nonparty system
Currency US dollar = 100 cents
Literacy rate 98%
Calorie consumption Not available

Palawan *139 E2 island* W Philippines
Palawan Passage *138 D2 passage* W Philippines
Paldiski *106 D2 prev.* Baltiski, *Eng* Baltic Port, *Ger.* Baltischport. Harjumaa, NW Estonia
Palembang *138 B4* Sumatera, W Indonesia
Palencia *92 D2 anc.* Palantia, Pallantia. Castilla-León, NW Spain
Palerme *see* Palermo
Palermo *97 C7 Fr.* Palerme; *anc.* Panhormus, Panormus. Sicilia, Italy, C Mediterranean Sea
Pāli *134 C3* Rājasthān, N India
Palikir *144 C2 country capital* (Micronesia) Pohnpei, E Micronesia
Palimé *see* Kpalimé
Palioúri, Ákrotírio *104 C4 var.* Akra Kanestron. *headland* N Greece
Palk Strait *132 C3 strait* India/Sri Lanka
Pallantia *see* Palencia
Palliser, Cape *151 D5 headland* North Island, New Zealand
Palma *93 G3 var.* Palma de Mallorca. Mallorca, Spain, W Mediterranean Sea
Palma del Río *92 D4* Andalucía, S Spain
Palma de Mallorca *see* Palma
Palmar Sur *53 E5* Puntarenas, SE Costa Rica
Palma Soriano *54 C3* Santiago de Cuba, E Cuba
Palm Beach *148 E1* New South Wales, E Australia
Palmer *154 A2 US research station* Antarctica
Palmer Land *154 A3 physical region* Antarctica
Palmerston *145 F4 island* S Cook Islands
Palmerston *see* Darwin
Palmerston North *150 D4* Manawatu-Wanganui, North Island, New Zealand
The Palmetto State *see* South Carolina
Palmi *97 D7* Calabria, SW Italy
Palmira *58 B3* Valle del Cauca, W Colombia
Palm Springs *47 D7* California, W USA
Palmyra Atoll *145 G2 US privately owned unincorporated territory* C Pacific Ocean
Palo Alto *47 B6* California, W USA

Paloe *see* Denpasar, Bali,
C Indonesia
Paloe *see* Palu
Palu *139 E4 prev.* Paloe. Sulawesi,
C Indonesia
Pamiers *91 B6* Ariège, S France
Pamir *123 F3 var.* Daryā-ye
Pāmīr, *Taj.* Dar''yoi Pomir. *river*
Afghanistan/Tajikistan
Pāmīr, Daryā-ye *see* Pamir
Pamir/Pāmīr, Daryā-ye *see* Pamirs
Pamirs *123 F3 Pash.* Daryā-ye Pāmīr,
Rus. Pamir. *mountain range* C Asia
Pāmiut *see* Paamiut
Pamlico Sound *43 G1 sound* North
Carolina, SE USA
Pampa *49 E1* Texas, SW USA
Pampa Aullagas, Lago *see* Poopó, Lago
Pampas *64 C4 plain* C Argentina
Pampeluna *see* Pamplona
Pamplona *58 C2* Norte de Santander,
N Colombia
Pamplona *93 E1 Basq.* Iruña, *prev.*
Pampeluna; *anc.* Pompaelo. Navarra,
N Spain
Panaji *132 B1 var.* Pangim, Panjim,
New Goa. *state capital* Goa, W India
Panamá *53 G4 var.* Ciudad de Panama,
Eng. Panama City. *country capital*
(Panama) Panamá, C Panama
Panama *53 G5 off.* Republic of Panama.
country Central America

PANAMA
Central America

Official name Republic of Panama
Formation 1903 / 1903
Capital Panama City
Population 3.2 million / 109 people per
sq mile (42 people per sq km) / 56%
Total area 30,193 sq miles
(78,200 sq km)
Languages Spanish*, English Creole,
Amerindian languages, Chibchan
languages
Religions Roman Catholic 86%,
Other 8%, Protestant 6%
Ethnic mix Mestizo 60%, White 14%,
Black 12%, Amerindian 8%, Asian 4%,
Other 2%
Government Presidential system
Currency Balboa = 100 centesimos
Literacy rate 92%
Calorie consumption 2272 calories

Panama Basin *35 C8 undersea feature*
E Pacific Ocean
Panama Canal *53 F4 shipping canal*
E Panama
Panama City *42 D3* Florida, SE USA
Panama City *see* Panamá
Panamá, Golfo de *53 G5 var.* Gulf of
Panama. *gulf* S Panama
Panama, Gulf of *see* Panamá, Golfo de
Panama, Isthmus of *see* Panama,
Istmo de
Panama, Istmo de *53 G4 Eng.* Isthmus
of Panama; *prev.* Isthmus of Darien.
isthmus E Panama
Panama, Republic of *see* Panama
Panay Island *139 E2 island* C Philippines
Pančevo *100 D3 Ger.* Pantschowa, *Hung.*
Pancsova. Vojvodina, N Serbia
Pancsova *see* Pančevo
Paneas *see* Bāniyās
Panevėžys *106 C4 var.* Panevėžys,
C Lithuania
Pangim *see* Panaji
Pangkalpinang *138 C4* Pulau Bangka,
W Indonesia
Pang-Nga *see* Phang-Nga
Panhormus *see* Palermo
Panjim *see* Panaji
Panopolis *see* Akhmîm
Pánormos *105 C7* Kríti, Greece,
E Mediterranean Sea
Panormus *see* Palermo
Pantanal *63 E3 var.* Pantanalmato-
Grossense. *swamp* SW Brazil
Pantanalmato-Grossense *see* Pantanal
Pantelleria, Isola di *97 B7 island*
SW Italy
Pantschowa *see* Pančevo
Pánuco *51 E3* Veracruz-Llave,
E Mexico
Pao-chi/Paoki *see* Baoji
Paola *102 B5* E Malta

Pao-shan *see* Baoshan
Pao-t'ou/Paotow *see* Baotou
Papagayo, Golfo de *52 C4 gulf*
NW Costa Rica
Papakura *150 D3* Auckland, North
Island, New Zealand
Papantla *51 F4 var.* Papantla de Olarte.
Veracruz-Llave, E Mexico
Papantla de Olarte *see* Papantla
Papeete *145 H4 dependent territory
capital* (French Polynesia) Tahiti,
W French Polynesia
Paphos *see* Páfos
Papilė *106 B3* Šiauliai, NW Lithuania
Papillion *45 F4* Nebraska, C USA
Papua *139 H4 var.* Irian Barat,
West Irian, West New Guinea, West
Papua; *prev.* Dutch New Guinea,
Irian Jaya, Netherlands New Guinea.
province E Indonesia
Papua and New Guinea, Territory of *see*
Papua New Guinea
Papua, Gulf of *144 B3 gulf* S Papua
New Guinea
Papua New Guinea *144 B3
off.* Independent State of Papua New
Guinea; *prev.* Territory of Papua and
New Guinea. *country* NW Melanesia

PAPUA NEW GUINEA
Australasia & Oceania

Official name Independent State of
Papua New Guinea
Formation 1975 / 1975
Capital Port Moresby
Population 5.9 million / 34 people per
sq mile (13 people per sq km) / 17%
Total area 178,703 sq miles
(462,840 sq km)
Languages Pidgin English*,
Papuan*, English, Motu,
750 (est.) native languages
Religions Protestant 60%, Roman
Catholic 37%, Other 3%
Ethnic mix Melanesian and mixed
race 100%
Government Parliamentary system
Currency Kina = 100 toeas
Literacy rate 57%
Calorie consumption 2193 calories

**Papua New Guinea, Independent State
of** *see* Papua New Guinea
Papuk *100 C3 mountain range*
NE Croatia
Pará *63 E2 off.* Estado do Pará. *state*
NE Brazil
Pará *see* Belém
Paracel Islands *125 E3 disputed territory*
SE Asia
Paracín *100 D4* Serbia, C Serbia
Paradise of the Pacific *see* Hawai'i
Pará, Estado do *see* Pará
Paragua, Rio *59 E3 river* SE Venezuela
Paraguay *64 C2 country* S Central
America

PARAGUAY
South America

Official name Republic of Paraguay
Formation 1811 / 1938
Capital Asunción
Population 6.2 million / 40 people per
sq mile (16 people per sq km) / 56%
Total area 157,046 sq miles (406,750
sq km)
Languages Guaraní*, Spanish*, German
Religions Roman Catholic 96%,
Protestant (including Mennonite) 4%
Ethnic mix Mestizo 90%, Other 8%,
Amerindian 2%
Government Presidential system
Currency Guaraní = 100 centimos
Literacy rate 92%
Calorie consumption 2565 calories

Paraguay *64 D2 var.* Río Paraguay. *river*
C South America
Paraguay, Río *see* Paraguay
Parahiba/Parahyba *see* Paraíba
Paraíba *63 G2 off.* Estado da Paraíba;
prev. Parahiba, Parahyba. *state*
E Brazil
Paraíba *see* João Pessoa
Paraíba, Estado da *see* Paraíba
Parakou *75 F4* C Benin

Paramaribo *59 G3 country capital*
(Suriname) Paramaribo, N Suriname
Paramushir, Ostrov *115 H3 island*
SE Russian Federation
Paraná *63 E4* Entre Ríos, E Argentina
Paraná *63 E5 off.* Estado do Paraná.
state S Brazil
Paraná *57 C5 var.* Alto Paraná. *river*
C South America
Paraná, Estado do *see* Paraná
Paranésti *104 C3 var* Paranestio.
Anatolikí Makedonía kai Thráki,
NE Greece
Paranestio *see* Paranésti
Paraparaumu *151 D5* Wellington, North
Island, New Zealand
Parchim *94 C3* Mecklenburg-
Vorpommern, N Germany
Parczew *98 E4* Lubelskie, E Poland
Pardubice *99 B5 Ger.* Pardubitz.
Pardubický Kraj, C Czech Republic
Pardubitz *see* Pardubice
Parechcha *107 B5 Pol.* Porzecze, *Rus.*
Porech'ye. Hrodzyenskaya Voblasts',
W Belarus
Parecis, Chapada dos *62 D3 var.* Serra
dos Parecis. *mountain range* W Brazil
Parecis, Serra dos *see* Parecis, Chapada
dos
Parenzo *see* Poreč
Parepare *139 E4* Sulawesi, C Indonesia
Párga *105 A5* Ípeiros, W Greece
Paria, Golfo de *see* Paria, Gulf of
Paria, Gulf of *59 E1 var.* Golfo de Paria.
gulf Trinidad and Tobago/Venezuela
Parika *59 F2* N Guyana
Paris *90 D1 anc.* Lutetia, Lutetia
Parisiorum, Parisii. *country capital*
(France) Paris, N France
Paris *49 G2* Texas, SW USA
Parisii *see* Paris
Parkersburg *40 D4* West Virginia,
NE USA
Parkes *149 D6* New South Wales,
SE Australia
Parkhar *see* Farkhor
Parma *96 B2* Emilia-Romagna, N Italy
Parnahyba *see* Parnaíba
Parnaíba *63 F2 var.* Parnahyba. Piauí,
E Brazil
Pärnu *106 D2 Ger.* Pernau, *Latv.*
Pērnava; *prev. Rus.* Pernov. Pärnumaa,
SW Estonia
Pärnu *106 D2 var.* Parnu Jõgi, *Ger.*
Pernau. *river* SW Estonia
Pärnu-Jaagupi *106 D2 Ger.* Sankt-
Jakobi. Pärnumaa, SW Estonia
Parnu Jõgi *see* Pärnu
Pärnu Laht *106 D2 Ger.* Pernauer Bucht.
bay SW Estonia
Paropamisus Range *see* Safīdkūh,
Selseleh-ye
Paroikia *105 D6* Kykládes, Greece,
Aegean Sea
Páros *105 C6 island* Kykládes,
Aegean Sea
Parral *64 B4* Maule, C Chile
Parral *see* Hidalgo del Parral
Parramatta *148 D1* New South Wales,
SE Australia
Parras *50 D3 var.* Parras de la Fuente.
Coahuila de Zaragoza, NE Mexico
Parras de la Fuente *see* Parras
Parsons *45 F5* Kansas, C USA
Pasadena *47 C7* California, W USA
Pasadena *49 H4* Texas, SW USA
Pașcani *108 C3 Hung.* Páskán. Iași,
NE Romania
Pasco *46 C2* Washington, NW USA
Pascua, Isla de *153 F4 var.* Rapa Nui,
Easter Island. *island* E Pacific Ocean
Pasewalk *94 D3* Mecklenburg-
Vorpommern, NE Germany
Pashkeni *see* Bolyarovo
Pasinler *117 F3* Erzurum, NE Turkey
Páskán *see* Pașcani
Pasłęk *98 D2 Ger.* Preußisch Holland.
Warmińsko-Mazurskie, NE Poland
Pasni *134 A3* Baluchistan, SW Pakistan
Paso de Indios *65 B6* Chubut,
S Argentina
Passarowitz *see* Požarevac
Passau *95 D6* Bayern, SE Germany
Passo Fundo *63 E5* Rio Grande do
Sul, S Brazil
Pastavy *107 C5 Pol.* Postawy, *Rus.*
Postavy. Vitsyebskaya Voblasts',
NW Belarus

Pastaza, Río *60 B2 river* Ecuador/Peru
Pasto *58 A4* Nariño, SW Colombia
Pasvalys *106 C4* Panevėžys,
N Lithuania
Patagonia *57 B7 semi arid region*
Argentina/Chile
Patalung *see* Phatthalung
Patani *see* Pattani
Patavium *see* Padova
Patea *150 D4* Taranaki, North Island,
New Zealand
Paterson *41 F3* New Jersey, NE USA
Pathein *see* Bassein
Pátmos *105 D6 island* Dodekánisa,
Greece, Aegean Sea
Patna *135 F3 var.* Azimabad. *state capital*
Bihār, N India
Patnos *117 F3* Ağrı, E Turkey
Patos, Lagoa dos *63 E5 lagoon* S Brazil
Pátra *105 B5 Eng.* Patras; *prev.* Pátrai.
Dytikí Ellás, S Greece
Pátrai/Patras *see* Pátra
Pattani *137 C7 var.* Patani. Pattani,
SW Thailand
Pattaya *137 C5* Chon Buri, S Thailand
Patuca, Río *52 D2 river* E Honduras
Pau *91 B6* Pyrénées-Atlantiques,
SW France
Paulatuk *37 E3* Northwest Territories,
NW Canada
Paungde *136 B4* Pegu,
C Myanmar (Burma)
Pautalia *see* Kyustendil
Pavia *96 B2 anc.* Ticinum. Lombardia,
N Italy
Pāvilosta *106 B3* Liepāja, W Latvia
Pavlikeni *104 D2* Veliko Tŭrnovo,
N Bulgaria
Pavlodar *114 C4* Pavlodar,
NE Kazakhstan
Pavlograd *see* Pavlohrad
Pavlohrad *109 G3 Rus.* Pavlograd.
Dnipropetrovs'ka Oblast', E Ukraine
Pawn *136 B3 river* C Myanmar (Burma)
Pax Augusta *see* Badajoz
Pax Julia *see* Beja
Paxoí *105 A5 island* Iónia Nisiá, Greece,
C Mediterranean Sea
Payo Obispo *see* Chetumal
Paysandú *64 D4* Paysandú,
W Uruguay
Pazar *117 E2* Rize, NE Turkey
Pazardzhik *104 C3 prev.* Tatar
Pazardzhik. Pazardzhik, SW Bulgaria
Peace Garden State *see* North Dakota
Peach State *see* Georgia
Pearl Islands *see* Perlas, Archipiélago
de las
Pearl Lagoon *see* Perlas, Laguna de
Pearl River *42 B3 river* Louisiana/
Mississippi, S USA
Pearsall *49 F4* Texas, SW USA
Peawanuk *38 C2* Ontario, C Canada
Peć *101 D5 Alb.* Pejë, *Turk.* Ipek.
Kosovo, S Serbia
Pechora *110 D3* Respublika Komi,
NW Russian Federation
Pechora *110 D3 river* NW Russian
Federation
Pechora Sea *see* Pechorskoye More
Pechorskoye More *110 D2
Eng.* Pechora Sea. *sea*
NW Russian Federation
Pecos *49 E3* Texas, SW USA
Pecos River *49 E3 river* New Mexico/
Texas, SW USA
Pécs *99 C7 Ger.* Fünfkirchen, *Lat.*
Sopianae. Baranya, SW Hungary
Pedra Lume *74 A3* Sal, NE Cape Verde
Pedro Cays *54 C3 island group* Greater
Antilles, S Jamaica North America
N Caribbean Sea W Atlantic Ocean
Pedro Juan Caballero *64 D2* Amambay,
E Paraguay
Peer *87 D5* Limburg, NE Belgium
Pegasus Bay *151 C6 bay* South Island,
New Zealand
Pegu *136 B4 var.* Bago. Pegu,
SW Myanmar (Burma)
Pehuajó *64 C4* Buenos Aires, E Argentina
Pei-ching *see* Beijing/Beijing Shi
Peine *94 B3* Niedersachsen, C Germany
Pei-p'ing *see* Beijing/Beijing Shi
Peipsi Järv/Peipus-See *see* Peipus, Lake
Peipus, Lake *106 E3
Est.* Peipsi Järv, *Ger.* Peipus-See,
Rus. Chudskoye Ozero. *lake*
Estonia/Russian Federation

Peiraías *105 C6 prev.* Piraiévs, *Eng.*
  Piraeus. Attikí, C Greece
Pejé *see* Peć
Pek *136 D4 var.* Xieng Khouang; *prev.*
  Xiangkhoang. Xiangkhoang, N Laos
Pekalongan *138 C4* Jawa, C Indonesia
Pekanbaru *138 B3 var.* Pakanbaru.
  Sumatera, W Indonesia
Pekin *40 B4* Illinois, N USA
Peking *see* Beijing/Beijing Shi
Pelagie, Isole *97 B8 island group*
  SW Italy
Pelagosa *see* Palagruža
Pelican State *see* Louisiana
Pelly Bay *37 G3* Nunavut, N Canada
Pélmonostor *see* Beli Manastir
Peloponnese/Peloponnesus *see*
  Pelopónnisos
Pelopónnisos *105 B6 var.* Morea, *Eng.*
  Peloponnese; *anc.* Peloponnesus.
  peninsula S Greece
Pematangsiantar *138 B3* Sumatera,
  W Indonesia
Pemba *79 F2 prev.* Port Amelia,
  Porto Amélia. Cabo Delgado,
  NE Mozambique
Pemba *73 D7 island* E Tanzania
Pembroke *38 D4* Ontario, SE Canada
Penang *see* George Town
Penang *see* Pinang, Pulau, Peninsular
  Malaysia
Penas, Golfo de *65 A7 gulf* S Chile
Penderma *see* Bandırma
Pendleton *46 C3* Oregon, NW USA
Pend Oreille, Lake *46 D2 lake* Idaho,
  NW USA
Peneius *see* Pineiós
Peng-pu *see* Bengbu
Penibético, Sistema *see* Béticos, Sistemas
Peniche *92 B3* Leiria, W Portugal
Peninsular State *see* Florida
Penninae, Alpes/Pennine, Alpi *see*
  Pennine Alps
Pennine Alps *95 A8 Fr.* Alpes Pennines,
  It. Alpi Pennine, *Lat.* Alpes Penninae.
  mountain range Italy/Switzerland
Pennine Chain *see* Pennines
Pennines *89 D5 var.* Pennine Chain.
  mountain range N England, UK
Pennines, Alpes *see* Pennine Alps
Pennsylvania *40 D3 off.* Commonwealth
  of Pennsylvania, *also known as*
  Keystone State. *state* NE USA
Penobscot River *41 G2 river* Maine,
  NE USA
Penong *149 A6* South Australia
Penonomé *53 F5* Coclé, C Panama
Penrhyn *145 G3 atoll* N Cook Islands
Penrhyn Basin *143 F3 undersea feature*
  C Pacific Ocean
Penrith *148 D1* New South Wales,
  SE Australia
Penrith *89 D5* NW England, UK
Pensacola *42 C3* Florida, SE USA
Pentecost *144 D4 Fr.* Pentecôte. *island*
  C Vanuatu
Pentecôte *see* Pentecost
Penza *111 C6* Penzenskaya Oblast',
  W Russian Federation
Penzance *89 C7* SW England, UK
Peoria *40 B4* Illinois, N USA
Perchtoldsdorf *95 E6* Niederösterreich,
  NE Austria
Percival Lakes *146 C4 lakes* Western
  Australia
Perdido, Monte *93 F1 mountain*
  NE Spain
Perece Vela Basin *see* West Mariana
  Basin
Pereira *58 B3* Risaralda, W Colombia
Peremyshl *see* Przemyśl
Pergamino *64 C4* Buenos Aires,
  E Argentina
Périgueux *91 C5 anc.* Vesuna.
  Dordogne, SW France
Perito Moreno *65 B6* Santa Cruz,
  S Argentina
Perlas, Archipiélago de las *53 G5 Eng.*
  Pearl Islands. *island group* SE Panama
Perlas, Laguna de *53 E3 Eng.* Pearl
  Lagoon. *lagoon* E Nicaragua
Perleberg *94 C3* Brandenburg,
  N Germany
Perlepe *see* Prilep
Perm' *114 C3 prev.* Molotov. Permskaya
  Oblast', NW Russian Federation
Pernambuco *63 G2 off.* Estado de
  Pernambuco. *state* E Brazil

Pernambuco *see* Recife
Pernambuco Abyssal Plain *see*
  Pernambuco Plain
Pernambuco, Estado de *see* Pernambuco
Pernambuco Plain *67 C5 var.*
  Pernambuco Abyssal Plain. *undersea
  feature* E Atlantic Ocean
Pernau *see* Pärnu
Pernauer Bucht *see* Pärnu Laht
Pērnava *see* Pärnu
Pernik *104 B2 prev.* Dimitrovo. Pernik,
  W Bulgaria
Pernov *see* Pärnu
Perote *51 F4* Veracruz-Llave, E Mexico
Pérouse *see* Perugia
Perovsk *see* Kyzylorda
Perpignan *91 C6* Pyrénées-Orientales,
  S France
Perryton *49 F1* Texas, SW USA
Perryville *45 H5* Missouri, C USA
Persia *see* Iran
Persian Gulf *120 C4 var.* The Gulf, *Ar.*
  Khalīj al 'Arabī, *Per.* Khalīj-e Fars.
  Gulf SW Asia
Perth *147 A6 state capital* Western
  Australia
Perth *88 C4* C Scotland, UK
Perth Basin *141 E6 undersea feature*
  SE Indian Ocean
Peru *60 D3 off.* Republic of Peru. *country*
  W South America

PERU
South America

Official name Republic of Peru
Formation 1824 / 1941
Capital Lima
Population 28 million / 57 people per sq
mile (22 people per sq km) / 73%
Total area 496,223 sq miles (1,285,200
sq km)
Languages Spanish*, Quechua*, Aymara*
Religions Roman Catholic 95%, Other 5%
Ethnic mix Amerindian 50%,
Mestizo 40%, White 7%, Other 3%
Government Presidential system
Currency New sol = 100 centimos
Literacy rate 88%
Calorie consumption 2571 calories

Peru *see* Beru
Peru Basin *67 A5 undersea feature*
  E Pacific Ocean
Peru-Chile Trench *56 A4 undersea
  feature* E Pacific Ocean
Perugia *96 C4 Fr.* Pérouse; *anc.* Perusia.
  Umbria, C Italy
Perugia, Lake of *see* Trasimeno, Lago
Peru, Republic of *see* Peru
Perusia *see* Perugia
Péruwelz *87 B6* Hainaut, SW Belgium
Pervomays'k *109 E3 prev.* Ol'viopol'.
  Mykolayivs'ka Oblast', S Ukraine
Pervyy Kuril'skiy Proliv *115 H3 strait*
  E Russian Federation
Pesaro *96 C3 anc.* Pisaurum. Marche,
  C Italy
Pescara *96 D4 anc.* Aternum, Ostia
  Aterni. Abruzzo, C Italy
Peshāwar *134 C1* North-West Frontier
  Province, N Pakistan
Peshkopi *101 C6 var.* Peshkopia,
  Peshkopija. Dibër, NE Albania
Peshkopia/Peshkopija *see* Peshkopi
Pessac *91 B5* Gironde, SW France
Petach-Tikva *see* Petah Tiqwa
Petah Tiqwa *119 A6 var.* Petach-Tikva,
  Petah Tiqva, Petakh Tikva. Tel Aviv,
  C Israel
Petakh Tikva/Petah Tiqva *see* Petah
  Tiqwa
Pétange *87 D8* Luxembourg,
  SW Luxembourg
Petchaburi *see* Phetchaburi
Peterborough *149 B6* South Australia
Peterborough *38 D5* Ontario,
  SE Canada
Peterborough *89 E6 prev.*
  Medeshamstede. E England, UK
Peterhead *88 D3* NE Scotland, UK
Peter I Island *154 A3 Norwegian
  dependency* Antarctica
Petermann Bjerg *83 E3 mountain*
  C Greenland
Petersburg *41 E5* Virginia, NE USA
Peters Mine *59 F3 var.* Peter's Mine.
  N Guyana

Petit St-Bernard, Col du *see* Little Saint
  Bernard Pass
Peto *51 H4* Yucatán, SE Mexico
Petoskey *40 C2* Michigan,
  N USA
Petra *see* Wādī Mūsá
Petrich *104 C3* Blagoevgrad,
  SW Bulgaria
Petrikau *see* Piotrków Trybunalski
Petrikov *see* Pyetrykaw
Petrinja *100 B3* Sisak-Moslavina,
  C Croatia
Petroaleksandrovsk *see* To'rtkol'
Petrodvorets *110 A4 Fin.* Pietarhovi.
  Leningradskaya Oblast', NW Russian
  Federation
Petrograd *see* Sankt-Peterburg
Petrokov *see* Piotrków Trybunalski
Petropavl *see* Petropavlovsk
Petropavlovsk *114 C4 Kaz.* Petropavl.
  Severnyy Kazakhstan, N Kazakhstan
Petropavlovsk-Kamchatskiy *115 H3*
  Kamchatskaya Oblast', E Russian
  Federation
Petroșani *108 B4 var.* Petroșeni,
  Ger. Petroschen, *Hung.* Petrozsény.
  Hunedoara, W Romania
Petroschen/Petroșeni *see* Petroșani
Petroskoi *see* Petrozavodsk
Petrovgrad *see* Zrenjanin
Petrovsk-Port *see* Makhachkala
Petrozavodsk *110 B3 Fin.* Petroskoi.
  Respublika Kareliya, NW Russian
  Federation
Petrozsény *see* Petroșani
Pettau *see* Ptuj
Pevek *115 G1* Chukotskiy Avtonomnyy
  Okrug, NE Russian Federation
Pezinok *99 C6 Ger.* Bösing, *Hung.* Bazin.
  Bratislavský Kraj, W Slovakia
Pforzheim *95 B6* Baden-Württemberg,
  SW Germany
Pfungstadt *95 B5* Hessen, W Germany
Phangan, Ko *137 C6 island*
  SW Thailand
Phang-Nga *137 B7 var.* Pang-Nga,
  Phangnga. Phangnga, SW Thailand
Phangnga *see* Phang-Nga
Phan Rang/Phanrang *see* Phan
  Rang-Thap Cham
Phan Rang-Thap Cham *137 E6 var.*
  Phanrang, Phan Rang, Phan Rang
  Thap Cham. Ninh Thuân, S Vietnam
Phan Thiêt *137 E6* Bình Thuân,
  S Vietnam
Pharnacia *see* Giresun
Pharus *see* Hvar
Phatthalung *137 C7 var.* Padalung,
  Patalung. Phatthalung, SW Thailand
Phayao *136 C4 var.* Muang Phayao.
  Phayao, NW Thailand
Phenix City *42 D2* Alabama,
  S USA
Phet Buri *see* Phetchaburi
Phetchaburi *137 C5 var.* Bejraburi,
  Petchaburi, Phet Buri. Phetchaburi,
  SW Thailand
Philadelphia *41 F4* Pennsylvania,
  NE USA
Philadelphia *see* 'Ammān
Philippine Basin *125 F3 undersea
  feature* W Pacific Ocean
Philippines *139 E1 off.* Republic of the
  Philippines. *country* SE Asia

PHILIPPINES
Southwest Asia

Official name Republic of the Philippines
Formation 1946 / 1946
Capital Manila
Population 83.1 million / 722 people per
sq mile (279 people per sq km) / 59%
Total area 115,830 sq miles
(300,000 sq km)
Languages Filipino*, English*, Tagalog,
Cebuano, Ilocano, Hiligaynon, many
other local languages
Religions Roman Catholic 83%,
Protestant 9%, Muslim 5%, Other
(including Buddhist) 3%
Ethnic mix Malay 96%, Other 3%,
Chinese 2%
Government Presidential system
Currency Philippine peso = 100 centavos
Literacy rate 93%
Calorie consumption 2379 calories

Philippines *139 E1 island group*
  W Pacific Ocean
Philippine Sea *125 F3 sea* W Pacific
  Ocean
Philippines, Republic of the *see*
  Philippines
Philippine Trench *142 A1 undersea
  feature* W Philippine Sea
Philippopolis *see* Plovdiv
Phitsanulok *136 C4 var.* Bisnulok,
  Muang Phitsanulok, Pitsanulok.
  Phitsanulok, C Thailand
Phlórina *see* Flórina
Phnom Penh *see* Phnum Penh
Phnum Penh *137 D6 var.* Phnom Penh.
  country capital (Cambodia) Phnum
  Penh, S Cambodia
Phoenix *48 B2 state capital* Arizona,
  SW USA
Phoenix Islands *145 E3 island group*
  C Kiribati
Phôngsali *136 C3 var.* Phong Saly.
  Phôngsali, N Laos
Phong Saly *see* Phôngsali
Phrae *136 C4 var.* Muang Phrae, Prae.
  Phrae, NW Thailand
Phra Nakhon Si Ayutthaya *see*
  Ayutthaya
Phra Thong, Ko *137 B6 island*
  SW Thailand
Phuket *137 B7 var.* Bhuket, Puket, *Mal.*
  Ujung Salang; *prev.* Junkseylon, Salang.
  Phuket, SW Thailand
Phuket, Ko *137 B7 island* SW Thailand
Phumî Kâmpóng Trâbêk *137 D5 prev.*
  Phum Kompong Trabek. Kâmpóng
  Thum, C Cambodia
Phumî Sâmraông *137 D5 prev.* Phum
  Samrong. Siĕmréab, NW Cambodia
Phum Kompong Trabek *see* Phumî
  Kâmpóng Trâbêk
Phum Samrong *see* Phumî Sâmraông
Phu Vinh *see* Tra Vinh
Piacenza *96 B2 Fr.* Plaisance; *anc.*
  Placentia. Emilia-Romagna, N Italy
Piatra-Neamţ *108 C4 Hung.*
  Karácsonkõ. Neamţ, NE Romania
Piauhy *see* Piauí
Piauí *63 F2 off.* Estado do Piauí; *prev.*
  Piauhy. *state* E Brazil
Piauí, Estado do *see* Piauí
Picardie *90 C3 Eng.* Picardy. *cultural
  region* N France
Picardie *90 C3 Eng.* Picardy. *region*
  N France
Picardy *see* Picardie
Piccolo San Bernardo, Colle di *see* Little
  Saint Bernard Pass
Pichilemu *64 B4* Libertador, C Chile
Pico *92 A5 var.* Ilha do Pico. *island*
  Azores, Portugal, NE Atlantic Ocean
Pico, Ilha do *see* Pico
Picos *63 F2* Piauí, E Brazil
Picton *151 C5* Marlborough, South
  Island, New Zealand
Piedmont *see* Piemonte
Piedras Negras *51 E2 var.* Ciudad
  Porfirio Díaz. Coahuila de Zaragoza,
  NE Mexico
Pielinen *84 E4 var.* Pielisjärvi. *lake*
  E Finland
Pielisjärvi *see* Pielinen
Piemonte *96 A2 Eng.* Piedmont. *region*
  NW Italy
Pierre *45 E3 state capital* South Dakota,
  N USA
Piešt'any *99 C6 Ger.* Pistyan, *Hung.*
  Pöstyén. Tranavský Kraj, W Slovakia
Pietarhovi *see* Petrodvorets
Pietari *see* Sankt-Peterburg
Pietarsaari *see* Jakobstad
Pietermaritzburg *78 C5 var.*
  Maritzburg. KwaZulu/Natal, E South
  Africa
Pietersburg *see* Polokwane
Pigs, Bay of *see* Cochinos, Bahía de
Pihkva Järv *see* Pskov, Lake
Pijijiápán *51 G5* Chiapas, SE Mexico
Pikes Peak *44 C5 mountain* Colorado,
  C USA
Pikeville *40 D5* Kentucky, S USA
Pikinni *see* Bikini Atoll
Piła *98 C3 Ger.* Schneidemühl.
  Wielkopolskie, C Poland
Pilar *64 C3 var.* Villa del Pilar.
  Ñeembucú, S Paraguay
Pilcomayo, Rio *57 C5 river* C South
  America

Pilos *see* Pýlos
Pilsen *see* Plzeň
Pilzno *see* Plzeň
Pinang *see* Pinang, Pulau, Peninsular Malaysia
Pinang *see* George Town
Pinang, Pulau *138 B3 var.* Penang, Pinang; *prev.* Prince of Wales Island. *island* Peninsular Malaysia
Pinar del Río *54 A2* Pinar del Río, W Cuba
Píndhos/Píndhos Óros *see* Píndos
Píndos *104 A4 var.* Píndhos Óros, *Eng.* Pindus Mountains; *prev.* Píndhos. *mountain range* C Greece
Pindus Mountains *see* Píndos
Pine Bluff *42 B2* Arkansas, C USA
Pine Creek *146 D2* Northern Territory, N Australia
Pinega *110 C3 river* NW Russian Federation
Pineiós *104 B4 var.* Piniós; *anc.* Peneius. *river* C Greece
Pineland *49 H3* Texas, SW USA
Pines, Akrotírio *104 C4 cape* N Greece
Pines, The Isle of the *see* Juventud, Isla de la
Pine Tree State *see* Maine
Pingdingshan *128 C4* Henan, C China
Pingkiang *see* Harbin
Ping, Mae Nam *136 B4 river* W Thailand
Piniós *see* Pineiós
Pinkiang *see* Harbin
Pinos, Isla de *see* Juventud, Isla de la
Pinotepa Nacional *51 F5 var.* Santiago Pinotepa Nacional. Oaxaca, SE Mexico
Pinsk *107 B7 Pol.* Pińsk. Brestskaya Voblasts', SW Belarus
Pinta, Isla *60 A5 var.* Abingdon. *island* Galapagos Islands, Ecuador, E Pacific Ocean
Piombino *96 B3* Toscana, C Italy
Pioneer Mountains *46 D3 mountain range* Montana, N USA North America
Pionerskiy *106 A4 Ger.* Neukuhren. Kaliningradskaya Oblast', W Russian Federation
Piotrków Trybunalski *98 D4 Ger.* Petrikau, *Rus.* Petrokov. Lodzkie, C Poland
Piraeus/Piraiévs *see* Peiraiás
Pírgos *see* Pýrgos
Pirineos *see* Pyrenees
Piripiri *63 F2* Piauí, E Brazil
Pirna *94 D4* Sachsen, E Germany
Pirot *101 E5* Serbia, SE Serbia
Piryatin *see* Pyryatyn
Pisa *96 B3 var.* Pisae. Toscana, C Italy
Pisae *see* Pisa
Pisaurum *see* Pesaro
Pisco *60 D4* Ica, SW Peru
Písek *99 A5* Budějovický Kraj, S Czech Republic
Pishan *126 A3 var.* Guma. Xinjiang Uygur Zizhiqu, NW China
Pishpek *see* Bishkek
Pistoia *96 B3 anc.* Pistoria, Pistoriæ. Toscana, C Italy
Pistoria/Pistoriæ *see* Pistoia
Pistyan *see* Piešťany
Pisz *98 D3* Olsztyn. Warmińsko-Mazurskie, NE Poland
Pita *74 C4* NW Guinea
Pitalito *58 B4* Huila, S Colombia
Pitcairn Island *143 G4 island* S Pitcairn Islands
Pitcairn Islands *143 G4 UK dependent territory* C Pacific Ocean
Piteå *84 D4* Norrbotten, N Sweden
Pitești *108 B5* Argeș, S Romania
Pitsanulok *see* Phitsanulok
Pitt Island *see* Makin
Pittsburg *45 F5* Kansas, C USA
Pittsburgh *41 E4* Pennsylvania, NE USA
Pittsfield *41 F3* Massachusetts, NE USA
Piura *60 B2* Piura, NW Peru
Pivdennyy Buh *109 E3 Rus.* Yuzhnyy Bug. *river* S Ukraine
Placentia *see* Piacenza
Placetas *54 B2* Villa Clara, C Cuba
Plaínview *49 E2* Texas, SW USA
Pláka *95 C5 prev.* Mílos. Kyládes, Greece, Aegean Sea
Planeta Rica *58 B2* Córdoba, NW Colombia
Planken *94 E1* C Liechtenstein Europe
Plano *49 G2* Texas, SW USA
Plasencia *92 C3* Extremadura, W Spain

Plata, Río de la *64 D4 var.* River Plate. *estuary* Argentina/Uruguay
Plate, River *see* Plata, Río de la
Platinum *36 C3* Alaska, USA
Plattensee *see* Balaton
Platte River *45 E4 river* Nebraska, C USA
Plattsburgh *41 F2* New York, NE USA
Plauen *95 C5 var.* Plauen im Vogtland. Sachsen, E Germany
Plauen im Vogtland *see* Plauen
Plavinas *106 D4 Ger.* Stockmannshof. Aizkraukle, S Latvia
Plây Cu *137 E5 var.* Pleiku. Gia Lai, C Vietnam
Pleasant Island *see* Nauru
Pleiku *see* Plây Cu
Plenty, Bay of *150 E3 bay* North Island, New Zealand
Plérin *90 A3* Côtes d'Armor, NW France
Plesetsk *110 C3* Arkhangel'skaya Oblast', NW Russian Federation
Pleshchenitsy *see* Plyeshchanitsy
Pleskau *see* Pskov
Pleskauer See *see* Pskov, Lake
Pleskava *see* Pskov
Pleszew *98 C4* Wielkopolskie, C Poland
Pleven *104 C2 prev.* Plevna. Pleven, N Bulgaria
Plevlja/Plevlje *see* Pljevlja
Plevna *see* Pleven
Pljevlja *100 C4 prev.* Plevlja, Plevlje. N Montenegro
Plocce *see* Ploče
Ploče *100 B4 It.* Plocce; *prev.* Kardeljevo. Dubrovnik-Neretva, SE Croatia
Płock *98 D3 Ger.* Plozk. Mazowieckie, C Poland
Plöcken Pass *95 C7 Ger.* Plöckenpass, *It.* Passo di Monte Croce Carnico. *pass* SW Austria
Plöckenpass *see* Plöcken Pass
Ploești *see* Ploiești
Ploiești *108 C5 prev.* Ploești. Prahova, SE Romania
Plomári *105 D5 prev.* Plomárion. Lésvos, E Greece
Plomárion *see* Plomári
Płońsk *98 D3* Mazowieckie, C Poland
Plovdiv *104 C3 prev.* Eumolpias; *anc.* Evmolpia, Philippopolis, *Lat.* Trimontium. Plovdiv, C Bulgaria
Plozk *see* Płock
Plunge *106 B3* Telšiai, W Lithuania
Plyeshchanitsy *107 D5 Rus.* Pleshchenitsy. Minskaya Voblasts', N Belarus
Plymouth *55 G3 dependent territory capital* (Montserrat) SW Montserrat
Plymouth *89 C7* SW England, UK
Plzeň *99 A5 Ger.* Pilsen, *Pol.* Pilzno. Plzeňský Kraj, W Czech Republic
Po *80 D4 river* N Italy
Pobedy, Pik *126 B3 Chin.* Tomür Feng. *mountain* China/Kyrgyzstan
Po, Bocche del *see* Po, Foci del
Pocahontas *42 B1* Arkansas, C USA
Pocatello *46 E4* Idaho, NW USA
Pochinok *111 A5* Smolenskaya Oblast', W Russian Federation
Pocking *95 D6* Bayern, SE Germany
Podbrodzie *see* Pabradė
Poděbrady *99 B5 Ger.* Podiebrad. Středočeský Kraj, C Czech Republic
Podgorica *101 C5 prev.* Titograd. *country capital* (Montenegro) S Montenegro
Podiebrad *see* Poděbrady
Podil's'ka Vysochina *108 D3 plateau* W Ukraine
Podium Anicensis *see* le Puy
Podol'sk *111 B5* Moskovskaya Oblast', W Russian Federation
Podravska Slatina *see* Slatina
Podujevo *101 D5* Kosovo, S Serbia
Podunajská Rovina *see* Little Alföld
Poetovio *see* Ptuj
Po, Foci del *96 C2 var.* Bocche del Po. *river* NE Italy
Pogradec *101 D6 var.* Pogradeci. Korçë, SE Albania
Pogradeci *see* Pogradec
Pohjanlahti *see* Bothnia, Gulf of
Pohnpei *144 C2 prev.* Ponape Ascension Island. *island* E Micronesia
Poictiers *see* Poitiers
Point de Galle *see* Galle

Pointe-à-Pitre *55 G3* Grande Terre, C Guadeloupe
Pointe-Noire *77 B6* Le Kouilou, S Congo
Point Lay *36 C2* Alaska, USA
Poitiers *90 B4 prev.* Poictiers; *anc.* Limonum. Vienne, W France
Poitou *90 B4 cultural region* W France
Pokharā *135 E3* Western, C Nepal
Pokrovka *see* Kyzyl-Suu
Pokrovs'ke *109 G3 Rus.* Pokrovskoye. Dnipropetrovs'ka Oblast', E Ukraine
Pokrovskoye *see* Pokrovs'ke
Pola *see* Pula
Pola de Lena *92 D1* Asturias, N Spain
Poland *81 E3* Kiritimati, E Kiribati
Poland *80 B4 off.* Republic of Poland, *var.* Polish Republic, *Pol.* Polska, Rzeczpospolita Polska; *prev. Pol.* Polska

POLAND
Northern Europe

Official name	Republic of Poland
Formation	1918 / 1945
Capital	Warsaw
Population	38.5 million / 328 people per sq mile (126 people per sq km) / 66%
Total area	120,728 sq miles (312,685 sq km)
Languages	Polish*
Religions	Roman Catholic 93%, Other and nonreligious 5%, Orthodox Christian 2%
Ethnic mix	Polish 97%, Other 2%, Silesian 1%
Government	Parliamentary system
Currency	Zloty = 100 groszy
Literacy rate	99%
Calorie consumption	3374 calories

Rzeczpospolita Ludowa, The Polish People's Republic. *country* C Europe
Poland, Republic of *see* Poland
Polatlı *116 C3* Ankara, C Turkey
Polatsk *107 D5 Rus.* Polotsk. Vitsyebskaya Voblasts', N Belarus
Pol-e Khomrī *123 E4 var.* Pul-i-Khumri. Baghlān, NE Afghanistan
Poli *see* Pólis
Polikastro/Polikastron *see* Polýkastro
Polikrayshte *104 D2* Veliko Tŭrnovo, N Bulgaria
Pólis *102 C5 var.* Poli. W Cyprus
Polish People's Republic, The *see* Poland
Polish Republic *see* Poland
Polkowice *98 B4 Ger.* Heerwegen. Dolnośląskie, W Poland
Pollença *93 G3* Mallorca, Spain, W Mediterranean Sea
Pologi *see* Polohy
Polohy *109 G3 Rus.* Pologi. Zaporiz'ka Oblast', SE Ukraine
Polokwane *78 D4 prev.* Pietersburg. Limpopo, NE South Africa
Polonne *108 D2 Rus.* Polonnoye. Khmel'nyts'ka Oblast', NW Ukraine
Polonnoye *see* Polonne
Polotsk *see* Polatsk
Polska/Polska, Rzeczpospolita/ Polska Rzeczpospolita Ludowa *see* Poland
Polsko Kosovo *104 D2* Ruse, N Bulgaria
Poltava *109 F2* Poltavs'ka Oblast', NE Ukraine
Poltoratsk *see* Aşgabat
Põlva *106 E3 Ger.* Pölwe. Põlvamaa, SE Estonia
Pölwe *see* Põlva
Polyarnyy *110 C2* Murmanskaya Oblast', NW Russian Federation
Polýkastro *104 B3 var.* Polikastro; *prev.* Polikastron. Kentrikí Makedonía, N Greece
Polynesia *143 F4 island group* C Pacific Ocean
Pomeranian Bay *94 D2 Ger.* Pommersche Bucht, *Pol.* Zatoka Pomorska. *bay* Germany/Poland
Pomir, Dar"yoi *see* Pamir/Pāmir, Daryā-ye
Pommersche Bucht *see* Pomeranian Bay
Pomorska, Zatoka *see* Pomeranian Bay
Pomorskiy Proliv *110 D2 strait* NW Russian Federation
Pompaelo *see* Pamplona
Pompano Beach *43 F5* Florida, SE USA
Ponape Ascension Island *see* Pohnpei

Ponca City *49 G1* Oklahoma, C USA
Ponce *55 F3* C Puerto Rico
Pondicherry *132 C2 var.* Puducherri, *Fr.* Pondichéry. Pondicherry, SE India
Ponferrada *92 C1* Castilla-León, NW Spain
Poniatowa *98 E4* Lubelskie, E Poland
Pons Aelii *see* Newcastle upon Tyne
Pons Vetus *see* Pontevedra
Ponta Delgada *92 B5* São Miguel, Azores, Portugal, NE Atlantic Ocean
Ponta Grossa *63 E4* Paraná, S Brazil
Pontarlier *90 D4* Doubs, E France
Ponteareas *92 B2* Galicia, NW Spain
Ponte da Barca *92 B2* Viana do Castelo, N Portugal
Pontevedra *92 B1 anc.* Pons Vetus. Galicia, NW Spain
Pontiac *40 D3* Michigan, N USA
Pontianak *138 C4* Borneo, C Indonesia
Pontisarae *see* Pontoise
Pontivy *90 A3* Morbihan, NW France
Pontoise *90 C3 anc.* Briva Isarae, Cergy-Pontoise, Pontisarae. Val-d'Oise, N France
Ponziane, Isole *97 C5 island* C Italy
Poole *89 D7* S England, UK
Poona *see* Pune
Poopó, Lago *61 F4 var.* Lago Pampa Aullagas. *lake* W Bolivia
Popayán *58 B4* Cauca, SW Colombia
Poperinge *87 A6* West-Vlaanderen, W Belgium
Poplar Bluff *45 G5* Missouri, C USA
Popocatépetl *51 E4 volcano* S Mexico
Popper *see* Poprad
Poprad *99 D5 Ger.* Deutschendorf, *Hung.* Poprád. Prešovský Kraj, E Slovakia
Poprad *99 D5 Ger.* Popper, *Hung.* Poprád. *river* Poland/Slovakia
Porbandar *134 B4* Gujarāt, W India
Porcupine Plain *80 B3 undersea feature* E Atlantic Ocean
Pordenone *96 C2 anc.* Portenau. Friuli-Venezia Giulia, NE Italy
Poreč *100 A2 It.* Parenzo. Istra, NW Croatia
Porech'ye *see* Parechcha
Pori *85 D5 Swe.* Björneborg. Länsi-Soumi, SW Finland
Porirua *151 D5* Wellington, North Island, New Zealand
Porkhov *110 A4* Pskovskaya Oblast', W Russian Federation
Porlamar *59 E1* Nueva Esparta, NE Venezuela
Póros *105 C6* Póros, S Greece
Póros *105 A5* Kefallinía, Iónia Nisiá, Greece, C Mediterranean Sea
Pors *see* Porsangenfjorden
Porsangenfjorden *84 D2 Lapp.* Pors. *fjord* N Norway
Porsgrunn *85 B6* Telemark, S Norway
Portachuelo *61 G4* Santa Cruz, C Bolivia
Portadown *89 B5 Ir.* Port An Dúnáin. S Northern Ireland, UK
Portalegre *92 C3 anc.* Ammaia, Amoea. Portalegre, E Portugal
Port Alexander *36 D4* Baranof Island, Alaska, USA
Port Alfred *78 D5* Eastern Cape, S South Africa
Port Amelia *see* Pemba
Port An Dúnáin *see* Portadown
Port Angeles *46 B1* Washington, NW USA
Port Antonio *54 B5* NE Jamaica
Port Arthur *49 H4* Texas, SW USA
Port Augusta *149 B6* South Australia
Port-au-Prince *54 D3 country capital* (Haiti) C Haiti
Port Blair *133 F2* Andaman and Nicobar Islands, SE India
Port Charlotte *43 E4* Florida, SE USA
Port Darwin *see* Darwin
Port d'Envalira *91 B8* E Andorra Europe
Port Douglas *148 D3* Queensland, NE Australia
Port Elizabeth *78 C5* Eastern Cape, S South Africa
Portenau *see* Pordenone
Porterville *47 C7* California, W USA
Port-Étienne *see* Nouâdhibou
Port Florence *see* Kisumu
Port-Francqui *see* Ilebo

Port-Gentil 77 A6 Ogooué-Maritime, W Gabon
Port Harcourt 75 G5 Rivers, S Nigeria
Port Hardy 36 D5 Vancouver Island, British Columbia, SW Canada
Port Harrison see Inukjuak
Port Hedland 146 B4 Western Australia
Port Huron 40 D3 Michigan, N USA
Portimão 92 B4 var. Vila Nova de Portimão. Faro, S Portugal
Port Jackson 148 E1 harbour New South Wales, E Australia
Portland 149 B7 Victoria, SE Australia
Portland 41 G2 Maine, NE USA
Portland 46 B3 Oregon, NW USA
Portland 49 G4 Texas, SW USA
Portland Bight 54 B5 bay S Jamaica
Portlaoighise see Port Laoise
Port Laoise 89 B6 var. Portlaoise, Ir. Portlaoighíse; prev. Maryborough. C Ireland
Portlaoise see Port Laoise
Port Lavaca 49 G4 Texas, SW USA
Port Lincoln 149 A6 South Australia
Port Louis 79 H3 country capital (Mauritius) NW Mauritius
Port-Lyautey see Kénitra
Port Macquarie 149 E6 New South Wales, SE Australia
Port Mahon see Mahón
Portmore 54 B5 C Jamaica
Port Moresby 144 B3 country capital (Papua New Guinea) Central/National Capital District, SW Papua New Guinea
Port Musgrave 149 B9 bay Queensland, N Australia Pacific Ocean Arafua Sea Gulf of Carpentaria
Port Natal see Durban
Porto 92 B2 Eng. Oporto; anc. Portus Cale. Porto, NW Portugal
Porto Alegre 63 E5 var. Pôrto Alegre. state capital Rio Grande do Sul, S Brazil
Porto Alegre 76 E2 São Tomé, S Sao Tome and Principe, Africa
Porto Alexandre see Tombua
Porto Amélia see Pemba
Porto Bello see Portobelo
Portobelo 53 G4 var. Porto Bello, Puerto Bello. Colón, N Panama
Port O'Connor 49 G4 Texas, SW USA
Porto Edda see Sarandë
Portoferraio 96 B4 Toscana, C Italy
Port-of-Spain 55 H5 country capital (Trinidad and Tobago) Trinidad, Trinidad and Tobago
Porto Grande see Mindelo
Portogruaro 96 C2 Veneto, NE Italy
Porto-Novo 75 F5 country capital (Benin) S Benin
Porto Rico see Puerto Rico
Porto Santo 70 A2 var. Ilha do Porto Santo. island Madeira, Portugal, NE Atlantic Ocean
Porto Santo, Ilha do see Porto Santo
Port Sudan 72 C3 Red Sea, NE Sudan
Porto Torres 97 A5 Sardegna, Italy, C Mediterranean Sea
Porto Velho 62 D2 var. Velho. state capital Rondônia, W Brazil
Portoviejo 60 A2 var. Puertoviejo. Manabí, W Ecuador
Port Pirie 149 B6 South Australia
Port Rex see East London
Port Said 72 B1 Ar. Būr Saʿīd. N Egypt
Portsmouth 89 D7 S England, UK
Portsmouth 41 G3 New Hampshire, NE USA
Portsmouth 40 D4 Ohio, N USA
Portsmouth 41 F5 Virginia, NE USA
Port Stanley see Stanley
Port Swettenham see Klang/Pelabuhan Klang
Port Talbot 89 C7 S Wales, UK
Portugal 92 B3 off. Republic of Portugal. country SW Europe

PORTUGAL
(continued)

OReligions Roman Catholic 97%, Other 2%, Protestant 1%
Ethnic mix Portuguese 98%, African and other 2%
Government Parliamentary system
Currency Euro = 100 cents
Literacy rate 93%
Calorie consumption 3741 calories

Portugal, Republic of see Portugal
Portuguese East Africa see Mozambique
Portuguese Guinea see Guinea-Bissau
Portuguese Timor see East Timor
Portuguese West Africa see Angola
Portus Cale see Porto
Portus Magnus see Almería
Portus Magonis see Mahón
Port-Vila 144 D4 var. Vila. country capital (Vanuatu) Éfaté, C Vanuatu
Porvenir 61 E3 Pando, NW Bolivia
Porvenir 65 B8 Magallanes, S Chile
Porvoo 85 E6 Swe. Borgå. Etelä-Suomi, S Finland
Porzecze see Parechcha
Posadas 64 D3 Misiones, NE Argentina
Poschega see Požega
Posen see Poznań
Posnania see Poznań
Postavy/Postawy see Pastavy
Posterholt 87 D5 Limburg, SE Netherlands
Postojna 95 D8 Ger. Adelsberg, It. Postumia. SW Slovenia
Postumia see Postojna
Pöstyén see Piešt'any
Potamós 105 C7 Antikýthira, S Greece
Potentia see Potenza
Potenza 97 D5 anc. Potentia. Basilicata, S Italy
P'ot'i 117 F2 W Georgia
Potiskum 75 G4 Yobe, NE Nigeria
Potomac River 41 E5 river NE USA
Potosí 61 F4 Potosí, S Bolivia
Potsdam 94 D3 Brandenburg, NE Germany
Potwar Plateau 134 C2 plateau NE Pakistan
Poŭthisăt 137 D6 prev. Pursat. Poŭthisăt, W Cambodia
Po, Valley of the see Po Valley
Po Valley 96 C2 It. Valle del Po. valley N Italy
Považská Bystrica 99 C5 Ger. Waagbistritz, Hung. Vágbeszterce. Trenčiansky Kraj, W Slovakia
Poverty Bay 150 E4 inlet North Island, New Zealand
Póvoa de Varzim 92 B2 Porto, NW Portugal
Powder River 44 D2 river Montana/Wyoming, NW USA
Powell 44 C2 Wyoming, C USA
Powell, Lake 44 B5 lake Utah, W USA
Požarevac 100 D4 Ger. Passarowitz. Serbia, NE Serbia
Poza Rica 51 F4 var. Poza Rica de Hidalgo. Veracruz-Llave, E Mexico
Poza Rica de Hidalgo see Poza Rica
Požega 100 D4 prev. Slavonska Požega, Ger. Poschega, Hung. Pozsega. Požega-Slavonija, NE Croatia
Poznań 98 C3 Ger. Posen, Posnania. Wielkopolskie, C Poland
Pozoblanco 92 D4 Andalucía, S Spain
Pozsega see Požega
Pozsony see Bratislava
Pozzallo 97 C8 Sicilia, Italy, C Mediterranean Sea
Prachatice 99 A5 Ger. Prachatitz. Jihočeský Kraj, S Czech Republic
Prachatitz see Prachatice
Prado del Ganso see Goose Green
Prae see Phrae
Prag/Praga/Prague see Praha
Prague 80 D3 Oklahoma, C USA
Praha 99 A5 Eng. Prague, Ger. Prag, Pol. Praga. country capital (Czech Republic) Středočeský Kraj, NW Czech Republic
Praia 74 A3 country capital (Cape Verde) Santiago, S Cape Verde
Prairie State see Illinois

PORTUGAL
Southwest Europe

Official name Republic of Portugal
Formation 1139 / 1640
Capital Lisbon
Population 10.5 million / 296 people per sq mile (114 people per sq km) / 64%
Total area 35,672 sq miles (92,391 sq km)
Languages Portuguese

Prathet Thai see Thailand
Prato 96 B3 Toscana, C Italy
Pratt 45 E5 Kansas, C USA
Prattville 42 D2 Alabama, S USA
Pravda 104 D1 prev. Dogrular. Silistra, NE Bulgaria
Pravia 92 C1 Asturias, N Spain
Preny see Prienai
Prenzlau 94 D3 Brandenburg, NE Germany
Prerau see Přerov
Přerov 99 C5 Ger. Prerau. Olomoucký Kraj, E Czech Republic
Preschau see Prešov
Prescott 48 B2 Arizona, SW USA
Preševo 101 D5 Serbia, SE Serbia
Presidente Epitácio 63 E4 São Paulo, S Brazil
Presidente Stroessner see Ciudad del Este
Prešov 99 D5 var. Preschau, Ger. Eperies, Hung. Eperjes. Prešovský Kraj, E Slovakia
Prespa, Lake 101 D6 Alb. Liqen i Prespës, Gk. Límni Megáli Préspa, Límni Prespa, Mac. Prespansko Ezero, Serb. Prespansko Jezero. lake SE Europe
Prespa, Limni/Prespansko Ezero/ Prespansko Jezero/Prespës, Liqen i see Prespa, Lake
Presque Isle 41 H1 Maine, NE USA
Pressburg see Bratislava
Preston 89 D5 NW England, UK
Prestwick 88 C4 W Scotland, UK
Pretoria see Tshwane
Preussisch Eylau see Bagrationovsk
Preußisch Holland see Pasłęk
Preussisch-Stargard see Starogard Gdański
Préveza 105 A5 Ípeiros, W Greece
Pribilof Islands 36 A3 island group Alaska, USA
Priboj 100 D4 Serbia, W Serbia
Price 44 B4 Utah, W USA
Prichard 42 C3 Alabama, S USA
Priekule 106 B3 Ger. Prökuls. Klaipėda, W Lithuania
Prienai 107 B5 Pol. Preny. Kaunas, S Lithuania
Prieska 78 C4 Northern Cape, C South Africa
Prijedor 100 B3 Republika Srpska, NW Bosnia and Herzegovina
Prijepolje 100 D4 Serbia, W Serbia
Prikaspiyskaya Nizmennost' see Caspian Depression
Prilep 101 D6 Turk. Perlepe. S FYR Macedonia
Priluki see Pryluky
Primorsk 106 A4 Ger. Fischhausen. Kaliningradskaya Oblast', W Russian Federation
Primorsko 104 E2 prev. Keupriya. Burgas, E Bulgaria
Primorsk/Primorskoye see Prymors'k
Prince Albert 37 F5 Saskatchewan, S Canada
Prince Edward Island 39 F4 Fr. Île-du Prince-Édouard. province SE Canada
Prince Edward Islands 69 E8 island group S South Africa
Prince George 37 E5 British Columbia, SW Canada
Prince of Wales Island 148 B1 island Queensland, E Australia
Prince of Wales Island 37 F2 island Queen Elizabeth Islands, Nunavut, NW Canada
Prince of Wales Island see Pinang, Pulau
Prince Patrick Island 37 E2 island Parry Islands, Northwest Territories, NW Canada
Prince Rupert 36 D4 British Columbia, SW Canada
Prince's Island see Príncipe
Princess Charlotte Bay 148 C2 bay Queensland, NE Australia
Princess Elizabeth Land 154 C3 physical region Antarctica
Príncipe 77 A5 var. Príncipe Island, Eng. Prince's Island. island N Sao Tome and Principe
Príncipe Island see Príncipe
Prinzapolka 53 E3 Región Autónoma Atlántico Norte, NE Nicaragua
Pripet 107 C7 Bel. Prypyats', Ukr. Pryp"yat'. river Belarus/Ukraine

Pripet Marshes 107 B7 forested and swampy region Belarus/Ukraine
Prishtinë see Priština
Priština 101 D5 Alb. Prishtinë. Kosovo, S Serbia
Privas 91 D5 Ardèche, E France
Privolzhskaya Vozvyshennost' 81 G3 var. Volga Uplands. mountain range W Russian Federation
Prizren 101 D5 Alb. Prizreni. Kosovo, S Serbia
Prizreni see Prizren
Probolinggo 138 D5 Jawa, C Indonesia
Probstberg see Wyszków
Progreso 51 H3 Yucatán, SE Mexico
Prokhladnyy 111 B8 Kabardino-Balkarskaya Respublika, SW Russian Federation
Prokletije see North Albanian Alps
Prökuls see Priekulė
Prokuplje 101 D5 Serbia, SE Serbia
Prome 136 B4 var. Pyè. Pegu, C Myanmar (Burma)
Promyshlennyy 110 E3 Respublika Komi, NW Russian Federation
Proscieskoye see Prościejów
Proskurov see Khmel 'nyts'kyy
Prossnitz see Prostějov
Prostějov 99 C5 Ger. Prossnitz, Pol. Prościejów. Olomoucký Kraj, E Czech Republic
Provence 91 D6 cultural region SE France
Providence 41 G3 state capital Rhode Island, NE USA
Providence see Fort Providence
Providencia, Isla de 53 F3 island NW Colombia South America
Providenya 172 B1 Chukotskiy Avtonomnyy Okrug, NE Russian Federation
Provo 44 B4 Utah, W USA
Prudhoe Bay 36 D2 Alaska, USA
Prusa see Bursa
Pruszków 98 D3 Ger. Kaltdorf. Mazowieckie, C Poland
Prut 108 D4 Ger. Pruth. river E Europe
Pruth see Prut
Pružana see Pruzhany
Pruzhany 107 B6 Pol. Prużana. Brestskaya Voblasts', SW Belarus
Prychornomor'ska Nyzovyna see Black Sea Lowland
Prydniprovs'ka Nyzovyna/ Prydnyaprowskaya Nizina see Dnieper Lowland
Prydz Bay 154 D3 bay Antarctica
Pryluky 109 F2 Rus. Priluki. Chernihivs'ka Oblast', NE Ukraine
Prymors'k 109 G4 Rus. Primorsk; prev. Primorskoye. Zaporiz'ka Oblast', SE Ukraine
Pryp"yat'/Prypyats' see Pripet
Przemyśl 99 E5 Rus. Peremyshl. Podkarpackie, C Poland
Przhevalsk see Karakol
Psará 105 D5 island E Greece
Psël 109 F2 river Russian Federation/Ukraine
Pskov 114 B2 Ger. Pleskau, Latv. Pleskava. Pskovskaya Oblast', W Russian Federation
Pskov, Lake 84 E3 Est. Pihkva Järv, Ger. Pleskauer See, Rus. Pskovskoye Ozero. lake Estonia/Russian Federation
Pskovskoye Ozero see Pskov, Lake
Ptich' see Ptsich
Ptich 107 C7 Rus. Ptich'. Homyel'skaya Voblasts', SE Belarus
Ptsich 107 C7 Rus. Ptich'. river SE Belarus
Ptuj 95 E7 Ger. Pettau; anc. Poetovio. NE Slovenia
Pucallpa 60 C3 Ucayali, C Peru
Puck 98 C2 Pomorskie, N Poland
Pudasjärvi 84 D4 Oulu, C Finland
Puebla 51 F4 var. Puebla de Zaragoza. Puebla, S Mexico
Puebla de Zaragoza see Puebla
Pueblo 44 D5 Colorado, C USA
Puerto Acosta 61 E4 La Paz, W Bolivia
Puerto Ángel 51 F5 Oaxaca, SE Mexico
Puerto Argentino see Stanley
Puerto Ayacucho 58 D3 Amazonas, SW Venezuela

Puerto Baquerizo Moreno 60 B5 *var.*
  Baquerizo Moreno. Galapagos Islands,
  Ecuador, E Pacific Ocean
Puerto Barrios 52 C2 Izabal,
  E Guatemala
Puerto Bello *see* Portobelo
Puerto Berrío 58 B2 Antioquia,
  C Colombia
Puerto Cabello 58 D1 Carabobo,
  N Venezuela
Puerto Cabezas 53 E2 *var.* Bilwi.
  Región Autónoma Atlántico Norte,
  NE Nicaragua
Puerto Carreño 58 D3 Vichada,
  E Colombia
Puerto Cortés 52 C2 Cortés,
  NW Honduras
Puerto Cumarebo 58 C1 Falcón,
  N Venezuela
Puerto Deseado 65 C7 Santa Cruz,
  SE Argentina
Puerto Escondido 51 F5 Oaxaca,
  SE Mexico
Puerto Francisco de Orellana 60 B1
  var. Coca. Orellana, N Ecuador
Puerto Gallegos *see* Río Gallegos
Puerto Inírida 58 D3 *var.* Obando.
  Guainía, E Colombia
Puerto La Cruz 59 E1 Anzoátegui,
  NE Venezuela
Puerto Lempira 53 E2 Gracias a Dios,
  E Honduras
Puerto Limón *see* Limón
Puertollano 92 D4 Castilla-La Mancha,
  C Spain
Puerto López 58 C1 La Guajira,
  N Colombia
Puerto Maldonado 61 E3 Madre de
  Dios, E Peru
Puerto México *see* Coatzacoalcos
Puerto Montt 65 B5 Los Lagos, C Chile
Puerto Natales 65 B7 Magallanes,
  S Chile
Puerto Obaldía 53 H5 San Blas,
  NE Panama
Puerto Plata 55 E3 *var.* San Felipe de
  Puerto Plata. N Dominican Republic
Puerto Presidente Stroessner *see* Ciudad
  del Este
Puerto Princesa 139 E2 *off.* Puerto
  Princesa City. Palawan, W Philippines
Puerto Princesa City *see* Puerto Princesa
Puerto Príncipe *see* Camagüey
Puerto Rico 55 F3 *off.* Commonwealth
  of Puerto Rico; *prev.* Porto Rico. *US
  commonwealth territory* C West Indies
Puerto Rico 56 B1 *island* C West Indies
Puerto Rico, Commonwealth of *see*
  Puerto Rico
Puerto Rico Trench 56 B1 *trench*
  NE Caribbean Sea
Puerto San José *see* San José
Puerto San Julián 65 B7 *var.* San Julián.
  Santa Cruz, SE Argentina
Puerto Suárez 61 H4 Santa Cruz,
  E Bolivia
Puerto Vallarta 50 D4 Jalisco,
  SW Mexico
Puerto Varas 65 B5 Los Lagos, C Chile
Puerto Viejo 53 E4 Heredia, NE Costa
  Rica
Puertoviejo *see* Portoviejo
Puget Sound 46 B1 *sound* Washington,
  NW USA
Puglia 97 E5 *var.* Le Puglie, *Eng.* Apulia.
  region SE Italy
Pukaki, Lake 151 B6 *lake* South Island,
  New Zealand
Pukekohe 150 D3 Auckland, North
  Island, New Zealand
Puket *see* Phuket
Pukhavichy 107 C6 *Rus.* Pukhovichi.
  Minskaya Voblasts', C Belarus
Pukhovichi *see* Pukhavichy
Pula 100 A3 *It.* Pola; *prev.* Pulj. Istra,
  NW Croatia
Pulaski 40 D5 Virginia, NE USA
Puławy 98 D4 *Ger.* Neu Amerika.
  Lubelskie, E Poland
Pul-i-Khumri *see* Pol-e Khomrī
Pulj *see* Pula
Pullman 46 C2 Washington, NW USA
Pułtusk 98 D3 Mazowieckie, C Poland
Puná, Isla 60 A2 *island* SW Ecuador
Pune 134 C5 *prev.* Poona. Mahārāshtra,
  W India
Punjab 134 C2 *prev.* West Punjab,
  Western Punjab. *province* E Pakistan

Puno 61 E4 Puno, SE Peru
Punta Alta 65 C5 Buenos Aires,
  E Argentina
Punta Arenas 65 B8 *prev.* Magallanes.
  Magallanes, S Chile
Punta Gorda 52 C2 Toledo, SE Belize
Punta Gorda 53 E4 Región Autónoma
  Atlántico Sur, SE Nicaragua
Puntarenas 52 D4 Puntarenas, W Costa
  Rica
Punto Fijo 58 C1 Falcón, N Venezuela
Pupuya, Nevado 61 E4 *mountain*
  W Bolivia
Puri 135 F5 *var.* Jagannath. Orissa,
  E India
Puriramya *see* Buriram
Purmerend 86 C3 Noord-Holland,
  C Netherlands
Pursat *see* Poŭthĭsăt, Poŭthĭsăt, W
  Cambodia
Purus, Rio 62 C2 *var.* Río Purús. *river*
  Brazil/Peru
Pusan 129 E4 *off.* Pusan-gwangyŏksi, *var.*
  Busan, *Jap.* Fusan. SE South Korea
Pusan-gwangyŏksi *see* Pusan
Pushkino *see* Bilǎsuvar
Püspökladány 99 D6 Hajdú-Bihar,
  E Hungary
Putorana, Gory/Putorana Mountains
  see Putorana, Plato
Putorana, Plato 114 D3 *var.* Gory
  Putorana, *Eng.* Putorana Mountains.
  mountain range N Russian Federation
Putrajaya 138 B3 *country capital*
  (Malaysia) Kuala Lumpur, Peninsular
  Malaysia
Puttalam 132 C3 North Western
  Province, W Sri Lanka
Puttgarden 94 C2 Schleswig-Holstein,
  N Germany
Putumayo, Río 58 B5 *var.* Içá, Río. *river*
  NW South America
Putumayo, Río *see* Içá, Rio
Puurmani 106 D2 *Ger.* Talkhof.
  Jõgevamaa, E Estonia
Pyatigorsk 111 B7 Stavropol'skiy Kray,
  SW Russian Federation
Pyatikhatki *see* P"yatykhatky
P"yatykhatky 109 F3 *Rus.* Pyatikhatki.
  Dnipropetrovs'ka Oblast', E Ukraine
Pyè *see* Prome
Pyetrykaw 107 C7 *Rus.* Petrikov.
  Homyel'skaya Voblasts', SE Belarus
Pýlos 105 B6 *var.* Pilos. Pelopónnisos,
  S Greece
Pyritz *see* Pyrzyce
P'yŏngyang 129 E3 *var.* P'yŏngyang-si,
  Eng. Pyongyang. *country capital*
  (North Korea) SW North Korea
P'yŏngyang-si *see* P'yŏngyang
Pyramid Lake 47 C5 *lake* Nevada,
  W USA
Pyrenaei Montes *see* Pyrenees
Pyrenees 102 B2 *Fr.* Pyrénées, *Sp.*
  Pirineos; *anc.* Pyrenaei Montes.
  mountain range SW Europe
Pýrgos 105 B6 *var.* Pírgos. Dytikí Ellás,
  S Greece
Pyritz *see* Pyrzyce
Pyryatyn 109 E2 *Rus.* Piryatin.
  Poltavs'ka Oblast', NE Ukraine
Pyrzyce 98 B3 *Ger.* Pyritz. Zachodnio-
  pomorskie, NW Poland
Pyu 136 B4 Pegu, C Myanmar (Burma)
Pyuntaza 136 B4 Pegu,
  SW Myanmar (Burma)

Q

Qā' al Jafr 119 C7 *lake* S Jordan
Qaanaaq 82 D1 *var.* Qânâq, *Dan.* Thule.
  Avannaarsua, N Greenland
Qabātiya 119 E6 N West Bank Asia
Qābis *see* Gabès
Qābis, Khalīj *see* Gabès, Golfe de
Qacentina *see* Constantine
Qafṣah *see* Gafsa
Qagan Us *see* Dulan
Qahremānshahr *see* Kermānshāh
Qaidam Pendi 126 C4 *basin* C China
Qal'aikhum 123 F3 *Rus.* Kalaikhum.
  S Tajikistan
Qalāt 123 E5 *Per.* Kalāt. Zābol,
  S Afghanistan
Qal'at Bīshah 121 B5 'Asīr, SW Saudi
  Arabia
Qalqīlya 119 D6 Central, W West
  Bank Asia

Qamdo 126 D5 Xizang Zizhiqu, W China
Qamishly *see* Al Qāmishlī
Qânâq *see* Qaanaaq
Qaqortoq 82 C4 *Dan.* Julianehåb.
  Kitaa, S Greenland
Qaraghandy/Qaraghandy Oblysy *see*
  Karaganda
Qara Qum *see* Garagum
Qarataū *see* Karatau, Zhambyl,
  Kazakhstan
Qarkilik *see* Ruoqiang
Qarokŭl 123 F3 *Rus.* Karakul'.
  E Tajikistan
Qarqannah, Juzur *see* Kerkenah, Îles de
Qars *see* Kars
Qarshi 123 E3 *Rus.* Karshi; *prev.*
  Bek-Budi. Qashqadaryo Viloyati,
  S Uzbekistan
Qasigiannguit *see* Qasigiannguit
Qasigiannguit 82 C3 *var.* Qasigianguit,
  Dan. Christianshåb. Kitaa,
  C Greenland
Qasr Farâfra 72 B2 W Egypt
Qaṣr al-Farāfra *see* Qasr Farâfra
Qaṭanā 119 B5 *var.* Katana. Dimashq,
  S Syria
Qatar 120 C4 *off.* State of Qatar, *Ar.*
  Dawlat Qatar. *country* SW Asia

QATAR
Southwest Asia

Official name	State of Qatar
Formation	1971 / 1971
Capital	Doha
Population	813,000 / 191 people per sq mile
	(74 people per sq km) / 93%
Total area	4416 sq miles (11,437 sq km)
Languages	Arabic*
Religions	Muslim (mainly Sunni) 95%, Other 5%
Ethnic mix	Arab 40%, Indian 18%, Pakistani 18%, Other 14%, Iranian 10%
Government	Monarchy
Currency	Qatar riyal = 100 dirhams
Literacy rate	89%
Calorie consumption	Not available

Qatar, State of *see* Qatar
**Qattara Depression/Qaṭṭārah,
  Munkhafaḍ al** *see* Qaṭṭāra,
  Monkhafad el
Qaṭṭāra, Monkhafad el 88 A1 *var.*
  Munkhafaḍ al Qaṭṭārah, *Eng.* Qattara
  Depression. *desert* NW Egypt
Qausuittuq *see* Resolute
Qazaqstan/Qazaqstan Respublikasy
  see Kazakhstan
Qazimāmmād 117 H3 *Rus.* Kazi
  Magomed. SE Azerbaijan
Qazris *see* Cáceres
Qazvīn 120 C2 *var.* Kazvin. Qazvīn,
  N Iran
Qena 72 B2 *var.* Qinā; *anc.* Caene,
  Caenepolis. E Egypt
Qeqertarssuaq *see* Qeqertarsuaq
Qeqertarsuaq 82 C3 *var.* Qeqertarssuaq,
  Dan. Godhavn. Kitaa, S Greenland
Qeqertarsuaq 82 C3 *island*
  W Greenland
Qeqertarsuup Tunua 82 C3 *Dan.* Disko
  Bugt. *inlet* W Greenland
Qerveh *see* Qorveh
Qeshm 120 D4 *var.* Jazireh-ye Qeshm,
  Qeshm Island. *island* S Iran
Qeshm Island/Qeshm, Jazīreh-ye
  see Qeshm
Qilian Shan 126 D3 *var.* Kilien
  Mountains. *mountain range* N China
Qimusseriarsuaq 82 C2
  Dan. Melville Bugt, *Eng.* Melville Bay.
  bay NW Greenland
Qinā *see* Qena
Qing *see* Qinghai
Qingdao 128 D4 *var.* Ching-Tao,
  Ch'ing-tao, Tsingtao, Tsintao, *Ger.*
  Tsingtau. Shandong, E China
Qinghai 126 C4 *var.* Chinghai, Koko
  Nor, Qing, Qinghai Sheng, Tsinghai.
  province C China
Qinghai Hu 126 C4 *var.* Ch'ing Hai,
  Tsing Hai, *Mong.* Koko Nor. *lake*
  C China
Qinghai Sheng *see* Qinghai
Qingzang Gaoyuan 126 B4 *var.* Xizang
  Gaoyuan, *Eng.* Plateau of Tibet.
  plateau W China
Qinhuangdao 128 D3 Hebei, E China

Qinzhou 128 B6 Guangxi Zhuangzu
  Zizhiqu, S China
Qiong *see* Hainan
Qiqihar 128 D2 *var.* Ch'i-ch'i-ha-
  erh, Tsitsihar; *prev.* Lungkiang.
  Heilongjiang, NE China
Qira 126 B4 Xinjiang Uygur Zizhiqu,
  NW China
Qita Ghazzah *see* Gaza Strip
Qitai 126 C3 Xinjiang Uygur Zizhiqu,
  NW China
Qīzān *see* Jīzān
Qizil Orda *see* Kyzylorda
Qizil Qum/Qizilqum *see* Kyzyl Kum
Qizilrabot 123 G3 *Rus.* Kyzylrabot.
  SE Tajikistan
Qogir Feng *see* K2
Qom 120 C3 *var.* Kum, Qum, Qom,
  N Iran
Qomolangma Feng *see* Everest, Mount
Qomul *see* Hami
Qo'qon 123 F2 *var.* Khokand,
  Rus. Kokand. Farg'ona Voliyati,
  E Uzbekistan
Qorveh 120 C3 *var.* Qerveh, Qurveh.
  Kordestān, W Iran
Qostanay/Qostanay Oblysy *see*
  Kostanay
Qoubaïyât 118 B4 *var.* Al Qubayyät.
  N Lebanon
Qoussantina *see* Constantine
Quang Ngai 137 E5 *var.* Quangngai,
  Quang Nghia. Quang Ngai,
  C Vietnam
Quangngai *see* Quang Ngai
Quang Nghia *see* Quang Ngai
Quan Long *see* Ca Mau
Quanzhou 128 D6 *var.* Ch'uan-chou,
  Tsinkiang; *prev.* Chin-chiang. Fujian,
  SE China
Quanzhou 128 C6 Guangxi Zhuangzu
  Zizhiqu, S China
Qu'Appelle 37 F5 *river* Saskatchewan,
  S Canada
Quarles, Pegunungan 139 E4 *mountain
  range* Sulawesi, C Indonesia
Quarnero *see* Kvarner
Quartu Sant' Elena 97 A6 Sardegna,
  Italy, C Mediterranean Sea
Quba 117 H2 Rus. Kuba.
  N Azerbaijan
Qubba *see* Ba'qūbah
Québec 39 E4 *var.* Quebec. *province
  capital* Québec, SE Canada
Québec 38 D3 *var.* Quebec. *province*
  SE Canada
Queen Charlotte Islands 36 C5
  Fr. Îles de la Reine-Charlotte. *island
  group* British Columbia, SW Canada
Queen Charlotte Sound 36 C5 *sea area*
  British Columbia, W Canada
Queen Elizabeth Islands 37 E1
  Fr. Îles de la Reine-Elisabeth. *island
  group* Nunavut, N Canada
Queensland 148 B4 *state* N Australia
Queenstown 151 B7 Otago, South Island,
  New Zealand
Queenstown 78 D5 Eastern Cape,
  S South Africa
Quelimane 79 E3 *var.* Kilimane,
  Kilmain, Quilimane. Zambézia,
  NE Mozambique
Quelpart *see* Cheju-do
Quepos 53 E4 Puntarenas, S Costa Rica
Que Que *see* Kwekwe
Quera *see* Chur
Querétaro 51 E4 Querétaro de Arteaga,
  C Mexico
Quesada 53 E4 *var.* Ciudad Quesada,
  San Carlos. Alajuela, N Costa Rica
Quetta 134 B2 Baluchistān, SW Pakistan
Quetzalcoalco *see* Coatzacoalcos
Quezaltenango 52 A2 *var.*
  Quetzaltenango. Quezaltenango,
  W Guatemala
Quibdó 58 A3 Chocó, W Colombia
Quilimane *see* Quelimane
Quillabamba 60 D3 Cusco, C Peru
Quilon 132 C3 *var.* Kolam, Kollam.
  Kerala, SW India
Quimper 90 A3 *anc.* Quimper Corentin.
  Finistère, NW France
Quimper Corentin *see* Quimper
Quimperlé 90 A3 Finistère, NW France
Quincy 40 A4 Illinois, N USA
Qui Nhon/Quinhon *see* Quy Nhơn
Quissico 79 E4 Inhambane,
  S Mozambique

Quito *60 B1 country capital* (Ecuador) Pichincha, N Ecuador
Qulyndy Zhazyghy *see* Kulunda Steppe
Qum *see* Qom
Qurein *see* Al Kuwayt
Qūrghonteppa *123 E3 Rus.* Kurgan-Tyube. SW Tajikistan
Qurlurtuuq *see* Kugluktuk
Qurveh *see* Qorveh
Quşayr *see* Al Quşayr
Quxar *see* Lhazê
Quy Nhơn *137 E5 var.* Quinhon, Qui Nhon. Bình Định, C Vietnam
Qyteti Stalin *see* Kuçovë
Qyzylorda/Qyzylorda Oblysy *see* Kyzylorda

R

Raab *100 B1 river* Austria/Hungary
Raab *see* Rába
Raab *see* Győr
Raahe *84 D4 Swe.* Brahestad. Oulu, W Finland
Raalte *86 D3* Overijssel, E Netherlands
Raamsdonksveer *86 C4* Noord-Brabant, S Netherlands
Raasiku *106 D2 Ger.* Rasik. Harjumaa, NW Estonia
Rába *99 B7 Ger.* Raab. *river* Austria/Hungary
Rabat *70 C2 var.* al Dar al Baida. *country capital* (Morocco) NW Morocco
Rabat *102 B5* W Malta
Rabat *see* Victoria
Rabbah Ammon/Rabbath Ammon *see* 'Ammān
Rabinal *52 B2* Baja Verapaz, C Guatemala
Rabka *99 D5* Małopolskie, S Poland
Râbniţa *see* Rîbniţa
Rabyānah, Ramlat *71 G4 var.* Rebiana Sand Sea, Şaḩrāʾ Rabyānah. *desert* SE Libya
Rabyānah, Şaḩrāʾ *see* Rabyānah, Ramlat
Răcari *see* Durankulak
Race, Cape *39 H3 cape* Newfoundland, Newfoundland and Labrador, E Canada
Rach Gia *137 D6* Kiên Giang, S Vietnam
Rach Gia, Vinh *137 D6 bay* S Vietnam
Racine *40 B3* Wisconsin, N USA
Rácz-Becse *see* Bečej
Rădăuţi *108 C3 Ger.* Radautz, *Hung.* Rádóc. Suceava, N Romania
Radautz *see* Rădăuţi
Rádóc *see* Rădăuţi
Radom *98 D4* Mazowieckie, C Poland
Radomsko *98 D4 Rus.* Novoradomsk. Łódzkie, C Poland
Radomyshl' *108 D2* Zhytomyrs'ka Oblast', N Ukraine
Radoviš *101 E6 prev.* Radovište. E Macedonia
Radovište *see* Radoviš
Radviliškis *106 B4* Šiauliai, N Lithuania
Radzyń Podlaski *98 E4* Lubelskie, E Poland
Rae-Edzo *see* Edzo
Raetihi *150 D4* Manawatu-Wanganui, North Island, New Zealand
Rafa *see* Rafah
Rafaela *64 C3* Santa Fe, E Argentina
Rafah *119 A7 var.* Rafa, Rafaḥ, *Heb.* Rafiaḥ, *var.* Raphiah. SW Gaza Strip
Rafaḥ *see* Rafah
Rafiaḥ *see* Rafah
Raga *73 A5* Western Bahr el Ghazal, SW Sudan
Ragged Island Range *54 C2 island group* S Bahamas
Ragnit *see* Neman
Ragusa *97 C7* Sicilia, Italy, C Mediterranean Sea
Ragusa *see* Dubrovnik
Rahachow *107 D7 Rus.* Rogachëv. Homyel'skaya Voblasts', SE Belarus
Rahaeng *see* Tak
Rahaţ, Ḩarrat *121 B5 lava flow* W Saudi Arabia
Rahīmyār Khān *134 C3* Punjab, SE Pakistan

Rāichūr *132 C1* Karnātaka, C India
Raidestos *see* Tekirdağ
Rainier, Mount *34 A4 volcano* Washington, NW USA
Rainy Lake *38 A4 lake* Canada/USA
Raipur *135 E4* Chhattisgarh, C India
Rājahmundry *135 E5* Andhra Pradesh, E India
Rajang *see* Rajang, Batang
Rajang, Batang *138 D3 var.* Rajang. *river* East Malaysia
Rājapālaiyam *132 C3* Tamil Nādu, SE India
Rājasthān *134 C3 state* NW India
Rājasthān *134 C3 cultural region* NW India
Rājkot *134 C4* Gujarāt, W India
Rāj Nāndgaon *135 E4* Chhattisgarh, C India
Rajshahi *135 G3 prev.* Rampur Boalia. Rajshahi, W Bangladesh
Rakahanga *145 F3 atoll* N Cook Islands
Rakaia *151 B6 river* South Island, New Zealand
Rakka *see* Ar Raqqah
Rakke *106 E2* Lääne-Virumaa, NE Estonia
Rakvere *106 E2 Ger.* Wesenberg. Lääne-Virumaa, N Estonia
Ralik Chain *144 D1 island group* Ralik Chain, W Marshall Islands
Ramadi *see* Ar Ramādī
Râmnicul-Sărat *see* Râmnicu Sărat
Râmnicu Sărat *108 C4 prev.* Râmnicul-Sărat, Rîmnicu-Sărat. Buzău, E Romania
Râmnicu Vâlcea *108 B4 prev.* Rîmnicu Vîlcea. Vâlcea, C Romania
Rampur Boalia *see* Rajshahi
Ramree Island *136 A4 island* W Myanmar (Burma)
Ramtha *see* Ar Ramthā
Rancagua *64 B4* Libertador, C Chile
Rānchī *135 F4* Jhārkhand, N India
Randers *85 B7* Århus, C Denmark
Rånes *see* Ringvassøya
Rangiora *151 B6* Canterbury, South Island, New Zealand
Rangitikei *150 D4 river* North Island, New Zealand
Rangoon *see* Yangon
Rangpur *135 G3* Rajshahi, N Bangladesh
Rankin Inlet *37 G3* Nunavut, C Canada
Rankovićevo *see* Kraljevo
Ranong *137 B6* Ranong, SW Thailand
Rapa Nui *see* Pascua, Isla de
Raphiah *see* Rafah
Rapid City *44 D3* South Dakota, N USA
Räpina *106 E3 Ger.* Rappin. Põlvamaa, SE Estonia
Rapla *106 D2 Ger.* Rappel. Raplamaa, NW Estonia
Rappel *see* Rapla
Rappin *see* Räpina
Rarotonga *145 G5 island* S Cook Islands, C Pacific Ocean
Ras al'Ayn *see* Ra's al 'Ayn
Ra's al 'Ayn *118 D1 var.* Ras al 'Ain. Al Ḩasakah, N Syria
Ra's an Naqb *119 B7* Ma'ān, S Jordan
Raseiniai *106 B4* Kaunas, C Lithuania
Rasht *120 C2 var.* Resht. Gīlān, NW Iran
Rasik *see* Raasiku
Râşnov *108 C4 prev.* Rişno, Rozsnyó, *Hung.* Barcarozsnyó. Braşov, C Romania
Rastenburg *see* Kętrzyn
Ratak Chain *144 D1 island group* Ratak Chain, E Marshall Islands
Ratan *85 C5* Jämtland, C Sweden
Rat Buri *see* Ratchaburi
Ratchaburi *137 C5 var.* Rat Buri. Ratchaburi, W Thailand
Ratibor/Ratisbona/Ratisbonne *see* Regensburg
Rat Islands *36 A2 island group* Aleutian Islands, Alaska, USA
Ratlām *134 D4 prev.* Rutlam. Madhya Pradesh, C India
Ratnapura *132 D4* Sabaragamuwa Province, S Sri Lanka
Raton *48 D1* New Mexico, SW USA
Rättvik *85 C5* Dalarna, C Sweden
Raudhatain *see* Ar Rawdatayn
Raufarhöfn *83 E4* Norðurland Eystra, NE Iceland
Raukawa *see* Cook Strait

Raukumara Range *150 E3 mountain range* North Island, New Zealand
Raurkela *151 F4 var.* Raurkela; *prev.* Rourkela. Orissa, E India
Rauma *85 D5 Swe.* Raumo. Länsi-Souni, SW Finland
Raumo *see* Rauma
Raurkela *see* Rāurkela
Ravenna *96 C3* Emilia-Romagna, N Italy
Rāvi *134 C2 river* India/Pakistan
Rāwalpindi *134 C1* Punjab, NE Pakistan
Rawa Mazowiecka *98 D4* Łódzkie, C Poland
Rawicz *98 C4 Ger.* Rawitsch. Wielkopolskie, C Poland
Rawitsch *see* Rawicz
Rawlins *44 C3* Wyoming, C USA
Rawson *65 C6* Chubut, SE Argentina
Rayak *118 B4 var.* Rayaq, Riyāq. E Lebanon
Rayaq *see* Rayak
Rayleigh *43 F1* UK
Rayong *137 C5* Rayong, S Thailand
Razāzah, Buḩayrat ar *120 B3 var.* Baḩr al Milḩ. *lake* C Iraq
Razdolnoye *see* Rozdol'ne
Razelm, Lacul *see* Razim, Lacul
Razgrad *104 D2* Razgrad, N Bulgaria
Razim, Lacul *108 D5 prev.* Lacul Razelm. *lagoon* NW Black Sea
Reading *89 D7* S England, UK
Reading *41 F4* Pennsylvania, NE USA
Realicó *64 C4* La Pampa, C Argentina
Reăng Kesei *137 D5* Bătdâmbâng, W Cambodia
Rebecca, Lake *147 C6 lake* Western Australia
Rebiana Sand Sea *see* Rabyānah, Ramlat
Rebun-tō *130 C2 island* NE Japan
Rechitsa *see* Rechytsa
Rechytsa *107 D7 Rus.* Rechitsa. Brestskaya Voblasts', SW Belarus
Recife *63 G2 prev.* Pernambuco. *state capital* Pernambuco, E Brazil
Recklinghausen *94 A4* Nordrhein-Westfalen, W Germany
Recogne *87 C7* Luxembourg, SE Belgium
Reconquista *64 D3* Santa Fe, C Argentina
Red Deer *37 E5* Alberta, SW Canada
Redding *47 B5* California, W USA
Redon *90 B3* Ille-et-Vilaine, NW France
Red River *45 E1 river* Canada/USA
Red River *36 C2 var.* Yuan, *Chin.* Yuan Jiang, *Vtn.* Sông Hồng Hà. *river* China/Vietnam
Red River *35 C6 river* S USA
Red River *42 D3 river* Louisiana, S USA
Red Sea *72 D3 var.* Sinus Arabicus. *sea* Africa/Asia
Red Wing *45 G2* Minnesota, N USA
Reefton *151 C5* West Coast, South Island, New Zealand
Reese River *47 C5 river* Nevada, W USA
Refahiye *117 E3* Erzincan, C Turkey
Regensburg *95 C6 Eng.* Ratisbon, *Fr.* Ratisbonne, *hist.* Ratisbona; *anc.* Castra Regina, Reginum. Bayern, SE Germany
Regenstauf *95 C6* Bayern, SE Germany
Reggane *70 D3* C Algeria
Reggio *see* Reggio nell'Emilia
Reggio Calabria *see* Reggio di Calabria
Reggio di Calabria *97 D7 var.* Reggio Calabria, *Gk.* Rhegion; *anc.* Regium, Rhegium. Calabria, SW Italy
Reggio Emilia *see* Reggio nell'Emilia
Reggio nell'Emilia *96 B2 var.* Reggio Emilia, *abbrev.* Reggio; *anc.* Regium Lepidum. Emilia-Romagna, N Italy
Reghin *108 C4 Ger.* Sächsisch-Reen, *Hung.* Szászrégen; *prev.* Reghinul Săsesc, *Ger.* Sächsisch-Regen. Mureş, C Romania
Reghinul Săsesc *see* Reghin
Regina *37 F5 province capital* Saskatchewan, S Canada
Reginum *see* Regensburg
Registan *see* Rīgestān
Regium *see* Reggio di Calabria
Regium Lepidum *see* Reggio nell'Emilia
Rehoboth *78 B3* Hardap, C Namibia
Rehoboth/Rehovoth *see* Reḩovot
Reḩovot *119 A6 var.* Rehoboth, Rekhovoth, Rehovoth. Central, C Israel
Reichenau *see* Bogatynia, Poland
Reichenberg *see* Liberec
Reid *147 D6* Western Australia

Reikjavik *see* Reykjavík
Ré, Île de *90 A4 island* W France
Reims *90 D3 Eng.* Rheims; *anc.* Durocortorum, Remi. Marne, N France
Reindeer Lake *37 F4 lake* Manitoba/Saskatchewan, C Canada
Reine-Charlotte, Îles de la *see* Queen Charlotte Islands
Reine-Élisabeth, Îles de la *see* Queen Elizabeth Islands
Reinga, Cape *150 C1 headland* North Island, New Zealand
Reinosa *92 D1* Cantabria, N Spain
Reka *see* Rijeka
Reḩovoth *see* Reḩovot
Reliance *37 F4* Northwest Territories, C Canada
Remi *see* Reims
Rendina *see* Rentína
Rendsburg *94 B2* Schleswig-Holstein, N Germany
Rengat *138 B4* Sumatera, W Indonesia
Reni *108 D4* Odes'ka Oblast', SW Ukraine
Rennell *144 C4 var.* Mu Nggava. *island* S Solomon Islands
Rennes *90 B3 Bret.* Roazon; *anc.* Condate. Ille-et-Vilaine, NW France
Reno *47 C5* Nevada, W USA
Renqiu *128 C4* Hebei, E China
Rentína *105 B5 var.* Rendina. Thessalía, C Greece
Reps *see* Rupea
Republika Srpska *see* Foča
Repulse Bay *37 G3* Northwest Terretories, N Canada
Reschitza *see* Reşiţa
Resht *see* Rasht
Resicabánya *see* Reşiţa
Resistencia *64 D3* Chaco, NE Argentina
Reşiţa *108 A4 Ger.* Reschitza, *Hung.* Resicabánya. Caraş-Severin, W Romania
Resolute *37 F2* Inuit. Qausuittuq. Cornwallis Island, Nunavut, N Canada
Resolution Island *39 E1 island* Nunavut, NE Canada
Resolution Island *151 A7 island* SW New Zealand
Réunion *79 H4 off.* La Réunion. *French overseas department* W Indian Ocean
Réunion *141 B5 island* W Indian Ocean
Reus *93 F2* Cataluña, E Spain
Reutlingen *95 B6* Baden-Württemberg, S Germany
Reuver *87 D5* Limburg, SE Netherlands
Reval/Revel *see* Tallinn
Revillagigedo Island *50 B5 island* Alexander Archipelago, Alaska, USA
Rexburg *46 E3* Idaho, NW USA
Reyes *61 F3* Beni, NW Bolivia
Rey, Isla del *53 G5 island* Archipiélago de las Perlas, SE Panama
Reykjanes Basin *82 C5 var.* Irminger Basin. *undersea basin* N Atlantic Ocean
Reykjanes Ridge *80 A1 undersea ridge* N Atlantic Ocean
Reykjavík *83 E5 var.* Reikjavik. *country capital* (Iceland) Höfuðhborgarsvaeðhi, W Iceland
Reynosa *51 E2* Tamaulipas, C Mexico
Rezé *90 A4* Loire-Atlantique, NW France
Rēzekne *106 D4 Ger.* Rositten; *prev. Rus.* Rezhitsa. Rēzekne, SE Latvia
Rezhitsa *see* Rēzekne
Rezovo *104 E3 Turk.* Rezve. Burgas, E Bulgaria
Rezve *see* Rezovo
Rhaedestus *see* Tekirdağ
Rhegion/Rhegium *see* Reggio di Calabria
Rheims *see* Reims
Rhein *see* Rhine
Rheine *94 A3 var.* Rheine in Westfalen. Nordrhein-Westfalen, NW Germany
Rheine in Westfalen *see* Rheine
Rheinisches Schiefergebirge *95 A5 var.* Rhine State Uplands, *Eng.* Rhenish Slate Mountains. *mountain range* W Germany
Rhenish Slate Mountains *see* Rheinisches Schiefergebirge
Rhin *see* Rhine
Rhine *80 D4 Dut.* Rijn, *Fr.* Rhin, *Ger.* Rhein. *river* W Europe
Rhinelander *40 B2* Wisconsin, N USA
Rhine State Uplands *see* Rheinisches Schiefergebirge

Rho *96 B2* Lombardia, N Italy
Rhode Island *41 G3 off.* State of Rhode Island and Providence Plantations, *also known as* Little Rhody, Ocean State. *state* NE USA
Rhodes *see* Ródos
Rhodesia *see* Zimbabwe
Rhodope Mountains *104 C3 var.* Rodhópi Óri, *Bul.* Rhodope Planina, Rodopi, *Gk.* Orosirá Rodhópis, *Turk.* Dospad Dagh. *mountain range* Bulgaria/Greece
Rhodope Planina *see* Rhodope Mountains
Rhône *91 D6 cultural region* E France
Rhône *91 D6 department* E France
Rhône *80 C4 river* France/Switzerland
Rhum *88 B3 var.* Rum. *island* W Scotland, UK
Ribble *89 D5 river* NW England, UK
Ribeira *92 B1* Galicia, NW Spain
Ribeirão Preto *63 F4* São Paulo, S Brazil
Riberalta *61 F2* Beni, N Bolivia
Râbniţa *108 D3 var.* Râbniţa, *Rus.* Rybnitsa. NE Moldova
Rice Lake *40 A2* Wisconsin, N USA
Richard Toll *74 B3* N Senegal
Richfield *44 B4* Utah, W USA
Richland *46 C2* Washington, NW USA
Richmond *151 C5* Tasman, South Island, New Zealand
Richmond *40 C5* Kentucky, S USA
Richmond *41 E5 state capital* Virginia, NE USA
Richmond Range *151 C5 mountain range* South Island, New Zealand
Ricobayo, Embalse de *92 C2 reservoir* NW Spain
Ricomagus *see* Riom
Ridgecrest *47 C7* California, W USA
Ried *see* Ried im Innkreis
Ried im Innkreis *95 D6 var.* Ried. Oberösterreich, NW Austria
Riemst *87 D6* Limburg, NE Belgium
Riesa *94 D4* Sachsen, E Germany
Rift Valley *see* Great Rift Valley
Rīga *106 C3 Eng.* Riga. *country capital* (Latvia) Rīga, C Latvia
Rigaer Bucht *see* Riga, Gulf of
Riga, Gulf of *106 C3 Est.* Liivi Laht, *Ger.* Rigaer Bucht, *Latv.* Rigas Jūras Līcis, *Rus.* Rizhskiy Zaliv; *prev. Est.* Riia Laht. *gulf* Estonia/Latvia
Rīgān *120 E4* Kermān, SE Iran
Rigas Jūras Līcis *see* Riga, Gulf of
Rigestân *122 D5 var.* Registan. *desert region* S Afghanistan
Riia Laht *see* Riga, Gulf of
Riihimäki *85 D5* Etelä-Suomi, S Finland
Rijeka *100 A2 Ger.* Sankt Veit am Flaum, *It.* Fiume, *Slvn.* Reka; *anc.* Tarsatica. Primorje-Gorski Kotar, NW Croatia
Rijn *see* Rhine
Rijssel *see* Lille
Rijssen *86 E3* Overijssel, E Netherlands
Rimah, Wâdī ar *120 B4 var.* Wâdī ar Rummah. *dry watercourse* C Saudi Arabia
Rimini *96 C3 anc.* Ariminum. Emilia-Romagna, N Italy
Râmnicu-Sărat *see* Râmnicu Sărat
Râmnicu Vîlcea *see* Râmnicu Vâlcea
Rimouski *39 E4* Québec, SE Canada
Ringebu *85 B5* Oppland, S Norway
Ringen *see* Rõngu
Ringkøbing Fjord *85 A7 fjord* W Denmark
Ringvassøya *84 C2 Lapp.* Ráneš. *island* N Norway
Río *see* Río de Janeiro
Riobamba *60 B1* Chimborazo, C Ecuador
Rio Branco *56 B3 state capital* Acre, W Brazil
Rio Branco, Território de *see* Roraima
Río Bravo *51 E2* Tamaulipas, C Mexico
Río Cuarto *64 C4* Córdoba, C Argentina
Rio de Janeiro *63 F4 var.* Rio. *state capital* Rio de Janeiro, SE Brazil
Rio de Janeiro *63 E5 var.* Rio. *state* SE Brazil
Río Gallegos *65 B7 var.* Gallegos, Puerto Gallegos. Santa Cruz, S Argentina
Río Grande *63 E5* San Pedro do Rio Grande do Sul. Rio Grande do Sul, S Brazil
Río Grande *50 D3* Zacatecas, C Mexico
Rio Grande do Norte *63 G2 off.* Estado do Rio Grande do Norte. *state* E Brazil

Rio Grande do Norte, Estado do *see* Rio Grande do Norte
Rio Grande do Sul *63 E5 off.* Estado do Rio Grande do Sul. *state* S Brazil
Rio Grande do Sul, Estado do *see* Rio Grande do Sul
Rio Grande Plateau *see* Rio Grande Rise
Rio Grande Rise *57 E6 var.* Rio Grande Plateau. *undersea plateau* SW Atlantic Ocean
Ríohacha *58 B1* La Guajira, N Colombia
Río Lagartos *51 H3* Yucatán, SE Mexico
Riom *91 C5 anc.* Ricomagus. Puy-de-Dôme, C France
Río San Juan *53 E4 department* S Nicaragua
Río Verde *51 E4 var.* Rioverde. San Luis Potosí, C Mexico
Rioverde *see* Río Verde
Ripoll *93 G2* Cataluña, NE Spain
Rishiri-tō *130 C2 var.* Risiri Tō. *island* NE Japan
Risiri Tō *see* Rishiri-tō
Rîşno *see* Râşnov
Risti *106 D2 Ger.* Kreuz. Läänemaa, W Estonia
Rivas *52 D4* Rivas, SW Nicaragua
Rivera *64 D3* Rivera, NE Uruguay
River Falls *40 A2* Wisconsin, N USA
Riverside *47 C7* California, W USA
Riverton *151 A7* Southland, South Island, New Zealand
Riverton *44 C3* Wyoming, C USA
Rivière-du-Loup *39 E4* Québec, SE Canada
Rivne *108 C2 Pol.* Równe, *Rus.* Rovno. Rivnens'ka Oblast', NW Ukraine
Rivoli *96 A2* Piemonte, NW Italy
Riyadh/Riyâḍ, Minţaqat ar *see* Ar Riyâḍ
Riyâq *see* Rayak
Rize *117 E2* Rize, NE Turkey
Rizhao *128 D4* Shandong, E China
Rizhskiy Zaliv *see* Riga, Gulf of
Rkîz *74 C3* Trarza, W Mauritania
Road Town *55 F3 dependent territory capital* (British Virgin Islands) Tortola, C British Virgin Islands
Roanne *91 C5* Rodumna. Loire, E France
Roanoke *41 E5* Virginia, NE USA
Roanoke River *43 F1 river* North Carolina/Virginia, SE USA
Roatán *52 C2 var.* Coxen Hole, Coxin Hole. Islas de la Bahía, N Honduras
Roat Kampuchea *see* Cambodia
Roazon *see* Rennes
Robbie Ridge *143 E3 undersea ridge* W Pacific Ocean
Robert Williams *see* Caála
Robinson Range *147 B5 mountain range* Western Australia
Robson, Mount *37 E5 mountain* British Columbia, SW Canada
Robstown *49 G4* Texas, SW USA
Roca Partida, Isla *50 B5 island* W Mexico
Rocas, Atol das *63 G2 island* E Brazil
Rochefort *87 C7* Namur, SE Belgium
Rochefort *90 B4 var.* Rochefort sur Mer. Charente-Maritime, W France
Rochefort sur Mer *see* Rochefort
Rochester *45 G3* Minnesota, N USA
Rochester *41 G3* New Hampshire, NE USA
Rochester *41 E3* New York, NE USA
Rocheuses, Montagnes/Rockies *see* Rocky Mountains
Rockall Bank *80 B2 undersea bank* N Atlantic Ocean
Rockall Trough *80 B2 trough* N Atlantic Ocean
Rockdale *148 E2* Texas, SW USA
Rockford *40 B3* Illinois, N USA
Rockhampton *148 D4* Queensland, E Australia
Rock Hill *43 E1* South Carolina, SE USA
Rockingham *147 A6* Western Australia
Rock Island *40 B3* Illinois, N USA
Rock Sound *54 C1* Eleuthera Island, C Bahamas
Rock Springs *44 C3* Wyoming, C USA
Rockstone *59 F3* C Guyana
Rocky Mount *43 F1* North Carolina, SE USA
Rocky Mountains *34 B4 var.* Rockies, *Fr.* Montagnes Rocheuses. *mountain range* Canada/USA
Roden *86 E2* Drenthe, NE Netherlands

Rodez *91 C5 anc.* Segodunum. Aveyron, S France
Rodhópi Óri *see* Rhodope Mountains
Ródhos/Rodi *see* Ródos
Rodopi *see* Rhodope Mountains
Ródos *105 E7 var.* Ródhos, *Eng.* Rhodes, *It.* Rodi; *anc.* Rhodos. *island* Dodekánisa, Greece, Aegean Sea
Rodosto *see* Tekirdağ
Rodunma *see* Roanne
Roermond *87 D5* Limburg, SE Netherlands
Roeselare *87 A6 Fr.* Roulers; *prev.* Rousselaere. West-Vlaanderen, W Belgium
Rogachëv *see* Rahachow
Rogatica *100 C4* Republika Srpska, SE Bosnia and Herzegovina
Rogers *42 A1* Arkansas, C USA
Roger Simpson Island *see* Abemama
Roi Ed *see* Roi Et
Roi Et *137 D5 var.* Muang Roi Et, Roi Ed. Roi Et, E Thailand
Roja *106 C2* Talsi, NW Latvia
Rokiškis *106 C4* Panevėžys, NE Lithuania
Rokycany *99 A5 Ger.* Rokytzan. Plzeňský Kraj, W Czech Republic
Rokytzan *see* Rokycany
Rólas, Ilha das *76 E2 island* S Sao Tome and Principe, Africa, E Atlantic Ocean
Rolla *45 G5* Missouri, C USA
Röm *see* Rømø
Roma *96 C4 Eng.* Rome. *country capital* (Italy) Lazio, C Italy
Roma *149 D5* Queensland, E Australia
Roman *104 C2* Vratsa, NW Bulgaria
Roman *108 C4 Hung.* Románvásár. Neamţ, NE Romania
Romania *108 B4 Bul.* Rumûniya, *Ger.* Rumänien, *Hung.* Románia, *Rom.* România, *SCr.* Rumunjska, *Ukr.* Rumuniya, *prev.* Republica Socialistă România, Roumania, Rumania, Socialist Republic of Romania, *prev. Rom.* Romînia. *country* SE Europe

ROMANIA
Southeast Europe

Official name Romania
Formation 1878 / 1947
Capital Bucharest
Population 21.7 million / 244 people per sq mile (94 people per sq km) / 56%
Total area 91,699 sq miles (237,500 sq km)
Languages Romanian*, Hungarian (Magyar), Romani, German
Religions Romanian Orthodox 87%, Roman Catholic 5%, Protestant 4%, Other 2%, Greek Orthodox 1%, Greek Catholic (Uniate) 1%
Ethnic mix Romanian 89%, Magyar 7%, Roma 3%, Other 1%
Government Presidential system
Currency Romanian leu = 100 bani
Literacy rate 97%
Calorie consumption 3455 calories

România, Republica Socialistă *see* Romania, Socialist Republic of *see* Romania
Românvásár *see* Roman
Rome *42 D2* Georgia, SE USA
Rome *see* Roma
Rominia *see* Romania
Romny *109 F2* Sums'ka Oblast', NE Ukraine
Rømø *85 A7 Ger.* Röm. *island* SW Denmark
Roncador, Serra do *56 D4 mountain range* C Brazil
Ronda *92 D5* Andalucía, S Spain
Rondônia *62 D3 off.* Estado de Rondônia. *state* W Brazil
Rondônia, Estado de *see* Rondônia
Rondônia, Território de *see* Rondônia
Rondonópolis *63 E3* Mato Grosso, W Brazil
Rongelap Atoll *144 D1 var.* Rönlap. *atoll* Ralik Chain, NW Marshall Islands
Röngu *106 D3 Ger.* Ringen. Tartumaa, SE Estonia
Rönlap *see* Rongelap Atoll

Rønne *85 B8* Bornholm, E Denmark
Ronne Ice Shelf *154 A3 ice shelf* Antarctica
Roosendaal *87 C5* Noord-Brabant, S Netherlands
Roosevelt Island *154 B4 island* Antarctica
Roraima *62 D1 off.* Estado de Roraima; *prev.* Território de Rio Branco, Território de Roraima. *state* N Brazil
Roraima, Estado de *see* Roraima
Roraima, Mount *59 E3 mountain* N South America
Roraima, Território de *see* Roraima
Røros *85 B5* Sør-Trøndelag, S Norway
Rosa, Lake *54 D2 lake* Great Inagua, S Bahamas
Rosario *64 D4* Santa Fe, C Argentina
Rosario *64 D2* San Pedro, C Paraguay
Rosarito *50 A1* Baja California, NW Mexico
Roscianum *see* Rossano
Roscommon *40 C2* Michigan, N USA
Roseau *55 G4 prev.* Charlotte Town. *country capital* (Dominica) SW Dominica
Roseburg *46 B4* Oregon, NW USA
Rosenau *see* Rožňava
Rosenberg *49 G4* Texas, SW USA
Rosenberg *see* Ružomberok
Rosengarten *93 B3* Niedersachsen, N Germany
Rosenheim *95 C6* Bayern, S Germany
Rosia Bay *93 H5 bay* W Gibraltar Europe W Mediterranean Sea Atlantic Ocean
Roşiori de Vede *108 B5* Teleorman, S Romania
Rositten *see* Rēzekne
Roslavl' *111 A5* Smolenskaya Oblast', W Russian Federation
Rosmalen *86 C4* Noord-Brabant, S Netherlands
Ross *151 B6* West Coast, South Island, New Zealand
Rossano *97 E6 anc.* Roscianum. Calabria, SW Italy
Ross Ice Shelf *154 B4 ice shelf* Antarctica
Rossiyskaya Federatsiya *see* Russian Federation
Rosso *74 B3* Trarza, SW Mauritania
Rossosh' *111 B6* Voronezhskaya Oblast', W Russian Federation
Ross Sea *154 B4* Antarctica
Rostak *see* Ar Rustâq
Rostock *94 C2* Mecklenburg-Vorpommern, NE Germany
Rostov *see* Rostov-na-Donu
Rostov-na-Donu *111 B7 var.* Rostov, *Eng.* Rostov-on-Don. Rostovskaya Oblast', SW Russian Federation
Rostov-on-Don *see* Rostov-na-Donu
Roswell *48 D2* New Mexico, SW USA
Rota *144 B1 island* S Northern Mariana Islands
Rotcher Island *see* Tamana
Rothera *154 A2 UK research station* Antarctica
Rotomagus *see* Rouen
Rotorua *150 D3* Bay of Plenty, North Island, New Zealand
Rotorua, Lake *150 D3 lake* North Island, New Zealand
Rotterdam *86 C4* Zuid-Holland, SW Netherlands
Rottweil *95 B6* Baden-Württemberg, S Germany
Rotuma *145 E4 island* NW Fiji Oceania S Pacific Ocean
Roubaix *90 C2* Nord, N France
Rouen *90 C3 anc.* Rotomagus. Seine-Maritime, N France
Roulers *see* Roeselare
Roumania *see* Romania
Round Rock *49 G3* Texas, SW USA
Rourkela *see* Räurkela
Rousselaere *see* Roeselare
Roussillon *91 C6 cultural region* S France
Rouyn-Noranda *38 D4* Québec, SE Canada
Rovaniemi *84 D3* Lappi, N Finland
Rovigno *see* Rovinj
Rovigo *96 C2* Veneto, NE Italy
Rovinj *100 A3 It.* Rovigno. Istra, NW Croatia

Rovno *see* Rivne
Rovuma, Rio *79 F2 var.* Ruvuma. *river*
  Mozambique/Tanzania
Rovuma, Rio *see* Ruvuma
Równe *see* Rivne
Roxas City *139 E2* Panay Island,
  C Philippines
Royale, Isle *40 B1 island* Michigan,
  N USA
Royan *91 B5* Charente-Maritime,
  W France
Rozdol'ne *109 F4 Rus.* Razdolnoye.
  Respublika Krym, S Ukraine
Rožňava *99 D6 Ger.* Rosenau, *Hung.*
  Rozsnyó. Košický Kraj, E Slovakia
Rózsahegy *see* Ružomberok
Rozsnyó *see* Râşnov
Rozsnyó *see* Rožňava
Ruanda *see* Rwanda
Ruapehu, Mount *150 D4 volcano*
  North Island, New Zealand
Ruapuke Island *151 B8 island*
  SW New Zealand
Ruatoria *150 E3* Gisborne, North Island,
  New Zealand
Ruawai *150 D2* Northland, North Island,
  New Zealand
Rubezhnoye *see* Rubizhne
Rubizhne *109 H3 Rus.* Rubezhnoye.
  Luhans'ka Oblast', E Ukraine
Ruby Mountains *47 D5 mountain range*
  Nevada, W USA
Rucava *106 B3* Liepāja, SW Latvia
Rudensk *see* Rudzyensk
Rūdiškės *107 B5* Vilnius, S Lithuania
Rudnik *104 E2* Varna, E Bulgaria
Rudny *see* Rudnyy
Rudnyy *114 C4 var.* Rudny. Kostanay,
  N Kazakhstan
Rudolf, Lake *see* Turkana, Lake
Rudolfswert *see* Novo mesto
Rudzyensk *107 C6 Rus.* Rudensk.
  Minskaya Voblasts', C Belarus
Rufiji *73 C7 river* E Tanzania
Rufino *64 C4* Santa Fe,
  C Argentina
Rugāji *106 D4* Balvi, E Latvia
Rügen *94 D2 cape* NE Germany
Ruggell *94 E1* N Liechtenstein Europe
Ruhja *see* Rūjiena
Ruhnu *106 C2 var.* Ruhnu Saar, *Swe.*
  Runö. *island* SW Estonia
Ruhnu Saar *see* Ruhnu
Rujen *see* Rūjiena
Rūjiena *106 D3 Est.* Ruhja, *Ger.* Rujen.
  Valmiera, N Latvia
Rukwa, Lake *73 B7 lake* SE Tanzania
Rum *see* Rhum
Ruma *100 D3* Vojvodina, N Serbia
Rumadiya *see* Ar Ramādī
Rumania/Rumänien *see* Romania
Rumbek *73 B5* El Buhayrat,
  S Sudan
Rum Cay *54 D2 island* C Bahamas
Rumia *98 C2* Pomorskie,
  N Poland
Rummah, Wādī ar *see* Rimah, Wādī ar
Rummelsburg in Pommern *see* Miastko
Rumuniya/Rumūniya/Rumunjska
  see Romania
Runanga *151 B5* West Coast, South
  Island, New Zealand
Rundu *78 C3 var.* Runtu. Okavango,
  NE Namibia
Runö *see* Ruhnu
Runtu *see* Rundu
Ruoqiang *126 C3 var.* Jo-ch'iang, *Uigh.*
  Charkhlik, Charkhliq, Qarkilik.
  Xinjiang Uygur Zizhiqu, NW China
Rupea *108 C4 Ger.* Reps, *Hung.*
  Kőhalom; *prev.* Cohalm. Braşov,
  C Romania
Rupel *87 B5 river* N Belgium
Rupella *see* la Rochelle
Rupert, Rivière de *38 D3 river* Québec,
  C Canada
Rusaddir *see* Melilla
Ruschuk/Rusçuk *see* Ruse
Ruse *104 D1 var.* Ruschuk, Rustchuk,
  Turk. Rusçuk. Ruse, N Bulgaria
Rusadir *see* Melilla
Russellville *42 A1* Arkansas, C USA
Russia *see* Russian Federation
Russian America *see* Alaska
Russian Federation *112 D2 off.* Russian
  Federation, *var.* Russia, *Latv.* Krievija,
  Rus. Rossiyskaya Federatsiya. *country*
  Asia/Europe

RUSSIAN FEDERATION
Europe / Asia

Official name Russian Federation
Formation 1480 / 1991
Capital Moscow
Population 143 million / 22 people per
sq mile (8 people per sq km) / 78%
Total area 6,592,735 sq miles (17,075,200
sq km)
Languages Russian*, Tatar, Ukrainian,
Chavash, various other national
languages
Religions Orthodox Christian 75%,
Other 15%, Muslim 10%
Ethnic mix Russian 82%, Other 10%,
Tatar 4%, Ukrainian 3%, Chavash 1%
Government Presidential system
Currency Russian rouble = 100 kopeks
Literacy rate 99%
Calorie consumption 3072 calories

Russian Federation *see* Russian
  Federation
Rustaq *see* Ar Rustāq
Rust'avi *117 G2* SE Georgia
Rustchuk *see* Ruse
Ruston *42 B2* Louisiana, S USA
Rutanzige, Lake *see* Edward, Lake
Rutba *see* Ar Ruţbah
Rutlam *see* Ratlām
Rutland *41 F2* Vermont,
  NE USA
Rutög *126 A4 var.* Rutog, Rutok.
  Xizang Zizhiqu, W China
Rutok *see* Rutög
Ruvuma *69 E5 var.* Rio Rovuma. *river*
  Mozambique/Tanzania
Ruvuma *see* Rovuma, Rio
Ruwenzori *77 E5 mountain range*
  Uganda/Dem. Rep. Congo
Ruzhany *107 B6*
  Rus. Ruzhany. Brestskaya Voblasts',
  SW Belarus
Ružomberok *99 C5 Ger.* Rosenberg,
  Hung. Rózsahegy. Žilinský Kraj,
  N Slovakia
Rwanda *73 B6 off.* Rwandese Republic;
  prev. Ruanda. *country* C Africa

RWANDA
Central Africa

Official name Republic of Rwanda
Formation 1962 / 1962
Capital Kigali
Population 9 million / 934 people per
sq mile (361 people per sq km) / 6%
Total area 10,169 sq miles
(26,338 sq km)
Languages Kinyarwanda*, French*,
Kiswahili, English
Religions Roman Catholic 56%,
Traditional beliefs 25%, Muslim 10%,
Protestant 9%
Ethnic mix Hutu 90%, Tutsi 9%, Other
(including Twa) 1%
Government Presidential system
Currency Rwanda franc = 100 centimes
Literacy rate 64%
Calorie consumption 2084 calories

Rwandese Republic *see* Rwanda
Ryazan' *111 B5* Ryazanskaya Oblast',
  W Russian Federation
Rybach'ye *see* Balykchy
Rybinsk *110 B4 prev.* Andropov.
  Yaroslavskaya Oblast', W Russian
  Federation
Rybnik *99 C5* Śląskie, S Poland
Rybnitsa *see* Rîbniţa
Ryde *148 E1* UK
Ryki *98 D4* Lubelskie, E Poland
Rykovo *see* Yenakiyeve
Rypin *98 C3* Kujawsko-pomorskie,
  C Poland
Ryssel *see* Lille
Rysy *99 C5 mountain* S Poland
Ryukyu Islands *see* Nansei-shotō
Ryukyu Islands *see* Nansei-shotō
Ryukyu Trench *125 F3*
  var. Nansei Syotō Trench. *trench*
  S East China Sea
Rzeszów *99 E5* Podkarpackie,
  SE Poland
Rzhev *110 B4* Tverskaya Oblast',
  W Russian Federation

S

Saale *94 C4 river* C Germany
Saalfeld *95 C5 var.* Saalfeld an der Saale.
  Thüringen, C Germany
Saalfeld an der Saale *see* Saalfeld
Saarbrücken *95 A6 Fr.* Sarrebruck.
  Saarland, SW Germany
Sääre *106 C2 var.* Sjar. Saaremaa,
  W Estonia
Saare *see* Saaremaa
Saaremaa *106 C2 Ger.* Oesel, Ösel; *prev.*
  Saare. *island* W Estonia
Saariselkä *84 D2 Lapp.* Suoločielgi.
  Lappi, N Finland
Sab' Ābār *118 C4 var.* Sab'a Biyar, Sa'b
  Bi'ār. Ḥimş, C Syria
Sab'a Biyar *see* Sab' Ābār
Šabac *100 D3* Serbia, W Serbia
Sabadell *93 G2* Cataluña, E Spain
Sabah *138 D3 prev.* British North
  Borneo, North Borneo. *state* East
  Malaysia
Sabanalarga *58 B1* Atlántico,
  N Colombia
Sabaneta *58 C1* Falcón, N Venezuela
Sabaria *see* Szombathely
Sab'atayn, Ramlat as *121 C6 desert*
  C Yemen
Sabaya *61 F4* Oruro, S Bolivia
Sa'b Bi'ār *see* Sab' Ābār
Şāberī, Hāmūn-e *122 C5 var.*
  Daryācheh-ye Hāmun, Daryācheh-ye
  Sīstān. *lake* Afghanistan/Iran
Sabḥā *71 F3* C Libya
Sabi *see* Save, Rio
Sabinas *51 E2* Coahuila de Zaragoza,
  NE Mexico
Sabinas Hidalgo *51 E2* Nuevo León,
  NE Mexico
Sabine River *49 H3 river* Louisiana/
  Texas, SW USA
Sabkha *see* As Sabkhah
Sable, Cape *43 E5 headland* Florida,
  SE USA
Sable Island *39 G4 island* Nova Scotia,
  SE Canada
Şabyā *121 B6* Jīzān, SW Saudi Arabia
Sabzawar *see* Sabzevār
Sabzevār *120 D2 var.* Sabzawar.
  Khorāsān-Razavī, NE Iran
Sachsen *94 D4 Eng.* Saxony, *Fr.* Saxe.
  state E Germany
Sachs Harbour *37 E2* Banks Island,
  Northwest Territories, N Canada
Sächsisch-Reen/Sächsisch-Regen
  see Reghin
Sacramento *47 B5 state capital*
  California, W USA
Sacramento Mountains *48 D2*
  mountain range New Mexico,
  SW USA
Sacramento River *47 B5 river*
  California, W USA
Sacramento Valley *47 B5 valley*
  California, W USA
Sá da Bandeira *see* Lubango
Şa'dah *121 B6* NW Yemen
Sado *131 C5 var.* Sadoga-shima. *island*
  C Japan
Sadoga-shima *see* Sado
Saena Julia *see* Siena
Safad *see* Zefat
Şafāqis *see* Sfax
Safed *see* Zefat
Säffle *85 B6* Värmland, C Sweden
Safford *48 C3* Arizona, SW USA
Safi *70 B2* W Morocco
Safīdküh, Selseleh-ye *122 D4 Eng.*
  Paropamisus Range. *mountain range*
  W Afghanistan
Sagaing *136 B3* Sagaing,
  C Myanmar (Burma)
Sagami-nada *131 D6 inlet* SW Japan
Sagan *see* Żagań
Sāgar *134 D4 prev.* Saugor. Madhya
  Pradesh, C India
Sagarmāthā *see* Everest, Mount
Sagebrush State *see* Nevada
Saghez *see* Saqqez
Saginaw *40 C3* Michigan,
  N USA
Saginaw Bay *40 D2 lake bay* Michigan,
  N USA
Sagua la Grande *54 B2* Villa Clara,
  C Cuba

Sagunto *93 F3 Cat.* Sagunt, *Ar.*
  Murviedro; *anc.* Saguntum. País
  Valenciano, E Spain
Sagunt/Saguntum *see* Sagunto
Sahara *68 B3 desert* Libya/Algeria
Sahara el Gharbiya *72 B2 var.* Aş Şaḥrāʾ
  al Gharbīyah, *Eng.* Western Desert.
  desert C Egypt
Sahara el Sharqiya *68 D3 var.* Aş Şaḥrāʾ
  ash Sharqīyah, *Eng.* Arabian Desert,
  Eastern Desert. *desert* E Egypt
Saharan Atlas *see* Atlas Saharien
Sahel *74 D3 physical region* C Africa
Sāḥiliyah, Jibāl as *118 B3 mountain*
  range NW Syria
Sāhīwāl *134 C2 prev.* Montgomery.
  Punjab, E Pakistan
Saïda *119 A5 var.* Şaydā, Sayida; *anc.*
  Sidon. W Lebanon
Sa'īdābād *see* Sīrjān
Saidpur *135 G3 var.* Syedpur. Rajshahi,
  NW Bangladesh
Saigon *see* Hồ Chí Minh
Saimaa *85 E5 lake* SE Finland
St Albans *89 E6 anc.* Verulamium.
  E England, UK
Saint Albans *40 D5* West Virginia,
  NE USA
St Andrews *88 C4* E Scotland, UK
Saint Anna Trough *see* Svyataya Anna
  Trough
St. Ann's Bay *54 B4* C Jamaica
St. Anthony *39 G3* Newfoundland,
  Newfoundland and Labrador,
  SE Canada
Saint Augustine *43 E3* Florida, SE USA
St Austell *89 C7* SW England, UK
S.Botolph's Town *see* Boston
St-Brieuc *90 A3* Côtes d'Armor,
  NW France
St. Catharines *38 D5* Ontario, S Canada
St-Chamond *91 D5* Loire, E France
Saint Christopher and Nevis,
  Federation of *see* Saint Kitts and Nevis
Saint Christopher-Nevis *see* Saint Kitts
  and Nevis
St. Clair, Lake *40 D3 var.* Lac à L'Eau
  Claire. *lake* Canada/USA
St-Claude *91 D5 anc.* Condate. Jura,
  E France
Saint Cloud *45 F2* Minnesota, N USA
Saint Croix *55 F3 island* S Virgin
  Islands (US)
Saint Croix River *40 A2 river*
  Minnesota/Wisconsin, N USA
St David's Island *42 B5 island*
  E Bermuda
St-Denis *79 G4 dependent territory*
  capital (Réunion) NW Réunion
St-Dié *90 E4* Vosges, NE France
St-Egrève *91 D5* Isère, E France
Sainte Marie, Cap *see* Vohimena,
  Tanjona
Saintes *91 B5 anc.* Mediolanum.
  Charente-Maritime, W France
St-Étienne *91 D5* Loire, E France
St-Flour *91 C5* Cantal, C France
St-Gall/Saint Gall/St. Gallen *see* Sankt
  Gallen
St-Gaudens *91 B6* Haute-Garonne,
  S France
Saint George *149 D5* Queensland,
  E Australia
St George *42 B4* N Bermuda
Saint George *44 A5* Utah, W USA
St. George's *55 G5 country capital*
  (Grenada) SW Grenada
St-Georges *39 E4* Québec, SE Canada
St-Georges *59 H3* E French Guiana
Saint George's Channel *89 B6 channel*
  Ireland/Wales, UK
St George's Island *42 B4 island*
  E Bermuda
Saint Helena *69 B6 UK dependent*
  territory C Atlantic Ocean
St. Helena Bay *78 B5 bay* SW South
  Africa
St Helier *89 D8 dependent territory*
  capital (Jersey) S Jersey, Channel
  Islands
St.Iago de la Vega *see* Spanish Town
Saint Ignace *40 C2* Michigan, N USA
St-Jean, Lac *39 E4* Québec,
  SE Canada
Saint Joe River *46 D2 river* Idaho,
  NW USA North America
St. John *39 F4* New Brunswick,
  SE Canada

Saint John 41 H1 Fr. Saint-John. river Canada/USA
Saint-John see Saint John
St John's 55 G3 country capital (Antigua and Barbuda) Antigua, Antigua and Barbuda
St. John's 39 H3 province capital Newfoundland, Newfoundland and Labrador, E Canada
Saint Joseph 45 F4 Missouri, C USA
St Julian's 102 B5 N Malta
Saint Kitts and Nevis 55 F3 off. Federation of Saint Christopher and Nevis, var. Saint Christopher-Nevis. country E West Indies

SAINT KITTS & NEVIS
West Indies

Official name Federation of Saint Christopher and Nevis
Formation 1983 / 1983
Capital Basseterre
Population 38,958 / 280 people per sq mile (108 people per sq km) / 34%
Total area 101 sq miles (261 sq km)
Languages English*, English Creole
Religions Anglican 33%, Methodist 29%, Other 22%, Moravian 9%, Roman Catholic 7%
Ethnic mix Black 94%, Mixed race 3%, Other and Amerindian 2%, White 1%
Government Parliamentary system
Currency Eastern Caribbean dollar = 100 cents
Literacy rate 98%
Calorie consumption 2609 calories

St-Laurent see St-Laurent-du-Maroni
St-Laurent-du-Maroni 59 H3 var. St-Laurent. NW French Guiana
St-Laurent, Fleuve see St. Lawrence
St. Lawrence 39 E4 Fr. Fleuve St-Laurent. river Canada/USA
St. Lawrence, Gulf of 39 F3 gulf NW Atlantic Ocean
Saint Lawrence Island 36 B2 island Alaska, USA
St-Lô 90 B3 anc. Briovera, Laudus. Manche, N France
St-Louis 90 E4 Haut-Rhin, NE France
Saint Louis 74 B3 NW Senegal
Saint Louis 45 G4 Missouri, C USA
Saint Lucia 55 E1 country SE West Indies

SAINT LUCIA
West Indies

Official name Saint Lucia
Formation 1979 / 1979
Capital Castries
Population 166,312 / 705 people per sq mile (273 people per sq km) / 38%
Total area 239 sq miles (620 sq km)
Languages English*, French Creole
Religions Roman Catholic 90%, Other 10%
Ethnic mix Black 90%, Mulatto (mixed race) 6%, Asian 3%, White 1%
Government Parliamentary system
Currency Eastern Caribbean dollar = 100 cents
Literacy rate 90%
Calorie consumption 2988 calories

Saint Lucia Channel 55 H4 channel Martinique/Saint Lucia
St-Malo 90 B3 Ille-et-Vilaine, NW France
St-Malo, Golfe de 90 A3 gulf NW France
Saint Martin see Sint Maarten
St.Matthew's Island see Zadetkyi Kyun
St. Matthias Group 144 B3 island group NE Papua New Guinea
St-Maur-des-Fossés 90 E2 Val-de-Marne, Ile-de-France, N France
St. Moritz 95 B7 Ger. Sankt Moritz, Rmsch. San Murezzan. Graubünden, SE Switzerland
St-Nazaire 90 A4 Loire-Atlantique, NW France
Saint-Nicolas see São Nicolau
St-Omer 90 C2 Pas-de-Calais, N France
Saint Paul 45 F2 state capital Minnesota, N USA

St-Paul, Île 141 C6 island Île St-Paul, NE French Southern and Antarctic Territories Antarctica Indian Ocea
St Peter Port 89 D8 dependent territory capital (Guernsey) C Guernsey, Channel Islands
Saint Petersburg 43 E4 Florida, SE USA
Saint Petersburg see Sankt-Peterburg
St-Pierre and Miquelon 39 G4 Fr. Îles St-Pierre et Miquelon. French territorial collectivity NE North America
St-Quentin 90 C3 Aisne, N France
Saint Thomas see São Tomé, Sao Tome and Príncipe
Saint Thomas see Charlotte Amalie, Virgin Islands (US)
Saint Ubes see Setúbal
Saint Vincent 55 G4 island N Saint Vincent and the Grenadines
Saint Vincent see São Vicente
Saint Vincent and the Grenadines 55 H4 country SE West Indies

SAINT VINCENT & THE GRENADINES
West Indies

Official name Saint Vincent and the Grenadines
Formation 1979 / 1979
Capital Kingstown
Population 117,534 / 897 people per sq mile (346 people per sq km) / 55%
Total area 150 sq miles (389 sq km)
Languages English*, English Creole
Religions Anglican 47%, Methodist 28%, Roman Catholic 13%, Other 12%
Ethnic mix Black 66%, Mulatto (mixed race) 19%, Asian 6%, Other 5%, White 4%
Government Parliamentary system
Currency Eastern Caribbean dollar = 100 cents
Literacy rate 88%
Calorie consumption 2599 calories

Saint Vincent, Cape see São Vicente, Cabo de
Saint Vincent Passage 55 H4 passage Saint Lucia/Saint Vincent and the Grenadines
Saint Yves see Setúbal
Saipan 142 B1 island/country capital (Northern Mariana Islands) S Northern Mariana Islands
Saishū see Cheju-do
Sajama, Nevado 61 F4 mountain W Bolivia
Sajószentpéter 99 D6 Borsod-Abaúj-Zemplén, NE Hungary
Sakākah 120 B4 Al Jawf, NW Saudi Arabia
Sakakawea, Lake 44 D1 reservoir North Dakota, N USA
Sak'art'velo see Georgia
Sakata 130 D4 Yamagata, Honshū, C Japan
Sakhalin see Sakhalin, Ostrov
Sakhalin, Ostrov 115 G4 var. Sakhalin. island SE Russian Federation
Sakhon Nakhon see Sakon Nakhon
Şäki 117 G2 Rus. Sheki; prev. Nukha. NW Azerbaijan
Saki see Saky
Sakishima-shotō 130 A3 var. Sakisima Syotō. island group SW Japan
Sakisima Syotō see Sakishima-shotō
Sakiz see Saqqez
Sakiz-Adasi see Chíos
Sakon Nakhon 136 D4 var. Muang Sakon Nakhon, Sakhon Nakhon. Sakon Nakhon, E Thailand
Saky 109 F5 Rus. Saki. Respublika Krym, S Ukraine
Sal 74 A3 island Ilhas de Barlavento, NE Cape Verde
Sala 85 C6 Västmanland, C Sweden
Salacgrīva 106 C3 Est. Salatsi. Limbaži, N Latvia
Sala Consilina 97 D5 Campania, S Italy
Salado, Río 62 D5 river E Argentina
Salado, Río 64 C1 river C Argentina
Şalālah 121 D6 SW Oman
Salamá 52 B2 Baja Verapaz, C Guatemala
Salamanca 64 B4 Coquimbo, C Chile
Salamanca 92 D2 anc. Helmantica, Salmantica. Castilla-León, NW Spain

Salamīyah 118 B3 var. As Salamīyah. Ḥamāh, W Syria
Salang see Phuket
Salantai 106 B3 Klaipėda, NW Lithuania
Salatsi see Salacgrīva
Salavan 137 D5 var. Saravan, Saravane. Salavan, S Laos
Salavat 111 D6 Respublika Bashkortostan, W Russian Federation
Sala y Gomez 153 F4 island Chile, E Pacific Ocean
Sala y Gomez Fracture Zone see Sala y Gomez Ridge
Sala y Gomez Ridge 153 G4 var. Sala y Gomez Fracture Zone. fracture zone SE Pacific Ocean
Salazar see N'Dalatando
Šalčininkai 107 C5 Vilnius, SE Lithuania
Saldus see Zaragoza
Saldus 106 B3 Ger. Frauenburg. Saldus, W Latvia
Sale 149 C7 Victoria, SE Australia
Salé 70 C2 NW Morocco
Salekhard 114 D3 prev. Obdorsk. Yamalo-Nenetskiy Avtonomnyy Okrug, N Russian Federation
Salem 132 C2 Tamil Nādu, SE India
Salem 46 B3 state capital Oregon, NW USA
Salerno 97 D5 anc. Salernum. Campania, S Italy
Salerno, Golfo di 97 C5 Eng. Gulf of Salerno. gulf S Italy
Salerno, Gulf of see Salerno, Golfo di
Salernum see Salerno
Salihorsk 107 C7 Rus. Soligorsk. Minskaya Voblasts', S Belarus
Salima 79 E2 Central, C Malawi
Salina 45 F5 Kansas, C USA
Salina Cruz 51 F5 Oaxaca, SE Mexico
Salinas 60 A2 Guayas, W Ecuador
Salinas 47 B6 California, W USA
Salisbury 89 D7 var. New Sarum. S England, UK
Salisbury see Harare
Sállan see Sørøya
Sallyana see Salyan
Salmantica see Salamanca
Salmon River 46 D3 river Idaho, NW USA
Salmon River Mountains 46 D3 mountain range Idaho, NW USA
Salo 85 D6 Länsi-Suomi, SW Finland
Salon-de-Provence 91 D6 Bouches-du-Rhône, SE France
Salonica/Salonika see Thessaloníki
Salonta 108 A3 Hung. Nagyszalonta. Bihor, W Romania
Sal'sk 111 B7 Rostovskaya Oblast', SW Russian Federation
Salt see As Salṭ
Salta 64 C2 Salta, NW Argentina
Saltash 89 C7 SW England, UK
Saltillo 51 E3 Coahuila de Zaragoza, NE Mexico
Salt Lake City 44 B4 state capital Utah, W USA
Salto 64 D4 Salto, N Uruguay
Salton Sea 47 D8 lake California, W USA
Salvador 63 G3 prev. São Salvador. state capital Bahia, E Brazil
Salween 124 C2 Bur. Thanlwin, Chin. Nu Chiang, Nu Jiang. river SE Asia
Şalyan 135 E3 var. Sallyana. Mid Western, N Nepal
Salzburg 95 D6 anc. Juvavum. Salzburg, N Austria
Salzgitter 94 C4 prev. Watenstedt-Salzgitter. Niedersachsen, C Germany
Salzwedel 94 C3 Sachsen-Anhalt, N Germany
Šamac see Bosanski Šamac
Samakhixai 137 E5 var. Attapu, Attopeu. Attapu, S Laos
Samalayuca 50 C1 Chihuahua, N Mexico
Samar 139 F2 island C Philippines
Samara 111 C6 prev. Kuybyshev. Samarskaya Oblast', W Russian Federation
Samarang see Semarang
Samarinda 138 D4 Borneo, C Indonesia
Samarkand see Samarqand
Samarkandski/Samarkandskoye see Temirtau
Samarobriva see Amiens
Samarqand 123 E2 Rus. Samarkand. Samarqand Viloyati, C Uzbekistan
Samawa see As Samāwah

Sambalpur 135 F4 Orissa, E India
Sambava 79 G2 Antsiranana, NE Madagascar
Sambir 108 B2 Rus. Sambor. L'vivs'ka Oblast', NW Ukraine
Sambor see Sambir
Sambre 90 D2 river Belgium/France
Samfya 78 D2 Luapula, N Zambia
Saminatal 94 E2 valley Austria/Liechtenstein Europe
Samnān see Semnān
Sam Neua see Xam Nua
Samoa 145 E4 off. Independent State of Western Samoa, var. Sāmoa, prev. Western Samoa. country W Polynesia

SAMOA
Australasia & Oceania

Official name Independent State of Samoa
Formation 1962 / 1962
Capital Apia
Population 185,000 / 169 people per sq mile (65 people per sq km) / 22%
Total area 1104 sq miles (2860 sq km)
Languages Samoan*, English*
Religions Christian 99%, Other 1%
Ethnic mix Polynesian 90%, Euronesian 9%, Other 1%
Government Parliamentary system
Currency Tala = 100 sene
Literacy rate 99%
Calorie consumption 2945 calories

Sāmoa see Samoa
Samoa Basin 143 E3 undersea basin W Pacific Ocean
Samobor 100 A2 Zagreb, N Croatia
Sámos 105 E6 prev. Limín Vathéos. Sámos, Dodekánisa, Greece, Aegean Sea
Sámos 105 D6 island Dodekánisa, Greece, Aegean Sea
Samothrace see Samothráki
Samothráki 104 D4 Samothráki, NE Greece
Samothráki 104 C4 anc. Samothrace. island NE Greece
Sampit 138 C4 Borneo, C Indonesia
Samsun 116 D2 anc. Amisus. Samsun, N Turkey
Samtredia 117 F2 W Georgia
Samui, Ko 137 C6 island SW Thailand
Samut Prakan 137 C5 var. Muang Samut Prakan, Paknam. Samut Prakan, C Thailand
San 74 D3 Ségou, C Mali
San 99 E5 river SE Poland
Şan'ā' 121 B6 Eng. Sana. country capital (Yemen) W Yemen
Sana 100 B3 river NW Bosnia and Herzegovina
Sanae 154 B2 South African research station Antarctica
Sanaga 77 B5 river C Cameroon
San Ambrosio, Isla 57 A5 Eng. San Ambrosio Island. island W Chile
San Ambrosio Island see San Ambrosio, Isla
Sanandaj 120 C3 prev. Sinneh. Kordestān, W Iran
San Andrés, Isla de 53 F3 island NW Colombia South America
San Andrés Tuxtla 51 F4 var. Tuxtla. Veracruz-Llave, E Mexico
San Angelo 49 F3 Texas, SW USA
San Antonio 52 B2 Toledo, S Belize
San Antonio 64 B4 Valparaíso, C Chile
San Antonio 49 F4 Texas, SW USA
San Antonio Oeste 65 C5 Río Negro, E Argentina
San Antonio River 49 G4 river Texas, SW USA
Sanāw 121 C6 var. Sanaw. NE Yemen
San Benedicto, Isla 50 B4 island W Mexico
San Benito 52 B1 Petén, N Guatemala
San Benito 49 G5 Texas, SW USA
San Bernardino 47 C7 California, W USA
San Blas 50 C3 Sinaloa, C Mexico
San Blas, Cape 42 D3 headland Florida, SE USA
San Blas, Cordillera de 53 G4 mountain range NE Panama
San Carlos 52 D4 Río San Juan, S Nicaragua

San Carlos 48 B2 Arizona, SW USA
San Carlos see Quesada, Costa Rica
San Carlos de Ancud see Ancud
San Carlos de Bariloche 65 B5 Río
 Negro, SW Argentina
San Carlos del Zulia 58 C2 Zulia,
 W Venezuela
San Clemente Island 47 B8 island
 Channel Islands, California, W USA
San Cristóbal 58 C2 Táchira,
 W Venezuela
San Cristobal 144 C4 var. Makira. island
 SE Solomon Islands
San Cristóbal de see San Cristóbal de
 Las Casas
San Cristóbal de Las Casas 51 G5 var.
 San Cristóbal. Chiapas, SE Mexico
San Cristóbal, Isla 60 B5 var. Chatham
 Island. island Galapagos Islands,
 Ecuador, E Pacific Ocean
Sancti Spíritus 54 B2 Sancti Spíritus,
 C Cuba
Sandakan 138 D3 Sabah, East Malaysia
Sandalwood Island see Sumba, Pulau
Sandanski 104 C3 prev. Sveti Vrach.
 Blagoevgradt, SW Bulgaria
Sanday 88 D2 island NE Scotland, UK
Sanders 48 C2 Arizona, SW USA
Sand Hills 44 D3 mountain range
 Nebraska, C USA
San Diego 47 C8 California, W USA
Sandnes 85 A6 Rogaland, S Norway
Sandomierz 98 D4 Rus. Sandomir.
 Świętokrzyskie, C Poland
Sandomir see Sandomierz
Sandoway 136 A4 Arakan State,
 W Myanmar (Burma)
Sandpoint 46 C1 Idaho, NW USA
Sand Springs 49 G1 Oklahoma,
 C USA
Sandusky 40 D3 Ohio, N USA
Sandvika 85 A6 Akershus, S Norway
Sandviken 85 C6 Gävleborg, C Sweden
Sandwich Island see Éfaté
Sandwich Islands see Hawaiian Islands
Sandy Bay 93 H5 Saskatchewan,
 C Canada
Sandy City 44 B4 Utah, W USA
Sandy Lake 38 B3 lake Ontario,
 C Canada
San Esteban 52 D2 Olancho, C Honduras
San Eugenio/San Eugenio del Cuareim
 see Artigas
San Felipe 58 D1 Yaracuy,
 NW Venezuela
San Felipe de Puerto Plata see Puerto
 Plata
San Félix, Isla 57 A5 Eng. San Felix
 Island. island W Chile
San Felix Island see San Félix, Isla
San Fernando 92 C5 prev. Isla de León.
 Andalucía, S Spain
San Fernando 55 H5 Trinidad, Trinidad
 and Tobago
San Fernando 46 D1 California, W USA
San Fernando 58 D2 var. San Fernando
 de Apure. Apure, C Venezuela
San Fernando de Apure see San
 Fernando
San Fernando del Valle de Catamarca
 64 C3 var. Catamarca. Catamarca,
 NW Argentina
San Fernando de Monte Cristi see
 Monte Cristi
San Francisco 47 B6 California, W USA
San Francisco del Oro 50 C2
 Chihuahua, N Mexico
San Francisco de Macorís 55 E3
 C Dominican Republic
San Fructuoso see Tacuarembó
San Gabriel 60 B1 Carchi, N Ecuador
San Gabriel Mountains 46 E1 mountain
 range California, W USA
Sangihe, Kepulauan see Sangir,
 Kepulauan
Sangir, Kepulauan 139 F3 var
 Kepulauan Sangihe. island group
 N Indonesia
Sāngli 132 B1 Mahārāshtra, W India
Sangmélima 77 B5 Sud, S Cameroon
Sangre de Cristo Mountains 48 D1
 mountain range Colorado/New Mexico,
 C USA
San Ignacio 52 B1 prev. Cayo, El Cayo.
 Cayo, W Belize
San Ignacio 61 F3 Beni, N Bolivia
San Ignacio 50 B2 Baja California Sur,
 W Mexico

San Joaquin Valley 47 B7 valley
 California, W USA
San Jorge, Golfo 65 C6 var. Gulf of San
 Jorge. gulf S Argentina
San Jorge, Gulf of see San Jorge, Golfo
San José 53 E4 country capital (Costa
 Rica) San José, C Costa Rica
San José 61 G3 var. San José de
 Chiquitos. Santa Cruz, E Bolivia
San José 52 B3 var. Puerto San José.
 Escuintla, S Guatemala
San José 47 B6 California, W USA
San José see San José del Guaviare,
 Colombia
San José de Chiquitos see San José
San José de Cúcuta see Cúcuta
San José del Guaviare 58 C4 var. San
 José. Guaviare, S Colombia
San Juan 64 B4 San Juan, W Argentina
San Juan 55 F3 dependent territory
 capital (Puerto Rico) NE Puerto Rico
San Juan see San Juan de los Morros
San Juan Bautista 64 D3 Misiones,
 S Paraguay
San Juan Bautista see Villahermosa
San Juan Bautista Tuxtepec see Tuxtepec
San Juan de Alicante 93 F4 País
 Valenciano, E Spain
San Juan del Norte 53 E4 var. Greytown.
 Río San Juan, SE Nicaragua
San Juan de los Morros 58 D2 var. San
 Juan. Guárico, N Venezuela
San Juanito, Isla 50 C4 island C Mexico
San Juan Mountains 48 D1 mountain
 range Colorado, C USA
San Juan River 48 C1 river Colorado/
 Utah, W USA
San Julián see Puerto San Julián
Sankt-Bartholomäi see Palamuse
Sankt Gallen 95 B7 var. St. Gallen, Eng.
 Saint Gall, Fr. St-Gall. Sankt Gallen,
 NE Switzerland
Sankt-Georgen see Sfântu Gheorghe
Sankt-Jakobi see Pärnu-Jaagupi,
 Pärnumaa, Estonia
Sankt Martin see Martin
Sankt Moritz see St. Moritz
Sankt-Peterburg 110 B4 prev.
 Leningrad, Petrograd, Eng.
 Saint Petersburg, Fin. Pietari.
 Leningradskaya Oblast', NW Russian
 Federation
Sankt Pölten 95 E6 Niederösterreich,
 N Austria
Sankt Veit am Flaum see Rijeka
Sankuru 77 D6 river C Dem. Rep. Congo
Şanlıurfa 117 E4 prev. Sanli Urfa, Urfa;
 anc. Edessa. şanlıurfa, S Turkey
Sanli Urfa see Şanlıurfa
San Lorenzo 61 G5 Tarija, S Bolivia
San Lorenzo 60 A1 Esmeraldas,
 N Ecuador
San Lorenzo, Isla 60 C4 island W Peru
Sanlúcar de Barrameda 92 C5
 Andalucía, S Spain
San Luis 64 C4 San Luis, C Argentina
San Luis 52 B2 Petén, NE Guatemala
San Luis 50 A1 var. San Luis Río
 Colorado. Sonora, NW Mexico
San Luis Obispo 47 B7 California,
 W USA
San Luis Potosí 51 E3 San Luis Potosí,
 C Mexico
San Luis Río Colorado see San Luis
San Marcos 52 A2 San Marcos,
 W Guatemala
San Marcos 49 G4 Texas, SW USA
San Marcos de Arica see Arica
San Marino 96 B1 country capital (San
 Marino) C San Marino
San Marino 96 D1 off. Republic of San
 Marino. country S Europe

SAN MARINO
(continued)

Currency Euro = 100 cents
Literacy rate 99%
Calorie consumption Not available

San Marino, Republic of see San Marino
San Martín 154 A2 Argentinian research
 station Antarctica
San Mateo 59 E2 Anzoátegui,
 NE Venezuela
San Matías 61 H3 Santa Cruz, E Bolivia
San Matías, Golfo 65 C5 var. Gulf of San
 Matías. gulf E Argentina
San Matías, Gulf of see San Matías, Golfo
Sanmenxia 128 C4 var. Shan Xian.
 Henan, C China
Sänmiclăuş Mare see Sânnicolau Mare
San Miguel 52 C3 San Miguel,
 SE El Salvador
San Miguel 50 D2 Coahuila de Zaragoza,
 N Mexico
San Miguel de Ibarra see Ibarra
San Miguel de Tucumán 64 C3 var.
 Tucumán. Tucumán, N Argentina
San Miguelito 53 G4 Panamá,
 C Panama
San Miguel, Río 61 G3 river E Bolivia
San Murezzan see St. Moritz
Sannär see Sennar
Sânnicolau-Mare see Sânnicolau Mare
Sânnicolau Mare 108 A4 var.
 Sânnicolau-Mare, Hung. Nagyszentmiklós; prev.
 Sânmiclăuş Mare, Sînnicolau Mare.
 Timiş, W Romania
Sanok 99 E5 Podkarpackie, SE Poland
San Pablo 61 F5 Potosí, S Bolivia
San Pedro 52 C1 Corozal, NE Belize
San-Pédro 74 D5 S Côte d'Ivoire
 (Ivory Coast)
San Pedro 50 D3 var. San Pedro de
 las Colonias. Coahuila de Zaragoza,
 NE Mexico
San Pedro de la Cueva 50 C2 Sonora,
 NW Mexico
San Pedro de las Colonias see San Pedro
San Pedro de Lloc 60 B3 La Libertad,
 NW Peru
San Pedro Mártir, Sierra 50 A1
 mountain range NW Mexico
San Pedro Sula 52 C2 Cortés,
 NW Honduras
San Rafael 64 B4 Mendoza, W Argentina
San Rafael Mountains 47 C7 mountain
 range California, W USA
San Ramón de la Nueva Orán 64 C2
 Salta, N Argentina
San Remo 96 A3 Liguria, NW Italy
San Salvador 52 B3 country capital
 (El Salvador) San Salvador,
 SW El Salvador
San Salvador de Jujuy 64 C2 var. Jujuy.
 Jujuy, N Argentina
Sansanné-Mango 75 E4 var. Mango.
 N Togo
Sansepolcro 96 C3 Toscana, C Italy
San Severo 97 D5 Puglia, SE Italy
Santa Ana 61 F3 Beni, N Bolivia
Santa Ana 52 B3 Santa Ana,
 NW El Salvador
Santa Ana 46 D2 California, W USA
Santa Ana de Coro see Coro
Santa Ana Mountains 46 E2 mountain
 range California, W USA
Santa Barbara 50 C2 Chihuahua,
 N Mexico
Santa Barbara 47 C7 California,
 W USA
Santa Catalina Island 47 B8 island
 Channel Islands, California, W USA
Santa Catarina 63 E5 off. Estado de
 Santa Catarina. state S Brazil
Santa Catarina, Estado de see Santa
 Catarina
Santa Clara 54 B2 Villa Clara, C Cuba
Santa Clarita 46 D1 California, USA
Santa Comba 76 D2 Galicia, NW Spain
Santa Cruz 76 E2 São Tomé, S São Tome
 and Principe, Africa
Santa Cruz 47 B6 California, W USA
Santa Cruz 61 G4 department E Bolivia
Santa Cruz Barillas see Barillas
Santa Cruz del Quiché 52 B2 Quiché,
 W Guatemala
Santa Cruz de Tenerife 70 A3 Tenerife,
 Islas Canarias, Spain, NE Atlantic Ocean

Santa Cruz, Isla 60 B5 var. Indefatigable
 Island, Isla Chávez. island Galapagos
 Islands, Ecuador, E Pacific Ocean
Santa Cruz Islands 144 D3 island group
 E Solomon Islands
Santa Cruz, Río 65 B7 river S Argentina
Santa Elena 52 B1 Cayo, W Belize
Santa Fe 64 C4 Santa Fe, C Argentina
Santa Fe 48 D1 state capital New Mexico,
 SW USA
Santa Fe see Bogotá
Santa Fe de Bogotá see Bogotá
Santa Genoveva 50 B3 mountain
 W Mexico
Santa Isabel 144 C3 var. Bughotu. island
 N Solomon Islands
Santa Isabel see Malabo
Santa Lucia Range 47 B7 mountain
 range California, W USA
Santa Margarita, Isla 50 B3 island
 W Mexico
Santa Maria 63 E5 Rio Grande do Sul,
 S Brazil
Santa Maria 47 B7 California, USA
Santa Maria 92 A5 island Azores,
 Portugal, NE Atlantic Ocean
Santa Maria del Buen Aire
 see Buenos Aires
Santa María, Isla 60 A5 var. Isla
 Floreana, Charles Island. island
 Galapagos Islands, Ecuador,
 E Pacific Ocean
Santa Marta 58 B1 Magdalena,
 N Colombia
Santa Maura see Lefkáda
Santa Monica 46 D1 California, W USA
Santana 76 E2 São Tomé, C Sao Tome
 and Principe, Africa
Santander 92 D1 Cantabria, N Spain
Santanilla, Islas 53 E1 island group
 NE Honduras North America
Santarém 63 E2 Pará, N Brazil
Santarém 92 B3 anc. Scalabis. Santarém,
 W Portugal
Santa Rosa 64 C4 La Pampa, C Argentina
Santa Rosa see Santa Rosa de Copán
Santa Rosa de Copán 52 C2 Santa
 Rosa. Copán, W Honduras
Santa Rosa Island 47 B8 island
 California, W USA
Sant Carles de la Rápida see Sant Carles
 de la Ràpita
Sant Carles de la Ràpita 93 F3 var. Sant
 Carles de la Ràpida. Cataluña, NE Spain
Santiago 64 B4 var. Gran Santiago,
 country capital (Chile) Santiago, C Chile
Santiago 55 E3 var. Santiago de los
 Caballeros. N Dominican Republic
Santiago 53 F5 Veraguas, S Panama
Santiago 92 B1 var. Santiago de
 Compostela, Eng. Compostella; anc.
 Campus Stellae. Galicia, NW Spain
Santiago 74 A3 var. São Tiago. island
 Ilhas de Sotavento, S Cape Verde
Santiago see Santiago de Cuba, Cuba
Santiago de Compostela see Santiago
Santiago de Cuba 54 C3 var. Santiago.
 Santiago de Cuba, E Cuba
Santiago de Guayaquil see Guayaquil
Santiago del Estero 64 C3 Santiago del
 Estero, C Argentina
Santiago de los Caballeros see Santiago,
 Dominican Republic
Santiago de los Caballeros see Ciudad de
 Guatemala, Guatemala
Santiago Pinotepa Nacional see
 Pinotepa Nacional
Santiago, Río 60 B2 river N Peru
Santi Quaranta see Sarandë
Santissima Trinidad see Chilung
Sant Julià de Lòria 91 A8 Sant Julià de
 Lòria, SW Andorra Europe
Santo see Espíritu Santo
Santo Antão 74 A2 island Ilhas de
 Barlavento, N Cape Verde
Santo Antònio 76 E1 Príncipe,
 N Sao Tome and Principe, Africa
Santo António 76 E1 Príncipe,
 N Sao Tome and Principe, Africa
Santo Domingo 54 D3 prev. Ciudad
 Trujillo. country capital (Dominican
 Republic) SE Dominican Republic
Santo Domingo de los Colorados
 60 B1 Pichincha, NW Ecuador
Santo Domingo Tehuantepec see
 Tehuantepec
San Tomé de Guayana
 see Ciudad Guayana
Santorini 105 D7 island Kykládes,
 Greece, Aegean Sea

SAN MARINO
Southern Europe

Official name Republic of San Marino
Formation 1631 / 1631
Capital San Marino
Population 28,880 / 1203 people per
 sq mile (473 people per sq km) / 94%
Total area 23.6 sq miles (61 sq km)
Languages Italian*
Religions Roman Catholic 93%, Other and
 nonreligious 7%
Ethnic mix Sammarinese 80%, Italian 19%,
 Other 1%
Government Parliamentary system

Santos 63 F4 São Paulo, S Brazil
Santos Plateau 57 D5 *undersea plateau* SW Atlantic Ocean
Santo Tomé 64 D3 Corrientes, NE Argentina
Santo Tomé de Guayana *see* Ciudad Guayana
San Valentín, Cerro 65 A6 *mountain* S Chile
San Vicente 52 C3 San Vicente, C El Salvador
São Francisco, Rio 63 F3 *river* E Brazil
Sao Hill 73 C7 Iringa, S Tanzania
São João da Madeira 92 B2 Aveiro, N Portugal
São Jorge 92 A5 *island* Azores, Portugal, NE Atlantic Ocean
São Luís 63 F2 *state capital* Maranhão, NE Brazil
São Mandol *see* São Manuel, Rio
São Manuel, Rio 63 E3 *var.* São Mandol, Teles Pirés. *river* C Brazil
São Marcos, Baía de 63 F1 *bay* N Brazil
São Miguel 92 A5 *island* Azores, Portugal, NE Atlantic Ocean
Saona, Isla 55 E3 *island* SE Dominican Republic
Saône 91 D5 *river* E France
São Nicolau 74 A3 *Eng.* Saint Nicholas. *island* Ilhas de Barlavento, N Cape Verde
São Paulo 63 E4 *state capital* São Paulo, S Brazil
São Paulo 63 E4 *off.* Estado de São Paulo. *state* S Brazil
São Paulo de Loanda *see* Luanda
São Paulo, Estado de *see* São Paulo
São Pedro do Rio Grande do Sul *see* Rio Grande
São Roque, Cabo de 63 G2 *headland* E Brazil
São Salvador *see* Salvador, Brazil
São Salvador/São Salvador do Congo *see* M'Banza Congo, Angola
São Tiago *see* Santiago
São Tomé 77 A5 *country capital* (Sao Tome and Principe) São Tomé, S Sao Tome and Principe
São Tomé 76 E2 *Eng.* Saint Thomas. *island* S Sao Tome and Principe
Sao Tome and Principe 76 D1 *off.* Democratic Republic of Sao Tome and Principe. *country* E Atlantic Ocean

---

SÃO TOMÉ & PRÍNCIPE
West Africa

Official name Democratic Republic of São Tomé and Príncipe
Formation 1975 / 1975
Capital São Tomé
Population 187,410 / 505 people per sq mile (195 people per sq km) / 47%
Total area 386 sq miles (1001 sq km)
Languages Portuguese*, Portuguese Creole
Religions Roman Catholic 84%, Other 16%
Ethnic mix Black 90%, Portuguese and Creole 10%
Government Presidential system
Currency Dobra = 100 centimos
Literacy rate 83%
Calorie consumption 2460 calories

Sao Tome and Principe, Democratic Republic of *see* Sao Tome and Principe
São Tomé, Pico de 76 D2 *mountain* São Tomé, C Sao Tome and Principe, Africa
São Vicente 74 A3 *Eng.* Saint Vincent. *island* Ilhas de Barlavento, N Cape Verde
São Vicente, Cabo de 92 B5 *Eng.* Cape Saint Vincent, *Port.* Cabode São Vicente. *cape* S Portugal
São Vicente, Cabo de *see* São Vicente, Cabo de
Sápai *see* Sápes
Sapele 75 F5 Delta, S Nigeria
Sápes 104 D3 *var.* Sápai. Anatolikí Makedonía kai Thráki, NE Greece
Sapir *see* Sappir
Sa Pobla 93 G3 Mallorca, Spain, W Mediterranean Sea
Sappir 119 B7 *var* Sapir. Southern, S Israel
Sapporo 130 D2 Hokkaidō, NE Japan
Sapri 97 D6 Campania, S Italy

Sapulpa 49 G1 Oklahoma, C USA
Saqqez 120 C2 *var.* Saghez, Sakiz, Saqqiz. Kordestän, NW Iran
Saqqiz *see* Saqqez
Sara Buri 137 C5 *var.* Saraburi. Saraburi, C Thailand
Saraburi *see* Sara Buri
Saragossa *see* Zaragoza
Saragt *see* Sarahs
Saraguro 60 B2 Loja, S Ecuador
Sarahs 122 D3 *var.* Saragt, *Rus.* Serakhs. Ahal Welaýaty, S Turkmenistan
Sarajevo 100 C4 *country capital* (Bosnia and Herzegovina) Federacija Bosna I Hercegovina, SE Bosnia and Herzegovina
Sarakhs 120 E2 Khorāsān-Razavī, NE Iran
Saraktash 111 D6 Orenburgskaya Oblast', W Russian Federation
Saran' 114 C4 *Kaz.* Saran. Karaganda, C Kazakhstan
Saranda *see* Sarandë
Sarandë 101 C7 *var.* Saranda, *It.* Porto Edda; *prev.* Santi Quaranta. Vlorë, S Albania
Saransk 111 C5 Respublika Mordoviya, W Russian Federation
Sarasota 43 E4 Florida, SE USA
Saratov 111 B3 Saratovskaya Oblast', W Russian Federation
Saravan/Saravane *see* Salavan
Sarawak 138 D3 *state* East Malaysia
Sarawak *see* Kuching
Sarcelles 90 D1 Val-d'Oise, Île-de-France, N France Europe
Sardegna 97 A5 *Eng.* Sardinia. *island* Italy, C Mediterranean Sea
Sardinia *see* Sardegna
Sarera, Teluk *see* Cenderawasih, Teluk
Sargasso Sea 66 B4 *sea* W Atlantic Ocean
Sargodha 134 C2 Punjab, NE Pakistan
Sarh 76 C4 *prev.* Fort-Archambault. Moyen-Chari, S Chad
Sārī 120 D2 *var.* Sari, Sāri. Māzandarān, N Iran
Saría 105 E7 *island* SE Greece
Sarıkamış 117 F3 Kars, NE Turkey
Sarikol Range 123 G3 *Rus.* Sarykol'skiy Khrebet. *mountain range* China/Tajikistan
Sark 89 D8 *Fr.* Sercq. *island* Channel Islands
Şarkışla 116 D3 Sivas, C Turkey
Sarmiento 65 B6 Chubut, S Argentina
Sarnia 38 C5 Ontario, S Canada
Sarny 108 C1 Rivnens'ka Oblast', NW Ukraine
Sarochyna 107 D5 *Rus.* Sorochino. Vitsyebskaya Voblasts', N Belarus
Sarov 111 C5 *prev.* Sarova. Respublika Mordoviya, SW Russian Federation
Sarova *see* Sarov
Sarpsborg 85 B6 Østfold, S Norway
Sarrebruck *see* Saarbrücken
Sartène 91 E7 Corse, France, C Mediterranean Sea
Sarthe 90 B4 *river* N France
Sárti 104 C4 Kentrikí Makedonía, N Greece
Saruhan *see* Manisa
Saryarqa *see* Kazakhskiy Melkosopochnik
Sarykol'skiy Khrebet *see* Sarikol Range
Sary-Tash 123 F2 Oshskaya Oblast', SW Kyrgyzstan
Saryyesik-Atyrau, Peski 123 G1 *desert* E Kazakhstan
Sasebo 131 A7 Nagasaki, Kyūshū, SW Japan
Saskatchewan 37 F5 *province* SW Canada
Saskatchewan 37 F5 *river* Manitoba/Saskatchewan, C Canada
Saskatoon 37 F5 Saskatchewan, S Canada
Sasovo 111 B5 Ryazanskaya Oblast', W Russian Federation
Sassandra 74 D5 *var.* Ibo, Sassandra (Ivory Coast)
Sassandra 74 D5 *var.* Ibo, Sassandra Fleuve. *river* S Côte d'Ivoire (Ivory Coast)
Sassandra Fleuve *see* Sassandra
Sassari 97 A5 Sardegna, Italy, C Mediterranean Sea
Sassenheim 86 C3 Zuid-Holland, W Netherlands
Sassnitz 94 D2 Mecklenburg-Vorpommern, NE Germany

Sathmar *see* Satu Mare
Sátoraljaújhely 99 D6 Borsod-Abaúj-Zemplén, NE Hungary
Sätpura Range 134 D4 *mountain range* C India
Satsunan-shotō 130 A3 *island group* Nansei-shotō, SW Japan Asia
Sattanen 84 D3 Lappi, NE Finland
Satu Mare 108 B3 *Ger.* Sathmar, *Hung.* Szatmárrnémeti. Satu Mare, NW Romania
Sau *see* Sava
Saudi Arabia 121 B5 *off.* Kingdom of Saudi Arabia, Al 'Arabiyah as Su'ūdīyah, *Ar.* Al Mamlakah al 'Arabīyah as Su'ūdīyah. *country* SW Asia

---

SAUDI ARABIA
Southwest Asia

Official name Kingdom of Saudi Arabia
Formation 1932 / 1932
Capital Riyadh
Population 24.6 million / 30 people per sq mile (12 people per sq km) / 86%
Total area 756,981 sq miles (1,960,582 sq km)
Languages Arabic*
Religions Sunni Muslim 85%, Shi'a Muslim 15%
Ethnic mix Arab 90%, Afro-Asian 10%
Government Monarchy
Currency Saudi riyal = 100 halalat
Literacy rate 79%
Calorie consumption 2844 calories

Saudi Arabia, Kingdom of *see* Saudi Arabia
Sauer *see* Sûre
Saugor *see* Ságar
Saulkrasti 106 C3 Rīga, C Latvia
Sault Sainte Marie 40 C1 Michigan, N USA
Sault Ste. Marie 38 C4 Ontario, S Canada
Saumur 90 B4 Maine-et-Loire, NW France
Saurimo 78 C1 *Port.* Henrique de Carvalho, Vila Henrique de Carvalho. Lunda Sul, NE Angola
Sava 100 E6 *Rus.* Sava. Mahilyowskaya Voblasts', E Belarus
Savá 52 D2 Colón, N Honduras
Sava 100 B3 *Eng.* Save, *Ger.* Sau, *Hung.* Száva. *river* SE Europe
Savai'i 145 E4 *island* NW Samoa
Savannah 43 E2 Georgia, SE USA
Savannah River 43 E2 *river* Georgia/South Carolina, SE USA
Savannakhet *see* Khanthabouli
Savanna-La-Mar 54 A5 W Jamaica
Savaria *see* Szombathely
Save *see* Sava
Save, Rio 79 E3 *var.* Sabi. *river* Mozambique/Zimbabwe
Saverne 90 E3 *var.* Zabern; *anc.* Tres Tabernae. Bas-Rhin, NE France
Savigliano 96 A2 Piemonte, NW Italy
Savigsivik *see* Savissivik
Savinski *see* Savinskiy
Savinskiy 110 C3 *var.* Savinski. Arkhangel'skaya Oblast', NW Russian Federation
Savissivik 82 D1 *var.* Savigsivik. Avannaarsua, N Greenland
Savoie 91 D5 *cultural region* E France
Savona 96 A2 Liguria, NW Italy
Savu Sea 139 E5 *Ind.* Laut Sawu. *sea* S Indonesia
Sawakin *see* Suakin
Sawdirī *see* Sodiri
Sawhāj *see* Sohâg
Şawqirah 121 D6 *var.* Suqrah. S Oman
Sawu, Laut *see* Savu Sea
Saxe *see* Sachsen
Saxony *see* Sachsen
Sayaboury *see* Xaignabouli
Sayanskiy Khrebet 112 D3 *mountain range* S Russian Federation
Saýat 122 D3 *Rus.* Sayat. Lebap Welaýaty, E Turkmenistan
Sayaxché 52 B2 Petén, N Guatemala
Şaydā/Sayida *see* Saïda
Sayhūt 121 D6 E Yemen
Saynshand 127 E2 Dornogovĭ, SE Mongolia
Sayre 41 E3 Pennsylvania, NE USA

Say'ūn 121 C6 *var.* Saywūn. C Yemen
Saywūn *see* Say'ūn
Scalabis *see* Santarém
Scandinavia 16 D2 *geophysical region* NW Europe
Scarborough 89 D5 N England, UK
Scarpanto *see* Kárpathos
Scebeli *see* Shebeli
Schaan 94 E1 W Liechtenstein Europe
Schaerbeek 87 C6 Brussels, C Belgium
Schaffhausen 95 B7 *Fr.* Schaffhouse. Schaffhausen, N Switzerland
Schaffhouse *see* Schaffhausen
Schagen 86 C2 Noord-Holland, NW Netherlands
Schaulen *see* Šiauliai
Schebschi Mountains *see* Shebshi Mountains
Scheessel 94 B3 Niedersachsen, NW Germany
Schefferville 39 E2 Québec, E Canada
Schelde *see* Scheldt
Scheldt 87 B5 *Dut.* Schelde, *Fr.* Escaut. *river* W Europe
Schell Creek Range 47 D5 *mountain range* Nevada, W USA
Schenectady 41 F3 New York, NE USA
Schertz 49 G4 Texas, SW USA
Schiermonnikoog 86 D1 *Fris.* Skiermûntseach. *island* Waddeneilanden, N Netherlands
Schijndel 86 D4 Noord-Brabant, S Netherlands
Schil *see* Jiu
Schiltigheim 90 E3 Bas-Rhin, NE France
Schivelbein *see* Świdwin
Schlackenwerth *see* Ostrov
Schleswig 94 B2 Schleswig-Holstein, N Germany
Schleswig-Holstein 94 B2 *state* N Germany
Schlettstadt *see* Sélestat
Schlochau *see* Człuchów
Schneekoppe *see* Sněžka
Schneidemühl *see* Piła
Schoden *see* Skuodas
Schönebeck 94 C4 Sachsen-Anhalt, C Germany
Schönlanke *see* Trzcianka
Schooten *see* Schoten
Schoten 87 C5 *var.* Schooten. Antwerpen, N Belgium
Schouwen 86 B4 *island* SW Netherlands
Schwabenalb *see* Schwäbische Alb
Schwäbisch Alb 95 B6 *var.* Schwabenalb, *Eng.* Swabian Jura. *mountain range* S Germany
Schwandorf 95 C5 Bayern, SE Germany
Schwarzwald 95 B6 *Eng.* Black Forest. *mountain range* SW Germany
Schwaz 95 C7 Tirol, W Austria
Schweidnitz *see* Świdnica
Schweinfurt 95 B5 Bayern, SE Germany
Schweiz *see* Switzerland
Schwerin 94 C3 Mecklenburg-Vorpommern, N Germany
Schwertberg *see* Świecie
Schwiebus *see* Świebodzin
Schwyz 95 B7 *var.* Schwiz. Schwyz, C Switzerland
Schyl *see* Jiu
Scilly, Isles of 89 B8 *island group* SW England, UK
Scio *see* Chíos
Scoresby Sound/Scoresbysund *see* Ittoqqortoormiit
Scoresby Sund *see* Kangertittivaq
Scotia Sea 57 C8 *sea* SW Atlantic Ocean
Scotland 88 C3 *cultural region* Scotland, U K
Scotland 88 C3 *national region* Scotland, U K
Scott Base 154 B4 NZ research station Antarctica
Scott Island 154 B5 *island* Antarctica
Scottsbluff 44 D3 Nebraska, C USA
Scottsboro 42 D1 Alabama, S USA
Scottsdale 48 B2 Arizona, SW USA
Scranton 41 F3 Pennsylvania, NE USA
Scrobesbyrig' *see* Shrewsbury
Scupi *see* Skopje
Scutari *see* Shkodër
Scutari, Lake 101 C5 *Alb.* Liqeni i Shkodrës, *SCr.* Skadarsko Jezero. *lake* Albania/Montenegro
Scyros *see* Skýros
Searcy 42 B1 Arkansas, C USA

Seattle *46 B2* Washington, NW USA
Sébaco *52 D3* Matagalpa, W Nicaragua
Sebaste/Sebastia *see* Sivas
Sebastián Vizcaíno, Bahía *50 A2 bay*
  NW Mexico
Sebastopol *see* Sevastopol'
Sebenico *see* Šibenik
Sechura, Bahía de *60 A3 bay* NW Peru
Secunderãbãd *134 D5 var.*
  Sikandarabad. Andhra Pradesh, C India
Sedan *90 D3* Ardennes, N France
Seddon *151 D5* Marlborough, South
  Island, New Zealand
Seddonville *151 C5* West Coast, South
  Island, New Zealand
Sédhiou *74 B3* SW Senegal
Sedlez *see* Siedlce
Sedona *48 B2* Arizona, SW USA
Sedunum *see* Sion
Seeland *see* Sjælland
Seesen *94 B4* Niedersachsen, C Germany
Segestica *see* Sisak
Segezha *110 B3* Respublika Kareliya,
  NW Russian Federation
Seghedin *see* Szeged
Segna *see* Senj
Segodunum *see* Rodez
Ségou *74 D3 var.* Segu. Ségou,
  C Mali
Segovia *92 D2* Castilla-León, C Spain
Segoviao Wangki *see* Coco, Río
Segu *see* Ségou
Séguédine *75 H2* Agadez, NE Niger
Seguin *49 G4* Texas, SW USA
Segura *93 E4 river* S Spain
Seinäjoki *85 D5 Swe.* Östermyra.
  Länsi-Suomi, W Finland
Seine *127 E1 river* N France
Seine, Baie de la *90 B3 bay* N France
Sekondi *see* Sekondi-Takoradi
Sekondi-Takoradi *75 E5 var.* Sekondi.
  S Ghana
Selânik *see* Thessaloníki
Selenga *127 E1 Mong.* Selenge Mörön.
  river Mongolia/Russian Federation
Selenge Mörön *see* Selenga
Sélestat *90 E4 Ger.* Schlettstadt.
  Bas-Rhin, NE France
Seleucia *see* Silifke
Selfoss *83 E5* Sudhurland,
  SW Iceland
Sélibaby *74 C3 var.* Sélibaby. Guidimaka,
  S Mauritania
Sélibaby *see* Sélibabi
Selma *47 C6* California, W USA
Selway River *46 D2 river* Idaho,
  NW USA North America
Selwyn Range *148 B3 mountain range*
  Queensland, C Australia
Selzaete *see* Zelzate
Semarang *138 C5 var.* Samarang. Jawa,
  C Indonesia
Sembé *77 B5* La Sangha, NW Congo
Semendria *see* Smederevo
Semey *see* Semipalatinsk
Semezhevo *see* Syemyezhava
Seminole *49 E3* Texas, SW USA
Seminole, Lake *42 D3 reservoir* Florida/
  Georgia, SE USA
Semipalatinsk *114 D4 Kaz.* Semey.
  Vostochnyy Kazakhstan, E Kazakhstan
Semnãn *120 D3 var.* Samnãn. Semnãn,
  N Iran
Semois *87 C8 river* SE Belgium
Sendai *131 A8* Kagoshima, Kyūshū,
  SW Japan
Sendai *130 D4* Miyagi, Honshū,
  C Japan
Sendai-wan *130 D4 bay* E Japan
Senec *99 C6 Ger.* Wartberg,
  Hung. Szenc; *prev.* Szempcz.
  Bratislavský Kraj, W Slovakia
Senegal *74 B3 off.* Republic of Senegal,
  Fr. Sénégal. *country* W Africa

SENEGAL
West Africa

Official name Republic of Senegal
Formation 1960 / 1960
Capital Dakar
Population 11.7 million / 157 people per
sq mile (61 people per sq km) / 47%
Total area 75,749 sq miles
(196,190 sq km)
Languages French*, Diola,
Mandinka, Malinke, Pulaar, Serer,
Soninke, Wolof

SENEGAL
(continued)

Religions Sunni Muslim 90%, Christian
(mainly Roman Catholic) 5%, Traditional
beliefs 5%
Ethnic mix Wolof 43%, Toucouleur 24%,
Serer 15%, Other 11%, Diola 4%,
Malinke 3%
Government Presidential system
Currency CFA franc = 100 centimes
Literacy rate 39%
Calorie consumption 2279 calories

Senegal *74 C3 Fr.* Sénégal. *river* W Africa
Senegal, Republic of *see* Senegal
Senftenberg *94 D4* Brandenburg,
  E Germany
Senia *see* Senj
Senica *99 C6 Ger.* Senitz, Hung. Szenice.
  Trnavský Kraj, W Slovakia
Seniça *see* Sjenica
Senitz *see* Senica
Senj *100 A3 Ger.* Zengg, It. Segna; anc.
  Senia. Lika-Senj, NW Croatia
Senja *84 C2 prev.* Senjen. *island*
  N Norway
Senjen *see* Senja
Senkaku-shotō *130 A3 island group*
  SW Japan
Senlis *90 C3* Oise, N France
Sennar *72 C4 var.* Sannãr. Sinnar,
  C Sudan
Senones *see* Sens
Sens *90 C3 anc.* Agendicum, Senones.
  Yonne, C France
Sensburg *see* Mragowo
Sên, Stœng *137 D5 river* C Cambodia
Senta *100 D3 Hung.* Zenta. Vojvodina,
  N Serbia
Seo de Urgel *see* La See d'Urgel
Seoul *see* Soul
Şepsi-Sângeorz/Sepsiszentgyörgy *see*
  Sfântu Gheorghe
Sept-Îles *39 E3* Québec, SE Canada
Seraing *87 D6* Liège, E Belgium
Serakhs *see* Sarahs
Seram, Laut *see* Ceram Sea
Seram, Pulau *139 F4 var.* Serang, Eng.
  Ceram. *island* Maluku, E Indonesia
Serang *138 C5* Jawa, C Indonesia
Serang *see* Seram, Pulau
Serasan, Selat *138 C3 strait*
  Indonesia/Malaysia
Serbia *100 D4 off.* Federal Republic
  of Serbia; prev. Yugoslavia, SCr.
  Jugoslavija. *country* SE Europe

SERBIA
Europe

Official name Republic of Serbia
Formation 2006 / 2006
Capital Belgrade
Population 9.11 million / 290 people per
sq mile (112 people per sq km) / 52%
Total area 34,116 sq miles
(88,361 sq km)
Languages Serbo-Croat*, Albanian,
Hungarian
Religions Orthodox Christian 85%,
Muslim 6%, Other 6%, Roman
Catholic 3%
Ethnic mix Serb 66%, Albanian 19%,
Hungarian 4%, Bosniak 2%, Other 9%
Government Parliamentary system
Currency Dinar (Serbia) = 100 para
Literacy rate 98%
Calorie consumption Not available

Serbia, Federal Republic of *see* Serbia
Sercq *see* Sark
Serdar *122 C2 prev. Rus.* Gyzyrlabat,
  Kizyl-Arvat. Balkan Welaýaty,
  W Turkmenistan
Serdica *see* Sofia
Serenje *78 D2* Central, E Zambia
Seres *see* Sérres
Seret/Sereth *see* Siret
Serhetabat *122 D4 prev. Rus.*
  Gushgy, Kushka. Mary Welaýaty,
  S Turkmenistan
Sérifos *105 C6 anc.* Seriphos. *island*
  Kykládes, Greece, Aegean Sea
Seriphos *see* Sérifos
Serov *114 C3* Sverdlovskaya Oblast',
  C Russian Federation

Serowe *78 D3* Central, SE Botswana
Serpa Pinto *see* Menongue
Serpent's Mouth, The *59 F2 Sp.* Boca
  de la Serpiente. *strait* Trinidad and
  Tobago/Venezuela
Serpiente, Boca de la *see* Serpent's
  Mouth, The
Serpukhov *111 B5* Moskovskaya Oblast',
  W Russian Federation
Sérrai *see* Sérres
Serrana, Cayo de *53 F2 island group*
  NW Colombia South America
Serranilla, Cayo de *53 F2 island
  group* NW Colombia South America
  Caribbean Sea
Serravalle *96 E1* N San Marino
Sérres *104 C3 var.* Seres; prev. Sérrai.
  Kentrikí Makedonía, NE Greece
Sesdlets *see* Siedlce
Sesto San Giovanni *96 B2* Lombardia,
  N Italy
Sesvete *100 B2* Zagreb, N Croatia
Setabis *see* Xátiva
Sète *91 C6 prev.* Cette. Hérault,
  S France
Setesdal *85 A6 valley* S Norway
Sétif *71 E2 var.* Stif. N Algeria
Setté Cama *77 A6* Ogooué-Maritime,
  SW Gabon
Setúbal *92 B4 Eng.* Saint Ubes, Saint
  Yves. Setúbal, W Portugal
Setúbal, Baía de *92 B4 bay* W Portugal
Seul, Lac *38 B3 lake* Ontario,
  S Canada
Sevan *117 G2* C Armenia
Sevana Lich *117 G3 Eng.* Lake Sevan,
  Rus. Ozero Sevan. *lake* E Armenia
Sevan, Lake/Sevan, Ozero *see* Sevana
  Lich
Sevastopol' *109 F5 Eng.* Sebastopol.
  Respublika Krym, S Ukraine
Severn *38 B2 river* Ontario, S Canada
Severn *89 D6 Wel.* Hafren. *river*
  England/Wales, UK
Severnaya Dvina *110 C4 var.* Northern
  Dvina. *river* NW Russian Federation
Severnaya Zemlya *115 E2 var.* Nicholas
  II Land. *island group* N Russian
  Federation
Severnyy *110 E3* Respublika Komi,
  NW Russian Federation
Severodonets'k *see* Syeverodonets'k
Severodvinsk *110 C3 prev.* Molotov,
  Sudostroy. Arkhangel'skaya Oblast',
  NW Russian Federation
Severomorsk *110 C2* Murmanskaya
  Oblast', NW Russian Federation
Severo-Sibirskaya Nizmennost'
  115 E2 var. North Siberian Plain,
  Eng. North Siberian Lowland. *lowlands*
  N Russian Federation
Seversk *114 D4* Tomskaya Oblast',
  C Russian Federation
Sevier Lake *44 A4 lake* Utah, W USA
Sevilla *92 C4 Eng.* Seville; anc. Hispalis.
  Andalucía, SW Spain
Seville *see* Sevilla
Sevlievo *104 D2* Gabrovo, N Bulgaria
Sevluš/Sevlyush *see* Vynohradiv
Seward's Folly *see* Alaska
Seychelles *79 G1 country* W Indian
  Ocean

SEYCHELLES
Indian Ocean

Official name Republic of Seychelles
Formation 1976 / 1976
Capital Victoria
Population 81,188 / 781 people per
sq mile (301 people per sq km) / 64%
Total area 176 sq miles (455 sq km)
Languages French Creole*, English,
French
Religions Anglican 8%,
Roman Catholic 90%,
Other (including Muslim) 2%
Ethnic mix Creole 89%, Indian 5%,
Other 4%, Chinese 2%
Government Presidential system
Currency Seychelles rupee = 100 cents
Literacy rate 92%
Calorie consumption 2465 calories

Seychelles *79 G1 island group*
  NE Seychelles
Seydhisfjördhur *83 E5* Austurland,
  E Iceland

Seýdi *122 D2 Rus.* Seydi; prev.
  Neftezavodsk. Lebap Welaýaty,
  E Turkmenistan
Seyhan *see* Adana
Sfákia *see* Chóra Sfakíon
Sfântu Gheorghe *108 C4 Ger.* Sankt-
  Georgen, Hung. Sepsiszentgyörgy;
  prev. Şepsi-Sângeorz, Sfîntu Gheorghe.
  Covasna, C Romania
Sfax *71 F2 Ar.* Şafãqis. E Tunisia
Sfîntu Gheorghe *see* Sfântu Gheorghe
's-Gravenhage *86 B4 var.* Den Haag,
  Eng. The Hague, Fr. La Haye.
  country capital (Netherlands-seat
  of government) Zuid-Holland,
  W Netherlands
's-Gravenzande *86 B4* Zuid-Holland,
  W Netherlands
Shaan/Shaanxi Sheng *see* Shaanxi
Shaanxi *128 B5 var.* Shaan, Shaanxi
  Sheng, Shan-hsi, Shenshi, Shensi.
  province C China
Shabani *see* Zvishavane
Shabeelle, Webi *see* Shebeli
Shache *126 A3 var.* Yarkant. Xinjiang
  Uygur Zizhiqu, NW China
Shacheng *see* Huailai
Shackleton Ice Shelf *154 D3 ice shelf*
  Antarctica
Shaddãdi *see* Ash Shadãdah
Shãhãbãd *see* Eslãmãbãd
Shahjahanabad *see* Delhi
Shahr-e Kord *120 C3 var.* Shahr Kord.
  Chahãr MaḤall va Bakhtiãrī, C Iran
Shahr Kord *see* Shahr-e Kord
Shãhrũd *120 D2 prev.* Emãmrũd,
  Emãmshahr. Semnãn, N Iran
Shalkar *114 B4 var.* Chelkar.
  Aktyubinsk, W Kazakhstan
Shãm, Bãdiyat ash *see* Syrian Desert
Shandí *see* Shendi
Shandong *128 D4 var.* Lu, Shandong
  Sheng, Shantung. *province* E China
Shandong Sheng *see* Shandong
Shanghai *128 D5 var.* Shang-hai.
  Shanghai Shi, E China
Shanghai Shi *129 D5 var.* Hu, Shanghai.
  municipality E China
Shanghai *see* Shanghai Shi
Shangrao *128 D5* Jiangxi, S China
Shan-hsi *see* Shaanxi, China
Shan-hsi *see* Shanxi, China
Shannon *89 A6 Ir.* an tSionainn. *river*
  W Ireland
Shan Plateau *136 B3 plateau*
  E Myanmar (Burma)
Shansi *see* Shanxi
Shantar Islands *see* Shantarskiye Ostrova
Shantarskiye Ostrova *115 G3*
  Eng. Shantar Islands. *island group*
  E Russian Federation
Shantou *128 D6 var.* Shan-t'ou, Swatow.
  Guangdong, S China
Shan-t'ou *see* Shantou
Shantung *see* Shandong
Shanxi *128 C4 var.* Jin, Shan-hsi, Shansi,
  Shanxi Sheng. *province* C China
Shan Xian *see* Sanmenxia
Shanxi Sheng *see* Shanxi
Shaoguan *128 C6 var.* Shao-kuan,
  Cant. Kukong; prev. Ch'u-chiang.
  Guangdong, S China
Shao-kuan *see* Shaoguan
Shaqrã' *120 B4* Ar Riyãd, C Saudi Arabia
Shaqrã *see* Shuqrah
Shar *130 D5 var.* Charsk. Vostochnyy
  Kazakhstan, E Kazakhstan
Shari *130 D2* Hokkaidō, NE Japan
Shari *see* Chari
Sharjah *see* Ash Shãriqah
Shark Bay *147 A5 bay* Western Australia
Sharqi, Al Jabal ash/Sharqi, Jebel esh
  see Anti-Lebanon
Shashe *78 D3 var.* Shashi. *river*
  Botswana/Zimbabwe
Shashi *see* Shashe
Shatskiy Rise *125 G1 undersea rise*
  N Pacific Ocean
Shawnee *49 G1* Oklahoma, C USA
Shaykh, Jabal ash *see* Hermon, Mount
Shchadryn *107 D7 Rus.* Shchedrin.
  Homyel'skaya Voblasts', SE Belarus
Shchedrin *see* Shchadryn
Shcheglovsk *see* Kemerovo
Shchëkino *111 B5* Tul'skaya Oblast',
  W Russian Federation
Shchors *109 E1* Chernihivs'ka Oblast',
  N Ukraine

Shchuchin *see* Shchuchyn
Shchuchinsk 114 C4 *prev.* Shchuchye.
  Akmola, N Kazakhstan
Shchuchye *see* Shchuchinsk
Shchuchyn 107 B5 *Pol.* Szczuczyn
  Nowogródzki, *Rus.* Shchuchin.
  Hrodzyenskaya Voblasts', W Belarus
Shebekino 111 A6 Belgorodskaya
  Oblast', W Russian Federation
Shebelē Wenz, Wabē *see* Shebeli
Shebeli 73 D5 *Amh.* Wabē Shebelē Wenz,
  It. Scebeli, *Som.* Webi Shabeelle. *river*
  Ethiopia/Somalia
Sheberghān 123 E3 *var.* Shibarghān,
  Shiberghan, Shibarghān. Jowzjān,
  N Afghanistan
Sheboygan 40 B2 Wisconsin, N USA
Shebshi Mountains 76 A4 *var.*
  Schebschi Mountains. *mountain range*
  E Nigeria
Shechem *see* Nablus
Shedadi *see* Ash Shadādah
Sheffield 89 D5 N England, UK
Shekhem *see* Nablus
Sheki *see* Şäki
Shelby 44 B1 Montana, NW USA
Sheldon 45 F3 Iowa, C USA
Shelekhov Gulf *see* Shelikhova, Zaliv
Shelikhova, Zaliv 115 G2
  Eng. Shelekhov Gulf. *gulf* E Russian
  Federation
Shendi 72 C4 *var.* Shandī. River Nile,
  NE Sudan
Shengking *see* Liaoning
Shenking *see* Liaoning
Shenshi/Shensi *see* Shaanxi
Shenyang 128 D3 *Chin.* Shen-yang, *Eng.*
  Moukden, Mukden; *prev.* Fengtien.
  province capital Liaoning, NE China
Shen-yang *see* Shenyang
Shepetivka 108 D2 *Rus.* Shepetovka.
  Khmel'nyts'ka Oblast', NW Ukraine
Shepetovka *see* Shepetivka
Shepparton 149 C7 Victoria,
  SE Australia
Sherbrooke 39 E4 Québec, SE Canada
Shereik 72 C3 River Nile, N Sudan
Sheridan 44 C2 Wyoming, C USA
Sherman 49 G2 Texas, SW USA
's-Hertogenbosch 86 C4 *Fr.* Bois-le-
  Duc, *Ger.* Herzogenbusch. Noord-
  Brabant, S Netherlands
Shetland Islands 88 D1 *island group*
  NE Scotland, UK
Shevchenko *see* Aktau
Shibarghān *see* Sheberghān
Shiberghan/Shibarghān *see* Sheberghān
Shibetsu 130 D2 *var.* Sibetu. Hokkaidō,
  NE Japan
Shibh Jazīrat Sīna *see* Sinai
Shibushi-wan 131 B8 *bay* SW Japan
Shigatse *see* Xigazê
Shih-chia-chuang/Shihmen *see*
  Shijiazhuang
Shihezi 126 C2 Xinjiang Uygur Zizhiqu,
  NW China
Shiichi *see* Shyichy
Shijiazhuang 128 C4 *var.* Shih-chia-
  chuang; *prev.* Shihmen. *province
  capital* Hebei, E China
Shikārpur 134 B3 Sind, S Pakistan
Shikoku 131 C7 *var.* Sikoku. *island*
  SW Japan
Shikoku Basin 125 F2 *var.* Sikoku Basin.
  undersea basin N Philippine Sea
Shikotan, Ostrov 130 E2 *Jap.* Shikotan-
  tō. *island* NE Russian Federation
Shikotan-tō *see* Shikotan, Ostrov
Shilabo 73 D5 Somali, E Ethiopia
Shiliguri 135 F3 *prev.* Siliguri. West
  Bengal, NE India
Shilka 115 F4 *river* S Russian Federation
Shillong 135 G3 *state capital* Meghālaya,
  NE India
Shimbir Berris *see* Shimbiris
Shimbiris 72 E4 *var.* Shimbir Berris.
  mountain N Somalia
Shimoga 132 C2 Karnātaka, W India
Shimonoseki 131 A7 *var.* Simonoseki,
  hist. Akamagaseki. Bakan. Yamaguchi,
  Honshū, SW Japan
Shinano-gawa 131 C5 *var.* Sinano Gawa.
  river Honshū, C Japan
Shindand 122 D4 Herāt, W Afghanistan
Shingū 131 C6 *var.* Singū. Wakayama,
  Honshū, SW Japan
Shinjō 130 D4 *var.* Sinzyô. Yamagata,
  Honshū, C Japan

Shinyanga 73 C7 Shinyanga,
  NW Tanzania
Shiprock 48 C1 New Mexico, SW USA
Shīrāz 120 D4 *var.* Shīrāz. Fārs, S Iran
Shishchitsy *see* Shyshchytsy
Shivpuri 134 D3 Madhya Pradesh,
  C India
Shizugawa 130 D4 Miyagi, Honshū,
  NE Japan
Shizuoka 131 D6 *var.* Sizuoka. Shizuoka,
  Honshū, S Japan
Shklov *see* Shklow
Shklow 107 D6 *Rus.* Shklov.
  Mahilyowskaya Voblasts', E Belarus
Shkodër 101 C5 *var.* Shkodra, *It.* Scutari,
  SCr. Skadar. Shkodër, NW Albania
Shkodra *see* Shkodër
Shkodrës, Liqeni i *see* Scutari, Lake
Shkumbinit, Lumi i 101 C6 *var.*
  Shkumbi, Shkumbin. *river* C Albania
Shkumbi/Shkumbin *see* Shkumbinit,
  Lumi i
Sholāpur *see* Solāpur
Shostka 109 F1 Sums'ka Oblast',
  NE Ukraine
Show Low 48 B2 Arizona,
  SW USA
Show Me State *see* Missouri
Shpola 109 E3 Cherkas'ka Oblast',
  N Ukraine
Shqipëria/Shqipërisë, Republika e
  see Albania
Shreveport 42 A2 Louisiana, S USA
Shrewsbury 89 D6 *hist.* Scrobesbyrig'.
  W England, UK
Shu 114 C5 *Kaz.* Shū. Zhambyl,
  SE Kazakhstan
Shū *see* Shu
Shuang-liao *see* Liaoyuan
Shumagin Islands 36 B3 *island group*
  Alaska, USA
Shumen 104 D2 Shumen, NE Bulgaria
Shumilina 107 E5 *Rus.* Shumilino.
  Vitsyebskaya Voblasts', NE Belarus
Shumilino *see* Shumilina
Shunsen *see* Ch'unch'ŏn
Shuqrah 121 B7 *var.* Shaqrā.
  SW Yemen
Shwebo 136 B3 Sagaing,
  C Myanmar (Burma)
Shyichy 107 C7 *Rus.* Shiichi.
  Homyel'skaya Voblasts', SE Belarus
Shymkent 114 B5 *prev.* Chimkent.
  Yuzhnyy Kazakhstan, S Kazakhstan
Shyshchytsy 107 C6 *Rus.* Shishchitsy.
  Minskaya Voblasts', C Belarus
Siam *see* Thailand
Siam, Gulf of *see* Thailand, Gulf of
Sian *see* Xi'an
Siang *see* Brahmaputra
Siangtan *see* Xiangtan
Šiauliai 106 B4 *Ger.* Schaulen. Šiauliai,
  N Lithuania
Siazan' *see* Siyäzän
Sibay 111 D6 Respublika Bashkortostan,
  W Russian Federation
Šibenik 116 B4 *It.* Sebenico. Šibenik-
  Knin, S Croatia
Siberia *see* Sibir'
Siberoet, Pulau *see* Siberut, Pulau
Siberut, Pulau 138 A4 *prev.* Siberoet.
  island Kepulauan Mentawai,
  W Indonesia
Sibi 134 B2 Baluchistān, SW Pakistan
Sibir' 115 E3 *var.* Siberia. *physical region*
  NE Russian Federation
Sibiti 77 B6 La Lékoumou, S Congo
Sibiu 108 B4 *Ger.* Hermannstadt, *Hung.*
  Nagyszeben. Sibiu, C Romania
Sibolga 138 B3 Sumatera, W Indonesia
Sibu 138 D3 Sarawak, East Malaysia
Sibut 76 C4 *prev.* Fort-Sibut. Kémo,
  S Central African Republic
Sibuyan Sea 139 E2 *sea* W Pacific Ocean
Sichon 137 C6 *var.* Ban Sichon. Si Chon.
  Nakhon Si Thammarat, SW Thailand
Si Chon *see* Sichon
Sichuan 128 B5 *var.* Chuan, Sichuan
  Sheng, Ssu-ch'uan, Szechwan,
  Szechwan. *province* C China
Sichuan Pendi 128 B5 *basin* C China
Sichuan Sheng *see* Sichuan
Sicilia 97 C7 *Eng.* Sicily; *anc.* Trinacria.
  island Italy, C Mediterranean Sea
Sicilian Channel *see* Sicily, Strait of
Sicily, Strait of 97 B7 *var.* Sicilian
  Channel. *strait* C Mediterranean Sea
Sicuani 61 E4 Cusco, S Peru

Sidári 104 A4 Kérkyra, Iónia Nisiá,
  Greece, C Mediterranean Sea
Sidas 138 C4 Borneo, C Indonesia
Siderno 97 D7 Calabria, SW Italy
Sidhirókastron *see* Sidirókastro
Sidi Barráni 72 A1 NW Egypt
Sidi Bel Abbès 70 D2 *var.* Sidi bel Abbès,
  Sidi-Bel-Abbès. NW Algeria
Sidirókastro 104 C3 *prev.*
  Sidhirókastron. Kentrikí Makedonía,
  NE Greece
Sidley, Mount 154 B4 *mountain*
  Antarctica
Sidney 44 D1 Montana, NW USA
Sidney 44 D3 Nebraska, C USA
Sidney 40 C4 Ohio, N USA
Sidon *see* Saïda
Sidra *see* Surt
Sidra/Sidra, Gulf of *see* Surt, Khalīj,
  N Libya
Siebenbürgen *see* Transylvania
Siedlce 98 E3 *Ger.* Sedlez, *Rus.* Sesdlets.
  Mazowieckie, C Poland
Siegen 94 B4 Nordrhein-Westfalen,
  W Germany
Siemiatycze 98 E3 Podlaskie, NE Poland
Siena 96 B3 *Fr.* Sienne; *anc.* Saena Julia.
  Toscana, C Italy
Sienne *see* Siena
Sieradz 98 C4 Sieradz, C Poland
Sierpc 98 D3 Mazowieckie, C Poland
Sierra Leone 74 C4 off. Republic of Sierra
  Leone. *country* W Africa

SIERRA LEONE
West Africa

Official name Republic of
Sierra Leone
Formation 1961 / 1961
Capital Freetown
Population 5.5 million / 199 people per
sq mile (77 people per sq km) / 37%
Total area 27,698 sq miles
(71,740 sq km)
Languages English*, Mende. Temne. Krio
Religions Muslim 30%, Traditional
beliefs 30%, Other 30%, Christian 10%
Ethnic mix Mende 35%, Temne 32%,
Other 21%, Limba 8%, Kuranko 4%
Government Presidential system
Currency Leone = 100 cents
Literacy rate 30%
Calorie consumption 1936 calories

Sierra Leone Basin 66 C4 *undersea basin*
  E Atlantic Ocean
Sierra Leone, Republic of *see* Sierra
  Leone
Sierra Leone Ridge *see* Sierra Leone Rise
Sierra Leone Rise 66 C4 *var.* Sierra
  Leone Ridge, Sierra Leone Schwelle.
  undersea rise E Atlantic Ocean
Sierra Leone Schwelle *see* Sierra
  Leone Rise
Sierra Madre 52 B2 *var.* Sierra
  de Soconusco. *mountain range*
  Guatemala/Mexico
Sierra Madre del Sur 51 E5 *mountain
  range* S Mexico
Sierra Madre Occidental 50 C3 *var.*
  Western Sierra Madre. *mountain range*
  C Mexico
Sierra Madre Oriental 51 E3 *var.*
  Eastern Sierra Madre. *mountain range*
  C Mexico
Sierra Nevada 47 C6 *mountain range*
  S Spain
Sierra Nevada 47 C6 *mountain range*
  W USA
Sierra Vieja 48 D3 *mountain range*
  Texas, SW USA
Sierra Vista 48 B3 Arizona, SW USA
Sífnos 105 C6 *anc.* Siphnos. *island*
  Kykládes, Greece, Aegean Sea
Sigli 138 A3 Sumatera, W Indonesia
Siglufjördhur 83 E4 Nordhurland
  Vestra, N Iceland
Signal Peak 48 A2 *mountain* Arizona,
  SW USA
Signan *see* Xi'an
Signy 154 A2 UK *research station* South
  Orkney Islands, Antarctica
Siguatepeque 52 C2 Comayagua,
  W Honduras
Siguiri 74 D4 NE Guinea
Sihanoukville *see* Kâmpóng Saôm
Siilinjärvi 84 E4 Itä-Suomi, C Finland

Siirt 117 F4 *var.* Sert; *anc.* Tigranocerta.
  Siirt, SE Turkey
Sikandarabad *see* Secunderābād
Sikasso 74 D4 Sikasso, S Mali
Sikeston 45 H5 Missouri, C USA
Sikhote-Alin', Khrebet 115 G4
  mountain range SE Russian Federation
Siking *see* Xi'an
Siklós 99 C7 Baranya, SW Hungary
Sikoku *see* Shikoku
Sikoku Basin *see* Shikoku Basin
Šilalė 106 B4 Tauragė, W Lithuania
Silchar 135 G3 Assam, NE India
Silesia 98 B4 *physical region*
  SW Poland
Silifke 116 C4 *anc.* Seleucia. Mersin,
  S Turkey
Siliguri *see* Shiliguri
Siling Co 126 C5 *lake* W China
Silinhot *see* Xilinhot
Silistra 104 E1 *var.* Silistria; *anc.*
  Durostorum. Silistra, NE Bulgaria
Silistria *see* Silistra
Sillamäe 106 E2 *Ger.* Sillamäggi. Ida-
  Virumaa, NE Estonia
Sillamäggi *see* Sillamäe
Sillein *see* Žilina
Šilutė 106 B4 *Ger.* Heydekrug. Klaipėda,
  W Lithuania
Sılvan 117 F4 Dıyarbakır, SE Turkey
Silva Porto *see* Kuito
Silver State *see* Colorado
Silver State *see* Nevada
Simanichy 107 C7 *Rus.* Simonichi.
  Homyel'skaya Voblasts', SE Belarus
Simav 116 B3 Kütahya, W Turkey
Simav Çayı 116 A3 *river* NW Turkey
Simbirsk *see* Ul'yanovsk
Simeto 97 C7 *river* Sicilia, Italy,
  C Mediterranean Sea
Simeulue, Pulau 138 A3 *island*
  NW Indonesia
Simferopol' 109 F5 Respublika Krym,
  S Ukraine
Simitla 104 C3 Blagoevgrad, SW Bulgaria
Şimlăul Silvaniei/Şimleul Silvaniei *see*
  Şimleu Silvaniei
Şimleu Silvaniei 108 B3 *Hung.*
  Szilágysomlyó; *prev.* Şimlăul Silvaniei,
  Şimleul Silvaniei. Sălaj, NW Romania
Simonichi *see* Simanichy
Simonoseki *see* Shimonoseki
Simpelveld 87 D6 Limburg,
  SE Netherlands
Simplon Pass 95 B8 *pass* S Switzerland
Simpson *see* Fort Simpson
Simpson Desert 148 B4 *desert* Northern
  Territory/South Australia
Sinai 72 C2 *var.* Sinai Peninsula, *Ar.*
  Shibh Jazīrat Sīna, Sīnā'. *physical
  region* NE Egypt
Sinaia 108 C4 Prahova, SE Romania
Sinano Gawa *see* Shinano-gawa
Sīnā'/Sinai Peninsula *see* Sinai
Sincelejo 58 B2 Sucre, NW Colombia
Sind 134 B3 *var.* Sindh. *province*
  SE Pakistan
Sindelfingen 95 B6 Baden-Württemberg,
  SW Germany
Sindh *see* Sind
Sindi 106 D2 *Ger.* Zintenhof. Pärnumaa,
  SW Estonia
Sines 92 B4 Setúbal, S Portugal
Singan *see* Xi'an
Singapore 138 A1 off. Republic of
  Singapore. *country* SE Asia

SINGAPORE
Southeast Asia

Official name Republic of Singapore
Formation 1965 / 1965
Capital Singapore
Population 4.3 million / 18220 people
per sq mile (7049 people per sq km)
/ 100%
Total area 250 sq miles (648 sq km)
Languages English*, Malay*, Mandarin*,
Tamil*
Religions Buddhist 55%, Taoist 22%,
Muslim 16%, Hindu, Christian,
and Sikh 7%
Ethnic mix Chinese 77%, Malay 14%,
Indian 8%, Other 1%
Government Parliamentary system
Currency Singapore dollar = 100 cents
Literacy rate 93%
Calorie consumption Not available

Singapore 138 B3 country capital
(Singapore) S Singapore
Singapore, Republic of see Singapore
Singen 95 B6 Baden-Württemberg,
S Germany
Singida 73 C7 Singida, C Tanzania
Singkang 139 E4 Sulawesi, C Indonesia
Singkawang 138 C3 Borneo, C Indonesia
Singora see Songkhla
Singü see Shingü
Sining see Xining
Siniscola 97 A5 Sardegna, Italy,
C Mediterranean Sea
Sinj 100 B4 Split-Dalmacija, SE Croatia
Sinkiang/Sinkiang Uighur
Autonomous Region see Xinjiang
Uygur Zizhiqu
Sinnamarie see Sinnamary
Sinnamary 59 H3 var. Sinnamarie.
N French Guiana
Sinneh see Sanandaj
Sinnicolau Mare see Sânnicolau Mare
Sinoe, Lacul see Sinoie, Lacul
Sinoie, Lacul 108 D5 prev. Lacul Sinoe.
lagoon SE Romania
Sinop 116 D2 anc. Sinope. Sinop,
N Turkey
Sinope see Sinop
Sinsheim 95 B6 Baden-Württemberg,
SW Germany
Sint Maarten 55 G3 Eng. Saint Martin.
island N Netherlands Antilles
Sint-Michielsgestel 86 C4 Noord-
Brabant, S Netherlands
Sîn-Miclăuş see Gheorgheni
Sint-Niklaas 87 B5 Fr. Saint-Nicolas.
Oost-Vlaanderen, N Belgium
Sint-Pieters-Leeuw 87 B6 Vlaams
Brabant, C Belgium
Sintra 73 E5 Nugaal, NE Somalia
Sintra 92 B3 prev. Cintra. Lisboa,
W Portugal
Sinuijiuf 73 E5 Nugaal, NE Somalia
Sinus Aelaniticus see Aqaba, Gulf of
Sinus Gallicus see Lion, Golfe du
Sinyang see Xinyang
Sinzyô see Shinjō
Sion 95 A7 Ger. Sitten; anc. Sedunum.
Valais, SW Switzerland
Sioux City 45 F3 Iowa, C USA
Sioux Falls 45 F3 South Dakota,
N USA
Sioux State see North Dakota
Siphnos see Sífnos
Siping 128 D3 var. Ssu-p'ing, Szeping;
prev. Ssu-p'ing-chieh. Jilin, NE China
Siple, Mount 154 A4 mountain Siple
Island, Antarctica
Siquirres 53 E4 Limón, E Costa Rica
Siracusa 97 D7 Eng. Syracuse. Sicilia,
Italy, C Mediterranean Sea
Sir Edward Pellew Group 148 B2 island
group Northern Territory, NE Australia
Siret 108 C3 var. Siretul, Ger.
Sereth, Rus. Seret, Ukr. Siret. river
Romania/Ukraine
Siretul see Siret
Siria see Syria
Sirikit Reservoir 136 C4 lake
N Thailand
Sirjān 120 D4 prev. Sa'īdābād. Kermān,
S Iran
Sirna see Sýrna
Şırnak 117 F4 Şırnak, SE Turkey
Síros see Sýros
Sirte see Surt
Sirti, Gulf of see Surt, Khalīj
Sisak 100 B3 var. Siscia, Ger. Sissek,
Hung. Sziszek; anc. Segestica. Sisak-
Moslavina, C Croatia
Siscia see Sisak
Sisimiut 82 C3 var. Holsteinborg,
Holsteinsborg, Holstenborg,
Holstensborg. Kitaa, S Greenland
Sissek see Sisak
Sīstān, Daryācheh-ye see Şāberī,
Hāmūn-e
Sitaş Cristuru see Cristuru Secuiesc
Siteía 105 D8 var. Sitía. Kríti, Greece,
E Mediterranean Sea
Sitges 93 G2 Cataluña, NE Spain
Sitía see Siteía
Sittang 136 B4 var. Sittoung. river
S Myanmar (Burma)
Sittard 87 D5 Limburg, SE Netherlands
Sitten see Sion
Sittoung see Sittang
Sittwe 136 A3 var. Akyab. Arakan State,
W Myanmar (Burma)

Siuna 52 D3 Región Autónoma Atlántico
Norte, NE Nicaragua
Siut see Asyūţ
Sivas 116 D3 anc. Sebastia, Sebaste.
Sivas, C Turkey
Siverek 117 E4 Şanlıurfa, S Turkey
Siwa 72 A2 var. Sīwah. NW Egypt
Sīwah see Siwa
Six Counties, The see Northern Ireland
Six-Fours-les-Plages 91 D6 Var,
SE France
Siyäzän 117 H2 Rus. Siazan'.
NE Azerbaijan
Sjælland 85 B8 Eng. Zealand, Ger.
Seeland. island E Denmark
Sjar see Säare
Sjenica 101 D5 Turk. Seniça. Serbia,
SW Serbia
Skadar see Shkodër
Skadarsko Jezero see Scutari, Lake
Skagerak see Skagerrak
Skagerrak 85 A6 var. Skagerak. channel
N Europe
Skagit River 46 B1 river Washington,
NW USA
Skalka 84 C3 lake N Sweden
Skarżysko-Kamienna 98 D4
Świętokrzyskie, C Poland
Skaudvilė 106 B4 Tauragė,
SW Lithuania
Skegness 89 E6 E England, UK
Skellefteå 84 D4 Västerbotten,
N Sweden
Skellefteälven 84 C4 river N Sweden
Ski 85 B6 Akershus, S Norway
Skíathos 105 C5 Skíathos, Vóreies
Sporádes, Greece, Aegean Sea
Skidal' 107 B5 Rus. Skidel'.
Hrodzyenskaya Voblasts',
W Belarus
Skidel' see Skidal'
Skiermûntseach see Schiermonnikoog
Skierniewice 98 D3 Łódzkie, C Poland
Skiftet 106 C1 strait Finland Atlantic
Ocean Baltic Sea Gulf of Bothnia/Gulf
of Finland
Skíros see Skýros
Skópelos 105 C5 Skópelos, Vóreies
Sporádes, Greece, Aegean Sea
Skopje 101 D6 var. Üsküb, Turk. Üsküp,
prev. Skoplje; anc. Scupi. country
capital (FYR Macedonia)
N FYR Macedonia
Skoplje see Skopje
Skovorodino 115 F4 Amurskaya Oblast',
SE Russian Federation
Skuodas 106 B3 Ger. Schoden, Pol.
Szkudy. Klaipėda, NW Lithuania
Skye, Isle of 88 B3 island NW Scotland,
UK
Skylge see Terschelling
Skýros 105 C5 var. Skíros. Skńyros,
Vóreies Sporádes, Greece, Aegean Sea
Skýros 105 C5 var. Skíros; anc. Scyros.
island Vóreies Sporádes, Greece,
Aegean Sea
Slagelse 85 B7 Vestsjælland, E Denmark
Slatina 100 C3 Hung. Szlatina; prev.
Podravska Slatina. Virovitica-
Podravina, NE Croatia
Slatina 108 B5 Olt, S Romania
Slavgorod see Slawharad
Slavonska Požega see Požega
Slavonski Brod 100 C3 Ger. Brod,
Hung. Bród; prev. Brod, Brod na Savi.
Brod-Posavina, NE Croatia
Slavuta 108 C2 Khmel'nyts'ka Oblast',
NW Ukraine
Slavyansk see Slov"yans'k
Slawharad 107 E7 Rus. Slavgorod.
Mahilyowskaya Voblasts', E Belarus
Sławno 98 C2 Zachodnio-pomorskie,
NW Poland
Slēmāni see As Sulaymānīyah
Sliema 102 N5 N Malta
Sligo 89 A5 Ir. Sligeach. Sligo,
NW Ireland
Sliven 104 D2 var. Slivno. Sliven,
C Bulgaria
Slivnitsa 104 B2 Sofiya, W Bulgaria
Slivno see Sliven
Slobozia 108 C5 Ialomiţa, SE Romania
Slonim 107 B6 Pol. Słonim, Rus. Slonim.
Hrodzyenskaya Voblasts', W Belarus
Słonim see Slonim
Slovakia 99 C6 off. Slovenská Republika,
Ger. Slowakei, Hung. Szlovákia, Slvk.
Slovensko. country C Europe

SLOVAKIA
Central Europe

Official name Slovak Republic
Formation 1993 / 1993
Capital Bratislava
Population 5.4 million / 285 people per
sq mile (110 people per sq km) / 57%
Total area 18,859 sq miles
(48,845 sq km)
Languages Slovak*, Hungarian (Magyar),
Czech
Religions Roman Catholic 60%,
Other 18%, Atheist 10%, Protestant 8%,
Orthodox Christian 4%
Ethnic mix Slovak 85%, Magyar 11%,
Other 2%, Roma 1%, Czech 1%
Government Parliamentary system
Currency Slovak koruna = 100 halierov
Literacy rate 99%
Calorie consumption 2889 calories

Slovak Ore Mountains see Slovenské
rudohorie
Slovenia 95 D8 off. Republic of Slovenia,
Ger. Slowenien, Slvn. Slovenija. country
SE Europe

SLOVENIA
Central Europe

Official name Republic of Slovenia
Formation 1991 / 1991
Capital Ljubljana
Population 2 million / 256 people per
sq mile (99 people per sq km) / 50%
Total area 7820 sq miles (20,253 sq km)
Languages Slovene*, Serbo-Croat
Religions Roman Catholic 96%,
Other 3%, Muslim 1%
Ethnic mix Slovene 83%, Other 12%,
Serb 2%, Croat 2%, Bosniak 1%
Government Parliamentary system
Currency Tolar = 100 stotinov
Literacy rate 99%
Calorie consumption 3001 calories

Slovenia, Republic of see Slovenia
Slovenija see Slovenia
Slovenská Republika see Slovakia
Slovenské rudohorie 99 D6
Eng. Slovak Ore Mountains,
Ger. Slowakisches Erzgebirge,
Ungarisches Erzgebirge. mountain
range C Slovakia
Slovensko see Slovakia
Slov"yans'k 109 G3 Rus. Slavyansk.
Donets'ka Oblast', E Ukraine
Słowakei see Slovakia
Slowakisches Erzgebirge see Slovenské
rudohorie
Slowenien see Slovenia
Słubice 98 B3 Ger. Frankfurt. Lubuskie,
W Poland
Sluch 108 D1 river NW Ukraine
Słupsk 98 C2 Ger. Stolp. Pomorskie,
N Poland
Slutsk 107 C6 Rus. Slutsk. Minskaya
Voblasts', S Belarus
Smallwood Reservoir 39 F2 lake
Newfoundland and Labrador,
S Canada
Smara 70 B3 var. Es Semara. N Western
Sahara
Smarhon' 107 C5 Pol. Smorgonie,
Rus. Smorgon'. Hrodzyenskaya
Voblasts', W Belarus
Smederevo 100 D4 Ger. Semendria.
Serbia, N Serbia
Smederevska Palanka 100 D4 Serbia,
C Serbia
Smela see Smila
Smila 109 E2 Rus. Smela. Cherkas'ka
Oblast', C Ukraine
Smilten see Smiltene
Smiltene 106 D3 Ger. Smilten. Valka,
N Latvia
Smola 84 A4 island W Norway
Smolensk 111 A5 Smolenskaya Oblast',
W Russian Federation
Smorgon'/Smorgonie see Smarhon'
Smyrna see İzmir
Snake 34 B4 river Yukon Territory,
NW Canada
Snake River 46 C3 river NW USA
Snake River Plain 46 D4 plain Idaho,
NW USA

Sneek 86 D2 Friesland, N Netherlands
Sneeuw-gebergte see Maoke,
Pegunungan
Snežka 98 B4 Ger. Schneekoppe,
Pol. Śnieżka. mountain N Czech
Republic/Poland
Śniardwy, Jezioro 114 D2 Ger.
Spirdingsee. lake NE Poland
Sniečkus see Visaginas
Śnieżka see Snežka
Snina 99 E5 Hung. Szinna. Prešovský
Kraj, E Slovakia
Snowdonia 89 C6 mountain range
NW Wales, UK
Snowdrift see Łutselk'e
Snow Mountains see Maoke,
Pegunungan
Snyder 49 F3 Texas, SW USA
Sobradinho, Barragem de see
Sobradinho, Represa de
Sobradinho, Represa de 63 F2 var.
Barragem de Sobradinho. reservoir
E Brazil
Sochi 111 A7 Krasnodarskiy Kray,
SW Russian Federation
Socialist People's Libyan Arab
Jamahiriya see Libya
Société, Archipel de la 145 G4 var.
Archipel de Tahiti, Îles de la Société,
Eng. Society Islands. island group
W French Polynesia
Société, Îles de la/Society Islands see
Société, Archipel de la
Society Islands see Société,
Archipel de la
Soconusco, Sierra de see Sierra Madre
Socorro 48 D2 New Mexico, SW USA
Socorro, Isla 50 B5 island W Mexico
Socotra see Suquṭrā
Soc Trăng 137 D6 var. Khanh Hung.
Soc Trăng, S Vietnam
Socuéllamos 93 E3 Castilla-La Mancha,
C Spain
Sodankylä 84 D3 Lappi, N Finland
Sodari see Sodiri
Söderhamn 85 C5 Gävleborg,
C Sweden
Södertälje 85 C6 Stockholm,
C Sweden
Sodiri 72 B4 var. Sawdirī, Sodari.
Northern Kordofan, C Sudan
Soekaboemi see Sukabumi
Soemba see Sumba, Pulau
Soengaipenoeh see Sungaipenuh
Soerabaja see Surabaya
Soerakarta see Surakarta
Sofia see Sofiya
Sofiya 104 C2 var. Sophia,
Eng. Sofia, Lat. Serdica. country capital
(Bulgaria) (Bulgaria) Sofiya-Grad,
W Bulgaria
Sogamoso 58 B3 Boyacá, C Colombia
Sognefjorden 85 A5 fjord NE North Sea
Sohâg 72 B2 var. Sawhāj, Suliag.
C Egypt
Sohar see Şuḩār
Sohm Plain 66 B3 abyssal plain
NW Atlantic Ocean
Sohrau see Żory
Sokal' 108 C2 Rus. Sokal. L'vivs'ka
Oblast', NW Ukraine
Söke 116 A4 Aydın, SW Turkey
Sokhumi 117 E1 Rus. Sukhumi.
NW Georgia
Sokodé 75 F4 C Togo
Sokol 110 C4 Vologodskaya Oblast',
NW Russian Federation
Sokółka 98 E3 Podlaskie, NE Poland
Sokolov 99 A5 Ger. Falkenau an
der Eger; prev. Falknov nad Ohří.
Karlovarský Kraj, W Czech Republic
Sokone 74 B3 W Senegal
Sokoto 75 F3 Sokoto, NW Nigeria
Sokoto 75 F4 river NW Nigeria
Sokotra see Suquṭrā
Solāpur 124 B3 var. Sholāpur.
Mahārāshtra, W India
Solca 108 C3 Ger. Solka. Suceava,
N Romania
Sol, Costa del 92 D5 coastal region
S Spain
Soldeu 91 B7 NE Andorra Europe
Solec Kujawski 98 C3 Kujawsko-
pomorskie, C Poland
Soledad 58 B1 Atlántico,
NE Venezuela
Isla Soledad see East Falkland
Soligorsk see Salihorsk

Solikamsk 114 C3 Permskaya Oblast',
NW Russian Federation
Sol'-Iletsk 111 D6 Orenburgskaya
Oblast', W Russian Federation
Solingen 94 A4 Nordrhein-Westfalen,
W Germany
Solka see Solca
Sollentuna 85 C6 Stockholm,
C Sweden
Solo see Surakarta
Solok 138 B4 Sumatera, W Indonesia
Solomon Islands 144 C3 prev. British
Solomon Islands Protectorate. country
W Solomon Islands N Melanesia
W Pacific Ocean

SOLOMON ISLANDS
Australasia & Oceania

Official name Solomon Islands
Formation 1978 /1978
Capital Honiara
Population 478,000 / 44 people per sq
mile (17 people per sq km) / 20%
Total area 10,985 sq miles
(28,450 sq km)
Languages English*, Melanesian Pidgin,
Pidgin English
Religions Anglican 34%,
Roman Catholic 19%, Methodist 11%,
Seventh-day Adventist 10%, South Seas
Evangelical Church 17%, Other 9%
Ethnic mix Melanesian 94%,
Polynesian 4%, Other 2%
Government Parliamentary system
Currency Solomon Islands dollar =
100 cents
Literacy rate 77%
Calorie consumption 2265 calories

Solomon Islands 144 C3 island group
Papua New Guinea/Solomon Islands
Solomon Sea 144 B3 sea W Pacific Ocean
Soltau 94 B3 Niedersachsen,
NW Germany
Solun see Thessaloníki
Sol'tsy 110 A4 Novgorodskaya Oblast',
W Russian Federation
Solwezi 78 D2 North Western,
NW Zambia
Sōma 130 D4 Fukushima, Honshū,
C Japan
Somalia 73 D5 off. Somali Democratic
Republic, Som. Jamuuriyada
Demuqraadiga Soomaaliyeed,
Soomaaliya; prev. Italian Somaliland,
Somaliland Protectorate. country
E Africa

SOMALIA
East Africa

Official name Somalia
Formation 1960 / 1960
Capital Mogadishu
Population 8.2 million / 34 people per
sq mile (13 people per sq km) / 28%
Total area 246,199 sq miles
(637,657 sq km)
Languages Somali*, Arabic*, English,
Italian
Religions Sunni Muslim 98%,
Christian 2%
Ethnic mix Somali 85%, Other 15%
Government Transitional regime
Currency Somali shilling = 100 centesimi
Literacy rate 24%
Calorie consumption 1628 calories

Somali Basin 69 E5 undersea basin
W Indian Ocean
Somali Democratic Republic see
Somalia
Somaliland 73 D5 disputed territory
N Somalia
Somaliland Protectorate see Somalia
Sombor 100 C3 Hung. Zombor.
Vojvodina, NW Serbia
Someren 87 D5 Noord-Brabant,
SE Netherlands
Somerset 42 A5 var. Somerset Village.
W Bermuda
Somerset 40 C5 Kentucky, S USA
Somerset Island 42 A5 island
W Bermuda
Somerset Island 37 F2 island
Queen Elizabeth Islands, Nunavut,
NW Canada

Somerset Village see Somerset
Somers Islands see Bermuda
Somerton 48 A2 Arizona,
SW USA
Someş 108 B3 river Hungary/Romania
Europe
Somme 90 C2 river N France
Sommerfeld see Lubsko
Somotillo 52 C3 Chinandega,
NW Nicaragua
Somoto 52 D3 Madriz,
NW Nicaragua
Songea 73 C8 Ruvuma, S Tanzania
Sŏngjin see Kimch'aek
Songkhla 137 C7 var. Songkla, Mal.
Singora. Songkhla, SW Thailand
Songkla see Songkhla
Sonoran Desert 48 A3
var. Desierto de Altar. desert
Mexico/USA
Sonoran Desert see Altar, Desierto de
Sonsonate 52 B3 Sonsonate,
W El Salvador
Soochow see Suzhou
**Soomaaliya/Soomaaliyeed,
Jamuuriyada Demuqraadiga** see
Somalia
Soome Laht see Finland, Gulf of
Sop Hao 136 D3 Houaphan, N Laos
Sophia see Sofiya
Sopianae see Pécs
Sopot 98 C2 Plovdiv, C Bulgaria
Sopron 99 B6 Ger. Ödenburg. Győr-
Moson-Sopron, NW Hungary
Sorau/Sorau in der Niederlausitz
see Żary
Sorgues 91 D6 Vaucluse, SE France
Sorgun 116 D3 Yozgat, C Turkey
Soria 93 E2 Castilla-León, N Spain
Soroca 108 D3 Rus. Soroki.
N Moldova
Sorochino see Sarochyna
Soroki see Soroca
Sorong 139 F4 Papua, E Indonesia
Sørøy see Sørøya
Sørøya 84 C2 var. Sørøy, Lapp. Sállan.
island N Norway
Sortavala 110 B3 Respublika Kareliya,
NW Russian Federation
Sotavento, Ilhas de 74 A3
var. Leeward Islands. island group
S Cape Verde
Sotkamo 84 E4 Oulu, C Finland
Souanké 77 B5 La Sangha, NW Congo
Soueida see As Suwaydā'
Souflí 104 D3 prev. Souflíon. Anatolikí
Makedonía kai Thráki, NE Greece
Souflíon see Souflí
Soufrière 55 F2 W Saint Lucia
Soukhné see As Sukhnah
Sŏul 129 E4 off. Sŏul-t'ŭkpyŏlsi,
Eng. Seoul, Jap. Keijō; prev. Kyŏngsŏng.
country capital (South Korea)
NW South Korea
Sŏul-t'ŭkpyŏlsi see Sŏul
Soûr 119 A5 var. Şūr; anc. Tyre.
SW Lebanon
Souris River 44 E1 var. Mouse River.
river Canada/USA
Soúrpi 105 B5 Thessalía, C Greece
Sousse 71 F2 var. Sūsah. NE Tunisia
South Africa 78 C4 off. Republic of
South Africa, Afr. Suid-Afrika. country
S Africa

SOUTH AFRICA
Southern Africa

Official name Republic of South Africa
Formation 1934 / 1994
Capital Pretoria; Cape Town;
Bloemfontein
Population 47.4 million / 101 people per
sq mile (39 people per sq km) / 55%
Total area 471,008 sq miles (1,219,912
sq km)
Languages English, isiZulu, isiXhosa,
Afrikaans, Sepedi, Setswana, Sesotho,
Xitsonga, siSwati, Tshivenda, isiNdebele
Religions Christian 68%, Traditional
beliefs and animist 29%, Muslim 2%,
Hindu 1%
Ethnic mix Black 79%, White 10%,
Colored 9%, Asian 2%
Government Presidential system
Currency Rand = 100 cents
Literacy rate 82%
Calorie consumption 2956 calories

South Africa, Republic of see
South Africa
South America 56 continent
Southampton 89 D7 hist. Hamwih, Lat.
Clausentum. S England, UK
Southampton Island 37 G3 island
Nunavut, NE Canada
South Andaman 133 F2 island Andaman
Islands, India, NE Indian Ocean
South Australia 149 A5 state S Australia
South Australian Basin 142 B5 undersea
basin SW Indian Ocean
South Bend 40 C3 Indiana, N USA
South Beveland see Zuid-Beveland
South Bruny Island 149 C8 island
Tasmania, SE Australia
South Carolina 43 E2 off. State of South
Carolina, also known as The Palmetto
State. state SE USA
South Carpathians see Carpaţii
Meridionali
South China Basin 125 E4 undersea
basin SE South China Sea
South China Sea 124 D4 Chin. Nan Hai,
Ind. Laut Cina Selatan, Vtn. Biển Đông.
sea SE Asia
South Dakota 44 D2 off. State of South
Dakota, also known as The Coyote
State, Sunshine State. state N USA
Southeast Indian Ridge 141 D7
undersea ridge Indian Ocean/Pacific
Ocean
Southeast Pacific Basin 153 E5 var.
Belling Hausen Mulde. undersea basin
SE Pacific Ocean
South East Point 149 C7 headland
Victoria, S Australia
Southend-on-Sea 89 E6 E England, UK
Southern Alps 151 B6 mountain range
South Island, New Zealand
Southern Cook Islands 145 F4 island
group S Cook Islands
Southern Cross 147 B6 Western
Australia
Southern Indian Lake 37 F4 lake
Manitoba, C Canada
Southern Ocean 67 B7 ocean Atlantic
Ocean/Indian Ocean/Pacific Ocean
Southern Uplands 88 C4 mountain
range S Scotland, UK
South Fiji Basin 142 D4 undersea basin
S Pacific Ocean
South Geomagnetic Pole 154 B3 pole
Antarctica
South Georgia 57 D8 island South
Georgia and the South Sandwich
Islands, SW Atlantic Ocean
South Goulburn Island 146 E2 island
Northern Territory, N Australia
South Huvadhu Atoll 132 A5 atoll
S Maldives
South Indian Basin 141 D7 undersea
basin Indian Ocean/Pacific Ocean
South Island 151 C6 island S New
Zealand
South Korea 129 E4 off. Republic of
Korea, Kor. Taehan Min'guk. country
E Asia

SOUTH KOREA
East Asia

Official name Republic of Korea
Formation 1948 / 1953
Capital Seoul
Population 47.8 million / 1254 people
per sq mile (484 people per sq km) /
82%
Total area 38,023 sq miles
(98,480 sq km)
Languages Korean*
Religions Mahayana Buddhist 47%,
Protestant 38%, Roman Catholic 11%,
Confucianist 3%, Other 1%
Ethnic mix Korean 100%
Government Presidential system
Currency South Korean won = 100 chon
Literacy rate 98%
Calorie consumption 3058 calories

South Lake Tahoe 47 C5 California,
W USA
South Orkney Islands 154 A2 island
group Antarctica
South Ossetia 117 F2 former autonomous
region SW Georgia
South Pacific Basin see Southwest
Pacific Basin

South Platte River 44 D4 river
Colorado/Nebraska, C USA
South Pole 154 B3 pole Antarctica
Antarctica
South Sandwich Islands 57 D8 island
group SE South Georgia and South
Sandwich Islands
South Sandwich Trench 57 E8 trench
SW Atlantic Ocean
South Shetland Islands 154 A2 island
group Antarctica
South Shields 88 D4 NE England, UK
South Sioux City 45 F3 Nebraska, C USA
South Taranaki Bight 150 C4 bight
SE Tasman Sea
South Tasmania Plateau see Tasman
Plateau
South Uist 88 B3 island NW Scotland,
UK
South-West Africa/South West Africa
see Namibia
South West Cape 151 A8 headland
Stewart Island, New Zealand
Southwest Indian Ocean Ridge see
Southwest Indian Ridge
Southwest Indian Ridge 141 B6 var.
Southwest Indian Ocean Ridge.
undersea ridge SW Indian Ocean
Southwest Pacific Basin 143 E4 var.
South Pacific Basin. undersea basin
SE Pacific Ocean
Sovereign Base Area 102 C5 uk military
installation S Cyprus
Soweto 78 D4 Gauteng, NE South Africa
Sôya-kaikyō see La Perouse Strait
Spain 92 D3 off. Kingdom of Spain, Sp.
España; anc. Hispania, Iberia, Lat.
Hispana. country SW Europe

SPAIN
Southeast Europe

Official name Kingdom of Spain
Formation 1492 / 1713
Capital Madrid
Population 43.1 million / 224 people per
sq mile (86 people per sq km) / 78%
Total area 194,896 sq miles (504,782
sq km)
Languages Spanish*, Catalan*, Galician*,
Basque*
Religions Roman Catholic 96%, Other 4%
Ethnic mix Castilian Spanish 72%,
Catalan 17%, Galician 6%, Basque 2%,
Other 2%, Roma 1%
Government Parliamentary system
Currency Euro = 100 cents
Literacy rate 98%
Calorie consumption 3371 calories

Spain, Kingdom of see Spain
Spalato see Split
Spanish Town 54 B5 hist. St.Iago de la
Vega. C Jamaica
Sparks 47 C5 Nevada, W USA
Sparta see Spárti
Spartanburg 43 E1 South Carolina,
SE USA
Spárti 105 B6 Eng. Sparta. Pelopónnisos,
S Greece
Spearfish 44 D2 South Dakota, N USA
Speightstown 55 G1 NW Barbados
Spencer 45 F3 Iowa, C USA
Spencer Gulf 149 B6 gulf
South Australia
Spey 88 C3 river NE Scotland, UK
Spice Islands see Maluku
Spiess Seamount 67 C7 seamount
S Atlantic Ocean
Spijkenisse 86 B4 Zuid-Holland,
SW Netherlands
Spili 105 C8 Kríti, Greece,
E Mediterranean Sea
Spīn Būldak 123 E5 Kandahār,
S Afghanistan
Spirdingsee see Śniardwy, Jezioro
Spitsbergen 83 F2 island NW Svalbard
Split 100 B4 It. Spalato. Split-Dalmacija,
S Croatia
Špogi 106 D4 Daugvapils, SE Latvia
Spokane 46 C2 Washington, NW USA
Spratly Islands 138 B2 Chin. Nansha
Qundao. disputed territory SE Asia
Spree 94 D4 river E Germany
Springfield 40 B4 state capital Illinois,
N USA
Springfield 41 G3 Massachusetts,
NE USA

Springfield 45 G5 Missouri, C USA
Springfield 40 C4 Ohio, N USA
Springfield 46 B3 Oregon, NW USA
Spring Garden 59 F2 NE Guyana
Spring Hill 43 E4 Florida, SE USA
Springs Junction 151 C5 West Coast, South Island, New Zealand
Springsure 148 D4 Queensland, E Australia
Sprottau see Szprotawa
Spruce Knob 41 E4 *mountain* West Virginia, NE USA
Srbinje see Foča
Srebrenica 100 C4 Republika Srpska, E Bosnia and Herzegovina
Sredets 104 D2 *prev.* Syulemeshlii. Stara Zagora, C Bulgaria
Sredets 104 E2 *prev.* Grudovo. Burgas, E Bulgaria
Srednerusskaya Vozvyshennost' 109 G1 *Eng.* Central Russian Upland. *mountain range* W Russian Federation
Srednesibirskoye Ploskogor'ye 114 D3 *var.* Central Siberian Uplands, *Eng.* Central Siberian Plateau. *mountain range* N Russian Federation
Sremska Mitrovica 100 C3 *prev.* Mitrovica, *Ger.* Mitrowitz. Vojvodina, NW Serbia
Srepok, Sông see Srêpôk, Tônle
Srêpôk, Tônle 137 E5 *var.* Sông Srepok. *river* Cambodia/Vietnam
Sri Aman 138 C3 Sarawak, East Malaysia
Sri Jayawardanapura 132 D3 *var.* Sri Jayawardenepura; *prev.* Kotte. Western Province, W Sri Lanka
Sri Jayawardenepura see Sri Jayawardanapura
Srīkākulam 135 F5 Andhra Pradesh, E India
Sri Lanka 132 D3 *off.* Democratic Socialist Republic of Sri Lanka; *prev.* Ceylon. *country* S Asia

---

SRI LANKA
South Asia

Official name Democratic Socialist Republic of Sri Lanka
Formation 1948 / 1948
Capital Colombo
Population 20.7 million / 828 people per sq mile (320 people per sq km) / 24%
Total area 25,332 sq miles (65,610 sq km)
Languages Sinhala, Tamil, Sinhala, Tamil, English
Religions Buddhist 69%, Hindu 15%, Muslim 8%, Christian 8%
Ethnic mix Sinhalese 74%, Tamil 18%, Moor 7%, Burgher, Malay, and Veddha 1%
Government Mixed presidential-parliamentary system
Currency Sri Lanka rupee = 100 cents
Literacy rate 90%
Calorie consumption 2385 calories

Sri Lanka, Democratic Socialist Republic of see Sri Lanka
Srinagarind Reservoir 137 C5 *lake* W Thailand
Srpska, Respublika 100 B3 *republic* Bosnia and Herzegovina
Ssu-ch'uan see Sichuan
Ssu-p'ing/Ssu-p'ing-chieh see Siping
Stabroek 87 B5 Antwerpen, N Belgium
Stade 94 B3 Niedersachsen, NW Germany
Stadskanaal 86 E2 Groningen, NE Netherlands
Stafford 89 D6 C England, UK
Staicele 106 D3 Limbaži, N Latvia
Staierdorf-Anina see Anina
Stájerlakanina see Anina
Stakhanov 109 H3 Luhans'ka Oblast', E Ukraine
Stalin see Varna
Stalinabad see Dushanbe
Stalingrad see Volgograd
Stalino see Donets'k
Stalinobod see Dushanbe
Stalinsk see Novokuznetsk
Stalinski Zaliv see Varnenski Zaliv
Stalin, Yazovir see Iskür, Yazovir

Stalowa Wola 98 E4 Podkarpackie, SE Poland
Stamford 41 F3 Connecticut, NE USA
Stampalia see Astypálaia
Stanislau see Ivano-Frankivs'k
Stanislav see Ivano-Frankivs'k
Stanisławów see Ivano-Frankivs'k
Stanke Dimitrov see Dupnitsa
Stanley 65 D7 *var.* Port Stanley, Puerto Argentino. *dependent territory capital* (Falkland Islands) East Falkland, Falkland Islands
Stanleyville see Kisangani
Stann Creek see Dangriga
Stanovoy Khrebet 113 E3 *mountain range* SE Russian Federation
Stanthorpe 149 D5 Queensland, E Australia
Staphorst 86 D2 Overijssel, E Netherlands
Starachowice 98 D4 Świętokrzyskie, C Poland
Stara Kanjiža see Kanjiža
Stara Pazova 100 D3 *Ger.* Altpasua, *Hung.* Ópazova. Vojvodina, N Serbia
Stara Planina see Balkan Mountains
Stara Zagora 104 D2 *Lat.* Augusta Trajana. Stara Zagora, C Bulgaria
Starbuck Island 145 G3 *prev.* Volunteer Island. *island* E Kiribati
Stargard in Pommern see Stargard Szczeciński
Stargard Szczeciński 98 B3 *Ger.* Stargard in Pommern. Zachodnio-pomorskie, NW Poland
Stari Bečej see Bečej
Starobel'sk see Starobil's'k
Starobil's'k 109 H2 *Rus.* Starobel'sk. Luhans'ka Oblast', E Ukraine
Starobin 107 C7 *var.* Starobyn. Minskaya Voblasts', S Belarus
Starobyn see Starobin
Starogard Gdański 98 C2 *Ger.* Preussisch-Stargard. Pomorskie, N Poland
Starokonstantinov see Starokostyantyniv
Starokostyantyniv 108 D2 *Rus.* Starokonstantinov. Khmel'nyts'ka Oblast', NW Ukraine
Starominskaya 111 A7 Krasnodarskiy Kray, SW Russian Federation
Staryya Darohi 107 C6 *Rus.* Staryye Dorogi. Minskaya Voblasts', S Belarus
Staryye Dorogi see Staryya Darohi
Staryy Oskol 111 B6 Belgorodskaya Oblast', W Russian Federation
State College 41 E4 Pennsylvania, NE USA
Staten Island see Estados, Isla de los
Statesboro 43 E2 Georgia, SE USA
States, The see United States of America
Staunton 41 E5 Virginia, NE USA
Stavanger 85 A6 Rogaland, S Norway
Stavers Island see Vostok Island
Stavropol' 111 B7 *prev.* Voroshilovsk. Stavropol'skiy Kray, SW Russian Federation
Stavropol' see Tol'yatti
Steamboat Springs 44 C4 Colorado, C USA
Steenwijk 86 D2 Overijssel, N Netherlands
Steier see Steyr
Steierdorf/Steierdorf-Anina see Anina
Steinamanger see Szombathely
Steinkjer 84 B4 Nord-Trøndelag, C Norway
Stejarul see Karapelit
Stendal 94 C3 Sachsen-Anhalt, C Germany
Stepanakert see Xankändi
Stephenville 47 F3 Texas, SW USA
Sterling 44 D4 Colorado, C USA
Sterling 40 B3 Illinois, N USA
Sterlitamak 114 B3 Respublika Bashkortostan, W Russian Federation
Stettin see Szczecin
Stettiner Haff see Szczeciński, Zalew
Stevenage 89 E6 E England, UK
Stevens Point 40 B2 Wisconsin, N USA
Stewart Island 151 A8 *island* S New Zealand
Steyerlak-Anina see Anina
Steyr 95 D6 *var.* Steier. Oberösterreich, N Austria

Stif see Sétif
Stillwater 49 G1 Oklahoma, C USA
Stirling 88 C4 C Scotland, UK
Stjørdalshalsen 84 B4 Nord-Trøndelag, C Norway
Stockach 95 B6 Baden-Württemberg, S Germany
Stockholm 85 C6 *country capital* (Sweden) Stockholm, C Sweden
Stockmannshof see Pļaviņas
Stockton 47 B6 California, W USA
Stockton Plateau 49 E4 *plain* Texas, SW USA
Stœng Trêng 137 D5 *prev.* Stung Treng. Stœng Trêng, NE Cambodia
Stoke see Stoke-on-Trent
Stoke-on-Trent 89 D6 *var.* Stoke. C England, UK
Stolbce see Stowbtsy
Stolbtsy see Stowbtsy
Stolp see Słupsk
Stolpmünde see Ustka
Stómio 104 B4 Thessalía, C Greece
Storebælt 85 B8 *var.* Store Bælt, *Eng.* Great Belt, Storebelt. *channel* Baltic Sea/Kattegat
Store Bælt see Storebælt
Storebelt see Storebælt
Støren 85 B5 Sør-Trøndelag, S Norway
Storfjorden 83 G2 *fjord* S Norway
Storhammer see Hamar
Stornoway 88 B2 NW Scotland, UK
Storsjön 85 B5 *lake* C Sweden
Storuman 84 C4 Västerbotten, N Sweden
Storuman 84 C4 *lake* N Sweden
Stowbtsy 107 C6 *Pol.* Stolbce, *Rus.* Stolbtsy. Minskaya Voblasts', C Belarus
Strabane 89 B5 *Ir.* An Srath Bán. W Northern Ireland, UK
Strakonice 99 A5 *Ger.* Strakonitz. Jihočeský Kraj, S Czech Republic
Strakonitz see Strakonice
Stralsund 94 D2 Mecklenburg-Vorpommern, NE Germany
Stranraer 89 C5 S Scotland, UK
Strasbourg 90 E3 *Ger.* Strassburg; *anc.* Argentoratum. Bas-Rhin, NE France
Strășeni 108 D3 *var.* Strasheny. C Moldova
Strasheny see Strășeni
Strassburg see Strasbourg, France
Strassburg see Aiud, Romania
Stratford 150 D4 Taranaki, North Island, New Zealand
Strathfield 148 E2 New South Wales, E Australia
Straubing 95 C6 Bayern, SE Germany
Strehaia 108 B5 Mehedinți, SW Romania
Strelka 114 D4 Krasnoyarskiy Kray, C Russian Federation
Strigonium see Esztergom
Strofiliá see Strofyliá
Strofyliá 105 C5 *var.* Strofilia. Évvoia, C Greece
Stromboli, Isola 97 D6 *island* Isole Eolie, S Italy
Stromeferry 88 C3 N Scotland, UK
Strömstad 85 B6 Västra Götaland, S Sweden
Strömsund 84 C4 Jämtland, C Sweden
Struga 101 D6 SW FYR Macedonia
Struma see Strymónas
Strumica 101 E6 E FYR Macedonia
Strumyani 104 C3 Blagoevgrad, SW Bulgaria
Strymónas 104 C3 *Bul.* Struma. *river* Bulgaria/Greece
Stryy 108 B2 L'vivs'ka Oblast', NW Ukraine
Studholme 151 B6 Canterbury, South Island, New Zealand
Stuhlweissenberg see Székesfehérvár
Stung Treng see Stœng Trêng
Sturgis 44 D3 South Dakota, N USA
Stuttgart 95 B6 Baden-Württemberg, SW Germany
Stykkishólmur 83 E4 Vesturland, W Iceland
Styr 108 C1 *Rus.* Styr'. *river* Belarus/Ukraine
Su see Jiangsu
Suakin 72 C3 *var.* Sawakin. Red Sea, NE Sudan
Subáčius 106 C4 Panevėžys, NE Lithuania

Subaykhān 118 E3 Dayr az Zawr, E Syria
Subotica 100 D2 *Ger.* Maria-Theresiopel, *Hung.* Szabadka. Vojvodina, N Serbia
Suceava 108 C3 *Ger.* Suczawa, *Hung.* Szucsava. Suceava, NE Romania
Su-chou see Suzhou
Suchow see Xuzhou, Jiangsu, China
Suchow see Suzhou, Jiangsu, China
Sucker State see Illinois
Sucre 61 F4 *hist.* Chuquisaca, La Plata. *country capital* (Bolivia-legal capital) Chuquisaca, S Bolivia
Suczawa see Suceava
Sudan 72 A4 *off.* Republic of Sudan, *Ar.* Jumhuriyat as-Sudan; *prev.* Anglo-Egyptian Sudan. *country* N Africa

---

SUDAN
East Africa

Official name Republic of the Sudan
Formation 1956 / 1956
Capital Khartoum
Population 36.2 million / 37 people per sq mile (14 people per sq km) / 36%
Total area 967,493 sq miles (2,505,810 sq km)
Languages Arabic*, Dinka, Nuer, Nubian, Beja, Zande, Bari, Fur, Shilluk, Lotuko
Religions Muslim (mainly Sunni) 70%, Traditional beliefs 20%, Christian 9%, Other 1%
Ethnic mix Other Black 52%, Arab 40%, Dinka and Beja 7%, Other 1%
Government Presidential system
Currency Sudanese pound or dinar = 100 piastres
Literacy rate 59%
Calorie consumption 2228 calories

Sudanese Republic see Mali
Sudan, Jumhuriyat as- see Sudan
Sudan, Republic of see Sudan
Sudbury 38 C4 Ontario, S Canada
Sudd 73 B5 *swamp region* S Sudan
Sudeten 98 B4 *var.* Sudetes, Sudetic Mountains, Cz./Pol. Sudety. *mountain range* Czech Republic/Poland
Sudetes/Sudetic Mountains/Sudety see Sudeten
Südkarpaten see Carpații Meridionali
Südliche Morava see Južna Morava
Sudostroy see Severodvinsk
Sue 73 B5 *river* S Sudan
Sueca 93 F3 País Valenciano, E Spain
Sue Wood Bay 42 B5 *bay* W Bermuda North America W Atlantic Ocean
Suez 72 B1 *Ar.* As Suways, El Suweis. NE Egypt
Suez Canal 72 B1 *Ar.* Qanāt as Suways. *canal* NE Egypt
Suez, Gulf of 72 B2 *Ar.* Khalīj as Suways. *gulf* NE Egypt
Suğla Gölü 116 C4 *lake* SW Turkey
Şuhār 121 D5 *var.* Sohar. N Oman
Sühbaatar 127 E1 Selenge, N Mongolia
Suhl 95 C5 Thüringen, C Germany
Suicheng see Suixi
Suid-Afrika see South Africa
Suidwes-Afrika see Namibia
Suixi 128 C6 *var.* Suicheng. Guangdong, S China
Sujāwal 134 B3 Sind, SE Pakistan
Sukabumi 138 C5 *prev.* Soekaboemi. Jawa, C Indonesia
Sukagawa 131 D5 Fukushima, Honshū, C Japan
Sukarnapura see Jayapura
Sukarno, Puntjak see Jaya, Puncak
Sukhne see As Sukhnah
Sukhona 110 C4 *var.* Tot'ma. *river* NW Russian Federation
Sukhumi see Sokhumi
Sukkertoppen see Maniitsoq
Sukkur 134 B3 Sind, SE Pakistan
Sukumo 131 B7 Kōchi, Shikoku, SW Japan
Sulaimaniya see As Sulaymānīyah
Sulaimān Range 134 C2 *mountain range* C Pakistan
Sula, Kepulauan 139 E4 *island group* C Indonesia
Sulawesi see Celebes
Sulawesi, Laut see Celebes Sea
Sulechów 98 B3 *Ger.* Züllichau. Lubuskie, W Poland
Suliag see Sohâg

Sullana 60 B2 Piura, NW Peru
Sullivan Island see Lanbi Kyun
Sulphur Springs 49 G2 Texas,
 SW USA
Sultānābād see Arāk
Sulu Archipelago 139 E3 island group
 SW Philippines
Sülüktü see Sulyukta
Sulu, Laut see Sulu Sea
Sulu Sea 139 E2 var. Laut Sulu. sea
 SW Philippines
Sulyukta 123 E2 Kir. Sülüktü.
 Batkenskaya Oblast', SW Kyrgyzstan
Sumatera 137 B8 Eng. Sumatra. island
 W Indonesia
Sumatra see Sumatera
Šumava see Bohemian Forest
Sumba, Pulau 139 E5 Eng. Sandalwood
 Island; prev. Soemba. island Nusa
 Tenggara, C Indonesia
Sumba, Selat 139 E5 strait Nusa
 Tenggara, S Indonesia
Sumbawanga 73 B7 Rukwa,
 W Tanzania
Sumbe 78 B2 var. N'Gunza, Port. Novo
 Redondo. Cuanza Sul, W Angola
Sumeih 73 B5 Southern Darfur, S Sudan
Sumgait see Sumqayıt, Azerbaijan
Summer Lake 46 B4 lake Oregon,
 NW USA
Summit 93 H5 Alaska, USA
Sumqayıt 117 H2 Rus. Sumgait.
 E Azerbaijan
Sumy 109 F2 Sums'ka Oblast',
 NE Ukraine
Sunbury 149 C7 Victoria,
 SE Australia
Sunda Islands see Greater Sunda Islands
Sunda, Selat 138 B5 strait Jawa/
 Sumatera, SW Indonesia
Sunda Trench see Java Trench
Sunderland 88 D4 var. Wearmouth.
 NE England, UK
Sundsvall 85 C5 Västernorrland,
 C Sweden
Sunflower State see Kansas
Sungaipenuh 138 B4 prev.
 Soengaipenoeh. Sumatera,
 W Indonesia   •
Sunnyvale 47 A6 California,
 W USA
Sunset State see Oregon
Sunshine State see Florida
Sunshine State see New Mexico
Sunshine State see South Dakota
Suntar 115 F3 Respublika Sakha
 (Yakutiya), NE Russian Federation
Sunyani 75 E5 W Ghana
Suoločielgi see Saariselkä
Suomenlahti see Finland, Gulf of
Suomen Tasavalta/Suomi see Finland
Suomussalmi 84 E4 Oulu, E Finland
Suông 137 D6 Kâmpóng Cham,
 C Cambodia
Suoyarvi 110 B3 Respublika Kareliya,
 NW Russian Federation
Supe 60 C3 Lima, W Peru
Supérieur, Lac see Superior, Lake
Superior 40 A1 Wisconsin, N USA
Superior, Lake 40 B1 Fr. Lac Supérieur.
 lake Canada/USA
Suqrah see Şawqirah
Suqutrā 121 C7 var. Sokotra, Eng.
 Socotra. island SE Yemen
Şūr 121 E5 NE Oman
Şūr see Soûr
Surabaja see Surabaya
Surabaya 138 D5 prev. Surabaja,
 Soerabaja. Jawa, C Indonesia
Surakarta 138 C5 Eng. Solo; prev.
 Soerakarta. Jawa, S Indonesia
Šurany 99 C6 Hung. Nagysurány.
 Nitriansky Kraj, SW Slovakia
Sūrat 134 C4 Gujarāt, W India
Suratdhani see Surat Thani
Surat Thani 137 C6 var. Suratdhani.
 Surat Thani, SW Thailand
Surazh 107 E5 Rus. Surazh. Vitsyebskaya
 Voblasts', NE Belarus
Surdulica 101 E5 Serbia, SE Serbia
Sûre 92 D7 var. Sauer. river W Europe
Surendranagar 134 C4 Gujarāt, W India
Surfers Paradise 149 E5 Queensland,
 E Australia
Surgut 114 D3 Khanty-Mansiyskiy
 Avtonomnyy Okrug, C Russian
 Federation
Surin 137 D5 Surin, E Thailand

Surinam see Surinam
Suriname 59 G3 off. Republic of
 Suriname, var. Suriname; prev. Dutch
 Guiana, Netherlands Guiana. country
 N South America

SURINAME
South America

Official name Republic of Suriname
Formation 1975 / 1975
Capital Paramaribo
Population 499,000 / 8 people per sq
mile (3 people per sq km) / 74%
Total area 63,039 sq miles
(163,270 sq km)
Languages Dutch*, Sranan (Creole),
Javanese, Sarnami Hindi, Saramaccan,
Chinese, Carib
Religions Hindu 27%, Protestant 25%,
Roman Catholic 23%, Muslim 20%,
Traditional beliefs 5%
Ethnic mix Creole 34%, South Asian 34%,
Javanese 18%, Black 9%, Other 5%
Government Parliamentary system
Currency Suriname dollar (guilder until
2004) = 100 cents
Literacy rate 88%
Calorie consumption 2652 calories

Suriname, Republic of see Surinam
Sūrīya/Sūriyah, Al-Jumhūrīyah al-
 'Arabīyah as- see Syria
Surkhab, Darya-i- see Kahmard,
 Daryā-ye
Surkhob 123 F3 river C Tajikistan
Surt 71 G2 var. Sidra, Sirte.
 N Libya
Surt, Khalīj 71 F2 Eng. Gulf of Sidra,
 Gulf of Sirti, Sidra. gulf N Libya
Surtsey 83 E5 island S Iceland
Suruga-wan 131 D6 bay SE Japan
Susa 96 A2 Piemonte, NE Italy
Sūsah see Sousse
Susanville 47 B5 California,
 W USA
Susitna 36 C3 Alaska, USA
Susteren 87 D5 Limburg,
 SE Netherlands
Susuman 115 G3 Magadanskaya Oblast',
 E Russian Federation
Sutlej 134 C2 river India/Pakistan
Suur Munamägi 106 D3
 var. Munamägi, Ger. Eier-Berg.
 mountain SE Estonia
Suur Väin 106 C2 Ger. Grosser Sund.
 strait W Estonia
Suva 145 E4 country capital (Fiji) Viti
 Levu, W Fiji
Suvalkai/Suvalki see Suwałki
Suwałki 98 E2 Lith. Suvalkai, Rus.
 Suvalki. Podlaskie, NE Poland
Suwār see Aş Şuwār
Suways, Khalīj as see Suez, Gulf of
Suways, Qanāt as see Suez Canal
Suweida see As Suwaydā'
Suzhou 128 D5 var. Soochow, Su-chou,
 Suchow; prev. Wuhsien. Jiangsu,
 E China
Svalbard 83 E1 Norwegian dependency
 Arctic Ocean
Svartisen 84 C3 glacier C Norway
Svay Riĕng 137 D6 Svay Riĕng,
 S Cambodia
Sveg 85 B5 Jämtland, C Sweden
Svenstavik 85 C5 Jämtland,
 C Sweden
Sverdlovsk see Yekaterinburg
Sverige see Sweden
Sveti Vrach see Sandanski
Svetlogorsk see Svyetlahorsk
Svetlograd 111 B7 Stavropol'skiy Kray,
 SW Russian Federation
Svetlovodsk see Svitlovods'k
Svetozarevo see Jagodina
Svilengrad 104 D3 prev. Mustafa-Pasha.
 Khaskovo, S Bulgaria
Svitlovods'k 109 F3 Rus. Svetlovodsk.
 Kirovohrads'ka Oblast', C Ukraine
Svizzera see Switzerland
Svobodnyy 115 G4 Amurskaya Oblast',
 SE Russian Federation
Svyataya Anna Trough 172 C4 var.
 Saint Anna Trough. trough N Kara Sea
Svyetlahorsk 107 D7 Rus. Svetlogorsk.
 Homyel'skaya Voblasts', SE Belarus
Swabian Jura see Schwäbische Alb
Swakopmund 78 B3 Erongo, W Namibia

Swansea 89 C7 Wel. Abertawe.
 S Wales, UK
Swarzędz 98 C3 Poznań, W Poland
Swatow see Shantou
Swaziland 78 D4 off. Kingdom of
 Swaziland. country S Africa

SWAZILAND
Southern Africa

Official name Kingdom of Swaziland
Formation 1968 / 1968
Capital Mbabane
Population 1 million / 151 people per
sq mile
(58 people per sq km) / 26%
Total area 6704 sq miles (17,363 sq km)
Languages English*, siSwati*, isiZulu,
Xitsonga
Religions Christian 60%, Traditional
beliefs 40%
Ethnic mix Swazi 97%, Other 3%
Government Monarchy
Currency Lilangeni = 100 cents
Literacy rate 79%
Calorie consumption 2322 calories

Swaziland, Kingdom of see Swaziland
Sweden 84 B4 off. Kingdom of Sweden,
 Swe. Sverige. country N Europe

SWEDEN
Northern Europe

Official name Kingdom of Sweden
Formation 1523 / 1905
Capital Stockholm
Population 9 million / 57 people per
sq mile (22 people per sq km) / 83%
Total area 173,731 sq miles
(449,964 sq km)
Languages Swedish*, Finnish, Sámi
Religions Evangelical Lutheran 82%,
Other 13%, Roman Catholic 2%,
Muslim 2%, Orthodox Christian 1%
Ethnic mix Swedish 88%, Foreign-born
or first-generation immigrant 10%, Finnish
and Sámi 2%
Government Parliamentary system
Currency Swedish krona = 100 öre
Literacy rate 99%
Calorie consumption 3185 calories

Sweden, Kingdom of see Sweden
Sweetwater 49 F3 Texas, SW USA
Świdnica 98 B4 Ger. Schweidnitz.
 Wałbrzych, SW Poland
Świdwin 98 B2 Ger. Schivelbein.
 Zachodnio-pomorskie,
 NW Poland
Świebodzice 98 B4 Ger. Freiburg in
 Schlesien, Swiebodzice. Wałbrzych,
 SW Poland
Świebodzin 98 B3 Ger. Schwiebus.
 Lubuskie, W Poland
Świecie 98 C3 Ger. Schwertberg.
 Kujawsko-pomorskie, C Poland
Swindon 89 D7 S England, UK
Swinemünde see Świnoujście
Świnoujście 98 B2 Ger. Swinemünde.
 Zachodnio-pomorskie, NW Poland
Swiss Confederation see Switzerland
Switzerland 95 A7 off. Swiss
 Confederation, Fr. La Suisse, Ger.
 Schweiz, It. Svizzera; anc. Helvetia.
 country C Europe

SWITZERLAND
Central Europe

Official name Swiss Confederation
Formation 1291 / 1857
Capital Bern
Population 7.3 million / 475 people per
sq mile (184 people per sq km) / 68%
Total area 15,942 sq miles (41,290 sq km)
Languages German*, French*, Italian*,
Romansch*, Swiss-German
Religions Roman Catholic 46%,
Protestant 40%, Other and
nonreligious 12%, Muslim 2%
Ethnic mix German 65%, French 18%,
Italian 10%, Other 6%, Romansch 1%
Government Parliamentary system
Currency Swiss franc = 100 rappen/
centimes
Literacy rate 99%
Calorie consumption 3526 calories

Swansea —

Sycaminum see Hefa
Sydenham Island see Nonouti
Sydney 148 D1 state capital New South
 Wales, SE Australia
Sydney 39 G4 Cape Breton Island,
 Nova Scotia, SE Canada
Sydney Island see Manra
Syedpur see Saidpur
Syemyezhava 107 C6 Rus. Semezhevo.
 Minskaya Voblasts', C Belarus
Syene see Aswān
Syeverodonets'k 109 H3 Rus.
 Severodonetsk. Luhans'ka Oblast',
 E Ukraine
Syktyvkar 110 D4 prev. Ust'-Sysol'sk.
 Respublika Komi, NW Russian
 Federation
Sylhet 135 G3 Sylhet, NE Bangladesh
Synel'nykove 109 G3 Dnipropetrovs'ka
 Oblast', E Ukraine
Syowa 154 C2 Japanese research station
 Antarctica
Syracuse 41 E3 New York,
 NE USA
Syracuse see Siracusa
Syrdar'ya 114 B4 Sirdaryo Viloyati,
 E Uzbekistan
Syria 118 B3 off. Syrian Arab Republic,
 var. Siria, Syrie, Ar. Al-Jumhūrīyah
 al-'Arabīyah as-Sūriyah, Sūrīya.
 country SW Asia

SYRIA
Southwest Asia

Official name Syrian Arab Republic
Formation 1941 / 1967
Capital Damascus
Population 19 million / 267 people per
sq mile (103 people per sq km) / 55%
Total area 71,498 sq miles (184,180 sq km)
Languages Arabic*, French, Kurdish,
Armenian, Circassian, Turkic languages,
Assyrian, Aramaic
Religions Sunni Muslim 74%, Other
Muslim 16%, Christian 10%
Ethnic mix Arab 89%, Kurdish 6%,
Other 3%, Armenian, Turkmen, and
Circassian 2%
Government One-party state
Currency Syrian pound = 100 piasters
Literacy rate 83%
Calorie consumption 3038 calories

Syrian Arab Republic see Syria
Syrian Desert 119 D5
 Ar. Al Hamad, Bādiyat ash Shām.
 desert SW Asia
Syrie see Syria
Sýrna 105 E7 var. Sirna. island Kykládes,
 Greece, Aegean Sea
Sýros 105 C6 var. Síros. island Kykládes,
 Greece, Aegean Sea
Syulemeshlii see Sredets
Syvash, Zaliv see Syvash, Zatoka
Syvash, Zatoka 109 F4 Rus. Zaliv Syvash.
 inlet S Ukraine
Syzran' 111 C6 Samarskaya Oblast',
 W Russian Federation
Szabadka see Subotica
Szamotuły 98 B3 Poznań, W Poland
Szászrégen see Reghin
Szatmárrnémeti see Satu Mare
Száva see Sava
Szczecin 98 B3 Eng./Ger. Stettin.
 Zachodnio-pomorskie,
 NW Poland
Szczecinek 98 B2 Ger. Neustettin.
 Zachodnio-pomorskie, NW Poland
Szczeciński, Zalew 98 A2 var.
 Stettiner Haff, Ger. Oderhaff. bay
 Germany/Poland
Szczuczyn Nowogródzki see Shchuchyn
Szczytno 98 D3 Ger. Ortelsburg.
 Warmińsko-Mazurskie,
 NE Poland
Szechuan/Szechwan see Sichuan
Szeged 99 D7 Ger. Szegedin, Rom.
 Seghedin. Csongrád, SE Hungary
Szegedin see Szeged
Székelykeresztúr see Cristuru Secuiesc
Székesfehérvár 99 C6 Ger.
 Stuhlweissenberg; anc. Alba Regia.
 Fejér, W Hungary
Szeklerburg see Miercurea-Ciuc
Szekler Neumarkt see Târgu Secuiesc
Szekszárd 99 C7 Tolna, S Hungary
Szempcz/Szenc see Senec

Szenice *see* Senica
Szeping *see* Siping
Szilágysomlyó *see* Şimleu Silvaniei
Szinna *see* Snina
Sziszek *see* Sisak
Szitás-Keresztúr *see* Cristuru Secuiesc
Szkudy *see* Skuodas
Szlatina *see* Slatina
Szlovákia *see* Slovakia
Szolnok 99 D6 Jász-Nagykun-Szolnok, C Hungary
Szombathely 99 B6 *Ger.* Steinamanger; *anc.* Sabaria, Savaria. Vas, W Hungary
Szprotawa 98 B4 *Ger.* Sprottau. Lubuskie, W Poland
Sztálinváros *see* Dunaújváros
Szucsava *see* Suceava

T

Tabariya, Bahrat *see* Tiberias, Lake
Table Rock Lake 49 G1 *reservoir* Arkansas/Missouri, C USA
Tábor 99 B5 Jihočeský Kraj, S Czech Republic
Tabora 73 B7 Tabora, W Tanzania
Tabrīz 120 C2 *var.* Tebriz; *anc.* Tauris. Āzarbāyjān-e Sharqī, NW Iran
Tabuaeran 145 G2 *prev.* Fanning Island. *atoll* Line Islands, E Kiribati
Tabūk 120 A4 Tabūk, NW Saudi Arabia
Täby 85 C6 Stockholm, C Sweden
Tachau *see* Tachov
Tachov 99 A5 *Ger.* Tachau. Plveňský Kraj, W Czech Republic
Tacloban 139 F2 *off.* Tacloban City. Leyte, C Philippines
Tacloban City *see* Tacloban
Tacna 61 E4 Tacna, SE Peru
Tacoma 46 B2 Washington, NW USA
Tacuarembó 64 D4 *prev.* San Fructuoso. Tacuarembó, C Uruguay
Tademaït, Plateau du 70 D3 *plateau* C Algeria
Tadmor/Tadmur *see* Tudmur
Tādpatri 132 C2 Andhra Pradesh, E India
Tadzhikistan *see* Tajikistan
Taegu 129 E4 *off.* Taegu-gwangyŏksi, *var.* Daegu, *Jap.* Taikyū. SE South Korea
Taegu-gwangyŏksi *see* Taegu
Taehan-haehyŏp *see* Korea Strait
Taehan Min'guk *see* South Korea
Taejŏn 129 E4 *off.* Taejŏn-gwangyŏksi, *Jap.* Taiden. C South Korea
Taejŏn-gwangyŏksi *see* Taejŏn
Tafassâsset, Ténéré du 75 G2 *desert* N Niger
Tafila/Ṭafilah, Muḥāfaẓat aţ *see* Aṭ Ṭafīlah
Taganrog 111 A7 Rostovskaya Oblast', SW Russian Federation
Taganrog, Gulf of 109 G4 *Rus.* Taganrogskiy Zaliv, *Ukr.* Tahanroz'ka Zatoka. *gulf* Russian Federation/Ukraine
Taganrogskiy Zaliv *see* Taganrog, Gulf of
Taguatinga 63 F3 Tocantins, C Brazil
Tagus 92 C3 *Port.* Rio Tejo, *Sp.* Río Tajo. *river* Portugal/Spain
Tagus Plain 80 A4 *abyssal plain* E Atlantic Ocean
Tahanroz'ka Zatoka *see* Taganrog, Gulf of
Tahat 71 E4 *mountain* SE Algeria
Tahiti 145 H4 *island* Îles du Vent, W French Polynesia
Tahiti, Archipel de *see* Société, Archipel de la
Tahlequah 49 G1 Oklahoma, C USA
Tahoe, Lake 47 B5 *lake* California/Nevada, W USA
Tahoua 75 F3 Tahoua, W Niger
Taichū *see* T'aichung
T'aichung 128 D6 *Jap.* Taichū; *prev.* Taiwan. C Taiwan
Taiden *see* Taejŏn
Taieri 151 B7 *river* South Island, New Zealand
Taihape 150 D4 Manawatu-Wanganui, North Island, New Zealand
Taihoku *see* T'aipei
Taikyū *see* Taegu
Tailem Bend 149 B7 South Australia

T'ainan 128 D6 *Jap.* Tainan; *prev.* Dainan. S Taiwan
T'aipei 128 D6 *Jap.* Taihoku; *prev.* Daihoku. *country capital* (Taiwan) N Taiwan
Taiping 138 B3 Perak, Peninsular Malaysia
Taiwan 128 D6 *off.* Republic of China, *var.* Formosa, Formo'sa. *country* E Asia

TAIWAN
East Asia

Official name Republic of China (ROC)
Formation 1949 / 1949
Capital Taipei
Population 22.9 million / 1838 people per sq mile (710 people per sq km) / 69%
Total area 13,892 sq miles (35,980 sq km)
Languages Amoy Chinese, Mandarin Chinese, Hakka Chinese
Religions Buddhist, Confucianist, and Taoist 93%, Christian 5%, Other 2%
Ethnic mix Han (pre-20th-century migration) 84%, Han (20th-century migration) 14%, Aboriginal 2%
Government Presidential system
Currency Taiwan dollar = 100 cents
Literacy rate 97%
Calorie consumption Not available

Taiwan *see* T'aichung
T'aiwan Haihsia/Taiwan Haixia *see* Taiwan Strait
Taiwan Strait 128 D6 *var.* Formosa Strait, *Chin.* T'aiwan Haihsia, Taiwan Haixia. *strait* China/Taiwan
Taiyuan 128 C4 *var.* T'ai-yuan, T'ai-yüan; *prev.* Yangku. *province capital* Shanxi, C China
T'ai-yuan/T'ai-yüan *see* Taiyuan
Ta'izz 121 B7 SW Yemen
Tajikistan 123 E3 *off.* Republic of Tajikistan, *Rus.* Tadzhikistan, *Taj.* Jumhurii Tojikiston; *prev.* Tajik S.S.R. *country* C Asia

TAJIKISTAN
Central Asia

Official name Republic of Tajikistan
Formation 1991 / 1991
Capital Dushanbe
Population 6.5 million / 118 people per sq mile (45 people per sq km)
Total area 55,251 sq miles (143,100 sq km)
Languages Tajik*, Uzbek, Russian
Religions Sunni Muslim 80%, Other 15%, Shi'a Muslim 5%
Ethnic mix Tajik 62%, Uzbek 24%, Russian 8%, Other 4%, Tatar 1%, Kyrgyz 1%
Government Presidential system
Currency Somoni = 100 diram
Literacy rate 99%
Calorie consumption 1828 calories

Tajikistan, Republic of *see* Tajikistan
Tajik S.S.R *see* Tajikistan
Tajo, Río *see* Tagus
Tak 136 C4 *var.* Rahaeng. Tak, W Thailand
Takao *see* Kaohsiung
Takaoka 131 C5 Toyama, Honshū, SW Japan
Takapuna 150 D2 Auckland, North Island, New Zealand
Takhiatash *see* Takhiatosh
Takhtakupyr *see* Taxtako'pir
Takikawa 130 D2 Hokkaidō, NE Japan
Takla Makan Desert *see* Taklimakan Shamo
Taklimakan Shamo 126 B3 *Eng.* Takla Makan Desert. *desert* NW China
Takow *see* Kaohsiung
Takutea 145 G4 *island* S Cook Islands
Talabriga *see* Aveiro
Talabriga *see* Talavera de la Reina
Talachyn 107 D6 *Rus.* Tolochin. Vitsyebskaya Voblasts', NE Belarus
Talamanca, Cordillera de 53 E5 *mountain range* S Costa Rica
Talara 60 B2 Piura, NW Peru
Talas 123 F2 Talasskaya Oblast', NW Kyrgyzstan
Talaud, Kepulauan 139 F3 *island group* E Indonesia

Talavera de la Reina 92 D3 *anc.* Caesarobriga, Talabriga. Castilla-La Mancha, C Spain
Talca 64 B4 Maule, C Chile
Talcahuano 65 B5 Bío Bío, C Chile
Taldykorgan 114 C5 *Kaz.* Taldyqorghan; *prev.* Taldy-Kurgan. Taldykorgan, SE Kazakhstan
Taldy-Kurgan/Taldyqorghan *see* Taldykorgan
Ta-lien *see* Dalian
Taliq-an *see* Tāloqān
Tal'ka 107 C6 *Rus.* Tal'ka. Minskaya Voblasts', C Belarus
Talkhof *see* Puurmani
Tallahassee 42 D3 *prev.* Muskogean. *state capital* Florida, SE USA
Tall al Abyaḍ *see* At Tall al Abyaḍ
Tallin *see* Tallinn
Tallinn 106 D2 *Ger.* Reval, *Rus.* Tallin; *prev.* Revel. *country capital* (Estonia) Harjumaa, NW Estonia
Tall Kalakh 118 B4 *var.* Tell Kalakh. Ḥimṣ, C Syria
Tallulah 42 B2 Louisiana, S USA
Talnakh 114 D3 Taymyrskiy (Dolgano-Nenetskiy) Avtonomnyy Okrug, N Russian Federation
Tal'ne 109 E3 *Rus.* Tal'noye. Cherkas'ka Oblast', C Ukraine
Tal'noye *see* Tal'ne
Taloga 49 F1 Oklahoma, C USA
Tāloqān 123 E3 *var.* Taliq-an. Takhār, NE Afghanistan
Talsen *see* Talsi
Talsi 106 C3 *Ger.* Talsen. Talsi, NW Latvia
Taltal 64 B2 Antofagasta, N Chile
Talvik 84 D2 Finnmark, N Norway
Tamabo, Banjaran 138 D3 *mountain range* East Malaysia
Tamale 75 E4 C Ghana
Tamana 63 E3 *prev.* Rotcher Island. *atoll* Tungaru, W Kiribati
Tamanrasset 71 E4 *var.* Tamenghest. S Algeria
Tamar 89 C7 *river* SW England, UK
Tamar *see* Tudmur
Tamatave *see* Toamasina
Tamazunchale 51 E4 San Luis Potosí, C Mexico
Tambacounda 74 C3 SE Senegal
Tambov 111 B6 Tambovskaya Oblast', W Russian Federation
Tambura 73 B5 Western Equatoria, SW Sudan
Tamchaket *see* Tâmchekket
Tâmchekket 74 C3 *var.* Tamchaket. Hodh el Gharbi, S Mauritania
Tamenghest *see* Tamanrasset
Tamiahua, Laguna de 51 F4 *lagoon* Veracruz-Llave, Mexico
Tamil Nādu 132 C3 *prev.* Madras. *cultural region* SE India
Tamil Nādu 132 C3 *prev.* Madras. *state* SE India
Tam Ky 137 E5 Quang Nam-ƒa Năng, C Vietnam
Tammerfors *see* Tampere
Tampa 43 E4 Florida, SE USA
Tampa Bay 43 E4 *bay* Florida, SE USA
Tampere 85 D5 *Swe.* Tammerfors. Länsi-Suomi, W Finland
Tampico 51 E3 Tamaulipas, C Mexico
Tamworth 149 D6 New South Wales, SE Australia
Tanabe 131 C7 Wakayama, Honshū, SW Japan
Tana Bru 84 D2 Finnmark, N Norway
T'ana Häyk' 72 C4 *var.* Lake Tana. *lake* NW Ethiopia
Tanais *see* Don
Tana, Lake *see* T'ana Häyk'
Tanami Desert 146 D3 *desert* Northern Territory, N Australia
Tananarive *see* Antananarivo
Ṭāndārei 108 D5 Ialomiţa, SE Romania
Tandil 65 D5 Buenos Aires, E Argentina
Tandjoengkarang *see* Bandar Lampung
Tanega-shima 131 B8 *island* Nansei-shotō, SW Japan
Tanen Taunggyi *see* Tane Range
Tane Range 136 B4 *Bur.* Tanen Taunggyi. *mountain range* W Thailand

Tanezrouft 70 D4 *desert* Algeria/Mali
Ṭanf, Jabal aţ 118 D4 *mountain* SE Syria
Tanga 69 E5 Tanga, E Tanzania
Tanga 73 C7 *region* E Tanzania
Tanganyika and Zanzibar *see* Tanzania
Tanganyika, Lake 73 B7 *lake* E Africa
Tanger 70 C2 *var.* Tangiers, Tangier, *Fr./Ger.* Tangek, *Sp.* Tánger; *anc.* Tingis. NW Morocco
Tangerk *see* Tanger
Tanggula Shan 126 C4 *mountain* W China
Tangier *see* Tanger
Tangiers *see* Tanger
Tangra Yumco 126 B5 *var.* Tangro Tso. *lake* W China
Tangro Tso *see* Tangra Yumco
Tangshan 128 D3 *var.* T'ang-shan. Hebei, E China
T'ang-shan *see* Tangshan
Tanimbar, Kepulauan 139 F5 *island group* Maluku, E Indonesia
Tanjungkarang/Tanjungkarang-Telukbetung *see* Bandar Lampung
Tanna 144 D4 *island* S Vanuatu
Tannenhof *see* Krynica
Tan-Tan 70 B3 SW Morocco
Tan-tung *see* Dandong
Tanzania 73 C7 *off.* United Republic of Tanzania, *Swa.* Jamhuri ya Muungano wa Tanzania; *prev.* German East Africa, Tanganyika and Zanzibar. *country* E Africa

TANZANIA
East Africa

Official name United Republic of Tanzania
Formation 1964 / 1964
Capital Dodoma
Population 38.3 million / 112 people per sq mile (43 people per sq km) / 33%
Total area 364,898 sq miles (945,087 sq km)
Languages English*, Kiswahili*, Sukuma, Chagga, Nyamwezi, Hehe, Makonde, Yao, Sandawe
Religions Muslim 33%, Christian 33%, Traditional beliefs 30%, Other 4%
Ethnic mix Native African (over 120 tribes) 99%, European and Asian 1%
Government Presidential system
Currency Tanzanian shilling = 100 cents
Literacy rate 69%
Calorie consumption 1975 calories

Tanzania, Jamhuri ya Muungano wa *see* Tanzania
Tanzania, United Republic of *see* Tanzania
Taoudenit *see* Taoudenni
Taoudenni 75 E2 *var.* Taoudenit. Tombouctou, N Mali
Tapa 106 E2 *Ger.* Taps. Lääne-Virumaa, NE Estonia
Tapachula 51 G5 Chiapas, SE Mexico
Tapaiu *see* Gvardeysk
Tapajós, Rio 63 E2 *var.* Tapajóz. *river* NW Brazil
Tapajóz *see* Tapajós, Rio
Taps *see* Tapa
Ṭarābulus 71 F2 *var.* Ṭarābulus al Gharb, *Eng.* Tripoli. *country capital* (Libya) NW Libya
Ṭarābulus al Gharb *see* Ṭarābulus
Ṭarābulus/Ṭarābulus ash Shām *see* Tripoli
Taraclia 108 D4 *Rus.* Tarakilya. S Moldova
Tarakilya *see* Taraclia
Taranaki, Mount 150 C4 *var.* Egmont. *volcano* North Island, New Zealand
Tarancón 93 E3 Castilla-La Mancha, C Spain
Taranto 97 E5 *var.* Tarentum. Puglia, SE Italy
Taranto, Golfo di 97 E6 *Eng.* Gulf of Taranto. *gulf* S Italy
Taranto, Gulf of *see* Taranto, Golfo di
Tarapoto 60 C2 San Martín, N Peru
Tarare 91 D5 Rhône, E France
Tarascon 91 D6 Bouches-du-Rhône, SE France
Tarawa 144 D2 *atoll* Tungaru, W Kiribati

Taraz *114 C5 prev.* Aulie Ata, Auliye-Ata, Dzhambul, Zhambyl. Zhambyl, S Kazakhstan
Tarazona *93 E2* Aragón, NE Spain
Tarbes *91 B6 anc.* Bigorra. Hautes-Pyrénées, S France
Tarcoola *149 A6* South Australia
Taree *149 D6* New South Wales, SE Australia
Tarentum *see* Taranto
Târgoviște *108 C5 prev.* Tirgoviște. Dâmbovița, S Romania
Târgu Jiu *108 B4 prev.* Tirgu Jiu. Gorj, W Romania
Târgul-Neamț *see* Târgu-Neamț
Târgul-Săcuiesc *see* Târgu Secuiesc
Târgu Mureș *108 B4 prev.* Oșorhei, Tîrgu Mures, Ger. Neumarkt, *Hung.* Marosvásárhely. Mureș, C Romania
Târgu-Neamț *108 C3 var.* Târgul-Neamț; *prev.* Tîrgu-Neamț. Neamț, NE Romania
Târgu Ocna *108 C4 Hung.* Aknavásár; *prev.* Tîrgu Ocna. Bacău, E Romania
Târgu Secuiesc *108 C4 Ger.* Neumarkt, Szekler Neumarkt, *Hung.* Kezdivásárhely; *prev.* Chezdi-Oșorheiu, Târgul-Săcuiesc, Tîrgu Secuiesc. Covasna, E Romania
Tar Heel State *see* North Carolina
Tarija *61 G5* Tarija, S Bolivia
Tarim *121 C6* C Yemen
Tarim Basin *see* Tarim Pendi
Tarim He *126 B3 river* NW China
Tarim Pendi *124 C2 Eng.* Tarim Basin. *basin* NW China
Tarma *60 C3* Junín, C Peru
Tarn *91 C6 cultural region* S France
Tarn *91 C6 department* S France
Tarn *91 C6 river* S France
Tarnobrzeg *98 D4* Podkarpackie, SE Poland
Tarnopol *see* Ternopil'
Tarnów *99 D5* Małopolskie, S Poland
Tarraco *see* Tarragona
Tarragona *93 G2 anc.* Tarraco. Cataluña, E Spain
Tarrasa *see* Terrassa
Tàrrega *93 F2 var.* Tarrega. Cataluña, NE Spain
Tarsatica *see* Rijeka
Tarsus *116 C4* Mersin, S Turkey
Tartous/Tartouss *see* Ṭarṭūs
Tartu *106 D3 Ger.* Dorpat; *prev. Rus* Yurev, Yur'yev. Tartumaa, SE Estonia
Tashqurghan *see* Kholm
Tasikmalaja *see* Tasikmalaya
Tasikmalaya *138 C5 var.* Tasikmalaja. Jawa, C Indonesia
Tasman Basin *142 C5 var.* East Australian Basin. *undersea basin* S Tasman Sea
Tasman Bay *151 C5 inlet* South Island, New Zealand
Tasmania *149 B8 prev.* Van Diemen's Land. *state* SE Australia
Tasmania *152 B4 island* SE Australia
Tasman Plateau *142 C5 var.* South Tasmania Plateau. *undersea plateau* SW Tasman Sea
Tasman Sea *142 C5 sea* SW Pacific Ocean
Tassili-n-Ajjer *71 E4 plateau* E Algeria
Tatabánya *99 C6* Komárom-Esztergom, NW Hungary
Tatar Pazardzhik *see* Pazardzhik
Tathlith *121 B5* 'Asir, S Saudi Arabia
Tatra Mountains *99 D5 Ger.* Tatra, *Hung.* Tátra, *Pol./Slvk.* Tatry. *mountain range* Poland/Slovakia

Tatra/Tátra *see* Tatra Mountains
Tatry *see* Tatra Mountains
Ta-t'ung/Tatung *see* Datong
Tatvan *117 F3* Bitlis, SE Turkey
Ta'ū *145 F4 island* Manua Islands, E American Samoa
Taukum, Peski *123 G1 desert* SE Kazakhstan
Taumarunui *150 D4* Manawatu-Wanganui, North Island, New Zealand
Taungdwingyi *136 B3* Magwe, C Myanmar (Burma)
Taunggyi *136 B3* Shan State, C Myanmar (Burma)
Taunton *89 C7* SW England, UK
Taupo *150 D3* Waikato, North Island, New Zealand
Taupo, Lake *150 D3 lake* North Island, New Zealand
Tauragė *106 B4 Ger.* Tauroggen. Tauragė, SW Lithuania
Tauranga *150 D3* Bay of Plenty, North Island, New Zealand
Tauris *see* Tabriz
Tauroggen *see* Tauragė
Taurus Mountains *see* Toros Dağları
Tavas *116 B4* Denizli, SW Turkey
Tavastehus *see* Hämeenlinna
Tavira *92 C5* Faro, S Portugal
Tavoy *137 B5 var.* Dawei. Tenasserim, S Myanmar (Burma)
Tavoy Island *see* Mali Kyun
Tawakoni, Lake *49 G2 reservoir* Texas, SW USA
Tawau *138 D3* Sabah, East Malaysia
Ṭawkar *see* Tokar
Tawzar *see* Tozeur
Taxco *51 E4 var.* Taxco de Alarcón. Guerrero, S Mexico
Taxco de Alarcón *see* Taxco
Takhiatosh *122 C2 Rus.* Takhiatash. Qoraqalpoghiston Respublikasi, W Uzbekistan
Taxtako'pir *122 D1 Rus.* Takhtakupyr. Qoraqalpg'iston Respublikasi, NW Uzbekistan
Tay *88 C3 river* C Scotland, UK
Taylor *49 G3* Texas, SW USA
Taymā' *120 A4* Tabūk, NW Saudi Arabia
Taymyr, Ozero *115 E2 lake* N Russian Federation
Taymyr, Poluostrov *115 E2 peninsula* N Russian Federation
Taz *114 D3 river* N Russian Federation
T'bilisi *117 G2 Eng.* Tiflis. *country capital* (Georgia) SE Georgia
Tchad *see* Chad
Tchad, Lac *see* Chad, Lake
Tchien *see* Zwedru
Tchongking *see* Chongqing
Tczew *98 C2 Ger.* Dirschau. Pomorskie, N Poland
Te Anau *151 A7* Southland, South Island, New Zealand
Te Anau, Lake *151 A7 lake* South Island, New Zealand
Teapa *51 G4* Tabasco, SE Mexico
Teate *see* Chieti
Tebingtinggi *138 B3* Sumatera, N Indonesia
Tebriz *see* Tabriz
Techirghiol *108 D5* Constanța, SE Romania
Tecomán *50 D4* Colima, SW Mexico
Tecpan *51 E5 var.* Tecpan de Galeana. Guerrero, S Mexico
Tecpan de Galeana *see* Tecpan
Tecuci *108 C4* Galați, E Romania
Tedzhen *see* Harīrūd/Tejen
Tedzhen *see* Tejen
Tees *89 D5 river* N England, UK
Tefé *62 D2* Amazonas, N Brazil
Tegal *138 C4* Jawa, C Indonesia
Tegelen *87 D5* Limburg, SE Netherlands
Tegucigalpa *52 C3 country capital* (Honduras) Francisco Morazán, SW Honduras
Teheran *see* Tehrān
Tehrān *120 C3 var.* Teheran. *country capital* (Iran) Tehrān, N Iran
Tehuacán *51 F4* Puebla, S Mexico
Tehuantepec *51 F5 var.* Santo Domingo Tehuantepec. Oaxaca, SE Mexico
Tehuantepec, Golfo de *51 F5 var.* Gulf of Tehuantepec. *gulf* S Mexico
Tehuantepec, Gulf of *see* Tehuantepec, Golfo de

Tehuantepec, Isthmus of *see* Tehuantepec, Istmo de
Tehuantepec, Istmo de *51 F5 var.* Isthmus of Tehuantepec. *isthmus* SE Mexico
Tejen *122 C3 Rus.* Tedzhen. Ahal Welāyaty, S Turkmenistan
Tejen *see* Harīrūd
Tejo, Rio *see* Tagus
Te Kao *150 C1* Northland, North Island, New Zealand
Tekax *51 H4 var.* Tekax de Álvaro Obregón. Yucatán, SE Mexico
Tekax de Álvaro Obregón *see* Tekax
Tekeli *114 C5* Almaty, SE Kazakhstan
Tekirdağ *116 A2 It.* Rodosto; *anc.* Bisanthe, Raidestos, Rhaedestus. Tekirdağ, NW Turkey
Te Kuiti *150 D3* Waikato, North Island, New Zealand
Tela *52 C2* Atlántida, NW Honduras
Telanaipura *see* Jambi
Tel Aviv-Jaffa *see* Tel Aviv-Yafo
Tel Aviv-Yafo *119 A6 var.* Tel Aviv-Jaffa. Tel Aviv, C Israel
Teles Pirés *see* São Manuel, Rio
Telish *104 C2 prev.* Azizie. Pleven, N Bulgaria
Tell Abiad/Tell Abyad *see* At Tall al Abyaḍ
Tell Kalakh *see* Tall Kalakh
Tell Shedadi *see* Ash Shadādah
Tel'man/Tel'mansk *see* Gubadag
Teloekbetoeng *see* Bandar Lampung
Telo Martius *see* Toulon
Telschen *see* Telšiai
Telšiai *106 B3 Ger.* Telschen. Telšiai, NW Lithuania
Telukbetung *see* Bandar Lampung
Temerin *100 D3* Vojvodina, N Serbia
Temeschburg/Temeschwar *see* Timișoara
Temesvár/Temeswar *see* Timișoara
Temirtau *114 C4 prev.* Samarkandski, Samarkandskoye. Karaganda, C Kazakhstan
Tempio Pausania *97 A5* Sardegna, Italy, C Mediterranean Sea
Temple *49 G3* Texas, SW USA
Temuco *65 B5* Araucanía, C Chile
Temuka *151 B6* Canterbury, South Island, New Zealand
Tenasserim *137 B6* Tenasserim, S Myanmar (Burma)
Ténenkou *74 D3* Mopti, C Mali
Ténéré *75 G3 physical region* C Niger
Tenerife *70 A3 island* Islas Canarias, Spain, NE Atlantic Ocean
Tengger Shamo *127 E3 desert* N China
Tengréla *74 D4 var.* Tingréla. N Côte d'Ivoire (Ivory Coast)
Tenkodogo *75 E4* S Burkina Faso
Tennant Creek *148 A3* Northern Territory, C Australia
Tennessee *42 C1 off.* State of Tennessee, *also known as* The Volunteer State. *state* SE USA
Tennessee River *42 C1 river* S USA
Tenojoki *see* Deatnu
Tenos *see* Tinos
Tepelena *see* Tepelenë
Tepelenë *101 C7 var.* Tepelena, *It.* Tepeleni. Gjirokastër, S Albania
Tepeleni *see* Tepelenë
Tepic *50 D4* Nayarit, C Mexico
Teplice *98 A4 Ger.* Teplitz; *prev.* Teplice-Šanov, Teplitz-Schönau. Ústecký Kraj, NW Czech Republic
Teplice-Šanov/Teplitz/Teplitz-Schönau *see* Teplice
Tequila *50 D4* Jalisco, SW Mexico
Teraina *145 G2 prev.* Washington Island. *atoll* Line Islands, E Kiribati
Teramo *96 C4 anc.* Interamna. Abruzzi, C Italy
Tercan *117 E3* Erzincan, NE Turkey
Terceira *92 A5 var.* Ilha Terceira. *island* Azores, Portugal, NE Atlantic Ocean
Terceira, Ilha *see* Terceira
Terekhovka *see* Tsyerakhowka
Teresina *63 F2 var.* Therezina. *state capital* Piauí, NE Brazil
Termez *see* Termiz
Termia *see* Kýthnos
Términos, Laguna de *51 G4 lagoon* SE Mexico
Termiz *123 E3 Rus.* Termez. Surkhondaryo Viloyati, S Uzbekistan

Termoli *96 D4* Molise, C Italy
Terneuzen *87 B5 var.* Neuzen. Zeeland, SW Netherlands
Terni *96 C4 anc.* Interamna Nahars. Umbria, C Italy
Ternopil' *108 C2 Pol.* Tarnopol, *Rus.* Ternopol'. Ternopil's'ka Oblast', W Ukraine
Ternopol' *see* Ternopil'
Terracina *97 C5* Lazio, C Italy
Terranova di Sicilia *see* Gela
Terranova Pausania *see* Olbia
Terrassa *93 G2 Cast.* Tarrasa. Cataluña, E Spain
Terre Adélie *154 C4 physical region* SE Antarctica Antarctica
Terre Haute *40 B4* Indiana, N USA
Terre Neuve *see* Newfoundland and Labrador
Terschelling *86 C1 Fris.* Skylge. *island* Waddeneilanden, N Netherlands
Teruel *93 F3 anc.* Turba. Aragón, E Spain
Tervel *104 E1 prev.* Kurtbunar, *Rom.* Curtbunar. Dobrich, NE Bulgaria
Tervueren *see* Tervuren
Tervuren *87 C6 var.* Tervueren. Vlaams Brabant, C Belgium
Teseney *72 C4 var.* Tessenei. W Eritrea
Tessalit *75 E2* Kidal, NE Mali
Tessaoua *75 G3* Maradi, S Niger
Tessenderlo *87 C5* Limburg, NE Belgium
Tessenei *see* Teseney
Testigos, Islas los *59 E1 island group* N Venezuela
Tete *79 E2* Tete, NW Mozambique
Teterow *94 C3* Mecklenburg-Vorpommern, NE Germany
Tétouan *70 C2 var.* Tetouan, Tetuán. N Morocco
Tetovo *101 D5* Razgrad, N Bulgaria
Tetschen *see* Děčín
Tetuán *see* Tétouan
Tevere *96 C4 Eng.* Tiber. *river* C Italy
Teverya *119 B5 var.* Tiberias, Tverya. Northern, N Israel
Te Waewae Bay *151 A7 bay* South Island, New Zealand
Texarkana *42 A2* Arkansas, C USA
Texarkana *49 H2* Texas, SW USA
Texas *49 F3 off.* State of Texas, *also known as* Lone Star State. *state* S USA
Texas City *49 H4* Texas, SW USA
Texel *86 C2 island* Waddeneilanden, NW Netherlands
Texoma, Lake *49 G2 reservoir* Oklahoma/Texas, C USA
Teziutlán *51 F4* Puebla, S Mexico
Thai, Ao *see* Thailand, Gulf of
Thai Binh *136 D3* Thai Binh, N Vietnam
Thailand *137 C5 off.* Kingdom of Thailand, *Th.* Prathet Thai; *prev.* Siam. *country* SE Asia

THAILAND
Southeastern Asia

Official name Kingdom of Thailand
Formation 1238 / 1907
Capital Bangkok
Population 64.2 million / 325 people per sq mile (126 people per sq km) / 22%
Total area 198,455 sq miles (514,000 sq km)
Languages Thai*, Chinese, Malay, Khmer, Mon, Karen, Miao
Religions Buddhist 95%, Muslim 4%, Other (including Christian) 1%
Ethnic mix Thai 83%, Chinese 12%, Malay 3%, Khmer and Other 2%
Government Parliamentary system
Currency Baht = 100 stang
Literacy rate 93%
Calorie consumption 2467 calories

Thailand, Gulf of *137 C6 var.* Gulf of Siam, *Th.* Ao Thai, *Vtn.* Vinh Thai Lan. *gulf* SE Asia
Thailand, Kingdom of *see* Thailand
Thai Lan, Vinh *see* Thailand, Gulf of
Thai Nguyên *136 D3* Bắc Thai, N Vietnam
Thakhèk *136 D4 var.* Muang Khammouan. Khammouan, C Laos
Thamarid *see* Thamarīt
Thamarīt *121 D6 var.* Thamarid, Thumrayt. SW Oman

Thames *150 D3* Waikato, North Island, New Zealand
Thames *89 B8* *river* S England, UK
Thanh Hoa *136 D3* Thanh Hoa, N Vietnam
Thanintari Taungdan *see* Bilauktaung Range
Thanlwin *see* Salween
Thar Desert *134 C3* *var.* Great Indian Desert, Indian Desert. *desert* India/Pakistan
Tharthär, Buhayrat ath *120 B3* *lake* C Iraq
Thásos *104 C4* Thásos, E Greece
Thásos *104 C4* *island* E Greece
Thaton *136 B4* Mon State, S Myanmar (Burma)
Thayetmyo *136 A4* Magwe, C Myanmar (Burma)
The Crane *55 H2* *var.* Crane. S Barbados
The Dalles *46 B3* Oregon, NW USA
The Flatts Village *see* Flatts Village
The Hague *see* 's-Gravenhage
Theodosia *see* Feodosiya
The Pas *37 F5* Manitoba, C Canada
Therezina *see* Teresina
Thérma *105 D6* Ikaría, Dodekánisa, Greece, Aegean Sea
Thermaic Gulf/Thermaicus Sinus *see* Thermaïkós Kólpos
Thermaïkós Kólpos *104 B4* *Eng.* Thermaic Gulf; *anc.* Thermaicus Sinus. *gulf* N Greece
Thermiá *see* Kýthnos
Thérmo *105 B5* Dytikí Ellás, C Greece
The Rock *93 H4* New South Wales, SE Australia
The Sooner State *see* Oklahoma
Thessaloníki *104 C3* *Eng.* Salonica, Salonika, *SCr.* Solun, *Turk.* Selânik. Kentrikí Makedonía, N Greece
The Valley *55 G3* *dependent territory capital* (Anguilla) E Anguilla
The Village *49 G1* Oklahoma, C USA
The Volunteer State *see* Tennessee
Thiamis *see* Kalamás
Thian Shan *see* Tien Shan
Thibet *see* Xizang Zizhiqu
Thief River Falls *45 F1* Minnesota, N USA
Thienen *see* Tienen
Thiers *91 C5* Puy-de-Dôme, C France
Thiès *74 B3* W Senegal
Thikombia *see* Cikobia
Thimbu *see* Thimphu
Thimphu *135 G3* *var.* Thimbu; *prev.* Tashi Chho Dzong. *country capital* (Bhutan) W Bhutan
Thionville *90 D3* *Ger.* Diedenhofen. Moselle, NE France
Thira *105 D7* Santoríni, Kykládes, Greece, Aegean Sea
Thíra *see* Santoríni
Thiruvanathapuram *see* Trivandrum
Thitu Island *128 C8* *island* NW Spratly Islands
Tholen *86 B4* *island* SW Netherlands
Thomasville *42 D3* Georgia, SE USA
Thompson *37 F4* Manitoba, C Canada
Thonon-les-Bains *91 D5* Haute-Savoie, E France
Thorenburg *see* Turda
Thorlákshöfn *83 E5* Sudhurland, SW Iceland
Thorn *see* Toruń
Thornton Island *see* Millennium Island
Thorshavn *see* Tórshavn
Thospitis *see* Van Gölü
Thouars *90 B4* Deux-Sèvres, W France
Thoune *see* Thun
Thracian Sea *104 D4* *Gk.* Thrakikó Pélagos; *anc.* Thracium Mare. *sea* Greece/Turkey
Thracium Mare/Thrakikó Pélagos *see* Thracian Sea
Three Kings Islands *150 C1* *island group* N New Zealand
Thrissur *see* Trichūr
Thuin *87 B7* Hainaut, S Belgium
Thule *see* Qaanaaq

Thumrayt *see* Thamarīt
Thun *95 A7* *Fr.* Thoune. Bern, W Switzerland
Thunder Bay *38 B4* Ontario, S Canada
Thuner See *95 A7* *lake* C Switzerland
Thung Song *137 C7* *var.* Cha Mai. Nakhon Si Thammarat, SW Thailand
Thýamis *see* Kalamás
Tianjin *128 D4* *var.* Tientsin. Tianjin Shi, E China
Tianjin *see* Tianjin Shi
Tianjin Shi *128 D4* *var.* Jin, Tianjin, T'ien-ching, Tientsin. *municipality* E China
Tian Shan *see* Tien Shan
Tianshui *128 B4* Gansu, C China
Tiba *see* Chiba
Tiber *see* Tevere, Italy
Tiber *see* Tivoli, Italy
Tiberias *see* Teverya
Tiberias, Lake *119 B5* *var.* Chinnereth, Sea of Bahr Tabariya, Sea of Galilee, *Ar.* Bahrat Tabariya, *Heb.* Yam Kinneret. *lake* N Israel
Tibesti *76 C2* *var.* Tibesti Massif, *Ar.* Tibistī. *mountain range* N Africa
Tibesti Massif *see* Tibesti
Tibet *see* Xizang Zizhiqu
Tibetan Autonomous Region *see* Xizang Zizhiqu
Tibet, Plateau of *see* Qingzang Gaoyuan
Tibistī *see* Tibesti
Tibnī *see* At Tibnī
Tiburón, Isla *50 B2* *var.* Isla del Tiburón. *island* NW Mexico
Tiburón, Isla del *see* Tiburón, Isla
Tichau *see* Tychy
Tichît *74 D2* *var.* Tichitt. Tagant, C Mauritania
Tichitt *see* Tichît
Ticinum *see* Pavia
Ticul *51 H3* Yucatán, SE Mexico
Tidjikdja *see* Tidjikja
Tidjikja *74 C2* *var.* Tidjikdja; *prev.* Fort-Cappolani. Tagant, C Mauritania
T'ien-ching *see* Tianjin Shi
Tienen *87 C6* *var.* Thienen, *Fr.* Tirlemont. Vlaams Brabant, C Belgium
Tiên Giang, Sông *see* Mekong
Tien Shan *126 B3* *Chin.* Thian Shan, Tian Shan, T'ien Shan, *Rus.* Tyan'-Shan'. *mountain range* C Asia
Tientsin *see* Tianjin
Tierp *85 C6* Uppsala, C Sweden
Tierra del Fuego *65 B8* *island* Argentina/Chile
Tiflis *see* T'bilisi
Tifton *42 D3* Georgia, SE USA
Tifu *139 F4* Pulau Buru, E Indonesia
Tighina *108 D4* *Rus.* Bendery; *prev.* Bender. E Moldova
Tigranocerta *see* Siirt
Tigris *120 B2* *Ar.* Dijlah, *Turk.* Dicle. *river* Iraq/Turkey
Tiguentourine *71 E3* E Algeria
Ti-hua/Tihwa *see* Ürümqi
Tijuana *50 A1* Baja California, NW Mexico
Tikhoretsk *111 A7* Krasnodarskiy Kray, SW Russian Federation
Tikhvin *110 B4* Leningradskaya Oblast', NW Russian Federation
Tiki Basin *143 G3* *undersea basin* S Pacific Ocean
Tikinsso *143 G3* *river* E Guinea
Tiksi *115 F2* Respublika Sakha (Yakutiya), NE Russian Federation
Tilburg *86 C4* Noord-Brabant, S Netherlands
Tilio Martius *see* Toulon
Tillabéri *75 F3* *var.* Tillabéry. Tillabéri, W Niger
Tillabéry *see* Tillabéri
Tílos *105 E7* *island* Dodekánisa, Greece, Aegean Sea
Timan Ridge *see* Timanskiy Kryazh
Timanskiy Kryazh *110 D3* *Eng.* Timan Ridge. *ridge* NW Russian Federation
Timaru *151 B6* Canterbury, South Island, New Zealand
Timbaki/Timbákion *see* Tympáki
Timbedgha *74 D3* *var.* Timbédra. Hodh ech Chargui, SE Mauritania

Timbédra *see* Timbedgha
Timbuktu *see* Tombouctou
Timiş *108 A4* *county* SW Romania
Timişoara *108 A4* *Ger.* Temeschwar, Temesvar, *Hung.* Temesvár; *prev.* Temeschburg. Timiş, W Romania
Timmins *38 C4* Ontario, S Canada
Timor *125 F5* *island* Nusa Tenggara, C Indonesia
Timor Sea *125 F5* *sea* E Indian Ocean
Timor Timur *see* East Timor
Timor Trench *see* Timor Trough
Timor Trough *125 F5* *var.* Timor Trench. *trough* NE Timor Sea
Timrå *85 C5* Västernorrland, C Sweden
Tindouf *70 C3* W Algeria
Tineo *92 C1* Asturias, N Spain
Tingis *see* Tanger
Tingo María *60 C3* Huánuco, C Peru
Tingréla *see* Tengréla
Tinhosa Grande *76 E2* *island* N Sao Tome and Principe, Africa, E Atlantic Ocean
Tinhosa Pequena *76 E1* *island* N Sao Tome and Principe, Africa, E Atlantic Ocean
Tinian *144 B1* *island* S Northern Mariana Islands
Tínos *105 D6* Tínos, Kykládes, Greece, Aegean Sea
Tínos *105 D6* *anc.* Tenos. *island* Kykládes, Greece, aegean Sea
Tip *101 E6* Papua, E Indonesia
Tipitapa *52 D3* Managua, W Nicaragua
Tip Top Mountain *38 C4* *mountain* Ontario, S Canada
Tirana *see* Tiranë
Tiranë *101 C6* *var.* Tirana. *country capital* (Albania) Tiranë, C Albania
Tiraspol *108 D4* *Rus.* Tiraspol'. E Moldova
Tiraspol' *see* Tiraspol
Tiree *88 B3* *island* W Scotland, UK
Tirgovişte *see* Târgovişte
Tîrgu Jiu *see* Târgu Jiu
Tîrgu Mureş *see* Târgu Mureş
Tîrgu-Neamţ *see* Târgu-Neamţ
Tîrgu Ocna *see* Târgu Ocna
Tîrgu Secuiesc *see* Târgu Secuiesc
Tirlemont *see* Tienen
Tírnavos *see* Týrnavos
Tirnovo *see* Veliko Tŭrnovo
Tirol *95 C7* *off.* Land Tirol, *var.* Tyrol, *It.* Tirolo. *state* W Austria
Tirol, Land *see* Tirol
Tirolo *see* Tirol
Tirreno, Mare *see* Tyrrhenian Sea
Tiruchchirāppalli *132 C3* *prev.* Trichinopoly. Tamil Nādu, SE India
Tiruppattūr *132 C2* Tamil Nādu, SE India
Tisa *see* Tisza
Tisza *103 F1* *Ger.* Theiss, *Rom./Slvn./SCr.* Tisa, *Rus.* Tissa, *Ukr.* Tysa. *river* SE Europe
Tiszakécske *99 D7* Bács-Kiskun, C Hungary
Titano, Monte *96 E1* *mountain* C San Marino
Titicaca, Lake *61 E4* *lake* Bolivia/Peru
Titograd *see* Podgorica
Titose *see* Chitose
Titova Mitrovica *see* Kosovska Mitrovica
Titovo Užice *see* Užice
Titu *108 C5* Dâmboviţa, S Romania
Titule *77 D5* Orientale, N Dem. Rep. Congo
Tiverton *89 C7* SW England, UK
Tivoli *96 C4* *anc.* Tiber. Lazio, C Italy
Tizimín *51 H3* Yucatán, SE Mexico
Tizi Ouzou *71 E1* *var.* Tizi-Ouzou. N Algeria
Tizi-Ouzou *see* Tizi Ouzou
Tiznit *70 B3* SW Morocco
Tjilatjap *see* Cilacap
Tjirebon *see* Cirebon
Tlaquepaque *50 D4* Jalisco, C Mexico
Tlascala *see* Tlaxcala
Tlaxcala *51 F4* *var.* Tlascala, Tlaxcala de Xicohténcatl. Tlaxcala, C Mexico
Tlaxcala de Xicohténcatl *see* Tlaxcala
Tlemcen *70 D2* *var.* Tilimsen, Tlemsen. NW Algeria
Tlemsen *see* Tlemcen
Toamasina *79 G3* *var.* Tamatave. Toamasina, E Madagascar

Toba, Danau *138 B3* *lake* Sumatera, W Indonesia
Tobago *55 H5* *island* NE Trinidad and Tobago
Tobol *114 C4* Kaz. Tobyl. *river* Kazakhstan/Russian Federation
Tobol'sk *114 C3* Tyumenskaya Oblast', C Russian Federation
Tobruch/Tobruk *see* Ţubruq
Tobyl *see* Tobol
Tocantins *63 E3* *off.* Estado do Tocantins. *state* C Brazil
Tocantins, Estado do *see* Tocantins
Tocantins, Rio *63 F2* *river* N Brazil
Tocoa *52 D2* Colón, N Honduras
Tocopilla *64 B2* Antofagasta, N Chile
Todi *96 C4* Umbria, C Italy
Todos os Santos, Baía de *63 G3* *bay* E Brazil
Toetoes Bay *151 B8* *bay* South Island, New Zealand
Tofua *145 E4* *island* Ha'apai Group, C Tonga
Togo *75 E4* *off.* Togolese Republic; *prev.* French Togoland. *country* W Africa

TOGO
Western Africa

Official name Republic of Togo
Formation 1960 / 1960
Capital Lomé
Population 6.1 million / 290 people per sq mile (112 people per sq km) / 33%
Total area 21,924 sq miles (56,785 sq km)
Languages French*, Ewe, Kabye, Gurma
Religions Traditional beliefs 50%, Christian 35%, Muslim 15%
Ethnic mix Ewe 46%, Kabye 27%, Other African 26%, European 1%
Government Presidential system
Currency CFA franc = 100 centimes
Literacy rate 53%
Calorie consumption 2345 calories

Togolese Republic *see* Togo
Tojikiston, Jumhurii *see* Tajikistan
Tokanui *151 B7* Southland, South Island, New Zealand
Tokar *72 C3* *var.* Ţawkar. Red Sea, NE Sudan
Tokat *116 D3* Tokat, N Turkey
Tokelau *145 E3* *NZ overseas territory* W Polynesia
Tőketerebes *see* Trebišov
Tokio *see* Tōkyō
Tokmak *123 G2* *Kir.* Tokmok. Chuyskaya Oblast', N Kyrgyzstan
Tokmak *109 G4* *var.* Velykyy Tokmak. Zaporiz'ka Oblast', SE Ukraine
Tokmok *see* Tokmak
Tokoroa *150 D3* Waikato, North Island, New Zealand
Tokounou *74 C4* C Guinea
Tokushima *131 C6* *var.* Tokusima. Tokushima, Shikoku, SW Japan
Tōkyō *130 A1* *var.* Tokio. *country capital* (Japan) Tōkyō, Honshū, S Japan
Tōkyō-wan *130 A2* *bay* S Japan
Tolbukhin *see* Dobrich
Toledo *92 D3* *anc.* Toletum. Castilla-La Mancha, C Spain
Toledo *40 D3* Ohio, N USA
Toledo Bend Reservoir *49 G3* *reservoir* Louisiana/Texas, SW USA
Toletum *see* Toledo
Toliara *79 F4* *var.* Toliary; *prev.* Tuléar. Toliara, SW Madagascar
Toliary *see* Toliara
Tolmein *see* Tolmin
Tolmino *see* Tolmin
Tolna *99 C7* *Ger.* Tolnau. Tolna, S Hungary
Tolnau *see* Tolna
Tolochin *see* Talachyn
Tolosa *93 E1* País Vasco, N Spain
Tolosa *see* Toulouse
Toluca *51 E4* *var.* Toluca de Lerdo. México, S Mexico
Toluca de Lerdo *see* Toluca
Tol'yatti *111 C6* *prev.* Stavropol'. Samarskaya Oblast', W Russian Federation

Tomah *40 B2* Wisconsin,
N USA
Tomakomai *130 D2* Hokkaidō,
NE Japan
Tomar *92 B3* Santarém, W Portugal
Tomaschow *see* Tomaszów Mazowiecki
Tomaschow *see* Tomaszów Lubelski
Tomaszów *see* Tomaszów Mazowiecki
Tomaszów Lubelski *98 E4*
Ger. Tomaschow. Lubelskie,
E Poland
Tomaszów Mazowiecka *see* Tomaszów
Mazowiecki
Tomaszów Mazowiecki *98 D4*
var. Tomaszów Mazowiecka;
prev. Tomaschow, *Ger.* Tomaschow.
Łódzkie, C Poland
Tombigbee River *42 C3* *river* Alabama/
Mississippi, S USA
Tombouctou *75 E3* *Eng.* Timbuktu.
Tombouctou, N Mali
Tombua *78 A2* *Port.* Porto Alexandre.
Namibe, SW Angola
Tomelloso *93 E3* Castilla-La Mancha,
C Spain
Tomini, Gulf of *139 E4* *var.* Teluk
Tomini; *prev.* Teluk Gorontalo. *bay*
Sulawesi, C Indonesia
Tomini, Teluk *see* Tomini, Gulf of
Tomsk *114 D4* Tomskaya Oblast',
C Russian Federation
Tomür Feng *see* Pobedy, Pik
Tonezh *see* Tonyezh
Tonga *145 E4* *off.* Kingdom of Tonga,
var. Friendly Islands. *country*
SW Pacific Ocean

TONGA
Australasia & Oceania

Official name Kingdom of Tonga
Formation 1970 / 1970
Capital Nuku'alofa
Population 112,422 / 404 people per
sq mile
(156 people per sq km) / 43%
Total area 289 sq miles (748 sq km)
Languages Tongan*, English
Religions Free Wesleyan 41%,
Roman Catholic 16%, Church of Jesus
Christ of Latter-day Saints 14%, Free
Church of Tonga 12%, Other 17%
Ethnic mix Polynesian 99%, Other 1%
Government Monarchy
Currency Pa'anga (Tongan dollar) =
100 seniti
Literacy rate 99%
Calorie consumption Not available

Tonga, Kingdom of *see* Tonga
Tongatapu *145 E5* *island* Tongatapu
Group, S Tonga
Tonga Trench *143 E3* *trench* S Pacific
Ocean
Tongchuan *128 C4* Shaanxi,
C China
Tongeren *87 D6* *Fr.* Tongres. Limburg,
NE Belgium
Tongking, Gulf of *128 B7* *Chin.*
Beibu Wan, *Vtn.* Vinh Bắc Bộ. *gulf*
China/Vietnam
Tongliao *127 G2* Nei Mongol Zizhiqu,
N China
Tongres *see* Tongeren
Tongshan *see* Xuzhou, Jiangsu, China
Tongtian He *126 C4* *river* C China
Tonj *73 B5* Warab, SW Sudan
Tônlé Sap *137 D5* *Eng.* Great Lake. *lake*
W Cambodia
Tonopah *47 C6* Nevada, W USA
Tonyezh *107 C7* *Rus.* Tonezh.
Homyel'skaya Voblasts', SE Belarus
Tooele *44 B4* Utah, W USA
Toowoomba *149 E5* Queensland,
E Australia
Topeka *45 F4* *state capital* Kansas,
C USA
Toplicza *see* Topliţa
Topliţa *108 C3* *Ger.* Töplitz, *Hung.*
Maroshevíz; *prev.* Topliţa Română,
Hung. Oláh-Topliza, Toplicza.
Harghita, C Romania
Topliţa Română/Töplitz *see* Topliţa
Topol'čany *99 C6* *Hung.* Nagytapolcsány.
Nitriansky Kraj, W Slovakia
Topolovgrad *104 D3* *prev.* Kavakli.
Khaskovo, S Bulgaria
Topolya *see* Bačka Topola

Top Springs Roadhouse *146 D3*
Northern Territory, N Australia
Torda *see* Turda
Torez *109 H3* Donets'ka Oblast',
SE Ukraine
Torgau *94 D4* Sachsen, E Germany
Torhout *87 A5* West-Vlaanderen,
W Belgium
Torino *96 A2* *Eng.* Turin. Piemonte,
NW Italy
Tornacum *see* Tournai
Torneå *see* Tornio
Torneträsk *84 C3* *lake* N Sweden
Tornio *84 D4* *Swe.* Torneå. Lappi,
NW Finland
Tornionjoki *84 D3* *river* Lappi/
Norrbotten, Finland/Sweden
Toro *92 D2* Castilla-León, N Spain
Toronto *38 D5* *province capital* Ontario,
S Canada
Toros Dağları *116 C4* *Eng.* Taurus
Mountains. *mountain range*
S Turkey
Torquay *89 C7* SW England, UK
Torrance *46 D2* California, W USA
Torre, Alto da *92 B3* *mountain*
C Portugal
Torre del Greco *97 D5* Campania,
S Italy
Torrejón de Ardoz *93 E3* Madrid,
C Spain
Torrelavega *92 D1* Cantabria, N Spain
Torrens, Lake *149 A6* *salt lake* South
Australia
Torrent *93 F3* *Cas.* Torrente, *var.*
Torrent de l'Horta. País Valenciano,
E Spain
Torrent de l'Horta/Torrente *see* Torrent
Torreón *50 D3* Coahuila de Zaragoza,
NE Mexico
Torres Strait *148 C1* *strait* Australia/
Papua New Guinea
Torres Vedras *92 B3* Lisboa,
C Portugal
Torrington *44 D3* Wyoming,
C USA
Tórshavn *83 F5* *Dan.* Thorshavn.
Dependent territory capital Streymoy,
N Faeroe Islands Europe
To'rtkok'l *122 D2*
var. Türtkül, *Rus.* Turtkul'; *prev.*
Petroaleksandrovsk. Qoraqalpog'iston
Respublikasi, W Uzbekistan
Tortoise Islands *see* Colón,
Archipiélago de
Tortosa *93 F2* *anc.* Dertosa. Cataluña,
E Spain
Tortue, Montagne *59 H3* *mountain*
range C French Guiana
Tortuga, Isla *see* La Tortuga, Isla
Toruń *98 C3* *Ger.* Thorn. Toruń,
Kujawsko-pomorskie, C Poland
Tõrva *106 D3* *Ger.* Törwa. Valgamaa,
S Estonia
Törwa *see* Tõrva
Torzhok *110 B4* Tverskaya Oblast',
W Russian Federation
Tosa-wan *131 B7* *bay* SW Japan
Toscana *96 B3* *Eng.* Tuscany. *region*
C Italy
Toscano, Arcipelago *96 B4*
Eng. Tuscan Archipelago. *island*
group C Italy
Toshkent *123 E2* *Eng./Rus.* Tashkent.
country capital (Uzbekistan) Toshkent
Viloyati, E Uzbekistan
Totana *93 E4* Murcia,
SE Spain
Tot'ma *see* Sukhona
Totness *59 G3* Coronie, N Suriname
Tottori *131 B6* Tottori, Honshū,
SW Japan
Touâjil *74 C2* Tiris Zemmour,
N Mauritania
Touggourt *71 E2* NE Algeria
Toukoto *74 C3* Kayes, W Mali
Toul *90 D3* Meurthe-et-Moselle,
NE France
Toulon *91 D6* *anc.* Telo Martius,
Tilio Martius. Var, SE France
Toulouse *91 B6* *anc.* Tolosa. Haute-
Garonne, S France
Toungoo *136 B4* Pegu,
C Myanmar (Burma)
Touraine *90 B4* *cultural region*
C France
Tourane *see* Đà Nẵng
Tourcoing *90 C2* Nord, N France

Tournai *87 A6* *var.* Tournay, *Dut.*
Doornik; *anc.* Tornacum. Hainaut,
SW Belgium
Tournay *see* Tournai
Tours *90 B4* *anc.* Caesarodunum,
Turoni. Indre-et-Loire, C France
Tovarkovskiy *111 B5* Tul'skaya Oblast',
W Russian Federation
Tower Island *see* Genovesa, Isla
Townsville *148 D3* Queensland,
NE Australia
Towoeti Meer *see* Towuti, Danau
Towraghoudi *122 D4* Herāt,
NW Afghanistan
Towson *41 F4* Maryland, NE USA
Towuti, Danau *139 E4* *Dut.* Towoeti
Meer. *lake* Sulawesi, C Indonesia
Toyama *131 C5* Toyama, Honshū,
SW Japan
Toyama-wan *131 B5* *bay* W Japan
Toyohara *see* Yuzhno-Sakhalinsk
Toyota *131 C6* Aichi, Honshū,
SW Japan
Tozeur *71 E2* *var.* Tawzar. W Tunisia
Trâblous *see* Tripoli
Trabzon *117 E2* *Eng.* Trebizond; *anc.*
Trapezus. Trabzon, NE Turkey
**Traiectum ad Mosam/Traiectum
Tungorum** *see* Maastricht
Traiskirchen *95 E6* Niederösterreich,
NE Austria
Trajani Portus *see* Civitavecchia
Trajectum ad Rhenum *see* Utrecht
Trakai *107 C5* *Ger.* Traken, *Pol.* Troki.
Vilnius, SE Lithuania
Traken *see* Trakai
Tralee *89 A6* *Ir.* Trá Lí. SW Ireland
Trá Lí *see* Tralee
Tralles Aydin *see* Aydın
Trang *137 C7* Trang, S Thailand
Transantarctic Mountains *154 B3*
mountain range Antarctica
Transilvania *see* Transylvania
Transilvaniei, Alpi *see* Carpaţii
Meridionali
Transjordan *see* Jordan
**Transsylvanische Alpen/Transylvanian
Alps** *see* Carpaţii Meridionali
Transylvania *108 B4* *Eng.* Ardeal,
Transilvania, *Ger.* Siebenbürgen, *Hung.*
Erdély. *cultural region* NW Romania
Trapani *97 B7* *anc.* Drepanum. Sicilia,
Italy, C Mediterranean Sea
Trâpeăng Vêng *137 D5* Kâmpóng
Thum, C Cambodia
Trapezus *see* Trabzon
Traralgon *149 C7* Victoria, SE Australia
Trasimenischersee *see* Trasimeno, Lago
Trasimeno, Lago *96 C4* *Eng.* Lake
of Perugia, *Ger.* Trasimenischersee.
lake C Italy
Traù *see* Trogir
Traverse City *40 C2* Michigan, N USA
Tra Vinh *137 D6* *var.* Phu Vinh. Tra
Vinh, S Vietnam
Travis, Lake *49 F3* *reservoir* Texas,
SW USA
Travnik *100 C4* Federacija Bosna
I Hercegovina, C Bosnia and
Herzegovina
Trbovlje *95 E7* *Ger.* Trifail.
C Slovenia
Treasure State *see* Montana
Trebič *99 B5* *Ger.* Trebitsch. Vysočina,
C Czech Republic
Trebinje *101 C5* Republika Srpska,
S Bosnia and Herzegovina
Trebišov *99 D6* *Hung.* Tőketerebes.
Košický Kraj, E Slovakia
Trebitsch *see* Trebič
Trebnitz *see* Trzebnica
Tree Planters State *see* Nebraska
Trélazé *90 B4* Maine-et-Loire,
NW France
Trelew *65 C6* Chubut, SE Argentina
Tremelo *87 C5* Vlaams Brabant,
C Belgium
Trenčín *99 C5* *Ger.* Trentschin,
Hung. Trencsén. Trenčiansky Kraj,
W Slovakia
Trencsén *see* Trenčín
Trengganu, Kuala *see* Kuala Terengganu
Trenque Lauquen *64 C4* Buenos Aires,
E Argentina
Trent *see* Trento
Trento *96 C2* *Eng.* Trent, *Ger.* Trient;
anc. Tridentum. Trentino-Alto Adige,
N Italy

Trenton *41 F4* *state capital* New Jersey,
NE USA
Trentschin *see* Trenčín
Tres Arroyos *65 D5* Buenos Aires,
E Argentina
Treskavica *100 C4* *mountain range*
SE Bosnia and Herzegovina
Tres Tabernae *see* Saverne
Treves/Trèves *see* Trier
Treviso *96 C2* *anc.* Tarvisium. Veneto,
NE Italy
Trichinopoly *see* Tiruchchirāppalli
Trichūr *132 C3* *var.* Thrissur. Kerala,
SW India
Tridentum/Trient *see* Trento
Trier *95 A5* *Eng.* Treves, *Fr.* Trèves; *anc.*
Augusta Treverorum. Rheinland-Pfalz,
SW Germany
Triesen *94 E2* SW Liechtenstein Europe
Triesenberg *94 E2* SW Liechtenstein
Trieste *96 D2* *Slvn.* Trst. Friuli-Venezia
Giulia, NE Italy
Trifail *see* Trbovlje
Tríkala *104 B4* *prev.* Trikkala. Thessalía,
C Greece
Trikkala *see* Tríkala
Trimontium
see Plovdiv
Trinacria *see* Sicilia
Trincomalee *132 D3* *var.* Trinkomali.
Eastern Province, NE Sri Lanka
Trindade, Ilha da *67 C5* *island* Brazil,
W Atlantic Ocean
Trinidad *61 F3* Beni, N Bolivia
Trinidad *64 D4* Flores, S Uruguay
Trinidad *47 C5* Colorado, C USA
Trinidad *55 H5* *island* C Trinidad and
Tobago
Trinidad and Tobago *55 H5* *off.*
Republic of Trinidad and Tobago.
country SE West Indies

TRINIDAD & TOBAGO
West Indies

Official name Republic of Trinidad
and Tobago
Formation 1962 / 1962
Capital Port-of-Spain
Population 1.3 million / 656 people per sq
mile (253 people per sq km) / 74%
Total area 1980 sq miles (5128 sq km)
Languages English*, English Creole, Hindi,
French, Spanish
Religions Christian 60%, Hindu 24%,
Other and nonreligious 9%, Muslim 7%
Ethnic mix East Indian 40%, Black 40%,
Mixed race 19%, White and Chinese 1%
Government Parliamentary system
Currency Trinidad and Tobago dollar
= 100 cents
Literacy rate 99%
Calorie consumption 2732 calories

Trinidad and Tobago, Republic of *see*
Trinidad and Tobago
Trinité, Montagnes de la *59 H3*
mountain range C French Guiana
Trinity River *49 G3* *river* Texas,
SW USA
Trinkomali *see* Trincomalee
Trípoli *105 B6* *prev.* Trípolis.
Pelopónnisos, S Greece
Tripoli *118 B4* *var.* Tarābulus, Ţarābulus
ash Shām, Trâblous; *anc.* Tripolis.
N Lebanon
Tripoli *see* Ţarābulus
Trípolis *see* Trípoli, Greece
Trípolis *see* Tripoli, Lebanon
Tristan da Cunha *69 B7* *dependency of*
Saint Helena SE Atlantic Ocean
Triton Island *128 B7* *island* S Paracel
Islands
Trivandrum *132 C3* *var.*
Thiruvananthapuram. *state capital*
Kerala, SW India
Trnava *99 C6* *Ger.* Tyrnau, *Hung.*
Nagyszombat. Trnavský Kraj,
W Slovakia
Trnovo *see* Veliko Tŭrnovo
Trogir *100 B4* *It.* Traù. Split-Dalmacija,
S Croatia
Troglav *100 B4* *mountain* Bosnia and
Herzegovina/Croatia
Trois-Rivières *39 E4* Québec, SE Canada
Troki *see* Trakai
Trollhättan *85 B6* Västra Götaland,
S Sweden

Tromsø *84 C2 Fin.* Tromssa. Troms, N Norway
Tromssa *see* Tromsø
Trondheim *84 B4 Ger.* Drontheim; *prev.* Nidaros, Trondhjem. Sør-Trøndelag, S Norway
Trondheimsfjorden *84 B4 fjord* S Norway
Trondhjem *see* Trondheim
Troódos *102 C5 var.* Troodos Mountains. *mountain range* C Cyprus
Troodos Mountains *see* Troódos
Troppau *see* Opava
Troy *42 D3* Alabama, S USA
Troy *41 F3* New York, NE USA
Troyan *104 C2* Lovech, N Bulgaria
Troyes *90 D3 anc.* Augustobona Tricassium. Aube, N France
Trst *see* Trieste
Trstenik *100 E4* Serbia, C Serbia
Trucial States *see* United Arab Emirates
Trujillo *52 D2* Colón, NE Honduras
Trujillo *60 B3* La Libertad, NW Peru
Trujillo *92 C3* Extremadura, W Spain
Truk Islands *see* Chuuk Islands
Trûn *114 B5* Pernik, W Bulgaria
Truro *39 F4* Nova Scotia, SE Canada
Truro *89 C7* SW England, UK
Trzcianka *98 B3 Ger.* Schönlanke. Pila, Wielkopolskie, C Poland
Trzebnica *98 C4 Ger.* Trebnitz. Dolnośląskie, SW Poland
Tsalka *117 F2* S Georgia Asia
Tsamkong *see* Zhanjiang
Tsangpo *see* Brahmaputra
Tsarevo *104 E2 prev.* Michurin. Burgas, E Bulgaria
Tsarigrad *see* Istanbul
Tsaritsyn *see* Volgograd
Tschakathurn *see* Čakovec
Tschaslau *see* Čáslav
Tschenstochau *see* Częstochowa
Tsefat *see* Zefat
Tselinograd *see* Astana
Tsetsen Khan *see* Öndörhaan
Tsetserleg *126 D2* Arhangay, C Mongolia
Tshela *77 B6* Bas-Congo, W Dem. Rep. Congo
Tshikapa *77 C7* Kasai Occidental, SW Dem. Rep. Congo
Tshuapa *77 D6 river* C Dem. Rep. Congo
Tshwane *78 D4 var.* Epitoli; *prev.* Pretoria. *country capital* (South Africa-administrative capital) Gauteng, NE South Africa
Tsinan *see* Jinan
Tsinghai *see* Qinghai, China
Tsing Hai *see* Qinghai Hu, China
Tsingtao/Tsingtau *see* Qingdao
Tsinkiang *see* Quanzhou
Tsintao *see* Qingdao
Tsitsihar *see* Qiqihar
Tsu *131 C6 var.* Tu. Mie, Honshū, SW Japan
Tsugaru-kaikyō *130 C3 strait* N Japan
Tsumeb *78 B3* Otjikoto, N Namibia
Tsuruga *131 C6 var.* Turuga. Fukui, Honshū, SW Japan
Tsuruoka *130 D4 var.* Turuoka. Yamagata, Honshū, C Japan
Tsushima *131 A7 var.* Tsushima-tō, Tusima. *island group* SW Japan
Tsushima-tō *see* Tsushima
Tsyerakhowka *107 D8 Rus.* Terekhovka. Homyel'skaya Voblasts', SE Belarus
Tsyurupinsk *see* Tsyurupyns'k
Tsyurupyns'k *109 E4 Rus.* Tsyurupinsk. Khersons'ka Oblast', S Ukraine
Tu *see* Tsu
Tuamotu, Archipel des *see* Tuamotu, Îles
Tuamotu Fracture Zone *143 H3 fracture zone* E Pacific Ocean
Tuamotu, Îles *145 H4 var.* Archipel des Tuamotu, Dangerous Archipelago, Tuamotu Islands. *island group* N French Polynesia
Tuamotu Islands *see* Tuamotu, Îles
Tuapi *53 E2* Región Autónoma Atlántico Norte, NE Nicaragua
Tuapse *111 A7* Krasnodarskiy Kray, SW Russian Federation
Tuba City *48 B1* Arizona, SW USA
Tubbergen *86 E3* Overijssel, E Netherlands
Tubeke *see* Tubize
Tubize *87 B6 Dut.* Tubeke. Walloon Brabant, C Belgium

Tubmanburg *74 C5* NW Liberia
Ṭubruq *71 H2 Eng.* Tobruk, *It.* Tobruch. NE Libya
Tubuai, Îles/Tubuai Islands *see* Australes, Îles
Tucker's Town *42 B5* E Bermuda
Tuckum *see* Tukums
Tucson *48 B3* Arizona, SW USA
Tucumán *see* San Miguel de Tucumán
Tucumcari *49 F2* New Mexico, SW USA
Tucupita *59 E2* Delta Amacuro, NE Venezuela
Tucuruí, Represa de *63 F2 reservoir* NE Brazil
Tudela *93 E2 Basq.* Tutera; *anc.* Tutela. Navarra, N Spain
Tudmur *118 C3 var.* Tadmur, Tamar, *Gk.* Palmyra, *Bibl.* Tadmor. Ḥimṣ, C Syria
Tuguegarao *139 E1* Luzon, N Philippines
Tuktoyaktuk *37 E3* Northwest Territories, NW Canada
Tukums *106 C3 Ger.* Tuckum. Tukums, W Latvia
Tula *111 B5* Tul'skaya Oblast', W Russian Federation
Tulancingo *51 E4* Hidalgo, C Mexico
Tulare Lake Bed *47 C7 salt flat* California, W USA
Tulcán *60 B1* Carchi, N Ecuador
Tulcea *108 D5* Tulcea, E Romania
Tul'chin *see* Tul'chyn
Tul'chyn *108 D3 Rus.* Tul'chin. Vinnyts'ka Oblast', C Ukraine
Tuléar *see* Toliara
Tulia *49 E2* Texas, SW USA
Tulle *91 C5 anc.* Tutela. Corrèze, C France
Tulln *95 E6 var.* Oberhollabrunn. Niederösterreich, NE Austria
Tully *148 D3* Queensland, NE Australia
Tulsa *49 G1* Oklahoma, C USA
Tuluá *58 B3* Valle del Cauca, W Colombia
Tulun *115 E4* Irkutskaya Oblast', S Russian Federation
Tumaco *58 A4* Nariño, SW Colombia
Tumba, Lac *see* Ntomba, Lac
Tumbes *60 A2* Tumbes, NW Peru
Tumkūr *132 C2* Karnātaka, W India
Tumuc-Humac Mountains *63 E1 var.* Serra Tumucumaque. *mountain range* N South America
Tumucumaque, Serra *see* Tumuc Humac Mountains
Tunca Nehri *see* Tundzha
Tunduru *73 C8* Ruvuma, S Tanzania
Tundzha *104 D3 Turk.* Tunca Nehri. *river* Bulgaria/Turkey
Tungabhadra Reservoir *132 C2 lake* S India
Tungaru *145 E2 prev.* Gilbert Islands. *island group* W Kiribati
T'ung-shan *see* Xuzhou
Tungsten *36 D4* Northwest Territories, W Canada
Tung-t'ing Hu *see* Dongting Hu
Tunis *71 E1 var.* Tûnis. *country capital* (Tunisia) NE Tunisia
Tunis, Golfe de *102 D3 Ar.* Khalīj Tūnis. *gulf* NE Tunisia
Tunisia *71 F2 off.* Republic of Tunisia, *Ar.* Al Jumhūrīyah at Tūnisīyah, *Fr.* République Tunisienne. *country* N Africa

TUNISIA
North Africa

Official name Republic of Tunisia
Formation 1956 / 1956
Capital Tunis
Population 10.1 million / 168 people per sq mile (65 people per sq km)
Total area 63,169 sq miles (163,610 sq km)
Languages Arabic*, French
Religions Muslim (mainly Sunni) 98%, Christian 1%, Jewish 1%
Ethnic mix Arab and Berber 98%, Jewish 1%, European 1%
Government Presidential system
Currency Tunisian dinar = 1000 millimes
Literacy rate 74%
Calorie consumption 3238 calories

Tunisia, Republic of *see* Tunisia
Tunisienne, République *see* Tunisia

Tūnisīyah, Al Jumhūrīyah at *see* Tunisia
Tūnis, Khalīj *see* Tunis, Golfe de
Tunja *58 B3* Boyacá, C Colombia
Tuong Buong *see* Tương Đương
Tương Đương *136 D4 var.* Tuong Buong. Nghệ An, N Vietnam
Tüp *see* Tyup
Tupelo *42 C2* Mississippi, S USA
Tupiza *61 G5* Potosí, S Bolivia
Turabah *121 B5* Makkah, W Saudi Arabia
Turangi *150 D4* Waikato, North Island, New Zealand
Turan Lowland *122 C2 var.* Turan Plain, *Kaz.* Turan Oypaty, *Rus.* Turanskaya Nizmennost', *Turk.* Turan Pesligi, *Uzb.* Turan Pasttekisligi. *plain* C Asia
Turan Oypaty/Turan Pesligi/Turan Plain/Turanskaya Nizmennost' *see* Turan Lowland
Turan Pasttekisligi *see* Turan Lowland
Ṭurayf *120 A3* Al Ḥudūd ash Shamālīyah, NW Saudi Arabia
Turba *see* Teruel
Turbat *134 A3* Baluchistān, SW Pakistan
Turčiansky Svätý Martin *see* Martin
Turda *108 B4 Ger.* Thorenburg, *Hung.* Torda. Cluj, NW Romania
Turek *98 C3* Wielkopolskie, C Poland
Turfan *see* Turpan
Turin *see* Torino
Turkana, Lake *89 C6 var.* Lake Rudolf. *lake* N Kenya
Turkestan *114 B5 Kaz.* Türkistan. Yuzhnyy Kazakhstan, S Kazakhstan
Turkey *116 B3 off.* Republic of Turkey, *Turk.* Türkiye Cumhuriyeti. *country* SW Asia

TURKEY
Asia / Europe

Official name Republic of Turkey
Formation 1923 / 1939
Capital Ankara
Population 73.2 million / 246 people per sq mile (95 people per sq km)
Total area 301,382 sq miles (780,580 sq km)
Languages Turkish*, Kurdish, Arabic, Circassian, Armenian, Greek, Georgian, Ladino
Religions Muslim (mainly Sunni) 99%, Other 1%
Ethnic mix Turkish 70%, Kurdish 20%, Other 8%, Arab 2%
Government Parliamentary system
Currency new Turkish lira = 100 kurus
Literacy rate 88%
Calorie consumption 3357 calories

Turkey, Republic of *see* Turkey
Turkish Republic of Northern Cyprus *102 D5 disputed territory* Cyprus
Türkistan *see* Turkestan
Türkiye Cumhuriyeti *see* Turkey
Türkmenabat *122 D3 prev. Rus.* Chardzhev, Chardzhou, Chardzhui, Lenin-Turkmenski, *Turkm.* Chärjew. Lebap Welaýaty, E Turkmenistan
Turkmen Aylagy *122 B2 Rus.* Turkmenskiy Zaliv. *lake gulf* W Turkmenistan
Turkmenbashi *see* Türkmenbaşy
Türkmenbaşy *122 B2 Rus.* Turkmenbashi; *prev.* Krasnovodsk. Balkan Welaýaty, W Turkmenistan
Türkmenbaşy Aylagy *122 A2 prev. Rus.* Krasnovodskiy Zaliv, *Turkm.* Krasnowodsk Aylagy. *lake Gulf* W Turkmenistan
Turkmenistan *122 B2; prev.* Turkmenskaya Soviet Socialist Republic. *country* C Asia

TURKMENISTAN
Central Asia

Official name Turkmenistan
Formation 1991 / 1991
Capital Ashgabat
Population 4.8 million / 25 people per sq mile (10 people per sq km) / 45%
Total area 188,455 sq miles (488,100 sq km)
Languages Turkmen*, Uzbek, Russian, Kazakh, Tatar

TURKMENISTAN
Central Asia

** OReligions** Sunni Muslim 87%, Orthodox Christian 11%, Other 2%
Ethnic mix Turkmen 77%, Uzbek 9%, Russian 7%, Other 4%, Kazakh 2%, Tatar 1%
Government One-party state
Currency manat = 100 tenga
Literacy rate 99%
Calorie consumption 2742 calories

Turkmenskaya Soviet Socialist Republic *see* Turkmenistan
Turkmenskiy Zaliv *see* Turkmen Aylagy
Turks and Caicos Islands *55 E2 UK dependent territory* N West Indies
Turlock *47 B6* California, W USA
Turnagain, Cape *150 D4 headland* North Island, New Zealand
Turnau *see* Turnov
Turnhout *87 C5* Antwerpen, N Belgium
Turnov *98 B4 Ger.* Turnau. Liberecký Kraj, N Czech Republic
Türnovo *see* Veliko Tŭrnovo
Turnu Măgurele *108 B5 var.* Turnu-Măgurele. Teleorman, S Romania
Turnu Severin *see* Drobeta-Turnu Severin
Turócszentmárton *see* Martin
Turoni *see* Tours
Turpan *126 C3 var.* Turfan. Xinjiang Uygur Zizhiqu, NW China
Turpan Depression *see* Turpan Pendi
Turpan Pendi *126 C3 Eng.* Turpan Depression. *depression* NW China
Turpentine State *see* North Carolina
Türtkül/Turtkul' *see* To'rtko'l
Turuga *see* Tsuruga
Turuoka *see* Tsuruoka
Tuscaloosa *42 C2* Alabama, S USA
Tuscan Archipelago *see* Toscano, Arcipelago
Tuscany *see* Toscana
Tusima *see* Tsushima
Tutela *see* Tulle, France
Tutela *see* Tudela, Spain
Tutera *see* Tudela
Tuticorin *132 C3* Tamil Nādu, SE India
Tutrakan *104 D1* Silistra, NE Bulgaria
Tutuila *145 F4 island* W American Samoa
Tuvalu *145 E3 prev.* Ellice Islands. *country* SW Pacific Ocean

TUVALU
Australasia & Oceania

Official name Tuvalu
Formation 1978 / 1978
Capital Fongafale, on Funafuti Atoll
Population 11,636 / 1164 people per sq mile (448 people per sq km) / 45%
Total area 10 sq miles (26 sq km)
Languages Tuvaluan, Kiribati, English
Religions Church of Tuvalu 97%, Other 1%, Baha'i 1%, Seventh-day Adventist 1%
Ethnic mix Polynesian 96%, Other 4%
Government Nonparty system
Currency Australian dollar and Tuvaluan dollar = 100 cents
Literacy rate 95%
Calorie consumption Not available

Ṭuwayq, Jabal *121 C5 mountain range* C Saudi Arabia
Tuxpan *50 D4* Jalisco, C Mexico
Tuxpan *50 D4* Nayarit, C Mexico
Tuxpán *51 F4 var.* Tuxpán de Rodríguez Cano. Veracruz-Llave, E Mexico
Tuxpán de Rodríguez Cano *see* Tuxpán
Tuxtepec *51 F4 var.* San Juan Bautista Tuxtepec. Oaxaca, S Mexico
Tuxtla *51 G5 var.* Tuxtla Gutiérrez. Chiapas, SE Mexico
Tuxtla *see* San Andrés Tuxtla
Tuxtla Gutiérrez *see* Tuxtla
Tuy Hoa *137 E5* Phu Yên, S Vietnam
Tuz Gölü *116 C3 lake* C Turkey

Tver' *110 B4 prev.* Kalinin. Tverskaya Oblast', W Russian Federation
Tverya *see* Teverya
Twin Falls *46 D4* Idaho, NW USA
Tyan'-Shan' *see* Tien Shan
Tychy *99 D5* var. Tichau. Śląskie, S Poland
Tyler *49 G3* Texas, SW USA
Tylos *see* Bahrain
Tympáki *105 C8 var.* Timbaki; *prev.* Timbákion. Kriti, Greece, E Mediterranean Sea
Tynda *115 F4* Amurskaya Oblast', SE Russian Federation
Tyne *88 D4 river* N England, UK
Tyósi *see* Chōshi
Tyras *see* Dniester
Tyre *see* Soûr
Tyrnau *see* Trnava
Týrnavos *104 B4 var.* Tírnavos. Thessalía, C Greece
Tyrol *see* Tirol
Tyros *see* Bahrain
Tyrrhenian Sea *97 B6 It.* Mare Tirreno. *sea* N Mediterranean Sea
Tyumen' *114 C3* Tyumenskaya Oblast', C Russian Federation
Tyup *123 G2 Kir.* Tüp. Issyk-Kul'skaya Oblast', NE Kyrgyzstan
Tywyn *89 C6* W Wales, UK
Tzekung *see* Zigong
Tziá *105 C6 prev.* Kéa, Kéos; *anc.* Ceos. *island* Kykládes, Greece, Aegean Sea

U

Uaco Cungo *78 B2* C Angola
UAE *see* United Arab Emirates
Uanle Uen *see* Wanlaweyn
Uaupés, Rio *see* Vaupés, Río
Ubangi *77 C5 Fr.* Oubangui. *river* C Africa
Ubangi-Shari *see* Central African Republic
Ube *131 B7* Yamaguchi, Honshū, SW Japan
Ubeda *93 E4* Andalucía, S Spain
Uberaba *63 F4* Minas Gerais, SE Brazil
Uberlândia *63 F4* Minas Gerais, SE Brazil
Ubol Rajadhani/Ubol Ratchathani *see* Ubon Ratchathani
Ubon Ratchathani *137 D5 var.* Muang Ubon, Ubol Rajadhani, Ubol Ratchani, Udon Ratchathani. Ubon Ratchathani, E Thailand
Ubrique *92 D5* Andalucía, S Spain
Ubsu-Nur, Ozero *see* Uvs Nuur
Ucayali, Río *60 D3 river* C Peru
Uchiura-wan *130 D3 bay* NW Pacific Ocean
Uchkuduk *see* Uchquduq
Uchquduq *122 D2 Rus.* Uchkuduk. Navoiy Viloyati, N Uzbekistan
Uchtagan Gumy/Uchtagan, Peski *see* Uçtagan Gumy
Uçtagan Gumy *122 C2 var.* Uchtagan Gumy, *Rus.* Peski Uchtagan. *desert* NW Turkmenistan
Udaipur *134 C3 prev.* Oodeypore. Rājasthān, N India
Uddevalla *85 B6* Västra Götaland, S Sweden
Udine *96 D2 anc.* Utina. Friuli-Venezia Giulia, NE Italy
Udintsev Fracture Zone *154 A5 tectonic feature* S Pacific Ocean
Udipi *see* Udupi
Udon Ratchathani *see* Ubon Ratchathani
Udon Thani *136 C4 var.* Ban Mak Khaeng, Udorndhani. Udon Thani, N Thailand
Udorndhani *see* Udon Thani
Udupi *132 B2 var.* Udipi. Karnātaka, SW India
Uele *77 D5 var.* Welle. *river* NE Dem. Rep. Congo
Uelzen *94 C3* Niedersachsen, N Germany
Ufa *111 D6* Respublika Bashkortostan, W Russian Federation
Ugâle *106 C2* Ventspils, NW Latvia
Uganda *73 B6 off.* Republic of Uganda. *country* E Africa

UGANDA
East Africa

Official name Republic of Uganda
Formation 1962 / 1962
Capital Kampala
Population 28.8 million / 374 people per sq mile (144 people per sq km) / 14%
Total area 91,135 sq miles (236,040 sq km)
Languages English*, Luganda, Nkole, Chiga, Lango, Acholi, Teso, Lugbara
Religions Roman Catholic 38%, Protestant 33%, Traditional beliefs 13%, Muslim (mainly Sunni) 8%, Other 8%
Ethnic mix Bantu tribes 50%, Other 45%, Sudanese 5%
Government Nonparty system
Currency New Uganda shilling = 100 cents
Literacy rate 69%
Calorie consumption 2410 calories

Uganda, Republic of *see* Uganda
Uglovka *110 B4 var.* Novgorodskaya Oblast', W Russian Federation
Uhorshchyna *see* Hungary
Uhuru Peak *see* Kilimanjaro
Uíge *78 B1 Port.* Carmona, Vila Marechal Carmona. Uíge, NW Angola
Uinta Mountains *44 B4 mountain range* Utah, W USA
Uitenhage *78 C5* Eastern Cape, S South Africa
Uithoorn *86 C3* Noord-Holland, C Netherlands
Ujda *see* Oujda
Ujelang Atoll *144 C1 var.* Wujlān. *atoll* Ralik Chain, W Marshall Islands
Ujgradiska *see* Nova Gradiška
Ujmoldova *see* Moldova Nouă
Ujungpandang *see* Makassar
Ujung Salang *see* Phuket
Újvidék *see* Novi Sad
UK *see* United Kingdom
Ukhta *114 C3* Respublika Komi, NW Russian Federation
Ukiah *47 B5* California, W USA
Ukmergė *106 C4 Pol.* Wiłkomierz. Vilnius, C Lithuania
Ukraina *see* Ukraine
Ukraine *108 C2 off.* Ukraine, *Rus.* Ukraina, *Ukr.* Ukrayina; *prev.* Ukrainian Soviet Socialist Republic, Ukrainskay S.S.R. *country* SE Europe

UKRAINE
Eastern Europe

Official name Ukraine
Formation 1991 / 1991
Capital Kiev
Population 46.5 million / 199 people per sq mile (77 people per sq km) / 68%
Total area 223,089 sq miles (603,700 sq km)
Languages Ukrainian*, Russian, Tatar
Religions Christian (mainly Orthodox) 95%, Other 4%, Jewish 1%
Ethnic mix Ukrainian 73%, Russian 22%, Other 4%, Jewish 1%
Government Presidential system
Currency Hryvna = 100 kopiykas
Literacy rate 99%
Calorie consumption 3054 calories

Ukraine *see* Ukraine
Ukrainian Soviet Socialist Republic *see* Ukraine
Ukrainskay S.S.R/Ukrayina *see* Ukraine
Ulaanbaatar *127 E2 Eng.* Ulan Bator; *prev.* Urga. *country capital* (Mongolia) Töv, C Mongolia
Ulaangom *126 C2* Uvs, NW Mongolia
Ulan Bator *see* Ulaanbaatar
Ulanhad *see* Chifeng
Ulan-Ude *115 E4 prev.* Verkhneudinsk. Respublika Buryatiya, S Russian Federation
Uleälv *see* Oulujoki
Uleträsk *see* Oulujärvi
Ulft *86 E4* Gelderland, E Netherlands
Ullapool *88 C3* N Scotland, UK

Ulm *95 B6* Baden-Württemberg, S Germany
Ulsan *129 E4 Jap.* Urusan. SE South Korea
Ulster *89 B5 province* Northern Ireland, UK/Ireland
Ulungur Hu *126 B2 lake* NW China
Uluru *147 D5 var.* Ayers Rock. *rocky outcrop* Northern Territory, C Australia
Ulyanivka *see* Ul'yanovka. Kirovohrads'ka Oblast', C Ukraine
Ul'yanovka *see* Ulyanivka
Ul'yanovsk *111 C5 prev.* Simbirsk. Ul'yanovskaya Oblast', W Russian Federation
Umán *51 H3* Yucatán, SE Mexico
Uman' *109 E3 Rus.* Uman. Cherkas'ka Oblast', C Ukraine
Uman *see* Uman'
Umanak/Umanaq *see* Uummannaq
'Umān, Khalīj *see* Oman, Gulf of
'Umān, Salṭanat *see* Oman
Umbrian-Machigian Mountains *see* Umbro-Marchigiano, Appennino
Umbro-Marchigiano, Appennino *96 C3 Eng.* Umbrian-Machigian Mountains. *mountain range* C Italy
Umeå *84 C4* Västerbotten, N Sweden
Umeälven *84 C4 river* N Sweden
Umiat *36 D2* Alaska, USA
Umm Buru *72 A4* Western Darfur, W Sudan
Umm Durmān *see* Omdurman
Umm Ruwaba *72 C4 var.* Umm Ruwābah, Um Ruwāba. Northern Kordofan, C Sudan
Umm Ruwābah *see* Umm Ruwaba
Umnak Island *36 A3 island* Aleutian Islands, Alaska, USA
Um Ruwāba *see* Umm Ruwaba
Umtali *see* Mutare
Umtata *78 D5* Eastern Cape, SE South Africa
Una *100 B3 river* Bosnia and Herzegovina/Croatia
Unac *100 B3 river* W Bosnia and Herzegovina
Unalaska Island *36 A3 island* Aleutian Islands, Alaska, USA
'Unayzah *120 B4 var.* Anaiza. Al Qaşim, C Saudi Arabia
Unci *see* Almería
Uncía *61 F4* Potosí, C Bolivia
Uncompahgre Peak *44 B5 mountain* Colorado, C USA
Undur Khan *see* Öndörhaan
Ungaria *see* Hungary
Ungarisches Erzgebirge *see* Slovenské rudohorie
Ungarn *see* Hungary
Ungava Bay *39 E1 bay* Québec, E Canada
Ungava, Péninsule d' *38 D1 peninsula* Québec, SE Canada
Ungeny *see* Ungheni
Ungheni *108 D3 Rus.* Ungeny. W Moldova
Unguja *see* Zanzibar
Üngüz Angyrsyndaky Garagum *122 C2 Rus.* Zaunguzskiye Garagumy. *desert* N Turkmenistan
Ungvár *see* Uzhhorod
Unimak Island *36 B3 island* Aleutian Islands, Alaska, USA
Union *43 E1* South Carolina, SE USA
Union City *42 C1* Tennessee, S USA
Union of Myanmar *see* Burma
United Arab Emirates *121 C5 Ar.* Al Imārāt al 'Arabiyah al Muttaḥidah, *abbrev.* UAE; *prev.* Trucial States. *country* SW Asia

UNITED ARAB EMIRATES
Southwest Asia

Official name United Arab Emirates
Formation 1971 / 1972
Capital Abu Dhabi
Population 4.5 million / 139 people per sq mile (54 people per sq km) / 86%
Total area 32,000 sq miles (82,880 sq km)
Languages Arabic*, Farsi, Indian and Pakistani languages, English
Religions Muslim (mainly Sunni) 96%, Christian, Hindu, and Other 4%

UNITED ARAB EMIRATES
(continued)

Ethnic mix Asian 60%, Emirian 25%, Other Arab 12%, European 3%
Government Monarchy
Currency UAE dirham = 100 fils
Literacy rate 77%
Calorie consumption 3225 calories

United Arab Republic *see* Egypt
United Kingdom *89 B5 off.* United Kingdom of Great Britain and Northern Ireland, *abbrev.* UK. *country* NW Europe

UNITED KINGDOM
Northwest Europe

Official name United Kingdom of Great Britain and Northern Ireland
Formation 1707 / 1922
Capital London
Population 59.7 million / 640 people per sq mile (247 people per sq km) / 90%
Total area 94,525 sq miles (244,820 sq km)
Languages English*, Welsh, Scottish Gaelic
Religions Anglican 45%, Roman Catholic 9%, Presbyterian 4%, Other 42%
Ethnic mix English 80%, Scottish 9%, West Indian, Asian, and other 5%, Northern Irish 3%, Welsh 3%
Government Parliamentary system
Currency Pound sterling = 100 pence
Literacy rate 99%
Calorie consumption 3412 calories

United Kingdom of Great Britain and Northern Ireland *see* United Kingdom
United Mexican States *see* Mexico
United Provinces *see* Uttar Pradesh
United States of America *35 B5 off.* United States of America, *var.* America, The States, *abbrev.* U.S., USA. *country*

UNITED STATES
North America

Official name United States of America
Formation 1776 / 1959
Capital Washington D.C.
Population 298 million / 84 people per sq mile (33 people per sq km) / 77%
Total area 3,717,792 sq miles (9,626,091 sq km)
Languages English*, Spanish, Chinese, French, German, Tagalog, Vietnamese, Italian, Korean, Russian, Polish
Religions Protestant 52%, Roman Catholic 25%, Muslim 2%, Jewish 2%, Other 19%
Ethnic mix White 69%, Hispanic 13%, Black American/African 13%, Asian 4%, Native American 1%
Government Presidential system
Currency US dollar = 100 cents
Literacy rate 99%
Calorie consumption 3774 calories

United States of America *see* United States of America
Unst *88 D1 island* NE Scotland, UK
Ünye *116 D2* Ordu, W Turkey
Upala *52 D4* Alajuela, NW Costa Rica
Upata *59 E2* Bolívar, E Venezuela
Upemba, Lac *77 D7 lake* SE Dem. Rep. Congo
Upernavik *82 C2 var.* Upernivik. Kitaa, C Greenland
Upernivik *see* Upernavik
Upington *78 C4* Northern Cape, W South Africa
Upolu *145 F4 island* SE Samoa
Upper Klamath Lake *46 A4 lake* Oregon, NW USA
Upper Lough Erne *89 A5 lake* SW Northern Ireland, UK
Upper Red Lake *45 F1 lake* Minnesota, N USA
Upper Volta *see* Burkina Faso
Uppsala *85 C6* Uppsala, C Sweden
Ural *112 B3 Kaz.* Zayyq. *river* Kazakhstan/Russian Federation
Ural Mountains *see* Ural'skiye Gory

Ural'sk *114 B3 Kaz.* Oral. Zapadnyy
 Kazakhstan, NW Kazakhstan
Ural'skiye Gory *114 C3*
 var. Ural'skiy Khrebet, *Eng.* Ural
 Mountains. *mountain range*
 Kazakhstan/Russian Federation
Ural'skiy Khrebet *see* Ural'skiye Gory
Uraricoera *62 D1* Roraima, N Brazil
Ura-Tyube *see* Üroteppa
Urbandale *45 F3* Iowa, C USA
Urdunn *see* Jordan
Uren' *111 C5* Nizhegorodskaya Oblast',
 W Russian Federation
Urga *see* Ulaanbaatar
Urganch *122 D2 Rus.* Urgench; *prev.*
 Novo-Urgench. Xorazm Viloyati,
 W Uzbekistan
Urgench *see* Urganch
Urgut *123 E3* Samarqand Viloyati,
 C Uzbekistan
Uroševac *101 D5 Alb.* Ferizaj. Kosovo,
 S Serbia
Üroteppa *123 E2 Rus.* Ura-Tyube.
 NW Tajikistan
Uruapan *51 E4 var.* Uruapan del
 Progreso. Michoacán de Ocampo,
 SW Mexico
Uruapan del Progreso *see* Uruapan
Uruguai, Rio *see* Uruguay
Uruguay *64 D4 off.* Oriental Republic
 of Uruguay; *prev.* La Banda Oriental.
 country E South America

URUGUAY
South America

Official name Eastern Republic of
Uruguay
Formation 1828 / 1828
Capital Montevideo
Population 3.5 million / 52 people per sq
mile (20 people per sq km) / 91%
Total area 68,039 sq miles (176,220 sq km)
Languages Spanish*
Religions Roman Catholic 66%, Other
and nonreligious 30%, Jewish 2%,
Protestant 2%
Ethnic mix White 90%, Mestizo 6%,
Black 4%
Government Presidential system
Currency Uruguayan peso = 100
céntsimos
Literacy rate 98%
Calorie consumption 2828 calories

Uruguay *64 D3 var.* Rio Uruguai, Río
 Uruguay. *river* E South America
Uruguay, Oriental Republic of *see*
 Uruguay
Uruguay, Rio *see* Uruguay
Urumchi *see* Ürümqi
Ürümqi *126 C3 var.* Tihwa,
 Urumchi, Urumqi, Urumtsi,
 Wu-lu-k'o-mu-shih, Wu-lu-mu-ch'i;
 prev. Ti-hua. Xinjiang Uygur Zizhiqu,
 NW China
Urumtsi *see* Ürümqi
Urundi *see* Burundi
Urup, Ostrov *115 H4 island* Kuril'skiye
 Ostrova, SE Russian Federation
Urusan *see* Ulsan
Urziceni *108 C5* Ialomiţa, SE Romania
Usa *110 E3 river* NW Russian Federation
Uşak *116 B3 prev.* Ushak. Uşak,
 W Turkey
Ushak *see* Uşak
Ushant *see* Ouessant, Île d'
Ushuaia *65 B8* Tierra del Fuego,
 S Argentina
Usinsk *110 E3* Respublika Komi,
 NW Russian Federation
Üsküb/Üsküp *see* Skopje
Usmas Ezers *106 B3 lake*
 NW Latvia
Usol'ye-Sibirskoye *115 E4*
 Irkutskaya Oblast', C Russian
 Federation
Ussel *91 C5* Corrèze, C France
Ussuriysk *115 G5*
 prev. Nikol'sk, Nikol'sk-Ussuriyskiy,
 Voroshilov. Primorskiy Kray,
 SE Russian Federation
Ustica, Isola d' *97 B6 island* S Italy
Úst'-Ilimsk *115 E4* Irkutskaya Oblast',
 C Russian Federation
Ústí nad Labem *98 A4*
 Ger. Aussig. Ústecký Kraj,
 NW Czech Republic

Ustinov *see* Izhevsk
Ustka *98 C2 Ger.* Stolpmünde.
 Pomorskie, N Poland
Ust'-Kamchatsk *115 H2* Kamchatskaya
 Oblast', E Russian Federation
Ust'-Kamenogorsk *114 D5 Kaz.*
 Öskemen. Vostochnyy Kazakhstan,
 E Kazakhstan
Ust'-Kut *115 E4* Irkutskaya Oblast',
 C Russian Federation
Ust'-Olenëk *115 E3* Respublika Sakha
 (Yakutiya), NE Russian Federation
Ustrzyki Dolne *99 E5* Podkarpackie,
 SE Poland
Ust'-Sysol'sk *see* Syktyvkar
Ustyurt Plateau *122 B1 var.* Ust
 Urt, *Uzb.* Ustyurt Platosi. *plateau*
 Kazakhstan/Uzbekistan
Ustyurt Platosi *see* Ustyurt Plateau
Usulután *52 C3* Usulután,
 SE El Salvador
Usumacinta, Río *52 B1 river*
 Guatemala/Mexico
Usumbura *see* Bujumbura
U.S./USA *see* United States of America
Utah *44 A1 off.* State of Utah,
 also known as Beehive State, Mormon
 State. *state* W USA
Utah Lake *44 B4 lake* Utah,
 W USA
Utena *106 C4* Utena, E Lithuania
Utica *41 F3* New York,
 NE USA
Utina *see* Udine
Utrecht *86 C4 Lat.* Trajectum ad
 Rhenum. Utrecht, C Netherlands
Utsunomiya *131 D5 var.* Utunomiya.
 Tochigi, Honshū, S Japan
Uttaranchal *135 E2 state* N India
Uttaranchal *135 E2 cultural region*
 N India
Uttar Pradesh *135 E3 prev.* United
 Provinces, United Provinces of Agra
 and Oudh. *cultural region* N India
Uttar Pradesh *135 E3 prev.* United
 Provinces, United Provinces of Agra
 and Oudh. *state* N India
Utunomiya *see* Utsunomiya
Uulu *106 D2* Pärnumaa,
 SW Estonia
Uummannaq *82 C3 var.* Umanak,
 Umanaq. Kitaa, C Greenland
Uummannarsuaq *see* Nunap Isua
Uvalde *49 F4* Texas, SW USA
Uvarovichi *107 D7 Rus.* Uvarovichi.
 Homyel'skaya Voblasts', SE Belarus
Uvarovichi *see* Uvarovichy
Uvea, Île *145 E4 island* N Wallis and
 Futuna
Uvs Nuur *126 C1 var.* Ozero Ubsu-Nur.
 lake Mongolia/Russian Federation
'Uwaynāt, Jabal al *88 A3 var.* Jebel
 Uweinat. *mountain* Libya/Sudan
Uweinat, Jebel *see* 'Uwaynāt, Jabal al
Uyo *75 G5* Akwa Ibom, S Nigeria
Uyuni *61 F5* Potosí, W Bolivia
Uzbekistan *122 D2 off.* Republic of
 Uzbekistan. *country* C Asia

UZBEKISTAN
Central Asia

Official name Republic of Uzbekistan
Formation 1991 / 1991
Capital Tashkent
Population 26.6 million / 154 people per
sq mile (59 people per sq km) / 37%
Total area 172,741 sq miles
(447,400 sq km)
Languages Uzbek*, Russian, Tajik,
Kazakh
Religions Sunni Muslim 88%,
Orthodox Christian 9%, Other 3%
Ethnic mix Uzbek 71%, Other 12%,
Russian 8%, Tajik 5%, Kazakh 4%
Government Presidential system
Currency Som = 100 tiyin
Literacy rate 99%
Calorie consumption 2241 calories

Uzbekistan, Republic of *see* Uzbekistan
Uzhgorod *see* Uzhhorod
Uzhhorod *108 B2 Rus.* Uzhgorod;
 prev. Ungvár. Zakarpats'ka Oblast',
 W Ukraine
Užice *100 D4 prev.* Titovo Užice. Serbia,
 W Serbia

V

Vaal *78 D4 river* C South Africa
Vaals *87 D6* Limburg, SE Netherlands
Vaasa *85 D5 Swe.* Vasa; *prev.*
 Nikolainkaupunki. Länsi-Soumi,
 W Finland
Vaassen *86 D3* Gelderland,
 E Netherlands
Vác *99 C6 Ger.* Waitzen. Pest,
 N Hungary
Vadodara *134 C4 prev.* Baroda. Gujarāt,
 W India
Vaduz *94 E2 country capital*
 (Liechtenstein) W Liechtenstein
Vág *see* Váh
Vágbeszterce *see* Považská Bystrica
Váh *99 C5 Ger.* Waag, *Hung.* Vág. *river*
 W Slovakia
Váhtjer *see* Gällivare
Väinameri *106 C2 prev.* Muhu Väin,
 Ger. Moon-Sund. *sea* E Baltic Sea
Vajdahunyad *see* Hunedoara
Valachia *see* Wallachia
Valday *110 B4* Novgorodskaya Oblast',
 W Russian Federation
Valdecañas, Embalse de *92 D3 reservoir*
 W Spain
Valdepeñas *93 E4* Castilla-La Mancha,
 C Spain
Valdés, Península *65 C6 peninsula*
 SE Argentina
Valdez *36 C3* Alaska, USA
Valdia *see* Weldiya
Valdivia *65 B5* Los Lagos, C Chile
Val-d'Or *38 D4* Québec, SE Canada
Valdosta *43 E3* Georgia, SE USA
Valence *91 D5 anc.* Valentia, Valentia
 Julia, Ventia. Drôme, E France
Valencia *46 D1* California, USA
Valencia *58 D1* Carabobo, N Venezuela
Valencia, Golfo de *93 F3 var.* Gulf of
 Valencia. *gulf* E Spain
Valencia, Gulf of *see* Valencia, Golfo de
Valencia/Valencia *see* País Valenciano
Valenciennes *90 D2* Nord, N France
Valentia *see* Valence, France
Valentia *see* País Valenciano
Valentia Julia *see* Valence
Valentine State *see* Oregon
Valera *58 C2* Trujillo, NW Venezuela
Valetta *see* Valletta
Valga *106 D3 Ger.* Walk, *Latv.* Valka.
 Valgamaa, S Estonia
Valira *91 A8 river* Andorra/Spain Europe
Valjevo *100 C4* Serbia, W Serbia
Valjok *see* Válljohka
Valka *106 D3 Ger.* Walk. Valka,
 N Latvia
Valka *see* Valga
Valkenswaard *87 D5* Noord-Brabant,
 S Netherlands
Valladolid *51 H3* Yucatán, SE Mexico
Valladolid *92 D2* Castilla-León,
 NW Spain
Vall D'Uxó *see* La Vall D'Uixó
Valle de la Pascua *58 D2* Guárico,
 N Venezuela
Valledupar *58 B1* Cesar, N Colombia
Vallejo *47 B6* California, W USA
Vallenar *64 B3* Atacama, N Chile
Valletta *97 C8 prev.* Valetta. *country
 capital* (Malta) E Malta
Valley City *45 E2* North Dakota,
 N USA
Válljohka *84 D2 var.* Valjok. Finnmark,
 N Norway
Valls *93 G2* Cataluña, NE Spain
Valmiera *106 D3 Est.* Volmari, *Ger.*
 Wolmar. Valmiera, N Latvia
Valona *see* Vlorë
Valozhyn *107 C5 Pol.* Wołożyn, *Rus.*
 Volozhin. Minskaya Voblasts',
 C Belarus
Valparaíso *64 B4* Valparaíso, C Chile
Valparaíso *40 C3* Indiana, N USA
Valverde del Camino *92 C4* Andalucía,
 S Spain
Van *117 F3* Van, E Turkey
Vanadzor *117 F2 prev.* Kirovakan.
 N Armenia
Vancouver *36 D5* British Columbia,
 SW Canada
Vancouver *46 B3* Washington,
 NW USA

Vancouver Island *36 D5 island* British
 Columbia, SW Canada
Vanda *see* Vantaa
Van Diemen Gulf *146 D2 gulf* Northern
 Territory, N Australia
Van Diemen's Land *see* Tasmania
Vaner, Lake *see* Vänern
Vänern *85 B6 Eng.* Lake Vaner; *prev.*
 Lake Vener. *lake* S Sweden
Vangaindrano *79 G4* Fianarantsoa,
 SE Madagascar
Van Gölü *117 F3 Eng.* Lake Van; *anc.*
 Thospitis. *salt lake* E Turkey
Van Horn *48 D3* Texas, SW USA
Van, Lake *see* Van Gölü
Vannes *90 A3 anc.* Dariorigum.
 Morbihan, NW France
Vantaa *85 D6 Swe.* Vanda. Etelä-Suomi,
 S Finland
Vanua Levu *145 E4 island* N Fiji
Vanuatu *144 C4 off.* Republic of
 Vanuatu; *prev.* New Hebrides. *country*
 SW Pacific Ocean

VANUATU
Australasia & Oceania

Official name Republic of Vanuatu
Formation 1980 / 1980
Capital Port Vila
Population 211,000 / 45 people per sq
mile (17 people per sq km) / 20%
Total area 4710 sq miles (12,200 sq km)
Languages Bislama* (Melanesian pidgin),
English*, French*, other indigenous
languages
Religions Presbyterian 37%, Other 19%,
Anglican 15%, Roman Catholic 15%,
Traditional beliefs 8%, Seventh-day
Adventist 6%
Ethnic mix Melanesian 94%, Other 3%,
Polynesian 3%
Government Parliamentary system
Currency Vatu = 100 centimes
Literacy rate 74%
Calorie consumption 2587 calories

Vanuatu, Republic of *see* Vanuatu
Van Wert *40 C4* Ohio, N USA
Vapincum *see* Gap
Varakļani *106 D4* Madona, C Latvia
Vārānasi *135 E3 prev.* Banaras,
 Benares, *hist.* Kasi. Uttar Pradesh,
 N India
Varangerfjorden *84 E2 Lapp.*
 Várjjatvuotna. *fjord* N Norway
Varangerhalvøya *84 D2 Lapp.*
 Várnjárga. *peninsula* N Norway
Varannó *see* Vranov nad Topl'ou
Varasd *see* Varaždin
Varaždin *100 B2 Ger.* Warasdin, *Hung.*
 Varasd. Varaždin, N Croatia
Varberg *85 B7* Halland, S Sweden
Vardar *101 E6 Gk.* Axiós. *river*
 FYR Macedonia/Greece
Varde *85 A7* Ribe, W Denmark
Vareia *see* Logroño
Varéna *107 B5 Pol.* Orany. Alytus,
 S Lithuania
Varese *96 B2* Lombardia, N Italy
Vârful Moldoveanu *108 B4*
 var. Moldoveanul; *prev.* Vîrful
 Moldoveanu. *mountain*
 C Romania
Várjjatvuotna *see* Varangerfjorden
Varkaus *85 E5* Itä-Suomi, C Finland
Varna *104 E2 prev.* Stalis; *anc.* Odessus.
 Varna, E Bulgaria
Varnenski Zaliv *104 E2 prev.* Stalinski
 Zaliv. *bay* E Bulgaria
Várnjárga *see* Varangerhalvøya
Varshava *see* Warszawa
Vasa *see* Vaasa
Vasiliki *105 A5* Lefkáda, Iónioi Nísoi,
 Greece, C Mediterranean Sea
Vasilishki *107 B5 Pol.* Wasiliszki,
 Rus. Vasilishki. Hrodzyenskaya
 Voblasts', W Belarus
Vasil'kov *see* Vasyl'kiv
Vaslui *108 D4* Vaslui,
 C Romania
Västerås *85 C6* Västmanland,
 C Sweden
Vasyl'kiv *109 E2 var.* Vasil'kov.
 Kyyivs'ka Oblast', N Ukraine
Vaté *see* Éfaté
Vatican City *97 A7 off.* Vatican City
 State. *country* S Europe

VATICAN CITY
Southern Europe

Official name State of the Vatican City
Formation 1929 / 1929
Capital Vatican City
Population 921 / 5418 people per sq mile
(2093 people per sq km) / 100%
Total area 0.17 sq miles (0.44 sq km)
Languages Italian*, Latin*
Religions Roman Catholic 100%
Ethnic mix The current pope is
German. Cardinals are from many
nationalities, but Italians form the
largest group. Most of the resident lay
persons are Italian.
Government Papal state
Currency Euro = 100 cents
Literacy rate 99%
Calorie consumption Not available

Vatican City State *see* Vatican City
Vatnajökull *83 E5 glacier* SE Iceland
Vatter, Lake *see* Vättern
Vättern *85 B6 Eng.* Lake Vatter; *prev.*
Lake Vetter. *lake* S Sweden
Vaughn *48 D2* New Mexico, SW USA
Vaupés, Río *58 C4 var.* Rio Uaupés.
river Brazil/Colombia
Vava'u Group *145 E4 island group*
N Tonga
Vavuniya *132 D3* Northern Province,
N Sri Lanka
Vawkavysk *107 B6 Pol.* Wołkowysk,
Rus. Volkovysk. Hrodzyenskaya
Voblasts', W Belarus
Växjö *85 C7 var.* Vexiö. Kronoberg,
S Sweden
Vaygach, Ostrov *110 E2 island*
NW Russian Federation
Veendam *86 E2* Groningen,
NE Netherlands
Veenendaal *86 D4* Utrecht,
C Netherlands
Vega *84 B4 island* C Norway
Veglia *see* Krk
Veisiejai *107 B5* Alytus, S Lithuania
Vejer de la Frontera *92 C5* Andalucía,
S Spain
Veldhoven *87 D5* Noord-Brabant,
S Netherlands
Velebit *100 A3 mountain range*
C Croatia
Velenje *95 E7* Ger. Wöllan. N Slovenia
Veles *101 E6 Turk.* Köprülü.
C FYR Macedonia
Velho *see* Porto Velho
Velika Kikinda *see* Kikinda
Velika Morava *100 D4 var.* Glavn'a
Morava, Morava, *Ger.* Grosse Morava.
river C Serbia
Velikaya *113 G2 river* NE Russian
Federation
Veliki Bečkerek *see* Zrenjanin
Velikiye Luki *110 A4* Pskovskaya
Oblast', W Russian Federation
Velikiy Novgorod *110 B4 prev.*
Novgorod. Novgorodskaya Oblast',
W Russian Federation
Veliko Túrnovo *see* Veliko Tŭrnovo
Veliko Tŭrnovo *104 D2 prev.* Tirnovo,
Trnovo, Tŭrnovo, *Eng.* Veliko Tŭrnovo.
Veliko Tŭrnovo, N Bulgaria
Velingrad *104 C3* Pazardzhik, C Bulgaria
Vel'ký Krtíš *99 D5* Banskobystrický
Kraj, C Slovakia
Vellore *132 C2* Tamil Nādu, SE India
Velobriga *see* Viana do Castelo
Velsen *see* Velsen-Noord
Velsen-Noord *86 C3 var.* Velsen.
Noord-Holland, W Netherlands
Vel'sk *110 C4 var.* Velsk.
Arkhangel'skaya Oblast',
NW Russian Federation
Velventós *see* Velvéntos
Velvéntos *104 B4 var.* Velvendós.
Dytiki Makedonía, N Greece
Velykyy Tokmak *see* Tokmak
Vendôme *90 C4* Loir-et-Cher,
C France
Venedig *see* Venezia
Vener, Lake *see* Vänern
Venetia *see* Venezia
Venezia *96 C2 Eng.* Venice, *Fr.* Venise,
Ger. Venedig; *anc.* Venetia. Veneto,
NE Italy
Venezia, Golfo di *see* Venice, Gulf of

Venezuela *58 D2 off.* Republic of
Venezuela; *prev.* Estados Unidos de
Venezuela, United States of Venezuela.
country N South America

VENEZUELA
South America

Official name Bolivarian Republic of
Venezuela
Formation 1830 / 1830
Capital Caracas
Population 26.7 million / 78 people per
sq mile (30 people per sq km) / 87%
Total area 352,143 sq miles
(912,050 sq km)
Languages Spanish*, Amerindian
languages
Religions Roman Catholic 89%,
Protestant and other 11%
Ethnic mix Mestizo 69%, White 20%,
Black 9%, Amerindian 2%
Government Presidential system
Currency Bolívar = 100 centimos
Literacy rate 93%
Calorie consumption 2336 calories

Venezuela, Estados Unidos de *see*
Venezuela
Venezuela, Golfo de *58 C1 Eng.* Gulf
of Maracaibo, Gulf of Venezuela. *gulf*
NW Venezuela
Venezuela, Gulf of *see* Venezuela,
Golfo de
Venezuelan Basin *56 B1 undersea basin*
E Caribbean Sea
Venezuela, Republic of *see* Venezuela
Venezuela, United States of *see*
Venezuela
Venice *42 C4* Louisiana, S USA
Venice *see* Venezia
Venice, Gulf of *96 C2 It.* Golfo di
Venezia, *Slvn.* Beneški Zaliv. *gulf*
N Adriatic Sea
Venise *see* Venezia
Venlo *87 D5 prev.* Venloo. Limburg,
SE Netherlands
Venloo *see* Venlo
Venta *106 B4 Ger.* Windau. *river*
Latvia/Lithuania
Venta Belgarum *see* Winchester
Ventia *see* Valence
Ventimiglia *96 A3* Liguria,
NW Italy
Ventspils *106 B2 Ger.* Windau.
Ventspils, NW Latvia
Vera *64 D3* Santa Fe, C Argentina
Veracruz *51 F4 var.* Veracruz Llave.
Veracruz-Llave, E Mexico
Veracruz Llave *see* Veracruz
Vercellae *see* Vercelli
Vercelli *96 A2 anc.* Vercellae.
Piemonte, NW Italy
Verdal *see* Verdalsøra
Verdalsøra *84 B4 var.* Verdal. Nord-
Trøndelag, C Norway
Verde, Cabo *see* Cape Verde
Verde, Costa *92 D1 coastal region*
N Spain
Verden *94 B3* Niedersachsen,
NW Germany
Veria *see* Véroia
Verkhnedvinsk *see* Vyerkhnyadzvinsk
Verkhneudinsk *see* Ulan-Ude
Verkhoyanskiy Khrebet *115 F3*
mountain range NE Russian Federation
Vermillion *45 F3* South Dakota,
N USA
Vermont *41 F2 off.* State of Vermont,
also known as Green Mountain State.
state NE USA
Vernal *44 B4* Utah, W USA
Vernon *49 F2* Texas, SW USA
Verőcze *see* Virovitica
Véroia *104 B4 var.* Veria,
Vérroia, *Turk.* Karaferiye. Kentrikí
Makedonía, N Greece
Verona *96 C2* Veneto, NE Italy
Vérroia *see* Véroia
Versailles *90 D1* Yvelines, N France
Verulamium *see* St Albans
Verviers *87 D6* Liège, E Belgium
Vesdre *87 D6 river* E Belgium
Veselinovo *104 D2* Shumen,
NE Bulgaria
Vesontio *see* Besançon
Vesoul *90 D4 anc.* Vesulium, Vesulum.
Haute-Saône, E France

Vesterålen *84 B2 island group*
N Norway
Vestfjorden *84 C3 fjord* C Norway
Vestmannaeyjar *83 E5* Sudhurland,
S Iceland
Vesulium/Vesulum *see* Vesoul
Vesuna *see* Périgueux
Vesuvio *97 D5 Eng.* Vesuvius. *volcano*
S Italy
Vesuvius *see* Vesuvio
Veszprém *99 C7 Ger.* Veszprim.
Veszprém, W Hungary
Veszprim *see* Veszprém
Vetrino *104 E2* Varna, E Bulgaria
Vetrino *see* Vyetryna
Vetter, Lake *see* Vättern
Veurne *87 A5 var.* Furnes. West-
Vlaanderen, W Belgium
Vexiö *see* Växjö
Viacha *61 F4* La Paz, W Bolivia
Viana de Castelo *see* Viana do Castelo
Viana do Castelo *92 B2 var.* Viana de
Castelo; *anc.* Velobriga. Viana do
Castelo, NW Portugal
Vianen *86 C4* Utrecht, C Netherlands
Viangchan *136 C4 Eng./Fr.* Vientiane.
country capital (Laos) C Laos
Viangphoukha *136 C3*
var. Vieng Pou Kha. Louang Namtha,
N Laos
Viareggio *96 B3* Toscana,
C Italy
Viborg *85 A7* Viborg, NW Denmark
Vic *93 G2 var.* Vich; *anc.* Ausa, Vicus
Ausonensis. Cataluña, NE Spain
Vicentia *see* Vicenza
Vicenza *96 C2 anc.* Vicentia. Veneto,
NE Italy
Vich *see* Vic
Vichy *91 C5* Allier, C France
Vicksburg *42 B2* Mississippi,
S USA
Victoria *79 H1 country capital*
(Seychelles) Mahé, SW Seychelles
Victoria *36 D3 province capital*
Vancouver Island, British Columbia,
SW Canada
Victoria *102 A5 var.* Rabat. Gozo,
NW Malta
Victoria *49 G4* Texas, SW USA
Victoria *149 C7 state* SE Australia
Victoria *see* Masvingo, Zimbabwe
Victoria Bank *see* Vitória Seamount
Victoria de Durango *see* Durango
Victoria de las Tunas *see* Las Tunas
Victoria Falls *78 C3* Matabeleland
North, W Zimbabwe
Victoria Falls *78 C2 waterfall*
Zambia/Zimbabwe
Victoria Falls *see* Iguaçu, Saltos do
Victoria Island *37 F3 island* Northwest
Territories, NW Canada
Victoria, Lake *73 B6 var.* Victoria
Nyanza. *lake* E Africa
Victoria Land *154 C4 physical region*
Antarctica
Victoria Nyanza *see* Victoria, Lake
Victoria River *146 D3 river* Northern
Territory, N Australia
Victorville *47 C7* California,
W USA
Vicus Ausonensis *see* Vic
Vicus Elbii *see* Viterbo
Vidalia *43 E2* Georgia,
SE USA
Videm-Krško *see* Krško
Viden *see* Wien
Vidin *104 B1 anc.* Bononia. Vidin,
NW Bulgaria
Vidzy *107 C5 Rus.* Vidzy. Vitsyebskaya
Voblasts', NW Belarus
Viedma *65 C5* Río Negro,
E Argentina
Vieng Pou Kha *see* Viangphoukha
Vienna *see* Wien, Austria
Vienna *see* Vienne, France
Vienne *91 D5 anc.* Vienna. Isère,
E France
Vienne *90 B4 river* W France
Vientiane *see* Viangchan
Vientos, Paso de los *see* Windward
Passage
Vierzon *90 C4* Cher, C France
Viesite *106 C4 Ger.* Eckengraf.
Jēkabpils, S Latvia
Vietnam *136 D4 off.* Socialist Republic of
Vietnam, *Vtn.* Công Hòa Xã Hội Chu
Nghia Viêt Nam. *country* SE Asia

VIETNAM
Southeast Asia

Official name Socialist Republic of
Vietnam
Formation 1976 / 1976
Capital Hanoi
Population 84.2 million / 670 people per
sq mile (259 people per sq km) / 20%
Total area 127,243 sq miles
(329,560 sq km)
Languages Vietnamese*, Chinese, Thai,
Khmer, Muong, Nung, Miao, Yao, Jarai
Religions Buddhist 55%, Other and
nonreligious 38%, Christian (mainly
Roman Catholic) 7%
Ethnic mix Vietnamese 88%, Other 6%,
Chinese 4%, Thai 2%
Government One-party state
Currency Dông = 10 hao = 100 xu
Literacy rate 90%
Calorie consumption 2566 calories

Vietnam, Socialist Republic of *see*
Vietnam
Vietri *see* Viêt Tri
Viêt Tri *136 D3 var.* Vietri. Vinh Phu,
N Vietnam
Vieux Fort *55 F2* S Saint Lucia
Vigo *92 B2* Galicia, NW Spain
Viipuri *see* Vyborg
Vijayawāda *132 D1 prev.* Bezwada.
Andhra Pradesh, SE India
Vila *see* Port-Vila
Vila Artur de Paiva *see* Cubango
Vila Bela da Santissima Trindade *see*
Mato Grosso
Vila da Ponte *see* Cubango
Vila de João Belo *see* Xai-Xai
Vila de Mocímboa da Praia *see*
Mocímboa da Praia
Vila do Conde *92 B2* Porto,
NW Portugal
Vila do Zumbo *78 D2 prev.*
Vila do Zumbu, Zumbo. Tete,
NW Mozambique
Vila do Zumbu *see* Vila do Zumbo
Vilafranca del Penedès *93 G2 var.*
Villafranca del Panadés. Cataluña,
NE Spain
Vila General Machado *see* Camacupa
Vila Henrique de Carvalho *see* Saurimo
Viļaka *106 D4* Balvi, NE Latvia
Vilalba *92 C1* Galicia, NW Spain
Vila Marechal Carmona *see* Uíge
Vila Nova de Gaia *92 B2* Porto,
NW Portugal
Vila Nova de Portimão *see* Portimão
Vila Pereira de Eça *see* N'Giva
Vila Real *92 C2 var.* Vila Rial.
Vila Real, N Portugal
Vila Rial *see* Vila Real
Vila Robert Williams *see* Caála
Vila Salazar *see* N'Dalatando
Vila Serpa Pinto *see* Menongue
Vileyka *see* Vilyeyka
Vilhelmina *84 C4* Västerbotten,
N Sweden
Vilhena *62 D3* Rondônia,
W Brazil
Vília *105 C5* Attikí, C Greece
Viliya *107 C5 Lith.* Neris,
Rus. Viliya. *river* W Belarus
Viliya *see* Neris
Viljandi *106 D2 Ger.* Fellin.
Viljandimaa, S Estonia
Vilkaviškis *106 B4 Pol.* Wyłkowyszki.
Marijampolé, SW Lithuania
Villa Acuña *50 D2 var.* Ciudad Acuña.
Coahuila de Zaragoza, NE Mexico
Villa Bella *61 F2* Beni, N Bolivia
Villacarrillo *93 E4* Andalucía,
S Spain
Villa Cecilia *see* Ciudad Madero
Villach *95 D7 Slvn.* Beljak. Kärnten,
S Austria
Villacidro *97 A5* Sardegna, Italy,
C Mediterranean Sea
Villa Concepción *see* Concepción
Villa del Pilar *see* Pilar
Villafranca de los Barros *92 C4*
Extremadura, W Spain
Villafranca del Panadés *see* Vilafranca
del Penedès
Villahermosa *51 G4 prev.* San Juan
Bautista. Tabasco, SE Mexico

Villajoyosa *93 F4 Cat.* La Vila Joíosa.
País Valenciano, E Spain
Villa María *64 C4* Córdoba,
C Argentina
Villa Martín *61 F5* Potosí,
SW Bolivia
Villa Mercedes *64 C4* San Juan,
Argentina
Villanueva *50 D3* Zacatecas,
C Mexico
Villanueva de la Serena *92 C3*
Extremadura, W Spain
Villanueva de los Infantes *93 E4*
Castilla-La Mancha, C Spain
Villarrica *64 D2* Guairá, SE Paraguay
Villavicencio *58 B3* Meta, C Colombia
Villaviciosa *92 D1* Asturias, N Spain
Villazón *61 G5* Potosí, S Bolivia
Villena *93 F4* País Valenciano,
E Spain
Villeurbanne *91 D5* Rhône,
E France
Villingen-Schwenningen *95 B6*
Baden-Württemberg, S Germany
Villmanstrand *see* Lappeenranta
Vilna *see* Vilnius
Vilnius *107 C5 Pol.* Wilno, *Ger.* Wilna;
prev. Rus. Vilna. *country capital*
(Lithuania) Vilnius, SE Lithuania
Vil'shanka *109 E3 Rus.* Olshanka.
Kirovohrads'ka Oblast', C Ukraine
Vilvoorde *87 C6 Fr.* Vilvorde. Vlaams
Brabant, C Belgium
Vilvorde *see* Vilvoorde
Vilyeyka *107 C5 Pol.* Wilejka, *Rus.*
Vileyka. Minskaya Voblasts',
NW Belarus
Vilyuy *115 F3 river* NE Russian
Federation
Viña del Mar *64 B4* Valparaíso,
C Chile
Vinaròs *93 F3* País Valenciano, E Spain
Vincennes *40 B4* Indiana, N USA
Vindhya Mountains *see* Vindhya Range
Vindhya Range *134 D4 var.* Vindhya
Mountains. *mountain range* N India
Vindobona *see* Wien
Vineland *41 F4* New Jersey, NE USA
Vinh *136 D4* Nghệ An, N Vietnam
Vinh Loi *see* Bac Liêu
Vinishte *104 C2* Montana,
NW Bulgaria
Vinita *49 G1* Oklahoma, C USA
Vinkovci *100 C3 Ger.* Winkowitz,
Hung. Vinkovcze. Vukovar-Srijem,
E Croatia
Vinkovcze *see* Vinkovci
Vinnitsa *see* Vinnytsya
Vinnytsya *108 D2 Rus.* Vinnitsa.
Vinnyts'ka Oblast', C Ukraine
Vinogradov *see* Vynohradiv
Vinson Massif *154 A3 mountain*
Antarctica
Viranşehir *117 E4* Şanlıurfa,
SE Turkey
Vîrful Moldoveanu *see* Vârful
Moldoveanu
Virginia *45 G1* Minnesota, N USA
Virginia *41 E5 off.* Commonwealth
of Virginia, *also known as* Mother
of Presidents, Mother of States, Old
Dominion. *state* NE USA
Virginia Beach *41 F5* Virginia,
NE USA
Virgin Islands *see* British Virgin Islands
Virgin Islands (US) *55 F3 var.* Virgin
Islands of the United States; *prev.*
Danish West Indies. *US unincorporated
territory* E West Indies
Virgin Islands of the United States *see*
Virgin Islands (US)
Viróchey *137 E5* Rôtânôkiri,
NE Cambodia
Virovitica *100 C2 Ger.* Virovititz,
Hung. Verőcze; *prev. Ger.* Werowitz.
Virovitica-Podravina, NE Croatia
Virovititz *see* Virovitica
Virton *87 D8* Luxembourg, SE Belgium
Virtsu *106 D2 Ger.* Werder. Läänemaa,
W Estonia
Vis *100 B4 It.* Lissa; *anc.* Issa. *island*
S Croatia
Vis *see* Fish
Visaginas *106 C4 prev.* Sniečkus. Utena,
E Lithuania
Visākhapatnam *135 E5* Andhra Pradesh,
SE India
Visalia *47 C6* California, W USA

Visby *85 C7 Ger.* Wisby. Gotland,
SE Sweden
Viscount Melville Sound *37 F2
prev.* Melville Sound. *sound*
Northwest Territories, N Canada
Visé *87 D6* Liège, E Belgium
Viseu *92 C2 prev.* Vízeu. Viseu,
N Portugal
Vislinskiy Zaliv *see* Vistula Lagoon
Visoko *100 C4* Federacija Bosna
I Hercegovina, C Bosnia and
Herzegovina
Visttasjohka *84 D3 River* N Sweden
Vistula *see* Wisła
Vistula Lagoon *98 C2 Ger.* Frisches Haff,
Pol. Zalew Wiślany, *Rus.* Vislinskiy
Zaliv. *lagoon* Poland/Russian
Federation
Vitebsk *see* Vitsyebsk
Viterbo *96 C4 anc.* Vicus Elbii. Lazio,
C Italy
Viti *see* Fiji
Viti Levu *145 E4 island* W Fiji
Vitim *115 F4 river* C Russian Federation
Vitória *63 F4 state capital* Espírito Santo,
SE Brazil
Vitoria *see* Vitoria-Gasteiz
Vitoria Bank *see* Vitória Seamount
Vitória da Conquista *63 F3* Bahia,
E Brazil
Vitoria-Gasteiz *93 E1 var.* Vitoria,
Eng. Vittoria. País Vasco, N Spain
Vitória Seamount *67 B5 var.* Victoria
Bank, Vitoria Bank. *seamount*
C Atlantic Ocean
Vitré *90 B3* Ille-et-Vilaine,
NW France
Vitsyebsk *107 E5 Rus.* Vitebsk.
Vitsyebskaya Voblasts', NE Belarus
Vittoria *97 C7* Sicilia, Italy,
C Mediterranean Sea
Vittoria *see* Vitoria-Gasteiz
Vizcaya, Golfo de *see* Biscay, Bay of
Vizianagaram *135 E5 var.* Vizianagram.
Andhra Pradesh, E India
Vizianagram *see* Vizianagaram
Vjosës, Lumi i *101 C7
var.* Vijosa, Vijosë, *Gk.* Aóos. *river*
Albania/Greece
Vlaanderen *see* Flanders
Vlaardingen *86 B4* Zuid-Holland,
SW Netherlands
Vladikavkaz *111 B8 prev.* Dzaudzhikau,
Ordzhonikidze. Respublika Severnaya
Osetiya, SW Russian Federation
Vladimir *111 B5* Vladimirskaya Oblast',
W Russian Federation
Vladimirovka *see* Yuzhno-Sakhalinsk
Vladimir-Volynskiy *see*
Volodymyr-Volyns'kyy
Vladivostok *115 G5* Primorskiy Kray,
SE Russian Federation
Vlagtwedde *86 E2* Groningen,
NE Netherlands
Vlasotince *101 E5* Serbia, SE Serbia
Vlieland *86 C1 Fris.* Flylân. *island*
Waddeneilanden, N Netherlands
Vlijmen *86 C4* Noord-Brabant,
S Netherlands
Vlissingen *87 B5 Eng.* Flushing,
Fr. Flessingue. Zeeland,
SW Netherlands
Vlodava *see* Włodawa
Vlonë/Vlora *see* Vlorë
Vlorë *101 C7 prev.* Vlonë, *It.* Valona,
Vlora. Vlorë, SW Albania
Vlotslavsk *see* Włocławek
Vöcklabruck *95 D6* Oberösterreich,
NW Austria
Vogelkop *see* Doberai, Jazirah
Vohimena, Tanjona *79 F4 Fr.* Cap
Sainte Marie. *headland* S Madagascar
Voiron *91 D5* Isère, E France
Vojvodina *100 D3 Ger.* Wojwodina.
Vojvodina, N Serbia
Volga *111 B7 river* NW Russian
Federation
Volga Uplands *see* Privolzhskaya
Vozvyshennost'
Volgodonsk *111 B7* Rostovskaya Oblast',
SW Russian Federation
Volgograd *111 B7 prev.* Stalingrad,
Tsaritsyn. Volgogradskaya Oblast',
SW Russian Federation
Volkhov *110 B4* Leningradskaya Oblast',
NW Russian Federation
Volkovysk *see* Vawkavysk
Volmari *see* Valmiera

Volnovakha *109 G3* Donets'ka Oblast',
SE Ukraine
Volodymyr-Volyns'kyy *108 C1
Pol.* Włodzimierz, *Rus.* Vladimir-
Volynskiy. Volyns'ka Oblast',
NW Ukraine
Vologda *110 B4* Vologodskaya Oblast',
W Russian Federation
Vólos *105 B5* Thessalía, C Greece
Volozhin *see* Valozhyn
Vol'sk *111 C6* Saratovskaya Oblast',
W Russian Federation
Volta *75 E5 river* SE Ghana
Volta Blanche *see* White Volta
Volta, Lake *75 E5 reservoir* SE Ghana
Volta Noire *see* Black Volta
Volturno *97 D5 river* S Italy
Volunteer Island *see* Starbuck Island
Volzhskiy *111 B6* Volgogradskaya
Oblast', SW Russian Federation
Võnnu *106 E3 Ger.* Wendau. Tartumaa,
SE Estonia
Voorst *86 D3* Gelderland, E Netherlands
Voranava *107 C5 Pol.* Werenów, *Rus.*
Voronovo. Hrodzyenskaya Voblasts',
W Belarus
Vorderrhein *95 B7 river* SE Switzerland
Vóreies Sporádes *105 C5
var.* Vóreioi Sporádes, Vórioi
Sporádhes, *Eng.* Northern Sporades.
island group E Greece
Vóreioi Sporádes *see* Vóreies Sporádes
Vórioi Sporádhes *see* Vóreies Sporádes
Vorkuta *111 C2* Respublika Komi,
NW Russian Federation
Vormsi *106 C2 var.* Vormsi Saar,
Ger. Worms, *Swed.* Ormsö. *island*
W Estonia
Vormsi Saar *see* Vormsi
Voronezh *111 B6* Voronezhskaya
Oblast', W Russian Federation
Voronovo *see* Voranava
Voroshilov *see* Ussuriysk
Voroshilovgrad *see* Luhans'k, Ukraine
Voroshilovsk *see* Stavropol', Russian
Federation
Võru *106 D3 Ger.* Werro. Võrumaa,
SE Estonia
Vosges *90 E4 mountain range*
NE France
Vostochno-Sibirskoye More
115 F1 Eng. East Siberian Sea. *sea*
Arctic Ocean
Vostochnyy Sayan *see* Eastern Sayans
Vostok Island *see* Vostok Island
Vostok *154 C3 Russian research station*
Antarctica
Vostok Island *145 G3
var.* Vostock Island; *prev.* Stavers
Island. *island* Line Islands, SE Kiribati
Voznesens'k *109 E3 Rus.* Voznesensk.
Mykolayivs'ka Oblast', S Ukraine
Vrangelya, Ostrov *115 F1 Eng.* Wrangel
Island. *island* NE Russian Federation
Vranje *101 E5* Serbia, SE Serbia
Vranov *see* Vranov nad Topl'ou
Vranov nad Topl'ou *99 D5 var.* Vranov,
Hung. Varannó. Prešovský Kraj,
E Slovakia
Vratsa *104 C2* Vratsa, NW Bulgaria
Vrbas *100 C3* Vojvodina, NW Serbia
Vrbas *100 C3 river* N Bosnia and
Herzegovina
Vsetín *99 C5 Ger.* Wsetin. Zlínský Kraj,
E Czech Republic
Vučitrn *101 D5* Kosovo, S Serbia
Vukovar *100 C3 Hung.* Vukovár.
Vukovar-Srijem, E Croatia
Vulcano, Isola *97 C7 island* Isole
Eolie, S Italy
Vung Tau *137 E6 prev. Fr.* Cape Saint
Jacques, Cap Saint-Jacques. Ba Ria-
Vung Tau, S Vietnam
Vyatka *111 C5 river* NW Russian
Federation
Vyatka *see* Kirov
Vyborg *110 B3 Fin.* Viipuri.
Leningradskaya Oblast', NW Russian
Federation
Vyerkhnyadzvinsk *107 D5 Rus.*
Verkhnedvinsk. Vitsyebskaya
Voblasts', N Belarus
Vyetryna *107 D5 Rus.* Vetrino.
Vitsyebskaya Voblasts', N Belarus
Vynohradiv *108 B3 Cz.* Sevluš, *Hung.*
Nagyszöllös, *Rus.* Vinogradov; *prev.*
Sevlyush. Zakarpats'ka Oblast',
W Ukraine

W

Wa *75 E4* NW Ghana
Waag *see* Váh
Waagbistritz *see* Považská Bystrica
Waal *86 C4 river* S Netherlands
Wabash *40 C4* Indiana, N USA
Wabash River *40 B5 river* N USA
Waco *49 G3* Texas, SW USA
Wad Al-Hajarah *see* Guadalajara
Waddān *71 F3* NW Libya
Waddeneilanden *86 C1 Eng.* West
Frisian Islands. *island group*
N Netherlands
Waddenzee *86 C1 var.* Wadden Zee. *sea*
SE North Sea
Wadden Zee *see* Waddenzee
Waddington, Mount *36 D5 mountain*
British Columbia, SW Canada
Wādī as Sīr *119 B6 var.* Wadi es Sir.
'Ammān, NW Jordan
Wadi es Sir *see* Wādī as Sīr
Wadi Halfa *72 B3 var.* Wādi Ḥalfā'.
Northern, N Sudan
Wādī Mūsā *119 B7 var.* Petra. Ma'ān,
S Jordan
Wad Madanī *see* Wad Medani
Wad Medani *72 C4 var.* Wad Madanī.
Gezira, C Sudan
Waflia *139 F4* Pulau Buru, E Indonesia
Wagadugu *see* Ouagadougou
Wagga Wagga *149 C7* New South Wales,
SE Australia
Wagin *147 B7* Western Australia
Wâh *134 C1* Punjab, NE Pakistan
Wahai *139 F4* Pulau Seram, E Indonesia
Wahaybah, Ramlat Al *see* Wahībah,
Ramlat Āl
Wahiawā *47 A8 var.* Wahiawa. O'ahu,
Hawai'i, USA
Wahībah, Ramlat Ahl *see* Wahībah,
Ramlat Āl
Wahībah, Ramlat Āl *121 E5 var.* Ramlat
Ahl Wahībah, Ramlat Āl Wahaybah,
Eng. Wahībah Sands. *desert* N Oman
Wahībah Sands *see* Wahībah, Ramlat Āl
Wahpeton *45 F2* North Dakota,
N USA
Wahran *see* Oran
Waiau *151 A7 river* South Island, New
Zealand
Waigeo, Pulau *139 G4 island* Maluku,
E Indonesia
Waikaremoana, Lake *150 E4 lake* North
Island, New Zealand
Wailuku *47 B8* Maui, Hawai'i, USA
Waimate *151 B6* Canterbury, South
Island, New Zealand
Waiouru *150 D4* Manawatu-Wanganui,
North Island, New Zealand
Waipara *151 C6* Canterbury, South
Island, New Zealand
Waipawa *150 E4* Hawke's Bay, North
Island, New Zealand
Waipukurau *150 D4* Hawke's Bay,
North Island, New Zealand
Wairau *151 C5 river* South Island, New
Zealand
Wairoa *150 E4* Hawke's Bay, North
Island, New Zealand
Wairoa *150 D2 river* North Island, New
Zealand
Waitaki *151 B6 river* South Island, New
Zealand
Waitara *150 D4* Taranaki, North Island,
New Zealand
Waitzen *see* Vác
Waiuku *150 D3* Auckland, North Island,
New Zealand
Wakasa-wan *131 C6 bay* C Japan
Wakatipu, Lake *151 A7 lake* South
Island, New Zealand
Wakayama *131 C6* Wakayama, Honshū,
SW Japan
Wake Island *152 C2 US unincorporated
territory* NW Pacific Ocean
Wake Island *142 D1 atoll* NW Pacific
Ocean
Wakkanai *130 C1* Hokkaidō,
NE Japan
Walachei/Walachia *see* Wallachia
Wałbrzych *98 B4 Ger.* Waldenburg,
Waldenburg in Schlesien. Dolnośląskie,
SW Poland
Walcourt *87 C7* Namur, S Belgium
Wałcz *98 B3 Ger.* Deutsch Krone.
Zachodnio-pomorskie, NW Poland

Waldenburg/Waldenburg in Schlesien
  see Wałbrzych
Waldia *see* Weldiya
Wales 36 C2 Alaska, USA
Wales 89 C6 *Wel.* Cymru. *cultural region*
  Wales, UK
Wales 89 C6 *Wel.* Cymru. *national*
  region Wales, UK
Walgett 149 D5 New South Wales,
  SE Australia
Walk *see* Valga, Estonia
Walk *see* Valka, Latvia
Walker Lake 47 C5 *lake* Nevada,
  W USA
Wallachia 108 B5 *var.* Walachia, *Ger.*
  Walachei, *Rom.* Valachia. *cultural*
  region S Romania
Walla Walla 46 C2 Washington,
  NW USA
Wallenthal *see* Haţeg
Wallis and Futuna 145 E4 *Fr.* Territoire
  de Wallis et Futuna. *French overseas*
  territory C Pacific Ocean
Wallis et Futuna, Territoire de *see*
  Wallis and Futuna
Walnut Ridge 42 B1 Arkansas, C USA
Waltenberg *see* Zalău
Walthamstow 89 B7 Waltham Forest,
  SE England, UK
Walvisbaai *see* Walvis Bay
Walvis Bay 78 A4 *Afr.* Walvisbaai.
  Erongo, NW Namibia
Walvish Ridge *see* Walvis Ridge
Walvis Ridge 69 B7 *var.* Walvish Ridge.
  undersea ridge E Atlantic Ocean
Wan *see* Anhui
Wanaka 151 B6 Otago, South Island,
  New Zealand
Wanaka, Lake 151 A6 *lake* South Island,
  New Zealand
Wanchuan *see* Zhangjiakou
Wandel Sea 83 E1 *sea* Arctic Ocean
Wandsworth 89 A8 Wandsworth,
  SE England, UK
Wanganui 150 D4 Manawatu-
  Wanganui, North Island, New Zealand
Wangaratta 149 C7 Victoria,
  SE Australia
Wankie *see* Hwange
Wanki, Río *see* Coco, Río
Wanlaweyn 73 D6 *var.* Wanle Weyn,
  It. Uanle Uen. Shabeellaha Hoose,
  SW Somalia
Wanle Weyn *see* Wanlaweyn
Wanxian *see* Wanzhou
Wanzhou 128 B5 *var.* Wanxian.
  Chongqing Shi, C China
Warangal 135 E5 Andhra Pradesh,
  C India
Warasdin *see* Varaždin
Warburg 94 B4 Nordrhein-Westfalen,
  W Germany
Ware 37 E4 British Columbia,
  W Canada
Waremme 87 C6 Liège, E Belgium
Waren 94 C3 Mecklenburg-
  Vorpommern, NE Germany
Wargla *see* Ouargla
Warkworth 150 D2 Auckland, North
  Island, New Zealand
Warnemünde 94 C2 Mecklenburg-
  Vorpommern, NE Germany
Warner 49 G1 Oklahoma, C USA
Warnes 61 G4 Santa Cruz, C Bolivia
Warrego River 149 C5 *seasonal river*
  New South Wales/Queensland,
  E Australia
Warren 40 D3 Michigan, N USA
Warren 40 D3 Ohio, N USA
Warren 41 E3 Pennsylvania, NE USA
Warri 75 F5 Delta, S Nigeria
Warrnambool 149 B7 Victoria,
  SE Australia
Warsaw *see* Warszawa
Warszawa 98 D3 *Eng.* Warsaw,
  Ger. Warschau, *Rus.* Varshava. *c*
  country capital (Poland) Mazowieckie,
  C Poland
Warta 98 B3 *Ger.* Warthe. *river*
  W Poland
Wartberg *see* Senec
Warthe *see* Warta
Warwick 149 E5 Queensland,
  E Australia
Washington 44 A2 NE England, UK
Washington DC 41 E4 *country capital*
  (USA) District of Columbia,
  NE USA

Washington Island *see* Teraina
Washington, Mount 41 G2 *mountain*
  New Hampshire, NE USA
Wash, The 89 E6 *inlet* E England, UK
Wasiliszki *see* Vasilishki
Waspam 53 E2 *var.* Waspán. Región
  Autónoma Atlántico Norte,
  NE Nicaragua
Waspán *see* Waspam
Watampone 139 E4 *var.* Bone. Sulawesi,
  C Indonesia
Watenstedt-Salzgitter *see* Salzgitter
Waterbury 41 F3 Connecticut,
  NE USA
Waterford 89 B6 *Ir.* Port Láirge.
  Waterford, S Ireland
Waterloo 45 G3 Iowa, C USA
Watertown 41 F2 New York, NE USA
Watertown 45 F2 South Dakota,
  N USA
Waterville 41 G2 Maine, NE USA
Watford 89 A7 E England, UK
Watsa 77 E5 Orientale, NE Dem. Rep.
  Congo
Watts Bar Lake 42 D1 *reservoir*
  Tennessee, S USA
Wau 73 B5 *var.* Wāw. Western Bahr el
  Ghazal, S Sudan
Waukegan 40 B3 Illinois, N USA
Waukesha 40 B3 Wisconsin, N USA
Wausau 40 B2 Wisconsin, N USA
Waverly 45 G3 Iowa, C USA
Wavre 87 C6 Walloon Brabant,
  C Belgium
Wāw *see* Wau
Wawa 38 C4 Ontario, S Canada
Waycross 43 E3 Georgia, SE USA
Wearmouth *see* Sunderland
Webfoot State *see* Oregon
Webster City 45 F3 Iowa, C USA
Weddell Plain 154 A2 *abyssal plain*
  SW Atlantic Ocean
Weddell Sea 154 A2 *sea* SW Atlantic
  Ocean
Weener 94 A3 Niedersachsen,
  NW Germany
Weert 87 D5 Limburg, SE Netherlands
Weesp 86 C3 Noord-Holland,
  C Netherlands
Węgorzewo 98 D2 *Ger.* Angerburg.
  Warmińsko-Mazurskie, NE Poland
Weichsel *see* Wisła
Weimar 94 C4 Thüringen, C Germany
Weissenburg *see* Alba Iulia
Weissenburg in Bayern 95 C6 Bayern,
  SE Germany
Weissenstein *see* Paide
Weisskirchen *see* Bela Crkva
Weiswampach 87 D7 Diekirch,
  N Luxembourg
Wejherowo 98 C2 Pomorskie,
  NW Poland
Welchman Hall 55 G1 C Barbados
Weldiya 72 C4 *var.* Waldia, *It.* Valdia.
  Amhara, N Ethiopia
Welkom 78 D4 Free State,
  C South Africa
Welle *see* Uele
Wellesley Islands 148 B2 *island group*
  Queensland, N Australia
Wellington 151 D5 *country capital*
  (New Zealand) Wellington, North
  Island, New Zealand
Wellington 45 F5 Kansas, C USA
Wellington *see* Wellington, Isla
Wellington, Isla 65 A7 *var.* Wellington.
  island S Chile
Wells 46 D4 Nevada, W USA
Wellsford 150 D2 Auckland, North
  Island, New Zealand
Wells, Lake 147 C5 *lake* Western
  Australia
Wels 95 D6 *anc.* Ovilava. Oberösterreich,
  N Austria
Wembley 89 A8 Alberta, W Canada
Wemmel 87 B6 Vlaams Brabant,
  C Belgium
Wenatchee 46 B2 Washington,
  NW USA
Wenchi 75 E4 W Ghana
Wen-chou/Wenchow *see* Wenzhou
Wendau *see* Võnnu
Wenden *see* Cēsis
Wenzhou 128 D5 *var.* Wen-chou,
  Wenchow. Zhejiang, SE China
Werda 78 C4 Kgalagadi, S Botswana
Werder *see* Virtsu
Werenów *see* Voranava

Werkendam 86 C4 Noord-Brabant,
  S Netherlands
Werowitz *see* Virovitica
Werro *see* Võru
Wesenberg *see* Rakvere
Weser 94 B3 *river* NW Germany
Wessel Islands 148 B1 *island group*
  Northern Territory, N Australia
West Antarctica *see* Lesser Antarctica
West Australian Basin *see* Wharton
  Basin
West Bank 119 A6 *disputed region*
  SW Asia
West Bend 40 B3 Wisconsin, N USA
West Bengal 135 F4 *cultural region*
  NE India
West Bengal 135 F4 *state* NE India
West Cape 151 A7 *headland* South
  Island, New Zealand
West Des Moines 45 F3 Iowa,
  C USA
Westerland 94 B2 Schleswig-Holstein,
  N Germany
Western Australia 146 B4 *state*
  W Australia
Western Bug *see* Bug
Western Desert *see* Sahara el Gharbīya
Western Dvina 85 E7 *Bel.* Dzvina, *Ger.*
  Düna, *Latv.* Daugava, *Rus.* Zapadnaya
  Dvina. *river* W Europe
Western Ghats 134 C5 *mountain range*
  SW India
Western Isles *see* Outer Hebrides
Western Punjab *see* Punjab
Western Sahara 70 B3 *disputed territory*
  N Africa
Western Samoa *see* Samoa
Western Samoa, Independent State
  of *see* Samoa
Western Sayans *see* Zapadnyy Sayan
Western Scheldt *see* Westerschelde
Western Sierra Madre *see* Sierra Madre
  Occidental
Westerschelde 87 B5 *Eng.* Western
  Scheldt; *prev.* Honte. *inlet* S North Sea
West Falkland 65 C7 *var.* Gran Malvina.
  island W Falkland Islands
West Fargo 45 F2 North Dakota,
  N USA
West Frisian Islands *see*
  Waddeneilanden
West Irian *see* Papua
Westliche Morava *see* Zapadna Morava
West Mariana Basin 142 B1 *var.* Perece
  Vela Basin. *undersea feature* W Pacific
  Ocean
West Memphis 42 B1 Arkansas,
  C USA
West New Guinea *see* Papua
Weston-super-Mare 89 D7
  SW England, UK
West Palm Beach 43 F4 Florida,
  SE USA
West Papua *see* Papua
Westport 151 C5 West Coast, South
  Island, New Zealand
West Punjab *see* Punjab
West River *see* Xi Jiang
West Siberian Plain *see* Zapadno-
  Sibirskaya Ravnina
West Virginia 40 D4 *off.* State of West
  Virginia, *also known as* Mountain State.
  state NE USA
Wetar, Pulau 139 F5 *island* Kepulauan
  Damar, E Indonesia
Wetzlar 95 B5 Hessen, W Germany
Wevok 36 C2 *var.* Wewuk. Alaska, USA
Wewuk *see* Wevok
Wexford 89 B6 *Ir.* Loch Garman.
  SE Ireland
Weyburn 37 F5 Saskatchewan, S Canada
Weymouth 89 D7 S England, UK
Wezep 86 D3 Gelderland, E Netherlands
Whakatane 150 E3 Bay of Plenty, North
  Island, New Zealand
Whale Cove 37 G3 Nunavut, C Canada
Whangarei 150 D2 Northland, North
  Island, New Zealand
Wharton Basin 141 D5 *var.* West
  Australian Basin. *undersea feature*
  E Indian Ocean
Whataroa 151 B6 West Coast, South
  Island, New Zealand
Wheatland 44 D3 Wyoming, C USA
Wheeler Peak 48 D1 *mountain* New
  Mexico, SW USA
Wheeling 40 D4 West Virginia,
  NE USA

Whitby 89 D5 N England, UK
Whitefish 44 B1 Montana, NW USA
Whitehaven 89 C5 NW England, UK
Whitehorse 36 D4 *territory capital*
  Yukon Territory, W Canada
White Nile 72 B4 *var.* Bahr el Jebel.
  river S Sudan
White Nile 72 B4 *Ar.* Al Baḥr al Abyaḍ,
  An Nīl al Abyaḍ, Bahr el Jebel. *river*
  SE Sudan
White River 44 D3 *river* South Dakota,
  N USA
White Sea *see* Beloye More
White Volta 75 E4 *var.* Nakambé,
  Fr. Volta Blanche. *river* Burkina
  Faso/Ghana
Whitianga 150 D2 Waikato, North
  Island, New Zealand
Whitney, Mount 47 C6 *mountain*
  California, W USA
Whitsunday Group 148 D3 *island group*
  Queensland, E Australia
Whyalla 149 B6 South Australia
Wichita 45 F5 Kansas, C USA
Wichita Falls 49 F2 Texas, SW USA
Wichita River 49 F2 *river* Texas, SW USA
Wickenburg 48 B2 Arizona, SW USA
Wicklow 89 B6 *Ir.* Cill Mhantáin. *county*
  E Ireland
Wicklow Mountains 89 B6 *Ir.* Sléibhte
  Chill Mhantáin. *mountain range*
  E Ireland
Wieliczka 99 D5 Małopolskie, S Poland
Wieluń 98 C4 Sieradz, C Poland
Wien 95 E6 *Eng.* Vienna, *Hung.*
  Bécs, *Slvk.* Vídeň, *Slvn.* Dunaj; *anc.*
  Vindobona. *country capital* (Austria)
  Wien, NE Austria
Wiener Neustadt 95 E6
  Niederösterreich, E Austria
Wierden 86 E3 Overijssel, E Netherlands
Wiesbaden 95 B5 Hessen, W Germany
Wieselburg und Ungarisch-Altenburg/
  Wieselburg-Ungarisch-Altenburg
  see Mosonmagyaróvár
Wiesenhof *see* Ostrołęka
Wight, Isle of 89 D7 *island* UK
Wigorna Ceaster *see* Worcester
Wijchen 86 D4 Gelderland,
  SE Netherlands
Wijk bij Duurstede 86 D4 Utrecht,
  C Netherlands
Wilcannia 149 C6 New South Wales,
  SE Australia
Wilejka *see* Vilyeyka
Wilhelm, Mount 144 B3 *mountain*
  C Papua New Guinea
Wilhelm-Pieck-Stadt *see* Guben
Wilhelmshaven 94 B3 Niedersachsen,
  NW Germany
Wilia/Wilja *see* Neris
Wilkes Barre 41 F3 Pennsylvania,
  NE USA
Wilkes Land 154 C4 *physical region*
  Antarctica
Wilkomierz *see* Ukmergė
Willard 48 D2 New Mexico,
  SW USA
Willcox 48 C3 Arizona, SW USA
Willebroek 87 B5 Antwerpen,
  C Belgium
Willemstad 55 E5 *dependent territory*
  capital (Netherlands Antilles) Curaçao,
  Netherlands Antilles
Williston 44 D1 North Dakota,
  N USA
Wilmington 41 F4 Delaware,
  NE USA
Wilmington 43 F2 North Carolina,
  SE USA
Wilmington 40 C4 Ohio, N USA
Wilna/Wilno *see* Vilnius
Wilrijk 87 C5 Antwerpen, N Belgium
Winchester 89 D7 *hist.* Wintanceaster,
  Lat. Venta Belgarum. S England, UK
Winchester 41 E4 Virginia, NE USA
Windau *see* Ventspils
Windau *see* Venta
Windhoek 78 B3 *Ger.* Windhuk.
  country capital (Namibia) Khomas,
  C Namibia
Windhuk *see* Windhoek
Windorah 148 C4 Queensland,
  C Australia
Windsor 38 C5 Ontario, S Canada
Windsor 89 D7 S England, UK
Windsor 41 G3 Connecticut,
  NE USA

Windward Islands 55 H4 *island group*
E West Indies
Windward Islands *see* Barlavento, Ilhas
de, Cape Verde
Windward Passage 54 D3 *Sp.* Paso de
los Vientos. *channel* Cuba/Haiti
Winisk 38 C2 *river* Ontario, S Canada
Winkowitz *see* Vinkovci
Winnebago, Lake 40 B2 *lake* Wisconsin,
N USA
Winnemucca 47 C5 Nevada, W USA
Winnipeg 37 G5 *province capital*
Manitoba, S Canada
Winnipeg, Lake 37 G5 *lake* Manitoba,
C Canada
Winnipegosis, Lake 38 A3 *lake*
Manitoba, C Canada
Winona 45 G3 Minnesota, N USA
Winschoten 86 E2 Groningen,
NE Netherlands
Winsen 94 B3 Niedersachsen,
N Germany
Winston Salem 43 E1 North Carolina,
SE USA
Winsum 86 D1 Groningen,
NE Netherlands
Wintanceaster *see* Winchester
Winterswijk 86 E4 Gelderland,
E Netherlands
Winterthur 95 B7 Zürich,
NE Switzerland
Winton 148 C4 Queensland,
E Australia
Winton 151 A7 Southland, South Island,
New Zealand
Wisby *see* Visby
Wisconsin 40 A2 *off.* State of Wisconsin,
also known as Badger State. *state*
N USA
Wisconsin Rapids 40 B2 Wisconsin,
N USA
Wisconsin River 40 B3 *river* Wisconsin,
N USA
Wisła 98 C2 *Eng.* Vistula, *Ger.* Weichsel.
river C Poland
Wiślany, Zalew *see* Vistula Lagoon
Wismar 94 C3 Mecklenburg-
Vorpommern, N Germany
Wittenberge 94 C3 Brandenburg,
N Germany
Wittlich 95 A5 Rheinland-Pfalz,
SW Germany
Wittstock 94 C3 Brandenburg,
NE Germany
W. J. van Blommesteinmeer 59 G3
reservoir E Suriname
Władysławowo 98 C2 Pomorskie,
N Poland
Włocławek 98 C3 *Ger./Rus.* Vlotslavsk.
Kujawsko-pomorskie, C Poland
Włodawa 98 E4 *Rus.* Vlodava. Lubelskie,
SE Poland
Włodzimierz *see* Volodymyr-Volyns'kyy
Wlotzkasbaken 78 B3 Erongo,
W Namibia
Wodonga 149 C7 Victoria, SE Australia
Wodzisław Śląski 99 C5 *Ger.* Loslau.
Śląskie, S Poland
Wojerecy *see* Hoyerswerda
Wójja *see* Wotje Atoll
Wojwodina *see* Vojvodina
Woking 89 D7 SE England, UK
Wolf, Isla 60 A4 *island* Galápagos,
Galapagos Islands, W Ecuador South
America
Wolfsberg 95 D7 Kärnten, SE Austria
Wolfsburg 94 C3 Niedersachsen,
N Germany
Wolgast 94 D2 Mecklenburg-
Vorpommern, NE Germany
Wołkowysk *see* Vawkavysk
Wollan *see* Velenje
Wollaston Lake 37 F4 Saskatchewan,
C Canada
Wollongong 149 D6 New South Wales,
SE Australia
Wolmar *see* Valmiera
Wołożyn *see* Valozhyn
Wolvega 86 D2 *Fris.* Wolvegea.
Friesland, N Netherlands
Wolvegea *see* Wolvega
Wolverhampton 89 D6 C England, UK
Wolverine State *see* Michigan
Wŏnsan 129 E3 SE North Korea
Woodburn 46 B3 Oregon,
NW USA
Woodland 47 B5 California,

Woodruff 40 B2 Wisconsin,
N USA
Woods, Lake of the 38 A3 *Fr.* Lac des
Bois. *lake* Canada/USA
Woodville 150 D4 Manawatu-
Wanganui, North Island,
New Zealand
Woodward 49 F1 Oklahoma, C USA
Worcester 78 C5 Western Cape,
SW South Africa
Worcester 89 D6 *hist.* Wigorna Ceaster.
W England, UK
Worcester 41 G3 Massachusetts,
NE USA
Workington 89 C5 NW England, UK
Worland 44 C3 Wyoming, C USA
Wormatia *see* Worms
Worms 95 B5 *anc.* Augusta Vangionum,
Borbetomagus, Wormatia. Rheinland-
Pfalz, SW Germany
Worms *see* Vormsi
Worthington 45 F3 Minnesota,
N USA
Wotje Atoll 144 D1 *var.* Wójjä.
atoll Ratak Chain, E Marshall Islands
Woudrichem 86 C4 Noord-Brabant,
S Netherlands
Wrangel Island *see* Vrangelya, Ostrov
Wrangel Plain 155 B2 *undersea feature*
Arctic Ocean
Wrocław 98 C4 *Eng./Ger.* Breslau.
Dolnośląskie, SW Poland
Września 98 C3 Wielkopolskie,
C Poland
Wsetin *see* Vsetín
Wuchang *see* Wuhan
Wuday'ah 121 C6 *spring/well* S Saudi
Arabia
Wuhai 127 E3 *var.* Haibowan. Nei
Mongol Zizhiqu, N China
Wuhan 128 C5 *var.* Han-kou, Han-k'ou,
Hanyang, Wuchang, Wu-han; *prev.*
Hankow. *province capital* Hubei,
C China
Wu-han *see* Wuhan
Wuhsien *see* Wuxi
Wuhsi/Wu-his *see* Wuxi
Wuhu 128 D5 *var.* Wu-na-mu. Anhui,
E China
Wujlän *see* Ujelang Atoll
Wukari 75 G4 Taraba, E Nigeria
Wuliang Shan 128 A6 *mountain range*
SW China
Wu-lu-k'o-mu-shih/Wu-lu-mu-ch'i
see Ürümqi
Wu-na-mu *see* Wuhu
Wuppertal 94 A4 *prev.* Barmen-
Elberfeld. Nordrhein-Westfalen,
W Germany
Würzburg 95 B5 Bayern, SW Germany
Wusih *see* Wuxi
Wuxi 128 D5 *var.* Wuhsi, Wu-hsi,
Wusih. Jiangsu, E China
Wuyi Shan 125 E3 *mountain range*
SE China
Wye 89 C6 *Wel.* Gwy. *river* England/
Wales, UK
Wyłkowyszki *see* Vilkaviškis
Wyndham 146 D3 Western Australia
Wyoming 40 C3 Michigan, N USA
Wyoming 44 B3 *off.* State of Wyoming,
also known as Equality State. *state*
C USA
Wyszków 98 D3 *Ger.* Probstberg.
Mazowieckie, NE Poland

X

Xaafuun, Raas 72 E4 *var.* Ras Hafun.
cape NE Somalia
Xaçmaz 117 H2 *Rus.* Khachmas.
N Azerbaijan
Xaignabouli 136 C4 *prev* Muang
Xaignabouri. *Fr.* Sayaboury.
Xaignabouli, N Laos
Xai-Xai 79 E4 *prev.* João Belo, Vila de
João Belo. Gaza, S Mozambique
Xalapa 51 F4 Veracruz-Llave, Mexico
Xam Nua 136 D3 *var.* Sam Neua.
Houaphan, N Laos
Xankändi 117 G3 *Rus.* Khankendi;
prev. Stepanakert. SW Azerbaijan
Xánthi 104 C3 Anatolikí Makedonía kai
Thráki, NE Greece
Xátiva 93 F3 *var.* Jativa; *anc.* Setabis.
País Valenciano, E Spain
Xauen *see* Chefchaouen

Xäzär Dänizi *see* Caspian Sea
Xeres *see* Jeréz de la Frontera
Xiaguan *see* Dali
Xiamen 128 D6 *var.* Hsia-men;
prev. Amoy. Fujian, SE China
Xi'an 128 C4 *var.* Changan, Sian,
Signan, Siking, Singan, Xian.
province capital Shaanxi, C China
Xiang *see* Hunan
Xianggang *see* Hong Kong
Xiangkhoang *see* Pèk
Xiangtan 128 C5 *var.* Hsiang-t'an,
Siangtan. Hunan, S China
Xiao Hinggan Ling 128 D2 *Eng.* Lesser
Khingan Range. *mountain range*
NE China
Xichang 128 B5 Sichuan, C China
Xieng Khouang *see* Pèk
Xieng Ngeun *see* Muong Xiang Ngeun
Xigazê 126 C5 *var.* Jih-k'a-tse, Shigatse,
Xigaze. Xizang Zizhiqu, W China
Xi Jiang 124 D3 *var.* Hsi Chiang, *Eng.*
West River. *river* S China
Xilinhot 127 F2 *var.* Silinhot. Nei
Mongol Zizhiqu, N China
Xilokastro *see* Xylókastro
Xin *see* Xinjiang Uygur Zizhiqu
Xingkai Hu *see* Khanka, Lake
Xingu, Rio 63 E2 *river* C Brazil
Xingxingxia 126 D3 Xinjiang Uygur
Zizhiqu, NW China
Xining 127 E4 *var.* Hsining, Hsi-ning,
Sining. *province capital* Qinghai,
C China
Xinjiang *see* Xinjiang Uygur Zizhiqu
Xinjiang Uygur Zizhiqu 126 B3
var. Sinkiang, Sinkiang Uighur
Autonomous Region, Xin, Xinjiang.
autonomous region NW China
Xinpu *see* Lianyungang
Xinxiang 128 C4 Henan, C China
Xinyang 128 C5 *var.* Hsin-yang,
Sinyang. Henan, C China
Xinzo de Limia 92 C2 Galicia,
NW Spain
Xiqing Shan 124 D2 *mountain range*
C China
Xiva 122 D2 *Rus.* Khiva, Khiwa. Xorazm
Viloyati, W Uzbekistan
Xixón *see* Gijón
Xizang *see* Xizang Zizhiqu
Xizang Gaoyuan *see* Qingzang Gaoyuan
Xizang Zizhiqu 126 B4 *var.* Thibet,
Tibetan Autonomous Region, Xizang,
Eng. Tibet. *autonomous region*
W China
Xolotlán *see* Managua, Lago de
Xuddur 73 D5 *var.* Hudur, *It.* Oddur.
Bakool, SW Somalia
Xuwen 128 C7 Guangdong, S China
Xuzhou 128 D4 *var.* Hsu-chou,
Suchow, Tongshan; *prev.* T'ung-shan.
Jiangsu, E China
Xylókastro 105 B5 *var.* Xilokastro.
Pelopónnisos, S Greece

Y

Ya'an 128 B5 *var.* Yaan. Sichuan,
C China
Yabēlo 73 C5 Oromo, C Ethiopia
Yablis 53 E2 Región Autónoma Atlántico
Norte, NE Nicaragua
Yablonovyy Khrebet 115 F4 *mountain
range* S Russian Federation
Yabraī Shan 127 E3 *mountain range*
NE China
Yafran 71 F2 NW Libya
Yaghan Basin 67 B7 *undersea feature*
SE Pacific Ocean
Yagotin *see* Yahotyn
Yahotyn 109 E2 *Rus.* Yagotin. Kyyivs'ka
Oblast', N Ukraine
Yahualica 50 D4 Jalisco, SW Mexico
Yakima 46 B2 Washington, NW USA
Yakima River 46 B2 *river* Washington,
NW USA
Yakoruda 104 C3 Blagoevgrad,
SW Bulgaria
Yaku-shima 131 B8 *island*
Nansei-shotō, SW Japan
Yakutat 36 D4 Alaska, USA
Yakutsk 115 F3 Respublika Sakha
(Yakutiya), NE Russian Federation
Yala 137 C7 Yala, SW Thailand
Yalizava 107 D6 *Rus.* Yelizovo.
Mahilyowskaya Voblasts', E Belarus

Yalong Jiang 128 A5 *river* C China
Yalova 116 B3 Yalova, NW Turkey
Yalpug, Ozero *see* Yalpuh, Ozero
Yalpuh, Ozero 108 D4 *Rus.* Ozero
Yalpug. *lake* SW Ukraine
Yalta 109 F5 Respublika Krym,
S Ukraine
Yalu 125 E2 *Chin.* Yalu Jiang, *Jap.*
Oryokko, *Kor.* Amnok-kang. *river*
China/North Korea
Yalu Jiang *see* Yalu
Yamaguchi 131 B7 *var.* Yamaguti.
Yamaguchi, Honshū, SW Japan
Yamal, Poluostrov 114 D2 *peninsula*
N Russian Federation
Yamaniyah, Al Jumhūriyah al *see*
Yemen
Yambio 73 B5 *var.* Yambiyo. Western
Equatoria, S Sudan
Yambiyo *see* Yambio
Yambol 104 D2 *Turk.* Yanboli. Yambol,
E Bulgaria
Yamdena, Pulau 139 G5 *prev.*
Jamdena. *island* Kepulauan Tanimbar,
E Indonesia
Yamoussoukro 74 D5 *country capital*
(Côte d'Ivoire (Ivory Coast)) C Côte
d'Ivoire (Ivory Coast)
Yamuna 134 D3 *prev.* Jumna. *river*
N India
Yana 115 F2 *river* NE Russian Federation
Yanboli *see* Yambol
Yanbu 'al Bahr 121 A5 Al Madīnah,
W Saudi Arabia
Yangambi 77 D5 Orientale, N Dem.
Rep. Congo
Yangchow *see* Yangzhou
Yangiyo'l 123 E2 *Rus.* Yangiyul'.
Toshkent Viloyati, E Uzbekistan
Yangiyul' *see* Yangiyo'l
Yangku *see* Taiyuan
Yangon 136 B4 *Eng.* Rangoon. Yangon,
S Myanmar (Burma)
Yangtze *see* Chang Jiang/Jinsha Jiang
Yangtze *see* Jinsha Jiang
Yangtze Kiang *see* Chang Jiang
Yangzhou 128 D5 *var.* Yangchow.
Jiangsu, E China
Yankton 45 E3 South Dakota, N USA
Yannina *see* Ioánnina
Yanskiy Zaliv 113 F2 *bay* N Russian
Federation
Yantai 128 D4 *var.* Yan-t'ai; *prev.*
Chefoo, Chih-fu. Shandong, E China
Yaoundé 77 B5 *var.* Yaunde. *country
capital* (Cameroon) Centre,
S Cameroon
Yap 144 A1 *island* Caroline Islands,
W Micronesia
Yapanskoye More East Sea/Japan, Sea of
Yapen, Pulau 139 G4 *prev.* Japen. *island*
E Indonesia
Yap Trench 142 B2 *var.* Yap Trough.
undersea feature SE Philippine Sea
Yap Trough *see* Yap Trench
Yapurá *see* Caquetá, Río, Brazil/Colombia
Yapurá *see* Japurá, Rio, Brazil/Colombia
Yaqui, Río 50 C2 *river* NW Mexico
Yaransk 111 C5 Kirovskaya Oblast',
NW Russian Federation
Yarega 110 D4 Respublika Komi,
NW Russian Federation
Yarkant *see* Shache
Yarlung Zangbo Jiang *see* Brahmaputra
Yarmouth 39 F5 Nova Scotia, SE Canada
Yarmouth *see* Great Yarmouth
Yaroslav *see* Jarosław
Yaroslavl' 110 B4 Yaroslavskaya Oblast',
W Russian Federation
Yarumal 58 B2 Antioquia,
NW Colombia
Yasyel'da 107 B7 *river* Brestskaya
Voblasts', SW Belorussia Europe
Yatsushiro 131 A7 *var.* Yatusiro.
Kumamoto, Kyūshū, SW Japan
Yatusiro *see* Yatsushiro
Yaunde *see* Yaoundé
Yavari *see* Javari, Rio
Yaviza 53 H5 Darién, SE Panama
Yavoriv 108 B2 *Pol.* Jaworów,
Rus. Yavorov. L'vivs'ka Oblast',
NW Ukraine
Yavorov *see* Yavoriv
Yazd 120 D3 *var.* Yezd. Yazd, C Iran
Yazoo City 42 B2 Mississippi, S USA
Ýding Skovhøj 85 A7 *hill* C Denmark
Ýdra 105 C6 *var.* Ídhra. *island* Ýdra,
S Greece

Ye *137 B5* Mon State,
S Myanmar (Burma)
Yecheng *126 A3 var.* Kargilik. Xinjiang
Uygur Zizhiqu, NW China
Yefremov *111 B5* Tul'skaya Oblast',
W Russian Federation
Yekaterinburg *114 C3 prev.* Sverdlovsk.
Sverdlovskaya Oblast', C Russian
Federation
Yekaterinodar *see* Krasnodar
Yekaterinoslav *see* Dnipropetrovs'k
Yelets *111 B5* Lipetskaya Oblast',
W Russian Federation
Yelisavetpol *see* Gäncä
Yelizavetgrad *see* Kirovohrad
Yelizovo *see* Yalizava
Yell *88 D1 island* NE Scotland, UK
Yellowhammer State *see* Alabama
Yellowknife *37 E4 territory capital*
Northwest Territories, W Canada
Yellow River *see* Huang He
Yellow Sea *128 D4 Chin.* Huang Hai,
Kor. Hwang-Hae. sea E Asia
Yellowstone River *44 C2 river* Montana/
Wyoming, NW USA
Yel'sk *107 C7 Rus.* Yel'sk. Homyel'skaya
Voblasts', SE Belarus
Yelwa *75 F4* Kebbi, W Nigeria
Yemen *121 C7 off.* Republic of Yemen,
Ar. Al Jumhuriyah al Yamaniyah,
Al Yaman. *country* SW Asia

YEMEN
Southwest Asia

Official name Republic of Yemen
Formation 1990 / 1990
Capital Sana
Population 21 million / 97 people per sq
mile (37 people per sq km) / 25%
Total area 203,849 sq miles (527,970
sq km)
Languages Arabic*
Religions Sunni Muslim 55%, Shi'a
Muslim 42%, Christian, Hindu, and
Jewish 3%
Ethnic mix Arab 95%, Afro-Arab 3%,
Indian, Somali, and European 2%
Government Presidential system
Currency Yemeni rial = 100 sene
Literacy rate 49%
Calorie consumption 2038 calories

Yemen, Republic of *see* Yemen
Yemva *110 D4 prev.* Zheleznodorozhnyy.
Respublika Komi, NW Russian
Federation
Yenakiyeve *109 G3 Rus.* Yenakiyevo;
prev. Ordzhonikidze, Rykovo.
Donets'ka Oblast', E Ukraine
Yenakiyevo *see* Yenakiyeve
Yenangyaung *136 A3* Magwe,
W Myanmar (Burma)
Yendi *75 E4* NE Ghana
Yengisar *126 A3* Xinjiang Uygur
Zizhiqu, NW China
Yenierenköy *102 D4 var.* Yialousa,
Gk. Agialoúsa. NE Cyprus
Yenisey *114 D3 river* Mongolia/Russian
Federation
Yenping *see* Nanping
Yeovil *89 D7* SW England, UK
Yeppoon *148 D4* Queensland,
E Australia
Yerevan *117 F3 Eng.* Erivan. *country
capital* (Armenia) C Armenia
Yeriho *see* Jericho
Yerushalayim *see* Jerusalem
Yeso *see* Hokkaidō
Yeu, Île d' *90 A4 island* NW France
Yevlakh *see* Yevlax
Yevlax *117 G2 Rus.* Yevlakh.
C Azerbaijan
Yevpatoriya *109 F5* Respublika Krym,
S Ukraine
Yeya *109 H4 river* SW Russian
Federation
Yezerishche *see* Yezyaryshcha
Yezo *see* Hokkaidō
Yezyaryshcha *107 E5 Rus.* Yezerishche.
Vitsyebskaya Voblasts', NE Belarus
Yialousa *see* Yenierenköy
Yiannitsá *see* Giannitsá
Yichang *128 C5* Hubei, C China
Yıldızeli *116 D3* Sivas, N Turkey
Yinchuan *128 B4 var.* Yinch'uan, Yin-
ch'uan, Yinchwan. *province capital*
Ningxia, N China

Yin-ch'uan/Yinch'uan *see* Yinchuan
Yinchwan *see* Yinchuan
Yindu He *see* Indus
Yin-hsien *see* Ningbo
Yining *126 B2 var.* I-ning, *Uigh.* Gulja,
Kuldja. Xinjiang Uygur Zizhiqu,
NW China
Yin-tu Ho *see* Indus
Yisrael/Yisra'el *see* Israel
Yithion *see* Gýtheio
Yogyakarta *138 C5 prev.* Djokjakarta,
Jogjakarta, Jokyakarta. Jawa,
C Indonesia
Yokohama *131 D5* Aomori,
Honshū, C Japan
Yokohama *130 A2* Kanagawa,
Honshū, S Japan
Yokote *130 D4* Akita, Honshū,
C Japan
Yola *75 H4* Adamawa, E Nigeria
Yonago *131 B6* Tottori, Honshū,
SW Japan
Yong'an *128 D6 var.* Yongan. Fujian,
SE China
Yongzhou *129 C6 var.* Lengshuitan.
Hunan, S China
Yonkers *41 F3* New York, NE USA
Yonne *90 C4 river* C France
Yopal *58 C3 var.* El Yopal. Casanare,
C Colombia
York *89 D5 anc.* Eboracum, Eburacum.
N England, UK
York *45 E4* Nebraska, C USA
York, Cape *148 C1 headland*
Queensland, NE Australia
York, Kap *see* Innaanganeq
Yorkton *37 F5* Saskatchewan, S Canada
Yoro *52 C2* Yoro, C Honduras
Yoshkar-Ola *111 C5* Respublika Mariy
El, W Russian Federation
Yösönbulag *see* Altay
Youngstown *40 D4* Ohio, N USA
Youth, Isle of *see* Juventud, Isla de la
Ypres *see* Ieper
Yreka *46 B4* California, W USA
Yrendagué *see* General Eugenio A. Garay
Yssel *see* IJssel
Ysyk-Köl *see* Issyk-Kul', Ozero
Ysyk-Köl *see* Balykchy
Yu *see* Henan
Yuan *see* Red River
Yuan Jiang *see* Red River
Yuba City *47 B5* California,
W USA
Yucatán, Canal de *see* Yucatan Channel
Yucatan Channel *51 H3 Sp.* Canal de
Yucatán. *channel* Cuba/Mexico
Yucatan Peninsula *see* Yucatán,
Península de
Yucatán, Península de *35 C7*
Eng. Yucatan Peninsula. *peninsula*
Guatemala/Mexico
Yuci *see* Jinzhong
Yue *see* Guangdong
Yue Shan, Tai *see* Lantau Island
Yueyang *128 C5* Hunan, S China
Yugoslavia *see* Serbia
Yukhavichy *107 D5 Rus.* Yukhovichi.
Vitsyebskaya Voblasts', N Belarus
Yukhovichi *see* Yukhavichy
Yukon *36 C2 river* Canada/USA
Yukon *see* Yukon Territory
Yukon, Territoire du *see* Yukon
Territory
Yukon Territory *36 D3 var.* Yukon,
Fr. Territoire du Yukon. *territory*
NW Canada
Yulin *128 C6* Guangxi Zhuangzu
Zizhiqu, S China
Yuma *48 A2* Arizona, SW USA
Yumen *128 A3 var.* Laojunmiao,
Yümen. Gansu, N China
Yun *see* Yunnan
Yungki *see* Jilin
Yung-ning *see* Nanning
Yunjinghong *see* Jinghong
Yunki *see* Jilin
Yunnan *128 A6 var.* Yun, Yunnan
Sheng, Yünnan, Yun-nan. *province*
SW China
Yunnan *see* Kunming
Yunnan Sheng *see* Yunnan
Yünnan/Yun-nan *see* Yunnan
Yurev *see* Tartu
Yuruá, Río *see* Juruá, Rio
Yury'ev *see* Tartu
Yushu *126 D4 var.* Gyêgu. Qinghai,
C China

Yuty *64 D3* Caazapá, S Paraguay
Yuzhno-Sakhalinsk *115 H4 Jap.*
Toyohara; *prev.* Vladimirovka. Ostrov
Sakhalin, Sakhalinskaya Oblast',
SE Russian Federation
Yuzhnyy Bug *see* Pivdennyy Buh
Yuzhou *see* Chongqing
Ÿylanly *see* Gurbansoltan Eje

Z

Zaandam *see* Zaanstad
Zaanstad *86 C3 prev.* Zaandam.
Noord-Holland, C Netherlands
Zabaykal'sk *115 F5* Chitinskaya Oblast',
S Russian Federation
Zabern *see* Saverne
Zabid *121 B7* W Yemen
Żabinka *see* Zhabinka
Ząbkowice *see* Ząbkowice Śląskie
Ząbkowice Śląskie *98 B4 var.*
Ząbkowice, *Ger.* Frankenstein,
Frankenstein in Schlesien.
Dolnośląskie, SW Poland
Zábřeh *99 C5 Ger.* Hohenstadt.
Olomoucký Kraj, E Czech Republic
Zacapa *52 B2* Zacapa, E Guatemala
Zacatecas *50 D3* Zacatecas, C Mexico
Zacatepec *51 E4* Morelos, S Mexico
Zacháro *105 B6 var.* Zaharo, Zakháro.
Dytikí Ellás, S Greece
Zadar *100 A3 It.* Zara; *anc.* Iader.
Zadar, SW Croatia
Zadetkyi Kyun *137 B6 var.* St.Matthew's
Island. *island* Mergui Archipelago,
S Myanmar (Burma)
Zafra *92 C4* Extremadura, W Spain
Żagań *98 B4 var.* Zagań, Żegań,
Ger. Sagan, Sprottau. W Poland
Zagazig *72 B1 var.* Az Zaqāzīq. N Egypt
Zágráb *see* Zagreb
Zagreb *100 B2 Ger.* Agram, *Hung.*
Zágráb. *country capital* (Croatia)
Zagreb, N Croatia
Zágros, Kühhâ-ye *120 C3*
Eng. Zagros Mountains. *mountain
range* W Iran
Zagros Mountains *see* Zágros, Kühhâ-ye
Zaharo *see* Zacháro
Zähedän *120 E4 var.* Zahidan; *prev.*
Duzdab. Sīstān va Balūchestān, SE Iran
Zahidan *see* Zähedän
Zahlah *see* Zahlé
Zahlé *118 B4 var.* Zaḥlah. C Lebanon
Záhony *99 E6* Szabolcs-Szatmár-Bereg,
NE Hungary
Zaire *see* Congo (river)
Zaire *see* Congo (Democratic Republic of)
** Zaječar** *100 E4* Serbia, E Serbia
Zakháro *see* Zacháro
Zakhidnyy Buh/Zakhodni Buh *see* Bug
Zákhō *120 B2 var.* Zākhū. N Iraq
Zākhū *see* Zákhō
Zakopane *99 D5* Małopolskie, S Poland
Zante *see* Zákynthos
Zákynthos *105 A6 var.* Zákinthos,
It. Zante. *island* Iónia Nísoi, Greece,
C Mediterranean Sea
Zalaegerszeg *99 B7* Zala, W Hungary
Zalău *108 B3 Ger.* Waltenberg, *Hung.*
Zilah; *prev. Ger.* Zillenmarkt. Sălaj,
NW Romania
Zalim *121 B5* Makkah, W Saudi Arabia
Zambesi/Zambeze *see* Zambezi
Zambezi *78 C2* North Western,
W Zambia
Zambezi *78 D2 var.* Zambesi, *Port.*
Zambeze. *river* S Africa
Zambia *78 C2 off.* Republic of Zambia;
prev. Northern Rhodesia. *country*
S Africa

ZAMBIA
Southern Africa

Official name Republic of Zambia
Formation 1964 / 1964
Capital Lusaka
Population 11.7 million / 41 people per sq
mile (16 people per sq km) / 45%
Total area 290,584 sq miles (752,614
sq km)
Languages English*, Bemba, Tonga,
Nyanja, Lozi, Lala-Bisa, Nsenga
Religions Christian 63%, Traditional
beliefs 36%, Muslim and Hindu 1%
Ethnic mix Bemba 34%, Other

ZAMBIA
(continued)

○African 26%, Tonga 16%, Nyanja 14%,
Lozi 9%, European 1%
Government Presidential system
Currency Zambian kwacha = 100 ngwee
Literacy rate 68%
Calorie consumption 1927 calories

Zambia, Republic of *see* Zambia
Zamboanga *139 E3 off.* Zamboanga City.
Mindanao, S Philippines
Zamboanga City *see* Zamboanga
Zambrów *98 E3* Łomża, E Poland
Zamora *92 D2* Castilla-León, NW Spain
Zamora de Hidalgo *50 D4* Michoacán
de Ocampo, SW Mexico
Zamość *98 E4 Rus.* Zamoste. Lubelskie,
E Poland
Zamoste *see* Zamość
Zancle *see* Messina
Zanda *126 A4* Xizang Zizhiqu,
W China
Zanesville *40 D4* Ohio, N USA
Zanjān *120 C2 var.* Zenjan, Zinjan.
Zanjān, NW Iran
Zante *see* Zákynthos
Zanthus *147 C6* Western Australia,
S Australia Oceania
Zanzibar *73 D7* Zanzibar, E Tanzania
Zanzibar *73 C7 Swa.* Unguja. *island*
E Tanzania
Zaozhuang *128 D4* Shandong,
E China
Zapadna Morava *100 D4*
Ger. Westliche Morava. *river*
C Serbia
Zapadnaya Dvina *110 A4* Tverskaya
Oblast', W Russian Federation
Zapadnaya Dvina *see* Western Dvina
Zapadno-Sibirskaya Ravnina *114*
C3 Eng. West Siberian Plain. *plain*
C Russian Federation
Zapadnyy Bug *see* Bug
Zapadnyy Sayan *114 D4 Eng.* Western
Sayans. *mountain range* S Russian
Federation
Zapala *65 B5* Neuquén, W Argentina
Zapiola Ridge *67 B6 undersea feature*
SW Atlantic Ocean
Zapolyarnyy *110 C2* Murmanskaya
Oblast', NW Russian Federation
Zaporozh'ye *see* Zaporizhzhya
Zaporizhzhya *109 F3*
Rus. Zaporozh'ye; *prev.* Aleksandrovsk.
Zaporiz'ka Oblast', SE Ukraine
Zapotiltic *50 D4* Jalisco, SW Mexico
Zaqatala *117 G2 Rus.* Zakataly.
NW Azerbaijan
Zara *116 D3* Sivas, C Turkey
Zara *see* Zadar
Zarafshan *see* Zarafshon
Zarafshon *122 D2 Rus.* Zarafshan.
Navoiy Viloyati, N Uzbekistan
Zarafshon *see* Zeravshan
Zaragoza *93 F2 Eng.* Saragossa; *anc.*
Caesaraugusta, Salduba. Aragón,
NE Spain
Zarand *120 D3* Kermān, C Iran
Zaranj *122 D5* Nīmrūz,
SW Afghanistan
Zarasai *106 C4* Utena, E Lithuania
Zárate *64 D4 prev.* General José
F.Uriburu. Buenos Aires,
E Argentina
Zarautz *93 E1 var.* Zarauz. País Vasco,
N Spain
Zarauz *see* Zarautz
Zaraza *59 E2* Guárico, N Venezuela
Zarghün Shahr *123 E4 var.* Katawaz.
Paktīkā, SE Afghanistan
Zaria *75 G4* Kaduna, C Nigeria
Zarós *105 D8* Kríti, Greece,
E Mediterranean Sea
Zarqa *see* Az Zarqā'
Żary *98 B4 Ger.* Sorau, Sorau in der
Niederlausitz. Lubuskie,
W Poland
Zaunguzskiye Garagumy *see* Üngüz
Angyrsyndaky Garagum
Zavertse *see* Zawiercie
Zavet *104 D1* Razgrad, NE Bulgaria
Zavidovići *100 C3* Federacija Bosna
I Hercegovina, N Bosnia and
Herzegovina
Zawia *see* Az Zāwiyah

Zawiercie 98 D4 *Rus.* Zavertse. Śląskie, S Poland
Zawilah 71 F3 *var.* Zuwaylah, *It.* Zueila. C Libya
Zaysan Köl *see* Zaysan, Ozero
Zaysan, Ozero 114 D5 *Kaz.* Zaysan Köl. *lake* E Kazakhstan
Zayyq *see* Ural
Zbarazh 108 C2 Ternopil's'ka Oblast', W Ukraine
Zduńska Wola 98 C4 Sieradz, C Poland
Zealand *see* Sjælland
Zeebrugge 87 A5 West-Vlaanderen, NW Belgium
Zeewolde 86 D3 Flevoland, C Netherlands
Zefat 119 B5 *var.* Safed, Tsefat, *Ar.* Safad. Northern, N Israel
Żegań *see* Zagań
Zeiden *see* Codlea
Zeist 86 C3 Utrecht, C Netherlands
Zele 87 B5 Oost-Vlaanderen, NW Belgium
Zelenoborskiy 110 B2 Murmanskaya Oblast', NW Russian Federation
Zelenograd 111 B5 Moskovskaya Oblast', W Russian Federation
Zelenogradsk 106 A4 *Ger.* Cranz, Kranz. Kaliningradskaya Oblast', W Russian Federation
Zelle *see* Celle
Zel'va 107 B6 *Pol.* Zelwa. Hrodzyenskaya Voblasts', W Belarus
Zelwa *see* Zel'va
Zelzate 87 B5 *var.* Selzaete. Oost-Vlaanderen, NW Belgium
Žemaičių Aukštumas 106 B4 *physical region* W Lithuania
Zemst 87 C5 Vlaams Brabant, C Belgium
Zemun 100 D3 Serbia, N Serbia
Zengg *see* Senj
Zenica 100 C4 Federacija Bosna I Hercegovina, C Bosnia and Herzegovina
Zenta *see* Senta
Zeravshan 123 E3 *Taj./Uzb.* Zarafshon. *river* Tajikistan/Uzbekistan
Zevenaar 86 D4 Gelderland, SE Netherlands
Zevenbergen 86 C4 Noord-Brabant, S Netherlands
Zeya 113 F3 *river* SE Russian Federation
Zgerzh *see* Zgierz
Zgierz 98 C4 *Ger.* Neuhof, *Rus.* Zgerzh. Łódź, C Poland
Zgorzelec 98 B4 *Ger.* Görlitz. Dolnośląskie, SW Poland
Zhabinka 107 A6 *Pol.* Żabinka, *Rus.* Zhabinka. Brestskaya Voblasts', SW Belarus
Zhambyl *see* Taraz
Zhanaozen 114 A4 *Kaz.* Zhangaözen; *prev.* Novyy Uzen'. Mangistau, W Kazakhstan
Zhangaözen *see* Zhanaozen
Zhangaqazaly *see* Ayteke Bi
Zhang-chia-k'ou *see* Zhangjiakou
Zhangdian *see* Zibo
Zhangjiakou 128 C3 *var.* Changkiakow, Zhang-chia-k'ou, *Eng.* Kalgan; *prev.* Wanchuan. Hebei, E China
Zhangzhou 128 D6 Fujian, SE China

Zhanjiang 128 C7 *var.* Chanchiang, Chan-chiang, *Cant.* Tsamkong, *Fr.* Fort-Bayard. Guangdong, S China
Zhaoqing 128 C6 Guangdong, S China
Zhdanov *see* Mariupol'
Zhe *see* Zhejiang
Zhejiang 128 D5 *var.* Che-chiang, Chekiang, Zhe, Zhejiang Sheng. *province* SE China
Zhejiang Sheng *see* Zhejiang
Zheleznodorozhnyy 106 A4 Irkutskaya Oblast', C Russian Federation
Zheleznodorozhnyy *see* Yemva
Zheleznogorsk 111 A5 Kurskaya Oblast', W Russian Federation
Zhëltyye Vody *see* Zhovti Vody
Zhengzhou 128 C4 *var.* Ch'eng-chou, Chengchow; *prev.* Chenghsien. *province capital* Henan, C China
Zhezkazgan 114 C4 *Kaz.* Zhezqazghan; *prev.* Dzhezkazgan. Karaganda, C Kazakhstan
Zhezqazghan *see* Zhezkazgan
Zhidachov *see* Zhydachiv
Zhitkovichi *see* Zhytkavichy
Zhitomir *see* Zhytomyr
Zhlobin 107 D7 Homyel'skaya Voblasts', SE Belarus
Zhmerinka *see* Zhmerynka
Zhmerynka 108 D2 *Rus.* Zhmerinka. Vinnyts'ka Oblast', C Ukraine
Zhodino *see* Zhodzina
Zhodzina 107 D6 *Rus.* Zhodino. Minskaya Voblasts', C Belarus
Zholkev/Zholkva *see* Zhovkva
Zholsaly *see* Dzhusaly
Zhonghua Renmin Gongheguo *see* China
Zhovkva 108 B2 *Pol.* Żółkiew, *Rus.* Zholkev, Zholkva; *prev.* Nesterov. L'vivs'ka Oblast', NW Ukraine
Zhovti Vody 109 F3 *Rus.* Zhëltyye Vody. Dnipropetrovs'ka Oblast', E Ukraine
Zhovtneve 109 E4 *Rus.* Zhovtnevoye. Mykolayivs'ka Oblast', S Ukraine
Zhovtnevoye *see* Zhovtneve
Zhydachiv 108 B2 *Pol.* Żydaczów, *Rus.* Zhidachov. L'vivs'ka Oblast', NW Ukraine
Zhytkavichy 107 C7 *Rus.* Zhitkovichi. Homyel'skaya Voblasts', SE Belarus
Zhytomyr 108 D2 *Rus.* Zhitomir. Zhytomyrs'ka Oblast', NW Ukraine
Zibo 128 D4 *var.* Zhangdian. Shandong, E China
Zichenau *see* Ciechanów
Zielona Góra 98 B4 *Ger.* Grünberg, Grünberg in Schlesien, Grüneberg. Lubuskie, W Poland
Zierikzee 86 B4 Zeeland, SW Netherlands
Zigong 128 B5 *var.* Tzekung. Sichuan, C China
Ziguinchor 74 B3 SW Senegal
Zilah *see* Zalău
Žilina 99 C5 *Ger.* Sillein, *Hung.* Zsolna. Žilinský Kraj, N Slovakia
Zillenmarkt *see* Zalău
Zimbabwe 78 D3 *off.* Republic of Zimbabwe; *prev.* Rhodesia. *country* S Africa

ZIMBABWE
Southern Africa

Official name Republic of Zimbabwe
Formation 1980 / 1980
Capital Harare
Population 13 million / 87 people per sq mile (34 people per sq km) / 35%
Total area 150,803 sq miles (390,580 sq km)
Languages English*, Shona, isiNdebele
Religions Syncretic (Christian/traditional beliefs) 50%, Christian 25%, Traditional beliefs 24%, Other (including Muslim) 1%
Ethnic mix Shona 71%, Ndebele 16%, Other African 11%, White 1%, Asian 1%
Government Presidential system
Currency Zimbabwe dollar = 100 cents
Literacy rate 90%
Calorie consumption 1943 calories

Zimbabwe, Republic of *see* Zimbabwe
Zimnicea 108 C5 Teleorman, S Romania
Zimovniki 111 B7 Rostovskaya Oblast', SW Russian Federation
Zinder 75 G3 Zinder, S Niger
Zinov'yevsk *see* Kirovohrad
Zintenhof *see* Sindi
Zipaquira 58 B3 Cundinamarca, C Colombia
Zittau 94 D4 Sachsen, E Germany
Zlatni Pyasǔtsi 104 E2 Dobrich, NE Bulgaria
Zlín 99 C5 *prev.* Gottwaldov. Zlínský Kraj, E Czech Republic
Złotów 98 C3 Wielkopolskie, C Poland
Znamenka *see* Znam"yanka
Znam"yanka 109 F3 *Rus.* Znamenka. Kirovohrads'ka Oblast', C Ukraine
Żnin 98 C3 Kujawsko-pomorskie, C Poland
Zoetermeer 86 C4 Zuid-Holland, W Netherlands
Zólkiew *see* Zhovkva
Zolochev *see* Zolochiv
Zolochiv 109 G2 *Rus.* Zolochev. Kharkivs'ka Oblast', E Ukraine
Zolochiv 108 C2 *Pol.* Złoczów, *Rus.* Zolochev. L'vivs'ka Oblast', W Ukraine
Zolote 109 H3 *Rus.* Zolotoye. Luhans'ka Oblast', E Ukraine
Zolotonosha 109 E2 Cherkas'ka Oblast', C Ukraine
Zolotoye *see* Zolote
Zomba 79 E2 Southern, S Malawi
Zombor *see* Sombor
Zongo 77 C5 Equateur, N Dem. Rep. Congo
Zonguldak 116 C2 Zonguldak, NW Turkey
Zonhoven 87 D6 Limburg, NE Belgium
Żory 99 C5 *var.* Zory, *Ger.* Sohrau. Śląskie, S Poland
Zouar 76 C2 Borkou-Ennedi-Tibesti, N Chad
Zouérate 74 C2 *var.* Zouérate, Zouïrât. Tiris Zemmour, N Mauritania
Zouérate *see* Zouérat
Zouïrât *see* Zouérat

Zrenjanin 100 D3 *prev.* Petrovgrad, Veliki Bečkerek, *Ger.* Grossbetschkerek, *Hung.* Nagybecskerek. Vojvodina, N Serbia
Zsil/Zsily *see* Jiu
Zsolna *see* Žilina
Zsombolya *see* Jimbolia
Zsupanya *see* Županja
Zubov Seamount 67 D5 *undersea feature* E Atlantic Ocean
Zueila *see* Zawilah
Zug 95 B7 *Fr.* Zoug. Zug, C Switzerland
Zugspitze 95 C7 *mountain* S Germany
Zuid-Beveland 87 B5 *var.* South Beveland. *island* SW Netherlands
Zuider Zee *see* IJsselmeer
Zuidhorn 86 E1 Groningen, NE Netherlands
Zuidlaren 86 E2 Drenthe, NE Netherlands
Zula 72 C4 E Eritrea
Züllichau *see* Sulechów
Zumbo *see* Vila do Zumbo
Zundert 87 C5 Noord-Brabant, S Netherlands
Zunyi 128 B5 Guizhou, S China
Županja 100 C3 *Hung.* Zsupanya. Vukovar-Srijem, E Croatia
Zürich 95 B7 *Eng./Fr.* Zurich, *It.* Zurigo. Zürich, N Switzerland
Zurich, Lake *see* Zürichsee
Zürichsee 95 B7 *Eng.* Lake Zurich. *lake* NE Switzerland
Zurigo *see* Zürich
Zutphen 86 D3 Gelderland, E Netherlands
Zuwārah 71 F2 NW Libya
Zuwaylah *see* Zawilah
Zuyevka 111 D5 Kirovskaya Oblast', NW Russian Federation
Zvenigorodka *see* Zvenyhorodka
Zvenyhorodka 109 E2 *Rus.* Zvenigorodka. Cherkas'ka Oblast', C Ukraine
Zvishavane 78 D3 *prev.* Shabani. Matabeleland South, S Zimbabwe
Zvolen 99 C6 *Ger.* Altsohl, *Hung.* Zólyom. Banskobystrický Kraj, C Slovakia
Zvornik 100 C4 E Bosnia and Herzegovina
Zwedru 74 D5 *var.* Tchien. E Liberia
Zwettl 95 E6 Wien, NE Austria
Zwevegem 87 A6 West-Vlaanderen, W Belgium
Zwickau 95 C5 Sachsen, E Germany
Zwolle 86 D3 Overijssel, E Netherlands
Żydaczów *see* Zhydachiv
Zyōetu *see* Jōetsu
Żyrardów 98 D3 Mazowieckie, C Poland
Zyryanovsk 114 D5 Vostochnyy Kazakhstan, E Kazakhstan

Key to map pages

North & West Asia 112-113

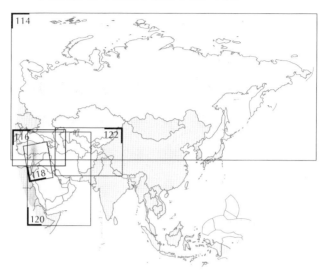

114

116 122

118

120

South & East Asia 124-125

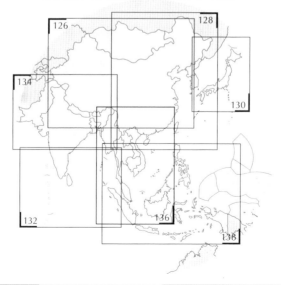

126 128

134

130

132 136

138